THE LAW OF WRECK

MARITIME AND TRANSPORT LAW LIBRARY

International Maritime Conventions
Volume Three
Protection of the Marine Environment
Francesco Berlingieri

Ship Building, Sale and Finance
Edited by Bariş Soyer and Andrew Tettenborn

The Modern Law of Marine Insurance
Volume Four
Edited by D Rhidian Thomas

Air Cargo Insurance
Malcom A. Clarke and George Leloudas

Offshore Oil and Gas Installations Security
An International Perspective
Mikhail Kashubsky

International Trade and Carriage of Goods
Edited by Bariş Soyer and Andrew Tettenborn

Maritime Law and Practice in China
Liang Zhao and Lianjun Li

Maritime Law
Fourth Edition
Edited by Yvonne Baatz

Maritime Cross-Border Insolvency
Under the European Insolvency Regulation and
the UNCITRAL Model Law
Lia Athanassiou

The Law of Yachts and Yachting
Second Edition
Edited by Filippo Lorenzon and Richard Coles

Maritime Liabilities in a Global and
Regional Context
Edited by Bariş Soyer and Andrew Tettenborn

New Technologies, Artificial Intelligence and
Shipping Law in the 21st Century
Edited by Bariş Soyer and Andrew Tettenborn

The Law of Wreck
Nicholas Gaskell and Craig Forrest

For more information about this series, please visit:
www.routledge.com/Maritime-and-Transport-Law-Library/book-series/MTLL

THE LAW OF WRECK

BY

NICHOLAS GASKELL
Professor of Maritime and Commercial Law
Marine and Shipping Law Unit
TC Beirne School of Law
University of Queensland
Barrister, Associate Tenant, Quadrant Chambers, London

and

CRAIG FORREST
Professor of Law
Director of the Marine and Shipping Law Unit
TC Beirne School of Law
University of Queensland

informa law
from Routledge

First published 2019
by Informa Law from Routledge
2 Park Square, Milton Park, Abingdon, Oxon OX14 4RN

and by Informa Law from Routledge
52 Vanderbilt Avenue, New York, NY 10017

Informa Law from Routledge is an imprint of the Taylor & Francis Group, an informa business

© 2019 Nicholas Gaskell and Craig Forrest

The right of Nicholas Gaskell and Craig Forrest to be identified as authors of this work has been asserted by them in accordance with sections 77 and 78 of the Copyright, Designs and Patents Act 1988.

All rights reserved. No part of this book may be reprinted or reproduced or utilised in any form or by any electronic, mechanical, or other means, now known or hereafter invented, including photocopying and recording, or in any information storage or retrieval system, without permission in writing from the publishers.

Whilst every effort has been made to ensure that the information contained in this book is correct, neither the author nor Informa Law can accept any responsibility for any errors or omissions or any consequences arising therefrom.

Trademark notice: Product or corporate names may be trademarks or registered trademarks, and are used only for identification and explanation without intent to infringe.

British Library Cataloguing-in-Publication Data
A catalogue record for this book is available from the British Library

Library of Congress Cataloging-in-Publication Data
Names: Gaskell, Nicholas, author. | Forrest, Craig, author.
Title: The law of wreck / by Nicholas Gaskell, Professor of Maritime and
  Commercial Law, Marine and Shipping Law Unit, TC Beirne School of Law,
  University of Queensland, Barrister, Associate Tenant, Quadrant
  Chambers, London, and Craig Forrest, Professor of Law, Director of the
  Marine and Shipping Law Unit, TC Beirne School of Law, University of
  Queensland
Description: Abingdon, Oxon ; New York : Informa Law from Routledge, 2019. |
  Series: Maritime and transport law library | Includes index. | Identifiers:
  LCCN 2019026304 (print) | LCCN 2019026305 (ebook) | ISBN 9781138208278 (cloth) |
  ISBN 9781315459578 (ebook)
Subjects: LCSH: Shipwrecks—Law and legislation. | Salvage. | Nairobi International
  Convention on the Removal of Wrecks (2007 May 23)
Classification: LCC K1188.A8 G37 2019 (print) | LCC K1188.A8 (ebook) |
  DDC 343.09/68—dc23
LC record available at https://lccn.loc.gov/2019026304
LC ebook record available at https://lccn.loc.gov/2019026305

ISBN: 978-1-138-20827-8 (hbk)
ISBN: 978-1-315-45957-8 (ebk)

Typeset in Times
by Apex CoVantage, LLC
Printed and bound by CPI Group (UK) Ltd, Croydon CR0 4YY

BRIEF CONTENTS

Preface	xxi
Acknowledgements	xxv
Table of abbreviations	xxvii
Table of cases	xli
Table of legislation	lv

Part I Wreck in national and international law

CHAPTER 1	INTRODUCTION TO WRECK CASUALTIES	3
CHAPTER 2	WRECK AND THE MARITIME COMMERCIAL ADVENTURE	35
CHAPTER 3	RIGHTS IN RELATION TO WRECK	211
CHAPTER 4	STATE RIGHTS AND WRECK	249
CHAPTER 5	LAW OF THE SEA AND WRECK	295
CHAPTER 6	UNDERWATER CULTURAL HERITAGE	325

Part II Wreck Removal Convention 2007

CHAPTER 7	WRECK REMOVAL CONVENTION 2007: CREATION	359
CHAPTER 8	WRECK REMOVAL CONVENTION 2007: SCOPE	393
CHAPTER 9	WRECK REMOVAL CONVENTION 2007: STATES' RIGHTS AND DUTIES	415
CHAPTER 10	WRECK REMOVAL CONVENTION 2007: SHIPOWNERS' AND INSURERS' LIABILITIES	437
CHAPTER 11	NATIONAL WRECK REMOVAL LAW AND THE MSA 1995 PART 9A	523

BRIEF CONTENTS

Part III Wreck removal contracts

CHAPTER 12 TRANSITION TO WRECK REMOVAL:
            SALVAGE AND SCOPIC   567

CHAPTER 13 WRECK REMOVAL OPERATIONS AND
            CONTRACTS   595

Part IV Wreck disposal

CHAPTER 14 WRECK DISPOSAL   655

Appendices   715
Index   801

DETAILED CONTENTS

Preface	xxi
Acknowledgements	xxv
Table of abbreviations	xxvii
Table of cases	xli
Table of legislation	lv

Part I Wreck in national and international law

CHAPTER 1 INTRODUCTION TO WRECK CASUALTIES — 3
1.1 Introduction — 3
    1.1.1 Wreck and maritime law — 3
    1.1.2 Wreck definitions — 4
    1.1.3 Scope of book — 5
1.2 Influential wreck casualties — 5
    1.2.1 *Torrey Canyon* (1967) — 6
        1.2.1(a) The casualty — 7
        1.2.1(b) Legal claims — 8
    1.2.2 Wrecks since 1967 — 10
        1.2.2(a) Tanker wrecks — 10
        1.2.2(b) Other wrecks — 14
    1.2.3 *MSC Napoli* (2007) — 15
        1.2.3(a) The casualty — 15
        1.2.3(b) Removal operations — 16
        1.2.3(c) Legal claims — 17
        1.2.3(d) Lessons — 18
    1.2.4 *Rena* (2011) — 18
        1.2.4(a) The casualty — 18
        1.2.4(b) Practical and legal problems — 20
        1.2.4(c) Legal claims — 21
        1.2.4(d) Full removal or consent for dumping? — 22
        1.2.4(e) 2017 consent order and indigenous factors — 24
        1.2.4(f) Lessons — 26
    1.2.5 *Costa Concordia* (2012) — 27
        1.2.5(a) The casualty — 27

		1.2.5(b)	Removal operations	28
		1.2.5(c)	Costs and liabilities	29
1.3	Cargo problems			30
	1.3.1	Changing environmental focus		30
	1.3.2	Particular problems with containers		30
		1.3.2(a)	Containers lost overboard	30
		1.3.2(b)	Weight and contents of containers	31
		1.3.2(c)	Increase in size of container ships	31
1.4	P&I Clubs' major incident analysis			32

CHAPTER 2 WRECK AND THE MARITIME COMMERCIAL ADVENTURE — 35

2.1	Wreck and carriage of goods contracts			35
	2.1.1	Overview of cargo's position after wreck		36
	2.1.2	Wreck and sale of goods contracts		37
	2.1.3	Cargo owners and salvage or wreck removal operations		37
		2.1.3(a)	Cargo owners and salvage	38
		2.1.3(b)	Removal by cargo interests themselves	38
	2.1.4	Carriage contracts and cargo forwarding costs		39
		2.1.4(a)	Transhipment costs under the carriage contract	40
		2.1.4(b)	Termination of the carriage contract	41
	2.1.5	Liability for cargo loss or damage caused by wreck		44
		2.1.5(a)	Hague/Visby Rules liability scheme	45
		2.1.5(b)	Error in navigation or management exception	48
		2.1.5(c)	Burden of proof under Art III and Art IV	50
		2.1.5(d)	Proof of loss or damage	51
		2.1.5(e)	Limitation of liability under the Hague/Visby Rules	53
		2.1.5(f)	Forum issues in carriage claims	55
	2.1.6	Cargo owner's liability for wreck		56
	2.1.7	Charterers and wreck		58
		2.1.7(a)	Bareboat charterers	58
		2.1.7(b)	Voyage charterers	61
		2.1.7(c)	Time charterers	63
		2.1.7(d)	Charterers' influence on wreck removal	69
2.2	Wreck and crew			70
	2.2.1	Master's concerns after casualty		70
	2.2.2	Criminalisation of seafarers after shipwreck		71
	2.2.3	Fair treatment of crew after shipwreck		72
	2.2.4	Maritime Labour Convention 2006		73
		2.2.4(a)	MLC 2006 and repatriation costs	74
		2.2.4(b)	Financial security for abandonment	74
		2.2.4(c)	Indemnity for unpaid wages	75
		2.2.4(d)	Compensation for injury and loss	75
		2.2.4(e)	Financial security for compensation	76
		2.2.4(f)	Implementation of MLC 2006 financial security provisions	76

2.3	Wreck and passengers		77
	2.3.1	Application of Athens Convention 2002	78
	2.3.2	Liability for death and injury	80
	2.3.3	Compensation and limits of liability for death and injury	83
	2.3.4	Passengers' luggage	85
	2.3.5	Compulsory insurance	86
	2.3.6	Domestic carriage	89
	2.3.7	Passenger claims and forum issues	89
2.4	Wreck and collision liability		90
	2.4.1	Liability	90
	2.4.2	Wreck and causation	91
	2.4.3	Damages for wreck	93
	2.4.4	Apportionment of liability	94
2.5	Wreck and limitation of liability		95
	2.5.1	Introduction to limitation of liability	96
	2.5.2	Craft for which limitation is available	97
	2.5.3	Persons who may limit	98
	2.5.4	Claims subject to limitation	99
		2.5.4(a) Property and personal claims	99
		2.5.4(b) Pollution claims	100
		2.5.4(c) Wreck and cargo removal claims	102
		2.5.4(d) Charterers and limitation claims	105
	2.5.5	Limitation for salvors and wreck removal contractors	106
	2.5.6	Calculating the limits	109
		2.5.6(a) Examples of limits	109
		2.5.6(b) Distinct occasion	111
	2.5.7	'Breaking' limitation	112
	2.5.8	LLMC opt-out for wreck and cargo removal claims	114
	2.5.9	Limitation procedure and forum shopping	116
		2.5.9(a) Establishing a limitation fund	116
		2.5.9(b) Multi-state limitation proceedings	117
		2.5.9(c) *Baltic Ace* litigation	119
		2.5.9(d) LLMC fund and the wreck removal reservation	122
		2.5.9(e) Limitation fund recognition and the EU	124
		2.5.9(f) Limitation forum shopping, the WRC 2007 and policy	128
2.6	Wreck and pollution liability		131
	2.6.1	International action after *Torrey Canyon*	131
	2.6.2	CLC and Fund Convention regime	132
		2.6.2(a) CLC 1992	133
		2.6.2(b) Fund Convention 1992	138
		2.6.2(c) Supplementary Fund Protocol 2003	140
	2.6.3	Bunkers Convention 2001	141
	2.6.4	HNSC 2010	144
	2.6.5	Environmental Liability Directive 2004	150
2.7	Wreck and the law of salvage		152
	2.7.1	Overview of salvage law	152

				Page
	2.7.2	Applicable salvage law		153
	2.7.3	Salvage terminology		154
	2.7.4	Professional salvage and wreck removal contractors		155
	2.7.5	Success in preventing a wreck		156
	2.7.6	Can a wreck be salved?		158
	2.7.7	Salvage reward		159
		2.7.7(a)	Size of reward	160
		2.7.7(b)	Liability to pay salvage	161
	2.7.8	Salvors' security for payment		162
	2.7.9	Salvage and the environment		163
		2.7.9(a)	Enhanced reward	164
		2.7.9(b)	Special compensation	164
		2.7.9(c)	SCOPIC 2018	167
2.8	Wreck and general average			169
	2.8.1	GA claims		170
	2.8.2	GA security		171
	2.8.3	Cutting away wreck		173
2.9	Wreck and marine insurance			173
	2.9.1	Role of marine insurance with shipwreck		173
	2.9.2	H&M cover: casualties and wreck		175
		2.9.2(a)	Risks covered	175
		2.9.2(b)	Wreck removal and liabilities	176
		2.9.2(c)	Proximate cause and defences	177
		2.9.2(d)	Mortgagee cover and wreck	178
	2.9.3	Cargo cover: casualties and wreck		179
		2.9.3(a)	Importance of cover	179
		2.9.3(b)	Levels of cover	179
		2.9.3(c)	Salvage, GA and wreck removal	182
		2.9.3(d)	Exclusions from cover	182
		2.9.3(e)	Forwarding after casualty	184
	2.9.4	Total loss		188
		2.9.4(a)	Actual total loss	188
		2.9.4(b)	Constructive total loss and notice of abandonment	190
		2.9.4(c)	Acceptance of notice of abandonment	191
	2.9.5	Wreck and the practice of underwriters		193
		2.9.5(a)	Information and evidence	193
		2.9.5(b)	Underwriters' decision time for total loss	195
	2.9.6	Insurance cover for liabilities		197
		2.9.6(a)	Availability of P&I Club cover for casualties	197
		2.9.6(b)	Typical P&I Club cover for casualties	198
		2.9.6(c)	'Pay to be paid' clause	201
		2.9.6(d)	P&I Club cover for wreck liabilities	204
		2.9.6(e)	P&I cover for crew claims	208
CHAPTER 3	RIGHTS IN RELATION TO WRECK			211
3.1	Conceptual development of wreck and interests in wreck			211

3.2	Ownership of wreck		213
	3.2.1	Choice of law in relation to ownership	214
	3.2.2	Identifying the owner	216
	3.2.3	Acquiring ownership of a wreck	220
	3.2.4	Human remains	222
3.3	Abandonment of rights		222
	3.3.1	Derelict	222
	3.3.2	Abandonment of ownership	224
3.4	Insurer's rights		231
	3.4.1	The insurer's rights to take over property	232
	3.4.2	Subrogation	234
	3.4.3	Reinsurance	234
	3.4.4	War risks	235
	3.4.5	Insurer's rights to long lost wrecks	237
3.5	Salvors' and finders' rights		239
	3.5.1	The salvors' rights to possession	239
	3.5.2	Possession of sunken wrecks	241
	3.5.3	*In specie* salvage award	245
	3.5.4	Finds	246

CHAPTER 4		STATE RIGHTS AND WRECK		249
4.1	Introduction			249
4.2	Wreck response and UK regulation			249
	4.2.1	Pollution preparedness and response in the UK		249
	4.2.2	Role of the SOSREP		250
	4.2.3	MSA 1995 Sch 3A and UK intervention powers		252
		4.2.3(a)	Directions to persons in control of the casualty	252
		4.2.3(b)	Recipients of directions	255
		4.2.3(c)	Directions to person in control of land	257
		4.2.3(d)	Directions to 'other' ships	258
		4.2.3(e)	Power to take action	260
		4.2.3(f)	Enforcement and procedure	261
		4.2.3(g)	Extent of powers over UK and foreign ships	262
		4.2.3(h)	Temporary exclusion zones	262
	4.2.4	Wreck and the relationship between public agencies		263
	4.2.5	Response coordination and the *MSC Napoli*		264
4.3	Shipping inquiries and wreck			266
4.4	State rights to wreck			268
	4.4.1	Right to wreck in UK territorial waters		268
	4.4.2	Right to wreck outside UK territorial waters		269
4.5	Receiver of Wreck			270
	4.5.1	Receiver of Wreck's function: vessels in distress		270
	4.5.2	Receiver of Wreck's function: salvage		271
	4.5.3	Receiver of Wreck's function: dealing with wreck		272
	4.5.4	Salvage of or by State vessels		276
	4.5.5	Modern practice of Receiver of Wreck		276

4.6	Coastguard and wreck claims	277
4.7	Wreck protection legislation	278
	4.7.1 Protection of Wrecks Act 1973	278
	4.7.2 Protection of Military Remains Act 1986	280
	4.7.3 Ancient Monuments and Archaeological Areas Act 1979	285
	4.7.4 Comparative US approach to protection of historic wreck	286
4.8	Sovereign immunity and wrecks	287

CHAPTER 5 LAW OF THE SEA AND WRECK — 295

5.1	Early law of the sea	295
5.2	Polluting wrecks and intervention beyond the territorial sea	296
5.3	Intervention Convention 1969	296
5.4	United Nations Convention on the Law of the Sea	299
	5.4.1 Development of UNCLOS	299
	5.4.2 Jurisdictional regime	300
5.5	UNCLOS and wrecks	306
	5.5.1 Marine pollution	306
	5.5.2 Obligations to report and inform	311
	5.5.3 Archaeologically and historically important wrecks	312
5.6	UNCLOS and jurisdiction with respect to wrecks that pose a pollution hazard	316
	5.6.1 Polluting wrecks in internal waters and territorial sea	316
	5.6.2 Polluting wrecks in EEZ and continental shelf	316
	5.6.3 Intervention beyond territorial sea	318
	5.6.4 Hazards that are not navigational or polluting	320
5.7	OPRC 1990	321

CHAPTER 6 UNDERWATER CULTURAL HERITAGE — 325

6.1	Protection of historic wrecks	325
6.2	Development of UCH 2001	325
6.3	Aim of UCH 2001	326
6.4	Salvage and historic wrecks	327
	6.4.1 Maritime archaeology and salvage	328
	6.4.2 UK position on salvage and historic wreck	331
	6.4.3 Salvage Convention and historic wreck	332
6.5	Defining "underwater cultural heritage"	332
6.6	Non-commercialisation and salvage	334
6.7	Activities to be regulated	336
6.8	Good archaeological practice	336
6.9	Jurisdictional structure	337
	6.9.1 Internal waters, archipelagic waters and territorial sea	338
	6.9.2 Contiguous zone	339
	6.9.3 Continental shelf and EEZ	339
	6.9.4 The Area	340
6.10	Regulatory and deterrent regime	341
	6.10.1 Competent authorities and authorisation	341

		6.10.2	Public awareness and training	342
		6.10.3	Sanctions and seizure	342
	6.11	International cooperation		344
	6.12	Other agreements		345
	6.13	Warships and other State-owned vessels		346
	6.14	Implementation through UNESCO		349
	6.15	State practice		349
		6.15.1	US position	350
		6.15.2	UK position	351
	6.16	Conclusion		355

Part II Wreck Removal Convention 2007

CHAPTER 7   WRECK REMOVAL CONVENTION 2007: CREATION — 359

7.1	Need for a Wreck Removal Convention			359
7.2	Development of WRC 2007			361
	7.2.1	Initial negotiations 1967–1990		361
	7.2.2	Renewed negotiations 1990–2002		368
	7.2.3	Drafting 2002–2007		370
7.3	WRC 2007 and the international legal order			370
	7.3.1	WRC 2007 and general principles of international law		371
	7.3.2	WRC 2007 and UNCLOS		371
	7.3.3	Avoidance of overlap with other IMO conventions		375
7.4	WRC 2007 and non-State parties			376
	7.4.1	Wrecks of non-State parties in territorial sea		376
	7.4.2	Binding nature of WRC 2007 for non-State parties and wreck in EEZ		377
	7.4.3	Coastal State action and non-State party wrecks in EEZ		380
	7.4.4	Insurance cover and non-State party wrecks in EEZ		381
	7.4.5	WRC 2007 as generally accepted international rules and standards		383
		7.4.5(a)	Laws and regulations for the prevention, reduction and control of pollution	384
		7.4.5(b)	Generally acceptable	385
7.5	Cooperation			387
7.6	Convention form			387
	7.6.4	Preamble		388
	7.6.5	Entry into force requirements		388
	7.6.6	Dispute settlement		389
	7.6.7	Annex		390
7.7	Participation			390

CHAPTER 8   WRECK REMOVAL CONVENTION 2007: SCOPE — 393

8.1	Introduction			393
8.2	Wrecks that pose a hazard			393
	8.2.1	Defining "wreck"		393
		8.2.1(a)	Maritime casualty	394
		8.2.1(b)	Sunken or stranded ship	395

		8.2.1(c)	Objects from ships	396
		8.2.1(d)	Objects and cargo lost at sea	396
		8.2.1(e)	Effective salvage of ships about to sink or strand	396
		8.2.1(f)	Derelict and abandoned ships	398
		8.2.1(g)	Fixed and floating platforms	400
		8.2.1(h)	Wrecked warships and other government non-commercial ships	402
		8.2.1(i)	Aircraft	403
	8.2.2	Defining "hazard"		404
	8.2.3	Defining "related interests"		405
	8.2.4	Defining "removal"		406
	8.2.5	Defining "Affected State"		406
8.3	Scope of WRC 2007			408
	8.3.1	Geographical scope		408
	8.3.2	Temporal scope		410
8.4	Extension of the WRC 2007 to territorial sea			410
	8.4.1	Coastal State rights in territorial sea		410
	8.4.2	Application of WRC 2007 to territorial sea		411

CHAPTER 9 WRECK REMOVAL CONVENTION 2007: STATES' RIGHTS AND DUTIES 415

9.1	Flag State obligations			415
	9.1.1	State of a ship's registry and flag State		415
	9.1.2	Flag State obligations		417
	9.1.3	Reporting		417
		9.1.3(a)	Who must report	418
		9.1.3(b)	What must be reported and to whom	420
		9.1.3(c)	Practical difficulties in reporting	420
	9.1.4	Cooperation in process of wreck removal		421
9.2	Affected States' powers and obligations			422
	9.2.1	Warning		422
	9.2.2	Determination of hazard		423
	9.2.3	Locating the wreck		424
	9.2.4	Marking the wreck		425
	9.2.5	Removal of the wreck		427
		9.2.5(a)	Hazard notice	427
		9.2.5(b)	Scope of "removal"	428
		9.2.5(c)	Removal of hazard by a salvor	429
		9.2.5(d)	Removal of hazard by the Affected State	430
		9.2.5(e)	Proportionality and reasonableness	431
		9.2.5(f)	Overlap with preventative measures	432
		9.2.5(g)	Cost of wreck removal	433
		9.2.5(h)	Ownership of wreck and power of sale	433
		9.2.5(i)	State obligation to remove	434
		9.2.5(j)	State liability	434
9.3	State powers in territorial sea			435

CHAPTER 10 WRECK REMOVAL CONVENTION 2007: SHIPOWNERS' AND INSURERS' LIABILITIES — 437

- 10.1 Introduction — 437
- 10.2 Registered shipowner's liability for costs — 437
    - 10.2.1 Strict liability for costs — 438
    - 10.2.2 Persons liable to pay costs — 439
    - 10.2.3 Persons who can claim costs — 440
    - 10.2.4 Costs recoverable — 441
    - 10.2.5 Full or partial removal? — 443
    - 10.2.6 Unusual and difficult locations — 447
    - 10.2.7 Ships covered — 448
        - 10.2.7(a) Types of ship — 448
        - 10.2.7(b) Ships flagged in non-State parties — 452
    - 10.2.8 Completion of removal under WRC 2007 — 453
- 10.3 Defences to shipowner liability — 456
    - 10.3.1 War and terrorism — 457
        - 10.3.1(a) War — 457
        - 10.3.1(b) Third party damage — 457
    - 10.3.2 Natural phenomena — 460
    - 10.3.3 Government negligence — 461
        - 10.3.3(a) Government navigational aids — 461
        - 10.3.3(b) Government negligence generally — 461
- 10.4 Time limits — 462
- 10.5 Triggers to liability — 464
    - 10.5.1 Art 1 triggers — 464
        - 10.5.1(a) Abandonment and WRC 2007 liability — 464
        - 10.5.1(b) Proof of hazard — 465
        - 10.5.1(c) Hazard to fishing vessels — 466
        - 10.5.1(d) Other hazards and human remains — 466
    - 10.5.2 Art 9 triggers: EEZ and territorial waters differences — 468
    - 10.5.3 Recovery of wreck removal costs: EEZ — 468
        - 10.5.3(a) Wreck removal notices — 469
        - 10.5.3(b) Notice in writing — 472
        - 10.5.3(c) Informing registered owner — 473
        - 10.5.3(d) Deadline — 474
        - 10.5.3(e) Determination of hazard by a State — 475
    - 10.5.4 Recovery of wreck removal costs: territorial waters — 476
    - 10.5.5 Recovery of costs of locating wrecks — 478
    - 10.5.6 Recovery of costs of marking wrecks — 479
    - 10.5.7 Recovery of wreck removal costs: high seas — 480
- 10.6 Cargo removal under the WRC 2007 — 481
    - 10.6.1 Uncertainty in the WRC 2007? — 481
    - 10.6.2 Cargo removal: history — 483
    - 10.6.3 Cargo removal: conclusion — 488
    - 10.6.4 Cargo removal: liability beyond existing conventions — 488

10.7	WRC 2007 and limitation of shipowners' liability		490
10.8	Compulsory insurance		491
	10.8.1	Need for compulsory insurance	491
	10.8.2	Introduction to WRC 2007 Art 12	492
		10.8.2(a) 300 gt threshold	492
		10.8.2(b) Ships without a tonnage measurement	493
	10.8.3	WRC 2007 compulsory insurance certificates	494
	10.8.4	Direct action and insurer defences	496
		10.8.4(a) Nature of direct liability	496
		10.8.4(b) Insurer defences	498
		10.8.4(c) Wilful misconduct as used in Art 12(10)	499
		10.8.4(d) Wilful misconduct in English law	499
		10.8.4(e) Prohibition of other insurer defences	501
	10.8.5	Relationship of WRC 2007 insurance liability cap and LLMC limitation	502
		10.8.5(a) Nature of the insurer's liability cap	503
		10.8.5(b) Shipowner and insurer limiting for wreck removal	503
		10.8.5(c) Applicable national or international regime	504
		10.8.5(d) Insurer's liability cap if shipowner cannot limit	505
		10.8.5(e) Calculating Art 12(1) cap: which LLMC version?	508
		10.8.5(f) Calculating the Art 12(1) cap: sdr conversion	510
		10.8.5(g) Direct action outside WRC 2007 to avoid Art 12(1) cap	511
	10.8.6	P&I Club practice after entry into force of WRC 2007	511
10.9	Overlaps with other maritime liability regimes		514
	10.9.1	Overlap with Salvage Convention 1989	514
	10.9.2	Overlap with maritime pollution liability conventions	515
		10.9.2(a) Conflict with CLC 1992	516
		10.9.2(b) Conflict with HNS Convention 2010	519
		10.9.2(c) Conflict with Bunkers Convention 2001	520
	10.9.3	Conflict with nuclear liability conventions	521

CHAPTER 11		NATIONAL WRECK REMOVAL LAW AND THE MSA 1995 PART 9A	523
11.1	Wreck removal in national law		523
	11.1.1	Introduction	523
	11.1.2	UK local harbour legislation	524
		11.1.2(a) Harbours Docks and Piers Clauses Act 1847 s 56	524
		11.1.2(b) Modern local harbour legislation	526
	11.1.3	Merchant Shipping Act 1995	527
		11.1.3(a) Harbour authorities: s 252	527
		11.1.3(b) General lighthouse authorities: s 253	528
11.2	Accession choices for States		530
	11.2.1	Merits of the WRC 2007	530
	11.2.2	Should States extend the WRC 2007 to territorial waters?	531
	11.2.3	Checklist when adopting the WRC 2007	532

11.3	MSA 1995 Part 9A		534
	11.3.1	UK method of enactment of WRC 2007	534
		11.3.1(a) Wreck Removal Convention Act 2011	534
		11.3.1(b) Incorporation of WRC 2007	535
	11.3.2	Extension of WRC 2007 into UK territorial waters	538
	11.3.3	Part 9A administrative provisions	539
		11.3.3(a) Wreck reports	540
		11.3.3(b) Locating and marking wrecks	540
		11.3.3(c) Removal by registered owner	541
		11.3.3(d) Removal in default by UK itself	544
		11.3.3(e) Compulsory insurance certificates	545
		11.3.3(f) Offences and enforcement	546
		11.3.3(g) Government ships	546
	11.3.4	Part 9A liability provisions	547
		11.3.4(a) Liability for UK wreck costs	547
		11.3.4(b) Direct action against insurer	551
		11.3.4(c) Relationship with existing UK wreck removal laws	555
	11.3.5	GLAs and wreck removal under Part 9A	556
11.4	Abandoned ships		559

Part III   Wreck removal contracts

CHAPTER 12   TRANSITION TO WRECK REMOVAL: SALVAGE AND SCOPIC — 567

12.1	Salvage and wreck removal		567
	12.1.1	Introduction	567
	12.1.2	Salvage contracts: commercial and legal choices	567
		12.1.2(a) Initial considerations	567
		12.1.2(b) Salvage contract or not?	568
		12.1.2(c) Salvage contract or a towage contract?	569
		12.1.2(d) Non-professional contractors	570
		12.1.2(e) Sub-contractor commercial pressure: duress and frustration	571
		12.1.2(f) Subcontracting on salvage basis	572
12.2	Termination of services		573
	12.2.1	Salvors operating without a contract	573
	12.2.2	Salvage contracts and the Salvage Convention 1989	578
	12.2.3	Termination by LOF salvor	579
	12.2.4	Termination by shipowner under LOF	580
12.3	SCOPIC and the transition from salvage to wreck removal		582
	12.3.1	SCOPIC caretaking role	582
	12.3.2	Special casualty representative	584
	12.3.3	Special representatives	585
	12.3.4	SCOPIC termination provisions	586

		12.3.4(a)	Termination of SCOPIC by salvor	586
		12.3.4(b)	Termination of SCOPIC by shipowner	589
		12.3.4(c)	Termination of SCOPIC and State intervention	590
	12.3.5	SCOPIC and preventing pollution from a wreck		593

CHAPTER 13 WRECK REMOVAL OPERATIONS AND CONTRACTS — 595

13.1	Introduction			595
	13.1.1	Urgency for wreck removal operations		595
	13.1.2	Public relations		595
	13.1.3	Recovery of bodies		596
13.2	Range of technical wreck removal options			600
13.3	Responsibility for arranging wreck removal contracts			602
	13.3.1	Shipowner and insurer		602
	13.3.2	State action to engage contractors		603
	13.3.3	Choice of contractor		603
13.4	Wreck removal tendering			604
	13.4.1	Tender process		604
	13.4.2	Quantitative risk assessment		605
13.5	Wreck removal and ancillary contracts			607
13.6	Wreck removal contracts			607
	13.6.1	Introduction to BIMCO wreck removal contracts		607
	13.6.2	Allocation of wreck removal risks and costs		608
	13.6.3	Wreckhire 2010: overview and risk allocation		610
		13.6.3(a)	Basic performance obligations	611
		13.6.3(b)	Hire payments and costs	613
		13.6.3(c)	Duration of services	616
		13.6.3(d)	Changes in services, personnel, craft or equipment	617
		13.6.3(e)	Delay	619
		13.6.3(f)	Termination or suspension	620
		13.6.3(g)	Claims and liabilities	622
		13.6.3(h)	Pollution risks	626
		13.6.3(i)	Wreck delivery and disposal	627
		13.6.3(j)	Collaboration and consultation	629
		13.6.3(k)	Arbitration, mediation and expert evaluation	631
	13.6.4	Wreckfixed 2010: overview and risk allocation		633
		13.6.4(a)	Introduction and comparison with Wreckhire 2010	633
		13.6.4(b)	Price and risk	634
		13.6.4(c)	Changes in services, personnel, craft or equipment	635
		13.6.4(d)	Termination	636
		13.6.4(e)	Wreck delivery and disposal	637
	13.6.5	Wreckstage 2010: overview and risk allocation		639
		13.6.5(a)	Introduction and comparison with other forms	639
		13.6.5(b)	Payment stages	641

13.6.5(c)	Extra costs	641
13.6.5(d)	Changes in services, personnel, craft or equipment	642
13.6.5(e)	Delay	643
13.6.5(f)	Termination	644
13.6.5(g)	Delivery and disposal	645

Part IV Wreck disposal

CHAPTER 14 WRECK DISPOSAL — 655

- 14.1 Dumping of ships and cargoes at sea — 656
  - 14.1.1 Introduction — 656
  - 14.1.2 London (Dumping) Convention 1972/1996 — 657
    - 14.1.2(a) London Convention 1972 — 658
    - 14.1.2(b) LC Protocol 1996 — 659
    - 14.1.2(c) Civil liability for dumping under the LC Protocol 1996 — 663
  - 14.1.3 OSPAR Convention 1992 — 663
  - 14.1.4 Dumping and the UK — 664
    - 14.1.4(a) Background — 664
    - 14.1.4(b) Marine and Coastal Access Act 2009 — 664
- 14.2 Dumping or abandonment? — 667
- 14.3 Scrapping of ships generally — 669
- 14.4 Transboundary waste disposal — 670
  - 14.4.1 Basel Convention 1989 — 670
  - 14.4.2 EU Waste Shipment Regulation 2006 — 673
- 14.5 Ship recycling — 676
  - 14.5.1 Hong Kong Ship Recycling Convention 2009 — 676
  - 14.5.2 EU Ship Recycling Regulation 2013 — 678
    - 14.5.2(a) Introduction and entry into force — 678
    - 14.5.2(b) Scope — 679
    - 14.5.2(c) UK Ship Recycling Requirements Regulations 2018 — 682
- 14.6 EU Waste Framework Directive 2008 — 685
  - 14.6.1 Background — 685
  - 14.6.2 Overview of Waste Framework Directive 2008 — 687
    - 14.6.2(a) Definitions — 687
    - 14.6.2(b) General duties — 688
  - 14.6.3 *Commune de Mesquer* — 689
  - 14.6.4 Wreck and the Waste Framework Directive — 690
    - 14.6.4(a) Who are waste producers or holders? — 691
    - 14.6.4(b) Relationship with LC 1972/LC Protocol 1996 — 692
    - 14.6.4(c) Relationship with WRC 2007 and LLMC — 693
  - 14.6.5 Waste disposal: adoption in the UK — 693
    - 14.6.5(a) Waste regulations 2011 — 694
    - 14.6.5(b) Marine waste licensing and exemptions — 696

	14.6.5(c) Environmental Protection Act 1900	701
	14.6.5(d) Practical compliance considerations for wreck waste	702
14.7	Commercial choices for wreck disposal	703
	14.7.1 Sale of wreck	703
	14.7.2 Wreck and ship deregistration	705
	14.7.3 BIMCO disposal voyage contracts	708
	14.7.4 *Rena* trust fund and finality	712

Appendices	715
Introduction	715
Weblinks	716
Merchant Shipping Act 1995: Extracts	717
Appendix 1: MSA 1995 Part IX, ss 252–255	717
Appendix 2: MSA 1995 Part 9A, ss 255A-255U	721
Appendix 3: MSA 1995 Schedule 3A Safety Directions	729
Appendix 4: MSA 1995 Sched 11ZA [Text of the WRC 2007]	735
Appendix 5: Wreck Removal Convention 2007:	
Annex (Certificate of Insurance)	747
Appendix 6: WRC 2007: Diplomatic Conference Resolutions	749
BIMCO Wreck Removal Contracts	753
Appendix 7: Wreckhire 2010	753
Appendix 8: Wreckfixed 2010	767
Appendix 9: Wreckstage 2010	779
Appendix 10: Wreckstage 2010 BIMCO explanatory notes	793
Index	801

PREFACE

This book was prompted by the entry into force of the Nairobi Wreck Removal Convention 2007 (which we abbreviate as WRC 2007), followed by its enactment in the UK in the Wreck Removal Convention Act 2011, and the increased attention given to removal of wrecks such as the *MSC Napoli, Rena* and *Costa Concordia*. Such casualties have had environmental impacts but have also caused real concern about the huge costs that must be borne by shipowners and insurers. In the course of writing an article on the "Wreck Removal Convention 2007" (in [2016] LMCLQ 49) we were aware of being able to present only part of the picture of the law relating to wrecks. We have both previously undertaken research into the legal issues arising from the efforts to locate, record and (in some cases) raise the remains of long-lost shipwrecks. Many of these have historic or cultural significance, others still have a commercial value, and in both cases there are difficult issues as to ownership and abandonment of rights. We have also been involved with State authorities concerning the international law issues concerning wreck and how to deal with it in national law. This book is, in a sense, the culmination of this work over many years.

Increasing technological capabilities have meant that search and recovery operations for all types of wreck are now in the realms of possibility (albeit at great cost), whereas not so long ago such wrecks were beyond all hope of discovery or recovery. Moreover, the wreck of a ship and its cargo may have profound implications on the commercial parties involved in a modern maritime adventure (as well as their insurers), eg through the chartering of ships and the carriage of cargo and passengers, in particular through liabilities in relation to cargo, passengers and pollution. We wanted to integrate into a larger text some of these wider issues of how the wreck of a ship could condition how the parties react to the casualty as well as the possible liabilities they may face. In doing so we hoped to show the links between the disparate legal subjects while attempting to capture some of the practical commercial issues faced by all parties, including maritime law practitioners. We have not tried to cover all the law relating to maritime casualties generally. As we explain in Chapter 2, this would be unnecessary if it merely replicated other standard works on particular aspects of marine casualty law. We only intend to deal in outline with issues such as charterparties, salvage, collision and pollution liabilities in order that a reader can have an overview of how wreck impinges on different areas of maritime law and be aware of the need to look in a number of different directions when handling wreck claims. For more detail readers should refer to other leading works in the Informa stable, in particular *Law of Tug Tow and Offshore Contracts*, but also others including *Shipping and the Environment, Time Charters, Voyage Charters* and *Marine Cargo Insurance*.

PREFACE

The book is divided into four parts. Part I introduces how wreck features in national and international law generally. Chapter 1 introduces a number of key wreck casualties so as to provide a link to later discussions of some of the practical and legal problems raised by them. Chapter 2 aims to give an overview of how wreck can affect the legal position of a whole variety of persons involved in the commercial maritime voyage. We then cover rights in relation to wreck, eg claims for ownership (Chapter 3) and the State rights in relation to wreck eg in national law (Chapter 4). This leads on to the treatment of wreck in international law, including rights of intervention (Chapter 5). Chapter 6 introduces the cultural heritage dimension in national and international law. Part II covers the WRC 2007, which is really the heart of the work. We have taken the opportunity in Part II to expand, reorder and completely revise the work in our earlier LMCLQ article. There are separate chapters on the genesis of the Convention (Chapter 7), its scope (Chapter 8), the rights and duties of States (Chapter 9) and the liability position for shipowners and insurers (Chapter 10). Chapter 11 examines the enactment of the Convention in UK national law. Part III considers the contractual aspects of wreck removal and examines the transition from salvage to wreck removal (Chapter 12) and BIMCO's wreck removal contracts (Chapter 13). Finally, Part IV (Chapter 14) completes the cycle by considering the complications involving disposal of wrecks, including the ship recycling provisions now applicable from 2019.

We considered that it was important to include factual wreck examples (eg in Chapters 1 and 10) to give some colour to our analysis, but it is not always possible to verify all information contained in web links—particularly relating to financial consequences that would inevitably be 'commercial in confidence'. While it has become common in some academic works to give footnotes with the date on which each web link was sourced, this adds considerably to the word length and is largely unnecessary as it is obvious to all readers that links can change. We therefore prefer simply to say here that we have endeavoured to check that all links were current as at 31 December 2018. Similarly, the wide availability of web sources means that it is not really necessary to include massive Appendices. We have therefore sought to include only those sources that are not easily available or which we consider to be vital to understand our analysis. Links to those readily available are provided in the Appendices.

To assist navigation through the work, we have included extensive cross-references to support the Index and detailed Table of Contents. Maritime law makes much use of abbreviations and acronyms and the appearance of these on a page can sometimes be daunting or confusing, yet they are necessary to reduce length. We have therefore included a Table of Abbreviations to assist readers. Finally, the Appendices contain the WRC 2007, relevant extracts from UK legislation and facsimiles of BIMCO wreck removal contracts. We have lightly annotated the text of the WRC 2007 with cross-references to the main discussion of its articles in the book and to its implementation in the MSA 1995.

We would of course be very grateful for any comments or corrections. We should note that there are inevitably gaps, caused by lack of space (or our ignorance). In particular, it is not possible to cover the law of every country, including the US. Nevertheless, we hope that the book will be useful to all with an interest in wreck, including the legal profession, insurers, P&I clubs, ship owners, ship operators, cargo owners, salvors, mariners, port operators, government regulators as well as academics.

We accept joint responsibility for the whole book, but record that: Nick Gaskell wrote Chapters 1, 2, 10–14; Craig Forrest wrote Chapters 5–7; Craig had primary responsibility

PREFACE

for Chapters 3 and 4 (based in part on earlier work by Sarah Dromgoole and Nick Gaskell) and Chapters 8 and 9 (based in part on joint work for the 2016 article).

We have endeavoured to state the law as at 31 December 2018, although with the assistance of the publishers we have been able to refer to some developments in 2019. The anticipated effects of Brexit are addressed briefly in the opening pages of Chapter 14.

Nick Gaskell and Craig Forrest
TC Beirne School of Law, University of Queensland, Brisbane
August 2019

Wreck Removal Convention Bill

Hansard 18 March 2011, Volume 525, Col 589

Dr Thérèse Coffey in moving the third reading of the Bill in the Commons stated:

> I will open with a quick question. What do you find lying on a seabed shivering? The answer is a nervous wreck. Perhaps I am a bit of a nervous wreck because I finally get to speak to the Bill that stands in my name.

If the authors are nervous wrecks it arises through exposing this book to a wider audience.

ACKNOWLEDGEMENTS

We would like to thank our colleagues in the TC Beirne School of Law at the University of Queensland and its Marine and Shipping Law Unit (MASLU), in particular Professor (now Justice) Sarah Derrington and Dr Michael White OAM QC. Without their stimulating support the book would not have been possible. We also thank our MASLU research assistants, Katelyn Lamont and Madeline Rodgers.

We would also acknowledge the tremendous input into the development of the law by the CMI and IMO, but also BIMCO whose balanced forms are now the basis of most offshore contracts. We are especially grateful to BIMCO for permission to reproduce its wreck contracts and accompanying notes. Extracts from SCOPIC are reproduced with the kind permission of Lloyd's. Crown copyright information is reproduced with the permission of the Controller of HMSO and the Queen's Printer for Scotland. Permission was also given by London Offshore Consultants to refer to their 2014 "Report on the comparisons between *Rena* and other wreck removal operations in recent years", and by the Standard Club and UK Club to refer to extracts from their 2018/19 P&I Rules.

We have benefited by being able to present our views to a variety of audiences around the world, including to the Maritime law Association of Australia and New Zealand (MLAANZ). We are particularly grateful to the many individuals who have given their time to respond to our questions about the law and to give us insights into commercial practice. There are almost too many to mention, but they include: Mariano Aznar, Andrew Angel, Patrick Archie, Rebecca Austin, David Baker, Andrew Bardot, Roger Barker, Paul Bender, Archie Bishop, David Bolomini, Tim Bowden, Dianne Bowles, Jan de Boer, Sarah Dromgoole (including for permission to refer to existing joint work), Patrick Griggs, Matthew Hockaday, Mark Hoddinot, Måns Jacobsson, Sam Kendall-Marsden, Alison Kentuck, George Koumpenas, Patrick Quirk, Deucalion Rediadis, Francis Rose, Paul Rowland, Hugh Shaw, Toby Stone, Mike Williams, Anna Wollin. We apologise if any names are omitted from this list. The views expressed in the book are, however, our own, and are not to be attributed to any of the above.

We are grateful to our publishers, especially Amy Jones and Caroline Church, for their patience and support in what has become a far more ambitious project than we had first envisaged, and to the whole editorial team.

We would also like to thank our families and friends for their tolerance and support throughout an extended writing process, and above all, Lindsay Gaskell and Kerry Forrest.

ABBREVIATIONS

1. Organisations, commercial and general abbreviations
2. Conventions, legislation and agreements
3. Books, articles and other publications

1. ORGANISATIONS, COMMERCIAL AND GENERAL ABBREVIATIONS

ADR:	alternative dispute resolution
ATL:	actual total loss
BEIS:	Department for Business Energy and Industrial Strategy
BIMCO:	Baltic and International Maritime Council [formerly, Conference]
BP:	British Petroleum
CEFAS:	Centre for Environment, Fisheries and Aquaculture Science
CIF:	cost insurance freight
CLCS:	Commission on the Limits of the Continental Shelf
CLIA:	Cruise Lines International Association
CMI:	Comité Maritime International
COP:	Conference of the Parties
CTL:	constructive total loss
DCMS:	Department of Digital, Culture, Media and Sport
DECC:	Department of Energy and Climate Change
DEFRA:	Department for Environment, Food and Rural Affairs
DfT:	Department for Transport
DOALOS:	United Nations Division of Ocean Affairs and the Law of the Sea
DWT:	deadweight tonnage
EEZ:	Exclusive Economic Zone
EG:	Environment Group
EMSA:	European Maritime Safety Agency
EU:	European Union
FCL:	full container load
FEU:	forty foot equivalent unit [container size]
FIATA:	International Federation of Freight Forwarders' Associations
FOB:	free on board
FONASBA:	Federation of National Associations of Shipbrokers and Agents
FPSO:	floating production, storage and offloading (vessel)
FSU:	floating storage unit

ABBREVIATIONS

GA:	general average
Gf:	gold francs
gt:	gross tons
H&M:	hull and machinery [insurance]
HFO:	heavy fuel oil
HNS:	hazardous and noxious substances
IACS:	International Association of Classification Societies
IALA:	International Association of Marine Aids to Navigation and Lighthouse Authorities
ICA:	Inter-Club NYPE Agreement 1996
ICC:	International Chamber of Commerce
ICOMOS:	International Council on Monuments and Sites
ICS:	International Chamber of Shipping
ILA:	International Law Association
ILO:	International Labour Organisation
ILU:	Institute of London Underwriters
IMO:	International Maritime Organisation
IMCO:	International Maritime Consultative Organisation
IMF:	International Monetary Fund
International Group:	International Group Association of P&I Clubs
IOPC Fund:	International Oil Pollution Compensation Fund(s)
ISA:	International Seabed Authority
ISU:	International Salvage Union
ITOPF:	International Tanker Owners Pollution Federation Limited
IUA:	International Underwriting Association of London
LGD:	lead government department
LIRMA:	London Insurance and Reinsurance Market Association
LNG:	liquefied natural gas
LOF:	Lloyd's Standard form of Salvage Agreement (Lloyd's Open Form)
LPG:	liquid petroleum gas
LRF:	Local Response Forum
MAIB:	Marine Accidents Investigation Branch
MAtoN:	Mobile Marine Aids to Navigation
MCA:	Maritime and Coast Guard Agency
MEPC:	Marine Environment Protection Committee
MERCOM:	Maritime Emergency Response Commander
MLAANZ:	Maritime Law Association of Australia and New Zealand
MMO:	Maritime Management Organisation
MOD:	Ministry of Defence
MOU:	Memorandum of Understanding
MRC:	Marine Response Centre
mt:	metric tonnes
nm:	nautical miles
NYPE:	New York Produce Exchange time charter
OECD:	Organisation for Economic Co-operation and Development
PCB:	polychlorinated biphenyls

ABBREVIATIONS

P&I Club:	Protection and Indemnity Club
PREMIAM:	Pollution Response in Emergencies Marine Impact Assessment and Monitoring
QRA:	Quantitative Risk Assessment
Reefer:	refrigerated container
RMST:	RMS Titanic Inc
ROV:	remotely operated vehicle
SCC:	Strategic Coordination Centre
SCG:	Strategic Coordinating Group
SCOPIC:	Special Compensation P&I Club
SCR:	Shipowners Casualty Representative
SCU:	Salvage Control Unit
SCUBA:	self-contained underwater breathing apparatus
SDR:	special drawing right [of IMF]
SOSREP:	Secretary of State's Representative for Maritime Salvage & Intervention
SRC:	Shoreline Response Centre
SSC:	single ship company
STAC:	Science and Technical Advice Cell
STOPIA:	Small Tanker Oil Pollution Indemnification Agreement
TCG:	Tactical Coordinating Group
TEU:	twenty foot equivalent unit [container size]
TOPIA:	Tanker Oil Pollution Indemnification Agreement
UNCITRAL:	United Nations Commission on International Trade Law
UNEP:	United Nations Environment Programme
UNESCO:	United Nations Educational, Scientific and Cultural Organisation
VGM:	verified gross mass
VOC:	Vereenigde Oostindische Compagnie (Dutch East India Company)
WG:	Working Group
WSC:	World Shipping Council

2. CONVENTIONS, LEGISLATION AND AGREEMENTS

Accident Reporting Regulations 2012: Merchant Shipping (Accident Reporting and Investigations) Regulations 2012

Athens Convention 1974: Convention Relating to the Carriage of Passengers and their Luggage by Sea 1974

Athens Convention 2002: Athens Convention 1974 as amended by 2002 Protocol

Basel Convention: Basel Convention on Transboundary Movement of Hazardous Wastes and their Disposal 1989

Bonn Agreement: Agreement for Cooperation in Dealing with Pollution of the North Sea by Oil and other Harmful Substances 1983, as amended in 2001

Brussels I Regulation Recast: Regulation (EU) No 1215/2012 of the European Parliament and of the Council of 12 December 2012 on jurisdiction and the recognition and enforcement of judgments in civil and commercial matters

Bunkers Convention 2001: International Convention on Civil Liability for Bunker Oil Pollution Damage 2001

ABBREVIATIONS

CLC 1969: International Convention on Civil Liability for Oil Pollution Damage
CLC 1992: CLC 1971 as amended by 1992 Protocol
COGSA: Carriage of Goods by Sea Act
Collision Convention 1910: Convention for the Unification of Certain Rules of Law with respect to Collisions between Vessels 1910
Commune de Mesquer: *Commune de Mesquer v Total France SA and Total International Ltd*, Case C-188/07, Judgment of the Court (Grand Chamber) of 24 June 2008, [2]]
Controlled Waste Regulations: Controlled Waste (England and Wales) Regulations 2012 (SI 2012/811)
ELD Regulations: Environmental Damage (Prevention and Remediation) (England) Regulations 2015 (SI 2015/810)
Environmental Liability Directive 2004: Directive 2004/35/CE of the European Parliament and of the Council of 21 April 2004 on environmental liability with regard to the prevention and remedying of environmental damage
EPA 1990: Environmental Protection Act 1990
Exempted Activities Order: Marine Licensing (Exempted Activities) Order 2011 (SI 2011/409)
Fund Convention 1971: International Convention on the Establishment of an International Fund for Compensation for Oil Pollution Damage 1971
Fund Convention 1992: 1971 Fund Convention as amended by 1992 Protocol
Gard Rules 2018: Gard Rules for Ships 2018
Hague Rules 1924: International Convention for the Unification of Certain Rules of Law relating to Bills of Lading 1924
Hague-Visby Rules 1968: Hague Rules as amended by Protocols of 1968 and 1979
Hague/Visby Rules: Hague Rules and/or Hague-Visby Rules
Hamburg Rules 1978: International Convention on the Carriage of Goods by Sea 1978
Hazardous Waste Directive: EC Council Directive 91/689/EEC on hazardous waste (OJ No L 377, 31 12 1991)
HDPCA: Harbours, Docks and Piers Clauses Act 1847
High Seas 1958: Geneva Convention on the High Seas 1958
HNSC: Convention on Liability and Compensation for Damage in Connection with the Carriage of Hazardous and Noxious Substances by Sea [1996/2010]
Hong Kong Convention: International Convention for the Safe and Environmentally Sound Recycling of Ships 2009
IMDG: International Maritime Dangerous Goods Code
Intervention Convention: International Convention relating to Intervention on the High Seas in Cases of Oil Pollution Casualties 1969 [and its 1973 Protocol]
ISM Code: International Management Code for the Safe Operation of Ships and for Pollution Prevention
LC 1972: Convention on the Prevention of Marine Pollution by Dumping of Wastes and Other Matter 1972 [sometimes "London 'Dumping' Convention"]
LC Protocol 1996: Convention on the Prevention of Marine Pollution by Dumping of Wastes and Other Matter (Protocol) 1996 [LC 1972 as amended by 1996 Protocol]
Limitation Convention 1924: International Convention for the Unification of Certain Rules relating to the Limitation of Liability of Owners of Sea-going Vessels 1924
LLMC 1976: Convention on Limitation of Liability for Maritime Claims 1976
LLMC 1996: Convention on Limitation of Liability for Maritime Claims 1996 [LLMC 1976 as amended by 1996 Protocol]

ABBREVIATIONS

LSSAC: Lloyd's Standard Salvage and Arbitration Clauses
MARPOL: International Convention for the Prevention of Pollution from Ships [1973/1978]
MIA: Marine Insurance Act [1906]
MLC 2006: Maritime Labour Convention 2006
Montreal Convention: Convention for the Unification of Certain Rules for International Carriage by Air 1999
MSA: Merchant Shipping Act [eg 1854, 1894, 1995]
MSMSA 1997: Merchant Shipping Marine Security Act 1997
MTA: Maritime Transport Act 1994 (NZ)
NCP: National Contingency Plan for Marine Pollution from Shipping and Offshore Installations 2014, updated 2017
Offshore Safety Directive 2013: Directive 2013/30/EU on safety of offshore oil and gas operations
OPRC: International Convention on Oil Pollution Preparedness Response and Co-operation 1990
OPRC-HNS Protocol: Protocol on Preparedness, Response and Co-operation to pollution Incidents by Hazardous and Noxious Substances, 2000
OPRS: Convention for the Protection of the Marine Environment of the North-East Atlantic 1992
OSPAR Convention: Convention for the Protection of the Marine Environment of the North-East Atlantic 1992
Paris Convention 1960: Convention on Third Party Liability in the Field of Nuclear Energy 1960
Registration Regulations 1993: Merchant Shipping (Registration of Ships) Regulations 1993 (S.I. No. 3138), as amended by the Merchant Shipping (Registration of Ships) (Amendment) Regulations 1994 S.I. No. (541)
RMA: Resource Management Act 1991 (NZ)
Rome II Regulation: Regulation (EC) No 864/2007 of the European Parliament and of the Council of 11 July 2007 on the law applicable to non-contractual relations (Rome II)
Rotterdam Rules 2008: United Nations Convention on Contracts for the International Carriage of Goods Wholly or Partly by Sea 2008
Salvage Convention 1910: Convention for the Unification of Certain Rules of Law relating to Assistance and Salvage at Sea 1910
Salvage Convention 1989: International Convention on Salvage 1989
SAR 1979: International Convention on Maritime Search and Rescue 1979
Ship Recycling Regulation 2013: Regulation (EU) No 1257/2013 of the European Parliament and of the Council of 20 November 2013
Ship Recycling Requirements Regulations 2018: Ship Recycling (Requirements in relation to Hazardous Materials on Ships) (Amendment etc) Regulations 2018 (SI 2018/122)
Ship Recycling Requirements (EU Exit) Regulations 2019: Ship Recycling (Facilities and Requirements for Hazardous Materials on Ships) (Amendment) (EU Exit) Regulations 2019SI 2019/277)
SOLAS: International Convention for the Safety of Life at Sea 1974
TOMPA: Transport Operations (Marine Pollution) Act 1995 (Qld)
TSWR Regulations: Transfrontier Shipment of Waste Regulations 2007 (SI 2007/1711)
UCH 2001: Underwater Cultural Heritage Convention 2001
UK Carriage of Passengers Regulations 2012: Merchant Shipping (Carriage of Passengers by Sea) Regulations (SI 2012/3152)
UK Club Rules 2018: UK P&I Club *Rules and Articles 2018*
UNCLOS: United Nations Convention on the Law of the Sea 1982

Vienna Convention: Vienna Convention on the Law of Treaties: Vienna Convention on the Law of Treaties 1969

Vienna Nuclear Damage Convention: Convention on Civil Liability for Nuclear Damage 1963

Warsaw Hague Convention 1955: Hague Protocol to Amend the Warsaw Convention for the Unification of Certain Rules Relating to International Carriage by Air 1929

Waste Framework Directive 2008: Directive 2008/98/EC of the European Parliament of the Council of 19 November 2008 on waste and repealing certain Directives [2008] OJ L 312/3 (OJ L 312), 22.11.2008

Waste Regulations 2011: Waste (England and Wales) Regulations 2011 (SI 2011/988)

Waste Shipment Regulation 2006: Regulation (EC) No 1013/2006 of the European Parliament and of the Council (OJ L 190, 12 July 2006)

WRC 2007: Nairobi International Convention on the Removal of Wrecks 2007

WRCA 2011: Wreck Removal Convention Act 2011

YAR: York Antwerp Rules [eg 1974, 2004, 2016]

3. BOOKS, ARTICLES AND OTHER PUBLICATIONS

AG's Rena Cabinet Paper: NZ Cabinet paper of 31 July 2014 by the Attorney General, C Finlayson, www.crownlaw.govt.nz/assets/Uploads/Reports/cabinet-paper.pdf

Aikens: R Aikens, R Lord, M Bools, *Bills of Lading* (2nd ed, Informa, 2015)

Altes: A Altes, "Submarine Antiquities: A Legal Labyrinth" (1976) 4 *Syracuse JICL* 76

Arend: A Arend, "Archaeological and Historical Objects: Implications of UNCLOS III" (1982) 22 *Virginia Journal of International Law* 777

Arnould: J Gilman, C Blanchard, M Templeman, P Hopkins, N Hart, *Arnould: Law of Marine Insurance and Average* (19th ed. Sweet & Maxwell, 2018)

Aznar "Contiguous zone": Aznar "The Contiguous Zone as an Archaeological Maritime Zone" (2014) 29 *International journal of Marine and Coastal Law* 1

Aznar, "Underwater cultural heritage": M Aznar, "The Legal protection of Underwater Cultural Heritage: Concerns and Proposals" in C Espósito, J Kraska, H Scheiber and Moon-Song Kwon, *Ocean Law and Policy: 20 Years under UNCLOS* (Brill Nijhoff, 2017)

Aznar-Gomez: M Aznar-Gomez, "Legal Status of Sunken Warships 'Revisited'" (2001–2002) 8 *Spanish YIL* 1

Aznar & Varmer: M Aznar and O Varmer, "The Titanic as Underwater Cultural Heritage: Challenges to its Legal International Protection" (2013) 44 ODIL 96.

Baltic Ace Wreck Removal: Boskalis website, https://magazine.boskalis.com/issue03/baltic-ace-wreck-removal

Bass: G Bass, *Archaeology under Water* (Penguin Books, 1966)

Bederman: D Bederman, "Rethinking the Legal Status of Sunken Warships" (2000) 31 ODIL 97.

Berlingieri Vol II: F Berlingieri, *International Maritime Conventions: Volume II* (Informa, 2015)

Berlingieri Vol III: F Berlingieri, *International Maritime Conventions: Volume III* (Informa, 2017)

Bills of Lading: Law and Contracts: N Gaskell, Y Baatz, R Asariotis, *Bills of Lading: Law and Contracts* (2000, Informa)

Bishop: A Bishop, "The Development of Environmental Salvage and Review of the London Salvage Convention 1989" (2012) 37 Tul Mar LJ 65.

Blot: J Blot, *Underwater Archaeology: Exploring the World Beneath the Sea* (Thames and Hudson, 1995)

ABBREVIATIONS

Boyle: A Boyle, "Marine pollution under the Law of the Sea Convention" (1985) 79 AJIL 347

Braekhus: S Braekhus, "Salvage of wrecks and wreckage: Legal issued arising from the Rhunde Find" (1976) 20 *Scandinavian Studies in Law* 39

Brice: J Reeder, *Brice on Maritime Law of Salvage* (5th ed, Sweet & Maxwell 2011)

Caflish: L Caflish, "Submarine Antiquities and the International Law of the Sea" (1982) 13 *Netherlands Yearbook of International Law* 3

Carver on Bills of Lading: G Treitel, F Reynolds, *Carver on Bills of Lading* (4th ed, Sweet & Maxwell, 2017)

Carver on Charter Parties: H Bennett et al (eds), *Carver on Charterparties* (2017, Sweet & Maxwell)

Chitty on Contracts: H Beale (ed), *Chitty on Contracts* (32nd ed, Sweet & Maxwell, 2015).

Churchill & Lowe: R Churchill and A Lowe, *The Law of the Sea* (3rd ed, Juris Publishing 1999)

Clarke, Ship Mortgages: A Clarke, "Ship Mortgages", Chap 26 of *Palmer & McKendrick, Interests in Goods*

CMI GA Guidelines: "*CMI Guidelines Relating to General Average*"

CMI Torrey Canyon Report: Report of International Sub-Committee on Torrey Canyon, CMI Documentation 1968 Vol I

Cogliati-Bantz & Forrest: V Cogliati-Bantz and C Forrest, "Consistent: The Convention on the Protection of the Underwater Cultural Heritage and the United Nations Convention on the Law of the Sea" (2013) 2(3) *Cambridge International and Comparative law Journal* 1

Conway: H Conway, *The Law and the Dead* (Routledge, 2016)

De La Rue & Anderson: C De La Rue, C Anderson, *Shipping and the Environment* (2nd ed, Informa, 2009)

Delgado, Encyclopaedia: JP Delgado (ed), *Encyclopaedia of Underwater and Maritime Archaeology* (London: British Museum Press, 1997)

Delgado & Varmer: J Delgado and O Varmer, "The Public Importance of World War I Shipwrecks: Why a State Should Care and the Challenges of Protection" in U Guérin, A Rey Da Silva and L Simmonds, *The Underwater Cultural Heritage from World War I: Proceedings of the Scientific Conference on the Occasion of the Centenary of World War I* (UNESCO, 2015)

Derrington & Turner: S Derrington and J Turner, *The Law and Practice of Admiralty Matters* (2nd ed, OUP, 2016)

DfT, Consultation on Implementation of WRC 2007: DfT, "Consultation on: The UK Implementation and Ratification of the Nairobi International Convention on the Removal of Wrecks, 2007" (May 2008)

DfT, Summary of Responses 2008: DfT, "Summary of Responses to the Consultation on the Draft Marine Navigation Bill" (October 2008)

Dicey & Morris: A Briggs, A Dickinson, J Harris, J McClean, P McEleavy, C McLaughlin and C Morse, *Dicey, Morris and Collins The Conflict of Laws* (15th ed, Sweet & Maxwell, 2012 and 2018 Supplement)

Donaldson Report 1994: *Safer Ships, Cleaner Seas*, Report of Lord Donaldson's Inquiry into the Prevention of Pollution from Merchant Shipping (Cm 2560, HMSO, 1994)

Donaldson Review 1999: Review of Salvage and Intervention and their Command and Control (Cm 4193, 1999).

Dorey: G Dorey, "Rights to wreck in Norman Customary law" (1993) 15 *Guernsey LJ* 63

Dromgoole, "Military Remains": S Dromgoole, "Military Remains On and Around the Coast of the United Kingdom" (1996) 2 IJMCL 23

Dromgoole, "Protection of Historic Wreck": S Dromgoole, "Protection of Historic Wreck: The UK Approach Part II: Towards reform" (1989) 4 IJECL 95

Dromgoole, "Reflections UNESCO": S Dromgoole, "Reflections on the position of the major maritime powers with respect to the UNESCO Convention on the Protection of the Underwater Cultural Heritage" (2013) 38 *Marine Pol*icy 116

Dromgoole, "Titanic": S Dromgoole "The International Agreement for the Protection of the Titanic: Problems and Prospects" (2006) 37 ODIL 1

Dromgoole, Underwater Cultural Heritage: S Dromgoole *Underwater Cultural Heritage and International Law* (CUP, 2013)

Dromgoole, "UNESCO Convention": S Dromgoole *The Protection of Underwater Cultural heritage: National Perspectives in Light of the UNESCO Convention 2001* (Martinus Nijhoff, 2006)

Dromgoole, "United Kingdom": S Dromgoole, "United Kingdom" in S Dromgoole (ed) *The Protection of the Underwater Cultural Heritage: National Perspectives in Light of the UNESCO Convention 2001* (Martinus Nijhoff Publishers, 2006)

Dromgoole & Forrest: S Dromgoole and C Forrest, "The 2007 Nairobi Wreck Removal Convention and Hazardous Historic Shipwrecks", [2009] LMCLQ 92

Dromgoole & Gaskell: S Dromgoole and N Gaskell, "Interests in wreck" in N. Palmer and E. McKendrick, *Interests in Goods* (2nd ed, LLP 1998)

Dromgoole & Gaskell, "Right to Historic Wrecks": S Dromgoole and N Gaskell, "Who has a Right to Historic Wrecks and Wreckage?" (1993) *Int J Cultural Property* 217

Dunt: J Dunt, *Marine Cargo Insurance* (2nd ed, Informa, 2016)

Edelman & Burns, Reinsurance: C Edelman and A Burns, *The Law of Reinsurance* (2nd ed. Oxford University Press, 2013)

Emergency Response and Recovery: HM Government, "Emergency Response and Recovery: Non-statutory guidance accompanying the Civil Contingencies Act 2004" (5th ed, 28 October 2013)

Environment Agency, Tenth anniversary of MSC Napoli: Environment Agency, Press release "Tenth anniversary of the MSC Napoli shipwreck disaster", 18 January 2017

Eustis: F Eustis III, "The Glomar Explorer Incident: Implications for the Law of Salvage" (1975) 16 *Virginia Journal of International Law* 177

Fletcher-Tomenius et al: P Fletcher-Tomenius, P O'Keefe and M Williams, "Salvor in Possession: Friend or Foe to Marine Archaeology" (2000) 9 *International Journal of Cultural Property* 263

Forrest, Protection of Cultural Heritage: C. Forrest, *International Law and the Protection of Cultural Heritage* (Routledge 2010)

Forrest, "South Africa": C Forrest, "South Africa" in S Dromgoole (ed), *The Protection of the Underwater Cultural Heritage: National Perspectives in Light of the UNESCO Convention 2001* (Martinus Nijhoff Publishers, 2006) 247

Gaskell, 1989 Salvage Convention: N Gaskell, "The 1989 Salvage Convention and the Lloyd's Open Form (LOF) Salvage Agreement 1990", 16 Tul Mar LJ 1

Gaskell, Amoco Cadiz I: N Gaskell "The Amoco Cadiz I: Liability Issues" (1985) 3 JENRL 169

Gaskell, Amoco Cadiz II: N Gaskell "The Amoco Cadiz II: Limitation and Legal Implications" (1985) 4 JENRL 225

Gaskell, The Amount of Limitation: N Gaskell, "The Amount of Limitation" in *Limitation of Shipowners' Liability: The New Law (1986)*

ABBREVIATIONS

Gaskell, Bunker Pollution Limitation: N Gaskell "The Bunker Pollution Convention 2001 and limitation of liability" (2009) 15 JIML 477

Gaskell, Compensation for Offshore Pollution: N Gaskell, "Compensation for Offshore Pollution: Ships and Platforms" in Malcolm Clarke (ed) *Maritime Law Evolving* (Hart 2013)

Gaskell, "Interpretation of Maritime Conventions": N. Gaskell, "The Interpretation of Maritime Conventions at Common Law", in J. Gardner (ed.), *United Kingdom Law in the 1990s* (1990)

Gaskell, Liability and Compensation Regimes: Pollution of the High Seas: N Gaskell "Liability and Compensation Regimes: Pollution of the High Seas", R Beckman, M McCreath, J Roach, Z Sun (eds), *High Seas Governance: Gaps and Challenges* (Brill/Nijhoff, 2018)

Gaskell, Limitation of Liability: N Gaskell, "Limitation of liability and division of loss in operation", Appendix 4 of *Marsden and Gault*

Gaskell, Lloyd's Open Form and Contractual Remedies: N Gaskell, "The Lloyd's Open Form and Contractual Remedies" [1986] LMCLQ 306

Gaskell, MSA 1995: N Gaskell, "Merchant Shipping Act 1995" in *Current Law Statutes 1995* (Sweet & Maxwell 1995)

Gaskell, MSMSA 1997: N Gaskell, "Merchant Shipping and Maritime Security Act 1997" in *Current Law Statutes 1997* (Sweet & Maxwell 1997)

Gaskell, Mont Louis Part One: N Gaskell, "Lessons of the Mont Louis Part One: Prevention of Hybrid Accidents" (1986) 1 IJECL 117

Gaskell, New Limits for Passengers: N Gaskell "New Limits for Passengers and Others in the United Kingdom" (1998) LMCLQ 312

Gaskell & Forrest, Marine Pollution Damage: N Gaskell and C Forrest, "Marine Pollution Damage in Australia: Implementing the Bunker Oil Convention 2001 and the Supplementary Fund Protocol 2003" (2008) 27 *UQLJ* 103

Gow: W Gow, *Marine Insurance* (3rd ed, Macmillan, 1903)

Griggs, Convention: P Griggs, "Wreck removal: Draft Convention" (2006) *CMI Yearbook 2005–2006*, 379

Griggs, Legislative Traps: P Griggs, "The Wreck Removal Convention 2007 (WRC 2007) – legislative traps"

Griggs et al: P Griggs, R Williams, J Farr, *Limitation of Liability for Maritime Claims* (4th ed, Informa, 2004)

Gurses, The Law of Marine Insurance: O Gurses, *The Law of Marine Insurance* (2nd ed, Routledge, 2017)

Hazelwood & Semark: S Hazelwood, D Semark, *P&I Clubs: Law and Practice* (4th ed, Informa, 2010)

Herbert, Challenges: J Herbert, *The challenges and implications of removing shipwrecks in the 21st century* (Lloyd's 2013)

House of Lords, WRC Bill Second Reading debate: Earl Attlee, Second Reading of the Wreck Removal Convention Bill in the House of Lords, Hansard Vol 727, col 1134 (13 May 2011)

Hudson & Harvey: G Hudson, M Harvey, *The York-Antwerp Rules: The Principles and Practice of General Average Adjustment* (4th ed, Informa, 2017);

IG MLC 2006 FAQs: International Group Circular of FAQs for Members on the MLC 2006 as amended, "Financial Security Requirements" (10 August 2018)

IMO Status of Treaties: IMO, *Status of IMO Treaties* (16 November 2018) [publication updated monthly: see eg www.imo.org/en/About/Conventions/StatusOfConventions/Pages/Default.asp]

International Sub-Committee Torrey Canyon: Report of International Sub-Committee on Torrey Canyon, CMI Documentation 1968 Vol IUNESCO Review, Underwater Cultural Heritage: UK

ABBREVIATIONS

UNESCO 2001 Convention Review Group, *The UNESCO Convention on the Protection of the Underwater Cultural Heritage 2001: An Impact Review for the United Kingdom* (2014)

Jackson: D Jackson, *Enforcement of Maritime Claims* (4th ed, LLP, 2000)

Kendall-Marsden & O'Donnell: S Kendall-Marsden, U O'Donnell, "Major Casualty Management: Wreck removal and salvage" (Standard Club, August 2018)

Kennedy & Rose: F. Rose, *Kennedy & Rose: Law of Salvage* (9th ed, Sweet & Maxwell, 2017)

Large Casualty Working Group: Executive Summary: IG Large Casualty Working Group Review of Casualties Involving Salvage/Scopic and Wreck Removal 2002–2016

Law of Ship Mortgages: G Bowtle, D Osbourne, C Buss, *Law of Ship Mortgages* (2nd ed, Informa, 2016).

Lewins: K Lewins, *The International Carriage of Passengers by Sea* (Sweet & Maxwell, 2016)

Lillington: S Lillington, "Wreck or wreccum maris?" [1987] LMCLQ 267

Limitation of Liability: The New Law: Institute of Maritime Law (N Gaskell, ed), *Limitation of Shipowners' Liability: The New Law* (Sweet & Maxwell, 1986)

Lobo-Guerrero: Luis Lobo-Guerrero *Insuring War: Sovereignty, security and risk* (Routledge, 2012)

LOC Report: London Offshore Consultants, "Report on the comparisons between Rena and other wreck removal operations in recent years" (9 July 2014): www.crownlaw.govt.nz/assets/Uploads/Reports/wreck-removal-report-3.pdf.

Lowndes & Rudolph: R Cornah, R Sarll, J Shield, *Lowndes & Rudolf: The Law of General Average and The York-Antwerp Rule* (Sweet & Maxwell, 15th ed, 2018)

Machum & Metcalf, Will Insurance Cover That?: A review of the Challenges faced by coastal States Seeking to Recoup Costs for the Removal of wrecks under the Nairobi Wreck Removal Convention" in Chircop et al (eds), *The Regulation of International Shipping: International and Comparative Perspectives*

MAIB, MSC Napoli Report: UK Marine Accident Investigation Board, 'Report on the investigation of the structural failure of *MSC Napoli*, English Channel on 18 January 2007', Accident Investigation Report 9/2008, April 2008

Marine Navigation Bill Consultation 2008: DfT, "Draft Marine Navigation Bill: Consultation Document" (May 2008)

"Marine Pollution Contingency Plan": MMO, Marine Pollution Contingency Plan (2014, updated 2018),

Marine War Risk: M Miller, *Marine War Risks* (3rd ed, LLP 2005)

Marsden: R. Marsden, "Admiralty Droits and Salvage – Gas Float Whitton, No.II" (1899) LX LQR 353

Marsden & Gault: S Gault, S Hazelwood (Gen eds), *Marsden and Gault on Collisions at Sea* (14th ed, Sweet and Maxwell, 2016)

Marten, Maritime Law NZ: B Marten, *Maritime Law in New Zealand*, Thomson Reuters, 2016)

Marten, Third Party Agreements: B Marten, "Third Party agreements in the salvage context" [2014] LMCLQ 497

Martinez Gutierrez: N Martinez Gutierrez, *Limitation of Liability in International Maritime Conventions* (Routledge, 2011)

MCA Response MSC Napoli: UK Maritime and Coastguard Agency 'MSC Napoli Incident, The Maritime and Coastguard Agency's Response', April 2008.

Meeson & Kimbell: N Meeson and J Kimbell, *Admiralty Jurisdiction and Practice* (5th ed, Informa, 2017)

M'Gonigle & Zacher: R M'Gonigle and M Zacher, *Pollution, Politics and International Law: Tankers at Sea* (University of California Press 1979)

Modern Treaty Law: A Aust, *Modern Treaty Law and Practice* (CUP, 2000)

M/S Erika Consequences: D E Somers, G Gonsaeles, "The Consequences of the Sinking of the M/S Erika In European Waters: Towards a Total Loss for International Shipping Law?" 41 JMLC 57

Newton: C Newton, "Finders Keepers? The Titanic and the 1982 Law of the Sea Convention" (1986) 10 *Hastings International and Comparative Law Review* 159

Noppen: R Noppen, *German Commerce Raiders 1914–18* (Osprey Publishers 2015)

Nordquist: M Nordquist, *United Nations Convention on the Law of the Sea 1982: A Commentary* Vol. V (Martinus Nijhoff, Dordrecht, 1989)

Official Records 1969: *Official Records of the International Legal Conference on Marine Pollution Damage* (IMCO, 1973)

Oxman: B Oxman, "The duty to respect generally accepted international standards' (1991) 24 *NYU J Int Law and Politics* 109

Oxman, "Marine Archaeology": B Oxman, "Marine Archaeology and the International Law of the Sea" (1988) 12(3) *Columbia VLA Journal of Law and the Arts* 353

Palmer & McKendrick, Interests in Goods: N Palmer and E McKendrick (eds), *Interests in Goods* (2nd ed, LLP, 1998)

Prott & Srong: L Prott, I Srong, *Background Materials on the Protection of the Underwater Cultural Heritage* (UNESCO Publishing, 1999)

Rainey: S Rainey, *Law of Tug Tow and Offshore Contracts* (4th ed, Informa, 2018)

Rena: Waitangi Final Report: Final Report on the MV Rena and Motiti Island Claims (Waitangi Tribunal Report 2015, WAI 2391, WAI 2393)

Rena: Crown Law 2017 Letter to Ombudsman, "Crown Law Letter of 2 March 2017 to Ombudsman re Final Decision into Inquiry into release of Rena Deeds", www.crownlaw.govt.nz/publications/reports/

Responding to Emergencies: Cabinet Office, "Responding to Emergencies, The UK Central Government Response: Concept of Operations" (updated 2013): https://assets.publishing.service.gov.uk/government/uploads/system/uploads/attachment_data/file/192425/CONOPs_incl_revised_chapter_24_Apr-13.pdf

Reynolds & Tsimplis: B Reynolds, M Tsimplis *Shipowners' Limitation of Liability* (Wolters Kluwer, 2012)

Roach: J Roach, "France Concedes United States has title to CSS Alabama" (1991) 85 AJIL 381

Ronzitti (2011): N Ronzitti, "The Legal regime of Wrecks of Warships and Other State-Owned Ships in International Law" (2011) 74 *Yearbook of the Institute of International Law* 131

Ronzitti (2015): N Ronzitti, "The Legal regime of Wrecks of Warships and Other State-Owned Ships in International Law" (2015) 76 *Yearbook of the Institute of International Law* 267

Rose, General Average: F Rose, *General Average: Law and Practice* (3rd ed, Informa, 2017)

Rose, Marine Insurance: F Rose, *Marine Insurance: Law and Practice* (2nd ed, Informa, 2012)

Rothwell & Stephens: D Rothwell and T Stephens, *The International Law of the Sea* (2nd ed, Hart Publishing 2016)

Rubin: A Rubin, "Sunken Soviet Submarines and Central Intelligence: Laws of Property and the Agency" (1975) 69 *American Journal of International Law* 855

Sassoon: F Lorenzon, Y Baatz, *Sassoon on CIF and FOB Contracts* (6th ed, Sweet & Maxwell, 2017)

Scovazzi: T Scovazzi, "Sunken Spanish Ships before American Courts" (2018) 33 *IJMCL* 1

ABBREVIATIONS

Scrutton: B Eder et al, *Scrutton on Charterparties and Bills of Lading* (23rd ed and 1st Supplement, 2017, Sweet & Maxwell, 2017)

Shearer: I Shearer (ed), D P O'Connell, *The International Law of the Sea, Vol II* (OUP, 2015)

Shipwreck in International and National Law: H Rak, P Wetterstein (eds), *Shipwreck in International and National Law* (Åbo Akademi University, 2008)

Skuld: Skuld, "Contractual wreck removal", 31 August 2018, www.skuld.com/topics/legal/pi-and-defence/contractual-wreck-removal/

Smeele: F Smeele, "International Civil Litigation and the Pollution of the Marine Environment" (with an Annex I translation of the decision by Hens Feilberg of Gorrisen Federspiel Kierkegaard); https://core.ac.uk/download/pdf/18513993.pdf

Somers & Gonsaeles: "The Consequences of the Sinking of the M/S Erika In European Waters: Towards a Total Loss for International Shipping Law?" 41 JMLC, 57

Strati: A Strati, *The Protection of the Underwater Cultural Heritage: An Emerging Objective of the Contemporary Law of the Sea* (Martinus Nijhoff Publishers, 1995)

Swedish Club P&I Guidelines 2012: Swedish Club, *P&I Rules and Exceptions 2012* (3rd ed, 2012)

Tan: A Khee-Jin Tan, *Vessel-Source Marine Pollution* (CUP, 2006)

Throckmorton: P Throckmorton, *The Sea Remembers: Shipwrecks and Archaeology* (Mitchell Beasley, 1987)

Time Charters: T Coghlin et al, *Time Charters* (7th ed, Informa, 2014)

Torrey Canyon Case Study: P Burrows, C Rowley, D Owen, "Torrey Canyon: A Case study In accidental Pollution" Scottish journal of Political Economy Vol XXI, No 3, November 1974

Torrey Canyon Scientific Report: "The Torrey Canyon (Report of the Committee of Scientists on the Scientific and Technical Aspects of the Torrey Canyon Disaster)", Cmnd 3246 (HMSO London 1967)

Transport Committee Ninth Report 2008: House of Commons Transport Committee, "Ninth Report of Session 2007–08, "The Draft Marine Navigation Bill" (19 July 2008)

Tsimplis: M Tsimplis, "Law and jurisdiction for English limitation of liability proceedings" (2010) 16 (4) JIML 289

Tsimplis, Hong Kong Convention: M Tsimplis, "The Hong Kong Convention on the Recycling of Ships" [2010] LMCLQ 305

Van der Kuil: V van der Kuil, "Limitation of liability for maritime claims and Politics: Curse or Cure?" in C Ryngaert, E Molenaar and S Nouwen (eds) *What's Wrong with International Law?* (Brill, 2015)

VanderZwaag: D VanderZwaag, "The International Control of Ocean Dumping" in R Rayfuse (ed) *Research Handbook on International Marine Environmental Law* (Edward Elgar, 2015)

Varmer "United States": O Varmer, "United States of America" in S Dromgoole *The Protection of Underwater Cultural heritage: National Perspectives in Light of the UNESCO Convention 2001* (Martinus Nijhoff, 2006)

Varmer & Blanco: O Varmer and C Blanco, "The Case for Using the Law of Salvage to preserve Underwater Cultural Heritage: The Integrated Marriage of the Law of Salvage and Historic Preservation" (2018) 49 JMLC 401

Vessel-Source Pollution: E Franckx (ed) Vessel-source Pollution and Coastal State Jurisdiction (Kluwer Law International, 2001)

Voyage Charters: J Cooke et al, *Voyage Charters* (4th ed, Informa, 2014)

Wilkinson: D Wilkinson, 'Time to discard the concept of waste?' (1999) 1 Environmental Law Review 172

Williams: M Williams, "War graves and Salvage: Murky Waters?" (2000) 5 IJML 151

Yorke, "UNESCO Convention": R Yorke "The UNESCO Convention and the Protection of Underwater Cultural Heritage in International Waters: The United Kingdom Situation" (2010) 5 *J Maritime Archaeology* 153

Zekala: M Zekala, "Liability and Salvage: Titanic Jurisprudence in United States Federal Court" (2012) 16 *Lewis & Clark LR* 1075

TABLE OF CASES

Ace Imports Pty Ltd v Companhia de Navegacao Lloyd Brasiliero
 (The Esmerelda 1) [1988] 1 Lloyd's Rep 206 (SC NSW)...52
Adamastos Co Ltd v Anglo Saxon Petroleum Co Ltd (The Saxon Star)
 [1959] AC 133, [1958] 1 Lloyd's Rep 73..58
Admiralty Commissioners (The Radstock) v Owners of the SS Volute
 [1922] 1 AC 129, (1921) 9 LL L L Rep 439..92
Aegean Sea Traders Corp v Repsol Petroleo SA (The Aegean Sea) [1998]
 2 Lloyd's Rep 39...12, 61, 100, 102, 104, 105, 137
Aegean Sea, The [1998] 2 Lloyd's Rep 39 ....12, 61, 100, 102, 104, 105, 137
A-G v Glen Line and Liverpool & London War Risks Association
 (1930) 37 Ll L Rep 55 (HL) 235
AIC Ltd v Marine Pilot Ltd (The Archimidis) [2008] 1 Lloyd's Rep 597 61
Akiba on Behalf of the Torres Strait Regional Seas Claim Group v Commonwealth of
 Australia [2013] HCA 33 27
Albionic, The [1941] P 99...223
Alexandra Towing Co Ltd v Millet and Egret (The Bramley Moore) [1964] P 200 107
Algrete Shipping Co Inc v IOPC Fund [2003] 1 Lloyd's Rep 123....................................140
Alhani, The [2018] 2 Lloyd's Rep 563 53
Allgemeine Versicherungs Gesellschaft Helvetia v Administrator of German Property [1931]
 1 KB 67...232
Allianz SpA and Generali Assicurazioni Generali SpA v West Tankers Inc (The Front
 Comor) (Case C-185/07) [2009] 1 AC 1138 203
Alstom Ltd v Liberty Mutual Insurance Co (No 2) [2013] FCA 116 (Fed Ct Australia) ...183
Altair, The [2008] 2 Lloyd's Rep 90..154, 163
Anders Maersk, The [1986] 1 Lloyd's Rep 483..41
Anglo-Algerian SS Co Ltd v Houlder Line Ltd [1908] 1 KB 659 93
Aquila, The (1798) 1 C Rob 36, 165 ER 87 ....211, 212, 223, 224, 240, 330
ARA Libertad Case (Argentina v Ghana), The [2012] ITLOS Rep 21 287
Arabert (No 2), The [1961] 1 Lloyd's Rep 363 104
Arrow Shipping Co Ltd v Tyne Improvement Commissioners (The Crystal)
 [1894] AC 508 ...., 525
Arthur Guinness, Son & Company (Dublin) Ltd v The Freshfield (Owners)
 (The Lady Gwendoleyn) [1965] P 294, [1965] 1 Lloyd's Rep 335......................47, 114
Asfar v Blundell (1895) 1 Com Cas 71, [1896] 1 QB 123 189

TABLE OF CASES

Assens Havn v Navigators Management (UK) Ltd Case C-368/16 (CJEU, 13 July 2017),
  [2018] Lloyd's Rep IR 10 203
Assicurazione Generali v Bessie Morris SS Co [1892] 2 QB 652 ....42, 43
Association and the Romney, The [1970] 2 Lloyd's Rep 5 ....224, 227, 241, 242, 328, 330
Athanasia Comninos, The [1990] 1 Lloyd's Rep 277 ....57, 62, 65
Atlantic Oil Carriers v British Petroleum Co (The Atlantic Duchess) [1957]
  2 Lloyd's Rep 54 62
Att. Gen. v Sir Henry Constable [1601] 5 Co Rep 106a, 77 ER 218 ....211, 212
Auguste Legembre, The [1902] P 123 240
Bahamas Oil Refining Company International Ltd v The Owners of the Cape Bari
  Tankschiffahrts GMBH & Co KG (The Cape Bari) [2016] UKPC 20,
  [2016] 2 Lloyd's Rep 469 ....61, 64, 106,108, 624, 711
Baltic Highway v Przybyla, 7 January 2014 (Isle of Man High Court;
  case ref 78): www.judgments.im/ Content/J1443.htm 120, 123
Baltic Shipping Co v Dillon (1991) 22 NSWLR (NSWCA) (1993) 136 CLR 344 (High
  Court of Australia) 79
Baltimore, Crisfeld & Onancock Line, Inc v United States, 140 F2d 230 (4th Cir 1944) 229
Bank of Nova Scotia v Hellenic Mutual War Risks Association Bermuda Ltd (The Good
  Luck) [1992] 1 AC 233, [1991] 2 Lloyd's Rep 191 179
Barameda Enterprises Pty Ltd v Ronald Patrick O'Connor and KFV Fisheries Pty Ltd
  (The Tiruna) [1987] 2 Lloyd's Rep 666 (Qld Sup Ct) 104
Barker v Janson (1867–1868) LR 3 CP 303 188
Barracuda Tanker Corp, In re, 281 F Supp 228, 231 (SDNY 1968) 9
Barracuda Tanker Corp, In re, 409 F 2d 1013 (2d Cir 1969) 7
Bemis v Lusitania [1995] AMC 1665 (E.D. Va.) 226, 242
Berger and Light Diffusers Pty v Pollock [1973] 2 Lloyd's Rep 442 189
Berkshire, The [1974] I Lloyd's Rep 185 68
Bernina (No 2), The (1886) 12 PD 36 40
Blane Steamships v Minister of Transport [1951] KB 96, [1951] 2 Lloyd's Rep 155 ....42, 59, 232
Blue Nile Shipping Co Ltd v Iguana Shipping and Finance Inc (The Darfur) [2004] 2
  Lloyd's Rep 469, ...105
Bold Buccleugh, The: Harmer v Bell (1850) 7 Moo PCC 267 162
Bosphorus Queen, The [2018] Lloyd's LR 493 ....309, 318
Boston Corporation v France, Fenwick and Co (1923) 28 Com Cas 367 232
Bougues Offshore SA v Caspian Shipping [1998] 2 Lloyd's Rep 461 ....116, 120
BP Exploration Operating Co Ltd v Chevron Shipping (The Chevron North
  America) [2002] 1 Lloyd's Rep 77 ....59, 91
Bradley v Newsom [1919] AC 16 (HL) 212, 223, 224, 330
Braer, Landcatch v IOPC Fund [1999] 2 Lloyd's Rep 316 140
Breydon Merchant, The [1992] 1 Lloyd's Rep 373 ....104, 105
Brondrett v Hentig (1816) Holt NP 149 189
Browner International Ltd v Monarch Shipping Co. Ltd (The European
  Enterprise) [1989] 2 Lloyd's Rep 185 ....55, 113
Cairns v Northern Light House and Calypso Marine [2013] ScotCS CSOH 22 79
Calliope, The [1970] 1 Lloyd's Rep 84 91
Caltex Singapore v BP Shipping Ltd [1996] 1 Lloyd's Rep 286 ....118, 119, 128

Cammell v Sewell (1858) 3 H&N 617; (1860) 5 H&N 728...........215
Canada Rice Mills Ltd v Union Marine & General Insurance Co Ltd (1940)
    67 Ll L Rep. 549...........183
Canadian Pacific Ry Co. v SS Storstad [1919] UKPC 124, [1920] AC 397...........81
Candlewood Navigation Corp v Mitsui OSK Line (The Mineral Transporter and The Ibaraki
    Maru) [1986] AC 1, [1985] 2 Lloyd's Rep 303...........66, 93
Cape Bari, The [2016] 2 Lloyd's Rep 469...........61, 64, 106, 108, 624, 711
Capella, The [1892] P 70 PDAD...........240
Capitan San Luis, The [1993] 2 Lloyd's Rep 573...........113
Caresse Navigation ltd v Zurich Assurances Maroc and Others (The Channel
    Ranger) [2015] 1 Lloyd's Rep 256...........53
Cargo ex Schiller [1877] 2 PD 145, 3 Asp MLC 439 (CA)...........212
Caspian Basin Specialised Emergency Salvage Administration v Bougues Offshore [1997] 2
    Lloyd's Rep 507...........104
Caspiana, The [1956] 2 Lloyd's Rep 379...........40
Cenargo Navigation Ltd and Merchant Ferries Ltd v Harbour of Carlingford Lough
    Improvement Commissioners (The Merchant Venture) [1997] 1 Lloyd's Rep 388...........461
Cendor Mopu, The [2011] 1 Lloyd's Rep 560...........178, 183
Chagos Marine Protected Area Arbitration, In re, Award 18 March 2015...........411
Champion, The (1856) Swa 129...........223, 240
Charlotta, The (1831) 2 Hagg 361...........277
Charlotte, The (1848) 2 W Rob 68...........152
Chevron North America, The [2002] 1 Lloyd's Rep 77...........525
China Pacific v Food Corp of India (The Winson) [1983] AC 939, [1982]
    1 Lloyd's Rep 117...........39, 44, 49
City of Lancaster, The (1929) 34 Ll L Rep 381 (CA)...........240
Clarke v Dunraven (The Satanita) [1897] AC 59...........108
Clifton, The (1834) 3 Hagg 117...........277
CMA CGM SA v Classica Shipping Co Ltd [2004] EWCA 114, [2004]
    1 Lloyd's Rep 460...........57, 61, 98, 105, 106
Cobb Coin Co. v Unidentified, Wrecked and Abandoned Sailing Vessel
    549 F Supp 540 (SD Fla 1982)...........229, 231, 246, 328, 329
Coltman and another v Bibby Tankers Ltd (The Derbyshire) [1988]
    1 Lloyd's Rep 109...........91
Columbus-America Discovery Group v The Unidentified, Wrecked and
    Abandoned Sailing Vessel [1989] AMC 1955, [1990] AMC 2409,
    [1992] AMC 2705, [1995] AMC 1985...........215, 225, 227, 242, 245, 330
Columbus-America Discovery Group, Inc v Atlantic Mutual
    Insurance Company, 42 F Supp 1327, 1990 (ED Va 1990);
    974 F2d 450 (4th Cir 1992)...........229, 237, 246, 247, 329
Comitas, The (1947) 80 Ll L Rep 672...........240
Commission v Italy, Case C-270/03...........695
Commune de Mesquer v Total France SA and Total International Ltd,
    Case C-188/07, Judgment of the Court (Grand Chamber) of
    24 June 2008, [2] [2008] 2 Lloyd's Rep 672...........689-692, 702
Compagnia Maritima San Basilio SA v Oceanus Mutual Underwriting Association

(Bermuda) Limited (The Eurysthenes) [1977] 1 QB 49, [1976]
  2 Lloyd's Rep 171..47, 112, 178
Continental Shelf (Libyan Arab Jamahiriya/Malta) [1985] ICJ Rep 13 304
Cosmopolitan, The (1848) 6 Notes of Cases Suppl. XVII..223
Cossman v West (1887) 13 App Cas 160, 6 Asp MLC 233 (PC) 212, 224, 240, 241, 330
CPC Consolidated Pool Carriers v CTM Cia Transmediterranea SA
  (The CPC Gallia) [1994] 1 Lloyd's Rep 68...709
Crystal, The [1894] AC 504...224, 232
CSAV Compania Sud Americana De Vapores SA v Hin-Pro International Logistics Ltd
  [2015] EWCA 401, [2015] 2 Lloyd's Rep 1..56
Czarnikow Ltd v Koufos (The Heron II) [1969] 1 AC 350, [1967] 2 Lloyd's Rep 457....51
Daina Shipping Co v Te Runanga o Ngati [2012] NZHC 3411, [2013] NZHC 500,
  [2013] 2 NZLR 799..22, 26
Danah, The [1993] 1 Lloyd's Rep 351..64, 69
Dantzic Packet, The (1837) 3 Hagg 383...240, 241
Davis v Stena Line Ltd [2005] EWHC 420 (QB), [2005] 2 Lloyd's Rep 13 82
DC Merwestone, The [2013] 2 Lloyd's Rep 131 (reversed on other grounds,
  [2016] 2 Lloyd's Rep 198)..178
Dee Conservancy Board v McConnell [1928] 2 KB 159 ....92, 524, 528, 555
Deep Sea Maritime Ltd v Monjasa A/S (The Alhani) [2018] EWHC 1495,
  [2018] 2 Lloyd's Rep 563..53
Deep Sea Resources Inc v The Brother Jonathan [1995] AMC 1682 (N.D. Cal.),
  102 F3d 379 (11th Cir.) 225, 226, 242
Delimitation of the Maritime Boundary in the Gulf of Maine (Canada/United
  States of America) [1984] ICJ Rep 246..304
Dominator Limited v Gilberson SL and Others 2009 MLR 161 ....120, 124
Doodeward v Spence (1908) 9 SR (NSW) 107 222
Dornoch Ltd & Ors v Westminster International BV & Ors (The WD
  Fairway (No 3)) [2009] EWHC 1782 (Admiralty), [2009] 2 Lloyd's
  Rep 420 ....192, 196, 233, 707
Dornoch Ltd & Ors v Westminster International BV & Ors (The WD
  Fairway) [2009] EWHC 889 (Admiralty), [2009] 2 Lloyd's Rep 191 ..190, 192, 193, 196,
  214, 215, 707, 708
Douglas, The (1882) 7 PD 751..92
Dunelmia, The [1970] 1 QB 289 62
Duthie v Hilton, LR 4 CP 138...189
Eads v Brazelton, 22 Ark 499 (1861)..330
Effort Shipping Co Ltd v Linden Management SA (The Giannis NK) [1998]
  1 Lloyd's Rep 337..57
Egypt, The (1932) 44 Ll L Rep 21 ....158, 159, 193, 225, 227
Elwes v Brigg Gas Co (1886) 33 Ch D 562...213, 225, 246
Emden, The [1920] 2 Ll L Rep 7 (PDAD)...218
Eridania SpA v Rudolf A Oetker (The Fjord Wind) [1999] 1 Lloyd's Rep 307 43
Esso Petroleum Corp v Southport Corp [1956] AC 218, [1955] 2 Lloyd's Rep 655 ....8, 94, 144
Eurasian Dream, The [2002] 1 Lloyd's Rep 719..48
European Enterprise, The [1989] 2 Lloyd's Rep 185 50

TABLE OF CASES

Eurysthenes, The [1976] 2 Lloyd's Rep 171 .... 47, 112, 178
Fairport International Exploration Inc v The Shipwrecked Vessel Known as
  the Captain Lawrence [1996] AMC 882, aff 'd US App. Lexis 1595 (6th Cir. 1997) 226
Falcke v Scottish Imperial Insurance Co (1886) 34 Ch D 234 152
Federal Commerce and Navigation Co Ltd v Tradax Export SA (The Maratha Envoy) [1978]
  AC 1; [1977] 2 Lloyd's Rep. 301 608
Federal Steam Navigation v Department of Trade and Industry (sub nom The Huntingdon)
  [1974] 1 WLR 505 546
Fibrosa Spolka Alcyna v Fairbairn Lawson Combe Barbour Ltd [1943] AC 32 42
Fibrosa v Fairbairn [1943] AC 32 .... 43, 621
Fiona, The [1993] 1 Lloyd's Rep 257, [1994] 2 Lloyd's Rep 506 58
Firma C-Trade SA v Newcastle Protection and Indemnity Association (The Fanti);
  Socony Mobil Oil Co Inc v West of England Shipowners Mutual Insurance
  Association (London) Limited (No 2) (The Padre Island) [1991] 2 AC 1,
  [1990] 2 Lloyd's Rep 191 .... 201, 202
Flore (1929) 34 Ll L Rep 172 240
Fothergill v Monarch Airlines Ltd [1981] AC 251, [1980] 2 Lloyd's Rep 295 538
Fraser Shipping Ltd v Colton (The Shakir II) [1997] 1 Lloyd's Rep 586 .... 189, 190
Fritz Thyssen, The [1967] 1 Lloyd's Rep 104 .... 70, 91
Fulham, The [1899] P 251 .... 260, 271
Gard Marine & Energy Ltd v China National Chartering Co Ltd (The Ocean
  Victory) [2017] UKSC 35, [2017] 1 Lloyd's Rep 521 .... 60, 62, 64, 105, 106, 176, 460, 624
George Cohen, Sons & Co. v Standard Marine Insurance Co Ltd (1925) 21 Ll L Rep 30 189
Georges Christos Lemos, The, Third Party Proceedings [1991] 2 Lloyd's Rep 107 65
Giannis NK, The [1998] 1 Lloyd's Rep 33 .... 57, 58
Glasgow Packet, The (1844) 2 W Rob 306 240
Glaucus, The (1948) 81 Ll L Rep 262 152
Glencore Energy UK Ltd v Freeport Holdings Ltd (The Lady M) [2017] EWHC 3348,
  [2018] Lloyd's Rep Plus 22, [2019] EWCA Civ 388, [2019] 2 Lloyd's Rep 109 .... 47, 458
Global Marine Exploration v The Unidentified, Wrecked and (for Finders-Right purposes)
  Abandoned Sailing Vessel [2018] AMC 1603 216
Goldman v Thai Airways International Ltd [1983] 1 WLR 1186 113
Good Luck, The [1988] 1 Lloyd's Rep 514 179
Goodwin, Ferreira & Co v Lamport & Holt (1929) 34 Ll L Rep 192 49
Gosse Millerd v Canadian Government Merchant Marine [1929] AC 726 48
Grand Champion Tankers v Norpipe A/S (The Marion) [1984] AC 563, [1984]
  2 Lloyd's Rep 1 47
Great Peace Shipping Ltd v Tsavliris International Ltd (The Great Peace) [2002] EWCA Civ
  1407, [2003] QB 679, [2002] 2 Lloyd's Rep 653 572
Gustaf, The (1862) Lush 506, 508, 167 ER 230 162
Happy Fellow, The [1997] 1 Lloyd's Rep 130 114
Hassel, The [1959] 2 Lloyd's Rep 82 .... 241, 574
Hatteras Inc v The USS Hatteras, 1984 AMC 1094 (SD Tex 1981), aff 'd 698
  F2d 1215 (5th Cir 1982) 229
Hedley Byrne v Heller & Partners Ltd [1964] AC 465 8
Hener v United States 525 F Supp 350 [1982] AMC 847 (SDNY 1981) 224

TABLE OF CASES

Her Majesty the Queen in Right of Ontario v Mar-Dive Corporation et al [1997] AMC 1000 .... 226, 269, 330
Herceg Novi, The and The Ming Galaxy [1998] 2 Lloyd's Rep 454 120
HMS Thetis (1835) 3 Hagg 229, 166 ER 312 .... 158, 212, 224, 330, 398
Homburg Houtimport BV v Agrosin Pte Ltd and Others (The Starsin) [2003] UKHL 12, [2004] 1 AC 715, [2003] 1 Lloyd's Rep 571 41
Hooper v Gumm (1867) LR 2 Ch App 282 214
Houston City, The [1954] 2 Lloyd's Rep 148 62
Industrie Chimiche Italia Centrale v Alexander G Tsavliris & Sons Maritime (The Choko Star No 1) [1987] 1 Lloyd's Rep 508 39
Integrated Container Services Inc v British Traders Insurance Co Ltd [1984] 2 Lloyd's Rep 154 187
Irene M, The [2014] 1 Lloyd's Rep 349 189
Irish Stardust, The (Fed Ct, Canada) [1977] 1 FC 485, [1977] 1 Lloyd's Rep 195 461
J Lauritzen AS v Wijsmuller BV (The Super Servant Two) [1990] 1 Lloyd's Rep 1 .... 40, 43
James Buchanan & Co Ltd v Babco Forwarding & Shipping (UK) Ltd [1978] AC 141, [1978] 1 Lloyd's Rep 119 538
JI Macwilliam Co Inc v Mediterranean Shipping Co SA (The Rafaela S) [20002] EWCA Civ 556, [2003] 2 Lloyd's Rep 113; on appeal [2005] UKHL 11, [2005] 2 AC 423, [2005] 1 Lloyd's Rep 347 .... 41, 45, 709
Johnson v Chapman (1865) 19 CB (NS) 563 173
Jupiter, The [1927] P 250 214
Kairos Shipping Limited v Enka & Co LLC and others (The Atlantik Confidence) [2014] EWCA 21, [2014] 1 Lloyd's Rep 586 120
Kapitan Sakharov, The [2000] 2 Lloyd's Rep 255 57
Kastor Navigations Co Ltd v AGF MAT (The Kastor Too) [2004] EWCA Civ 277; [2004] 2 Lloyd's Rep 119 .... 192, 232, 233
Kenya Railways v Antares Co Pte Ltd (The Antares No.2) [1987] 1 Lloyd's Rep 424 50
KH Enterprise, The (Cargo Owners) v Pioneer Container (Owners) (The Pioneer Container) [1994] 2 AC 324 41
King and Anor v The Owners and All Person Claiming an Interest in the La Lavia, Juliana and Santa Maria de la Vision [1990] 3 IR 413 230
Klein v Unidentified, Wrecked and Abandoned Sailing Vessel, 568 F Supp 1562, 1568 (SD Fla 1983) 329
Klein v Unidentified, Wrecked and Abandoned Sailing Vessel, 758 F2d 1515 (11th Cir 1985) 330
Kodro Shipping Corp v Empresea Cubana de Fletes (The Evia No. 2) [1982] 2 Lloyd's Rep 307 64
Königsberg, The [1920] 2 Ll L Rep 7 218
Kos, The [2012] 2 Lloyd's Rep 292 .... 41, 44, 49, 65
Kulukundis v Norwich Union Fire Insurance Society [1937] KB 1 (1936) 55 Ll L Rep 55 42
Kuwait Maritime Transport Co v Rickmers Linie KG (The Danah) [1993] 1 Lloyd's Rep 351 37
Kuwait Petroleum Corp v I & D Oil Carriers Ltd (The Houda) [1994] 2 Lloyd's Rep 541 64
Kylix, The and the Rustringen [1979] Lloyd's Rep 133 525

TABLE OF CASES

Kyokuyo Co Ltd v AP Moller-Maersk A/S Trading as Maersk Line [2018 EWCA Civ 778, [2018] 2 Lloyd's Rep 59 55
La Lavia, Juliana and Santa Maria de la Vision, In re [1996] 1 Irish Law Reports Monthly 194 331
Lady M, The [2019] 2 Lloyd's Rep 109 .... 47, 458
Lawrence v NCL(Bahamas) Ltd (The Norwegian Jade) [2917] EWCA Civ 2222, [2018] 1 Lloyd's Rep 607 82
Lee v Airtours Holidays Ltd [2004] 1 Lloyd's Rep 683; 80
Leeds Shipping Co Ltd v Société Francaise Bunge (The Eastern City) [1958] 2 Lloyd's Rep 127 61
Leerort, The [2001] 2 Lloyd's Rep 291 113
Lennards v Asiatic Petroleum [1915] AC 705 113
Leon Blum, The [1915] P 290 570
Liffey, The (1887) 6 Asp MLC 255 245
Limnos, The [2008] 2 Lloyd's Rep 166 54
Lindsay v The Wrecked and Abandoned Vessel RMS Titanic, No. 97 Civ. 9248(HB), 1998 WL 557591 (SDNY Sept. 2, 1998) 244
Liver Alkali Co v Johnson (1875) LR 9 Ex 338 67
Loch Tulla, The (1950) 84 Ll L Rep 62 240
London Steamship Owners' Mutual Insurance Association Ltd v Kingdom of Spain & Anor (The Prestige No 2) [2015] EWCA Civ 333, [2015] 2 Lloyd's Rep 33 203
Lucullite, The (1929) 33 Ll L Rep 186 112
Lusitania, The [1986] 1 QB 384 .... 212, 217, 226, 227, 247, 269, 270, 330, 398
Lyrma, The (No.2) [1978] 2 Lloyd's Rep 30 162
Maersk Olie and Gas A/S v Firma M de Haan and W de Boer Case C-39/02, [2005] 1 Lloyd's Rep 210 126
Mahkutai, The [1996] AC 650, [1996] 2 Lloyd's Rep 1 41
Manifest Shipping Co Ltd v Uni-Polaris Insurance Co Ltd and La Réunion Européene Co Ltd (The Star Sea) [2001] UKHL 1, [2003] 1 AC 465, [2001] 1 Lloyd's Rep 389113, 137, 178, 502
Maralunga [1995] Int ML 176 114
Marbig Rexel Pty Ltd v ABC Container Line NV (The TNT Express) [1992] 2 Lloyd's Rep 636 (SCNSW) 52
Marco Gambazzi v DaimlerChrysler Canada Inc (Case C-394/07) [2010] QB 388; [2009] 1 Lloyd's Rep 647 125
Marex Titanic Inc v Wrecked & Abandoned Vessel, 805 F Supp 375 (ED Va 1992) ... 243
Maria, The (1834) 166 ER 364 241
Marion, The [1984] 2 Lloyd's Rep 1 114
Maritime Fish v Ocean Trawlers [1935] AC 524 43
Martha's Vineyard Scuba Headquarters, Inc v Unidentified, Wrecked and Abandoned Steam Vessel, 833 F2d 1059 (1st Cir 1987) 247, 329
Masefield AG v Amlin Corporate Member Ltd (The Bunga Melati Dua) [2011] EWCA Civ 24; [2011] 1 Lloyd's Rep 630 189
Maude, The (1893) 7 Asp 400 239
Mayhew Foods Ltd v Overseas Containers Ltd [1984] 1 Lloyd's Rep 317 49
MDM Salvage, Inc v Unidentified, Wrecked and Abandoned Sailing Vessel, 631 F Supp 308 329

Mediterranean Freight Services Ltd v BP Oil International Ltd (The Fiona) [1993] 1 Lloyd's Rep 257, [1994] 2 Lloyd's Rep 506 57
Merannio, The (1927) 28 Ll L Rep 352 ....156, 157
Meridian Global Funds Management Asia Ltd v Securities Commission [1995] 2 AC 500 114
Metvale Ltd and Another v Monsanto International SARL and Others (The MSC Napoli) [2009] 1 Lloyd's Rep 246 17
Michael v Musgrave (Trading as YNYS Ribs) (The Sea Eagle) [2011] EWHC 1438 (Admlty), [2012] 2 Lloyd's Rep 37 79
Milan, The (1861) Lush 388 95
Millie, The (1939) 64 Ll L R 318 104
Mineral Transporter, The and The Ibaraki Maru [1985] 2 Lloyd's Rep 303 ....66, 93
Miraflores (Owners) v George Livanos (Owners) (The Miraflores and The Abadesa) [1967] 1 AC 826, [1967] 1 Lloyd's Rep 191 92
Mitsui & Co Ltd v Beteiligungsgesellschaft LPG Tankerflotte MBH & Co KG (The Longchamp) [2017] UKSC 68, [2018] 1 Lloyd's Rep 1 171
Morris v Lyonesse Salvage Co Ltd (The Association and The Romney) [1970] 2 Lloyd's Rep 59 ....224, 227, 241, 242, 328, 330
Mostyn, The [1928] AC 57 91
Mount Isa Mines Ltd v The Ship "Thor Commander" [2018] FCA 1326 [2019] 1 Lloyd's Rep 167 ....254, 256, 259, 542, 591
Moyer v Wrecked and Abandoned Vessel, Known as the Andrea Doria, 836 F Supp 1099, (DNJ 1993) 242, 243
MSC Napoli [2009] 1 Lloyd's Rep 246 ....17, 56, 98, 105, 110
MSC Rosa M [2000] 2 Lloyd's Rep 339 113
MT Tojo Maru (Owners) (her cargo & freight) v NV Bureau Wijsmuller, The Tojo Maru [1972] AC 242, sub nom. NV Bureau Wijsmuller v Tojo Maru (Owners), The Tojo Maru [1971] 1 Lloyd's Rep 341 ....47, 106, 143, 153, 158, 556, 574, 578
MV Brillante Virtuoso, The [2015] 1 Lloyd's Rep 651 ....186, 187, 190, 196
Nagasaki Spirit, The [1997] 1 Lloyd's Rep 323 ....161, 575, 582
National Justice Companiera Naviera SA v Prudential Assurance Co Ltd (The Ikarian Reefer) [1995] 1 Lloyd's Rep 455 177
Nema, The [1982] AC 724 621
New Hampshire Insurance Company v MGN Ltd [1996] EWHC 398 (Comm), [1997] LRLR 24 179
Ngai Te Hapu Inc v Bay of Plenty Regional Council [2017] NZEnvC 073 ....19-26, 320
Niarchos v Shell Tankers [1961] 2 Lloyd's Rep 496 43
Nissos Amorgos: see Assuranceforeningen Gard Gjensidig v The International Oil Pollution Compensation Fund 1971 [2014] EWHC 3369 (Comm), [2014] 2 Lloyd's Rep 219 139
Noble Resources Ltd and Unirise Development Ltd v Greenwood (The Vasso) [1993] 2 Lloyd's Rep 309 187
Nordsjø Dykker Co v Høvding Skipsopphugging (1970) 135 Norsk Retstidende 346 (Norwegian Supreme Court) 229
Norfolk v Mytravel [2004] 1 Lloyd's Rep 106 80
Norman, The [1960] 1 Lloyd's Rep 1 113
North Sea Continental Shelf Case [1969] ICJ Rep 3 303
Northern Shipping Co v Deutsche Seereederei GmBH (The Kapitan Sakharov) [2000] 2

TABLE OF CASES

Lloyd's Rep 255...51
Northern Territory v Mr A Griffiths (deceased) and Lorraine Jones on Behalf of the
 Ngaliwurru and Nungali Peoples [2019] HCA 7..24
Nugent v Smith (1876) 1 CPD 421..67
Ocean Crown, The [2010] 1 Lloyd's Rep 468...160
Ocean St. Nav. Co Ltd v Evans (1934) 40 Com Cas 108 232
Ocean Victory, The [2017] 1 Lloyd's Rep 521 ....60, 62, 64, 105, 106, 176, 460, 624
Oceangas Gibraltar Ltd v Port of London Authority (The Cavendish) [1993]
 2 Lloyd's Rep 292...438
Oceanic Co. v Evans (1934) 40 Com Cas 111..232
Odyssey Marine Exploration, Inc v Unidentified Shipwrecked Vessel 675 F Supp 2d 1126
 (MD Fla 2009), aff 'd 657 F3d 1159 (11th Cir 2011)....................................221, 227, 231, 242, 293
Oil Spill by the Amoco Cadiz, In re, 954 F2d 1279 (7th Cir 1992)...11
Olympic, The [1913] P 92...211
Owners of Cargo Lately Laden on Board the Tatry v Owners of the Maciej Rataj (Case
 C-406/92) [1999] QB 515, [1995] 1 Lloyd's Rep 302 125
Owners of Cargo on Board The Merak v The Merak (Owners) (The Merak) [1965] P 223
 [1965] 2 Lloyd's Rep 527..53
Owners of Mitero Marigo v Owners of Fritz Thyssen (The Fritz Thyssen) [1967] 1 Lloyd's
 Rep 104, 112, [1967] 2 Lloyd's Rep 199...70, 91
P & O Braer [1999] 2 Lloyd's Rep 534 140
P Samuel & Co Ltd v Dumas [1924] AC 431..179
Paal Wilson & Co v Partenreederei Hannah Blumenthal (The Hannah Blumenthal) [1983] 1
 AC 854, 909, [1983] 1 Lloyd's Rep 103 42
Palm Branch, The [1916] P 230, [1919] AC 272..234
Papera Traders Co. Ltd v Hyundai Merchant Marine Co Ltd (The Eurasian Dream) [2002]
 EWHC 118 (Comm), [2002] 1 Lloyd's Rep 719...46
Parker v British Airways Board [1982] QB 1004..246
Parlement Belge, The (1880), 5 PD 197..287
Parsons Corporation v CV Scheepvaartonderneming "Happy Ranger" (The Happy Ranger)
 [2002] EWCA Civ 694, [2002] 2 Lloyd's Rep 357...709
Pegase, The [1981] 1 Lloyd's Rep 175..52
Pergo, The [1987] 1 Lloyd's Rep 582 (Ct Sn)..223
Perks v Clark (Inspector of Taxes) [2001] 2 Lloyd's Rep 431 98
Petroleo Brasileiro SA v ENE Kos 1 Ltd (The Kos) [2012] UKSC 17, [2012] 2 AC 164,
 [2012] 2 Lloyd's Rep 292...41, 44, 49, 65
Pierce v Bemis (The Lusitania) [1986] QB 384 ....212, 217, 226, 227, 247, 269, 270, 330, 398
Pioneer Shipping v BTP Tioxide (The Nema) [1982] AC 724, [1981] 2 Lloyd's Rep 239................43

Platoro Ltd, Inc v The Unidentified Remains of a Vessel, 614 F2d 1051, 1055–56 (5th Cir
 1980); (1981) 518 F Supp 816; 1981 AMC 1087,...229, 231, 329
Polemis v Furness, Withy and Co Ltd, In re [1921] 3 KB 560..66
President of India v Metcalfe Shipping Co. (The Dunelmia) [1970] 1 QB 289......................45, 709
Prins Frederick, The (1820) 2 Dod 451 289
Product Star, The (No 2), [1991] 2 Lloyd's Rep 468..66
Provincial Insurance Co of Canada v Leduc (1874) LR 6 PC 224..192

TABLE OF CASES

Case	Pages
Putbus, The [1969] P 136, 150, 153, [1969] 1 Lloyd's Rep 253	104, 524, 536
Pyrene Ltd v Scindia Steam Navigation Co Ltd [1954] 2 QB 402	49
Qenos Pty v Ship APL Sydney [2009] FCA 1090	93, 101
R (On the Application of Fogg) v The Secretary of State for Defence [2006] 2 Lloyd's Rep 576	282
R v Forty-Nine Casks of Brandy (1836) 3 Hagg Adm 257, 166 ER 401	212, 268
R v Goodwin [2006] 1 Lloyd's Rep 432	98
R.M.S. Titanic, Inc v The Wrecked and Abandoned Vessel ("Titanic I"), 924 F Supp 714 (ED Va 1996) 1106 (DNJ 1993)	243
R.M.S. Titanic, Inc v The Wrecked and Abandoned Vessel, 435 F3d 521 (4th Cir 2006)	244, 247
R.M.S. Titanic, Inc v The Wrecked and Abandoned Vessel, 531 F Supp 2d 691 (ED Va 2007)	244
R.M.S. Titanic, Inc v The Wrecked and Abandoned Vessel, 742 F Supp 2d 784 (ED Va 2010)	237
R.M.S. Titanic, Inc v The Wrecked and Abandoned Vessel, 804 F Supp 2d 508 (ED Va 2011)	245, 246
R.M.S. Titanic, Inc v The Wrecked and Abandoned Vessel, 9 F Supp 2d 624 (ED Va 1998)	244
R.M.S. Titanic, Inc v The Wrecked and Abandoned Vessel, Civ. No. 2:93cv902 (ED Va July 28, 2000)	244
R.M.S. Titanic, Inc v The Wrecked and Abandoned Vessel, No. 2:93CV902, 1996 WL 650135 (ED Va Aug. 3, 1996)	244
Rafaela S, The [2005] UKHL 11, [2005] 2 AC 423, [2005] 1 Lloyd's Rep 347	45, 709
Reardon Smith Line v Australian Wheat Board (The Houston City) [1956] AC 266, [1954] 2 Lloyd's Rep 14	61
Renos, The [2019] UKSC 29 [2019] 2 Lloyd's Rep 78 (SC), [2018] 1 Lloyd's Rep 285 (CA)	168, 169, 190, 191, 196
Renton GH & Co Ltd v Palmyra Trading Corp (The Caspiana) [1957] AC 149, [1956] 2 Lloyd's Rep 379	40
River Gurara, The [1996] 2 Lloyd's Rep 53	55
River Wear Commissioners v Adamson (1877) 2 App Cas 743	91, 525
Riverstone Meat Co Pty v Lancashire Shipping Co (The Muncaster Castle) [1961] AC 807	46
Robinson v Western Australian Museum (1977) 51 ALJR 806, (1977) 138 CLR 283	225, 227, 229, 245
Rosa S, The [1988] 2 Lloyd's Rep 574	54
Rose v Miles (1815) 4 M&S 101	94, 524
Roux v Salvador (1836) 3 Bing NC 266	188
Royal Boskalis Westminster NV v Mountain [1997] 1 Lloyd's Reins L Rep 523	191
Russland, The [1924] P 55	162
Saint Jacques II, The [2003] 1 Lloyd's Rep 203	113
Saipem SpA v Dredging VO2 BV (The Volvox Hollandia (No 1)) [1988] 2 Lloyd's Rep 361	125
Salem, The [1983] 1 Lloyd's Rep 342	182, 184, 656
Salt Union Ltd v Wood [1893] 1 QB 370	449
Salvage Association, Re The [2003] EWCH (Ch) 1028	216
Sarah Bell, The (1845) 4 Notes of Cases 144	223

Schooner Exchange v McFaddon (1812) 7 Cranch 116 287
Sea Angel, The [2007] EWCA Civ 547; [2007] 2 Lloyd's Rep 517..........................42, 572, 591, 592
Sea Eagle, The [2012] 2 Lloyd's Rep 37 ....79, 89, 97, 449
Sea Hunt Inc v The Unidentified Shipwrecked Vessel or Vessels etc 47 F Supp
  2d 678 (ED Va 1999)..221, 231, 247
Sea Hunt, Inc v Unidentified Shipwrecked Vessel or Vessels, 221 F3d 634
  (4th Cir 2000), cert. denied, 148 L Ed 2d 956, 121 S Ct 1079 (2001) 221, 227, 229
Seawheel Rhine/Assi Eurolink case Hoge Raad First Chamber, 29 September
  2006, No C05/147 HRJ MH/MK (2007) Schip & Schade 1 ....123, 126, 128
Select Commodities Ltd v Valdo SA (The Florida) [2007] 1 Lloyd's Rep 1 43
Sellers Fabrics Pty Ltd v Hapag-Lloyd AG (The Encounter Bay) [1998] NSWSC 644................113
Semco Salvage & Marine Pte Ltd v Lancer Navigation Co Ltd (The Nagasaki Spirit) [1997]
  1 Lloyd's Rep 323..165
Seven Seas Transportation Ltd v Pacifico Union Marina Corp (The Satya Kailash) [1984] 1
  Lloyd's Rep 588..66
Shakir II, The [1997] 1 Lloyd's Rep 586 195
Shell International Petroleum Co Ltd v Gibbs (The Salem) [1983] 1 Lloyd's Rep 342 181
Shipowners' Mutual Protection and Indemnity Association (Luxembourg) v Containerships
  Denizcilik Nakliyat Ve Ticaret A.S. (The Yusuf Cepnioglu) [2015] EWHC 258 (Comm),
  [2015] 1 Lloyd's Rep 267; on appeal [2016] EWCA Civ 386, [2016] 1 Lloyd's
  Rep 641..202, 203
Sidhu v British Airways Plc [1997] AC 430, [1997] 2 Lloyd's Rep 76..................................80, 82
Silver Bullion (Cargo ex Sir Robert Peel) (1854) 2 Spinks E&A 70...277
Simon v Taylor [1975] 2 Lloyd's Rep 338 ....217, 223, 224, 226, 227, 229, 291, 331
Simpson v Thompson (1877) 3 App Cas 279 232
Smit Tak Offshore Services v Youell and General Accident Fire & Life Assurance
  Co PLC [1992] 1 Lloyd's Rep 154...207
Smit v Joseph Mobius [2001] 2 All ER (Comm) 265...109
Smjeli, The [1982] 2 Lloyd's Rep 74..107
Societe Anonyme des Minerals v Grant Trading Inc (The Ert Stephanie) [1989] 1 Lloyd's
  Rep 349..113
Spar Shipping AS v Grand China Logistics Holding (Group) Co Ltd (The Star Capella, Spar
  Vega and Spar Draco) [2016] EWCA CIV 982 [2016] 2 Lloyd's Rep 447..........................622
Spiliada Maritime Corp v Cansulex Ltd (The Spiliada) [1987] AC 460, [1987]
  1 Lloyd's Rep 1...56
Spiliada, The [1987] AC 460, [1987] 1 Lloyd's Rep 1 118
Stag Line v Foscolo Mango [1932] AC 328 50
Standard Steamship Owners' Protection and Indemnity Association (Bermuda) Ltd v GIE
  Vision Bail & Ors [2004] EWHC (Comm) 2919 208
Star Sea, The [1997] 1 Lloyd's Rep 360, [2001] 1 Lloyd's Rep 38..........................113, 137, 178, 502
Starsin, The [2004] 1 AC 715, [2003] 1 Lloyd's Rep 571 68
State by Erwin v Massachusetts Co., 95 So 2d 902 (Fla 1956)..229
Steamship Imo v La Compagnie Generale Transatlantique (1920) 2 Ll L Rep 188 (PC) 144
Steedman v Scofield [1992] 2 Lloyd's Rep 163 79
Stonedale No 1, The [1956] AC 1..104
Stoormvaart Maatschappy Nederland, The v Peninsular and Oriental Steam Navigation

Company (The Voorwaarts and The Khedive) (1880) 5 App Cas 795 94
Strong Wise Limited v Esso Australia Resources Pty Ltd [2010] FCA 240, [2010] 2 Lloyd's
    Rep 555 .... 111, 112
Subaqueous Exploration & Archaeology Ltd v The Unidentified, Wrecked and Abandoned
    Vessel, 577 F Supp 597 (D Md 1983) 330
Subro Valour, The [1995] 1 Lloyd's Rep 509 52
Suez Fortune Investments Ltd and Piraeus Bank AE v Talbot Underwriting Ltd [2016]
    EWHC 1085 (Comm) 178, 187
Suez Fortune Investments Ltd and Piraeus Bank AE v Talbot Underwriting Ltd and Anor
    [2018] EWHC 2929 (Comm) 178, 187
Suez Fortune Investments Ltd v Talbot Underwriting Ltd (The M/V Brillante Virtuoso)
    [2015] 1 Lloyd's Rep 651 ....178, 187
Sveriges Angfartygs Assurans Forening (The Swedish Club) v Connect Shipping
    (The Renos) [2019] UKSC 29 [2019] 2 LLoyd's Rep 78 ....168, 169, 190, 191, 196
Svitzer Salvage BV v Z Energy Ltd (recall) [2013] NZHC 3541 (20 December 2013) 571
Svitzer Salvage BV v Z Energy Ltd (reissue) [2013] NZHC 2584 ....19, 20, 571
Sylvia, The [2010] 2 Lloyd's Rep 81 66
Tasman Orient Line CV v New Zealand China Clays Ltd (The Tasman Pioneer) [2010] 2
    Lloyd's Rep 13 48-49
Tasman Pioneer, The [2010] 2 Lloyd's Rep 13 48-49
Tate & Lyle Food Distribution Ltd v Greater London Council [1983] 2 AC 509 [1983] 2
    Lloyd's Rep 117 ....94, 524
Texaco Southampton, The [1983] 1 Lloyd's Rep 94 (NSWCA) 570
Thomas v Harrowing SS Co [1915] AC 58 40
Thompson v One Anchor and Two Anchor Chains, 221 F 770 (WD Wis 1916) 330
Thor Commander, The [2019] 1 Lloyd's Rep 167 ....254, 256, 542, 259, 591
Thor Shipping A/S v Ship Al Duhail (2008) 173 FCR 524 214
Through Transport Mutual Insurance Association (Eurasia) Ltd v New India Assurance Co.
    Ltd (The Hari Blum No 1) [2003] EWHC 3158 (Comm), [2004] 1 Lloyd's Rep 206,
    [2005] 1 Lloyd's Rep 67 203
Thyssen Inc v Calypso Shipping Corporation SA [2000] 2 Lloyd's Rep 243 53
Tisand Pty Ltd v Owners of the Ship MV Cape Morton (ex Freya) (2005) 143 FCR 43 214
Titanic, The, 209 F. 501 (1913 SDNY 2d Cir.), aff'd 233 U.S. 718 (1914) 96
Tojo Maru, The [1972] AC 242 ....47, 106, 143, 153, 158, 556, 574, 578
Tracomin v Sudan Oil Seeds (No 2) [1983] 3 All E.R. 140 56
Tramontana II, The [1969] 2 Lloyd's Rep 94 525
Transfield Shipping Inc v Mercator Shipping Inc (The Achilleas) [2009] AC 61, [2008] 2
    Lloyd's Rep 275 66
Treasure Salvors Inc v The Unidentified, Wrecked and Abandoned Sailing Vessel [1981]
    AMC 1529 (Salvors II), [1981] AMC 1857 (Salvors III) 215, 229, 230, 245, 247, 269, 286
Treasure Salvors, Inc v Unidentified, Wrecked and Abandoned Sailing Vessel, 408 F Supp
    907 (SD Fla 1976) 231
Treasure Salvors, Inc v Unidentified, Wrecked and Abandoned Sailing Vessel, 569 F2d 330,
    337 (5th Cir 1978) 229, 230, 329
Trustees Executors and Agency Cp Ltd v Inland Revenue Commissioners [1973] Ch 254 214
Tsilhqot'in Nation v British Columbia [2014] SCC 44 442

Tubantia, The (1924) P 78, 18 Ll L Rep 158 .... 159, 212, 224, 226, 241, 242, 287, 330, 398
Unique Mariner (No 2), The [1979] 1 Lloyd's Rep 37 .... 153, 239, 572, 574, 578, 580
Unique Mariner, The [1978] 1 Lloyd's Rep 438...153, 572
United Kingdom v Albania, [1949] ICJ Rep 4 422
United States v Steinmetz, 763 F Supp 1293 (DNJ 1991), aff 'd 973 F2d 212 (3d Cir 1992),
    cert. denied 113 S Ct 1578 (1993) 217, 229
Universe Tankships of Monrovia v International Transport Workers Federation
    [1983] 1 AC 366 637
Uno case Decision of 11 May 2005 ....122, 123, 126
Venetico Marine SA v International General Insurance Co Ltd (The Irene M) [2014] 1
    Lloyd's Rep 349..189
Veritas, The [1901] P 304..162
Vinnlustodin HF v Sea Tank Shipping AS (The Aqasia) [2018] EWCA Civ 276, [2018] 1
    Lloyd's Rep 530...54, 710
Vishbha Abha, The [1990] 2 Lloyd's Rep 3112; The Herceg Novi and The Ming Galaxy
    [1998] 2 Lloyd's Rep 254 119
Volcafe Ltd and others v Compania Sud Americana de Vapores SA [2018]
    UKSC 61, [2019] 1 Lloyd's Rep 21 ....46, 50, 51, 63, 64
Volvox Hollandia [1988] 2 Lloyd's Rep 361 120
WD Fairway [2009] EWHC 889 (Admiralty); [2009] 2 Lloyd's Rep 191 ....192, 233
Wells v The Gas Float Whitton No 2 [1897] AC 337, 8 Asp MLC 272 (HL) 212
West Tankers Inc v Allianz SpA (The Front Comor) (Case C-185–07) [2009]
    AC 1138...56
Western Regent, The [2005] EWCA (Civ), [2005] 2 Lloyd's Rep 359 .... 116, 119, 120
Whistler International v Kawasaki Kisen Kaisha (The Hill Harmony) [2001]
    1 AC 638, [2001] 1 Lloyd's Rep 147..64
White v Crisp (1854) 10 Ex 312 224
Wiggins v 1100 Tons, More or Less, of Italian Marble (The Clythia), 186 F Supp
    452 (ED Va 1960) 330
Winpenny and Chedester v Philadelphia 65 Pa. 135 (1870)...224
World Harmony, The [1967] P 341 ....66, 93
Yemgas FZCO v Superior Pescadores SA Panama (The Superior Pescadores) [2016]
    EWCA Civ 101, [2016] 1 Lloyd's Rep 561..54
Yusuf Cepnioglu, The [2016] 1 Lloyd's Rep 641 203
Zaanland, The [1918] P 303..234
Zeta, The (1875) 21 TLR 648 ....223, 245, 272
Zych v Unidentified, Wrecked and Abandoned Vessel Believed to be
    The Seabird [1993] AMC 2201 (ND Ill) [1994] AMC 2672 (7th Cir.) 225, 227
Zych v Unidentified, Wrecked and Abandoned Vessel, 755 F Supp 213 (ND Ill 1990)................247

TABLE OF LEGISLATION

Abandoned or Hazardous Vessels Act 2019 (Can) 523, 548
Abandoned Shipwreck Act 1987 (US)..229, 269, 286, 350
   s 2102...213
Administration of Justice Act 1956..8
Aircraft (Wreck and Salvage) Order 1938 (SR & O 1938/136)
   Art 2 159
   Art 3 159
Aircraft (Wrecks and Salvage) Order (1938), Art 2(b) (SR&O 1938/136) 212
Ancient Monuments and Archaeological Areas Act 1979 ....285, 286
   s 2 285
   s 53(1) 285
   s 53(2) 285
   s 61(7) 285
Antiquities Act (US) 350
Arbitration Act 1996
   s 12 53
Archaeological Resources Protection Act (US)...350
Basel Convention on Transboundary Movement of Hazardous
   Wastes and their Disposal 1989 (Basel Convention)..........669, 670, 673, 674, 675, 676, 679, 680
   Art 1.1 671
   Art 1.3 672
   Art 2 672
   Art 2.1 671
   Art 2.3 671
   Art 2.8 671
   Art 2.10 671
   Art 4.7(c) 671
   Art 6 671
   Art 6.3 671
   Art 6.9 671
   Art 7 672
Bonn Agreement for cooperation in dealing with pollution of the North Sea by oil
   and other harmful substances 1983 ....249, 657
Brussels Convention for the Unification of Certain Rules Concerning the Immunity
   of State-owned Ships 1926 288

Brussels Convention on the Liability of Operators of Nuclear Ships 1962 ... 521
Carriage of Goods by Sea Act 1936 (US) ... 54, 67
Carriage of Goods by Sea Act 1971 ... 44, 710
 s 1A ... 54
 s 1(3) ... 45
Carriage of Goods by Sea Act 1991 (Cth, Australia)
 s 11 ... 53
Carriage of Goods by Sea Act 1992 ... 51
 s 1(3) ... 45
 s 3(1) ... 58
 s 3(3) ... 58
Carriage of Passengers Regulations 2012 ... 78, 89
Chichester Harbour Conservancy Act 1971 ... 527
 ss 43–44 ... 528
Civil Aviation Act 1982
 s 87 ... 159
 s 87(4) ... 159
Civil Contingencies Act 2004 ... 263, 265
Civil Procedure Rules 1998 (SI 1998/3132)
 r 61.11(18) ... 120
 r 61.11(19) ... 116
Coast Protection Act 1949 ... 665
Comhairle nan Eilean Siar (Ardveenish) Harbour Revision Order 2000 (SI 2000/233) ... 561
 Art 33(1) ... 528
 Art 33(2) ... 528
 Art 34 ... 529
 Art 34(7) ... 529
 Art 35 ... 560
Commission Decision 96/350/EC of 24 May 1996 adapting Annexes IIA and IIB to Council
 Directive 75/442/EEC on waste [1996] OJ L 135/32 ... 686
Companies Act 2006 (Consequential Amendments, Transitional Provisions and
 Savings) Order 2009 (SI 2009/2860) ... 732
 Art 152(5) ... 261
Constitutional Reform Act 2005 Sch 11 ... 734
Consumer Insurance (Disclosure and Representations) Act 2012 ... 174, 193
Consumer Protection Act 2015
 s 2 ... 607
 s 224(1) ... 154
Consumer Rights Act 2015 ... 80, 89
Continental Shelf (Designation of Areas) Order 2013 (SI 2013/3162) ... 665
Contracts (Rights of Third Party) Act 1999 ... 172
 s 1 ... 614
Control of Pollution (Amendment) Act 1989 ... 693, 696
Controlled Waste (England and Wales) Regulations 2012 (SI 2012/811) ... 701
 reg 3 ... 701
 Sch 11 ... 701

TABLE OF LEGISLATION

Controlled Waste (Registration of Carriers and Seizure of Vehicles) Regulations 1991 (SI 1991/1624) 693
Convention for the Prevention of Marine Pollution by Dumping from Ships and Aircraft (Oslo Convention) 1972 663
Convention for the Protection of the Marine Environment of the North-East Atlantic 1992 (OSPAR) 249, 321, 660, 663, 667
Art 1(f) 664
Art 1(o) 664
Art 2 ....663, 664
Art 3(1) 664
Art 3(2) 664
Art 4 664
Art 7 664
Art 8 664
Art 9 664
Art 21 664
Art 22 664
Convention for the Suppression of Unlawful Acts Against the Safety of Maritime Navigation 1988 369
Convention for the Unification of Certain Rules for International Carriage by Air 1999 (Montreal Convention 1999) 78, 83, 88, 112
Art 52 86
Convention for the Unification of Certain Rules of Law relating to Assistance and Salvage at Sea 1910 (Salvage Convention 1910) 153, 581
Art 3 ....577, 578
Art 7 153
Art 8 152
Art 11 152
Art 14 289
Convention for the Unification of Certain Rules of Law with respect to Collisions between Vessels 1910 (Collision Convention) 94, 95
Convention on Civil Liability for Nuclear Damage 1963 (Nuclear Damage Convention) 132, 375, 521
Convention on Conditions for Registration of Ships 1986 416
Convention on Fishing and Conservation of the Living Resources of the High Seas 1958 ....295, 299
Convention on International Civil Aviation 1944 403
Convention on Limitation of Liability for Maritime Claims 1976 (LLMC 1976) 21, 25, 84, 90, 96, 97, 111, 119, 122, 126, 128, 158, 395, 502, 505, 514, 532, 535
Art 1(2) 97
Art 1(6) 503, 504, 508
Art 2 ....8, 526
Art 2(1)(d) 115, 440
Art 2(1)(e) 115, 440
Art 2(2) 440

Art 2(d) 399
Art 4 506
Art 6 493
Art 6(1)(b) 493, 503, 508
Art 6(5) 493, 494
Art 15(5)(b) 401
Art 18 ...... 22, 503
Art 18(1) 119
Art 20 ...... 508, 509
Art 21 508
Convention on Limitation of Liability for Maritime Claims 1996 as amended by
    1996 Protocol (LLMC 1996) 21, 46, 55, 57, 84, 90,
    96, 97, 100, 111, 119, 125, 126, 131, 133, 142–147, 151, 158, 364, 369, 402, 439, 493, 505, 509,
    513–517, 520, 521, 531, 532, 535, 554, 690, 693
Art 1 ...... 109, 137, 448
Art 1(1) 98
Art 1(2) 98
Art 1(3) 106, 107, 256
Art 1(4) 98, 106
Art 1(6) 98, 203, 498, 503, 504, 508, 552
Art 2 ...... 8, 98–101, 105, 107, 109, 116, 129, 526
Art 2(1)(a) 91, 99, 100, 101, 104, 115, 116, 130, 489, 516
Art 2(1)(c) 100, 115, 130, 489, 516, 575
Art 2(1)(d) 100–107, 114–116, 121–124, 130, 206, 440, 489, 516, 562
Art 2(1)(e) 100–107, 114, 115, 123, 124, 130, 206, 440, 490, 516, 554
Art 2(1)(f) 100–102, 107
Art 2(2) 103, 105, 108, 440
Art 3 ...... 112, 129, 130
Art 3(5) 107
Art 3(a) 103, 104, 108, 575
Art 3(b) 100
Art 3(e) 72, 99
Art 4 ...... 113, 119, 506
Art 6 ...... 72, 99, 109, 122, 545
Art 6(1)(a) 77, 111
Art 6(1)(b) 54, 111, 117, 490, 492, 503, 508, 510–514, 553
Art 6(1)(d) 108
Art 6(1)(e) 108
Art 6(1)(f) 108
Art 6(2) 77, 554
Art 6(4) 107, 624
Art 6(5) 109
Art 6(a)(b) 109
Art 7 ...... 84, 85, 86, 99, 109
Art 7(1) 84
Art 8 ...... 109, 510

TABLE OF LEGISLATION

Art 8(6) 514
Art 10 122
Art 10(1) 116
Art 10(2) 115
Art 11 ....116, 118
Art 11(1) 120, 127
Art 11(3) 117
Art 12 118
Art 12(2) 119
Art 12(4) 119
Art 13 118
Art 13(1) 118, 122, 123, 124, 124, 127
Art 13(2) 118, 124
Art 14 117
Art 15 ....130, 503
Art 15(1) 123
Art 15(2)(b) 130
Art 15(3)bis 85
Art 15(4) 97
Art 15(5) 448
Art 15(5)(a) 97
Art 15(5)(b) 97, 129
Art 18 ....105, 119, 121, 122, 124, 490, 503, 506, 508, 510, 532, 553
Art 18(1)(b) 100, 103, 114, 119, 130
Art 19 125
Art 25(1) 112
Convention on the Continental Shelf 1958 ....295, 299
Art 2(1) 303
Convention on the High Seas 1958 ....295, 298, 299, 305
Art 10 307
Art 24 295
Convention on the Means of Prohibiting and Preventing the Illicit Import,
    Export and Transfer of Ownership of Cultural Property 1970
Art 5 341
Art 10 342
Art 13 341
Art 14 341
Convention on the Prevention of Marine Pollution by Dumping of Wastes
    and Other Matter (Protocol) 1996 [LC 1972 as amended by 1996
    Protocol] (LC Protocol) 396, 661, 662, 667, 692, 693
Art 1(4).2.1 661
Art 1.4.2.2 660
Art 2 658
Art 3 658
Art 4 658
Art 4(2) 661

Art 5	658
Art 8	658
Art 10	658
Art 12	663
Art 15	663
Art 23	657
Annex 2	658
Convention on the Prevention of Marine Pollution by Dumping of Wastes and Other Matter 1972 (LC 1972)	396, 657, 660, 662, 663, 667, 692, 693
Art I(5)	658
Art III	657
Art III(1)(b)(i)	657, 661
Art IV	657
Art IV(3)	657
Art V	658
Art VII	658
Art VIII	663
Art 10(4)	288
Annex I	657
Annex III	657, 658
Convention on the Protection of the Underwater Cultural Heritage (UCH 2001))	213, 293, 306, 315, 316, 325, 326, 332, 333, 340, 348, 351, 354, 355, 363
Art 1(1)(b)	334
Art 1(1)(c)	334
Art 1(6)	353
Art 1(7)	336
Art 1(8)	346
Art 2	335, 337
Art 2(2)	352
Art 2(3)	343
Art 2(8)	346, 348, 351
Art 2(9)	349
Art 3	338, 346, 352
Art 4	335, 341
Art 5	336
Art 6	345
Art 6(2)	345
Art 7	342, 352
Art 7(1)	338
Art 7(2)	338, 347, 351
Art 7(3)	338, 344, 347, 348, 351, 352
Art 8	339, 342
Art 9	339
Art 9(1)(a)	339
Art 9(1)(b)	340, 420
Art 9(3)	340

Art 9(4) 340
Art 9(5) 340, 344, 352
Art 10 ....339, 352
Art 10(2) 340
Art 10(3) 340
Art 10(4) 340
Art 10(5) 340
Art 10(7) 351
Art 11(4) 344, 352
Art 12 ....341, 352
Art 12(6) 344
Art 13 ....341, 347
Art 14 341
Art 15 ....337, 341
Art 16 ....337, 341
Art 17 ....338, 341, 342
Art 17(3) 344, 352
Art 18 344
Art 18(1) 343
Art 18(2) 338, 343
Art 18(3) 343
Art 18(4) 343
Art 19 ....344, 352
Art 19(1) 344
Art 19(2) 344
Art 19(3) 344
Art 20 342
Art 21 ....342, 344, 352
Art 22 341
Art 27 ....325, 349
Art 33 337
Annex 341

Convention on the Territorial Sea and the Contiguous Zone 1958 ....295, 299
Convention on Third Party Liability in the Field of Nuclear Energy 1960
    (Paris Convention) 132, 375, 521
Convention Relating to the Carriage of Passengers and their Luggage by
    Sea 1974 (Athens Convention 1974) 6, 78, 84, 85, 89
Convention Relating to the Carriage of Passengers and their Luggage by Sea 1974 as amended by
    2002 Protocol (Athens Convention 2002) 53, 78, 84, 85, 89, 94, 99, 112, 202, 369, 385, 386,
    440, 459, 535, 54
Art 1(1) 79, 80
Art 1(4) 79
Art 1(6) 85
Art 1(8) 82
Art 1(8)(a) 82

Art 2	78, 449
Art 3	80
Art 3(1)	80, 81
Art 3(1)(b)	88
Art 3(2)	81
Art 3(5)(a)	81
Art 3(5)(c)	81
Art 3(5)(d)	81, 83
Art 3(6)	82, 83
Art 4bis(10)	87
Art 4bis(12)	87
Art 4bis(13)	87
Art 5	86
Art 6	80
Art 7	81, 83
Art 7(1)	83
Art 7(2)	85
Art 8	83, 86
Art 10(1)	87
Art 13	83
Art 14	80
Art 16	89
Art 16(2)(a)	90
Art 16(2)(b)	90
Art 17(1)	90
Art 17(2)	90
Art 17bis	90
Art 17bis(3)	90
Art 18	78, 90
Art 41(2)	80
Coroners (Investigations) Regulations 2013 (SI 2013/1629)	599
Coroners and Justice Act 2009	599
Council Decision 2002/971/EC authorising Member States to ratify or accede to the HNSC	145
Council Decision 2012/22/EU of 12 December 2011 concerning the accession of the EU to the Athens Convention 2002 etc	90
Council Directive 75/439/EEC of 16 June 1975 on the disposal of waste oils [1975] OJ L 194/23	686
Council Directive 91/156/EEC of 18 March 1991 amending Directive 75/442/EEC on waste [1991] OJ L 078/32	686
Council Directive 91/689/EEC of 12 December 1991 on hazardous waste (the Hazardous Waste Directive) [1991] OJ L 377/20	686
Council Directive 91/692/EEC of 23 December 1991 standardizing and rationalizing reports on the implementation of certain Directive relating to the environment [1991] OJ L 377/48	686

TABLE OF LEGISLATION

Council Directive 1999/35/EC of 29 April 1999 on a system of mandatory surveys for the safe operation of regular ro-ro ferry and high-speed passenger craft services 266
Council Directive 2002/59/EC of the European Parliament and of the Council of 27 June 2002 establishing a community vessel traffic monitoring and information system 253, 257, 266
Art 20 323
Council Directive 2004/35/CE of the European Parliament and of the Council of 21 April 2004 on environmental liability with regard to the prevention and remedying of environmental damage
....131, 144, 150, 151, 451, 490, 516, 626, 689
Art 1(6) 151
Art 1(7) 151
Art 1(16) 151
Art 2(1) 151
Art 2(2) 151
Art 4 150
Art 4(1) 151
Art 4(2) 151
Art 8 151
Art 8(3)(a) 151
Art 8(3)(b) 151
Art 10 151
Art 14 151
Council Directive 2006/12/EC of the European Parliament and of the Council of 5 April 2006 on waste [2006] OJ L 114/9 ....686, 687, 690, 694
Art 8 688
Art 15 689
Council Directive 2008/98/EC of the European Parliament of the Council of 19 November 2008 on waste and repealing certain Directives [2008] OJ L 312/3 137, 616, 665, 674, 681, 683, 685, 690, 692, 694, 695, 698, 703
Art 2(1) 701
Art 2(1)(c) 693
Art 2(2) 701
Art 2(3) 701
Art 3 687
Art 3(1) 701
Art 3(5) 691
Art 3(8) 702
Art 6 688
Art 12 688
Art 13 ....688, 698
Art 14(1) 688, 691
Art 14(2) 689, 693
Art 15 ....688, 696
Art 15(1) 688
Art 17 688
Art 23–35 697

Art 24 ....688, 697
Art 26 ....688, 697
Art 26(3)..688
Art 35 688
Art 36 ....688, 696
Art 42 686
Annex III 687
Council Directive 2008/99/EC of the European Parliament and of the Council of
 19 November 2008 on the protection of the environment through criminal law 71
Council Directive 2009/13/EC of 16 February 2009 implementing the Agreement
 concluded by the European Community Shipowners' Associations (ECSA) and
 the European Transport Workers' Federation (ETF) on the Maritime Labour
 Convention, 2006 (O.J. L124, 20.5.2009, 30)..73
Council Directive 2009/17/EC of the European Parliament and of the Council of
 23 April 2009 amending Directive 2002/59/EC establishing a Community vessel traffic
 monitoring and information system..253
Council Directive 2009/18/EC of the European Parliament and of the Council of
 23 April 2009 establishing the fundamental principles governing the investigation
 of accidents in the maritime transport sector and amending Council Directive
 1999/35/EC and Directive 2002/59/EC of the European Parliament and of the Council 266
Council Directive 2009/20/EC of the European Parliament and of the Council of
 23rd April 2009 on the insurance of shipowners for maritime claims O.J. L. 131/128
 (28 May 2009...14, 197
Council Directive 2009/21/EC of the European Parliament and of the Council of
 23rd April 2009 on compliance with flag State requirements 681
Council Directive 2009/45/EC (Recast) of 25 June 2009 on safety rules and standards
 for passenger ships...89
Council Directive 2011/92/EU of the European Parliament and of the Council of 13
 December 2011 on the assessment of the effects of certain public and private
 projects on the environment 660
Council Directive 2012/23/EU amending Directive 2009/138/EC (Solvency II) as
 regards the date for its transposition and the date of its application, and the date
 of repeal of certain Directives 90
Council Directive 2013/30/EU of the European Parliament and of the Council of
 12 June 2013 on safety of offshore oil and gas operations and amending Directive
 2004/35/EC 150, 451
Council Directive 2015/2302 of the European Parliament and of the Council of
 25 November 2015 on package travel and linked travel arrangements 80
Crimes Act 1961 71
Cross-Border Insolvency Regulations 2006 (SI 2001/1030)..668
Crown Proceedings Act 1947..288
s 29 ....276, 290
Dangerous Substances in Harbour Areas Regulations (SI 1987/37) 526
Dangerous Vessels Act 1985..257, 526
s 6A..257
Dumping at Sea Act 1974 664

TABLE OF LEGISLATION

Dutch Civil Code
Art 8:75 5(1)(c) 121
Enterprise Act 2016 196
Environment Act 1990 693
Environment Act 1995
s 108 675
Environmental Damage (Prevention and Remediation) (England) Regulations 2015
    (SI 2015/810) 150
reg 7(2) 151
Environmental Permitting (England and Wales) Regulations 2010 (SI 2010/675) ...694, 695
reg 12 696
Environmental Protection Act 1990
s 33 ....696, 702
s 34 702
s 57(8) 701
s 75(2) 701
s 75(4) 701
s 98(5A) 701
s 141 701
s 156 701
European Communities (Definition of Treaties) (Maritime Labour Convention)
    Order 2009 (SI 2009/1757) 73
European Communities Act 1972
s 2(2) 694
European Convention on the Protection of the Archaeological Heritage 1992 345
European Union (Withdrawal) Act 2018 ....655, 656
European Union (Withdrawal) Act 2018 (Exit Day) (Amendment) (No. 2)
    Regulations 2019 (SI 2019/859) 655
European Union (Withdrawal) Act 2018 (Exit Day) (Amendment)
    Regulations 2019 (SI 2019/718) 655
Exclusive Economic Zone Order 2013 (SI 2013/3161) 262, 538, 665
Food and Environment Protection Act 1985 ....665, 695
s 5 ....664, 695
s 6 ....664, 695
s 7 695
Foreign States Immunity Act 293
Fund Convention 1971 as amended by 1992 Protocol (Fund Convention 1992) 6, 133, 138, 144,
    145, 146, 148, 149, 321, 375, 404, 453, 461, 515–518, 535, 663, 690
Art 1(2) 139, 140
Art 2 138
Art 4(1) 519
Art 4(1)(a) 138, 386
Art 4(1)(b) 138, 519
Art 4(1)(c) 138, 519
Art 4(2)(a) 139
Art 4(2)(b) 138

Art 4(3) 139
Art 4(4)(a) 138
Art 4(5) 134, 139
Art 7(6) 139
Arts 10–15 138
Geneva Convention on the High Seas 1958
Art 5 415
Art 6 415
Government of India Act 1858
s 39 219
Great Barrier Reef Marine Park Act 1975
s 28GA 102
Hague Convention for the Protection of Cultural Property in the Event of Armed
    Conflict 1954
Art 7 .... 341, 342
Art 15 341
Hague Rules as amended by Protocols of 1968 and 1979 (Hague-Visby
    Rules) 45, 68, 78, 112, 179, 709, 712
Art I(a) 45
Art I(b) 45
Art I(c) 45
Art I(e) 49
Art III
r 1 51
r 2 68
r 6 53
r 1 .... 46, 48, 58
r 2 .... 46, 48, 50, 51, 57
r 4 52
r 6 .... 53, 56
r 8 .... 40, 45, 53, 63
Art IV 45, 171, 662, 710
r 1 .... 46, 50
r 2 .... 46, 50, 51, 67
r 2(a) 44, 48, 49, 50, 51, 67
r 2(b) 47, 67
r 2(c) 47, 50, 51
r 2(f) 47
r 2(I) 47
r 2(j) 47
r 2(m) 47
r 2(n) 47
r 2(p) 47
r 2(q) 47, 51
r 2(q) 49, 57
r 4 50

r 5	46, 53, 54
r 5(a)	54
r 5(b)	51, 52
r 5(c)	55
r 6	57, 58, 62, 65
Art V	710
Art VII	49
Art VIII	54
Art IX	54
Art X	45, 449

Harbours Act (Northern Ireland) 1970 527
Harbours Act 1964

s 14	528
s 40A	257, 526
s 40B–40D	257
s 14	526

Harbours, Docks and Piers Clauses Act 1847 .... 91, 526, 527

s 52	526
s 56	159, 224, 524, 525, 528, 529, 538, 544, 555, 556
s 57	560
s 74	91, 525

Hazardous Waste (England and Wales) Regulations 2005 (SI 2005/894) 694, 701
reg 2 694
Hazardous Waste (Wales) Regulations 2005 (SI 2005/1806) 694
Health and Safety at Work Act 1974 683
Historic Monuments and Archaeological Objects (Northern Ireland)
　Order 1995 (SI 1995/1625) 285
Hong Kong International Convention for the Safe and Environmentally
　Sound Recycling of Ships (Hong Kong Convention) 2009 ......658, 659, 660, 669, 672, 676, 678,
　679, 680, 682, 705

Art 1(1)	678
Art 4	676
Art 5	676
reg 1(4)	677
reg 4(2)	677
reg 8	677
reg 8.4	677
reg 9	677

Hovercraft (Application of Enactment) Order 1972 (SI 1972/971)
Art 8(1) 212, 395
Hovercraft (Civil Liability) Order 1986 (SI 1986/1305) 79, 98
Hovercraft (Convention on Limitation of Liability for Maritime Claims
　(Amendment)) Order 1998 (SI 1998/1257) 79, 98
Hovercraft Act 1968 ....98, 395
Insurance Act 2015 ....174, 178, 193, 199
s 13A 196

s 13A(3)(a) 196
s 15 174
s 16 174
s 17 174
s 18 174
International Convention for the Control and Management of Ships' Ballast
    Water and Sediments 2004 307
International Convention for the Prevention of Pollution from Ships [1973/1978]
    (MARPOL) 10, 71, 307–309, 400, 401, 418, 420, 422, 673, 674
Art 1(2) 312
Art 2(2) 404
Art 2(4) 395, 401
Art 2(5) 407
Art 8 ....312, 407, 417, 419
Art 16(2) 300
Annex V 661, 662
Protocol 312
International Convention for the Prevention of Pollution of the Sea by Oil 1954 308
International Convention for the Safety of Life at Sea 1974 (SOLAS) 10, 52, 71, 307, 309, 312,
    418–420, 426, 449
reg 33 ....152, 259
Art VIII(b) 300
International Convention for the Unification of Certain Rules of Law relating
    to Bills of Lading 1924 (Hague Rules) 44, 45, 68, 179, 710
Art III 45
r 1 67
Art IV 45
r 5 53
Art X 45
International Convention for the Unification of Certain Rules Relating to Assistance
    and Salvage of Aircraft or by Aircraft at Sea 1938 212
International Convention for the Unification of Certain Rules relating to the Limitation
    of Liability of Owners of Sea-Going Vessels 1924 (Limitation Convention 1924) 96
International Convention on Civil Liability for Bunker Oil Pollution Damage 2001
    (Bunkers Convention 2001) 6, 21, 30, 61, 64, 80, 86, 101, 116, 134, 137, 141, 144, 147, 157,
    202, 206, 258, 321, 369, 371, 381, 385, 404, 432, 440, 441, 453, 456, 490, 496, 502, 504–507,
    515, 516, 521, 532, 545, 549, 553, 555, 583, 626, 668
Art 1(1) 141, 142
Art 1(3) 59, 440, 520
Art 1(5) 141
Art 1(7) 375
Art 1(8) 142
Art 1(9) 141
Art 1(10) 415
Art 2 141
Art 2(a) 408

Art 2(a)(ii) 409
Art 3(1) 141–143
Art 3(2) 59
Art 3(3) 141, 142
Art 3(3)(a) 142, 460
Art 3(3)(b) 141
Art 3(5) 520, 521
Art 3(6) 142, 627
Art 4(1) 375
Art 6 ....130, 143, 520
Art 7 ....142, 509
Art 7(1) 142, 382, 386
Art 7(6) 668
Art 7(10) 130, 142, 663
Art 8 141
Art 10 117
Art 11 144
International Convention on Civil Liability for Oil Pollution Damage 1969 (CLC 1969) 6, 100,
    132–134, 363, 371, 501, 517
Art III(2)(b) 458
International Convention on Civil Liability for Oil Pollution Damage 1969 as
    amended by 1992 Protocol (CLC 1992) 6, 10, 59, 61, 64, 86, 100, 101, 112, 129–134, 138,
    141–148, 157, 197, 202, 206, 258, 321, 385, 386, 399, 404, 411, 423, 431, 433, 435, 440, 442,
    453, 490, 499, 502, 515–517, 535, 548, 549, 555, 592, 626
Art I(1) 134
Art I(4) 415
Art I(5) 134
Art I(6) 134, 139, 441, 517
Art I(7) 140, 375, 432, 518
Art I(8) 663
Art II 134
Art II(a) 408
Art II(a)(ii) 409
Art II(b) 397, 399
Art III(2) 139, 141
Art III(4) 136, 137, 142, 439, 440, 456, 511, 518–520, 690
Art III(4)(d) 137, 626
Art III(4)(e) 626
Art III(5) 137, 627
Art IV 135, 439
Art V(2) 203, 663
Art V(3) 135
Art V(4) 134
Art V(9) 135
Art VI(4) 136
Art VII 135

Art VII(1) 135, 381
Art VII(2) 494
Art VII(5) 668
Art VII(8) 135, 136, 496, 502, 663
Art VII(9) 135, 502, 507
Art VII(11) 382, 386
Art VIII 134, 463
Art IX 134
Art X 117
Art XII 137
International Convention on Liability and Compensation for Damage in
    Connection with the Carriage of Hazardous and Noxious Substances by
    Sea 1996 (HNSC 1996) 141, 145, 150, 369, 433, 486, 489, 490, 513, 521
International Convention on Liability and Compensation for Damage in
    Connection with the Carriage of Hazardous and Noxious Substances by
    Sea 2010 (HNSC 2010) 6, 30, 59,
    61, 64, 93, 100, 101, 103, 112, 129, 130, 134, 145, 149, 150, 202, 321, 385, 404, 432, 435, 440,
    441, 453, 489, 490, 490, 502, 515, 516, 519, 520, 530, 545, 549, 592, 626, 663, 689
    Art 1(5) 146
    Art 1(6) 145, 146
    Art 1(7) 375
    Art 1(v) 146
    Art 3 149
    Art 3(b) 408, 409
    Art 4(2) 375
    Art 4(2)(b) 521
    Art 4(5) 149
    Art 5 145
    Art 7 .... 145, 147
    Art 7(2)(a) 145
    Art 7(2)(b) 145
    Art 7(2)(c) 145
    Art 7(2)(d) 146
    Art 7(4) 146, 519
    Art 7(5) 146, 440, 446
    Art 9 147
    Art 9(1)(a) 148
    Art 9(1)(b) 148
    Art 9(2) 147
    Art 12(5) 668
    Art 12(8) 502
    Art 12(9) 502, 507
    Art 13 .... 148, 415
    Art 14(1)–(4) 149
    Art 14(3)(b) 149
    Art 14(5)(a) 148

Art 37(3) 149
Art 37(4) 149
Art 38 149
Art 39 149
Art 40 ....117, 149
Art 41(2) 58
International Convention on Load Lines 1966
Art VI(2) 300
International Convention on Maritime Liens and Mortgages 1993
Art 16 416
International Convention on Maritime Search and Rescue 1979 152
International Convention on Oil Pollution Preparedness Response and Co-operation 1990 (OPRC
    1990) 321, 387, 417, 418, 420, 595
Art 1(1) 322
Art 1(3) 322
Art 2(1) 322
Art 2(2) 322
Art 2(3) 322
Art 2(4) 322
Art 3 322
Art 4 .... 312, 418, 422
Art 4(1) 322
Art 4(1)(c) 322
Art 4(1)(d) 322
Art 4(1)(e) 322
Art 4(2) 322, 323
Art 5(1) 322
Art 5(1)(c) 322
Art 5(2) 323
Art 6 322
Art 7(1) 323
Art 7(3) 323
Art 8 ....323, 422
Art 9 323
Art 9(1) 323
Annex 323
International Convention on Salvage 1989 (Salvage
    Convention 1989) 103, 132, 144, 149, 153–158, 170, 213, 300, 348, 363, 397, 398, 401, 429,
    433, 440, 485, 520, 535–537, 583, 592
Art 1 ....255, 576
Art 1(2) 578
Art 1(a) 137, 154, 158, 166, 167, 575, 698
Art 1(b) 159, 400
Art 1(c) 159
Art 1(d) 166, 626, 698
Art 1(e) 578

Art 3	240, 400, 402, 451
Art 4	289, 403
Art 4(2)	289, 402
Art 5	549
Art 5(1)	430
Art 5(2)	613
Art 6	154, 168, 581
Art 6(1)	578, 582
Art 6(2)	38, 39, 580
Art 6(3)	154, 579, 591
Art 7	154, 161, 254, 570, 572, 579
Art 8	577
Art 8(1)	106, 157, 164, 573
Art 8(1)(a)	157, 574, 611
Art 8(1)(b)	164, 579, 580, 611
Art 8(1)(c)	574
Art 8(1)(d)	574, 577
Art 8(2)(b)	579
Art 9	319
Art 10	152, 573, 581
Art 11	387
Art 12	181, 579, 580, 582
Art 12(1)	575
Art 12(2)	166, 578
Art 13	108, 157, 159, 160, 165, 168, 181, 204, 514, 515, 568, 569, 575, 576, 579, 582, 595, 597
Art 13(1)	164
Art 13(1)(b)	160, 164
Art 13(1)(e)	595
Art 13(1)(f)	579, 595
Art 13(1)(i)	155
Art 13(1)(j)	155
Art 13(2)	161, 164
Art 13(b)	177
Art 14	108, 159, 164–168, 172, 188, 205, 254, 515, 570, 575, 576, 577, 581, 582, 589, 590, 698
Art 14(1)	166, 575, 578
Art 14(2)	165–168
Art 14(3)	165, 167, 575, 597
Art 17	154
Art 18	82
Art 19	240, 294, 577, 578, 581, 582
Art 19	167
Art 20(1)	162
Art 21	162, 165
Art 21(3)	162
Art 23(1)	162

Art 25	289
Art 30(1)(d)	332
International Convention on Standards of Training, Certification and Watchkeeping for Seafarers 1978 (STCW)	307, 309
Art XII(1)(a)	300
International Convention on the Control of Harmful Anti-Fouling Systems on Ships 2001	307
International Convention on the Establishment of a Supplementary Fund for Oil Pollution Damage 1982 as amended by Protocol of 2003	133, 141
Art 6	140
International Convention on the Establishment of an International Fund for Compensation for Oil Pollution Damage 1971 (Fund Convention 1971)	6, 132–134, 139, 371
International Convention on the Establishment of an International Fund for Compensation for Oil Pollution Damage 1971 as amended by 1992 Protocol	10, 440
International Convention on Tonnage Measurement of Ships 1969	109, 110
International Convention relating to Intervention on the High Seas in Cases of Oil Pollution Casualties 1969 (and its 1973 Protocol)	6, 132, 252, 261, 262, 296, 298, 361, 363, 375–380, 401, 406, 408, 410, 411, 423, 438, 543
Art I	296, 297, 405
Art I(2)	297
Art II	399
Art II(1)	296, 319, 394
Art II(2)(a)	296
Art II(2)(b)	400, 402
Art II(3)	297
Art II(4)	407
Art III(a)	297, 427
Art V(1)	431
Art V(2)	297
Art VI	431, 434
Protocol	
Art 1(2)	297
Art 1(3)	297
International Convention Relating to the Arrest of Sea-Going Ships 1952 (Arrest Convention 1952)	162
International Convention Relating to the Limitation of Liability of Owners of Sea-Going Ships 1957 (Limitation Convention 1957)	96, 104, 112–114, 119, 134, 158, 490
Art 1(1)	119
International Waste Shipments (Amendment) (EU Exit) Regulations 2019 (SI 2019/590)	656, 673
Law Reform (Frustrated Contracts) Act 1943	42
Legal Aid, Sentencing and Punishment of Offenders Act 2012 (Fines on Summary Conviction) Regulations 2015 (SI 2015/664)	Sch 4
	546, 722, 723, 725, 731
Limitation Act 1980	
s11	89

TABLE OF LEGISLATION

Lloyd's Act 1871
s 34 239
s 35 238
s 41 239
Luggage by Sea (Domestic Carriage) Order 1987 (SI 1987/670) 89
Magistrates' Court Act 1980 267
Marine (Scotland) Act 2010 ....279, 665
Marine and Aviation Insurance (War Risks) Act 1952 236
Marine and Coastal Access Act 2009 ....264, 561, 664, 666, 695
s 41 538
s 65 696
s 65(1) 665
s 66 696
s 66(1) 665, 695–699
s 66(2) 697
s 67 666
s 68 666
s 69 666
s 70 666
s 71 666
s 72 666
s 73 666
s 74 ....666, 695
s 85 667
s 88 667
s 90 667
s 91 667
s 107(2) 700
Sch 7 667
Marine Environment (Amendment) (EU Exit) Regulations 2018 (SI 2018/ 1399) 656
Marine Insurance Act 1906 (MIA 1906) 174, 190, 198
s 9(1) 234
s 9(2) 234
s 14(1) 178
s 18(2) 175
s 25(1) 176
s 27(1) 175
s 31(2) 185
s 39 177
s 39(5) 178
s 40(2) 184
s 48 185
s 55 177
s 55(2) 181, 199
s 55(2)(a) 136, 176, 177, 499
s 55(2)(b) 177

s 55(2)(c)	177
s 57(1)	188
s 57(2)	190
s 58	188
s 60(1)	190
s 61	190
s 62(1)	190
s 62(2)	191
s 62(3)	191
s 62(5)	191, 192
s 62(7)	191
s 62(8)	191
s 63	525
s 63(1)	192, 232, 233
s 64(2)	181
s 65	181
s 65(2)	181
s 66	169
s 68(1)	175
s 78	181, 187
s 79	233, 525
s 79(1)	192, 232, 234
s 81	175
s 85(3)	198
s 85(4)	198
s 88	191
Marine Licensing (Exempted Activities) (Amendment) Order 2013 (SI 2013/526)	699
Marine Licensing (Exempted Activities) (Amendment) Order 2019 (SI 2019/893)	666
Marine Licensing (Exempted Activities) Order 2011 (Exempted Activities Order) (SI 2011/409)	666, 697
Art 3	697
Art 5	698
Art 6(2)(c)	699
Art 7	697
Art 8	697
Art 9	698
Art 10	698
Art 11	700
Art 15	700
Art 16	700
Art 17B	699
Art 21	700
Art 24	698
Art 28	698, 699
Art 32	698
Marine Navigation Act 2013	534

s 5 ....257, 526
s 8(1) 557
s 8(2) 557
s 8(2)(a) 541
s 8(2)(b) 722
s 8(3) 723
s 9 558
s 9(2) 557
s 11 527
Marine Safety Act 2003 ....258, 262
s 1 ....251, 252, 729
s 2 729
Sch 2 257
Sch 3A 251
Maritime Code of the People's Republic of China 1992 97
Maritime Conventions Act 1911
s 6 153
s 7 153
s 8 153
Maritime Labour Convention 2006 (MLC 2006) 73, 77, 202, 209
reg 2.5 74
reg 2.6 75
reg 4.2 ....75, 76
reg 5.1 73
reg 5.1.6 72
Art VI 74
Maritime Transport Act 1994 (NZ) 21, 71, 145, 212
s 86 22
s 100 571
s 248 20
Maritime Transport Amendment Act 1999 (NZ) 212
Maryport Harbour Revision Order 2007 (SI 2007/3463) (Maryport Order) 561
Art 25 528
Art 26 ....528, 560
Art 27 ....528, 560
Medway Ports Authority Act 1973 s 4 524
s 46(6) 526
Mental Health Act 1983 238
Merchant Shipping (Accident Reporting and Investigations) Regulations 2012 (SI 2012/1743)
    (Accident Reporting Regulations 2012) 266
reg 3(1) 267
reg 4 267
reg 5 266
reg 6(1) 267
reg 6(2) 267
reg 6(4) 267

reg 7(2)..267
reg 7(4)..267
reg 8 267
reg 10 267
reg 11 267
reg 14 267
reg 19 267
Merchant Shipping (Accident Reporting and Investigations) Regulations 2013
    (SI 2013/2882)...266
Merchant Shipping (Amendment and Extension) Act 2011 (Mal) 532
Merchant Shipping (Carriage of Passengers by Sea) Regulations (SI 2012/3152) 78
Merchant Shipping (Compulsory Insurance of Shipowners for Maritime Claims)
    Regulations 2012 (SI 2012/2267)...197
Merchant Shipping (Convention on Limitation of Liability for Maritime Claims)
    (Amendment) Order 1998 (SI 1998/1258) 85, 109, 110
Merchant Shipping (Convention on Limitation of Liability for Maritime Claims)
    (Amendment) Order 2004 (SI 2004/1273) 109, 110
Merchant Shipping (Convention Relating to the Carriage of Passengers and their
    Luggage by Sea) Order 2014 (SI 2014/1361) 78
Merchant Shipping (Dangerous Goods and Marine Pollutants) Regulations 1997
    (SI 1997/2367)..257
Merchant Shipping (Flag State Directive) Regulations 2011 (SI 2011/2667)................681
Merchant Shipping (Formal Investigations) Rules (SI 1985/1001)........................... r 4
   268
Merchant Shipping (Liability of Shipowners and Others) Act 1958 8
Merchant Shipping (Liability of Shipowners and Others) (Calculation of Tonnage)
    Order 1986 (SI 1986/1040)...109
reg 2 494
Merchant Shipping (Maritime Labour Convention) (Compulsory Financial Security)
    (Amendment) Regulations 2018 (SI 2018/667) 73
Merchant Shipping (Maritime Labour Convention) (Consequential and Minor Amendments)
    Regulations 2014 (SI 2014/1614)..73
Merchant Shipping (Maritime Labour Convention) (Minimum Requirements for
    Seafarers etc.) Regulations 2014 (SI 2014/1613)...73–75
Merchant Shipping (Maritime Labour Convention) (Miscellaneous Amendments)
    Regulations 2018 (SI 2018/242)..73
Merchant Shipping (Miscellaneous Provisions) (Amendments etc) (EU Exit)
    Regulations 2018 (SI 2018/1221)..656
Merchant Shipping (Oil Pollution Preparedness, Response and Cooperation Convention)
    (Amendment) Regulations 2001 (2001/1639)...321
Merchant Shipping (Oil Pollution Preparedness, Response and Co-operation Convention)
    (Amendment) Regulations 2015 (SI 2015/386) 321
Merchant Shipping (Oil Pollution Preparedness, Response and Cooperation Convention) Order
    1997 (1997/2567) 321
Merchant Shipping (Oil Pollution Preparedness, Response Co-operation Convention)
    Regulations 1998 (SI 1998/1056) (OPRC Regulations)...321

TABLE OF LEGISLATION

Merchant Shipping (Oil Pollution) (Bunkers Convention) Regulations 2006
(SI 2006/1244) 141, 551
Merchant Shipping (Oil Pollution) (Supplementary Fund Protocol) Order 2006
(SI 2006/1265) 133
Merchant Shipping (Passengers' Rights) (Amendment etc.) (EU Exit) Regulations
2019 (SI 2019/649) 78, 80
Merchant Shipping (Pollution) Act 2006
s 1 133
s 3 535
Merchant Shipping (Port State Control) Regulations 2011 (SI 2011/2601) 683
Merchant Shipping (Prevention of Oil Pollution) Regulations 1996 (SI 1996/2154) 257
Merchant Shipping (Prevention of Pollution (Intervention) (Foreign Ships) Order 1997
(SI 1997/1869) 262
Merchant Shipping (Prevention of Pollution) (Intervention) (Foreign Ships) Order 1997
(SI 1997/2568) 262
Merchant Shipping (Prevention of Pollution) (Law of the Sea Convention) Order 1996
(SI 1996/282) 262
Merchant Shipping (Prevention of Pollution) (Limits) Regulations 2014
(SI 2014/3306) 262, 665, 673
Merchant Shipping (Prevention of Pollution: Substances Other than Oil) (Intervention)
Order 1997 (SI 1997/1869) 262
Merchant Shipping (Registration etc.) Act 1993
Sch 4 .... 245, 272
Merchant Shipping (Registration of Ships) Regulations 1993 (SI 1993/3138)
reg 56(1) 705
reg 56(1)(c) 706
reg 56(2) 706
Merchant Shipping (Registration, etc.) Act 1993 277
Merchant Shipping (Reporting Requirements for Ships Carrying Dangerous or
Polluting Goods) Regulations 1995 (SI 1995/2498) 257
Merchant Shipping (Safety of Navigation) Regulations 2002 (SI 2002/1473) ... 257, 449
Sch 3 152
Merchant Shipping (Salvage and Pollution) Act 1994 154
Merchant Shipping (Tonnage) Regulations 1997 (SI 1997/1510) 109
Merchant Shipping (United Kingdom Wreck Convention Area) Order 2015 (SI 2015/172) 721
Art 2 538
Merchant Shipping (Vessel Traffic Monitoring and Reporting Requirements)
Regulations 2004 (SI 2004/2110) 257
r 22(1) 256, 729
Merchant Shipping Act 1854 212
s 2 .... 212, 268
Merchant Shipping Act 1894 .... 108, 158, 212, 217, 528
s 30 527
s 503 .... 8, 112, 526
s 518 272
s 530 .... 483, 526, 527

s 531	483, 527, 528
s 532	483, 526

Merchant Shipping Act 1906
s 72	269
Pt IV	72

Merchant Shipping Act 1970
s 62	72
s 67	72

Merchant Shipping Act 1981 44

Merchant Shipping Act 1995 .... 115, 133, 145, 153, 155, 159, 234, 246, 266, 267, 270, 279, 280, 290, 331, 395, 535–537, 700

s 1	321, 683, 697
s 1(3)	721
s 9	216, 705
s 9(3)	705
s 16(3)	706
s 17	216
s 39	570
s 73–75	72
s 85	71
s 92	152
s 93	152
s 98	71
s 100	71
s 100C-100E	252
s 100C	259
s 108A	251, 543, 729
s 129(2)(b)	262, 529
s 137–141	252
s 137(1)(c)	253
s 137(9)	394
s 141	298
s 151(1)	257
s 153A	101, 141
s 154	101, 134, 141, 144
s 154(2A)	141
s 156(1)	555
s 160	100
s 165(3)	553
s 168	102, 116, 143, 502
s 170(1)	141
s 176A	133
s 176B	133
s 182A	145
s 182B	145
s 182C	145

s 183	78, 535
s 185	535, 551, 552
s 185(4)	99, 115
s 187–190	94
s 187(1)	94
s 187(5)	95
s 187(7)	94
s 188	72, 77, 99
s 189	95
s 191	98
s 192	94
s 192A	197, 386
s 193	529
s 193(1)	529
s 193(2)	529
s 193(3)	529
s 193(4)	722
s 193(5)	529
s 193(6)	529
s 195	529, 558
s 197	557
s 197(2)	529
s 197(8)–(11)	557
s 197A	527, 558
s 197A(3)(a)	558
s 197A(3)(b)	558
s 197A(6)	558, 559
s 201	529
s 210	557
s 211	724
s 213	557
s 223(1)	529
s 224	535, 579
s 224(1)	154
s 225	272, 276
s 226	245, 271, 276
s 226(1)	271
s 226(2)	272
s 226(3)	272
s 227(2)	272, 276
s 228	272, 276
s 230	289, 293
s 230(1)	276, 289, 290, 293
s 230(2)	276m 290
s 231	271, 277
s 231(2)	271

s 231(3)	271
s 231(4)	271
s 232	277
s 232(1A)	271
s 232(2)	270
s 232(3)	271
s 232(4)	270
s 233	277
s 233(1)	260, 270
s 233(2)	270
s 234	271, 277
s 234(1)	271
s 234(4)–(6)	271
s 234(7)	271
s 235	271, 277
s 236	245, 272
s 236(1)	245, 272
s 236(2)	272, 275
s 236(3)	275
s 236(4)	275
s 237	245, 272
s 238(1)	274
s 238(3)	274
s 239(1)	274, 275
s 239(3)	274
s 240(1)	275
s 241	247, 268, 269, 275
s 242	275
s 242(1)	269
s 242(2)	269
s 243(2)	269, 276
s 243(6)	275
s 244(1)	275
s 245	274, 275
s 246(1)	274
s 246(3)(a)	270, 275
s 246(4)	274
s 247	275
s 248	270
s 248(2)	277
s 249	277
s 249(1)	275
s 249(2)	275
s 249(3)	276
s 250	277
s 250(1)	277

s 250(2) 277
s 250(3) 277
s 252 ....525, 527–529, 538, 541, 544, 555–557, 560, 717
s 252(1) 527
s 252(2)(a) 669
s 252(2)(b) 527
s 252(2)(c) 669
s 252(2)(d) 669
s 252(3) 527
s 252(3A) 461, 527, 541
s 252(4) 527
s 252(10) 527
s 253 ....527–529, 538, 541, 544, 555–557, 559, 560, 718
s 253(1) 529
s 253(1)(a) 529
s 253(1)(b) 669
s 253(2) 529, 669
s 253(2)(b) 529
s 253(3) 557
s 253(4) 529
s 254 718
s 255 ....213, 222, 330, 483, 719
s 255(1) 4, 212, 268
s 255(2) 268
s 255A–255U 535, 536
s 255A 721
s 255B 537, 540, 721
s 255B(1) 540
s 255B(2) 540
s 255B(3) 540
s 255B(4) 540
s 255B(6) 540
s 255B(7) 540, 546
s 255C 541, 544, 547–550, 556, 557, 559, 722
s 255C(1) 543
s 255C(2) 92, 537
s 255C(3) 540, 555
s 255C(4) 541, 555, 556
s 255C(6) 541, 546
s 255C(7) 540
s 255D 475, 541, 543, 544, 722
s 255D(1) 537, 541, 543
s 255D(2) 207, 537, 541, 543
s 255D(3) 537
s 255D(4) 542, 543, 546
s 255E 468, 543, 723

s 255E(2)	537, 541, 542
s 255E(4)	546
s 255F	441, 478, 539, 544, 547, 548, 550, 556, 557, 559, 723
s 255F(1)	537, 544, 549, 559
s 255F(2)	252, 544, 555, 559
s 255F(3)	544
s 255F(5)	544
s 255F(6)	544
s 255G	252, 437, 441, 500, 510, 522, 539, 545, 547–551, 555, 556, 724
s 255G(1)	547
s 255G(1)(a)	548
s 255G(1)(b)	548, 549, 556
s 255G(2)	456, 537, 547, 549, 550, 552, 727
s 255G(3)	537, 549
s 255G(3)(c)	549, 724
s 255G(4)	550
s 255G(5)	115, 551, 552
s 255H	462, 550, 551, 552, 723
s 255H(4)(b)	550
s 255I	537, 545, 556, 557, 557, 724, 725,
s 255J(3)	545, 548
s 255J(4)	545
s 255J(5)	545
s 255J(6)	451, 492
s 255J(7)	554
s 255K	537, 545–547, 725,
s 255K(1)	546
s 255L	546, 725
s 255M	537, 545, 547, 725
s 255M(3)	537, 546
s 255M(4)	545
s 255N	545, 726
s 255N(5)	540
s 255O	545, 726
s 255O(2)	546
s 255O(3)	545, 546, 553
s 255P	537, 551, 553, 554, 726
s 255P(1)	548, 551
s 255P(1)(b)	498, 551, 553
s 255P(1)(c)	553
s 255P(2)	549, 551, 552
s 255P(3)	552
s 255P(4)	552
s 255P(5)	115, 552–554
s 255P(6)	552–554
s 255Q	545, 727

s 255Q(1)	554
s 255R	727
s 255R(1)	540, 547, 721, 722
s 255R(2)	252, 253, 536, 540, 547, 555, 721
s 255R(3)	545, 546
s 255R(4)	439, 539, 548, 556
s 255R(5)	537, 722
s 255R(6)	538, 721
s 255R(7)	545
s 255S	539, 546, 728
s 255S(1)	534, 548
s 255S(2)	537
s 255S(4)	547, 554
s 255S(6)	548
s 255S(7)	548
s 255T	462, 550, 728
s 255U	728
s 255U(1)	728
s 258(1)	683
s 258(2)	683
s 258(3)	683
s 259	267
s 267	266
s 267(2)(b)	266
s 268	266, 267
s 268(3)	267
s 268(5)	267
s 269(2)	268
s 269(3)	268
s 270	267
s 271	266
s 284	725
s 306(2A)(c)	535, 724, 727, 728
s 308	528
s 309	528
s 311	98, 706
s 313	98, 255, 539
s 313(1)	527, 540, 721, 722, 726
s 313(2)	262, 269, 538
s 313(2)(a)	278
s 313A	262
s 315(2)	535, 539
s 315(3)	535, 539
s 315(4)	535, 539
s 315(5)	535, 539
s 315(6)	535

s 503	104, 106
s 518	245, 269
Pt 9A	202, 252, 260, 439, 481
Sch 3A	252, 253, 254, 255, 256, 257, 258, 259, 260, 261, 536, 542, 543, 543, 729
para 1	252, 258, 260
para 1(2)	255–257
para 1(3)	253, 257
para 1(4)	253
para 2	257–261
para 2(3)	258
para 2(3)(b)	258
para 3	259, 260
para 4	260
para 5	261
para 6	261
para 6(2)	257
para 6(2)(b)	255
para 7	261
para 8	261
para 9	261
para 11	261
para 11(2)	261
para 12	261
para 13	261
para 14	261
para 15	261
para 15(2)	258
para 15(3)	258
para 15(6)	258
para 17	262
para 19	262
para 20(2)	259
para 22(1)	253
para 22(2)	253, 256, 257
para 22(2)(c)	256
para 23	253
Sch 5A	145
Sch 5ZA	133
Sch 6	78, 79, 535
Sch 7	85, 98, 100, 109, 110, 115, 128, 256, 510, 535, 545, 552, 554, 554
Sch 11	152, 154, 165, 255, 535, 581, 595
Sch 11ZA	535, 537, 735
Merchant Shipping Act 1995 (Act of Tynwald) s 503	120
Merchant Shipping Act 1995 (Amendment) Order 2016 (SI 2016/1061)	85, 109, 115
Merchant Shipping and Maritime Security Act 1997	252, 262, 284, 321, 527
s 14	145

s 16	197, 386
s 19	557
s 24	283
s 24(1)	284
s 24(2)	284
s 24(8)	284
Sch 6	527
Mersey Docks Acts Consolidation Act 1858	526
Model Law on Cross Border Insolvency 1997	668

Nairobi International Convention on the Removal of Wrecks 2007 (WRC 2007) 4, 21, 30, 35, 59, 61, 63, 86, 87, 99, 101, 116, 122, 128, 132–134, 137–143, 147, 149, 157, 159, 167, 181, 195–199, 202, 204, 205, 252, 254, 300, 306, 311, 316, 318, 323, 359–373, 378, 380–393, 398–404, 410–415, 433, 434, 438, 458, 481, 493, 502, 513, 515, 520–523, 524, 527, 530, 533–535, 561, 562, 614, 621, 628, 630, 643, 663, 666, 668, 693, 704, 712

Preamble	388
Art 1	367, 437, 448, 456, 468, 536, 547, 735
Art 1(1)	409, 455, 480, 538, 540
Art 1(2)	376, 395, 402, 448, 449, 450, 451, 493, 494, 533, 538
Art 1(3)	176, 296, 394, 421, 450, 463, 464, 465, 481, 482, 488, 536, 540, 547, 555, 556, 559
Art 1(4)	394, 400, 430, 450, 451, 463, 465, 48–488, 541
Art 1(4)(a)	395, 396
Art 1(4)(b)	396, 479, 482, 484, 487
Art 1(4)(c)	396, 420, 421, 450, 482, 487
Art 1(4)(d)	397, 488, 547
Art 1(5)	405, 407, 410, 423, 431, 442, 450, 454, 465, 466, 469, 475, 482, 536, 599, 722
Art 1(5)(a)	466
Art 1(5)(b)	466, 483, 488, 489, 543
Art 1(6)	405, 407, 429, 441, 442, 466, 599, 722
Art 1(6)(a)	466
Art 1(7)	406, 428, 429, 441, 443, 453, 454, 488, 655
Art 1(8)	419, 439, 539, 548, 722
Art 1(9)	137, 419, 440, 540, 548, 721
Art 1(10)	407, 468
Art 1(11)	415
Art 2	380, 421, 431, 456, 466, 470, 471, 475, 537, 547, 736
Art 2(1)	404, 434, 453, 494,
Art 2(2)	379, 414, 431, 433, 436, 441–443, 475, 479, 480, 531, 547
Art 2(3)	379, 416, 429, 431, 433, 436, 441, 443, 453, 454, 475, 518, 531, 547
Art 2(4)	379, 413, 435, 436, 480, 533
Art 2(5)	387, 407, 408, 410, 410, 424
Art 3	737
Art 3(1)	410
Art 3(2)	376, 377, 413, 449, 533, 538, 543
Art 3(3)	533
Art 3(4)	533

TABLE OF LEGISLATION

Art 3(5)...533
Art 4 737
Art 4(1)...375, 543
Art 4(2)..288, 402, 451, 516, 528, 539, 548
Art 4(3)..402, 456, 537
Art 4(4)...377, 413, 435, 436, 468, 476, 479, 533
Art 4(4)(a)...260, 414, 436, 533, 533, 544
Art 4(4)(a)(ii)..477, 534
Art 4(4)(a)(iii)...533
Art 4(4)(b)..413, 429, 435, 437, 455, 477, 533, 542, 543
Art 5 ....92, 417, 440, 473, 478, 540, 721, 738
Art 5(1)...312, 416, 418–421, 452
Art 5(2)...419, 420, 473, 537, 540
Art 5(d)...482
Art 6 ....33, 406, 424, 427, 443, 462, 463, 473, 479, 537, 599, 738
Art 6(1)(a)...425, 475
Art 6(1)(b)..491
Art 6(1)(h)..482, 486, 488
Art 6(1)(o)...424, 467
Art 7 ....92, 206, 424, 440, 441, 468, 473, 476, 478, 479, 518, 540, 541, 547, 739
Art 7(1)..422, 424
Art 7(2)..425, 453, 478, 479
Art 8 ....92, 206, 424, 440, 441, 473, 476, 479, 540, 541, 547, 612, 739
Art 8(1)..453, 480
Art 8(2)..425, 480
Art 8(3)..426, 480
Art 9 ....374, 379, 406, 425, 427, 429, 431, 437, 440, 441, 462, 468, 469,
    473–476, 479, 541, 547, 555, 739
Art 9(1)...413, 421, 427, 435, 453, 475, 477, 533, 537, 547
Art 9(1)(a)...416, 476
Art 9(2)....................................422, 428, 429, 452, 467, 470, 475, 477, 516, 534, 537, 541, 543, 722
Art 9(3)..422, 453, 475, 477, 495, 534, 537, 541, 543, 545
Art 9(4)..........................156, 251, 260, 413, 429, 430, 435, 437, 453, 455, 466–470, 475, 477, 514,
    531, 533, 537, 538, 542, 543, 550
Art 9(5)...397, 413, 430, 435, 466, 467, 470, 471, 477, 533, 534, 538
Art 9(6)...208, 469–477, 537, 541
Art 9(6)(a)..429, 469
Art 9(6)(b)...427, 429, 469
Art 9(6)(c)...428, 469, 471, 472
Art 9(7)...208, 413, 430, 435, 467, 470–478, 533, 534, 537, 539, 544, 547
Art 9(8)....................................208, 413, 416, 428, 429, 435, 467, 469–478, 515, 533, 534, 537, 539, 544, 547
Art 9(9)..413, 429, 435, 477, 533, 534, 537, 546
Art 9(10)...374, 379, 388, 413, 417, 435, 477, 533, 537
Art 9(11)..473, 477, 545
Art 10 ....206, 374, 377, 413, 437, 438, 468, 471, 472, 475, 476, 479, 490, 491,
    510, 515, 533, 547, 576, 740

TABLE OF LEGISLATION

Art 10(1)..134, 433, 437–441, 452, 453, 456, 459, 464, 468–470, 472, 474, 476–480, 482, 498, 517, 550, 552
Art 10(1)(a) 456, 457, 460, 547, 550
Art 10(1)(b) 456, 457, 459, 500, 547, 550
Art 10(1)(c) 438, 456, 457, 461, 462, 547, 550
Art 10(2) 130, 395, 490, 506, 517, 520, 532
Art 10(2)(a) 460
Art 10(3) 39, 456, 498, 517, 535, 537, 555, 556
Art 10(4) 438, 439, 462, 472, 550
Art 10(5) 485
Art 11 ....377, 413, 437, 476, 484, 514, 516, 521, 741
Art 11(1) 375, 432, 516, 518, 519, 520, 537, 549
Art 11(1)(a) 140, 518, 519
Art 11(2) 486, 535, 537, 549
Art 11(5) 416
Art 12 ....377, 413, 417, 437, 440, 476, 478, 492, 493, 496, 501, 502, 509, 511, 512, 545, 548, 669, 741
Art 12(1) 97, 128, 381, 382, 395, 416, 449, 450, 452, 493, 494, 497, 503–511, 531, 544, 545, 547, 553, 554, 725
Art 12(2) 401, 416, 493, 494, 554
Art 12(3)(a) 495
Art 12(3)(b) 495
Art 12(5) 416, 495
Art 12(6) 495
Art 12(7) 416
Art 12(9) 495, 496
Art 12(10) 128, 130, 200, 206, 207, 459, 465, 468–471, 474–479, 493, 496–513, 532–535, 537, 551–554, 667, 726
Art 12(11) 416, 494
Art 12(12) 382, 387, 494, 497, 544, 545
Art 12(13) 495
Art 12(14) 416
Art 13 ....207, 410, 437, 462, 463, 465, 469, 509, 551, 552, 744
Art 14 744
Art 15 ....386, 389, 435, 533, 537, 744
Art 15(2) 389, 390
Art 15(4) 390
Art 15(5)(a) 395
Art 16 ....371, 386, 540, 745
Art 17 ....387, 745
Art 18 ....387, 464, 745
Art 19 ....387, 745
Art 20 ....387, 746
Art 21 ....387, 746
National Marine Sanctuaries Act (US) 350
Navigation Act 2012 (Cth) (Aus) s 14 ....213, 222

s 14(1) 212
Offshore Installations (Emergency Pollution Control) Regulations 2002 (SI 2002/1861) 250
Oil Pollution Act 1971
s 12 252
Oil Pollution Act 1990 (US) 133
s 1003(a) 459
Package Travel and Linked Travel Arrangements Regulations 2018 (SI 2018/634) 80
Pilotage Act 1987
s 16 438
Planning and Compulsory Purchase Act 2004 694
Pollution Prevention and Control Act 1999
s 2 694
Poole Harbour Revision Order 2012 (SI 2012/1777)
Art 3 524
Port of London Authority Act 1968
s 120 526
s 120(1) 560
s 120(5) 526
Prevention of Oil Pollution Act 1971 ....260, 298
Protection of Military Remains Act 1986 ....220, 222, 249, 280, 284, 331, 338, 666
s 1(1) 281
s 1(2) 282
s 1(2)(a) 281
s 1(2)(b) 281
s 1(3)(a) 281
s 1(3)(b) 283
s 1(4)(a) 282
s 1(6) 281
s 2 282
s 2(1)(b) 281
s 2(2) 281, 282
s 2(3) 281, 282
s 2(3)(b) 281
s 3(1) 283
s 4 282
Protection of Military Remains Act 1986 (Designation of Vessels and Controlled Sites) Order 2012 (SI 2012/1110) 283
Protection of the Sea (Powers of Intervention) Act 1981 (Cth) (Aus) s 11(1)(h) 256
Protection of Wrecks (RMS Titanic Order) Order 2003 (SI 2003/2496) 284
Art 4 346
Protection of Wrecks Act 1973 ....213, 249, 262, 278, 286, 325, 338, 346
s 1 ....278, 279
s 1(2) 279
s 1(2)(a) 331
s 1(3) 279
s 1(4) 278

s 1(5) 279
s 1(5)(b) 279
s 1(5)(c) 279
s 2(1) 280
s 3(1) 278
s 3(3) 279
Railway (Accident Reporting and Investigations) (Amendment) (EU Exit)
  Regulations 2018 (SI 2018/1400) 266
Regulation (EC) No. 1346/2000 of 29 May 2000 on insolvency proceedings,
  and some of the issues that arise in maritime law 668
Regulation (EC) No 44/2001 (Brussels I Regulation)
Art 33 122
Regulation (EC) No 1882/2003 of the European Parliament and of the Council
  [2003] OJ L 284/1 686
Regulation (EC) No 1013/2006 of the European Parliament and of the Council
  of 14 June 2006 on shipments of waste 673–675, 705, 706
Art 1(3) 679
Art 2(9) 675
Art 2(10) 674
Art 2(13) 675
Art 2(15) 674
Art 4 674
Art 4(1) 675
Art 5 675
Art 6 675
Art 9 674
Art 10 675
Art 16 675
Art 18 674
Art 34(1) 674
Art 34(2) 674
Art 35 674
Art 36 674
Art 40 674
Art 41 674
Art 41(2) 674
Art 42 674
Art 43 674
Art 44 674
Art 45 674
Regulation (EC) No 864/2007 of the European Parliament and of the Council
  of 11 July 2007 on the law applicable to non-contractual obligations (Rome II)
Art 14(1) 204
Art 15 127
Art 16 128
Art 18 204

Art 26	128
Art 41(2)	83
Regulation (EC) No 392/2009 of the European Parliament and of the Council of 23 April 2009 on the liability of carriers of passengers by sea in the event of accidents	14, 78, 89
Art 2	78
Art 6	80
Regulation (EU) No 1177/2010 of the European Parliament and of the Council of 24 November 2010 concerning the rights of passengers when travelling by sea and inland waterway	80, 89
Regulation (EU) No 1215/2012 of the European Parliament and of the Council of 12 December 2012 on jurisdiction and the recognition and enforcement of judgments in civil and commercial matters (Brussels I Regulation Recast)	90, 118
Art 1.2(d)	204
Art 9	124, 125
Art 25(1)	55
Art 29	56
Art 29	125
Art 30	56, 125, 127
Art 33	125
Art 37–43	120
Art 39	127
Art 45(1)(a)	125, 127
Art 45(1)(c)	125, 127
Art 45(1)(d)	125
Art 45(2)	127
Art 45(3)	125
Regulation (EU) No 1257/2013 of the European Parliament and of the Council of 20 November 2013 on ship recycling and amending Regulation (EC) No 1013/2006 and Directive 2009/16/EC	656, 674, 678, 679, 683, 685, 705, 706
Art 1	680
Art 2	682
Art 2(2)(c)	681
Art 3(1)	680
Art 3(2)	680
Art 3(6)	681
Art 3(14)	681
Art 5	679, 683
Art 6	679
Art 6(1)	684
Art 6(2)	681, 684
Art 6(3)	680, 684
Art 6(4)	684
Art 7	680
Art 8	680
Art 8	683
Art 12	682, 683

Art 16	680
Art 22	682
Art 27	673, 679
Art 32	678
Removal of Wreck Act 1877	527
Renewable Energy Zone (Designation of Area) Order 2004 (SI 2004/2668)	673
Resource Management Act 1991 (NZ)	22, 23, 71
s 2	20
s 6(e)	24
s 15(1)	21
s 15A	20, 21
s 15B	21
Rotterdam Convention on the Prior Informed Consent Procedure for Certain Hazardous Chemicals and Pesticides in International Trade	671
Senior Courts Act 1981	
s 20	162
s 21	162
s 21(4)	8
s 24(2)(c)	290
Ship Recycling (Facilities and Requirements for Hazardous Materials on Ships) (Amendment) (EU Exit) Regulations 2019 (SI 2019/277)	679
Ship Recycling (Requirements in relation to Hazardous Materials on Ships) (Amendment etc.) Regulations 2018 (SI 2018/1122)	679
reg 7	683
reg 8	683–685
reg 51	683
Ship Recycling Facilities Regulations (Northern Ireland) 2015 (SI 2015/229)	682
Ship Recycling Facilities Regulations 2015 (SI 2015/430)	682, 699
Ship Recycling Requirements Regulations (EU Exit) Regulations 2019 (SI 2019)	680, 683
Shipping Registration Act 1981 (Cth) s 12(1)	300
State Immunity Act 1976	288
Stockholm Convention on Persistent Organic Pollutants 2001	671
Strasbourg Convention on Limitation of Liability in Inland Navigation 1988	151
Sunken Military Craft Act 2004 (US)	284, 287
s 1401	228
Territorial Sea (Limits) Order 1989 (SI 1989/482)	538
Territorial Sea Act 1987	538
s 1(1)(a)	269
Third Parties (Rights Against Insurers) Act 1930	
s 9(5)	202
s 9(6)	202
Third Parties (Rights against Insurers) Act 2010	551
s 9(6)	86
Third Parties (Rights against Insurers) Act 2010 (Commencement) Order 2016 (SI 2016/550)	202

TABLE OF LEGISLATION

Tonnage Convention 1969	494
Town and Country Planning Act 1990	694
Transfrontier Shipment of Waste (Amendment) Regulations 2014 (SI 2014/861)	673
Transfrontier Shipment of Waste (TSWR) Regulations 2007 (SI 2007/1711)	673
reg 48	675
reg 49	675
reg 51	675
Sch 4	675
Sch 5	675
Transport Infrastructure Act 1994 (Qld) s 281E	91
Transport Operations (Marine Safety) Act 2004 (Qld) s 91	466, 599

Treasure Act 1996

s 3(7)	213

Treaty of St. Germain

Art 136	221
Art 141	221

Treaty of Versailles

Art 184	221
Treaty of Waitangi	20
UN Convention on Contracts for the International Carriage of Goods Wholly or Partly by Sea 2008 (Rotterdam Rules)	44

UN Convention on Jurisdictional Immunities of States and Their Property 2004

Art 21(1)(b)	289
UN International Convention on the Carriage of Goods by Sea 1978 (Hamburg Rules)	44
UNESCO Convention for the Safeguarding of the Intangible Cultural Heritage 2003	27

UNESCO Recommendation Concerning the Protection at National Level of the Cultural and Natural Heritage

Art 1–17	341
Art 12	342

Unfair Contract Terms Act 1977

Sch 11	154
United Nations Agreement for the Implementation of the Provisions of the United Nations Convention on the Law of the Sea of 10 December 1982 relating to the Conservation and Management of Straddling Fish Stocks and Highly Migratory Fish Stocks	300
United Nations Convention on the Law of the Sea 1982 (UNCLOS)	213, 249, 262, 299, 300, 316, 340, 351, 353, 372, 375, 379, 385–390, 403, 406, 407, 410, 412, 413, 416, 431, 658
Art 1(1)(1)	305, 313
Art 1(3)	305
Art 2	301
Art 2(1)	316, 407
Art 2(3)	376, 377, 410, 411
Art 3	301
Art 4	301
Art 6(2)	316
Art 8	538

Art 9	301
Art 10	301
Art 11	301
Art 12	301
Art 13	301
Art 15(1)	301
Art 17	316, 411
Art 18(2)	301, 316
Art 19	301, 316
Art 19(1)	301
Art 19(2)(l)	302
Art 20	301
Art 21	259, 411
Art 21(4)	310
Art 24	411
Art 24(1)	434
Art 24(2)	422, 434
Art 29	290, 402
Art 32	288
Art 33	302, 313, 314
Art 39(2)(a)	310
Art 41(3)	310
Art 47	301
Art 48	301
Art 49	301
Art 53(8)	310
Art 55	316
Art 56	316, 317, 374, 408
Art 56(1)	303
Art 56(1)(b)	304
Art 56(1)(b)(iii)	304, 373, 384
Art 56(1)(c)	304
Art 56(2)	431
Art 56(3)	304
Art 56(3)	316
Art 58	304, 316, 374, 408
Art 59	304
Art 60	400, 405
Art 60(3)	310, 400
Art 60(6)	310
Art 76(1)	303
Art 76(5)	303
Art 77	303
Art 77(3)	409
Art 78(2)	431
Art 87	305

Art 91	300, 415, 681
Art 92	305, 415, 681
Art 94	300, 305, 415
Art 94(2)(a)	310
Art 94(5)	310
Art 95	288, 290, 305
Art 96	288, 290
Art 97–206	321
Art 98	152, 259
Art 98(1)	259
Art 123	410
Art 133(a)	305
Art 136	305
Art 137	305
Art 145	306
Art 149	299, 306, 313, 315, 325
Art 157(1)	305
Art 157(2)	306
Art 192	373
Art 194	374
Art 194(3)(b)	307, 373, 378, 384
Art 194(3)(b)(iii)	384
Art 194(4)	431
Art 198	312
Art 210(6)	310, 657
Art 207(1)	310
Art 211	309, 310, 373, 374, 384
Art 211(1)	307, 308, 317, 371, 384
Art 211(2)	308, 309, 384
Art 211(3)	309, 384
Art 211(4)	309, 316, 378, 384
Art 211(5)	309, 310, 316, 317, 378, 384, 530
Art 211(6)	310, 423
Art 211(7)	312, 384, 418, 422, 530
Art 212(1)	310
Art 217	317, 378
Art 217(1)	311, 317
Art 217(4)	317
Art 217(6)	317
Art 218(1)	311, 317
Art 219	311, 317
Art 220	309, 317, 374, 378, 384
Art 220(1)	311
Art 220(2)	311
Art 220(3)	311, 317
Art 220(4)	317

Art 220(5)	317
Art 220(6)	318
Art 220(7)	318
Art 221	317–321, 361, 368, 373, 411, 480
Art 221(1)	320
Art 221(2)	394, 399
Art 222	311, 317
Art 223–233	384
Art 225	431
Art 228	318
Art 229	380
Art 234	310
Art 235	402, 480
Art 235(1)	308
Art 236	288, 480
Art 237	372, 373
Art 271	310
Art 287	389, 390
Art 303	299, 313–315, 325
Art 303(1)	325
Art 303(2)	314, 339
Art 303(4)	315, 338, 353
Art 311	378
Art 311(2)	373, 374
Art 311(3)	373, 374
Art 312	372
Art 322	338
Vienna Convention on the Law of Treaties 1969	374, 377
Art 11	371
Art 28	410
Art 31–33	538
Art 31	388
Art 31(1)	511
Art 34	371, 374, 378, 379
Art 38	383
Art 41(3)	372, 374
Warsaw-Hague Convention 1955	112
Art 25(1)	113
Waste (England and Wales) (Amendment) Regulations 2014 (SI 2014/656)	696
Waste (England and Wales) Regulations 2011 (SI 2011/988)	694, 696, 702
reg 3(1)	694
reg 3(2)	694
reg 4	694
reg 7	694
reg 10	694
reg 12	694

reg 12(1)(a) 695
reg 12(1)(b) 695
reg 12(1)(c) 695
reg 12(1)(d) 695
reg 12(1)(e) 695
reg 24(5)(e) 695
reg 25 694
reg 26 694
reg 26(1)(a) 695
reg 26(1)(b) 695
reg 35(6) 695, 703
Waste (Miscellaneous Amendments) (EU Exit) (No. 2) Regulations 2019 (2019)
reg 17 701
Waste Management Licensing Regulations 1994 (SI 1994/1056) 694
World Heritage Convention 1972
Art 5 341
Wreck and Salvage Act 1846 ....212, 268
Wreck Removal Convention Act 2011 ....523, 524, 527, 534–539, 553
s 1 534
s 1(3) 535, 724, 727, 728
s 1(5) 535, 539
s 2 534
Wreck Removal Convention Act 2011 (Commencement) Order 2015 (SI 2015/133) 534
Wrecked, Abandoned or Hazardous Vessels Act 2019 (Can) 449, 532, 561
s 27 562
s 30 561
s 32 561
s 33 561
s 34 561
s 47 562
s 90 562
York Antwerp Rules 1994 170
York Antwerp Rules 2004 170
York Antwerp Rules 2016 ....63, 69, 108, 170
r 12 170
r A 171
r D 171
r I 173
r V 170
r VI 172, 173
r VI(b) 172
r VI(c) 172
r VI(d) 172
r VIII 171

PART I

WRECK IN NATIONAL AND INTERNATIONAL LAW

CHAPTER 1

Introduction to wreck casualties

1.1 Introduction

1.1.1 Wreck and maritime law

Shipwrecks have long been the subject of romantic tales (in fact and fiction), conjuring up images of sailors confronting the natural elements of wind and sea where, despite the heroic efforts of crew and salvors, the ship ultimately succumbs to those forces.[1] While those forces have not really changed from antiquity, the ability to resist them has developed along with the practices of shipbuilding and navigation. The physical risks from any casualty involving a ship remain the same, namely the loss of the ship and its cargo and, more importantly, possible loss of life and personal injury. In the last 50 years, the risks to the environment have become more apparent, mainly as a result of the volume and variety of cargoes carried. As will be seen, the environmental factor now plays an increasing role in wreck removal.

The law relating to wreck reflects the problems of how to deal with the ending of the life of a ship (usually by accident or inadvertence). It is merely one aspect of maritime law which itself has many unique principles that do not exist or apply on land, including the principles of salvage and general average. Maritime (including wreck) law also intersects with most general principles of law, including property law (eg raising ownership issues), torts law (eg dealing with interference with rights) and contract law. Contract law, in particular, governs the relationships of the many commercial parties to the maritime commercial adventure that might end in a wreck. Maritime law recognises such private law rights, but also public maritime law duties (eg to regulate safety and protect the environment). Such rights and duties may arise through international law (eg conventions) and/or national law (eg statutes or the common law).

While the aim of this book is to provide an analysis of the "law of wreck", it has to be recognised at the outset that its subject matter is not so distinct or easily identifiable as, say, the law of salvage which has developed its own unique principles. In fact, wreck law intersects with most of that general body of maritime law (outlined above) which deals with the *consequences* of a maritime casualty, including how to prevent that casualty from resulting in the wreck (and total loss) of a ship. Many specialist maritime law texts touch incidentally on the wreck of a ship and its cargo while looking at broader issues (eg the carriage of goods generally). The aim of Part I is not to repeat the detailed coverage of

---

1 Maritime libraries are full of accounts of ships being wrecked and the attempts to salve or raise them. For a relatively recent example of the genre, see T. Redding, *Best Endeavours* (ABR, 2004), a book commissioned by the ISU for its 50th general meeting. It recounts some 150 cases, some of which involved unusual wreck raising examples, eg the raising of a China Airlines Boeing 747 and that of the Russian submarine *Kursk*. More graphic images are freely available on the web, eg on YouTube videos produced by the major salvage and wreck removal companies.

such works but, rather, to provide a legal and (where possible) practical overview of the issues which arise more generally when ships are wrecked during the maritime commercial adventure.[2] Before there can be detailed consideration of wreck removal, in particular the Nairobi Wreck Removal Convention (WRC) 2007,[3] it is necessary to set the scene in public international law[4] and appropriate to discuss private and State rights in wreck (including ownership),[5] as well as historic wrecks that have a cultural significance.[6]

1.1.2 Wreck definitions

English maritime law has sometimes struggled with broad definitions (eg of ship or wreck).[7] Thus, care has to be taken to identify the particular purpose or statute for which a definition is being used. There is an ancient definition of *wreccum maris*, dating back to jurisdictional disputes between the common law courts and the Court of Admiralty,[8] but it may have limited modern relevance. Some of the ancient concepts are still reflected in the definition of "wreck" in s 255(1) of the MSA 1995,[9] but this definition applies *only* to wreck as referred to in Part IX of the Act. That Part still contains echoes from another era, when sailing ships were wrecked with all hands, presenting legal and administrative problems of dealing with the remains. Part IX is still relevant[10] but forms only a relatively small aspect of modern wreck law.

The 19th century, in particular, saw renewed interest in the ancient provisions dealing with the ownership of wreck[11] and the related issue of compensation for salvors.[12] This coincided with increasing concerns from the 1840s about the safety of the new steamships and the number of wrecks involving them. Those concerns led to considerable merchant shipping legislation throughout the later 1800s designed to prevent wrecks or to investigate the causes of them.[13] These wider aspects of the public regulation of maritime safety are generally beyond the scope of the present book.

Apart from some contexts where "wreck" is given a special meaning,[14] we will refer more generally in this book to a 'wreck' in the factual sense of a ship and its cargo which have met with a casualty that is so severe that it has seriously affected, and often terminated, the planned voyage. The sinking of the ship with its cargo is the easiest example of wreck. There may, though, be circumstances where a ship strands—creating a risk of

---

2 See Chapter 2.
3 See Part II.
4 See Chapter 5.
5 See Chapters 3 and 4.
6 See Chapters 4 and 6.
7 See S Dromgoole and N Gaskell, "Interests in Wreck" [*Dromgoole & Gaskell, Interests in Wreck*], Chapter 7 in N Palmer and E McKendrick (eds), *Interests in Goods* (2nd ed, LLP, 1998) 185–186.
8 See 3.1.
9 See 3.1, 3.3.1.
10 See further Chapters 3 and 4.
11 See eg W Palmer, *The Law of Wreck: Considered with a View to Its Amendment* (Butterworth, London, 1843); W Marvin, *A Treatise on the Law of Wreck and Salvage* (Little, Brown, Boston, 1858).
12 See further 2.7.
13 See eg W Murton, *Wreck Inquiries: The Law and Practice Relating to Formal Investigations in the United Kingdom [etc]* (Stevens, London, 1884), especially 1–29; see now 4.3.
14 Eg in Part IX of the MSA 1995, and see 3.1.

sinking or total loss—but where there is a possibility (however remote) that the ship or cargo may be saved. In common parlance this may be described as a shipwreck, but the legal issues here are not quite so clear as with a total loss by sinking. Principles relating to salvage (and general average)[15] may apply rather than those relating eg to wreck removal,[16] and the book will deal separately with the effect of the transition from salvage to wreck removal.[17]

1.1.3 Scope of book

The remainder of Chapter 1 will identify some major casualties that have influenced the wreck law discussed elsewhere in the book.

Chapter 2 will then consider the normal commercial voyage and examine the potential effects of a casualty resulting in a wreck upon the various interests involved in the ship. That may involve a transitional period after the immediate casualty during which the ship and cargo cease to be things of value and gradually become potential liabilities (eg where they sink and the cost of raising them exceeds any value that they might have). While wreck law used to be largely an issue for private interests, ie the owners of ships and cargoes (with their insurers), wreck removal has become of increasing concern to States; to that extent it forms the main focus of this book in Parts II–IV. Even if a ship is not raised and remains on the seabed for many years, it may later be perceived to have a historic or cultural value, and different policies may be applied to it. Dramatic improvements in technology mean that many sunken ships once thought lost forever can now be located and, in some circumstances, it may even be feasible to recover a valuable cargo. Here the law of cultural property meets new commercial entrepreneurs and together they may awake the interest of owners who had long given up on, or forgotten, their sunken property (usually cargo).[18]

1.2 Influential wreck casualties

Wreck law has most recently been influenced by the focus on the environmental consequences of wreck and the increasing costs of wreck removal.[19] In that context it is appropriate to introduce some key casualties that have influenced the development of the law or which provide illustrations of the modern problems facing all those involved with dealing with wrecks.

Apart from the specific wreck casualties highlighted below, there are many other examples that could be given. A Belgian company maintains a website that claims to be the world's largest online wreck database, with over 180,000 wrecks recorded.[20] National

---

15 See 2.7, 2.8.
16 See Parts II and III.
17 See Chapter 12.
18 See Chapters 3, 4 and 6.
19 See 1.4, and J Herbert, *The Challenges and Implications of Removing Shipwrecks in the 21st Century* (Lloyd's, 2013) [*Herbert, Challenges*], available at www.lloyds.com/news-and-insight/risk-insight/library/technology/wreck-report.
20 www.wrecksite.eu/. The company does not own copyright in most of the texts and illustrations, but mainly uses links to text and illustrations belonging to others. See also https://shipwrecklog.com/.

hydrographic services also maintain details of wreck locations, although they contain few details about wreck removal operations or costs. The European Maritime Safety Agency (EMSA)[21] publishes an annual maritime accident review which contains details of many recent casualties,[22] although most do not result in wrecks where there is a total loss. Other data can be found in reports compiled by the IMO.[23] One insurer, Allianz, publishes an annual "Safety and Shipping Review" which in 2018 had a table showing all causes of total loss in the period 2008–2017.[24] This separated the broad category of wreck into two: foundered (sunk, submerged), 593; wrecked/stranded (grounded), 229. The IOPC Fund also publishes annual reports about tanker casualties and maintains a database of incidents.[25] The web contains many news articles about contemporary casualties, but they vary greatly in accuracy, especially where legal issues and claims settlements are discussed.[26]

The list of possible examples is therefore vast, but the focus here is on those that have been influential and are referred to elsewhere in the book.

1.2.1 Torrey Canyon (1967)

The *Torrey Canyon* disaster in 1967 did not involve wreck removal, and is a 'wreck' case in the general sense, as described above, of being a marine 'casualty' involving a total loss. Still, it acted as the catalyst for the development of modern marine pollution law, as well as stimulating debate on ship design and operation. Within a relatively short time (in international terms) it gave rise to significant conventions on the right of States to intervene in an environmental casualty,[27] and on liability for oil pollution from tankers.[28] Those latter conventions themselves have been hugely influential in later conventions dealing with liabilities.[29] The International Maritime Organisation [IMO][30] has been able to develop a suite of liability conventions, largely using boilerplate text derived to deal with the problems revealed by the *Torrey Canyon*. Eventually, the WRC 2007 became part of this suite and, as will be seen,[31] owes its origin to debates started after the *Torrey Canyon* disaster.

---

21 See www.emsa.europa.eu/ and the European Marine Casualty Information Platform.
22 See eg *Annual Overview of Marine Casualties and Incidents 2018*. It is noticeable that fishing vessels figure highly in the statistics.
23 See eg Maritime Facts and Figures: Casualties, at https://imo.libguides.com/c.php?g=659460&p=4655524.
24 Safety and Shipping Review 2018, 14. See www.agcs.allianz.com/assets/PDFs/Reports/AGCS_Safety_Shipping_Review_2018.pdf.
25 See www.iopcfunds.org/incidents/incident-map/ and 2.6.2(b).
26 As noted in the Preface, this book contains illustrations of wrecks and the costs of removal, but we emphasise that these are provided from information publicly available to us from a variety of sources. Exact details of claims and settlements are often kept strictly confidential, but the most reliable sources will usually be P&I Clubs or the IOPC Fund.
27 See the Intervention Convention 1969; also 5.3.
28 See the CLC 1969/1992 and Fund Convention 1971/1992: see 2.6.2.
29 See the Bunkers Convention 2001 (see 2.6.3), the HNSC 2010 (see 2.6.4) and the Athens Convention 2002 (see 2.3).
30 Until 1982, this body was known as the International Maritime Consultative Organisation [IMCO].
31 See Part II.

The history of the *Torrey Canyon* and its place in marine environmental law have been extensively discussed over the years.[32] It is not necessary here to rehearse all those discussions, although few have focused on wreck law, but the problems caused by the disaster illustrate many of the underlying issues with maritime casualties and, for that reason, it is appropriate to set out the basic facts and legal issues.

1.2.1(a) The casualty

The *Torrey Canyon* was one of the new generation of supertankers, of 61,623 gt and registered in Liberia. The ship was owned by the Liberian company Barracuda Tanker Co, and time chartered for 20 years to the US company Union Oil (the parent company of Barracuda).[33] *Torrey Canyon* was carrying 119,328 tons of crude oil shipped by BP Trading for Milford Haven, under a sub-voyage charter. On 18 March 1967 the master took an ill-advised short cut and ran aground on the Seven Stones Reef, 11 miles off the UK mainland.

Dutch salvors Bureau Wijsmuller were contracted on an LOF (no cure no pay basis) to save the vessel, but at that time (before the 1973 increases in oil prices) the oil cargo was worth nearly one-tenth of the value of the ship. So it was in the salvor's interest to save the ship, even if that meant discharging the cargo into the sea to lighten the load.[34] In fact, it became clear that neither refloating of the ship nor lightening it was realistic.[35] It proved impossible to use the ship's own power and, after several days' dangerous work, there was an explosion on 21 March that killed the chief salvage officer. Plans were considered for cutting the ship in two so that part could be towed away, but this would have been too dangerous. Even had it been possible, towage would have been impractical, and it would have been difficult to find a suitable location for lightening.[36] On 27 March the salvor's tugs were ordered to leave the area and they decided to abandon salvage operations.[37] All towing operations had failed and on 29 March the ship broke its back and was wrecked.

Of the oil cargo, some 30,000 tons were lost in the first few hours of the casualty, and by 25 March a further 20,000 tons had leaked out.[38] By that stage 100 miles of coastline had been affected. It became apparent that the coastal States were ill-equipped to deal with a wreck of that size and, in particular, its large cargo. This gave rise to uncertainty about the extent of the UK's powers to intervene in relation to the private property in a foreign ship wrecked on rocks that were almost certainly beyond the UK territorial waters (generally accepted as 3 miles in 1967) and therefore on the high seas. Eventually, when it was clear

---

32 See eg, "The Torrey Canyon (Report of the Committee of Scientists on the Scientific and Technical Aspects of the Torrey Canyon Disaster)", Cmnd 3246 (HMSO, 1967) [*Torrey Canyon Scientific Report*]; "Liberia: Report of the Board of Investigation in the Matter of the Stranding of the SS Torrey Canyon on March 18, 1967" (1967) 6 ILM 480–487; P Burrows, C Rowley, D Owen, "*Torrey Canyon*: A Case Study in Accidental Pollution", Scottish Journal of Political Economy Vol. 21, No. 3, November 1974 [*Torrey Canyon Case Study*] 237; C De La Rue, C Anderson, *Shipping and the Environment* (2nd ed, Informa, 2009) [*De La Rue & Anderson*] 10–12; S Rares, "Ships that Changed the Law: The *Torrey Canyon* Disaster" [2018] LMCLQ 336.

33 See *In re Barracuda Tanker Corp*, 409 F2d 1013 (2d Cir 1969).

34 In this century, governments would almost certainly insist that after saving the crew, shipowners and salvors should concentrate next on reducing pollution by offloading cargo and bunkers: see 12.3.1.

35 *Torrey Canyon Scientific Report*, 12–13; *Torrey Canyon Case Study*, 243.

36 *Torrey Canyon Scientific Report*, 11–12. If refloating had been possible, the ship would probably have been towed into the Atlantic and sunk. Today that would raise issues of dumping: see 14.1.

37 www.zeesleepvaart.com/torreycanyon.eng.htm.

38 *Torrey Canyon Scientific Report*, 6.

that salvage had failed, the UK government on 28–30 March ordered the ship to be bombed by the RAF in an attempt to burn off the cargo. At the time this was thought to be partially effective,[39] but is rarely considered today as, although some lighter fractions can burn off, there will be much heavy residue left which will soon emulsify and be difficult to remove. At the peak of the recovery operations there were some 53 ships using 90,000 gallons of detergents per day. Again, in retrospect, the type of chemicals being used could themselves be harmful to marine life.[40]

1.2.1(b) Legal claims

The size of the operation and the extent of damage meant that very large legal claims were likely. In the initial period after the wreck, in 1967, the UK's cost estimates were some £1.6 million, but overall costs were estimated at £6 million, even before French claims were taken into account (and property claims were still to be assessed).[41] Later modelling estimated the total costs as being at least £14.24 million, of which the hull claim was £5.89 million and the cargo claim was £600,000.[42] These property claims contrasted with the response and ecological damage claims for the UK and France, which varied from £7.75 million to £10 million.[43]

At the time, the basis of liability would have been in negligence[44] or public nuisance,[45] and fault in navigation of the shipowner could hardly be doubted on the facts. Still, many liability questions faced the UK and French government claimants. Which courts would have jurisdiction? Who could claim? Who were the appropriate defendant(s)? What damages were recoverable? Was there contributory negligence of the UK?[46] Could the defendants limit liability under maritime law? Did the defendants have any assets or financial security (including insurance) against which a claim could be brought?

In practice, enforcement issues will always be at the forefront of any maritime claim, especially where foreign defendants are involved. Union Oil was a potentially wealthy defendant but was neither the registered owner nor a bareboat charterer, so it would not be responsible in principle for the crew's negligence as they were employed by

---

39 *Torrey Canyon Scientific Report*, 32–33.

40 ITOPF case studies, eg www.itopf.com/in-action/case-studies/case-study/torrey-canyon-united-kingdom-1967/.

41 By the time a Working Group of CMI's International Sub-committee met in Rome on 4–5 Oct 1967, the French claims were estimated as 40 million francs: Report of International Sub-committee on Torrey Canyon, CMI Documentation 1968 Vol I, [TC-2, 10–67] 96.

42 *Torrey Canyon Case Study*, 241.

43 *Torrey Canyon Case Study*, 242.

44 There may have been difficulties in 1967 about establishing a duty of care. This would not have been a problem for any property owners claiming damage, but may have been for a government claiming clean-up expenses incurred in respect of the high seas. And in all cases, at the time there would have been serious doubts about whether any economic losses could be claimed, eg by hoteliers, despite the relatively recent decision of the House of Lords in *Hedley Byrne v Heller & Partners Ltd* [1964] AC 465.

45 The UK government claims for the actual costs to clean up beaches may have been special damage in public nuisance at common law: cf *Esso Petroleum Corp v Southport Corp* [1956] AC 218, [1955] 2 Lloyd's Rep 655, and 2.4.3. The position may have been less clear for activities on the high seas.

46 It was reported that Barracuda claimed that the oil pollution was mainly due to the bombing of the ship without the consent of the owners: see *The Times*, 4 April 1968, 8.

Barracuda.[47] The shipowner Barracuda was a foreign company, but its assets would probably consist only of the ships it owned (and any insurance proceeds represented by their loss). The *Torrey Canyon* was a total loss, so could not realistically have a value that could be realised through arrest and sale in an action in rem in the UK. According to Lloyd's Register at the time, Barracuda only owned two other ships: the *Sansinena* and the *Lake Palourde*. A sister ship arrest[48] might have been possible, provided that one of these two ships came into the jurisdiction of the UK (or courts applying similar rules), but the security that would have been required to release the ships would only have been to their value, not the full extent of any claim.[49] It appears that the *Lake Palourde* was arrested by the UK government in Singapore to secure its claims but, after security was provided for the UK government's claims, the ship apparently sailed before the French government could arrest it to secure its claims.[50] France later arrested the same ship in proceedings in Rotterdam.[51] Even if Barracuda could have been sued in the UK, it would probably have been entitled to limit its liability, eg under the existing UK legislation.[52] The CMI reported that with a limitation tonnage of 59,350 tons there would be appropriate property limits of US$4,746,000.[53]

Meanwhile, in order to forestall any actions in the US, Barracuda and Union initiated proceedings to limit liability under the then US law to the sum of US$50, based in effect on the value of the ship after the incident (effectively nothing, apart from one lifeboat). UK and French government negligence claims were then brought against Union on the basis that a time charterer was not then entitled to limit liability under US law.[54] Although as parent company Union had established Barracuda as a subsidiary, would that be enough to create a liability through a form of indirect ownership or control, eg through participation

---

47 Similarly, the cargo owners (BP) were clearly not negligent.

48 Under the Administration of Justice Act 1956, since replaced by what is now the Senior Courts Act 1971 s 21(4): see N Meeson and J Kimbell, *Admiralty Jurisdiction and Practice* (5th ed, Informa, 2017) [*Meeson and Kimbell*] 102–108.

49 Further, it is unlikely that any claim could have been brought against any P&I liability insurer of this ship, as the Club might have sought to rely on a "pay to be paid" clause if the shipowner had failed to pay the full claim itself: see 2.9.6(c).

50 *The Times*, 4 April 1968, 8.

51 See Hansard, HC Deb 11 November 1969 vol 791 cols 199–200. *The Times* (4 April 1968, 8) reported that the French government agreed to the release of the ship against a bond provided by Phoenix Assurance for £3.2 million in damages, and that a similar bond had been provided to the UK for £3 million (the total sum being the approximate value of the ship).

52 The MSA 1894 s 503 (as amended by the Merchant Shipping (Liability of Shipowners and Others) Act 1958). Had this been a simple wreck removal claim, the position might have been different: see further 2.5.1.

53 Probably around £1.5 million at the time, although when the settlement was eventually announced it was said that the owners had claimed to limit to about £750,000: see Hansard, HC Deb 11 November 1969 vol 791 col 200. It is assumed that the CMI calculation was based on the 1957 Limitation Convention limits of 1,000 gf per limitation ton. Interestingly, the CMI Report noted that if one were allowed to take the deadweight tonnage (ie reflecting cargo size), the limit would have been $9,463,000. The need to have adequate limits and to focus on the cargo's contribution to the pollution can be seen in the subsequent provisions of the CLC and Fund Convention: see 2.6.2(a) and (b).

54 By contrast, under the then MSA 1894, as amended, a time charterer could limit liability. That is also the position under the LLMC 1976/1996 Art 2: see 2.5.3, 2.5.4(d).

in design or manufacture?[55] And, in any event, was limitation possible for Union under US law?[56]

On 11 November 1969, it was announced[57] that Barracuda and Union had settled both governments' claims for £1.5 million each (about US$7.2 million in total),[58] plus another £25,000 (about US$60,000) as an ex gratia payment for other potential claimants.[59] The attorney general, Sir Elwyn Jones, told the House of Commons that although a claim had been lodged for £6 million (about US$22 million), the settlement was made in view of the "uncertainties, inevitable delays and expense of litigation, complex and unique points of law involved in proving liability, and finally the difficulty in qualifying and proving damages".

On the very date of this 1969 announcement, IMCO was holding a diplomatic conference to try to deal with some of the legal problems that had become apparent.[60]

1.2.2 Wrecks since 1967

1.2.2(a) Tanker wrecks

After the *Torrey Canyon*, IMCO (and later IMO) legislated to minimise pollution from oil tankers being wrecked by introducing a series of conventions regulating the design and operation of such tankers.[61] These pollution prevention conventions provided traditional public law remedies, through the criminal law, to enforce their provisions. In the same period, the IMO introduced parallel conventions which provided typical private law remedies, through compensation mechanisms, designed to pay for losses after a casualty.[62] What is significant about these developments is that most of them were a reaction to the wreck of particular tankers—in what might be called a 'disaster reaction syndrome'.[63] Nevertheless, these measures have contributed to a progressive downward trend in oil spills.[64]

It is appropriate to note briefly some of the key tanker wrecks which have influenced the way that compensation arrangements have been developed since *Torrey Canyon*.[65]

---

55 Although it would have been hard to prove from the known facts that there was any causative link between this and the casualty, given the obvious negligence of the master.

56 At first instance, *In re Barracuda Tanker Corp*, 281 F Supp 228, 231 (SDNY 1968), the judge had held that in effect there was a form of sale and leaseback, so that Union might be an "owner" entitled to limit. On appeal, *In re Barracuda Tanker Corp*, 409 F2d 1013 (2d Cir 1969), the court doubted if Union could be an "owner" for limitation purposes (nor was it a bareboat charter entitled to limit), but the tricky issue of Union's liability was sent to trial. It appears that the case settled beforehand.

57 Hansard, HC Deb 11 November 1969 vol 791 cols 199–206.

58 This was in effect the amount of security the owners had to put up to release the sister ship *Lake Palourde* in Singapore, but did not include any additional security given to the French. US$ figures in Congressional Record, Senate, November 12, 1969, p. 33854.

59 But if this sum was exceeded the governments actually agreed to indemnify the owner for any excess.

60 See 2.6.1 for the action taken.

61 See eg International Convention for the Prevention of Pollution from Ships, 1973 (MARPOL), as modified by Protocols of 1978 and 1997 and the International Convention for the Safety of Life at Sea (SOLAS) 1974; De la Rue & Anderson, 807–853.

62 Eg the CLC and Fund Convention compensation regimes that provided, inter alia, for strict liability up to agreed limits and provisions dealing with financial security for claims: see 2.6.2.

63 For the legislative reaction to passenger shipwrecks in the 1980s and 1990s, see 1.2.2(b) and 2.3.

64 ITOPF, Oil Tanker Spill Statistics 2017: www.itopf.org/knowledge-resources/data-statistics/statistics/.

65 Detailed accounts of the compensation claims generated by these wrecks can be found in the documentation of the IOPC Funds, eg in the Annual Reports: see also 2.6.2(b).

Together, they have permanently changed the financial focus of wreck law away from mere commercial loss to the ship and cargo owners and onto environmental damage—and the economic losses that may flow from that.[66]

The *Amoco Cadiz* (109,700 gt), carrying 220,000 tons of oil, was wrecked off the French coast in 1978 after a steering failure.[67] The size of the ensuing claims was not only because of the massive amount of oil that leaked from the wreck and needed to be cleaned up, but also because of the economic impact on the French tourist and fishing industries. The sums available under the CLC 1969 would not have been enough to meet all claims, and the Fund Convention 1971 was not then in force, so the French claimants forum shopped by bringing litigation in the US.[68] Some 14 years after the wreck, in 1992, a US court eventually awarded some US$61 million to the French claimants (plus interest) and US$21.7 million to the cargo owner (plus interest), without limitation of liability.[69] The main legal consequence of the wreck was a call to increase the sums available under the international regimes. Significant increases were agreed in 1984 Protocols to both the CLC 1969 and Fund Convention 1971, but these never entered into force.[70] Eventually, these 1984 Protocols were largely reproduced by two further Protocols in 1992, which produced what are now referred to as the CLC 1992 and Fund Convention 1992—still the main international tanker compensation regime.[71]

In 1980, the Malagasy tanker *Tanio* (18,048 gt) broke up off the French coast and the bow section sank in 90 m with about 5,000 mt of oil cargo. It took 16 months to pump out the oil, while it appears that the wrecked hull remained on the seabed. The financial settlement was long and complex.[72]

The *Exxon Valdez* (112,088 gt) went aground off Alaska in 1989 with the loss of some oil cargo.[73] Although it was eventually refloated, this wreck was significant not only for the difficulty and cost of clean-up in a sensitive area, but also because it put an end to US moves to join the international CLC and Fund Convention system (then in the form of the 1984 Protocols) and led to the unique US national solution of the Oil Pollution Act 1990.

The *Haven* (109,977 gt) exploded and sank in 1991 off Genoa, Italy, with an oil cargo of about 144,000 mt. Part of the deck section separated and sank in about 80 m, the bow section sank in about 500 m, and the remainder was towed inshore but eventually sank in about 90 m. About 10,000 mt of oil was spilled. Initial claims exceeded £284 million but

---

66 See generally IOPC Funds *Summary of Incidents 2018* (https://www.iopcfunds.org/incidents/incidents-summary-table/), showing details of the other 41 major incidents under the 1992 Fund, and the 107 under the 1971 Fund.

67 See *De La Rue & Anderson*, 27–28.

68 See N Gaskell "The Amoco Cadiz I: Liability Issues" (1985) 3 JENRL 169, "The Amoco Cadiz II: Limitation and Legal Implications" (1985) 4 JENRL 225–242.

69 See *In re Oil Spill by the Amoco Cadiz*, 954 F2d 1279 (7th Cir 1992). The calculation of pre-judgment interest was US$33 million for the cargo claim alone: see 4 F3d 997 (7th Cir 1992). There is apparently no report of the interest payable on the French claims, but the total payable to them would presumably have been over US$150 million, so that a rough overall total might be in excess of US$200 million.

70 Largely owing to concerns about the burden of contributions to the IOPC Fund.

71 See 2.6.2.

72 See IOPC Fund, *Annual Report 1988*, 25; www.cedre.fr/en/spill/tanio/tanio_threat.php; and 10.2.5.

73 See *De La Rue & Anderson*, 48–52.

a complicated global settlement was reached for about £43 million.[74] The wreck was not raised, but oil apparently leaked from it many years afterwards.

In 1992, the *Aegean Sea* (57,801 gt) with a cargo of 79,082 mt of oil was wrecked while entering La Coruña in Spain.[75] There was a large fire and the forward section sank, but oil from the stern section was removed by salvors working from the shore. An estimated amount of about 73,500 mt of cargo was lost (some by fire). There was large-scale pollution and damage to property and a total of £45 million was paid out.[76]

Two UK wrecks were particularly influential as they also illustrated that the CLC and Fund system was not adequate to deal with large clean-up and compensation claims. The *Braer* (44,989 gt) went aground off Scotland in 1993, but at that stage the CLC 1992 and Fund Convention 1992[77] were not in force. The compensation claims exceeded the existing CLC 1969 and Fund Convention 1971 limits and the UK government agreed to put its claims behind those of private economic loss claimants. Many shortcomings were recognised by the Donaldson Report.[78] The *Sea Empress* (77,356 gt) grounded in Milford Haven in Wales in 1996 while carrying 130,018 mt of oil. Again, the 1992 regime was not in force. The compensation paid was some £36.6 million.[79] Negligence and public nuisance recourse claims were brought by the IOPC Fund against the port authority for its alleged failures in relation to the port operations, including proper channel marking, and this claim was ultimately settled for £20 million. One significant result of the casualty was the Donaldson Review,[80] which highlighted the need for greater national coordination of responses to such incidents.[81]

The tanker *Erika* (19,666 gt) was carrying a cargo of 30,884 mt of heavy fuel oil in December 1999 on a voyage from Dunkirk to Livorno when it encountered heavy weather. Although it made for a port of refuge, it experienced a major hull failure and eventually broke in two about 45 nm off the French coast.[82] The bow section then sank, and an attempt to tow the stern section into deeper waters away from the coast failed after a day; this too sank. Some 400 km of coastline was affected by pollution. This was one of the first cases under the CLC 1992 and Fund Convention 1992.[83] The significance of this wreck was that it showed how even the 1992 compensation regime might not provide sufficient funds to compensate for pollution that affected a wide area of coast in a developed state.[84] This led

---

74 IOPC Funds, *Annual Report 1989*, 42–48.

75 The value of the ship, bunkers and lost freight amounted to about US65 million and spawned its own litigation between shipowner and charterer: see *Aegean Sea Traders Corp v Repsol Petroleo SA (The Aegean Sea)* [1998] 2 Lloyd's Rep 39, and 2.4.4(c), 2.5.4(b).

76 See IOPC Funds, *Incidents Involving the IOPC Funds 2013*.

77 See 2.6.2(a) and (b).

78 Lord Donaldson, *Safer Ships, Cleaner Seas*, Report of Lord Donaldson's Inquiry into the Prevention of Pollution from Merchant Shipping (Cm 2560, HMSO, 1994) [*Donaldson Report 1994*].

79 IOPC Funds, *Annual Report 2003*, 58–63; SEEEC, "The Environmental Impacts of the *Sea Empress* Oil Spill" (1998).

80 Lord Donaldson, *Review of Salvage Intervention and their Command and Control* (CM 4193, HMSO, 1999) [*Donaldson Review 1999*].

81 In particular by the creation of the SOSREP: see 4.2.2.

82 IOPC Fund, *Fund Annual Report 2007*, 77–90.

83 See 2.6.2(a) and (b).

84 In the end it appeared that the 1992 regime was able to pay all claims within the limits and a complex global settlement of claims was reached in 2011: see IOPC Funds, *Incidents Involving the IOPC Funds 2013*, 6–11.

to calls for even more compensation amounts to be made available, if not from the international system, then outside it[85] or through new EU legislation. As an immediate result of the disaster the EU introduced a series of packages (*Erika* I and II)[86] dealing with regulation and safety.[87] It also raised the possibility of dealing with pollution damage compensation both generally and in relation to marine pollution.

While the EU was still considering the *Erika* packages, the Bahamas-registered tanker *Prestige* (42,820 gt) broke in two in 2002 and sank some 260 km west of Vigo (Spain) at depths of over 3,500 m.[88] Some 63,200 mt of oil were lost. Like the *Erika*, the resulting pollution caused great loss to the tourism and fishing industries in Spain and France. Some oil, perhaps 100 mt, was left in the after part of the wreck after clean-up operations.[89] Once again, it appeared that the limits of liability under the Fund Convention 1992 might not be enough to meet all possible claims.[90] As with previous cases (eg *Amoco Cadiz* and *Erika*), claimants sought to avoid the shipowner and Fund's limits of liability. In December 2018, the Spanish Supreme Court delivered a final judgment[91] ordering that the Spanish State, the French State and other claimants be awarded some €1.6 billion in compensation, later reduced to about €1.4 billion.[92] The IOPC Fund responded by agreeing to make pro rata payments up to its applicable limit of liability of €171.5 million.[93] The Supreme Court also found that the London P&I Club was liable for all the damages caused by the incident beyond the CLC limits and up to the limit of its policy of US$1 billion.[94] It remains to be seen how far the judgment can be enforced against the Club.[95]

The international significance of the *Prestige* wreck is that it gave added impetus to ensure that additional funds were available to pay compensation—particularly for economic loss claims. The EU Commission considered that the *Erika* I and II packages were

---

85 There were also attempts to sue the classification society, in a bid to satisfy claims that exceeded the CLC and Fund 1992 limits, and Total as seller of the cargo and charterer. Total agreed to pay the French State €153.9, an amount awarded by a criminal court, taking into account sums already received from the IOPC Fund: see IOPC Funds, *Incidents Involving the IOPC Funds 2011*, 49; also 14.6.3.

86 See COM(2000) 142 COM(2000) 802 and *De La Rue & Anderson*, 75.

87 Eg on the enhancement of port state control; accelerated phasing out of single-hull vessels; vessel traffic monitoring; a notification system for ships bound for or leaving EU ports and carrying dangerous or polluting goods; the establishment of the European Maritime Safety Agency [EMSA]. See Directive 2005/35/EC of the European Parliament and of the Council of 7 September 2005 on ship-source pollution and on the introduction of penalties for infringements. D Somers, G Gonsaeles, "The Consequences of the Sinking of the M/S *Erika* in European Waters: Towards a Total Loss for International Shipping Law?" 41 JMLC 57 [*Somers & Gonsaeles*], 82.

88 IOPC Funds, *Incidents involving the IOPC Funds 2013*, 12.

89 For disputes about whether the removal costs for this last oil were unrecoverable as being disproportionate, see IOPC Funds, *Annual Report 1996*, 112, 92FUND/EXC.30/9/2, 29 September 2005, 92FUND/EXC.32/4/Add.1, 7 February 2006; 92FUND/EXC.32/6, para 3.2.80; also 9.2.5(e), 10.2.4.

90 By 31 December 2018 the total claims paid by the IOPC Fund were over £107 million (about €121 million): see IOPC Funds, *Annual Report 2018*, 16, 45.

91 Supreme Court (Penal Chamber), Cassation Appeal/606/2018, available on the IOPC Funds website in Spanish with extracts in English: www.iopcfunds.org/incidents/incident-map/#126-13-November-2002.

92 This consisted of €885 million for losses and €553 million for 'moral' damages: see IOPC Funds, IOPC/APR19/3/2, 15 March 2019; IOPC/APR19/3/2/1, 25 March 2019.

93 For the calculation of Fund limits more generally, see 2.6.2(b).

94 IOPC Funds, *Annual Report 2018*, 16; IOPC/APR19/3/2, 15 March 2019: see also 2.9.6(b). For the ramifications of this for the WRC 2007, see 10.8.5(g); also 10.8.6 for Club reinsurance cover.

95 See also 2.9.6(c).

insufficient and worked on proposals for a third maritime safety package (*Erika* III),[96] which by 2008 included proposals for a Directive on the civil liability and financial guarantees of shipowners. These moves raised the risk of a regional EU compensation regime that might have overlapped, or conflicted, with the IMO compensation regimes.[97] That was a significant driver for the creation of the Supplementary Fund Protocol in 2003.[98] Although negotiations for the Supplementary Fund Protocol 2003 had already started after the *Erika* disaster, this was of no immediate help to *Prestige* claimants. This *Erika* III package was eventually adopted on 11 March 2009. It included two Regulations and five Directives[99] but no new EU maritime compensation regime.

There have been other significant tanker wrecks since the *Prestige*,[100] but the P&I Clubs and the IOPC Fund have developed enormous experience in handling spills and dealing with compensation claims under the CLC and Fund Convention system.[101] That experience has also been important in dealing with the environmental impact of dealing with wreck cases more generally (including bunker spills and cargo loss).

1.2.2(b) Other wrecks

The wrecks described above have been only some of the main tanker casualties, but incidents involving the loss of the bunkers (fuel) from the wreck of all types of ships can also be very damaging and expensive. Most of the concerns were about operational spills from ships, particularly given the relatively small size of the spills and their frequency,[102] but by the 1990s, States were also concerned by bunker pollution from wrecks.[103] These concerns led to the Bunkers Convention 2001.[104]

There have, of course, been significant post-1967 wrecks involving many different types of ship. The wreck of passenger ship can involve the loss (or threat) of considerable loss of life.[105] The ferry *Herald of Free Enterprise* foundered in the English Channel in March 1987 after sailing with its bow door open, with the loss of 150 passengers and 38 crew. The ferry *Scandinavian Star* suffered a severe fire in April 1990 in the Baltic Sea, and 158 died. In 1994, the *MV Estonia* also foundered in the Baltic Sea with the loss of 878

---

96 See COM(2005)585 Final (23 November 2005).

97 Eventually, the EU agreed not to enact measures conflicting with the CLC/Fund system and the EC Directive on Environmental Liability 2004/35/EC Art 4(2) now contains exceptions so as to avoid such conflicts with the IMO liability Conventions: see 2.6.5. For other possible areas of conflict between EU law and the international regimes, see eg 14.6.3.

98 See 2.6.2(c).

99 One draft directive had proposed civil liability provisions (see COM/2007/0674 final), but by 2008 the EU Council agreed to withdraw these from what became Directive 2009/20/EC so that it only dealt with issues such as compulsory insurance of shipowners: see 2.9.6(a). See also Regulation (EC) No 392/2009, which extends to liabilities after the wreck of passenger ships: see 1.2.2(b), 2.3.1, 2.3.6.

100 Eg the *Hebei Spirit* (140,848 gt) off Korea in 2007.

101 See further 2.6.2(a) and (b).

102 See eg ITOPF paper at LEG 74/4/2, 9 August 1996, Annex. See also *De La Rue & Anderson*, 255–256.

103 Eg the wreck of the small container ship *Cita* off the Scilly Isles in 1997 involved clean-up operations of over £100,000.

104 See N Gaskell and C Forrest, "Marine Pollution Damage in Australia: Implementing the Bunker Oil Convention 2001 and the Supplementary Fund Protocol 2003" (2008) 27 UQLJ 103 [*Gaskell & Forrest*], 125–143, and 2.6.3.

105 Some of the casualties are listed in 2.3.1. See also 1.2.5.

INTRODUCTION TO WRECK CASUALTIES

lives after a failure of its bow visor.[106] In 2014, the *Sewol* sank in South Korea with the loss of 304 lives.[107] All these were ferries, but there have been significant incidents with cruise ships, including the sinking of the *Mikhail Lermontov* in New Zealand in 1986, fortunately with the loss of only one life, and the *Costa Concordia* in 2012 with 32 deaths.[108] Small river craft are also vulnerable to wreck, with the *Marchioness* sinking in 1989, with 51 lives lost after a collision in the Thames with a larger ship. The largest loss of life has usually occurred in the developing world, with the loss of the *Dona Paz* with 4,386 souls in the Philippines in 1987, the *Salem Express* in Egypt in 1991 (over 450 lost) and the *Neptune* in Haiti in 1993 (possibly over 2,000 drowned). The IMO has reacted to these wrecks by creating a convention to provide compensation, using elements of the CLC model.[109]

Examples of incidents involving wreck removal are given throughout the book,[110] but three specific wrecks will now be considered as they have also been influential in a variety of ways: the *MSC Napoli*, the *Rena* and the *Costa Concordia*.

1.2.3 MSC Napoli *(2007)*

The wreck of the *MSC Napoli* illustrates how a casualty can move from being a search and rescue (SAR) operation to salvage, government intervention, pollution prevention and ultimately wreck removal. The boundaries between these stages may not always be clear-cut.

1.2.3(a) The casualty

The *MSC Napoli* (53,409 gt) was a 1991 built UK flagged container ship (capacity 4,419 TEU) owned by Metvale Ltd and on charter to the Mediterranean Shipping Company (MSC).[111] When launched, it was one of the largest container ships ever built.[112] On 18 January 2007 it was en route from Antwerp to Portugal[113] with a cargo of 2,318 containers weighing 41,473 mt;[114] 159 containers weighing some 1,684 mt were classified as dangerous cargo. Some 3,800 mt of bunkers and lubricating oil were on board.[115] While in the English Channel it suffered a catastrophic hull failure in heavy seas. In effect, there was a

---

106 See also 4.6.2, 10.2.5.
107 See also 13.1.3, 13.6.2.
108 See 1.2.5.
109 See the Athens Convention 2002 and 2.3.
110 See eg 2.5.9(c) and 10.2.5.
111 See UK Marine Accident Investigation Board, *Report on the investigation of the structural failure of MSC Napoli, English Channel on 18 January 2007*, Accident Investigation Report 9/2008, April 2008 [*MAIB, MSC Napoli Report*], 4: https://assets.publishing.service.gov.uk/media/547c703ced915d4c0d000087/NapoliReport.pdf. The precise ownership arrangements are not entirely clear as there was also a Metvale Limited Partnership, apparently a British Virgin Islands entity, which was also described in reports as the owner. The registered operator, ie ship manager, was Zodiac Maritime Agencies Ltd of London.
112 MAIB, *MSC Napoli Report*, 16.
113 MAIB, *MSC Napoli Report*, 4.
114 Maritime and Coastguard Agency 'MSC Napoli Incident, the Maritime and Coastguard Agency's Response', April 2008 [*MCA Response MSC Napoli*], 11: http://webarchive.nationalarchives.gov.uk/20090510130332/www.redensigngroup.org/lrgtxt/197-299_napoli_report_final-redux.pdf.
115 A total of 3,512 mt of fuel oil and 152 mt of diesel: *MCA Response MSC Napoli*, 11; Environment Agency, press release, "Tenth anniversary of the *MSC Napoli* shipwreck disaster", 18 January 2017 [*Environment Agency, Tenth anniversary of MSC Napoli*].

large crack in the port side of the hull caused by a lack of buckling strength in the engine room region.[116]

The crew abandoned ship and were picked up by Royal Navy helicopters. French tugs towed the ship towards Portland but, in view of the risk of sinking, it was ordered by the Secretary of State's Representative for Maritime Salvage and Intervention (SOSREP)[117] to be deliberately beached in Branscombe Bay (ie a 'place of refuge'). A Temporary Exclusion Zone (TEZ) was established for the sea around the *MSC Napoli*, and a Temporary Danger Area (TDA) declared in the air (within 3 miles distance and 2,000 feet altitude).[118]

A consortium of professional salvors including Smit were engaged on the basis of a Lloyd's Open Form (LOF) contract including SCOPIC.[119] Smit divers drilled into the hull and from day 6 transferred more than 3,500 mt of bunker fuel (including diesel) into a chartered products tanker, the *Forth Fisher* (3368 gt), and oil was skimmed from the submerged holds and spaces; but about 302 mt of oil escaped along with oil residues (including lubricating oil and bilge oil).[120] Some washed up on local beaches, often mixed up with debris. Extensive resources were mobilised (eg tugs with booms and dispersants), and monitoring and clean-up continued for some 225 days; but overall the pollution was not major. One thousand seabirds were collected and sent to the RSPCA for treatment and 600 were later released. After the beaching some 117 containers were lost overboard, and 80 were washed ashore in the UK (two in France).[121] Some contents (eg light plastics) were carried by the tide to more remote beaches. Some 854 containers were removed from the deck of the ship by 25 February (39 days after the incident), but the main holds were flooded and it was not until 17 May (day 120) that the 1,358 below deck containers were removed.[122]

Although Portland had no dedicated container facilities (eg container cranes and stackers), the SOSREP[123] determined that the containers be shuttled there, having first been removed by a crane barge. Here a process was established for surveying the damaged containers, separating out that which could be salvaged; storage space was at a premium. This activity was overseen by the Environment Agency.[124]

1.2.3(b) Removal operations

Once the bunkers and containers had been removed, the issue became what to do with the hull of the wreck. Some idea of the choices that might be considered in such a case can be seen from the potential options for disposal that were discussed.[125] These included

---

116 *MAIB, MSC Napoli Report*, 39. As a result of the incident, screening took place of some 1,500 container ships and at least 12 were identified as needing remedial action, with a further ten being borderline.
117 See 4.2.2.
118 *MCA Response MSC Napoli*, 58. For the UK's intervention powers, see 4.2.3.
119 SCOPIC (see 2.7.9(c)) was invoked by Smit on 20 January: *MCA Response MSC Napoli*, 22.
120 *MCA Response MSC Napoli*, 54.
121 None of the dangerous goods containers was in fact lost overboard: *MCA Response MSC Napoli*, 43. Some of the cargo in containers washed ashore was 'liberated' by locals until measures were taken to inform the public that this was theft: see 3.5.3, 4.2.5, 4.5. For insurance coverage for theft, see 2.9.3(b).
122 *MCA Response MSC Napoli*, 13–14; cf at 72, where it is stated that 1,351 containers were recovered from below deck; in all, 2,199 containers were recovered from *MSC Napoli*.
123 See 4.2.2.
124 See 4.2.4.
125 *MCA Response MSC Napoli*, 81.

(a) leaving the vessel at the site and allowing a natural break-up; (b) dismantling the vessel in its current location; (c) dismantling the stern section and refloating the bow; (d) refloating the entire vessel and towing to a ship-recycling facility; (e) stripping the vessel, refloating it and towing it away for eventual seabed placement. By 18 June, discussions were still continuing with all interested parties. The commercial interests naturally wanted the ship refloated and moved as quickly as possible, but the SOSREP insisted on his approval of the ship's fate. Comprehensive environmental impact assessments (EIAs) had been prepared over several months and potential small pollutants (paint, batteries, etc) were removed.

After an attempt to refloat the ship on 9 July 2007, the hull damage was revealed to be worse than expected. To avoid the risk of breaking up at sea, and in the absence of any approval for disposal, the SOSREP ordered it to be beached again. On 20 July the forward part of the ship was separated by explosives in an operation by the Salvage and Marine Operations IPT (S&MO), a part of the Ministry of Defence. This bow section was towed to Belfast for scrapping and recycling.[126] The after section was dealt with under a different contract in 2008.[127] The accommodation section was cut away and removed and the remainder was cut into sections of about 300 mt to be recycled in the Netherlands. By July 2009 the Environment Agency was satisfied that all traces of the *MSC Napoli* had been removed.

1.2.3(c) Legal claims
The ship had Protection and Indemnity Club (P&I) Club cover with the London Steamship Owners Mutual Insurance Association. The eventual cost of the wreck removal operation to the shipowner (and Club) was variously reported to be in excess of £120 million,[128] or around US$135 million, although it is said that this would have been less if the ship could have been disposed of immediately after refloating.[129]

Claims were made against the shipowners in excess of £100 million from cargo owners and also from the UK government. The government's cost was approximately £2.7 million, of which only £1.3 million was recovered.[130] The only litigation that reached court was in relation to limitation of liability.[131] On 27 February 2007 the shipowners constituted a limitation fund under the LLMC 1996 for £14,710,000 in England, in respect of which a limitation decree was granted. It seems unlikely that any UK government claims relating to wreck removal would have been subject to limits, but those for bunker pollution may have been.[132] Major claims against the limitation fund were made by cargo owners and it was decided that, in principle, slot charterers from MSC were entitled to limit liability under the LLMC,[133] presumably in addition to any container limits under the Hague-Visby Rules.[134] The details of any final settlements are not publicly available.

---

126 On scrapping generally, see 14.1–14.3.
127 *Herbert, Challenges,* 18.
128 *Environment Agency, Tenth anniversary of MSC Napoli.*
129 *Herbert, Challenges,* 18.
130 See Earl Attlee, Second Reading of the Wreck Removal Convention Bill in the House of Lords, Hansard Vol 727, col 1134 (13 May 2011) [*House of Lords, WRC Bill Second Reading debate*]: see also 11.3.1.
131 *Metvale Ltd and Another v Monsanto International SARL and Others (The MSC Napoli)* [2009] 1 Lloyd's Rep 246; also 2.5.3.
132 See 2.5.3, 2.5.4(b), 2.5.5.
133 *The MSC Napoli* [2009] 1 Lloyd's Rep 246.
134 See 2.1.5(e).

1.2.3(d) Lessons

A number of significant lessons arise from the *MSC Napoli* casualty, some practical, some legal. The *MSC Napoli* is a typical example of how a casualty starts as a commercial salvage operation, then is affected by government intervention, and then moves into more of a wreck removal operation, depending on the value of the property saved relative to the costs of removal. This transition has a series of consequences for all parties involved. The financial motivations of the various commercial parties are affected along with their legal rights and liabilities.[135]

The actions of the SOSREP have generally been praised, in that the decision to bring the ship inshore and beach it might have appeared counter-intuitive, but was a "least worst" option.[136] It involved discussions between the French and UK authorities under the joint maritime contingency plan, Mancheplan, as to an appropriate place,[137] including factors such as whether nearby ports (eg Falmouth and Plymouth) had sufficient depth of water for the ship and whether the large number of containers could be offloaded and stored.[138]

As with oil tanker disasters, the *MSC Napoli* showed that there were real practical and legal problems in disposing of the residue of the cargo which was contaminated (eg with oil and mud).[139] There was little space to store the containers in Portland as they were brought ashore and then they had to be cleaned. In the event, MSC provided a feeder vessel to take undamaged containers away.[140] Options for final disposal had to be discussed and environmental impact assessments (EIAs) prepared.[141]

The *MSC Napoli* casualty was significant because it gave a concrete example to governments of how the effects of a wreck might be mitigated by coordinated action. In particular, it shows that bringing a ship to a place of relative safety enabled the removal of almost the entire quantity of cargo and bunkers on board. Had the ship been sunk in the English Channel, it would have been much harder (and more expensive) to deal with the safety and environmental threats. The environmental threat from container ships was further illustrated by the wreck of the *Rena*.

1.2.4 Rena *(2011)*

1.2.4(a) The casualty

The Liberian registered MV *Rena* grounded on 5 October 2011 on Otaiti (Astrolabe) Reef, some 12 km from New Zealand's coast (close to Motiti Island). The *Rena* was a 37,209 gt

---

135 See Chapters 12 and 13.

136 There have been other disasters, including the *Prestige* (see 1.2.2(a)), where it had been alleged that the failure to provide a place of safety may have caused a more serious total loss where cargo removal was not possible: see *De La Rue & Anderson*, 905–921; A Morrison, *Places of Refuge for Ships in Distress: Problems and Methods of Resolution* (Martinus Nijhoff, 2012).

137 The *MCA Response MSC Napoli*, 20, is rather coy about the reaction of the French authorities who "were unable to identify a suitable place of refuge for the *MSC Napoli* on the French coast within about 200 miles".

138 T Stone, "The UK Response to the *Napoli* Incident", International Oil Spill Conference Proceedings: May 2008, Vol. 2008, No. 1, 1037–1042.

139 *MCA Response MSC Napoli*, 14. For the UK response coordination and the casualty, see 4.8.5. For particular problems concerning containers, see 1.3.2. For disposal issues, see Chapter 14.

140 Cf 2.5.4.

141 *MCA Response MSC Napoli*, 15.

container ship owned by Daina Shipping Company, incorporated in Liberia (as a single ship company, but part of the fleet of Greek-controlled Costamare Shipping Inc, incorporated in the Marshall Islands).[142] She was on charter to MSC, with a cargo of 1,368 containers (547 on deck and 821 below deck). Thirty-seven of the containers were identified as containing potentially harmful cargo, including cryolite (a by-product of aluminium smelting), copper clove, and plastic beads. Eighty-six containers were lost overboard on the night of the grounding.[143] The *Rena* also had 1,733 mt of heavy fuel oil as bunkers on board and 200 mt of marine diesel oil.[144] A major oil spill response was activated by Maritime New Zealand under the Maritime Transport Act (MTA) 1994. On 6 October, Svitzer was appointed as a Lloyd's Open Form (LOF) salvor, with SCOPIC invoked.[145]

As with most modern disasters, the first priority was to remove bunkers, as 350 mt of bunkers leaked into the sea in the months after the grounding.[146] Some 8,000 volunteers helped to collect over 1,000 mt of oily waste from coastlines.[147] By 2014, 1,053 of the 1,368 containers had been recovered,[148] along with 4,500 mt of containers and debris.[149] A Long-term Environmental Recovery Plan was developed by 2012 to try to restore the general area of the casualty to its previous state, and by 2013 it appeared that the general environment was recovering well.[150]

Initially, the ship was aground forward, with the aft section floating freely. However, bad weather caused the vessel to move, resulting in gradual structural failure.[151] Significant breaking up occurred from March 2013 after a further major storm,[152] while much cargo and some oil remained on board. The aft and bow sections broke between the third and fifth holds, and by 2014 the remains of the ship were in broadly three parts.

Although large parts of the ship were removed over the next two years, the remains of the stern section sank over 50 m as a result of Cyclone Lusi in March 2014, making diving difficult and dangerous. Cyclone Pam in March 2015 caused significant changes to the wreck site, including the moving of the aft section into deeper water.[153] Substantial recovery work continued until 2016, involving the removal of 4,000 mt of material including

---

142 Information about the *Rena* can be gained from a variety of decisions and reports, not all of which are entirely consistent as to details. See www.crownlaw.govt.nz/publications/reports/ for the text of many reports commissioned by the New Zealand government. The following are of particular relevance: 'Crown Position on the Resource Consent Application for the Rena Wreck', NZ Cabinet paper of 31 July 2014 by the Attorney General, C Finlayson (available at www.crownlaw.govt.nz/assets/Uploads/Reports/cabinet-paper.pdf) [*AG's Rena Cabinet Paper*]; the Final Report on the MV Rena and Motiti Island Claims (Waitangi Tribunal Report 2015, WAI 2391, WAI 2393), 5 [*Rena: Waitangi Final Report*], www.waitangitribunal.govt.nz.
143 *Rena: Waitangi Final Report*, 5.
144 *Svitzer Salvage BV v Z Energy Ltd* (reissue) [2013] NZHC 2584 [6] records 1,700 mt of HFO.
145 For LOF and SCOPIC generally, see 2.8 (eg 2.8.9(c)). See 12.1.2(e) for litigation between Svitzer and a sub-contracted tanker, where Svitzer argued that it had agreed to pay an exorbitant amount under duress.
146 *Rena: Waitangi Final Report*, 5.
147 Ibid., 6.
148 *AG's Rena Cabinet Paper*, [10].
149 Ibid., [11].
150 Ibid., [16–17].
151 The ship eventually broke in two in January 2012.
152 *Ngai Te Hapu Inc v Bay of Plenty Regional Council* [2017] NZEnvC 73 [10].
153 Ibid., [13].

some 14 mt of exposed copper clove cargo deposits.[154] A major issue became how far it was possible, reasonable or economically viable to remove every trace of the vessel from the wreck (ie full removal). At that stage the aft section was gradually collapsing on itself (flat packing) with associated debris in even deeper water; there were remains of holds 3–5 and some containers; remains of the bow section were on and around the reef.[155]

The major remaining contaminants were TBT (tributyltin) paint flakes and the copper clove cargo in one container; by this stage there was still probably some unrecovered oil, but risks from this could be dealt with by monitoring and response.

1.2.4(b) Practical and legal problems

The *Rena* involved wreck removal operations concerning a container ship, like the *MSC Napoli*, but presented a number of different or contrasting issues. The location of the wreck posed problems that contributed significantly to the costs incurred by the shipowner. The site of the casualty was more remote than the *MSC Napoli*, but it was also in an area that had an importance to the indigenous Maori community. The widespread pollution from the bunkers, containers and debris was of particular concern to the indigenous Maori living in or affiliated to Motiti. This gave rise to proceedings under the Treaty of Waitangi (in relation to alleged failings in consultation by the State with Maori). Wreck removal notices were issued by Maritime New Zealand and, although large parts of the ship were removed, a significant dispute arose as to what to do with the wreck of the ship itself, in particular because of the cultural implications of the wreck. This gave rise to further proceedings as to whether the remains of the ship could be left *in situ*—in effect, dumped.

Thus, in addition to the normal maritime legal framework (eg regarding safety[156] and the environment[157]) there was another legislative layer involving the Treaty of Waitangi (broadly reflecting Maori rights). The resolution of the complex relationships between these laws added to the costs of an already difficult operation.

The civil legal framework that applied once the ship had grounded initially involved an interplay between traditional wreck removal provisions and those dealing with dumping.[158] Wreck removal notices were issued under the MTA 1994,[159] as the wreck was both hazardous (through pollution) and a hazard to navigation.[160] The default position under these notices was for the entire wreck to be removed. Under the Resource Management Act 1991 s 15A, consent was needed to leave (ie dump) any part of the wreck on the reef.[161] Section 2

---

154 Ibid., [14].
155 Ibid., [17].
156 Eg the MTA 1994.
157 Eg the Resource Management Act 1991.
158 B Marten, "International Recent Developments: New Zealand" (2014) 38 Tul Mar LJ 623, 623–631. B Marten, *Maritime Law in New Zealand* (Thomson Reuters, 2016) [*Marten, Maritime Law*]; W Irving, 'The Nairobi Convention: Reforming Wreck Removal in New Zealand' (2010) 24 ANZMLJ 76.
159 s 248: see *Svitzer Salvage BV v Z Energy Ltd (reissue)* [2013] NZHC 2584 [5].
160 The ship interests had suggested that that the MTA 1994 notices may have been invalid in so far as they did not relate to protect navigation [215], but the only practical effect of such a ruling might have been that dumping consent was required earlier [215]. In other circumstances, such an argument might be important.
161 *Ngai Te Hapu Inc v Bay of Plenty Regional Council* [2017] NZEnvC 073 [212], *Rena*; *Waitangi Final Report*, 6. The Act gave effect to anti-dumping obligations under UNCLOS Art 210 as well as the London (Dumping) Convention: see 14.1.2. See generally *Marten, Maritime Law*, 107.

defined dumping "(a) in relation to waste or other matter its deliberate disposal; and (b) in relation to a ship or an offshore installation, its deliberate disposal or abandonment". There was an argument as to whether the *Rena* had ceased to be a "ship" at some stage (eg after 2016),[162] but as a matter of interpretation of the dumping provision, s 15A, this was irrelevant: the remains were either "other matter from a ship" or it continued to be a ship with its cargo. In any event, a consent was needed from the time the wreck removal notices issued under the MTA 1994 were lifted in April 2016. Discharge of contaminants required consent under s 15(1) or s 15B.[163]

1.2.4(c) Legal claims

Accounts as to the total costs of the casualty vary, depending on which costs are included (and when conversions are made between US$ and NZ$).[164] Government response and clean-up costs were NZ$47 million.[165] In 2017 an estimate of the total cost of "salvage works" was US$650 million (about NZ$900 million).[166] This made it the second largest wreck removal operation after the *Costa Concordia* and has given rise to considerable concern in insurance and reinsurance markets.[167]

The potential liabilities involved pollution damage (including clean-up) and wreck removal.[168] At the time, New Zealand was not a party to the Bunkers Convention 2001[169] or the Wreck Removal Convention 2007,[170] but it was a party to the LLMC 1976 (not the LLMC 1996).[171] Domestic law, however, provided a liability regime though the Maritime Transport Act 1994. This covered wreck removal[172] and reflected elements of international liability conventions, eg for pollution damage (including that caused by harmful substances other than oil).[173] The provisions have not been without difficulties of interpretation or application,[174] but provided the basis for negotiations with the shipowner and its insurer, the Swedish Club,[175] a member of the International Group. A significant feature of the casualty was that the shipowner (through its Club) incurred the direct costs of salvage and wreck removal. This relieved the State to some extent of the need to engage contractors itself and then to claim against the shipowner. It was probably relevant that the Maritime

---

162 Eg using typical definitions of a ship in merchant shipping legislation such as the MTA 1994 (NZ) s 2(1) "every description of boat or craft used in navigation": *Ngai Te Hapu Inc v Bay of Plenty Regional Council* [2017] NZEnvC 073 [213].
163 Ibid., [224].
164 In *Ngai Te Hapu Inc v Bay of Plenty Regional Council* [2017] NZEnvC 073 [14].
165 *Rena: Waitangi Final Report*, 6.
166 *Ngai Te Hapu Inc v Bay of Plenty Regional Council* [2017] NZEnvC 073 [14].
167 See 1.2.5 and 1.4.
168 For potential cargo and charterparty issues, see 2.1.
169 See 2.6.3: accession occurred in 2014.
170 See Part II of the book (Chapters 7–10). The WRC 2007 only entered into force in 2015.
171 See 2.5: accession to the LLMC 1996 came only in 2014. See also B Marten, "Limitation of Liability in Maritime Law and Vessel-Source Pollution: A New Zealand Perspective" [2013] NZ L Rev 199.
172 See Parts 3A (added in 2013) and 9, as explained by *Marten, Maritime Law*, 155–161.
173 See Part 25, and cf 2.6.4.
174 See in particular *Marten, Maritime Law*, 186–188.
175 The Swedish Club was not only the liability insurer but also the hull and machinery insurer. This would greatly simplify claims handling, eg concerning notice of abandonment: see 2.9.4(b).

Transport Act 1994 s 86 provided that there would be no limit of liability for wreck removal operations.[176]

In October 2012 the State agreed a complex settlement with the *Rena*'s owners, comprising three deeds: relating to claims, indemnity and wreck removal.[177] The first settled the State's claim for NZ$27.6 million, but the second deed involved an indemnity *from* the State (up to NZ$38 million) if there were claims against the *Rena* by New Zealand public and local authorities.[178] This left open what was to happen to the sunken remains of the *Rena*. The *Rena*'s owners and insurers had indicated a preference to leave part of the hull underwater owing to the difficulties and costs in removing it. It was recognised that this needed a dumping or abandonment application to be made under the Resource Management Act [RMA] 1991, which might ultimately be decided in the Environmental Court. As part of the 2012 settlement, the State therefore agreed to "consider" making "good faith" submissions in support of such a consent application; and in so doing it could take into account "the environmental, cultural and economic interests of New Zealand and the likely costs and feasibility of complete removal of the Wreck".[179] Moreover, if there was such support and the application succeeded, with the result that the owners made a 'substantial costs saving', then the owners would pay NZ$10.4 million to the State for public purposes.[180]

This highly unusual provision was part of an overall compromise, and probably reflected a State recognition that the final removal was difficult and dangerous, and that there might be little to stop the shipowner and insurers from abandoning the wreck and leaving the State to such remedies as it might have against a foreign shipowner and insurer.[181] To the outsider, the remarkable feature of the *Rena* incident is that the shipowner and Club did stay and incur huge expenditure, when less reputable operators might simply have walked away at the start or sought to limit liability.

1.2.4(d) Full removal or consent for dumping?
Once the major part of the wreck had been removed, it became necessary for there to be a decision about what to do with the remainder. The position of the shipowner and Club was

---

176 Although no notification had been made to the IMO of the decision to opt out of wreck removal limitation under Art 18 of the LLMC 1976 (see 2.5.8), to which New Zealand was then a party. The absence of such a reservation might have left New Zealand open to a complaint by a State party to the LLMC 1976 that it was in breach of treaty obligations. Liberia (the flag State of *Rena* and State of incorporation of Daina), Marshall Islands (State of incorporation of Costamare) and Greece (State connected with control of Costamare) were parties to the LLMC 1976. In international law, it may well have been the position that the *Rena* was entitled to limit under the LLMC 1976 (and see *Daina Shipping Co v Te Runanga O Ngati Awa* [2012] NZHC 3411, [2013] NZHC 500). This doubt may have conditioned the State in its settlement negotiations. See also 2.5.1 (fn 552), 2.5.8 (fn 711).

177 *AG's Rena Cabinet Paper*, [22–25]. The deeds (with some redactions) are set out in "Crown Law Letter of 2 March 2017 to Ombudsman re Final Decision into Inquiry into release of Rena Deeds" [*Rena: Crown Law 2017 Letter to Ombudsman*]: www.crownlaw.govt.nz/publications/reports/.

178 *Rena: Waitangi Final Report*, 7. The exact figure is redacted in the Deed of Indemnity text in *Rena: Crown Law 2017 Letter to Ombudsman*.

179 *AG's Rena Cabinet Paper*, [24].

180 *AG's Rena Cabinet Paper*, [25]. In the event, this sum was not paid as a result of the position ultimately taken by the State on the resource consent application: see *Rena: Crown Law 2017 Letter to Ombudsman* [4.2].

181 Ibid., [114, 123].

clearly that, after huge expenditure, they wanted to declare the operation at an end, and they created an "Astrolabe Community Trust" to facilitate this.[182] The political problem was that strong indigenous concerns were raised about leaving any vestige of the ship on the Astrolabe Reef; similar views were expressed by others with environmental concerns. From a tactical viewpoint it is understandable that the shipowner and Club did not want to have an ongoing liability, with no discernible time limit. This no doubt conditioned their desire for an overall settlement with the government. But it seemed clear that there would be a need for independent permission to dump (or abandon) the remains under the RMA 1991. The Trust then made an application in 2013 to dump the remains under the RMA 1991, but the application was later amended to allow for 'abandonment' of the remains and for future discharges of identified contaminants subject to comprehensive conditions of consent.[183] One of the reasons for the amendment was that the government had taken the position that the application could not be fully supported as full data had not yet been supplied and it appeared some of the bow remains could be removed.[184]

This raised the question of whether a State could or should be entitled to full removal of every vestige of the ship and debris from it.[185] Should there be an absolute or relative solution? The government recognised this dilemma at the time of the original dumping application. While it wanted significant parts of the bow section still on the reef to be removed, this was estimated to take 410 days and cost NZ$79 million; the debris down to 30 m would take 184 days to clean up for about NZ$29 million.[186] By contrast, the aft section lying between 35 m and 70 m was more difficult and dangerous to remove. The applicants' experts had estimated that this could take between 2.6 and 7.1 years at a cost of between US$314 million and US$759 million.[187] The government's experts considered these estimates to be exaggerated,[188] but it seems clear at this stage that the issue was not one of whether the remains could physically be removed in a safe manner, but what the cost would be. All were aware that the costs so far had already made the removal costs the second most expensive in the world, and that reinsurers might be unhappy.

In the AG's Cabinet Paper, there is a revealing admission by the government that it was, to some extent, dependent on the goodwill of the shipowner and Club. The shipowner made it clear that if the consent was not forthcoming, it would reserve its position on 'full wreck removal', even though that might be the default position under the RMA 1991.[189] In other words, there was a veiled threat that the State might be left with its remedy against a single ship Liberian shipowning company with no assets. An alternative course of action of suing the Club might face a 'pay to be paid' defence,[190] or perhaps that the Club had paid its full

---

182 See also 14.7.4.
183 *Ngai Te Hapu Inc v Bay of Plenty Regional Council* [2017] NZEnvC 073, [1]. "Abandonment" as used in the RMA 1991 creates a less pejorative impression than dumping: cf 14.4.
184 *AG's Rena Cabinet Paper*, [119–125].
185 The government's own consultants produced a table showing international comparisons of ten wreck removal operations, where 'full' wreck removal orders had been issued. *AG's Rena Cabinet Paper*, [108–111], Appendix 7; and see 10.2.5 for the WRC 2007.
186 *AG's Rena Cabinet Paper*, [93–95].
187 Ibid., [97].
188 Ibid., [99].
189 Ibid., [113–115].
190 See 2.9.6(c), 2.5.9 and 10.8.6.

policy liability; claims against foreign reinsurers might also be difficult. The government concluded that it would not be viable to enforce the legal requirement of full removal.[191] Faced with this reality, the government decided to support the consent application on a partial basis.

1.2.4(e) 2017 consent order and indigenous factors
It is significant that by the time of the amended consent application, considered in 2017, the applicants based it on two propositions: (a) that all works that were feasible for wreckage removal had been done, and (b) all works that could safely be done had been done.[192] In the interim period, much additional removal work had been done, so that the application was pressed on a basis that was as close to 'full removal' as was reasonably possible.

On 17 May 2017, the Environment Court issued an interim decision granting consent to the abandonment of the vessel.[193] The court examined in detail the cultural environment to the "complex array" of indigenous groups all vying for recognition of their relationship to Otaiti, the reef.[194] Thus involved assessing a mass of oral sources in order to give effect to the requirements of s 6(e) of the RMA 1991 to recognise and provide for the relationship of Maori with their culture and traditions with their ancestral lands, water, sites, "*waahi tapu*" and other "*taonga*".[195] In addition, the Treaty of Waitangi had to be taken into account, as the reef was a site of cultural, spiritual and historical importance to a range of Maori groups.[196]

From the perspective of claims settlement, this level of investigation poses many difficulties, particularly for defendants. Collection of the evidence is time-consuming and can involve considerable differences in approach by difference indigenous groups. The Environment Court's decision shows that many of the cultural values are way beyond the expertise of traditional maritime lawyers. But where there is legislation protecting these values, it is necessary to identify those claiming cultural rights or wanting a say in how wreck removal operations are handled. Moreover, an assessment of impacts may involve cultural values that are strange to traditional compensation systems.[197]

In the Environment Court, there was much discussion of the "*mauri*" of the reef, a form of life force connection between traditional Maori gods and earthly matter that included spiritual and mortal elements.[198] The latter could include the value of a fishery as part

---

191 *AG's Rena Cabinet Paper*, [114]. This dilemma for States is at the heart of the discussions about the WRC 2007; see 10.2.5.
192 *Ngai Te Hapu Inc v Bay of Plenty Regional Council* [2017] NZEnvC 073, [27].
193 *Ngai Te Hapu Inc v Bay of Plenty Regional Council* [2017] NZEnvC 073.
194 Ibid., [35].
195 Ibid., [38].
196 Ibid., [106].
197 Cf *Northern Territory v Mr A Griffiths (deceased) and Lorraine Jones on Behalf of the Ngaliwurru and Nungali Peoples* [2019] HCA 7 (13 March 2019), where the High Court of Australia (in a case involving native title to land) had to consider, *inter alia*, how to ascertain compensation for loss or diminution of traditional attachment to the land, or connection to 'country', and for loss of rights to gain spiritual sustenance from the land. It awarded an amount for cultural loss "which society would rightly regard as an appropriate award for the loss" in the sum of Au$1.3 million in respect of an area of about 1.27 km^2: [2019] HCA 7 [3], see also [152–237], [304–325].
198 *Ngai Te Hapu Inc v Bay of Plenty Regional Council* [2017] NZEnvC 073 [94–95].

of the imperative to underpin the sustainable management of the natural resource.[199] The main threat to the *mauri* was caused by the grounding and salvage efforts. Remediation of the *mauri* could take the form of traditional activities, including atonement and various traditional rituals (ie activities way beyond the contemplation of normal pollution and wreck removal incidents). A crucial issue was how far the continued presence on the reef of remains of the wreck would could still affect the *mauri* in the future. The Environment Court concluded that the reef was gradually recovering its *mauri*.[200] It also found that nothing more could be done to protect the cultural context without endangering lives or risking damage to the reef.[201] To this extent, "full removal" of all remains was not reasonably required,[202] but it is clear from the evidence that the contractors, working with cultural advisers, had come as close to full removal as was physically possible.

It seems that it was the safety of the reef and human lives that were eventually more important than the cost of any further removal operations. The court declared that it would take an appropriate practical real-world approach to consent,[203] recognising that if consent was not granted, it was uncertain if there was any prospect of total removal of all remains.[204] There had been considerably more of the wreck removed between 2013 (when the owner and salvor were first suggesting leaving the remains) and the hearing in 2017. This is perhaps significant for States, as it appears that a degree of persistence may work— presupposing that there is a cooperative shipowner and insurer. Some 4,000 mt of additional material was apparently recovered after 2017 at a cost of over NZ$80 million.[205] Still, at some stage it has to be recognised that no more can be done without creating worse effects.[206] The court noted that the prospect of removing the aft section was negligible.[207] The mid-section of the *Rena* might involve removal of pieces of up to 600 mt, but this would be technically difficult and have adverse effects on the reef.[208] The bow section, on the reef, might break up into pieces of under 20 mt that might be removed, but wholesale removal was not appropriate.[209]

There was a debate about how far the consent to abandon would retrospectively legitimise the wreck in some way. The court answered this by granting consent subject to conditions. It is not appropriate here to analyse all those conditions,[210] but they centred around (a) enabling provision of information to the public; (b) making provision for removal of any contaminants or smaller parts of the vessel if and when they can be appropriately removed; (c) providing information to locals; and (d) recognising the role of "*kaitaki*"

---

199 Ibid., [95].
200 Ibid., [105].
201 Ibid., [109].
202 Ibid., [109].
203 Ibid., [125].
204 Ibid., [134].
205 Ibid., [141].
206 The court received evidence [148] about the attempt to raise the *Vinca Gorthon* which had sunk off Ijmuiden in the Netherlands in 1988, resting on pipelines. Owing to navigational issues, attempts had been made in 2010 and 2011 to raise the vessel, but these had failed (despite loss of life and damage to equipment).
207 *Ngai Te Hapu Inc v Bay of Plenty Regional Council* [2017] NZEnvC 073 [150].
208 Ibid., [151–152].
209 Ibid., [155].
210 See [389] et seq. for details, and also the Appendices.

(effectively those with a particular cultural connection to the reef) and making provision to strengthen their role.[211] To this end, the court required that there be a Monitoring Plan of the wreck site, with annual studies (eg to check for contamination, or wreck movements) and comparisons with a nearby reference site.

A *kaitaki* Reference Group would have a role in assessing any improvement to the *mauri* of the reef. A bond would be established in favour of the Regional Council in the provisional sum of NZ$6,350,000, depending on the final conditions that were agreed.[212] It would generally cover the monitoring and other costs as well as any environmental contingencies. There would also be a separate letter of undertaking from the Club, to last for ten years, that was to cover any further wreck removal of the bow section. The consent would last for ten years with a further ten years' maintenance provision (making 25 years in total since the casualty).[213]

In exercising its discretion to give consent the court considered the New Zealand Coastal Policy statement and other natural resource documents.[214] Many of these are peculiar to New Zealand, but they are indicative of the detailed factors taken into account by a court and which have to be addressed by applicants. Appendix D of the judgment shows an interesting comparison of the differences between the consent terms sought by the ship interests and those by claimants.

The court assumed that the owner would transfer to the Trust the title to the vessel but also sufficient funds to complete the tasks the subject matter of the consent.[215] It rejected an argument that somehow the shipowner could rely on limitation of liability to a sum less than the NZ$30 million offered to claimants.[216] After a number of amendments to the interim conditions,[217] the final consent order to the Astrolabe Community Trust was approved on 15 December 2017.[218]

1.2.4(f) Lessons

The lesson for a coastal State is that there can be problems if a State does not keep its maritime legislation up to date (eg through adherence to the LLMC 1976). As the UK has found, there are dangers of inconsistency if States try to paraphrase maritime liability conventions when enacting them in domestic legislation.[219]

The cultural factor raised its head in a number of contexts. It clearly inhibited claims settlement, in that the government was criticised for settling the claim without appropriate consultation with Maori interests. It also affected the exact parameters of the wreck

---

211 *Ngai Te Hapu Inc v Bay of Plenty Regional Council* [2017] NZEnvC 073 [162].
212 Ibid., [399] and Appendix D.
213 Ibid., [402].
214 Ibid., [227] et seq.
215 Ibid., [373], and see 14.7.4.
216 Cf 1.2.4(c) and the government views about the practicality of squeezing more from the shipowner and Club. See also 2.5, especially 2.5.9 for some of the practical and legal difficulties concerning limitation. For cargo claims generally, see 2.1.
217 See eg *Ngai Te Hapu Inc v Bay of Plenty Regional Council* [2017] NZEnvC 169 (13 October 2017) and *Ngai Te Hapu Inc v Bay of Plenty Regional Council* [2017] NZEnvC 180 (31 October 2017).
218 See *Ngai Te Hapu Inc v Bay of Plenty Regional Council* [2017] NZEnvC 206.
219 See eg *Daina Shipping Co v Te Runanga o Ngati* [2013] NZHC 500, [2013] 2 NZLR 799, referred to in Marten, *Maritime Law*, 50, 189.

removal task through the need to ensure consents. New Zealand's indigenous laws may have features that are not common to other States, even those with indigenous populations, but there is an increasing recognition of indigenous rights[220] and intangible cultural heritage,[221] and it must be acknowledged that their existence can greatly complicate wreck removal operations. At the very least, the lesson will be that the ship interests cannot rely exclusively on dealing with governments, and that consultation with local indigenous groups may be necessary.[222] Such a process is not likely to be easy or quick. But the desire for local communities to be involved does not only arise with indigenous populations such as the Maori. It seems that local communities in most parts of the world will want to be involved, and the extent to which they can intervene will vary according to local law. The *MSC Napoli* shows that efficient national disaster planning can help by identifying possible local interests in advance so that communities can feel that they have been involved.

1.2.5 Costa Concordia *(2012)*

1.2.5(a) The casualty

The *Costa Concordia* was a 114,147 gt cruise ship (with around 4,250 passengers and crew) that grounded off the island of Giglio in Italy and sank in January 2012. She was owned by Costa Crociere, part of Carnival Corporation and entered in the Standard P&I Club.

Thirty-two passengers and crew were killed, and the Club handled claims in more than 50 jurisdictions.[223] The master was subsequently prosecuted and imprisoned for 16 years,[224] while four crew members and the shipowner's crisis coordinator received sentenced of under three years. The *Costa Concordia* casualty is worthy of specific note here as it is known to be the most expensive wreck removal operation ever.

Removal of bunkers and wastes was undertaken by Smit Salvage and an Italian partner, Fratelli Neri. They deployed within two days and some 2,000 mt of bunkers were removed using modern 'hot tapping',[225] and tanks were sealed in a 'caretaking' operation.[226]

---

220 The Australian High Court has recognised native title rights in relation to waters, but accepting that they were not exclusive: *Akiba on Behalf of the Torres Strait Regional Seas Claim Group v Commonwealth of Australia* [2013] HCA 33.

221 See eg the UNESCO Convention for the Safeguarding of the Intangible Cultural Heritage 2003; L Lixinski, *Intangible Cultural Heritage and International Law* (OUP, 2013); M Stefano, P Davis, G Corsanne (eds), *Safeguarding Intangible Cultural Heritage* (Boydell Press, 2012); C Bell, R Paterson (eds), *Protection of First Nations Cultural Heritage: Laws, Policy and Reform* (UBC Press, 2009).

222 In fact, the Environment Court acknowledged that the owners and insurers did take expert advice from an early stage, so that particular groups were consulted and included in settlements [164].

223 Standard Club, "Major Casualty Management: Wreck removal and salvage", Standard Club (June 2018), [*Standard Club, Major Casualty Management*], www.standard-club.com/media/2767644/30178_sc_goto_35_casualty_wreckremovalsalvage_aw.pdf.

224 www.theguardian.com/world/2017/may/12/costa-concordia-captain-hands-himself-into-prison (May 2017). NB: there are not as many publicly available sources in English for information about the *Costa Concordia* as there are for the *Torrey Canyon*, *MSC Napoli* and *Rena*. Some sources are summaries in https://en.wikipedia.org/wiki/Costa_Concordia_disaster, but the 'official' website (www.theparbucklingproject.com/) is no longer available.

225 Involving a steam plant on a barge to run steam through inserts in to bunker tanks to create a flow of fuel, with temperature adjusted to according to the oil grades. The same technique was used with the car carrier *Baltic Ace*, sunk off Rotterdam in 2012: see 10.2.5; also 2.5.4(b), 2.5.9(c) and 14.3.

226 See 12.3.1.

It appeared that there was relatively little pollution, but this was of great significance to the Italian authorities as the area was heavily dependent on tourism. These sensitivities, expressed by national and local authorities, heavily influenced what was to happen to the wreck, which was soon recognised to be a total loss.

1.2.5(b) Removal operations

The removal operation for the hull went out to tender and, from the six tenders received, a wreck removal contract was signed with another major contractor, Titan Maritime (again with an Italian company, Micoperi[227]). It appears that one reason that Titan was the successful tenderer for the removal project was because it was willing to remove the wreck in one piece. The Italian authorities apparently expressed very strong views that this method was to be preferred, although some industry sources indicated that the cost of cutting up and removing the ship *in situ* (as with the *Tricolor*[228] and the Russian submarine *Kursk*) might have been US$150–$200 million.[229] *Costa Concordia* was twice the size of *Tricolor* and there would have been much more debris (eg furniture) from a cruise ship which could cause pollution. But even the technique of parbuckling carried with it the risk that the ship might break up in the process. At times the operation was costing US$1 million a day.

Indeed, all reports about the operation indicate that there was a very heavy involvement of the Italian State throughout the planning and removal operation, in particular as to the imposition of strict environmental requirements but also (it appears) as to the involvement of local Italian industries in the removal and ultimate scrapping. A *Costa Concordia* Emergency Commissioner's Office was established, and this liaised closely with the contractors, owners and Club. Titan's salvage master has indicated that complete cooperation with the authorities was vital and necessary to complete the operation; following government wishes, though, can be expensive for the owners and Club who will foot the bill.

The actual removal method was a marvel of engineering practice, whose details are perhaps not directly relevant in a law book. They involved[230] stabilising the ship while the extent of damage was assessed; constructing underwater steel platforms for the ship to rest on after righting; rotating (parbuckling) the ship to bring it upright on the platform (involving the use of jacks to provide a parbuckling force of over 6,800 mt); refloating the ship (with the aid of locally manufactured sponsons and blister tanks attached to each side of the hull); and towing the hull for a scrapping voyage.

Graphic videos of the removal operation are freely available on the internet,[231] but the refloating was a massive logistical exercise involving over 500 workers and some

---

227 www.micoperi.com/en/capabilities/removal-costa-concordia-has-been-awarded-micoperi.
228 See 10.2.5.
229 For a description of the cutting method, see "*Baltic Ace* Wreck Removal", Boskalis website: https://magazine.boskalis.com/issue03/baltic-ace-wreck-removal [*Baltic Ace Wreck Removal*]. Boskalis concluded that the wreck of the *Baltic Ace* could not be lifted intact and so it was planned to cut it into six sections of 1,500–2,000 mt and to lift these from the seabed with sheerlegs onto a barge for removal and recycling. Later, the deteriorating condition of the wreck required that it be cut into eight pieces, taking 30 hours each.
230 See eg, www.ardentglobal.com/2015/08/17/raising-the-costa-concordia/; *Herbert, Challenges*, 24.
231 Eg National Graphic Channel, "The raising of the *Costa Concordia*" (2014, Windfall Films), www.youtube.com/watch?v=WwtcoxQGHmc, including interviews with salvage master Nick Sloane.

30,000 mt of steel just in the fabrication of components. In July 2014 *Costa Concordia* was towed to Genoa for scrapping; dismantling and recycling was complete in July 2017.[232]

One example that has been given of strict environmental requirements is that when the granite seabed had to be drilled to secure the three platforms to stabilise the ship, the cuttings were taken to the surface and treated as waste, even though the raw material was essentially the same as that forming local beaches; as it had a higher density than natural sand, it was thought that it would change local ecosystems.[233]

1.2.5(c) Costs and liabilities

There has not been much public discussion about the liability of the shipowner, it being assumed that there was liability under Italian law for wreck removal, and there appears to have been no attempt to limit liability.[234] It may have been significant that the ship was registered in Italy, to an Italian company that itself was part of the largest passenger ship operator in the world, namely Carnival. Such an owner is likely to have significant public relations reasons for being seen to settle claims reasonably. It is also likely to be in good stead with the Club, although it is not known how far the entire claim was covered by the Club (and its reinsurers) or whether Carnival had agreed to substantial retentions for its own account (either initially, or as claims mounted).

Initial estimates of a cost of $300 million ballooned, partly as a result of weather delays and the need to have more extensive engineering solutions as the removal work progressed. Various estimates as to the total costs have been given, eg that the total exposure of the insurance market could be as high as US$2.5 billion (presumably including the hull claim), but the most reliable information available to the authors is that the wreck removal operation (combined with passenger compensation) has amounted to about US$1.5 billion. On this basis, the removal operation could have cost nearly three times the original building cost of the vessel. Most of the claims for wreck removal and associated costs have now settled,[235] although it is understood that some passenger claims are still to be resolved.

What is apparent from an overview of the removal operation is that modern technology can raise a ship of this size, whereas in previous generations such an operation would have been unthinkable. Although the ability to raise a ship completely will vary considerably, eg according to its size and location, the major constraint now appears to be the cost of mounting such an operation. It would not be a surprise if many States have seen the size of the insurance payout, and the fact that total removal was effected, and drawn the conclusion that this is the new paradigm. This has itself become a matter of real concern to the insurance and reinsurance markets.[236]

---

232 This involved one million work hours, with over 53,000 mt being recycled: https://worldmaritimenews.com/archives/225190/costa-concordia-saga-comes-to-an-end/. See also Chapter 14.

233 See W Laursen, "The Costa Effect", *The Maritime Executive* (25/11/2014), www.maritime-executive.com/magazine/The-Costa-Effect-2014-11-25#gs.cSBXV68.

234 Italy is not a party to the LLMC: see further 2.5.

235 See also 10.2.5 in relation to remediation and restoration.

236 See 1.4. For statistics on the number of sea passengers carried in the UK and internationally, see 2.3.

1.3 Cargo problems

1.3.1 Changing environmental focus

Oil pollution from tankers was the major concern after *Torrey Canyon*, and the concern about fuel oil in cargo ships generally has been manifested in a convention to deal with bunkers.[237] By the 1980s, though, it was recognised that there were likely to be an increasing number of environmental risks caused by substances other than oil.[238] While clean-up of oil (whether cargo or bunkers) after a ship is wrecked is often a first concern of modern salvage and wreck removal operations,[239] attention has shifted in many cases to the problems caused by the cargo rather than the ship herself. As will be seen, the WRC 2007 will now allow its provisions to be used to cover the cost of removing cargo,[240] but there are still real practical problems caused by cargoes and these are increasing.

Some cargoes may be extremely hazardous or noxious to humans or the environment, particularly if they are persistent.[241] Where a ship is wrecked it may be impossible or extremely difficult in many cases to remove bulk cargoes, such as coal or foodstuffs that might be easily contaminated by seawater. Such cargoes may not be inherently dangerous but present practical problems of removal; and that may translate either into great delay or cost and, increasingly, both. Other bulk cargoes, especially bulk chemicals, may be inherently hazardous or noxious.[242] So far, the world has been relatively lucky in avoiding a *Torrey Canyon* size of disaster for such substances.

An increasing concern is how to deal with container ships, as demonstrated by the *MSC Napoli*, the *Rena* and more recent casualties such as the *Kea Trader* in 2017.[243]

1.3.2 Particular problems with containers

1.3.2(a) Containers lost overboard

The UNCTAD "Review of Maritime Transport 2018"[244] records the staggering amount of international trade and shipping and reported that containerised trade accounted for 17.1% of total seaborne trade in 2017 and global volumes reached 148 million TEUs.[245]

The World Shipping Council (WSC) estimated that the value of containers transported in 2016 by the international liner shipping industry was more than US$4 trillion.[246] In surveys of its members as to the number of containers lost at sea, more than half were as a result

---

237 See 2.3.3 for the Bunkers Convention 2001.
238 See 2.3.4 for the HNSC 2010.
239 See eg 1.2.3–1.2.5, 2.8 and Chapter 12.
240 See 10.6.4; ie even before the HNSC 2010 (26.4) is in force.
241 The HNSC 2010 will aim to provide compensation for pollution damage in respect of many, but not all of these: see 2.6.4 and wrecks of coal carriers such as the *Smart*: see 10.2.5, 10.6.4.
242 See eg the cargo of styrene in the chemical tanker *Ievoli Sun* sunk in 2000: and see 14.1.2(b). Such substances should be covered by the HNSC 2010: see 2.6.4.
243 See 10.2.6.
244 https://unctad.org/en/PublicationsLibrary/rmt2018_en.pdf.
245 Twenty foot equivalent units; these are the smaller containers used in transport. Most containers seen on trucks and ships are FEUs (40 foot equivalent units). Although standardisation is vital, there is now a multiplicity of sizes and designs.
246 WSC, "Containers Lost At Sea – 2017 Update" (2017). The WSC claims that its members account for about 90% of global liner capacity.

of catastrophic (if rare) events. Between 2010 and 2013, the average annual loss was about 2,683 containers. Between 2014 and 2016, the average number lost was 1,390, although in 2014 alone some 1,683 were lost.[247] A single casualty can have a significant loss; eg there were 5,578 containers lost in 2013, some 77% of which came from the wreck of the *MOL Comfort* in the Indian Ocean. There is therefore a distinction to be made between containers lost from shipwrecks and from those washed overboard. The latter can still present significant navigational[248] and environmental risks, and may be very difficult (and expensive) to locate[249] and remove.[250] Containers are still being lost, despite the availability of industry guidelines for their safe carriage and an increase in ISO standards for container lashings.[251]

1.3.2(b) Weight and contents of containers
One particular problem faced by salvors or wreck removal contractors in dealing with a container ship is in knowing what the containers weigh and, indeed, what they actually contain. On leaving Antwerp the *MSC Napoli* had a 'deadload' of some 1,250 mt[252]—in effect the difference between the actual weight of cargo on board and the estimated weight as derived from shipper information in the ship's manifest (ie as recorded in bills of lading and waybills). At the time there was no requirement for containers to be weighed, and when 660 dry containers on deck were removed and weighed, some 137 (20%) were more than 3 mt different from their declared weight.[253] These 137 containers alone were 312 mt heavier than the manifest, and it was clear that this was a common problem in the container ship industry.[254] This overloading did not cause the hull failure, but it reduced safety margins.[255] Apart from the general effect on navigational stability, this sort of discrepancy is significant for salvors and wreck removal contractors who may have to remove the containers.[256] Moreover, 53 (7%) of the 700 deck containers on *MSC Napoli* were not in their planned positions, apparently within a 10% industry tolerance,[257] but again a potential difficulty for salvors contractors in dealing with containers of dangerous cargo.

1.3.2(c) Increase in size of container ships
Although *MSC Napoli* was large for its time, there has been an enormous increase in the size of container ships since. The latest generation of very large container ships can carry

---

247 These figures may be conservative in that they do not represent all owners. The IMO estimated in 2011 that 3,000 to 4,000 containers are lost overboard each year: see "Work Programme Proposed measures to prevent loss of containers", MSC 89/22/11 (2011).
248 See eg the *Pacific Adventurer*: see 2.6.3.
249 See eg the *YM Efficiency* that lost 81 containers overboard off New South Wales in 2018: www.amsa.gov.au/marine-environment/incidents-and-exercises/locating-containers-lost-ym-efficiency; also 10.5.5 and 11.3.5 for UK problems.
250 Such cargo can be subject to the wreck removal provisions of the WRC 2007: see 8.2.1(d), 10.6.
251 See eg International Chamber of Shipping and WSC, Safe Transport of Containers by Sea (2008).
252 *MAIB, MSC Napoli Report*, 15.
253 Ibid., 28–29.
254 Ibid., 42.
255 Ibid., 45.
256 Partly as a result of the *MSC Napoli* findings, SOLAS was amended in 2014 to require shippers, as from 1 July 2016, to provide a verified gross mass (VGM) of a container with cargo: see MSC.1/Circ 1475, and eg TT Club, *Verified Gross Mass Industry FAQs*, December 2015.
257 *MAIB, MSC Napoli Report* 29.

in excess of 18,000 TEUs. This increase in size is a feature of many ship types,[258] and these 'megaships' have given rise to a so-called salvage capability gap.[259] That is, the salvage industry, itself under increased financial pressure, may have difficulty in providing the technical means to deal with a wreck, eg by having heavy lift capacity to reach up to the top level of some of these container ships. Moreover, it has become clear that it is increasingly difficult to remove containers from the cells of a container ship when that ship is listing—a common feature of a casualty. Further, the ability to mobilise suitable equipment may vary greatly depending in which part of the world the casualty occurs.[260] That is even before the localised factors of access are considered, eg whether the casualty is aground on a dangerous reef prone to heavy seas or is far from a suitable port.

While governments may assume that the shipping industry can respond to all casualties that result in wrecks, there are doubts about the extent to which wreck removal contractors, and insurers,[261] can do so. The more sensitive question is how far it is reasonable or realistic to expect them to do so. In many environmental disasters, from *Torrey Canyon* onwards, governments have found that they have had to absorb financial costs, eg as a result of the operation of limits of liability.[262] This is unpopular politically but may be part of the price to be paid for encouraging a consumer society that requires such vast quantities of cargo to be carried by sea. It is controversial even to suggest that there is a balance to be struck between funding through industry liability and that from default expenditure by governments. It remains to be seen if wreck removal operations like *Rena* and *Costa Concordia* (in particular) will be the paradigms, or whether there are other more difficult outcomes for governments.[263]

1.4 P&I Clubs' major incident analysis

As a result of the increasing cost of wreck removal expenditure,[264] the International Group of Protection and Indemnity Clubs (International Group)[265] set up a "Large Casualty Working Group" to review the factors which had led to such an escalation of costs in the period 2002–2012. The initial Review was based on the 20 most significant casualties which resulted in claims on the Group pool occurring in the 10-year period from 2002 to 2012 involving removal of wreck (ROW) and SCOPIC liabilities. The Review was updated in March 2016 to reflect a further six casualties.[266] Many factors are outside the control of the parties, such as the location of the wreck, water depth, weather, availability of response equipment and its mobilisation. It is here though that proper operational planning can enable the appointment of risk consultants and technical experts at an early stage.

---

258 See *Herbert, Challenges*, 23.
259 Ibid., 26. See also 2.7.4.
260 See also 10.2.6.
261 See *Herbert, Challenges*, 29–31.
262 See 2.5 and 2.5.2(a).
263 See 1.4 and also 2.5.9, 7.1 and 10.8.6.
264 Including related SCOPIC expenditure: see 2.8.9(c), 12.3.
265 See www.igpandi.org/.
266 See Executive Summary (updated 2016) "IG Large Casualty Working Group Review of Casualties Involving Salvage/Scopic and Wreck Removal 2002–2016" [*Large Casualty Working Group: Executive Summary*].

INTRODUCTION TO WRECK CASUALTIES

The most significant cost impact of all the key factors considered was the intervention by government or other authority in large casualties involving SCOPIC and wreck removal.[267] The Review recommended that the best way to counter the disproportionate application of operational requirements was through an outreach program to governments, eg by the use of a Memorandum of Agreement (MOU), such as had been agreed with South Africa, Australia and New Zealand. Although the content of those MOUs is very general, with no binding content,[268] they form part of a trust building exercise in advance of any casualty, so that States can have some confidence when International Group members are involved. The education exercise would be well worth the time spent. The Review did conclude though that where there are disproportionate or unreasonable requirements imposed by States, the owner or Club should really consider challenging such action in the courts. It is perhaps significant that the Review drew specific attention to the fact that the hazard criteria set out in the WRC 2007 Art 6 might be useful in mounting such a challenge, eg to show that measures taken by the State or authority were proportionate and reasonably necessary in accordance with Art 2.[269]

The Review noted the increasing cost of bunker removal operations and a generally lower tolerance of pollution. It also recorded an increased focus on casualties involving laden container vessels. The condition of the vessel and weather conditions could have significant impacts on costs, especially where containers break loose. Subsequent storage and unstuffing of containers, and cargo disposal, were significant potential cost drivers. But other cargoes presented problems, eg disposing of vehicles and parts. The handling of scrap and steel cargoes also involved increased costs. There were increasing requirements of States to remove bulk cargoes, presumably other than the obvious pollutants such as oil and chemicals carried in bulk (which might previously have been left with the wreck).

The identification by the Clubs of the most significant cost factor in rising claim levels as being the involvement of States in wreck removal is linked to the WRC 2007. There seems little doubt that the Clubs see some of its key provisions as a means of limiting some claims. Not only must WRC 2007 measures be reasonable and proportionate, but the deadline for removal must also be reasonable, taking into account the nature of the hazard.[270] The Review also recognised that wreck removal contract provisions could also be significant cost drivers.[271]

---

267 In the *Fedra* sinking in 2008, it was estimated that costs were increased by 50% as a result of intervention by the Gibraltarian and Spanish authorities: see 10.2.5 and the LOC report (www.crownlaw.govt.nz/assets/Uploads/Reports/wreck-removal-report-3.pdf), 43. See also 4.2.3, 5.3, 5.5.
268 See also 10.8.6.
269 See further 9.2.5(e), 10.2.4.
270 See 9.2.5(e), 10.2.4. 10.8.6.
271 See 13.4.2, 13.6.2, 13.6.5(a).

CHAPTER 2

Wreck and the maritime commercial adventure

The wreck of a ship will have serious implications for all those involved in a normal commercial maritime adventure. This chapter will consider the perspective of such persons who may be interested if a ship is involved in a casualty and (eventually) wrecked, and the legal consequences for them. The aim is to help understand their reactions (and provide a wider context) as the full implications of a casualty become apparent, eg where a wreck removal operation is later required. The chapter therefore examines wreck in its wider sense, eg as affecting the maritime commercial adventure, and is not immediately concerned with wreck removal under the Nairobi International Convention on the Removal of Wrecks (WRC) 2007.[1] It is evident that many maritime law principles can interact when a wreck occurs, and one of the aims of this chapter is to show the links between them and with the sort of casualties highlighted in Chapter 1. As explained in the Preface and Chapter 1, the discussion that follows cannot provide exhaustive commentaries on every area of law involving maritime casualties.[2]

2.1 Wreck and carriage of goods contracts

The legal regimes governing liabilities of the shipowner to third parties arising out of wreck, eg for pollution damage or wreck removal, are essentially tortious or arise under statute.[3] By contrast, the position of many commercial parties to the maritime adventure who are affected by a shipwreck will be regulated by contract law.[4] This applies in particular to charterparty contracts and also to those carriage of goods contracts covered by bills of lading or non-negotiable instruments, such as waybills. In order to understand the position of the various parties it is necessary to be aware of the terms of the particular contract but also the governing (or applicable) law and the legal principles applied by that law. Such principles will include the formation of contract, the ascertainment of its terms, how to interpret those terms, the effect of vitiating facts such as (misrepresentations), when the contractual obligations may be terminated (eg for breach or frustration) and what remedies are available (eg damages). An examination of these general topics is beyond this book and reference should be made to general texts on contract law[5] or, more particularly, those governing shipping contracts.[6]

---

1 See Part II.
2 Where appropriate, references will be made throughout the chapter to specialist texts.
3 For pollution liabilities after a wreck, see 2.6; for wreck removal liabilities, see Chapter 10 and 11.3.4; for liabilities for a collision resulting in a wreck of one or both ships, see 2.4.
4 Contracts will also usually be relevant to the claims of crew and passengers affected by wreck: see 2.2, 2.3.
5 See eg H Beale, *Chitty on Contracts* (32nd ed, Sweet & Maxwell, 2015) [*Chitty on Contracts*].
6 See eg, T Coghlin et al, *Time Charters* (7th ed, Informa, 2014) [*Time Charters*]; J Cooke et al, *Voyage Charters* (4th ed, Informa, 2014) [*Voyage Charters*]; H Bennett at al (eds), *Carver on Charterparties* (2017,

2.1.1 Overview of cargo's position after wreck

Where a ship is wrecked, a number of issues will arise between the cargo owner and the owners or operators of the ship, depending on what has actually happened to the cargo. The cargo may have been totally lost, eg where the ship and cargo have sunk and are unrecoverable. If the ship is stranded, the cargo may be physically recoverable but could still be a constructive total loss,[7] eg if seawater has penetrated the holds of a cargo of wheat, or if refrigerated containers lose power resulting in the thawing of frozen meat. Alternatively, a salvage operation may recover the cargo, eg where oil is recovered from undamaged cargo tanks.[8] Some cargo may be lost or damaged during the salvage; eg while containers are being lifted off the deck there is a partial collapse of the stow, causing damage to the contents.

In some circumstances the cargo may be recovered physically intact, but its subsequent disposal is rendered more difficult or expensive as it is considered by the market as a 'distressed' cargo; eg where a bulk cargo of grain for human consumption is suspected by the market to be contaminated so that it has to be on-sold as animal feed. And even if the cargo is recovered physically and commercially intact, the disruption to the contract voyage may mean that a whole series of economic losses may follow, eg where an ultimate buyer refuses to take delivery under the sale contract, or where salved cargo is taken to a port of safety and has to be on-shipped to the intended port of discharge (or agreed alternative place of delivery).[9] In all these cases of damage or loss, issues will arise as to whether the carrier is in breach of the contract of carriage, eg as evidenced by a bill of lading or waybill.[10]

The position is further complicated if the ship is subject to one or more charterparties. Indeed, it would be rather surprising if there were not a string of charterers involved, especially concerning bulk cargoes. There may be a registered shipowner (perhaps owning a single ship), with a head bareboat charter,[11] a time charter[12] and below that one or more voyage sub-charters.[13] A container ship such as the *MSC Napoli* or *Rena* may have contractual carriers who have slot-chartered space from a shipowner that is part of a pool or consortium of owners. In many cases charterers will probably not be owners of cargo, except eg in bulk trades where a voyage charterer may be an FOB seller or buyer. But all charterers will be acutely aware of the financial consequences of a shipwreck, either in relation to their rights and liabilities to the shipowner 'above' them in a chain, or to the sub-charterers and cargo owners 'below' to whom they may also have liabilities.[14] Charterers, like owners,

---

Sweet & Maxwell); B Eder et al, *Scrutton on Charterparties and Bills of Lading* (23rd ed and 1st Supplement, 2017, Sweet & Maxwell, 2017); R Aikens, R Lord, M Bools, *Bills of Lading* (2nd ed, Informa, 2015); G Treitel, F Reynolds, *Carver on Bills of Lading* (4th ed, Sweet & Maxwell, 2017) [*Carver on Bills of Lading*]; N Gaskell, Y Baatz, R Asariotis, *Bills of Lading: Law and Contracts* (2000, Informa) [*Bills of Lading: Law and Contracts*]; S Girvin, *Carriage of Goods by Sea* (2nd ed, OUP, 2011); S Rainey, *The Law of Tug and Tow and Offshore Contracts* (4th ed, Informa, 2018).

7 See 2.9.4(b).
8 See 2.7 and 2.1.3.
9 See 2.1.4.
10 See 2.1.5; see also 2.9.5.
11 See 2.1.7(a).
12 See 2.1.7(c).
13 See 2.1.7(b).
14 See 2.1.7.

will be concerned to deliver as much of the cargo to final destination as quickly as they can to try to mitigate their exposure to cargo claims.

2.1.2 Wreck and sale of goods contracts

Where cargo is lost, damaged or delayed by a wreck of the carrying ship, this will also affect any underlying sale of goods contract. The sale of goods contract will regulate whether the seller or buyer bears the risk of such loss during the carriage contract. Thus, in an FOB or CIF sale the buyer will effectively assume all risks after shipment,[15] eg if the ship strands and is wrecked. Where the contract of sale takes place after the goods have been shipped, eg in a commodity sale, this may mean that the buyer retrospectively takes the risk that the ship has already been wrecked along with its cargo.[16] The result may be that, as between buyer and seller, the former cannot complain if the goods never arrive.[17] The sellers or buyers of the cargo will expect to have a contract of carriage that will regulate their relations with the contractual carrier, and may be able to claim under that contract if the wreck was caused through a breach by the carrier.[18] The sellers or buyers will probably have cargo insurance in order to cover the risks of a shipwreck, eg for where the carrier is not liable, and will look to their insurer first.[19]

2.1.3 Cargo owners and salvage or wreck removal operations

After a wreck, individual owners of cargo are unlikely to be held liable to third parties (eg States) for the costs of removal of their cargo[20] or for pollution caused by it,[21] and so the concerns of such owners and their insurers will be the saving of the cargo and accumulating evidence to justify a claim under a bill of lading or waybill against the contracting carrier (which might be the registered owner or a charterer), or under a charter against the registered or disponent owner.[22]

---

15 See eg Incoterms 2010, FOB A5, B5; CIF A5, B5; and F Lorenzon, Y Baatz, *Sassoon on CIF and FOB Contracts* (6th ed, Sweet & Maxwell, 2017) [*Sassoon*], Chapter 2.

16 See the discussion in *Sassoon*, 20–22. The contract may even expressly provide that the purchase price is to be paid "ship lost or not lost".

17 There are exceptions, eg where under a CIF contract the seller obtains a carriage contract that is not on reasonable or usual terms: see *Sassoon*, 22–35.

18 See 2.1.4, 2.1.5.

19 See 2.9.3. In an FOB contract this insurance will usually have been arranged by the buyer; in a CIF contract the insurance will have been arranged by the seller for the benefit of the buyer.

20 See eg 2.1.6, 10.2.2, 10.6, 11.1. Cf *Kuwait Maritime Transport Co v Rickmers Linie KG (The Danah)* [1993] 1 Lloyd's Rep 351, where charterers agreed with owners to meet in the first instance any claims of Dutch authorities in locating and salving lost and dangerous cargo in containers, and were entitled to reclaim such sums against owners through breach of the charter. For costs of forwarding, see 2.1.4.

21 Oil cargo owners are not liable under the CLC 1992, although they may have to contribute indirectly to any payments made under the Fund Convention 1992: see 2.6.2; similarly, under the HNSC 2010 when in force: see 2.6.4. Note that under EU law there is a possibility of liability under the Waste Framework Directive: see 14.6.3. National law might conceivably place liabilities on cargo owners, but this would generally be difficult as the cargo owner would not normally be at fault for any pollution caused by the ship being wrecked: cf where the cargo owner is also a charterer, see 2.1.6, 2.1.7.

22 See also 2.9.5(a).

2.1.3(a) Cargo owners and salvage

The owners of cargo and their insurers are often in an invidious position when there is a casualty. Individual cargo owners will rarely have representatives on board the ship for the voyage and will be heavily reliant on the shipowner (or contracting carrier) both for the provision of information and for any action to save their cargo. The position may be a little different where voyage charterers are involved, eg as owners of a large bulk cargo, as they may well expect a greater degree of consultation about operations that might affect their cargo. Once a salvor performs services, the cargo interests will be reliant on the efforts of the salvor, as regulated by the Salvage Convention 1989.[23]

Under Art 6(2) of the Salvage Convention 1989, the shipowner and master have authority to enter salvage contracts on behalf of property on board the vessel, eg the cargo, even without the express permission of the cargo owner.[24] In these circumstances the cargo owner may find that it is bound by, say, an LOF 2011 contract to arbitrate in London a claim of which it may have had little notice.[25] Nevertheless, as the cargo owners will now be parties to the LOF contract they will be entitled to enforce its terms, eg to require salvors to use their best endeavours to salve the cargo.[26]

It is unlikely that cargo owners will be consulted by shipowners when a decision is made to engage salvors, and in many cases knowledge about the casualty may come very late (especially perhaps with container cargoes).[27] In the initial stages of operations, particularly, there will be little communication with cargo interests by the salvor, which will be relying on the ship's manifest for information about the cargo. When it becomes necessary to remove intact cargo from a wrecked ship, the salvor may need to contact cargo interests to obtain safety and other handling information about the cargo. This may be more easily be done with the relatively few owners of large specialised bulk cargoes (eg chemicals) but may often be impractical where thousands of containers are involved.

2.1.3(b) Removal by cargo interests themselves

If the shipowner (or contracting carrier) fails to assist in the removal of the cargo from the ship,[28] what happens next may depend on whether cargo can be salved, ie where its

---

23 See 2.7.

24 Under the LOF 2011 cl K, the shipowner and master warrant to the salvor that they have such authority: see also F Rose, *Kennedy & Rose: Law of Salvage* (9th ed, Sweet & Maxwell, 2017) [*Kennedy & Rose*], 353–356. It is possible that a powerful charterer may expressly withdraw the authority of the master under Art 6.2 so as to make local salvage arrangements, and it appears that this might be allowed by the Salvage Convention 1989: see N Gaskell, "Merchant Shipping Act 1995" in *Current Law Statutes 1995* [*Gaskell, MSA 1995*], 21/385–21/386. Even if the cargo owner is not bound by a particular salvage *contract*, it would still be liable to pay a salvage reward under the *Convention* for any success in saving its property: see 2.7.7(b). See also 12.2.1.

25 Authority under Art 6 can only apply to "salvage" services. This means that the property must have been in "danger". Cargo owners have sometimes disputed authority on the basis that there was never any danger to their cargo: and see *Gaskell, MSA 1995*, 21/384–21/386. In the context of casualties leading to wreck this is less likely to be an issue, as there should be little dispute as to the danger to all interests. In the event of a dispute about authority, the parties may agree to an ad hoc arbitration.

26 Under LOF 2011 cl A, and cf the "due care" obligation under the Salvage Convention 1989 Art 8(1): see eg *Kennedy & Rose*, 355-356, *Gaskell, MSA 1995*, 21/389–21/393, and 12.2.

27 Indeed, some individual consignees may be heavily reliant on freight forwarders and may not even know the identity of the actual carrying ship when there have been transhipments under a combined transport bill. See also 2.9.5(a) and 12.3.3.

28 See 2.1.4(a). See also 2.8.

recovered value is greater than the removal costs. Here, any salvor will have a direct salvage claim against the cargo owner for taking the cargo to a place of safety.[29]

Where the removal costs are likely to exceed the salved value, the cargo owner will have little direct interest to engage contractors to recover the cargo. A State may still require the wreck of the cargo (and, perhaps, the ship) to be removed by issuing a wreck removal order against the *shipowner*.[30] As will be seen, an order under the WRC 2007 is made against the shipowner alone; there is no joint or several liability of the cargo owner.[31] Thus, even if the shipowner may not be liable to the cargo owner for the loss of the cargo,[32] it (and indirectly its P&I Club) will have to pay the costs of removal. The Salvage Convention 1989 Art 6(2) only gives the master (or shipowner) the authority to contract on behalf of cargo for *salvage* services, not other services, so the master would have no authority under Art 6(2) to enter a wreck removal contract that binds cargo owners to pay for the costs.[33] In practice, though, the standard wreck removal contracts[34] are agreed directly with the shipowner on whom liability for wreck removal falls, and do not purport to bind cargo interests.[35]

Moreover, in addition to the costs of the operation, there is also the practical issue of having to deal with governments and wreck removal contractors (not to mention the media)[36] in order to raise cargo (and, possibly, the ship). This of itself will involve considerable management time and consequent cost. To some extent this means that cargo owners and charterers[37] can stand back and expect the shipowner to deal with the mechanics of the removal and disposal[38] of valueless wrecked cargo, while they can concentrate on their potential rights and liabilities under their contracts.[39]

2.1.4 Carriage contracts and cargo forwarding costs

While the shipowner might be able to rely on an exclusion of liability for loss or damage caused after a wreck,[40] there is a separate question under the contract of carriage as to who will bear the responsibility for any subsequent expenses for the removal and/or forwarding of that cargo.

---

29 See 2.7.7(b), also 2.9.3(c) for the insurance position.
30 See 9.2.5, 10.5.3(a), 11.1, 11.3.3(c).
31 See 10.2.2.
32 See 2.1.5(b)–(d).
33 It seems unlikely that there could be an agency of necessity in circumstances where the cargo is valueless and there is no direct liability on cargo owners to pay for removal: cf *China Pacific SA v Food Corp of India (The Winson)* [1982] AC 3339, *Industrie Chimiche Italia Centrale v Alexander G Tsavliris & Sons Maritime (The Choko Star No 1)* [1987] 1 Lloyd's Rep 508; and see *Kennedy & Rose*, 353–356.
34 See 13.6.
35 Cf 13.6.5(g). There may be contractual liabilities under charterparties to indemnify the shipowner for wreck removal costs: see eg 2.1.7(a).
36 See also 13.1.2.
37 Eg a slot charterer in the *MSC Napoli*: see 1.2.3, 2.5.3, 2.5.4(d).
38 For disposal, see Chapter 14.
39 Eg in the *Rena*, a charterer operated as a contractual carrier by issuing bills of lading and waybills in its name (with London jurisdiction clauses) to owners of cargo in particular containers. It could then establish a limitation fund under the LLMC 1996 (see fn 177 and 2.5) in the UK to deal with those particular cargo claims.
40 See 2.1.5(a), (b).

2.1.4(a) Transhipment costs under the carriage contract

Where the ship is permanently wrecked (eg a CTL) and sound cargo (eg containers) is taken to a place of safety, it may still be possible to tranship the cargo to the intended port of destination under the carriage contract. The question then arises as to who pays for the costs of transhipment, and the answer may depend heavily upon the terms of the relevant contract of carriage. In principle, a shipowner (as contracting carrier) that tranships cargo at its own expense, but completes the contractual voyage, will usually be entitled to its agreed freight.[41] Large container lines may actually arrange for transhipment onto their own vessels in order to reduce costs.[42]

In view of the uncertainties caused by the doctrine of frustration,[43] most carriage contracts contain liberty clauses[44] designed for circumstances that occur beyond the control of the carrier, and these may give the carrier a number of options. Bills of lading might include an express right to carry the goods to the contracted discharge port (eg by transhipment) but to charge extra freight; to suspend the voyage, but to charge for storage and extra freight; or to abandon a voyage, eg after a wreck, and make the cargo available at a port other than the contracted destination, but still earning full freight.[45] The extent to which such clauses are effective will depend on questions of contractual interpretation,[46] and whether they offend against, eg the Hague/Visby Rules.[47] Where the contract of carriage continues, the contracting carrier would in principle remain liable under the contract and the Hague/Visby Rules.[48] There may be a question as to whether the Hague or Hague-Visby Rules apply where where the State of the initial port of loading and the place of transhipment apply different versions of the Rules.[49] This would affect limitation of liability, in particular. Where the transhipment is a continuation of a single contract of carriage, it would seem that the Rules compulsorily applicable in the port of loading might apply (eg under English law

---

41 See eg *Thomas v Harrowing SS Co* [1915] AC 58; *Voyage Charters*, 311–312.

42 This may be relatively straightforward if the port of safety is one at which its vessels regularly call. Where that port is not one where container ships regularly called, it may be necessary to divert another ship from the fleet, or charter in tonnage: cf *The MSC Napoli*, 1.2.3.

43 See 2.1.4(b).

44 Variously described, eg as "force majeure", "hindrances", "methods of carriage" etc: see *Bills of Lading, Law and Contracts*, 372–376. Rather than having a single force majeure clause, it is becoming more common (eg in charters) to make use of separate BIMCO war, strikes and ice clauses.

45 See eg Maersk Terms of Carriage (2018) cl 20: https://terms.maersk.com/carriage. See also Conlinebill 2016 cll 6–7 for transhipment (and 2.1.4(b)). Conlinebill 2016 cl 14(e) provides that extra expenses incurred exercising liberties under the '*Caspiana*' clause (cl 17) would be payable in addition to freight, but this clause only covers government orders, war, ice strikes etc, and not the sinking of the ship. For such clauses see *Renton GH & Co Ltd v Palmyra Trading Corp (The Caspiana)* [1957] AC 149, [1956] 2 Lloyd's Rep 379; *Bills of Lading, Law and Contracts*, 373–376.

46 The courts will tend to interpret such liberty clauses against the carrier, eg so as not to apply if the event (eg a wreck) was caused by the prior negligence of the shipowner: cf *J Lauritzen AS v Wijsmuller BV (The Super Servant Two)* [1990] 1 Lloyd's Rep 1, 9.

47 Art III r 8 of the Rules would strike down any clause in a bill of lading that removed liabilities of the carrier, eg if a wreck was caused by unseaworthiness, but not for events beyond the control of the carrier: see *The Caspiana* [1956] 2 Lloyd's Rep 379.

48 See 2.1.5. In *The Bernina (No 2)* (1886) 12 PD 36, after a collision the carrier arranged with other owners to tranship cargo, but they failed to deliver it. The carrier was still held liable under its own carriage contracts as they had continued in force with the election by the carriers not to terminate the voyage: see also 2.1.4(b).

49 See 2.1.5(e).

if that shipment was from the UK).[50] If the transhipment represented an entirely new and separate voyage, then it might be appropriate to apply the Rules applicable in the place of transhipment.[51] The extent to which sub-contractors engaged to complete the voyage might be sued, eg in tort or bailment, will probably depend upon whether they can take advantage of a Himalaya clause in the carriage contract[52] or could rely on the doctrine of sub-bailment on terms.[53]

In a time charter that has not yet been terminated following a stranding, a shipowner that obeyed the orders of the time charterer to complete the carriage of cargo owned by third parties (eg under bills of lading) might be entitled to an implied indemnity at market rates; likewise if the shipowner was directly bound to the third parties because it had issued bills in its own name, as ordered, and was obliged to continue the carriage.[54] However, in both these examples, it is much more likely that the respective contracts of carriage will have been terminated.

2.1.4(b) Termination of the carriage contract

Apart from the case where the shipowner (or contracting carrier) is unable (physically or financially) to complete the contracted voyage, its decision whether to attempt to complete that voyage, eg by transhipment from the wreck site, is most likely to depend upon whether the cost is greater than any expected freight or expenses that it might be able to receive, or the possibility of claiming general average.[55] If the financial comparison is disadvantageous, the shipowner may decide to treat the contractual voyage as at an end. It will therefore be crucial to decide whether the contract of carriage has terminated by operation of law, eg by frustration, or as a result of an express clause[56] or a liberty given in the contract of carriage. Either way, this will affect the obligation of the shipowner (or contracting carrier) to ensure that the cargo arrives at its destination.

While some early case law about when a shipowner was entitled to abandon the voyage does not use the language of the modern doctrine of frustration,[57] it is now clear that when a supervening event renders performance of the contract impossible or radically different from that agreed, the contract will be frustrated. Frustration will result in the

---

50 Cf *The Anders Maersk* [1986] 1 Lloyd's Rep 483.
51 Cf *JI MacWilliam Co v Mediterranean Shipping Co (The Rafaela S)* [20002] EWCA Civ 556, [2003] 2 Lloyd's Rep 113 (not appealed to the HL on this issue). See *Voyage Charters*, 1009–1011; *Bills of Lading: Law and Contracts*, 314–320.
52 Eg Maersk Terms of Carriage (2018) cl 4 and the International Group of P&I Clubs/BIMCO Himalaya Clause for bills of lading and other contracts 2014 (incorporated eg in Conlinebill 2016 cl 15). See also cases such as *The Mahkutai* [1996] AC 650, [1996] 2 Lloyd's Rep 1; *Homburg Houtimport BV v Agrosin Pte Ltd and Others (The Starsin)* [2003] UKHL 12, [2004] 1 AC 715, [2003] 1 Lloyd's Rep 571; *Carver on Bills of Lading*, 443–472, 737–744; *Bills of Lading: Law and Contracts*, Chapter 12.
53 *The KH Enterprise (Cargo Owners) v Pioneer Container (Owners) (The Pioneer Container)* [1994] 2 AC 324; *Bills of Lading: Law and Contracts* 291–293, 398–401.
54 *The Kos* [2012] 2 Lloyd's Rep 292, [50, 79].
55 See 2.8.
56 See eg Shelltime 4 cl 20, which declares the time charter terminated when the ship is lost, including where there is a constructive total loss: see 2.9.4(b).
57 See *Bills of Lading, Law and Contracts*, 368–372.

automatic termination of future contractual obligations.[58] An example of where there would be a radical difference would be where a vessel is so damaged that the cost of repair and freight are greater than its market value.[59] In *Assicurazione Generali v Bessie Morris SS Co*,[60] a ship went aground and much of the cargo was jettisoned or heavily damaged. The shipowner was in breach for abandoning the voyage when the ship could have been repaired and taken the sound cargo to destination. Where a ship is wrecked through no actionable breach by the shipowner[61] this could generally be expected to result in frustration of a charterparty or bill of lading contract.[62] However, it has been suggested that if the ship was wrecked at the entrance to the port of discharge and the cargo could be unloaded into lighters and brought to port, the situation might be different.[63] Presumably, in this example the required performance would not be radically different in *nature* from normal lightering that might take place in a port with restricted quay facilities. By contrast, transhipment at a remote wreck site might involve radically different extra risks and duties; the mere fact that one method is more expensive than another is not of itself sufficient to frustrate a contract, so any extra cost to the shipowner would not be decisive.[64]

Where there is frustration, the common law position was that freight due before the frustrating event was still payable, but not that payable on delivery.[65] Freight payable in advance (eg on loading) is often expressly stated to be "deemed earned and non-returnable, [v]essel and/or cargo lost or not lost"[66] or "non-returnable in any event".[67] Hire payable under frustrated bareboat and time charters would be subject to equitable adjustments under the Law Reform (Frustrated Contracts) Act 1943, but note that an express clause might provide that hire was returnable after a total loss.[68]

---

58 See eg *Paal Wilson & Co v Partenreederei Hannah Blumenthal (The Hannah Blumenthal)* [1983] 1 AC 854, 909, [1983] 1 Lloyd's Rep 103.
59 See *Scrutton*, 40.
60 [1892] 2 QB 652. See also *Kulukundis v Norwich Union Fire Insurance Society* [1937] KB 1 (1936) 55 Ll L Rep 55 (an insurance on freight case) where the ship became a CTL, but a salvor took the hull and some sound cargo to destination. In *Kulukundis*, the repair costs would have exceeed the ship's value plus freight, but the fact that the ship is a CTL under the insurance contract is not determinative of the obligations under the carriage contract. It is quite common for a ship to be insured for greater than its market value, eg insured for US$20 million, but with a market value of US$15 million: see 2.9.4(b).
61 A breach, eg from unseaworthiness, that caused the ship to be wrecked would-be self-induced frustration. If the ship was wrecked because of negligent navigation that could be self-induced; but if there was an exception for such navigation, eg under the Hague/Visby Rules Art IV r 2(a) (see 2.1.5(b)) or charterparty (see 2.1.7(b) and (c)) the contract could still be frustrated: cf *Jackson v The Union Marine Insurance Co Ltd* (1874) LR 10 CP 125. See also *Voyage Charters*, 697–698, *Time Charters*, 495–497.
62 See eg *Blane Steamships v Minister of Transport* [1951] KB 96, [1951] 2 Lloyd's Rep 155.
63 See *Kulukundis v Norwich Union Fire Insurance Society* [1937] KB 1, 17 (1936) 55 LL L Rep 55, 62 (per Greene LJ, *obiter*).
64 It may be correct to say that the doctrine of frustration requires a "multi-factorial approach" (*The Sea Angel* [2007] EWCA Civ 547, [2007] 2 Lloyd's Rep 517, [111]), but this does not exactly assist in predictability.
65 See *Fibrosa Spolka Alcyna v Fairbairn Lawson Combe Barbour Ltd* [1943] AC 32.
66 See Gencon 1994 cl 4(b).
67 See Conlinebill 2016 cl 10.
68 See eg the NYPE 2015 cl 20 and 2.1.7(c).

Where a charter gives the shipowner the right to substitute a vessel, this right may survive the loss of the ship so that the contract is not automatically frustrated.[69] The authors of *Voyage Charters*[70] consider that if the owner then declines to use a substitute (or tranship) this would not be self-induced frustration. This approach may be justified, perhaps on the basis that the owner is given an unrestricted commercial option rather than having a duty, although such a conclusion sits rather uneasily with the case law.[71] Similar issues may arise with bills of lading which give carriers the option to substitute or tranship.[72] The difficulty is that frustration normally occurs automatically, but here there would need to be a period of time in which the shipowner might consider its choices. The frustration delay cases[73] show that it may not always be easy to define the exact moment of frustration, so where the option to substitute or tranship is unfettered it does not seem unreasonable for the carrier to be able to rely on frustration from the moment that an election is made not to substitute or tranship. If there was inordinate delay, the charterer or bill of lading holder might itself claim frustration. A wrongful abandonment of the carriage might leave the shipowner or carrier open to a claim by the cargo owner for damages for breach as a result of having to pay for separate transhipment itself.

If the shipowner relies on termination based upon the frustration of the voyage, eg because the completion of the voyage is physically impossible because of the wreck of the ship,[74] it might still separately arrange and pay for transhipment, eg for commercial reasons in the container trade. Here the shipowner has a liberty (but not an obligation) to tranship the cargo in order to earn its freight.[75] It may then have a number of ways in which to claim extra sums from cargo owners. First, if the ship is stranded (but not yet totally lost), and the shipowner itself incurs direct and extra costs to remove the cargo, eg by transhipment, this may be the basis for a claim by the shipowner for general average [GA];[76] the assumption here is that the cargo has a residual value against which the expenses can be charged, and that there was at that stage a common danger to all property including the ship at the time of transhipment, eg where cargo is offloaded so as lighten the ship for possible refloating.[77]

---

69 In *Niarchos v Shell Tankers* [1961] 2 Lloyd's Rep 496, a total loss was said to frustrate the time charter so that the shipowner no longer had the duty *or right* to make a substitution. The authors of *Time Charters* consider that a 'substitution' clause would need clear words if it was to be interpreted to apply after a total loss: see 477–479. This question of interpretation is central, but it is unclear if the approach (or inference) in *Niarchos* can be applied to contracts of carriage in voyage charters or bills of lading.

70 See 82–83, 703.

71 Eg *Maritime Fish v Ocean Trawlers* [1935] AC 524 and *J Lauritzen v Wijsmuller (The Super Servant Two)* [1990] 1 Lloyd's Rep 1.

72 See eg Conlinebill 2016 cll 6 and 7. Such clauses do not exclude frustration, eg where the contemplated voyage has been prevented by the wreck of the ship: cf *Fibrosa v Fairbairn* [1943] AC 32; *Select Commodities Ltd v Valdo SA (The Florida)* [2007] 1 Lloyd's Rep 1.

73 Such as *Pioneer Shipping v BTP Tioxide (The Nema)* [1982] AC 724, [1981] 2 Lloyd's Rep 239.

74 The entitlement of the carrier to terminate the contract of carriage will also be relevant to the extent to which cargo insurers may pay for transhipment: see 2.9.2(b).

75 See eg *Assicurazione Generali v Bessie Morris SS Co* [1892] 2 QB 652; *Eridania SpA v Rudolf A Oetker (The Fjord Wind)* [1999] 1 Lloyd's Rep 307, 332–335 (issues not considered when affirmed on appeal, [2000] 2 Lloyd's Rep 191, 204).

76 See 2.8.

77 It seems that it will be difficult to claim in general average the full costs of transhipment to the intended port of destination, as the common adventure will normally have ended at the wreck site: see 2.8 and *Lowndes & Rudolf*, 211–212.

Secondly, after the termination of a carriage contract, the shipowner (or carrier) has a continuing duty in bailment to look after the cargo.[78] This means that it will be entitled to its reasonable expenses for so doing[79] or, apparently, to be remunerated at market rates.[80] The payments here should cover discharge and storage locally, and might extend to on-carriage to the contractual destination. Thirdly, where the ship is already a wreck, the shipowner that undertakes on-carriage may seek to rely on a contractual claim against the cargo interests, perhaps relying on express liberties in a bill of lading or on agency.[81]

If the cargo owners pay for the transhipment from the wreck site themselves, this would not appear to be a GA act, but they may be covered under the forwarding charges provisions of their cargo insurance.[82] They and their insurers may then seek to seek to recoup the additional costs from the shipowner (or contracting carrier) if the wreck was caused by an actionable breach, eg unseaworthiness.[83]

It seems fair to say that the contractual position about responsibility for forwarding costs after a wreck is complex, and is made more so once GA and cargo insurance are taken into account.

2.1.5 Liability for cargo loss or damage caused by wreck

A cargo claim may be framed in contract, tort or bailment but, in addition to any terms contained in a bill of lading or waybill,[84] there is a heavy overlay of mandatory terms imposed by the Hague Rules,[85] the Hague-Visby Rules[86] or other provisions.[87]

---

78 *Petroleo Brasileiro SA v ENE Kos 1 Ltd (The Kos)* [2012] UKSC 17, [2012] 2 AC 164, [2012] 2 Lloyd's Rep 292 [28]. See also *Voyage Charters*, 709–710.

79 *China Pacific v Food Corp of India (The Winson)* [1983] AC 939, [1982] 1 Lloyd's Rep 117.

80 See *Cargo ex Argos* (1872) LR 5 PC 134, applied in the *The Kos* [2012] 2 Lloyd's Rep 292 [29]. *The Kos* was a charterparty withdrawal case where the issue was whether the shipowner was entitled to the cost of fuel and hire for two days after the withdrawal when the cargo was still on board. The case was decided on the basis of an express indemnity clause (see also 2.1.7(c)), so that strictly the conclusions on bailment are *obiter*. The decision that an agency of necessity is not required to cover expenses is less radical than the finding that such an agency is not a precondition for recovering remuneration: see the dissenting speech of Lord Mance; also Allsop CJ, "Recent Charterparty Decisions" (26 June 2013), 11, www.fedcourt.gov.au/digital-law-library/judges-speeches/chief-justice-allsop/allsop-cj-20130626

81 Either express agency, where the shipowner offers to carry the cargo on for extra freight and the cargo interests agree, or because there is an agency of necessity (but see *The Kos* [2012] 2 Lloyd's Rep 292 and the previous footnote).

82 On the basis that the forwarding charges are reasonable (albeit greater than under the original contract), see 2.9.3(b).

83 See 2.1.5(a).

84 Claims by charterers against shipowners for the loss of their cargo will be governed by the terms of the charterparty in which there is complete freedom to include any contractual terms, although in practice such claims are often made subject to the Hague/Visby Rules: see eg 2.1.7(b) and (c).

85 International Convention for the Unification of Certain Rules of Law relating to Bills of Lading 1924.

86 Ie the Hague Rules as amended by a Protocol of 1968; there is a further Protocol of 1979 introducing the sdr for limitation purposes. The Hague-Visby Rules are enacted in the UK in the Carriage of Goods by Sea Act (COGSA) 1971, as amended by the MSA 1981 to give effect to the 1979 Protocol.

87 Eg in national law or more recent carriage conventions. The UN International Convention on the Carriage of Goods by Sea [Hamburg Rules] 1978 is in force in 34 States, particularly in Africa: see also *Bills of Lading: Law and Contracts*, 6–7. The UN Convention on Contracts for the International Carriage of Goods Wholly or Partly by Sea [Rotterdam Rules] 2008 has not entered into force internationally.

2.1.5(a) Hague/Visby Rules liability scheme

After a wreck, the scheme of liability that would apply under the Hague Rules or Hague-Visby Rules is broadly similar.[88] Liabilities under the "Hague/Visby Rules"[89] are placed on the contracting carrier, ie the company that entered into the contract of carriage with the shipper of the cargo.[90] The contracting carrier could be the shipowner, but might also be a voyage or time charterer.[91] The Hague/Visby Rules Art III r 8 would render void any attempt to use a contract clause in a bill of lading[92] to reduce the carrier's liability below the minimum standards set out in the Rules.

Where a bill of lading is issued under or pursuant to a charterparty, the Hague and Hague-Visby Rules will apply to the contract of carriage only from the moment at which such bill regulates the relations between the carrier and the holder of the bill of lading.[93] This moment would occur when a person became the lawful holder of the bill under the Carriage of Goods by Sea Act 1992. For that person, Art III r 8 would render void any charterparty clause that reduced the liability of the carrier.[94] Not all carriage contracts require a negotiable bill of lading, and many containerised cargoes are carried on the basis of waybills. These are not bills of lading and it seems that they are not "similar documents of title" so as to fall within the Hague/Visby Rules mandatory provisions.[95] In theory this might allow carriers to exclude all liabilities, but in practice the container market would not allow this and most bills will incorporate the Hague Rules or, more usually, the Hague-Visby Rules.[96]

Not all cargo is given the protections of the Hague/Visby Rules, eg live animals and deck cargo.[97] It would not be unusual, for instance, to exclude all liability to a charterer or bill of lading holder for deck cargo washed overboard,[98] eg a cargo of timber or pipes carried on

---

88 See eg *Bills of Lading: Law and Contracts*, 272–283, *Carver on Bills of Lading*, Chapter 9. Although both sets of Rules apply to international carriage under Art X, it is common for States to apply them to domestic carriage: see eg COGSA 1971 s 1(3).

89 "Hague/Visby Rules" will be used as a simple expression to encompass the "Hague Rules" *and* the "Hague-Visby Rules", eg when their provisions are practically identical, as in most instances (eg under Arts III and IV). Reference to the individual sets of Rules will only be made when necessary, eg where limits differ: see eg 2.1.5(e).

90 Art I(a).

91 See 2.1.7(b) and (c).

92 The Hague/Visby Rules apply to straight bills, eg documents that might be based on a normal bill, but not made out "to order" of the consignee: see *The Rafaela S* [2005] UKHL 11, [2005] 2 AC 423, [2005] 1 Lloyd's Rep 347.

93 Arts 1(b), V. Where the bill is in the hands of the charterer it will usually operate as a receipt only, as the charterparty is the governing contract and the Hague/Visby Rules do not apply to charterparties (Art V) unless contractually incorporated: see 2.1.7(b) and eg *President of India v Metcalfe Shipping Co. (The Dunelmia)* [1970] 1 QB 289; *Voyage Charters*, 506–510; *Carver on Bills of Lading*, 106–138; *Bills of Lading: Law and Contracts*, Chapter 21.

94 Eg under Gencon 1994 cl 2: see 2.1.7(b).

95 See *Carver on Bills of Lading*, 636–639; *Bills of Lading: Law and Contracts* 713–725.

96 See eg Genwaybill 2016 cl 2, Combiconwaybill 2016 cl 11(2), and cf Bimco Blank Back Form of Non-Negotiable Liner Waybill 2016; *Bills of Lading: Law and Contracts*, 726–735. The form of the 'clause paramount' used for incorporation may give rise to some uncertainty as to which version of the Rules is incorporated in a waybill: cf *Voyage Charterers*, 947–948, 995–997, 107–109.

97 See Art I(c). Deck cargo is only outside the Hague/Visby Rules if the bill of lading states on its face that the goods are (not may be) carried on deck and that they are in fact so carried. See also 2.9.2(b) and *Voyage Charterers*, 167–172; *Time Charters*, 363–364.

98 See eg Conlinebill 2016 cl 3.

hatch covers. Such complete exclusions would be rare in a modern container bill of lading, as ships are designed for above deck container carriage. Where such a container is damaged or washed overboard, carriers would normally assume some contractual responsibility.[99]

Proof of fault by the carrier will usually be a major component of any claim, but (unlike the Hamburg Rules 1978) the Hague/Visby Rules do not have a single rule of liability based on fault. The liability responsibilities are split, rather confusingly, depending on whether there is a breach of an obligation of seaworthiness under Art III r 1, or of a duty to take care under Art III r 2.

The carrier would be liable under the Hague/Visby Rules Art III r 1 if the wreck was caused by any unseaworthiness of the vessel that existed at the start of its voyage,[100] eg if there was a defect in the hull plating, engines or navigational equipment, or if an incompetent crew had been employed.[101] The carrier has a defence under Art IV r 1 if it can prove that it exercised "due diligence" to make the ship seaworthy. This duty can only be discharged if the carrier proves that it, or its employees or agents, were not at fault. It is not enough for the carrier to prove that it chose competent surveyors, repairers or ship managers; these independent contractors must use due diligence.[102] Apart from the due diligence defence, the carrier will have no complete defence to an unseaworthiness claim, and for this reason unseaworthiness will always be at the forefront of any cargo claim after a wreck.[103]

If the cargo claimant cannot prove that unseaworthiness caused loss by a wreck it must show that the carrier failed *"properly and carefully to* load, handle, stow, *carry, keep, care for,* and discharge the goods carried" under Art III r 2.[104] Where the goods were loaded in apparent good order and condition, as recorded in the bill of lading or waybill, and either totally lost or damaged in a shipwreck, there would be evidence of a breach of Art III r 2. The carrier then has the burden of proving that it took reasonable care of the goods during the voyage.[105]

Article III r 2 is, however, made expressly subject to the list of exceptions in the Hague/Visby Rules Art IV r 2. Most of these are merely examples of where the carrier is not at

---

99 Container operators may well accept liability for containers on deck, but perhaps subject to the Hague Rules, while excluding liability for all other deck cargo: see eg the Maersk Terms for Carriage (2018), cl 18. See also *Bills of Lading: Law and Contracts*, Section 10B. Thus, liability would require proof by a cargo owner of breach of the obligations of seaworthiness or due care, and would be subject to the usual Art IV r 2 defences, eg peril of the sea or negligent navigation: see 2.1.5(b). Limitation of liability under the Hague Rules would be calculated differently to that under the Hague-Visby Rules: see 2.1.5(e).

100 An engine breakdown in the middle of a voyage could still result from unseaworthiness if the defect existed at the start of the voyage.

101 By contrast with a crew that was generally competent; see the summary of the authorities in *Papera Traders Co. Ltd v Hyundai Merchant Marine Co Ltd (The Eurasian Dream)* [2002] EWHC 118 (Comm), [2002] 1 Lloyd's Rep 719 [128–129].

102 *Riverstone Meat Co Pty v Lancashire Shipping Co (The Muncaster Castle)* [1961] AC 807; see also 2.1.5(b).

103 It will also be significant if the cargo owner wants to resist a claim for general average: see 2.8. The carrier will be able to limit liability, though, under the LLMC 1996 (see 2.5.4(a)), and the Hague/Visby Rules Art IV r 5 (see 2.1.5(e)).

104 The italicised words are those most likely to be relevant in a wreck case.

105 *Volcafe Ltd and Others v Compania SudAmericana De Vapores SA* [2018] UKSC 61, [2019] 1 Lloyd's Rep 21, discussed below.

fault, eg where the loss is caused by acts of the shipper,[106] third parties,[107] or events beyond the carrier's control.[108] There is a specific exception Art IV r 2(c) for "perils, dangers and accidents of the sea or other navigable waters", which covers fortuities and could apply where a ship is wrecked by hitting an unchartered reef, by being driven aground by hurricane force winds, or as a result of a collision with another ship.[109]

There is also an exception in Art IV r 2(b) for "fire, unless caused by the actual fault or privity of the carrier". This exception could apply where a fire broke out in cargo and spread to the ship, causing it to be wrecked.[110] The "carrier" will not be able to rely on the exception if the fire was caused by the fault or recklessness of a person whose misconduct could be considered as that of the shipowner itself, eg someone at board level.[111] In *The Lady M*[112] the fire exception was also held to apply to fires even if started negligently or deliberately (or barratrously[113]) by a member of the crew, in that case the chief engineer. The effect of this exception could therefore be quite wide in a wreck case where the cargo or bunkers catch fire, either before a grounding or after a stranding. The latter could include circumstances where the fire started as a result of actions by the salvor.[114] There might still be questions of causation or interpretation relating to "fire", eg where there is an explosion.[115] The cargo claimant would still be able to rely on initial unseaworthiness if that

---

106 Eg Art IV r 2(i): similarly, if the cargo was insufficiently packed, Art IV r 2(n).

107 Eg an "act of war" (Art IV r 2(e)), or "restraints of princes" (Art IV r 2(f)), or "strikes" (Art IV r 2(j)), or "riots" (Art IV r 2(j)).

108 Eg "inherent defect, quality or vice of the goods" (Art IV r 2(m)), or "latent defects" (Art IV r 2(p)). There is also a 'catch all' Art IV r 2(q) exception for "any other cause arising without the actual fault or privity of the carrier, or without the fault or neglect of the agents or servants of the carrier". In *Glencore Energy UK Ltd v Freeport Holdings Ltd (The Lady M)* [2017] EWHC 3348, [2018] Lloyd's Rep Plus 22, the Art IV r 2(q) exception was held not to apply to barratrous acts of chief engineer. There was no appeal on the Art IV r 2(q) point, but the carrier was able to rely on Art IV r 2(b): see *The Lady M* [2019] EWCA Civ 388, [2019] 2 Lloyd's Rep 109 and below; also *Carver on Bills of Lading*, 706–707.

109 For burden of proof issues where there is fault, see 2.1.5(c), but note the effect of Art IV r 2(a) where the wrecked ship is guilty of negligent navigation.

110 As happened to the *Maersk Honam* in March 2018.

111 There is much case law on the phrase "actual fault or privity", as used in the MSA 1894 s 503; see *Bills of Lading: Law and Contracts*, 344 and eg *Arthur Guinness, Son & Company (Dublin) Ltd v The Freshfield (Owners) (The Lady Gwendoleyn)* [1965] P 294, [1965] 1 Lloyd's Rep 335, *Grand Champion Tankers v Norpipe A/S (The Marion)* [1984] AC 563, [1984] 2 Lloyd's Rep 1, and cf *The Eurysthenes* [1976] 2 Lloyd's Rep 171. "Privity" essentially means knowledge, including 'blind eye' knowledge: see 2.5.7, 2.9.2(c) and cf 10.8.4(d). The burden of proof in Art IV r 2(b) is on the cargo claimant.

112 [2019] EWCA Civ 388 [2019] 2 Lloyd's Rep 109.

113 Barratry for these purposes can be taken from the MIA 1906, Sch "Rules for the Construction of the Policy", para 11, to include "every wrongful act wilfully committed by the master or crew to the prejudice of the owner, or, as the case may be, the charterer": [2019] EWCA Civ 388 [1].

114 Cf *The Motor tanker Tojo Maru (Owners) (her cargo & freight) v NV Bureau Wijsmuller, The Tojo Maru* [1972] AC 242, *sub nom. NV Bureau Wijsmuller v Tojo Maru (Owners), The Tojo Maru* [1971] 1 Lloyd's Rep 341: see also 2.5.5.

115 Consider the Halifax explosion in 1917: see 2.6.4 (fn 961). After a collision there was a small fire before the devastating explosion. It would be difficult to say that this explosion (and the total loss of cargo as one consequence) were not caused by the fire. In other cases, the existence of a spark or flame may have to be inferred: cf *Aikens*, paras 10.232–10.233, *Voyage Charters*, 1083–1084.

caused the fire.[116] This could include circumstances where the crew were not competent or trained to be able to deal with the fire.[117]

2.1.5(b) Error in navigation or management exception
However, there is one well-known (and controversial) exception that is particularly significant to wreck, namely Art IV r 2(a): "act, neglect, or default of the master, mariner, pilot, or the servants of the carrier in the navigation or in the management of the ship".[118] Put simply, if the wreck is caused by negligent navigation the carrier has a complete defence,[119] and this would have applied to many of the major wreck cases such as the *Torrey Canyon* and the *Rena*.[120] In *Tasman Orient Line CV v New Zealand China Clays Ltd (The Tasman Pioneer)*,[121] the ship grounded after the master negligently navigated by taking a dangerous short cut and began taking on water. For a while he concealed the location of the casualty, claimed he had hit a floating object and sailed on for several hours. It was alleged that the delay prevented salvors from arriving in time to offload the deck cargo from the partially submerged vessel.[122] The cargo interests tried to argue that the conduct of the master after the grounding was not negligent navigation within Art IV r 2(a) as his actions were done in bad faith to save his reputation. This attempt to circumvent the rule by importing a notion of navigation in 'good faith' was rightly rejected by the New Zealand Supreme Court, and the deck cargo loss fell within the exception.

It is the "management" part of the Art IV r 2(a) defence that has caused most problems of interpretation, as almost every failure to care for cargo under Art III r 2 could be an error in management. The courts have given a narrow meaning these words. In *Gosse Millerd v Canadian Government Merchant Marine*,[123] it was held that the exception applied to the management of the ship as a navigable entity rather than to acts that were referable to the management of the cargo alone (ie a duty within Art III r 2). It would be relevant to inquire whether the negligence occurred in the caring for the safety of the ship, or in preventing damage to it, or otherwise for the ship's purposes. In the wreck context, the defence would apply to non-navigational decisions or actions by the master and crew, eg failure to ballast the ship properly (leading to a capsize) or to maintain the engine or other machinery or equipment while at sea (leading to a loss of power or steering).[124]

Even where Art IV r 2(a) appears to apply, there may still be questions of causation where, after a ship grounds, the cargo is damaged some time later. Cargo lost or damaged

---

116 Unless this were a UK ship and there was no intent or recklessness of senior management: see the MSA 1995 s 186 and 2.5.7.
117 See eg *The Eurasian Dream* [2002] 1 Lloyd's Rep 719, where a car carrier became a total loss after a fire started in port when jump leads were used by stevedores to start cars at the same time as car refuelling took place. The crew were ignorant of the fire risks and inadequately trained in firefighting, and there was also a shortage of walkie-talkies.
118 See eg *Voyage Charters*, 1078–1083.
119 There is no equivalent defence in the Hamburg Rules 1978 or the Rotterdam Rules 2008.
120 See 1.2.1, 1.2.4 and eg B Marten, *Maritime Law in New Zealand* (Thomson Reuters, 2016), 176.
121 [2010] 2 Lloyd's Rep 13.
122 Presumably it was accepted that any below deck cargo fell within the exception.
123 [1929] AC 726.
124 If there was a defect at the start of the voyage, the ship would be unseaworthy under Art III r 1 and this would be the cause of any later wreck, if eg the steering failed.

by the action of wind and waves while the ship is aground would clearly be "loss or damage arising or resulting from" the negligent navigation that put the ship aground.[125] The same conclusion is likely where the cargo is damaged or lost during risky attempts to salve it.[126] In either case, if the cargo is washed overboard, it cannot be argued that the Hague/Visby Rules have ceased to operate once the goods 'left' the ship. Under Art 1(e) the Rules only cease to operate when the goods are "discharged" from the ship, which clearly would not cover an involuntary loss; moreover, the operative cause of the loss occurred while the goods were on board.

Where the further performance of the contract of carriage has been terminated, eg for frustration,[127] the parties will still be entitled to rely on rights that had accrued beforehand. On this basis, the carrier could continue to rely on Art IV r 2(a) in respect of cargo loss that arose from the negligent navigation or management but occurred after the termination. There may come a time when this causative link is broken, and the question may arise as to whether the carrier is liable under any residual duties of reasonable care, eg in bailment while the cargo is still in its possession.[128]

Where the carrier has *not* terminated the contract of carriage,[129] its Hague/Visby Rules obligations will continue in principle until the goods are finally discharged at the port of destination. Most liner bills of lading will expressly permit the carrier to sub-contract the contractual carriage "on any terms whatsoever".[130] The carrier's contractual and Hague/Visby obligations would continue to apply while the goods are on board a salvor's barge, or a ship that has been chartered in to complete the voyage.[131] There may be difficult questions about whether the Hague/Visby Rules would apply continuously even during periods of transhipment when the goods are no longer on a ship but ashore pending on-shipment.[132]

---

125 See *The Tasman Pioneer* [2010] 2 Lloyd's Rep 13 [37] where refrigerated containers on deck had their generator power turned off by the salvors for some days prior to the removal of the containers from the grounded ship. This appeared to be because the cables from a temporary generator were running through water, or because the ship's generator was turned off in order to conserve fuel for pumping efforts. The dairy cargo was actually damaged by heat, not seawater. This was also held to be caused by an error in navigation or management: see also [2009] 2 Lloyd's Rep 308 [93].

126 Eg if the salvors were not themselves negligent as the carrier might also rely then on Art IV r 2(q): see 2.1.5(a). If the salvors were negligent in the way they cared for the cargo they might have liabilities in tort (subject to limitation, see 2.5.5), unless brought within a Himalaya clause in the bill of lading: see *Bills of Lading: Law and Contracts*, 283–397; *Carver on Bills of Lading*, 443–460.

127 See 2.1.4(b).

128 Cf *China Pacific v Food Corp of India (The Winson)* [1983] AC 939 and *The Kos* [2012] 2 Lloyd's Rep 292; and 2.1.4(b).

129 See 2.1.4(b).

130 See eg the Maersk Terms for Carriage (2018) cl 4(a).

131 Cf *Goodwin, Ferreira & Co v Lamport & Holt* (1929) 34 Ll L Rep 192; *Voyage Charters*, 1019–1020.

132 See *Mayhew Foods Ltd v Overseas Containers Ltd* [1984] 1 Lloyd's Rep 317, where the Hague-Visby Rules were applied even while the cargo was temporarily ashore. This decision raises some difficult questions about how the Rules can be applied when the cargo is not on a ship when damaged. The normal 'tackle to tackle' assumptions arising from Art 1(e) and Art VII (see *Pyrene Ltd v Scindia Steam Navigation Co Ltd* [1954] 2 QB 402) allow for freedom of contract after goods are discharged from the ship, and it is common for bills of lading to exclude all liability after "discharge"; combined transport bills may provide some alternative basis of liability, eg the Hague Rules: cf the Maersk Terms for Carriage (2018) cll 5–6. It seems that where the transhipment voyage is a continuation of the contracted carriage, "discharge" will refer to the final port of destination: see *Voyage Charters*, 1022–1023, 1032; also *Bills of Lading: Law and Contracts*, 260–261, 310–313.

Where normal on-carriage is involved, there will come a stage where the causative effects of the original negligent navigation will cease to operate, so that any subsequent loss or damage may not be excepted under Art IV r 2(a).

The Art IV r 2(a) exception will therefore often have a decisive effect on any cargo claim after a shipwreck. Apart from alleging unseaworthiness as the cause of the loss, one way in which claimants have tried to avoid exceptions in carriage contracts, including those in Art IV r 2, is to allege that there has been an unjustified "deviation" by the carrier from the contractual voyage. "Deviation" has developed as a special rule of maritime law and has been held to prevent a carrier from relying on the Art IV r 2 defences. Thus, in *Stag Line v Foscolo Mango*,[133] a decision by a master to take an unreasonable short cut when leaving port[134] was held to be a deviation that was not justified as being reasonable under Art IV r 4. The result was that the carrier could not rely on the error in navigation defence. The precise reason for depriving the carrier of its defence is still controversial, as it might be justified on the basis of causation, but the history of the doctrine suggests that it may operate in maritime law even if the deviation was not causative.[135]

2.1.5(c) Burden of proof under Art III and Art IV

The burden of proving due diligence to make a ship seaworthy is clearly placed on the carrier by Art IV r 1. There had been many doubts about how the burden of proving fault was to operate when considering the interplay of Art III r 2 and Art IV r 2, particularly those exceptions that did not specifically exclude the fault of the carrier, eg "perils of the sea" and, to a limited extent, "fire". Could the carrier rely, eg, on the Art IV r 2(c) defence where there might also have been concurrent fault of the employees, and who had to prove whether there was any fault of the carrier? One view was that the cargo owner always had to prove fault and that it was not for the carrier to have to prove the absence of fault in order to show, eg, that it had properly taken care of the cargo, or that a "peril of the sea" had not occurred though its fault. This view was decisively rejected by the Supreme Court on 5 December 2018 in *Volcafe Ltd and others v Compania Sud Americana de Vapores SA*.[136] This case has conclusively decided that the carrier has the legal burden of disproving negligence if it wants to invoke an exception under Art IV r 2 (eg inherent vice), as it would under Art III r 2.

In wreck cases, the *Volcafe v CSAV* decision will have less impact, except where there may be disputes as to whether cargo was damaged before the shipwreck. The existence of the error in navigation or management defence in Art IV r 2(a) means that the carrier will

---

133 [1932] AC 328.

134 Deviation does not appear to have been run in *The Tasman Pioneer*. The shortcut taken there may have not have been the conventional route, but was possible with care and the use of a pilot. The master's decision to use this route was probably unwise for the size of vessel, especially as rain squalls could and did blank out the radar, but it is understood that the evidence may not have proved deviation.

135 For a discussion of the controversy and how the doctrine might operate in different contexts, see *Bills of Lading: Law and Contracts*, 172–204. It seems clear that the doctrine cannot deprive the carrier of its Hague-Visby limits under Art IV r 5 (see *The European Enterprise* [1989] 2 Lloyd's Rep 185), or the time bar under Art III r 6 (see *Kenya Railways v Antares Co Pte Ltd (The Antares No.2)* [1987] 1 Lloyd's Rep 424). See also *Voyage Charters*, Chapter 12 and 1058–1060.

136 [2018] UKSC 61, [2019] 1 Lloyd's Rep 21.

not need to rely on eg a "peril of the sea" under Art IV r 2(c), as "loss or damage arising or resulting from" the error is already excepted.

By contrast, if the operative cause of the wreck was initial unseaworthiness, there would be liability under Art III r 1, as the Art IV r 2 exceptions only apply to Art III r 2. Even if a defect occurred *after* sailing, and was not corrected or dealt with by the master, this would still be a "neglect . . . in the management of the ship" within Art IV r 2(a). That provision also excepts faults of other "servants of the carrier". The context of Art IV r 2(a) suggests that these are servants (ie employees not agents) performing carrier functions on board the ship itself rather than managers or other staff ashore, although this distinction is not made expressly.

If Art IV r 2(a) were *not* to apply to employees ashore, then it is possible that the *Volcafe v CSAV* approach might be relevant if such shore employees became aware of a defect or problem after the ship had sailed, eg where tests had shown bunkers to be contaminated or where a particular engine part had failed in a sister ship, but the master was not aware of the problem so as to be at fault within Art IV r 2(a). Here the ship would not be unseaworthy, as the defect did not exist at the start of the voyage. If the ship went aground owing to engine failure caused by the defective bunkers or engine parts, the carrier might seek to claim that there was a peril or accident of the sea within Art IV r 2(c). After *Volcafe v CSAV*, it would be required to show that the grounding was not caused by the fault of its employees (here, presumably, including the shore-based employees). This result in fact reproduces the effect of the 'catch-all' exception in Art IV r 2(q). Another example might be where there is an explosion in a container of undeclared dangerous cargo. The ship would not be unseaworthy if the carrier exercising due diligence could not have known about the cargo, but the carrier would have the burden of showing that any subsequent fire or explosion was not caused by its fault.[137]

2.1.5(d) Proof of loss or damage

Cargo claimants must always show that they have the right to sue, eg by being a lawful holder of a bill of lading, or being named as a consignee under a waybill.[138] They will also have to prove their loss or damage. Under a charterparty (that does not incorporate the Hague/Visby Rules) the compensation will be calculated on common law principles, designed to put the cargo owner in the position it would have been in if the contract had been performed. This would include the value of the cargo at the contracted port of delivery; it might also take into account a reduced market value if the particular cargo was delayed, if that was in the reasonable contemplation of the shipowner.[139] After a wreck where the goods are completely lost, the calculation under the Hague-Visby Rules Art IV r 5(b) is by reference to the value of the goods at the time and place where they should have

---

137 Cf *Northern Shipping Co v Deutsche Seereederei GmBH (The Kapitan Sakharov)* [2000] 2 Lloyd's Rep 255, where the explosion in an on-deck container caused a fire that was exacerbated by underdeck inflammable cargo that had been wrongly stowed so as to make the ship unseaworthy. Had it not been for this, the carrier should have been able to rely on eg Art IV r 2(b).

138 See the Carriage of Goods by Sea Act 1992; *Carver on Bills of Lading*, Chapter 5; *Bills of Lading: Law and Contracts*, Chapter 4.

139 *Czarnikow Ltd v Koufos (The Heron II)* [1969] 1 AC 350, [1967] 2 Lloyd's Rep 457, *Voyage Charters*, 628–633, 665–667.

been discharged in accordance with the contract. That will normally be the contracted port of delivery.[140]

In order for the calculation to be made, the cargo owner would also need to prove the quantity or weight of cargo that was shipped, as well as its condition. The condition on shipment is usually evidenced by a 'clean' bill of lading (or waybill) from the carrier recording that the goods were shipped in "apparent good order and condition".[141] Although a bill of lading or waybill may appear to record the quantity or weight of goods shipped, it will usually be qualified by carrier reservations, eg as to "weight unknown", "said to contain" or "shipper's load stow and count". These qualifications are often entirely reasonable, as it is not the carrier but the shipper that declares quantities and weights in the documents.[142] The effectiveness of such reservations may vary internationally but depends on whether the carrier has reasonable grounds for suspecting a discrepancy or has no reasonable means of checking.[143] It is clear in most legal systems that where a statement appears in a bill as to the quantity of goods within an FCL container (sealed by the shipper), a carrier's reservation as to the contents being unknown will be effective.[144] That is, the bill will be no evidence as to the contents of the container and the cargo owner will have to bring independent evidence as to what was shipped. Where the container is salved but delivered damaged, an inspection will reveal the contents, but proof of contents could be a particular problem where the container is totally lost after the shipwreck. Although a bill of lading in the hands of a consignee will be conclusive evidence of what was shipped,[145] the effect of the reservation as to the contents of the container means that there was no evidence in the first place.

Where the ship is disabled as a result of unseaworthiness the cargo owner may suffer consequential loss. In *The Subro Valour*,[146] it was held that under the Hague-Visby Rules the shipowner would be liable for salvage and transhipment expenses incurred by the cargo owner as well as the loss of an EEC financial subsidy caused by delay. There is still debate about whether the Hague/Visby Rules allow for financial or economic losses caused by delay, assuming it is within the contemplation of the parties,[147] or whether the reference to "the total amount recoverable" in the Hague-Visby Rules Art IV r 5(b) definitively excludes delay (or other consequential loss) by failing to mention it.[148] Most carriers have

---

140 This will also be the relevant time and place where goods are transhipped by the carrier and forwarded to the destination: see 2.1.4.

141 See *Bills of Lading: Law and Contracts*, 213–217. With a sealed container, this expression refers to the external condition of the container itself, and there is no evidence as to condition of goods inside: see *Marbig Rexel Pty Ltd v ABC Container Line NV (The TNT Express)* [1992] 2 Lloyd's Rep 636 (SCNSW). Cargo claimants must bring independent evidence of the condition on shipment.

142 Including, now, the "verified gross mass" of shipping containers, following amendments to SOLAS Chapter VI reg 2, introduced with effect from 2016 by the IMO to deal with problems of under-declaration of weight revealed after the wreck of the *MSC Napoli*: see 1.3.2(b).

143 See the Hague/Visby Rules Art III r 4 and *Bills of Lading: Law and Contracts*, 218–248.

144 See eg *Ace Imports Pty Ltd v Companhia de Navegacao Lloyd Brasiliero (The Esmerelda 1)* [1988] 1 Lloyd's Rep 206 (SC NSW).

145 See the Hague/Visby Rules Art III r 4.

146 [1995] 1 Lloyd's Rep 509.

147 As in *The Subro Valour*. See also *The Pegase* [1981] 1 Lloyd's Rep 175, a case involving a charterparty bill incorporating the Hague Rules, where lost resale profits were recovered after a deviation and delay.

148 See *Carver on Bills of Lading*, 719–720; *Bills of Lading: Law and Contracts*, 500–506, *Voyage Charters*, 111–1121.

express bill of lading clauses excluding delay, on the assumption that this is not prohibited by Art III r 8.[149]

The time bar under the Hague/Visby Rules Art III r 6 is notoriously short, at 12 months from the date of cargo delivery (eg if transhipped after a wreck) or of the date when it ought to have been delivered (eg if the ship is a total loss). This will probably be the shortest of the time limits after a wreck, eg by comparison with charterparty claims,[150] collision claims,[151] or those under one of the IMO liability conventions.[152] In order to avoid the time bar, cargo claimants either need to seek an extension of time from the carrier (or insurer) or to "bring suit" within the one-year period.[153] Although the case law is complicated, it seems that a suit in any competent court would suffice, but suit in a foreign court in breach of an exclusive English jurisdiction clause would not stop the time bar,[154] nor would commencement of court proceedings where there was an arbitration clause.[155] This may cause particular difficulty if a foreign court does not recognise the incorporation of arbitration clauses in bills of lading in the same manner as English courts,[156] or if the law of that State did not recognise that foreign jurisdiction or arbitration clause in bill of lading claims.[157]

2.1.5(e) Limitation of liability under the Hague/Visby Rules

The carrier will also be entitled to limit its liability to the cargo owner, both under the global limits of liability of conventions such as the LLMC 1996, and the limits in the Hague or Hague-Visby Rules Art IV r 5.

The global LLMC limit will not usually be relevant if there are few claims, eg where a single container is washed overboard owing to defective lashings. It will be very relevant in the case of a total loss shipwreck where there will be very many property or financial

---

149 See *Bills of Lading: Law and Contracts*, 339–343.

150 Eg six years for breach of contract. There may be dangers in a cargo claimant (including a charterer) delaying a cargo claim if there is a prospect of the shipowner bringing a claim not governed by the Hague/Visby Rules, eg for freight (or breach of a more general charterparty clause): see *Aries Tanker Corp. v Total Transport (The Aries)* [1977] 1 WLR 185, [1977] 1 Lloyd's Rep 334.

151 Eg two years: see 2.4; and passenger claims under the Athens Convention 2002, see 2.3.7.

152 Eg three or six years under the CLC 1992 or Fund Convention 1992 and the Bunkers Convention 2001: see 2.6.2(a)–(b), 2.6.3. Cf the HNSC 2010, 2.6.4, and the WRC 2007, 10.4.

153 Art III r 6.

154 See eg *Deep Sea Maritime Ltd v Monjasa A/S (The Alhani)* [2018] EWHC 1495, [2018] 2 Lloyd's Rep 563 [88–130] where the authorities are summarised. See also *Voyage Charters*, 1050–1055.

155 See eg *Owners of Cargo on Board The Merak v The Merak (Owners) (The Merak)* [1965] P 223 [1965] 2 Lloyd's Rep 527.

156 The Congenbill 1978 only incorporated charterparty terms generally, but the courts have held that this would not be sufficient to incorporate a charterparty arbitration or jurisdiction clause: see eg *Caresse Navigation ltd v Zurich Assurances Maroc and Others (The Channel Ranger)* [2015] 1 Lloyd's Rep 256 [15]. In *Thyssen Inc v Calypso Shipping Corporation SA* [2000] 2 Lloyd's Rep 243 the arbitration clause was in a charter (constituted only via a recap telex) and the charterer refused to provide a copy of the Congenbill bill of lading to the receiver/importer (that appears to have been a Congenbill 1994 that expressly incorporated the law and arbitration clause). The court might have granted an extension of time under the Arbitration Act 1996 s 12, had the claimant reacted quickly enough when it finally was given notice of the charter clause after litigation had started.

157 Cf the Carriage of Goods by Sea Act 1991 (Cth, Australia) s 11 and see *The Alhani* [2018] 2 Lloyd's Rep 563 [126–128]. While an English court might issue an anti-suit injunction to prevent the continuance of a foreign action, it might decline to issue a declaration that the time limit had expired for the purposes of the foreign proceedings (*The Alhani*, [128]).

claims against the ship, including all cargo claims, those from any other ship which might have been negligently damaged in a collision, and bunker pollution claims. All these claims will have to compete pro rata against the amount available under the LMLC 1996 Art 6(1)(b).[158]

The Hague/Visby Rules (in Art VIII) preserve the carrier's global limits but also apply their own limits (in Art IV r 5) calculated in relation to each individual contract of carriage and by reference to statements in the bill of lading or waybill. The calculation of the limits is different under the two sets of Rules. Under the Hague Rules Art IV r 5, there is no limit of liability for bulk cargo,[159] but there is a limit of £100 gold value per package or unit.[160] Under the Hague-Visby Rules (as amended by a Protocol of 1979) the limits are calculated using the special drawing right (sdr) of the IMF, which can be converted into national currencies on a daily basis by consulting the IMF website.[161] There is a Hague-Visby Rules Art IV r 5(a) limit of 666.67 sdr per package or unit or 2 sdr per kilo of gross weight of the goods lost or damaged,[162] whichever is greater. The weight alternative will produce a higher figure when packages are greater than 333.33 kg.[163] Table 2.1 illustrates the limits.

The weight alternative limit, shown per tonne, is so high that it would not operate to limit claims in relation to most bulk commodities such as oil, coal and grain; it might apply to high-value bulk products such as nickel or tin.

Table 2.1 Hague-Visby Rules limits of liability

Hague-Visby Rules sdr amounts	**£ sterling[1]**	**US$[2]**
667.67 sdr per package or unit	£1,331.91	$1,841.36
2 sdrs per kilo [2,000 sdrs per tonne]	£2.17 [£2,173.24]	$2.77 [$2,765]

[1] The calculation uses the IMF figures at 3 December 2018 with the rate of conversion of 1 sdr = £1.08662.

[2] As the international currency of shipping is the US$, this column gives comparative US$ figures for 3 December 2018 based on 1 sdr = US$1.3825. The US is *not* party to the Hague-Visby Rules, so the US$ figures are given by way of example only. Under the US Carriage of Goods by Sea Act 1936 there is a Hague Rules limit of $500 per package or customary freight unit.

---

158 See 2.5.4; also 2.5.6(a) for examples. Note also that these other claims might include wreck removal claims, unless the Affected State has made the reservation under LLMC Art 18: see 2.5.8.

159 *Vinnlustodin HF v Sea Tank Shipping AS (The Aqasia)* [2018] EWCA Civ 276, [2018] 1 Lloyd's Rep 530.

160 The 'gold value' reference in Art IX requires a complicated conversion into sterling by reference to the Coinage Acts and the equivalent value of £100 in gold in 1924: see *The Rosa S* [1988] 2 Lloyd's Rep 574, where the conversion produced a figure of £6,630 per package or unit. The gold price is highly volatile, but in 2018 the figure could have exceeded £20,000.

161 www.imf.org/en/data, where exchange rate data is available for the last five days and archived for previous periods. For conversion date, see COGSA 1971 s 1A.

162 See *The Limnos* [2008] 2 Lloyd's Rep 166 where only 262 mt of a bulk cargo of 44,000 mt of corn was damaged, but the whole cargo was then considered as "distressed" in the market and reduced in value; the 2 sdr limit was still to be calculated on the basis of the smaller amount.

163 The result of *The Rosa S* [1988] 2 Lloyd's Rep 574 is that the older Hague Rules limit may sometimes be higher than the package limit under the Hague-Visby Rules, but lower than the weight limits under the latter: see *Yemgas FZCO v Superior Pescadores SA Panama (The Superior Pescadores)* [2016] EWCA Civ 101, [2016] 1 Lloyd's Rep 561.

The carrier often has no means of knowing whether the shipper has made an accurate declaration of contents of a sealed container,[164] but the Hague Rules had no specific rule as to how to calculate the limits for goods in containers.[165] The Hague-Visby Rules introduced a specific container rule in Art IV r 5(c) based on the number of packages or units "enumerated" in the bill.[166] If the bill merely recorded "1 container said to contain frozen chicken", then there would be no "enumeration" other than of the one container, but in this case the alternative 2 sdr per kilo weight limit would apply.

It follows that the value of cargo lost over these limits could not be recovered against the carrier, even in cases of unseaworthiness.[167] Moreover, in a major wreck case, these limits would be applied to each carriage contract *before* all 'property' claims were made subject to a global limit, eg under the LLMC 1996;[168] ie there could be a double limit. In such cases, as with the total exclusions such as nautical fault, it is vital for the cargo owner to have obtained cargo insurance.[169]

2.1.5(f) Forum issues in carriage claims

After a wreck, there can be complex jurisdictional questions as the various claimants and potential defendants contemplate litigation in a variety of venues. The cargo owner bringing a claim under the bill of lading or waybill after a wreck will often find that the settlement of its claim is greatly complicated by these proceedings taking place elsewhere and between other parties. Thus, the collision, pollution or wreck removal liability claims may be brought in different States.[170] Meanwhile, the contractual claims may be subject to express jurisdiction, arbitration or choice of law clauses.

In principle, all these express clauses may be enforceable but are subject to controls and restrictions in both national and EU law.[171] The detailed conflict of laws rules are beyond this book,[172] but it can be noted that there may be potential conflicts between courts in

---

164 See 2.1.5(d) for proof issues.

165 In *The River Gurara* [1996] 2 Lloyd's Rep 53, the court decided that limitation should be based upon the number of packages that were proved to have been loaded within the containers, although the description in the bill will naturally be a basis for the calculation (unless contested by the carrier).

166 See eg *Kyokuyo Co Ltd v AP Moller-Maersk A/S Trading as Maersk Line* [2018 EWCA Civ 778, [2018] 2 Lloyd's Rep 59.

167 Unless the cargo owner was able to prove intent or recklessness of the carrier within Art IV r 5(e) of the Hague-Visby Rules. The right of the carrier to limit is not lost by such conduct of its employees generally, only those at a more senior level or with greater functional authority: see *Browner International Ltd v Monarch Shipping Co. Ltd (The European Enterprise)* [1989] 2 Lloyd's Rep 185, and see 2.5.7 for the similar test in the LLMC Art 4.

168 See 2.5.

169 See 2.9.2(b).

170 Eg the wreck liability proceedings may take place in the "Affected State" where the casualty occurred (see 8.2), and pollution claims are likely to arise in the same place; but if the pollution is in a neighbouring State that State's courts may hear the claim, eg under the CLC 1992 (see 2.6.2(a)). Collisions arising on the high seas could be litigated in a variety of States, but the parties (and their insurers) may well decide to choose an experienced convenient forum, eg London or Singapore.

171 See eg Regulation (EU) No 1215/2012 of the European Parliament and of the Council of 12 December 2012 on jurisdiction and the recognition and enforcement of judgments in civil and commercial matters [Brussels I Regulation Recast] Art 25(1) permitting exclusive jurisdiction clauses: also 2.5.9(e).

172 See Lord Collins of Mapesbury, J Harris (gen eds), *Dicey, Morris & Collins on the Conflict of Laws* (15th ed and Supplement, Sweet & Maxwell, 2018) [*Dicey & Morris*]; D Jackson, Enforcement of Maritime Claims

different jurisdictions that might be resolved on the basis of which court was first seised,[173] or whether proceedings in one jurisdiction should be stayed pending related litigation in another State,[174] perhaps on the basis of *forum non conveniens*.[175] There is much scope for forum shopping, especially where there may also be separate proceedings for determining liability and limitation of that liability.[176]

In order to try to minimise such forum issues, bills of lading will commonly contain an express choice of law and jurisdiction clause.[177] Cargo claimants that sue in places other than as specified in an exclusive English jurisdiction clause may find that they face an anti-suit injunction.[178] Most charterparties will contain an arbitration clause specifying that disputes between the charterer and shipowner will be subject to arbitration in London, New York or Singapore.[179] Modern charterparty bills will expressly incorporate law and arbitration clauses from the charterparty,[180] so that a consignee of a bulk cargo of ore that was due to be delivered in China but was wrecked en route may find that its claim is subject to arbitration in, say, London. Moreover, to proceed elsewhere might risk an anti-suit injunction, but may also mean that there has not been a "suit" brought to stop the operation of the Art III r 6 time bar.[181]

Allied to forum issues will be those by which the cargo claimant might seek to obtain security for any claim. It might be possible to arrest a sister ship to that wrecked,[182] but this remedy is unlikely to be available if the ship is owned by a single ship company. The cargo claimant will have difficulty suing a P&I insurer owing to the "pay to be paid" clause,[183] but might be able to seek a freezing injunction against any H&M insurance proceeds it can trace (eg in London).

2.1.6 Cargo owner's liability for wreck

The individual owner of cargo is highly unlikely to be directly responsible for a shipwreck, although as a voyage (or time) charterer it may be in breach if it orders the ship to an unsafe

---

(4th ed, LLP, 2000) [*Jackson*]; N Meeson, J Kimbell, *Admiralty Jurisdiction and Practice* (5th ed, Informa, 2017) [*Meeson & Kimbell*], 120–141.

173 See eg Brussels I Regulation Recast Art 29.
174 See eg Brussels I Regulation Recast Art 30.
175 *Spiliada Maritime Corp v Cansulex Ltd* (*The Spiliada*) [1987] AC 460, [1987] 1 Lloyd's Rep 1. This discretionary principle cannot be used where the Brussels I Regulation Recast is applicable.
176 See 2.5.9 and 10.8.5(g).
177 See eg the Maersk Terms for Carriage (2018) cl 26, choosing English law and the High Court in London. In the *Rena*, it is understood that there were London jurisdiction clauses in the bills issued by MSC as charterer and contracting carrier and that may have influenced LLMC 1996 limitation proceedings in the UK: and see 1.2.4. Cf *The MSC Napoli* [2009] 1 Lloyd's Rep 246 where two slot charterers had bills providing for German law and jurisdiction, but the limitation fund was established in London: see 2.5.4(d).
178 See eg *CSAV Compania Sud Americana De Vapores SA v Hin-Pro International Logistics Ltd* [2015] EWCA 401, [2015] 2 Lloyd's Rep 1. Where EU law applies such anti-suit injunctions may not be permitted: see *West Tankers Inc v Allianz SpA* (*The Front Comor*) (Case C-185-07) [2009] AC 1138.
179 See eg Gencon 1994 cl 19; NYPE 2015 cl 54.
180 See eg Congenbill 2016 cl 1, and eg *The Nerano* [1996] 1 Lloyd's Rep 1.
181 See eg *Tracomin v Sudan Oil Seeds (No 2)* [1983] 3 All E.R. 140; also 2.1.5(b).
182 As with the *Torrey Canyon*, 1.2.1(b).
183 See 2.9.6(c).

port.¹⁸⁴ It is possible, though, that dangerous cargo might catch fire or explode.¹⁸⁵ Provided that the nature of the cargo has been fully declared prior to shipment,¹⁸⁶ the carrier should be prepared to handle it correctly (or reject it). Sometimes dangerous cargo is not properly declared,¹⁸⁷ perhaps to avoid paying extra freight. This may lead to it being improperly stowed, eg underdeck next to a heat source.

Express obligations not to ship dangerous or injurious cargo may be inserted in charterparties or bills of lading,¹⁸⁸ and liabilities can arise for any breach.¹⁸⁹ There is also an absolute duty implied at common law for the shipper not to ship dangerous goods without giving notice of their dangerous nature to the carrier.¹⁹⁰ This implied duty is practically identical to that under the Hague/Visby Rules Art IV r 6, which provides that the shipper "shall be liable for all damages and expenses directly or indirectly arising out of or resulting from the shipment" of "goods of an inflammable, explosive or dangerous nature" where the carrier has not consented to such shipment "with knowledge of their nature or character". The liability of the shipper is strict and arises irrespective of any fault on their part.¹⁹¹ As between the carrier and the shipper, the carrier will have a defence if the goods are damaged as a result of the non-declaration. More seriously, the carrier will also have a claim against the shipper for any loss caused, eg if the vessel is wrecked, or if there are liabilities to other cargo interests.¹⁹² Such claims against the shipper will not be subject to limitation of liability under the LLMC 1996.¹⁹³ Moreover, the shipper remains liable even if the cargo

---

184 See 2.1.7(b)–(c).
185 See eg *The Athanasia Comninos* [1990] 1 Lloyd's Rep 277; also the Halifax explosion in 1917: see 2.9.2(b) (fn 961).
186 As required under the Hague/Visby Rules Art IV r 6.
187 See the *MSC Napoli* experience, 1.2.3 and 1.3.2(b).
188 See eg NYPE 2015 cl 16, Shelltime 4 cl 38: 2.1.7(c). Also Maersk Terms of Carriage (2018) cl 21.
189 See eg *CMA CGM SA v Classica Shipping Co Ltd* [2004] 1 Lloyd's Rep 460 and now the NYPE 2015 cl 16. See also the Maersk Terms of Carriage (2018) cl 21, which requires the cargo merchant to indemnify the carrier against all claims, even if the merchant was unaware of the nature of the goods; cl 21.4 preserves other rights of the carrier, eg under the Hague/Visby Rules Art IV r 6.
190 *Effort Shipping Co Ltd v Linden Management SA (The Giannis NK)* [1998] 1 Lloyd's Rep 337. Cf *Time Charters*, 187–189 where doubts are expressed as to whether the implied duty arises under a time charter (where there is an obligation to ship lawful merchandise), but it is noted that the same result in practice can be reached as a result of an implied indemnity for obeying the order to load a particular cargo.
191 *The Giannis NK* [1998] 1 Lloyd's Rep 337, 342. Moreover, the reference to "directly or indirectly" means that the indemnity could apply when the shipment had merely provided an occasion for something else to cause the damage, eg if gas had been deliberately ignited by an arsonist or there was an explosion caused by some highly abnormal accident: see *Mediterranean Freight Services Ltd v BP Oil International Ltd (The Fiona)* [1993] 1 Lloyd's Rep 257, [1994] 2 Lloyd's Rep 506, 522. See also *Voyage Charters*, 1130–1141; *Time Charters*, 180–188.
192 That liability to other cargo owners might arise from a failure properly care for the cargo under the Hague/Visby Rules Art III r 2, although the carrier might have a defence if it was not at fault (Art IV r 2(q)), or if there was an onboard error in managing the safety of the ship (Art IV r 2(a)). Such defences would not apply if the ship was unseaworthy: see *The Fiona* [1994] 2 Lloyd's Rep 506. See also *The Kapitan Sakharov* [2000] 2 Lloyd's Rep 255, where an Art IV r 6 claim for the sinking of a ship after an explosion in a container of undeclared dangerous cargo failed because of a break in the chain of causation when the fire was exacerbated by unseaworthiness: and see 2.1.5(d).
193 Cargo owners are not given limitation rights under the LLMC 1996: see 2.5.3. For the position of shipper that may also be charterers, see 2.5.4(d) and 2.5.5. Cargo owners would not be covered for liabilities to third parties under normal cargo insurance policies, see 2.9.2(b). Charterers may have liability cover, see 2.9.6(a).

has been sold in transit and the bill of lading has been transferred to a new holder.[194] Where the Hague/Visby Rules are incorporated into a charter, the liability of the "shipper" might also extend to the charterer.[195] The liability under Art IV r 6 does not arise if the effective (or contributory) cause of loss was the unseaworthiness of the ship under Art III r 1.[196]

If the ship is wrecked because of the shipper's failure to supply information about the hazardous and noxious substances, the carrier would expect to have a defence to a negligence claim from third parties (eg where there is an explosion in a port), unless it ought to have known about the nature of the cargo. If the HNSC 2010 enters into force, the carrier may have a defence to any claims made under it where it was not informed about the nature of the cargo.[197] However, the HNS Fund would be liable for the whole of any loss (eg pollution) caused if the ship were wrecked,[198] but it would then have a right of recourse against the shipper.[199]

2.1.7 Charterers and wreck

Charterers may become involved in wrecks in a number of ways and their rights and liabilities will vary depending on the type of charter that was agreed. Almost certainly, though, any disputes between the shipowner and charterer will be made subject to arbitration, eg in London, New York or Singapore.[200] Those disputes following a wreck will often be fought out at the same time as other claims (eg cargo and wreck removal claims) are being made in different fora (and often different States). Charterers, in particular, will be wary about the financial ability of a single ship owning company to pay a claim if its only asset has been wrecked and will be keen to ascertain the shipowner's insurance coverage.[201] Both charterers and shipowners will also be aware of the effect of limitation of liability on claims following a wreck.[202] Ultimately, though, their respective rights and liabilities will be regulated by the terms of the particular charterparty they have agreed, as this will seek to distribute and apportion commercial and legal risks between them, including those arising out of a wreck.

2.1.7(a) Bareboat charterers

Under standard bareboat charters,[203] such as BIMCO's Barecon 2017 cl 13, the bareboat charterer is the employer of the master and crew and would have tortious liabilities to third

---

194 See the Carriage of Goods by Sea Act 1992 s 3(3). It is less clear whether when the new lawful holder becomes liable under s 3(1) for the "same liabilities" as the shipper, it also assumes liabilities under Art IV r 6: cf *The Giannis NK* [1998] 1 Lloyd's Rep 337, 333–334; *Carver on Bills of Lading*, 281–297; *Bills of Lading: Law and Contracts*, 137–140. In a wreck case where the cargo is completely lost the holder may decide not to trigger s 3(1) by declining to demand delivery of the goods, but then it could not claim under the contract of carriage for any loss.
195 Using the reasoning in *Adamastos Co Ltd v Anglo Saxon Petroleum Co Ltd (The Saxon Star)* [1959] AC 133, [1958] 1 Lloyd's Rep 73: see *Time Charters*, 184, 624–626.
196 *The Fiona* [1993] 1 Lloyd's Rep 257, [1994] 2 Lloyd's Rep 506 (explosion of an unusually flammable fuel oil partly caused by failure to clean residues of previous cargo prior to loading).
197 See the HNSC 2010 Art 7(2)(d): also 2.6.4.
198 HNSC 2010 Art 14: also 2.6.4.
199 See the HNSC 2010 Art 41(2). See also 2.1.3 for other potential cargo liabilities.
200 See eg Gencon 1994 cl 19; Asbatankvoy 1977 cl 24; NYPE 2015 cl 54; Shelltime 4 (2003) cl 46.
201 See 2.9.1, 2.9.6(a).
202 See 2.5.4(d).
203 See M Davis, *Bareboat Charters* (2nd ed, Informa/LLP, 2005).

parties, eg for negligent navigation causing a wreck,[204] although it will usually be able to limit its liability.[205]

Whether the bareboat charterer (rather than the shipowner) has any direct liability for wreck removal may depend on local legislation,[206] but under the WRC 2007 wreck removal liabilities are those of the registered owner only, not the bareboat charterer.[207] The same principle applies to the CLC 1992 and the HNSC 2010,[208] but under the Bunkers Convention 2001[209] the bareboat charterer will be jointly and severally liable for bunker pollution damage, although it is only the registered owner that is obliged to insure. However, whether or not the charterer is *directly* liable, it is *contractually* liable under Barecon 2017 cl 22 to indemnify the shipowner against "any loss, damage or expense arising out of or in relation to any international convention which may impose liability upon the Owners".

An express wreck removal clause, Barecon 2017 cl 24, makes the charterer contractually liable for "any and all expenses in connection with the raising, removal, destruction, lighting or marking" of the ship; ie the shipowner can call on the charterer to pay first. As it will usually be the registered shipowner that is directly liable for wreck removal, the clause also obliges the charterer to indemnify the shipowner "against any sums whatsoever" which the shipowner becomes liable[210] to pay. The clause applies not only to where the ship becomes a wreck, but also where any part of it is lost or abandoned. If a ship is wrecked and becomes a CTL in the course of a bareboat charter, this might frustrate the charter[211] but would leave unaffected any pre-existing liabilities. It would seem that where the charter included a wreck removal indemnity clause the shipowner's right would have accrued *before* the frustrating event, even if the expenses were incurred afterwards.[212]

Under standard bareboat charters, such as Barecon 2017, the bareboat charterer is liable for any damage or loss that occurs to the ship,[213] and cl 19 expressly makes the charterer liable to the shipowner for a total loss.[214]

It naturally follows that the charterer will need the benefit of insurance, eg both H&M and P&I cover.[215] BIMCO's Barecon 89 (and 2001) cl 12 required the charterer to take

---

204 It may not be liable under strict liability legislation, eg for damage to harbours, where that liability is placed on the" owner": see *BP Exploration Operating Co Ltd v Chevron Shipping* [2002] 1 Lloyd's Rep 77 and 2.4.1.

205 See 2.5.3, 2.5.4(d). Where the ship is wrecked, there would be little point in bringing an action in rem against it, but in some circumstances it may be possible to arrest a sister ship owned by the charterer: for such admiralty law questions, see eg S Derrington and J Turner, *The Law and Practice of Admiralty Matters* (2nd ed, OUP, 2016) [*Derrington & Turner*] 86–97; and *Meeson & Kimbell*, 102–108.

206 Such legislation may create strict liability for wreck removal or, indeed, damage to harbour facilities: see eg 11.1.

207 See 10.2.2, 10.8.

208 See 2.6.2(a), 2.6.4. Under cl 25 the shipowner is not to contribute to general average: see also 2.8.

209 Arts 1(3) and 3(2): and see 2.6.3.

210 The liability has to arise from the lawful orders of an authority in relation to obstructions or a "hazard". This liability should cover all types of liability under the WRC 2007: see 8.2, 10.2.

211 See also 2.1.4(b).

212 Cf *Blane Steamships v Minister of Transport* [1951] 2 Lloyd's Rep 155.

213 Under Barecon 2017 cl 10, the ship has to be redelivered in the same condition as on delivery (fair wear and tear excepted), and cl 18 requires the charterer to effect all repairs.

214 See also 2.9.4. Based on its possession of the ship, the bareboat charterer would be able to maintain a claim in tort against a colliding ship in the same way as a shipowner.

215 See 2.9.2 and 2.9.6.

out such insurance, as approved by the shipowner, in their joint names. It was held in *The Ocean Victory*[216] that the effect of the clause was to operate as a complete code to regulate claims between the parties for insured losses; ie if the ship is wrecked by being ordered by the charterer to an unsafe port, the shipowner has no separate damages claim against the charterer for the value of the ship.[217] By contrast, it was accepted in the case[218] that this argument did not apply to the large claims for SCOPIC expenses, wreck removal costs or loss of hire[219] after the ship was wrecked in bad weather on leaving port.[220] In any event, the loss in *The Ocean Victory* fell on the H&M insurer, and its inability to seek redress by subrogation led to concerns in the market.[221] As a result, a reworded Barecon 2017 cl 17 now makes it clear that the obligatory co-insurance[222] "shall neither exclude nor discharge liability between the Owners and Charterers" but is intended to provide a first resort payment to shipowners. The bareboat charterer's liability will be satisfied by any insurance payment to the shipowner, but the new clause preserves any rights the shipowner (or its insurer) will have by way of indemnity or subrogation. This will mean that if the bareboat charterer (as disponent owner) receives an unsafe port order from a sub-charterer, the latter will now face a subrogation claim.

As the employer of master and crew, the bareboat charterer will be treated as a disponent owner in relation to sub-charterers and cargo owners, so it will effectively be in the same position as a shipowner as regards liability under any bill of lading[223] or sub-charter.

Barecon 2017 cl 31(c) deals with termination of the charter on the loss of the vessel. There is deemed termination when there is an actual total loss[224] or when agreement is

---

216 *Gard Marine & Energy Ltd v China National Chartering Co Ltd (The Ocean Victory)* [2017] UKSC 35, [2017] 1 Lloyd's Rep 521, albeit *obiter* and by a 3–2 majority.

217 This meant that the owners had to look only to the H&M insurance, but the insurer (by assignment) was unable to claim from the bareboat charterer. On that basis, as there was no liability of the bareboat charterer upwards, it was unable to claim any loss against sub-charterers who might give an unsafe order. Somewhat tantalisingly, the court left open two other means by which the bareboat charterer might have recovered directly against the sub-charterers that had passed on the port order; these were claims by way of bailment or transferred loss, in effect claiming not so much for its own loss but for that of the owner: see Lord Mance [124–126], Lord Sumption [94].

218 See Lord Sumption, [2017] 1 Lloyd's Rep 521 [93]; see also [2015] 1 Lloyd's Rep 381 [72] (CA); [2014] 1 Lloyd's Rep 59 [185] (Teare J).

219 The hull claim was for US$88.5 million, the SCOPIC claim was for US$12 million, wreck removal expenses were US$34.5 million and the loss of hire claim was for US$2.7 million. It was only the H&M insurer that was party to the case, as assignee of the interest of the shipowner and bareboat charterer (which were related).

220 Cl 12 also required the charterer to take out joint P&I cover, and it may have been arguable that the provision also created a complete code so as to preclude a claim for such expenses against the bareboat charterer. However, cl 18 expressly obliged the charterer to indemnity the shipowner "against any sums whatsoever" that the owner had to pay in consequence of the ship becoming a wreck.

221 Both generally and in relation to long term bareboat charters under Barecon 89, where renegotiation of cl 12 was not commercially possible.

222 Under cl 17 there is an option as to whether the charterer or shipowner actually takes out and pays for H&M, war and P&I cover. The need to protect mortgagees is expressly mentioned: and see 2.9.2(d).

223 See 2.1.1, 2.1.5. Under Barecon 2017 cl 22, the charterer may also have to indemnify the shipowner against expenses arising during the operation of the ship, including all consequences or liabilities arising from the master signing bills of lading.

224 See 2.9.4(a).

reached with the H&M insurers in respect of a constructive total loss.[225] Although obligations such as payment of hire will cease on termination, the termination is without prejudice to accrued rights,[226] eg for indemnities.

2.1.7(b) Voyage charterers

A voyage charterer does not employ the master and crew, unlike a bareboat charterer, and is therefore not generally liable to third parties for their faults, eg if the master's negligent navigation caused a collision resulting in the wreck of both ships.[227] Voyage charterers are not liable for wreck removal costs under the WRC 2007,[228] nor would they have any direct liability for pollution damage under the CLC 1992, the HNSC 2010 or the Bunkers Convention 2001.[229]

However, the voyage charterer may be liable to indemnify the shipowner under the charterparty, typically for giving an order to the master to proceed to an unsafe port. There will often be an express term that the charterer will nominate a safe port, place or berth.[230] In any event, a term will usually be implied that the voyage charterer undertakes that a ship can reach use and return from a nominated port (or berth) without, in the absence of some abnormal occurrence, being exposed to danger that cannot be avoided by good seamanship and navigation on the part of ship's master.[231] The consequences of being sent to an unsafe port can be catastrophic, involving not only loss of the vessel but also pollution damage, as with the *Aegean Sea* in 1992.[232] This might lead to a claim by the shipowner either for breach of the safe port term or for an implied indemnity for following the charterer's orders.[233] Where the shipowner does have a claim against the charterer for damage to the ship, the charterer may not be able to limit liability[234] unless it has included a clear contractual provision in the charter to that effect.[235]

Where a ship is wrecked in a normal commercial port, it may not be easy for the shipowner to prove that the port was unsafe unless it can point to some particular features of the

---

225 See 2.9.4(b). In the absence of such agreement, the relevant date is when a competent tribunal has adjudged upon the issue.
226 Barecon 2017 cl 31(e).
227 A voyage charterer itself might conceivably be guilty of causative negligence, eg in loading dangerous undeclared cargo that caused an explosion leading to the wreck of a ship, although the obvious claimants would then be the shipowner and other cargo owners: cf *CMA CGM SA v Classica Shipping Co Ltd* [2004] 1 Lloyd's Rep 460.
228 See 10.2.2.
229 See 2.6.2, 2.6.4; but cf 2.6.5.
230 See eg Bimchemvoy 2008 cl 3, Asbatankvoy 1977 cl 9. Charters such as Gencon 1994 have no pre-printed safe port provision, but this will often be added. The variety of ways in which the description can be added means that there may be uncertainty as to whether the charterer did assume responsibility for a safe nomination (see eg *AIC Ltd v Marine Pilot Ltd (The Archimidis)* [2008] 1 Lloyd's Rep 597), but if there is only reference to the named port, then there can be no implication and the risk falls on the owner who has agreed to go there (see *Reardon Smith Line v Australian Wheat Board (The Houston City)* [1956] AC 266, [1954] 2 Lloyd's Rep 148, 153).
231 *Leeds Shipping Co Ltd v Société Francaise Bunge (The Eastern City)* [1958] 2 Lloyd's Rep 127, 132.
232 See 1.2.2(a).
233 See *The Aegean Sea* [1998] 2 Lloyd's Rep 39.
234 See 2.5.4(d).
235 See *The Cape Bari* [2016] 2 Lloyd's Rep 469 and 2.5.5.

port that made it generally unsafe, or unsafe for the particular ship. In *The Ocean Victory*,[236] a ship was wrecked while trying to leave a nominated Japanese port to avoid damage at its berth during a very severe storm. The Supreme Court held that this was an "abnormal occurrence" (as opposed to a normal characteristic of the port) for which the charterer was not liable. That expression was not a term of art, but referred to an event that was "something well removed from the normal . . . out of the ordinary course and unexpected. It was something which the notional charterer would not have in mind".[237] It was not enough that the events were reasonably foreseeable, and the crucial issue was that it was rare for there to be a *combination* of vulnerability to long swells at the berth *and* northerly gales in the fairway. Even if the port was unsafe,[238] the charterer might still try to argue that the effective cause of the wreck was the negligence of the master, not the wrongful order of the charterer, but the courts are reluctant to come to such a conclusion where the master is operating under difficulties presented by the nature of the port.[239]

A charterer may also be liable to the shipowner for shipping a dangerous cargo, either at common law, or as a result of an express term, or through incorporation of the Hague/Visby Rules (including Art IV r 6).[240] If the cargo is one expressly listed for carriage, eg "crude oil" or "petroleum products",[241] its generally inflammable or explosive qualities would be known to a reasonable shipowner, and so notice by the charterer would relate to extra precautions or dangers that exceeded what was expected and which could not be dealt with by applying ordinary safety standards.[242]

Where a voyage charterer owns the cargo on board a wrecked ship, it may have a claim for loss of or damage to the cargo against the shipowner. As this will be a claim under the charterparty, and not under any bill of lading issued to the charterer,[243] there is freedom of contract as to the terms of carriage. Voyage charter terms may vary greatly, but it is possible in English law for the shipowner to exclude all liability for the loss of that cargo, eg a shipwreck caused by the negligence of the master. Asbatankvoy 1977 cl 19 is a wide general exceptions clause for oil charters that follows many of the Hague Rules exclusions, eg for error in navigation or management of the ship. It adds the words "collision" and

---

236 [2017] 1 Lloyd's Rep 521 (a time charter case, but applying the same principles).
237 [2017] 1 Lloyd's Rep 521 [16].
238 In *The Ocean Victory* a sub-charterer passed on voyage orders up a chain via a time charterer to the bareboat charterer. Had the court found the port to be unsafe, the liability would have been passed down the chain to the sub-charterer, with the time charterer hoping that the sub-charterer was financially secure, eg insured for charterer's liabilities: see 2.9.6(b). That sub-charter was on a time charter trip, but the position would have been the same if it had been a voyage charterer. For limitation of the liability of charterers, see 2.5.4(d).
239 See eg *The Ocean Victory* [2014] 1 Lloyd's Rep 59 [173–174] (Teare J; there was no appeal against this issue, see [2015] 1 Lloyd's Rep 381 [12]); *The Houston City* [1954] 2 Lloyd's Rep 148, 158; see also *Time Charters*, 215–217.
240 See 2.1.6 and *Voyage Charters*, 175–182. See Bimchemvoy 2008 for an example of where detailed specifications of bulk chemical cargoes have to be supplied by charterers (eg Box 13 and cll 22–24); cl 28 confirms that the owners, master and crew are familiar with the cargo and that a signed Material Data Safety Sheet is provided to the master before loading.
241 See Asbatankvoy 1977 cl 1.
242 See eg *Atlantic Oil Carriers v British Petroleum Co (The Atlantic Duchess)* [1957] 2 Lloyd's Rep 54 (fire and explosions to butanised crude oil cargo but no liability as no special hazards and Art IV r 6 not incorporated into charter); *The Athanasia Comninos* [1990] 1 Lloyd's Rep 277 (explosions from methane gas in coal).
243 *The Dunelmia* [1970] 1 QB 289, *Bills of Lading: Law and Contracts*, 685–689.

"stranding" to the traditional exception for "peril, danger or accident of the sea".[244] The clause also excludes the liability of the charterer for loss, damage or delay for a similar variety of events, including "perils of the seas".[245]

Gencon 1994 cl 2 is a well-known example of a very wide exclusion of the shipowner's liability for cargo loss damage or delay, caused eg by the negligence of the master which led to a shipwreck.[246] The exception would also extend to unseaworthiness causing the loss, eg where there was an engine failure caused by poor maintenance. The only liability would be for unseaworthiness caused by the "personal want of due diligence on the part of the Owners or their Manager" to make the vessel seaworthy. A deliberate cost-saving decision to delay repairs that led to a wreck would be a good example of such lack of due diligence, as occurred in *The Amoco Cadiz*.[247] But the word "personal" means that this would normally require proof of complicity by senior management, eg at director level, rather than a lack of care by someone lower in the hierarchy.[248] In practice, charterers commonly negotiate to delete such an extreme provision[249] and it may well be that a clause paramount is used to incorporate the Hague Rules to apply as between the shipowner and charterer.[250] Such incorporation raises well-known problems if there is a conflict with other charter terms such as Gencon 1994 cl 2, but the contractual incorporation of the Hague Rules Art III r 8 would render void those parts of cl 2 that reduced the non-delegable duty of due diligence to make the ship seaworthy.[251]

Most voyage charters have extensive provisions dealing with war risks,[252] and would contain a "both to blame collision clause"[253] and incorporate a version of the York Antwerp Rules with a "New Jason" clause.[254]

2.1.7(c) Time charterers

The time charterer, like the voyage charterer, does not employ the master and crew and would not normally be liable to third parties for their negligence in causing a wreck. Likewise, time charterers are not liable for wreck removal costs under the WRC 2007,[255]

---

244 As noted by *Voyage Charters*, 940, these words would already be covered within perils of the sea in English law.
245 This exception is made subject to other express charter provisions and would raise familiar causation issues, eg where the ship was wrecked after being ordered to an unsafe berth. The exception should in any event require the charterer to prove that the perils of the sea did not result from its own fault: cf *Volcafe Ltd and Others v Compania SudAmericana De Vapores SA* [2018] UKSC 61, [2019] 1 Lloyd's Rep 21, 2.1.5(c). See also *Voyage Charters*, Chapter 69.
246 See *Voyage Charters*, Chapter 11.
247 [1984] 2 Lloyd's Rep 304; and see 2.6.2(a), 1.2.2.
248 Cf 2.5.7. *Voyage Charters*, 247–253.
249 It is understood that a Gencon 2019 will make changes to cl 2, perhaps to reduce its extensive protection for shipowners.
250 See 2.1.5 for the Hague Rules liability scheme. A clause paramount is express in cl 20(b)(i) of Asbatankvoy 1977.
251 See 2.1.5(a) and *The Saxon Star* [1958] 1 Lloyd's Rep 73; *Voyage Charters*, 229 and 995–1002.
252 See eg Gencon cl 17 (Voywar 1993); Asbatankvoy cl 20(b)(vi).
253 See eg Gencon cl 11; Asbatankvoy cl 20(b)(iv); and 2.4; see 2.9.2(b).
254 See eg Gencon cl 12; Asbatankvoy cl 20(b)(ii) and (iii); see 2.8.1.
255 See 10.2.2.

nor would they have any direct liability for pollution damage under the CLC 1992,[256] the HNSC 2010[257] or the Bunkers Convention 2001.[258] It is theoretically possible that a charterer's negligent orders as to matters such as loading or stowage might contribute to a ship later being wrecked, eg where undeclared or unapproved dangerous cargo explodes, but third party tort claims against the charterer would be subject to limitation of liability.[259] Time charterers might be liable for the salvage of any of their property on board, eg bunkers.[260]

A time charterer has greater control over the commercial use of the vessel than a voyage charterer,[261] but operational decisions as to navigation would be a matter for the master.[262] The power to give voyage or other orders to the shipowner or master could result in the time charterers being liable to the shipowner, eg for ordering the ship to an unsafe port or place.[263] In *The Ocean Victory*,[264] a sub-charterer (under a time charter trip) passed on voyage orders up a chain via a time charterer to the bareboat charterer. Had the court found the port to be unsafe,[265] the liability would have been passed down the chain to the sub-charterer, with the time charterer hoping that the sub-charterer was financially secure, eg insured for charterer's liabilities.[266] The charterparty might, though, make the nomination obligation one that is not strict, but eg qualified by a duty only to use "due diligence" to employ the ship between and at safe places.[267] Where the shipowner does have a claim against the charterer for damage to the ship, the charterer may not be able to limit liability,[268] unless it has included a clear contractual provision in the charter to that effect.[269]

---

256 See 2.6.2. Oil charters such as Shelltime 4 would contain provisions dealing with pollution issues, eg requiring that the owner has International Group P&I cover up to US$1 billion, and as well as H&M cover: see cll 39, 44. See also *Time Charters*, 366 for the effect of additional clauses giving the charterer the benefit of the shipowner's P&I cover.

257 See 2.6.4.

258 See 2.6.3. This is the case even if the time charterer owned the bunkers that caused the pollution. The charter may expressly require the shipowner to obtain convention certificates of financial responsibility, eg under the Bunkers Convention 2001, in addition to normal insurance cover: see eg NYPE 2015 cl 6(a) and (b). Cf possible liabilities of the charterer as a holder of "waste" if bunkers leak: see 14.6.3.

259 See 2.5.3 and 2.5.4(d).

260 See 2.7.7(b) and cf *The Danah* [1993] 1 Lloyd's Rep 351.

261 See eg NYPE 2015 cl 8(a); Shelltime 4 (2003) cl 13(a) and cf 2.1.7(b). *Time Charters*, Chapter 19.

262 See eg NYPE 2015 cl 26 and *Whistler International v Kawasaki Kisen Kaisha (The Hill Harmony)* [2001] 1 AC 638, [2001] 1 Lloyd's Rep 147.

263 See also 2.1.7(b). The liability might arise by way of breach of an express safe port/berth clause in the charter, as in the amended NYPE charter in *The Ocean Victory* [2014] 1 Lloyd's Rep 59 [16]. It may also arise as a result of an implied indemnity for obeying a charterer's orders: *Kodro Shipping Corp v Empresea Cubana de Fletes (The Evia No. 2)* [1982] 2 Lloyd's Rep 307. See also *Kuwait Petroleum Corp v I & D Oil Carriers Ltd (The Houda)* [1994] 2 Lloyd's Rep 541 and *Time Charters*, Chapter 10.

264 [2017] 1 Lloyd's Rep 521; see also the discussion on liability in 2.1.7(a) and (b).

265 See 2.1.7(b).

266 See 2.9.6(b); and see also the discussion on charterers' right to limit liability in 2.5.4(d).

267 See eg Shelltime 4 cl 4(c), which expressly states that the charterer does not warrant the safety of any place and will have no liability for damage or loss unless caused by the failure to exercise due diligence; also *Time Charters*, 669–674.

268 See 2.5.4(d).

269 See *The Cape Bari* [2016] 2 Lloyd's Rep 469 and 2.5.5.

Charterers may well also be liable to the shipowner under implied indemnities[270] or express indemnities,[271] provided there is a direct causal link between the orders and the loss.[272] These indemnities could arise eg from explosions caused by the shipment of dangerous or injurious cargo,[273] from stevedore damage to the ship[274] or from any liabilities owed to third party bill of lading holders.[275]

Time charterers normally own and pay for the ship's bunkers,[276] so the charterer would have a keen interest if the bunkers could be salved[277] after a wreck and, if they were lost or contaminated, would look to recover the cost from the shipowner if the latter was in breach.[278] Similarly, if the charterers supplied substandard bunkers that led to an engine breakdown, that would be a breach for which they could be liable.[279]

Time charterers may have their own cargo on board a ship, but the ship is much more likely to be carrying the cargo of others. The time charterer may be operating merely as a disponent owner in a chain, ie making its profit as an intermediary from sub-time or sub-voyage charterers below it in the chain. It may have no direct contractual relationship with the cargo owners at all, unless it is a contracting carrier under bills of lading

---

270 As a result of obeying a charterer's commercial orders as to voyages or cargoes: see eg *The Athanasia Comninos* [1990] 1 Lloyd's Rep 277; *The Georges Christos Lemos Third Party Proceedings* [1991] 2 Lloyd's Rep 107 (explosion in coal cargo). See also *Time Charters*, 338–348; N Gaskell, "Charterers' Liability to Shipowner—Orders, Indemnities and Vessel Damage" in, J. Schelin (ed.) *Modern Law of Charterparties* (Stockholm, 2003) 19.

271 See Baltime 1939 (revised 2001) cl 9; and *The Kos* [2012] 2 Lloyd's Rep 292, where cl 13 of the Shelltime 3 charter provided for charterers to indemnify owners "against all consequences or liabilities that may arise . . . from the master . . . complying with Charterers' or their agents' orders"; Shelltime 4 cl 13 is to the same effect. This provision, though, would be subject to the "due diligence" restriction in cl 4(c) in so far as it referred to nominations of port or berths, and is mainly concerned with commercial orders, eg as to the bill of lading: see also *Time Charters*, 341.

272 See *Time Charters*, 344–346.

273 NYPE 2015 cl 16 prohibits the carriage of goods that are "dangerous, injurious, flammable or corrosive", unless carried in accordance with requirements or recommendations of competent authorities; it also excludes completely the carriage of arms, ammunition or explosives. Shelltime 4 (designed for oil and oil products) prohibits in cl 38 the shipment of "acids, explosives or cargoes injurious to the vessel" and expressly provides that any damage to the vessel caused by such shipment are for the charterer's account. Note that the inclusion of a clause paramount may also carry with it obligations concerning dangerous cargo under Art IV r 6 of the Hague/Visby Rules: see 2.1.6 and *Time Charters*, 180–188. It may be that that the effect of Shelltime 4 is that Art IV r 6 only applies to cargo claims under cl 27, while cl 28 applies to claims for damage to the vessel: *Time Charters*, 701.

274 NYPE 2015 cl 37 requires a charterer to pay for any damage to the ship caused by stevedores, provided notice is given to the charterers in 24 hours or when it could have been discovered by due diligence. It is possible that hidden damage (eg to valves or fuel lines) might only manifest itself at sea, and even cause the wreck of the ship.

275 For such liabilities, see 2.1.5(a).

276 See eg NYPE 2015 cl 9, although bunkers used while a ship is off hire would be for the owner's account: NYPE 2015 cl 17.

277 The charterers would be obliged to contribute to any salvage reward in proportion to the value of their property saved: see 2.7.7(b).

278 Shelltime 4 cl 20 provides that if the vessel is lost or missing the shipowner must reimburse the charterers for the estimated quantity of bunkers on board, at the price paid at the last bunkering port.

279 See eg NYPE 2015 cl 9(d), unless this was excepted on the basis that the wreck was caused by the exception in cl 21 for "accidents of the seas". As a matter of interpretation, it could be said that the effective cause of the loss was the defective bunkers. See also 2.5.4(d) for limitation of liability and *Time Charters*, 249.

or waybills.[280] After a wreck, therefore, the time charterer might have a claim for loss of its own cargo against the shipowner, but is more likely to be at risk of financial loss, eg from lost or wasted hire,[281] lost freight from sub-charterers, or having to meet cargo claims brought directly against it by cargo owners.

As with voyage charterers, the shipowner will have express obligations about the fitness of the vessel, and it is usual for these to continue throughout the charter period.[282] There are usually similar obligations in respect of the crew.[283] When a ship is grounded, the off-hire clause will normally operate to suspend payment of hire.[284] If the ship strands so as to become a wreck, ie a total loss, the contract will usually be frustrated[285] because the contract will be for a particular ship.[286] The NYPE 2015 cl 20 provides that any hire paid in advance is returnable as from the total loss. Shelltime 4 cl 20 also provides that such hire payments shall be returned to the charterer if the vessel is lost, but is more specific in stating that the charter will terminate if the vessel is lost, becomes a constructive total loss[287] or is missing.[288]

Where the time charterer suffers financial loss from the wreck as a result of breach by the shipowner,[289] the charterer would expect to have an action for damages if they are not too remote.[290] Most time charters, though, will contain exceptions that will operate as between shipowner and charterer.[291] Thus, the NYPE 2015 cl 21 now has a list of events that are mutually excepted, including "act of God ... fire ... and all dangers and accidents of the seas, rivers, machinery, boilers and navigation". These would normally be interpreted to apply to circumstances not caused by the faults of the parties,[292] but the clause also excepts "errors of navigation". This has been interpreted as not being wide enough to cover negligent navigation,[293] so

---

280 See below.
281 In English law, the time charterer will not be able to claim consequential loss in negligence from a third party that collided with chartered ship, eg for lost profit or any wasted hire: see *The World Harmony* [1967] P 341, *Candlewood Navigation Corp v Mitsui OSK Line (The Mineral Transporter and The Ibaraki Maru)* [1986] AC 1, [1985] 2 Lloyd's Rep 303.
282 See eg NYPE 2015 cl 6 (to keep the ship in a "thoroughly efficient state"); Shelltime 4 cl 1 ("in every way fit for the service") and cl 3 (duty to maintain).
283 See eg Shelltime 4 cl 2; cf NYPE 2015 cl 6(a), which refers only to the "full complement" of crew.
284 See eg NYPE 2015 cl 17; Shelltime 4 cl 21; *Time Charters*, Chapter 25 and 686–691.
285 See also 2.1.4(b); *Time Charters*, Chapter 26.
286 Any additional 'substitution' clause would need to specify that it was intended to apply after a loss: *Time Charters*, 477–479.
287 See 2.9.4.
288 The off-hire provisions are unaffected by the wide general exceptions (discussed below): see cl 27(d).
289 Eg if the vessel has not been properly maintained under NYPE cl 6(a) and it is this that caused the wreck. See also Shelltime 4 cl 1.
290 Cf *Transfield Shipping Inc v Mercator Shipping Inc (The Achilleas)* [2009] AC 61, [2008] 2 Lloyd's Rep 275, *The Sylvia* [2010] 2 Lloyd's Rep 81. On termination of the charter by owner's breach the time charterer would be expected to mitigate any loss by chartering substitute tonnage and claiming for any increase in hire rates: see eg *The Product Star (No 2)* [1991] 2 Lloyd's Rep 468; *Time Charters*, 103–1112; cf *Voyage Charters*, 628–633.
291 *Time Charters*, Chapter 27.
292 See eg *Polemis v Furness, Withy and Co Ltd, In re* [1921] 3 KB 560.
293 See *Seven Seas Transportation Ltd v Pacifico Union Marina Corp (The Satya Kailash)* [1984] 1 Lloyd's Rep 588; *Time Charters*, 513.

the shipowner would have to rely on the incorporation[294] of the Hague Rules with its Art IV r 2(a) defence.[295] In any event, if the vessel was not seaworthy (under cl 2) or properly maintained (under cl 6(a)) and that contributed to the negligent navigation, eg through a defective radar, it would seem on normal principles of interpretation that any exception would not apply.[296] Note that as cl 21 states that its exceptions are "mutually excepted" the charterer can also rely on them, although the "fire" exception might not apply if the effective cause was loading injurious cargo, nor would "accidents of the seas" if there had been a nomination of an unsafe port.[297]

Shelltime 4 cl 27 also contains very wide exceptions for "loss or damage or delay or failure", including from "act, neglect or default . . . in the navigation or management of the vessel",[298] "fire unless caused by the actual fault or privity of the owners",[299] "collision or stranding",[300] "dangers or accidents of the sea",[301] "explosion[302] . . . or any latent defect in hull, equipment or machinery".[303] These provisions go further than the NYPE in specifically excluding negligent navigation or management and effectively mean that after a wreck a charterer cannot recover from the shipowner most of the financial loss it suffers, eg lost profits or expenses caused by delay.[304] The clause also excludes the liability of shipowner *and* charterer from loss damage and delay arising from other causes that would not normally involve fault and are unlikely to result in a wreck.[305] Two major categories of claim by a charterer are expressly removed from the wide exceptions by cl 27(c). The first, cl 27(c)(i), relates to any liability of the shipowner for loss or damage to a wide variety of harbour facilities, including jetties, pipes or equipment near where a vessel may proceed under the charter. This is designed to cover oil terminal facilities that either may be owned by the charterer (or associated companies), or in respect of which it might have it might have liabilities (or owe indemnities) to the actual owner. The shipowner's liability might

---

294 See eg the clause paramount in NYPE 2015 cl 33(a) incorporating the US COGSA 1936 to apply the Hague Rules. Although the clause refers to "this bill of lading", it was held in *The Saxon Star* [1958] 1 Lloyd's Rep 73 that this was meant to apply as between the shipowner and charterer, not simply in any bills issued under the charter. See also *Time Charters*, 623–635.

295 See 2.1.5(b).

296 The incorporation of the Hague Rules would mean that the shipowner only had a duty of due diligence to make the ship seaworthy under Art III r 1.

297 See also *Time Charters*, 513.

298 Ie the Hague/Visby Art IV r 2(a) defence: see 2.1.5(b).

299 Ie the Hague/Visby Art IV r 2(b) defence: see 2.1.5(a).

300 These events could also fall within the neglect in navigation exception, but are expressly excepted even if there is no fault of the shipowner.

301 This exception would normally be interpreted to cover perils of the sea not arising from fault (see 2.1.5(c)) but the neglect in navigation or management exception would cover most fault leading to a wreck.

302 The context suggests that this refers to explosions of the ship's equipment rather than explosions of cargo, causing a wreck. These may be within the "management of the ship" exception if the cause of the explosion was in some way the responsibility of the crew.

303 The clause makes an express distinction between latent defects and those that arise from unfitness of the ship at delivery (cl 1), or failure to exercise due diligence to maintain the ship (cl 2); the exceptions do not appear to apply to the latter two.

304 They will be subject to the express duties of fitness in cll 1–3: see *Time Charters*, 699–670.

305 Apart from eg "war". The "Act of God" exception would not allow the charterer to point to bad weather (eg fog) as an exception if the ship was wrecked where the effective cause was an order to an unsafe port: cf *Liver Alkali Co v Johnson* (1875) LR 9 Ex 338; *Nugent v Smith* (1876) 1 CPD 421.

arise from negligent navigation, but may also be imposed as a strict liability under harbour legislation.[306] The second major carve-out from the wide exceptions for negligence relates to cargo claims, whether brought by the charterer or others. Under cl 27(c)(ii), these claims will be subject to one of the applicable international regimes, eg the Hague or Hague-Visby Rules.[307]

The extent to which a time charterer has any liability to cargo interests after a wreck will largely depend upon whether it or the shipowner was named as contracting carrier under the individual contract in the bill of lading or waybill.[308] In the container trade, the time charterer may have chartered in extra tonnage to fulfil its liner schedules and may want to issue bills of lading or waybills in its own name as part of its normal service; similarly if it has slot-chartered space on the ship as part of a pooling arrangement. The time charter will usually give the charterer great flexibility about issuing bills.[309] The charterer may require the master to issue bills of lading or waybills "as presented" that name the charterer as contracting carrier, so that as disponent owner it will have liabilities to cargo interests after a wreck.[310] Alternatively, the charterer may prefer to require the master to issue bills of lading or waybills that name the shipowner as contracting carrier, so that it is the latter which is contractually liable to the cargo interests. The charter provision, though, may also give the charterer an option to sign bills or waybills itself on behalf of the master.[311] Where the issuing of bills of lading or waybills creates liabilities for the shipowner that exceed that which has been agreed in the charter, the charterer may be liable to indemnify the shipowner for the excess,[312] eg where it has failed to ensure that bills of lading are issued that have the agreed clause paramount.[313]

Cargo loss claims between shipowner and time charterer would be subject to the Hague Rules as a result of the clause paramount.[314] There have been many problems in practice with the NYPE, particularly because it is usually the charterer that has the responsibility to engage stevedores,[315] and it may be unclear whether cargo damage was caused by them or the failings of the crew under Art III r 2, eg in their supervision of the stevedores. For this reason, the charterer and shipowner may agree to settle such claims on the basis of the allocation of risks set out in the Inter-Club NYPE Agreement [ICA] 1996,[316] now expressly

---

306 See 2.4.1, 11.1.1. The shipowner would expect to have P&I cover for damage to such fixed objects: see 2.9.6(b).
307 See 2.1.5, *Time Charters*, 699–670, 710.
308 *The Starsin* [2004] 1 AC 715, [2003] 1 Lloyd's Rep 571.
309 See eg NYPE 2015 cl 31; Shelltime 4 cl 13.
310 Eg subject to the Hague/Visby Rules: see 2.1.5.
311 See eg NYPE 2015 cl 31(a), which now requires the prior written authority of the master. Under cl 8 of the NYPE 1946, the authority of agents to sign was implied: see *The Berkshire* [1974] I Lloyd's Rep 185.
312 See eg NYPE 2015 cl 31(b). This itself involves difficult questions about whether the shipowner would be able to complain simply because the bills of lading exposed the owner to Hague/Visby liabilities to cargo owners in circumstances where it might (through freedom of contract) have assumed no liability to the charterer for the loss of its own cargo.
313 Required by Shelltime 4 cl 38 and see cl 27(c)(ii). See also the NYPE 2015 cl 31(a).
314 NYPE 2015 cl cl 31(a). This will apply to charterer-shipowner claims even though (unlike the Shelltime 4 provision) it does not expressly apply the Rules to the charterer's own cargo. Note also cl 27, below.
315 See eg NYPE 2015 cl 8(a); *Time Charters*, 356–362.
316 Most recently amended in 2011. See *Time Charters*, 366–377.

incorporated into the NYPE 2015.[317] In wreck cases it is unlikely that the loading and stowage was a cause of the wreck,[318] and where the claim arose out of the unseaworthiness or error in navigation or management of the vessel it is the shipowner that will be fully liable rather than the charterer.[319]

The time charterer may itself incur expenses after a casualty, eg in in paying for stevedoring, storage and transhipment; this may also involve extra insurance costs. The charterer may also incur costs in paying for salvage[320] and settling claims by cargo owners (eg for deviation, delay or damage to cargo).[321] All of these costs may ultimately be claimed by way of indemnity from the shipowner, but only if the casualty was caused by breach, there was no operative exception in the charter and the ICA 1996 did not apply. Most time charters have extensive provisions dealing with war risks[322] and would contain a "both to blame collision clause"[323] and incorporate a version of the York Antwerp Rules with a "New Jason" clause.[324]

2.1.7(d) Charterers' influence on wreck removal

A major operator in the position as charterer may wish to exert an influence on wreck removal operations for commercial reasons (including public relations)[325] as well as legal reasons. That influence may extend to encouraging the owner as to a particular course of action in dealing with the wreck as ship and cargo, eg MSC in the case of the *MSC Napoli*[326] and the *Rena*.[327] Although a charterer may have P&I liability cover (perhaps extending to liability in relation to wreck of the cargo), it may well be keen to ensure that wreck removal costs are directly borne by the shipowner. There may be operational costs associated with forwarding cargo, eg getting containers off the ship, de-stuffing, cleaning and re-stuffing.[328] The charterers will try to get the shipowner to pay directly for such costs, bearing in mind that any claim for these costs against the shipowner might be subject to limitation. To that extent, the charterers may well prefer to take a more withdrawn role, eg when State authorities are demanding action.

It is apparent that many powerful charterers (eg in the offshore sector) are including clauses in their charters that impose extensive obligations on shipowners to remove wrecks on the basis of orders given *by* the charterers. The P&I Clubs have always maintained that they will respond to wreck removals only when required by compulsion of law, eg by wreck removal orders issued by public authorities. So any contractual obligations assumed

---

317 NYPE 2015 cl 27. There is effectively a type of knock for knock allocation in the ICA cl 8, based on 100% liability for shipowner or charterer, or a 50%–50% split. It also has an independent two-year time bar in cl 6. The ICA will also take priority over other clauses in the charter, eg general exceptions or time limits.
318 If it was, see the express indemnity in the NYPE 2015 cl 37 in respect of damage to the ship.
319 The ICA assumes that the carriage was governed eg by the Hague/Visby Rules.
320 Cf *The Danah* [1993] 1 Lloyd's Rep 351.
321 See eg *The Darfur* [2004] 2 Lloyd's Rep 469; and 2.5.4(d) for limitation of such claims.
322 See eg NYPE 2015 cl 34 (Conwartime 2013); Shelltime cll 27(a), 33–35.
323 See eg NYPE 2015 cl 33(b); Shelltime 4 cl 36; also 2.4.4, 2.9.2(b).
324 See eg NYPE 2015 cll 25, 33(c); Shelltime 4 cl 37; also 2.8.1.
325 See also 13.1.2.
326 See 1.2.3.
327 See 1.2.4.
328 See 2.1.4.

by owners to charterers will be outside normal Club cover and thus a commercial risk for owners, unless the latter take out additional fixed premium cover.[329]

2.2 Wreck and crew

The master and crew of a ship will be directly affected by wreck in a number of ways. Their most immediate concern will be for their own safety, and this will also be a first priority of salvors.

2.2.1 Master's concerns after casualty

On a personal level, a casualty will be a particularly stressful time for the master. This may have been the most traumatic event in his career and he will be anxious about its effects on his future employment. He will be concerned about the reaction of his employers and whether he will be held to blame. This anxiety may have a number of effects on his conduct in the course of the casualty. He may be reluctant to take salvage services, fearing that the owners will object to the expense.[330] In some circumstances, failure to take prompt assistance might prejudice a claim against a guilty colliding ship, eg where the failure was deemed to be a *novus actus interveniens*.[331]

The master may initially be suspicious of those seeking to come aboard his ship immediately after a casualty, including potential salvors. While efforts are being made to save the ship, there may be many potential visitors. These will include salvors and others (such as surveyors or engineers) engaged by the owners or their insurers (P&I Club and H&M underwriters) who are there to help the master. Government representatives may be aboard to monitor operations and actually to give orders under intervention powers.[332] But there may be others who try to come aboard for purposes which are not directly in the interests of the master and owners. Lawyers, experts and investigators may be appointed by cargo interests or by those from a colliding ship; these persons will try to come on board not so much to help with salvage operations but to gain evidence for future legal claims against the owners. From the perspective of such claimants, this may be their only opportunity to get reliable evidence of the cause of the casualty (eg by interviewing the crew or inspecting the ship), especially if the ship eventually becomes a total loss. The master, though, may well prefer that these claimant representatives do not come aboard, and while he remains in charge of his vessel he will normally have the power to do so. Otherwise, although nominally in charge of his vessel, he may increasingly find that this control is gradually being

---

329 See Skuld, "Contractual Wreck Removal", 31 August 2018: www.skuld.com/topics/legal/pi-and-defence/contractual-wreck-removal/.
330 Although the master on the spot ought to be able to take urgent decisions about salvage, the reality with modern communications is often that such matters are often referred back to the owners or ship managers. Where a ship is grounded, it may well be that there is more time for the owners to arrange for expert assistance: see also 12.1.
331 See eg *Owners of Mitero Marigo v Owners of Fritz Thyssen (The Fritz Thyssen)* [1967] 1 Lloyd's Rep 104, 112, [1967] 2 Lloyd's Rep 199, and 2.4.
332 See 4.2.3, 5.3.

affected by the advice of salvors (often dealing directly with owners), and the orders of government officials.[333]

2.2.2 Criminalisation of seafarers after shipwreck

Seafarers may not only be concerned about immediate welfare issues but also about how they may be treated by the State in which the shipwreck occurred. They may face investigations, prosecutions and punishment in circumstances where they are particularly vulnerable. Casualties like the *Rena* will often result in criminal proceedings. Its master and second officer were prosecuted and served prison sentences.[334] The range of possible offences is enormous but mostly have to do with the unsafe operation of the ship[335] or from pollution.[336] After the wreck of the tanker *Tasman Spirit* in Pakistan in 2003, seven crew members were detained in prison for some nine months pending a compensation claim.[337] Shipowning companies may also be prosecuted, eg for poor maintenance or operation of the ship,[338] but senior managers will rarely be in the country of the casualty and it is likely that the company will be fined. Those fines might be quite heavy but can be covered by P&I insurance.[339]

The criminalisation of seafarers (sometimes as proxies for owners) has been a matter of increasing concern. Shortly after the agreement of the Maritime Labour Convention [MLC] 2006,[340] a Joint IMO/ILO Expert Working Group prepared "Guidelines on Fair Treatment of Seafarers in the Event of a Maritime Accident", which were adopted by the ILO and IMO.[341] These reflected the adoption of the MLC 2006 itself and deal with the particular practical concerns of seafarers where there have been accidents such as shipwrecks. Although soft law, the guidelines do provide a sensible checklist for those involved after

---

333 The presence of too many people on board the casualty is well recognised as being a hindrance to salvors and is one reason for the Code of Practice between the International Salvage Union [ISU] and International Group (allowing a Club observer in salvage operations). Under the SCOPIC agreement, there can be the appointment of the Special Casualty Representative (SCR) for the owners (see 12.3.2), one "Special Hull Representative" on behalf of Hull and Machinery underwriters and one "Special Cargo Representative" on behalf of cargo underwriters (see 12.3.3).

334 They were convicted in May 2012 of offences under the MTA 1994 for operating a vessel in a manner likely to cause danger, under the RMA 1991 for discharging a contaminant, and under the Crimes Act 1961 for altering ship documents. Daina was convicted in October 2012 of an offence under the RMA 1991 for the discharge of harmful substances from a ship in the coastal marine area and was fined $300,000 of a maximum $600,000. See 1.2.4 and *Rena Final Report*, 6; *AG Cabinet Paper*, [22].

335 See eg the MSA 1995 s 98 and the many safety regulations made eg under the MSA 1995 s 85 to give effect to IMO conventions such as SOLAS. These would include the Collision Regulations: see *Marsden & Gault*, 73–76, Chapter 22.

336 See eg the MSA 1995 s 131 and the many pollution regulations made, eg under the MSA 1995 s 128 to give effect to IMO conventions such as MARPOL.

337 See https://shipwrecklog.com/log/history/tasman-spirit/. Even a salvage master was imprisoned; see also 13.4.2.

338 See eg the MSA 1995 ss 98, 100, in addition to specific pollution offences. See also the Protection of the Environment through Criminal Law Directive 2008/99/EC (OJ L 328), 6.12.2008, p. 28.

339 That cover may also extend to paying any fines of the seafarer if the employer is obliged to do so, eg under the employment contract or general law, see 2.9.6(b).

340 See 2.2.4.

341 Resolution LEG.3(91), 27 April 2006.

accidents; they are addressed not only to the coastal State and the flag State, but also to the seafarer State, the shipowner and seafarer. So far as port and coastal States are concerned, there are 20 specific guidelines covering matters such as preserving the rights of seafarers, ensuring they have adequate provisions, access to interpreters and legal advice. In particular, a number of provisions emphasise the difficulties of detention, eg by that ensuring means of communication during detention, the need to gather evidence and promptly interview seafarers to minimise the need for them to remain, and to consider non-custodial alternatives to detention before trial (including bonds or other security, eg for fines). Flag States are enjoined to undertake their UNCLOS obligations, eg to conduct investigations expeditiously, and to ensure shipowners honour their obligations. Seafarer States (eg those such as the Philippines, which supply much of the world's maritime labour for employment on others' ships) are given seven guidelines, eg to fund repatriation if the shipowner and flag State fail to do so. Shipowners are also given seven guidelines in respect of investigations,[342] where their overriding duty to protect the rights of seafarers is emphasised. Seafarers themselves are given a number of guidelines including taking steps to ensure that they fully understand their right not to self-incriminate.

2.2.3 Fair treatment of crew after shipwreck

When the crew have been rescued from the ship, some (especially the master and officers) may have concerns about whether they may face investigation, detention and prosecution by a coastal State.[343] Otherwise, their immediate concerns will be repatriation and payment of wages; later there may be claims against the shipowner for injury or death.[344] At one time the premature end of the voyage might have meant that no wages were legally payable (as they were only earned on the completion of the voyage when freight was earned).[345] That position has been reversed by statute,[346] and the UK had long provided some relief for seamen shipwrecked on UK ships.[347] Reputable shipowners will take care of their crews, but the more practical problem is likely to be that the shipowner fails to respond after a major shipwreck.

These types of issues were investigated and addressed within the IMO and ILO, and the two bodies ultimately established a series of Joint IMO/ILO Ad Hoc Working Groups, in particular one on "Liability and Compensation Regarding Claims for Death, Personal Injury and Abandonment of Seafarers"[348] and another on "Fair Treatment of Seafarers in

---

342 Regulation 5.1.6 of the MLA 2006 puts an obligation on member States to hold an official inquiry into any serious marine casualty involving their flagged ships.

343 See 2.2.2.

344 See N Gaskell, C Smith, "Private Law Rights Applicable to Seafarers," Chapter 5 of D Fitzpatrick, M Anderson (eds) *Seafarers' Rights* (OUP, 2005). In the event of a claim against another ship responsible for the wreck, eg after a collision, the seafarer's tort claims may be brought jointly and severally against that other ship: see eg the MSA 1995 s 188, and 2.4.4. However, such claims may be subject to the other ship's limits of liability, eg under the LLMC 1996 Art 6, whereas a tort claim against the employing ship may not be subject to limits because of the LLMC 1996 Art 3(e): see 2.5.4(a).

345 See eg *Cutter v Powell* (1795) 101 ER 573.

346 See now the MSA 1995 s 38 (for UK ships).

347 See eg the MSA 1906 Part IV and the MSA 1970 ss 62, 67 (re-enacted in the MSA 1995 ss 73–75).

348 Established in 1998. See the Final Report in March 2009 of the WG: ILO/IMO/WGPS/9/2009/10.

the Event of a Maritime Accident".[349] In addition to commissioning research,[350] the Working Groups produced some soft law guidelines and, ultimately, drafts of convention text.[351] Thus, in 2001 the IMO and ILO resolved to adopt two sets of guidelines. The "Guidelines on Provision of Financial Security in Case of Abandonment of Seafarers"[352] and the "Guidelines on Shipowners' Responsibilities in Respect of Contractual Claims for Personal Injury to or Death of Seafarers" were adopted on 29 November 2001.[353] The aim was to encourage IMO member States to ensure that there was financial security to cover repatriation, maintenance, remuneration and expenses after abandonment.

2.2.4 Maritime Labour Convention 2006

The main underlying convention is now the ILO's MLC 2006.[354] It has been given effect in the UK.[355] To some extent its detailed requirements have overtaken some of the earlier soft law.[356] The MLC (and its amendments) have achieved a very wide degree of acceptance, eg among flag States, but its reach is much greater because of the possibility of port State control over the "maritime labour certificate" issued under it.[357]

The MLC 2006 now provides minimum employment standards which ILO member states should enforce for ships flying their flags, although it gives a great degree of flexibility as to how they will do that. The basic rights and obligations are set out in the 16 (relatively short) articles of the convention, but mostly in binding regulations. There is also a corresponding "Code", dealing with implementation of the regulations, which consists of Part A "Standards" (which must be enacted, but in a form to achieve functional

---

349 The first session of this Working Group met in January 2005.
350 A database was established about reported incidents of abandonment of seafarers: www.ilo.org/dyn/seafarers/seafarersbrowse.home.
351 For the latter see eg the 2014 amendments: 2.2.4.
352 A 22/Res.930, 17 December 2001.
353 See A 22/Res.931, 17 December 2001. These guidelines extended to issues that were not directly addressed in the earlier IMO Assembly Resolution A898(21) on "Guidelines on Shipowners' Responsibilities in Respect of Maritime Claims".
354 Entry into force on 20 August 2013, as amended in 2014 and 2016. There are some 84 ratifications, including the UK: see the ILO website, www.ilo.org.
355 Through delegated legislation (and see Merchant Shipping Notice 1850(M)), including the European Communities (Definition of Treaties) (Maritime Labour Convention) Order 2009 (SI 2009/1757). Note also the Agreement set out in the Annex to Council Directive 2009/13/EC of 16 February 2009 implementing the Agreement concluded by the European Community Shipowners' Associations (ECSA) and the European Transport Workers' Federation (ETF) on the Maritime Labour Convention, 2006 (O.J. L124, 20.5.2009, 30). The main UK implementation provisions were in the Merchant Shipping (Maritime Labour Convention) (Minimum Requirements for Seafarers etc.) Regulations 2014 (SI 2014/1613), but substantial amendments to existing UK legislation have been made by the Merchant Shipping (Maritime Labour Convention) (Consequential and Minor Amendments) Regulations 2014 (SI 2014/1614). See also the Merchant Shipping (Maritime Labour Convention) (Compulsory Financial Security) (Amendment) Regulations 2018 (SI 2018/667), The Merchant Shipping (Maritime Labour Convention) (Miscellaneous Amendments) Regulations 2018 (SI 2018/242).
356 Note the Joint ILO/IMO Working Group "Guidelines on Fair Treatment of Seafarers and on Liability and Compensation for Seafarers" issued after the MLC 2006 in order to support its aims; see eg IMO Resolution LEG.3(91) adopted on 27 April 2006, LEG/91/12.
357 See Regulation 5.1, as amended in 2016.

equivalence) and Part B "Guidelines" (which are not binding).[358] The relevant provisions on repatriation, abandonment and compensation for injury are scattered somewhat in the Convention.

2.2.4(a) MLC 2006 and repatriation costs

MLC Regulation 2.5, as amended in 2014, deals with repatriation. It provides that "Seafarers have a right to be repatriated at no cost to themselves in the circumstances and under the conditions specified in the Code" and that each ILO member state party to the MLC "shall require ships that fly its flag to provide financial security to ensure that seafarers are duly repatriated in accordance with the Code".[359] The circumstances are set out in Standard A2.5.1 and include "when the seafarers are no longer able to carry out their duties under their employment agreement or cannot be expected to carry them out in the specific circumstances".[360] This is supplemented by Guideline B2.5.1(b)(ii), which specifically includes "shipwreck" in this standard. Guideline B2.5.1 para 3 also lists the type of repatriation expenses to be covered, including passage with luggage, accommodation, food, medical treatment, pay and allowances from leaving the ship to destination,[361] Shipowners are not allowed to deduct costs of repatriation from wages.[362]

The MLC 2006 thus made a significant advance in the rights of seafarers, but it is dependent to some extent on national implementing legislation and more so as to the willingness or ability of the shipowner to pay for the expenses. In the aftermath of a shipwreck the owner may be in financial difficulties (eg because its freight or hire income has ceased, and it faces many new costs); and, where it is a single ship company, the availability of its assets may be severely limited from the perspective of all claimants. The MLC 2006 Standard A2.5.1 para 5(a) deals with this by putting an obligation on the flag State to arrange for repatriation of the seafarers if the shipowner fails to make arrangements for or to meet the cost of repatriation. The State may then seek reimbursement from the shipowner.[363]

2.2.4(b) Financial security for abandonment

Given the unstable financial position of many shipowners, it was inevitable that a crucial issue was going to how to achieve the "financial security" required by Regulation 2.5. It was here that the International Group of P&I Clubs became closely involved in the negotiations between the ILO and IMO, as it would be important for the Clubs to be able to give effect to the form of any cover and certification.[364] The original MLC 2006 left the issue of repatriation insurance somewhat in the air. The 2014 amendments have dealt with this by having a new Standard A2.5.2 on financial security to "ensure the provision of an

---

358 Article VI of the MLC sets out the obligations of states as to how they are to implement the various provisions. See also the Explanatory Note to the regulations and code of the MLC, reproduced with the text of the convention.

359 See eg the Merchant Shipping (Maritime Labour Convention) (Minimum Requirements for Seafarers etc.) Regulations 2014 (SI 2014/1613) Part 6 "Repatriation".

360 Standard A2.5.1(c) as amended in 2014.

361 The latter is subject to the important caveat "if provided for by national laws or regulations or collective agreements".

362 See Standard A2.5.1 para 3.

363 Standard A2.5.1 para 5(b).

364 The implementation of these provisions by the Clubs is dealt with in 2.9.6(e).

expeditious and effective financial security system to assist seafarers in the event of their abandonment". The IMO Guidelines have largely been supplanted by this new provision. It deems that there is an abandonment when the shipowner (a) fails to cover the cost of the seafarer's repatriation; (b) has left the seafarer without the necessary maintenance and support; or (c) has otherwise unilaterally severed their ties with the seafarer including failure to pay contractual wages for a period of at least two months.[365]

The Standard leaves the type of financial security to the member State, eg to provide for social security, or insurance, or a national fund. There is a requirement that flag States ensure that there is an appropriate certificate (or other documentary evidence) of financial security.[366] It should cover (a) outstanding wages and other entitlements due from the shipowner to the seafarer under their employment agreement, the relevant collective bargaining agreement or the national law of the flag State, limited to four months of any such outstanding wages and four months of any such outstanding entitlements; (b) all expenses reasonably incurred by the seafarer, including the cost of repatriation referred to in para 10; and (c) the essential needs of the seafarer including such items as adequate food, clothing where necessary, accommodation, drinking water supplies, essential fuel for survival on board the ship, necessary medical care and any other reasonable costs or charges from the act or omission constituting the abandonment until the seafarer's arrival at home.[367]

2.2.4(c) Indemnity for unpaid wages

The MLC 2006 also now provides generally, in Regulation 2.6, for seafarers to be entitled to adequate compensation in the case of "injury, loss or unemployment arising from the ship's loss or foundering". Despite the general reference to "injury and loss from foundering" in the title and content of Regulation 2.6, its Standard A2.6 and Guideline B2.6 concentrate only on the consequences for wages of unemployment following a wreck.[368] They require ILO member States to ensure that the shipowner pays to each seafarer on board an indemnity against unemployment resulting from the loss or foundering, but limited to two months' wages.[369] The seafarers' claims for wages generally would give rise to a maritime lien,[370] but with a wreck which is a total loss this is practically worthless, as there is no *res* to which the lien can attach.

2.2.4(d) Compensation for injury and loss

Although Regulation 2.6, above, speaks generally about seafarers being entitled to adequate compensation in the case of injury or loss "arising from the ship's loss or foundering", it is Regulation 4.2 that deals with a shipowner's liability for sickness, injury or death.[371] Regulation 4.2 obliges ILO member States to ensure that seafarers have a "right to material

---

365 Standard A2.5.2 para 2.
366 See eg the Merchant Shipping (Maritime Labour Convention) (Minimum Requirements for Seafarers etc.) Regulations 2014 (SI 1613) Part 6 "Repatriation", reg 26.
367 Standard A2.5.2 para 9.
368 The injury and loss issues are dealt with separately in reg 4.2, below.
369 Where the seafarer is injured, there may be a liability to pay wages for the duration of the injury, see reg 4.2, below.
370 And the MLC 1996 Guideline B2.6.1 requires states to ensure that such remedy applies to the indemnity.
371 Regulation 2.6 para 2 simply leaves the rights in respect of losses or injuries arising from a ship's loss or foundering to national law and, presumably, to the provisions in reg 4.2.

assistance and support from the shipowner with respect to the financial consequences of sickness, injury or death" arising from their employment. In particular, under Standard A4.2.1 laws should be adopted requiring shipowners to be responsible for the costs of sickness and injury while on board or until repatriated, including medical and burial expenses, as well as wages until repatriated. The extent of implementation will depend on national laws[372] which are given much leeway, eg where there are national social security schemes, and which may in any event restrict the liability of the shipowner to pay medical expenses (including board and lodging) and wages to 16 weeks.[373]

2.2.4(e) Financial security for compensation
The risk of impecuniosity or insolvency of the shipowner is now addressed in the amended Standard A4.2.1 para 1(b), which requires national laws to ensure that "shipowners shall provide financial security to assure compensation in the event of the death or long-term disability of seafarers due to an occupational injury, illness or hazard, as set out in national law, the seafarers' employment agreement or collective agreement". As noted, the MLC 2006 had been rather vague about the detail concerning financial security,[374] but the 2014 amendments now provide minimum requirements in Standard A4.2.1 para 8,[375] and also the express requirement in para 11 that ships carry a certificate of financial security, which has to contain information prescribed in a new Appendix A4-I of the MLC 2006. This information is of a very basic nature, eg name of ship, name and address of the provider of the financial security and the period of validity of the security. There does have to be an "attestation from the financial security provider that the financial security meets the requirements of Standard A4.2.1. The MLC 2006 provisions do not specifically address the typical policy defences which exist in Club cover, although under Standard A4.2.1 para 12 an insurer that wanted to cancel the security has to give at least 30 days' notice to the flag State.

2.2.4(f) Implementation of MLC 2006 financial security provisions
The 2014 amendments to the MLC 2006 came into force on 18 January 2017 and apparently caused some uncertainty.[376] It is not appropriate to go into the reasons here, but it can be noted that the MLC does not prescribe a particular form for certificates and so the International Group has developed a form of wording with States which is similar to the "Blue Cards" issued by Clubs under the IMO conventions. The financial security system shall provide "*direct access*, sufficient coverage and expedited financial assistance, in

---

372 The ILO issued in 2012 a handbook on "Guidance on Implementing the Maritime Labour Convention, 2006 Model National Provisions", see eg 74–76 on implementing Regulation 4.2. For the UK see the Merchant Shipping (Maritime Labour Convention) (Minimum Requirements for Seafarers etc.) Regulations 2014 (SI 2014/1613) Part 10, "Shipowners' Liability".
373 Standard A4.2.1 paras 2, 4.
374 The 2012 handbook suggested simply that model provisions in a "Schedule III" should be developed by national administrations, but no content details were provided.
375 Including cover for contractual compensation claims, ie those arising under the contract of employment. See also the new Standard A4.2.2. There is also a model Receipt and Release Form which may be used after payment of a contractual claim: see Guideline B4.2.2 and Appendix B4-I.
376 See eg International Group Circular of FAQs for Members on the MLC 2006 as amended, "Financial Security Requirements" (10 August 2018) [*IG MLC 2006 FAQs*]: www.ukpandi.com/fileadmin/uploads/uk-pi/Documents/2018/Ciruclars/MLC_FAQs_External_-_v_10_08_18.pdf.

accordance with this Standard, to any abandoned seafarer".[377] In the insurance context it is not clear whether direct access requires a form of direct action against the insurer,[378] or whether something less is possible. The assumption has been that a form of direct action is required, and this appears to be the case with the International Group form. It seems probable that the only insurance contract exclusions that can be relied on are those in the MLC Extension Clause 2016,[379] and relate to war, nuclear, biochem and cyber risks and sanctions. In some circumstances it is clear that MLC type claims may fall in ordinary Club cover but, because of the nature of typical cover, shipowners may need to rely on additional cover which may be provided as an extra by their Club.

2.3 Wreck and passengers

An enormous number of passengers are carried on ferries and cruise ships. For the UK alone, in 2017[380] there were 19.5 million passengers carried on international short sea ferry routes; cruise passenger numbers were 1.9 million; sea passengers on domestic routes were 44 million, of which 21.5 million were on river ferries and 3.5 million were on domestic sea crossings. Internationally, the largest industry association expected 30 million passengers to cruise in 2019 in over 272 cruise ships, with more being added each year.[381] Royal Caribbean's *Symphony of the Seas* (228,081 gt) was the world's largest cruise ship in 2018. Registered in the Bahamas, it can carry 5,518 passengers (double occupancy) and 6,680 in total; it has an international crew of 2,200.[382]

Passengers killed or injured in a collision owing to negligent navigation of the carrying ship and another vessel will be able to claim in tort against a colliding vessel as it will be jointly and severally liable.[383] This ship will be able to limit its liability under Art 6(1)(a) of the LLMC 1996.[384] That limit might be quite low, and there could be the usual difficulties of enforcement if it is wrecked and owned by a single ship company. The passengers would normally find it easier to make claims against the carrying ship. A claim in tort is possible if there was negligence, but the relationship between the passengers and the owners or operators of the carrying ship will usually be regulated by contract.[385] That contract itself will in many cases be subject to consumer protection provisions in national law and also by

---

377 Standard A2.5.2 para 4.
378 As with the pollution conventions: see 2.6.2.
379 See 2.9.6(e).
380 DfT, "Sea Passenger Statistics: All Routes 2017 (Final)" (7 November 2018), 1.
381 Cruise Lines International Association (CLIA), "2019 Cruise Trends & Industry Outlook" (December 2018), 18–19.
382 Royal Caribbean International, Ship Fact Sheet: www.royalcaribbeanpresscenter.com/fact-sheet/31/symphony-of-the-seas/.
383 See the MSA 1995 s 188 and 2.4.4.
384 These 'personal' limits are set at twice the level of the 'property' limits under Art 6(1)(b), but are separate from them; if the 'personal' fund is insufficient to meet all the injury and death claims, then claimants can share in the 'property' amount: see LLMC 1996 Art 6(2). For examples of the 'property limits' see Table 2.5, 2.5.6(a), and for the combined limits see N Gaskell, "Limitation of Liability and Division of Loss in Operation" [*Gaskell, Limitation of Liability*], Appendix 4 of *Marsden & Gault*, 973–1020.
385 See generally, K Lewins, *The International Carriage of Passengers by Sea* (2016, Sweet & Maxwell) [*Lewins*]; N Martinez Gutierrez, *Limitation of Liability in International Maritime Conventions* (Routledge, 2011) [*Martinez Gutierrez*], Chapter 4.

the Convention Relating to the Carriage of Passengers and their Luggage by Sea [Athens Convention] 1974, as amended. The Athens Convention is broadly similar in concept to the Hague/Visby Rules in that it sets out mandatory liabilities for the carriage of passengers by sea.[386]

2.3.1 Application of Athens Convention 2002

The Athens Convention 1974 entered into force on 28 April 1987, but following a series of disasters in the 1980s and 1990s[387] it was revised and replaced by the "Athens Convention 2002";[388] this is the original 1974 Convention as amended by a Protocol in 2002. The Athens Convention 2002 entered into force internationally on 23 April 2014[389] but had already been given regional effect in the EU.[390] The UK gave full effect to the Athens Convention 2002 as from 28 May 2014.[391] The Athens Convention 2002 contains major new liability provisions and introduces compulsory insurance and direct action against the insurer. Any attempts in the passenger contract to reduce the carrier's liability under the Convention will be void.[392]

Under Art 2,[393] States party to the Convention must apply it if the ship is flying the flag of a State party; this may be common for ferries, but will be rarer for cruise ships as many are flagged in non-State parties. Alternatively, the Convention will apply if the contract of carriage has been made in a State party; this may raise difficult questions of private international law, especially where internet bookings are made.[394] Finally, the Convention will apply under Art 2 when the contractual place of departure or destination is in a State party; again, this will be easier to satisfy for ferry services in Europe then for 'fly-cruises' to more exotic parts of the world. In the absence of an Art 2 connection, the Athens Convention 2002 may not apply unless it is applied by national or regional law[395] or contractually incorporated in the passenger ticket.

---

386 Cf the Convention for the Unification of Certain Rules for International Carriage by Air (Montreal Convention) 1999 that governs the carriage of passengers by air.
387 Eg the *Herald of Free Enterprise* (1987), the *Scandinavian Star* (1990), the *Estonia* (1994): see 1.2.2(b).
388 It is enacted in the MSA 1995 s 183, Schedule 6, as amended.
389 It has 28 contracting States, mostly in Europe: *IMO Status of Treaties* (November 2018). Some major flag States, such as Greece, Malta, the Marshall Islands and Panama are parties, but some prominent flag States used by cruise ship companies, such as the Bahamas, are not parties.
390 See Regulation (EC) No 392/2009 of the European Parliament and of the Council of 23 April 2009 on the liability of carriers of passengers by sea in the event of accidents. This was passed to give effect to the Protocol (and Guidelines on Implementation, see 2.3.5). In effect the Regulation applied most of the Convention within the EU prior to its entry into force internationally, but some of its provisions still apply to supplement the Convention: see 2.3.6. See also the Merchant Shipping (Carriage of Passengers by Sea) Regulations (SI 2012/3152) [the UK Carriage of Passengers Regulations 2012]. See now the Merchant Shipping (Passengers' Rights) (Amendment etc.) (EU Exit) Regulations 2019 (SI 2019/649) aimed at maintaining the existing EU derived obligations after Brexit: see also 14.1 for Brexit issues.
391 See the Merchant Shipping (Convention Relating to the Carriage of Passengers and their Luggage by Sea) Order 2014 (SI 2014/1361). This inserted the text of the new convention into the MSA 1995 Sch 6 Part I and made consequential amendments to Part II.
392 Art 18.
393 See *Lewins*, 103–105.
394 See also 2.3.7.
395 Eg Regulation (EC) No 392/2009 Art 2, applying the convention to international carriage or that within a single member State.

The Athens Convention 2002 applies to passengers[396] who have contracts of carriage.[397] It will cover not only the person who made the contract, eg a parent, but also those who are carried "under" the contract, eg a spouse or children for whom the parent has acted as agent in buying a ticket.[398] It will therefore extend not only to cruise ships but also ferries, provided that these are "seagoing" vessels[399] engaged on international voyages.[400]

The expression "seagoing" is an unfortunate one, as it could mean a ship that is physically capable of going to sea, one that is legally capable of going to sea or one that actually in fact goes to sea (eg at the time of a relevant incident). The English courts have tended to favour the last criterion, eg to require there to be a "ship" that did go to "sea".[401] The Athens Convention has been applied to a RIB,[402] but almost certainly would not apply to a jet ski.[403] What is "sea" will probably vary according to the legislation of particular States; UK merchant shipping legislation tends to refer to waters beyond harbour or river mouths, but may extend to exposed coastal waters.[404] River craft, such as the *Marchioness* that sank in the River Thames in 1989 after a collision with the *Bowbelle*, would almost certainly not be seagoing, so the Athens Convention 2002 would not apply if they were wrecked.[405]

The Athens Convention 2002 does not cover all liabilities relating to passengers but merely death and personal injury, and loss of or damage to luggage. This means that for passengers who are rescued from a wreck the Convention would not deal with issues such as refunds of fares, damages for disappointment at a ruined holiday[406] and claims for additional expenditure after the rescue (eg hotels and air fares). These issues would be regulated by the ordinary rules of contract, including the passenger ticket and any applicable

---

396 It could also apply to truck drivers who do not have contracts separate from the contract for their vehicle; it also applies to vets or others accompanying live animals: see Art 1(4).

397 The UK has added a requirement that the contract be "for reward": see the MSA 1995 Sch 6 Part II para 9; *Gaskell, MSA 1995*, 21/360–21/261; *Lewins* 99. Friends merely on board the owner's yacht wrecked at sea would not normally be within the Convention. The position of volunteers on a sailing boat might need closer examination to see if a contractual relationship existed.

398 'Crew' on board an ocean-going yacht might be covered by a contract of employment, not carriage, but see *Cairns v Northern Light House and Calypso Marine* [2013] ScotCS CSOH 22 where a rigid inflatable boat [RIB] was used to transport an employee where it was the employer that had a contract of carriage. It was held that the employee was carried "under" the contact of carriage.

399 Art 1(3), which excludes hovercraft. In the UK, liabilities to passengers are governed by the Hovercraft Act 1968 and delegated legislation, in particular the Hovercraft (Civil Liability) Order 1986 (SI 1986/1305), as amended by SI 1987/1835. In effect, there is a curious hybrid liability system whereby passenger claims are dealt with under air law (with per passenger limits apparently still at £80,009), but with additional merchant shipping 'global' limits of liability based on the LLMC 1996, although calculated on the weight of the hovercraft (see SI 1998/1257, and 2.5): cf 2.3.3.

400 See Art 2. See 2.3.6 for domestic carriage.

401 See *Michael v Musgrave (Trading as YNYS Ribs) (The Sea Eagle)* [2011] EWHC 1438 (Admlty), [2012] 2 Lloyd's Rep 37, summarising the case law; *Lewins*, 100–102, 154–155; *Martinez Gutierrez*, 37. See also 10.2.7(a) for the equivalent expression under the WRC 2007.

402 *The Sea Eagle* [2012] 2 Lloyd's Rep 37.

403 Cf *Steedman v Scofield* [1992] 2 Lloyd's Rep 163.

404 See *The Sea Eagle* [2012] 2 Lloyd's Rep 37 [10–15].

405 The owners of the ship could however limit liability: see 2.3.3. For a more extensive discussion of "seagoing", see 10.2.7(a).

406 See *Lewins*, 243–256 and eg *Baltic Shipping Co v Dillon* (1991) 22 NSWLR (NSWCA) (1993) 136 CLR 344 (High Court of Australia).

consumer protection laws.⁴⁰⁷ EU law, in particular, provides extensive remedies for stranded or delayed passengers and the provision of alternative arrangements at no extra cost.⁴⁰⁸ EU law would provide an additional remedy after a wreck as it provides for an advance payment sufficient to cover immediate economic needs.⁴⁰⁹

2.3.2 Liability for death and injury

The primary liability under the Athens Convention 2002 is placed on the carrier (ie the "contracting carrier" with whom the contract of carriage was made), but the "performing carrier" (eg the shipowner) can also be jointly and severally liable.⁴¹⁰ This means that tour operators who may have chartered the ship can be liable as carrier if they make the contracts of carriage as principals.⁴¹¹ Claims against a carrier or performing carrier can only be brought in accordance with the Convention.⁴¹²

The Athens Convention 2002 Art 3 introduced a rather complicated liability scheme based partly on strict liability and partly on fault. There is a strict liability regime for the death or injury to passengers caused by a "shipping incident". Apart from the case where the passenger was guilty of contributory negligence,⁴¹³ the only defences for the carrier in Art 3(1) are two of the boilerplate IMO defences, ie where it proves that the incident "resulted from an act of war, hostilities, civil war, insurrection or a natural phenomenon of an exceptional, inevitable and irresistible character" or "was wholly caused by an act or omission done with the intent to cause the incident by a third party".⁴¹⁴ There is no defence

---

407 Eg under the Consumer Rights Act 2015; *Lewins* 205–216. The authors agree with *Lewins*, 115–119, that the Athens Convention 2002 does not provide an exclusive code in the same way as air carriage under the Warsaw Convention 1929 (as held by the House of Lords in *Sidhu v British Airways Plc* [1997] AC 430, [1997] 2 Lloyd's Rep 76).

408 See eg Directive (EU) 2015/2302 of the European Parliament and of the Council of 25 November 2015 on package travel and linked travel arrangements [the EC Package Travel Directive 2015] in force from 1 July 2018, as enacted in the UK in the Package Travel and Linked Travel Arrangements Regulations 2018 (SI 2018/634); Regulation (EU) No 1177/2010 of the European Parliament and of the Council of 24 November 2010 concerning the rights of passengers when travelling by sea and inland waterway [EU Passenger Rights Regulation 2010]; *Lewins*, 116–117, 206–216, 249–256.

409 Regulation (EC) No 392/2009 Art 6. The payment should be proportionate to the damage suffered and made within 15 days of the identification of the person entitled to damages; in the event of the death, the payment should not be less than €21,000. See SI 2019/649 (fn 390) for post-Brexit sterling figures.

410 See Arts 1(1), 4. Rights of recourse are preserved as between the charterer or operator and the shipowner. For charter liabilities, see 2.1.7, but note that the terms for charters of passenger ships may be very different to those for cargo ships.

411 In some circumstances, package holiday operators that are not contracting carriers within the Athens Convention 2002 might be liable under the EC Package Travel Directive 2015 Part 4; cf *Norfolk v Mytravel* [2004] 1 Lloyd's Rep 106, *Lee v Airtours Holidays Ltd* [2004] 1 Lloyd's Rep 683; *Lewins*, 249–256.

412 See Art 14; cf 2.6.2(a) for channelling under the CLC 1992; also *Lewins*, 117–119.

413 See Art 6. It is difficult to see how passengers might contribute to a wreck or stranding (apart from disobeying crew evacuation instructions), but there may be examples on small passenger craft where passengers interfere with operations.

414 Cf 10.3 (WRC 2007); also 2.6.2(a) (CLC 1992), 2.6.3 (Bunkers Convention 2001). The Athens Convention 2002 does not provide a defence to strict liability of the carrier where the incident was caused by the negligence of a State in relation to navigational aids such as buoys or markers; cf 10.3.3. If a ship were wrecked because of such negligence the carrier might be able to disprove its own fault in so far as the passenger's claims exceeded 250,000 sdrs, as explained below.

for negligent navigation or management of the ship; the "natural phenomenon" defence places a heavy evidential burden on the carrier and is much more difficult to satisfy than showing mere bad weather was involved with the wreck.

The concept of "shipping incident" is particularly important and is defined in Art 3(5)(a) to mean "shipwreck, capsizing, collision or stranding of the ship, explosion or fire in the ship, or defect in the ship". "Defect" is itself further defined in Art 3(5)(c) to refer to "malfunction, failure or non-compliance with applicable safety regulations" in respect of the ship or its equipment when used for purposes connected with the ship as a nautical entity,[415] both for ordinary navigation[416] and when dealing with emergencies.[417] However, the passenger would not need to point to a "defect" where death or injury to the passenger is "caused by" a "shipwreck".[418] Indeed, the wide definition of "shipping incident" means that it would apply to virtually every aspect of a major casualty involving a passenger ship[419] and the claimants would not have to prove that there was fault of the carrier.

The catch with strict liability under Art 3(1) is that it only extends up to 250,000 sdr per passenger.[420] The 250,000 sdr figure is not strictly a limit of liability,[421] but the first tier of a two-tier liability system. If the passenger's proven injury or death claim[422] exceeds this figure in a shipping incident then, for the excess, the carrier will still be liable[423] if it is at fault, but on the basis of a reversed burden of proof. That is it will have to prove that the incident which caused the loss occurred without its fault or that of its employees; here it could point to the fault of a colliding ship as being the entire cause of the wreck.[424]

Where the passenger is injured in a non-shipping incident, the liability of the carrier will be based on fault, with the burden of proof on the claimant.[425] This is designed to apply for 'hotel type' liabilities, eg food poisoning, and will not be directly relevant to wreck cases. Although it is arguable that a trip on a loose-fitting carpet or a fall down stairs in heavy seas would not technically be a "shipping incident",[426] it has been noted that the definition of "defect" in Art 3(5)(d) covers malfunctions or failures in the ship or equipment when

---

415 The Art 3(5)(c) definition is designed to exclude many defects in the parts of the ship that passengers might occupy, eg lounges, bedrooms or bars; ie the sort of facilities that might be found in hotels or leisure facilities on land. The effect of these being 'non-shipping incidents' is that there is no strict liability and the passenger must prove fault under Art 3(2).
416 Eg when the part of the ship is used for "propulsion, steering, safe navigation, mooring, anchoring, arriving at or leaving berth or anchorage".
417 Eg when the part of the ship is used for "escape, evacuation, . . . and disembarkation of passengers; or . . . damage control after flooding; or . . . for the launching of life saving appliances".
418 Or any of the other events listed in Art 3(5)(a).
419 Including the major recent passenger shipwrecks, eg: *Herald of Free Enterprise* (capsizing after bow door left open); *Scandinavian Star* (fire); *Estonia* (sinking after apparent defect in ship's bow door); *Costa Concordia* (stranding and capsizing after striking a rock).
420 £271,655 (US $345,625) at the IMF rates on 3 December 2018: as explained in 2.5.6(a), Table 2.5 and footnotes.
421 For which see 2.3.4.
422 For calculation of damages, see 2.3.3.
423 Subject to the limit of liability of 400,000 sdrs under Art 7: see 2.3.3.
424 As occurred when the *Empress of Ireland* was wrecked in 1914 owing entirely to the negligence of the collier *Storstad*: see *Canadian Pacific Ry Co. v SS Storstad* [1919] UKPC 124, [1920] AC 397.
425 Art 3(2).
426 As narrowly defined in Art 3(5)(a) and (c).

used for the "escape" or "evacuation" of passengers. A loose-fitting carpet could be such a failure if a passenger tripped during an orderly emergency evacuation, resulting in strict liability. Where the ship had taken on a list on stranding, a fall down stairs or a trip could be caused by the "stranding" and therefore would also be a shipping incident, again resulting in strict liability.

Similar issues of causation may arise if passengers are killed or injured after being evacuated from the ship. The Athens Convention 2002 applies only to incidents occurring in "the course of carriage".[427] That is defined in Art 1(8) to include the period when the passenger is on board the ship or "in the course of . . . disembarkation, and the period during which the passenger [is] transported by water from [the ship to land], if the sort of such transport is included in the fare or if the vessel used for this purpose of auxiliary transport has been put at the disposal of the passenger by the carrier". This provision is designed for normal transport, ie where there are ship to shore excursions, or where the passenger has finally disembarked at the port of destination. It seems unlikely that the fare would cover any "cost" for evacuating passengers, eg on a salvage or rescue vessel, and the carrier may have had no hand in making available auxiliary transport in the immediate aftermath of a casualty.[428]

In *Davis v Stena Line Ltd*[429] a passenger fell overboard from a ferry and died in the sea. It was common ground before the judge that the death occurred in the "course of carriage", and this was clearly a sensible concession in relation to an involuntary departure from the ship. Any other interpretation would deprive the liability provisions of their bite after a wreck, eg when many *Titanic* survivors died in the sea after jumping overboard. Their decision to jump overboard was hardly a consensual end to the anticipated contractual voyage.[430] In the language of the Athens Convention 2002, their loss was caused by a shipping incident in the course of carriage.

The question then arises as to when the Athens Convention 2002 ceases to apply, ie where death or injury occurs at later stages after a wreck. The mere fact that a passenger dies while ashore in hospital does not prevent the Convention from applying if the death was caused by the wreck or stranding. It is also clear that if the passenger is safely rescued and taken to land, then any subsequent injury, eg on a quayside or in a vehicle, will not be governed by the Convention,[431] and more general principles may apply.[432] A harder

---

427 See Art 3(6), which places upon the claimant the burden of proving that incidents occurred in the course of carriage.

428 It is inconceivable that passengers would be charged for the rescue. Salvors might be entitled to 'life salvage', but this would only be payable by those responsible for paying a salvage reward: see the Salvage Convention 1989 Art 18. In other circumstances auxiliary transport will be the responsibility of the contracting carrier and it is irrelevant that the passengers do not take luggage with them: see *Lawrence v NCL(Bahamas) Ltd (The Norwegian Jade)* [2017] EWCA Civ 2222, [2018] 1 Lloyd's Rep 607.

429 [2005] EWHC 420 (QB), [2005] 2 Lloyd's Rep 13 [36].

430 In the same way that cargo would not have been "discharged" under the Hague/Visby Rules if it was lost from the vessel after sinking: see 2.1.5(b).

431 Art 1(8)(a) concludes by stating that "carriage does not include the period during which [the passenger] is in a marine terminal or station or on a quay or in or on any other port installation". Although this is again contemplating normal disembarkation, it must surely apply after a wreck when a passenger is safely ashore and no longer at risk from the maritime voyage.

432 The assumption here is that the Athens Convention 2002 does not provide a complete code which excludes death and injuries not falling within the convention: see *Lewins* 118, and cf *Sidhu v British Airways Plc* [1997] 2

example would be where the passenger is injured in circumstances where the causative effects of the wreck are still being felt, eg where a passenger swims ashore from the wreck but is injured while climbing up a rocky cliff face. It is submitted that this could exceptionally be considered as an injury caused by the wreck and in the course of carriage.[433] A determination that the Athens Convention 2002 will apply in these post-wreck situations will not always be to the advantage of passengers. Although they can take advantage of the strict liability provisions and compulsory insurance, they can also be met by the Athens Convention's limits of liability and two-year time bar.

2.3.3 Compensation and limits of liability for death and injury

The Athens Convention 2002 refers to liability for "loss suffered" as a result of death or personal injury.[434] The burden of proving the extent of loss lies with the claimant under Art 3(6) but, with one exception, the Convention does not define or regulate the calculation of that loss. The exception is in Art 3(5)(d) which provides that "loss" shall not include punitive or exemplary damages. Apart from this, the damages for death or injury to which a passenger claimant will be entitled will be a matter for governing law as applied by the forum. During negotiations for the Convention it was apparent that the level of awards varied greatly between States. This reflected different standards of living and the level of damages awarded by courts to dependents of those killed or injured, but also the extent to which their national social insurance schemes provided cover for medical expenses or disability. For example, the level of damage awards following the death of a 40-year-old doctor with two children would in general be very considerably higher than that of a 20-year-old shop assistant with no children; it is cheap to kill the young. These disparities between States might also affect forum shopping.[435]

The Athens Convention 2002 Art 7(1) provides that there is a limit of liability of 400,000 sdr[436] per passenger, ie this is a limit applied in relation to each passenger killed or injured.[437] This figure would probably bite in the UK for the type of death claim by the family of a

---

Lloyd's Rep 76. Any liabilities may then have to be determined by any contract law provisions applicable after discharge, in so far as they are not inconsistent with general consumer protection laws (eg under the Consumer Rights Act 2015); and by any applicable tort laws (eg at the place of injury). See also Regulation (EC) No 864/2007 of the European Parliament and of the Council of 11 July 2007 on the law applicable to con-contractual relations (Rome II) [Rome II Regulation], Art 4.

433 Cf *Collins v Lawrence* [2017] EWCA Civ 2268, [2018] 1 Lloyd's Rep 603 [18], where the process of disembarkation was said to cover "the whole period of moving from the vessel to a *safe position* on the shore" (emphasis added). That case concerned a normal fishing trip and steps to a shingle beach.

434 The Athens Convention 2002 contains no equivalent to Art 17 of the Montreal Convention 1999 which restricts claims to "bodily injury", thereby excluding claims for psychological or emotional loss: and see *Lewins*, 111–112.

435 See 2.3.7.

436 £434,648 (US $553,000) at the IMF rates on 3 December 2018: cf 2.5.6(a), Table 2.5 and footnotes. Under Art 10, interest and legal costs are not included in the limits, and carriers can agree to higher limits under both Arts 7 and 8. Under Art 13, the limits can be broken by the familiar intent or recklessness test also used in the LLMC: see 2.5.7.

437 By contrast, the Montreal Convention 1999 provides for a strict liability first tier of up to 113,110 sdrs, and fault based liability *without limit* above that.

prosperous professional (eg doctor or lawyer), or where there was a serious injury needing long-term care. Like the LLMC 1996,[438] the limit applies to each "distinct occasion".[439]

It is important also to take into account the effect of Art 18. This makes the Athens Convention 2002 subject to global limits in other international conventions. In a similar manner to the Hague/Visby Rules, this means that in a major casualty such as a shipwreck, the passenger might face two limits: one under the Athens Convention 2002 and one under the LLMC 1976 or LLMC 1996.[440] The relationship between the Athens Convention 2002 and one of the global limitation conventions is complicated by the permutations presented as a result of a State's ability (i) to be a party to one, all, or none of these conventions; (ii) to elect to have unlimited liability under the Athens Convention 2002, or the LLMC 1996, or both. These permutations have to be borne in mind when considering the limits that might apply to a passenger claim.

The LLMC 1976 introduced an LLMC Art 7 *global* limit for the *whole* ship in respect of passenger claims—separate from the normal Art 6 limits.[441] The Art 7 limit was calculated by taking the certified number of passengers that the ship was certified to carry and multiplying this by 46,666 sdrs.[442] This was itself subject to a 25 million sdr cap.[443] For a major disaster with several thousand passengers this overall cap was potentially punitively low.[444] The LLMC 1996 Art 7(1) replaced this global limit for passenger claims with higher figures of 175,000 sdrs[445] and abolished the 25 million sdr cap. Table 2.2 shows the limits available under Art 7 for ships of different carrying capacities.

Table 2.2 LLMC 1996 Art 7 passenger limits of liability

Ship's passenger capacity	LLMC 1996 sdr amounts	£ sterling[1]	US$[2]
20 passengers	3,500,000 sdrs	£3,803,170	$4,838,750
500 passengers	87,500,000 sdrs	£95,079,250	$120,968,750
1,000 passengers	175,000,000 sdrs	£190,158,500	$241,937,500
2,000 passengers	350,000,000 sdrs	£380,317,000	$483,875,000
5,000 passengers	875,000,000 sdrs	£950,792,500	$1,209,687,500

[1] The calculation uses the IMF figures at 3 December 2018 with the rate of conversion of 1 sdr = £1.08662.

[2] As the international currency of shipping is the US$, this column gives comparative figures for 3 December 2018 based on 1 sdr = US$1.3825. The US is *not* party to the LLMC, so the US$ figures are given by way of example only.

---

438 See 2.5.6(b).

439 Art 7(1) and 2.5.6(b). In the case of wreck, it is hard to see that there would be more than one such occasion (unless a passenger had already been injured in a separate incident earlier in the voyage).

440 See generally, N Gaskell "New Limits for Passengers and Others in the United Kingdom" (1998) LMCLQ 312 [*Gaskell, New Limits for Passengers*]; *Martinez Gutierrez*, Chapter 4.

441 See generally 2.5.4(a).

442 £50,708 (US $64,516) at the IMF rates on 3 December 2018: cf 2.5.6(a), Table 2.5 and footnotes.

443 £27,165,500 (US $34,562,500) at the IMF rates on 3 December 2018.

444 Particularly when combined with the Athens Convention 1974 limits of 46,000 sdr per passenger—before global limits under the LLMC 1976 were applied.

445 £190,159 (US$241,938) at the IMF rates on 3 December 2018.

These limits again apply to the overall theoretical carrying *capacity* of the vessel. They are available if only one passenger is killed or injured, but they only really bite when there is a major disaster. As the question of limitation of liability for death or injury after shipwrecks was controversial, States were given the ability in the LLMC 1996, in a new Art 15(3)bis, to have a higher (or unlimited liability) in their national law. In the UK, the government decided to take advantage of this option so as to provide that there was to be no limit for passenger claims in respect of seagoing ships under the LLMC 1996 in UK law.[446] The reason was that it proposed to allow carriers to limit instead under the Athens Convention 1974 (and later 2002).[447] The limit was retained in part, however, for small non-seagoing ships[448] but their Art 7 LLMC passenger limit in the UK is now 175,000 sdrs *per passenger*,[449] ie there is no *global* passenger limit for such ships but one closer in nature to that under Athens Convention 2002 Art 7.[450]

The result of these complicated legislative choices in the UK is that after the wreck of a large passenger ship, UK courts will only apply the limits of the Athens Convention 2002 to passenger claims against the carrying ship. The potential exposure of carriers (and their insurers) is still very high, even with the limits. Some examples of that exposure, and the need to create separate limits to deal with terrorism risks, are dealt with in relation to compulsory insurance.[451]

2.3.4 Passengers' luggage

The Athens Convention 2002 also regulates liability for loss of or damage to passengers' "luggage",[452] but has a particular set of rules for "cabin luggage".[453] However, Art 5

---

446 This was originally achieved by inserting a new para 6 into the MSA 1995 Sch 7 Part II which makes clear that the LLMC 1996 Art 7 does not apply to seagoing ships: see *Gaskell, New Limits for Passengers*, 325–330.

447 The government decided not to take advantage of Art 7(2) of the Athens Convention 2002 which also gives States the right to elect to have higher (or unlimited) liability under *that* Convention in its national law; ie the UK applies the Athens Convention 2002 limits to seagoing ships.

448 The small ship (under 300 gt) limits were not increased when the UK gave effect to the 2012/2015 increases in the LLMC 1996 limits: see DfT, "Government Response to Consultation: Changes to Domestic Legislation Implementing Certain International Maritime Liability Conventions" (2016); Merchant Shipping Act 1995 (Amendment) Order 2016 (SI 2016/1061) and 2.5.6(a). The original 2016 Consultation appeared to assume that LLMC 1996 Art 7 had already been disapplied to seagoing ships, which is an indication of the complexity of the legislation.

449 See the the MSA 1995 Sch 7 Part II para 1, as inserted by the Merchant Shipping (Convention on Limitation of Liability for Maritime Claims) (Amendment) Order 1998 (SI 1998/1258). Had this not been done there would have been no limit at all for such non-seagoing ships, as the Athens Convention 2002 only applies to seagoing ships and there was no equivalent in the MSA 1995 Sch 6 (Athens Convention) to Sch 7 Part II para 1 (LLMC applied to ships whether seagoing or not): see *Gaskell, New Limits for Passengers*, 328–329.

450 Albeit set at a lower level than the 400,000 sdr per passenger limit for seagoing ships. Moreover, it seems that the limit would also reduce the strict liability tier 1 level from 250,000 sdrs to 175,000 sdrs.

451 See 2.3.5.

452 Defined in Art 1(5) to mean any article or vehicle carried by the carrier under a contract of carriage. This would cover cars on a ferry, but the provision specifically excludes articles and vehicles that are themselves carried under a contract of *carriage*. Eg, trucks on ferries would normally be carried on the basis of a contract in a consignment note or waybill in which the Hague/Visby Rules may be incorporated: see 2.1.5(a).

453 Defined in Art 1(6) to mean luggage which the passengers have in their cabins or is otherwise in their possession, custody or control, including that which is in or on a vehicle (eg a ferry). This should include eg suitcases, clothing, sports equipment, computers and phones.

specifically excludes liability for valuables[454] unless deposited with the *carrier* for safe-keeping.[455] For cabin luggage, liability is based on the fault or neglect of the carrier, but there is a reverse burden of proof for shipping incidents.[456] That is the carrier must prove that the loss or damage was not caused by its fault. This might be difficult to prove after most wrecks, where some form of negligent navigation is usually involved, but not where a sinking was caused wholly by the negligence of a colliding ship.[457] For loss or damage to other luggage (eg a car on a ferry), the passenger must prove fault.

Passengers may often need to rely on personal travel insurance as, after a wreck, they may not always be able to claim for all their property loss, particularly as there are quite low limits of liability for luggage, especially for vehicles. The Athens Convention 2002 Art 8 provides the following limits of liability in relation to luggage: vehicles, 12,700 sdrs;[458] cabin luggage, 2,250 sdrs;[459] other luggage, 3,375 sdrs.[460] The limit applies to the total in each category, not per item of luggage.

2.3.5 Compulsory insurance

During negotiations for the Athens Convention 2002, there was serious consideration as to whether any insurance liability scheme should be based on personal accident insurance of the type obtained by passengers themselves before travelling or going on holiday (and sourced from the general insurance market).[461] In the event, Art 4bis largely follows the model of other IMO liability conventions,[462] but requires the (contracting) carrier to obtain insurance for its liabilities when passengers are carried in a ship carrying more than 12 passengers.[463] The minimum level of insurance is 250,000 sdrs per passenger, ie the level of strict liability.[464] As usual, a certificate of financial or other security will be required for

---

454 Valuables includes "monies, negotiable securities, gold, silverware, jewellery, ornaments, works of art", but there is also a catch-all "or *other* valuables", which is not defined. A very expensive watch could be a "valuable", like jewellery, but if it is generally worn on the person for functional rather than decorative purposes it should perhaps be treated as normal personal luggage, like phones, rather than valuable property being incidentally carried on board. In any event there is a limit of liability for luggage which would act as a delimiter in cases of doubt.
455 Ie not in a cabin safe: see *Lee v Airtours Holidays Ltd* [2004] 1 Lloyd's Rep 683 [38].
456 See 2.3.2.
457 Here the passenger's claim would be against the colliding ship: see 2.4.
458 £13,800 (US $17,558), including luggage in the vehicle. The carriage contract can agree a deductible (ie the amount the passenger must pay first) per vehicle of 330 sdrs (£359, US$456): calculations at the IMF rates on 3 December 2018..
459 £2,445 (US $3,111), with possible deductibles of £162 (US$206); calculations as in previous fn.
460 £3,667 ($4,666), with possible deductibles of £162 (US$206); calculations as in previous fns.
461 By contrast, the Montreal Convention 1999 Art 52 only requires States to ensure there is "adequate insurance" for liabilities, and does not provide for direct action. The EU provided in 2004 that there was a minimum insurance requirement of 250,000 sdrs per passenger.
462 Eg the CLC 1992 (see 2.6.2(a), the Bunkers Convention 2001 (see 2.6.3) and the WRC 2007 (see 10.8).
463 Art 4bis(1).
464 But not the level of maximum per passenger liability under Art 7 of 400,000 sdrs. In fact, carriers will probably have insurance cover beyond the 250,000 figure; see 2.9.6(b). Where that cover exists, passengers might be able to use the Third Parties (Rights Against Insurers) Act 2010 to proceed against the insurer for the excess and s 9(6) would prevent the insurer from relying on a 'pay or be paid' clause in in respect of liability for death or personal injury: see 2.9.6(c).

ships flying the flag of State parties,[465] but State parties are also required to exercise port state control measures to ensure that ships, wherever registered, carry the appropriate certificate.[466] There is also provision for direct action against the insurer, with the usual IMO restrictions on insurer defences.[467]

Table 2.3 gives an idea of the possible exposure of the insurers if sued under the direct action provisions[468] after a passenger ship sinks with the death of all passengers and the 250,000 sdr per passenger insurance cap applies.

Table 2.4 gives an idea of the possible exposure of carriers (and their insurers) if a passenger ship sinks with the death of all passengers and the carrier can limit to 400,000 sdrs per passenger.

Table 2.3 Athens Convention 2002: maximum exposure with direct insurer liability

Number of passengers	250,000 sdr insurer's direct action limit	£ sterling[1]	US$[2]
500 passengers	125,000,000 sdr	£135,827,500	$172,812,500
1,000 passengers	250,000,000 sdr	£271,655,000	$345,625,000
2,000 passengers	500,000,000 sdr	£543,310,000	$691,250,000
5,000 passengers	1,250,000,000 sdr	£1,358,275,000	$1,728,125,000

[1] The calculation uses the IMF figures at 3 December 2018 with the rate of conversion of 1 sdr = £1.08662.

[2] As the international currency of shipping is the US$, this column gives comparative figures for 3 December 2018 based on 1 sdr = US$1.3825. The US is *not* party to the Athens Convention 2002, so the US$ figures are given by way of example only.

Table 2.4 Athens Convention 2002: maximum exposure with passenger limits

Number of passengers	400,000 sdr per passenger limits	£ sterling[1]	US$[2]
500 passengers	200,000,000 sdrs	£217,324,000	$276,500,000
1,000 passengers	400,000,000 sdrs	£434,648,000	$553,000,000
2,000 passengers	800,000,000 sdrs	£869,296,000	$1,106,000,000
5,000 passengers	2,000,000,000 sdrs	£2,173,240,000	$2,765,000,000

[1] The calculation uses the IMF figures at 3 December 2018 with the rate of conversion of 1 sdr = £1.08662.

[2] As the international currency of shipping is the US$, this column gives comparative figures for 3 December 2018 based on 1 sdr = US$1.3825. The US is *not* party to the Athens Convention 2002, so the US$ figures are given by way of example only.

---

465 Art 4bis(12). It is noticeable that many passenger ships are flagged in, or have been transferred to, non-State parties.
466 Art 4bis(13).
467 Art 4bis(10); see also 2.6.2(a), 10.8.4 for discussion of such defences.
468 Art 10(1), (10). Cf the insurer 'cap' under the WRC 2007: see 10.8.5.

These tables obviously show worst case scenarios, but it can be seen that the potential exposure of carriers can be huge. During the drafting stage of the Athens Convention 2002, the P&I Clubs were concerned about the overall exposure, which partly explains why there was agreement to the relatively low limit of 400,000 sdr.[469]

During the negotiations the Clubs were particularly concerned about the absence of a specific "terrorism" defence, partly because such risks are treated as war risks outside normal Club cover[470] and subject to separate market insurance. The defence in Art 3(1)(b) only relates to third party acts, eg a bomb explosion, that "wholly" cause the incident. Although this is the same defence as in the other IMO liability conventions, the wreck of a large modern passenger ship carries with it not only the risk of large wreck removal claims[471] but also the potential for thousands of passenger claims. Moreover, by comparison with oil tankers or container ships, there is greater scope for access to passenger ships by unauthorised persons or passengers with terrorist intent; any failure in security measures would mean that the incident was not "wholly" caused by terrorism.

The final version of the Athens Convention 2002 was not changed to meet the terrorism concerns; States in effect called the bluff of the Clubs (and to some extent lost). The terrorism issue threatened to prevent the entry into force of the Convention as the Clubs indicated that they might not be able to provide the Convention certificates if they were unable to obtain market cover or reinsurance. Some Clubs were also concerned that large passenger risks might no longer be mutual enough for the vast majority of shipowners operating mainly cargo ships.

Negotiations took place at the IMO Legal Committee and "Guidelines for Implementation of the Athens Convention" were agreed in 2006.[472] In effect, these are like an amendment to the 2002 Protocol dressed up as implementation guidelines, albeit theoretically allowing States to change their position if the state of the insurance market improves. The Guidelines provide that, when adopting the Convention, States should make reservations allowing insurers to provide them with separate 'Blue Card' insurance certificates covering non-war risks and war risks. In respect of specified war and terrorist risks, States should accept that a carrier's liability is limited to 250,000 sdrs per passenger on each distinct occasion,[473] or 340 million sdrs[474] overall per ship for each distinct occasion. States adopting the convention have in fact made such reservations[475] so that these are now the operative figures.

Some P&I Clubs have traditionally provided cover for passenger liabilities within their Rules, while others only make it available as an additional agreed cover.[476] Owing to the limits of the insurance market, overall Club cover for passenger liabilities is normally

---

469 By comparison with the Montreal Convention 1999 where there was no such limit for passengers, but where the maximum number of passengers in a plane would be much lower than in most ships: see fn 461 above and 2.3.3 (fn 437).

470 See 2.9.6(a)–(b).

471 As with *Costa Concordia*: see 1.2.5.

472 See IMO Circular Letter No 1758, 20 November 2006; see E Røsaeg, "Passenger liabilities and insurance: terrorism and war risks", Chapter 12 in R Thomas (ed), *Liability Regimes in Contemporary Maritime Law* (Informa Law/Routledge, 2007); *Martinez Gutierrez*, 142–144.

473 Ie the strict liability limit: see also 2.5.6(b).

474 £369,450,800 (US$470,050,000) at the sdr rate for 3 December 2018.

475 See eg *IMO Status of Treaties* (November 2018) for examples of reservations.

476 See 2.9.6(b) for the cover; cf the reinsurance position, 10.8.6.

restricted to US$2 billion per event, or US$3 billion if combined with seafarer claims.[477] For the largest passenger ship shown in Table 2.4,[478] it may be necessary for carriers to arrange additional insurance for liabilities under the Athens Convention 2002.

2.3.6 Domestic carriage

The Athens Convention 2002 only applies to international carriage (ie between different States). In fact, the UK had long applied the Athens Convention 1974 to domestic carriage in seagoing ships, where the place of departure and destination under the contract was in the UK.[479]

As with any convention, a State can always apply the whole of the Athens Convention 2002 regime to carriage in that single State (ie domestic carriage). The EU Regulation (EC) No 392/2009 did this for all EU States by phasing in the application of the Athens Convention liability regime to apply to domestic carriage on ships of different sizes (Classes A, B, C and D),[480] ie to allow a transition period for smaller operators.[481] The UK Carriage of Passengers Regulations 2012 support the EU Regulation by applying it to ships in two categories (A and B) for the carriage of passengers by sea solely within the UK.[482] Where a passenger craft is wrecked that is not seagoing and not within Classes A and B, liability to the passengers will fall outside the Athens Convention 2002 and will therefore have to be decided under ordinary principles of negligence and contract law, but as regulated by consumer legislation.[483] Note, however, that limitation of liability may still be available to the shipowner.[484] The EU Passenger Rights Regulation 2010 also provides additional rights that can also apply to seagoing ships under 300 gt operating in domestic transport.

2.3.7 Passenger claims and forum issues

The Athens Convention 2002 Art 16 has a two-year time bar which is shorter than the normal three-year time limit for injury or death claims on land.[485] For injured passengers this

---

477 See 2.9.6(b) (fn 1429).
478 Cf the passenger capacity of the *Symphony of the Seas*: see 2.3.
479 Eg for trips to the Channel Islands: see the Carriage of Passengers and their Luggage by Sea (Domestic Carriage) Order 1987 (SI 1987/670). For non-seagoing ships (necessarily restricted to domestic carriage), the UK applied limits of liability not under the Athens Convention but under the LLMC 1996: see 2.3.3.
480 Defined in Directive 2009/45/EC (Recast) of 25 June 2009 on safety rules and standards for passenger ships. Class A ships are those engaged on domestic voyages operating at greater distances from the coast than B, C or D. Class B ships are passenger ships engaged on domestic voyages where they are at no point more than 20 miles from the line of coast. Class C are ships engaged on domestic voyages operating in seas where expected wave heights are low and they are never more than 15 miles from a place of refuge or 5 miles from a line of coast where shipwrecked persons can land. Class D are never more than 6 or 3 miles from refuge or coastline.
481 After 31 December 2018 the transition period has ended for ships in Classes A and B. The EU undertook a Consultation in 2016 on the effect of the Regulation, but no report has yet eventuated, only a summary of responses: https://ec.europa.eu/transport/modes/maritime/consultations/2016-maritime-liability_en.
482 For Class A ships, as from 30 December 2016, and for Class B ships after 30 December 2018: see reg 4.
483 Eg the Consumer Rights Act 2015.
484 See 2.3.3.
485 See the Limitation Act 1980 s 11. Many of the reported cases on the Convention have involved the time bar (eg *The Sea Eagle* [2012] 2 Lloyd's Rep 37) and it could be a trap for practitioners.

runs from the "date of disembarkation".[486] In the case of death "during carriage" the time runs from "the date when the passenger should have disembarked", ie at the intended final port of destination. Where a passenger is injured "during carriage" and dies "after disembarkation", the time runs from the date of death, but with a maximum of three years from the "date of disembarkation". These provisions are not really designed for shipwrecks where the carriage terminates involuntarily, eg when the ship sinks and the passenger jumps overboard, but it would seem that this would be in the course of "carriage".[487] The law of the Court seised of the case governs the grounds for suspending or interrupting the time bar, but there is a backstop of five years from disembarkation, or (if earlier) a period of three years from when the claimant knew or ought reasonably to have known of the injury, loss or damage caused by the incident.

The Athens Convention 2002 Art 17(1) gives passengers a wide choice of jurisdictions in which to sue,[488] provided the court is located in a State party. The result of this wide choice is that the passengers on a wrecked cruise ship will often be able to sue in a wide variety of States. Carriers cannot restrict this choice by a contractual choice of jurisdiction clause.[489] A foreign shipowner can be sued in its principal place of business, but the choices to sue it in the passenger's home State may be more restricted.[490] Passengers could sue in the place of departure or destination according to the contract of carriage, but this will not include the home State of the passenger who has flown to join a cruise elsewhere. Likewise, although passengers can sue in the court of their permanent residence, or where the contract of carriage is made,[491] these options are only available if the defendant "has a place of business and is subject to jurisdiction in that State". Passengers may also face possible jurisdictional conflicts where carriers seek to limit liability, eg under the LLMC 1976 or 1996 in a different State to that where the liability hearing is held.[492]

Recognition and enforcement of judgments in State parties is the general rule under Art 17bis, but Art 17bis(3) allows States to apply their own equivalent rules. This caveat was designed for the EU which applies its internal rules.[493]

2.4 Wreck and collision liability

2.4.1 Liability[494]

A collision between ships may result in the wreck of one or both of them, along with any cargo, and respective liabilities will need to be unravelled. Liability for collisions between

---

486 See Art 16(2)(a). Presumably this includes the date of a forced disembarkation after a wreck (rather than the planned date at the end of the voyage), although this sits uneasily with Art 16(2)(b).
487 See 2.3.2.
488 The choice applies also to the direct action claim under Art 4bis: see Art 17(2) and 2.3.5.
489 See Art 18.
490 See *Lewins*, 300–324.
491 This itself may cause uncertainties with email bookings when an electronic message is "received" in a foreign State according to e-commerce legislation.
492 See 2.3.3 and cf 2.5.9.
493 See eg EU Council Decision of 12 December 2011 concerning the accession of the EU to the Athens Convention 2002 etc, 2012/23/EU and Brussels Regulation I Recast; *Lewins*, 304–305.
494 See generally, S Gault, S Hazelwood (gen eds), *Marsden & Gault on Collisions at Sea* (14th ed, Sweet and Maxwell, 2016) [*Marsden & Gault*].

ships is merely an example of the default position in most systems of tort law, ie a claim is usually based on proof of negligence causing loss.[495] That negligence will usually arise from faults in navigation, but can also arise from negligence in the preparation, planning or supervision of a voyage. In all these cases the burden of proof will be on the person alleging negligence.

In some circumstances strict liability regimes might operate in the maritime context. Wreck removal is a prime example of where strict liability has been applied in maritime law.[496] There are other examples of strict liability in the context of incidents of navigation,[497] which might be relevant to some claimants when there is a wreck. One example is where there is damage to harbour facilities. Thus, the Harbours Docks and Piers Clauses Act (HDPCA) 1847 s 74 provides that a shipowner whose ship damages listed harbour facilities will be "answerable" (ie liable) to the authority owning the facility.[498] Such provisions are typical internationally.[499] In the context of wreck law, this simply means that a shipowner that is without fault when its ship is blown into a jetty and sinks may end up paying not only for wreck removal[500] but also for the costs of repairing the jetty.[501]

2.4.2 Wreck and causation

The ship *C* may be damaged in a collision with the *D*, but later is wrecked because its master negligently refuses to take prompt salvage assistance, eg by accepting pumps or taking a tow.[502] In these circumstances it might be held that the actions of the *C*'s master constituted a *novus actus interveniens*, so that the *D* was relieved of all liability on the basis that it was the fault of the *C*'s master that caused his ship to be wrecked.[503]

---

495 An innocent ship may go aground while taking action to avoid the negligent navigation of another, but no actual collision occurs. The same general principles apply, based on negligence.

496 See 7.1, 7.2, 10.2.1, 11.1.2, 11.1.3, 11.3.4.

497 Strict liability might arise in national labour laws, or for product liability (eg where defective parts are supplied to a ship). These are beyond the scope of this book, but note *Coltman and another v Bibby Tankers Ltd (The Derbyshire)* [1988] 1 Lloyd's Rep 109 where crew members sought to rely on the Employer's Liability (Defective Equipment) Act 1969 in order to raise a presumption that a ship was defective and that its owners were responsible. See also 2.2 for crew claims.

498 A defence was recognised where a ship had been abandoned and later drifted into harbour facilities: see *River Wear Commissioners v Adamson* (1877) 2 App Cas 743. This rather strange decision could undermine what is an early form of strict liability and has since been confined to cases where no human agency was involved: see *The Mostyn* [1928] AC 57, *BP Exploration Operating Co Ltd v Chevron Shipping (The Chevron North America)* [2002] 1 Lloyd's Rep 77, 99.

499 Eg in Australia, there are equivalents, such as the Transport Infrastructure Act 1994 (Qld) s 281E.

500 See 10.2, 11.1,.

501 Although note that, depending on the wording of the applicable local legislation, this liability may only be for the reinstatement costs rather than consequential losses while the jetty or other facility is out of action. Further, the damage to "harbour works, basins and waterways and aids to navigation" would be subject to limitation under the LLMC 1996 Art 2(a): see 2.5.4(a).

502 See eg the Government of Gibraltar, "Report on the Investigation of the Grounding of the MV *Fedra*", and 10.2.5.

503 See eg *The Fritz Thyssen* [1967] 1 Lloyd's Rep 104, 112, [1967] 2 Lloyd's Rep 199. If the fault of Ship *C* was held still to be weighing on Ship *B*'s master (eg forcing him to make difficult decisions in a hurry), then it might be possible to sub-apportion the liability: see *The Calliope* [1970] 1 Lloyd's Rep 84; *Marsden & Gault*,

Similar issues of causation may arise when a ship sinks, eg after a collision, but a third ship is then damaged by striking the wreck. If the colliding ships were negligent, they could expect to be liable for the damage to the third ship,[504] as the original negligence was the cause of the later striking. It will be relevant to ask whether the third ship could have avoided the collision by the exercise of good navigation (eg through a proper lookout). If this subsequent collision was in broad daylight and the wreck was only partly submerged, but clearly visible over a long distance, the owner of the third ship might be held completely responsible for its subsequent damage as it could be said that there was a clear line between the two acts of negligence.[505] Where the navigation was not so straightforward, eg in limited visibility or in a narrow channel, it is more likely that the third ship will have been contributorily negligent.[506]

Where a ship sinks and is wrecked without the fault of its owner, the latter may be strictly liable for wreck removal costs,[507] but without more it would have no automatic liability to another ship that was damaged by striking the wreck.[508] A failure by the shipowner to report the wreck as required[509] so that it could be marked or buoyed by a public authority could itself be an act of negligence giving rise to liability to the other ship.[510] Where the owner or operator[511] of the ship that is wrecked has given taken all reasonable steps immediately after the casualty to warn other users (eg by giving all appropriate notices), it would be difficult to find that it has been negligent; but this would not excuse it if the original cause of the sinking was negligence.[512]

In some circumstances it may be possible to sue a harbour or other public authority for failing to mark the wreck, either for breach of a statutory duty or at common law. Most such public authorities in the UK have powers, not duties, in relation to wreck removal,[513] which would make such a statutory claim more difficult.[514] The case law shows that there

---

604–614, 639–645. Note the difficulties that this solution can cause when limitation of liability is also involved: see 2.5.6(b); *Gaskell, Limitation of Liability*, 1013–1020.

504 *Dee Conservancy Board v McConnell* [1928] 2 KB 159, 163, 166, 168–169; cf *The Douglas* (1882) 7 PD 751, where the only issue was negligence after the sinking; *Marsden & Gault*, 552–553.

505 Cf *Admiralty Commissioners (The Radstock) v Owners of the SS Volute* [1922] 1 AC 129, 144 (1921) 9 LL L L Rep 439. Cf also the *Tricolor*, sinking in 2002 when three other ships collided with the wreck before buoys could be laid: see I Brynildsen, "Tricolor—The Collision, Sinking and Wreck Removal", 178 Gard News Insight (2005) and 10.2.5.

506 It will then be necessary to apportion liability between the colliding vessels and the third ship, all of which were negligent: see *Miraflores (Owners) v George Livanos (Owners) (The Miraflores and The Abadesa)* [1967] 1 AC 826, [1967] 1 Lloyd's Rep 191; also 2.4.4.

507 See eg 10.2, 11.1, 11.3.4(a). There may also be liability in negligence or nuisance: see 11.1.1.

508 There would be no liability to the other ship under the WRC 2007: see 10.2.2.

509 See now the WRC 2007 Art 5, and 9.1.3; also the MSA 1995 s 255B; 11.3.3(a).

510 *Dee Conservancy Board v McConnell* [1928] 2 KB 159.

511 Note that the WRC 2007 Art 5 imposes obligations to report on the master and "operator", which includes the owner and ship's managers: see Art 1(9); also 9.1.3(a), 11.3.3(a).

512 See also *Marsden & Gault*, 553.

513 See 11.1.2, 11.1.3, but cf 11.3.5; also *Marsden & Gault*, 411.

514 The WRC 2007 Arts 7 and 8 impose obligations on States to warn mariners of wrecks of which they are aware and to mark the wreck. The obligations are not absolute but refer to "practicable" or "reasonable" steps, which gives much leeway to authorities faced with limited resources. It is arguable that a failure to comply could give rise to an action for negligence, but it is not clear that a breach of the statutory duty under the MSA 1995 s

are difficult questions arising both under the many local statutory provisions as well as at common law.[515]

2.4.3 Damages for wreck

The damages that might be claimed in an ordinary collision action[516] resulting in a wreck could include the cost of replacing the sunken or wrecked vessel; the cost of hiring a temporary replacement until a new vessel can be bought; and the costs of salving or removing a sunken or grounded ship; the consequential losses, such as lost profits, that the sunken ship would have made until a replacement is found. In addition, there will be costs of replacing or repairing lost or damaged cargo.

Negligent navigation leading to a wreck might sometimes involve persons other than those directly involved in commercial shipping. A ship might catch fire and explode in a port with catastrophic consequences, eg massive loss of life damage and damage to property.[517] Here claimants would have the burden of proving negligence but may also face the same difficulties facing States in wreck removal claims, ie single ship companies, with few assets or insurance, but always with an ability to limit liability. Such claimants would benefit from an international liability convention backed by compulsory insurance.[518]

All parties involved in a collision resulting in a wreck may suffer various consequential or economic losses, eg dislocation to commercial operations caused by delay. The extent to which these are recoverable in English law is limited where the claimant is not actually the owner or bareboat charterer of the ship damaged or lost.[519] Thus, a time charterer of a ship wrecked in a collision will not normally be owed a duty of care by the negligent owner of the other ship; so there could be no claim for lost profit or even wasted hire. This approach was upheld by the Privy Council in a 1985 appeal from Australia,[520] although it is noticeable that Australian law now recognises maritime economic loss claims in many circumstances.[521] This approach might allow a negligence claim where a ship was trapped (but undamaged) in a harbour owing to the negligent sinking of another ship, whereas such a claim would apparently not be allowed in England.[522] It is possible that an English 'blocking' claim would be more successful if framed in public nuisance as special

---

255C(2) was intended to give rise to civil liability as opposed to being a public law obligation: see 9.2.1, 9.2.3, 11.3.3(b).

515 See *Marsden & Gault*, 411.

516 See *Marsden & Gault*, Chapter 17. There is no international convention on collision damages, although discussions were undertaken in the Comité Maritime International (CMI) in the 1980s. These gave rise to a set of non-binding guidelines called the Lisbon Rules 1985. These are useful as guidelines, but care must be taken by English lawyers as in some areas (eg on economic loss) the Rules are phrased in a manner inconsistent with, or go further than, English law.

517 Eg the explosion in Halifax (Nova Scotia) in 1917: see 2.6.4 (fn 961).

518 Eg the HNSC 2010, if it comes into force: see 2.6.4.

519 *The World Harmony* [1967] P 341; *Marsden & Gault*, 650–651; also 2.1.7(c).

520 *The Mineral Transporter and The Ibaraki Maru* [1985] 2 Lloyd's Rep 303; N Gaskell, "Economic Loss in the Maritime Context" [1985] LMCLQ 81, N Gaskell, "Economic Loss in Collision Cases" [1985] LMCLQ 407.

521 See *Quenos Pty Ltd v Ship APL Sydney* [2009] FCA 1090.

522 See *Anglo-Algerian SS Co Ltd v Houlder Line Ltd* [1908] 1 KB 659. The harbour authority might have a claim in negligence.

damage suffered from the blocking of a public waterway.[523] As a result of the restrictive approach to economic loss, it may be necessary for those suffering it to look to contractual arrangements.[524]

2.4.4 Apportionment of liability

Where both ships are at fault for a collision, the liability of their owners will be apportioned in States such as the UK according to the Convention for the Unification of Certain Rules of Law with respect to Collisions between Vessels (Collision Convention) 1910[525] on the basis of the degree to which each ship was at fault. For instance, if the ship L was 10% at fault for a collision resulting in the sinking of T, the L would be responsible for 10% of T's loss. If the owners of T claimed for its total loss and wreck removal (eg amounting to, say, $20 million), the L would be liable to pay $2 million.[526] So, a small proportion of liability can still result in a substantial liability, especially where the damages claimed by each are very different; eg in the above example, if the L had sustained only insignificant damage herself. At this stage statutory limitation of liability will become relevant, as each ship may be able to limit its liability to the other.[527] Counterclaims will normally be set off against each other before limits of liability are applied,[528] so the size of each ship (and therefore its limit) may be very significant. If the L were a small ship with a low limit, that might result in the T bearing most of its loss itself. If the L were large with a high limit, its owners would be very vulnerable to a collision action in which the T would be the claimant.[529]

Cargo owners involved in a wreck will also be affected by the proportionate fault rule in the Collision Convention 1910.[530] This means that when a carrying ship, the C, sinks after a collision, the owner whose cargo is lost may be forced to bring its tort of negligence claim against the colliding ship, the D, that was at wholly fault.[531] If the carrying ship, the C, were wholly at fault, the cargo owner would have no claim against the D. If the C and the D were

---

523 *Rose v Miles* (1815) 4 M&S 101, *Tate & Lyle Food Distribution Ltd v Greater London Council* [1983] 2 AC 509 [1983] 2 Lloyd's Rep 117; *Marsden & Gault*, 553–554. Cf *Esso Petroleum Corp v Southport Corp* [1956] AC 218, [1955] 2 Lloyd's Rep 655.

524 Eg insurance, or through charterparty or bill of lading provisions.

525 As now enacted in the MSA 1995 ss 187–190; under s 192 these provisions can apply to Royal Navy and other government ships. See also H Brandon, "Apportionment in British Courts" (1977) Tul L Rev 1025.

526 Under the MSA 1995 s 187(7) the proportionate fault rules apply not only to the normal collision damages claim (eg for repairs or total loss) but also to "any salvage or other expenses, consequent upon that fault, recoverable at law by way of damages". Those other expenses would clearly include wreck removal expenses.

527 See 2.5.

528 *The Stoormvaart Maatschappy Nederland v Peninsular and Oriental Steam Navigation Company (The Voorwaarts and The Khedive)* (1880) 5 App Cas 795; *Marsden & Gault*, 639–640; LLMC 1996 Art 5. A different system for dealing with cross claims may apply in hull insurance: see 2.9.2(b).

529 Forum shopping might then become relevant, as T's owners would then be seeking a suitable jurisdiction in which to bring suit, while Ship X's owners might be considering establishing a limitation fund as a pre-emptive defence: see 2.5.9.

530 See MSA 1995 s 187(1). As are the owners of any other property on board eg owners of communication equipment lashed to the ship, or even the belongings of crew and passengers, but note that passengers' luggage may in any event be covered under the Athens Convention 2002: 2.3.4.

531 That ship would be entitled to limit its liability: see 2.5.4(a).

jointly at fault, the cargo owner, though wholly innocent, would not be entitled to claim all of its loss against the *C* or the *D* arguing that they were joint tortfeasors who, on general tort principles, would each be liable for the whole loss. This is because the cargo owner is in effect identified by the Collision Convention 1910 with the faults of the *C*.[532] The cargo owner could in theory claim against the *C* for its proportion of the loss, but in practice the contract of carriage will give the owner of the *C* a complete defence of negligent navigation.[533] In some legal systems that do not apply the Collision Convention 1910, eg the US, the cargo owner might be able to bring a claim for 100% of its loss against the *D* as a joint tortfeasor. In turn, in the collision action, the *D* would be likely to seek recourse for the *C*'s proportion of that sum from the *C*. The *C* may then seek to recover that amount from the cargo owner under a "both to blame collision clause" in the bill of lading or charterparty contract.[534] For this reason, owners of cargo in ships that are wrecked may need to look to a variety of remedies against different defendants. In relation to the carrying ship, they may seek to avoid contract of carriage defences by proving a breach of the contract through unseaworthiness.[535] It is such difficulties that show the importance to cargo interests of obtaining insurance.[536]

There are slightly different apportionment rules where two or more ships are at fault resulting in personal injury and death claims. Here the Collision Convention 1910[537] provides for joint and several liability; ie the claimants could sue either or both ships for 100% of their loss.[538] The personal claimants are thus given some preference,[539] but the shipowner sued for 100% can then reclaim from the other ship the latter's proportion of loss.[540]

2.5 Wreck and limitation of liability

The detailed history and development of limitation of liability is beyond this book,[541] but it is necessary to explain its significance as the topic is a major factor in marine casualty disputes, including those involving wrecks and their removal.[542]

---

532 This is an application by the Convention of the rule in *The Milan* (1861) Lush 388. See *Marsden & Gault*, 637–639.

533 See 2.1.5(b). The MSA 1995 s 187(5) preserves the owner's right to a complete exclusion under any carriage contract, as well as any right to limit liability (see 2.5).

534 See eg Conlinebill 2016 cl 13 and 2.1.5(a) and (b); or Gencon 1994 cl 11 and 2.1.7(b); NYPE 2015 cl 33(b) and 2.1.7(c).

535 See 2.1.5(a).

536 See 2.9.3(a) for the Both to Blame Collision Clause in the *cargo* insurance policy.

537 See the MSA 1995 s 188.

538 The tactical choice may depend on factors such as amenability to suit and solvency of the shipowners. Limitation will also affect this choice, especially for crew members: see 2.5.4(a).

539 They will, though, face limits of liability, albeit higher than those applicable to property claimants: see 2.5.4(a) and 2.5.6(a).

540 See the MSA 1995 s 189.

541 See P Griggs, R Williams, J Farr, *Limitation of Liability for Maritime Claims* (4th ed, Informa, 2004) [*Griggs et al*]; B Reynolds and M Tsimplis, *Shipowners' Limitation of Liability* (Wolters Kluwer, 2012) [*Reynolds and Tsimplis*]; *Marsden & Gault*, Chapter 18 and App 4; *Martinez Gutierrez*; Institute of Maritime Law (N Gaskell, ed), *Limitation of Shipowners' Liability: The New Law* (Sweet & Maxwell, 1986) [*Limitation of Shipowners' Liability: The New Law*].

542 See also 10.7, 10.8.5.

2.5.1 Introduction to limitation of liability

The ability of a shipowner to limit its liability is of long standing and in the UK dates back to 1733. It was originally designed as a form of trade protection or encouragement, but the modern justification mostly relies on the need to provide and obtain insurance cover. Limitation of liability is a principle that now runs through all of maritime law, not simply to cases involving wreck, and it has been at the core of maritime liability conventions. In essence, a shipowner may be entitled to limit its liability where there is a collision or cargo loss, or death or injury to passengers. In principle, the shipowner may also be entitled to limit liability for wreck or cargo removal. The right to limitation under consideration here arises not by contract, but by operation of national law which may or may not give effect to a convention on limitation of liability.

Two distinct limitation systems emerged since the 18th century; one based on the value of the vessel itself[543] and the other on an artificial (but more certain) figure calculated by reference to its tonnage.[544] There have been three international conventions in 1924, 1957 and 1976. Those limitation conventions of 1924[545] and 1957[546] have largely been superseded.[547] The key convention is now the Convention on Limitation of Liability for Maritime Claims (LLMC) 1976. It has 54 contracting States[548] and was amended by a Protocol in 1996[549] that significantly increased the limits of liability.[550] The consolidated version of the LLMC 1976 with the 1996 amendments is known as the "LLMC 1996". The LLMC 1996 has over 56 contracting States, including the UK.[551] These represent 61.89% of the gross tonnage of the world's merchant fleet, but it is clear that acceptance of the LLMC 1976 or LLMC 1996 systems is by no means universal.[552] There is a strong membership amongst

---

543 The valuation system was relevant to the US litigation involving the wreck of the *Titanic*: see *The Titanic*, 209 F. 501 (1913 SDNY 2d Cir.), *aff'd* 233 U.S. 718 (1914). See also *Martinez Gutierrez*, Chapter 1.

544 The tonnage system was based on legislation in 1854 and 1862 that became the UK MSA 1894 s 503 and has been used in the limitation conventions from 1957 onwards (see below). See also N Gaskell, "The Amount of Limitation", in *Limitation of Liability: The New Law*, 45–49.

545 International Convention for the Unification of Certain Rules relating to the Limitation of Liability of Owners of Sea-Going Vessels 1924 [Limitation Convention 1924].

546 International Convention Relating to the Limitation of Liability of Owners of Sea-Going Ships 1957 [Limitation Convention 1957].

547 See CMI Yearbooks and J Hjalmarsson, Institute of Maritime Law, *The Ratification of Maritime Conventions* (Informa Law, loose-leaf).

548 *IMO Status of Treaties* (November 2018). Entry into force: 1 December 1986.

549 Protocol of 1996 to Amend the Convention on Limitation of Liability for Maritime Claims 1976: see N Gaskell, "New Limits for Passengers and Others in the United Kingdom" (1998) LMCLQ 312 [*Gaskell, New Limits*]. For a table of comparisons between the various limitation regimes, see Tables 4 and 5 in *Gaskell, Limitation of Liability*; *Marsden & Gault*, 984–986.

550 That limit has itself been increased internationally under a rapid amendment procedure as from 2015: see 2.5.6.

551 *IMO Status of Treaties* (November 2018). Entry into force: 13 May 2004.

552 Note that there are many LLMC 1996 States that have remained parties to the LLMC 1976 (eg Greece and Liberia). Sometimes this may be by oversight rather than conscious choice. The effect is that such States may have international obligations to LLMC 1976 flag states (eg Singapore) to recognise the lower LLMC 1976 limits. Following the *Rena* sinking in 2011 (see 1.2.4) New Zealand only acceded to the LLMC 1996 in 2014, but failed to denounce the LLMC 1976 until October 2017; see also 2.5.8.

the developed world, especially in Europe,[553] but the LLMC is less popular in the Americas: the US is not a party; neither are most South American States. Most of the non-parties have national limitation of liability laws. Some of these may mirror the LLMC,[554] but others may have significant differences to the LLMC, eg in the size of limits, the type of claims to which they apply and the ease with which the limits can be 'broken'. In the developing world, in particular, there may be uncertainty about whether States continue to enforce limitation regimes dating back to colonial days. All this means that there is a lack of uniformity giving scope for forum shopping.[555]

The emphasis in this book will be on the LLMC 1976, as amended (ie the LLMC 1996)—particularly because there is a key reference to it in the WRC 2007 Art 12(1).[556] Limitation is relevant in this chapter for three main reasons. First, there is its impact on maritime casualties generally and the associated (mainly commercial) claims, eg by shipowners claiming for the wreck of their ships after a collision, and by cargo owners for loss of cargo. Secondly, general limitation principles are referenced in the pollution conventions and how they deal with wreck.[557] Thirdly, there are specific provisions directly relevant both to salvage and wreck removal operations.[558]

The LLMC does not *create* liabilities; it merely *limits* any liability that might arise under common law or by statute. The LLMC therefore assumes that there is a liability that has been proven, eg for negligence.[559]

In most limitation regimes, including the LLMC 1996, there are a number of key common questions which arise. For which craft is limitation available? Who may limit? Which claims are subject to limitation? How are the limits calculated? How to establish a limitation fund? How to 'break' limitation.

2.5.2 Craft for which limitation is available

Under the LLMC Art 1(2), there is limitation of liability for all "seagoing" ships,[560] which means that the principle can apply to most craft involved in maritime casualties leading to shipwreck. But the LLMC does not apply to hovercraft[561] or floating platforms.[562] In theory, there is nothing to prevent a State giving more extensive rights to limitation in its national law, eg to non-seagoing ships, hovercraft or platforms. The UK has done this for

---

553 Although Italy is not a party to either LLMC 1976 or 1996 (and never ratified the 1924 or 1957 Limitation Conventions): this factor may have been relevant in settling the *Costa Concordia* claims: see 1.2.5(c).
554 The Maritime Code of the People's Republic of China 1992, Chapter XI, is virtually identical to the key provisions of LLMC 1976. Hong Kong-China, by contrast, is party to the LLMC 1996.
555 See 2.5.9.
556 See 10.7, 10.8.5.
557 See 2.6.
558 See 2.5.4(c), 2.5.5, 2.5.8.
559 By contrast, the CLC 1992 (2.6.2(a)) and HNSC 2010 (2.6.4) both create liabilities and provide their own limits of liability separate from the LLMC.
560 "Seagoing" is not defined. See the *The Sea Eagle* [2012] 2 Lloyd's Rep 37; also the discussion at 10.2.7(a), 2.3.1.
561 Art 15(5)(a).
562 Art 15(5)(b). Nor does it apply to drilling ships (Art 15(4)), but only, for instance, where there is not a higher limit in national legislation.

non-seagoing ships[563] and for hovercraft.[564] By contrast, there is no specific provision in the MSA 1995 for floating platforms, which means that UK law depends upon whether such craft would fall within the general inclusionary definition of "ship".[565]

2.5.3 Persons who may limit

The LLMC Art 1(1) and (2) lists those entitled to limit as owners, managers, operators,[566] parent companies and charterers.[567] The broad definitions in Art 1 mean that where there are maritime casualties, most of the commercial parties concerned will in some way be able to limit liability for claims brought by the others, but they must still show that the claims fall within Art 2.[568] Amongst those not specifically listed as entitled to limit are cargo owners (unless they are charterers), eg where their dangerous cargo causes damage to a ship,[569] or classification societies, eg where failure to inspect allows an unseaworthy ship to sail.[570] Once again, national law may grant limitation rights to others not covered by the LLMC, and the UK has retained a strange provision that gives dock owners and repairers the right to limit liability to shipowners (eg where there is a fire in a repair yard that wrecks a ship).[571]

There are two categories of persons whose rights to limit are particularly relevant to wreck, in addition to those mentioned above, namely salvors (including wreck removal contractors) and insurers. Salvors are dealt with separately, below.[572] Liability insurers, if sued directly, are entitled to limit *provided* that the assured itself can limit[573] but, as will

---

563 The MSA 1995, Sch 7 Pt II para 2.

564 Hovercraft Act 1968 and the Hovercraft (Civil Liability) Order 1986, as amended; Hovercraft (Convention on Limitation of Liability for Maritime Claims (Amendment)) Order 1998 (SI 1998/1257).

565 The MSA 1995 s 311; Sch 7 Pt I; Art 15, Pt II paras 2, 12 (note also s 313 of the MSA 1995). The s 311 definition of ship includes any "vessel used in navigation". See eg cases such as *Perks v Clark (Inspector of Taxes)* [2001] 2 Lloyd's Rep 431 (jack-up rigs were ships for income tax purposes). Pleasure craft are specifically excluded from limitation in the laws of some states, but not in the UK. On ordinary principles they could be considered as ships, but note that there must apparently be planned or ordered movement from one place to another. This would include yachts, but not jet skis used for having fun in the water without going anywhere (*R v Goodwin* [2006] 1 Lloyd's Rep 432). See also S Gahlen "Ships Revisited: A Comparative Study" (2014) 20 JIML 252.

566 Cf 2.6.2(a).

567 The latter includes a slot charterer: *The MSC Napoli* [2009] 1 Lloyd's Rep 246: see also 2.5.4(d) and *Marsden & Gault*, 704.

568 See 2.5.4.

569 See eg *CMA CGM SA v Classica Shipping Co Ltd* [2004] EWCA 114, [2004] 1 Lloyd's Rep 460, where a charterer was liable for shipping containers with bleaching powder that exploded, causing over $26 million in damage to the vessel. See also 2.1.6.

570 They would almost certainly not fall within Art 1(4), which allows persons such as employees to limit if sued directly, as they are not normally persons for whose faults the shipowner is responsible (eg vicariously).

571 MSA 1995 s 191 (reproducing the Merchant Shipping (Liability of Shipowners and Others) Act 1900: see *Gaskell, MSA 1995*, 21/216 for the restrictions on the operation of the provision. Such a provision has only marginal relevance to wreck law, but it is conceivable that a wrecked vessel is refloated (or loaded onto a heavy lift barge) and towed to a UK dock for scrapping (or a later scrapping voyage). The hull or might have some residual value and the barge could be worth a considerable amount. In these circumstances, it will be important to cover such potential liabilities in the scrapping contract: see also 14.3, 14.7.

572 See 2.5.5.

573 LLMC Art 1(6).

be seen, this caveat will be particularly important in the case of direct actions against the insurer under the WRC 2007.[574]

2.5.4 Claims subject to limitation

2.5.4(a) Property and personal claims

Article 2 of the LLMC lists the claims for which limitation is allowed. The list is long[575] and includes most claims arising out of maritime incidents, including death and injury, property damage, wreck raising and cargo raising, and consequential (eg economic) losses.

In the context of a casualty leading to a wreck, the shipowner can therefore expect to limit liability for 'property' claims made in particular by owners of cargo in its ship (whether under charters, bills of lading or waybills); owners of other ships (and their cargoes) damaged or lost in a collision; owners of harbour facilities, eg wharves or jetties.[576] Many 'pollution' related claims could also be limitable, provided that they did not overlap or conflict with other IMO maritime conventions such as the CLC.[577]

Somewhat controversially, shipowners are still entitled to limit liability to those killed or injured on board the ship or elsewhere.[578] Crew claims against the owner of the ship on which they are employed are not subject to limitation, ie they are treated in the same way as employees on land, *but* this exclusion only applies if the law governing the contract of employment expressly forbids limitation for such claims.[579] This means that LLMC limitation for crew claims is referable to another system, but the default position is that there is limitation. In general, then, crew claimants will be looking to sue their own ship, hoping to avoid the limits of liability of a colliding ship.[580]

Passenger injury and death claims are also subject to limitation in two ways. First, if passengers sue the carrying ship there is a special limit in LLMC 1996 Art 7, calculated according to the number of passengers the ship is certified to carry.[581] Secondly, if they sue a non-carrying ship (eg after a collision), then that ship will be entitled to limit under Art 6 according to its own tonnage. Tactically, although passengers could sue both ships as joint tortfeasors under the MSA s 188, it may be easier to sue the carrying ship.[582]

---

574 See 10.8.5 and the wreck removal opt-out, 2.5.8.
575 See also *Marsden & Gault*, 705–710.
576 All are covered in Art 2(1)(a).
577 These issues are addressed in 2.5.4(b).
578 Art 2(1)(a).
579 See Art 3(e). There is no limit in UK law under the MSA 1995 s 185(4) where persons are on board the ship or employed in connection with the ship or with salvage operations under a contract of service governed by UK law. While the number of UK crews is relatively small, there may be salvors or surveyors who are injured while on board a wrecked ship while salvage or removal operations are being undertaken.
580 Although both ships will be jointly and severally liable: see 2.4.4.
581 That limit is 175,000 sdrs multiplied by the number of passengers that the ship is authorised to carry according to its certificate: £190,159 (US$241,938) at the IMF rates on 3 December 2018: see 2.3.3, Table 2.2 and footnotes. The passengers may also be subject to a double limitation through the application of the Athens Convention 2002: see 2.3.3 on the relationship between the two sets of limits.
582 Eg under the Athens Convention 2002: see 2.3.3.

2.5.4(b) Pollution claims

Claims involving 'pollution' could theoretically fall within the LLMC as property damage,[583] economic loss,[584] measures to remove a wreck (or render harmless its cargo)[585] or measures to avert or minimise loss.[586] However, oil tanker pollution damage claims are excluded from the LLMC by Art 3(b) if there is oil pollution damage "within the meaning of [the CLC 1969] or of any amendment or Protocol thereto which is in force" (eg the 1992 Protocol creating the CLC 1992).[587] The applicable limits should be those of the registered shipowner under the CLC itself,[588] certainly in a State like the UK[589] which is party to the LLMC 1996 and the CLC 1992.[590]

Until the HNSC 2010 enters into force,[591] pollution (and damage) from hazardous and noxious substances[592] will be subject to the LLMC if the claims fall within the categories outlined above, eg property damage (and consequential loss), economic losses,[593] or as measures to remove a wreck or render harmless its cargo, or to avert or minimise loss.[594] The wreck of a chemical tanker could cause enormous pollution clean-up expenses as well as economic losses to tourism and fishing—in a similar manner to oil that is covered under the CLC. The loss of thousands of containers from the latest mega container ship could also involve massive losses and expense.[595] This means that those claims would compete with all other claimants in the sums available under the LLMC limits,[596] which could be grossly inadequate for major chemical pollution incidents. When, or if, the HNSC 2010 enters into force, the LLMC Art 18(1(b) will enable a State "to exclude claims for damage within the

---

583 Under Art 2(1)(a), eg where oil contaminates a desalination plant, boats in a port, or a fish farm.

584 Under Art 2(1)(a) as consequential loss resulting from property damage (eg damaged fishing nets); or under Art 2(1)(c) as pure economic loss (eg suffered by fishing vessels unable to operate because of bans, or hotels suffering a loss of trade).

585 Under Art 2(1)(d) or (e): see 2.5.4(c), 2.5.5 and 10.7.

586 Under Art 2(1)(f). This would not cover clean-up costs undertaken by the shipowner itself (see *The Aegean Sea* [1998] 2 Lloyd's Rep 39, 53), nor should there be an overlap with Art 2(1)(c): see also N Gaskell, "The Bunker Pollution Convention 2001 and Limitation of Liability" (2009) 15 JIML 477 [*Gaskell, Bunker Pollution Limitation*], 488–490.

587 Apparently whether or not the CLC is in force in a particular State; see *Martinez Gutierrez*, 185–188.

588 See 2.6.2(a), 2.5.4(b).

589 See the MSA 1995 s 160, Sch 7 Pt II para 4(2), *The Aegean Sea* [1998] 2 Lloyd's Rep 39, 54; *De La Rue & Anderson*, 795; *Marsden & Gault*, 711–712.

590 More generally, it is not entirely clear if the Art 3(b) exclusion only applies where the CLC is in force in the State in which the limitation action is being heard (ie so that there is a clear alternative remedy available), or whether it is a complete exclusion from the LLMC even for non-CLC states—of which there are relatively few). The reference to any amendments "in force" refers to whether the Protocol has achieved the necessary number of ratifications or accessions to come into force internationally, and not whether the Protocol is in force for the limitation State. The wording of Art 3(b) unfortunately indicates that there is a complete exclusion, and this is somewhat reinforced by the alternative, and better, solution adopted for the HNSC 2010; see 2.6.4.

591 See 2.6.4. Then States will make a reservation under Art 18(1)(b) of the LLMC 1996 (as amended by the 1996 Protocol) so as to exclude HNS claims from the LLMC 1996.

592 Other than persistent oil within the CLC.

593 Here the chemical pollution victims would also have to pass the hurdle of proving that economic loss claims were recoverable at common law: see 2.4.3.

594 Again, such claims would presently fall within LLMC Art 2(1)(a), (c), (d) or (e) and possibly (f).

595 See eg 1.3.2. It may be that some clean-up and wreck or cargo removal claims under Art 2(1)(d) or (e) are excepted from limitation by a State opt-out: see 2.5.8.

596 See the examples in 2.5.6(a).

meaning of" [the HNSC 2010] "or of any amendment or Protocol thereto". This will enable HNS State parties to ensure that the LLMC does not apply, but for non-HNS States the default position is that the LLMC would continue to apply to such claims.

Bunker pollution claims under the Bunkers Convention 2001[597] are capable of being limited under the LLMC. These would include property damage claims (with their consequential losses) as well as any economic loss claims (eg by the tourist and fishing industries).[598] Claims to "render harmless anything that is or has been on board" the ship would include bunkers under LLMC Art 2(1)(d).[599] Clean-up measures to avert or minimise loss might fall within Art 2(1)(f).[600] There had been doubts about whether bunker pollution clean-up claims could be considered as "property" damage in Art 2(1)(a).[601] The UK had enacted a temporary strict liability regime in the MSA 1995 s 154 to cover bunker pollution prior to the entry into force of the Bunkers Convention 2001,[602] and had provided in s 168 that any liability was "deemed to be a liability to damages" under the LLMC Art 2(1)(a). This deeming provision was extended to claims arising under the Bunkers Convention 2001 when it entered into force in the UK.[603] The effect, for the UK, is to ensure that all claims within the Bunkers Convention 2001 are potentially subject to limitation under the LLMC.[604]

The WRC 2007 may create liabilities for the costs of removing cargo that is an environmental threat.[605] Like the Bunkers Convention 2001,[606] it links the right to limit to other national or international regimes such as the LLMC 1996.[607] For both conventions, this linkage creates problems where the liability insurer seeks to limit.[608]

It should be noted that States might seek to bypass limits of liability in the pollution liability conventions by giving wide powers to courts to impose very large criminal fines. These would not seem to be claims within the LLMC Art 2, as the phrase "whatever the

---

597 See 2.6.3.

598 Whether such economic losses are recoverable is a separate question to whether limitation is available: see 2.4.3 and eg *Qenos Pty v Ship APL Sydney* [2009] FCA 1090. As with the practice under the CLC 1992 (2.6.2(a)), the Bunkers Convention 2001 recognises that some economic losses are recoverable: see 2.6.3.

599 As bunkers are part of the ship, not cargo under Art 2(1)(e): and see 2.5.4(b). State bunker clean-up expenses may well not be subject to limitation as a result of a State opt-out from paras (d) and (e): see 2.5.5, 2.5.8. There would be no opt-out, though, for property damage or economic losses cause by bunker spill. See *Gaskell, Bunker Pollution Limitation*, 489–490.

600 These claims are limitable if the measures are to avert or minimise loss "for which the person liable [eg the shipowner or charterer] may limit his liability in accordance with this Convention". This linkage of para (f) to liability assumes particular significance if there is a State opt-out from paras (d) and (e): see 2.5.8.

601 See *Gaskell, Bunker Pollution Limitation*, 484–489.

602 See the MSA 1996 s 154 and 2.6.3; *De La Rue & Anderson*, Chapter 6; *Gaskell, MSA 1995*, 21/180.

603 See the Merchant Shipping (Oil Pollution) (Bunkers Convention) Regulations 2006 (SI 2006/1244), inserting the MSA 1995 s 153A (giving effect to the Bunkers Convention 2001) and amending s 168. This is permissible under international law under the Bunkers Convention 2001 which leaves limitation to State parties, and probably also under the LLMC.

604 The caveat is because of the potential effect of the limitation opt-out in respect of Art 2(1)(d) and (e): see 2.5.8. See also *Martinez Gutierrez*, 193.

605 See 10.6.4. To the extent that this will "render harmless" the cargo, it can fall within LLMC Art 2(1)(e).

606 See above and 2.6.3.

607 See 10.7 for discussion of the WRC 2007 and limitation.

608 See 10.8.5. See also LEG 74/2/2, 9 August 1996.

basis of liability may be" is surely referring to civil and not criminal liability.[609] The difficulty for a State may be that the shipowner is not amenable to the jurisdiction (eg where the ship is wrecked and owned by a foreign single ship company) and insurance cover for fines may be non-existent or discretionary.[610] For large companies with a major presence in a particular jurisdiction, the risk of large fines as a supplement to civil liability can be very real.[611]

2.5.4(c) Wreck and cargo removal claims
It is LLMC Art 2(1)(d) and (e) that are most important for wreck and cargo removal. They are specifically listed as claims for which limitation is available. Article 2(1)(d) provides that there is limitation of liability for "claims in respect of the raising, removal, destruction or the rendering harmless of a ship which is sunk, wrecked, stranded or abandoned, including anything that is or has been on board such ship". States may opt out of these provisions,[612] but where they do not, the provisions will be very important to owners of a wreck as well as to salvage and wreck contractors.[613]

Although it is convenient to summarise the contents of (d) as 'wreck removal', the wording is much wider. It would clearly cover direct claims against a ship that was wrecked and itself caused costs (eg incurred by a State) in dealing with the aftermath. Not only would the costs of raising be limited, but also its removal and later destruction (eg scrapping if that yielded no value).[614] It would also cover cases where the wreck could not be removed but needed to be destroyed *in situ*, or rendered harmless, eg by reducing its remaining height underwater. Removal of bunkers from the tanks of a wrecked ship,[615] and the rendering harmless of bunkers that had escaped,[616] as they would be something that "is or has been on board" the ship. The latter expression would cover debris from the ship itself.

Literally, it could also cover cargo such as cars or containers, but cargo is specifically mentioned in (e). There is a degree of overlap within Art 2(1) and it generally accepted that a claim may fall under a number of heads. It may not normally make much difference whether "cargo" falls under (d) or (e), or both, but it might make a difference where States exercise an opt-out.[617] For that reason, the better interpretation is probably that (d) is confined to those items which naturally form part of the ship or its equipment and stores, and that "cargo" is dealt with exclusively in (e). There is a forceful argument, however, that Art 2(1)(d) applies to the cargo of a ship that is sunk, wrecked, stranded or abandoned, whereas Art 2(1)(e) only applies to cargo of a ship that is afloat. But this would mean that "cargo" removal separate from the ship might not be within (d) and the costs of doing so could thus be unlimited. It seems better to give a plain meaning to the two provisions and

---

609 The position may be rather blurred when the provision is called a civil or administrative penalty: cf Australia's Great Barrier Reef Marine Park Act 1975 (Cth), s 38GA.
610 See 2.9.6(a).
611 See also 2.9.6(b), 2.2.2, 1.2.2(a).
612 See 2.5.8.
613 See also 2.5.5.
614 See 14.3, 14.5.
615 Cf 12.3.1, 12.3.4(c).
616 Ie clean-up, if this was not within Art 2(1)(a) or (f): see *The Aegean Sea* [1998] 2 Lloyd's Rep 39, 52–53, and note the effect of the MSA 1995 s 168: see 2.5.4(b), 2.6.3.
617 This is particularly relevant as the UK has done so for (d) but not (e): see 2.5.8.

there seems no reason why there cannot be "removal" of the cargo of a floating or sunken ship within (e).[618] On that basis, the personal luggage of thousands of passengers that is wrecked with a cruise ship, such as *Costa Concordia*, is best considered as debris falling within (d).[619]

The trigger for the Art 2(1)(d) claim to limit must be that the ship is "sunk, wrecked, stranded or abandoned". As a matter of interpretation of this paragraph there is no room for an argument that a wrecked ship ceases to be a "ship" once sunk so that the LLMC does not apply.[620] A ship that is stranded may not necessarily be wrecked in the sense of being totally lost, as it may be refloated. In so far as the removal of such a ship succeeded in saving anything of value then a claim against its owner (and cargo) would be a salvage claim covered by the Salvage Convention 1989. These are excluded from limitation by LLMC Art 3(a),[621] The inclusion of the word "abandoned" in para (d) is significant because a ship may be intact, but left in a port when the owners become insolvent, and so be in such poor condition that it has no value. As will be seen, the WRC 2007 may not apply to ships abandoned in this sense,[622] so the ability to limit may be relevant to any liability created by a national statute[623] to remove such ships.

As noted, Art 2(1)(e) provides that there is limitation of liability for claims in respect of the "removal, destruction or the rendering harmless of the cargo of the ship". The distinction here is between the claim by the cargo owner for the value of the lost cargo itself, which would be subject to limitation under Art 2(1)(a), and claims to deal with problems caused by the cargo after a casualty, eg removal or clean-up claims by a State. This would include the costs of recovery of containers, whether washed overboard or lost from the ship after it sank,[624] as well as bulk cargo such as coal. If the clean-up involved oil subject to the CLC the claims would be excluded from the LLMC by Art 3.[625] If the HNSC 2010 enters into force it is expected that claims for the clean-up of chemicals (including those in containers) will also be excluded from the LLMC 1996.[626]

Article 2 makes the scope of the LLMC very wide as not only does Art 2(1) apply limitation to the listed claims "whatever the basis of liability may be", but Art 2(2) applies limitation "even if brought by way of recourse or for indemnity under a contract or otherwise".[627] Together this means that however a claimant frames its claim (eg in tort, under statute or in

---

618 Cf the discussion in *Martinez Gutierrez*, 45–46, 91–99, 210–211; also *Griggs et al*, 24.

619 As it is accompanying passengers subject to a contract of carriage of passengers, not cargo being carried under a contract for the carriage of goods.

620 Cf 14.7.2.

621 And see 2.5.5 and 2.7.

622 See 10.5.1(a); also 11.4, 14.2.

623 See eg the *Rena*, 1.2.4(d); also 11.1.2(a), 11.1.3(a), 11.4, 14.2.

624 Cf 10.6 and 2.9.3(b). If a ruined or distressed cargo was dumped overboard, it would literally be "destruction" within Art 2(1)((e), even if the dumping were illegal or contrary to international orders: see 14.6 and 4.8.3 and cf *Reynolds and Tsimplis*, 62. Clean-up costs caused by the dumping might still be recoverable without limit if this was reckless conduct within the LLMC Art 4.

625 Eg if there were persistent hydrocarbon mineral oils within the meaning of Art I(5) of the CLC 1992: see 2.6.2(a) and 2.5.4(b).

626 Through States making a reservation under Art 18(1)(b) of the LLMC 1996 (as amended by the 1996 Protocol): see 2.6.4, 2.5.4(c).

627 Claims by salvors and wreck removal contractors for payment by the person liable are not subject to limitation: see Art 2(2). See also 2.5.5 and 13.6.3(g).

contract) the shipowner can limit; even though the basis of a wreck removal claim may be statutory, there is still limitation.[628]

More difficult is the question of whether para (d) can apply to claims made not against the ship which itself is "sunk, wrecked, stranded or abandoned", but also where a claim is made against a colliding ship that caused or contributed to the wreck of the other.

Take the example of the *Corvus J* which collided with the *Baltic Ace* in 2014, as a result of which the latter was wrecked.[629] A wreck removal claim by the State against the *Baltic Ace* would clearly fall in para (d). If the *Baltic Ace* brought a recourse claim against the *Corvus J* for its own value, that would be a claim for damage to property within Art 2(1)(a).[630] Would it also be a claim falling within (d), ie a claim "*in respect of* the . . . removal . . . of *a* ship which is . . . wrecked"? (emphasis added). The words "in respect of" have to be interpreted without recourse to national precedents, but are very wide and the mention of "a" ship indicates that the paragraph does not require that the claim is actually brought against the ship that is wrecked, eg the *Baltic Ace*.[631] As noted, it would not normally matter if the shipowner could limit under more than one paragraph of Art 2(1), but States may opt out of paras (d) and (e) so that there is no limitation of liability for claims falling within those paragraphs. So, in a recourse action by *Baltic Ace* against *Corvus J*, the latter could limit liability under para (a) for a claim relating to the replacement value of the *Baltic Ace*, but could the latter claim that the *Corvus J* was unable to limit for any proportion of the wreck removal expenses for which *Corvus J* was indirectly liable (eg as a result of negligent navigation)? In other words, could that part of the claim be categorised as a wreck removal claim in respect of the wreck removal of the *Baltic Ace*?

This issue arose under the pre LLMC law in a number of English cases in which it was held that the colliding vessel could limit against the recourse claim, even if it did include a wreck removal element.[632] *Marsden & Gault*[633] take the view that the position under the LLMC is the same as the wreck claim is a "consequential loss" claim within Art 2(1)(a) and is brought by way of "recourse or for indemnity" under Art 2(2).[634] It is submitted that this

---

628 Under the Limitation Convention 1957 claims could only be limitable if they were for "damages" and case law under the MSA 1894 s 503 held that this did not include statutory wreck removal claims if they were expressed to create a debt: see *The Stonedale No 1* [1956] AC 1; *The Millie* (1939) 64 Ll L R 318, *The Putbus* [1969] P 136. As the LLMC refers to "whatever the basis of claim", these cases would not be decided the same way under the LLMC. States that would like to have the same result, ie for wreck removal claims not to be subject to limitation, must now use the opt-out under the LLMC: see 2.5.8.

629 See also 2.5.9(c), 10.2.5.

630 As would a recourse claim for bunkers lost with the ship, and for pollution liabilities of the *Baltic Ace*: see *The Aegean Sea* [1998] 2 Lloyd's Rep 39, 52–53.

631 Cf the wording in para (a) which does make a linkage between loss or damage and "*the* ship" in respect of which the claim to limit is made: See *Caspian Basin Specialised Emergency Salvage Administration v Bougues Offshore* [1997] 2 Lloyd's Rep 507, 522.

632 See *The Arabert (No 2)* [1961] 1 Lloyd's Rep 363, *The Putbus* [1969] P 136; cf *Barameda Enterprises Pty Ltd v Ronald Patrick O'Connor and KFV Fisheries Pty Ltd (The Tiruna)* [1987] 2 Lloyd's Rep 666 (Qld Sup Ct).

633 At 710.

634 It is also inconsistent with the treatment of recourse claims that include an element of salvage. See *The Breydon Merchant* [1992] 1 Lloyd's Rep 373, where a cargo claim against shipowners for salvage expenses resulting for unseaworthiness was also categorised as a recourse claim and not one for "salvage" (and not excluded by Art 3(a). Likewise, in *The Aegean Sea* [1998] 2 Lloyd's Rep 39, where a recourse claim by a tanker against a colliding ship for CLC damages paid to environmental claimants was treated as a recourse claim subject to

is the correct approach, as it is somewhat artificial to categorise this recourse claim as one for wreck (or cargo) removal.[635] Article 2(1)(d) and (e) were designed to deal with direct claims by the person who actually suffered loss or expense as a result of the wreck, and the reservation power in Art 18 was designed to ensure that States had a cause of action against the wrecked ship that was not subject to limitation.

2.5.4(d) Charterers and limitation claims

As noted in 2.5.3, "charterers" can limit, and *The MSC Napoli*[636] decided that this phrase includes slot charterers, eg for claims after a wreck made by cargo owners against a charterer (as contracting carrier). This does not mean that there is a separate fund for claims against the charterers and an additional one for shipowners;[637] there will be one fund calculated according to the ship's tonnage. This will be available to third parties in the sense of those external (or not connected) to the ship herself, eg collision damage claimants[638] or cargo claimants.

However, the Supreme Court held in *The Ocean Victory*[639] that a charterer will not be able to limit liability for a claim against it by the shipowner for loss of or damage to the very ship by reference to whose tonnage the limit is to be calculated. If the charterer ordered the ship to an unsafe port, the claim by the shipowner for the wreck of the ship would not be subject to limitation[640] – even if brought by way of indemnity under a contract.[641] Moreover, it has been held that consequential loss arising from the loss of that vessel would also not be limitable by the charterer, eg the shipowner's claim against the charterer for the shipowner's proportion of salvage remuneration or its contribution to general average.[642] On that basis, it would also seem that the charterer might not be able to limit a shipowner's claim for wreck and cargo removal expenses incurred in respect of the

---

limitation): see also N Gaskell, "Pollution Limitation and Carriage in the Aegean Sea", Chapter 5 of F. Rose (ed), *Lex Mercatoria: Essays on International Commercial Law in Honour of Francis Reynolds* (2000, LLP).

635 See *Gaskell, Bunker Pollution Limitation*, 484–6.

636 [2009] 1 Lloyd's Rep 246.

637 See also 2.5.6(b).

638 Eg where there is a bareboat charterer. Similarly, if a charterer loaded dangerous cargo and this caused an explosion resulting in third parties suffering loss (eg a terminal operator), the charterer could limit: see *CMA CGM SA v Classica Shipping Co Ltd* [2004] 1 Lloyd's Rep 460 [24].

639 [2017] 1 Lloyd's Rep 521, and 2.1.7.

640 In *Blue Nile Shipping Co Ltd v Iguana Shipping and Finance Inc (The Darfur)* [2004] 2 Lloyd's Rep 469, the logic of this approach was applied to a claim by a *shipowner* to limit a time charterer's claim for consequential losses arising out of damage to the vessel *itself* after a collision caused entirely by the owner's fault: the claims did not fall in Art 2 and the shipowner was unable to limit. By contrast, it was agreed that it could limit for claims by the time charterer for an indemnity in relation to payments made for settling cargo claims (as held in *CMA CGM SA v Classica Shipping Co Ltd* [2004] 1 Lloyd's Rep 460 [31–32]), and to salvors for saving the cargo (see also *The Breydon Merchant* [1992] 1 Lloyd's Rep 373).

641 As provided for in the LLMC Art 2(2). By contrast, a wreck owner that charters *another* ship, eg a tug, to assist with salvage or wreck removal operations is not faced by *The Ocean Victory* interpretation and could limit in the ordinary way.

642 *CMA CGM SA v Classica Shipping Co Ltd* [2004] 1 Lloyd's Rep 460 [29–30]; the decision was generally approved by the Supreme Court in *The Ocean Victory* [2017] 1 Lloyd's Rep 521 [87], [128]. It has also been held that the charterer could not limit either for claims by the shipowner for loss of freight, although it could limit for the value of the ship's bunkers: *Aegean Sea Traders Corp v Repsol Petroleo SA (The Aegean Sea)* [1998] 2 Lloyd's Rep 39, 51–52.

ship.⁶⁴³ This again entails reading Art 2(1)(d) and (e) as referring only to wreck and cargo removal claims from third parties.⁶⁴⁴

The Ocean Victory approach may seem somewhat surprising in the overall context of the LLMC, but is now settled in English law. It means that charterers are particularly exposed to claims for unlimited liability if the ship is wrecked by their actionable breach.⁶⁴⁵ To that extent they should be advised to ensure that they have full charterer's liability cover, eg with a P&I Club, or to include a contractual limitation provision (eg based on LLMC limits).⁶⁴⁶

2.5.5 Limitation for salvors and wreck removal contractors

Salvors are specifically included in LLMC Art 1(3)⁶⁴⁷ as persons who can limit, in wording that was meant to reverse in part the decision in *The Tojo Maru*⁶⁴⁸ which had prevented salvors from limiting liability in some circumstances. That case involved salvage operations to a grounded tanker where, owing to negligence by a salvage diver there was an explosion causing damage to the ship.⁶⁴⁹ Under the wording of the Limitation Convention 1957, as enacted in the MSA 1894 s 503, the salvage company could only limit liability in effect for faults committed on the salvage tug; so a diver's faults when operating *on* the casualty itself would not have been limitable. As a matter of policy, this decision caused great alarm to the salvage industry as it meant that, while operating as a voluntary emergency service, salvors could be liable for sums far greater than any salvage reward they could have earned.

The LLMC Art 1(3) definition now covers "any person rendering services in direct connection with salvage operations". This would allow limitation to be available not only for the actions of divers operating in the water alongside the casualty, but also those who are transferred to the casualty (eg by helicopter⁶⁵⁰ or launch). The individuals would either be considered as salvors themselves under Art 1(3) or as employees of the salvor (or persons for whose faults the salvor or shipowner is responsible) under Art 1(4).

---

643 As this would still result from "loss" of the ship within Art 2(1)(a) *CMA CGM SA v Classica Shipping Co Ltd* [2004] 1 Lloyd's Rep 460 [29–30]. Cf the recourse claim against a colliding ship, made by the owners of a ship sunk in a collision, that included a component for wreck removal on the basis that it was "brought by way of recourse or for an indemnity under a contract or otherwise" under Art 2(2): see 2.5.4(c).

644 To that extent this is consistent with the approach to these provisions in relation to recourse claims: see 2.5.4(c).

645 See 2.1.6 and 2.1.7.

646 For an example based on the LOF 1980, see *Martinez Gutierrez*, 203–204. It is possible to waive a right to limit liability, provided that this is done clearly: see *The Cape Bari* [2016] 2 Lloyd's Rep 469 and 2.5.5. This might be relevant where a wreck owner charters a vessel to assist in a salvage or wreck removal operation: see also 13.6.3(g).

647 And "salvage operations" within Art 2.

648 [1972] AC 242.

649 See now the also the duty of the salvor to take due care under Art 8(1) of the Salvage Convention 1989: also *Gaskell MSA 1995* 21/391; and 2.7, 12.2.1.

650 Note that a salvor not operating from a ship (eg where helicoptered onto a casualty from land,) or where the salvor is solely operating on the casualty the actual amount of limit will be calculated according to Art 6(4) on the basis of a deemed tonnage of 1,500 gt (and not according to the tonnage of a salvage tug that happens to be in attendance): see fn 657.

The protection is not restricted to employees of the salvor but could include independent experts such as surveyors or marine engineers.[651] Moreover, although *The Tojo Maru* was a case where the ship was ultimately salved, Art 1(3) is phrased so as to include as a "salvor" those who undertake wreck removal, cargo removal or clean-up operations.[652] This is important, because it means that wreck removal contractors and those that they employ will be entitled to limit liability for any liabilities they might incur for the wide categories of claim listed in Art 2.[653] There may be property damage, eg to the casualty itself, so that any residual value is diminished. There may also be loss of cargo, eg caused by negligence in transhipping it, including consequential loss (such as loss of market or profit). There may also be injury or death, eg to the crew of the casualty or other ships involved in the operation,[654] to government officials, or to experts working at the scene.

From the perspective of salvage or wreck removal personnel injured or killed in the course of a wreck removal operations, their claims will also be affected by the extended rights given by Art 1(3) to salvage and wreck removal contractors to limit liability. These personnel would need to prove liability (eg by negligence), and if they claimed against their own employer (eg a removal contractor) then they may be faced with the relatively low limit of liability of the vessel on which they are working (eg a tug).[655] If they are working on a chartered-in barge then the issue will probably be whether they have a cause of action against the barge owner (eg for unseaworthiness of the barge), in which case the barge owner will be the one to limit. Where there is a tug and tow together, eg when a tug is trying to tow a grounded ship off rocks to avoid a total loss, the issue will be whether to treat the two units as one for limitation purposes. The LLMC gives no guidance on this flotilla issue, but in principle if the only fault is in relation to the tug it should be that vessel's limit that applies, not some aggregate of tonnages of vessels in different ownership.[656]

In all cases where the salvor or wreck removal personnel are not operating from any ship at all, or on the ship to which the salvage or removal services are being offered, the limit of liability is calculated at a deemed tonnage of 1,500 gt[657]—the size in 1976 of a relatively large salvage vessel.

There are a number of claims related to salvage and wreck removal that might have been subject to limitation, given the wide wording of Art 2. First, direct claims by the

---

651 More difficult would be the case of those not at the scene of the casualty, such as engineers performing flotation calculations perhaps thousands of miles away, or the shipyard that fabricated buoyancy tanks of the type used with the *Costa Concordia*. In principle, these are both services upon which the salvage operation directly depends, so should be within the definition. The position might be different for those who supply goods or services to such sub-contractors, but are unaware of their ultimate destination or purpose (eg non-specialist lighting or generators).

652 This is because Art 1(3) refers to a salvor that renders services in direct connection with "salvage operations", and then goes on to state that these "shall also include operations referred to" in Art 2(1)(d),(e) and (f). See 2.5.4(c).

653 See 2.5.4.

654 But not those employed (within Art 3(5)) by the salvor or contractor who is liable.

655 Whether a claim against their employer is excluded from limitation under Art 3(e) depends on the law of the contract of employment: see 2.5.4(a).

656 See eg *Alexandra Towing Co Ltd v Millet and Egret (The Bramley Moore)* [1964] P 200; *The Smjeli* [1982] 2 Lloyd's Rep 74; Gaskell, *The Amount of Limitation*, 61–63. For an authoritative discussion of the flotilla issue, see *Rainey*, Chapter 12.

657 See Art 6(4) and cf Table 2.5, 2.5.6(a); also fn 650, above.

salvor against a ship or cargo owner for salvage[658] are excluded from limitation by Art 3(a), whether these claims arise by way of the general law (eg under Art 13 or 14 of the Salvage Convention 1989), or by contract (eg under the LOF or SCOPIC). This means in particular that any salvage reward, eg under the LOF, or any SCOPIC payment, will be paid in full and cannot be subject to a cap. The same applied to claims for general average,[659] whether under the York Antwerp Rules or not.

Secondly, the last sentence of Art 2(2) provides that claims set out in Art 6(1)(d) (broadly wreck removal), Art 6(1)(e) (broadly cargo removal) and Art 6(1)(f) (broadly clean-up) "shall not be subject to limitation of liability to the extent that they relate to remuneration under a contract with the person liable". This excludes such claims from limitation, even if they would otherwise have fallen within Art 2;[660] ie claims for payment by the wreck removal contractor which arise by contract with the "person liable"[661] are not subject to limitation. Thus, if a contractor is engaged on a daily rate Wreckhire 2010 contract and the operation is extended for longer than expected (but not terminated),[662] the shipowner cannot claim later to limit that contractual liability for hire by using the limit under the LLMC. The same principle would apply to those contractors working on cargo removal, or clean-up operations falling within Art 6(1)(e) or (f). By contrast, if craft or equipment belonging to a wreck removal contractor is damaged owing to the actions of the owner of the casualty (or those for whom it is responsible), the latter owner could expect to be able to limit any liability[663] for that claim using the first sentence of Art 2(2). It would seem that this claim would not be a claim for "remuneration" under the second sentence of Art 2(2), namely the basic payment for the services provided.

A particular issue arises in relation to wreck removal contracts where there are extensive knock for knock indemnities,[664] which would fall within the express coverage of Art 2(2) as claims brought by way of recourse or for indemnity under a contract or otherwise.[665] The LLMC does not specify whether the right to limitation is one that can be given up voluntarily by contract or not. The English practice dating back to the MSA 1894 was that limitation could be waived,[666] but it was unclear whether the same approach would be taken towards the LLMC. In *The Cape Bari*,[667] the Privy Council reaffirmed the ability to contract out of limitation but emphasised that the contract

---

658 See 2.7.
659 See 2.8.
660 Eg as "wreck removal" claims, or contract claims within the chapeau to Art 2(1) and the first sentence of Art 2(2).
661 Eg the shipowner liable to pay a State for wreck removal expenses: see Art 2(2).
662 See 13.6.3(c)–(e).
663 Note that the standard wreck removal contracts such as Wreckhire 2010 cl 16(c) may in any event exclude all liability for damage to the contract's vessel or those that are hired in: and see 13.6.3(g). It is assumed here that the owner of the hired-in craft would not be bound directly by such a contractual provision, owing to privity of contract (cl 26(b) would not be relevant as it deals with benefits not burdens affecting third parties). And (unlike cl 16(a)) there is no provision whereby the contractor has to indemnify the owner if such a claim is made against the owner. It is possible that the sub-contract may itself allow for some form of indemnity in these circumstances.
664 See 13.6.3(g).
665 See 2.5.4(c).
666 *Clarke v Dunraven (The Satanita)* [1897] AC 59.
667 *Bahamas Oil Refining Company International Ltd v The Owners of the Cape Bari Tankschiffahrts GMBH & Co KG (The Cape Bari)* [2016] UKPC 20, [2016] 2 Lloyd's Rep 469; *Rainey*, 180–181, 557–559.

must clearly and unequivocally abandon such valuable rights arising by operation of law. The court was not prepared to find that general words in the commercial contract were enough to oust limitation in that case.[668] In order to ensure that limitation was waived contractually in offshore contract operations, including wreck removal, parties would need to include a provision in their knock for knock clauses that expressly excluded limitation of liability, eg, "under Arts 1 or 2 of the LLMC". Clause 25(d) of Towcon 2008 and Towhire 2008 is not clear enough to achieve a waiver,[669] and none of the three wreck removal contracts[670] has any equivalent express provision, eg in Wreckhire 2010 cl 16. The indemnity in respect of "loss or damage of whatsoever nature" in cl 16 would still be too general to affect the right to limit.

2.5.6 Calculating the limits

The LLMC 1996 limits of liability are calculated according to tables set out in Arts 6 and 7, using the sdr of the IMF.[671] In 2012, the original LLMC 1996 limits were amended internationally (to come into effect on 8 June 2015)[672] and provided increases of 51% over the LLMC 1976, although these increases only took effect in the UK from 30 November 2016.[673] Limitation tonnage is calculated using the gross tonnage (gt) measurement under the International Convention on Tonnage Measurement of Ships 1969.[674]

2.5.6(a) Examples of limits
To illustrate the limits that might be applicable in wreck cases, Table 2.5 shows the appropriate limits for certain sizes of ship on the basis of Art 6(1)(b) of the LLMC 1996 (as amended by the 2012 increases that came into effect internationally in 2015). Table 2.6 shows ships involved in some of the wrecks discussed in 1.2.[675]

---

668 Some charters, such as Asbatankvoy 1977 cl 20(b)(v), expressly reaffirm the right to limit: see *Voyage Charters*, 968–969.

669 See *Smit v Joseph Mobius* [2001] 2 ALL ER (Comm) 265; *Rainey*, 180–181, 557–559.

670 Eg in Wreckhire 2010 cl 16, Wreckfixed 2010 cl 12, Wreckstage 2010 cl 13: and see 13.6.

671 For conversion date see the LLMC Art 8, the MSA 1995 Sch 7 Pt II para 7; *Gaskell, The Amount of Limitation*, 38–39. For limitation procedure, see *Marsden & Gault*, 727–739, 844–856.

672 Using a tacit amendment procedure LEG 99/14, 24 April 2012, 7–11. For the *Pacific Adventurer* incident and its influence on the increases, see 2.6.3.

673 See the Merchant Shipping Act 1995 (Amendment) Order 2016 (SI 2016/1061). This was an apparent breach by the UK of international obligations to LLMC 1996 State parties (perhaps caused by Brexit time pressures). But for casualties before 30 November 2016, UK courts would presumably continue to apply the previous limits in the MSA 1995 Sch 7, as amended by the Merchant Shipping (Convention on Limitation of Liability for Maritime Claims) Amendment Order 1998 (SI 1998/1258), and the Merchant Shipping (Convention on Limitation of Liability for Maritime Claims) Amendment Order SI 2004/1273. Note that the UK did not increase the limits for ships under 300 gt.

674 See the LLMC Art 6.5, the MSA 1995 Sch 7 Pt II para 5 and the Merchant Shipping (Tonnage) Regulations 1997 (SI 1997/1510). If there are still any ships not measured under the Tonnage Convention 1969, the best evidence available can be sued to produce the gt: see the Merchant Shipping (Liability of Shipowners and Others) (Calculation of Tonnage) Order 1986 (SI 1986/1040); *Gaskell, The Amount of Limitation*, 45–49.

675 The references to the named ships are for illustration, on the basis that these are the limits that might apply to ships of those sizes in 2018.

Table 2.5 LLMC 1996 'property' limits of liability: illustrative tonnages

Ship tonnage	LLMC 1996 sdr amounts	£ sterling[1]	US$[2]
250 gt ship [UK][3]	[500,000]	[£543,310]	[$691,250]
2,000 gt ship[4]	1,510,000 sdr	£1,640,796	$2,087,575
5,000 gt ship	3,322,000 sdr	£3,609,752	$4,592,665
10,000 gt ship	6,342,000 sdr	£6,891,344	$8,767,815
25,000 gt ship	15,402,000 sdr	£16,736,121	$21,293,265
80,000 gt ship	39,562,000 sdr	£42,988,860	$54,694,465
150,000 gt ship	60,702,000 sdr	£65,960,007	$83,920,515
200,000 gt ship	75,802,000 sdr	£82,367,969	$104,796,265

[1] The calculation uses the IMF figures at 3 December 2018 with the rate of conversion of 1 sdr = £1.08662.

[2] As the international currency of shipping is the US$, this column gives comparative figures for 3 December 2018 based on 1 sdr = US$1.3825. The US is *not* party to the LLMC, so the US$ figures are given by way of example only.

[3] The default minimum tonnage under the LLMC 1996 is 2000 gt (see following row and fn), but the LLMC: Art 15(2) gives States the right to adopt lower limitation tonnages for ships of 0–299 gt. The UK used this in the MSA 1995 Sch 7 Part II, para 5, as amended by Merchant Shipping (Convention on Limitation of Liability for Maritime Claims) (Amendment) Order 1998 (SI 1998/1258), as itself amended by SI 2004/1273. When the UK eventually gave effect to the 2012/2015 LLMC 1996 increases, it decided (after a consultation in 2016) not to increase these 0–299 gt small ship limits. See also Gaskell, *Limitation of Liability*, 973–974, 981–983.

[4] This is the minimum tonnage under the LLMC 1996 (as amended in 2012/2015) for States that have not exercised the option described above. That is, any seagoing ship of 0–2000 gt will have the minimum limits in this row.

Table 2.6 LLMC 1996 'property' limits of liability: major casualties (2018 figures)[1]

Ship and tonnage	LLMC 1996 sdr amounts	£ sterling[2]	US$[3]
Torrey Canyon 61,623 gt[4]	32,747,219 sdr	£35,583,783	$45,273,030
MSC Napoli[5] 53,409 gt	29,026,277 sdr	£31,540,533	$40,128,828
Rena 38,788 gt[6]	22,402,964 sdr	£24,343,509	$30,972,098
Costa Concordia 114,000 gt[7]	49,830,000 sdr	£54,146,275	$68,889,975

[1] As explained, the limits shown here represent the theoretical limits as at 3 December 2018, not the limits that would have applied in litigation involving those ships (see 1.2 generally on that litigation). The present table merely shows what the 2018 limits would be for a ship of that particular size.

[2] The calculation is made using the LLMC 1996 (as increased from 2015) and uses the IMF figures at 3 December 2018 with the rate of conversion of 1 sdr = £1.08662.

[3] As the international currency of shipping is the US$, this column gives comparative figures for 3 December 2018 based on 1 sdr = US$1.3825. The US is *not* party to the LLMC, so the US$ figures are given by way of example only.

[4] This figure was measured under the system in force prior to the Tonnage Convention 1969 and the limitation tonnage for the purposes of the Limitation Convention 1957 would have been a figure between the then net and gross tonnages: see Gaskell, *The Amount of Limitation*, 45–49; for the effect that this tonnage difference alone had on limitation, see Gaskell, *Limitation of liability*, Tables 2.4 and 2.5, 984–986. The figure in the table is therefore only illustrative.

[5] See 1.2.3. A limitation fund was established on 26 February 2007 for £14,710,000, calculated from the IMF figures for the previous day: *The MSC Napoli* [2009] 1 Lloyd's Reports 246.

[6] See 1.2.4.

[7] See 1.2.5. Note that passenger claims against the carrying ship could be subject to the separate limits in Art 7 of the LLMC: see 2.3.3.

The figures in both tables represent the sums available for *all* 'property' claims,[676] not only for wreck or cargo removal; these other claims would include, eg, cargo loss claims against the shipowner,[677] collision damage claims[678] and most bunker pollution claims.[679] Given the size of 'property' claims likely to follow from a wreck,[680] it can be seen that the limits can operate so as to severely restrict claims, particularly in relation to small ships.[681] Moreover, these limitation illustrations represent the highest available amounts under the latest international regime, the LLMC 1996 (with the 2012/2015 increases). The limits would be considerably lower for States party to the LLMC 1976, or which apply previous conventions, or have their own national regimes. This is of great significance when it comes to forum shopping, eg to find a more 'shipowner friendly' State that applies lower limits,[682] or a State that applies a more 'claimant friendly' test for breaking limits.[683]

2.5.6(b) Distinct occasion

The limits apply to the aggregate of claims that arise on "distinct occasion".[684] Thus, if there were a collision on leaving port but a ship was later wrecked for unconnected reasons, there would be two separate limits that were applicable. If the later wreck were causatively connected to the initial collision, so as to involve sub-apportionment of liability, there could be a debate about whether there were one or two limits.[685]

By contrast, claimants have looked to the Australian decision in *Strong Wise Limited v Esso Australia Resources Pty Ltd*[686] to dissect what might appear to a maritime observer as a single incident, so as to create separate "distinct occasions" and thereby an increased number of applicable limitation 'funds'. The approach in a wreck incident might be to try to sub-divide the casualty into stages with separate acts of causative negligence giving rise to more than one 'occasion', for instance initial negligence causing a ship to go aground, followed by a separate act of negligence in reacting to the situation; eg a decision to move the ship a day later that led to a total loss. Each case will be fact sensitive as to causation,

---

676 Strictly, these are called "other" claims in the LLMC to distinguish them from personal injury and death claims. For these 'personal' claims Art 6(1)(a) provides separate and higher limits which are approximately double those available for 'property' claims; see eg the tables in *Gaskell, Limitation of liability*. In a major disaster, if the Art 6(1)(a) amounts are insufficient, the personal claimants can share in the Art 6(1)(b) amounts, thereby diminishing even more the fund for 'property' claimants—including those claiming for the costs of wreck removal.

677 See 2.1.1, 2.1.5.

678 See 2.4. Note that under the LLMC Art 5 where there are counterclaims, eg after a collision, limitation is applied *after* the respective claims are set off, ie the limit is applied to the ship of the net defendant: see 2.4.4. This can make a considerable difference where there are disparities between the size of ships and their degrees of fault. A different system for dealing with cross claims may apply in hull insurance: and see 2.9.2(b).

679 See 2.6.3 and 2.5.4(b).

680 See the examples in 1.2.

681 If there were personal injury and death claimants, they would have twice the above limits available to them alone under the LLMC Art 6(1)(a) before being entitled to share in the property sums available under Art 6(1)(b). Ie the property claimants could have their 'share' reduced even further if there are significant unmet claims. For illustrations, see *Gaskell, Limitation of Liability*, 991–992.

682 See 2.5.9.

683 See 2.5.7.

684 Art 9. See *Rainey*, 554–555; *Marsden & Gault*, 725–727.

685 See 2.4 and *Gaskell, Limitation of Liability*, 1013–1020.

686 [2010] FCA 240, [2010] 2 Lloyd's Rep 555. This was not a wreck case but one involving damage to a pipeline by an anchor.

but it seems unlikely that an English court would be very willing to divide up the circumstances of a stranding leading to a total loss in the manner suggested in *Strong Wise*. The negligent actions of master and shipowner would really be an attempt to deal with the continuing consequences of what might be termed a single 'casualty', or occasion. It might only be where there is a clear separation in time and causation that *Strong Wise* might be followed;[687] eg where the ship is firmly aground, but it is possible safely to offload bunkers, and a week after the grounding in calm conditions the master negligently opens a valve allowing bunkers to leak onto the shore. The *Strong Wise* decision has not been easy to apply in subsequent disputes,[688] and if it is applied too liberally it could undermine the assumptions made in the always delicate negotiations at IMO over limitation amounts in conventions.

2.5.7 'Breaking' limitation

One of the ways in which claimants may try to avoid limits[689] is to prove that a shipowner has committed conduct that is so serious that it must be deprived of its right to limit. The old rules under the MSA 1894 s 503 and the Limitation Convention 1957 depended on a test which required proof only of "actual fault or privity"[690] and which meant that it was comparatively easy to break the limits in the UK. The test for 'breaking' limits in Article 4 of the LLMC States that a "person liable shall not be entitled to limit his liability if it is proved that the loss resulted from his personal act or omission, committed with the intent to cause such loss, or recklessly and with knowledge: that such loss would probably result". This test is largely derived from that used in the Warsaw-Hague Convention 1955 (as amended) on air transport[691] and has been used as a template in other maritime Conventions.[692]

The intent/recklessness test should mean that limitation will only be denied where the damage has been inflicted deliberately or by conduct that is virtually equivalent to such deliberate action. Mere negligence can give rise to liability,[693] but the limits should still be available. It will be rare that there is deliberate loss, except perhaps in cases of scuttling. Recklessness is used to denote circumstances beyond negligence where a person knows of a risk and is prepared to take it, even if he does not necessarily want or desire the natural consequences of running that risk. It is sometimes called "blind eye" knowledge, after Lord Nelson put a telescope to his blind eye and declared that he saw nothing, after being told that there was a flag signal from a superior. In the same way, one who is aware of risks

---

687 See eg *The Lucullite* (1929) 33 Ll L Rep 186.

688 Eg the damage or loss for each distinct occasion has to be allocated to that occasion. An attempt to use the multiple limitation "occurrences" argument in the *Shen Neng 1* litigation seemed likely to fail on the evidence given and the case settled at the single limitation figure: see 10.6.4.

689 See also the approach in *Strong Wise*, 2.5.6(b). Other ways are to show that the claim is excluded completely by Art 3 or does not fit within the various LLMC definitions: see eg 2.5.2, 2.5.3, 2.5.4.

690 "Fault" is straightforward, but "privity" in essence meant with knowledge and consent: see *The Eurysthenes* [1976] 2 Lloyd's Rep 171; cf 2.5.7, 2.9.2(c); cf 10.8.4(d), (e).

691 Art 25, since replaced by the Montreal Convention 1999: see also 2.3.3.

692 Such as such as the Hague-Visby Rules 1968, the CLC 1992, the HNSC 2010, the Athens Convention 2002.

693 Eg for a collision leading to a wreck.

but chooses to take them is reckless. Awareness of risk is the key, and the test is a subjective one, depending on actual (not constructive) knowledge.[694] The knowledge of loss is required to be probable and not merely 'possible', and the reference in Art 4 to "such loss" indicates that the knowledge must relate to the very loss that actually occurred and not loss generally.[695] Moreover, the burden of satisfying the Art 4 test is clearly on the claimant (ie victim). This itself makes the test even harder to satisfy.[696]

It is crucial to note that not only must the conduct be proved but, as the shipowner will invariably be a company, the intent or recklessness will need to be attributed to someone in the corporate structure. Recklessness of the master or crew can create liabilities for the employer but will not normally deprive the shipowner of limits.[697] There has been over 100 years of case law in the UK on who in the corporate structure is considered as the shipowner for these purposes.[698] If there is a single "directing mind and will", then that person's conduct will suffice.[699] If there is the necessary misconduct by a board of directors, then that is probably high enough.[700] It is where there is misconduct below this level that there are difficulties. Who in effect is performing the functions of an individual (ie non-corporate) shipowner? English law has long accepted that if the functions of a shipowner (ie the top decision-making functions) are delegated to a firm of ship managers, then one looks to that company (eg to its board of directors).[701] In *Meridian Global Funds Management Asia*

---

694 *Goldman v Thai Airways International Ltd* [1983] 1 WLR 1186; *The Leerort* [2001] 2 Lloyd's Rep 291; *The Saint Jacques II* [2003] 1 Lloyd's Rep 203; *The MSC Rosa M* [2000] 2 Lloyd's Rep 339.

695 *The Leerort* [2001] 2 Lloyd's Rep 291. Eg some knowledge of engine problems is unlikely to amount to the intent/recklessness likely to produce a collision. A deliberate and repeated flagrant breach of the Collision Regulations (eg navigating the wrong way in a traffic separation scheme) could be reckless: see *The Saint Jacques II* [2003] 1 Lloyd's Rep 20. A master might still claim that a collision would not have been probable if he had 'got away with it' in the past, but a court may be unlikely to believe such an assertion.

696 *The Capitan San Luis* [1993] 2 Lloyd's Rep 573; cf *The Norman* [1960] 1 Lloyd's Rep 1 for the contrary position under the 1957 Limitation Convention.

697 This is because of the reference to *personal* act or omission and the fact that the LLMC test differs crucially from the Warsaw-Hague Convention 1955 Art 25 where the air carrier lost limits for acts of "the carrier, his *servants or agents*". The italicised words are omitted from the maritime conventions, which must emphasise that the shipowner does not lose the right to limit *merely* because somebody employed by the company was guilty of misconduct (and see *Browner International Ltd v Monarch Shipping Co. Ltd (The European Enterprise)* [1989] 2 Lloyd's Rep 185).

698 Care is needed in reading the pre-LLMC cases, as the level of misconduct (actual fault or privity) was lower than that under the LLMC test and the burden of proof was different.

699 *Lennards v Asiatic Petroleum* [1915] AC 705.

700 See eg *Societe Anonyme des Minerals v Grant Trading Inc (The Ert Stephanie)* [1989] 1 Lloyd's Rep 349.

701 See eg *Lennards v Asiatic Petroleum* [1915] AC 705; *Grand Champion Tankers v Norpipe AS (The Marion)* [1984] AC 563, [1984] 2 Lloyd's Rep 1. See also *The Star Sea* [1997] 1 Lloyd's Rep 360, for a marine insurance case where the court had to consider who were the relevant persons in a single ship company (SSC) structure where the ship was unseaworthy when sent to sea. The decision makers whose conduct could be attributed to the SSC were the SSC's sole director, the board of directors of the ship management company and the latter's "technical director". The relevant question was "who was involved in the decision making processes required for sending the *Star Sea* to sea?": [1997] 1 Lloyd's Rep 360, 375 (see on appeal, [2001] 1 Lloyd's Rep 389, 395, 414). See also 2.9.2(c) and 10.8.4(d) for wilful misconduct. Where it is a charterer (or manager) that is seeking to limit (eg to meet a bill of lading claim), the focus should primarily be on its employees: see *Sellers Fabrics Pty Ltd v Hapag-Lloyd AG (The Encounter Bay)* [1998] NSWSC 644.

Ltd v Securities Commission,⁷⁰² the need to look at functional equivalence was reaffirmed. The mere recklessness of a junior manager or ship superintendent may not be high enough, but if the shipowners have devolved all decision-making powers to that person, then the shipowners risk that conduct being attributed to them.⁷⁰³

The approach taken by the English courts as to recklessness and corporate responsibility may not be one that comes so easily to judges in other systems. "Recklessness" is hard to translate as a concept, and some systems may equate it simply to "gross negligence", which could be less strict than the subjective English approach. The policy behind limitation may also not so obvious to judges less experienced in maritime law, or in cases where there are large claims and low limits.⁷⁰⁴ The differences between judicial approaches can again be a factor in forum shopping.⁷⁰⁵

In a wreck case, 'breaking limitation' will be relevant to recourse claims against other ships that caused the collision⁷⁰⁶ but will also be significant in pollution and cargo claims⁷⁰⁷ against the shipowner. It may also be relevant in wreck raising claims where shipowners are entitled to limit.⁷⁰⁸

2.5.8 LLMC opt-out for wreck and cargo removal claims

In theory, there is a limit for wreck and cargo removal claims falling under the LLMC Art 2(1)(d) and (e),⁷⁰⁹ but Art 18(1) of the LLMC allows a State to make a reservation (ie an opt-out) in relation to these paragraphs. The main reason was to protect the financial position of States, and dated back to the Limitation Convention 1957. States such as Australia and Germany have taken advantage of this right⁷¹⁰ so as to allow them to prevent shipowners relying on any limits for wreck or cargo removal claims, and to ensure that the owners will be liable for the full cost of the removal. Whether the power given by the reservation has been fully implemented into national law is another matter.⁷¹¹

---

702 [1995] 2 AC 500. This was a non-maritime case, but where the shipping cases were reviewed and the House of Lords decided that special rules of attribution are required to decide whose act (or knowledge or state of mind) was *for this purpose* intended to count as the acts of the company.

703 Cf *The Marion* [1984] 2 Lloyd's Rep 1; *Arthur Guinness Son & Co Ltd v Owners of the MV Freshfield (The Lady Gwendolen)* [1965] P 294, [1965] 1 Lloyd's Rep 335. The Korean Supreme Court has declined to treat the conduct of an agent, pilot or master as 'personal' to a shipowner (see *Maralunga* [1995] Int ML 176), but a later decision of 26 October 2006 shows that it may be easier to break limits where there are smaller (and sometimes more informal) management structures than with larger companies.

704 Some courts are perceived as being readier to break limits: see Gard, "Limitation of Liability Is Upheld by French Courts—22 Years On", Insight 2010 (17 April 2013) and cf *The Happy Fellow* [1997] 1 Lloyd's Rep 130, 137. There may still be procedural differences in non-common law systems, eg in the ability to obtain discovery to support 'breaking' claims.

705 See 2.5.9.

706 See 2.4.

707 See 2.6 and 2.1.1, 2.1.5.

708 See 2.5.8 and 10.7.

709 See 2.5.4(c).

710 See *IMO Status of Treaties* (November 2018).

711 New Zealand became a party to the LLMC 1976 and, in 2014 (after *Rena*), the LLMC 1996, but maintained provisions in its national law disallowing limitation for wreck removal: see 1.2.4(c). Unfortunately, the reservation was not made in international law to the IMO and this could have posed problems in the settlement of the *Rena* claims and in any future claims (if involving LLMC 1996 flag States). New Zealand only notified the

When ratifying the LLMC 1976 the UK, significantly, only made the reservation in respect of wreck removal under Art 2(1)(d) and *not* cargo removal under Art 2(1)(e)[712] (except as regards Gibraltar). At the ratification of the LLMC 1996, the UK reserved the right to exclude both provisions, but even when increasing the limits in 2016[713] has continued with the reservation only in respect of Art 2(1)(d), not (e).[714] The legislative enactment is the MSA 1995 Sch 7 Part 2 para 3.[715] From the perspective of the State, this seems an unduly favourable concession to shipowners if Art 2(1)(e) applies to cargo from sunken as well as floating ships.[716] Not only is cargo recovery likely to be increasingly expensive,[717] but there may be difficult distinctions required to be made between hull and cargo removal.[718] Norway, by contrast, made the reservation for both and elected to have stand-alone limits for wreck removal.[719] This UK anomaly seems inexplicable and, in the absence of some confidential assurances from owners and their insurers, it ought to be rectified, given the potential losses to the State. When the UK enacted the WRC 2007, a new s 255G(5) of the MSA 1995 was created to give effect to the liability provisions in Art 10 of the WRC 2007.[720] Section 255G(5) States expressly that the section "does not prevent the exercise of the right (if any) to limit liability by virtue of [the MSA 1995 s 185]". This provision is intended to give effect to Art 10(2) of the LLMC[721] and is neutral in that it does not affect the LLMC provisions applicable in the UK that are described here in section 2.5.8.[722]

The effect of making the full opt-out should be fairly clear; wreck removal costs and cargo removal costs should not be subject to limitation, nor should costs to clean up cargo.[723] This should follow, even if the claims also happened to fall within one of the other Art 2(1) paragraphs (eg (a) or (c)), as the express removal of the right to limit for claims falling in (d) and/or (e) must be intended to prevail for claims falling within those paragraphs. The reservation would not seem to apply to recourse claims that contained a component

---

IMO about the opt-out with effect from 15 October 2018. This emphasises the need for States to take an integrated view of the interaction of limitation of liability and wreck removal: see also 11.2.3, and *Martinez Gutierrez* 95.

712 Canada is another State that has not excluded cargo removal under (e), as has China (for the Hong Kong special region).

713 See the Merchant Shipping Act 1995 (Amendment) Order 2016 (SI 2016/1061) and 2.5.6(a).

714 Although this was raised by one consultee at the time of the belated 2016 increases, the government "did not consider it necessary to take this point forward at this time": see "Government response to consultation: Changes to domestic legislation implementing certain international maritime liability conventions" (2016), 9.

715 Uder the LLMC Art 2(1)(d) "shall not apply" unless a separate fund has been set up for harbour and conservancy authorities financed by dues from vessels; no such scheme has ever been established.

716 See 2.5.4(b). However, see 11.3.5(b) for some uncertainty about whether the UK has achieved unlimited direct action insurer liability under the WRC 2007 for the hull removal claims.

717 See 1.3.2.

718 Cf 2.5.8, 10.6.

719 K-J Gombrii, "Limitation of Liability—The Norwegian Solution", in H Rak, P Wetterstein (eds), *Shipwreck in International and National Law* (Åbo Akademi University, 2008) [*Shipwreck in International and National Law*].

720 See 11.3.4(a).

721 See 10.7.

722 See also s 255P(5), which appears to preserve the opt-out in relation to a direct action against the insurer, allowing unlimited liability in that claim: see 11.3.5(b).

723 On the basis that these are claims for the rendering harmless of the cargo within Art 2(1)(e): see 2.5.4(b). In the UK there is no opt-out for cargo removal within (e), but some uncertainty about its full extent: see 2.5.4(b).

for wreck removal.[724] Where the WRC 2007 applies, the effect of the opt-out may be more complicated, particularly for direct action claims against the insurer.[725]

Liability for bunker removal and clean-up costs, eg under the Bunkers Convention 2001, would also be limitable under the LLMC Art 2(1)(d) unless a reservation had been made.[726] Again, the effect of the reservation should be to remove the right to limit for claims falling precisely in (d) even if, as above, the claim also fell within another paragraph, eg (a).[727] It may be that not all aspects of 'clean-up' can be considered as "rendering harmless" of the bunkers. Thus, it might be arguable that environmental reinstatement, eg introducing replacement plants or species, goes beyond the neutralisation of the bunkers by physical removal and later cleaning.

For the UK the position is rather more complicated in relation to bunker pollution owing to the deeming provision in s 168 of the MSA 1995.[728] It may be said that s 168 (as amended), coming after the opt-out, is intended to be definitive in allowing for limitation for all claims arising from the Bunkers Convention. The alternative view is that s 168 should be interpreted to preserve rights to limit for property damage and economic loss, but that it leaves untouched any application of the opt-out in relation to Art 2(1)(d). In so far as the clean-up after a bunker spill is a form of wreck removal,[729] then the opt-out should be interpreted as taking effect notwithstanding s 168—again for claims falling precisely in (d).

The apparent advantage given to States that make the reservation(s) may, however, be undermined by forum shopping.[730]

2.5.9 Limitation procedure and forum shopping

2.5.9(a) Establishing a limitation fund[731]

Limitation can be invoked as a defence to any direct claim under LLMC Art 10, and this might be appropriate in simple cases where there are few parties.[732] Where the shipowner is likely to face claims from many parties, it will usually seek to establish a limitation fund under Art 11 of the LLMC in a State party (eg to LLMC 1996), provided that "legal proceedings are instituted there in respect of claims subject to limitation" under Art 2. It might be thought that this provision requires a clamant to bring a claim against a shipowner before the latter can institute limitation proceedings, but the English approach is that the "legal proceedings" can be instituted *by* the shipowner[733] (eg in the limitation action or for

---

724 See 2.5.4(c) and *Martinez Gutierrez*, 99–102.
725 See 10.7 and 10.8.5.
726 See 2.5.4(b).
727 Cf *Martinez Gutierrez*, 193–196.
728 See 2.5.4(b) and *Gaskell, Bunker Pollution and Limitation*, 489–490.
729 Ie removal of "anything that is or has been on board" the ship, within Art 2(1)(d): see 2.5.4(c).
730 See 2.5.9.
731 For the English practice generally, see *Marsden & Gault*, 727–739, 844–861; *Reynolds & Tsimplis*, Chapter 9; *Derrington & Turner*, 290–304; *Meeson & Kimbell*, Chapter 8.
732 Art 10(1) makes it clear that limitation may be invoked even without constitution of a fund.
733 See eg *Bougues Offshore SA v Caspian Shipping* [1998] 2 Lloyd's Rep 461, 474; *The Western Regent* [2005] EWCA (Civ), [2005] 2 Lloyd's Rep 359, CPR r 61.11(19) and *Reynolds and Tsimplis*, 119–122. Cf V van der Kuil, "Limitation of Liability for Maritime Claims and Politics: Curse or Cure?", Chapter 8 in C Ryngaert, E

a declaration of non-liability). In effect, this allows the shipowner some degree of forum shopping as it can make a pre-emptive strike.[734]

The fund can then be distributed to claimants pro rata; ie where the limit operates, every claimant suffers a proportionate loss. This can mean that there is a significant shortfall when there are large claims against the 'property' fund in Art 6(1)(b):[735] eg a combination of large bunker pollution economic loss claims, large cargo claims and claims from another high value ship sunk in a collision. All these claims will be competing against one another, as the limits apply to the aggregate of all claims,[736] whichever of the potential defendants to a liability action has constituted the fund.[737]

As with the enforcement of most maritime claims, limitation proceedings will be part of a number of stages: there may have been provisional remedies (such as arrest) to obtain security, and the shipowner (and Club) will be anxious to release this once a limitation fund has been established; there may be formal limitation proceedings (including establishing the fund and distributing it); there may be a hearing on the underlying merits of a dispute (eg whether there is liability for wreck removal costs); there may be separate enforcement proceedings to enforce any liability judgment. The interplay of these proceedings, sometimes involving jurisdictional questions, is particularly complex where proceedings take place in different States.

2.5.9(b) Multi-state limitation proceedings

In order to avoid multiplicity of proceedings, and conflicts between courts of different States, the CLC 1992, HNSC 2010 and Bunkers Convention 2001 specifically provide for which courts of State parties shall have jurisdiction to hear claims and also for courts of one State party to recognise and enforce judgments given in other State parties.[738] Unlike these conventions, the LLMC has no equivalent express provisions on jurisdiction, nor on recognition and enforcement. All this has meant that there is uncertainty about how to deal with potential limitation conflicts, thereby giving scope for differences in States' approaches about how far they will exercise their own jurisdiction. Although the LLMC does not expressly forbid the courts of one State party from establishing a fund if there is already one elsewhere, or compel them to recognise limitation judgments in other States parties, the LLMC rather assumes that a single fund will be established in one State party. Article 14 uses the governing law of that State to determine the constitution and distribution of

---

Molenaar and S Nouwen (eds) *What's Wrong with International Law?* (2015, Brill) [*Van der Kuil*], 85. Note the possible significance of an action brought by the master in the *Baltic Ace* litigation, 2.5.9(c).

734 See further 2.5.9(f).

735 See Table 2.5: 2.5.6(a).

736 See the LLMC Art 9.

737 See Art 11(3). Where a shipowner claims the right to establish a fund, it is customary in English practice to describe it as the limitation "claimant"(although, somewhat confusingly, it is often the defendant in the underlying liability action and Art 13(3) of the LLMC assumes that the "claimant" is a person who brings a claim against the fund.

738 See eg the CLC 1992 Art X and HNSC 2010 Art 40. These provisions would seem to extend to liability *and* limitation of the shipowner's liability under those conventions. The Bunkers Convention 2001 Art 10 is similar, but there is no *separate* right to limit provided by that convention (see 2.5.4(b) and 2.6.3).

the fund.[739] Articles 11–13 also place restrictions on the extent to which other limitation proceedings may be instituted.

Thus, under Art 13(1), once "a limitation fund" has been constituted, claimants against the fund are barred from "exercising any right in respect of such a claim against any other assets" of those who constituted the fund.[740] This means that the claimants cannot execute judgment against other assets of the defendant shipowner, such as a bank account within any State party. Nor can the claimants arrest or attach[741] a ship for security (including a sister ship if the casualty itself became a total loss wreck). If a ship *has* been arrested it *may* be released by the courts of another State party, but *must* be released in circumstances set out in Art 13(2), eg where the fund has been established in a place, in effect, where claimants might be. These places are at the port where the occurrence (eg a sinking) took place; or (where the occurrence did not occur in a port) the first port of call after the occurrence;[742] the port of disembarkation[743] for injury and death claims; the port of discharge in respect of damaged cargo;[744] or the State where the arrest is made.

The point of discussing these provisions is to indicate that they are not completely clear as to what courts in State parties are to do, eg where a fund is established elsewhere and there is no arrest of a vessel for security. The approach that a national court may take to potential conflicts of jurisdiction may depend on its own national law on how to deal with competing proceedings in other States. The EU has its own jurisdiction and judgments regime.[745]

English courts have tended to view limitation proceedings as procedural rather than substantive[746] and (outside the EU regime) have applied the principle of *forum non conveniens*[747] to decide whether to stay or dismiss English proceedings in favour of foreign

---

739 But that of itself can be viewed as the reaffirmation that procedural matters are an issue for the forum, rather than a statement that only one State party's courts can hear limitation matters after the fund is constituted.

740 The fund would normally be established in the name of the shipowner, but others could be joined, eg insurers.

741 It seems that attachment is used here in the civil law sense and may not extend to a freezing injunction, which is not an attachment but a personal remedy.

742 This would normally be irrelevant in the case of a sunken ship, but if the wreck is removed it would seem that the first port of call would be either the port or place of scrapping (see Chapter 14, eg 14.7), or a temporary intermediate port of call. In the context of a wreck removal claim the value of arresting the vessel to be scrapped may be limited, and there may be arguments in some States that the remains are no longer a "ship" capable of arrest: see 14.7.2.

743 In the context of a passenger ship wreck it is rather unclear what this means as the carrying vessel never arrives at a port. It probably cannot refer to the intended port of disembarkation, as although this may make sense for passengers, it does not for crew members. Unless there is no "disembarkation" at all after a wreck, the expression probably refers to any port where any individual (or possibly body) is taken ashore—even if by another vessel.

744 As with disembarkation, there is uncertainty about how this applies in a wreck case, but it probably applies to any port where damaged cargo is taken including where cargo is removed from a wreck and taken to a nearby port (eg Portland with the *MSC Napoli*). Where containers are removed at sea they may well be removed and shipped to a far distant port, eg where the wreck occurs in a remote location: see eg 10.2.6.

745 See Brussels I Regulation Recast and 2.5.9(e): also M Tsimplis, "Law and Jurisdiction for English Limitation of Liability Proceedings" (2010) 16 (4) JIML, 289 [*Tsimplis*].

746 See eg *Caltex Singapore v BP Shipping Ltd* [1996] 1 Lloyd's Rep 286, 296–7, and below.

747 As settled in *The Spiliada* [1987] AC 460, [1987] 1 Lloyd's Rep 1.

liability and limitation proceedings. In a series of cases,[748] English courts have varied in the importance to be attached to the fact that a foreign court might apply a lower limit than that applicable in an English court. In *The Herceg Novi and The Ming Galaxy*,[749] English liability proceedings following a collision in Singapore were stayed by the Court of Appeal in favour of Singapore proceedings where the 1957 Limitation Convention was then applied. The discretionary factor of juridical advantage to the claimant in having access to higher LLMC limits in England was not considered decisive. While in one sense such decisions pay respect to variances in international maritime law, they can also undermine it. The leading English cases have not yet had to grapple with the wreck reservation issue, which arguably raises wider public policy issues[750] than the mere allocation of risk as between two commercial parties. Such decisions do, though, tend to reinforce what might be termed a pro-shipowner (and insurer) approach.

These complications in limitation law have led to forum shopping by shipowners in particular, eg by starting limitation proceedings in an LLMC 1976 State to take advantage of its lower limits than under the LLMC 1996.[751] Although a State party to LLMC 1996 would not be bound in international law to recognise a limitation fund established under the LLMC 1976,[752] its courts may decide to stay their own limitation proceedings[753] in favour of a foreign jurisdiction that may be the more suitable place to hear the liability and limitation issues together. Claimants might similarly try to influence matters by starting a liability action in a State that is perceived to be more favourable to them, but they cannot force the constitution of a limitation fund in that State as its creation is a right given to the shipowner.

The resolution of all possible limitation conflicts is beyond a book on wreck law, but there is a real possibility of conflict of laws in relation to the wreck removal reservation in Art 18 of the LLMC.[754] This will be examined in the following sections.

2.5.9(c) *Baltic Ace* litigation

The tactics in relation to limitation and wreck claims are illustrated by the sinking outside Dutch territorial waters of the *Baltic Ace* (23,498 gt) on 5 December 2012 following a collision with the container ship *Corvus J*.[755] Wreck removal work started in 2014 and was completed in 2015.[756] The Netherlands had exercised the LLMC 1996 Art 18 reservation

---

748 See eg *Caltex Singapore v BP Shipping Ltd* [1996] 1 Lloyd's Rep 286; *The Vishbha Abha* [1990] 2 Lloyd's Rep 3112; *The Herceg Novi and The Ming Galaxy* [1998] 2 Lloyd's Rep 254; *The Western Regent* [2005] EWCA 985, [2005] 2 Lloyd's Rep 359. Reynolds and Tsimplis, 172–178, 190–193; Derrington & Turner, 286–297; F. Berlingieri (ed), *Travaux Préparatoires of the LLMC Convention, 1976, and of the Protocol of 1996* (CMI, 2000).

749 [1998] 2 Lloyd's Rep 254.

750 The public policy arguments in favour of giving more recognition to the rights of the 'reservation State' are developed more in 2.5.9(f). Such arguments are relevant also to EU law: see 2.5.9(e).

751 Where there is a conflict between the Limitation Convention 1957 and the LLMC 1976 the shipowner might actually prefer an LLMC jurisdiction as it is more difficult to break limits under the LLMC Art 4 than under the "actual fault or privity" rules in Art 1(1) of the former: see further 2.5.7 and eg *The Herceg Novi and Ming Galaxy* [1998] 2 Lloyd's Rep 454.

752 Subject to giving credit where appropriate for claims paid: see Arts 12(2) and (4).

753 Eg on *forum non conveniens* grounds in common law States, where the EU regime does not apply.

754 See 2.5.8. Strictly, the reservation for LLMC 1976 is made under Art 18(1), while under the LLMC 1996, the reservation is made under Art 18(1)(b) (as a result of the amendments made in the LLMC 1996 Protocol).

755 See also 2.5.4(c), 10.2.5, 13.1; also *Van der Kuil*.

756 See *Baltic Ace Wreck Removal* and 1.2.5(a).

in respect of wreck and cargo removal,[757] and the Dutch government incurred estimated wreck removal costs of some €67 million. There were also anticipated claims from others, including the cargo owners and the owners of the other ship involved in the collision, the *Corvus J*. The latter had been arrested in Flushing by the Netherlands, and its owners had created a limitation fund there while also seeking declarations of non-liability.[758]

The ship was flagged in the Bahamas,[759] but the registered shipowner, Baltic Highway Ltd, was a private company incorporated (and domiciled) in the Isle of Man.[760] Two days after the collision, the master of the *Baltic Ace* filed a claim for the loss of personal effects in the High Court of the Isle of Man.[761] Six days after the collision, the shipowner brought a limitation action[762] in the same court, based on the LLMC 1996 as applied in the Isle of Man.[763] On 3 May 2013 the North of England P&I Club constituted a fund by way of an irrevocable letter of credit undertaking.[764] The *Corvus J* owners argued that the Manx court should dismiss or stay its limitation action in favour of the Dutch proceedings, but the Isle of Man High Court refused the application and allowed the limitation claim to proceed. A justifiable basis for this was that limitation proceedings were separate from liability proceedings, ie a Dutch court could decide liability and the net claimants could come to the Isle of Man to compete for the fund there.[765] This is consistent with English authorities that recognise the right of the shipowner to choose the forum for limitation, eg in its place of incorporation.[766]

Of particular significance, though, are the observations made by the court in relation to any exercise of discretion to stay on the basis that this would cause a substantial injustice[767]

---

757 See 2.5.8.

758 Such negative declarations are a well-recognised attempt by potential defendants to pre-empt claimants who might otherwise start liability proceedings in a jurisdiction of their choice. In EU law the starting of an action for such a declaration of non-liability would make the court hearing the claim the first seised so as to trigger the rules of recognition of such proceedings in other States: see Brussels I Regulation Recast Arts 37–34.

759 And the Bahamas Maritime Authority carried out an accident investigation: see Report, 26 May 2016.

760 The Isle of Man is an internally self-governing British Crown Dependency, like Jersey and Guernsey. Although it is not part of the UK, the UK is responsible for international relations. The territory is not part of the EU or EEA: see www.gov.im/media/624101/protocol3relationshipwiththeeu.pdf. Like the Channel Islands, though, it may voluntarily use EU legislation.

761 The Polish master's relatively small claim at this early stage seems rather unusual. At the least, it enabled the shipowner to assert that there was a substantive claim on the merits in the Isle of Man, so as to facilitate an argument both that a limitation fund could be established under Art 11(1) (see 2.5.9(a)) and that it was a convenient forum for the limitation action. If shipowners are able to persuade crew members to launch tactical claims in friendly jurisdictions, their limitation forum shopping possibilities are enhanced.

762 *Baltic Highway v Przybyla*, 7 January 2014 (Isle of Man High Court; case ref 78): www.judgments.im/Content/J1443.htm.

763 Enacted in the Merchant Shipping (Convention on Limitation for Maritime Claims) Application Order 2000 (SD 386/00) made under section 5 of the Merchant Shipping Act 1995 (Act of Tynwald).

764 Club guarantees in the form of a letter of undertaking are cheaper and are also accepted in the English system as an alternative to the creation of a cash fund: *Kairos Shipping Limited v Enka & Co LLC and others (The Atlantik Confidence)* [2014] EWCA 21, [2014] 1 Lloyd's Rep 586. See now CPR 61.11(18).

765 The court followed an earlier Manx Appeal Division judgment in *Dominator Limited v Gilberson SL and Others 2009* MLR 161; www.judgments.im/Content/J1153.htm.

766 See eg *The Volvox Hollandia* [1988] 2 Lloyd's Rep 361; *Bougues Offshore SA v Caspian Shipping* [1998] 2 Lloyd's Rep 461, 474; *The Western Regent* [2005] 2 Lloyd's Rep 359.

767 A factor recognised by English courts in cases such as *The Herceg Novi and The Ming Galaxy* [1998] 2 Lloyd's Rep 454.

to the registered shipowner if it had to instigate limitation proceedings in the Netherlands. The judge[768] noted that in the Dutch implementation of the LLMC 1996 wreck removal costs were excluded but that a shipowner could establish a second limitation "wreck fund" under Dutch law for such costs.[769] In the *Baltic Ace* case it was said that this second limit would apparently have been about £9 million. This, not surprisingly, would have been similar to the Manx LLMC 1996 'property' limitation fund of about £9,873,641,[770] but this would have to cover all physical damage claims, eg including cargo loss, collision damage and (according to the judge) the wreck removal expenses. In other words, the Isle of Man court would apply the limit without regard to the Dutch position under the LLMC 1996 that there was no limit for wreck removal.

Such a conclusion may well be understandable from the perspective of the Manx (non-reservation) perspective,[771] but it undermines the important power of reservation given by the LLMC Art 18. It raises the broader question as to whether owners—even those entered in an International Group Club—will be able to avoid a State's LLMC Art 18 wreck and cargo raising reservations through the simple expedient of establishing a limitation fund in a State that has not exercised the reservations. It could make States or territories such as the Isle of Man a real choice for forum shopping[772] to reduce a registered shipowner's wreck removal liabilities.[773]

There are two problems with this aspect of the decision. The first is that it is not clear why the Isle of Man would not have applied the wreck removal reservation, as its acceptance had been earlier notified to the IMO by the UK on behalf of the Isle of Man.[774] There does not appear to have been any argument about whether the Manx court should in any way recognise the Art 18 position of the Netherlands, but it might not be surprising if a non-reservation State simply ignored that fact in applying its own domestic version of the LLMC.[775]

The second problem is, what would be the position in the Netherlands, ie a 'reservation State'. Would it have been obliged by the LLMC 1996 to bring its wreck removal liability

---

768 His Honour The Deemster Doyle, First Deemster and Clerk of the Rolls, at para 61.

769 Art 8:75 5(1)(c) of Dutch Civil Code, with the amount apparently being equal to the property fund: see *Van der Kuil*, 88. A similar provision apparently existed in German law: see the *Uno* case 2.5.9(d) and (e).

770 Authors' calculation based on 1 sdr = £1.02859 as at 2 May 2013.

771 See also the *Uno* and *Assi Eurolink* cases, 2.5.9(d) and (e).

772 R Butler, "Awareness of Global Limitation Regimes Key to Curbing Wreck Removal Exposure", *TradeWinds* (11 April 2014), available at www.hfw.com/Awareness-of-global-limitation-August-2014. Butler suggests that "the decision is likely to give a further boost to the Manx Register—now in the world's top 15 by tonnage, and ahead of Germany—and to Manx-registered owners. Other parties able to show a Manx 'jurisdictional link' might also be able to benefit".

773 See *Van der Kuil*.

774 The LLMC 1976 had been extended by the UK to the Isle of Man until denunciation with effect from 1 May 2012. The LLMC 1996 was extended with effect from 13 May 2004, although it was not until 25 May 2012 that the IMO was informed by the UK of the application to the Isle of Man of the UK's Art 18 reservations (eg as to Art 2(1)(d), but not (e): see 2.6.9). *IMO Status of Treaties* (November 2018). It may be that the reservations had not been effectively incorporated into Manx domestic law, but the authors have not been able to verify the position.

775 See also 2.5.9(f).

judgment to the Isle of Man and submit to the limit?[776] Or, could it effectively ignore the Manx fund as being irrelevant, on the basis that its international obligations under the LLMC 1996 allowed it to have unlimited liability in its own courts? Either way, there is a potential conflict of decisions which is not really resolved by the LLMC itself, and the position may differ depending on whether the relevant States are subject to the separate EU rules on jurisdiction and judgments. The position under the LLMC will first be considered, before taking into account the added difficulties in EU law.

2.5.9(d) LLMC fund and the wreck removal reservation

The LLMC itself is silent on what is supposed to happen when a limitation fund is established in a State party which has not exercised the reservation (ie a 'non-reservation State'), but a wreck liability claim can be brought in another State party, eg the Netherlands[777] or Australia. It is significant that many large open registry States are party to the LLMC 1976 and/or the LLMC 1996,[778] but few have made the Art 18 reservation.[779]

In the *Uno* case,[780] a Danish owned and registered ship (1,937 gt) sank in Germany in 2002 and a German State authority [WSN] paid €770,000 to raise it. After selling the remains there was a net claim of €746,528 and WSN obtained a German court judgment for wreck removal liability for 406,979 sdrs.[781] The judgment became binding and conclusive on 3 July 2003, and on 6 February 2004, a Danish court endorsed the judgment so that it could be enforced.[782] On 29 March 2004, the shipowner invoked limitation in the Maritime and Commercial Court of Copenhagen (on the basis of security provided by the P&I Club, Skuld), having indicated in the German proceedings that it would seek this further limitation. On the basis that Denmark was a non-reservation State, the Danish court allowed the shipowner to limit liability to the normal LLMC Art 6 amount of 406,979 sdr (plus interest). Such a fund was of course available to other claimants, eg in relation to cargo loss and bunker pollution, although WSN was able to put forward its full claim of 979,856 sdrs. As the shipowner had declined to establish a fund in Germany, the Art 13(1) bar to further

---

776 Butler, fn 772, concluded that the Dutch claim in the Isle of Man would be a "recourse claim" subject to the LLMC limits, although strictly the Dutch claim would be a direct claim, whereas any claim against the *Corvus J* for contributing to the collision would have been by way of recourse. For the difficulties of limitation for that claim, see 2.5.4(c).

777 The WRC 2007 did not come into force for the Netherlands until 19 April 2016, so it did not apply, but the position would have been no different if it had: cf 10.7. As the Netherlands is an EU State, its position is complicated by the EU rules on jurisdiction and judgments, so Australia will be taken as an example of a 'reservation State' (although it is not party to the WRC 2007).

778 Eg Bahamas, Liberia, the Marshall Islands, and a number of small island States. Liberia, Cyprus and Malta are LLMC 1996 States, but only the latter two have made the Art 18 reservation.

779 Of those with large registered fleets, Cyprus (LLMC 1976 and 1996) and Malta (LLMC 1996) have done so.

780 Decision of 11 May 2005, cited in F Smeele, "International Civil Litigation and the Pollution of the Marine Environment", 17 [*Smeele*] (with an Annex I translation of the decision by Hens Feilberg of Gorrisen Federspiel Kierkegaard); available at https://core.ac.uk/download/pdf/18513993.pdf.

781 The full claim was for as much as 979,856 sdrs, but apparently the German implementation of the Art 18 reservation allowed a separate limitation for wreck claims in the same amount as property claims—similar to that in Dutch law—and this produced the 406,979 sdr figure. WSN withdrew its claim for the difference in the German court, presumably on the basis that LLMC Art 10 allowed limitation as a defence without the establishment of a fund.

782 Under the then applicable Brussels I Regulation (Regulation (EC) No 44/2001) Art 33.

actions did not apply. It did not matter that the fund was set up after the final liability judgment had been given in Germany. The decision seems right as a matter of Danish law, but the more difficult question is how far the German authority would have been able to avoid this decision, eg first seeking a declaration in the German courts that the shipowner was not entitled to limit liability,[783] or (after the Danish judgment) returning to the German courts to enforce the first judgment (assuming there were assets in Germany).

While 'non-reservation States' can validly apply the Art 2(1)(d) and (e) wreck limits,[784] is the State party that has made such a reservation (ie a 'reservation State') bound by the way that the other State applied the limitation fund? Article 15(1) dealing with scope of application, obliges the courts of State parties to apply the convention if an application is made (i) to limit in *that* State or (ii) to release security held in that State.[785]

A literal reading of Art 13(1) would mean that once a fund has been established in a State party then there is a bar on the claimant exercising rights against the shipowner or its insurer, eg elsewhere. It is clear that such a bar can apply to wreck claims brought in the 'non-reservation State' (eg Liberia or Sweden[786]), but how can it be interpreted to apply to the courts of the 'reservation State' (eg Australia)? There are two scenarios here.

First, the wreck claimant may claim (perhaps mistakenly) against a fund in the 'non-reservation State' (even though the claim is not limitable); there is a difference of opinion on whether Art 13(1) generally bars a clamant whose claim is not subject to limitation from seeking to "claim" from other assets. *Griggs et al*[787] take the view that the bar operates, while *Reynolds and Tsimplis* disagree to the extent that the claimant is only prevented from pursuing other assets "during the period the claim is pursued against the limitation fund".[788] The latter view has some merit in that it avoids giving effect to an error, and it would make sense for courts to allow claimants to withdraw a claim against the fund in order to seek assets elsewhere;[789] but it is not clear if the authors mean that the claimant has in effect to elect *either* to claim against the fund *or* to seek the assets elsewhere. The idea that the claimant could claim against the fund (pro rata with other claimants) and then seek to 'top-up' its claim against other assets has a certain merit, but the wording of Art 13(1) suggests that this option is not open; ie that an election has to be made. This may have the unfortunate consequence that the wreck claimant may have to risk opting for the bird in the hand (ie a share of the limitation fund) rather than the one in the bush (ie an unlimited claim elsewhere, but with uncertainty about whether assets are available).[790]

---

783 See *Smeele*, 18.
784 As did the Manx court did with *Baltic Ace* and the Danish court with the *Uno*.
785 To that extent, it would seem to cover releasing security to support a limitation action in another State: see Art 13(2).
786 The Isle of Man is not given here as an example, owing to the uncertainty raised above as to whether there is a reservation applicable to it: see fn 774.
787 At 69.
788 At 127.
789 In the *Seawheel Rhine/Assi Eurolink* case (see 2.5.9(e)), owners made a conditional claim on a limitation fund in Sweden, denying in particular the competence of the Swedish court. This seems an appropriate course of action.
790 In a wreck claim the ship itself cannot practically be arrested for security, and it may be rare that a sister ship is available (but cf the *Torrey Canyon*, 1.2.1(b)). It is for such reasons that the WRC 2007 compulsory insurance provisions are relevant: see 2.5.9(f) and 10.8.

Secondly, what should be the approach of the 'reservation State's' courts to the limitation fund established in the non-reservation State? The Art 13(1) bar seems to be personal to the liability claimant, not a requirement on a State party itself to recognise the judgment.[791] If a claimant did elect to bring its wreck removal claim in a 'reservation State', the shipowner might seek an anti-suit injunction in the non-reservation State to prevent the claim being brought in the 'reservation State'. As a wreck claimant is likely to be the State itself, that would also raise issues of sovereign immunity as well as practicality.

The view of the LLMC 1996 'reservation State' (eg Australia) would simply be that there may well be an LLMC 1996 limitation fund validly established, and it may well limit claims brought in the State in which it is constituted (eg Liberia or Sweden); these could include normal claims like cargo damage, but also wreck and cargo raising claims arising that are brought in that State.[792] But it would have no effect on wreck removal claims brought in the 'reservation State' (eg Australia), as that State recognises no wreck removal limits and, by making the international reservation, it has given notice to all other State parties that it does not recognise limitation for wreck removal. It is significant that the reservation applies to all wreck removal (d) and (e) claims—not simply those arising in the 'reservation State' itself. So even a foreign State (or authority, or company) that claimed wreck removal expenses in the 'reservation State' would not face any shipowner's LLMC limit in that State.

The courts of the 'reservation State' may decide to exercise their own limitation jurisdiction to hear the wreck claims, and to decline any application for a stay in favour of the courts of the 'non-reservation State'. The Art 13(1) bar would not operate unless the wreck claimant has actually made a claim against the fund in the 'non-reservation State'.[793] The Art 13(2) restriction on arresting or attaching assets only applies to a provisional remedy to obtain security;[794] it would not apply to a claim to enforce an unlimited *judgment* in the 'reservation State'. The 'reservation State' judgment would only have a value, of course, if the shipowner had assets within the jurisdiction, or if that judgment could be enforced in a place where the shipowner did have assets. For EU States the position is more complicated.

2.5.9(e) Limitation fund recognition and the EU
The issue of resolving conflicts between LLMC 'reservation' and 'non-reservation States' is affected by the EU jurisdiction and judgments regime.[795] Within the EU, it appears that the following LLMC 1996 States have exercised the Art 18 reservation: Belgium, Croatia, Cyprus, France, Germany, Lithuania, Malta, the Netherlands, Poland, Spain and the

---

791 This is further complicated by the EU jurisdiction and judgments regime. See eg Article 6A of the Brussels Convention on Jurisdiction and the Enforcement of Judgments in Civil and Commercial Matters 1968 as applied in *Dominator Limited v Gilberson SL and Others 2009* MLR 161 (2.5.9(c)). See now Brussels I Regulation Recast Art 9 and 2.5.9(e).

792 These would include wreck claims arising for or in relation to that State or territory (eg a wreck in the Isle of Man), as well as wreck claims occurring elsewhere.

793 Because Art 13(1) refers to a "person having made a claim against the fund": see also 2.5.9(b). As noted, the claimant may have to elect whether to claim against the fund, or to proceed only in the 'reservation State'.

794 And, as noted in 2.5.9(b), it almost certainly does not apply to a common law freezing (or *Mareva*) injunction.

795 See *Tsimplis*.

UK.[796] The following EU States have not exercised the LLMC 1996 Art 18 reservation: Bulgaria, Denmark, Estonia, Finland, Greece, Hungary, Ireland, Latvia, Luxembourg, Portugal, Romania, Slovenia and Sweden.[797] Note that although a State has reserved the *right* to make a reservation, it may not necessarily have exercised that right in its national law: the UK is an example of such a State.[798] Some States are not party to the LLMC at all.[799]

The Brussels I Regulation Recast Art 9 provides that where EU Member States have jurisdiction in relation to liability they also have jurisdiction over claims for limitation of liability. The Regulation also contains well known rules on related actions in different Member States. Under Art 29 where proceedings involving the same cause of action and between the same parties are brought in the courts of different Member States, a court is obliged to stay its proceedings in favour of the court first seised. This has sometimes led to a rush to establish jurisdiction, and defendants might seek to do so by claiming relief in the form of a declaratory judgment of non-liability.[800] Where actions are merely related, courts have a discretion to stay under Art 30. Where there are proceedings in a Member State but also those in a third (ie non-EU) State (involving the same cause of action and between the same parties, the Member State's court may stay its own proceedings under Art 33, but must dismiss them if those in the third State have been concluded and have resulted in a judgment capable of enforcement.

Judgments given in a Member State must be recognised under Chapter III of Brussels I Regulation I Recast, but under Art 45(1)(a) such recognition must be refused if "such recognition is manifestly contrary to public policy (ordre public)" in the recognising Member State. This expression is interpreted restrictively by the CJEU,[801] but it is at least open for argument in a limitation case, eg in the conflict between limitation actions in 'reservation States' and claims brought in 'non-reservation States'.[802] But the public policy exception cannot be applied to the jurisdictional rules,[803] only those relating to recognition. Refusal of recognition must also occur under Art 45(1)(c) and (d) if the foreign Member State judgment is irreconcilable with an earlier judgment in the Member State. This means that (subject to Brexit) an English court would not enforce a foreign limitation decree if an earlier one had already been granted in the UK. However, it is likely that before this stage

---

796 In addition, the following LLMC 1996 have exercised the reservation: Canada, Hong Kong (China) (and only for para (d)), the Russian Federation and Turkey.

797 Norway, as an EEA member, has also not made a reservation. Other LLMC 1996 'non-reservation States' include: Antigua and Barbuda, Iceland, China (PRC), Comoros, Cook Islands, India, Jamaica, Japan, Kenya, Liberia, Madagascar, Malaysia, the Marshall Islands, Mongolia, New Zealand (and see 1.2.4(d)), Niue, Palau, Saint Lucia, Samoa, Saudi Arabia, Serbia, Sierra Leone, Syria, Tonga and Tuvalu.

798 See 2.5.8.

799 Eg Austria, Czech Republic, Italy and Slovakia.

800 Cf *Saipem SpA v Dredging VO2 BV (The Volvox Hollandia (No 1))* [1988] 2 Lloyd's Rep 361; *Owners of Cargo Lately Laden on Board the Tatry v Owners of the Maciej Rataj (Case C-406/92)* [1999] QB 515, [1995] 1 Lloyd's Rep 302 [*sub nom. the Maciej Rataj*].

801 See eg *Marco Gambazzi v DaimlerChrysler Canada Inc (Case C-394/07)* [2010] QB 388; [2009] 1 Lloyd's Rep 647; *Reynolds and Tsimplis*, 205–206.

802 See 2.5.9(c) and (d). For arguments in favour of a State exercising this public policy exception see 2.5.9(f). It might even be possible for a State expressly to declare its public policy in legislation, eg in its enactment of the LLMC or WRC 2007: see 11.2.3.

803 Art 45(3).

of irreconcilable judgments has been reached, there will have been applications for a jurisdictional stay.

In the *Uno* case,[804] the Danish court applied the judgment of the ECJ in *Maersk Olie and Gas A/S v Firma M de Haan and W de Boer*.[805] In that case a Dutch trawler (*Comelis Simon*) damaged Maersk's oil and gas pipelines in June 1985. A limitation claim was brought in the Dutch courts under the Limitation Convention 1957 in April 1987 and Maersk was notified of the provisional decree on 5 June; the order was upheld in 1988, but Maersk declined to claim against the fund. Meanwhile, on 20 June 1987 Maersk brought a liability claim in a Danish court. The ECJ held that under the then jurisdiction and judgments regime,[806] the liability action on the merits was separate from proceedings for the establishment of a limitation fund so that the pendente lite provisions did not apply; there were different causes of action and different subject matter. The Danish court was first seised only in respect of the liability issues. Moreover, the limitation judgment was one that had to be recognised in Denmark. The case appeared to be about a conflict of limitation conventions, as it appeared that by 1987 the Danish court would have applied the LLMC 1976, although the Netherlands did not apply the LLMC until 1990. The broad result was that a Member State was bound to recognise a judgment establishing a limitation fund in another Member State even in circumstances where that might lead to a different result to that in the other Member State. As the two sets of proceedings are related, it would have been possible for whichever court was first seised to stay its own proceedings in favour of the other,[807] but once there has been a limitation judgment it must be enforced. The position does not appear to be different under Brussels I Regulation Recast, even though the *Maersk Olie* case was not concerned with the wreck removal reservations.

A similar result was reached by the Netherlands Supreme Court in 2006 in the *Seawheel Rhine/Assi Eurolink* case.[808] Following a collision in January 2003, the *Assi Eurolink* became a wreck and on 10 February 2003 its Dutch owners gave notice to the Swedish owners and charterers[809] of the *Seawheel Rhine* of proceedings in the Netherlands to recover collision losses and payments for wreck removal. On 19 February, the *Seawheel Rhine* owners started Swedish arbitration proceedings against the charterers and in 24 February the charterers started a limitation action in Sweden. A fund was constituted though a guarantee from the Swedish Club and Alandia (the hull underwriter) in the sum of 1,800,093 sdr. On 12 March 2003 the *Assi Eurolink*'s owners arrested the *Seawheel Rhine* in Rotterdam and security was given for 1,800,093 sdrs (a normal property fund) and for 2,628,375 sdrs (wreck removal). As noted,[810] the Netherlands was an LLMC 'reservation State' that required a second 'wreck fund' rather than having unlimited liability for wreck

---

804 Decision of 11 May 2005: see 2.5.9(d).
805 Case C-39/02, [2005] 1 Lloyd's Rep 210.
806 The Convention on Jurisdiction and the Enforcement of Judgments in Civil and Commercial Matters 1968.
807 On the basis of what is now Art 30 of Brussels Regulation I (Recast).
808 Hoge Raad First Chamber, 29 September 2006, No C05/147 HRJ MH/MK (2007) Schip & Schade 1. Cited in *Smeele*,, 23 (with an Annex II unofficial translation of the decision by *Smeele* of the Rotterdam law firm Van Traa Advocaten). See also *Van der Kuil*, 77, 89.
809 It is assumed that they were bareboat charterers and thus liable for navigation and to indemnify the owner against loss or damage.
810 See 2.5.9(d).

removal. By contrast Sweden, while also an LLMC State, had not made the Art 18 reservation, with the effect that in Swedish law the basic property fund limit applied to all property claims, including wreck removal. The *Seawheel Rhine* owners therefore applied to the Dutch courts for the extra 'wreck' security to be released. At first instance and in the Court of Appeal, this application was dismissed for a variety of grounds[811] that were later overturned in the Netherlands Supreme Court. That court held that it was bound to recognise the Swedish limitation judgment under the then Brussels I Regulation,[812] with the result that the LLMC Art 13(1) 'immunity' extended to the Netherlands. This meant that extra security provided in the Netherlands had to be released, despite the conditional nature of the Dutch owners' "claim against the fund" under LLMC Art 13(1). The decision rested squarely on the EU regime under which the Dutch courts could not investigate the accuracy of the Swedish court's decision, eg whether it had jurisdiction.

The consequence is that the LLMC wreck removal reservation is seriously undermined by the application of the EU jurisdiction and judgement rules, particularly where a State has opted for unlimited liability. It may be possible to try to persuade a court in the 'non-reservation State' (eg Sweden or Denmark) to stay its proceedings under Brussels I Regulation Recast Art 30, provided that another court (eg in the Netherlands) has been first seised in a "related matter" (eg the liability action). As usual with the EU regime, there appears to be an imperative to rush to court in order to be first seised. It is not quite clear how far a court in, say, Germany or the Netherlands could be asked in a liability action also to make a definitive declaratory ruling about limitation, so as to make this enforceable in a non-reservation State such as Denmark or Sweden. Here, there might be the possibility of irreconcilable decisions so as to allow the 'non-reservation State' to refuse recognition under Art 45(1)(c). So far, it does not appear to have been argued that recognition of the non-reservation limitation is manifestly contrary to public policy under Brussels I Regulation Recast Art 45(1)(a). The merits of limitation in the commercial context can be debated,[813] but it is worth noting that where States are claimants in (essentially) environmental actions a public policy argument may be stronger. This EU regime would not apply to limitation funds established in non-EU States (eg Australia, Singapore) or in territories such as the Isle of Man where more purposive LLMC arguments[814] may well be proffered.

The Rome II Regulation Art 15 further complicates the matter by providing that the law applicable to non-contractual obligations (eg tort claims) also governs limitation of liability. Where the wreck removal claim was governed by, say, Swedish law, it might be argued that the English court would be obliged to apply the limitation regime of Sweden. *Marsden & Gault*[815] suggest that such a conclusion could be avoided by applying English

---

811 Eg that the arbitration proceedings were not legal proceedings within LLMC Art 11(1), so that the Swedish court had no jurisdiction to decide on limitation; or that the shipowner could not refer to such a proceeding in which it was the claimant (cf 2.5.9(a)); or that the 10 February proceedings came before the arbitration proceedings (ie so that the Dutch courts were first seised); or that enforcement proceedings should be refused as the Dutch claimants had not been given the opportunity to contest the competence of the Swedish courts.

812 See now Brussels I Regulation Recast Art 39. It did not matter that the initial limitation decree was made ex parte provided it was served or notified and there was an opportunity to challenge it (see now Art 45(2) of Brussels I Regulation Recast).

813 See also 2.5.9(f).

814 See eg 2.5.9(d).

815 At 846.

limitation law under the MSA 1995 Sch 7 as a mandatory law for the purposes of Art 16 of the Rome II Regulation, or by applying the public policy exception in Art 26 of Rome II. Although English law may prefer to categorise limitation rights as procedural[816] and outside Rome II,[817] it is by no means clear that this is an approach that would be adopted by other legal systems or the CJEU.[818]

2.5.9(f) Limitation forum shopping, the WRC 2007 and policy
The resolution of this limitation forum shopping issue would be particularly important if the WRC 2007 were also in force in a particular State and the limitation issue arose there. Here there is a difficult intersection of the WRC 2007 regime and that under the LLMC, particularly as the WRC 2007 would make the insurer directly liable under that State's law.[819] If the State's own limitation law allowed the shipowner to limit for wreck removal claims, ie it was a 'non-reservation State', then both the shipowner and insurer could limit liability in the ordinary way.[820] Even here, the shipowner and insurer might seek to limit liability in another State, eg one that was party to the LLMC 1976.[821] The possibility that the shipowner member itself could forum shop to achieve a limit for WRC 2007 wreck removal claims[822] might be a significant bargaining chip to a Club that otherwise might have stood behind the member (as in *Rena* and *Costa Concordia*)—even without direct liability.[823] To this extent, cases such as the *Baltic Ace, Uno* and *Seawheel Rhine/Assi Eurolink* suggest that there are some gaps in the protection that States may expect from wreck removal law.

If the Affected State did not allow the shipowner to limit (ie because it was a 'reservation State'), then the insurer would be directly liable up to the cap in Art 12(10)).[824] It is arguable that the insurer would not be able to forum shop for limitation purposes, eg to a 'non-reservation' LLMC 1976 State.[825] However, it would only be directly liable in that Affected State up to the LLMC 1996 limits under WRC 2007 Art 12(1) and (10).[826]

It is here that the WRC 2007 at least offers some minimum protection levels. If States find that an 'Isle of Man' defence is being used regularly, then they may decide that global limitation under the LLMC is no longer tolerable;[827] their difficulty is that even if they denounce the LLMC they may create unlimited liability but against an impecunious single ship company, and within the EU regime they would still be stuck with recognising a limitation fund in another Member State. The fear will be that cases such as *Baltic Ace* may be

---

816 See *Caltex Singapore v BP Shipping Ltd* [1996] 1 Lloyd's Rep 286, 296–7.
817 See Art 1(3).
818 See *Reynolds and Tsimplis*, 207–211.
819 See 10.8.
820 See 10.8.5(b).
821 See 10.8.5(c).
822 But see 10.8.5(c) for a possible restriction on forum shopping under the WRC 2007.
823 An Affected State may seek to 'top up' sums claimed directly from the insurer under the WRC 2007 Art 12(10) by suing the registered shipowner for any excess liability, eg where it was not entitled to limit because of the LLMC Art 18 reservation: see 2.5.8, 10.8.5(d).
824 See 10.8.4 and 10.8.5(d).
825 See 10.8.5(c) and (d). The reason is that the WRC Art 12(10) liability cap is technically separate from the LLMC limits, albeit that it borrows an LLMC 1996 calculation: see also 10.8.5(a).
826 See 10.8.5(d).
827 Cf 11.2.1, 11.2.3.

more of a guide as to the future practice of shipowners and insurers than cases such as the *Rena*[828] and *Costa Concordia*.[829]

There is here not only a conflict of laws but also of underlying policies; the shipowner's right to limit, against the State's right to have a wreck removal claim not subject to limitation. Some commentators have rather welcomed the principle that LLMC States parties should be bound to recognise the legal effects of foreign limitation decisions,[830] or that the EU rules have helpfully extended the scope of limitation.[831] The recognition of the foreign limitation proceedings in all cases gives effect to the idea of a concursus to which all claims should be brought; here there are parallels with the Model Law on Cross Border Insolvency, where there is a recognition of the need for a single place where the debtor has the centre of its main interests.[832]

By contrast, where a convention specifically allows for wreck limitation to be excluded in a State—and that right is recognised by all other contracting States—it would undermine that international agreement if the 'non-reservation State' was obliged to give up that significant right (which directly affects its own interests) in its own law simply because a shipowner in effect avoids that right by forum shopping elsewhere. Given the uncertainty in the LLMC itself, it is arguable that, where there is doubt about whether a shipowner can limit, the courts ought to err on the side of the default position, ie no limits—if only in the wider environmental context of wreck removal.

As a matter of broad principle, it is submitted that consideration of the 'reservation State's' position is the more important, and would be relevant in any assessment of public policy. It is also submitted that the absence of express recognition and enforcement provisions in the LLMC[833] gives rise to sufficient uncertainty as to the proper interpretation of the LLMC for a court in an LLMC reservation State to refuse to be bound by a decree in a non-reservation State limiting liability for wreck removal—unless bound by EU law to do so. It would be as if that non-reservation State had allowed a claim for limitation that clearly did not fall within LLMC Art 2 at all.[834] Unless the reservation State was bound by that 'wrong' interpretation by the 'non-reservation State', eg as a result of the EU jurisdiction and judgment rules,[835] the 'reservation State' would not seem to be bound in international law by an incorrect interpretation of the convention. In a similar manner, it can be argued that the foreign decree is simply irrelevant in the 'reservation State' which, in international law, is entitled to have unlimited liability for wreck and cargo removal in its national law.

---

828 In the *Rena*, there was always the possibility that the shipowner might claim to limit under the LLMC 1976, and this may have influenced the eventual settlement: see 1.2.4(e).

829 See 1.2.5(c).

830 *Van der Kuil*, 85.

831 *Smeele*, 25.

832 But even here there is a recognition that the pre-existence of a maritime lien in another State may be a special maritime security that may have to be recognised: see S Derrington, "The Interaction between Admiralty and Insolvency Law" (2009) 5 ANZ MLJ 30; M Hafeez-Baig, "The Interaction of the Statutory Right of Action In Rem and the Cross-Border Insolvency Act 2008 (Cth)" (2018) 26 Insolv LJ 22.

833 Cf the CLC 1992 and HNSC 2010: 2.6.2(a), 2.6.4.

834 Eg a claim for salvage under LLMC Art 3, or a claim to limit for a floating platform (excluded by LLMC Art 15(5)(b)).

835 See 2.5.9(e). It may be that this is the conclusion to be reached in EU law, although for the reasons given in this section the authors consider that courts in the EU may have taken a wrong turn.

It should be recalled that LLMC Art 2(1)(d) may also cover bunker clean-up costs, in so far as this is a form of rendering harmless something that has been on the ship.[836] If the non-'reservation State' establishes a limitation fund, this would also apply to limit bunker clean-up claims. If the 'reservation State' that suffered bunker pollution was bound to recognise that fund, its reservation in respect of a major claim with national significance would again be seriously undermined (or, indeed, made worthless). Of course, in a Bunkers Convention 2001 case the State would still have access to the direct action claim against the insurer (under Art 7(10)).

A more serious example would be if the HNSC 2010 enters into force. Unlike the CLC 1992, claims within the meaning of the HNSC 2010 are not automatically excluded from the LLMC under Art 3.[837] The LLMC Protocol 1996 inserted a new power of reservation in Art 18(1)(b) so that States had the option to reserve the right to exclude claims within the meaning of the HNSC from LLMC limitation. Otherwise, such HNS claims would fall within the LLMC Art 2(1)(a) (for property damage), Art 2(1)(c) (for economic loss claims) or Art 2(1)(e) (clean-up of HNS). In future, a 'non-reservation State' (ie here non-reservation under Art 18(1)(b)) that was not party to the HNSC 2010 could apply its LLMC fund to HNS claims in another State.[838] Again, if the forum shopping argument were to prevail, the major advances made by the HNSC could be bypassed. At the original HNS diplomatic conference in 2006, the shipowners and P&I Clubs failed to obtain a direct linkage between the HNSC and the LLMC[839] and States opted for stand-alone HNS limits (as with the CLC). It would be ironic if an indirect linkage had been achieved by dealing with the HNSC 2010 as a reservation rather than an exception in the LLMC 1996.

Similar issues can arise in relation to the various options given to States under Art 15 of the LLMC, eg to have lower limits in national law for ships under 300 gt.[840] There is no doubt that a national court, eg in the UK, would apply its own lower limits for such ships. But does that "national law" also bind another State party (which applied the higher convention limits based on 500 gt) to accept such a lower limit in international law; or could this State allow a claim to be brought in its courts for the difference between the 300–500 gt calculations? It is theoretically possible for a State to use Art 15(2)(b) to have unlimited liability for ships under 300 gt,[841] although this would be highly unusual (as the idea is to protect owners of smaller ships). In that case, there might be a limitation decision establishing a fund, combined with a declaration that a particular small shipowner could not limit. Could that shipowner then seek to establish a fund in a State that had not exercised the option?

---

836 See 2.5.4(b).
837 See 2.5.4(b).
838 If the 'non-reservation State' was also a party to the HNSC 2010, that might result in a conflict between the two conventions, as each would purport to apply limits to the same claim, but in these circumstances Art 42 of the HNSC 2010 (the "supersession clause") would mean that the 2010 Convention would take priority between the two conventions (as between State parties to both). The supersession clause by its own terms would not apply to States that were not party to the HNSC 2010.
839 As was later almost entirely achieved with the Bunker Convention 2011 Art 6 (see 2.6.3), and achieved by the WRC 2007 Art 10(2) and Art 12(10) (see 10.7, 10.8.5).
840 Art 15(2)(b).
841 See the tailpiece to Art 15(2), which refers generally to the need to notify the IMO of "the limits of liability adopted in its national legislation *or of the fact that there are none*" (emphasis added).

If forum shopping to a 'non-reservation State' is generally effective, this might lead 'reservation States' to consider that they had been misled about the LLMC bargain and would give them a strong incentive to denounce the LLMC. This would further undermine the universality of international maritime law.[842]

2.6 Wreck and pollution liability

Since the wreck of the oil tanker *Torrey Canyon* in 1967, the legal focus of attention has shifted significantly from the commercial losses of the shipping parties directly involved in the maritime adventure (eg shipowners, cargo owners and charterers) and to the environmental and consequential economic losses caused by pollution. This section aims to provide the background to, and an overview[843] of, the suite of IMO conventions that provide for liability for pollution following a wreck.[844] The conventions do not deal exclusively with wrecks, as they may also provide liability for leaks from ships that are not in distress, as well as from ships that may ultimately be salved. However, in the context of a casualty that threatens or leads to a wreck, pollution liability will be at the forefront of those trying to deal with the casualty—whether as potential defendant or claimant.

2.6.1 *International action after* Torrey Canyon

As noted in Chapter 1,[845] in November 1969 a settlement was announced of the government claims in respect of the *Torrey Canyon* disaster. Meanwhile, IMCO was holding a diplomatic conference to produce conventions to try to solve some of the legal problems faced by the States. In fact, IMCO had met as soon as 4 May 1967, and among the matters for further study was Item 16 on compensation and compulsory insurance. On 26 May 1967 the CMI set up an International Sub-committee to consider the legal issues posed by the casualty.[846] On 21 June 1967 IMCO for the first time formed an ad hoc Legal Committee. That Legal Committee was later formally included as a permanent part of the IMCO/IMO structure and has been responsible for drafting the suite of liability conventions of which the WRC 2007 is one. That June 1967 meeting asked the CMI to cooperate on Item 16, with a view to meeting jointly on 25 September 1967 on the basis of a preliminary CMI report.[847]

This cooperation between a private body of maritime lawyers and an international organisation representing governments became the pattern for the drafting of maritime liability conventions thereafter, including eg the Salvage Convention 1989 and the WRC 2007. The

---

842 See also 11.2.1, 11.2.3.
843 For a comprehensive analysis of the conventions see *De La Rue & Anderson*. See also N Gaskell, "Compensation for Offshore Pollution: Ships and Platforms", in Malcolm Clarke (ed) *Maritime Law Evolving* (Hart 2013) 63–93 [*Gaskell, Compensation for Offshore Pollution*].
844 It is not possible here to assess all national laws that provide for pollution liability, eg for States where the conventions do not apply, although many will replicate features of liability. Within the EU, see also 2.6.5 (Environmental Liability Directive 2004) and 14.6 (Waste Framework Directive 2008).
845 See 1.2.1(b).
846 See eg the Preliminary Report of Chairman of International Sub-committee on *Torrey Canyon*, CMI Documentation 1968 Vol I, [TC-1, 8–67], 25 August 1967, 68.
847 On 25–26 September, Working Group II of IMCO's Legal Committee also made a study.

CMI, which had for some 70 years been the focus for the drafting of maritime convention, recognised that governments now viewed IMCO as the main forum for reform rather than the essentially commercial forum of the CMI.[848] The difference in approach can be seen in the conservative responses of the member associations of the CMI to a questionnaire sent out by its Working Group, when most were against strict liability and favoured the retention of limitation of liability to facilitate insurance.[849] Although a preliminary draft of a CMI convention emerged over the next two years,[850] by that time there was also an IMCO draft for a November 1969 diplomatic conference.

As is now well known, at that 1969 conference IMCO agreed a convention dealing with the right of states to intervene in casualties.[851] It also agreed another convention[852] dealing with the liability of shipowners; in 1971 a further liability convention was agreed.[853] Together, these liability conventions tackled the main legal deficiencies highlighted by the *Torrey Canyon*. These included (i) the need for claimant states to resort to ordinary fault-based principles of liability in national law; (ii) the low limits of liability under general maritime law; (iii) the difficulties of deciding what types of environmental damage were recoverable; (iv) how to deal with transboundary pollution affecting different States; and (iv) how to ensure that there was financial security for any claim. It was the latter that was the most important, as it raised questions about what mechanisms were needed to deal with an insolvent (often foreign) shipowner (often a single ship company whose only asset was a ship now sunk) and whether oil companies should be liable in addition to shipowners.

After the agreement of the Intervention Convention 1969, the CLC 1969 and Fund Convention 1971, IMCO envisaged that there ought to be discussion about a convention dealing with the salvage and wreck removal aspects of disasters such as *Torrey Canyon*.[854]

2.6.2 CLC and Fund Convention regime

The International Convention on Civil Liability for Oil Pollution Damage (CLC) 1969 entered into force on 19 June 1975. It was most significantly amended[855] in 1992 by a Protocol[856] to create the "CLC 1992". The CLC has to be read together with the International

---

848 Report of International Sub-committee on *Torrey Canyon*, CMI Documentation 1968 Vol I, [TC-2, 10–67], 98.

849 Yet, as noted in the CMI Report, such issues were not completely new as they had arisen in respect of the nuclear conventions; eg the Convention on Third Party Liability in the Field of Nuclear Energy 1960 [Paris Convention], as amended and the Convention on Civil Liability for Nuclear Damage 1963 [Nuclear Damage Convention], as amended: see also 10.9.3.

850 With a compromise proposal based on a reverse burden of proof, but noting that liability insurance was in practice compulsory for ships with mortgages: see Vol IV 1968, [TC 22, 8–68], 132; Tokyo Conference in April 1969, 1969 Vol V; Documentation 1970, Vol I, where a text was adopted, p76 [TC to T-26]. IMCO's conference was in November 1969.

851 See 5.3.

852 The "Civil Liability Convention" [CLC]; see 2.6.2(a).

853 The "Fund Convention" 1971; see 2.6.2(b).

854 For the ensuing Salvage Convention 1989, see 2.7.2; for the development of the WRC 2007, see Chapter 7.

855 For earlier attempts in 1984: see *De La Rue & Anderson*, 29–30.

856 "Protocol of 1992 to Amend the International Convention on Civil Liability for Oil Pollution Damage 1969", adopted 27 November 1992, entry into force 30 May 1996. There are 137 Contracting States, the

Convention on the Establishment of an International Fund for Compensation for Oil Pollution Damage [Fund Convention] 1971 that entered into force on 16 October 1978.[857] It was also amended in 1992 by a Protocol to create the "Fund Convention 1992".[858] In addition, a "Supplementary Fund" was adopted in 2003 by a Protocol[859] to the Fund Convention 1992 and entered into force internationally on 3 March 2005. The UK has adopted these three main current oil tanker pollution conventions:[860] the CLC 1992,[861] the Fund Convention 1992[862] and the Supplementary Fund 2003.[863] There has been widespread international adoption of the first two, although the US is a significant absentee.[864] Many of the basic concepts and principles have been adopted as boilerplate text in the other IMO liability conventions, and were particularly influential in the drafting of the WRC 2007.[865]

2.6.2(a) CLC 1992

The CLC 1992[866] creates strict (ie no-fault) liability of a registered shipowner; eg the shipowner is liable even if the oil tanker is wrecked following a collision with a container ship and the latter is 100% at fault.[867] While 'shipwreck' is not specifically mentioned, the CLC

---

combined merchant fleets of which constitute approximately 97.69% of the gross tonnage of the world's merchant fleet: *IMO Status of Treaties* (November 2018).

857 The 1971 Fund ceased to exist with effect from 31 December 2014: see IOPC/2014/Circ.5, 17 November 2014.

858 Protocol of 1992 to Amend the International Convention on the Establishment of an International Fund for Compensation for Oil Pollution Damage, 1971, adopted 27 November 1992, entry into force 30 May 1996. There are 115 Contracting States, the combined merchant fleets of which constitute approximately 95.05% of the gross tonnage (gt) of the world's merchant fleet: *IMO Status of Treaties* (November 2018).

859 Protocol of 2003 to the International Convention on the Establishment of a Supplementary Fund for Oil Pollution Damage 1982. There are 32 Contracting States (mostly developed States in Europe): *IMO Status of Treaties* (November 2018).

860 In its implementing legislation the UK has unfortunately not included the complete text of the conventions in their original form in schedules (as with other IMO conventions), but has adopted the drafting technique of rewriting them within the MSA 1995 in a piecemeal manner that is often less clear than the original: cf 11.3.1. For convenience, references will be made to the convention provisions rather than specific sections of the MSA 1995. Care is also needed when questions arise concerning UK Overseas Territories (such as Bermuda) and Crown Dependencies (such as the Channel Islands and Isle of Man). It is necessary to check both whether the UK has ratified or acceded on behalf of them, *and* whether that action has been given effect in the local law of particular Territory or Dependency: cf 2.5.9(c).

861 Enacted in the UK in the MSA 1995 Part VI Chapter III (as amended).

862 Enacted in the UK in the MSA 1995 Part VI Chapter IV (as amended).

863 Enacted in the UK in the MSA 1995 Part VI Chapter IV (as amended), including in particular, a new s 176A, 176B and Sch 5ZA: see the Merchant Shipping (Pollution) Act 2006, s 1 and the Merchant Shipping (Oil Pollution) (Supplementary Fund Protocol) Order 2006 2006 No. 1265. The Order entered into force in the UK on 8 September 2006.

864 For the US position under the Oil Pollution Act 1990, see *De La Rue & Anderson*, 52–64 and Chapter 4. China is party to the CLC 1992, but not the Fund Convention 1992 (although Hong Kong (China) is party to the latter).

865 See Chapters 7–9.

866 The CLC 1969 is still in force for 34 States, some of which are also party to the CLC 1992: see *IMO Status of Treaties* (November 2018). It is not possible to deal with all the differences between the CLC 1969 and the CLC 1992, but it can be noted that the limits of liability are significantly lower in the former.

867 Cf 2.4. The tanker owner would be entitled to make a tort recourse claims against the container ship (see Art III(5)), but the latter could limit its liability under the LLMC 1996 to an amount that is likely to be considerably less than the tanker owner's CLC liability: see 2.5.4(a) and 2.5.6(a).

would clearly include pollution from oil tankers running aground, stranding or sinking—as it applies generally to an "incident", ie an "occurrence" causing (or threatening) pollution damage.[868] The liability is for oil[869] "pollution damage",[870] caused in the territorial waters (or the 200 nm EEZ) of Contracting States,[871] from a seagoing oil tanker[872] when it is actually carrying oil in bulk as cargo.[873]

There are certain limited defences available to the shipowner under Art III(2).[874] These include war; "exceptional, inevitable and irresistible" natural phenomena (eg tsunamis); deliberate harm by third parties (eg most terrorist activities);[875] and wrongful acts of governments in maintaining navigational aids (eg buoys).[876] There is also a time bar of three years from the pollution damage (with a maximum of six years from the first occurrence causing the incident).[877]

The CLC 1992 has its own 'stand-alone' limits of liability that are separate from (and higher than) the limits of liability available to shipowners under general limitation of liability conventions.[878] Limitation was appropriate because the shipowner was being made liable even in the absence of fault. Experience since the CLC 1969 and Fund Convention 1971 has shown that, at whatever the level the limits are set, major tanker wrecks have produced claims that are greatly in excess of the limits. As the total fund is distributed pro rata,[879] many claims will only be partly met (at least in the first instance). At the same time, the nature of claims has evolved significantly since the *Torrey Canyon*. An initial focus on State clean-up costs has now widened to include the economic losses faced by fishing

---

868 See Art I(8).

869 The CLC Art I(5) covers "persistent hydrocarbon mineral oil, such as crude oil, fuel oil, heavy diesel oil and lubricating oil" whether carried in an oil tanker as cargo *or* bunkers. Non-persistent oils, such as gasoline, light diesel oil, kerosene are not covered, and pollution from them would need to be covered by national law or the HNSC 2010, see 2.6.4.

870 For the definition in Art I(6), see 2.6.2(b). For possible conflicts with the WRC 2007 as to liability and damages, see 10.9.2(a).

871 Art II. It is those States that have jurisdiction to hear claims: see Art IX. If a tanker is wrecked on a shoal that is outside territorial waters or the EEZ, then the CLC does not apply: see N Gaskell, "Liability and Compensation Regimes: Pollution of the High Seas", in R Beckman, M McCreath, J Roach, Z Sun (eds), *High Seas Governance: Gaps and Challenges* (Brill/Nijhoff, 2018) [Gaskell, *Liability and Compensation Regimes: Pollution of the High Seas*].

872 See Art I(1) and cf 2.5.3. Non-seagoing ships fall outside the CLC and oil pollution from their wreck would need to be covered by national law: see eg the MSA 1995 s 154, and 2.6.3. Bunker oil pollution from non-tankers is dealt with in the Bunkers Convention 2001: see 2.6.3.

873 See the rather convoluted definition in Art I(1), that also applies the CLC when a tanker is in ballast after a carrying voyage, provided that it still has oil residues on board. On a ballast run the tanker may have a large quantity of bunkers on board which would be the real environmental risk: these are within the definition of "oil". A tanker that did not qualify under Art I(1) (eg after drydocking and lay-up voyages in ballast) may be covered for bunker pollution under the Bunkers Convention 2001: see 2.6.3.

874 For a more extensive discussion of the equivalent provisions in the WRC 2007 Art 10(1), see 10.3.

875 The pollution damage must have been "wholly caused" by the third party's actions. This leaves open the possibility of an allegation that terrorists or pirates were allowed to board the ship owing, in part, to defective security arrangements on board: see also 10.3.1.

876 Again, the damage must have been "wholly" caused by this fault.

877 See Art VIII.

878 See Art V. It was recognised after the *Torrey Canyon* that the existing limits of liability under the Limitation Convention 1957 would not be enough to cover large oil pollution claims: see 1.2.1(a), 2.6.1. For the LLMC 1996, see, 2.5.1, 2.5.4(a).

879 See the CLC 1992 Art V(4) and the Fund Convention 1992 Art Art 4(5).

and tourist industries. Indeed, the scale of the major wrecks in Europe, eg *Amoco Cadiz*, *Braer*, *Erika* and *Prestige*,[880] has meant that the impact has been felt along huge areas of coastlines and is often transboundary. An increase in economic loss claims (some of which are often highly speculative), combined with limits, means that there are inevitable delays in paying out genuine claims. This has sometimes prompted States to postpone their own legitimate clean-up claims in favour of economic loss claimants, eg after the *Braer* and *Erika* wrecks.[881] The CLC and Fund limits have been progressively increased after each disaster. After the *Erika* wreck in 1999, the CLC 1992 limits were increased in 2000 by the IMO Legal Committee, with effect from 1 November 2003.[882]

The limits are calculated in a similar manner to the LLMC,[883] eg using the sdr of the IMF to enable the shipowner to constitute a CLC limitation fund in a contracting State.[884] The minimum shipowner liability is 4,510,000 sdr for ships not exceeding 5,000 gt; this increases by 631 sdr per gt up to a maximum CLC 1992 liability of 89,770,000 sdr. Table 2.7 illustrates these figures by reference to some hypothetical ship sizes. For the total amounts available to claimants, the limits have to be aggregated with those available under the Fund Convention 1992.[885]

Note that tankers are often described commercially in terms of their deadweight tonnage but limitation is based on their gross tonnage, which is often considerably less. The *Erika* was only 19,666 gt but the wreck caused enormous loss.[886] The right to limit is lost if the pollution damage was caused intentionally or recklessly by the shipowner.[887]

The CLC deals with the single ship company problem by providing for compulsory insurance for the owners of tankers carrying more than 2,000 tons of bulk oil cargo.[888] The pollution damage victim can bring a direct action against the insurer,[889] instead of having to chase a reluctant shipowner. This protection is underpinned by the issuance of an insurance certificate, which will usually be required by CLC coastal States as a condition of entry into ports.[890] The vast majority of tankers are entered with International Group P&I Clubs who provide the necessary insurance cover in 'Blue Cards' which enable Contracting States to issue CLC certificates, which are essential to trade. The insurer cannot rely

---

880 See 1.2.2(a) for these and other major casualties.
881 See *Gaskell and Forrest*, 13.
882 IMO Legal Committee Resolution LEG.1 (82), 18 October 2000.
883 See 2.5.6(a).
884 See Art V(3) and (9).
885 See Table 2.8, 2.6.2(b).
886 For the gt of tankers in other major wrecks, see 1.2.2(a). Because of the relatively low limits of small tankers (and the resulting higher potential liability of the 1992 Fund), the Small Tanker Oil Pollution Indemnification Agreement (STOPIA) was agreed by owners and P&I insurers of small tankers (of 29,548 gt or below). In effect, it operates as form of refund between the Clubs and the 1992 Fund up to a maximum of 20 million sdr. This commercial arrangement has no direct effect for pollution claimants after a tanker wreck. See also the Tanker Oil Pollution Indemnification Agreement (TOPIA), 2.6.4(c) and eg IOPC Funds, *Annual Report 2017*, 7.
887 Art IV. For a fuller explanation of this test and whose misconduct in the corporate structure is attributed to the owning company, see 2.5.7.
888 Art VII(1). A wrecked tanker under this tonnage will still be subject to CLC liability and may well be insured, but there would be no right of direct action against the insurer under the CLC.
889 Art VII(8). Sums made available by the insurer are exclusively for the benefit of the CLC claimants: see Art VII(9) and cf 10.8.5.
890 See Art VII.

Table 2.7 CLC 1992 shipowner limits

Tanker tonnage	CLC 1992 sdr amounts	£ sterling[1]	US$[2]
5,000 gt tanker (eg 7,500 dwt)[3]	4,510,000 sdr	£4,900,656	$6,235,075
20,000 gt tanker (eg 30,000 dwt)	13,975,000 sdr	£15,185,515	$19,320,438
Panamax 40,000 gt (eg 70,000 dwt)	26,595,000 sdr	£28,898,659	$36,767,588
Aframax 60,000 gt (eg 110,000 dwt)	39,215,000 sdr	£42,611,803	$54,214,738
Suezmax 84,000 gt (eg 160,000 dwt)	54,359,000 sdr	£59,067,577	$75,151,318
VLCC 160,000 gt (eg 300,000 dwt)	*[102,315,000 sdr]*[4] 89,770,000 sdr	*[£111,177,525]* £97,545,877 sdr	*[$141,450,488]* $124,107,025 sdr

[1] The calculation uses the IMF figures at 3 December 2018 with the rate of conversion of 1 sdr = £1.08662.

[2] As the international currency of shipping is the US$, this column gives comparative figures for 3 December 2018 based on 1 sdr = US$1.3825. The US is *not* party to the CLC, so the US$ figures are given by way of example only.

[3] This is the minimum tonnage under the CLC 1992, ie any seagoing ship of 0–5,000 gt will have the minimum limits in this row, eg a 200 gt bunker barge (of about 500 dwt). However, a ship of that size would not be obliged to have CLC insurance: see Art VII. The deadweight tonnage (dwt) figures for tankers in this column are rough estimates for illustration purposes only, in order to give some idea of the tonnage of oil that might be carried.

[4] Figures in square brackets and italics show the limitation figures that would have applied had there not been an overall CLC 1992 maximum of 89,770,000 sdr. It is the latter figure that represents the limit for a ship of this gt.

on common policy defences, eg the insolvency of the shipowner, or the 'pay to be paid' clause,[891] although it can rely on the "wilful misconduct" of the shipowner.[892] It can also avail itself of the shipowner's limits.[893] Where the insurer does have these defences, the claimant may still be able to claim from the IOPC Fund.[894]

Given this relatively solid insurance protection, it was decided to avoid costly satellite litigation by 'channelling' claims to the registered owner only.[895] Further, oil pollution damage claims within the CLC cannot be brought against a long list of other potential defendants.[896] This exclusion of liability will be particularly important in the fall-out from a tanker wreck. Those excluded are specifically listed in Art III(4): (a) the master and crew

---

891 See Art VII(8) and 2.9.6(c).

892 Art VII(8) and see the MIA 1906 s 55(2)(a), eg deliberate action to scuttle the ship taken by the senior management of the assured: and see 2.9.2(c), 10.8.4(d) and (e).

893 Ie those under Art V: see Art VII(4).

894 See 2.6.2(b).

895 Art III(4). Further, the shipowner cannot be sued otherwise than under the CLC (eg under some wider national law): cf 14.6.3.

896 Unless the pollution damage resulted from their own personal act or mission committed intentionally or recklessly: Art III(4). This test will be almost impossible to satisfy unless there is conduct that is akin to scuttling, see 2.5.7.

(or other servants or agents of the shipowner);[897] (b) pilots or others performing services for the ship;[898] (c) charterers,[899] operators[900] or managers;[901] (d) salvors;[902] (e) those taking preventive measures;[903] and (f) all servants or agents of those in paras (c), (d) and (e). Nor can persons in the list be sued outside of the CLC (eg in national tort law) for any "pollution damage" that falls within the CLC definition.[904]

There is an issue as to whether actions to save cargo and bunkers are to be considered as pollution prevention (under the CLC) or salvage (eg governed by the Salvage Convention 1989). In general, it may be necessary to ask whether a primary propose of the activity can be identified.[905]

---

897 "Agents" covers traditional agents such as brokers, but might be interpreted more widely to cover those acting generally with the authority of the shipowner; this might include wreck removal contractors: see also (b), (d) and (e).

898 This might also include wreck removal contractors tasked to pump out oil cargo or bunkers from a wreck, as well as others such as expert engineers or surveyors who are dealing with wreck removal issues but who are not employed by salvors.

899 Bareboat charterers are specifically excluded from liability, even though they will employ the master and crew and normally be liable for them: see 2.1.7(a). It was thought clearer to make only the registered owner liable. For the same reason, voyage and time charterers are also excluded from liability, even though they may have some responsibility for a wreck, eg if they order a ship to an unsafe port or load dangerous cargo: see 2.1.7(b)–(c). This sort of conduct is unlikely to come within the intent/recklessness proviso: see Art III(4). For the potential overlap with the EU Waste Framework Directive, see 14.6.3.

900 "Operators" is not a concept that fits easily into English maritime law as it probably overlaps with "charterers"; cf the WRC 2007 Art 1(9), and 9.1.3(a), 11.3.3.

901 Ship managers would include independent firms of ship managers, or the managing company that takes all the operational decisions within a corporate group of single ship companies: see eg *The Star Sea* [1997] 1 Lloyd's Rep 360 and 2.5.7. The operational decisions of all such companies might have a causal connection to a wreck, eg where repairs are deliberately delayed: cf *The Amoco Cadiz* [1984] 2 Lloyd's Rep 304; N Gaskell, "The Amoco Cadiz I: Liability Issues" (1985) 3 JENRL 169, "The Amoco Cadiz II: Limitation and Legal Implications" (1985) 4 JENRL 225–242; also 1.2.2(a).

902 Art III(4)(d) actually refers rather restrictively to those performing "salvage operations with the consent of the owner or on the instructions of a competent public authority". This would not include the volunteer salvor that starts operations prior to any contact with owner or master, but that would be rare. "Salvage operations" is not separately defined, but Art 1(a) of the Salvage Convention 1989 defines it very widely to include any act or activity to assist a vessel in danger; taken alone, this could also include a wreck removal contractor: see 2.7.4 and *Gaskell, MSA 1995*, 21/374.

903 This could cover wreck removal contractors, if they are not within (a), (b) or (d), above. "Preventive measures" means any "reasonable measures" taken to prevent or minimise pollution. A negligent action while pumping out cargo or bunkers, eg failing to connect hoses properly, would not be covered unless it be said that the pumping measures were reasonable, albeit that their particular operation in the exigencies of a wreck was not. This is why it might be necessary for such contractors to rely on the other paras of Art III(4).

904 See 2.6.2(b) for the definition. There is nothing in Art III(4) that expressly excludes suit against a cargo owner that is not a charterer. In some circumstances, cargo owners might be negligent in a way that causes a wreck, eg in loading undeclared dangerous cargo that explodes, but probably not for nominating an unsafe port in a bill of lading: cf *The Aegean Sea* [1998] 2 Lloyd's Rep 39, 76–69 and 2.1.6. If there was liability in national law outside of the CLC, there is nothing in Art III(4) to prevent such an action. It is also unlikely that a cargo owner would be entitled to limit that liability under the LLMC 1996, as it is not within LLMC Art 1: see 2.5.3.

905 See also the CLC supersession clause, Art XII, aimed to give it priority over any pre-existing convention if there is a conflict between them. For convenience, this issue is also addressed in the context of the Bunkers Convention 2001: see 2.6.3. For overlap and conflicts between the CLC 1992 and the WRC 2007, see 10.9.2(a).

2.6.2(b) Fund Convention 1992

The Fund Convention 1992 supplements the CLC 1992 in the event of a tanker pollution disaster, including shipwreck, by providing for significant additional amounts to be made available to claimants. As part of the post-*Torrey Canyon* compromise, it was agreed that oil cargo interests would contribute to a second tier of liability, as it was obviously the oil cargo that was the major pollutant (not the ship itself). There is no liability of the individual owners of the oil cargo aboard the tanker involved in the casualty, but the International Oil Pollution Compensation (IOPC) Fund was created with legal personality[906] and based in London. After a casualty, such as the wreck of a tanker, the IOPC Fund collects contributions from all major oil importers worldwide (in States party to the convention) in order to be able to provide a second tier of liability.[907] In this way the loss and damage caused by tanker pollution is spread between the two commercial interests broadly represented in the maritime commercial adventure, namely the registered shipowner of the particular tanker (but insured usually by a P&I Club representing shipowners more widely) and the oil majors who required the transportation of oil cargoes that might become pollutants. This concept of the sharing of liabilities between shipowning interests and cargo owning interests was at the heart of the compromise which led to the CLC and Fund Convention,[908] and there have been commercial adjustments since.[909]

The main liability of the 1992 Fund is to pay compensation for pollution damage in excess of the CLC 1992 limits[910] up to the Fund's limit of liability of 203 million sdr,[911] as illustrated in Table 2.8. The Fund limit is aggregated with the CLC 1992 limits to produce a single total, ie the shipowner pays up to its limit, and the Fund pays above that.

The Fund's liability can also arise in two other circumstances, but in these cases the Fund may end up paying the *whole* of the claim, eg down to the first sdr that would otherwise be the shipowner's responsibility—provided that the pollution damage was caused by a tanker.[912] The first circumstance is where the shipowner is insolvent and its insurance is insufficient to cover the claim.[913] The second is because "no liability for the damage arises under" the CLC 1992.[914] Examples of this would be where the CLC exceptions operate, eg for a natural phenomenon (such as after a tsunami); or where there are deliberate acts of

---

906 Fund Convention 1992 Art 2. See www.iopcfunds.org for a wealth of information on the Fund system.
907 See Arts 10–15.
908 It was also to re-emerge on the negotiations for the HNSC, see 2.6.4. A similar problem was to recur in the negotiations for the WRC 2007, when there were long debates about how far the cargo on board a wrecked ship should contribute to the costs of its removal: see 10.6.2.
909 See STOPIA and TOPIA, 2.6.2(c) (fn 886).
910 See the Fund Convention 1992 Art 4(1)(c), and Table 2.7, 2.6.2(a). There may also be unusual circumstances where the ship is not registered in a State party to the CLC but is party, eg, to the 1957 Limitation Convention. In these circumstances, the State suffering the pollution might be obliged to recognise the 1957 limits and the IOPC Fund would pay compensation above that figure.
911 See Art 4(4)(a), as increased in 2000 along with the CLC 1992 (with effect from 2003): see 2.6.2(a). The total amount could be increased to 300,740,000 sdr if three State parties had imported 600 million tons of oil in a given year: in 2017, the relevant figure was only 548 million tons, see IOPC Funds, *Annual Report 2017*, 20.
912 Art 4(2)(b); ie the oil had not come from land-based sources. If the oil was proved to be from the bunkers of a non-tanker, the Bunkers Convention 2001 would be engaged: see 2.6.3.
913 See Art 4(1)(b). This might include circumstances where the insurer can avoid the cover because of wilful misconduct: see also 2.6.2(a), 2.9.2(c) and 10.8.4(d).
914 See Art 4(1(a).

Table 2.8 Fund Convention 1992 limits

Fund Convention 1992 sdr amounts	£ sterling[1]	US$[2]
203 million sdr	£220,583,860	$280,647,500

[1] The calculation uses the IMF figures at 3 December 2018 with the rate of conversion of 1 sdr = £1.08662. The conversion into local currency is made on its sdr value on the day that the IOPC Fund Assembly decides on the first date of payment of compensation: see Art 4(5).

[2] As the international currency of shipping is the US$, this column gives comparative figures for 3 December 2018 based on 1 sdr = US$1.3825. The US is *not* party to the Fund Convention 1992, so the US$ figures are given by way of example only.

third parties causing the wreck, eg sabotage or terrorism; or where defective State navigational aids caused the ship to go aground.[915] However, the Fund is not liable for pollution caused by war, warships or State ships on non-commercial service.[916]

This inter-relationship between the CLC 1992, its insurer and the IOPC Fund means that the insurer and Fund have to work quite closely together after a tanker wreck, as it may not be known at the outset exactly where ultimate responsibility will lie.[917] The degree of cooperation is one of the successes of the regime,[918] and both P&I Club and the Fund secretariat will be actively involved with the salvage and wreck removal operations involving tankers.

This cooperation will be focused upon the admissibility of "pollution damage" claims under the CLC 1992 and Fund Convention.[919] This expression covers contamination, clean-up measures taken by States and individuals[920] as well as reasonable measures of environmental reinstatement.[921] Financial losses, including lost profits from the impairment of the environment, are specifically included and this is of particular benefit to the tourism and fishing industries that suffer loss after major shipwrecks, such as the *Erika* and *Prestige*.[922] The IOPC Fund has issued an authoritative guide[923] to the type of claim that has been approved within the CLC and Fund regime. In many ways, international

---

915 See the CLC 1992 Art IIII(2), 2.6.2(a). In the event of the State's own negligence causing pollution damage, the Fund may be exonerated wholly or partly, but this would not extend to the cost of preventive measures, as opposed eg to economic losses: see the Fund Convention Art 4(3).

916 Fund Convention Art 4(2)(a).

917 From the claimant's perspective, they need to be aware, though, that the liabilities under the CLC and Fund Convention are legally separate, and the latter has its own time bar in Art 6. Although this is identical in length to that under the CLC (see 2.6.2(a)), a separate claim must be brought against the Fund, or it must be formally notified under Art 7(6) so that it can participate in proceedings.

918 It is underpinned by an MOU, although the relationship has been strained following claims under the Fund Convention 1971 involving the *Nissos Amorgos*: see *Assuranceforeningen Gard Gjensidig v The International Oil Pollution Compensation Fund 1971* [2014] EWHC 3369 (Comm), [2014] 2 Lloyd's Rep 219.

919 As defined in the CLC 1992 Art I(6), replicated in Art 1(2) of the Fund Convention 1992.

920 Including preventive measures such as 'threat removal' measures taken after an incident but before a spill.

921 These must be actually undertaken (or really planned) and the IOPC Fund does not admit theoretical damage claims, eg based on abstract economic models.

922 See 1.2.2(a) for these and other major tanker wreck cases.

923 See IOPC, *Claims Manual* (October 2016).

practice under the regime goes beyond the rather narrow notions of economic losses at common law, although ultimately the application of the Art I(9) definition will be a matter for national courts[924] as there is no separate CLC/Fund tribunal.

The entry into force of the WRC 2007 means that there is a potential overlap between preventive measures that fall within the CLC and Fund regime and wreck and cargo removal under the WRC 2007. In principle, the WRC 2007 will not apply if it is in conflict with the CLC and Fund regime.[925] Thus, the costs of pumping out an oil cargo and bunkers from the wreck of a tanker (and disposing of them) would usually be "preventive measures" covered within Art I(7) of the CLC, and Art 1(2) of the Fund Convention 1992. The costs of physically raising the hull of the ship would not be covered by the CLC and Fund Convention unless it was necessary to do so in order to prevent further pollution with the oil in its tanks. Given modern oil pumping and recovery techniques,[926] this may be unlikely, but it is possible that there are unpumpable residues that might eventually leak.

2.6.2(c) Supplementary Fund Protocol 2003

The Supplementary Fund 2003 operates as a third tier of liability for those States that consider that the Fund Convention 1992 does not provide enough compensation in the event of a major disaster, such as those involving the *Erika* and *Prestige*. It operates when if a claimant has not been able to obtain full and adequate compensation under the Fund Convention 1992. Its aggregate liability (taking into account CLC 1992 and Fund 1992 payments is a maximum of 750 million sdr), as illustrated in Table 2.9.

The time limit for claims is the same as that for the CLC 1992 and Fund Convention 1992, but a claimant does not have to make a separate claim against the Supplementary Fund as notification to the 1992 Fund is enough.[927] The Supplementary Fund 2003 is financed in the same way as the Fund Convention 1992, but in this case only by contributions

Table 2.9 Supplementary Fund 2003 limits

Supplementary Fund sdr amounts	**£ sterling[1]**	**US$[2]**
750 million sdr	£814,965,000	$1,036,875,000

[1] The calculation uses the IMF figures at 3 December 2018 with the rate of conversion of 1 sdr = £1.08662. The conversion into local currency is made on its sdr value on the day that the IOPC Fund 1992 Assembly decides on the first date of payment of compensation: see Art 4(5).

[2] As the international currency of shipping is the US$, this column gives comparative figures for 3 December 2018 based on 1 sdr = US$1.3825. The US is *not* party to the Supplementary Fund 2003, so the US$ figures are given by way of example only.

---

924 See eg two cases resulting from the wreck of the *Braer*, *Landcatch v IOPC Fund* [1999] 2 Lloyd's Rep 316; *P & O Braer* [1999] 2 Lloyd's Rep 534, and cf the somewhat narrower approach taken in *Algrete Shipping Co Inc v IOPC Fund* [2003] 1 Lloyd's Rep 123 (the *Sea Empress* wreck, see 1.2.2(a)). As a matter of principle courts ought to respect the massive experience developed within the international regime and reflect its enhanced (if cautious) practice on pollution damage claims.

925 See the WRC 2007 Art 11(1)(a). On conflicts generally with the WRC 2007, and the possible relevance of Art 11(1)(a) not specifically mentioning the Fund Convention 1992, see 10.9.2(a).

926 See techniques used with *Costa Concordia* and *Baltic Ace*, 1.2.5(b).

927 See the Supplementary Fund Protocol, Art 6.

from those States party to the Supplementary Fund Protocol 2003.[928] So far there have been no incidents involving the Supplementary Fund.

2.6.3 Bunkers Convention 2001

The CLC and Fund regime was designed to cover bunker pollution from oil tankers,[929] but that left open the risk of bunker pollution from all other ships. This was a significant problem, given that bulk carriers might be carrying several thousand tonnes of heavy fuel oil as bunkers that would be very difficult to clean up in the event of a wreck.

The International Convention on Civil Liability for Bunker Oil Pollution Damage [Bunkers Convention] 2001 was designed to remedy this gap[930] and entered into force on 21 November 2008.[931] It is enacted in the UK in the MSA 1995 s 153A,[932] and largely replaced an interim regime designed for bunker pollution under the MSA 1995 s 154.[933]

The Bunkers Convention 2001 filled the gap left by the CLC 1992 (and the HNSC 1996), by providing for strict liability[934] for pollution damage[935] from the bunkers[936] of all seagoing ships that are not oil tankers.[937] This means that in almost every wreck case there

---

928 There is also a commercial arrangement between the P&I Clubs and the Supplementary Fund 2003 that indemnifies the latter for 50% of amounts paid involving tankers. This is similar to STOPIA, see 2.6.2(b): see IOPC Funds, *Annual Report 2017*, 7. STOPIA does not directly affect pollution claimants after a tanker wreck.

929 For the limited circumstances when an oil tanker in ballast might not fall within the CLC 1992, see 2.6.2(a).

930 See N Gaskell and C Forrest, "Marine Pollution Damage in Australia: Implementing the Bunker Oil Convention 2001 and the Supplementary Fund Protocol 2003" (2008) 27 UQLJ 103 [*Gaskell & Forrest, Marine Pollution Damage*], 125–143; *Gaskell, Bunker Pollution Limitation; De La Rue & Anderson*, Chapter 6.

931 It has 91 Contracting States, the combined fleets of which constitute approximately 92.85% of the world's merchant fleet: *IMO Status of Treaties* (November 2018).

932 As inserted by the Merchant Shipping (Oil Pollution) (Bunkers Convention) Regulations 2006 (SI 2006/1244). As with the CLC and Fund Convention, the existing legislation has been amended piecemeal, and in 2018 the text had not been fully integrated into the MSA 1995 on the website www.legislation.gov.uk.

933 See *Gaskell, MSA 1995*, 21/178–21/181. Although not repealed, s 154 seems to have a largely historical or residual function as it cannot apply when s 153A applies (see the new s 154(2A)). The MSA 1995 s 154 will apply to non-seagoing ships that carry persistent hydrocarbon mineral oil (see s 170(1)), apparently whether as bunkers or cargo. This provision will therefore be relevant to clean-up operations following the wreck of ships not subject to the CLC 1992, Bunkers Convention 2001 or the WRC 2007.

934 Ie liability without fault: see Art 3(1). There are the usual limited defences in Art 3(3) based on Art III(2) of the CLC 1992 (see 2.6.2(a)), ie for war third party damage government failings in relation to navigational aids: see also 10.3.1. There is also a similar time limit for claims of three years from the bunker pollution damage or six years from the date of the first incident which caused the damage: see the Bunkers Convention 2001 Art 8.

935 The definition of "pollution damage" under the Bunkers Convention 2001 Art 1(9) is broadly similar to that in the CLC and Fund regime: see 2.6.2(b). It therefore includes contamination damage to property, loss of profit from environmental impairment (eg fishing and tourism losses), as well as reasonable environmental reinstatement. Attempts to widen the definition were rejected in negotiations: see LEG 79/6/3, 18 March 1999, and LEG 79/11, 22 April 1999, 15–16. The scope of application of the Bunkers Convention 2001 Art 2 also follows the CLC and Fund by applying to the territorial sea and EEZ of contracting states to the 2001 Convention.

936 Defined widely in the Bunkers Convention 2001 Art 1(5) to mean hydrocarbon mineral oil (including lube oil) used for the operation or propulsion of the ship; it includes generating fuel as well as that used in engines.

937 Ie ships not subject to the CLC: see the Bunkers Convention 2001 Arts 1(1), 3(b), and 2.6.2(a). For non-seagoing ships, see the MSA 1995 s 154; cf 2.5.3.

will be the potential for liability not only for damage and loss caused by bunker spills, but also for the cost of preventive measures.

Unlike the CLC and Fund regime, there is no second tier of liability in the Bunkers Convention 2001.[938] Article 3(1) therefore imposes the strict liability on the "shipowner at the time of an incident".[939] The "shipowner" is here defined to include the registered owner but also (and unlike the CLC) the "bareboat charterer, manager and operator of the ship".[940] Each of these persons is jointly and severally liable for the bunker pollution damage, so the claimant may be able to proceed against some others where the shipowner is insolvent.

In fact, the single ship company problem is less of an issue as the Bunkers Convention 2001 follows the CLC model by requiring the registered shipowner (only) to have insurance to cover bunker pollution damage, but only for ships over 1,000 gt.[941] Claimants also have a right of direct action against the insurer, with equivalent restrictions on insurer defences to those in the CLC.[942] Under the Bunkers Convention 2001, though, the insurer would not have a direct liability greater than the limit under the LLMC 1996.[943]

The Bunkers Convention potentially applies to huge numbers of ships and, in effect, requires most which trade worldwide to have Bunkers Convention 2001 certificates—even if registered in non-parties to the Convention. In a wreck case, bunker pollution claimants will normally sue the shipowner and its insurer, eg a P&I Club or fixed premium liability insurer. Charterers, managers and operators who are potentially liable under the Bunkers Convention 2001 may need their own insurance protection,[944] although the direct action provisions would not apply to claims against their insurers.[945] This is the same position with regard to small ships of under 1,000 gt; if they are wrecked, bunker pollution liabilities may be uninsured or, if insured, the insurer may be able to rely on policy defences. Such small ships might still have several hundred mt of bunkers on board, and even small spills can be very expensive to clean up.

One of the defects of the Bunkers Convention 2001 is that it does not have full channelling provisions like the CLC Art III(4) to prevent claims against third parties such as

---

938 This not only reduces the overall funds available, but also means that there is no second-tier Fund to cover some of the Bunkers Convention 2001 Art 3(3) exceptions: cf 2.6.2(b).

939 An "incident" is defined in Art 1(8) to mean any occurrence causing pollution damage or creating a grave and imminent danger of it. In the wreck context, this would obviously include a grounding, stranding or sinking. Expense in mobilising and deploying pollution prevention equipment (eg booms) for a grounded ship would be within this definition (and that of "preventive measures" in Art 1(9)), even if no bunker oil actually leaked—owing to the successful effects of salvors or wreck removal contractors. Claims for salvage, special compensation and general average are not affected by the Bunkers Convention 2001: see Art 3(a), and 2.7.9(a) and (b).

940 For a related discussion of managers and operators, see 2.6.2(a). For bareboat charterers generally, see 2.1.7(a), and cf 2.5.3, 2.5.4(a) and 2.5.4(d).

941 Bunkers Convention 2001 Art 7.

942 Bunkers Convention 2001 Art 7(10).

943 Bunkers Convention 2001 Art 7(1), 7(10). These provisions are not strictly limits of liability under the LLMC, but a cap on liability under the Bunkers Convention 2001 itself, eg if the insurer cannot take advantage of the shipowner's LLMC right to limit: see *Gaskell, Bunker Pollution Limitation*, 490–492. This issue is examined more comprehensively in relation to the WRC 2007: see 10.8.5.

944 Although they, like the registered shipowner, are strictly liable (ie even if not at fault), Art 3(6) preserves rights of recourse in contract and tort.

945 Ie from the claimant's perspective there are greater risks as the insurer may rely on policy defences such as the 'pay to be paid' clause: see 2.9.6(c).

salvors.[946] This means that there is nothing to prevent a bunker pollution victim from instituting a normal tort action for negligence against others who might be involved in a wreck, such as salvors and wreck removal contractors. They could potentially be liable for pollution, eg where a pipe is coupled incorrectly to a manifold during operations to remove bunkers from a stranded ship—resulting in the leak of bunker oil. Even allowing for some leeway when judging what is reasonable in the face of bad weather aboard a wreck,[947] the risk of liability is considerable. For this reason, such contractors would need to rely on their own liability insurance, obtain contractual indemnities[948] or seek to rely on statutory limitation of liability.[949] Such limitation is also crucial to those "shipowners" liable under the Bunkers Convention 2001 itself.

There are no stand-alone limits for bunker pollution under the Bunkers Convention 2001, as Art 6 merely states that nothing in the convention shall affect the right of the "shipowner" (as widely defined) to limit liability under any applicable national or international regime, such as the LLMC 1996. By this means, shipowning and insurance interests were able to achieve linkage of bunker pollution claims to the existing limits in conventions such as the LLMC 1996.[950] This means that, in principle, not only will there be limitation for most bunker pollution claims,[951] but that these claims must share in a fund for other 'property' claims—including extensive collision damage and cargo claims.

It did not take long for States to realise that apparent benefits of the Bunkers Convention 2001 were considerably reduced when the LLMC limits were applied to relatively ordinary bunker claims. An example was the casualty in 2009 involving the Hong Kong–registered container ship *Pacific Adventurer* (18,391 gt), where containers lost overboard in heavy seas holed the ship's bunker tanks, causing pollution on the Australian coastline. A limitation fund of Au$17.5 million was insufficient to meet the various claims of about Au$30 million caused by the spillage of only 270 mt of bunkers. A settlement was agreed of about Au$25 million, but the effects of the LLMC 1996 on bunker claims in particular prompted Australia to press for higher limits at the IMO.[952] Partly to assuage such State concerns, the IMO agreed in 2012 to an increase in the LLMC 1996 limits.[953]

As with the CLC 1992, the Bunkers Convention 2001 does not apply to claims for salvage or special compensation made *by* a salvor.[954] Salvage claims are unlimited, so it might be advantageous for a salvor to classify any claim for pumping undamaged oil from a

---

946 See 2.6.2(a).
947 Cf *The Tojo Maru* [1972] AC 242, and see 2.5.5.
948 Cf the limited indemnities in the wreck removal contracts, eg Wreckhire 2010: see 13.6.3(g).
949 See 2.5.5.
950 See *Gaskell, Bunker Pollution*, 2–3. A similar solution was followed in the WRC 2007, see 10.7.
951 The issue of which bunker pollution claims are limitable under the LLMC 1996 is dealt with in 2.5.4(b). The issue is complicated by the possibility of an LLMC opt-out for claims for the rendering harmless of the contents of a ship (see 2.5.8) and, for the UK, of a deeming provision under the MSA 1995 s 168 in respect of limitation under the Bunkers Convention 2001: see 2.5.4(b). Cf "Limitation of Liability for Pollution Clean-Up Costs in China" (2013) 211 Gard News 7, for the somewhat surprising approach of the Chinese Supreme Court in the *Zeus* case.
952 *Gaskell, Compensation for Offshore Pollution*, 72–77.
953 LEG 99/14, 24 April 2012, 7–11; see 2.5.4(b); also 2.5.6(a) for examples of limits for particular sizes of ships.
954 See the Bunkers Convention 2001 Art 3(a) and 2.7.7, 2.7.9(b).

wrecked ship as salvage rather than the prevention of pollution.[955] The general practice of the IOPC Fund in relation to oil tankers has been to assess whether the primary purpose of such efforts by salvors has been to save the valuable bunkers or to prevent pollution.[956] This is not an easy distinction to make and, where it is not possible to assess the primary purpose, the costs may well be apportioned between pollution prevention (under the CLC 1992 or Bunkers Convention 2011) and salvage (under the Salvage Convention 1989).[957] It will be easier to classify the expenses as for pollution prevention where the bunkers are already contaminated by seawater after a grounding, and the removal operation will result in disposal rather than reuse.[958] Salvors and wreck removal contractors may be more likely to perform such operations under contract,[959] but the issue remains as to whether the ship-owner can claim credit for payments in any limitation proceedings.[960]

2.6.4 HNSC 2010

While the CLC and Fund Convention have successfully operated to provide a liability regime for oil tanker pollution, the glaring gap has been for an equivalent regime to deal with liability for damage (including pollution damage) caused by the carriage of hazardous and noxious substances (HNS), eg bulk or packaged chemicals, LPG or LNG. The wreck of a bulk chemical carrier or large container ship presents very real environmental and safety risks, especially on sensitive coasts or in heavily populated ports. Those risks include explosions in a port, which might result in devastating loss of life and damage.[961]

In the absence of a convention, liability for death and injury, clean-up, environmental reinstatement, property damage and economic losses will depend on national laws that may vary greatly. At worst, claimants may suffer the same sort of legal and practical restrictions evidenced by the *Torrey Canyon*,[962] through reliance on the ordinary law of tort, eg for negligence and nuisance to give a remedy for such HNS claims.[963] In the EU it is possible that the Environmental Liability Directive 2004 might apply.[964] Other States may have general

---

955 Which might be subject to a CLC or LLMC limit, as the case may be: see 2.6.2(a) and 2.5.4(b). In practice, bunker removal is most likely to be covered as a SCOPIC expense: see 2.7.9(c), 12.3.1.

956 See eg the IOPC Funds, *Claims Manual* (October 2016 ed), para 31.15. The costs of mobilising salvage equipment to deal with a threat are routinely covered within the CLC 1992 and Bunkers Convention 2011.

957 The Bunkers Convention 2001 Art 11 is a supersession clause which provides that it supersedes preceding conventions (eg the Salvage Convention 1989), but only to the extent that there would be conflict with it. For possible overlaps and conflicts between the Bunkers Convention 2011 and the WRC 2007, see 10.9.2(c).

958 For disposal, see 14.6.

959 See eg SCOPIC 2018, 2.7.9(c) and 12.3.

960 See also 2.5.4(b) and 2.5.5.

961 See eg the wreck of the munitions ship *Mont Blanc* (3,121 gt) which exploded in Halifax (Nova Scotia) in 1917, after a collision with the *Imo* (5,043 gt). Over 2,000 were killed and large parts of the city were destroyed: see *Steamship Imo v La Compagnie Generale Transatlantique* (1920) 2 Ll L Rep 188 (PC) (a case only involving hull claims; death and injury were dealt with through charity and welfare relief). See also 2.1.5(a) (fn115), 2.1.6 (fn 185), 2.4.3 (fn 517), 2.9.2(b) (fn 1265).

962 See 1.2.1, 2.6.1, eg difficulties in proving fault, low (general) limits of liability, insolvency of single ship companies, and jurisdictional restrictions.

963 See eg *Esso Petroleum Corp v Southport Corp* [1955] 2 Lloyd's Rep 655. The MSA 1995 s 154 only applies a fall-back regime for oil pollution and is not a general liability provision covering all types of pollution damage: see 2.6.3.

964 See 2.6.5.

environmental liability legislation that could apply to a wreck involving pollution from HNS.[965] Such legislation may have a narrower scope than an international convention and lack safeguards such as compulsory insurance and direct action; it may also be subject to low general limits of liability (eg under the LLMC).

To fill the international gap, the IMO created the International Convention on Liability and Compensation for Damage in Connection with the Carriage of Hazardous and Noxious Substances by Sea [HNSC] 1996. It was designed to provide a similar regime to that in the CLC and Fund Convention, but for hazardous and noxious substances (other than oil cargoes in tankers), eg where there is chemical pollution after the wreck of a bulk carrier or container ship. Owing to insuperable difficulties with its second tier contribution system, the HNSC 1996 has never entered into force.[966] It was therefore amended by the HNS Protocol 2010.[967] The "HNSC 2010" is the HNSC 1996, as amended by the 2010 Protocol, and is designed to supersede the 1996 version.[968] It is not yet in force,[969] although active steps to facilitate entry into force have been underway at the IMO[970] and within the EU.[971]

The HNSC 2010 produces a regime very like the CLC and Fund Convention, but in a single (albeit complex) instrument. Given the similarities with the CLC and Fund regime, it is only necessary here to set out key features of the HNSC 2010. It will create strict liability[972] of the registered owner of any seagoing ship[973] for damage[974] caused by hazardous and noxious substances. There are the usual CLC-type defences,[975] but with the addition of a specific defence for the shipowner where it has not been informed about the nature of

---

965 See eg the New Zealand's MTA 1994 Part 25 and the *Rena*, 1.2.4(c). Australian State legislation may also give remedies: see eg the Transport Operations (Marine Pollution) Act 1995 (Qld), ss 115, 132F.

966 In anticipation of its adoption, the UK enacted facilitating legislation in the form of a new Chapter V of Part VI of the MSA 1995: see the Merchant Shipping and Maritime Security Act [MSMSA] 1997, s 14. The MSA 1995 Part V contains the text of the HNSC 1996 in a new Sch 5A (rather than being rewritten piecemeal, like the CLC and Fund Convention). Wide powers are provided in new ss 182(A)–(C) to give effect by Order to the Convention when it enters into force; these powers also apply to any *amendment* to the 1996 Convention and would thus include the HNS Protocol 2010. See N Gaskell, "Merchant Shipping and Maritime Security Act 1997" in *Current Law Statutes 1997* (Sweet & Maxwell, 1997) [*Gaskell, MSMSA 1997*], 28/64-28/69, 28/131-28/142.

967 The Protocol of 2010 to the International Convention on Liability and Compensation for Damage in Connection with the Carriage of Hazardous and Noxious Substances by Sea 1996.

968 See IMO LEG 99/14, para 3.2.

969 It has four Contracting States, and needs another eight (provided they meet a threshold of about an additional 11.5 million tonnes of cargo contributing to the general account): *IMO Status of Treaties* (November 2018).

970 See eg IMO, "Facilitation of the entry into force and harmonized interpretation of the 2010 HNS Protocol", IMO Doc LEG 105/3 (16 February 2018); also www.hnsconvention.org/.

971 See EU Council Decision (Council Decision of 18 November 2002, 2002/971/EC) authorising Member States to ratify or accede to the HNSC.

972 HNSC 2010 Art 7.

973 Cf 10.2.7. Note that Art 5 gives a State the option not to apply the HNSC to ships up to 200 gt doing cabotage with packaged HNS while on intra-State voyages. This exclusion can be extended to neighbouring States.

974 Defined in Art 1(6) more widely than "pollution damage" under the CLC 1992, so as also to cover injury and death (eg by poisoning or explosions).

975 Eg for war, third party damage, or government negligence with navigational aids: see Art 7(2)(a)–(c) and cf 2.6.2(a), 10.3.

the HNS, eg by the shipper.[976] Claims are channelled to the shipowner,[977] who is only liable under the HNSC 2010.[978]

The liability does not arise from any HNS, but only those listed.[979] The list is made by reference to generic IMO categories, covering bulk *and* packaged HNS cargoes.[980] Bulk cargoes will present broadly similar problems to oil under the CLC and Fund regime, but the inclusion of packaged HNS[981] is highly significant in relation to wreck, because it will cover HNS in containers. This means that after the loss of containers overboard from a ship,[982] or when a container ship is wrecked, the HNSC can apply so as to create liability for the "damage".[983] There could be property damage caused by contamination, explosion or fire.[984] Preventive measures would be covered, including mobilisation of equipment to deal with threats; search and efforts to find sunken, floating or beached containers of HNS; recovery of such containers and clean-up of any contents that have been spilled; and disposal of the waste remains of the HNS.[985] Where necessary, environmental reinstatement would be covered, as would economic loss suffered by tourism and fishing industries. It might be thought that container cargoes lost after a wreck would be messy but hardly likely to result in the sort of widespread environmental and economic losses caused by the major oil disasters.[986] But the loss of containers of pesticides could result in contamination of marine resources over a considerable area. There may well be difficult questions about apportioning costs between wrecked containers with cargoes of HNS and non-HNS goods.[987]

The compilation of a more specific practical reference list of HNS, to give flesh to the generic IMO categories of HNS, has been extremely difficult, as there are thousands of substances that might be within the IMO categories with new chemicals being created all the time. A useful online "HNS Finder" list has been created through the IOPC Funds and the IMO.[988] Most harmful chemicals are included, but not all potentially noxious ones.[989]

---

976 HNSC 2010 Art 7(2)(d). See also 2.5.4.

977 See Art 7(5); ie claims for HNS damage may not be brought against others such as the crew, charterers, salvors (including wreck removal contractors) and those taking preventive measures; and cf 2.6.2(a).

978 See Art 7(4). Rights of recourse are preserved by Art 7(6), eg a shipowner liable for HNS damage may bring a cross claim against a colliding ship; see also 2.4. The recourse claim may be subject to limitation under the LLMC 1996; see 2.5.4(b).

979 See Art 1(5).

980 A crucial distinction was made in the negotiations for the HNSC 2010 between liability for packaged HNS and the extent to which the HNS cargo industry should contribute to the second-tier HNS Fund. In the end, there was to be liability for packaged HNS, but no responsibility for its importers to contribute to the HNS Fund. This is one reason for the potential fragility of the HNS Fund itself.

981 Within the International Maritime Dangerous Goods (IMDG) Code: see the HNSC 2010 Art 1(v)(iv). Note also the possibility of a State opting out of applying the Convention to small cabotage ships carrying packed goods.

982 See 1.3.2(a), 10.6.

983 As defined in Art 1(6).

984 Physical damage caused by collision with floating containers would not be "caused" by the HNS (unless perhaps the container's cargo then caught fire or exploded): cf the *Pacific Adventurer* incident, 2.6.3.

985 Cf 14.6.

986 Eg *Erika* and *Prestige*, see 1.2.2(a).

987 See also 10.9.2(b).

988 See www.hnsconvention.org/hns-finder/. A simple search reveals that "picric acid" which exploded in the *Mont Blanc* in Halifax in 1917 (see fn 961) would be covered as packaged cargo.

989 Moreover, some are excluded by Art 4(3), including certain radioactive material: see *Gaskell, MSMSA 1997*, 28/64-28-65, 28/132-28-133; also 2.9.6(b), 10.9.3.

Coal was deliberately excluded from the HNS list, along with iron ore, grain, bauxite, alumina and phosphate rock. It is arguable that a cargo of coal could have deleterious environmental consequences in sensitive sea areas. On 3 April 2010, the Chinese registered bulk carrier *Shen Neng 1* (36,575 gt), carrying a cargo of 68,052 mt of coal, grounded on the Great Barrier Reef. The ship was eventually refloated after part of the cargo was transhipped. If the ship had been completely wrecked, the HNSC 2010 (even if in force) would not have applied to its cargo, eg to cover preventive measures generally,[990] the removal of any coal debris on the sea floor,[991] environmental reinstatement or economic losses. Moreover, the main damage to the reef in the incident was actually caused by *physical contact* (the ship grounding on the reef itself), so this would not have been damage "caused" by any HNS being carried in the ship within Art 7.[992]

The HNSC 2010 (when in force) will, like the CLC, have its own stand-alone limits for shipowners,[993] ie not linked to the LLMC 1996 like the Bunkers Convention 2001 and the WRC 2007.[994] The limits were altered in 2010 so as to produce a higher limit for ships where the damage is caused by packaged cargo as opposed to bulk cargo. This reflects, in part, a recognition of the potentially large claims that might come from the wreck of a big container ship. For damage caused by bulk HNS (eg bulk chemicals), the minimum shipowner liability is 10 million sdr for ships not exceeding 2,000 gt; this increases in stages[995] up to a maximum shipowner liability of 100 million sdr. For damage caused by packaged HNS (eg in containers) or by both bulk HNS and packaged HNS, the liability of the shipowner is a minimum of 11.5 million sdr for ships not exceeding 2,000 gt; this increases in stages[996] up to a maximum shipowner liability of 115 million sdr. Table 2.10 illustrates these figures by reference to some hypothetical ship sizes.

It can be seen that these figures are generally higher than those available under the CLC 1992[997] and greatly in excess of those under the LLMC 1996.[998] This is in part to reflect the possibility of death and injury under the HNSC 2010. The right to limit is lost if the pollution damage was caused intentionally or recklessly by the shipowner.[999]

---

990 The Bunkers Convention 2001 might have been relevant to cover preventive measures and clean-up of the very small amount of bunkers that leaked out, had such a claim been made within the relevant time limit.

991 By contrast, wreck removal legislation (eg the WRC 2007) might be used to remove the coal: cf the *Smart* grounding and see 10.6.4.

992 In the event, a claim was brought in negligence at common law for Au$70–194 million to pay for the removal of rubble and the scrapings of tributyltin paint from the ship's hull. The claim settled at the LLMC 1996 limits to cover Au$35 million for the cost of removing polluted rubble and Au$4.3 million for immediate clean-up costs. See *Gaskell, Liability and Compensation Regimes: Pollution of the High Seas*, 240–241.

993 HNSC 2010 Art 9.

994 See 2.6.3, 2.5.4(b) and (c), 10.7, 10.8.5.

995 From 2,001 gt to 50,000 gt, the minimum figure is increased by 1,500 sdrs; over 50,000 gt, the latter is increased by 360 sdrs per gt.

996 From 2,001 gt to 50,000 gt, the minimum figure is increased by 1,725 sdrs; over 50,000 gt, the latter is increased by 414 sdrs per gt.

997 See Table 2.7, 2.6.2(a).

998 See Tables 2.5, 2.6 and 7, 2.5.6(a). It is these LLMC limits that could apply to claims for bunker pollution (see 2.6.3, 2.5.4(b)) and wreck removal (see 10.7, 2.5.8).

999 Art 9(2). For a fuller explanation of this test and whose misconduct in the corporate structure is attributed to the owning company, see 2.5.7.

Table 2.10 HNSC 2010 shipowner limits

Tonnage	HNSC 2010 sdr amounts	£ sterling[1]	US$[2]
2,000 gt bulk carrier[3] (eg 3,000 dwt)	10,000,000 sdr	£10,866,200	$13,825,000
2,000 gt container ship[4] (eg 100 TEU)	11,500,000 sdr	£12,496,130	$15,898,750
20,000 gt bulk carrier (eg 35,000 dwt)	37,000,000 sdr	£40,204,940	$43,163,740
20,000 gt container ship (eg 2,000 TEU)	42,550,000 sdr	£46,235,681	$58,825,375
40,000 gt bulk carrier (eg 70,000 dwt)	67,000,000 sdr	£72,803,540	$92,627,500
40,000 gt container ship (eg 4,000 TEU)	77,050,000 sdr	£83,724,071	$106,521,625
90,000 gt bulk carrier (eg 175,000 dwt)	96,400,000 sdr	£104,750,168	$133,273,000
90,000 gt container ship (eg 9,000 TEU)	110,860,000 sdr	£120,462,693	$153,263,950
200,000 gt bulk carrier (eg 400,000 dwt)	*[136,000,000 sdr]*[5] 100,000,000 sdr	*[£147,780,320]* £108,662,000	*[$188,020,000]* $138,250,000
200,000 gt container ship (eg 20,000 TEU)	*[156,400,000 sdr]*[6] 115,000,000 sdr	*[£169,947,368]* £124,961,300	*[$216,223,000]* $158,987,500

[1] The calculation uses the IMF figures at 3 December 2018 with the rate of conversion of 1 sdr = £1.08662.

[2] As the international currency of shipping is the US$, this column gives comparative figures for 3 December 2018 based on 1 sdr = US$1.3825. The US is *not* party to the HNSC, so the US$ figures are given by way of example only.

[3] The bulk carrier entries show the limits where the damage is caused by bulk HNS. This row shows the minimum tonnage under the HNSC 2010 Art 9(1)(a). Any seagoing bulk carrier of 0–2,000 gt (eg a 200 gt ship) will have the minimum limits in this row. The deadweight tonnage (dwt) figures for bulk carriers in this column are estimates for illustration purposes only in order to give some idea of the tonnage of cargo that might be carried.

[4] The container ship entries show the limits where the damage is caused by packaged HNS, or by bulk and packaged HNS, or where it is not possible to determine whether the damage was caused by bulk or packaged HNS. This row shows the minimum tonnage under the HNSC 2010 Art 9(1)(b). The figures as to the number of TEUs carried by container ships in this column are rough estimates for illustration purposes only.

[5] Figures in square brackets and italics show the limitation figures that would have applied had there not been an overall HNS Art 9(1)(a) maximum limit of 100 million sdr. It is the latter figure that represents the limit for a ship of this gt.

[6] Figures in square brackets and italics show the limitation figures that would have applied had there not been an overall HNS Art 9(1)(b) maximum limit of 115 million sdr. It is the latter figure that represents the limit for a ship of this gt.

In order to follow the CLC and Fund two-tier liability scheme,[1000] the HNSC 2010 will create an HNS Fund.[1001] Its main purpose is to provide for a second tier of liability for HNS claims that exceed the shipowner's limits under the convention[1002] up to a maximum of 250 million sdr,[1003] as illustrated in Table 2.11.

1000 See 2.6.2(b).
1001 See Art 13.
1002 See eg Table 2.10.
1003 See Art 14(5)(a). This is aggregated with the shipowner's limit.

Table 2.11 HNS Fund 2010 limits

HNS Fund 2010 sdr amounts	£ sterling[1]	US$[2]
250 million sdr	£271,655,000	$345,625,000

[1] The calculation uses the IMF figures at 3 December 2018 with the rate of conversion of 1 sdr = £1.08662. The conversion into local currency is made on its sdr value on the day that the IOPC Fund Assembly decides on the first date of payment of compensation: see Art 4(5).

[2] As the international currency of shipping is the US$, this column gives comparative figures for 3 December 2018 based on 1 sdr = US$1.3825. The US is *not* party to the HNSC 2010, so the US$ figures are given by way of example only.

These HNS Fund figures have not changed since 1996, but although they are higher than those under the Fund Convention 1992, they are already considerably below those under the Supplementary Fund 2003.[1004] As with the Fund Convention 1992, the HNS Fund can also be liable for the whole of the HNS claim (including those amounts in the first tier), eg because of the insolvency of the shipowner or the inadequacy of its insurance or because there is no liability of the shipowner under the first tier.[1005]

The HNS Fund is more favourable to the claimant than the IOPC Fund where the source of any HNS damage is unclear. The HNS Fund can only deny liability if "the claimant cannot prove that there is a reasonable probability that the damage resulted from an incident involving one or more ships".[1006] The HNSC 2010 has time limits similar to those in the CLC and Fund regime, but more favourable to claimants as in a claim chemical pollution after a wreck might not be so obvious as oil pollution. The time limit against the shipowner is therefore three years from the date when "the person suffering the damage knew or ought reasonably to have known of the damage and of the identity of the owner".[1007] Moreover, the 'backstop' is ten years from the date of the incident which caused the damage.[1008]

Like the CLC and Fund regime, courts in contracting States to the HNSC 2010 will be given jurisdiction to hear claims for damage in their territorial seas and EEZ, and there are also provisions for mutual recognition and enforcement of judgments.[1009] There is a typical provision to ensure that the HNSC 2010 supersedes any prior convention if there is a conflict.[1010]

The major obstacle to the entry into force of the HNSC 2010 is its very complicated contribution provisions for the second tier. This arises because of the more segmented

---

1004 See Table 2.8 (2.6.2(b)) and Table 2.9 (2.6.2(c)).
1005 See Art 14(1)–(4); cf 2.6.2(b), for examples of where similar exceptions might operate. The HNS Fund will have a right of recourse against the shipowner or insurer (Art 41(1)), or against a shipper that failed to give appropriate notice to the shipowner of the HNS cargo (Art 41(2)).
1006 Art 14(3)(b); cf the Fund Convention 1992 Art 4(2)(b).
1007 See Art 37(1). Claims against the HNS Fund must be brought within a similar three-year period from the damage (without reference to the owner's identity: see Art 37(2)). Claimants will still need to start a separate action against the HNS Fund or give it notification under Art 39(7).
1008 See Art 37(3) and (4).
1009 See Arts 3, 38–40. This avoids some of the forum shopping issues, eg with the LLMC: cf 2.5.9.
1010 See Art 42. For overlap and conflicts between the HNSC 2010 and the WRC 2007, see 10.9.2(b). Cf 2.6.3, 2.6.2(a). 2.5.5 for overlaps with the Salvage Convention 1989.

nature of the industry contributors, by comparison with the oil industry, and the reluctance for there to be cross subsidisation. The HNS Fund is accordingly divided into four accounts, a General Account and Separate Accounts for oil (not in the CLC), LNG and LPG. Compensation under the HNS Fund will only be contributed to, in effect, by substances within that account. Packaged goods were excluded from the definition of contributing cargo in the 2010 HNS Protocol, although there is liability in respect of them, so they may fall within the General Account (which itself has separate sectors for bulk solids and other HNS). None of these administrative details should directly concern claimants after a wreck to which the HNSC 2010 will apply. However, the difficulties of ensuring that the various accounts and sectors are viable not only delays entry into force of the whole convention but may also call into question the solvency of a particular account after a major HNS incident.

2.6.5 Environmental Liability Directive 2004

After the *Erika*[1011] the EU enacted a wave of environmental legislation, some of which will affect maritime casualties,[1012] including wrecks. In particular, the Environmental Liability Directive 2004[1013] might apply to marine pollution and is applicable in the UK.[1014] In order to avoid international law conflicts, the Directive contains exceptions so that it does not apply to environmental damage (or imminent threat of such damage) arising from an incident in respect of which liability or compensation falls within the scope of specified international agreements on civil liability.[1015] These include the CLC 1992, the Fund Convention 1992 and the Bunkers Convention 2001.[1016] The HNSC 1996 (as amended) is also listed, but the exception would only apply when it is in force. This means that the Directive as enacted in the UK might presently apply to HNS incidents.[1017] It should be noted that the Offshore Safety Directive 2013 has extended the scope of the Environmental Liability Directive 2004 so that it applies more widely to offshore oil and gas operations, ie to deal with a *Deepwater Horizon* or *Montara* type of well wreck or blowout.[1018]

1011 See 1.2.1(a).
1012 See eg Directive 2008/56/EC of the European Parliament and of the Council of 17 June 2008 establishing a framework for community action in the field of marine environmental policy (Marine Strategy Framework Directive); also 14.4.2, 14.5.2, 14.6.
1013 Directive 2004/35/CE of the European Parliament and of the Council of 21 April 2004 on environmental liability with regard to the prevention and remedying of environmental damage; also Directive 2013/30/EU on safety of offshore oil and gas operations and amending Directive 2004/35/EC [Offshore Safety Directive]. See generally L Bergkamp, B Goldsmith, *The EU Environmental Liability Directive: A Commentary* (OUP 2013).
1014 It is enacted in England mainly in the Environmental Damage (Prevention and Remediation) (England) Regulations [ELD Regulations] 2015 (SI 2015/810): see also the Explanatory Memorandum. The ELD Regulations apply out to the limits of the EEZ and continental shelf; equivalent provisions exist for the devolved administrations in the UK, eg in Wales and Scotland. For post-Brexit issues, see 14.1.
1015 See Art 4(2) and Annex I; also *Somers & Gonsaeles*, 82.
1016 As well as the UNECE Convention on Civil Liability for Damage Caused during Carriage of Dangerous Goods by Road, Rail and Inland Navigation Vessels (CRTD) 1989; this is not in force.
1017 The Directive naturally makes no reference to the later WRC 2007: for possible overlaps, see 10.9.2.
1018 See the Offshore Safety Directive Art 7 and cf 10.2.7. The Offshore Safety Directive, recital 63, recognises the inadequacy of existing insurance systems for such losses.

The Directive has a very different liability structure to the IMO conventions, eg it makes an "operator" of activities that cause environmental damage strictly liable[1019] for prevention and remediation costs. The definition of "operator" is quite wide so as to cover a person who "operates or controls the occupational activity" or someone who under national legislation has delegated to them "decisive economic power over the technical functioning of such an activity".[1020] The "activity" itself can be virtually any economic or business activity and includes transport by sea of dangerous or polluting goods.[1021] The Directive could therefore cover not only shipowners, but possibly also managers and charterers,[1022] and possibly even a wreck removal contractor.[1023] There is also a more open definition of environmental damage[1024] than under the IMO conventions, and a generously expressed five-year time limit for cost recovery.[1025]

However, there are some familiar defences, including war and a CLC-type "natural phenomenon" defence.[1026] The operator can also rely on a defence where the damage was caused by third parties (eg terrorists),[1027] or resulted from compliance with a government order (given prior to the incident).[1028] The most significant defence for shipowners and others is that liability under the Directive is without prejudice to the right of a shipowner to limit liability under national legislation implementing the LLMC.[1029] There are no explicit compulsory insurance or direct action provisions, but the Directive enjoins member States to encourage development of financial security instruments to enable operators to use financial guarantees to cover their responsibilities.[1030]

1019 See Art 8(1). See generally the Commission's website for application and development of the Directive: http://ec.europa.eu/environment/legal/liability/index.htm.

1020 See Art 1(6).

1021 See Art 1(7) and Annex III, para 8.

1022 Cf 14.6.3.

1023 See also 13.6.3(h).

1024 See Art 2(1) and (2). The Directive does, though, set out a number of thresholds dependent upon whether the damage has "significant adverse effects" (see Annex I), and guidance on an appropriate remediation framework (see Annex II). The costs can also cover environmental impact assessments and a range of administrative costs:" see Art 1(16).

1025 See Art 10. The period runs not from the date of the original incident, but from the date on which remediation measures have been *completed*, or when the operator liable (or third party) has been identified.

1026 See Art 4(1) and cf 10.3.2.

1027 See Art 8(3)(a). Unlike the IMO Conventions, the operator does not have to prove that the third party "wholly" caused the damage: cf 10.3.1(b).

1028 See Art 8(3)(b). The defence would not therefore apply to the results of obeying an intervention order (see eg 4.2.3(a), or apparently one under the WRC 2007 Art 9(2) to remove a wreck.

1029 See Art 4(2) and the ELD Regulations 2015 reg 7(2); also 10.9.2. Article 4(2) also refers to limitation under the Strasbourg Convention on Limitation of Liability in Inland Navigation (CLNI) 1988, itself based on the LLMC. This latter convention was denounced by its four parties with effect from 1 July 2019. On that date it will be replaced by the Strasbourg Convention on the Limitation of Liability in Inland Navigation (CLNI) 2012, designed to be more attractive to States without direct access to the Rhine or Moselle. Both conventions allow for limitation for wreck removal, but also with an identical opt-out for wreck and cargo removal to the LLMC: cf 2.5.8. As the 2012 Convention is not an amendment of the 1988 Convention, it does not formally fall within the exception of Art 4(2) of the 2004 Directive.

1030 See Art 14. On the effectiveness of insurance measures, see Commission Report COM(2010) 581 final, 12 October 2010, 7–9.

2.7 Wreck and the law of salvage

This section will introduce the concept of salvage as it affects the many parties involved in a casualty leading to a wreck. It needs to be read with Chapter 12, which concentrates on the commercial and legal issues that arise as a salvage operation transitions towards one for wreck removal.

The details of salvage law are examined in the standard texts on the subject,[1031] and it is only necessary here to set out some basic principles in so far as they are relevant to a casualty that may lead to a wreck.

2.7.1 Overview of salvage law

The law of salvage developed from a time when maritime journeys were much more perilous than at present and also from the absence of any public rescue service to come to the aid of mariners and ships in distress. Salvage law recognises that it has always been necessary to encourage seafarers to go to the assistance of others, not only to save life[1032] but also to save valuable property (eg ship and cargo) in danger[1033] from shipwreck and total loss. The encouragement takes the form of a reward to a voluntary salvor for saving the property. The reward has traditionally been generous—far more than, say, the daily hire cost of a tug.[1034]

The drawback for the potential salvor is that this salvage reward is only payable if there has been success, ie that property has been saved; the underlying principle is one of "no cure no pay". A service which may have taken much time and involved much expense will not be rewarded if the ship and cargo sinks and becomes a total loss. The reward can only be payable out of the value of the property saved. So, if a salvor only manages to retrieve some containers of cargo from a ship wrecked on a reef, the maximum reward for the salvor would be the value (if any) that the containers and their contents have at a place of safety. A salvor that has saved valuable property, eg the containers of cargo, will have a maritime lien on that property; ie it can refuse to release the containers from its possession

---

1031 See eg *Kennedy & Rose*, Chapter 16; J Reeder, *Brice on Maritime Law of Salvage* (5th ed, Sweet & Maxwell 2011) [*Brice*], 154–205.

1032 International public law duties to assist vessels in distress have long existed: see eg the Collision Convention 1910 Art 8 and the Salvage Convention 1910 Art 11. See now UNCLOS 1982 Art 98; the International Convention for the Safety of Life at Sea (SOLAS), 1974 Chapter V reg 33; the International Convention on Maritime Search and Rescue (SAR) 1979 Annex, para 2.1.10; the Salvage Convention 1989 Art 10; IMO "Guidelines on the Treatment of Persons Rescued at Sea", Resolution MSC.167(78), 20 May 2004. See also the MSA 1995 ss 92–93 and Sched 11 Part I Art 10 and Part II para 3; the Merchant Shipping (Safety of Navigation) Regulations 2002 (SI 2002/1473, as amended), Sch 3 para 6. The MSA 1995 s 93 (as amended by the Merchant Shipping (Distress Messages) Regulations 1998 (SI 1998/1691)) extends the duty to assist aircraft in distress.

1033 See generally *Kennedy & Rose*, 153–161. If the salvor cannot prove there is danger to the property salved then there can be no salvage claim. It is not necessary that any distress should be actual or immediate or that the danger should be imminent and absolute (eg *The Charlotte* (1848) 2 W Rob 68, 71). The danger that the vessel faces includes immobilisation, eg where there is an engine failure but the vessel is not in immediate danger (eg *The Glaucus* (1948) 81 Ll L Rep 262, 266). It would be relevant to know if the ship was drifting towards dangerous shores: see eg *Fedra*, 10.2.5.

1034 In English law, salvage is a uniquely maritime concept and no equivalent exists for the saving of property on land: *Falcke v Scottish Imperial Insurance Co* (1886) 34 Ch D 234, 248.

until security is provided for its salvage claim. It is an essential characteristic of a salvage service, though, that the salved property was in danger, although this is largely a question of fact and not law.

2.7.2 Applicable salvage law

In English law, the law of salvage developed as an independent principle of maritime law through the case law of the Admiralty Court,[1035] particularly in the 19th century. The Convention for the Unification of Certain Rules of Law Respecting Assistance and Salvage at Sea[1036] (the Salvage Convention) 1910, to which the UK was a party, was largely considered to be declaratory of existing principles of admiralty law—to the extent that few provisions were given direct effect through statute.[1037] One key feature of salvage law was that the right of a salvor to claim a reward did not depend on any contract with the owners of the salved property, or even that there was consent of the owners; the legal basis was the performance of a service which benefited the property of another. If a salvor voluntarily provided a service which succeeded in saving property (eg ship and cargo) of value, then it was entitled to a reward assessed by the court on broad principles. The assessment of the reward depended not on a simple calculation of work and labour performed but reflected a broader intention to encourage future salvors by being generous in assessing a reward and relating it to a variety of factors—including in particular the value of property saved. It was always possible, though, to introduce the law of contract into a salvage service governed by admiralty law. This was mainly to settle in advance an agreed sum for the performance of a traditional no cure no pay admiralty salvage service; ie the basis of the claim was still in salvage law, but the amount could be regulated to some extent by contract.[1038] The development of the Lloyd's Standard Form of Salvage Agreement from 1892 presented the possibility of avoiding disputes at the scene of a casualty by leaving the salvage reward to be fixed by arbitration at Lloyd's. The fact that the reward was left open was reflected by the abbreviation "Lloyd's Open Form" (LOF). The precise relationship between the principles of admiralty salvage law and the contractual terms introduced by the LOF was not settled until the 1970s and 1980s. It was held that there was no special maritime magic about an LOF, as it was an ordinary contract for work and services,[1039] albeit with increasingly complicated provisions to deal with environmental implications of salvage.

1035 On the history and role of the Admiralty Court in salvage, see *Kennedy & Rose*, 49–63; *Brice*, 8–9.

1036 For an overview of the Salvage Convention 1910, see F Berlingieri, *International Maritime Conventions*: Vol II (Informa, 2015) [*Berlingieri, Vol II*], Chapter 4.

1037 See the Maritime Conventions Act 1911 ss 6–8, since repealed by the MSA 1995; the latter, by contrast, has given full effect to the successor Salvage Convention 1989.

1038 In fact, the Admiralty Court itself developed principles to review the validity of such agreements, anticipating to some extent modern principles of duress, and these powers were recognised in Art 7 of the Salvage Convention 1910 and Salvage Convention 1989.

1039 *The Tojo Maru* [1972] AC 242, 92; *The Unique Mariner* [1978] 1 Lloyd's Rep 438; *The Unique Mariner (No 2)* [1979] 1 Lloyd's Rep 37; also *Gaskell, MSA 1995*, 21/244; N Gaskell "The Lloyd's Open Form and Contractual Remedies" [1986] LMCLQ 306 [*Gaskell, Lloyd's Open Form and Contractual Remedies*], *Kennedy & Rose*, 5; also 12.2.1.

The adoption of the International Convention on Salvage [Salvage Convention] 1989[1040] effected a significant change in the form and content of salvage law in England. The Convention was enacted specifically by being given the force of law in the Merchant Shipping (Salvage and Pollution) Act 1994, now re-enacted through s 224(1) and Schedule 11 of the MSA 1985.[1041] Although the Salvage Convention 1989 still reflected many principles of existing salvage law, as a matter of formality the source of that law is now the convention (via the statute) rather than from the admiralty case law. If there is a conflict between the pre-existing case law and the convention (via the statute) then the convention should prevail.[1042] The Salvage Convention 1989 did, though, retain the ability to make salvage contracts and Art 6 provides that "the convention shall apply to any salvage operation save to the extent that a salvage contract provides expressly or by implication".[1043] This liberty is made use of in the modern LOF 2011 and SCOPIC 2018,[1044] but is subject to certain limitations regarding the environment,[1045] and quite wide discretionary power is given to a court to review any unfair terms.[1046]

In practice this means that even where such a contract is agreed, the underlying principles of the convention will normally apply, eg to assess the reward in a successful operation, but that the parties to the salvage contract may be free to agree their own terms. The most significant example of this is in relation to SCOPIC and its replacement of Art 14.[1047]

2.7.3 Salvage terminology

It is necessary to be clear about terminology when considering the applicable principles of salvage law in relation to wreck. "Salvage" is used variously to mean the reward obtained for the service, the service actually rendered[1048] and the cause of action arising out of that service.

The crucial distinction is between salvage performed under a contract such as the LOF and salvage without such a contract. Where there is no contract, the salvage reward is now

---

1040 Adopted 28 April 1989, entered into force 14 July 1996. For overviews of the Salvage Convention 1989, N Gaskell, "The 1989 Salvage Convention and the Lloyd's Open Form (LOF) Salvage Agreement" (1991) 16 Tul Mar LJ 1 [*Gaskell, 1989 Salvage Convention*]; *Berlingieri, Vol II*, Chapter 5.

1041 See generally *Gaskell, MSA 1995*, 21/238, 21/242–21/244.

1042 Note that an English court would apply the convention irrespective of whether the flag State was a party to it: *The Altair* [2008] 2 Lloyd's Rep 90 [42].

1043 See also 2.1.3(a) and 12.2.

1044 See 2.7.9(c), 12.2.2, 12.3.

1045 Art 6.3, Art 7; *Gaskell, MSA 1995*, 21/386–21/389.

1046 See Arts 7, 17, and cf 12.1.2(e). Note that commercial salvage and towage contracts are not generally subject to the powers to review contract terms; see the Unfair Contract Terms Act 1977 Sch 1 para 2, as amended by the Consumer Protection Act 2015. The latter Act now deals comprehensively with claims by a "consumer" that contract terms (including maritime contracts) are unfair and gives effect to a number of EU Directives, including Directive 93/13/EEC of the Council on unfair terms in consumer contracts. A "consumer" is defined in s 2 of the Consumer Protection Act 2015 to be an "individual acting for purposes that are wholly or mainly outside that individual's trade, business, craft or profession". These provisions might be theoretically be relevant, eg to contracts for the salvage of wrecked yachts, although they are much more likely in practice to 'bite' the sort of exculpatory terms found in towage and wreck removal contracts.

1047 See 2.7.9(c), 12.2.2 and 12.3.

1048 "Salvage operation" is defined in the 1989 Salvage Convention Art 1(a) as "any act or activity undertaken to assist a vessel or any other property in danger in navigable waters or in any other waters whatsoever".

based on rights and obligations set out in the Salvage Convention 1989 as applied by the MSA 1995. This might be termed 'convention salvage' or even 'pure salvage'. The first of these is now probably the most accurate description. The expression "common law salvage" is sometimes used, but can be misleading for a variety of reasons. First, it seems to hark back to the days when salvage law was sourced in case law rather than the Convention (via the MSA 1995). Secondly, it risks confusion with the (largely historical) question of whether there can be salvage under the principles of applied by the common law courts (as opposed to those applied by the Admiralty Court). It is doubtful if there ever really was any possibility of bringing a salvage claim at "common law" in this sense, but this is a largely theoretical question of little contemporary significance.[1049]

So, when the expression "common law salvage" is used at all, it is usually meant to signify that there is no applicable contract. In other words, the principles to apply are the basic principles of salvage law, now derived from the Salvage Convention 1989. The practical consequences of there being a 'no-contract' salvage are, for instance, the absence of an agreed arbitration and law clause and the fact that any reward for removing an environmental hazard will be entirely governed by the principles of Arts 13 and 14 of the Salvage Convention 1989 and not the LOF 2011 and SCOPIC 2018.

2.7.4 Professional salvage and wreck removal contractors

The salvage business is one that has always involved a high degree of risk, both technically (in dealing with a dangerous situation) and financially (through the no cure no pay principle). For this reason, professional salvors have always been part of a rather specialised industry, usually distinguished from those who merely operate tugs for mainly harbour service. A "salvor", though, can be any person or company that provides a valuable service, and to succeed in a salvage claim a person or company need not be a professional salvor.[1050] The maritime world, though, still depends on the expertise and resources of a private professional salvage industry. Most States have national plans for dealing with maritime emergencies[1051] and do maintain stockpiles of anti-pollution equipment, but there is a heavy reliance on the professional salvors to supply salvage vessels and, equally important, skilled salvage personnel to handle casualties.[1052]

The salvage industry has complained about falling income and increased costs, particularly since the 1970s and 1980s[1053] and that this has affected its ability to maintain dedicated salvage teams and equipment. The increased capabilities of harbour tugs and the availability of powerful offshore supply vessels has meant that specialist salvage tugs do not dominate the market as perhaps they once did. It also means that smaller operators may offer salvage services as an occasional lucrative adjunct to ordinary commercial services.

1049 See *Kennedy & Rose*, 64–71. As noted above, even the Admiralty Court can apply ordinary common law principles relating to contract (eg as to performance and breach).

1050 Although a professional salvor that maintains dedicated personnel and equipment will have that recognised in any salvage reward: see eg the Salvage Convention 1989 Art 13(1)(i) and (j).

1051 See 4.8.1, 5.7.

1052 States such as the UK and Australia have maintained a limited number of emergency towing vessels on charter (eg in the English Channel and the Great Barrier Reef), and some national Coast Guards have vessels and equipment that may be available in an emergency, but these are limited in number and location.

1053 With the major tanker disasters of that era; see 1.2.2(a).

Recent years have seen a rise in the number of smaller salvage operators, but also much consolidation amongst the bigger players[1054] and even suggestions that salvage expertise is being dissipated by a movement into offshore rig dismantling. Apart from these players, there have been some concerns about a decline in the number of experienced salvage personnel, in line with a decline in the employment of developed world (eg Western) seafarers. The rise of China, with a State supported salvage industry, has also raised some fears that its expansion into the salvage and wreck industry might affect international competition,[1055] but (as in other spheres) there can also be advantages in expanding capacity. Indeed, the major salvage and wreck contractors have for many years offered salvage services using a combination of their own equipment and that chartered in from other operators, albeit managed by their own salvage masters. Of real concern to some governments is that very specialised equipment may only be available in key hubs, eg Rotterdam, Cape Town and Singapore, from which it may take some time to be mobilised.[1056] The advent of the new breeds of super container ships such as the *Maersk Madrid* (214,286 gt with a capacity of 20,568 TEUs) has raised real concerns about the existence and availability of heavy lift crane barges with the capacity to offload containers from such ships.[1057]

In this context there is still a major concern for the international contractors in the application of cabotage principles by coastal States faced with a maritime casualty. In essence, this means that the State may require that any vessels operating in its waters must fly the flag of that State. While this is understandable in general commercial terms, it poses particular problems when highly specialised salvage services are required. Although this is perceived to be a particular issue in some Asian states, the tendency also applies elsewhere.[1058] The risk for a State is that the use of inexperienced local contractors may prolong operations or, worse, the operations may result in a complete wreck of ship and cargo with possible pollution consequences.

2.7.5 Success in preventing a wreck

An obvious example of where salvage principles are relevant to wreck is where there is a successful salvage service which *prevents* the ship being completely wrecked along with its cargo.[1059] Here the salvor will earn a reward for the services. The reward will be paid by hull and cargo interests in proportion to the value of what is saved, although the salvor's claim may be met indirectly by the hull and cargo insurers (subject to any policy excess).[1060]

1054 Eg Titan and Svitzer became part of Ardent in 2015 as a result of a merger between Crowley and Svitzer (which itself had acquired Wijsmuller in 2001 and Adsteam in 2007 while being part of the Maersk Group); Boskalis acquired Smit in 2012; Mammoet is part of BigLift (itself part of the Spliethoff Group).
1055 The raising of the wreck of the *Sewol* in 2014 was performed by the Shanghai Salvage Company apparently for a fixed price, but it potentially faced significant losses as the operation became more difficult: see 13.1.1, 13.1.2, 10.8.1.
1056 See 10.2.6.
1057 See 1.3.2(c).
1058 The *Costa Concordia* wreck removal notably involved the use of Italian contractors and disposal of the wreck in an Italian yard: see 1.2.5(b). See also 4.2.3(a) and the WRC 2007 Art 9(4): eg 10.5.2.
1059 The risk of total loss might also arise from the 'danger' that a port authority might order the vessel to be destroyed if it could cause an obstruction: *The Merannio* (1927) 28 Ll L Rep 352.
1060 See 2.9.2(a), 2.9.3(c).

Where a salvor prevents a ship from becoming a wreck, not only will the owners of ship and cargo benefit by having their property saved, but the shipowner may also avoid potential liabilities both for pollution (eg under the CLC 1992 or Bunkers Convention 2001)[1061] or for wreck removal, eg under the WRC 2007.[1062] It seems that a court may take this into account in a general way when fixing a reward[1063] in order to reflect the meritoriousness of the service,[1064] but attempts by salvors to try to add "saved liabilities" to the salved value were rejected in the negotiations for the Salvage Convention 1989.

The reward position is more complicated where the salvage operation is only partially successful. For example, a wrecked ship may be refloated, but it may have suffered damage that requires repairs. Those repairs may diminish the salvage fund available to the salvors; likewise, if only part of the cargo is recovered (eg containers on deck), or the cargo that is recovered has been contaminated. In these circumstances, there will be a salvage reward, but it may be significantly lower than the salvor might have expected for the work performed.

At some stage in the salvage operation it may become clear to the salvor that the salvage operations are unlikely to be successful, ie to give rise to a "useful result" under Art 13. Given the no cure no pay principle, the salvor has no immediate incentive to continue with the work, ie to prevent the ship and cargo becoming wrecked and a total loss. Where there is a no-contract "convention salvage", the salvor has limited obligations to continue with the service. Article 8(1) of the Salvage Convention 1989 provides that the salvor has a number of duties which are owed to "the owner of the vessel or other property in danger". These are not some wider public obligation but duties owed only to the property interests. In particular there is a duty in Art 8(1)(a) to carry out the salvage operations with due care". Given that the salvor is a volunteer, this provision does not oblige a salvor to carry out operations which are uneconomic.[1065] The obligation is to ensure that anything that the salvor decides to do must be done with due care; it does not mean that there will be a failure to exercise due care merely because a salvor decides that it would be too expensive to remove every item of cargo.[1066] If the salvor is in breach of any of the Art 8 obligations, so that for instance the ship and cargo become wrecked when with due care they might have been saved, there are two possible consequences under the convention. First, any overall reward may be reduced under Art 18; but if the ship and cargo become a total loss, there would be no reward anyway. Secondly, it is arguable that breach of Art 8 might sound in damages under the convention.[1067]

Where the salvage operations are governed by a contract such as the LOF, the salvor's obligations are arguably more onerous. The traditional term now in cl 1 is for the salvor to

---

1061 See 2.6.2(a), 2.6.3.
1062 See Chapter 10.
1063 See *Kennedy & Rose*, 161–164; *Brice*, 399–404.
1064 In *The Merannio* (1927) 28 Ll L Rep 352, a ship with valuable cargo was prevented from sinking in the Thames by being beached. It appears that the ship was a CTL, but the cargo saved was valuable. Lord Merivale mentioned the possible wreck raising expenses, or even destruction of vessel and cargo, as a consequence of port authority action to remove an obstruction. In a short extemporary judgment, the context was merely part of the process of producing a "fair and moderate" reward; there was no attempt to try to value the saving of liability.
1065 See further 12.2.1.
1066 *Gaskell, MSA 1995*, 21/390.
1067 Ibid., 21-391.

use "best endeavours" to salve. It is arguable that this goes beyond the exercise of due care and imposes some obligation to continue with the service; at least the salvor runs the risk of being in breach if it decides to leave the job, eg to take on a more lucrative operation elsewhere. Further, a failure to use best endeavours, eg leading to the wreck of a ship, would result in the salvor being in breach and liable to contractual damages. In *The Toju Maru*,[1068] a salvage diver negligently caused an explosion in the ship which resulted in a total loss when the ship could have been salved. The House of Lords held that the salvors were liable for the negligent performance of the best endeavours obligation.[1069]

The precise rights of salvors (but also shipowners) to bring the salvage service to an end without legal recourse caused some uncertainty in the 1980s and 1990s. In order to try to solve these problems, specific clauses relating to the termination of contractual salvage services were introduced into LOF and SCOPIC.[1070]

2.7.6 Can a wreck be salved?

A broader and more fundamental question is whether a ship[1071] and cargo can be subject to the law of salvage once they have sunk, ie they have become wrecked in a general sense. It might be thought obvious that there is no difference between salving a ship that is aground, and saving one that has sunk; provided that the saved property has a value, a 'salvor' ought to be rewarded in the same manner. This had long been the law and practice of the Admiralty Court.[1072] It appears that some civil law States treated the salvage of wrecks (*épaves* in French law) differently, although Berlingieri took the view that the Salvage Convention 1910 impliedly accepted the English approach that there could be salvage of sunken ships and wrecks.[1073]

This issue arose again during the negotiations for the Salvage Convention 1989 when there were debates about how to define the property which was subject to salvage. The discussion seemed to confuse two separate issues, ie how to treat the raising and removal of property that had a value from that which had no value. Wreck removal law is concerned with the latter, but it is in effect a default position which it is only necessary to apply when the law of salvage cannot benefit a salvor as there is nothing of value to be saved. The debates before and during the 1989 diplomatic conference clearly confirmed that the law of salvage can apply to sunken ships and cargoes.[1074] The key definition is now Art 1(a), which defines 'salvage operation' as 'any act or activity undertaken to assist a vessel or any other

---

1068 [1972] AC 242.
1069 It was also held that, under the legislation then in force (the MSA 1894 applying the Limitation Convention 1957) the salvors were not entitled to limit liability. That position has been changed in the LLMC 1976/1996: see 2.5.5.
1070 See 12.2–12.3.
1071 The Salvage Convention 1989 applies to any ship or craft or any structure capable of navigation (see Art 1(b)), but Art 3 excludes its application to platforms and drilling units when they are on location engaged in the exploration, exploitation or production of seabed mineral resources; ie salvage can only occur to such rigs when in transit.
1072 See eg *HMS Thetis* 166 ER 312; *The Egypt* (1932) 44 Ll L Rep 21; *Kennedy & Rose*, 107; *Brice*, Chapter 4 (especially 270–279).
1073 See *Berlingieri, Vol II*, 50.
1074 See *Berlingieri, Vol II*, 74–76, *Gaskell, 1989 Salvage Convention*, 34–37.

property in danger in navigable waters or in any other waters whatsoever'. A sunken ship is still a vessel,[1075] but would any event be "property". The latter is defined in Art 1(c) to mean "any property not permanently and intentionally attached to the shoreline and includes freight at risk".[1076] Proposals to allow States to make reservations over sunken property were rejected, with the consequence that the Salvage Convention 1989 can be applied to wrecks, however defined.[1077] This would appear to be the position even if national law considers generally that a sunken vessel ceases to be a "ship" in maritime law,[1078] as that wreck would be a "vessel" or "other property" for the purposes of *this* convention.

This conclusion is subject to some caveats. First, it can still be debated whether wrecked property at the bottom of the sea is still in "danger"; however the better view is that there is still danger in a broad sense while the property is, in effect, unavailable to its owners owing to its otherwise indefinite location on the seabed.[1079] Secondly, for the convention to provide an Art 13 salvage reward to a salvor there must be a "useful result", ie property of value must be saved sufficient to pay such a reward. Thirdly, if the wrecked property is raised or recovered but has no value, then the 'salvage' contractor would normally need to rely on a contract for wreck removal to recover any expenses;[1080] ie unlike salvage proper, there would need to be an advance agreement for remuneration. Fourthly, the only other mechanism under the Salvage Convention 1989 under which the salvage contractor could claim a payment for removing a wrecked ship or cargo would be to claim it as special compensation under Art 14.[1081]

The discussion in this section has focused on modern shipwrecks of commercial vessels.[1082] The application of salvage principles to long lost or historic wrecks raises difficult questions of proof as well as cultural heritage issues.[1083]

2.7.7 Salvage reward

There are two relevant aspects to the salvage reward:[1084] how it is calculated and who is bound to pay it.

1075 Defined in Art 1(b) as "any ship or craft, or any structure capable of navigation". There is no qualification here about the vessel not being sunk. Moreover, it is clear that craft such as semi-submersible drilling ships are capable of salvage, but not fixed platforms: see Art 3.

1076 The definition clearly excludes fixed pipelines. "Freight" here refers to the technical maritime law expression payment for carriage under a bill of lading or charterparty, and not to the more popular meaning, ie cargo more generally. Cargo would be "other property" in any event.

1077 *Berlingieri, Vol II*, 75. Cf 6.4.3.

1078 See 14.7.2.

1079 This would apply eg to a cargo, such as gold, that does not degrade while underwater: see eg *The Egypt* (1932) 44 Ll L Rep 21; *The Tubantia* [1924] P 78. See also 3.5.

1080 See the WRC 2007 and eg 10.2.3, 12.1, but note 2.7.9(c).

1081 See 2.7.9(b).

1082 The Civil Aviation Act 1982 s 87 allows for the salvage of aircraft in the same way as with vessels: and see *Kennedy & Rose*, 120-121. The Civil Aviation Act 1982 s 87(4) allows for an Order in Council to be made extending laws relating to wreck and salvage to be applied (with modifications) to aircraft in the same way as vessels. The Aircraft (Wreck and Salvage) Order 1938 (SR & O 1938/136) continues in force and applies through Art 2 to the MSA 1995 Part IX (Salvage and Wreck) and through Art 3 to the HDPCA 1847 s 56 (see 11.1.2(a); the Order is not available from www.legislation.gov.uk, but is reproduced in *Kennedy & Rose*, 805–807.

1083 See Chapter 3 and 6.4.1, 6.4.3.

1084 Note that "reward" and "award" are sometimes used interchangeably; the latter strictly refers to the decision made by an arbitrator on the amount of payment.

2.7.7(a) Size of reward

The size of the reward will ultimately be fixed by a judge or arbitrator, based on the criteria listed in Art 13 of the Salvage Convention 1989. These include the salved value of the vessel and other property; the skill and effort of the salvor; the nature and degree of the danger; time used and expenses of the salvor; and the measure of success of the salvage operation.[1085] The assessment of the reward will vary greatly according to circumstances and is rather more of an art than a science. There is no set scale of payment, although experienced maritime lawyers will rely heavily on the practice of Lloyd's arbitrators.[1086] A key starting component in any assessment will be the size of the salved fund. From the salvors' perspective, they will be focused not only on the final US$ figure awarded but also on what percentage this represents of the total salved value. The size of the salved fund must not be allowed to raise the amount of a salvage reward out of all proportion to the services rendered,[1087] eg where there is a relatively straightforward service to a ship in danger. The more complex the services required and the greater the danger to all parties, the higher the reward is likely to be. Thus, a prolonged but ultimately successful operation to remove thousands of containers from a wrecked container ship could be expected to result in a reward that was a relatively high percentage of their salved value.

The size of the potential reward is increased with the high value of modern cargo and passenger ships. A large container ship might easily be worth $100 million and its cargo could be valued at many times more than that. Indeed, the heaviest burden of a salvage reward will often fall on the cargo owners. From the salvor's perspective, this presents practical problems, eg in exercising a maritime lien, and obtaining security, in respect of potentially thousands of owners. By contrast, the cargo owners may often have little knowledge of the casualty and the efforts to save ship and cargo.[1088]

Between 1990 and 2008, the average percentage of awards to salved values in LOF cases varied from 4.9% (1990) to 18.8% (1999) with an average of 10.8%. By contrast, the average percentage awarded over a ten-year period from 2004 to 2013 was 23%, with container vessel cases amounting to 15.33%.[1089] The average salved value of container ships per award was higher than any other category of ship (eg bulk carriers) and the increasing size of container ships suggests that this trend will continue. The number of LOF cases has fallen in the period 2013–2017 by comparison with earlier years and the International Salvage Union (ISU) 2017 statistics for all salvage awards show that the average income (excluding SCOPIC payments) for each LOF case was 5.6% of salved value—the lowest

---

1085 Also included are the skill and efforts of the salvor in preventing or minimising damage to the environment: see the Salvage Convention 1989 Art 13(1)(b), and 2.7.9(a).

1086 Access to information about Lloyd's awards is by subscription: www.lloyds.com/market-resources/lloyds-agency/salvage-arbitration-branch/.

1087 *The Ocean Crown* [2010] 1 Lloyd's Rep 468, 475.

1088 See 2.1.3(a), 12.3.3.

1089 See Lloyd's Open Form Report 2015, 9. Caution needs to be exercised with the figures between 2009 and 2016, as they were affected by complex low value cases requiring reasonable rewards that necessarily amount to a high proportion of the salved value. By contrast, in 2017 property amounting to US$170 million was salved, but the percentage figure of awards to salved value was 4.7%.

on record.¹⁰⁹⁰ Interestingly, wreck removal income of ISU members amounted to 58% (US$264 million) of their total income.¹⁰⁹¹

The average percentage figures have to be treated with much care, as they are not really a guide in individual cases which can vary greatly depending on risk and what would be a fair reward for the salvor. In a case where the risk to ship and cargo is very high, eg where stranding and total loss is very likely without salvage intervention, an award might well be as much as 60%–65% of salved value.¹⁰⁹² Those with no experience of salvage law and practice may be surprised at the level of potential rewards by comparison with ordinary contracts for service—where payment may be calculated on a daily basis. The important point, though, is that in a casualty that might become a wreck, there may be a perception from the master or owners that the level of reward will not only be uncertain but also high. It is this fear that may cause delay in agreeing a salvage contract, which may in turn contribute to a ship being wrecked.¹⁰⁹³ Although fixed price salvage contracts have always been possible,¹⁰⁹⁴ the use of a fixed price 'capped' LOF has been raised more recently.

2.7.7(b) Liability to pay salvage
The basic principle of English law, enshrined in Art 13(2) of the Salvage Convention 1989, is that once the reward has been determined, it shall be paid by all of the vessel and other property interests in proportion to their respective salved values. This means that it is not only the shipowner that must contribute but also each of the separate cargo owners (as well as time charterers that might own bunkers). That liability is separate, which is why the salvor needs to obtain security from each interests.¹⁰⁹⁵ Where the ship and cargo are salved in the container trade, in particular, the shipowner (or contracting carrier) may decide to assume liability to pay the whole reward¹⁰⁹⁶ (providing security to the salvor accordingly) and then claim the cargo's proportion of salvage in general average.¹⁰⁹⁷ This may remove delays to the ship's continuing sailing schedule, although the shipowner may need to secure general average security from cargo. From the salvor's perspective, this may save it considerable time and trouble in trying to make contact with thousands of cargo interests whose contact details are more readily available to the shipowner, but it presents burdens and risks to the shipowner.¹⁰⁹⁸ Where the ship is wrecked and a CTL, and all or part of the cargo is salved, the shipowner may have less interest in assuming full liability. The ship's sailing

---

1090 See www.marine-salvage.com/media-information/our-latest-news/isu-statistics-for-2017-show-show-the-salvage-industry-continues-to-experience-weak-revenues/.
1091 Ibid.
1092 Cf *The Nagasaki Spirit* [1997] 1 Lloyd's Rep 323. These levels of percentages are likely to influence the amount of security demanded by salvors: see 2.7.8.
1093 See 12.1.2 and eg the *Fedra*, 10.2.5.
1094 Subject to the power under the Salvage Convention 1989 Art 7 to regulate excessive prices.
1095 See 2.7.8.
1096 This alternative is also open to States under Art 13(2) when enacting the convention, ie to make the reward payable by one interest only—usually the shipowner. This was to accommodate the Netherlands: see *Gaskell, MSA 1995*, 21/405.
1097 See 2.8. Alternatively, the shipowner may provide initial security to the salvor, until a lien can be exercised at the port of final destination under the contract of carriage.
1098 See 2.8.

schedule is no longer an issue and, if the cargo is taken to an intermediate port, freight may not be payable.

2.7.8 Salvors' security for payment

During and after the salvage operation, the salvor will be acutely conscious of the need to obtain security for payment of its reward, given the difficulty of enforcing claims against international defendants in foreign courts—especially with containerised cargoes belonging to thousands of different owners. The salvor may lose all practical means to enforce its claims once the salved cargo is delivered in a port of refuge to the many individual owners who then remove it. To protect its security, the salvor may have a number of remedies,[1099] bearing in mind that the claim will be time-barred if judicial or arbitration proceedings are not instituted two years after the salvage services were completed.[1100]

The salvor may well have assumed possession of items of cargo and will seek to retain that possession in the place of safety until security is provided.[1101] In some circumstances, salvors may have possessory rights that they can assert against other competing salvors, eg where they salve a "derelict", ie a ship abandoned by its master and crew without hope of recovering it or returning to it.[1102]

The strongest remedy available to the salvor is the right to a assert a maritime lien for a salvage claim.[1103] This privileged right over the salved property can be enforced through an Admiralty action in rem, and by the arrest of the salved property.[1104] A maritime lien does not depend on possession, and is not affected by any change in ownership or possession of the salved property;[1105] ie the claim travels with the ship or cargo and will bind a buyer even without notice of the claim. A maritime lien for salvage has priority over all other maritime liens that have attached to the vessel before the salvage, including earlier salvage, as without that service, no property would exist to secure any of the earlier liens.[1106]

The Salvage Convention 1989 Art 20(1) leaves unaffected the salvor's right to a maritime lien, but in Art 20(2) provides that the lien shall not be exercised when "satisfactory security" for the claim has been offered or provided.[1107] The Convention introduced a new provision, Art 21, which actually creates a duty on the person liable to pay for salvage (eg the shipowner and individual cargo owners) to provide "satisfactory security" for the claim (including for interest and costs). Art 21(3) recognises that the salved property shall not be removed from the first port of refuge without the salvor's consent.

In wreck cases where the ship is a total loss, it is likely that the salvor will be focusing on the recovery of cargo, hoping that enough can be recovered in sound condition so as to provide a sufficient fund to reward its services. In order to deter collusion between

---

1099 Note eg the powers of the receiver of wreck in relation to salvage: 4.5.2.
1100 1989 Salvage Convention Art 23(1).
1101 See the Salvage Convention Art 21(3), below.
1102 See 3.5.1 and *Kennedy & Rose*, 104, 516–523.
1103 See D Thomas, *Maritime Liens* (London, Stevens, 1980); *Jackson*, 17.35–17.63.
1104 Eg under the Senior Courts Act 1981 ss 20–21, giving effect to the Arrest Convention 1952.
1105 *The Bold Buccleugh: Harmer v Bell* (1850) 7 Moo PCC 267.
1106 *The Veritas* [1901] P 304; *The Russland* [1924] P 55; *The Gustaf* (1862) Lush 506, 508, 167 ER 230, 231; See also *The Lyrma (No.2)* [1978] 2 Lloyd's Rep 30 with respect to this priority if were to lead to an unjust result.
1107 See also 2.8.2.

shipowners and cargo owners, Art 21(2) puts an obligation on the shipowner to use best endeavours to ensure that cargo owners provide security to the salvor, but there may not be a lot that the shipowner can do once the cargo has been removed from the wrecked ship. In the container ship wreck cases, such as the *MSC Napoli*,[1108] it is likely that a lot of the cargo will be ruined and of no value. While the salvor can expect to claim salvage for the sound cargo, it is here that the salvor and shipowner will be thinking about the transition to wreck removal;[1109] the salvor in particular will be concerned about the problems of ruined cargo that has to be disposed of as waste.[1110]

Salvage contracts now contain extensive provisions on security.[1111] The LOF 2011 incorporates the Lloyd's Standard Salvage and Arbitration Clauses (LSSAC) 2014. Clause 4 of LSSAC in effect provides a security code which reflects in contractual form the provisions of the Convention. The salvors notify Lloyd's of the amount of their reasonable security demands. The amount of the security will reflect a guess as to the highest level of reward that might follow. This will not be 100% of the salved value, but might initially be a figure as high as 40%–65% in the type of case where a total loss was averted by the salvors. The level of security can be adjusted later. LSSAC cl 4.5 imposes fairly strict restrictions on the type of security that will be acceptable to Lloyd's or the salvor, and may need to be provided by a UK resident company or one with a high S&P rating. This can be difficult for some foreign insurers, while a guarantee insured at Lloyd's might be costly, eg at 0.5%–0.8% of the guaranteed amount. Until the security is provided, salved property cannot be removed from the place of safety to which it was taken. The salvors agree not to detain or arrest the property unless the security is not provided within 21 days of the termination of the salvage service.[1112]

In some cases, the realities of the political situation in the port of delivery may mean that it is impossible for the salvors to exercise any lien. The salvors may then have to use other methods of enforcement, eg by seeking a freezing (*Mareva*) injunction over other assets of the cargo owners.[1113]

2.7.9 Salvage and the environment

The *Torrey Canyon* and some of the later tanker disasters[1114] involved salvors in responding to casualties and incurring expenditure that was ultimately wasted when the ships became wrecks and nothing could be salved. Salvors complained that their efforts might have prevented pollution, eg by towing a ship away from sensitive coastlines, and thus 'saved' pollution liabilities for shipowners. As noted, attempts to have this 'value' recognised as a form of 'liability salvage' were rejected in the negotiations for the Salvage Convention 1989. However, it was recognised that salvors needed some extra encouragement to

---

1108 See 1.2.3.
1109 See Chapter 12.
1110 See Chapter 13.
1111 See *Kennedy & Rose*, 530–536; *Brice*, 549–556.
1112 For SCOPIC security, see 2.7.9(c).
1113 See eg *The Altair* [2008] 2 Lloyd's Rep 90, where the court issued such an injunction after rejecting a claim by the cargo owner for State immunity.
1114 See 1.2.1, 1.2.2(a).

become involved in tanker casualties in particular, but also where environmental damage was threatened by any cargo. This was achieved in two broad ways: firstly, by an 'enhanced reward'; secondly, by "special compensation".

2.7.9(a) Enhanced reward[1115]

The 'enhanced reward' becomes relevant when some property is salved. In the event of a wreck, this is most likely to be cargo or bunkers; eg the salvor may pump bunkers or oil cargoes into a transhipment tanker, or intact containers may be offloaded onto barges for transport to a nearby port. Article 8(1) of the Salvage Convention 1989 imposed an obligation on the salvor in performing the salvage operations, not only to exercise due care generally but also (in Art 8(1)(b)) to exercise due care to prevent or minimise "damage to the environment".[1116] This additional duty was recognised in Art 13(1)(b) whereby the traditional salvage reward may also reflect the skill and efforts of the salvor in preventing or minimising damage to the environment. The following features should be noted. First, there is no set figure to reflect this skill; in effect, the usual reward based on the list of Art 13(1) factors may be enhanced at the discretion of the judge or arbitrator, taking into account the causal effect of the salvor's actions on the environment. Secondly, the salvage reward can never exceed the salved value, which is relevant where little or no property is saved; in these cases "special compensation" may be relevant.[1117] Thirdly, as there is a normal salvage service, the reward is payable under Art 13(2) by those interests whose property has been saved.[1118] In the example of where the ship is wrecked, but some or all of the cargo is salved, the burden of paying the reward will fall pro rata on the individual cargo owners. In practice, this reward (including any enhancement) will be covered by their normal cargo insurance (subject to any deductibles).[1119]

2.7.9(b) Special compensation[1120]

The most controversial aspect of the major compromise finally agreed in 1989 was the introduction of Art 14. This was designed primarily to deal with the situation where there was no salved property, eg where ship and cargo were ultimately completely wrecked, but at the outset there had been a threat of damage to the environment. The idea was to encourage the salvor to become involved in a salvage operation even when it appeared that there was a high risk that there would be a wreck—ie where for obviously commercial reasons the salvor might be reluctant to gamble on property 'success'. The incentive to get involved where there was such an environmental threat was that the salvor would be guaranteed at least to recover its expenses in the operation—even if its efforts did not in the event succeed in preventing pollution. Where the salvor had actually prevented damage

---

1115 *Gaskell, MSA 1995*, 21/401–21/403; *Kennedy & Rose*, 179–184, 629; A Bishop, "The Development of Environmental Salvage and Review of the London Salvage Convention 1989" (2012) 37 Tul Mar LJ 65 [*Bishop*], 66–68.

1116 The latter expression was defined narrowly in Art 1(d), in particular by references to "major incidents" and "substantial" damage occurring in "coastal or inland waters or areas adjacent thereto": see *Gaskell, MSA 1995*, 21/377–21/378.

1117 See 2.7.9(b).

1118 See 2.7.7(b).

1119 See 2.9.3(c).

1120 *Gaskell, MSA 1995*, 21/404–21/416; *Kennedy & Rose*, 184–195; *Bishop*, 69–76.

to the environment, it would be entitled to claim its expenses plus an increment that might be up to 30% of those expenses (or in exceptional circumstances, up to 100%).[1121] A typical example might be where a tanker was towed away from an environmentally sensitive shore (but it later sank on the high seas), or where the bunkers of a stranded cargo ship were offloaded before the ship broke up.

Special compensation under Art 14 is payable only by the "owner of the ship" – not the owners of bunkers (eg time charterers) or cargo.[1122] The P&I Clubs, who stood to benefit if there was reduced pollution liability, agreed that they would provide cover to pay for special compensation. This was part of the 'Montreal Compromise', dating back to a CMI meeting in 1981 whereby underwriters agreed to cover the enhanced reward.

The position is slightly more complicated when some property is salved, as this might involve both Art 13 and Art 14—with questions about which insurer would ultimately pay. This was ultimately be a matter of balance for a judge or arbitrator, but a "common understanding"[1123] was that it was not necessary for the salved property to be 'used up' before special compensation is to be considered.

After the convention entered into force a number of problems arose in practice, in particular about how the salvor's expenses[1124] were to be calculated in the context of the balance between the underwriters and P&I insurance interests.[1125] These problems were resolved, somewhat unsatisfactorily from the salvor's perspective, by the House of Lords in *Semco Salvage & Marine Pte Ltd v Lancer Navigation Co Ltd (The Nagasaki Spirit)*.[1126] The result of that case was the need for salvors to prove (through a potentially expensive accounting exercise) what was a fair rate for their equipment used in any operation. Salvors also had difficulties in obtaining security for the special compensation, given that there was nothing against which a maritime lien could be exercised when the ship was wrecked.[1127] Meanwhile the P&I Clubs became concerned about a loss of control over expenditure, where special compensation payments were not fixed in the same way as a contract. There was some concern that salvors might drag out operations in order to incur special compensation in circumstances where the Club and owners might not have full access to information. In the end, the ISU and International Group of P&I Clubs decided to negotiate a new contractual solution to replace Art 14, namely SCOPIC.[1128]

Before considering where SCOPIC applies, it is necessary, though, to examine how far salvors might be able to use Art 14 to compensate them for wreck and cargo removal, eg where ship and cargo are wrecked and neither has any residual value to create a salved fund.[1129] It is highly unlikely that any salvor would wish to incur recovery costs without a wreck removal contract and financial security,[1130] but it is not inconceivable that a

---

1121 See Art 14.2.
1122 Nor is it allowable in general average: see 2.8.
1123 See the MSA 1995 Sch 11 Pt II para 4; *Gaskell, MSA 1995*, 21/433.
1124 Defined in Art 14(3).
1125 See generally *Bishop*, 69–76.
1126 [1997] 1 Lloyd's Rep 323.
1127 Despite an obligation under Art 21 on the shipowner (not insurer) to provide security. Where the ship was wrecked, it would be difficult to enforce the obligation on a single ship owning company with no assets.
1128 See 2.7.9(c).
1129 See also *Gaskell, MSA 1995*, 21/409–21/410.
1130 See Chapter 13, eg Wreckhire 2010 cl 15, 13.6.3(b).

contractor makes efforts to refloat a stranded ship, eg a fishing vessel, and then claims special compensation for removing the ship (and its bunkers) from a site of special scientific interest. This could be a classic Art 14 case, but the salvor does not strictly require permission from the shipowner or Club. Nor is there a specific right on the part of the shipowner to order the salvor to terminate Art 14 operations.[1131]

The issue about whether the salvor can use Art 14 in wreck cases seems more likely to arise in respect of cargo recovery—and there are a number of possible situations. A container ship may lose containers overboard in a storm but not be in danger itself.[1132] The recovery of those containers (and ruined cargo) from the shoreline or seabed may avert damage to the environment, eg if they contained pesticides or other dangerous chemicals. It seems doubtful that the salvor can have been carrying out salvage operations "in respect of a vessel" so as to utilise Art 14(1); ie cargo recovery work, unconnected with vessel salvage, is not covered. By contrast, if the vessel herself was in danger and containers were washed overboard during a salvage attempt, then a salvor might qualify for special compensation if it then recovered and removed the 'wrecked' containers with environmentally threatening cargo.[1133] Here, the salvor "*has* carried out salvage operations in respect of a vessel which . . . by its *cargo* threatened damage to the environment" (emphasis added).[1134] Presumably, the commercial incentive for the salvor would be to earn the Art 14(2) increment so as to recover its expenses 'plus' up to 30% (or even 100%). Again, if Art 14 is engaged it is the shipowner (*not* the cargo owner) that would pay the special compensation.

A more difficult example would be where, during salvage operations, the ship sinks with an environmentally threatening cargo (whether in bulk or in containers) and bunkers. The salvor might consider mounting a major operation either to raise the ship (with contents) or to remove the cargo or bunkers alone.[1135] In these examples, as the salvor "*has* carried out salvage operations" within Art 14(1) it would be entitled to special compensation for the expenses incurred up to the time of sinking. If the vessel had been wrecked, in the sense of being permanently stranded, it is conceivable that some parts of the vessel or the cargo might still have a residual value so as to justify normal salvage operations; in that case cargo and bunker removal would seem to fall within Art 14 if it later turned out that they had little or no value.

But where the ship is sunk, it may be clear that there is no reasonable prospect of anything of value being recovered so as to justify continued salvage operations; ie there was no prospect of a "useful result" within Art 12(1). It could then be argued that Art 14(1) is

---

1131 See further 12.2.1 on termination of services.

1132 See 1.3.2(a).

1133 Provided that the container containers together could satisfy the tests in Art 1(d), eg that there be substantial physical damage by pollution or contamination. It is not inconceivable that a single container with a particularly noxious cargo might satisfy the tests in sensitive areas. By contrast, the removal of small parcels of cargo might not pass the Art 1(d) thresholds.

1134 Cf where there are services to a vessel which sinks with such cargo, even where there is no attempt to salvage the ship: see *Gaskell, 1989 Salvage Convention*, 56–57.

1135 Again, if there has not already been salvage services in respect of the vessel, Art 14(1) is not engaged; so a salvor would have difficulty using Art 14 where it had arrived at the scene after the sinking. It would have to argue that it had provided assistance within Art 1(a) by responding to a distress signal, albeit that there was no useful result under Art 12(2).

not triggered as there is no longer any property in "danger" within Art 1(a);[1136] ie that the "salvage" operation had come to an end. The factual circumstances are so varied that it may sometimes be difficult to say whether there is anything of value to make the necessary connection between the 'salvage' and the 'raising' operations. Although the Salvage Convention 1989 does not clearly resolve such issues, it seems clear that it was not designed to provide for wreck removal unconnected to the salving of valuable property. So Art 14 would not seem to apply in the more extreme example where a salvor arrived at the scene of a casualty after the ship had already been wrecked and sunk, with no prospect of anything of value being saved. Here there is not even the connecting factor of salvage operations that have *already* been carried out.

An alternative, and simpler, argument in these examples (that are closer to wreck removal than salvage) is that special compensation would not be allowed under Art 14(3) as the expenses "were not reasonably incurred by the salvor in the salvage operation" or that equipment and personnel were not "reasonably used" in the salvage operation. It is not clear if the reasonableness relates only to the salvage operation or can be viewed more broadly; the latter is probably the better view. Even here, the 'environmental perspective' may be that operations to remove, say, bunkers may be reasonably incurred in most circumstances—especially as such products may well have some residual value. It may unreasonable within Art 14(3) to incur millions of dollars to remove bunkers of little value from a sunken wreck. In fact, many of the costs of removing potentially polluting cargo are better covered now by one of the pollution liability conventions.[1137]

In these cargo removal examples, the possibility of special compensation might theoretically be attractive to the salvor (where security is not an issue) as it does not need express permission to carry out the service:[1138] provided there was initially a salvage operation, the right to the compensation arises from the performance of the service within Art 14. By contrast, the shipowner (and Club) would be concerned about a lack of control over such removal operations and might either seek to rely on Art 19[1139] or decline to provide security for payment. Salvors are therefore highly unlikely to commit large resources in the hope of using Art 14 for what is in effect a wreck removal operation. Where the WRC 2007 is in force, the shipowner could have a liability to remove cargo and bunkers,[1140] but a contractor itself would have no right itself to perform the service and claim payment under the WRC 2007; a State might engage a contractor itself or order the shipowner to do so.

2.7.9(c) SCOPIC 2018

In order to provide a commercial solution to some of the problems experienced with Art 14, the ISU and International Group of P&I Clubs agreed the "Special Compensation P and

---

1136 Of course, there mere fact that the ship and contents are sunk (and on the seabed) does not mean that that they have no value. Thus, some cargo may not necessarily be ruined by sinking, eg gold, copper and aluminium bars, or valuable hardwoods. English law clearly contemplates that there can be salvage of such wrecked items: see 2.7.6.

1137 See 2.6.

1138 For termination, eg using Art 19, see 12.2.1.

1139 See 12.2.1.

1140 See 10.6.

I Club" (SCOPIC)[1141] clause.[1142] There have been various versions of SCOPIC, reflecting continuous negotiations between insurers, shipowners, and the ISU. The latest version is SCOPIC 2018. SCOPIC 2018 operates as a supplement to the LOF and in essence provides a replacement for Art 14 of the Salvage Convention 1989.[1143] Clause C (and Box 7) of LOF 2011 require an express incorporation of SCOPIC into the LOF. Nevertheless, the operative terms of SCOPIC do not apply unless invoked specifically by the salvor. It is generally in the salvor's interest to invoke SCOPIC in difficult casualties where traditional salvage success may be in doubt.[1144] In particular, the salvor does not have to show that there is a threat of damage to the environment, as with Art 14.[1145] Like Art 14, though, SCOPIC is payable only by the shipowner and is a part of its normal P&I cover, but not covered by normal H&M insurance;[1146] it is not payable by cargo interests nor covered by normal cargo insurance policies. In order to avoid SCOPIC remuneration being delayed, sub-clause 8 provides for payments to be made relatively quickly, eg within one month of presentation; this will be important for cash flow. In the more complicated scenario where there may be both an Art 13 salvage claim and a SCOPIC claim, a proportion of the assessed SCOPIC remuneration is also due within a month (presumably of presentation).

The key to SCOPIC is sub-clause 5, which provides for (i) the payment of set tariff rates for the salvor's personnel, tugs and equipment; (ii) the repayment of the salvor's "out of pocket" expenses; and (iii) a bonus normally of 25% on top of those rates and expenses.[1147] The tariff rates are revised regularly and currently set out in SCOPIC Appendix A (2017). The "out of pocket" expenses means "all those monies reasonably paid by or for and on behalf of the Contractor to any third party and in particular includes the hire of men, tugs, other craft and equipment used and other expenses reasonably necessary for the operation". They will generally be agreed at a cost basis with no separate mark-up by the salvor (as the bonus will be payable), but the Appendix A rates will be used for craft and equipment hired from other ISU members.[1148] If in order to offload cargo or bunkers the salvor has to charter in a ship from non-ISU members, the actual costs are in theory allowable, but where that cost is very high the salvor will have to show that the expense was reasonable.[1149]

As with special compensation under Art 14, questions can arise as to the scope of SCOPIC remuneration.[1150] One is whether to allow the costs of storing off-loaded cargo,

---

1141 See *Bishop*, 76; *Kennedy & Rose*, 181, 406–415; *Brice*, 612–630.

1142 "Clause" is somewhat of a misnomer, as SCOPIC 2018 contains 16 "sub-clauses", which are really separate provisions. There are also three appendices, two Codes of Conduct, a guarantee and other documents, guidance and lists; this all contrasts with the four paragraphs of Art 14.

1143 As allowed by Art 6 of the Convention: and see 12.2.2.

1144 Sub-clause 7 operates a slight disincentive, eg where the traditional Art 13 reward is greater than any SCOPIC remuneration the reward will be discounted.

1145 See 2.7.9(b).

1146 See sub-clause 6(i). This reflected the Montreal Compromise 1981 see (2.7.9(b)), but SCOPIC expenses (unlike salvage costs) cannot be taken into account in calculating repair costs for the purposes of CTL calculations: see *Sveriges Angfartygs Assurans Forening (The Swedish Club) v Connect Shipping (The Renos)* [2019] UKSC 29 [2019] 2 LLoyd's Rep 78 (SC, reversing CA)

1147 The bonus is in effect an additional profit element, reflecting the "increment" concept in Art 14(2).

1148 If the tugs or equipment are hired from non-ISU members, the salvor may have to demonstrate under sub-clause 5(iii)(b) the reasonableness of the expense to a Special Casualty Representative (SCR): for SCRs, see 12.3.2.

1149 Salvors may be under commercial pressure to pay very high rates for such charters, but attempts to argue duress may be very difficult: see the litigation arising out of the *Rena* casualty, 12.1.2(e).

1150 For termination, see 12.3.

eg where containers have to be stored in a port while their disposal is being considered. It seems that these costs are most likely allowable,[1151] but there may come a time when the shipowner and Club consider that it is no longer reasonable for the expenses to be incurred. This is an example of the somewhat unclear dividing line between salvage operations and wreck removal/disposal.[1152] It does not seem appropriate for a salvor to have a continuing unpaid responsibility to store and then dispose of distressed, valueless cargo once ashore—especially where a wreck removal order has been issued to the shipowner.

Salvors have complained that the Clubs and owners are accepting fewer SCOPIC agreements and that overall their income and capacity to respond is declining. In 2003 there were 89 new LOF cases, and in 27 (33%) of these SCOPIC was invoked.[1153] This appears to have been the highest by number and percentage. By contrast, in 2017, there were 63 new LOF cases in which 13 had SCOPIC invoked (21%). Although the percentage of SCOPIC cases since has averaged about 18% since 1999, it is true that the number of SCOPIC cases per year (averaging about 16%) has fallen since 2010.

The confidence of underwriters in how the Montreal Compromise was working through SCOPIC had been undermined by *The Renos*.[1154] The amended SCOPIC 2018 forms part of a continuing industry dialogue about the control of costs and risks, particularly in wreck removal operations, in which fixed price contracts are supplanting traditional salvage contracts.[1155] For the time being SCOPIC does seem to have a continuing function in relation to the transition between salvage and wreck removal.[1156]

2.8 Wreck and general average[1157]

In some circumstances involving a shipwreck a shipowner or cargo owner may be entitled to claim for general average (GA) sacrifices or expenditure incurred by them.[1158] In effect, GA is a mechanism by which some extraordinary losses and expenses from emergencies can be spread across the parties to the commercial maritime adventure. Like salvage,

---

1151 See SCR Digest No 5, 2–3. Where the containers of cargo are damaged and leaking, there may still be a need for the "prevention of pollution" within cl 14 of SCOPIC—even when they are ashore. The absence of punctuation in the clause makes it unclear whether "prevention" is also qualified by a need for the pollution to be in the "immediate vicinity" of the vessel, or whether that restriction applies only to the "*removal* of pollution". The restriction was presumably designed to exclude, from SCOPIC, operations to clean oil from coastlines a long way from the casualty. Such operations would more naturally fall within the CLC: see 2.6.2(a). It is less appropriate for the care of cargo that has been removed from the ship as part of a continuous salvage operation overall. A better reading to the clause might be to make "prevention of pollution" unqualified, or subject only to the requirement in the latter part of the clause that it be "necessary".

1152 See Chapter 12.

1153 Cf 2.7.7(a).

1154 [2018] 1 Lloyd's Rep 285 (CA) until its partial reversal [2019] 2 LLoyd's Rep 78 (SC). See 2.9.4(b).

1155 See 13.4.2, 13.6.2, 13.2.5.

1156 See Chapter 12.

1157 See R Cornah, R Sarll, J Shield, *Lowndes & Rudolf: The Law of General Average and the York-Antwerp Rules* (Sweet & Maxwell, 15th ed, 2018) [*Lowndes & Rudolf*]; F Rose, *General Average: Law and Practice* (3rd ed, Informa, 2017); G Hudson, M Harvey, *The York-Antwerp Rules: The Principles and Practice of General Average Adjustment* (4th ed, Informa, 2017) [*Hudson & Harvey*]; J Gilman, C Blanchard, M Templeman, P Hopkins, N Hart, *Arnould: Law of Marine Insurance and Average* (19th ed, Sweet & Maxwell, 2018) [*Arnould*], Chapter 26; *Voyage Charters*, Chapter 20.

1158 See s 66 of the MIA 1906.

general average only arises where valuable property has been saved and can contribute rateably to the loss or expenditure incurred by another party to the maritime adventure. In the light of the modern availability of insurance, it has long been questioned whether the concept of general average is needed, but it is still a reality in most legal systems (including the English) and its application in charterparties and bills of lading is usually through the contractual incorporation of the York Antwerp Rules (YAR). There have been regular revisions of the YAR,[1159] in particular the YAR 1994 which took account of the Salvage Convention 1989, and the YAR 2004.[1160] The latest version is the YAR 2016[1161] and these have achieved a wide measure of support and are now included in most of the latest BIMCO standard form carriage contracts.

2.8.1 GA claims

In the context of a ship which is stranded, GA sacrifices and expenditure would be relevant to acts by a shipowner to save the ship and cargo. Examples[1162] might include the letting slip of anchors and chains (eg to lose weight); the unusual straining of equipment such as pumps and engines in successful attempts to refloat the ship; the jettison of hatch covers so as to get to the seat of a fire; water damage to electrics caused by water pumped into the ship to put out a fire on a stranded ship; damage caused to a ship when it is voluntarily run aground in order to prevent foundering.[1163] The shipowner might also incur costs in refloating a ship (eg under a towage or salvage contract), or additional expenses in entering a port of refuge (eg harbour dues, agents' fees, costs of unlading hazardous cargo).

Cargo owners may be GA claimants, eg if their cargo is jettisoned to lighten a ship for refloating, or so that access may be gained to the seat of a fire lower in a hold; or if it is damaged by water in firefighting efforts when a hold is flooded to put out a fire; or damaged in the course of discharge to enable the ship to be refloated.[1164] There is an overriding "Rule Paramount" in the YAR 2016 that was first introduced in the YAR 1994. It provides that in "no case shall there be any allowance for sacrifice or expenditure unless reasonably made or incurred". This would require consideration both of the type of expenditure and the level of any fixed price contract, eg for lighterage of cargoes. Where a ship goes aground but is eventually taken to a place of safety for repairs, there may be costs of discharging, storing and reloading cargo so that it can be carried to the contractual destination. This may raise complicated issues about whether such expenses should be considered as general average

---

1159 The YAR are neither a convention nor a statute. and care must be taken to see which version of the Rules is incorporated by the particular bill of lading or charterparty.

1160 The YAR 2004 were not very popular with shipowners, who often preferred to incorporate earlier versions, such as the YAR 1994, into their charters and bills.

1161 With minor revisions in 2017: see documents available from the CMI website at https://comitemaritime.org/recent-work/general-average-2/, including a set of non-binding "*CMI Guidelines Relating to General Average*" on the YAR 2016 [*CMI GA Guidelines*]. See also the *CMI Yearbook* 2017–2018.

1162 *CMI GA Guidelines* B(3); *Hudson & Harvey* 4–5.

1163 See YAR 2016 r V and cf the *MSC Napoli*, 1.2.3(a).

1164 YAR 2016 r 12.

or should fall on those who paid for them;[1165] in some circumstances the costs of forwarding the cargo on a substitute vessel might be allowable.[1166]

The underlying assumption in a book about wreck is of a ship which itself is a total loss and is not taken for repairs, but only scrapping,[1167] with the assumption being that the scrap value is worth less than the costs of removal. However, even if the ship is a CTL at the wreck site, it might still be possible to save cargo from the wreck. Where the ship itself is completely wrecked at sea, the common adventure[1168] will usually end there, so that subsequent expenses (eg in transhipping cargo to a place of destination) would not be expected to give rise to GA; they will lie where they fall, subject to contractual principles concerning the completion of the voyage (or its frustration)[1169] or cargo insurance.[1170] It may be unclear whether the ship is a CTL until it is taken to a place of safety and delivered by salvors, and GA could continue until that point. The owners and Club might prefer to delay giving a notice of abandonment for a CTL[1171] while the ship is on that voyage,[1172] so as to be able to continue with a GA claim against cargo.[1173] Once the wrecked 'CTL ship' is safely alongside, the removal of the cargo ashore would not normally be a GA act, and the allocation of discharge costs may depend on the contract.[1174]

Rule D of the YAR 2016 provides that GA can arise irrespective of fault or breach of contract (eg by the shipowner), but makes clear that this does not affect remedies or defences that might otherwise be available, eg under the contract of carriage. Cargo owners (or their insurers) will be particularly alert to their rights to deny ultimate contributions where there is evidence of unseaworthiness or other actionable breach that caused the wreck.[1175]

2.8.2 GA security

As GA is potentially an unforeseen additional cost in the commercial voyage, it is usual for it (like salvage) to be covered in H&M and (particularly) cargo insurance policies.[1176]

1165 Se eg *Arnould*, 1402–1404. See also YAR 2016 r VIII.

1166 The issue of substituted expenses under the YAR is complicated and affected by the Supreme Court decision in *Mitsui & Co Ltd v Beteiligungsgesellschaft LPG Tankerflotte MBH & Co KG (The Longchamp)* [2017] UKSC 68, [2018] 1 Lloyd's Rep 1; see *Lowndes & Rudolf*, 180–195. Under Rule G forwarding costs may be allowable, but usually where the ship is in a place of safety undergoing repairs, rather than when it has been completely wrecked (as the common adventure will usually end then): see *Lowndes & Rudolf*, 211–218, 298–299, 326–328; *Arnould*, 1392–1395.

1167 See eg 14.3, 14.5.

1168 See YAR 2016 Rule A.

1169 See 2.1.4.

1170 See 2.9.3(e) and ICC 2009 cll 9 and 12 for the extent to which forwarding charges may be recovered under the cargo policy.

1171 See 2.9.4(b) and (c).

1172 Perhaps keeping the salvor on SCOPIC for the voyage to convey the cargo to safety, later converting that to a daily rate wreck removal contract, eg Wreckhire 2010: see 13.6.3.

1173 See YAR 1016 Rule VIII. The ship's proportion of values would probably be very low, given its scrap value.

1174 See 2.1.4(a) and (b).

1175 See 2.1.5(a)-(b). Note, though, that if fault or neglect by the shipowner, is excepted under the contract of carriage it will not bar a GA claim; eg negligent navigation causing a ship to be wrecked will be a defence for a carrier under Art IV r 2(a) of the Hague/Visby Rules and many charterparties: see 2.1.5(b), 2.1.7(b) and (c). This position is reiterated in the New Jason Clause found in many charterparties and bills in order to overcome difficulties in US law: see *Voyage Charters*, 603–604, 613, 963.

1176 See 2.9.2(a), 2.9.3(c).

Cargo owners would therefore look to their insurers to provide GA security to have any cargo released once it has been delivered. The cargo receiver may need to supply a GA bond, backed by a guarantee signed by the cargo insurer, as well as a commercial invoice with evidence of a CIF value.

Where a ship in liner service has stranded it may be more convenient for the shipowner (and its container clients) for it to engage and pay salvors for the entire salvage service, including any contribution that might technically be due from cargo owners.[1177] The shipowner would then claim back from individual cargo owners their proportions of the expenditure, having taken care to obtain GA security from them before any salved cargo is released to them.[1178] This expenditure is generally allowable under a reworded r VI of the YAR 2016, even if the salvage reward theoretically includes a component to represent an enhanced award to reflect prevention of damage to the environment.[1179] However, special compensation under Art 14 of the Salvage Convention 1989 is not allowable in GA, nor is "any other provision similar in substance (such as SCOPIC)".[1180] Note that a new YAR 2016 Rule VI(b) now imposes five listed restrictions on claiming salvage expenditure where shipowners, bunker owners and cargo owners may have separate contractual or legal liabilities to salvors (including for example under the LOF). It seeks to deal with particular problems such as the cost of reapportionment, eg where there are differences between the salved values (for salvage claims) and contributory values (for GA claims); the former are assessed at a place of safety while the latter are assessed at the termination of the adventure—and these may differ. The new restrictions are aimed to prevent the need for a costly reapportionment exercise unless it is apparent to adjusters that there would otherwise be significant differences.[1181] "Salvors in some jurisdictions will only accept cash by way of security. Their initial demands are typically very high, and are routinely negotiated down to more reasonable levels. Expenses incurred during these negotiations will now be allowable under Rule F".[1182]

In order to avoid the cost of collecting security from possibly thousands of cargo claimants, the H&M insurer may agree to 'absorb' cargo's proportion of GA by the use of absorption clauses (perhaps up to a specified financial amount) or special insurances (with additional premiums) to provide higher levels of cover.[1183] These examples are, of course, mainly related to circumstances where the ship is ultimately saved and not wrecked, but

---

1177 See 2.7.7(b).

1178 Instead of actually paying the salvor for cargo's proportion of salvage, the shipowner may simply provide interim security to the salvor for cargo once it has been taken to a place of safety. At the contractual destination the cargo interests may then need to give both GA and salvage guarantees: see *CMI GA Guidelines*, C(2).

1179 See YAR 2016 Rule VI(c) and 2.7.9(a). See also *Arnould*, 1400–1404; and cf 2.9.2(a) for hull insurance.

1180 See YAR 2016 Rule VI(d) and 2.7.9(b). SCOPIC cl 15 itself reinforces this position, as the shipowner promises not to bring claims in GA (eg against cargo) or under its own H&M policy; cargo owners are party to the LOF with SCOPIC, as a result of cl K of the LOF 2011. The H&M insurers are not parties, but presumably could rely on the Contracts (Rights of Third Party) Act 1999, or estoppel.

1181 See further *CMI GA Guidelines* F(1) and *Lowndes & Rudolf*, 265–288 (especially 284–288).

1182 See R Tomlinson, "UK Supreme Court Surprises Adjusters in the Longchamp Decision", Insight (20 February 2018), www.gard.no/web/updates/content/25015258/uk-supreme-court-surprises-adjusters-in-the-longchamp-decision. The Rule F allowance is a result of *The Longchamp* [2017] [2018] 1 Lloyd's Rep 1 (a piracy rather than a shipwreck case).

1183 See *Lowndes & Rudolf*, 15–16, 619–622.

will be considerations affecting the parties at the time of a casualty when its outcome is not known.

While LOF salvage claims need to be paid to the salvor relatively quickly after an award in order to avoid penalty interest charges, the settlement of GA is often a more long-drawn-out process, especially where unseaworthiness is alleged. Where there is a long delay, the shipowner's P&I Club may step in to assist with unrecovered GA.

2.8.3 Cutting away wreck

For the sake of completeness mention should be made of YAR Rule IV, dealing with "Cutting Away Wreck".[1184] This ancient provision states that "loss or damage sustained by cutting away wreck or parts of the ship which have been previously carried away or are effectively lost by accident shall not be allowed" as GA. The typical example was when parts of the ship such as masts and rigging had been lost overboard in heavy weather, but the master then had to decide whether to cut them away (or abandon them) in order to prevent danger to the ship. A decision to do so would not be treated as a GA sacrifice as it was already "wreck" in the general sense as used in the title to the Rule.

The principle applies, though, not only to "parts of the ship" but also "wreck" – which is not otherwise defined. In theory it could include cargo already accidentally washed overboard, such as containers or other deck cargo.[1185] The limited case law[1186] indicates that for the Rule to apply (and deny GA), the item must be virtually or inevitably lost; eg that a floating container was gradually sinking, so that any attempt to cut any connection with the ship[1187] merely hastened the inevitable. The Rule would not apply to cases where cargo was jettisoned after a grounding so as to assist in refloating; here GA would be allowed. Of course, if the ship sank anyway, there would not be any values to contribute to GA. Where cargo is washed ashore from a wreck, the cost of removing it would not seem to constitute a GA expense, nor would the costs of disposal.[1188]

2.9 Wreck and marine insurance

2.9.1 Role of marine insurance with shipwreck

Marine insurance was always designed to protect ship and cargo owners from the loss of their own property by shipwreck. Today, such cover is central to hull and machinery (H&M) and cargo policies.[1189] By contrast, in the 19th century Lloyd's underwriters were typically reluctant to offer cover for shipowners against *liabilities* they may have

---

1184 See *Lowndes & Rudolf*, 247–253.
1185 Note that YAR 2016 Rule I does not allow for jettison of cargo as GA unless carried in accordance with the custom of the trade. This might exclude some types of deck cargo: see *Voyage Charters*, 172.
1186 See *Johnson v Chapman* (1865) 19 CB (NS) 563; *Lowndes & Rudolf*, 248.
1187 Or, seemingly, a decision not to attempt recovery using the ship's derricks. The scenario seems unlikely, but not impossible. Moreover, containers lost overboard can pose serious threats to a ship: see eg the *Pacific Adventurer* casualty off Australia in 2009, when such containers holed the ship, causing bunker pollution: see 2.6.3.
1188 Cf *Lowndes & Rudolf*, 298–304, 343–344.
1189 See 2.9.2, 2.9.3. Other risks are also commonly insured, such as the loss of freight.

to third parties, despite the increasing need of shipowners for such cover. The limited protection offered by the optional running down clause (RDC), added to most policies,[1190] did not extend to wreck raising.[1191] It is well known that the difficulties faced by shipowners in obtaining cover for liabilities generally led to the formation of the mutual protection and indemnity clubs (P&I Clubs) that are today central to the coverage of liabilities worldwide.[1192]

The law of marine insurance governs the contractual relations between the assured (eg shipowner or cargo owner) and the insurer and has been underpinned by the Marine Insurance Act (MIA) 1906. The MIA 1906 has been heavily reformed by the Insurance Act 2015[1193] so as to remove some of the defences upon which insurers have often relied[1194] while imposing on insureds a new duty of "fair presentation".[1195]

The details of the law on marine insurance (including the significant 2015 reforms), and the infinite variety of policy terms, are beyond this book.[1196] Nevertheless, it is important to understand the role of insurers in relation to wreck, because they will have a significant influence on the settlement of claims arising out of casualties.[1197] First, the ship and cargo insurers will compensate owners of ship and cargo for the value of lost property, and they will usually cover salvage and general average costs in respect of valuable property which is recovered.[1198] Later, these insurers may want to assert rights in relation to sunken remains (even if found centuries later).[1199] Secondly, the Clubs (or other liability insurers) may have to pay for shipowners' liabilities to third parties,[1200] eg for cargo loss, ships damaged by collision or crew claims. In addition, they will usually be the ones paying for environmental

---

1190 See eg W Gow, *Marine Insurance* (3rd ed, Macmillan, 1903) [*Gow*], 255–259. The clause still exists today, eg the Institute Time Clauses-Hulls (1983) cl 8: see 2.9.2(b).

1191 In 1886, three company insurers were prepared to offer a fuller protection, but even this had its own internal contractual limit of liability for all claim on any one occasion of £30 per gross ton (see *Gow*, 255, 330). For modern exclusions, see 2.9.2(b).

1192 See further 2.9.6.

1193 The 2015 Act entered into force on 12 August 2016 and was amended by the Enterprise Act 2016 in relation to late payment of claims. The 2015 Act also separated insurance contracts into "consumer insurance" contracts (and see the Consumer Insurance (Disclosure and Representations) Act 2012) and "non-consumer insurance" contracts. The latter are the type of commercial contracts with which this book is mainly concerned. See *Arnould*, 1–3, Chaps 18A and 18B.

1194 Eg non-disclosure, misrepresentation or breach of policy "warranties" where insurers have in the past often declined to pay claims because of breaches (often minor or technical) unrelated to the actual loss: see now the Insurance Act 2015 s 11. There is some evidence that London market underwriters tended to rely on such technical defences when they suspected, but could not prove, fraud (eg scuttling): see now ss 12–13 on fraudulent claims.

1195 However, under ss 15–18 of the Insurance Act 2015 parties are allowed to contract out of some of the new obligations in non-consumer contracts. It is not clear how often this is now done in the London underwriting market, but it is typically done by the P&I Clubs in their rules: see eg 2.9.6(b).

1196 See eg *Arnould*; F Rose, *Marine Insurance: Law and Practice* (2nd ed, Informa, 2012) [*Rose, Marine Insurance*]; H Bennett, *Law of Marine Insurance* (2nd ed, OUP, 2006); J Dunt, *Marine Cargo Insurance* (2nd ed, Informa, 2016) [*Dunt*]; J Dunt, *International Cargo Insurance* (2012, Informa).

1197 See also 2.9.5.

1198 See 2.7, 2.8.

1199 See 3.2, 3.4.

1200 See 2.9.6(b) and (e).

liabilities, eg for oil pollution damage.[1201] In the particular context of this book, though, the Clubs will also be involved in paying for wreck removal.[1202]

There is a wide variety of insurance coverage worldwide,[1203] but reference here will be made (in outline) to that available from the London market.[1204] Since 2007, the placing of insurance will be according to the standards in the Market Reform Contract (MRC).[1205] Standard Hull or Cargo Clauses for incorporation into marine polices have been regularly produced by the Institute of London Underwriters (ILU) and by its successor the International Underwriting Association of London (IUA);[1206] they are still generally called "Institute Clauses"[1207] and are subject to English law and practice.[1208] The main parties requiring insurance will obviously be the shipowner and cargo owners in respect of the loss of their property, although others (such as charterers and banks)[1209] may also take out cover.

2.9.2 H&M cover: casualties and wreck

2.9.2(a) Risks covered

The shipowner will want insurance cover for the value[1210] of its ship, including both the "hull" and its "machinery". That machinery will, for example, include the engine, pumps and equipment such as derricks and anchors.[1211] The cover will include partial loss after a casualty in the general sense, eg where a ship is damaged in a collision and then salved and repaired. In the context of shipwreck, though, we are mainly concerned with the ship becoming a total loss.[1212]

In all policies it will be expected that the owner will bear a deductible, ie it will pay the first part of a claim itself. The amount will vary, but the bigger the deductible (ie risk borne by the shipowner) the cheaper the policy. This is important in settling any case arising, eg a wreck following a collision, because the insured owner will not simply be expecting to

---

1201 See 2.9.6(b).
1202 See 2.9.6(d) and 10.8.
1203 See eg that offered under the Nordic Marine Insurance Plan of 2013, Version 2019: www.nordicplan.org/The-Plan/. The website also contains a detailed commentary on the clauses.
1204 Including both Lloyd's and the company market. For information about the market, eg modern electronic processing of premiums, policies and claims, see the London Market Group, www.londonmarketgroup.co.uk.
1205 MRC v 1.9, September 2018: www.londonmarketgroup.co.uk/mrc.
1206 The ILU was the trade association for marine insurance companies from 1884, but became the International Underwriting Association of London (IUA) from 1999, following a merger so as to represent non-marine companies.
1207 See the IUA website (www.iuaclauses.co.uk/) for the hundreds of individual clauses that are available for particular circumstances. The clauses are designed for use with the modern policy forms, eg the Lloyd's Marine Policy (Mar 91), or the IUA Marine Policy, rather than the antiquated Lloyd's SG form. For the background to the replacement of the latter, see *Arnould*, 32–47.
1208 Strictly, the IUA 2003 Hull Clauses are prefaced by the word "International", although perversely the IUA 2009 Cargo Clauses are still prefaced by "Institute": see 2.9.2(a) and (b): see *Rose, Marine Insurance*, 4.
1209 See 2.1.7(a), 2.9.6(b), 2.9.2(d).
1210 As agreed in the insurance policy: MIA ss 27(1), 68(1). If the policy is unvalued then the measure of indemnity is the "insurable value of the subject matter insured": MIA s 18(2). If the owner under insures then it is deemed to be its own insurer for the excess: MIA s 81.
1211 It would also cover bunkers, certainly when owned by the shipowner assured, or at its risk (eg as bailee, as in time and voyage charters).
1212 See 2.9.4.

pocket the insurance proceeds but will have a real interest in finding out if there is someone who can be sued for liability.[1213]

The type of risks that the policy will cover will depend on the level of cover specified and paid for by the shipowner. There are three sets of modern hull clauses[1214] available—the Institute Hull Clauses of 1983 and 1995 and the International Hull Clauses 2003. It appears that the 1983 version is still most widely used;[1215] in any event there may be many variations agreed to the standard clauses.[1216] The Institute Time Clauses-Hulls (ITC-Hulls) 1983 list in cl 6 a series of marine perils that are covered if they cause loss or damage to the ship. In the context of shipwreck these would include most fortuitous risks likely to cause a "maritime casualty"[1217] leading to grounding, stranding or sinking: eg "perils of the sea";[1218] "fire" and "explosion";[1219] "earthquake volcanic eruption[1220] or lightning". Also covered[1221] are "latent defect" in the ship's machinery or hull; "negligence of master, officers, crew or pilots";[1222] and "negligence of repairers[1223] or charterers".[1224]

2.9.2(b) Wreck removal and liabilities
Most H&M policies will exclude liability for wreck removal. Thus, the ITC-Hulls 1983 cl 8.4.1 makes it clear that liability under the RDC shall not extend to "removal or disposal of obstructions, wrecks, cargoes or any other thing whatsoever".[1225] Although such cover may be provided by some underwriters, it is more usual for this loss to be covered by a P&I Club—along with other liabilities (above) excluded from hull cover.[1226] The

---

1213 See 2.4.1.
1214 For the replacement of the Lloyd's SG policy and development of the modern Clauses and practice, see *Arnould*, 41–43, 1118–1210.
1215 *Arnould*, 41. The 1995 and 2003 forms are very relevant for comparison purposes as they often deal expressly with practical and legal problems that might affect the ITC-Hulls 1983, and may even serve as a source for amendments to the 1983 form, eg as to whether leased equipment can be covered (see cl 3 of the ITC-Hulls 2003). It is not possible here to consider every alternative clause that might be available.
1216 Note that under the MIA 1906 s 25(1) the duration of cover may be specified by the voyage or by a period of time. Thus, in addition to the Institute Time Clauses-Hulls (1983) there are the Institute Voyage Clauses-Hulls (1983), of which the former are most commonly used: see *Arnould*, 433–435 for the key differences. There are also Institute Freight Clauses (Time and Voyage) which cover the risk of the shipowner losing its freight, ie the income earned from carriage; it seems that loss of hire or earnings insurance is now more common: see *Arnould*, 389–392.
1217 Note the use of this expression in Art 1(3) of the WRC: see 8.2.1(a) and Chapter 10 (eg 10.4).
1218 Eg bad weather, or other fortuitous action wind and waves.
1219 Eg where leaking engine oil is ignited, or where cargo overheats.
1220 Perhaps causing a tsunami.
1221 But subject to the loss or damage not resulting from want of due diligence by the assured, the shipowner or ship managers—ie those controlling corporate affairs, not the ship's personnel.
1222 Eg in navigation of the ship, or in leaving valves open. Employee negligence is one of the main risks for which a shipowner needs cover, but the insurer will not pay out where there is wilful misconduct of the senior management of the shipowning company: see the MIA s 55(2), and 10.8.4(d).
1223 Eg who cause breakdowns to engines, without the fault of the crew, leading to a stranding.
1224 Eg where they nominate an unsafe port and the ship sinks while entering or leaving. The assured and insurer (by subrogation) might then bring a contractual indemnity claim against the charterer: cf *The Ocean Victory* [2017] 1 Lloyd's Rep 521, where the owner failed in any event to prove that the port was unsafe: see 2.1.7(b) and (c).
1225 There is a similar provision in cl 13.1(i) of the Nordic Marine Insurance Plan of 2013.
1226 See 2.9.6(c).

shipowner's proportion of salvage and general average[1227] is expressly covered in the ITC-Hulls 1983 cl 11.[1228]

While the H&M policy will cover the shipowner after a shipwreck for the loss of the ship itself (eg for its value),[1229] there is only very limited cover for liabilities to third parties. The 3/4th collision liability clause, cl 8, provides for the underwriter to pay for a proportion only of any collision damage[1230] or loss to another ship or its cargo.[1231] Death and personal injury claims are specifically excluded by cl 8.4.4. Pollution or contamination is also a specific exclusion.[1232] Where there is a casualty that threatens the environment, States may intervene and, in extreme circumstances, may even order that the ship in question be destroyed.[1233] This loss is expressly covered by the ITC-Hulls 1983 cl 7, provided that the owners themselves had not caused the government action by their own want of due diligence to prevent or mitigate the pollution hazard.[1234]

2.9.2(c) Proximate cause and defences

Under s 55 of the MIA 1906 the insurer is only liable for loss proximately caused by the insured peril. In particular, this means that the insurer is not liable for the "wilful misconduct" of the assured,[1235] delay[1236] or ordinary wear and tear.[1237] The latter two examples are specifically subject to the policy providing otherwise. The proximate cause doctrine means that there often difficult questions of causation, eg when there is ingress of water after a crack develops in the ship,[1238] is the dominant cause an undiscoverable "latent defect" (covered) or "wear and tear" (not covered)?[1239] Where there are concurrent (or combinations of)

1227 See 2.7, 2.8.

1228 The 1983 form does not reflect (or allow for) the possible enhancement of a salvage reward under Art 13(b) of the Salvage Convention 1989 for preventing or minimising damage to the environment: see 2.7.9(a). It is highly unlikely that a salvage arbitrator would separately identify an amount for an enhancement, so the point may be difficult for insurers to raise. Modern practice is more clearly represented by the 1995 Hull Clauses, cl 10.6, and the 2003 Hull Clauses, cl 8.6. The enhanced reward would be covered if there was a general average claim for salvage remuneration: see 2.8.1.

1229 Under the ITC-Hulls 1983 cl 14 there is no deduction of new for old.

1230 Unless the assured agrees to 4/4 cover for an extra premium: see eg ITC-Hulls 2003 cl 38, and *Arnould*, 1148–1157. There is 4/4 cover under cl 13 of the Nordic Marine Insurance Plan of 2013.

1231 As between shipowner and H&M insurer claims may be settled not on the basis of a single liability but on cross liabilities: see ITC-Hulls cl 8.2.1; *Arnould*, 1148–1157; *Marsden & Gault*, 292–395, 642. Cf the approach in cl 4–14 of the Nordic Marine Insurance Plan of 2013 (and see the commentary at www.nordicplan.org/Commentary).

1232 ITC-Hulls 1983 cl 8.5. See also cl 13.1(f)–(g) of the Nordic Marine Insurance Plan of 2013.

1233 See further 4.8.3 and 5.3; note the modern restrictions on dumping, see 14.1.

1234 Cf the position for cargo, 2.9.2(d).

1235 See the MIA 1906 s 55(2)(a) and 10.8.4(d). This covers eg deliberate action to scuttle the ship taken by the senior management of the assured, rather than deliberate actions by the master and crew alone (barratry): see eg *National Justice Companiera Naviera SA v Prudential Assurance Co Ltd (The Ikarian Reefer)* [1995] 1 Lloyd's Rep 455; *Arnould*, 1107–1115; also 2.1.5(a) (fn113), 10.8.4(d).

1236 The MIA 1906 s 55(2)(b), eg delay causing economic loss beyond the value of the ship, such as loss of future contracts.

1237 The MIA 1906 s 55(2)(c), eg rusty hull plating that collapses in ordinary weather, without any particular fortuity being involved: and see *Arnould*, 1081–1083.

1238 Cf the *MSC Napoli*: see 1.2.3.

1239 Or is the cause a breach of the separate implied obligation of the assured under the MIA 1906 s 39 in a voyage policy that the ship is seaworthy at the start of the voyage: see *Arnould*, Chapter 20. In a time policy, the

causes, the question of which is the most proximate has been subject to much litigation,[1240] but all that is necessary to note here is that at the scene of the casualty it will be important to obtain evidence about what actually happened, and that there may be some uncertainty about whether the claim can be proved.[1241]

The H&M insurer might also seek to rely on other potential defences under the policy,[1242] or exclusions from cover. The latter would include loss or damage caused by war, strikes or malicious acts (eg terrorism).[1243] Modern instances of shipwrecks caused by war or terrorism are relatively rare, but their possibility means that a war risks insurer may be involved, rather than the H&M insurer.

2.9.2(d) Mortgagee cover and wreck

In practice, most shipowners will have arranged the purchase of their ship through the use of bank finance. The bank will look to secure for its loan in a variety of ways[1244] but will almost certainly have taken out a mortgage on the vessel.[1245] When the ship is wrecked, that mortgage will be practically worthless, so the bank will want to ensure that it has access to the proceeds of an H&M or loss of hire policy.[1246] It may have sought to do this in a variety or combination of ways, eg by taking out a separate mortgagee's interest policy;[1247] being a co-assured under the H&M policy; or being an assignee and named loss payee. It may be very concerned about the conduct of the assured in relation to the policy, eg where there is an allegation of wilful misconduct or a breach of the policy allowing the insurer to cancel cover or decline payment.[1248] In principle, though, the misconduct of the shipowner may not allow the insurer to prevent the innocent mortgagee from recovering on the policy (to

---

MIA 1906 s 39(5) provides that although there is no implied warranty of seaworthiness, the insurer is not liable for any loss attributable to unseaworthiness if the ship is sent to sea "with the privity of the assured". This is a similar test to that required to 'break' limitation, in that it requires knowledge or recklessness (including 'blind eye knowledge') of those in the senior management of the assured: see *Compagnia Maritima San Basilio SA v Oceanus Mutual Underwriting Association (Bermuda) Limited (The Eurysthenes)* [1977] 1 QB 49, [1976] 2 Lloyd's Rep 171; *Manifest Shipping Co Ltd v Uni-Polaris Insurance Co Ltd and La Réunion Européene Co Ltd (The Star Sea)* [2001] UKHL 1, [2003] 1 AC 465, [2001] 1 Lloyd's Rep 389 [27, 112]; cf 2.5.7.

1240 See *Arnould*, Chapter 22; eg *The Cendor Mopu* [2011] 1 Lloyd's Rep 560; *The DC Merwestone* [2013] 2 Lloyd's Rep 131 (reversed on other grounds, [2016] 2 Lloyd's Rep 198).

1241 See also 2.9.5.

1242 Eg breaches of express warranties (promises) by the assured (unless 'held covered' under cl 3), but note that the insurer's remedies may now be limited by the 2015 Act.

1243 Eg ITC-Hulls 1983 cl 23–25. Separate war and strike cover is available, eg under the Institute War and Strikes Clauses. See M Miller, *Marine War Risks* (3rd ed, Informa, 2005).

1244 Including personal and cross-corporate guarantees, particularly with single ship companies managed as a group.

1245 See G Bowtle, D Osbourne, C Buss, *Law of Ship Mortgages* (2nd ed, Informa, 2016) [*Law of Ship Mortgages*].

1246 The mortgagee has an insurable interest under the MIA 1906 s 14(1). See *Law of Ship Mortgages*, Chapter 16. The mortgagee will also insist that the owner takes out P&I liability cover: see 2.9.6(a).

1247 Eg under the Institute Mortgagees' Interest Clauses-Hulls 1997 and *Law of Ship Mortgages*, 466–472. See also Gard, "The Shipping Financier's Need for Mortgagees' Interest Insurance", (2004) Insight 175.

1248 See eg the *Brillante Virtuoso* casualty litigation: *Suez Fortune Investments Ltd v Talbot Underwriting Ltd (The M/V Brillante Virtuoso)* [2015] 1 Lloyd's Rep 651; *Suez Fortune Investments Ltd and Piraeus Bank AE v Talbot Underwriting Ltd* [2016] EWHC 1085 (Comm), *Suez Fortune Investments Ltd and Piraeus Bank AE v Talbot Underwriting Ltd and Anor* [2018] EWHC 2929 (Comm).

the extent of its loan).[1249] Bank mortgagees may insist that the shipowner obtains from its insurer a letter of undertaking that the insurer will notify the bank if cover has ceased, and this may create contractual liabilities between insurer and bank.[1250]

2.9.3 Cargo cover: casualties and wreck

2.9.3(a) Importance of cover

Cargo insurance is particularly vital to the cargo owner,[1251] as the contract of carriage will usually allow the carrier to exclude or limit its liability in a wide variety of circumstances, especially those permitted by the Hague and Hague-Visby Rules.[1252] Of these, the most significant are the defence of nautical fault and the financial limits of liability. Thus, even where the ship is wrecked owing to the negligent navigation of the master, the contracting carrier will not be liable for the loss of cargo; and even if the carrier cannot avoid liability for unseaworthiness causing the sinking or stranding, it will be able to limit its liability.[1253] In practice, the cargo owner will turn immediately to its insurer for recovery[1254] and may leave it to the insurer to try to bring a subrogated claim against the carrier.[1255]

Cargo insurance is naturally arranged in relation to particular voyages, although regular shippers will often have floating or open cover enabling them to nominate ('declare') cargoes for particular voyages rather than having to negotiate separate policies each time.[1256] So, after a wreck it will be important to check that appropriate declarations have been made.

2.9.3(b) Levels of cover

The latest Institute Cargo Clauses (ICC) 2009[1257] provide three alternative levels of cover, (A), (B) and (C), with different risks set out in cl 1 of each.[1258]

1249 See *P Samuel & Co Ltd v Dumas* [1924] AC 431 (scuttling by owners, without knowledge of mortgagee); *New Hampshire Insurance Company v MGN Ltd* [1996] EWHC 398 (Comm), [1997] LRLR 24; *Arnould*, 1109; also 10.8.4(d).

1250 See eg *Bank of Nova Scotia v Hellenic Mutual War Risks Association Bermuda Ltd (The Good Luck)* [1992] 1 AC 233, [1991] 2 Lloyd's Rep 191 (a war risks rather than an H&M case). See the description (by Hobhouse J at first instance) of typical financing and insurance arrangements in *The Good Luck* [1988] 1 Lloyd's Rep 514, 521; also *The Law of Ship Mortgages*, Chapter 16.

1251 See also 2.1.3.

1252 See 2.1.2, 2.1.5.

1253 See 2.1.5(e) and 2.5.4(a).

1254 As with H&M cover (2.9.2(a)), there will usually be a policy deductible for the insured, so to that extent it will always have some interest in recoveries against the carrier. Of course, some cargo owners, especially large traders, may decide to self-insure or maintain a very high deductible. The peculiar maritime risks presented by GA and salvage claims mean that even such large traders may choose to have full cover for these risks.

1255 In the event of a collision, the insurer might then seek to recover in tort against the other ship, eg if it had also been negligent. If, contrary to the Collision Convention 1910 (but, say, under US law), the insurer was able to recover 100% of the loss, the other ship might then seek an indemnity in a collision action against the carrying ship: see 2.4.4. If, in turn, the carrier then sued the cargo owner under a "Both to Blame Collision Clause" in the *carriage* contract, the assured would be protected by cl 3 of all three of the ICC 2009: see also *Dunt*, 14.39–14.42.

1256 See *Dunt*, Chapter 3; *Arnould*, Chapter 9.

1257 See *Dunt*, generally, for authoritative treatment of the 2009 clauses, their development and for analysis of the previous 1982 clauses; also, *Arnould*, 43–46 (on the somewhat confusing levels of cover previously available) and 1211–1230 (for modern practice under the 2009 Clauses).

1258 As with H&M cover, there are many specific clauses designed as policy additions to cover particular trades or commodities, eg oil or frozen food: see *Dunt*, paras 9.52–9.81; also N Hudson, T Madge, K Sturges, *Marine Insurance Clauses* (5th ed, Informa, 2012).

The ICC 2009 (A) effectively provide for a type of 'all risks'[1259] cover for loss of or damage to the cargo insured,[1260] but with the exception of specific claims excluded by cll 4–7.[1261] Cargo lost or damaged in a shipwreck would be covered in almost all instances, even if it is not known exactly how or why a ship sank, as this would be a classic example of a fortuity (rather than eg inherent vice[1262]). Cover would also extend to any theft of the cargo while ashore or to any malicious damage to it.[1263]

The ICC 2009 (B) and (C), by contrast, cover loss or damage to the cargo "reasonably attributed" to a list of specific risks only – with (B) being more extensive than (C).[1264] The ICC 2009 (B) cl 1 covers (in particular) "fire or explosion";[1265] "vessel or craft being stranded grounded sunk or capsized";[1266] "overturning or derailment of land conveyance";[1267] "collision or contact of vessel . . . with any external object";[1268] "discharge of

---

1259 See *Dunt*, Chapter 8.

1260 Shipping containers themselves are rarely owned by the cargo owner, but rather by the shipping line or a leasing company; separate cover can be obtained under the Institute Container Clauses 1987: see *Arnould*, 332. The mutual TT Club insures about 80% of maritime containers both for loss and in relation to liabilities (see www. ttclub.com/about-us/). Deck carriage of containers in purpose built containers ships should certainly be within the risk contemplated by the insurer but, otherwise, insurers may need to be informed of the deck carriage for the risk to attach, or alternatively to use a specific on-deck clause: see *Dunt*, paras 3.40–3.43, 11.75; *Arnould*, 329–331; *Rose, Marine Insurance*, 24–25.

1261 See below.

1262 Once the assured proves a fortuity in the all risks policy, the burden would be on the insurer to prove inherent vice: see *The Cendor Mopu* [2011] 1 Lloyd's Rep 160; *Dunt*, para 8.9.

1263 This would include any plundering by local inhabitants when cargo is washed ashore: see eg the *MSC Napoli* 1.2.3(a), 3.5.3, 4.5, 4.8.5. Cf the cover under (B) and (C), below.

1264 *Dunt* notes that even though (C) complies with Incoterms 2010 para A3(b) for CIF contracts, all risks cover is more usual: see para 9.3. As will be seen, there are instances where (B) and (C) cover is not entirely satisfactory to cover all wreck losses.

1265 Clause 1.1.1. Eg when the ship catches fire and an oil cargo is consumed before the ship sinks. Note that arson is not covered as a result of the exclusion in cl 4.7, although intervention action may be: see below and *Dunt*, paras 9.12–9.16. An "explosion" could cover the type of cargo loss caused when the *Mont Blanc* blew up in Halifax, Nova Scotia, in 1917: see also 2.6.4 (fn 961)2.1.5(a), 2.6.4. An explosion caused by terrorism is specifically excluded by cl 7.3: see below.

1266 Clause 1.1.2, and *Dunt*, paras 9.17–9.21. The combination of expressions would obviously cover most shipwrecks. This means that it may not be necessary to examine the extensive case law on the meaning of "stranding" under old forms of policy. "Stranding" has generally been confined to fortuitous taking of the ground, by action of wind and waves, rather than planned grounding in the ordinary course of navigation (eg on a mud mooring, where no hidden obstacles are expected): see, generally, *Arnould*, 1142–1143 and cf 8.2.1(b). Where a ship has been deliberately grounded in shallow water as a result of salvage efforts, or in obedience to a government order designed to stop a sinking in deep water (as with the *MSC Napoli*, 1.2.3), it is submitted that there is sufficient fortuity for the cover to apply. *Arnould* suggests (at 1219, fn 538) that "sunk" does not include a partially submerged ship, but this would normally be "stranded" or "grounded" and it would not seem appropriate or intended that there should be a gap between the concepts.

1267 Clause 1.1.3 and *Dunt*, para 9.22. This might be relevant if the cargo has to be moved at a place of safety after being discharged from a wreck.

1268 Clause 1.1.4 and *Dunt*, paras 9.22–9.24. This would include cargo loss or damage after a ship is damaged following a collision with another ship, or a bridge or jetty. A sinking would be covered by cl 1.2.2, but the vessel might become be wrecked in the sense of becoming a CTL without sinking.

cargo at a port of distress";[1269] and "earthquake, volcanic eruption or lightening".[1270] In addition, it covers loss or damage caused[1271] by "general average sacrifice",[1272] "jettison or washing overboard"[1273] and "entry of sea lake or river water into vessel craft hold conveyance container or place of storage".[1274] Finally, it covers "total loss of any package lost overboard or dropped while loading on to, or unloading from, vessel or craft".[1275] The latter is the only restriction requiring total loss claims rather than for partial loss or damage ("average").

The ICC 2009 (C) cl 1 has a similar list of risks to (B), but does not cover "earthquake, volcanic eruption or lightening", "entry of sea lake or river water [etc]", "washing overboard", or "total loss of any package lost overboard [etc]". In the context of wrecks, it is perhaps only the last two or three omissions that may be of significance. Neither (B) nor (C) cover theft of cargo, eg by the shipowner[1276] or where looters seek to take cargo

---

1269 Clause 1.1.5 and *Dunt*, para 9.25. There is no specific mention of a "place" of distress, ie where cargo is discharged onto a remote shore where a ship has stranded. This, however, might be already covered as "reasonably attributable" to stranding (and in some circumstances might be general average, see 2.8). There is no express requirement that the cargo has to be off-loaded from the original carrying ship. So, provided that the cover has not otherwise ended, this provision could cover, eg, damage to containers occurring during unloading from a salvor's barge, where proper discharge equipment may not be available in a small local port. For theft from a port of distress, see fn 131.

1270 Clause 1.1.6. This risk is more apt to apply to loss on land, but might cover a tsunami, although any subsequent loss is likely to fall within one of the other risks, eg stranding.

1271 As with H&M policies, the principles of proximate cause will be relevant, eg whether losses were caused by the entry of seawater or defective packing of the cargo (see the exclusion in cl 4, below). Where a ship is aground it may be particularly vulnerable to heavy waves which are more than a normal container might expect to resist. See generally *Dunt*, Chapter 7 for causation principles relating to cargo and for the significance between the variety of expressions used, eg "attributable to" or "arising from".

1272 Clause 1.2.1 and *Dunt*, para 9.28. General average *charges* are covered by cl 2, see below.

1273 Clause 1.2.2 and *Dunt*, para 9.29–9.31. "Jettison" is the deliberate casting overboard of cargo, eg in order to save the ship. This might also give rise to a general average claim for the sacrifice. "Washing overboard" would cover, eg, the value of containers (or other deck cargo) washed overboard in heavy weather, even if the ship herself is not a casualty. For liability for *recovery* costs and possible sue and labour claims, see below and cf 10.6.

1274 Clause 1.2.3 and *Dunt*, paras 9.32–9.36. While this expression may be narrower than the traditional "peril of the seas" (see *Arnould*, 1220), in the case of shipwreck it could cover water damage caused by any fortuity, eg where a ship suffers bottom damage on a reef and water enters a hold. In most circumstances the loss to cargo will almost certainly fall within one of the other risks, eg stranding, grounding or capsizing. Rain (not sea) water entering a container would not be covered, and in any event might be caused by defective packing (see cl 4.3); but if the container had been damaged when the ship was wrecked (or in necessary salvage operations) then any rain water damage (eg while ashore in a place of safety) could be reasonably attributable, eg to a stranding or collision.

1275 Clause 1.2.3 and *Dunt*, para 9.36. The provision may have been designed for normal discharging operations from the original carrying ship. Literally, though, it might also cover loss of containers being transferred to a barge during a salvage operation, as the reference to "vessel" is not expressly restricted to the original carrying ship. Alternatively, the loss might be attributable to a stranding, especially if discharging conditions were difficult, or be covered under cl 9, below.

1276 Cf *Shell International Petroleum Co Ltd v Gibbs (The Salem)* [1983] 1 Lloyd's Rep 342.

from containers washed ashore,[1277] although it is possible to purchase additional cover for this.[1278]

2.9.3(c) Salvage, GA and wreck removal

Clause 2 of all three of the ICC 2009 ((A), (B) and (C)) automatically covers the cargo owner for "general average[1279] and salvage charges".[1280] There is no specific exclusion for any legal *liability* to pay for the costs to remove wrecked cargo,[1281] for two reasons: first, cargo owners are not normally held liable for such removal under national law or the WRC 2007;[1282] secondly, the cover is for "loss *of* or damage *to*" the cargo, and not for the costs of removal as such. However, if (after a sinking) cargo is washed ashore and 'recovered' by salvors, this could result in a normal salvage claim.[1283] If that cargo were, instead, recovered by (and at the expense of) its owners, then associated costs might be recoverable either as "forwarding charges" or as a "sue and labour" expense.[1284]

2.9.3(d) Exclusions from cover

The (A), (B) and (C) Clauses all have exclusions from cover, as set out in cll 4–7 of each, some of which might be relevant in a wreck case. Thus, under cl 4 of ICC (A) the insurance does not cover "loss damage or expense" "attributable" to the "wilful misconduct of the assured";[1285] "caused by insufficiency or unsuitability of

---

1277 As with the *MSC Napoli*: see 1.2.3 and 3.5.3, 4.5. It may be hard to argue that theft by locals is "reasonably attributable" to stranding (a covered risk), unless perhaps a particular piece of coastline is notorious for lawlessness and 'wreckers'. A similar question of attribution may arise where there is theft after cargo is "discharge[d] at a [remote] port of distress" – a covered risk. If the port has inherently poor security features, then it may be easier to equate theft with damage caused during discharge by the lack of suitable equipment or storage facilities. NB: malicious *damage* caused by looters would be excluded in the (B) and (C) clauses: see below.

1278 See the Institute Theft, Pilferage and Non-Delivery Clause 1/12/82: *Dunt*, paras 9.37–9.38, *Arnould*, 1224.

1279 See *Dunt*, 9.39–9.40, 14.31–14.38; also 2.8, and 2.9.2(b). The cover is to avoid loss from "any cause" except those excluded in cll 4–7 (see below). In a normal wreck case, most of the exclusions would not restrict a general average claim, eg for salvage expenses, even when the salvors are trying to save cargo from theft by looters—a risk that would not otherwise be covered under the ICC 2009 (B) and (C): see below and cf *Dunt*, 14.37. Cf the slightly different issue about whether the assured could claim for security costs incurred ashore after the end of the common adventure: see 2.9.3(e), below.

1280 See *Dunt*, 9.39–9.40, 14.24–14.30; also 2.7 and 2.9.2(b). The specific reference to "salvage charges" means those recoverable by a salvor under general maritime law (eg Arts 12–13 of the Salvage Convention 1989), rather than under a contract (eg the LOF): see the MIA 1906 s 65. Under the MIA 1906 s 65(2) these contractual costs might be recovered either as a general average loss, or as particular charges, ie sue and labour expenses (see ss 64(2), 78). In a wreck case, the end result will normally be that the cargo assured is covered for any form of salvage, although technically sue and labour expenses can be claimed over and above the insured value: see *Dunt*, 14.24, 14.29; cf the H&M cover, where all forms of salvage are covered *within* the policy (see 2.9.2(b)).

1281 Cf the express provision in cl 8.4 of the ITC-Hulls 1983, 2.9.2(b).

1282 See 2.1.6, 2.4.1, 10.2.2, 11.2.

1283 Assuming it had a value, see 2.7.5; but probably not a general average claim owing to the ending of the common adventure, see 2.8.1.

1284 See 2.9.3(e).

1285 Clause 4.1. Eg if the cargo owners conspired with the owners to scuttle the ship: cf the MIA s 55(2) and 10.8.4(d). If the cargo was lost by scuttling of which the cargo assured had no knowledge, the loss would be covered in an all risks policy unless there had been a change of voyage: cf *The Salem* [1983] 1 Lloyd's Rep 342, and the (B) and (C) cover, below. See *Dunt*, paras 8.48–8.56, generally, and at 8.55–8.57 for the suggestion that

packing";[1286] "caused by inherent vice";[1287] "caused by delay";[1288] or "caused by insolvency or financial default of the owners, managers, charterers or operators".[1289] Under the ICC 2009 (A) cl 5, the insurer waives any breach of implied insurance obligations of

---

where an assured cargo seller arranges cover on behalf of (or assigns the policy to) an innocent CIF buyer, the latter ought not to be tainted by the wilful misconduct of the former. It is submitted that there is much commercial common sense in such an approach, although it might be said that in principle (given the difficulties faced by insurers) the buyer ought to have the burden of showing that it was ignorant of the misconduct of the seller (once that had been proved by the insurer).

1286 Clause 4.3. See *Dunt*, paras 8.35–8.45, and inherent vice, below. The packing, including container stowage, has to be sufficient to withstand "the ordinary incidents" of the transit, rather than any extraordinary stresses caused during a salvage or transhipment operation. The exclusion only applies where the packing is "carried out" by the assured or its employees, eg where they stuff FCL containers, rather than where independent contractors (eg in a container terminal) perform the packing: the position may be different where the third parties act under the control, or according to the instructions, of the assured: and see *Dunt*, paras 8.38–8.39. In practice, the strictness of the exclusion may be reduced by using special packing clauses which exclude cover only when there is fault, knowledge (or "privity") or consent of the assured: see *Dunt*, para 8.45, and eg *Alstom Ltd v Liberty Mutual Insurance Co (No 2)* [2013] FCA 116 (Fed Ct Australia). In that case, a mere contractual right to inspect the packing was not enough to fix an assured with knowledge where it had entrusted the task to a foreign packing company, and there was no indication of blind eye knowledge (eg if contractors had been engaged who were known to take shortcuts).

1287 Cl 4.4. See *Dunt*, paras 7.28–7.29, 8.24–8.34 and *The Cendor Mopu* [2011] 1 Lloyd's Rep 560. This exclusion can always raise difficult causation questions, eg where cargo is affected by condensation when exposed to heat or humidity in bad weather. In an 'all risks' wreck case, the exclusion seems less likely to apply where cargo is properly packed. Clearly, where perishable goods in a refrigerated container are damaged owing to a loss of power after a casualty, the proximate cause of loss would be, say, the stranding (covered as a peril) rather than the inherent susceptibility of the cargo; see also next fn, 1288. Note that there may be specific clauses to cover such risks, eg the Institute Frozen Food Clauses; *Dunt*, para 9.64. There is a separate, though related, exclusion in cl 4.2 that covers "ordinary" leakage, loss in weight or volume, and wear and tear: see *Dunt*, paras 8.14–8.23. In a casualty leading to a wreck, the stresses may easily exceed the "ordinary", but will also relate to the packing exclusion, cl 4.3.

1288 Clause 4.5. This would exclude loss of market, or other economic losses: and see *Dunt*, para 8.58. In some circumstances, though, delay from an insured risk (eg stranding) may result in physical damage to cargo. If electrical supply is then interrupted to a refrigerated container, the effective cause of loss to perishable cargoes would be the stranding, not delay or inherent vice. A similar result could apply where de-humidifying or ventilation equipment could not operate and steel, or other cargo susceptible to damp, is damaged: cf *Canada Rice Mills Ltd v Union Marine & General Insurance Co Ltd* (1940) 67 Ll L Rep. 549. The position may be more difficult where the cargo in an unventilated hold is affected by damp endured during a stranding that lasted considerably more than the expected voyage. In principle, the dominant cause here could still be the stranding. See *Dunt*, paras 7.19.7.27, considering some of the older case law, and 9.35.

1289 Clause 4.6. After a casualty involving the wreck of a ship owned by a single ship company, it would not be surprising if any of those listed became insolvent. This might mean that the shipowner (particularly if uninsured or faced by potential policy defences from the H&M insurer) ceased to take an active part in attempts to deal with the casualty. This might result in cargo's interests being ignored immediately after the casualty, eg if no attempt is made by owners to try to save the cargo, or if no care is taken by them of any cargo that has been landed. The cl 4 exclusion, though, only applies where the cargo assured should have been aware "*at the time of loading*" that the financial difficulty could prevent the "normal prosecution of the voyage"; this would not seem to apply to abnormal events, such as shipwreck. Moreover, the exclusion would not apply to an assignee in good faith (eg a CIF buyer). Where shipowners or charterers 'go missing' after a casualty, the cargo owners will have to rely on salvors whose costs should be covered by the policy: see also 2.7.7(b), 12.1.3 and *Dunt*, paras 8.59–8.68, and note the effect of cl 12, below.

seaworthiness of the vessel.[1290] This means that even where the ship is unseaworthy or unfit to carry the cargo, there is no exclusion of cover *unless* the assured cargo owner was "privy" to that state of the vessel at the time of loading.[1291] In a similar way to H&M policies, the ICC 2009 (A) excludes loss, damage or expense caused by war,[1292] strikes or terrorism.[1293] These risks might be most relevant to cargo involved in a wreck when it is taken to a place of safety in a war-torn country.

The exclusions in ICC 2009 (B) and (C) cll 4–7 are almost identical to those in (A), but note that in their cl 4.7 there is an additional exclusion for "deliberate damage to or deliberate destruction" of the cargo by the wrongful act of "any person or persons".[1294] This is designed for third party malicious damage,[1295] although additional cover can be purchased.[1296] This exclusion might apply to looters who try to plunder cargo washed ashore in containers but do not succeed in stealing any.[1297] It might also apply where cargo is lost through scuttling by the shipowner, even if the cargo assured is not involved.[1298] Where an oil cargo is deliberately set on fire as part of efforts to reduce pollution, this should fall within the "fire" peril and may not be excluded as "wrongful", especially if authorised by a State under its intervention powers.[1299]

2.9.3(e) Forwarding after casualty

Normal cargo cover does not end once the cargo physically leaves the ship but under cl 8 (the "Transit Clause") can extend beyond the carrying voyage to include storage at a warehouse in the intended port of destination.[1300] Where a casualty intervenes, the

---

1290 Arising under the MIA 1906 s 40(2). Note that there may be an additional express clause in open cover (eg the Institute Classification Clause 01/01/2001) that impose requirements that vessels be of a maximum age and classed with a recognised classification society (eg Lloyd's Register of Shipping or other Member of the International Association of Classification Societies (IACS)): see *Dunt*, paras 8.82–18.90.

1291 See cl 5.1.1 and *Dunt*, paras 8.73–8.81. It is not enough that the assured ought to have known of any problems; what is required is actual knowledge or recklessness (eg awareness of a risk, and a willingness to run it). Charterer's employees may well have greater knowledge about the state of the ship than individual shippers of containers, but it is not clear how far the knowledge of agents such as freight forwarders and brokers may be attributed to the assured. The assured cargo owner (and the insurer by subrogation) may have a recourse claim against the contractual carrier for breach of the contract of carriage if the ship is unseaworthy: see 2.1.5(a). As with the wilful misconduct provision, 2.9.3(d), the exclusion does not apply to an innocent assignee (eg a CIF buyer): see cl 5.2.

1292 Clause 6. See also 3.4.3 for insurers' rights including those resulting from war where the government might act as a reinsurer.

1293 Clause 7. Separate war and strike cover is available for damage or loss to cargo, eg under the Institute War Clauses (Cargo) 2009 and Institute Strikes Clauses (Cargo) 2009. See *Dunt*, Chapter 10.

1294 See *Dunt*, paras 9.41–9.48.

1295 As opposed to wilful misconduct of the assured which is already excluded: see 2.9.3(d) (above); also 10.8.4(d).

1296 The Institute Malicious Damage Clause 1/8/82 which is, though, subject to the policy exclusions (eg terrorism): see *Dunt*, paras 9.45–9.47, *Arnould*, 1224–1225.

1297 As already noted, theft is not a risk covered under ICC 2009 (B) and (C), although, again, additional cover is available: see 2.9.3(b).

1298 Cf *The Salem* [1983] 1 Lloyd's Rep 342, and also the position under the all risks cover, 2.9.3(b). Note that loss, damage or expense caused by terrorism is specifically excluded by cl 7.3.

1299 See 5.3, 4.8.3 and cf the *Torrey Canyon* casualty, 1.2.1. Cf cl 7 of the ITC-Hulls 1983, 2.9.2(b).

1300 There are equivalent provisions in (A), (B) and (C). These clauses were previously known as 'warehouse to warehouse' clauses: see *Dunt*, paras 11.6–11.64; *Arnould*, 465–468.

cargo interests will want to ensure that their cover continues for as long as possible. In principle, the insurance remains in force under cl 8.3 "during delay beyond the control of the assured, any deviation, forced discharge, reshipment or transhipment and during any variation of the adventure arising from any variation of the adventure".[1301] This covers the sort of case where, after the ship is wrecked, the shipowner (or contracting carrier) arranges itself for the forwarding of sound cargo to the port of destination in order to earn the contractual freight.[1302] This transhipment might involve various stages that might not otherwise be in the ordinary course of transit, such as an initial offloading from the wreck and transport to a place of safety undertaken by salvors,[1303] before on-shipment to the intended port of destination under the contract of carriage.[1304] At the final destination the cargo owner may find that, before delivery, it has to give security to meet any salvage or general average claims,[1305] but in the meantime its cargo insurance should have continued to provide cover for whatever risks have been agreed under the policy.[1306]

The scenario above envisages a continuation of the underlying contract of carriage, but is subject to ICC 2009 cl 9 ("Termination of the Contract of Carriage").[1307] If, "owing to circumstances beyond the control" of the assured cargo owner, "the contract of carriage is terminated at a port or place other than that named" in the contract of carriage,[1308] then the insurance will also terminate. This drastic consequence is avoided if the assured cargo owner gives "prompt notice" to the insurers and requests continuation of cover (subject to any required additional premium). Once the notice and request are made, the cargo insurance continues in force[1309] until one of two times. First, under cl 9.1, it continues until the

---

1301 See *Dunt*, paras 11.65–11.75, *Arnould*, 477–479; also the MIA 1906 s 59. Under cl 18 the assured has a general obligation "act with reasonable despatch" (ie avoid delay) in circumstances *within* their control; see also the MIA 1906 s 48.

1302 See *Dunt*, paras 11.73–11.74. See also 2.1.4(a) 2.1.4(b).

1303 It may be a question of degree whether an emergency detour is still an attempt to further the goods to the ultimate destination and within the "ordinary course of transit" under cl 8.1–8.2 (see *Dunt*, paras 1.29–11.33), but cl 8.3 is presumably definitive where it applies.

1304 See eg the *MSC Napoli*, 1.2.2. At the final destination the insurance would terminate in the ordinary way under cl 8.1, eg in a final warehouse.

1305 See 2.7.8, 2.8.

1306 Eg, under all risks (A) cover if the cargo is damaged during transhipment or storage at the place of safety; under (B) or (C) cover theft or malicious damage may be excluded.

1307 There are equivalent provisions in ICC 2009 (A), (B) and (C). See *Dunt*, 12.11–12.12; *Arnould*, 478–479, 544–548.

1308 This contractual termination could often apply after a shipwreck where the shipowner (or contracting carrier) is unable or unwilling to complete the contracted voyage. For frustration of the carriage contract, and contractual liberties to terminate or cancel, see 2.1.3(b).

1309 The wording of cl 9 ("shall remain in force") does not appear strictly to give the insurer a right to refuse to extend the cover—unlike cl 10.1, dealing with changes of voyage generally, where further agreement of the insurer is required: cf *Dunt*, 12.7–12.10, 12.12, and *Arnould*, 544–548. However, cl 9 does allow the insurer to require an "additional premium". In theory, this would mean that the insurer could quote an unreasonably high figure in order to avoid the risk, yet that would defeat the "right" to the cover that is recognised both in the wording of cl 9 and in the italicised "Note" that appears at the end of all the Clauses (where the only qualification is prompt notice). Clause 10.1 has an express reference to "reasonable commercial market rate", but no such wording appears in cl 9. To give effect to the "right" in cl 9, the assured can rely on the MIA s 31(2) which gives a right to a "reasonable additional premium". Alternatively, it may be necessary to imply a term, eg that the additional premium in cl 9 should be at a reasonable commercial market rate, unless the insurer can show that it is not

cargo is sold and delivered at the port or place (other than the named destination) where the contract is terminated, or 60 days (or any agreed extension) after arrival of the cargo at that place (if sooner).[1310] Secondly, under cl 9.2, if the cargo is forwarded within that 60 days (or any agreed extension) to the insured destination (or even to "any other destination"),[1311] the insurance will continue until the normal end of transit. It is clear that after a major casualty, cargo owners must be astute to be aware of the 60-day period and to keep their insurers informed.[1312]

Clause 9.2 has to be read with cl 12, "Forwarding Charges",[1313] which applies where the insured transit terminates at a port or place other than the original insured destination, eg a place of safety after a shipwreck. Then, the insurer will reimburse the assured cargo owners for "any extra charges properly and reasonably incurred in unloading storing and forwarding the cargo" to the destination to which it is insured.[1314] *Dunt*[1315] notes that the clause merely confirms that the forwarding charges are recoverable as sue and labour expenses,[1316] but this is expressly subject to the exclusions in cll 4–7; the effect of the latter was originally designed to exclude the commercial risk of insolvency of the shipowner.[1317] Nor does cl 12 apply to general average or salvage charges.[1318]

It seems unlikely that forwarding charges would be "reasonably incurred" under cl 12 by the cargo owners if, at the stage of forwarding, they knew that the cargo was worthless

---

possible for any reasonable insurer to produce a quotation for that risk. That would seem unlikely as the insurer would continue to have the benefit of existing limits on cover and exclusions (eg terrorism).

1310 It is possible that cargo, eg containers, may be moved to a place of storage that is very remote and that the salvors have either claimed to redeliver the goods or, for some reason, are no longer taking care of them (cf *The M/V Brillante Virtuoso* [2015] 1 Lloyd's Rep 651 [296–297]. Provided that the appropriate notice and request have been made, the cargo owners can still have coverage against loss of or damage to the goods.

1311 There is no express requirement that this "other" destination has to be agreed by the insurer, but presumably this is where it will demand an appropriate increase in premium.

1312 Cargo owners often have particular difficulties about finding out what is going on after a casualty: see 2.1.3, 2.9.5, 2.7.9(c), 12.1.1, 12.3.3. The clause does not make clear whether the need to be "prompt" is judged objectively or subjectively, but it would seem appropriate that it took into account the knowledge of the particular assured cargo owner, especially as the opening words of cl 9 recognise that the clause operates when there are circumstances beyond the control of the assured. Once the assured has some reliable information that would trigger action by a reasonable assured (eg a notice of termination from the shipowner), then the promptness criterion should certainly operate.

1313 See *Dunt*, paras 13.62–13,73; *Arnould*, 1342–1345.

1314 As set out in cl 8. Where cl 9.2 operates, this presumably could include a changed (ie "other") destination.

1315 *Dunt*, para 8.64.

1316 See cl 16.

1317 Itself a separate exclusion under cl 4.6: see above and *Dunt*, para 8.64. The effect of this insolvency exclusion in a wreck case seems somewhat removed from a mischief involving the use of substandard ships and abandonment of the voyage even without a casualty. That is why the current cl 4.6 only operates where the assured is aware of the insolvency (and does not apply to an assignee). Clause 12 also excludes any unloading, storage or forwarding "charges arising from the fault negligence insolvency or financial default of the assured" itself. As the clause only covers "reimbursement" for extra charges, it would seem that it would not apply to a cargo owner that had no funds to hand as a result of financial pressures caused by the wreck; this might not be fanciful, as a cargo seller might be dependent upon payment at destination. It would therefore exclude extra storage charges, perhaps while the assured raised additional finance.

1318 As noted, these are covered separately. So, for example, it would seem that salvage principles and payments would normally apply to the period from when the salvor saves the cargo from the wreck and takes it to the place of safety; while forwarding costs thereafter would fall under cl 12.

or likely to be so; ie that the forwarding costs would exceed its value. To interpret the provision otherwise would mean that the cargo insurer would be held indirectly liable for removal of wrecked cargo that would normally be a liability of the shipowner (and its P&I insurer).

The existence of cl 12 means that it may not be necessary for cargo owners to claim forwarding expenses separately as a "sue and labour" expense[1319] under ICC 2009 cl 16 ("Minimising Losses"), although there might possibly be other expenses not within cl 12. Clause 16 places an express duty on the assured (i) to take reasonable measures to avert or minimise any loss recoverable under the policy and (ii) to ensure that all rights against carriers, bailees or other third parties are properly preserved and exercised.[1320] In exchange, the insurer will reimburse any charges properly and reasonably incurred.

It is not always clear when the rights and duties in respect of sue and labour come to an end,[1321] but it seems that while there is a continuation of the peril to any cargo transferred onshore, expenses incurred are recoverable up until a notice of abandonment is given[1322] or even up to the issue of a claim form for a total loss.[1323] As already explained, cl 9 provides a regime for when the "contract of carriage is terminated" short of the contractual destination or the "transit is otherwise terminated". It is possible that neither of these events have been triggered, eg there is no formal termination notice given by the shipowner (or contracting carrier), or it is difficult to say that the transit has terminated when the ship is still aground. The cargo assured might still be able to use the 'sue and labour' clause to reclaim any extra costs incurred reasonably to recover the cargo, or to prevent it from deteriorating or being damaged.[1324] There probably needs to be at least a "significant risk" that the loss would otherwise fall on the insurer,[1325] and this will condition what is reasonable. In a place of safety with few facilities it may be necessary to provide temporary cover, although the extent to

---

[1319] Under the MIA 1906 s 78 a sue and labour clause is supplementary rights and duties to sue and labour come to an end to the policy and expenses can be claimed even if the insurer has paid for a total loss. General average and salvage cannot be recovered under the clause, nor can expenses to avert losses not covered by the policy. See *Dunt*, 14.1–14.33; *Arnould*, Chapter 25, especially 1301–1302.

[1320] Eg in making an unreasonable settlement of a claim against the carrier. Failure by the assured gives rise to a contractual claim for damages by the insurer: see *Noble Resources Ltd and Unirise Development Ltd v Greenwood (The Vasso)* [1993] 2 Lloyd's Rep 309. In that case the cargo assured was not automatically in breach by failing to obtain a *Mareva* (freezing) injunction to prevent the proceeds of an H&M policy being removed from the UK by a single ship company (whose ship was sunk with the cargo and which had no other assets in the jurisdiction). Such an injunction is a common tactic to try to bring claims against single ship companies after a total loss, but in this case the assured had taken reasonable steps to consider obtaining one: a failure to consider the matter at all might have led to a breach. The classic example of failure to protect rights would be making an insurance claim after failing to ensure that the one-year Hague/Visby time bar (see 2.1.1, 2.1.5) had not expired, thereby depriving he insurer of a subrogated claim against the carrier: see *Dunt*, paras 14.17–14.20.

[1321] See *Arnould*, 1665–1666.

[1322] See 2.9.4(b).

[1323] See *Suez Fortune Investments Ltd v Talbot Underwriting Ltd (The M/V Brillante Virtuoso)* [2015] 1 Lloyd's Rep 651 [280–297]. For the sequel to that H&M case, involving allegations of wilful misconduct, see *Suez Fortune Investments Ltd and Piraeus Bank AE v Talbot Underwriting Ltd* [2016] EWHC 1085 (Comm); *Suez Fortune Investments Ltd and Piraeus Bank AE v Talbot Underwriting Ltd and Anor* [2018] EWHC 2929 (Comm).

[1324] Cf *Integrated Container Services Inc v British Traders Insurance Co Ltd* [1984] 2 Lloyd's Rep 154; *Arnould*, 1215–1216.

[1325] *The M/V Brillante Virtuoso* [2015] 1 Lloyd's Rep 651 [293]; *Dunt*, para 14.10.

which security costs can be reimbursed may depend on whether the policy covers theft or malicious damage.[1326] Where the cargo is already damaged, eg where containers are off-loaded with seawater damage, the assured may have to make difficult judgments about how much money should be expended before the cargo is a CTL. Liability for wreck removal, including disposal of waste, is not covered under the policy, so any expenses related to that would not be recoverable as sue and labour, nor would expenses directly incurred in minimising pollution from leaking containers[1327] (as opposed to preserving the cargo).

2.9.4 Total loss

When a ship is wrecked, it is likely that the shipowner and cargo owners will want to claim for the complete loss of their property against their respective underwriters.[1328] The law distinguishes in essence between two types of total loss: a physical loss and a financial loss (ie a 'write-off').

2.9.4(a) Actual total loss
A ship was said to be an actual total loss (ATL) when "it becomes totally destroyed or annihilated, or if it be placed, by reasons of perils . . . in such a position, that it is wholly out of the power of the assured or of the underwriters to procure its arrival" at its destination.[1329] This is now reflected in the MIA 1906 in s 57(1), which provides that "[w]here the subject-matter insured is destroyed, or so damaged as to cease to be a thing of the kind insured, or where the assured is irretrievably deprived thereof, there is an actual total loss". Ships that have been wrecked, eg by sinking, might fall within one or more of the categories reflected in s 57(1); eg being considered "destroyed", "ceasing" to be a ship[1330] or lost in depths such that the assured was "irretrievably deprived thereof".[1331] When a ship becomes a wreck in this sense, so that the remains no longer qualify as a ship, there is an ATL.[1332]

In the era of wooden sailing ships, it was easier to equate a sunken ship to one that had been completely destroyed by fire.[1333] This notion no longer necessarily holds true,

---

1326 See 2.9.3(c) and fn 1279.

1327 It is possible that some environmental mitigation expenses incurred by salvors (eg under State instruction) might be recoverable under Art 14 of the Salvage Convention 1989, or SCOPIC, but these would normally be claimed by the salvor from the shipowner and covered by its P&I insurer: see 2.7.9(b) and (c), and above. Where valuable cargo is salved, any salvage reward could include recognition of the skill and efforts of the salvor in preventing pollution (see 2.7.9(a) and above) and (to the extent that the salvor's expenditure is 'buried' in an overall salvage award) it might be that such expenses would be indirectly covered as "salvage" under the cargo policy.

1328 Of course, if the ship is merely damaged (eg it is refloated) there would be a claim for partial loss, ie for cost of repairs. Such a claim is not the main focus of this book, although the possibility of saving the ship will be prominent at the time of the casualty, and is directly relevant to salvage operations (see 2.7). It is more likely, though, that cargo may be saved in a damaged state from a wreck and so, after a casualty, cargo owners will also be considering partial loss claims for damage to their goods: see 2.9.3(b) and (e).

1329 *Roux v Salvador* (1836) 3 Bing NC 266, 286. See generally, *Arnould*, Chapter 28.

1330 *Barker v Janson* (1867–1868) LR 3 CP 303, 305. See also O Gurses, *The Law of Marine Insurance* (2nd ed, Routledge, 2017) [*Gurses*], 330.

1331 Where a ship is missing, an ATL may be presumed if no news has been received after the lapse of a reasonable time: MIA 1906 s 58.

1332 *Arnould*, 1509–1510.

1333 *Gurses*, 328.

given increases in salvage capability, as many sunken wrecks are capable of being raised and made operational again. If the ship is not completely destroyed, the wrecked remains might still be considered as no longer a ship if it ceased to be a thing of the kind insured; this turns on the facts of each case.[1334] The degree to which a stranded[1335] ship might be salvaged, refloated and then made capable again of navigation might determine whether, while stranded, it is still a ship.[1336] The ship cannot be an ATL if it is physically and legally possible to repair the damage.[1337]

Similar principles apply to cargo,[1338] so that if cargo from a wreck is washed ashore and then plundered (ie stolen) by local inhabitants, there may still be an ATL; the cargo owner would have been irretrievable deprived of the goods although they were initially 'saved'.[1339] Likewise, perishable cargo that has been immersed in seawater when the ship is wrecked may be recovered, but in such as state that its nature has been wholly changed so as to be an ATL. Thus, in *Asfar v Blundell*,[1340] after a collision in the Thames a ship was almost entirely submerged for two or three tides (although later raised and docked). A cargo of dates was "simply a mass of pulpy matter impregnated with sewage and in a state of fermentation" but, although condemned for human use, still had considerable value and was sold for distillation into spirit. Although the dates had not been totally destroyed, there was an ATL as the nature of the cargo had changed and it was unmerchantable as dates.[1341]

The test for an ATL has been applied strictly with the "utmost rigour", given the possibility of finding a constructive total loss.[1342] The distinction between the two types of loss

---

1334 See eg *Fraser Shipping Ltd v Colton (The Shakir II)* [1997] 1 Lloyd's Rep 586, 591. In that case a heavylift ship, on a scrapping voyage, stranded and was "almost in two"; this would have required salvage in two pieces. Still, it was held that the ship had not lost its "essential character"; the need to have two halves for towage was an issue that went to cost rather than identity, ie pointing more towards a CTL: see 2.6.3(b). This is perhaps an exceptional example where the subject matter of the insurance was *already* in effect a hulk of floating metal, and this identity had not changed. Moreover, a CTL was not covered under the policy; cf *Venetico Marine SA v International General Insurance Co Ltd (The Irene M)* [2014] 1 Lloyd's Rep 349.

1335 NB: a stranded ship is a 'wreck' for the purposes of the WRC 2007, Art 4(a): see further 8.2.1(b).

1336 See eg *The Irene M* [2014] 1 Lloyd's Rep 349, [398–406], where the judge accepted that if the vessel could not be moved except for scrapping then it was no longer a thing of the kind insured; on the facts it could have been moved for repair and there was not an ATL.

1337 *The Irene M* [2014] 1 Lloyd's Rep 349, [400]. See also *George Cohen, Sons & Co. v Standard Marine Insurance Co Ltd* (1925) 21 Ll L Rep 30.

1338 See *Dunt*, 13.23.13.38.

1339 See eg *Brondrett v Hentig* (1816) Holt NP 149, *Arnould*, 1503–1504. As to an ATL by destruction of cargo, see *Arnould* 1508–1509, 1512–1520. As to whether such theft is covered under the ICC (A), (B) or (C), see 2.9.2(b).

1340 See eg *Asfar v Blundell* (1895) 1 Com Cas 71, [1896] 1 QB 123, 127 (a case on insurance of freight).

1341 Similarly, cement solidified by seawater would have been so changed as to lose its properties as cement (*Duthie v Hilton*, LR 4 CP 138); or where machinery designed for a particular purpose only has a scrap value (cf *Berger and Light Diffusers Pty v Pollock* [1973] 2 Lloyd's Rep 442; *Arnould*, 1517). There may be difficult questions of degree, eg whether goods are merely damaged (as where distressed foodstuffs intended for human consumption could be sold on as feedstuffs for animal consumption). Modern cargo insurance cover will now usually extend to partial loss (ie damage), so the distinctions may be less important: see 2.9.3(b).

1342 See eg. *Masefield AG v Amlin Corporate Member Ltd (The Bunga Melati Dua)* [2011] EWCA Civ 24 [16]; [2011] 1 Lloyd's Rep 630 [16] and 2.6.3(b).

might be important for a variety of reasons, eg if the policy only covered an ATL,[1343] and the ensuing rights and obligations of the parties differ.[1344]

2.9.4(b) Constructive total loss and notice of abandonment
As seen, it is not necessarily straightforward to determine whether a wreck is an ATL—especially when commercial considerations, such as the salvage expenses, are taken into account.[1345] The MIA 1906 therefore also provides for another form of total loss: a constructive total loss (CTL). There is a CTL "where the subject-matter insured is reasonably abandoned on account of its actual total loss appearing to be unavoidable, or because it could not be preserved from an ATL without an expenditure which would exceed its value when the expenditure had been incurred".[1346] This includes, for example, cases where the recovery of a sunken or stranded ship would be more expensive than the value of the ship itself.[1347] The same principle applies to cargo, eg where the cost of recovering, reconditioning and forwarding the goods to the port of destination would exceed its value on arrival.[1348] The insurance is therefore for the maritime adventure, ie the cargo itself and its arrival at destination.[1349]

Where the total loss of a vessel appears unavoidable, or where it is not commercially viable to preserve a vessel from total loss, the owner can claim a CTL by 'abandoning'[1350] the ship to the insurer, treating the loss as if it were an ATL[1351] and thereby being indemnified in full. To be able to claim for a CTL a "notice of abandonment" is necessary,[1352] whereby the owner voluntarily offers to cede its entire interest in the vessel to the insurer. The notice of abandonment is essentially an election[1353] by the assured to claim as a total loss that which, in reality, is only a partial loss (in that the wreck has some potential residual value). In the case of an ATL, no such notice of abandonment is necessary[1354] since, in theory, there is nothing left to abandon. At

---

1343 As in *Fraser Shipping Ltd v Colton (The Shakir II)* [1997] 1 Lloyd's Rep 586 (fn 1334, above). Note that, historically, some cargo policies were issued to cover total losses only, and not partial losses (or 'free of average'); modern policies do not usually apply this restriction, see *Arnould*, 1512–1520.

1344 In particular as to the notice of abandonment and the right of the insurer to take over the remains. See also 3.4.1.

1345 See eg. *Fraser Shipping Ltd v Colton* [1997] 1 Lloyd's Rep 586.

1346 MIA 1906 s 60(1); *Arnould*, 1528–1528. See also cl 19 of the ITC-Hulls 1983 and cl 13 of the ICC 2009.

1347 See MIA 1906 s 60(2); and see the ITC-Hulls 1983 cl 19, which specifically the insured value as the repaired value and leaves out of account the damaged or break-up value of the vessel or wreck. The CTL calculation may include general average and salvage costs (prior to any notice of abandonment, and estimated thereafter), but not SCOPIC expenses (see 2.7.9(c)) incurred by the shipowner: see The Renos [2019] 2 LLoyd's Rep 78 (SC). The CA decision had been criticised and its reversal on this issue may remove any need for hull underwriters to change policy wordings to exclude SCOPIC from CTL calculations: see UK P&I Club Quarterly Review, Issue 6, Summer 2018.

1348 See ICC 2009 cl 13; also *Dunt*, paras 13.45–13.55; *Arnould*, 1583–1592.

1349 See *Dunt*, paras 13.56–13.61.

1350 On the concept of 'abandonment' generally in marine insurance, see *The WD Fairway* [2009] EWHC 889 (Admiralty); [2009] 2 Lloyd's Rep 191; *Arnould*, Chapter 30; Rose, *Marine Insurance*, Chapter 24.

1351 MIA 1906 s 61.

1352 MIA 1906 ss 60(1), 62(1).

1353 MIA 1906 s 62(1).

1354 MIA 1906 s 57(2).

the time of the casualty, eg where the ship has sunk or stranded, it may be uncertain whether there is an ATL or CTL. In practice, where an owner wishes to claim for a total loss, it may be advisable to issue a notice of abandonment and the determination as to whether the loss amounts to an ATL or CTL can be left for a later stage.[1355]

Thus, to be entitled to claim for a CTL, the assured must give a timely, unequivocal, valid notice of abandonment.[1356] The notice of abandonment must reflect the unconditional abandonment of the assured's interests, eg in the ship.[1357] The MIA 1906 s 62(2) provides that the "notice of abandonment may be given in writing, or by word of mouth[1358] . . . and may be given in terms which indicate the intention of the assured to abandon his insured interest in the subject-matter insured unconditionally to the insurer".[1359] The notice must be given in a reasonable time[1360] to allow the insurer to take immediate steps to do what is best for the vessel.[1361] What is reasonable is a question of fact and obviously dependent on the reliability of the information received by the assured.[1362] An insurer may waive a notice of abandonment[1363] and, in any event, it is unnecessary where the assured receives information of the loss at a time when there would be no possible benefit to the insurer of receiving a notice.[1364]

2.9.4(c) Acceptance of notice of abandonment
The insurer is not bound to accept the notice of abandonment, which is in effect a contractual offer.[1365] Where the insurer has not accepted the notice of abandonment, the assured that wishes to maintain the right to treat the loss as a CTL must continue to treat the ship as abandoned. Any act inconsistent with this, such as selling the wreck for its own benefit, could be a waiver or revocation of the notice that would negate the claim for a total loss (as opposed to a partial loss).[1366]

There is no particular form by which an insurer must accept a notice of abandonment in the case of an assured's claim for a CTL, and abandonment is essentially a question of fact.[1367] The mere silence of the insurer after notice is not an acceptance[1368] as the notice

---

1355 *Arnould*, 1494–1495; *Rose, Marine Insurance*, 446, 456 and 497. See also 2.9.5.
1356 See further *Rose, Marine Insurance*, 498–502.
1357 MIA 1906 s 62(2); *Arnould*, 1526–1528, 1628–1630.
1358 This would now include by email or phone.
1359 Thus, it would not be enough for the assured merely to give an indication that it was thinking about abandoning: see also *Arnould*, 1494–1495, 1628–1630.
1360 MIA 1906 ss 62(3) and 88.
1361 Eg by taking ownership and arranging for sale for scrap. See also 3.2.
1362 Cf *The Renos* [2018] 1 Lloyd's Rep 285 [2019] 2 LLoyd's Rep 78, where a delay of five months was reasonable. However, that was not a wreck case, eg where a ship is stranded and where there is a degree of urgency or a need for immediate decisions to be made. In practice the courts may allow a large margin of error when assessing the costs of repair, bearing in mind what a prudent uninsured owner would do: *The M/V Brillante Virtuoso* [2015] 1 Lloyd's Rep 651 [92]; *Arnould*, 1557–1560, 1640–1642.
1363 MIA s 62(8).
1364 MIA s 62(7).
1365 *The WD Fairway* [2009] EWHC 889 (Admiralty); [2009] 2 Lloyd's Rep 191; *Arnould*, 1650–1652; *Dunt*, 16.24; *Rose, Marine Insurance*, 496. Cf MIA s 62(4), (5) and (6).
1366 *Arnould*, 1652–1654; see *Royal Boskalis Westminster NV v Mountain* [1997] 1 Lloyd's Reins L Rep 523, 555–559; (appealed on other grounds, [1997] EWCA Civ 1140).
1367 *Arnould*, 1531–1532, 1635–1637; *Rose, Marine Insurance*, 505.
1368 MIA 1906 s 62(5).

of abandonment amounts to an offer by the assured and the insurer is under no duty to accept, reject or otherwise respond to it.[1369] Indeed, mere payment is insufficient to amount to acceptance of the notice of abandonment.[1370] The acceptance of an abandonment by the insurer may be either express, or implied from conduct.[1371] In order for acceptance to be implied from conduct, it is necessary for the insurer to act in ways consistent with the exercise of rights of ownership. It is unclear what type or level of conduct is sufficient but, for example, where an insurer took possession of the wrecked ship, undertook repairs and kept the ship in its possession it was found to have accepted the notice of abandonment.[1372] Not all acts by the insurer necessarily reflect the exercise of any proprietary right and they may merely be acts to minimise losses on behalf of the assured owner; an example might be where the insurer declines the notice expressly, but takes up salvage on behalf of the *owner*,[1373] but presumably the position would be different if the insurer agreed a salvage contract in its *own* name. Implied acceptance of the notice of abandonment may be difficult to prove, but in some circumstances the conduct of the insurer might estop it from denying acceptance, even if it did not in fact intend to accept the abandonment.[1374]

Acceptance of the notice of abandonment along with payment for a CTL loss can have the effect of transferring property to the insurer.[1375] After paying for a CTL, the insurer would have an unfettered and unilateral entitlement to any remains recovered by a salvage or wreck removal operation.[1376] It will usually be a matter of agreement between assured and underwriter as to whether the assured arranges for the sale of the wreck for recycling on behalf of the insurer, or reimburses the insurer later for any proceeds.[1377]

The main reason why insurers may settle a CTL claim but decline a notice of acceptance (and also decline to take over the property) is in order to avoid the risk that (as owners) they may be faced with liabilities, in particular for wreck removal.[1378] Given the risk of such

---

1369 See *Rose, Marine Insurance*, 505.

1370 *The WD Fairway* [2009] EWHC 889 (Admiralty); [2009] 2 Lloyd's Rep 191; *Rose, Marine Insurance*, 511.

1371 MIA 1906 s 62(5).

1372 *Provincial Insurance Co of Canada v Leduc* (1874) LR 6 PC 224, *Arnould*, 1650–1652.

1373 *Rose, Marine Insurance*, 507.

1374 See *Arnould*, 1650–1652. There is a standard provision in the sue and labour clause (eg cl 13.3 of the ITC-Hulls 1983), whereby measures taken to save protect or recover the property shall not be considered as a waiver or acceptance of abandonment. There are doubts as to the effectiveness of the provision, but it should have some evidentiary effect: see *Rose, Marine Insurance*, 506; *Arnould*, 1651–1652.

1375 See the MIA ss 63(1), 79(1), *Kastor Navigation C Ltd v AGF MAT (The Kastor Two)* [2004] 2 Lloyd's Rep 119; *Arnould*, 1623–1626, 1656–1657, 1661–1663.

1376 *Dornoch Ltd & Ors v Westminster International BV & Ors (The WD Fairway)* [2009] EWHC 889 (Admiralty), [2009] 2 Lloyd's Rep 191 [10]; *Dornoch Ltd & Ors v Westminster International BV & Ors (The WD Fairway (No 3))* [2009] EWHC 1782 (Admiralty), [2009] 2 Lloyd's Rep 420 [55].

1377 See *The WD Fairway* [2009] 2 Lloyd's Rep 191 [10], where there was an "unprecedented" dispute about the residual open market value of the wreck, which was a very large dredger that the assured did not want to see pass into the hands of a competitor. The assured purported to sell to an associated company so as to prevent an open market sale: and see 14.7.2. See also *The WD Fairway (No 3)* [2009] 2 Lloyd's Rep 420 [11–18], where the CTL settlement documentation did not evidence an election by the insurers not to exercise their rights to take over the vessel, and where an estoppel by convention also operated; see also 14.7.3 and *Arnould*, 1623–1626. In the event, Tomlinson J set aside the transfer under the Insolvency Act 1986 s 423, as it was at an undervalue: see [2009] 2 Lloyd's Rep 420 [129–135]. The final order [166] was that ownership be transferred back to the insurers.

1378 See further 2.9.5(b) on the practice of underwriters, and 11.1.1.

liability, insurers will usually make their rejection of the notice explicit.[1379] Underwriters would be more likely to accept title to valuable cargoes, for example bullion,[1380] but may face an evidential difficulty if they attempt to do this many years after a sinking.[1381]

The rejection by the insurer of the notice of abandonment is not irrevocable,[1382] but where the insurer does not accept the notice of abandonment, the property continues to vest in the assured, at least for insurance purposes.[1383] Issues about the proprietary rights in a wreck, and whether the insurer has gained an interest, are particularly important in the case of ancient or historic wreck and will be dealt with later.[1384]

2.9.5 Wreck and the practice of underwriters

Looking more broadly, the effect of all these insurance arrangements is that in the event of a shipwreck, the hull and cargo insurers will also be keenly concerned in the events leading *up to* the sinking or stranding. They will want to be sure that the hull and cargo is a total loss (whether actual or constructive). Then they will be concerned to discover whether there is any evidence that may enable them to refuse the claims, eg non-payment of premium, misrepresentation, non-disclosure, breach of a policy warranty, fraud (eg scuttling), or simply that the loss was not a risk covered by the policy.[1385] The extent to which insurers can rely on such defences has been limited by the recent amendments made to the MIA 1906[1386] but the point is that the involvement of underwriters in the wreck casualty will normally be limited to issues relating to reimbursement of the ship and cargo owners for the insured value of their property. There may, though, be some insurers who have provided full cover for hull or cargo loss *and* for liabilities.[1387]

2.9.5(a) Information and evidence

The H&M underwriters would have been notified by the shipowners (perhaps via brokers) of a casualty and a possible claim for loss. Many insurance policies would have provisions requiring prompt notification.[1388] Insurers will have a direct initial interest, though, in attempts to salve the ship and cargo.[1389] Not only will a successful operation reduce any insurance claim but, as seen already,[1390] salvage itself is covered as a risk by the hull and cargo insurers (as is general average). In other words, when a salvor makes a direct

---

1379 *Arnould*, 1625–1626.
1380 See eg *The Egypt* (1932) 44 Ll L Rep 21, 31.
1381 See 3.3, 3.4.5.
1382 See MIA 1906 s 62(4), and eg *The WD Fairway* [2009] 2 Lloyd's Rep 191 [33].
1383 *Arnould*, 1661–1663.
1384 See 3.4; also *Dunt*, 16.24.
1385 "Hull Claims Guidelines" are regularly issued by the Joint Hull Committee (of Lloyd's and the IUA) to assist assureds in dealing with insurers: see eg JH2012/009A (2012) and www.lmalloyds.com/lma/jointhull.
1386 See the Consumer Insurance (Disclosure and Representations) Act 2012 and the Insurance Act 2015: see further *Arnould*, 2–3, Chaps 18A and 18B.
1387 Eg under the Nordic Marine Insurance Plan of 2013, Version 2019.
1388 The ITC-Hulls 1983 does not use the word "prompt" in its notice of claim provision, cl 10(1), but the ITC-Hulls 1995 cl 11.1 requires the notice to be given "promptly". The ICC 2009 cl 9 require prompt notice where the carriage contract is terminated: see 2.9.3(e).
1389 See generally 2.7.
1390 See 2.9.2(b) and 2.9.3(c).

claim for a reward against the hull or cargo owner, the latter will seek to be indemnified by their insurer who will be liable to pay the assured up to the value of the salved property.[1391] The H&M underwriters, in particular, may be consulted about (or even be involved in) the appointment of salvors, although in many circumstances decisions may need to be taken by the master or shipowner before underwriters can be notified. The degree of involvement of H&M underwriters in any salvage operation may vary, depending in part in their confidence in the actions taken by the owners. In practice, many underwriters will be more concerned with maintaining a close watching brief on activities and would probably appoint their own surveyors to report on and assess the claim. This may have the aim of obtaining evidence of the salvage operation, so as to be able to assess later if any claimed reward is justified; if the salvage operation is not being pursued efficiently, the underwriter might be prejudiced, eg if the ship sinks when it could have been saved or if the operations are unduly prolonged.

At the time and scene of the casualty, the hull and cargo insurers will also have an interest in gathering evidence about what had happened beforehand in order to resist (if appropriate) a claim by the insured, eg if scuttling is suspected or (in the case of cargo insurers) whether the loss was caused by a breach of the contract of carriage, such as unseaworthiness.[1392] In this sense, their representatives will not necessarily be assisting in efforts to salve or remove the wreck. This can sometimes cause tensions with government officials and salvors who are trying to carry out dangerous operations and do not always want to have superfluous persons on board who might get in the way (and whose lives may be at risk). Shipowners who are nervous about what evidence may be found (eg about unseaworthiness) may actively wish to discourage the presence on board of underwriters' representatives.

The extent to which the H&M underwriters can obtain information, monitor activities and (sometimes) influence them will depend on whether they have any representatives at the casualty to represent them. In the immediate aftermath of a casualty the flow of information may be dependent on the shipowner and salvors; later the underwriters might seek to appoint a representative such as a surveyor to attend and may be suspicious if they are denied access to a casualty. The shipowner will be particularly aware that it will be making a commercial insurance claim, so may not wish to antagonise the underwriters. Whether the H&M underwriters can insist upon such representation has been somewhat controversial, given concerns by salvors that their task may be made more difficult by the presence on board the ship of representatives of commercial interests. This issue is now dealt with contractually in SCOPIC 2018, which allows the appointment of a "Special Hull Representative".[1393]

The position of cargo owners[1394] and their underwriters[1395] may be slightly different. Cargo underwriters may hear about the casualty later than other interests, and in most cases

---

1391 If the cargo has been salved and taken to a port of refuge, the salvor will exercise its maritime lien until the cargo is released against a bond or other security provided by the insurer: see 2.7.8. In the event that such security is provided the insurer may then have assumed a direct contractual liability to the salvor to pay any amount later decided by a court or arbitrator.
1392 As they may want to instigate recovery claims against the carrier: see 2.1.1, 2.1.5.
1393 See 12.3.3.
1394 See also 2.1.1, 2.1.3.
1395 See 2.9.3, 2.9.5.

are unlikely to be able to influence events greatly, especially where there are very many insurers of a container cargo. Cargo owners and underwriters will, though, be as keen as other parties to gather evidence at the scene of a casualty because they will almost certainly be looking for ways to sue the shipowner or carrier.[1396] For this reason, the master (and shipowners) will be keen to keep cargo surveyors and lawyers away from the scene—in addition to the concerns of the salvors about having more people on board who are not assisting in saving the casualty.[1397] Part of the industry compromise with H&M and cargo underwriters in SCOPIC was to allow a "Special Cargo Representative" to be appointed for cargo interests.[1398]

2.9.5(b) Underwriters' decision time for total loss

The general law and practice on ATLs and CTLs will be directly relevant to how insurers handle wreck claims, but there is a practical issue that arises with most wrecks, which is how long it will take the H&M insurer to decide whether (i) there is a loss for which it will pay under the policy and (ii) the ship has any residual value that means that it is worth salving. If the ship sank immediately, there would be an obvious claim for an ATL. In the case of a stranding or grounding, where a notice of abandonment (for a CTL) has been served on the insurer, the position is more uncertain. At this stage, the shipowner (and the P&I Club) would be fairly convinced that thereafter there was no possibility of salvage of the vessel and that it was possible that a wreck removal might be involved (eg if the ship was aground or likely to sink in coastal waters). But in order to be able to carry out that operation, the shipowner and Club would need to be sure that the H&M underwriters would be willing to pay as for a total loss and would not be asserting any rights of ownership of the vessel.

The practice is almost invariably for the H&M underwriters to reject any notice of abandonment, mainly to avoid any potential liabilities if the insurer assumed rights of ownership of the vessel, including wreck removal or environmental damage. Whether the underwriter would really be exposed to statutory liabilities, eg for wreck removal, under national law may depend upon the extent to which that legislation fixes a time at which ownership is judged for liability purposes.[1399] Either way, unless there was some clear future value in the vessel there would be little interest in assuming ownership of it; had there been any value, then salvage operations might have been expected to continue. The tactical position of cargo underwriters might be slightly different, as portions of cargo might have a value if raised later, but again there might be concerns about potential liabilities in national law, eg in respect of waste.[1400]

1396 See 2.1.1, 2.1.5.

1397 There may be circumstances where the salvors would welcome those with technical cargo expertise, eg where there is dangerous cargo in containers, or where it is not clear how seawater contamination will affect a particular cargo.

1398 See 2.7.9(c), 12.3.3.

1399 Eg whether the legislation attached to the owner at the point of a casualty, or at the time of any wreck removal operations or expenditure: see also 11.1 for some of the issues arising before the WRC 2007; also *Arnould*, 1661. An insurer that elected to take over the property would not become liable under the WRC 2007 per se as the liabilities attach to the registered owner or compulsory insurer: see 10.2.2. The position might be different if the wrecked ship were raised and then sank on a towage voyage to the scrapyard; cf *The Shakir II* [1997] 1 Lloyd's Rep 586 (see 2.9.6(a) and 14.7.3).

1400 Cf 14.6.

While the H&M underwriters might reject the notice of abandonment, the "time honoured and common if not universal practice" is for them to agree to place the assured in the position as if a writ/claim form had been issued.[1401] They will be expected to agree (or not) to pay as for a CTL. This decision may involve a variety of considerations, and resultant investigations. For instance, the ship may be firmly aground and have suffered significant damage, but may possibly be refloated and removed. The decision of whether the ship is in fact a CTL at this stage may involve enquiries of ship repairers and towage companies (as to the cost of removal and repair) and of ship brokers (as to the value of such a ship if repaired). These enquiries may take some time to conduct, and for decisions to be made upon them. As noted, there may be other enquiries that underwriters will be making, eg about the terms of the policy, and any breaches, non-disclosures or misrepresentations made by the insured shipowner.

Apparently, in practice, these underwriters' decisions may take some time. It might take at least four weeks if the ship is aground at a remote location—often considerably longer.[1402] Meanwhile the shipowner, Clubs and States may be wanting to take wreck removal operations. From the shipowner's perspective, any premature actions might cause a problem with the CTL claim. If, for instance, the actions were taken to cut away part of the ship, so that it could be refloated, the underwriters might later claim that this action was technically wrong and that all or part of the vessel might have been completely saved. This might raise difficult issues of causation or quantification of loss.

A more recent pressure for insurers is the introduction of Part IVA in the Insurance Act 2015[1403] which has created in s 13A a new implied term in every contract of insurance that insurers pay valid claims within a "reasonable time". This includes a reasonable time to "investigate and assess the claim". An assessment of what is a "reasonable time" will depend on many varied circumstances but the Act provides a non-exhaustive list of factors including (a) the type of insurance; (b) the size and complexity of the claim; (c) compliance with any relevant statutory or regulatory rules or guidance; and (d) factors outside the insurer's control.[1404] In the event of a shipwreck, many examples show that there may be great uncertainty in CTL cases in working out what residual value a ship might have, eg whether it is financially worth repairing.[1405] It may be hard for a claimant insured to prove that there was an unreasonable delay while CTL investigations are taking place. But once the insurer has effectively withdrawn from salvage operations (eg through communications with salvors, Club and Affected State) it may be obvious that the ship is a total loss. Thereafter, claims payment might only depend on other matters (eg as to values or wilful misconduct allegations).

In practice, therefore, there is often a somewhat uncertain transition from salvage to wreck removal that may also represent a transition between the risks and tasks assumed by H&M insurers and the Clubs.[1406]

1401 *The WD Fairway* [2009] 2 Lloyd's Rep 191 [6].

1402 See eg *The M/V Brillante Virtuoso* [2015] 1 Lloyd's Rep 651. There may also be disputes between assured and insurer as to the residual value of the hull, even where a CTL has been agreed: see eg *The WD Fairway (No 3)* [2009] 2 Lloyd's Rep 420 [55].

1403 As amended by the Enterprise Act 2016 as from 4 May 2017.

1404 S 13A(3)(a).

1405 Quotations from shipyards as to the cost of repair may vary greatly: see eg *The Renos* [2018] 1 Lloyd's Rep 285 (CA) [2019] 2 LLoyd's Rep 78 (SC).

1406 These operational and contractual issues are addressed in more detail in Chapter 12.

2.9.6 Insurance cover for liabilities

2.9.6(a) Availability of P&I Club cover for casualties

P&I cover for liabilities developed in the 19th century to deal with the increasing risks caused by the navigation of steamships, in particular passenger ships.[1407] Since then, the P&I Clubs have played an increasingly important role both in international law and commercially. International conventions have been drafted taking into account the role of P&I Clubs.[1408] Regional legislation regulation has also sought to impose minimum insurance standards.[1409] The 13 members of the International Group of P&I Clubs[1410] are said to provide indemnity cover for the liabilities[1411] of owners (and many charterers) of the majority[1412] of the world's ocean-going fleets, but such cover could be offered by any insurance company. Some insurers[1413] may offer liability cover as part of a total insurance package (ie including H&M cover); this may make claims settlement more straightforward.[1414] Some companies[1415] may offer liability cover as a fixed premium product, and this is quite common for small ships such as fishing vessels. Fixed premium insurance companies may not be quite so flexible as International Group Clubs when covering claims, eg for wreck removal. Club boards retain significant discretionary powers[1416] to pay certain claims and the International Group Clubs have generally assumed responsible political positions with States.[1417]

Clubs provide cover on a mutual, sharing basis, where shipowner members usually are asked to pay an initial "call" (ie estimated pro rata payment request, like a premium) at the start of the policy year at noon GMT on 20 February.[1418] If the Club receives an unexpectedly large number of claims from all members, there will be a "supplementary call". The professional managers of the Clubs will try to ensure that such supplementary calls are

---

1407 See 2.9; S Hazelwood, D Semark, *P&I Clubs: Law and Practice* (4th ed, Informa, 2010) [*Hazelwood & Semark*], Chapter 1; *Arnould*, 103–113.

1408 Eg the conventions dealing with pollution (see 2.6), limitation of liability (see 2.5), salvage (see 2.7), carriage of passengers (see 2.3) and wreck removal (see 10.8).

1409 See eg Directive 2009/20/EC of the European Parliament and of the Council of 23rd April 2009 on the insurance of shipowners for maritime claims O.J. L. 131/128 (28 May 2009), part of the *Erika* package of reforms (see 1.2.2(a)), which covers matters such as the acceptance of insurance certificates. In the UK, general powers to require compulsory insurance are found in the MSA 1995 s 192A, introduced s 16 of the MSMSA 1997: see *Gaskell, MSMSA 1997*, 28/72–28/78; also the Merchant Shipping (Compulsory Insurance of Shipowners for Maritime Claims) Regulations 2012 (SI 2012/2267).

1410 https://www.igpandi.org.

1411 Clubs also provide proactive assistance under "freight demurrage and defence" (FDD) cover, eg to recover freight or salvage from cargo owners. They may also offer war risk cover, excluded from the H&M policy.

1412 Figures well in excess of about 90% are often quoted, but the exact number will vary depending on the type of craft: see www.igpandi.org/about. For tankers the figure may be as high as 95% or more, as such ships will usually need Club cover to provide 'Blue Cards' to enable them to obtain insurance certificates from States, eg for the CLC 1992 (see 2.6.2(a)), or WRC 2007 (see 10.8.3).

1413 See eg the Swedish Club's *Rules for P&I Insurance 2018/2019*, r 11.

1414 See the *Rena* where the Swedish Club covered both H&M and liabilities: 1.2.4(a).

1415 Some Clubs may offer the option of a fixed premium policy, see eg *Gard Rules for Ships 2018* [*Gard Rules 2018*], r 10(2).

1416 See the omnibus clause, 2.9.6(b), and 10.8.5(d).

1417 Eg through the IMO and relationships built up with particular States eg through MOUs: see 10.8.6.

1418 Historically the date when the Baltic Sea is supposed to thaw, allowing timber trading ships to sail from Russia.

rare or minimised. Large casualties with high claims payments can have a major effect on a Club's need to make such calls, even when such claims are spread between International Group members and then reinsured. This is why high wreck removal claims are such a concern.[1419]

The nature and content of such liability cover could vary greatly, but the rules of the major P&I Clubs in the International Group are broadly similar, which is not surprising given their pooling and reinsurance arrangements.[1420] This book will concentrate on the role of the P&I Clubs.[1421] It is not possible to provide a detailed analysis of Club cover,[1422] but in the context of wreck there are really two broad perspectives about the role of the Clubs. The first concerns the cover that it will be offering to all those involved in a casualty (ie relevant to a wreck in the broadest sense). The second concerns specific cover for wreck removal, including that under the WRC 2007.[1423]

The MIA 1906 applies generally to mutual insurance, but this allows modification by the terms of the Club Rules.[1424] Club Rules are freely available on the web.[1425]

2.9.6(b) Typical P&I Club cover for casualties[1426]

Most Club Rules cover a "mixed bag of risks that has developed in an unplanned empirical and piecemeal fashion",[1427] but will allow a shipowner to have cover for a huge variety of liabilities. These will include those arising from most marine casualties leading to shipwreck. They will include personal injury, death and repatriation claims from seafarers;[1428] passenger death and injury claims;[1429] collision liabilities[1430] and

---

1419 See 1.4.
1420 For details of reinsurance cover, see 10.8.6.
1421 In places, in order to avoid repetition, it will be more convenient to refer to liability cover being provided by a "Club" as shorthand for any "liability insurer", but the role of other providers should not be ignored.
1422 See *Hazelwood & Semark*, Chaps 9–12; E Gold, *Gard Handbook on P&I Insurance* (5th ed., 2002); also the Swedish Club's helpful guidelines as to the practical application of its rules, Swedish Club, *P&I Rules and Exceptions 2012* (3rd ed., 2012) [*Swedish Club P&I Guidelines 2012*].
1423 See 2.9.6(d).
1424 See MIA 1906 s 85(3)–(4). In practice the Club Rules are fairly exhaustive, but note the effect of the s 55(3) wilful misconduct defence: 2.9.6(b) and 10.8.4(d).
1425 See eg UK P&I Club *Rules and Articles 2018* [*UK Club Rules 2018*]; Standard Club, *P&I and Defence Rules and Correspondents 2018/19; Gard Rules 2018*; Swedish Club, *Rules for P&I Insurance 2018/2019.*.
1426 See *Hazelwood & Semark*, Chaps 9 and 10.
1427 *Hazelwood & Semark*, 124. Most Rules will have a definitions clause that must be consulted as it often expands or restricts the apparent cover: see eg Standard Club, *P&I Rules* r 2 (Definitions).
1428 See 2.9.6(e).
1429 Not all Clubs are as keen on insuring passenger ships as others. The Standard Club's *P&I Rules 2018/19* include passenger claims within r 3. The *UK Club Rules 2018* deal with passenger ships in a separate r 4, Section 3, simply indicating that passenger claims may be insured on terms and conditions as may be agreed by the Club. The Clubs apply an aggregate policy limit of US$2 billion for one event for liability to passengers and US$3 billion to passengers and seafarers together: see eg *UK Club Rules 2018* r 5Biii; *Gard Rules 2018* App IV. See also 2.3.5.
1430 Only to the extent that these are not covered by the RDC under the H&M policy: see 2.9.2(b) and eg *UK Club Rules 2018*, r 2, Section 10 cf.

damage to other property generally;[1431] cargo liabilities;[1432] pollution liabilities;[1433] and towage.[1434]

Most of the Rules are hedged around with many exceptions and restrictions, and these may vary greatly. International Group Clubs generally exclude some key provisions of the Insurance Act 2015, eg so as to allow the Club to avoid the policy for member breaches of fair presentation (or utmost good faith) or of a warranty—even if the breach could not have increased the risk of loss.[1435] Rights to terminate the cover could therefore arise from a variety of circumstances,[1436] eg through non-compliance with the Club's recommendations after a ship survey,[1437] or for failing to give notice that the ship has returned from lay-up.[1438] Other typical exclusions might relate to potential liability of the shipowner to cargo interests after a wreck, eg if there has been a deviation that has led to the shipowner losing defences or rights under the carriage contract.[1439] War risks will normally be excluded unless there is separate cover agreed,[1440] and there is not normally cover for liabilities for the carriage of nuclear substances.[1441] In addition, claims are not recoverable if the liability is incurred owing to the privity or wilful misconduct of the insured.[1442] The express exclusion for this may go further than that applied by s 55(2) of the MIA 1906,[1443] eg by an expansive definition[1444] or by making the decision about whether the misconduct occurred subject to the opinion of the Club's board.[1445]

1431 Including damage to fixed or floating property such as pipelines or jetties. See also 2.4.1.

1432 Including liability not only for the loss of the cargo (including from unseaworthiness) but also eg the disposal of damaged or sound cargo from a damaged ship: see 2.1.1 and eg *UK Club Rules 2018* r 2, Section 17.

1433 Eg for liabilities caused through the discharge or escape of oil or other substances, including liability for loss, damage or contamination and costs of reasonable measures to minimise pollution; costs or liabilities incurred as a result of compliance with State pollution intervention powers (but not including normal salvage operations and that the costs are not recoverable under the H&M policy): see eg *UK Club Rules 2018* r 2, Section 12 (as limited by r 5B to US$1 billion for 2018); also 2.6, 4.8.3, 5.4, 2.9.2(b).

1434 This would typically cover liability arising out of ordinary towage, eg where ship and tug are wrecked while entering a port. Where there is a non-customary towage, eg after a wrecked hull is raised, the terms will have to be agreed with the Club, but LOF, SCOPIC and knock for knock towage contracts (eg Towhire or the UK Standard Towing Conditions) would normally be covered: see 13.5 and eg *UK Club Rules 2018* r 2, Section 13; also 12.1.2(c).

1435 See eg the Standard Club's *P&I Rules 2018/19* r 1.5.2, which excludes ss 8, 10, 11 13, 13A and 14. This rule also allows for termination for fraud. Note that these policy exclusions would not apply where the Club is directly liable through issuing a certificate under one of the IMO conventions, eg the WRC 2007: see eg 10.8.4.

1436 Note that there might be a separate obligation to notify H&M insurers or mortgagees if a policy is terminated: see 2.9.2(d).

1437 See eg *UK Club Rules 2018* r 5Q.

1438 See eg *UK Club Rules 2018* r 5R.

1439 See eg the Standard Club's *P&I Rules 2018/19* r 3.13, exclusion (2).

1440 See eg the *UK Club Rules 2018* r 5E and the War Risks P&I Excess Cover Clause; for wreck removal claims, r 5E matches the exclusion in the WRC 2007 Art 10(a), see 10.3. See also M Miller, *Marine War Risks* (3rd ed, Informa, 2005).

1441 *De la Rue & Anderson*, 748, eg the Standard Club's *P&I Rules 2018/19* r 4.4.

1442 See 10.8.4(e).

1443 See also 2.9.2(a) and 10.8.4(d).

1444 The Standard Club's *P&I Rules 2018/19* r 6.19 refers to "privity or wilful misconduct", and defines the latter in r 26 as "an act intentionally done or a deliberate omission by an insured party with knowledge that the performance or omission will probably result in injury or loss, or an act done or omitted in such a way as to allow an inference of a reckless disregard for the probable consequences"; ie virtually identical to the test for breaking limits in the LLMC Art 4: 2.5.7; and see 10.8.4(d).

1445 See Standard Club's *P&I Rules 2018/19* r 6.19; and see 10.8.4(c).

The extent to which a Club can rely on defences, eg to terminate cover, will be restricted when there is direct liability under one of the IMO liability regimes, such as the WRC 2007.[1446]

One of the most controversial aspects of Club cover is that for fines imposed on the shipowner,[1447] in particular for the accidental discharge or escape of oil or other substances.[1448] There may also be a discretionary cover for any fine, if the owner took reasonable steps to avoid the event giving rise to the fine.[1449] The cover may extend to seafarers if the shipowner is legally obliged to reimburse them.[1450] In order to try to restrict States from adding fines to damages so as to circumvent limits, the Rules may provide that the overall Club oil pollution exposure aggregates fines and damages.[1451] It might be thought that, even with deductibles,[1452] such protection undermines the deterrent effect of any penalty imposed or threatened.[1453] Although the Club may decline to pay a fine on the general grounds of illegality, the continued existence and use of the cover suggests that actually paying such fines may not be illegal in most legal systems.[1454]

In addition to cover for shipowners, most Clubs offer optional insurance cover for others involved in a casualty, including charterers.[1455] This cover may be very important where the charterer owes contractual duties to the shipowner to indemnify the latter for losses incurred by the shipowner, including loss of or damage to the entered ship.[1456]

Finally, most Clubs have an "omnibus" clause, which is a form of catch-all discretionary provision whereby the board of the Club (itself consisting of shipowner members) may decide to cover a particular liability.[1457] A Club would only apply any discretion to reimburse after all litigation against the member has been concluded.[1458]

1446 See eg the WRC 2007 Art 12(10); and see 10.8.4.

1447 See *Hazelwood & Semark*, 169–175.

1448 See eg *UK Club Rules 2018* r 2 Section 22E, and r 44 (definition). The cover does not apply when the fine arose from construction or equipment provisions of MARPOL 1973/78, but would apparently apply to operational violations of MARPOL.

1449 See eg *UK Club Rules 2018* r 2, Section 22F and 2.5.4(b); and see 2.6.2(a).

1450 See *UK Club Rules 2018* r 2, Section 22A; and see 2.2.2.

1451 See eg *UK Club Rules 2018* r 2 Section 22 (additional note referring to the limit in r 5B).

1452 See *Hazelwood & Semark*, 170.

1453 The *Donaldson Report* (paras 18.24–18.25) noted the criticism while acknowledging that the matter was more complex than might appear.

1454 An amendment at the Report Stage of the Merchant Shipping and Maritime Security Bill 1997 in the Lords proposed that the practice be made illegal, but it was later withdrawn. At the 75th Session of the IMO Legal Committee in April 1997, eight governments, including the UK, presented a paper advocating the discontinuation of the practice of including in P&I Club insurance cover fines for illegal discharges under MARPOL, but the proposal does not seem to have gone further: see LEG/75/10/1, 4 March 1997, LEG/75/12.

1455 See eg *UK Club Rules 2018* r 4, Section 1 (and Addendum for Charterers, 130–131). Also *Hazelwood & Semark*, Chapter 25.

1456 The charterer may not be able to limit liability for damage to the ship itself (see 2.5.5(b), 2.5.4(d)), but the insurance cover for the charterer may well be limited in amount, either to the deemed limit of liability of the ship under the LLMC, or to a maximum amount (eg $300 million): see *Hazelwood & Semark*, 377–378, Chapter 25.

1457 See eg r 3.20 of the Standard Club's *P&I Rules 2018/19*; also *Hazelwood & Semark*, 191–193 and 10.8.5(d).

1458 See, eg the Standard Club, "Discretionary Claims: An Overview", June 2018.

It is typical to find a clause providing for the governing law of the policy[1459] and for all disputes to be subject to arbitration.[1460] These choices may be significant for direct action wreck claims against the Clubs under national law.[1461]

2.9.6(c) 'Pay to be paid' clause

The 'pay to be paid' clause[1462] is found in the Rules of most P&I Clubs, albeit worded differently in each. The traditional wording is in the form of a pre-condition to cover, eg the *UK Club Rules 2018*, rule 5A:

> ***Payment first by the Owner***
>
> Unless the Directors in their discretion otherwise decide, it is a condition precedent of an Owner's right to recover from the funds of the Association in respect of any liabilities, costs or expenses that he shall first have discharged or paid the same out of funds belonging to him unconditionally and not by way of loan or otherwise.[1463]

It was held in the House of Lords in *The Fanti*[1464] litigation that, where the insurance policy is governed by English law,[1465] the rule is a pre-condition of the insurer's liability.[1466] The commercial significance of the 'pay to be paid' clause is that the Clubs have used it to refuse to pay claimants directly for maritime claims, eg where the insured owner is insolvent and has not paid the claim itself.[1467] In practice, the Clubs may sometimes use their discretion to pay claims directly to third parties even where the shipowner has not paid first.[1468] This would only be done on an ad hoc basis, eg if a Club has negotiated an out-of-court settlement of a large claim and part of the agreement is that settlement amounts are paid directly (sometimes urgently) by the Club.[1469]

1459 Eg English law for UK Clubs, eg *UK Club Rules 2018* r 42; and eg Norwegian Law in r 90 of the *Gard Rules 2018*, and Swedish law in the Swedish Club's *Rules for P&I Insurance 2018/2019* rr 2 and 18.

1460 Eg London arbitration in the *UK Club Rules 2018* r 40C, and Oslo arbitration in the *Gard Rules 2018* r 9.

1461 See 2.9.6(c) (fn 1479).

1462 See *Hazelwood & Semark*, Chapter 20; Swedish Club, *P&I Rules and Exception 2012*, 33–35.

1463 Rule 2 Section 4 contains an exception in relation to liabilities to crew under the Maritime Labour Convention 2006: see also 2.2.3. Other UK Clubs have similar clauses: eg Standard Club's *P&I Rules 2018/19* rr 16.5, 16.16.1. Gard's *Rules for Ships 2018* r 87 has a similar condition precedent pay first clause, with an MLC 1996 exception. The Swedish Club's *Rules for P&I Insurance 2018/2019* r 2 characterises the pay to be paid clause as part of the description (or "nature") of cover, rather than an exception or pre-condition.

1464 *Firma C-Trade SA v Newcastle Protection and Indemnity Association (The Fanti); Socony Mobil Oil Co Inc v West of England Shipowners Mutual Insurance Association (London) Limited (No 2) (The Padre Island)* [1991] 2 AC 1, [1990] 2 Lloyd's Rep 191.

1465 Eg under the *UK Club Rules 2018* r 42. Under the *Swedish Club Rules 2018/2019* r 18, disputes are to be settled under Swedish law with arbitration.

1466 Nor can the *claimant* satisfy the condition by incurring expenditure itself (ie 'paying first') and then claiming from the Club.

1467 The clause is regarded as particularly important to Clubs because they have traditionally offered cover to members without a policy limit, although there are now limits for pollution and passenger claims: for Club reinsurance cover see 10.8.6. The mutuality of membership also means that members need to be able to rely on the financial probity of other members.

1468 *Swedish Club P&I Guidelines 2012*, 34. This discretionary payment will probably require the shipowner to pay any deductible to the Club. See also *Hazelwood & Semark*, 336–338.

1469 It is not known if this has happened in some of the major wreck claims, such as *Rena* and *Costa Concordia*.

But the underlying effect of the clause is that where the owner is a single ship company whose only asset is wrecked, claimants (such as cargo owners) may have difficulty in claiming directly against the insurer in the UK. The same difficulty would in theory apply to other third party claimants after a wreck, eg pollution claimants, unless they are given additional rights by statute. The IMO liability conventions[1470] do so through compulsory insurance with direct action against the insurer that has provided insurance to enable a State to issue a convention certificate.[1471] Wreck removal claimants could be met by the 'pay to be paid' rule, unless States have adopted the WRC 2007 with its direct action provisions.[1472]

Many States have 'consumer protection' provisions allowing direct action against an insurer where the insured is insolvent, and restricting technical insurer defences. In the UK, it was held in *The Fanti* that the Third Parties (Rights Against Insurers) Act 1930 would not to apply where there was a 'pay to be paid' clause, as there never *was* a liability of the insurer which could be accessed by a claimant. It followed that no action could be brought against the Club where the shipowner was insolvent; and by definition, the insolvent shipowner will not pay the claim itself. The Third Parties (Rights Against Insurers) Act 2010[1473] produced reforms that state clearly in s 9(5) that "rights are not subject to a condition requiring the prior discharge by the insured of the insured's liability to the third party". But this is subject to s 9(6), which states that "[i]n the case of a contract of marine insurance, subsection (5) applies only to the extent that the liability of the insured is a liability in respect of death or personal injury". In other words, apart from death or injury claims,[1474] there has been no change to the 'pay to be paid' rule as it affects the various maritime claims after a wreck—such as cargo claims, wreck removal[1475] or pollution claims not governed by the direct action provisions of the IMO conventions.[1476]

This UK approach to the 'pay to be paid' rule will not necessarily be followed in all jurisdictions,[1477] where State national direct action legislation may treat the clause as an exception in the policy that can be disregarded.[1478] The claimant may then obtain judgment

---

1470 Eg the CLC 1992 (2.6.2(a)), the Bunkers Convention 2001 (2.6.3), the HNSC 2010 (2.6.4), the Athens Convention 2002 (2.3.5), the WRC 2007 (10.8). See also the requirements of the Maritime Labour Convention 2006, 2.2.3.

1471 The Club will issue a 'Blue Card' addressed to a State confirming that an owner has in place insurance to cover convention liabilities. It thereby accepts that it will be liable to pay claims directly: see eg *UK Club Rules 2018* r 5U.

1472 See 10.8.4.

1473 The 2010 Act entered fully into force on 1 August 2016 (see SI 2016/550), but does not apply to prior insolvencies or liabilities: see generally *Arnould*, 289–306.

1474 See 2.3.5.

1475 Note that the new Part 9A of the MSA 1995 disapplies the Third Party Rights legislation in respect of wreck removal certificates: see 11.3.4(b).

1476 Eg where there is a claim against the Club in a State not party to one of the conventions, or as (with HNS claim) where the relevant convention is not yet in force internationally. The personal injury and death exception in s 9(6) was drafted to protect the most vulnerable individuals (rather than companies), such as passengers and crew, and at a time when (i) it was not clear if the Athens Convention 2002 would enter into force and (ii) the MLC 2006 had not yet been agreed: see also 2.2.3.

1477 See *Swedish Club P&I Guidelines 2012*, 33–34.

1478 Ie the clause may not be regarded as a pre-condition, but against public policy: see eg *Shipowners' Mutual Protection and Indemnity Association (Luxembourg) v Containerships Denizcilik Nakliyat Ve Ticaret A.S. (The Yusuf Cepnioglu)* [2015] EWHC 258 (Comm), [2015] 1 Lloyd's Rep 267, [87]. Cf the Swedish Club's characterisation of the pay to be paid clause as part of the description of cover rather than an exception or pre-condition.

against the insurer in that jurisdiction and seek to enforce the judgment where the insurer has assets.[1479] The Club may try to prevent such action by the use of an anti-suit injunction, relying, eg on an English arbitration clause in the Club Rules.[1480] *The Prestige No 2*[1481] was a decision arising out of the 2002 sinking of the tanker *Prestige*.[1482] France and Spain tried to avoid the shipowner's CLC limit of liability[1483] by suing a UK-based Club under Spanish national direct action legislation, even though the Club was entitled to a cap on its *own* direct liability under the CLC insurance it had provided. The Club sought to resist such enforcement by obtaining a UK arbitration award under the Club Rules, which declared that it was not liable. It succeeded in obtaining an award based on the 'pay to be paid' clause, and the Court of Appeal agreed to enforce that as a judgment against the French and Spanish States.[1484] The effectiveness of such a defence may depend on whether the claim is characterised as one under the insurance contract, or an independent statutory claim. In the former case, the arbitration clause would apply (and defeat the claim, given that English law was the governing law);[1485] in the latter case, the foreign law would provide an independent right of recovery, to which the contractual arbitration clause would not apply.[1486]

The effectiveness of an English court jurisdiction clause was undermined in the EU by *Assens Havn v Navigators Management (UK) Ltd*,[1487] where the CJEU (8th Chamber) held that a marine liability insurer (which was not a Club) could not rely on an exclusive English jurisdiction clause in its marine liability policy when sued in another EU State (Denmark) under the latter's direct action provisions by a third party claimant (which had been faced by an insolvent assured). The result, although somewhat surprising, is consistent with the type of expansive 'pro-victim' approach taken by EU courts in relation to its

---

1479 National direct action statutes may also be used as a means to avoid the shipowner's limit of liability. The LLMC Art 1(6) prevents this by allowing the insurer to limit: see 2.5.3 and cf 10.8.5. States not party to the LLMC may find that the insurance cover is limited to an amount to which the shipowner would have been entitled to limit: see eg Swedish Club, *Rules for P&I Insurance 2018/2019* r 2 and *Swedish Club P&I Guidelines 2012*, 37.

1480 *Shipowners' Mutual Protection and Indemnity Association (Luxembourg) v Containerships Denizcilik Nakliyat VE Ticaret AS (The Yusuf Cepnioglu)* [2016] 1 Lloyd's Rep 641, a case involving Turkey. Such actions may not be possible to prevent claims in other EU states because of EU legislation on jurisdiction and judgments: see *Allianz SpA and Generali Assicurazioni Generali SpA v West Tankers Inc (The Front Comor)* (Case C-185/07) [2009] 1 AC 1138, and now Brussels Regulation I Recast.

1481 *The London Steamship Owners' Mutual Insurance Association Ltd v The Kingdom of Spain & Anor (The Prestige No 2)* [2015] EWCA Civ 333, [2015] 2 Lloyd's Rep 33.

1482 See 1.2.2(a) for the Spanish liability proceedings.

1483 In part by relying on a possible criminal conviction of the master. Under the CLC Art V(2), the shipowner's limit could only be broken if there was deliberate or reckless conduct on behalf of the shipowning company: see also 2.6.2(a), 2.5.7.

1484 Who were also held bound by the arbitration clause between the shipowner and Club.

1485 See eg *Through Transport Mutual Insurance Association (Eurasia) Ltd v New India Assurance Co. Ltd (The Hari Blum No 1)* [2003] EWHC 3158 (Comm), [2004] 1 Lloyd's Rep 206, [2005] 1 Lloyd's Rep 67, where an arbitration clause has been held to be binding on a third party under the Finnish direct action provisions: see also H Lund, "Shipwrecks in National and International Law – Insurance Issues and Direct Actions", in *Shipwreck in International and National Law*, 227–228.

1486 *The Yusuf Cepnioglu* [2016] 1 Lloyd's Rep 641 [1], although the court found that a 'pay to be paid' clause was unenforceable in Turkey the nature of the third party claimant's right was characterised as essentially contractual [19–21].

1487 Case C-368/16 (CJEU, 13 July 2017), [2018] Lloyd's Rep IR 10.

insurance jurisdiction rules.[1488] The case did not directly concern arbitration clauses[1489] of the type that would apply in relation to P&I Club 'pay to be paid' clauses, nor choice of law clauses.[1490] The resolution of these issues is beyond this book,[1491] but is another example of where EU law may affect wreck claims.[1492]

The *Prestige* litigation seems likely to go further, and there are difficult issues of sovereign immunity, but it illustrates a number of points that may be relevant after a shipwreck. First, under existing law, an ordinary claimant (or State) may face considerable difficulties and delays if it tries to sue a Club (or liability insurer) directly, outside of the IMO liability regimes. Secondly, while the attempts by the States to bypass the CLC limits by bringing a form of parallel action may be outside the spirit (or the provisions) of the CLC,[1493] the *Prestige* action shows that coastal States dissatisfied with the caps on liability of the insurer under an IMO convention will go to great lengths to avoid them.[1494] Thirdly, English law preferences for the strict legal rights of insurers (often with UK links) over third party claimants may not be followed in many States, particularly where EU law applies.

The existence of the 'pay to be paid' clause, like limitation of liability, is part of the tactical armoury of a P&I Club. There is little evidence about how often the Clubs fall back on the clause in practice, but perhaps it is sometimes used if a Club feels that the claimant is trying in some way to gain an unfair tactical advantage, eg avoiding limits or choice of forum (or law).[1495]

2.9.6(d) P&I Club cover for wreck liabilities

P&I cover extends to liabilities relating to wreck generally, so the normal collision damage cover would usually extend to salvage or wreck removal costs incurred by another ship with which the entered ship is in collision.[1496] The owners of professional salvage and wreck removal vessels would expect to have their own P&I cover for risks involving their vessels and personnel.[1497] Clubs will normally exclude cover for liability to pay any salvage reward,[1498] as this is usually covered in the H&M and cargo policies.[1499] However, the Clubs

---

1488 See *Arnould*, 112, for a suggestion that insurers might seek to rely on jurisdiction clauses in non-EU States.
1489 See the Brussels Regulation I Recast Art 1.2(d) and recital 12.
1490 See the Rome II Regulation, Arts 14(1) and 18. In the *Assens Havn v Navigators* case, the Danish Supreme Court subsequently applied Danish law as the one most closely connected to the claim, despite the insurance policy being governed by English law: see G Gjelsten, H Steen, "Jurisdiction Clauses and Choice of Law in Direct Actions" (4 December 2017), www.wr.no/aktuelt/publications/so-update/jurisdiction-clauses-and--choice-of-law-in-direct-actions/.
1491 See also *Arnould*, Chapter 5, especially 132–133.
1492 Cf 2.5.9(e) and Chapter 14.
1493 See 14.6.3 on the use of the EU waste liability rules.
1494 Cf 2.5.9, also the insurance 'cap' under the WRC 2007, 10.8.5.
1495 In a similar way to underwriters who suspected fraud but could not prove it: see 2.9.1 (fn 1194).
1496 See eg the Standard Club's *P&I Rules 2018/19* r 3.7. For recourse claims and limitation, see eg 2.5.4.
1497 Apart from where the saving of life is involved, vessels conducting salvage or wreck removal themselves may be excluded from general cover, but covered by a special agreement: see eg *UK Club Rules 2018* r 5H. Likewise if a ship is used for waste disposal operations and a claim arises out of them: see r 5H(iv) and 14.6.
1498 Eg under the Salvage Convention 1989 Art 13: see 2.7 and eg the Standard Club's *P&I Rules 2018/19* r 5.9.
1499 See 2.9.2(b), 2.9.3(c).

will provide cover for special compensation to the salvor.[1500] Likewise the Clubs would not normally cover general average.[1501]

More specifically, there has been long-standing Club cover for wreck raising and removal.[1502] Although the wording of terms may differ between Clubs, there is a degree of commonality in them. A typical example of Club cover is found in the Standard Club's *P&I Rules 2018/19* r 3.11:

> 3.11.1 Liabilities for or incidental to the raising, removal, destruction, lighting or marking of the wreck of the ship. The value of the wreck and all stores and materials saved must be deducted from any reimbursement and only the balance is recoverable.
> 3.11.2 Liabilities resulting from the actual or attempted raising, removal or destruction of the wreck of the ship, cargo or any other property on board.
> 3.11.3 Liabilities resulting from the presence or involuntary shifting of the wreck of the ship, cargo or any other property on board caused by the casualty which led to the loss of the ship, cargo or any other property on board. Unless the board otherwise determines, a member is not entitled to be reimbursed by the club in respect of any liability incurred more than two years after the ship, cargo or any other property on board became a wreck.
> 3.11.4 Liabilities for or incidental to the raising, removal, destruction or disposal of cargo or any other property which is being, or has been, carried on the ship. The value of all cargo or any other property saved accruing to the member must be deducted from any reimbursement and only the balance is recoverable.
>
> **Exclusions to rule 3.11**
>
> (1) There shall be no recovery if the member has, without the agreement of the managers, transferred his interest in the wreck other than by abandonment, at any time after the ship became a wreck.
> (2) There shall be no recovery unless the raising, removal, destruction, lighting or marking of the wreck, or the raising, removal, destruction or disposal of cargo or any other property, was compulsory by law or was undertaken with the agreement of the managers.
> (3) Unless the board otherwise determines, a member is not entitled to reimbursement in respect of any liability unless he took reasonable measures to raise, remove, destroy, light or mark the wreck, or raise, remove, destroy or dispose of cargo or any other property.
> (4) Unless the board otherwise determines, there shall be no recovery unless the member has contracted for removal of the wreck on terms which have been approved by the managers.
> (5) There shall be no recovery in respect of liabilities for or incidental to the raising, removal, destruction, lighting or marking of the wreck of the ship unless the ship became a wreck as a result of a casualty. For the purpose of this rule, 'casualty' means collision, stranding, explosion, fire or similar fortuitous event, but excludes any wreck caused by dereliction or neglect.

This extensive type of cover was designed for wreck removal liabilities arising under national provisions,[1503] but can be applied to those under the WRC 2007, albeit with some

---

1500 Under the Salvage Convention 1989 Art 14 or its equivalent in the LOF and SCOPIC: see 2.7.9(b)–(c) and eg *UK Club Rules 2018* r 2, Section 21.

1501 Except in the limited circumstances when not all of this is recoverable under the H&M policy owing to differences between the ship's H&M valuation and its value for salvage or general average: see eg *UK Club Rules 2018* r 2, Section 20. Under Section 19, the shipowner may be able to claim for unrecovered salvage or general average contributions from cargo interests, eg where the shipowner has paid the salvor directly for 100% of its claim: and see 2.7.7(b), 2.7.8, 2.8.2.

1502 See *Hazelwood & Semark*, 178–179.

1503 See eg 11.1.

care.[1504] It covers raising and removal of the wreck of the hull as well as ancillary (but often expensive) liabilities, such as the lighting or marking of the ship.[1505] Cargo raising and removal is specifically covered, whether that cargo has been lost from a floating ship, or has sunk with the wreck.[1506] The cover extends to the "disposal" of the cargo (and other property on board such as bunkers),[1507] but not (expressly) to the disposal of the ship; only "destruction" of the ship is mentioned.[1508] Waste incineration or disposal operations carried out by the ship itself can be excluded,[1509] eg where attempts are made to burn cargo or bunkers on the wreck. If there are doubts about whether any particular expenses are covered, eg for surveyors or other experts, they may fall within the sue and labour provision, r 3.19. This would cover extraordinary costs and expenses after a casualty, but does need approval of the Club.

Wreck removal operations may themselves result in liabilities, eg where damage is caused to the vessels of wreck removal contractors, or where there is a fire or explosion causing death and property damage; these should be covered.[1510] The Club may cover the member for the negligence of wreck removal contractors, provided that the member acted reasonably to employ them (eg by using independent contractors, rather than a related company which was not adequate), and that there are contracts in place under which the contractors carry insurance and accept risks of liability.[1511]

Rule 3.11 makes no specific mention of pollution liabilities arising during a wreck removal operation, eg where oil cargo leaks from a wrecked tanker, or bunkers are spilled from a bulk carrier, or where pesticide in containers is lost into the sea. These may be covered by the word "incidental" in rr 3.11.1 and 3.11.4, or be attempted removal operations in r 3.11.2. More likely they are covered under the general rule covering pollution.[1512] It

---

1504 See below (eg fn 1514), for the effect of the direct liability of insurer under the WRC 2007 Art 12(10) and, more generally, Skuld, "Contractual Wreck Removal" (31 August 2018), www.skuld.com/topics/legal/pi-and-defence/contractual-wreck-removal/.

1505 Rule 3.11.2. There is no specific mention of *"locating"* the wreck, which is one of the specific liabilities under the WRC 2007 Art 10: and see 10.2.1, 10.5.6. Yet the WRC 2007 treats "locating" (in Art 7) separately from "Marking" (in Art 8). It may be arguable that the insurance wording (pre-dating the convention) could be interpreted so that the costs of "locating" are "incidental" expenses to the marking of a wreck, but the omission is curious. It would not prevent the insurer being directly liable in respect of a certificate covering WRC 2007 liabilities: see 10.8.4.

1506 Rule 3.11.4 and see 10.6. Cf the question about the interpretation of the LLMC Art 2(1)(d) and (e): see 2.5.4(c).

1507 See r 3.11.4. See also r 3.13.12(1) dealing with cargo liabilities and covering extra costs in disposing of damaged or worthless cargo if those costs cannot be recovered from, eg the cargo owner or charterer. This rule is more relevant to ordinary carriage contracts where the cargo interests are insolvent or uncommunicative.

1508 Cf rr 3.11.1 and 3.11.4 and see fn 1518. Destruction might more naturally refer to destruction in situ or at sea rather than recycling: see 14.5 and 14.6. If the ultimate "disposal" of the wreck is not covered, there may be problems about defining when a wreck removal operation comes to an end, even under the WRC 2007: see 10.2.8, 13.6.5(g), 14.7.

1509 See r 5.16.

1510 Rule 3.11.2.

1511 S Kendall-Marsden, U O'Donnell, "Major Casualty Management: Wreck Removal and Salvage" (Standard Club, August 2018) [*Kendall-Marsden & O'Donnell*], 2: www.standard-club.com/media/2767807/major-casualty-management-wreck-removal-and-salvage.pdf.

1512 Rule 3.8 in the Standard Club's *P&I Rules 2018/19*. The Club may well have direct liability to a pollution claimant for the full extent of any pollution liability arising eg under the CLC 1992 (see 2.6.2(a)), Bunkers Convention 2001 (see 2.6.3) or the HNSC 2010 (see 2.6.4) when in force.

may take some time to remove a wreck, or that removal may not be possible. If some time after the wreck the hull or cargo shifts it may become an obstruction to navigation (risking damage to other ships) or even an environmental or cultural threat.[1513] These are covered within r 3.11.3, although there is a time limit on the cover of two years (unless the Club agrees otherwise).[1514]

Traditionally, the Clubs have imposed a number of restrictions on wreck cover, and the exclusions to r 3.11 are fairly typical. These have been summarised by a leading industry expert: "The most important provisos to this aspect of P&I club cover are that the wreck must have arisen out of a casualty (and not mere neglect), there must be a legal obligation on the member to remove the wreck (voluntary wreck removal is not covered) and the member cannot recover costs if they have transferred their interest in the wreck to a third party without the club's consent (other than by abandonment)".[1515]

These principles follow from the wording of Club rules and industry practice, but some care is needed with specific rules when the compulsory insurance provisions of the WRC 2007 apply. Whether the wording of the particular wreck removal rule fully covers a ship-owner for WRC 2007 liabilities is in a sense irrelevant if the Club has issued a policy and presented a Blue Card enabling a Contracting State to issue a WRC 2007 certificate, thereby creating a direct liability for the Club under the WRC 2007 Art 12(10).[1516] The Club becomes directly liable to the claimant Affected State for all liabilities of the registered shipowner *under the Convention*.[1517] Thus, even if the Club rule falls short of the liability under the WRC 2007, the insurer will still be directly liable.[1518] Further, the only policy defence that the insurer can rely on is wilful misconduct.[1519] Still, the Club would not expect to respond unless there was a wreck removal order issued by the relevant State.[1520] While the WRC 2007 contemplates the issuing of a type of wreck removal notice under

---

1513 Cf the *Rena*, 1.2.4 and 8.2.2.

1514 This is an understandable provision to prevent costs in relation to ships long lost, but it does not map on to the three- or six-year time limit of the WRC 2007 Art 13 (see 10.4), nor eg the potentially longer limit in respect of the HNSC 2010 when in force. The Swedish Club, r 7 section 5 has a three-year limit from the date of the insurance ceasing. Again, a Club would be liable under the direct action provision in the WRC 2007 Art 12(10) for the full period under the convention: see 10.8.

1515 S Kendall-Marsden, "Wreck removal liability unravelled" International Tug and OSV, May/June 2017 (available at www.standard-club.com/media/2533695/tug-osv-wreck-removal-liability-unravelled.pdf).

1516 For WRC 2007 insurance certificates see 10.8.3.

1517 See 10.8.4.

1518 Eg if the rule does not extend to the costs of "locating" the wreck (see fn 1505), or has a shorter time bar (see fn 1514). The question about whether the cover extends to the disposal of the ship (see fn 1508) raises difficult questions under the WRC 2007 itself: see 10.2.8. Given that Club cover extends to disposal of cargo, it may be that Club practice may also extend to hull disposal, at least to a voyage to a recycling facility: see also 14.5, 14.7.3.

1519 See Art 12(10) and 10.8.4(c) and (d).

1520 *Kendall-Marsden & O'Donnell*, 2; also the MSA 1995 s 255D(2), 11.3.3(c) and 11.3.4(b). It would not expect to respond to commercial pressure: see *Smit Tak Offshore Services v Youell and General Accident Fire & Life Assurance Co PLC* [1992] 1 Lloyd's Rep 154; *Hazelwood & Semark*, 178. Nor would it respond where a charterparty (eg in the offshore sector) requires an owner to remove a wreck (or other material) when this is ordered by the *charterer*: see Skuld, "Contractual Wreck Removal" (31 August 2018). The shipowner may need to obtain additional fixed premium cover for indemnities arising from such terms.

Art 9(6), there are circumstances in Art 9(7) and (8) where a WRC 2007 liability can arise where the Affected State takes action itself to remove the wreck.[1521]

In practice, there is often a difficulty in deciding if a ship is a CTL under the H&M policy[1522] and not yet commercially a wreck (eg where it is still afloat, or abandoned). Clubs have waited to reimburse the costs of removal until the H&M underwriters have formally declined to pay for removal (eg as part of a salvage operation).[1523] Strictly, such a notice is irrelevant where the WRC 2007 applies to create a direct liability of the Club. The transition from salvage to wreck removal is not always easy to delineate,[1524] and the views of the two sets of insurers will form part of the factual basis to decide when a ship is a wreck under the WRC 2007.

2.9.6(e) P&I cover for crew claims
Although most International Group Clubs will provide cover to shipowners for their liabilities in respect of crew injuries and death,[1525] it is apparent that many registered shipowners may not actually engage the crew directly under contracts of employment, but may employ ship managers who may themselves make the contract of employment. Under the management contract, it may be that these managers undertake to procure insurance for crew liabilities.[1526] Sometimes those employed in shops on cruise ships may be employed by a company having a concession from the cruise line and the latter may agree to include the concessionaire in its P&I cover.[1527] It is possible that some fixed premium insurers of such liabilities may not be prepared to issue MLC 2006 certificates.[1528] In such cases the shipowner member may have to ask the Club for discretionary cover to issue the certificates, which may involve the Club in seeking an indemnity from the other insurer.[1529]

Where the shipowner is liable to pay for injury and death of a seafarer, Club cover will normally extend to the payment of damages and compensation, as well as ancillary expenses such as hospital, medical and funeral bills.[1530] Most Club Rules would cover liabilities to crew who lose their personal effects, eg after a wreck.[1531] Likewise, liability to pay wages may be covered generally where seafarers are injured or killed,[1532] or by specific

---

1521 Notice should be given to the flag State and registered owner: see eg Art 9(8) and 10.5.3, 11.3.3(c)(c).

1522 See 2.9.4(b), 2.9.5(b).

1523 *Kendall-Marsden & O'Donnell*, 2; see also *Hazelwood & Semark*, 178; London Arbitration No 4/88 (LMNL 227).

1524 See 12.1.

1525 Note the overall Club limit of cover for passenger and crew claims of US$3 billion: see 2.3.5 and cf 10.8.6.

1526 See eg Shipman 2009 cll 5(b), 7 and 10. Although in theory a shipowner might exclude crew risks in its normal P&I cover, the managers and owners might expect to become joint assureds for crew risks.

1527 See eg *Standard Steamship Owners' Protection and Indemnity Association (Bermuda) Ltd v GIE Vision Bail & Ors* [2004] EWHC (Comm) 2919. Cf *Gard Rules 2018* r 56.

1528 See 2.2.4(e).

1529 See *IG MLC 2006 FAQs*, para 18.

1530 See eg *UK Club Rules 2018* r 2, Section 2. *Gard Rules 2018* rule 27 provides more detail, eg to include the sending home of an urn or coffin.

1531 See eg *UK Club Rules 2018* r 2, Section 5. This would cover clothes, but not cash or valuables (unless the shipowner took out special cover).

1532 See eg *Gard Rules 2018* r 27.1(e).

reference to loss of employment by reason of the total loss of the ship.[1533] Liability to pay the repatriation expenses of seafarers is usually covered generally,[1534] or by reference to circumstances such as the total loss of the vessel necessitating the signing off of the crew.[1535] Liabilities arising only by contract under a crew agreement, and not eg by statute, might not be covered unless the terms have previously been agreed by the Club.[1536]

References in Club rules to the MLC 2006 seem to appear rather by accretion than by full integration. For example, there is usually an additional repatriation provision making express reference to liability under the MLC 2006,[1537] although there are sometimes exceptions to it.[1538] In the 2018 rules of most Clubs there is a separate provision for where the Club has issued a certificate of insurance or financial liability for liability under the MLC 2006. This cover is usually set out in the MLC Extension Clause 2016.[1539] The Club here undertakes to pay on behalf of the shipowner the latter's MLC liabilities for outstanding wages and repatriation[1540] or compensation for long-term disability;[1541] ie there is in effect a form of direct liability and another exception to the pay to be paid clause.[1542] The International Group has stated that its understanding is that "[r]epatriation and unpaid wages will be covered under the [Club] Rules in some cases, including when due to a shipwreck. However, repatriation and overdue wages fall outside the scope of P&I cover when arising from abandonment under Standard A2.5.2 due to, for example, a shipowner's financial default".[1543] However, "The MLC Extension Clause provides that Clubs will discharge and pay claims made by seafarers pursuant to the Certificates. The Clause imposes an obligation on Members to reimburse their Club if the claims which the Club has paid to seafarers fall outside the scope of cover provided by the Rules".[1544]

1533 See eg *UK Club Rules 2018* r 2, Section 6; *Gard Rules 2018* r 27.1(b).
1534 Eg *UK Club Rules 2018* r 2, Section 4A.
1535 See eg *Gard Rules 2018* r 27.1(b).
1536 See eg *Gard Rules 2018* rule 27.1 (proviso).
1537 See eg *UK Club Rules 2018* r 2, Section 4B; *Gard Rules 2018* r 27.3.
1538 Eg termination of the employment contract generally, or sale of the ship. The exceptions do not apply for repatriation expenses that fall within the MLC 2006, eg if the ship were wrecked and the contract terminated, or if the wrecked ship was sold for scrap.
1539 See eg *Gard Rules 2018* Appendix IV, Section 4; *UK Club Rules 2018* r 5U (and Owner's Addendum to the Rule Book).
1540 In accordance with MLC 2006 Regulation 2.5 Standard A2.5 and Guideline B2.5.
1541 In accordance with MLC 2006 Regulation 4.2, Standard A4.2 and Guideline B4.2.
1542 See eg *Gard Rules 2018* r 87(3).
1543 *IG MLC 2006 FAQs*, para 10.
1544 *IG MLC 2006 FAQs*, para 11.

CHAPTER 3

Rights in relation to wreck

3.1 Conceptual development of wreck and interests in wreck

In common terms 'wreck' has a very wide meaning, and when pertaining to a vessel usually means one that has been "broken, ruined, or totally disabled by being driven on rocks, cast ashore, or stranded; a wrecked or helpless ship" or which has sunk.[1] It is used both to describe the event and the result. Buckley LJ in *The Olympic*[2] understood 'wreck' to mean broadly "anything happening to the ship which renders her incapable of carrying out the maritime adventure".[3] The resulting wreck usually extends to the vessel (hull, machinery, fixtures and fittings) as well as its cargo and to all the crew and passenger's belongings associated with the vessel.[4] This common meaning is also reflected in the Institute of International Law's 2015 resolution on the wrecks of State vessels, defining a wreck as a "sunken State ship which is no longer operational, or any part thereof, including any sunken object that is or has been on board such ship".[5]

This common understanding of the term 'wreck' underpins the various legal meanings of 'wreck', which differ depending on the context within which it is used. The earliest meanings were concerned not so much with what constituted wreck, but rather who had an interest in the wreck. 'Wreck' is said to derive from the old Danish word '*varech*', whose original meaning is lost, but which was used in Normandy to refer to "all those things which the sea has thrown ashore by chance or stress of weather".[6] Early English admiralty pronouncements of the meaning of wreck were concerned with rights to wreck, particularly that cast ashore within the ebb and flow of the tide, termed *wreccum maris*, and if unclaimed by an owner, passed to the Crown[7] or to the Crown's assignee, such as the Lord of the local manor.[8] This limited meaning of 'wreck' was extended by statute to cover a separate Crown prerogative, that pertaining to maritime property that had not reached shore—*adventurae maris*—but if recovered and unclaimed passed to the Crown as a droit in the office of admiralty.[9] This applied to flotsam, jetsam and lagan, where flotsam, is when a ship is sunk

---

1 *Oxford English Dictionary* (2nd ed, OUP 1989). See also 1.1.
2 [1913] P 92.
3 [1913] P 92, 107. See S Lillington, "Wreck or *wreccum maris*?" [1987] LMCQ 267 [*Lillington*], 268.
4 Wreck excludes buoys, such as data buoys and mooring buoys. See "Wreck and Salvage Law", www.gov.uk/guidance/wreck-and-salvage-law.
5 Institute of International Law, www.idi-iil.org/app/uploads/2017/06/2015_Tallinn_09_en-1.pdf; N Ronzitti, "The Legal Regime of Wrecks of Warships and Other State-Owned Ships in International Law" (2015) 76 *Yearbook of the Institute of International Law* [*Ronzitti* (2015)] 267, 371.
6 G Dorey, "Rights to Wreck in Norman Customary Law" (1993) 15 *Guernsey LJ* [*Dorey*] 63.
7 *Att. Gen. v Sir Henry Constable* [1601] 5 Co Rep 106a; *The Aquila* (1798) 1 C Rob 36, 41.
8 *Kennedy & Rose*, 102.
9 On the history of the Crown's right to wreck, see *Dromgoole & Gaskell "Interest in Wreck"*, 178; *Brice*, 270–275; R Marsden, "Admiralty Droits and Salvage — Gas Float Whitton, No. II" (1899) 15 LQR [*Marsden*]

or otherwise perished, and the goods float on the sea; jetsam, is when the ship is in danger of being sunk, and to lighten the ship the goods are cast into the sea, and afterwards, notwithstanding, the ship perish perishes. Lagan, *vel potius ligan*, is when the goods which are so cast into the sea, and afterwards the ship perishes, and such goods are so heavy that they sink to the bottom and the mariners, to the intent to have them again, tie them to a buoy or cork, or such other thing that will not sink, so that they may find them again.[10]

Wreck also included derelict, being a vessel that has been abandoned at sea by the master and crew, without an intention of returning to it (*sine animo revertendi*) or hope of recovery (*sine spe recuperandi*).[11] It was thus not restricted to a vessel that had actually succumbed to any danger and been driven ashore or sunk, but without a crew such an eventuality is highly likely. A derelict that does sink does not cease to be derelict merely because it lies on the bottom of the sea, and sunken vessels are more accurately termed 'derelict', and 'wreck' in a broader sense.[12]

Early and subsequent statutory enactment dealing with 'wreck' did not in fact define the term; indeed, the Wreck and Salvage Act 1846 contains no definition of 'wreck' at all. The 1854 MSA was the first to attempt something like a definition, but did no more than recognise the scope of *wrecccum maris* and to add to that, *adventurae maris*.[13] This has essentially been repeated in both the 1894 and 1995 MSAs such that s 255(1) provides simply that 'wreck' "*includes* jetsam, flotsam, lagan and derelict found in or on the shores of the sea or any tidal water".[14] To the extent that it is not covered within this definition, wreck also includes fishing boats and fishing gear lost or abandoned at sea and either found or taken possession of within UK waters, or beyond those waters but brought within UK waters.[15] It has also been extended to include aircraft[16] and hovercraft.[17]

The lack of a uniform meaning of the term "wreck" is also evident in the legislation of other common law jurisdictions—whether general shipping legislation or specific legislation relating to wreck or historic wreck.[18] The various historic accretions do not provide

---

353; S Braekhus, "Salvage of Wrecks and Wreckage: Legal Issues Arising from the Rhunde Find" (1976) 20 *Scandinavian Studies in Law* [*Braekhus*] 39; and *Dorey*, 63.

10 *Att. Gen. v Sir Henry Constable* [1601] 5 Co Rep 106a, 77 ER 218. See also *Cargo ex Schiller* [1877] 2 PD 145, 3 Asp MLC 439 (CA); *R v Forty-Nine Casks of Brandy* (1836) 3 Hagg Adm 257, 166 ER 401; *Wells v The Gas Float Whitton No 2* [1897] AC 337, 8 Asp MLC 272 (HL).

11 *The Aquila* (1798) 1C Rob 36, 165 ER 87; *Cossman v West* (1887) 13 App Cas 160, 6 Asp MLC 233 (PC); *Bradley v Newsom* [1919] AC 16 (HL); *The Tubantia* (1924) P 78, 18 Ll L Rep 158. See 3.3.1; see further *Kennedy & Rose*, 104–107.

12 HMS *Thetis* (1834) 2 Knapp 390 (PC); 3 Hagg 229, 166 ER 390; *The Tubantia* (1924) P 78, 18 Ll L Rep 158; *The Lusitania* [1986] QB 384.

13 MSA 1854 s 2.

14 Emphasis added.

15 MSA s 255(2).

16 Aircraft (Wrecks and Salvage) Order (1938), Art 2(b) (SR&O 1938/136). International Convention for the Unification of Certain Rules Relating to Assistance and Salvage of Aircraft or by Aircraft at Sea, adopted 28 September 1938, never entered into force, but enacted in the UK. *Brice*, 17, 236, 656–685; *Kennedy & Rose*, 104, 118–123.

17 Hovercraft (Application of Enactments) Order 1972 (S.I. 1972, No. 971) Art 8(1). *Kennedy & Rose*, 104, 123–124. On the inclusion of hovercraft in the scope of the WRC 2007 see 8.2.1(b), and the exclusion of aircraft see 8.2.1(i).

18 See eg Australia's Navigation Act 2012 (Cth), s 14(1), and New Zealand's Maritime Transport Act 1994 (as amended by the Maritime Transport Amendment Act 1999).

much modern guidance and, in effect, such legislation for the most part simply provides that the term "wreck" includes certain forms of maritime property. The US Abandoned Shipwrecks Act 1987 is similarly sparse, defining "shipwreck" merely as "a vessel or wreck, its cargo and other contents", and without then defining the term 'wreck'.[19] A more expansive and recent statutory definition is to be found in the Australian Navigation Act 2012, defining wreck as including "a vessel that is wrecked, derelict, stranded, sunk or abandoned or that has foundered; and . . . any thing that belonged to or came from [that vessel]; . . . any thing that belonged to or came from a vessel in distress; and . . . jetsam, flotsam and lagan".[20] Reference to "wreck" usually arises within these legislative provisions in the context of salvage. The difficulty in arriving at the meaning of wreck in this context is reflected in the fact that the Salvage Convention 1989 also fails to set out a meaning for "wreck", although there can be salvage of wrecked maritime property.[21]

This definition of wreck is not limited in time and applies to all wreck irrespective of when the wrecking event occurred. It thus applies to the remains of vessels and its cargo from antiquity.[22] The archaeological and historical importance of a number of these wrecks[23] was such that protective regimes were adopted in a number of jurisdictions as early as the 1970s, such as the UK's Protection of Wrecks Act 1973.[24] These regimes modify the general laws applicable to wrecks especially salvage law, and the term 'historic wrecks' is used in a general sense to refer to wrecks of an archaeological and historical importance, some of which may be subject the these statutory protective regimes.

Historic wrecks also falls within a broader category of archaeological and historical material, referred to in UNCLOS as objects of an archaeological and historical nature.[25] More recently this broader category of archaeological and historical material has achieved some protection in the UNESCO Convention on the Protection of the Underwater Cultural Heritage (UCH 2001), addressed in detail in Chapter 6.

3.2 Ownership of wreck

The wreck of a vessel, its cargo and other property on board remain chattel. In *Elwes v Brigg Gas Co*[26] Chitty J considered whether a 2,000-year-old boat buried on land close to a river ought to be considered as a mineral and part of the soil in which it was embedded[27] or as a chattel. While the question did not need to be addressed to resolve the case, Chitty J

---

19 Abandoned Shipwrecks Act 1987 s 2102. See also 6.15.2.
20 Navigation Act 2012 (Cth) s 14.
21 See *Gaskell, "The 1989 Salvage Convention"*, 34–38; *Kennedy & Rose*, 112. See 2.7.6.
22 Treasure Act 1996 s 3(7) provides that an object is not treasure as defined in the Act if it is wreck within the meaning of s 255 of the MSA 1995.
23 For a history and development of underwater archaeology, see GF Bass, *Archaeology under Water* (Penguin Books, 1966) [*Bass*]; P Throckmorton, *The Sea Remembers: Shipwrecks and Archaeology* (Mitchell Beasley, 1987) [*Throckmorton*]; C Forrest, *International Law and the Protection of Cultural Heritage* (Routledge 2010) [*Forrest, Protection of Cultural Heritage*] 287–300; S Dromgoole, *Underwater Cultural Heritage and International Law* (CUP, 2013) [*Dromgoole, Underwater Cultural Heritage*] 2–7.
24 See 4.6.1.
25 See 5.5.3.
26 (1886) 33 Ch D 562.
27 The US Abandoned Shipwrecks Act 1987 is expressly applied to shipwrecks 'embedded' in the submerged lands of a State or coraline formations.

was of the view that the boat remained a chattel, rather than becoming part of the soil, as it had preserved its original character. Thus, ownership of wreck is not fundamentally different to ownership of any other property.

3.2.1 Choice of law in relation to ownership

The determination of who the owner of a vessel, cargo or personal belongings of passengers and crew that becomes wreck is, follows the usual rules for ownership of chattels.[28] This includes how ownership is maintained, lost or transferred. However, wreck, by its nature, may be connected to different jurisdictions with different laws on ownership. For example, the vessel itself may be flagged in one State, owned by a national of another, be carrying cargo of a third State, and have crew who are nationals of and resident in a fourth State. When that vessel then becomes a wreck off the coast of a fifth State, and is found and salved by a salvor in that State, the question of ownership of property may arise, and requires a consideration of the private intentional law rules applied by the forum in which the dispute is to be settled. As such, "a ship is not like an ordinary personal chattel".[29]

The choice of law rule for chattels is the *lex situs*—the law of the place where the chattel is situated.[30] However, a generally accepted view is that a ship may be said to be situated in the place of its registry, irrespective of where it actually lies.[31] In such a case, the law of the State of registry (flag State) of the ship determines the question of ownership, including whether ownership has been abandoned.[32] This at least appears a useful solution where ships are situated in the high seas at the relevant time, or may merely be passing through the territorial seas of a number of States during its passage. Dicey and Morris, however, suggest that this rule ought not to apply when the vessel is clearly situated in a particular territorial sea at the given time.[33]

Moreover, that the law of the flag should determine questions of ownership is problematic given the rise of the use of flags of convenience.[34] The beneficial owner of the vessel will usually have no real connection with the flag State and the application of that law to issues of ownership would be to ignore the laws that would originally have applied to the acquisition of ownership of the vessel, being the law of the place where the vessel was situated when ownership was acquired (*lex situs*).[35] While the *lex situs* may be the State of registry if purchasing a registered vessel, this is not necessarily the case.[36]

---

28 *The Jupiter* [1927] P 250.
29 *Hooper v Gumm* (1867) LR 2 Ch App 282, 290. A Briggs, A Dickinson, J Harris, J McClean, P McEleavy, C McLaughlin and C Morse, *Dicey, Morris & Collins on The Conflict of Laws* (15th ed, vol II, Sweet & Maxwell 2012) [*Dicey & Morris*], 1300.
30 *Dicey & Morris*, 1300.
31 Ibid.; *Tisand Pty Ltd v Owners of the Ship MV Cape Morton* (2005) *(ex Freya)* (2005) 143 FCR 43 (Fed Ct Aust).
32 Ibid., 79. *Dicey & Morris*, 1300. See further I Shearer (ed), DP O'Connell, *The International Law of the Sea. Vol II* (OUP, 2015) [*Shearer*], 750–757.
33 *Dicey & Morris*, 1300; *The WD Fairway* [2009] 2 Lloyd's Rep 191, 219; *Trustees Executors and Agency Cp Ltd v Inland Revenue Commissioners* [1973] Ch 254.
34 See *The WD Fairway* [2009] 2 Lloyd's Rep 191.
35 *Tisand Pty Ltd v Owners of the Ship MV Cape Morton (ex Freya)* (2005) 143 FCR 43, 78–79. See also *Thor Shipping A/S v Ship Al Duhail* (2008) 173 FCR 524.
36 *Dicey & Morris*, 1301.

Where a vessel is not registered it may still have a nationality. A ship that is not registered may nevertheless be recognised as having a nationality is accordance with the domestic laws of a State—usually that of the ship's owners.[37] Where registration is voluntary and the vessel was not registered,[38] determining the nationality of the ship is more problematic. Usually nationality will follow the owner of the vessel, and in cases where there are joint owners, that of the majority.[39] Despite unregistered ships having a possible nationality (including deregistered vessels)[40] the *lex situs*—being the place where the ship is actually situated—applies to questions of ownership etc. In *The WD Fairway*, Tomlinson J held that the sale of a deregistered dredger was governed by the law of place where the dredger physically was at the time of sale (Thailand) rather than the law of the ship's last place of registration (the Netherlands).[41]

The same problem arises with respect to choice of law rule for addressing proprietary interests in cargo on the ship, or the effects belonging to its passengers or crew. The nationalities of these persons may be numerous, even supposing they can be traced, and the flag of the carrying ship is a more convenient and pragmatic choice of law rule than that referenced to the properties' owners. Alternatively, while the cargo has a closer connection with the ship and the flag State than that of the owners, the place where the cargo is physically situated at the relevant time has arguably the closest connection; however fortuitous that may be. In *Cammell v Sewell*,[42] a ship carrying timber from Russia was wrecked off Norway, and the cargo sold at auction in Norway. The purchaser then sold the timber to a second buyer in England. The cargo insurer acquired ownership pursuant to subrogation under the insurance policy and sought to recover the timber from the second buyer. The court held that the first buyer had obtained good title in Norway which could validly be passed to the English buyer.[43]

In some cases, other choice of law rules have been proposed. Where, for example, there are doubts as to the law of the flag, it would also be possible to consider the law of the salvor or finder. This is perhaps less attractive, because of the possibility that salvors could be seen to manipulate a court by 'flag shopping', ie by utilising vessels of a flag State with a convenient law of salvage or finds. There are also difficulties in assigning a single nationality to a salvor when there is a multi-national joint venture. An often used alternative is merely to apply the law of the forum, particularly where a wreck is found within the internal waters or territorial sea of the forum State, but also in cases where the vessel is found beyond national jurisdiction. Indeed, while the law of the flag or the physical location of the ship is a convenient choice of law rule for modern wrecks, it is less clear that this should be applied to historic wrecks. In a number of US cases dealing with historic shipwrecks in US waters, the law of the flag has been overlooked and the assumption made that the only relevant law is that of the forum.[44]

---

37 See for example Shipping Registration Act 1981 (Australia) s 29.
38 See the MSA 1995 s 9(1).
39 *Shearer*, 753.
40 *The WD Fairway* [2009] 2 Lloyd's Rep 191, 193.
41 Ibid., 219–223.
42 (1858) 3 H&N 617; (1860) 5 H&N 728.
43 *Dicey & Morris*, 716; P Torremans (ed), *Cheshire, North and Fawcett Private International Law* (15th ed, OUP, 2017) 1268.
44 *Treasure Salvors Inc v The Unidentified, Wrecked and Abandoned Sailing Vessel* [1981] AMC 1857, *Columbus-America Discovery Group v The Unidentified, Wrecked and Abandoned Sailing Vessel* [1989] AMC 1955, [1990] AMC 2409, [1992] AMC 2705, [1995] AMC 1985.

3.2.2 Identifying the owner

Prima facie, the strongest interest in wreck is the proprietary interest of the owner. In modern casualties this is not usually problematic where the wreck has value, and any dispute as to ownership will be addressed no differently to that applicable to any other chattel, subject to specific statutory requirement related to vessels.[45] It is perhaps more difficult to ascertain ownership where the wreck is a liability, given the complex and notoriously secretive mechanism for holding proprietary interest in ships in the modern shipping industry. It may be even more difficult to identify the owner when a wreck is discovered some time, perhaps centuries, after its sinking or stranding.[46]

The older the wreck is the more difficult establishing ownership will be. Ownership claims to vessels and their contents which were wrecked since the middle of the 19th century are easier to establish partly because of the recording of ownership with the vessel's registration and because commercial interests maintained records, particularly insurance interests. The Salvage Association,[47] for example, operating with Lloyd's and the ILU,[48] maintained records dating back to 1860 of vessels lost and claims made. When a potential purchaser or salvor expresses an interest in a wreck, the Association would endeavour to discover the existence of any commercial (particularly insurance) interests. For instance, many vessels lost during the two World Wars may have been insured or reinsured for war risks, including by the UK government, and these commercial and government interests, assisted by the Salvage Association, may subsequently contract with, or sell the wreck or cargo, to salvors. Although the Association no longer exists, its records have been archived and can be accessed.[49] Both Lloyd's and the IUA[50] are able to assist members in tracing corporate succession from forerunners who may have underwritten a loss many years ago.

Establishing the ownership of wrecks than foundered earlier than the mid-19th century is much more problematic and often gives rise to inferences of abandonment. This also applies to cargo and personal possessions on board a wreck. Original owners of such items can rarely be identified in these older wrecks, and consequently there are far fewer claims by descendants claiming such property than there is to those claiming the wreck itself. This is exemplified in the lack of claims to the cargo or personal belongings of crew and passengers recovered from the wreck of the *Lusitania*, sunk by *U-20* in 1915 with the loss

---

45 Such as MSA 1995 ss 9 and 17.

46 See for example *Global Marine Exploration v The Unidentified, Wrecked and (for Finders-Right purposes) Abandoned Sailing Vessel* [2018] AMC 1603, where France had to prove ownership of *la Trinit*, a warship sunk in 1565 off Florida.

47 The Salvage Association was incorporated by Royal Charter in 1867 (as The Association for the Protection of Commercial Interests as Respects Wrecked and Damaged Property) but amended in 1971 with the principal objects to protect the interests of members and others in respect of shipping, cargoes and marine, non-marine and aviation insurance; and to carry out salvage operations, including in particular surveys of shipping, cargoes and investigations into the causes of loss, damage or injury to such interests. Its membership has comprised Lloyd's underwriters and insurance companies. The Salvage Association was wound up in 2003 but some if its functions appear to have been taken over by Braemar Shipping Services. See *Re The Salvage Association* [2003] EWCH (Ch) 1028.

48 See 2.9.1.

49 Centre for Archival Collections https://lib.bgsu.edu/finding_aids/collections/show/23.

50 See 2.9.1.

of 1,198 passengers and crew. In 1982, cargo and personal belonging were raised from the wreck, brought into the UK directly from the wreck site and deposited with the Receiver of Wreck as required by the MSA 1894.[51] However, no owners or descendants came forth to claim that property within the one-year statutory period provided for, and thus a dispute arose as to whether the finder or the Crown was entitled to the artefacts.[52] The Crown's right to wreck was found to be limited to that found within UK territorial waters and as the wreck of the *Lusitania* did not lie in such waters, the Crown had no right to the abandoned artefacts.

States own not only warships and other governmental vessels but may also own commercial vessels used for commercial services. Whether that ownership persists after the vessel has sunk depends on a variety of factors, including where the vessel sank.[53] Questions of abandonment, in particular, arise in these situations.[54] In the case of a warship, there should be few problems in establishing ownership and thus nationality, although the increasing fragmentation of larger States may give rise to problems as to which is the legitimate successor. Questions of State succession do arise where the original State has either been subsumed into a new larger State, or more likely, the original State has broken up into one or more newly constituted States. In *Simon v Taylor*,[55] for example, whether the Federal Republic of Germany (West Germany) or the German Democratic Republic (East Germany) was the legitimate successor of Nazi Germany after World War II was raised in the context of ownership of a German U-boat. Sheen J did not have to decide the question specifically, holding that the assertion of ownership by the Federal Republic of Germany was legitimate as "there is only one Germany which has survived the cataclysm of 1945 intact though there are two regimes competing for control of its territory".[56]

Disputes concerning the ownership of sunken State owned vessels have often been resolved by States on a bilateral basis.[57] This includes, for example, US recognition of French ownership of the wreck of the *La Belle*, a French vessel sunk in US territorial waters in 1686 and the French recognition of US ownership of the *CSS Alabama*, sunk off Cherbourg in 1868.[58] Indeed, ownership of the ship's bell, which had been recovered and was on sale with a private dealer, was held to remain with the State.[59] Canada recognised British ownership of *HMS Erebus* and *HMS Terror*, sunk in 1848. Similarly, Norway recognised the Dutch ownership of the Dutch East India Company (Vereenigde Oostindische Compagnie—VOC) wreck *Akerendam*, sunk in 1725, and German ownership of *U-76*

---

51 On the role of the Receiver of Wreck see 4.4.
52 *Pierce v Bemis (The Lusitania)* [1986] QB 384; *Lillington*, 267. See 4.3.
53 For some of the problems caused when one State tries to recover the warship of another, see M Collins, "Salvage of Sunken Military Vessels. Project Jennifer: A Dangerous Experiment" (1977) 8 JMLC 433.
54 See 3.3.
55 [1975] 2 Lloyd's Rep 338.
56 Ibid., 343.
57 See generally M Aznar-Gomez, "Legal Status of Sunken Warships 'Revisited'" (2001–2002) 8 *Spanish YIL* 1 [*Anzar-Gomez*], 12–16.
58 The Exchange of Notes between US and France does not, in fact, recognise US ownership, though it was acknowledge in other correspondence. JA Roach, "France Concedes United States Has Title to *CSS Alabama*" (1991) 85 *AJIL* [*Roach*] 381.
59 *United States v Richard Steinmetz* 763 F Supp 1293 (DNJ 1991), aff'd 973 F2d 212 (3d Cir 1992), *cert denied* 113 S Ct 1578 (1993).

sunk in 1917.[60] Other agreements have not specifically recognised ownership of the original flag State but the relevant States have nevertheless managed to reach agreement on how the wreck was to be managed. For example, the UK and South Africa reached agreement on the salvage of the *Birkenhead*, a UK vessel sunk in South African territorial waters in 1852, without having to address the issue of ownership.[61] Similarly, the Exchange of Notes between Australian and the Netherlands concerning the VOC wreck off Western Australia does not specifically recognise Dutch ownership, though transfers whatever rights the Dutch have to Australia.[62]

Though establishing ownership of warships and other governmental vessels is usually not difficult, this may be complicated by the laws applicable to transfer of ownership in war. Ownership of warships and other auxiliary ships were, according to the law of war, transferred to the belligerent State following capture or surrender.[63] For example, during the battle of Tsushima in 1905, the czarist cruiser *Admiral Nakhimov* was substantially damaged and abandoned by its crew. Before it sank, it was boarded by Japanese sailors from the cruiser *Sadomaru* and the Japanese flag hoisted on the foremast. Despite efforts to keep it afloat, it sank. In 1980, Japan undertook salvage operations on the wreck of the *Admiral Nakhimov* that the Soviet government objected to. Japan's response set out the applicable international law: "[i]n accordance with international law, the rights with respect to the captured enemy ships and property aboard them are transferred immediately and finally to the captor State, therefore, all the rights of the Russian side with respect to the *Admiral Nakhimov* became extinct at the time when the vessel was captured by the Japanese Imperial Navy".[64] Transfer of ownership by prize was also prevalent in the Great War. The German commerce raider *Comoran*, for example, had originally been the Russian merchant ship *Ryazan* until captured in 1914.[65] In certain circumstances, this might include the capture of what may be regarded as a wreck. The German cruiser *Emden*, for example, was so badly damaged by *HMAS Sydney* that it was beached and wrecked. The wreck was subsequently considered captured and condemned as prize.[66] Similarly, the *Königsberg*, sunk in the Rufiji Delta, was considered captured and ownership transferred to Britain.[67] So too were 26 German U-boats that surrendered to the Royal Navy and were subsequently scuttled off Kent. As owners, the British government sold the wrecks of the U-boats to a

---

60 *Braekhus*, 39.
61 On the wreck, see A Kayle, *Salvage of the Birkenhead* (Southern Book Publishers, 1990).
62 The Netherlands and Australia reached agreement on a number of VOC wrecks in Australia including *Batavia, Vergulde Draeck, Zuytdorp* and the *Zeewijck*. In the agreement, the Netherlands transferred to Australia "all its right, title and interest in and to wrecked vessels lying on or off the coast of the State of Western Australia" in return for Australia recognising that the Netherlands had an interest in articles recovered from these wrecks. However, the Agreement does not actually state that the Netherlands did have title to the vessels and therefore does not constitute an acknowledgement of their claim by Australia. See Agreement Between the Netherlands and Australia concerning Old Dutch Shipwrecks in L Prott and I Srong, *Background Materials on the Protection of the Underwater Cultural Heritage* (UNESCO Publishing, 1999) [*Prott & Srong*] 75).
63 C Colombos, *A Treatise on the Law of Prize* (Grotius Society, 1940) 45.
64 *Aznar-Gomez*, 1, 12.
65 Wreck Site, www.wrecksite.eu/wreck.aspx?16015.
66 *The Emden* [1920] 2 Ll L Rep 7 (PDAD). See also R Noppen, *German Commerce Raiders 1914–18* (Osprey, 2015) [*Noppen*], 14.
67 *The Königsberg* [1920] 2 Ll L Rep 7. See also *Noppen*, 18–20.

private company to be salvaged by the new owners.[68] Ownership of the German fleet scuttled at Scapa Flow in 1918 also vested in the British government.

Similarly, ownership of merchant vessels in war may be transferred by virtue of being condemned as prize. The *Lutine* (whose bell now hangs at Lloyd's) was, for example, originally French, but had been captured by the English and claimed as prize. While sailing under the English flag with specie valued at £1 million, it was wrecked off the Netherlands in 1799 and again claimed as prize, this time by the Dutch. The specie was insured at Lloyd's, which paid out in full on the claim. The conflict which arose between Lloyd's and the Dutch government as to who was the rightful owner of the specie was resolved in 1857 when they came to an arrangement whereby Lloyd's received half of the amount recovered.[69]

State ownership may arise in unusual circumstances and apply to historic wrecks. For example, the Dutch government took over the assets and liabilities of the VOC when it was liquidated in 1798 and has claimed ownership of vessels belonging to the company.[70] In the UK, the Dutch government secured its interest in a number of wrecks including the *Amsterdam*, the *de Leifde*, the *Hollandia*, the *Lastdrager*, the *Adelaar*, the *Princess Maria*, the *Cuaçcao* and the *Slot ter Hoge*.[71] The Dutch government has also made claims to VOC wrecks in other jurisdictions, including South Africa[72] and, as already discussed, Australia.

Similarly, unusual circumstances surround the ownership of wrecks of the English East India Company such as the *Grosvenor*, lost off South Africa in 1782.[73] The Government of India Act 1858 s 39 vested in the Crown the "monies, stores, goods, chattels and other . . . personal estate" of the East India Company "to be applied and disposed of . . . for the purposes of the government of India". Following the Indian Independence Act 1947, the property rights and interests of the former colony were divided between India and Pakistan.[74] Who then had a right to the wrecks of the English East India Company was not clear. Exactly what property might have passed on independence is unclear, as the British government, for example, considered that some company property, such as the India Office Library, remained vested in the Crown. However, it could be that such property though still owned by the Crown, is subject to a statutory trust to be used "for the "purposes" (ie benefit) of India".[75] It is also not clear whether wrecks were covered in the original Act and if so, whether it applied to all company wrecks or only to those in UK waters. Given these difficulties, including whether Pakistan or India might assert a right, the UK has not made claim to English East India Company wrecks.

---

68 See UNESCO, www.unesco.org/new/en/culture/themes/underwater-cultural-heritage/the-underwater-heritage/world-war-i/a-heritage-under-threat/.

69 *Dromgoole & Gaskell, "Interest in Wreck"*, 170.

70 A Altes, "Submarine Antiquities: A Legal Labyrinth" (1976) 4 *Syracuse JICL* 76 [*Altes*], 85.

71 *Altes*, 76, 85.

72 C Forrest, "South Africa" in S Dromgoole (ed), *The Protection of the Underwater Cultural Heritage: National Perspectives in Light of the UNESCO Convention 2001* (Martinus Nijhoff Publishers, 2006) [*Forrest, "South Africa"*] 247. See also M Turner, *Shipwrecks and Salvage in South Africa: 1505 to the Present* (1988) 77–78.

73 *Turner*, 77–78. Other examples include the *Earl of Abergavenny* sunk off Weymouth in 1805; the *Admiral Gardner*, sunk in the Goodwin Sands in 1809; and the *Hindostan*, which sank off Margate in 1803.

74 *Dromgoole & Gaskell, "Interest in Wreck"*, 155.

75 Ibid.

3.2.3 Acquiring ownership of a wreck

As with all other forms of property, there are many ways of acquiring ownership of wreck from an original identifiable owner.[76] Wrecks can, and are, bought and sold, and in some cases, given away. Indeed, in many cases salvors would prefer to purchase a wreck and recover what is then its own property rather than undertake a salvage operation subject to salvage law. As such, salvors regularly purchase wrecks from the original owner or more commonly, from insurance interests that have obtained ownership following payment for an actual or constructive total loss of the vessel.[77]

Governments may also sell their wrecks, including wrecks of warships. *HMS Natal*, for example, sunk by accident in the shallow waters of Cromarty Firth with the loss of 405 men in 1915, was sold in 1921 to salvors.[78] Similarly, *HMS Aboukir*, *HMS Cressy* and *HMS Hogue*, famously sunk by *U-9*, with the loss of 1,495 men, appears to have been sold by the British government to salvors for scrap in the 1950s.[79] The British government also sold off enemy ships, such as the *Königsberg*, initially sold in 1924 and subsequently sold a number of other times throughout the 1950s and 1960s.[80] In some cases, ships have been sold by the State to entities that intend to protect the ship for its archaeological or historical value or simply donated to such an entity.[81] For example, the wreck of what is believed to be the *Grace Dieu*, the biggest ship ever built in England at the time of its construction in 1416, lies in the river Hamble in Hampshire. On the basis that it may be the *Grace Dieu* and thus a Crown vessel, the MOD, acting on behalf of the Crown, transferred all such right, title or interest as the Crown may have had in the wreck to the University of Southampton, acting on behalf of the Society for Nautical Research, for the nominal sum of £5 in 1970.[82] Similarly, the *Mary Rose*, sunk in 1545 was donated by the MOD to the Mary Rose Trust, while the *Anne*, sunk in 1690 was donated to the Nautical Museums Trust.[83] Much more controversially, the MOD entered into a deed of transfer for *HMS Victory*, sunk in 1744, with a charity called the Maritime Heritage Foundation.[84] However, the charity then entered into a contract with a US commercial salvage company—Odyssey Marine Exploration—to excavate the wreck site. This has drawn significant criticism and led to the initiation of litigation in 2019 when the MOD then tried to prevent the salvage operation proceeding.[85]

---

76 Rights acquired to abandoned property are addressed further in 3.3.

77 See 3.4.

78 The wreck of *HMS Natal* is now a designated controlled site under the Protection of Military Remains Act 1986. See Wreck Site, www.wrecksite.eu/wreck.aspx?432.

79 R York, "World War I Underwater Cultural heritage and the Loss of the *HMS Aboukir*, *HMS Cressy* and *HMS Hogue* 1914" in U Guérin, A Rey Da Silva and L Simmonds, *The Underwater Cultural Heritage from World War I: Proceedings of the Scientific Conference on the Occasion of the Centenary of World War I* (UNESCO, 2015) 86.

80 K Patience, *Shipwrecks and Salvage on the East African Coast* (2006) 157.

81 S Dromgoole and N Gaskell, "Who Has a Right to Historic Wrecks and Wreckage?" (1993) *Int J Cultural Property* [*Dromgoole & Gaskell, "Right to Historic Wrecks"*] 217, 224.

82 V Fenwick and A Gale, *Historic Shipwrecks: Discovered, Protected and Investigated* (Tempus 1999) 35.

83 *Dromgoole & Gaskell, "Right to Historic Wrecks"*, 224; See *Dromgoole, Underwater Cultural Heritage*, 99.

84 D Alberge "Archaeologists accuse MoD of allowing US company to 'plunder' shipwreck", *Guardian*, www.theguardian.com/uk/2012/may/06/hms-victory-shipwreck-odyssey-excavation.

85 See R Byrne, "HMS Victory: The English Channel's 'abandoned shipwreck'", BBC, www.bbc.com/news/uk-england-47044932.

Wrecks may also be transferred by way of treaty, though in some cases, this was not necessarily intentional. The Treaty of Versailles, for example, had not expressly dealt with wrecks, but in Art 184 provided that "all the German surface warships which are not in German ports cease to belong to Germany, who renounces all rights over them". Arguably this included the wrecks of German vessels, especially those scuttled in Scapa Flow. Certainly, the Admiralty dealt with these as British property without objection from Germany.[86] A similar position appears to apply to Germany's ally Austria-Hungary. The 1919 Treaty of St. Germain provided that "all Austro-Hungarian warships, submarines included [were] declared to be finally surrendered to the Principal Allied and Associated Powers", as were "all arms, ammunitions and other naval war material, including mines and torpedoes".[87] Like the Treaty of Versailles, there is no evidence of any intent to include wrecks within this scope.[88]

Other treaties have also impacted on State ownership of wrecks. For example, all German property in Norway as at 9 May 1945 was taken over by the Norwegian government, including wrecked German warships and merchant ships off the Norwegian coast. So too did the Treaty of Paris in 1763 that ended the seven-year war, concluded between Spain, France and UK. In *Sea Hunt Inc v The Unidentified Shipwrecked Vessel or Vessels etc*,[89] the court at first instance found that the treaty constituted an abandonment of ownership of the warship *La Galga*, sunk in 1750, though this was reversed on appeal.[90]

Ownership of a wreck or its contents may also be acquired by succession, even centuries after the original loss. For example, Baron Bentinck of Gorssel, descendant of a passenger on board the Dutch East Indiaman *Hollandia* which sank in 1743, declared his interest in a copper-gilt shoe buckle and silver cutlery bearing his family arms.[91] More recently, 24 individuals claimed right as successors in title to cargo carried on board the Spanish frigate *Nuestra Señora de las Mercedes*, sunk in 1804 and recovered in 2007 off the Straits of Gibraltar.[92]

Ownership of a wreck may also pass by way of subrogation, and indeed many merchant vessels sunk in the two World Wars were covered by the war risk insurance scheme and passed by way of subrogation to either one of the marine insurance companies involved in the scheme or the British government itself as the insurer or reinsurer.[93] Salvors may acquire property in lieu of a salvage award[94] or through the law of finds.[95] Another, more

---

86 SC George, *Jutland to Junkyard* (Birlinn, 2003) plates 44–45. Nevertheless, some iconic property was returned to Germany, including, in 1965, the bells of the *Derfflinger* and *Friedrich der Grosse* as well as the *Derfflinger*'s seal.

87 Treaty of St. Germain Arts 136 and 141. See *Ronzitti 2015*, 314.

88 For a contrary view, see MM Hafner in *Ronzitti 2015*, 314.

89 47 F Supp 2d 678 (ED Va 1999).

90 *Sea Hunt, Inc v Unidentified Shipwrecked Vessel or Vessels*, 221 F3d 634 (4th Cir 2000), *cert. denied*, 148 L Ed 2d 956, 121 S Ct 1079 (2001).

91 Dromgoole & Gaskell, "Interest in Wreck", 154.

92 *Odyssey Marine Exploration, Inc v Unidentified Shipwrecked Vessel*, 675 F Supp 2d 1126 (MD Fla 2009), *aff'd*, 657 F3d 1159 (11th Cir 2011). These claims were not addressed as the court found that it did not have jurisdiction to adjudicate the matter on the basis that the wreck was Spanish property and entitled to immunity from arrest. See further 4.7.

93 See 3.4.

94 See 3.5.3.

95 See 3.5.4.

theoretical method of acquisition might be through accretion. A number of ancient wrecks have been found on land which was once part of the seabed or a river floor.[96] Finally owners, including cargo owners, may be deprived of ownership which is transferred to the State through overriding legislation.[97]

3.2.4 Human remains

A great many wrecks entomb the remains of their crew or passengers, especially those that sank in conflicts such as the two World Wars. Depending on the environmental conditions at the wreck site, human remains can be found several hundred years after a sinking.[98] The question of the existence of rights over the human remains is particularly problematic, and while debated, the general principles is that the law recognises no property rights in human remains.[99] It does not appear though that the relatives or the personal representatives of a deceased entombed in a wreck have clearly recognised rights at common law to require that a wreck and its human contents be raised, or to restrict or prohibit salvage operations.[100] Nevertheless, in this context, it would raise particular problems in relation to the extent of 'wreck' itself, but also to the application of salvage law and the law of finds.[101] Whilst not recognised as being wreck, human remains are often so intricately connected to a wreck that these considerations need to be taken into account of the human remains when addressing wreck. Indeed, it was the concern with human remains that promoted the enactment of the Protection of Military Remains Act 1986.[102]

3.3 Abandonment of rights

3.3.1 Derelict

Wreck is defined in s 255 of the MSA as including "derelict", though that is not defined.[103] In the law of salvage, derelict refers to a vessel that has been abandoned at sea by the master and crew, without any intention of returning to it (*sine animo revertendi*) or hope

---

96 For example, in September 1992 a wooden ship possibly dating from the stone age was found 23 ft below street level during road construction work in Dover. Archaeologists believed that it was left on the edge of a river estuary that once flowed through the area: *The Independent*, 17 October 1992. One boat found near Whitstable in Kent has been dated to about ad 870. P Marsden, "Archaeology at Sea" (1972) 46 Antiquity 198.
97 See further 11.1.3.
98 For example, in 1995 the remains of an Elizabethan soldier were recovered from a Tudor warship which sank off the Channel Island of Alderney in 1592: *The Times*, 8 July 1995. The remains of a sailor lost in the Battle of the Nile in 1798 were also found during excavations. See L Foreman and E Blue Phillips, *Napoleon's Lost Fleet: Bonaparte, Nelson and the Battle of the Nile* (Roundtable Press, 1999) 204.
99 *Doodeward v Spence* (1908) 9 SR (NSW) 107. See *Conway* 2–3. See also R Marusyk and M Swain, "A Question of Property Rights in the Human Body" (1989) 21 *Ottawa LR* 351; P Skegg, "Human Corpses, Medical Specimens and the Law of Property" (1975) 4 *Anglo-American LR* 412; P Matthews, "Whose Body? People as Property" (1983) 36 *Current Legal Problems* 193.
100 Dromgoole & Gaskell, "Interest in wreck", 159. See 13.1.3.
101 See 3.5, 10.5.1(d).
102 See 4.6.2.
103 See also Navigation Act 2012 (Cth) (Australia) s 14.

of recovery (*sine spe recuperandi*).[104] It is also applied to cargo from such a vessel.[105] The abandonment of a derelict usually occurs in the face of imminent peril where the master expects the vessel to be lost, and thus no hope exists of returning to it. If the master or crew do expect to return once the peril has passed, then the vessel is not derelict.[106] This may be the case, for example, where the master and crew temporarily abandon the vessel in order to seek assistance.[107] Whether possession has been abandoned depends on the circumstances and there is no form by which the order to abandon ship is given, or indeed, any necessity for such an order.[108] It turns simply on the evidence as to the intention of the master and crew, however subsequently ascertained or implied.[109]

What "no hope of recovery" (*sine spe recuperandi*) actually means is not clear. The requirement that there be no hope of recovery for a vessel to be rendered derelict reflects the difficulties in times past of recovering vessels from the perils of the sea, particularly once sunk. With modern recovery and salvage technology virtually any wreck can be found and recovered. A more modern interpretation might mean that it refers only to the more immediate hope of recovering a vessel before it sinks or is stranded.

It is the intent to abandon the vessel that renders it derelict and where no intent can be found, no abandonment can be found. For example, in *Bradley v Newscom*[110] the crew of a merchant ship were forced to leave the ship as a result of a German submarine attack. The ship was later found afloat and brought to port by naval ships. In claiming for freight—since the voyage had effectively been completed—the court held that the crew had not abandoned the ship as they had been forced to leave the ship and had not formed the requisite intention to abandon it; and were therefore able to claim freight.[111] Where all the crew have died in the wrecking, for example, no intent to abandon may be found at the time of the wrecking.[112] Where the master and crew do abandon a vessel with the intent not to return, but subsequently have a change of heart and do return, the original intent stands and the vessel remains a derelict.[113] In such circumstances the crew may be eligible for a salvage award.[114]

The difficulty of determining the intent to abandon at the time of the wrecking event usually arises in circumstances where the vessel has been salved but in circumstances where it was not necessary to do so.[115] Where, however, a vessel found at sea is in a position of danger and without any crew, it is *prima facie* a derelict.[116] To the extent that a wreck remains in peril once sunk, this presumption will apply and where all the crew may have

---

104 *Kennedy & Rose*, 104.
105 Ibid., 105.
106 *The Zeta* (1875) LR 4 A&E 460; *The Aquila* (1798) IC Rob 36, 165 ER 87, 88–89;
107 *The Champion* (1856) Swa 129, at 130.
108 *The Albionic* [1941] P 99 at 112.
109 *Kennedy & Rose*, 105.
110 [1919] AC 16.
111 See *Simon v Taylor* [1975] 2 Lloyd's Rep 338.
112 *Bradley v H Newsom Sons & Co* [1919] AC 16, 24–25; *Brice*, 276.
113 *The Sarah Bell* (1845) 4 Notes of Cases 144, 145. *Brice*, 279.
114 *Kennedy & Rose*, 216.
115 On the process of abandonment itself, see *Kennedy & Rose*, 247.
116 *The Cosmopolitan* (1848) 6 Notes of Cases Suppl. XVII; *The Pergo* [1987] 1 Lloyd's Rep 582 (Ct Sn). *Kennedy & Rose*, 106.

perished, the presumption will stand in the absence of evidence to the contrary. Certainly, all old wrecks will therefore be derelict.[117]

3.3.2 Abandonment of ownership

Derelict does not involve the loss of the owner's property in the vessel[118] and does not then render the wreck *res nullius*.[119] Owners may however, voluntarily divest themselves of their ownership rights in the wreck.[120] Abandonment of ownership requires intent (*animus derelinquendi*) on the owner's part to relinquish rights of ownership.[121] Indeed, at one stage owners could abandon ownership and therefore avoid liabilities that arise after abandonment. In *White v Crisp*,[122] the court concluded that "[i]t is clear that the original owner, or the transferee of the wreck may abandon it and so put an end to his liability". Similarly, in *Winpenny and Chedester v Philadelphia*,[123] the court held:

> When a vessel is lost by the act of God, or by accident, the owner suffers oftentimes great damage, and when she becomes a total loss, it seems to be a great hardship to add to his misfortunes the duty of removing the wreck. It would discourage commerce to hold him to so severe a duty; for who would engage in trade, if, when he had lost his vessel, he might be forced to incur an expense of more than her original cost in removing the wreck from some difficult position? If compelled by the accident to abandon his property, the duty to remove should rather fall on the public, who are interested in the navigation, than on him.[124]

In *The Crystal*,[125] the owners of a vessel sunk in a river entrance after a collision had given notice of abandonment to their underwriters. The wreck was a navigation hazard. The local authority, in accordance with s 56 of the Harbours, Docks and Piers Clauses Act 1847, blew the wreck up to remove the hazard and sought to recover the cost of doing so from the owners. The court found that the owners had, through the notice of abandonment, formed the intent to abandon ownership, rendering the wreck *res nullius*. Since the owners had abandoned the ship prior to this action, they were not the owners at the time and thus not liable.

Such abandonment of ownership is best evidenced by some expressed form. In *Hener v United States*, Sofaer J held that "a finding that title to [a wreck] has been lost requires strong proof, such as the owner's express declaration abandoning title".[126] At least with

---

117 As to the application of salvage law to sunken derelicts as wreck, see 2.7.6.
118 In civil law systems, the term 'dereliction' is used to denote abandonment or relinquishment of the right of ownership: see *Braekhus*, 47.
119 *The Aquila* (1798) 1C Rob 36, 165 ER 87, 88–89; *HMS Thetis* (1835) 3 Hagg 229, 166 ER 390, 393; *Cossman v West* (1887) 13 App Cas 160, 180, 181; *Bradley v Newsom* [1919] AC 16 (HL) 27–28; *The Tubantia* (1924) P 78, 87; *The Association and the Romney* [1970] 2 Lloyd's Rep 5, 60; *Simon v Taylor* [1975] 2 Lloyd's Rep 338, 342, 343; *Brice*, 275–277.
120 See A Hudson, "Abandonment", in N Palmer and E McKendrick, *Interests in Goods* (2nd ed, LLP, 1998), 595; K Roberts, "Sinking, Salvage and Abandonment" (1977) 51 *Tulane LR* 1196, 1199.
121 *Dromgoole & Gaskell, "Interest in Wreck"*, 163.
122 (1854) 10 Ex 312, 322.
123 65 Pa. 135 (1870).
124 This position was reversed in *Wyandotte Company v United States*, 389 U.S. 191 (1967). R Lanier, "Abandon Ship? The Utility of Abandonment" (1977–1978) 9 JMLC 131.
125 [1894] AC 508, 516.
126 525 F Supp 350 [1982] AMC 847 (SDNY 1981).

respect to express abandonment of ownership of wrecks other than in relation to insurers, there appears to be little case law (or academic comment).[127]

Where there is no express abandonment of ownership, it may nevertheless be inferred or implied from the surrounding circumstances. This requires evidence not only of the physical relinquishment of possession or control over the vessel but also of the intent to abandon ownership.[128] Great difficulty exists in determining the circumstances from which an intent to relinquish the rights of ownership can be inferred or implied. The question arises most often in relation to vessels that sank, or were stranded, sometime before their discovery and salvage, and the extent to which the intent to abandon ownership can be inferred from the owner's inaction, and whether the duration of that inaction is a factor.[129]

It is with respect to the owner's inaction in searching for and recovering a wreck that gives rise to inferred abandonment. It is not clear what actions might be expected of an owner over time, particularly when the location of the wreck is not known, and may have sunk in deep water beyond the technology to recover at the time of sinking or for some period after that. These issues have arisen in a number of US cases. In *Zych v The Unidentified, Wrecked and Abandoned Vessel Believed to be The Lady Elgin*,[130] an underwriter had paid for the actual loss of the vessel after it had sunk in Lake Michigan in 1860 and by subrogation acquired ownership of the wreck. The company's successors sold their interest in the wreck in 1990, but at no time over the intervening 130 years had the company or its successors taken any steps to find and recover the wreck. Nevertheless, the court held that in those circumstances, ownership had not been abandoned. Similarly, the insurer that had acquired a subrogated interest in the wreck of the *Central America* was able to assert its proprietary interests despite having made no attempt to find the wreck after it sank in 1857.[131] Given that it had sunk well beyond the coast in deep waters, no such attempt could have been expected.[132] It appears that insurance companies take the view that subrogated title to a wreck never lapses through mere inactivity.[133]

Where a wreck is long lost, abandonment can easily be inferred, as was the case in respect of the 2,000-year-old boat in *Elwes v Brigg Gas Co.*[134] In cases where the time period between sinking and discovery or recovery has been relatively short, courts have not easily inferred abandonment. In *The Egypt*,[135] for example, the court held that a cargo of gold that had lain on the seabed for four years prior to recover had not been abandoned by its owners. Langton J held that "[s]o long as the underwriters had not abandoned it

---

127 P Fletcher-Tomenius, P O'Keefe and M Williams, "Salvor in Possession: Friend or Foe to Marine Archaeology" (2000) 9 *Int J Cultural Property* 263 [*Fletcher-Tomenius et al*], 277.
128 *Fletcher-Tomenius et al*, 263, 278.
129 See *Robinson v Western Australian Museum* (1977) 51 ALJR 806, 820–821. See *Dromgoole & Gaskell, "Interests in Wreck"*, 167.
130 [1991] AMC 359, 1254, 1259 (ND Ill). Cf *Zych v The Unidentified, Wrecked and Abandoned Vessel Believed to be The Seabird* [1993] AMC 2201 (ND Ill) [1994] AMC 2672 (7th Cir.).
131 *Columbus-America v The Unidentified Wrecked and Abandoned Sailing Vessel* [1992] AMC 2705, [1995] AMC 1985.
132 See also *Deep Sea Resources Inc v The Brother Jonathan* [1995] AMC 1682 (ND Cal), 102 F3d 379 (11th Cir.).
133 *Dromgoole & Gaskell, "Interests in Wreck"*, 166.
134 (1886) 33 Ch D 562, 568–569.
135 (1932) 44 Ll L Rep 21, 39.

I think it was their property and remained their property, even though it was not actually accessible to them at the time". Similarly, in *The Tubantia*[136] the court held that the owners of the vessel or the cargo had not lost their ownership right where the vessel had sunk only eight years previously. In *Simon v Taylor*,[137] although the issue of the passage of time was not explicitly raised, the Singapore High Court recognised the German Federal Republic's ownership over a U-boat which had sunk 28 years earlier. In another case concerning a German U-boat, which came before the Norwegian Supreme Court in 1970,[138] Eckhoff J stated:

> It is possible that an owner's inactivity over a long period, taking into account the circumstances, can be a sufficient reason for considering that the proprietary right to a wrecked vessel has been relinquished. If so, this must depend on a total evaluation of the circumstances after the shipwreck, and a balancing of the owner's interest, on the one hand, against a potential appropriator's interest, on the other. I agree . . . that inactivity over a certain number of years cannot in itself be conclusive.

In *The Lusitania*,[139] Sheen J held that so "far as the owners of the contents are concerned, it is a necessary inference from the agreed facts and from the lapse of 67 years before any attempt was made to salve the contents that the owners of the contents abandoned their property".[140] An important factor in inferring abandonment from the evidence in this case was the failure of any claimant to come forth within the statutory one-year period to make a claim. Where the owners of the hull has asserted their ownership rights, despite also not having made any attempt to recover their property over that same 67 years, this was not challenged and abandonment not inferred from the lapse of time and inactivity during that time.[141]

The passage of time and the owners' inactivity are but two factors from which abandonment might be inferred. It is the sum of the evidence that goes to the intent to abandon. For example, in *Fairport International Exploration Inc v The Shipwrecked Vessel Known as the Captain Lawrence*,[142] the vessel stranded in 40–60 ft of water close to shore. The captain and owner of the vessel was a salvage diver, and the salvage capacity in 1933 when it stranded was such that a salvage attempt could have been made, but none was. The owner had also declined Coast Guard assistance when it was offered after the stranding. The owner valued the vessel at no more than $200 at the time, had no insurance and made no provision for the future of the vessel when he died intestate. The court was held that this circumstantial evidence showed an intention to abandon. Similarly, in the Canadian case *Her Majesty the Queen in Right of Ontario v Mar-Dive Corporation et al*,[143] the court was required to determine whether the owner had abandoned ownership of a ship that had sunk in Lake Erie in 1852 due to a collision. The owner had sued the other vessel for the total

---

136 [1924] P 78, 87.
137 [1975] 2 Lloyd's Rep 338.
138 N Rt 346 (1970 ND 107). *Braekhus*, 54.
139 [1986] 1 QB 384.
140 Ibid., 389.
141 See also *Bemis v Lusitania* [1995] AMC 1665 (E.D. Va.). Cf *Deep Sea Resources Inc v The Brother Jonathan* [1995] AMC 1682 (N.D. Cal.), 102 F3d 379 (11th Cir.), where the court considered it premature to make a general declaration of abandonment of cargo and effects which had not yet been raised.
142 [1996] AMC 882, *aff'd* US App. Lexis 1595 (6th Cir. 1997).
143 *Her Majesty The Queen in Right of Ontario v Mar-Dive Corporation et al*, 1997 AMC 1000.

loss of the ship, and had not objected when divers had removed the safe from the ship in 1856. This, the court concluded, amounted to the "giving up", "total desertion" and "absolute relinquishment" of private goods amounting to abandonment. In this case, the owner had, by its actions, impliedly abandoned ownership.

An important factor in inferring abandonment is whether an ownership claim is being made.[144] In *Columbus-America v The Unidentified Wrecked and Abandoned Sailing Vessel*,[145] the US court held that "where a previous owner claims long lost property that was involuntary taken from his control, the law is hesitant to find abandonment and such must be proved by clear and convincing evidence". It is much harder to infer the intent to abandon when the owner denies such intent. Usually though, the claimant derives their proprietary interest from the owner of the vessel when it sank, either by way of purchase,[146] succession (especially when the owner is a corporate entity), or by way of subrogation.[147] The question arises then whether the original owner had abandoned ownership such that these entities could not have acquired any ownership rights, or whether the subsequent owner had abandoned ownership.

Where the vessel is State owned, further complications arise. It has been said that a "State owner of a warship or commercial vessel might be expected to retain an interest longer than a private owner, if only because it is more likely to have the physical, financial and political means to assert rights".[148] It is also the case that States exist in perpetuity such that ownership does not change by way of succession. It is not surprising then that in cases such as *Simon v Taylor*,[149] the court held that the State had not, merely through the passage of time, abandoned ownership. Similarly, State ownership of vessels sunk in the 17th and 18th centuries and only recently discovered have been recognised.[150]

The US in particular has argued that ownership of State vessels can only be abandoned by a clearly expressed intention to that effect.[151] The US Policy for the Protection of Sunken Warships in 2001 declares:

> United States retains title indefinitely to its sunken State craft unless title has been abandoned or transferred in the manner Congress authorized or directed. The United States recognizes the rule of international law that title to foreign sunken State craft may be transferred or abandoned

---

144 [1986] 1 QB 384.

145 [1992] AMC 2705, 2727.

146 In *The Lusitania* [1986] 1 QB 384, the claimant was also the owner of the hull, having purchased the rights from the insurer who had acquired those rights by way of subrogation. This ownership was not disputed and not raised in the proceedings, as it was the ownership of the personal belonging of the passengers and crew, and the cargo that was being claimed.

147 In *The Egypt* (1932) 44 Ll L Rep 21, 39, the owner of the wreck was the insurer. See also *Zych v The Unidentified, Wrecked and Abandoned Vessel Believed to be The Lady Elgin* 1991] AMC 359, 1254, 1259 (N.D. Ill.); *Columbus-America v The Unidentified Wrecked and Abandoned Sailing Vessel* [1992] AMC 2705, [1995] AMC 1985.

148 *The Association and The Romney* [1970] 2 Lloyd's Rep 59, 61.

149 [1975] 2 Lloyd's Rep 338.

150 See *Sea Hunt, Inc v Unidentified Shipwrecked Vessel or Vessels*, 221 F3d 634 (4th Cir 2000), 2000 AMC 2113 (Spanish ownership of *La Galga* sunk in 1750 and Juno sunk in 1802 recognised); *Robinson v Western Australian Museum* (1977) 51 ALJR 806 (Dutch ownership of the *Vergulde Draeck* sunk in 1665 as successor in title of VOC recognised); *Odyssey Marine Exploration, Inc v Unidentified Shipwrecked Vessel*, 675 F Supp 2d 1126 (MD Fla 2009), aff'd 657 F3d 1159 (11th Cir 2011) (Spanish ownership in Mercedes sunk in 1804 recognised).

151 See 4.7.

only in accordance with the law of the foreign flag State. Further, the United States recognizes that title to a United States or foreign sunken State craft, wherever located, is not extinguished by passage of time, regardless of when such sunken State craft was lost at sea.[152]

In relation to the many Japanese wrecks littering the Pacific Ocean, the Japanese government has declared that:

> According to international law, sunken State vessels, such as warships and vessels on government service, regardless of location or of the time elapsed remain the property of the State owning them at the time of their sinking unless it explicitly and formally relinquishes its ownership. Such sunken vessels should be respected as maritime graves. They should not be salvaged without the express consent of the Japanese Government.[153]

Germany, Russia, UK and France have all expressed similar views.[154] The German government declared that it "retains ownership of any German State ship or aircraft owned by it or the German Reich at the time of its sinking." So too Russia, declaring that "Under international law of the sea all the sunken warships and government aircraft remain the property of their flag State. The Government of the Russian Federation retains ownership of any Russian sunken warship, including the warships of the Russian Empire and the Soviet Union, regardless the time they sank".[155] The UK declared that "flag State's rights are not lost merely by the passage of time", while France stated:

> [t]he primacy of the title of ownership is intangible and inalienable: no intrusive action may be taken regarding a French sunken State craft, without the express consent of the French Republic, unless it has been captured by another State prior to sinking. But this primacy does not forbid the State to freely renounce, whenever it wants to and in a formal way, to use some of its right on the wreck (except its ownership).[156]

Indeed, the official policy of the US is that it is a well-established rule of international law "that title to military vessels and aircraft can be lost only by capture or surrender during battle (before sinking), by international agreement, or by an express act of abandonment, gift or sale by the sovereign in accordance with relevant principles of international law and the law of the flag State governing the abandonment of Government property".[157] However, US State practice has not been as unequivocal.[158] For example, while the text

---

152 See Sunken Military Craft Act 2004, s 1401. See 4.6.4 and 6.15.1.
153 R Pixa, "In Defense of Perpetual Title to Sovereign Wrecks" (2009) *Department of the Navy*, www.history.navy.mil/branches/org12-7m.htm.
154 Federal Register, Vol 69 No 24, February 5, 2005, 5647–5648 [*Federal Register 69/24*], www.qpo.gov and https://coast.noaa.gov/data/Documents/OceanLawSearch/President's%202001%20Statement%20on%20 Sunken%20Warships,%2069%20Fed.%20Reg.%205647%20(Feb.%205,%202004).pdf
155 The UK makes the point that it retains both ownership and possession of the wreck of the *HMS Repulse* and *HMS Prince of Wales*, which were sunk off the coast of Malaya in 1941 with the loss of 840 men and rest in comparatively shallow waters, by regularly having navy divers replacing the White Ensigns on the wrecks.
156 France further noted that "[t]hese principles have been applied in the Agreement between the Government of the USA and the Government of the French Republic regarding the wreck of *La Belle*, signed at Washington, DC, March 31st, 2003, and the Agreement between the Government of the USA and the Government of the French Republic concerning the wreck of the *CSS Alabama*, signed at Paris, October 4th, 1989". Federal Register, 69/24.
157 See J Roach, "Sunken Warships and Military Aircraft" (1996) 20 *Marine Policy* 351. See 4.7.
158 For a detailed discussion, see D Bederman, "Rethinking the Legal Status of Sunken Warships" (2000) 31 ODIL [*Bederman*] 97.

and legislative history of the US Abandoned Shipwreck Act 1987 clearly evinces an intention to apply the express abandonment theory to US vessels, it does not do so for foreign vessels. This is also reflected in US Admiralty Court decisions that have found that State vessels of Spain and the UK found in US waters had been impliedly abandoned.[159] Similarly, with regard to US State vessels, little consistency can be found in US Admiralty Court decisions, with implied abandonment found in the case of both the *USS Texas* and *USS Massachusetts*,[160] while an express abandonment was required in the case of the *CSS Alabama*[161] and the *USS Hatteras*.[162] More recent decisions in US jurisprudence has however, coincided with the development of an express theory of abandonment. In *Sea Hunt, Inc v Unidentified Shipwrecked Vessel or Vessels*,[163] the court was required to determine whether Spain had abandoned title to the wrecks of the *La Galga* and *Juno*. While many Spanish vessels have been the subject of litigation in the US, Spain had never made any claim of ownership in the past.[164] Spain's appearance in the litigation to claim ownership was pivotal in the determination of the appropriate test of abandonment. The Court of Appeal referred to the decision in *Columbus-America Discovery Group v Atlantic Mutual Ins Co*,[165] in which it had been held that although abandonment could be inferred in the case of 'long lost' shipwrecks, such an inference would not be sustained where a previous owner came forward and asserted a proprietary interest. Although this case concerned the wreck of a private merchant vessel, the court in the *Sea Hunt* case relied on this precedent to assert that the appearance of Spain in claiming ownership required the application of the express abandonment theory.

While US courts has grappled with the problem of abandonment of warships, few other States have had cause to do so. In the limited cases that have arisen, little consistency can be ascertained.[166] Few cases have reached national courts, and in most cases, the issue has been resolved through bilateral agreements between the claimant flag State and the State in whose waters the wreck was found.[167] In some cases, the agreement does not necessary

---

159 US courts on occasion have found State vessels to have been impliedly abandoned, see *Platoro Limited Inc v The Unidentified Remains of a Vessel* (1981) 518 F Supp 816.

160 *Baltimore, Crisfeld & Onancock Line, Inc v United States*, 140 F2d 230 (4th Cir 1944); and *State by Erwin v Massachusetts Co.*, 95 So 2d 902 (Fla 1956).

161 *United States v Steinmetz*, 763 F Supp 1293 (DNJ 1991), aff'd 973 F2d 212 (3d Cir 1992), cert. denied 113 S Ct 1578 (1993).

162 *Hatteras Inc v The USS Hatteras*, 1984 AMC 1094 (SD Tex 1981), aff'd 698 F2d 1215 (5th Cir 1982).

163 *Sea Hunt, Inc v Unidentified Shipwrecked Vessel or Vessels*, 221 F3d 634 (4th Cir 2000), 2000 AMC 2113.

164 See for example *Treasure Salvors, Inc v Unidentified, Wrecked and Abandoned Sailing Vessel*, 569 F2d 330, 337 (5th Cir 1978); *Cobb Coin Co. v Unidentified, Wrecked and Abandoned Sailing Vessel*, 549 F Supp 540, 561, 557 (SD Fla 1982).

165 *Columbus-America Discovery Group v Atlantic Mutual Ins Co.*, 974 F2d 450 (4th Cir 1992).

166 See *Simon v Taylor and Others* [1975] 2 Lloyd's Rep 338; *Nordsjø Dykker Co v Høvding Skipsopphugging* (1970) 135 Norsk Retstidende 346 (Norwegian Supreme Court) (holding that a German U-boat sunk off Norway had not been impliedly abandoned by Germany); and *Robinson v Western Australian Museum* (1977) 138 CLR 283 (holding that the Netherlands, as successor in title to the Dutch East India Company, had not impliedly abandoned the wreck of the *Vergulde Draeck* off Western Australia).

167 Disputes concerning the ownership of sunken State owned vessels include the *CSS Alabama*, a US vessel sunk in French territorial waters; the *HMS Spartan*, a UK vessel sunk in Italian territorial waters; the *Admiral Nakhimov*, a captured Russian vessel sunk in Japanese territorial waters; the *Juno* and *La Galga*, Spanish vessels sunk in US territorial waters; the *La Belle*, a French vessel sunk in US territorial waters; the *Akerendam*, a VOC vessels sunk in Norwegian waters, and the *Birkenhead*, a British vessel sunk in South African territorial waters.

recognise the claim of ownership of the flag State at all, and the agreements simply proceed on the basis that the States will cooperate in the recovery of the vessel, and in some way share the proceeds or artefacts recovered.[168]

States do not always assert their ownership right to their warships, particularly those from past centuries where its status as a warship may be questionable, or the circumstances of its sailing and sinking, especially in colonial times, may be unpalatable by today's mores.[169] This is further complicated by the time span of any particular nation's maritime history and the context of its use of naval vessels. Spain, for example, had numerous wrecks scattered over the world's oceans, many the result of wars fought with a range of different belligerent States and impacting upon its many colonies. When Spanish wrecks were found, Spain was hesitant to raise claims given its colonial history. For example, in 1969 the Spanish Armada vessel the *Sante Maria de la Rosa* was found off the Republic of Ireland's coast. While Spain expressed interest, no claim of ownership or other right was asserted. It was also not always clear that Spain did, in fact have clear ownership of the wreck. For example, it appears that in relation to three Spanish Armada ships off Streedagh Ireland—*La Lavia, Juliana* and *Santa Maria de la Vision*—none actually belonged to Spain and had been private merchant ships commandeered by Spain when in Spanish ports.[170] In the case of the Armada galleon *Girona*, which was discovered in 1967 off the Northern Irish Coast, the vessel had been engaged at war with the British when it sank and it may be that when sunk it was considered a prize of war.[171] When Spanish vessel were first discovered off the Americas, many with significant cargoes of gold and other valuables on board that had been obtained from its colonies, such as the *Nuestra Senora Atocha* off Florida, Spain made no claim.[172] Instead the US government, individual States and salvors fought

---

168 In the cases of the *Birkenhead* and *CSS Alabama*, it is interesting to note that the flag State claims of ownership were not recognised in the Exchange of Notes. In the case of the *CSS Alabama*, France did acknowledge the US's claim in other correspondence. *Roach,* 381. Similarly, the agreement between the Netherlands and Australia regarding VOC vessels does not actually acknowledge the Dutch government's ownership of these vessels prior to the conclusion of the agreement. *Prott & Strong,* 75–78.

169 O Varmer, "United States of America", in S Dromgoole, *The Protection of Underwater Cultural Heritage: National Perspectives in Light of the UNESCO Convention 2001* (Martinus Nijhoff, 2006) [*Varmer, "United States"*], 351, 368.

170 *King and Anor v The Owners and All Person Claiming an Interest in the La Lavia, Juliana and Santa Maria de la Vision* [1990] 3 IR 413. See further S Birch and DM McElvogue, "*La Lavia, Juliana* and *Santa Maria de la Vision*: Three Spanish Armada Transports Lost Off Streedagh Strand, Co Sligo: An Interim Report" (1999) 28 *Int J Nautical Archaeology* 265.

171 *Dromgoole & Gaskell, "Interests in Wrecks",* 157. See also N O'Conner, "Ireland", in S Dromgoole, *The Protection of Underwater Cultural Heritage: National Perspectives in Light of the UNESCO Convention 2001* (Martinus Nijhoff, 2006), 127; S Kirwan, "Ireland and the UNESCO Convention on the Protection of the Underwater Cultural Heritage" (2010) 5 *J Maritime Archaeology* 105.

172 *Treasure Salvors, Inc v Unidentified, Wrecked and Abandoned Sailing Vessel,* 569 F2d 330, 337 (5th Cir 1978). The wreck was that of the *Nuestra Señora de Atocha,* a Spanish galleon en route to Spain that sank in 1622 on the continental shelf off Florida, had arguably the greatest haul of gold, precious stones and other treasure ever recovered from a Spanish wreck. There is a considerable amount of academic commentary on these issues. See, for example, D Owen, "Some Legal Troubles with Treasure" (1985) 16 JMLC 139; D Owen, "The Abandoned Shipwreck Act of 1987" (1988) 19 JMLC 499; B Alexander, "Treasure Salvage beyond the Territorial Sea" (1989) 20 JMLC 1.

for rights to the wrecks.[173] However, in the late 1990s Spain did intervene and claim ownership when salvors attempted to apply the law of finds to lay claim to the wrecks of the Spanish vessels *Juno*, sunk in 1750, and the *La Galga*, sunk in 1802, both in the waters of Virginia.[174] With Spain as a claimant, the court required an express abandonment which in this case did not exist. Spain too made a claim to the *Mercedes* when US salvors, contrary to Spanish wishes, salvaged artefacts from the wreck.[175]

While many States do insist on the application of an express abandonment theory to State vessels, there is no clear indication that customary international law endorses this theory and certainly no conventional international law that does so. This prompted the Institute of International Law[176] to address specifically the "Legal Regime of Wrecks of Warships and Other State-Owned Ships in International Law".[177] Following a draft report in 2011,[178] a Resolution was adopted in 2015.[179] The purpose of the Resolution is to promote the progress of international law through clarifying the existing law and opining on what the law ought to be if the existing law is uncertain.[180] On the question of ownership and abandonment, the Resolution declared: "Sunken State ships remain the property of the flag State, unless the flag State has clearly stated that it abandoned the wreck or relinquished or transferred title to it".[181] International consensus therefore seems to be converging on this point.

3.4 Insurer's rights

As noted earlier,[182] in many cases where a ship has become a wreck an insurer will have compensated the owner for an ATL or a CTL. An insurer that has compensated an owner for a ship may acquire an interest in whatever remains of the ship—the wreck.

As explained,[183] the almost invariable practice is for an insurer to decline a notice of abandonment given when a ship is claimed to be a CTL. Where the insurer does not accept

---

173 *Treasure Salvors, Inc v Unidentified, Wrecked and Abandoned Sailing Vessel*, 408 F Supp 907 (SD Fla 1976). See also *Platoro Ltd Inc v The Unidentified Remains of a Vessel* (1981) 518 F Supp 816; *Cobb Coin Co. v Unidentified, Wrecked and Abandoned Sailing Vessel*, 549 F Supp 540, 561, 557 (S.D. Fla. 1982).

174 *Sea Hunt, Inc v Unidentified, Shipwrecked Vessel or Vessels*, 47 F Supp 2d 678 (ED Va 1999), 221 F3d 634 (4th Cir. 2000), *cert. denied* 121 S Ct 1079 (2001). For US cases involving Spanish vessels off the coast of the US, see T Scovazzi, "Sunken Spanish Ships before American Courts" (2018) 33 IJMCL [*Scovazzi*], 1; *Bederman*, 117; *Varmer, "United States"*, 351.

175 *Odyssey Marine Exploration, Inc v Unidentified Shipwrecked Vessel*, 675 F Supp 2d 1126 (MD Fla 2009), *aff'd* 657 F3d 1159 (11th Cir 2011). For a full account of litigation concerning Spanish vessel in the US admiralty courts, see *Scovazzi*, 1.

176 The Institute of International Law (*Institut de droit international*) was founded in 1873 at an institution independent of any governmental influence which would be able both to contribute to the development of international law and act so that it might be implemented. See www.idi-iil.org/en/a-propos/.

177 Santiago Session in 2007, 9th Scientific Commission. See N Ronzitti, "The Legal Regime of Wrecks of Warships and Other State-Owned Ships in International Law" (2011) 74 *Yearbook of the Institute of International Law* [*Ronzitti* (2011)], 131.

178 *Ronzitti* (2011), 131.
179 Institute of International Law, www.idi-iil.org/app/uploads/2017/06/2015_Tallinn_09_en-1.pdf.
180 *Ronzitti* (2015), 267.
181 Resolution Art 4; *Ronzitti* (2015), 267, 372.
182 See 2.9.4.
183 See 2.9.4(b), 2.9.5.

the notice of abandonment, the property continues to vest in the assured. That is, the notice of abandonment is merely an offer made by the assured to the insurer and does not amount to abandonment of all proprietary interests such as to render the ship *res nullius*.[184] Indeed, a shipowner may show an intention not to abandon even after giving notice of abandonment.[185] On the other hand, a notice of abandonment may have some evidentiary value as to abandonment of ownership,[186] and though not decisive, might be combined with other evidence such as inactivity over a passage of time.[187]

3.4.1 The insurer's rights to take over property

In the case of an ATL, or the acceptance of a valid notice of abandonment for a CTL, the MIA provides in s 63(1) that "the insurer is entitled to take over the interest of the assured in whatever may remain of the subject matter insured and all proprietary rights incidental thereto".[188] Moreover, irrespective of the acceptance of the notice of abandonment, s 79(1) provides that "[w]here the insurer pays for a total loss . . . he thereupon becomes entitled to take over the interest of the assured in whatever may remain of the subject-matter so paid for, and he is thereby subrogated to all the rights and remedies of the assured in and in respect of that subject-matter as from the time of the casualty causing the loss". On settlement, for example, the insurer becomes entitled to take over the interest of the shipowner in whatever may remain of the ship, such as the benefit of any salvage or the proceeds of sale of any wreck.

It is clear that insurers are "entitled" to take over these rights and that, unless the insurer elects to exercise their rights, they are not forced to accept them.[189] Indeed, in practice it is usual for hull insurers not to accept a notice of abandonment, because the hull may be of little commercial value and may pose liabilities such as wreck removal or pollution costs.[190] However, there is some dicta to the effect that property passed to the insurer from the time of the disaster in respect of which the loss was claimed for and paid,[191] and the MIA 1906 provisions were in part designed to overcome some of the adverse consequences for an insurer of such a finding. If the dicta are correct, it may be necessary to draw distinctions between insured wrecks which sank before and after the passing of the MIA 1906.

The insurer's rights in the ship are not realised until such time as the insurer accepts the notice of abandonment, agrees to indemnify the assured and in fact does so.[192] The abandonment of the assured's interest only crystallises at the time of acceptance and payment,

---

184 *Oceanic Co. v Evans* (1934) 40 Com Cas 111; *Blane S.S. Co. v Minister of Transport* [1951] 2 KB 965, 990. But see *Boston Corporation v France, Fenwick and Co* (1923) 28 Com Cas 367. See further *Rose, Marine Insurance*, 513.
185 See *Ocean St. Nav. Co Ltd v Evans* (1934) 40 Com Cas 108, at 111.
186 See *The Crystal* [1894] AC 508.
187 See 2.9.5(b).
188 See *Kastor Navigations Co Ltd v AGF MAT (The Kastor Too)* [2004] EWCA Civ 277; [2004] 2 Lloyd's Rep 119.
189 See *Arnould*, 1624.
190 *Rose, Marine Insurance*, 517; See *Arnould*, 1662.
191 *Simpson v Thompson* (1877) 3 App Cas 279, 292; *Allgemeine Versicherungs Gesellschaft Helvetia v Administrator of German Property* [1931] 1 KB 672, 687. See *Arnould*, 1661.
192 *Rose, Marine Insurance*, 496.

but operates retrospectively to the time of the actual casualty.[193] The MIA 1906 lays down no time limit in which the insurer must exercise the option, and as such there appears to be no reason why this could not be done many years after the casualty, provided that the assured still has an interest that can be taken over (and not have abandoned the wreck), and the insurer has not acted in a way that could be deemed as a waiver of its rights.[194]

As to the first issue, since s 63(1) addresses the insurer's right to take over "the interest of the assured in whatever may remain of the subject-matter insured", the risk arises that after notice of abandonment is given in the case of a CTL, but not yet accepted by the insurer, the assured abandons all proprietary rights in the wreck or may transfer rights to a third party. This abandonment is not one in relation to the insurer, but one of a proprietary interest in general.[195] An assured's abandonment of a wreck rendering it *res nullius* will allow a third party to acquire a right that will defeat those that the insurer may wish to "take over". Such an action immediately after settlement would seem to defeat one purpose of the MIA 1906, which is to preserve the residual value of the wreck for the insurer.[196] The MIA 1906 is equivocal on the issue, which essentially addresses the relationship between the assured and the insurer, and not those of third parties. Insurers therefore need to ensure they unequivocally elect to take over the interest of the assured pursuant to s 63(1) or 79 and in a timely manner and actually give effect to that election. In *WD Fairway*, the court held that although the insurer's acceptance of the notice of abandonment entitled the insurer to take over the assured's right, and which apply retrospectively to the casualty, until such time as the insurer actually exercises that election and the rights of the assured, the assured retains the right to transfer the wreck to a third party.[197]

As to the second issue, while an insurer can expressly waive its rights pursuant to ss 63(1) and 79, whether a waiver can be implied is less certain. It has been submitted, for example, that where the "insurer settles the assured's claim for an amount which consists of the full value, but with a deduction for the residual value of the wreck, there is *some* evidence that it does not intend to exercise its right (at some future stage) to take over the wreck as it has, effectively, returned its right to the owner".[198] However, given the statutory entitlement to take over the assured's interest in the wreck, it is unlikely that the insurer would be found to have elected to waive this right without an express disclaimer of their entitlement.[199] It might be possible for an insurer to 'hedge its bets' by expressly reserving its rights to take over the wreck at some time in the future.[200]

On acceptance of the notice of abandonment, the insurer is entitled to take over the interest of the assured, and, on payment of the indemnity, the latter is personally liable to transfer the relevant interest to the insurer.[201] The transfer thus depends on the interest of

---

193 *Kastor Navigation Co Ltd v AGF MAT (The Kastor Too)* EWCA Civ 277; [2004] 2 Lloyd's Rep 119.
194 Dromgoole & Gaskell, "Interest in Wreck", 173.
195 See 3.3.
196 Dromgoole & Gaskell, "Interest in Wreck", 174. It is argued that the insurer may have an action against the assured for prejudicing the insurer's interest.
197 *WD Fairway* [2009] EWHC 889 (Admlty); [2009] 2 Lloyd's Rep 191.
198 Dromgoole & Gaskell, "Interest in Wreck", 175.
199 *The WD Fairway (No.3)* [200] EWHC 1782 (Admiralty); [2009] 2 Lloyd's Rep 420. Rose, *Marine Insurance*, 519.
200 Dromgoole & Gaskell, "Interest in Wreck", 175. See 2.9.4(b).
201 Rose, *Marine Insurance*, 520.

the assured. Where the assured has legal title to what amounts to a chattel, the acceptance of the notice of abandonment effectively transfers ownership. Where there are statutory registration requirements, such as the MSA 1995, the insurer will have to comply with these to acquire full title.[202] Until such time as the legal interest is transferred, the insurer will acquire an equitable interest.[203]

Once the notice of abandonment is accepted, the rights of the underwriters are retrospective, operating from the moment of the casualty. This 'clothes' the underwriters with all the rights and responsibilities of the owner from the moment of the loss, including the right to salvage the wreck.[204] Where the underwriters have accepted the notice of abandonment, they will also be liable for a salvage reward when the wreck is recovered by third party salvors.[205]

3.4.2 Subrogation

Section 79(1) of the MIA 1906 provides that "[w]here the insurer pays for a total loss . . . he thereupon becomes entitled to take over the interest of the assured in whatever may remain of the subject-matter so paid for, and he is thereby subrogated to all the rights and remedies of the assured in and in respect of that subject-matter as from the time of the casualty causing the loss". This address not only the proprietary rights the assured might have had in the wreck but also those rights the assured might have had against third parties.[206]

3.4.3 Reinsurance

Many marine risks will be reinsured and it is possible that underwriters may have reinsured a particularly valuable ship or its cargo, either as to a part of its value or (exceptionally) its whole.[207] Section 9(1) of the MIA 1906 provides for reinsurance, declaring "the insurer under a contract of marine insurance has an insurable interest in his risk and may re-insure in respect of it". Such reinsurance contracts are, for the most part, subject to the same principles as those of primary marine insurance contracts.[208] Section 9(2) of the MIA 1906 provides that "[u]nless the policy otherwise provides, the original assured has no right or interest in respect of such reinsurance". However, the reinsurer has an interest in the subject matter insured. The risk insured against has been held to be that in relation to the subject matter of the insurance policy rather than in the primary insurer's liability.[209] The reinsurer thus has an interest in the settlement of claims with the assured,

---

202 Ibid., 523.
203 Ibid., 515.
204 *Arnould*, 1656. An exception applies in the case of prize where insurers cannot claim an interest in the prize when they have accepted a notice of abandonment after the seizure and paid out on the claim. *The Palm Branch* [1916] P 230, [1919] AC 272; *The Zaanland* [1918] P 303.
205 *Arnould*, 1661.
206 See further ibid., 1669.
207 A detailed consideration of reinsurance is beyond the scope of his work. A full account can be found in C Edelman and A Burns, *The Law of Reinsurance* (2nd ed. Oxford University Press, 2013) [*Edelman & Burns, Reinsurance*].
208 *Arnould*, 1745.
209 Ibid., 1750.

and usually, through the use of cooperation clauses or claim control clauses, can participate in the settlement process.[210] The reinsurer is entitled under the principle of subrogation to exercise the insurer's rights of subrogation to claim rights or benefits.[211] A reinsurer could be entitled, for example, to a proportion of any sum later realised by the insurer in respect of the sale of a wreck which had been abandoned as a CTL to the insurer.[212] The reinsurer is thus entitled to exercise in its own name the insurer's right to take over the property on the insurer paying for a loss.

3.4.4 War risks

Marine insurance evolved continually from its original in the 17th century to a point where a clear distinction was made between 'maritime risks' and 'war risks'.[213] Increasingly, 'war risks' were being excluded from general cover.[214] In 1898, a General Meeting of Lloyd's decided that the two risks should be insured by separate policies.[215] This led to the development of separate War Risk Insurance Associations that specialised in war risk policies.[216]

Shortly before the outbreak of World War I, the government concluded that the existing market arrangements would be inadequate to facilitate continued trade and adopted a War Risks Insurance Scheme to shore up the existing cover.[217] This scheme required the existing War Risk Associations to cover all war risks, though the State would then act as reinsurer for 80% of the Associations' liabilities. In some cases, the government acted as the primary war risk insurer. For example, the government standard charterparty (T99) provided for marine risks to be covered by the shipowner and war risks to be covered by the government.[218] With respect to cargo, a State Insurance Office was established that offered a flat rate for cargo war risk insurance.

With the commencement of World War II, the War Risk Insurance Act 1939 and government policy reintroduced a similar reinsurance regime to that which had applied in World War I, but with coverage of up to 96%.[219] In the case of requisitioned ships, the government Tonnage Replacement Scheme provided that vessels would be chartered on terms that insured the vessel with a listed Group of War Risks Associations, with the government paying the premiums.[220] The commercial insurers in World War II continued to provide cover, for example to the Ministry of Food and Supply, under a Food and Supply Master Slip which covered a large proportion of imports.[221] The Ministry of Transport War Risks

---

210 *Edelman & Burns, Reinsurance*, 117.
211 Ibid., 133; *Arnould*, 1772.
212 See *A-G v Glen Line and Liverpool & London War Risks Association* (1930) 37 Ll L Rep 55 (HL).
213 M Miller, *Marine War Risks* (3rd ed, LLP 2005) [*Marine War Risks*], 3.
214 For the modern position especially in relation to terrorism, see 2.3.5 and 2.9.6(b).
215 *Marine War Risks*, 4.
216 A Hurd, *The Merchant Navy: Volume 1* (John Murray, 1921) 229.
217 See further L Lobo-Guerrero, *Insuring War: Sovereignty, Security and Risk* (Routledge, 2012) [*Lobo-Guerrero*].
218 *Arnould*, 1237.
219 Ibid.
220 *Lobo-Guerrero*, 89–96.
221 Dromgoole & Gaskell, "Interest in Wreck", 177.

Insurance Office also provided cargo cover for British and (later) foreign ships where the facilities provided by the commercial market were inadequate.[222]

The lessons of the World Wars were then reflected in the Marine and Aviation Insurance (War Risks) Act 1952, which allows prompt government participation in war risk insurance and reinsurance at the outbreak of war. The division between the two risks was, however, exceptionally difficult to determine, and by 1983 significant reform was needed to address the complex situation. This led to the adoption of new forms and Institute Clauses for use in a variety of circumstances.[223] This applied to the particular risk insured against, and did not affect the essential principles discussed above with respect to the insurers' interest. The 1988 "Agreement on War Risks Reinsurance with Her Majesty's Government" was adopted to further facilitate war risk insurance.[224] Against the background of this complex and changing historical arrangements, it is often difficult to determine what interest the government may have with respect to a wreck that it insured either as the primary war risk insurer or the reinsurer.

As noted in the earlier discussion, in the case of an ATL, or the acceptance of a valid notice of abandonment for a CTL, "the insurer is entitled to take over the interest of the assured in whatever may remain of the subject matter insured and all proprietary rights incidental thereto".[225] Where the UK government has acted as the primary insurer under a War Risk insurance scheme, for a vessel or cargo, it can thus take over the interests of the assured and have an interest in the wreck.

In the case of reinsurance, the manner on which the government as reinsurer has participated in proceedings has changed somewhat. In the working of the World War I War Risks Insurance Scheme, Admiralty representatives would participate in the War Risk Associations' claims committee, but it was the War Risk Association itself that settled the claim with the assured. If the Admiralty representative on the claims committee did not agree with the proposed settlement, then the Admiralty's liability would be settled by arbitration or in court, but this liability, it appears, would be with respect to the Association, rather than with the assured.[226] Nevertheless, the reinsurer (the government) had a continuing interest in the wreck (or cargo) by way of subrogation. The reinsurer is thus entitled to exercise in its own name the insurer's right to take over the property on the insurer paying for a loss.

The 1988 "Agreement on War Risks Reinsurance with Her Majesty's Government" recognises this and further clarifies the principle of subrogation by providing that recoveries under subrogated claims by the UK Mutual War Risks Association against third parties is to be divided proportionately with the Secretary of State. If the Association fails to exercise its powers of subrogation within 30 days of being given notice by the Secretary of State, the latter may institute "proceedings in the name of the Association and/or the name of the owner of the reinsured ship". The agreement goes on to require the Association "to execute such formal assignment or such formal deed of subrogation of all or any rights, and shall take all reasonable steps generally, including production of all information documents and evidence, as the Secretary of State may require".

---

222 Ibid.
223 See *Arnould*, 1231; *Rose, Marine Insurance*, 349.
224 Reprinted in K Michel, *War, Terror and Carriage by Sea* (Informa, 2004); *Marine War Risks*, 573.
225 MIA 1906 s 63(1).
226 *Dromgoole & Gaskell, "Interest in Wreck"*, 176.

3.4.5 Insurer's rights to long lost wrecks

Difficult issues with respect to total losses are exacerbated with respect to long lost wrecks which have subsequently been discovered and found to have some value, indeed often extensive value. For example, the discovery in 1989 of the American Civil War—era *SS Central America* with a purported US$1 billion in gold cargo, led to ownership claims by a number of insurance companies that had paid the owners for its loss in 1857.[227] A US court found that the insurers had acquired an interest in the wreck and cargo through payment of a total loss, and had not abandoned those claims in the intervening years.[228] The insurance interests ultimately obtained 10% of the value of the cargo with the salvors being awarded a 90% salvage award.[229]

Whilst less commercially valuable but of great historical importance, the discovery of the *RMS Titanic* also raised difficult questions concerning the rights of insurers. The *RMS Titanic*'s hull, fixtures and fittings were insured for £1 million and the insurance claim made by White Star Line for the ATL was met in full. A number of the 80 signatories on the Lloyd's slip underwriting the risk of loss, some of which may have represented several underwriters, were either indecipherable or unidentifiable.[230] In any event, no claim to the hull was made by any of the underwriters. Liverpool & London Steamship Protection and Indemnity Association, an insurer of passenger property on the *Titanic*, did assert a claim, which was settled with the salvor out of court.[231]

Subject to the discussion above regarding the insurer taking over the rights of the assured in the wreck, the usual rules of abandonment of those rights and succession of rights applies.[232] Marine insurance though is a particularly complex arrangement, the more so when the insurer is an underwriter or syndicate of Lloyd's of London, the premier marine insurance market, and the likely source of marine insurance for vessels sunk some time ago. Although created as a statutory corporation by the Lloyd's Act 1871,[233] Lloyd's itself is not an insurer but facilitates the provision of marine insurance through its individual underwriting members (or names).[234] Members are companies or limited liability partnerships, as well as individuals, though no new individuals have been admitted since 2003. Members group together into syndicates, managed by a managing agent, as a practical way of sharing the burden of insurer. However, the syndicates are neither a partnership nor any form of body corporate, and each member thus continues to be an individual insurer subject to the MIA 1906. A syndicate that has insured a vessel is therefore in fact a number

---

227 Dromgoole, *Underwater Cultural Heritage*, 103. For an account of the recovery of the *SS Central America*, see G Kinder, *Ship of Gold in the Deep Blue Sea* (Atlantic Monthly Press, 1998).

228 In *Columbus-America Discovery Group v The Unidentified, Wrecked and Abandoned Sailing Vessel*, 974 F2d 450 (4th Cir 1992), the court required a cargo insurer to prove title by showing, *inter alia*, the name of the shipper, the assured, identification of the specific property shipped and the value of each shipment.

229 *Columbus-America Discovery Group v The Unidentified, Wrecked and Abandoned Sailing Vessel*, 1993 WL 580900, at *15 (ED Va Nov. 18, 1993).

230 Dromgoole & Gaskell, "Interest in Wreck", 172.

231 *R.M.S. Titanic, Inc v The Wrecked and Abandoned Vessel*, 742 F Supp 2d 784, 789 (ED Va 2010). See M Zekala, "Liability and Salvage: *Titanic* Jurisprudence in United States Federal Court" (2012) 16 *Lewis & Clark LR* 1075.

232 See 3.3.

233 Still in force. See Lloyd's Act 1982 Sch 3.

234 J Burling, *Lloyd's: Law and Practice* (Informa, 2014), 1.

of separate members that have insured part of the risk. In practice then, the market operates through agents who will act on behalf of the underwriters or syndicates. In respect of syndicate underwriting, the individual members still retain full liabilities under the policy.

The focus of the membership at Lloyd's is usually on the member's liability under the policies underwritten by the member or a syndicate the member is party to. The current Lloyd's Members' Agent's Agreements (both General and for Corporate Members)[235] have detailed provisions dealing with matters such as the death and insolvency of a member during a particular year of account.[236] Neither of the agreements appears to deal specifically with the position where benefits may accrue to the underwriters many years after the particular year of account has been closed. Since the liabilities of deceased members survive as liabilities of their estates,[237] so benefits accruing to members accrue to the estate. Indeed, the Lloyd's standard Managing Agent's Agreement defines a 'name' to include "the Name's executors or administrators, trustees in bankruptcy and any receiver appointed under the Mental Health Act 1983 and any person performing similar functions in any jurisdiction".[238] So in the case of long lost wrecks where the insurers paid for a total loss (or may have paid for a CTL, accepted a notice of abandonment and taken over the rights of the assured) and has not abandoned their rights to the wreck, each individual insurer's estate will have a claim to a relative portion of the wreck. In many cases, however, it may be difficult to identify the individual insurers given that often it is merely a signature on a slip, or if they can be identified to trace their ultimate beneficiaries. Since the onus is on interested parties to assert their interest in a wreck, in practice the interests of these individual insurers are simply not given effect. Such was the case with the *RMS Titanic* in terms of the hull insurers, where no claimants came forward, and in the case of the *Lusitania*, where no claimants for the belonging of any of the passengers made a claim.

Interestingly though, Lloyd's itself has provided for a direct interest in at least one wreck. *HMS Lutine* sank in 1799 off Holland with a cargo worth over £1 million in specie, insured by a Lloyd's syndicate.[239] At the time of Lloyd's incorporation, the prospect of further recoveries from *HMS Lutine* still existed, but by then all the individual names were dead. As such, s 35 of the Lloyd's Act 1871 provided that Lloyd's could "do or join in doing all such lawful things as they think expedient with a view to further salving from the wreck of the *Lutine*" and to hold sums obtained for "purposes connected with shipping or marine insurance", subject to possible claims being made by individual insurer's beneficiaries should they come forward to make a claim. This, however, was only provided for in the specific case of the *Lutine*, and does not appear to apply to any other wreck. A conclusion that has been drawn from this is that "Lloyd's would probably not have any right to

---

235 Lloyd's Standard Managing Agent's Agreement, www.lloyds.com/market-resources/market-services/lloyds-standard-agency-agreements.

236 Clause 14.2 of the Managing Agent's Agreement states that in such cases, the profit or loss of a given year shall be apportioned proportionately amongst the other members of the syndicate, as if the particular name had not been an underwriter for that year.

237 *Lloyd's: Law and Practice*, 86.

238 Lloyd's Standard Managing Agent's Agreement, www.lloyds.com/market-resources/market-services/lloyds-standard-agency-agreements.

239 See *Dromgoole & Gaskell, "Interest in Wreck"*, 171, citing R Flowers, M Wynn Jones, *Lloyd's of London: An Illustrated History* (1974), 114–118, and H Lay, *A Textbook of the History of Marine Insurance* (1925), 58.

claim on behalf of such untraceable underwriters in the absence of an equivalent statutory sanction for other wrecks".[240]

Section 34 of Lloyd's Act 1871 does allow Lloyd's to aid or undertake the discovery, recovery, protection or removal of wrecks, although s 41 leaves unaffected "any interest or right of any shipowner or other person" in the wreck.

As discussed earlier, Lloyd's, the IUA and use of the Salvage Association archives[241] enables insurance interests to trace possible rights in relation to long lost but recently found wrecks.

3.5 Salvors' and finders' rights

The rendering of a salvage service usually gives rise to a salvage reward if property of value has been saved.[242] In certain circumstances, salvors will be entitled to a reward where no property of value has been saved but damage to the marine environment has been averted or minimised by the salvor.[243] Importantly, the salvor is granted a maritime lien to secure the payment of the salvage reward.[244] While the maritime lien does not depend on possession, salvors may—and often do—assume possession of recovered objects and may seek to retain that possession until security for the payment of the salvage reward is provided.[245] In some circumstances (eg where they salve a 'derelict'), salvors may have possessory rights that can be asserted against competing salvors. In other circumstances, a 'salvor' might be regarded as a finder such that the finder acquires a proprietary right in the objects recovered.[246]

3.5.1 The salvors' rights to possession

While the maritime lien does not require the salvor to be in possession of the salved property, salvors do have rights in relation to that property which will be protected as against the owners of the property and against third parties that interfere, or attempt to interfere, with the property of the salvage operations.[247] If the salvage services are rendered under contract, then any action by the contracting owner of the property that interferes with the salvors' ability to complete its contractual obligations is a breach of contract giving rise to damages.[248] On the other hand, a contract such as the LOF[249] 2011 requires the salvor to rely on the contractual provisions for security and cannot take possession of, or detain, the salved property other than in accordance with the contract.

---

240 *Dromgoole & Gaskell "Interest in Wreck"*, 171. "It would also seem that the provision was not designed to enable the proceeds to be spread amongst existing members, but to further more general, if not charitable, aims".
241 See 3.2.2.
242 See 2.7.1 and 2.7.7.
243 See 2.7.1.
244 See 2.7.8.
245 Salvage Convention 1989 Art 21(3).
246 See 3.5.4.
247 *Brice*, 207.
248 Ibid. *The Maude* (1893) 7 Asp 400, 401.
249 *Kennedy & Rose*, 517; LSSAC 2014 cl 4.9.

Absent a salvage contract, a salvor that is replaced by the owner with another salvor is entitled to a salvage award for the service rendered up until replaced, but is not entitled to compensation for dispossession on the basis of *restitution in integrum*.[250] Nevertheless, the determination of the salvage award has, in a number of cases, taken into account the fact that the salvor was dispossessed and replaced with another salvor, enhancing the salvage award.[251] If the salvage services were rendered under contract, then any action by the contracting owner of the property that prevents the salvor from completing his contractual obligations is a breach of contract giving rise to damages.[252]

In the normal course of events where the master retains control of a vessel but salvors rendered a salvage service, the right to possession of both the vessel and the cargo remain with the shipowner. Where the master remains in control of the vessel, he continues to make decisions as to its operation, including whether to accept or reject any offer of salvage services.[253] In *The Dantzic Packet*,[254] the court held that the master in charge of the vessel is entitled to "employ whom he pleases, and to take what measures he thinks proper for the preservation of the ship".[255] Where the master refuses the offer of salvage, but salvage services are nevertheless rendered, the right to salvage may arise if the refusal was unreasonable under the circumstances.[256] Similarly, where the owners have not allowed the master to accept salvage services when it was appropriate that he do so, salvage has been awarded.[257] This is reflected in Art 19 of the Salvage Convention 1989, which provides that "Services rendered notwithstanding the express and reasonable prohibition of the owner or master of the vessel . . . shall not give rise to payment under this Convention".[258] In all these circumstances, provided the master remain in possession and control of the vessel, salvors acquire no possessory interest in the vessel or cargo.[259]

Where the master has temporarily left the ship in order, for example, to obtain assistance, and the master then returns to the ship and takes control, salvors are bound to hand over control to the master and have at no time any possessory right.[260] Exceptionally, however, a salvor may retain possession in such circumstances where the salvor's security may be at risk if the salvor does return the property to the master.[261]

If the master and crew have abandoned the vessel so as to render it derelict, the salvor acquires a possessory right enforceable against both the owner and against third parties such as competing salvors. Where the vessel is derelict, but remains afloat and in the continued possession of the salvor, the possessory rights of the salvor are protected. In *Cossmann v West*, the court held that the salvors who first takes possession of the vessel "have the

---

250 *The Unique Mariner (No.2)* (1831) 166 ER 275.
251 *The City of Lancaster* (1929) 34 Ll L Rep 381 (CA); *The Comitas* (1947) 80 Ll L Rep 672; *The Loch Tulla* (1950) 84 Ll L Rep 62, 69.
252 *The Unique Mariner (No.2)* (1831) 166 ER 275.
253 Kennedy & Rose, 519; Brice, 40–43; Gaskell, "The Lloyd's Open Form and Contractual Remedies", 306.
254 (1837) 3 Hagg 383.
255 See also *The Champion* (1863) 3 Br & Lush 69, 71; *The Glasgow Packet* (1844) 2 W Rob 306, 312.
256 *The Auguste Legembre* [1902] P 123.
257 *The Flore* (1929) 34 Ll L Rep 172, 176.
258 See also Salvage Convention 1910 Art 3.
259 *Cossmann v West* (1887) 13 App Cas 160, 181.
260 Ibid.; *The Capella* [1892] P 70 PDAD; *The Aquila* (1798) 1 C Rob 36, 165 ER 87, 88.
261 Kennedy & Rose, 520.

entire and absolute possession and control of the vessel, and no one can interfere with them except in the case of manifest incompetence".[262] Similarly, in *The Dantzic Packet*,[263] the court held that "where there is a set of salvors who are in actual possession of a vessel found derelict . . . they cannot be extruded by other persons strangers to the vessel".[264]

In the case of a derelict that has sunk or stranded (wreck), it is much harder for a salvor to continue to possess the wreck in the conventional sense. The nature of the marine environment is such that the salvor is likely to have to leave the wreck site and return to shore on numerous occasions. When this occurs, problems may arise with respect of the owner's attempts to stop, or to control, the salvage operations or where other competing salvors attempt to take possession when the first salvors have left the wreck site. The possessory rights of the first salvor are therefore of some importance.

3.5.2 Possession of sunken wrecks

Where the vessel is derelict and sunk so as to make continued actual possession difficult, if not impossible, the crucial question is whether the nature and extent of the acts of the salvor in relation to the wreck are sufficient to constitute possession. In order to establish that they are in possession of a derelict the salvors must show "firstly, that they have *animus possidendi*, and secondly, that they have exercised such use and occupation as is reasonably practicable having regard to the subject matter of the derelict, its location, and the practice of salvors".[265] Where there are salvors competing over a derelict, the first salvor is entitled to protect its possessory rights by using the normal civil law remedies, for example by seeking damages or an injunction. The effectiveness of an injunction, in particular, will depend on the extent to which the second salvor is legally or practically amenable to the control of the court.[266] The law of salvage has therefore developed the status of salvor-in-possession, or "right of first salvor", whereby the court will recognise the first salvors exclusive right to salvage the discovery.[267] This was comprehensively addressed in *The Tubantia*.[268]

The *Tubantia* was a Dutch-flagged steamship torpedoed by *UB-13* in 1916 in international waters in the North Sea whilst carrying a valuable cargo owned by the German government that was being sent to Argentina. Six years after it sink, the plaintiff undertook an expedition to recover its cargo. They buoyed the site when first finding it and undertook salvage operations when the weather permitted. The weather allowed only about 8 minutes per day in the

---

262 *Cossmann v West* (1887) 13 App Cas 160, 181. Dromgoole and Gaskell hold that where an owner wants to resume possession in circumstances where the salvor is not incompetent, which might undermine the salvor's security where it is not possible to perfect it through an action *in rem*, the best approach is to allow the owner to resume possession, by itself or through its agents, but to preserve any salvage claims of the first salvor. The lien might not be perfected if the vessel travels to a State where the maritime lien cannot be enforced in practice, eg where a State owned vessel is concerned. It is submitted that the possessory lien should not be extended. *Dromgoole & Gaskell, "Interest in Wreck"*, 189. The mechanism does exist in salvage law to compensate superseded salvors: see eg *The Hassel* [1959] 2 Lloyd's Rep 82.
263 (1835) 166 ER 447.
264 See also *The Maria* (1834) 166 ER 364.
265 *Morris v Lyonesse Salvage Co Ltd (The Association and The Romney)* [1970] 2 Lloyd's Rep 59, 61.
266 *Dromgoole & Gaskell, "Interest in Wreck"*, 190.
267 On the status of salvor in possession in the UK, see *Fletcher-Tomenius et al*, 263.
268 [1924] P 78.

holds, and only 25 days were available in 1923. The plaintiff had not contacted the owners and therefore had no contract or other salvage agreement. The defendants had not been aware of the plaintiff's salvage operation until they arrived at the site, but on finding salvors already there nevertheless began to undertake their own salvage operation. This, the plaintiff argued, interfered with their rights to the wreck. The court agreed and granted an injunction on the basis that the first salvor had sufficient possessory rights arising from the salvor having initiated salvage operations first and, through their activities and buoying the wreck, had effective possession.[269] The interference of the defendant amounted to a trespass to goods.

Together with the requisite *animus possidendi*, the salvors must have exercised "such use and occupation as is reasonably practicable having regard to the subject matter of the derelict, its location, and the practice of salvors".[270] This is a matter of fact and degree. In *Bemis v Lusitania*,[271] the US court found that while the plaintiff has undertaken an initial successful expedition to the known site of the wreck of the *Lusitania*, a subsequent photographic expedition with the National Geographic Society and a failed expedition in 1994 were insufficient to establish possession, dominion or control, and the court refused an injunction to restrain others from the wreck site.[272]

Where a wreck lies beyond the territorial waters of a State, that State no longer has jurisdiction over the actual site and it may be difficult for a salvor to assert possessory right in relation to that wreck. While a coastal State may have *in personam* jurisdiction over the salvor, the State does not have jurisdiction over the *res*—the wreck. In the UK, the court's jurisdiction is limited by its *in personam* jurisdiction. In the US, however, admiralty courts have developed the concept of *quasi in rem* jurisdiction, which is a form of extra-territorial jurisdiction over wreck sites in international waters. *Quasi in rem* jurisdiction is underpinned by the principle of constructive possession which allows the use of the fiction that the wreck and all artefacts constitute a single *res* that can be in the salvor's possession[273] By brining part of the *res*, in the form of a single artefact from the wreck, into the court's jurisdiction, the fiction is established that the whole wreck is then subject to the court's jurisdiction. For example, in *J. F. Moyer v The Wreck of the Andrea Doria*,[274] salvors recovered mosaic friezes from the wreck of the *Andrea Doria* that had sunk in international waters in 1956 following a collision, and brought them into the US. The court, whilst recognising that the wreck site lay in international waters, granted the salvor protective relief over the site itself on the basis that the material brought into the court's jurisdiction was a substitute for the wreck itself, and represented the wreck, it being impossible to have brought the wreck itself into the jurisdiction. Thus, the salvor was recognised as a salvor-in-possession and the court recognised the salvor's exclusive right to salvage the wreck. Similarly, following the discovery of the *Central America*, the salvor recovered a lump of coal and brought this to the court in order to invoke the court's *quasi in rem* jurisdiction.[275]

---

269 *The Tubantia* [1924] P 78.
270 *Morris v Lyonesse Salvage Co Ltd (The Association and The Romney)* [1970] 2 Lloyd's Rep 59, 61.
271 [1995] AMC 1665 (E.D. Va.).
272 Cf *Deep Sea Resources Inc v The Brother Jonathan* [1995] AMC 1682 (ND Cal), 102 F3d 379 (11th Cir), where an injunction was granted to a first finder.
273 See *Odyssey Marine Exploration, Inc v Unidentified Shipwrecked Vessel*, 657 F3d 1159 (11th Cir 2011).
274 *Moyer v The Wreck of the Andrea Doria*, 836 F Supp 1099 (DNJ 1993).
275 *Columbus-America Discovery Group, Inc v Unidentified Wreck of the S.S. Central America* [1989] AMC 1955.

More famously, US admiralty courts have also exercised *quasi in rem* jurisdiction over the site of the *Titanic*, which lies on the outer limits of the Canadian continental shelf, and granted the salvor possessory rights to the wreck.[276] Following the discovery of the wreck in 1985 a US company, Titanic Ventures, recovered approximately 1,800 artefacts from the wreck site. A further expedition was undertaking in 1993 by RMS Titanic Inc (RMST), the successor in title to Titanic Ventures, recovering a further 800 artefacts. Subsequently, RMST sought exclusive salvage rights to the wreck.[277] While the wreck site lay outside the geographical jurisdiction of the court, RMST sought to invoke the court's *in rem* jurisdiction by presenting a single artefact recovered from the wreck before the court. This the court considered sufficient to invoke a *quasi in rem* jurisdiction, allowing it to declare RMST to be salvor in possession.[278] Only one other party, Liverpool & London Steamship Protection and Indemnity Association, had filed a claim asserting an interest in the wreck. Later RMST entered into a settlement agreement with the Association, and the District Court dismissed the Association's claim.[279] Since no other claims were made to the recovered artefacts, the court declared RMST the "true, sole and exclusive owner of any items salvaged from the wreck".[280]

In 1994, RMST undertook another expedition to the wreck site and recovered further artefacts from the debris field. However, RMST's failure to undertake an expedition during the 1995 'weather window' prompted a rival salvor to request a rescission of the court's order granting RMST exclusive salvage rights on the grounds that RMST had failed to diligently salvage the *Titanic*, had evidenced no intention to salvage it in the future and, at that time, was financially incapable of utilising its rights.[281] The test as to the continuation of the salvor's status as salvor in possession required the salvor to show that the salvage operations were ongoing, undertaken with due diligence and has some prospects of success.[282] For salvage operations to be ongoing, "the possession need not be continuous, but only as such the nature and situation of the salvage operations permit. . . . Possession is not defeated, however, when the salvor leaves the wreck for a justifiable reason and with an intention of returning".[283] The court reviewed the activities of RMST and held that RMST had done enough to maintain its status as salvor in possession, particularly given the short weather window.

---

276 *R.M.S. Titanic, Inc v The Wrecked and Abandoned Vessel ("Titanic I")*, 924 F Supp 714, 716 (ED Va 1996). On the discovery of the *Titanic*, see RD Ballard, *The Discovery of the Titanic* (Madison Publishing, 1987); RD Ballard, *Explorations: An Autobiography* (Wiedenfeld & Nicolson, 1995).

277 For an overview of the litigation regarding the *Titanic*, see C Forrest, "Salvage Law and the Wreck of the Titanic" (2000) 1 LMCLQ 1.

278 *R.M.S. Titanic, Inc v The Wrecked and Abandoned Vessel*, 924 F Supp 714, 716 (ED Va 1996). For a discussion on the ownership of the wreck and artefacts, see MS Timpany, "Ownership Rights in the *Titanic*" (1986) 37 *Case Western Law Review* 72; D Cyclon, "Who owns the *Titanic*?" (1985) 28 *Oceanus* 94.

279 *R.M.S. Titanic, Inc v The Wrecked and Abandoned Vessel*, 920 F Supp 96, 97 (ED Va 1996). Another rival salvor had earlier sought to challenge RMSTs status as salvor in possession but withdrew its challenge when it appeared unlikely to succeed. See *Marex Titanic Inc v Wrecked & Abandoned Vessel*, 805 F Supp 375 (ED Va 1992); *Marex Titanic Inc v Wrecked & Abandoned Vessel*, 2 F3d 544 (4th Cir 1993). See also *Zekala*.

280 *R.M.S. Titanic, Inc v The Wrecked and Abandoned Vessel*, 924 F Supp 714, 716 (ED Va 1996).

281 Ibid., 716.

282 Ibid., 722–724.

283 Ibid., 720, citing *Moyer v Wrecked and Abandoned Vessel, Known as the Andrea Doria*, 836 F Supp 1099, 1106 (DNJ 1993).

The extent to of the salvor right as salvor in possession was further tested when, having lost the ability to salvage the wreck, the rival salvor decided to undertake an expedition to the wreck site for the sole purpose of photographing the wreck. RMST immediately sought an injunction preventing the rival from undertaking this expedition.[284] In granting the injunction, the court indicated that "photographs can be marketed like any other physical artefact and, therefore, the rights to images, photographs, videos, and the like belong to [RMST]".[285] Indeed, the court found that allowing a party to access the wreck to take photographs was "akin to allowing another salvor to physically invade the wreck and take artefacts themselves".[286]

In 1998, the British company Deep Ocean Expeditions began marketing an expedition called "Operation Titanic" that would take tourists to visit the wreck whilst accompanying a scientific expedition from the Russian Academy of Sciences. When RMST learned of the expedition, it filed another motion for a preliminary injunction. The court, continuing to exercise *in rem* jurisdiction granted the injunction, preventing in other party from (i) interfering with the rights of RMST, as salvor in possession; (ii) conducting search, survey or salvage operations of the wreck; (iii) obtaining any image, video or photograph of the wreck or wreck site; and (iv) entering the wreck.[287] This was reversed on appeal. The Fourth Circuit limited the application of its constructive *in rem* jurisdiction that allowed it to grant possessory rights to the salvor. The court ruled that constructive *in rem* jurisdiction in relation to a wreck site beyond its geographical jurisdiction was 'imperfect' or 'inchoate' and was underpinned by some artefact that represented the wreck being within the court's jurisdiction.[288] This limitation on the court's jurisdiction reflects the limits of the possessory rights that can be granted with respect to wrecks beyond a court's territorial jurisdiction, and the inability to apply these to foreign vessels and nationals.

In 2000 the court further ordered the salvor not to penetrate or cut into the *Titanic* or to sell any of the artefacts.[289] RMST then sought to be declared owner of the wreck and all the artefacts, including many that were taken to France after the initial 1987 expedition, on the basis of the law of finds. This the court rejected.[290] As such, the salvor's possessory rights were limited to that of salvor in possession and to the artefacts recovered from the wreck and actually in the salvor's possession.[291] RMST was regarded as the salvor in possession of those recovered artefacts, not the owner thereof. RMST therefore initiated a salvage claim for US$110,859,200. Since there was no identifiable owner, and no suitable purchaser for the collection could be found, the court awarded *in specie* the entire collection to RMST subject to the existing covenants—that is, that the collection could only be sold

---

284 *R.M.S. Titanic, Inc v The Wrecked and Abandoned Vessel*, No. 2:93CV902, 1996 WL 650135 (ED Va Aug. 3, 1996).

285 Ibid., at *3.

286 Ibid., at *2. See also *Lindsay v The Wrecked and Abandoned Vessel RMS Titanic*, No. 97 Civ. 9248(HB), 1998 WL 557591 (SDNY Sept. 2, 1998) in relation to a photographer's claim to be recognised a salvor in possession—though settled before determination.

287 *R.M.S. Titanic, Inc v The Wrecked and Abandoned Vessel*, 9 F Supp 2d 624, 640 (ED Va 1998).

288 Ibid., 633.

289 *R.M.S. Titanic, Inc v The Wrecked and Abandoned Vessel*, Civ. No. 2:93cv902 (ED Va July 28, 2000).

290 *R.M.S. Titanic, Inc v The Wrecked and Abandoned Vessel*, 435 F3d 521 (4th Cir 2006).

291 *R.M.S. Titanic, Inc v The Wrecked and Abandoned Vessel*, 531 F Supp 2d 691, 693 (ED Va 2007).

by RMST as a collection, and that RMST's salvor in possession status was subject to the court's continued oversight.[292]

Although discovery of a wreck site without recovering an artefact has, at least in the US, been insufficient to vest exclusive salvage rights, telepresence may offer an alternative method of constructive possession for a salvor, alleviating the salvors need to proffer an artefact from the wreck site. Telepresence refers to the ability of the salvors to locate and to investigate the wreck site using remotely operated vehicles (ROVs) and to provide real-time imaging of the wreck. In *Columbus-America Discovery Group v the Unidentified, Wrecked and Abandoned Sailing Vessel*,[293] the court held that the "exercise of effective control is achieved not through physical presence of a human being at the ocean bottom" but instead through a combination of four factors: (i) locating the object searched for; (ii) real-time imaging of the object; (iii) placement or the capability to place teleoperated or robotic manipulators on or near the object (capable of manipulating it as directed by human beings exercising control from the surface); and (iv) present intent to control (including deliberately not disturbing) the location of the object. This 'telepresence' or 'telepossession' was an important component of the salvor's possession of the wreck site.[294] However, the mere discovery of a wreck does not give a right to possession.[295]

The salvor's right to possession of recovered artefacts is, however, limited by the MSA 1995. Sections 226, 236 and 237 provided for the Receiver of Wreck to take possession of wreck found or recovered in UK waters or found in other waters but brought directly into the UK.[296] More specifically, s 236(1) provides that any person who finds or takes possession of wreck in UK waters or brings wreck found elsewhere into UK waters must "if he is the owner of it, give notice to the receiver stating that he has found or taken possession of it, and describing the marks by which it may be recognised" or "if he is not the owner of it, give notice to the receiver that he has found or taken possession of it and, as directed by the receiver, either hold it to the receiver's order or deliver it to the receiver".[297] It is an offence to fail to report a find to the receiver.[298] It does not, however, apply to salvors who remain in possession of a ship in order to ensure the safety of the vessel.[299]

3.5.3 In specie *salvage award*

The determination of the salvage award, and the obligation to pay, was addressed in 2.8.7. US courts have awarded *in specie* awards rather than a monetary award, particularly in

---

292 *R.M.S. Titanic, Inc v The Wrecked and Abandoned Vessel*, 804 F Supp 2d 508, 509 (ED Va 2011).

293 *Columbus-America Discovery Group v the Unidentified, Wrecked and Abandoned Sailing Vessel* [1989] AMC 1955, reversed on other grounds [1992] AMC 2705.

294 [1989] AMC 1955, 1958. See *Dromgoole & Gaskell, "Interest in Wreck"*, 193.

295 *Robinson v Western Australian Museum* (1977) 51 ALJR 806, 821; *Treasure Salvors Inc v The Unidentified, Wrecked and Abandoned Sailing Vessel* [1981] AMC 1857.

296 On the Receiver of Wreck see 4.4.

297 Under the MSA 1894 s 518, there was an obligation to deliver the wreck to the Receiver, but this requirement was removed and the present text in paragraph (b) was inserted by the Merchant Shipping (Registration etc.) Act 1993 Sch 4 para 22. Indeed, the policy now is that in most cases the salvor will be asked to hold the material to the Receiver's order. Wreck and Salvage Law, www.gov.uk/guidance/wreck-and-salvage-law.

298 See *The Zeta* (1875) 21 TLR 648. The salvor will still be entitled to salvage, even though not complying with this section, if in the end, the property is returned to the owner. See *Brice*, 306. See 4.4.3.

299 *The Liffey* (1887) 6 Asp MLC 255; *Kennedy & Rose*, 525.

relation to the recovery of historic wrecks. In *Cobb Coin Co. v Unidentified, Wrecked and Abandoned Sailing Vessel*,[300] the court made an *in specie* award on the basis that "the property saved is uniquely and intrinsically valuable beyond its monetary value".[301] More recently, as discussed above, the court awarded *in specie* the entire collection to RMST, the salvors in possession of the *Titanic* wreck site.[302] While the result may appear to be the same as that achieved through an application of the law of finds, the difference lies in the capacity of the court making the *in specie* award in accordance with salvage law to ensure that it continues to have oversight over the activities of the salvor on the wreck through the recognition of the salvor as salvor in possession. The law of finds would not recognise any ongoing possessory rights to the wreck site itself; only to the recovered artefacts.

The MSA 1995 does not provide for an *in specie* award. However, the discretion granted to the Receiver of Wreck does allow the Receiver to essentially make an *in specie* award. This is commonly done when the recovered artefact has a low monetary value and is not historically or archaeologically important—such as a plate or ordinary porthole. The salvor is offered the artefact in lieu of a salvage award, as the cost of selling the artefact at auction would exceed the value of the artefact.[303]

If the recovered artefact has some archaeological or historical value[304] and was found within UK territorial waters such that it is vested in the Crown[305] the Receiver of Wreck may obtain expert advice as to whether the artefact ought to be placed in a museum or similar public institution. Where possible, the Receiver of Wreck will try to keep collections of recovered artefacts from the same wreck together and offer newly recovered material to the institution holding the collection. However, unless the salvor voluntary waves their salvage claim, it is usually that institution that then has to pay the salvage award to the salvor. If the institution cannot or does not wish to pay the salvage award, the artefact can be offered to the salvor in lieu of the salvage award. In cases of high-value historic wreck material where a museum cannot be found to take the artefact, it may be auctioned.[306]

Where an owner of recovered artefacts is identified, but the owner does not want the property back and does not, therefore, want to pay a salvage award, the Receiver of Wreck may also offer the salvor the artefacts in lieu of a salvage award.[307]

3.5.4 Finds

The common law recognises that a finder of property should be entitled to claim property not claimed by anyone else. In *Parker v British Airways Board*,[308] the court recognised that

---

300 549 F Supp 540, 560 (SD Fla 1982).

301 See also *Columbus-America Discovery Group, Inc v Atlantic Mutual Insurance Co*, 974 F2d 450, 469 (4th Cir 1992).

302 *R.M.S. Titanic, Inc v The Wrecked and Abandoned Vessel*, 804 F Supp 2d 508, 509 (ED Va 2011).

303 See 4.4.5.

304 Whilst the MSA 1995 does not differentiate between modern and historic wreck, the Receiver of Wreck considers that any wreck that sank over 100 years ago is historic.

305 See 4.3.

306 See 4.4.5.

307 See 4.4.5.

308 [1982] QB 1004. See also *Elwes v Brigg Gas Co* (1886) 13 Ch D 562; see 1.2, which concerned a prehistoric boat embedded in the land rather than at sea.

a number of persons might have a right to claim an interest in lost goods, including the occupier of land, although the finder may have a greater interest than all but the true owner.

In the case of wreck, the Crown has a right to unclaimed wreck as either *wreccum maris* or *adventurae maris*, now reflected in s 241 of the MSA 1995, which declares that "Her Majesty and Her Royal successors are entitled to all unclaimed wreck found in the United Kingdom or in United Kingdom waters except in places where Her Majesty or any of Her Royal predecessors has granted the right to any other person". In *Pierce v Bemis (The Lusitania)*,[309] the court held that property found outside of the UK territorial waters and brought into the UK was not subject to the Crown's right, and that, in the absence of a claim by the true owners of the property, the finder had good title to that property.[310]

In the US, the court in *Treasure Salvors Inc v The Unidentified, Wrecked and Abandoned Sailing Vessel*[311] held that the Crown's prerogative right to wreck had not been inherited and was thus not a part of US law. The court went on to hold that "in extraordinary cases, such as this one, where the property has been lost or abandoned for a very long period . . . the maritime law of finds supplements the possessory interest normally granted to a salvor and vests title by occupancy in one who discovers such abandoned property and reduces it into possession".[312] The law of finds was applied in a number of subsequent cases.[313] The US government's unsuccessful claim that the English Crown's right to wreck had been inherited in US law led to the adoption of the *Abandoned Shipwreck Act* in 1987.[314] However, more recent Admiralty Court decisions have sought to limit the application of the law of finds.[315] In *R.M.S. Titanic, Inc v The Wrecked and Abandoned Vessel*, the US Fourth Circuit regarded the law of finds as "a disfavoured common-law doctrine rarely applied to wrecks and then only under limited circumstances".[316] The court was concerned to maintain control over the salvor's activities on the wreck of the *Titanic*, and could only do so by the application of salvage law that recognised the salvor as salvor in possession. Moreover, by applying salvage law and awarding the salvor an *in specie* award of all the recovered artefacts rather than applying the law of finds and vesting ownership in the finder, the court was able to continue to impose on the salvor the covenants that regulated the activities of the salvor on the wreck site and the salvor's possession of the recovered artefacts.[317]

---

309 [1986] QB 384.
310 See 4.3.
311 [1978] AMC 1404 (*Salvors I*), [1981] AMC 1529 (*Salvors II*), [1981] AMC 1857 (*Salvors III*).
312 [1981] AMC 1857, 1865.
313 *Zych v Unidentified, Wrecked and Abandoned Vessel*, 755 F Supp 213 (ND Ill 1990); *Martha's Vineyard Scuba Headquarters, Inc v Unidentified, Wrecked and Abandoned Steam Vessel*, 833 F2d 1059 (1st Cir 1987). See also *Columbus-America Discovery Group, Inc v Atlantic Mutual Insurance Company*, 974 F2d 450 (4th Cir 1992); *Sea Hunt, Inc v Unidentified, Shipwrecked Vessel or Vessels*, 47 F Supp 3d 678 (ED Va 1999).
314 See further Chapter 6.
315 See further W Dunlap, "Ownership of Underwater Cultural Heritage" (2018) 49 JMLC 425.
316 *R.M.S. Titanic, Inc v The Wrecked and Abandoned Vessel*, 435 F3d 521, 530 (4th Cir 2006).
317 Ibid.

CHAPTER 4

State rights and wreck

4.1 Introduction

Chapter 5 addresses States' jurisdictional capacity to regulate wreck within the various maritime zones provided for in UNCLOS. This chapter addresses the exercise of those rights by the UK (and other States by way of comparison) as well as State rights arising from national law. This begins with a consideration of the UK's regulatory capacity to respond to wrecks that pose a hazard.

The UK's regulatory regime also addresses the right of the State to claim ownership of wreck and of the regulation of existing wrecks—as opposed to wrecks that pose an immediate hazard at the time of the wrecking event.[1] Further regulatory provisions are addressed in the Protection of Wrecks Act 1973 and in the Protection of Military Remains Act 1986, which addresses issues relevant to wreck within UK territorial waters and those in international waters.

The extent of the State's right, particularly in its internal waters and territorial sea, are limited by the application of the principle of sovereign immunity. This is an important principle with respect to the salvage of State vessels, and more particularly to wrecks, especially those that sank some time ago. This chapter ends with a consideration of this international law principle, which bridges the consideration of State rights in national law in this chapter and the State's rights as provided for in international law in the next chapter.

4.2 Wreck response and UK regulation

4.2.1 Pollution preparedness and response in the UK

When a casualty occurs, States will need to respond. The experience of the *Torrey Canyon* and subsequent disasters has shown overwhelmingly that pollution and costs can be significantly reduced by proper advance planning.[2] At the national level, the UK's operational response to marine casualties has been heavily influenced by the *Donaldson Report*,[3] which followed the *Braer* disaster in 1993 and later in Lord Donaldson's "Review of Salvage and Intervention and their Command and Control", following the *Sea Empress* disaster in

---

1 On States' right to wreck removal itself, see Chapter 11.

2 The international framework for responding to marine casualties, including wrecks, is dealt with in Chapter 5. Relevant conventions include eg UNCLOS (see 5.4), the Intervention Convention 1969 (see 5.3) and the OPRC Convention 1990 (see 5.5). See also the Bonn Agreement (14.1.1) and the OSPAR Convention (14.1.3).

3 *Safer Ships, Cleaner Seas*, Report of Lord Donaldson's Inquiry into the Prevention of Pollution from Merchant Shipping (Cm 2560, HMSO, 1994) [*Donaldson Report 1994*]; Government Response (Cm 2766, 1995).

1996.[4] Both the *Donaldson Report* and *Review* gave rise to a series of recommendations which are embodied both in legislation and guidance documents.

The Lead Government Departments (LGDs) for counter-pollution preparedness, regulation and response are the Department for Transport (DfT) for shipping and the Department of Business, Energy and Industrial Strategy (BEIS) for offshore installations.[5] The Maritime and Coastguard Agency (MCA) is an executive agency of DfT and is in effect the LGD for marine pollution incidents from shipping. It is designated as the UK Competent Authority for counter-pollution response, and has primary responsibility for the "National Contingency Plan for Marine Pollution from Shipping and Offshore Installations" (NCP).[6] The NCP is subtitled "A Strategic Overview for Responses to Marine Pollution from Shipping and Offshore Installations", but in fact it also has a significant section on operational matters.

The NCP adopts a three-tiered approach to oil pollution contingency planning, where Tier 1 is local, Tier 2 is regional and Tier 3 is national (requiring a response coordinated by the MCA). For a Tier 3 response to a major wreck it will normally be appropriate to establish 'response cells', eg a Marine Response Centre (MRC) and a Salvage Control Unit (SCU).[7] The MRC (under the MCA's Head of Counter Pollution and Salvage Branch) would deal with the most appropriate means to contain, disperse and remove potential pollutants from the scene. The SCU (headed by the Secretary of State's Representative for Maritime Salvage & Intervention—SOSREP), has a role to monitor salvage operations and proposals in order to ensure that they do not have an adverse effect on safety and the environment.

4.2.2 Role of the SOSREP

One of the main results of the *Donaldson Review* was the creation in 1999 of the post of Secretary of State's Representative for Maritime Salvage & Intervention (SOSREP) as a national coordinator for marine emergencies.[8] The powers available to the SOSREP are described in more detail in 4.2.3, but extend to UK territorial waters for safety issues and in the EEZ for pollution from shipping related incidents.[9] Note that the MSA 1995 Part 9A now gives additional powers to the Secretary of State in the EEZ in relation to wrecks,

---

4 Cm 4193, presented to Parliament by the Secretary of State for the Environment, Transport and the Regions, March 1999 [*Donaldson Review 1999*]. See also the MAIB *Report into the Grounding and Subsequent Salvage of the Tanker Sea Empress* (HMSO, 1997), and 1.2.2.

5 BEIS superseded the Department of Energy and Climate Change (DECC) in July 2016. See generally the Offshore Installations (Emergency Pollution Control) Regulations 2002 (SI 2002/1861). Note that the EU's reaction to the *Deepwater Horizon* blowout in 2010 was to issue an Offshore Safety Directive (013/30/EU of 12 June 2013), which has been given effect through eg the Offshore Installations (Offshore Safety Directive) Regulations 2015 (SI 2015/385). The OPRC Regulations 1998 were amended as a result because oil pollution emergency plans cover the response that an offshore installation or oil handling facility will make in the event of releases.

6 2014, updated 2017: see www.gov.uk/government/publications/national-contingency-planncp.

7 For liaison with other bodies, see 4.4.4.

8 The concept has been used elsewhere, see eg Maritime Emergency Response Commander (MERCOM) in Australia. Cf the slightly different role of an on-scene commander for search and rescue operations to be designated under the International Convention on Maritime Search and Rescue (SAR) 1979, Annex, para 5.7.

9 For pollution incidents from offshore installations the powers extend to the UK continental shelf. This might only be relevant to wreck cases where there was a collision with a rig.

and these powers will in practice be exercised by the SOSREP.[10] The SOSREP's role is described in the NCP[11] as being "empowered to make crucial and often time-critical decisions, without delay and without recourse to higher authority, where such decisions are in the overriding UK public interest". In particular, the SOSREP "has the ultimate and decisive voice for maritime salvage, offshore containment and intervention", although the position "does not include any responsibility for either at sea or shoreline clean-up activities".[12]

The SCU is used regularly by the SOSREP and is a way of bringing together key people to discuss issues as an incident escalates. When a wreck incident is reported, the SOSREP will consider whether there is a safety and navigational issue requiring consultation with a General Lighthouse Authority (GLA) such as Trinity House. Where there is a safety issue, as with the *Fluvius Tamar* in 2017,[13] the remedial options will be examined, eg whether the clearance above the wreck can be achieved by partial removal of the upper works or, as in that case, if complete removal was required. Trinity House would then undertake buoying or marking in the interim, while the SOSREP consulted with the shipowner or, in practice, its P&I Club about organising and paying for the wreck removal. The Club would be asked whether or not it was going to engage contractors directly to remove the wreck. If so, the SOSREP would monitor both competence and timeliness. At the other end of the scale, where small fishing vessels are involved (without P&I Club cover but perhaps with cover from a fixed premium insurer), it may be necessary to monitor the activities of removal contractors who are appointed by owners or insurers but who may be smaller, less experienced, diving companies. In any event, the SOSREP would expect to be presented with a wreck removal plan for approval, and all stakeholders would be consulted before the SOSREP gives final approval.

During a wreck removal operation, the SOSREP would have regular meetings to discuss progress. In the *MSC Napoli* wreck[14] there were sometimes two meetings a day, later reduced to one. With the *Fluvius Tamar* there were a few meetings, but the remainder were done by conference call. For vessels sunk in deeper waters, eg over 60 m, the SOSREP might be prepared to let the wreck remain on the seabed where it is not a risk to navigation, but would insist at a minimum that hydrocarbons such as bunkers be removed and may require the Club to arrange for an ROV to be mobilised. Where there are environmental threats, the SOSREP would consult the Environment Agency. A wreck may have a relatively small amount of bunkers on board, eg 70 mt, but when the vessel is raised there will always be some residue in vents which would leave a sheen. Experience with vessels like trawlers shows that while it may sometimes be possible to remove bunkers, there might be bunker pollution risks in attempting a full wreck removal rather than leaving the vessel on the seabed. These will be the sort of cases where the Clubs will argue as to

---

10 See 11.3.3 and note that the Marine Safety Act 2003 s 1 inserted a new s 108A of the MSA 1995 which makes clear that other provisions of the MSA 1995 shall have no effect in so far as they are (i) inconsistent with the exercise of powers under Sch 3A, or (ii) would interfere with a person's compliance with a direction under Sch 3A, or (iii) would interfere with action taken by virtue of Sch 3A. See also 11.3.3(c) on the possible limiting effects of the WRC 2007 Art 9(4) and its relationship with intervention powers.
11 NCP para 5.5.
12 For the responsibilities of the Environment Agency and MMO, see 4.2 and 14.1.4(b).
13 See 11.3.5.
14 See 1.2.3(b).

the reasonableness of full wreck removal[15] and a pragmatic view may need to be taken. It might still be appropriate to monitor vessels left on the seabed, and if they do deteriorate it may be necessary to return to consider full removal for safety or environmental reasons.

A wreck removal direction under the MSA 1995 Part 9A may not always be necessary if there is a cooperative shipowner, but where the insurance is with a P&I Club the latter will normally require a direction so as to trigger the liability.[16] Sometimes the SOSREP's enquiry of the shipowner will reveal that there is no wreck removal insurance. This may be more likely with very small vessels, eg the *MV Ella*, which was a decommissioned tug bought privately and under tow from Hartlepool to Rochester when it foundered near Lowestoft in 2017 and became a hazard to navigation. The SOSREP apparently served a wreck removal direction on the owner, who had provided little information previously, and also preserved the position in respect of liability for marking, arranging a survey and dive inspection. Having discovered there was no insurance, the SOSREP then issued a direction to Trinity House under the MSA 1995 s 255F(2)[17] to remove the wreck, an important step in triggering liability on the shipowner under the WRC 2007 as enacted in the MSA 1995 s 255G.[18]

Disposal of cargo after a wreck is a particular problem for the SOSREP as well as other parties.[19] The *MSC Napoli* experience showed that it was a costly, time-consuming exercise, eg after containers were discharged in Portland it was necessary to systematise the sorting process, eg as to what could be saved and what went to landfill.

4.2.3 MSA 1995 Sch 3A and UK intervention powers

Chapter 5 deals with the right under international law to intervene in marine casualties, eg under the International Convention relating to Intervention on the High Seas in Cases of Oil Pollution Casualties 1969, and its 1973 Protocol (the Intervention Convention 1969).[20] National law may vary both as to the form and content of legislation dealing with these powers, but also as to the way they are exercised administratively. In the UK, legislation was introduced following the *Torrey Canyon* to give effect to these powers and has been progressively amended since.[21] The current provisions are now contained in the MSA 1995 Sch 3A (safety directions) as inserted by the Marine Safety Act 2003.[22]

4.2.3(a) Directions to persons in control of the casualty

The MSA 1995 Sch 3A para 1 sets out a series of very wide powers given to the Secretary of State for Transport (in practice exercised by the SOSREP)[23] to intervene by way of

---

15 See 10.2.4, 10.2.5.
16 See also 10.8.
17 See 11.3.3(d).
18 Ibid. The MSA 1995 s 5255R(2) extends the liability to unregistered ships.
19 See generally Chapter 14.
20 See 5.3.
21 See the Prevention of Oil Pollution Act 1971, s 12, replaced by ss 137–141 of the MSA 1995, as amended. These gave the power to give directions. The MSMSA 1997 added ss 100C-100E, giving powers to require ships be moved (with associated penalties). See generally *Gaskell, MSA 1995*, 21/161.
22 Marine Safety Act 2003 s 1. The Marine Safety Act 2003 also repealed the MSA 1995 ss 100C–100E (movement of ships) and 137–141 (pollution directions).
23 See 4.2.2.

giving directions to those in control of the ship in distress, while being careful to reserve any underlying rights in international law.[24]

The threshold for intervention has gradually been reduced over the years. The direction powers under Sch 3A para 1 are now conditional upon (i) some "accident" happening to a ship[25] that (ii) creates a risk to safety or a risk of pollution by a hazardous substance[26] and (iii) that the direction is necessary[27] to remove or reduce the risk. There is no longer any restriction requiring the pollution to be on a "large scale", but it must be "significant".[28] In relation to the sort of marine casualties likely to lead to a wreck, these requirements may not be difficult to satisfy, as nearly all casualties now involve the risk of bunker pollution—and even relatively small quantities of bunkers can have significant effects, especially in marine sensitive areas.[29]

The type of direction that can be given is expressed very broadly, eg to "take or refrain from taking any specified action" in relation to the ship itself, its cargo or bunkers, the ship's equipment, any craft being towed, or persons on board.[30] Specific instances of the direction powers are also given,[31] eg to require a person to ensure that a ship is moved or not moved; or that it be moved from a specified place or area or over a specified route; that cargo or other substance is or is not unloaded or discharged; that specified salvage measures are taken or not taken; or that a person is put ashore or on board a ship.

A series of casualties[32] identified that a refusal to grant entry into ports of refuge for vessels in distress might lead to their wreck. As a result, both the IMO[33] and EU[34] have issued guidance to States. An EU Directive[35] requires Member States to set up national plans to deal with places of refuge for vessels in distress. The SOSREP is the competent authority to assign UK places of refuge[36] and can use intervention powers to give effect to them.[37] This

---

24 See MSA 1995 Sch 3A para 23. Note also the Salvage Convention 1989 Art 5.

25 As defined in Sch 3A para 22(1) to mean a collision of ships, a stranding, another incident of navigation or another event (whether on board a ship or not), which results in material damage to a ship or its cargo or in an imminent threat of material damage to a ship or its cargo. The same expression is used in the MSA 1995 Part 9A s 255R(2): see 11.3.1.

26 Defined very widely in para 22(2) to include oil and "any other substance which create a hazard to human health, harms living resources or marine life, damages amenities or interferes with lawful use of the sea". This goes far beyond notions of poisonous chemicals to cover eg plastic packaging in containers. The reference to "amenities" requires "damage" rather than interference, but it is not hard to consider debris on a beach as damaging the amenity.

27 There is no specific requirement that the powers are needed "urgently" as under the repealed MSA 1995 s 137(1)(c).

28 Sch 3A para 22(1).

29 See 1.2.2, 2.6.3.

30 Sch 3A para 1(3).

31 Ibid., para 1(4).

32 Including the *Erika* and *Prestige*; see 1.2.2(a).

33 IMO Resolution A.949 (23), "Guidelines on Places of Refuge for Ships in Need of Assistance".

34 "EU Operational Guidelines", Version 5—Final 1 February 2018 and www.emsa.europa.eu/implementation-tasks/places-of-refuge.html.

35 Vessel Traffic Monitoring and Information System Directive 2002/59/EC of 27 June 2002, as amended by Directive 2009/17.

36 And risk assessment is addressed in s 16 of the NCP (see 4.8.5).

37 See T Stone, "The Experience of the United Kingdom", Chapter 16 of A Chircop, O Linden (eds) *Places of Refuge for Ships—Emerging Environmental Concerns of a Maritime Custom* (Martinus Nijhoff, 2006).

was done with the *MSC Napoli*[38] and, in 2016, a fire in a cargo of wood pellets (ie biomass) in the *V Due* (23,689 gt) caused the SOSREP to order that the ship be taken back to the port of Liverpool as a place of refuge.

In the context of salvage and wreck removal operations, it is hard to think of many restrictions on the powers that may be exercised. Thus, in the *MSC Napoli* casualty,[39] there was clear authorisation for directions about beaching the ship in a place of refuge and as to which route might be taken to a recycling facility. Although "wreck removal" is not specifically mentioned in Sch 3A, it is clearly covered by the powers in relation to movement, which are not limited by whether the vessel is afloat or not. Thus, directions about the type of wreck removal operations, eg how they are to be carried out, would seem to be allowed. There may be an overlap in the content of directions under Sch 3A and those for wreck removal under Part 9A,[40] but they are much more likely now to include specific references to the WRC 2007 (and Part 9A) in order to trigger cost recovery.[41]

In both salvage and wreck removal operations, a direction can be made to remove bunkers before any other action is taken to save ship and cargo, even if this leads to loss of that property and a diminution in the prospects of a large salvage reward.[42] What is a little more unclear is the extent to which the powers to direct that "specified salvage measures are taken" could be used to insist upon particular contractual terms being used. This may be relevant when the shipowner is trying to negotiate a non-salvage towage contract, but the contractor at the scene wants a salvage contract (eg LOF with SCOPIC).[43] Given the risks caused by delay,[44] the SOSREP could direct the shipowner that operations to save the ship should start immediately and should be done in a certain way (and perhaps even that a particular contractor be used or not), but it does not seem that there is power to direct the commercial terms on which this is done. The contractor cannot in general be forced to take part unless it is already a "salvor", so a direction to the shipowner may assist it to obtain salvage terms.[45]

The reference to "salvage measures" is an example, not a limitation. In theory, it could cover any decision to demobilise salvage equipment, eg when it appears that the ship will become a wreck.[46] More difficult is whether there are any restrictions on the persons to whom directions may be given.

Sometimes the service of a direction under the MSA 1995 Sch 3A, eg to take towage or salvage assistance, may take the pressure off a master who is reluctant to engage a tug (for salvage or towage); eg where the vessel is adrift after an engine breakdown. The direction takes the matter out of his hands and he cannot be criticised by owners.

---

38 See 1.2.3(a).
39 See 1.2.3.
40 See 11.3.3(c).
41 See 10.5 and 11.3.4(a).
42 The salvor thus affected is compensated either under the Salvage Convention 1989 Art 14 or SCOPIC: see 2.7.9, 12.1.2.
43 See 12.1.2.
44 See eg *The Fedra*; 10.2.5.
45 This is without prejudice to any rights to set aside a contract for duress under Art 7 of the Salvage Convention 1989. Cf *Mount Isa Mines Ltd v The Ship "Thor Commander"* [2018] FCA 1326 [2019] 1 Lloyd's Rep 167, 4.2.3(b).
46 See also 12.3.4(c).

4.2.3(b) Recipients of directions

Directions under Sch 3A para 1 may be given not only to the master or shipowner[47] but also to an extended list of persons who might have some control over the ship.[48] These include a person in possession of the ship (eg a bareboat charterer), a pilot, and a salvor in possession (including servants or agents of the salvor who are in charge of the salvage operation).[49] Taken together, these enable the SOSREP to give orders to most persons engaged in salvage operations. In particular, the salvor in possession can apparently be ordered not to demobilise equipment.[50]

At what stage, though, does the salvor cease to be in possession; ie how far can a salvor that is already engaged on a salvage operation determine that for safety or financial reasons (or both) it wishes to terminate its involvement? Its rights to terminate vis-à-vis the ship and cargo owner[51] are separate from the present public law question of whether it can be compelled, in effect, to continue its operations. A salvor would have a defence to any prosecution for refusing to obey a direction if it reasonably believed that compliance with the direction would involve a serious risk to human life[52] and, of course, the SOSREP could issue its direction to the *shipowner*. But once a salvor ceases to be in possession of a ship, it does not appear that *it* can then be given directions. Nor perhaps could directions be given to a salvor that had signed an LOF and had not performed any work, or had agreed to salve (without any contract) but had not yet started on salvage operations. There may even be cases where a salvor is actually engaged on a salvage operation but is not in possession of the casualty (eg where it is still under the control of its master and crew).[53]

The possibility of termination by salvors could presumably be avoided if the SOSREP issues an early direction about the salvage operation and includes in it a requirement that the salvor notifies the SOSREP before taking any action to terminate, or (more simply) forbids demobilisation without permission once a salvage operation is underway.[54]

The list in Sch 3A para 1(2) is definitive and not open-ended (unlike the type of directions that may be given). Strictly, the list does not include a wreck removal contractor, even if in possession of the ship, unless it can be called a "salvor". There is no separate definition of "salvor" for the purposes of Sch 3A,[55] and where the ship and cargo are a total loss with no residual value it might be said that such contractors cannot be salvors, as there is nothing of value to save. However, it might be possible to refer to the wide definition of "salvage operation" in Art 1 of the Salvage Convention 1989 as the vessel might still be in

---

47 Including the owner at the time of the accident; ie where the ship is sold after the casualty or becomes the property of the insurer: see 14.7.1 and 3.4. For "master", see s 313(1).

48 Sch 3A para 1(2), further extending a list made by the amendments originally introduced by the MSMSA 1997, s 2.

49 Eg a salvage master.

50 See further 12.2.4, 12.3.4(c).

51 See 12.2, 12.3.4(a).

52 Sch 3A para 6(2)(b).

53 While the salvor may have a maritime lien on the casualty this does not give the salvor the right to take possession when it does not already have possession. See *Kennedy & Rose*, 527.

54 There are powers to vary or revoke a direction: see para 10.

55 Nor under s 313 of the MSA 1995 or Art 1 the Salvage Convention 1989 (as incorporated in Sch 11 of the MSA 1995).

"danger" in a broad sense.[56] In any event, directions can be given to the master or owner of the casualty that is controlling operations and they would be obliged to give instructions to the salvor engaged by them.[57]

The point is that the powers under para 1 are not exercisable in relation to any vessel that happens to be in the vicinity; they are focused on the ship in respect of which the accident occurred.[58] There is no power under para 1[59] to give directions to a salvage or wreck removal contractor's vessel that happened to be in the vicinity but was not yet engaged upon any salvage services. This may also be relevant to sub-contractors involved in wreck removal operations. Although, it may be tempting to try in effect to "commandeer" a tug that is nearby, it does not appear there is power to give a direction to do so under para 1.[60] Directions cannot be given to a hull or cargo insurer unless it becomes the owner,[61] nor to a P&I Club as it never owns the ship and will be careful not to take possession. Again, though, directions can be given indirectly, ie to the shipowner.

There was originally no specific power to give directions to cargo owners, or eg time or voyage charterers, even though they may have knowledge or facilities that might assist a salvage or wreck removal operation. In 2004 the list in Sch 3A was amended to include a new para 1(2)(da) naming "the owner of a hazardous substance in the ship" as a person to whom directions could be given.[62] "Hazardous substance" is itself defined widely to include oil and "any other substance which creates a hazard to human health, harms living resources or marine life, damages amenities or interferes with lawful use of the sea".[63] The additional para 1(2)(da) power is useful but not entirely free from ambiguity. There may be uncertainty as to who is the "owner" of a cargo in transit that is subject to a negotiable bill of lading, which may have been transferred a number of times, or even pledged. It might have been more helpful if the provision was more widely worded to include a named shipper or consignee. With an oil cargo, or with certain specialised types of cargo, the cargo

---

56 Moreover, under the LLMC 1996 Art 1(3) a "salvor" includes a wreck removal contractor: see the MSA 1995 Sch 7 Part I and 2.5.5.

57 They would have to show that they tried as hard as they could to comply with the direction to have a defence to a charge of failing to obey it: see para 16(2)(a). That would include exercising contractual or other rights in relation to the salvor.

58 Cf the Australian Protection of the Sea (Powers of Intervention) Act 1981 (Cth) s 11(1)(h), which gives power for the authorities to "require another ship to be made available for purposes in connection with" towing the casualty. In *Mount Isa Mines Ltd v The Ship "Thor Commander"* [2018] FCA 1326 [2019] 1 Lloyd's Rep 167 [Fed Court] [275–276, 309] it was assumed that this entitled orders to be given to a foreign flag bulk carrier that had responded to an emergency call from a casualty and was standing by, perhaps to take a tow under contract. Both the casualty and the bulk carrier were given orders that a tow should be accepted, if safe to do so, until relieved by emergency towage craft. The direction specified that it applied "irrespective of whether or not a Lloyd's Open form or other similar agreement has been signed". The only relevant issue was whether the bulk carrier was entitled to salvage (it was) and the quantum of the reward. The validity of the order was not challenged, but it may be doubted whether (i) in English law the bulk carrier was *already* a "salvor" subject to Sch 3A orders or (ii) under international law such an order could be given to a foreign flag ship (at least in the EEZ).

59 But see 4.8.3(d).

60 And there would clearly be difficulties in international law where a foreign tug was exercising rights of navigation. See also 5.6.

61 See 3.4.1.

62 See the Merchant Shipping (Vessel Traffic Monitoring and Reporting Requirements) Regulations 2004 (SI 2004/2110) r 22(1).

63 See Sch 3A para 22(2). The Secretary of State can also prescribe substances by order: para 22(2)(c).

owner may well be a company with refining, processing or storage facilities. A direction could be given to it as an owner, but it may be that the reception facilities are owned by another (perhaps associated) company and different powers may be needed where it owns or controls land or premises.[64]

Major container lines such as MSC (with the *MSC Napoli*, or the *Rena*) will not own the cargo and may only be time or voyage charterers and thus not in possession of the ship. It is possible that they might own or have possession of the physical containers and be subject to a para 1(2)(da) direction in that capacity. It would also seem that the new power could allow a direction to a time charterer in respect of the ship's bunkers.[65]

With a container ship, individual cargo owners are unlikely to be able to assist much after a wreck, except in relation to providing information about cargo properties. The powers under para 1 emphasise action rather than assistance in the form of information or advice. While there is no express power to direct cargo owners or other cargo interests to supply information, it is arguable that such a direction might fall within the words "take any action" in para 1(3), obliging the recipients to try as hard as they could to comply with the relevant direction.[66] There are additional sources of information about cargoes, particularly in the EU.[67] Notification may already have been required about dangerous or polluting goods carried by ships, for ships to carry a manifest of such goods, and for the reporting of incidents and accidents at sea.[68]

4.2.3(c) Directions to person in control of land

Following experience with the wreck of the *Sea Empress* in 1996,[69] it was apparent that powers were needed in relation to ports and land facilities. This has been dealt with in two ways. First, Sch 3A para 1 directions may also be issued to the harbour authority or the harbour master where the ship in distress is in, or has been directed to move into, waters which are regulated or managed by a harbour authority.[70] It is clear that powers of harbour masters[71] are subject to the MSA 1995 Sch 3A powers exercisable by the SOSREP.[72]

Secondly, a separate recommendation in the *Donaldson Review* resulted in what is now Sch 3A para 2. This allows directions to be given to those in control of land to make their land or certain facilities used by ships (eg berths, wharves, jetties) available where it is necessary in order to remove or reduce risks of pollution or to safety. This is a significant

---

64 See 4.2.3(c).
65 Bunkers would fall within the definition of oil in the MSA 1995 s 151(1), as applied by Sch 3A para 22(2).
66 See the defence in Sch 3A para 6(2): see 4.2.3(f).
67 Under eg Directive 2002/59/EC of the European Parliament and of the Council of 27 June 2002 establishing a community vessel traffic monitoring and information system.
68 See eg (as amended) the Merchant Shipping (Reporting Requirements for Ships Carrying Dangerous or Polluting Goods) Regulations 1995 (SI 1995/2498); the Merchant Shipping (Prevention of Oil Pollution) Regulations 1996 (SI 1996/2154); the Merchant Shipping (Dangerous Goods and Marine Pollutants) Regulations 1997 (SI 1997/2367); the Merchant Shipping (Safety of Navigation) Regulations 2002 (SI 2002/1473); the Merchant Shipping (Vessel Traffic Monitoring and Reporting Requirements) Regulations 2004 (SI 2004/2110).
69 See 1.2.2(a).
70 Sch 3A para 1(2)(g).
71 The Dangerous Vessels Act 1985 gives certain powers for harbour masters to intervene, eg if there is a wreck in a harbour involving dangerous cargo. There may also be local harbour legislation: see also the Harbours Act 1964 s 40A–40D (as added by the Marine Navigation Act 2013 s 5), and 11.1.2.
72 See eg s 6A of the Dangerous Vessels Act 1985, inserted by Sch 2 of the Marine Safety Act 2003.

power of considerable relevance to wreck cases. "It may, for instance, be necessary or appropriate for a ship in danger to make use of facilities for berthing and repair, or for the landing of passengers or discharge of potentially polluting cargoes".[73] To some extent this power may be relevant to the type of cargo owner to whom para 1 directions could be given[74] but that owns or controls coastal[75] facilities such as storage tanks, a container terminal or container storage facilities in a nearby port. The definition of persons in charge of land or premises refers to whether they are "wholly or partly able to control the use made of the land or premises".[76] As the emphasis is on "control" rather than ownership, the powers could be used in relation to oil companies, terminal operators, harbour authorities and charterers—even if they only have contractual rights to use facilities.

The agreement of the harbour authority, landowner or person in control of premises is now no longer required. They would, though, be entitled first to be able to make representation,[77] and secondly to the costs of compliance from the shipowner.[78]

This type of power can also be very important when a ship is stranded on a shore and the only access to it is via coastal land, eg to transfer containers to land when a sea approach is too dangerous. International experience[79] shows that those with control over the land may demand a high fee for access by contractors, in addition to remediation costs. The Sch 3A powers could prevent contractors being 'held to ransom' in this way, and there would be no power under Sch 3A to require the shipowner to pay a fee unrelated to actual costs. The Sch 3A powers would not allow for there to be any double recovery, eg if there was payment under the CLC 1992 and the Bunker Convention 2001, by contract or, indeed, if the landowner claimed salvage.[80]

The Sch 3A para 2 powers would also be relevant to wreck removal operations, provided that there was a safety or pollution risk. This might present a difficulty where the ship has had bunkers and cargo removed and the only operation for which access is required is to dismantle all or part of the structure. Even here, it is possible that the wide definition of "pollution by a hazardous substance"[81] could be interpreted to include damage to amenities such as a beach.

Contractors who wanted access to remove wrecks and debris from a beach might still need to obtain separate licensing approval under waste legislation.[82]

4.2.3(d) Directions to 'other' ships
The powers given in relation to Sch 3A paras 1 and 2[83] require there to be an accident to a particular ship, and give very wide powers—albeit limited as to the persons to whom directions can be given. But there may be circumstances where the SOSREP does want to

---

73 Marine Safety Act 2003, Explanatory Memo, para 12.
74 See 4.2.3(b).
75 Ie those adjacent to or accessible from UK waters: see para 2(3)(b).
76 See para 2(3).
77 Para 13, unless not reasonably practicable.
78 Sch 3A para 15(2) and 15(3).
79 Eg the *Rena*; 1.2.4.
80 Sch 3A para 15(6) and see 2.6.2(a), 2.6.3 and 2.7.
81 Sch 3A para 15(2) and fn 18 above.
82 See 14.6.5(b).
83 See 4.2.3(a)–(c).

give directions to ships *other* than the casualty itself; Sch 3A para 3 addresses this issue, but in a very circumscribed way.

Directions can be given to the master or owner (or eg bareboat charterer) of these 'other' ships, but only that they be moved (or not moved) from particular places, or by particular routes, within the UK—or out of the UK waters altogether.[84] The trigger for such a direction is that it is necessary (a) to secure the safety of the ship itself *or of other ships*; (b) to secure the safety of persons or property; (c) to prevent or reduce pollution. This power might be used, eg to control access by wreck removal contractors' vessels to a wreck site; to prevent particular barges being used to transport offloaded containers or oil; or to require that a heavy-lift barge (with wreck remains on board) take a particular route away from the removal site. The direction could also be that the remains of the hull and cargo on board a contracted ship should leave the UK altogether, eg to be recycled elsewhere.[85] It does not appear that Sch 3A para 3 of itself gives the power to direct that a wreck be taken to a particular port or recycling facility and certainly not once the carrying or towing ship is outside UK waters.[86] Nor is there power to commandeer a passing salvage tug (or other vessel) to force it to tow the ship in distress.[87]

The para 3 powers cannot be exercised against foreign ships unless they are exercising neither the right of innocent passage nor the right of transit passage through straits used for international navigation.[88] In the examples of wreck removal contractors' vessels given above, they would not be exercising rights of innocent passage in UK waters as that passage is not continuous and expeditious if they are stopping to take action in respect of a UK wreck site. On that basis, para 3 would apply to them.[89] Where the vessel is exercising the right of innocent passage, it is hardly likely that any direction need be given other than routing directions, these directions that the coastal State has the power to direct, in any event.[90]

While this power to give directions to foreign ships on innocent passage through the territorial sea is limited, those ships are under a duty to render assistance in any event pursuant to UNCLOS Art 98[91] and SOLAS V regulation 33.[92] Moreover, the Receiver

---

84 A removal direction to beyond the UK is not possible for UK ships: Sch 3A para 20(2). See also the MSA 1995 s 100C (repealed).

85 Such orders would have to take into account the UK's obligations in relation to exporting wastes generally: see eg 14.4–14.6.

86 Cf 10.2.8, 14.7.3.

87 Ie to go beyond the underlying duty to provide assistance to a casualty in order to save life: see 2.7.1 and 4.2.3(b). Cf the Australian position, *The Thor Commander* [2019] 1 Lloyd's Rep 167.

88 Sch 3A para 20(1). A qualifying foreign ship is defined in MSA 1995 s 313A as meaning "any ship other than (a) a British ship, or (b) ship which is not registered under Part II and which (although not by virtue of section 1(1)(d) a British ship) (i) is wholly owned by persons falling within subsection (2) below, and (ii) is not registered under the law of a country outside the United Kingdom".

89 For geographical restrictions over foreign ships outside territorial waters, see 4.8.3(g).

90 UNCLOS Art 21.

91 UNCLOS Art 98(1) provides that "[e]very State shall require the master of a ship flying its flag, in so far as he can do so without serious danger to the ship, the crew or the passengers: (a) to render assistance to any person found at sea in danger of being lost; (b) to proceed with all possible speed to the rescue of persons in distress, if informed of their need of assistance, in so far as such action may reasonably be expected of him". See also 2.7.1 (fn 1032).

92 SOLAS V regulation 33(1) provides that "the master of a ship at sea which is in a position to be able to provide assistance on receiving information from any source that persons are in distress at sea, is bound to

of Wreck may, for the purpose of the preservation of shipwrecked persons, or of the vessel, cargo and equipment, require such persons as he thinks necessary to assist him; require the master, or other person having the charge, of any vessel near at hand to give such assistance with his men, or vessel, as may be in his power; and require the use of any vehicle that may be near at hand[93] in circumstances where a UK or foreign vessel is wrecked, stranded, or in distress at any place on or near the coasts of the UK or any tidal water within UK waters.[94] Not only is the geographical scope of this more limited than the territorial sea[95] but the practical involvement of the Receiver of Wreck in these circumstances differs to that of SOSREP in that the Receiver's functions would be aimed at preserving property. This significantly limits the directions that the Receiver might give a foreign ship pursuant to s 233.

4.2.3(e) Power to take action

It may be that the *direction* powers set out in Sch 3A paras 1–3 are inadequate or ineffective. In those circumstances, Sch 3A para 4 gives even wider power to the Secretary of State (ie SOSREP) to take such *action* "as appears to him necessary or expedient" for the purpose for which a direction could have been given or was given. In effect, this gives powers to take over an operation. Four specific examples are given: (a) to authorise a person to enter land or make use of facilities; (b) to authorise a person to do anything which the Secretary of State could require a person to do by a direction; (c) to authorise a person to assume control of a ship; and (d) to make arrangements or authorise the making of arrangements for the sinking or destruction of a ship.

The type of example relevant to wreck is where a single ship—owning company is insolvent or untraceable and there is no insurer to respond. Here the DfT (through the SOSREP) might need to engage contractors itself; they may need access to land or facilities, to move a grounded ship, or to go aboard and take control of the wreck.[96]

These powers seem to pre-suppose that directions, eg to a shipowner, would not work so that someone else has to be authorised to take action. Yet in the case of destruction of the ship, eg by planned scuttling, the shipowners may be only too ready to accept a direction (even though destruction of the ship is not listed in para 1), as this may be cheaper than recycling.[97] The destruction power was specifically included in the original Prevention of Oil Pollution Act 1971 in order to deal with the potential problems

---

proceed with all speed to their assistance, if possible informing them or the search and rescue service that the ship is doing so. This obligation to provide assistance applies regardless of the nationality or status of such persons or the circumstances in which they are found. If the ship receiving the distress alert is unable or, in the special circumstances of the case, considers it unreasonable or unnecessary to proceed to their assistance, the master must enter in the log-book the reason for failing to proceed to the assistance of the persons in distress, taking into account the recommendation of the Organization, to inform the appropriate search and rescue service accordingly".

93 MSA 1995 s 233(1).
94 See further 4.4.1.
95 *The Fulham* [1899] P 251.
96 Cf the restriction on powers under the WRC 2007 Art 9(4) (and Art 4(4)(a)): see the MSA 1995 Part 9A and 11.3.3(c).
97 See 14.1.4, 14.3, 14.5.

identified with the *Torrey Canyon*.⁹⁸ Note also international restrictions on the UK authorising such dumping.⁹⁹

4.2.3(f) Enforcement and procedure

The MSA 1995 Sch 3A, paras 5–9 set out a whole series of offences to reinforce its powers, eg for failure to obey a direction. Here it is a defence for a person to show that that they tried as hard as they could to comply with the relevant direction, or that they reasonably believed that compliance with the direction would involve a serious risk to human life. This would be dependent on expert evidence, eg of a salvage master, and obviously has to be in the context of the knowledge of persons at the time. It is also an offence to obstruct those carrying out directions or authorised actions.

There are obvious practical problems in communicating directions to a casualty at sea, or to foreign owners or operators, and paras 11–13 address procedural issues. A ship may be boarded for a direction to be served, and in respect of companies the direction may generally be served in accordance with normal company law procedures, eg for UK companies or those operating in the UK. For other companies, eg those overseas with no connection to the UK, the direction may be served "in such manner as he thinks most suitable".¹⁰⁰ There is no requirement that directions be in a particular form, or even in writing, but in practice it can be expected that oral communications will be backed up by faxes or emails.

In some circumstances, eg in relation to para 2 land directions and para 4 actions, a person may be entitled to recover its costs of compliance.¹⁰¹ Apart from this, there is no automatic right to be compensated for obeying a direction, which is a public law duty justified by urgency. A right of compensation is only given if the remedial action required was not reasonably necessary for the purpose for which the direction was given, or caused loss or damage which could not be justified by reference to that purpose.¹⁰² This is, nevertheless, a powerful restraint on the exercise of public power, but the actions of the SOSREP have to be considered in context, eg given the lack of clear information at early stages of a casualty and the need for quick action. Account specifically has to be taken of the extent of the risk to safety or threat of pollution, the likelihood of the remedial action being effective, and the extent of the loss or damage caused by the remedial action.

---

98 See 1.2.1. It seems that the bombing of the ship was agreed by the owners. For the insurance position of the shipowner, see 2.9.2(b); 2.9.3(d).

99 See 14.1.2, 14.1.3 and eg cases such as the *Christos Bitas*, which ran aground in 1978 off the Pembrokeshire coast, initially losing 4,000 mt of crude oil. The master refloated the vessel, but once it was discovered that it was badly damaged and leaking further oil, it was stopped and 26,000 mt of crude oil was transferred to two other tankers. The cost of repairing the vessel after cleaning and emptying the fuel tanks appeared excessive and the shipowner agreed to sink the vessel. It was towed 500 km west of Fastnet Rocks in the Atlantic and sunk in very deep water. www.shipspotting.com/gallery/photo.php?lid=2480758. See also 14.1, 14.2.

100 Sch 3A para 11(2) as substituted by the Companies Act 2006 (Consequential Amendments, Transitional Provisions and Savings) Order 2009 (SI 2009) para 152(5).

101 See Sch 3A para 15 and the discussion in 4.2.3(c).

102 Sch 3A para 14. This is broadly similar to the Intervention Convention provisions: see 5.3.

4.2.3(g) Extent of powers over UK and foreign ships

There has always been a distinction made in the UK legislation between those powers exercisable against foreign and UK ships in order to comply with UNCLOS.[103] This means that distinctions have to be made between powers exercised under international law in the EEZ, continental shelf and high seas and those created and authorised by national law within territorial waters.

The UK will apply the pollution risk direction powers to a UK ship anywhere in the world, and to any ship (eg foreign flagged) in UK waters[104] or an area of the sea specified under the MSA 1995 s 129(2)(b).[105] The latter refers to the UK's EEZ where the UK exercises jurisdiction under UNCLOS to protect and preserve the marine environment.[106] Where there are pollution risks, the UK will also apply its intervention direction powers outside these areas to any ship, but subject to an Order in Council—ie to ensure compliance with international law, eg the Intervention Convention 1969 and its 1973 Protocol.[107] The language used for these high seas powers is more restricted, eg to conform with the international law requirement that there be a level of threat involving "grave and imminent danger".[108]

Where there is a risk only to safety (and not of pollution), the powers over foreign ships are more circumscribed,[109] although as already noted this is unlikely to be relevant to most casualties where there will nearly always be a risk of pollution from bunkers, cargo or debris from a wreck.

4.2.3(h) Temporary exclusion zones

The *Donaldson Report* noted that the Protection of Wrecks Act 1973 had been used to create a restricted area around the wreck of the *Braer*, but that powers might have been needed before the ship was wrecked.[110] Sections 100A and 100B were added to the MSA 1995[111] to allow temporary exclusion zones to be created in the event of a casualty (to ships or other structures) in order to restrict access by uninvolved vessels. Such access might otherwise hinder operations to save a ship, personnel on board and cargo. In particular, pollution

---

103 See Chapter 5 generally, and eg the Intervention Convention, 5.3. As international law has developed, so UK merchant shipping legislation has been adjusted to take advantage of the wider powers of States, eg in relation to the EEZ and continental shelf.

104 Under the MSA 1995 s 313(2), this means the sea or other waters within the seaward limits of the territorial sea of the UK; ie the 12 mile limit and internal waters such as the Thames Estuary.

105 Sch 3A, para 17.

106 See the Merchant Shipping (Prevention of Pollution) (Law of the Sea Convention) Order 1996 (SI 1996/282), the Exclusive Economic Zone Order 2013 (SI 2013/3161); also the Merchant Shipping (Prevention of Pollution) (Limits) Regulations 2014 (SI 2014/3306). For maps of the UK's EEZ (and continental shelf), see NCP (see 4.2.5).

107 Sch 3A para 18. See the Merchant Shipping (Prevention of Pollution) (Intervention) (Foreign Ships) Order 1997 (SI 1997/2568), Merchant Shipping (Prevention of Pollution: Substances Other than Oil) (Intervention) Order 1997 (SI 1997/1869).

108 See the Merchant Shipping (Prevention of Pollution (Intervention) (Foreign Ships) Order 1997 (SI 1997/1869) and 5.2.

109 See MSA 1995 Sch 3A para 19 and s 313A.

110 *Donaldson Report 1994* para 21.105.

111 By the MSMSA 1997: see *Gaskell, MSMSA 1997*, 28/12–28/16. These provisions were left unaffected by the Marine Safety Act 2003, above, and although not part of Sch 3A it is convenient to deal with them here.

prevention operations might be endangered or delayed if other vessels entered the area. These zones have been regularly used by the SOSREP.

4.2.4 Wreck and the relationship between public agencies

The multiplicity of agencies that might be involved in a casualty leading to a wreck is a major complicating factor in wreck removal operations. It can result in delay in decision-making, which in turn increases risks and costs.[112] To some extent this is an inevitable consequence of overlapping administrative responsibilities, whether regional, national or local. While administrators should be able to coordinate responses, their tasks are often made more difficult by politicians at the various levels. Though usually well meaning, they often have a tendency to want to be seen to be "doing something" and doing it immediately, even when more considered judgment may be needed. But when immediate decisions are needed, eg about bringing casualties to an inshore place of safety, they may well procrastinate. These responses are increasingly driven by the need to deal with the media.[113]

Although the MCA has the primary responsibility for shipping incidents, there are inevitably roles for other agencies and bodies (including devolved administrations and commercial organisations) and these are described in the NCP in particular.[114] A bewildering number of acronyms will be encountered, which leads to suspicions of bureaucracy, but at least displays a structured response to a crisis.

At the highest strategic level, government responses to emergencies generally are organised subject to the Civil Contingencies Act 2004.[115] It is at this level that LGDs are identified. Here and in the NCP, it is recognised that a Strategic Coordinating Group (SCG) may be needed to coordinate a local multi-agency response, located in a Strategic Coordination Centre (SCC). The group will normally be chaired by a senior police officer in the "response" phase[116] and may sometimes be grandly described as the "Gold Commander". The SCG will be triggered by a Civil Contingency (Gold Level) under the 1994 Act, ie where there is likely to be significant on-shore consequential impacts on health, the economy or environment, or where significant public and media interest has been generated.[117] The SCG may itself create sub-groups.[118] Where there is a Civil Contingency (Silver and/

---

112 See 1.4 for P&I Club findings about these costs.

113 See 13.1.2 and Cabinet Office, "Responding to Emergencies, the UK Central Government Response: Concept of Operations" (updated 2013) [*Responding to Emergencies*], para 3.40: https://assets.publishing.service.gov.uk/government/uploads/system/uploads/attachment_data/file/192425/CONOPs_incl_revised_chapter_24_Apr-13.pdf.

114 Indeed, a list of NCP stakeholders runs to 11 closely typed pages: see https://assets.publishing.service.gov.uk/government/uploads/system/uploads/attachment_data/file/478669/151026_Stakeholders_List.pdf.

115 See HM Government, "Emergency Response and Recovery: Non-statutory guidance accompanying the Civil Contingencies Act 2004" (5th ed, 28 October 2013) [*Emergency Response and Recovery*], https://assets.publishing.service.gov.uk/government/uploads/system/uploads/attachment_data/file/253488/Emergency_Response_and_Recovery_5th_edition_October_2013.pdf. Also *Responding to Emergencies*. See also two guidance volumes, "Guidance on Part 1 of the Civil Contingencies Act 2004, Its Associated Regulations and Non-statutory Arrangements" and "Non-statutory Guidance to Complement Emergency Preparedness": www.gov.uk/government/publications/emergency-preparedness.

116 Or perhaps a Local Authority Chief Executive in the "recovery" phase, or if there are no threats to life.

117 NCP para 9.12.

118 *Responding to Emergencies*, para 5.5.

or Bronze), a Tactical Coordinating Group (TCG) may be established, comprising senior officers of each agency, to coordinate the on-shore operational response plan.[119] After the acute phase of an incident, recovery may be coordinated by a Recovery Co-ordinating Group, usually chaired by a local authority official.

Most wrecks and other serious maritime casualties will cause the MCA to trigger the formation of an Environment Group (EG) to provide a single advisory line on public health and environmental issues where advice is required for a local, regional or national response.[120] The SCG may establish a Science and Technical Advice Cell (STAC) to work within the EG. There are standing Environment Groups for the whole UK coastline. The Marine Management Organisation (MMO)[121] will brief the Department for Environment, Food and Rural Affairs (DEFRA), ensure local participation in an EG and approve use of oil spill treatment products if appropriate.[122] The MMO has issued guidance as to its response to major pollution incidents and the use of oil spill dispersants.[123] Its plan provides a table of authorisation hierarchies and targets for approvals.

The use of equipment for controlling, containing or recovering oil is exempt from marine licensing under the Marine and Coastal Access Act 2009. The use of booms, mats and pillows which are completely recovered from the sea after they have absorbed oil are considered to fall under this heading and do not therefore require a licence to be put in the sea.[124]

While the NCP provides guidance as to the immediate impact of casualties, there has apparently been less focus on later monitoring.[125] Guidance and standards for post-spill environmental marine monitoring is to be provided through a DEFRA initiative (Pollution Response in Emergencies Marine Impact Assessment and Monitoring), which is intended as a resource for UK government agencies advising incident environment groups and others.[126]

4.2.5 Response coordination and the MSC Napoli

In 2008, when the wreck operations concerning the *MSC Napoli*[127] were nearly finished, the MCA produced a very detailed and thorough report into the response that it (and other government agencies) took to the wreck.[128] From a government perspective, the wreck

---

119 NCP para 9.13, *Emergency Response and Recovery*, para 4.2.2 notes that Gold and Silver should properly be used to describe single-agency levels of command. The SCG and TCG effectively replace what was previously known as a Marine Response Centre.
120 NCP para 9.14.
121 See 14.1.4(b).
122 *Emergency Response and Recovery*, para 8.2.
123 See MMO, Marine Pollution Contingency Plan (2014, updated 2018),
https://assets.publishing.service.gov.uk/government/uploads/system/uploads/attachment_data/file/737259/Marine_pollution_contingency_plan_2018.pdf. Also MMO Guidance, "How We Respond to Marine Pollution Incidents", www.gov.uk/guidance/how-we-respond-to-marine-pollution-incidents.
124 MMO, Marine Pollution Contingency Plan (2014, updated 2018), para 7.2. See also 14.1.4(b).
125 This was a particular issue for New Zealand with the *Rena*: see 1.2.4.
126 See www.cefas.co.uk/premiam/.
127 See 1.2.3.
128 UK Maritime and Coastguard Agency, "MSC Napoli Incident, The Maritime and Coastguard Agency's Response", April 2008 [*MCA Napoli Response*], http://webarchive.nationalarchives.gov.uk/20090510130332/www.redensigngroup.org/lrgtxt/197-299_napoli_report_final-redux.pdf.

highlighted the intersection of three different UK response mechanisms, each designed to deal with slightly different situations: (i) the response specifically to marine pollution under the NCP;[129] (ii) the response to major UK land-based incidents generally; and (iii) the organisation of civil protection in the UK as required by the Civil Contingencies Act in 2004.[130] Taken together, these all require cooperation, sharing of information, emergency planning, risk management, public information and (where necessary) business continuity management. The potential problems are exacerbated by the interaction of different layers of public administration, eg national or local, and when a country has devolved powers (as in the UK) or a federal structure (as in Australia). In a *marine* incident, though, the *Sea Empress* disaster highlighted the need for there to be a clear command structure rather than a 'decision by committee' approach.[131]

Under the NCP, the MCA established an SCU to deal with the salvage operation and a MRC[132] to manage the pollution response at sea. A multi-agency EG was also convened to advise on how to minimise the environmental and public health impact of the wreck and to assist in the coordination of the land-based response. Organisations represented on the group included the Environment Agency, Natural England, the Health Protection Agency, the Centre for Environment, Fisheries and Aquaculture Science (CEFAS) and the RSPB. On the land side, the NCP identifies the possibility of a local authority establishing a Shoreline Response Centre (SRC), but this did not happen—partly because the shipowners and Club had arranged directly for contractors to clean up the beaches.[133] The casualty illustrated the number of land-based organisations that might want to become involved, with the risk that there might be too many cooks spoiling the broth. This need to deal with many agencies (national, regional and local) with differing jurisdictions and levels of marine knowledge has become a common feature of international casualties that might have an environmental impact. This is especially so where the land-based interests may not have a full appreciation of the role of casualty response leaders such as the MCA and SOSREP.[134] The MCA's Response Report noted that the "land co-ordinated response was a complex operation, involving two Local Response Forums (LRFs); two County Councils; two District Councils directly (and others indirectly); Devon and Cornwall Constabulary; Devon Fire and Rescue Service; the MCA; the landowners (the National Trust) and the Environment Agency".[135]

On 20 January 2007, the Devon and Cornwall Constabulary made use of contingency planning to declare a 'Critical Incident'[136] under the Civil Contingencies Act in 2004 and opened

---

129 See 4.8.2.
130 *MCA Napoli Response*, 27.
131 *Donaldson Review 1999*.
132 See Table of Abbreviations for these acronyms.
133 *MCA Napoli Response*, 26.
134 Decision making on a place of refuge is an obvious point of tension where local interests who do not want the risk of a ship near their costs may delay maritime decision-making and result in a worse environmental outcome. After the *Sea Empress* disaster, the powers of national intervention were strengthened so that eg the SOSREP could give orders to countermand a decision of a local harbour master to refuse access. Once an appropriate hierarchy is established it is probably easier in practice to consult with local interests in order to resolve problems in a sensible way.
135 *MCA Napoli Response*, 25.
136 Ibid., 24.

a strategic 'Gold Control'.[137] This facilitated coordination with Local Response Forums set up under the Act and enabled the police to deal with land-based consequences of the casualty, eg when containers were washed ashore. Not only had there to be access through narrow roads to remove the contents, but also there had to be some control over the crowds which, in the glare of TV cameras, flocked to the beach to 'liberate' valuable property such as BMW motorbikes. There was a mistaken belief that somehow this wrecked property was available on the basis of 'finders' keepers'. The police and the Receiver of Wreck soon made clear that there were strict legal provisions regulating the finding of such cargo.[138]

The wreck of the *MSC Napoli* presented a multitude of problems, but in hindsight was actually a relatively successful operation.

4.3 Shipping inquiries and wreck

An aspect of a State's response to a shipping casualty, including that which leads to a wreck, is to inquire as to its cause, particularly to prevent further incidences occurring from similar causes.[139] The MSA 1995 makes provision for a number of shipping inquiries, the two of direct importance to wreck is the investigation by a Chief Inspector of Marine Accidents[140] and a formal investigation of marine accidents by a wreck commissioner (or sheriff in Scotland).[141]

An accident involving a ship or a ship's boat in UK waters, or which are UK ships (or boats) in other waters, is subject to investigation by such persons, including a Chief Inspector of Marine Accidents, as appointed by the Secretary of State pursuant to MSA 1995 s 267. The entity so appointed is the Marine Accident Investigation Branch (MAIB) of DfT.[142] While the MAIB is within DfT, it acts independently since it may be required to consider the role of DfT in maritime accidents. The sole objective of these investigations is to prevent future accidents and not to determine liability.[143] The Secretary of State can also refer any other accidents involving ships or ship's boats to the MAIB, such as accidents in internal waters and rivers.[144] The investigations undertaken by the MAIB are governed by the Merchant Shipping (Accident Reporting and Investigations) Regulations 2012 (Accident Reporting Regulations 2012).[145] These give effect to a number of EU Directives.[146] However, the 2018 Amendments make provision for the UK's exit from the EU and especially in relation to these EU Directives, but these amendments will only take effect on exit day.[147]

---

137 Ibid., 34.
138 Ibid., 32; see 3.5, 4.4.
139 *Marsden & Gault*, 903.
140 MSA 1995 s 267.
141 Ibid. s 268. The other inquiries relate to the fitness or conduct of officers and seamen (MSA 1995 ss 61–63) and to deaths of those aboard a UK ship or UK seamen abroad (MSA 1995 s 271).
142 *Marsden & Gault*, 904.
143 Accident Reporting Regulations 2012 reg 5.
144 MSA 1995 s 267(2)(b).
145 (SI 2012/1743) and amended by the Merchant Shipping (Accident Reporting and Investigations) Regulations 2013 (SI 2013/2882).
146 Council Directive 1999/35/EC; 2009/18/EC and 2002/59/EC.
147 Merchant Shipping (Accident Reporting and Investigations) and the Railway (Accident Reporting and Investigations) (Amendment) (EU Exit) Regulations 2018 (SI 2018/1400).

"Accident" is defined to mean an event that has occurred directly by or in connection with the operation of a ship leading to death; serious injury; loss of a person from a ship; material damage to a ship; the loss, abandonment, stranding, collision or disablement of a ship; material damage to marine infrastructure external of a ship that could seriously endanger the safety of the ship, another ship or any individual; or pollution, or the potential for such pollution to the environment caused by damage to a ship.[148] When such an accident has occurred, the master, a senior officer or the ship's owner must, as soon as is practicable after the accident and by the quickest means possible, notify the Chief Inspector of the accident and provide a report that sets out the circumstances of the accident, findings from any investigation and any measure to be adopted to prevent future accidents of the same sort.[149] Others, such as harbour masters, waterway authorities and the MCA also have to report accidents.[150] This duty to report does not, however apply to accidents on pleasure vessels or recreational craft hired on a bareboat basis and in some circumstances, smaller craft less than 8 m in length.[151]

The Chief Inspector must carry out a preliminary investigation in the case of serious marine casualties, such as collisions, groundings, pollution or explosion, to determine whether a safety investigation should be undertaken.[152] In cases involving wreck there will almost certainly be an investigation undertaken by MAIB. The Accident Reporting Regulations 2012 sets out the process for this investigation, including preservation of evidence,[153] interview witnesses,[154] etc. On completion of an investigation, the report is sent to the Secretary of State and made public.[155]

The MSA 1995 also provides for a formal investigation into an accident—irrespective of whether one had been undertaken by MAIB—by a wreck commissioner (or sheriff in Scotland).[156] This is a more formal investigation, being public and usually with an Admiralty Judge or QC as the wreck commissioner, and subject to aspects of the evidentiary rules of the Magistrates' Court Act 1980.[157] While the primary purpose of such an inquiry is purely investigatory and seeks to identify the cause of the accident, it may also seek to determine whether any penalties should be imposed on any person whose wrongful act or default was the cause or a contributory cause of the accident.[158] This may include the cancellation or suspension of an officer's certificates. Where such a determination is a consideration in the investigation, the wreck commissioner is assisted by one or two assessors

---

148 Accident Reporting Regulations 2012 reg 3(1).

149 Accident Reporting Regulations 2012 reg 6(1) and (4).

150 Ibid. reg 6(2).

151 Ibid. reg 4.

152 Ibid. reg 7. See also the powers of the Chief Inspector as provided for in MSA 1995 s 259 (Accident Reporting Regulations 2012 reg 7(4)).

153 Accident Reporting Regulations 2012 regs 8, 10.

154 Ibid. reg 11. Various offences in relation to withholding or altering evidence, obstructing the investigation etc are provided for, eg reg 19.

155 Accident Reporting Regulations 2012 reg 14.

156 MSA 1995 s 268.

157 Ibid. ss 268(3), 270. Merchant Shipping (Formal Investigations) Rules (SI 1985/1001) as amended by SI 1990/123 and SI 2000/1623. On the implementation and interpretation of these procedure see Report of Clarke LJ into the *Marchioness/Bowbelle* (February 2001, Cm 4558).

158 MSA 1995 s 268(5). See *Marsden & Gault*, 908.

THE LAW OF WRECK

who are usually experts in the field under consideration, such as engineers, master mariners, naval architects, etc.[159]

The Secretary of State has the power to order re-hearings, particularly when new evidence comes to light. This is important in the case of wrecks, as the actual wreck may be discovered some time after the first hearing or subsequent investigations of a wreck using new technology reveals new important evidence. Such was the case with the investigation of the *MV Derbyshire*[160] and the *Gaul*.[161] The re-hearing may be by the original wreck commissioner, a new wreck commissioner or the High Court.[162]

The reports of the MAIB or the wreck commissioner do not have a direct effect on any subsequent litigation that may arise between parties eg in the case of a collision. Indeed, the report of the wreck commissioner cannot be used in evidence in subsequent litigation—though this position has been criticised.[163] However, since it is unlikely that the outcome in such litigation will differ to that in the formal investigation on the same evidence put to the wreck commissioner, in practice matters are often settled after the report of the formal investigation has been published.[164] It is therefore of some import for those with an interest in wreck arising from a maritime casualty.

4.4 State rights to wreck

4.4.1 Right to wreck in UK territorial waters

Section 241 MSA 1995 provides that "Her Majesty and Her Royal successors are entitled to all unclaimed wreck found in the UK or in UK waters except in places where Her Majesty or any of Her Royal predecessors has granted the right to any other person". As discussed in Chapter 3, 'wreck' is not defined as such, merely providing that it "includes jetsam, flotsam, lagan and derelict[165] found in or on the shores of the sea or any tidal water".[166] It is thus that which constituted *wreccum maris* to which is added *adventurae maris*.[167]

The Crown may grant and indeed has granted its right to wreck to others, usually to the Lord of the Manor whose lands bordered the coastline.[168] The MSA 1995 recognises this by providing a mechanism by which any reported wreck found in the relevant area and

---

159 Merchant Shipping (Formal Investigations) Rules reg 4.
160 See also 2.4.1.
161 See 13.1.3.
162 MSA 1995 s 269(2)–(3).
163 *Marsden & Gault*, 914.
164 Ibid.
165 S 255(2) provides that "Fishing boats or fishing gear lost or abandoned at sea and either—(a) found or taken possession of within United Kingdom waters; or (b) found or taken possession of beyond those waters and brought within those waters; shall be treated as wreck for the purposes of this Part".
166 The origin of this section was the MSA 1854 s 2. The 1854 Act was a consolidating statute. The earlier Wreck and Salvage Act 1846 had no definition of wreck.
167 MSA 1995 s 255(1). On the distinction between *wrecccum maris* and *adventurae maris* see *R v Forty-Nine Casks of Brandy* [1836] 3 Hagg Adm 257. On the history of the Crown's right to wreck, see *Dromgoole & Gaskell, "Interest in wreck"*, 179; *Marsden*, 353; *Braekhus*, 43; KS Goddard, "Is There a Right to Wreck?" [1983] LMCLQ 625; *Dorey*, 63.
168 For example, it appears that the Crown's right to wreck in the Whitstable area on the Thames Estuary was ceded to the local manorial lord, and his successors are now entitled to personal possessions on board the wreck of a Roman ship lying in the area. *Dromgoole & Gaskell, "Interest in wreck"*, 180.

reported to the Receiver of wreck, can then be reported to those entitled to the wreck.[169] The claimant's entitlement must be proved by a formal statement containing the particulars of their title, as well as an address to which notices of finds may be sent.[170] If such title is proved to the satisfaction of the Receiver, she must notify that person when wreck is found in the relevant area. If no ownership claim is made to the property within the one-year statutory period, then the entitlement derived from the Crown's grant is entitled to possession of that property after payment of all expenses, costs, fees and salvage due in respect of that property.[171]

Whether this Royal prerogative to wreck, both *wreccum maris* and *adventurae maris*, has been inherited by the legal systems of former British colonies has been the subject of some litigation. In *HM v Mar-Dive*,[172] the Canadian court held that the Royal prerogative did survive and vested in Her Majesty in Right of Ontario. On the other hand, in the US, the court in *Treasure Salvors Inc v The Unidentified, Wrecked and Abandoned Sailing Vessel*[173] held that the Crown's prerogative to wreck had not been inherited and was not a part of US law. In that case, the ownership rights rested with the finder in the case of abandoned wrecks.[174]

4.4.2 Right to wreck outside UK territorial waters

The Crown's right to wreck applies only to that "found in the United Kingdom or in United Kingdom waters",[175] meaning the "sea or other waters within the seaward limits of the territorial sea of the United Kingdom".[176] In *Pierce v Bemis (The Lusitania)*,[177] the wreck lay in international waters just outside the territorial waters of Ireland, but the artefacts recovered were brought directly into the UK. After the expiry of the one-year statutory claim period,[178] no claim to the recovered property had been made and Sheen J had to determine whether the salvors or the Crown had a better title to these unclaimed artefacts. As there was no duty to bring wreck recovered in international waters into the UK, Sheen J held that the Crown could have no right to such wreck under the Act, and the finders would be entitled to the artefacts.[179] It appears that the Crown may have had rights to wreck

---

169 MSA 1995 s 242(2).
170 Ibid. s 242(1).
171 Ibid. s 243(2).
172 [1997] AMC 1000 (Ontario, Canada).
173 [1978] AMC 1404 (*Salvors I*), [1981] AMC 1529 (*Salvors II*), [1981] AMC 1857 (*Salvors III*).
174 This has subsequently been amended to the extent that the Abandoned Shipwreck Act 1987 vests certain abandoned shipwrecks (but not all) in the federal government which may then transfer those rights to a particular State of the US. See further *Varmer, "United States"*, 355.
175 MSA 1995 s 241.
176 Ibid. s 313(2). The Territorial Sea Act 1987 s 1(1)(a) provides for a territorial sea of 12 nautical miles in breadth.
177 [1986] QB 384.
178 MSA 1894 s 518; see further below.
179 The duty to report wreck found or taken possession of within UK territorial limits was extended by MSA 1906 s 72 to apply to wreck found or taken possession of outside UK limits but later brought within those limits. *Dromgoole & Gaskell, "Right to Historic Wrecks"*, 379.

found outside territorial waters and brought within the UK, but Sheen J concluded that as a consolidating statute, the MSA 1995 had removed any such pre-existing Crown rights.[180]

4.5 Receiver of Wreck

Section 248 of the MSA 1995 provides that the Secretary of State "shall have the general superintendence throughout the United Kingdom of all matters relating to wreck" but that one or more persons may be appointed as "Receiver of Wreck" for the purposes of the Act, and to discharge such functions as are assigned to the Receiver by the Secretary of State.[181] The position of Receiver of Wreck is of long standing[182] and arose in the days of numerous casualties of wooden sailing vessels that necessitated a mechanism to control the plundering of wrecked vessels by local communities.[183] The intent was to provide for the safekeeping of property from vessels in distress or recently wrecked and the return to its owners. That did not extend to wreck that did not come ashore, and as such, many of the provisions relating to the Receiver of Wreck were not designed originally to apply to sunken wrecks.[184]

4.5.1 Receiver of Wreck's function: vessels in distress

The Receiver of Wreck has responsibilities with respect to UK or foreign vessels that are wrecked, stranded, or in distress "at any place on or near the coasts of the United Kingdom or any tidal water within United Kingdom waters".[185] On being informed that a vessel is in distress, the Act requires the Receiver to "forthwith proceed to the place where the vessel is; take command of all persons present; and assign such duties and give such directions to each person as he thinks fit for the preservation of the vessel and of the lives of the shipwrecked persons".[186] Moreover, the Receiver may, for the purpose of the preservation of shipwrecked persons or of the vessel, cargo and equipment, "require such persons as he thinks necessary to assist him; require the master, or other person having the charge, of any vessel near at hand to give such assistance with his men, or vessel, as may be in his power; and require the use of any vehicle that may be near at hand".[187] It is an offence to intentionally disobey the direction of the Receiver in these circumstances[188] or to refuse, without reasonable excuse, to comply with any requirement made by the Receiver.[189] That

---

180 [1986] QB 384, 395. See *Dromgoole & Gaskell, "Interest in Wreck"*, 181. See also ML Nash, "The Lusitania and Its Consequences" (1986) 4 *New LJ* 317; J Gibson, "The Lusitania and Ownership of Wreck" (1986) 1 IJECL 323.
181 The Receiver of Wreck sits within the MCA, which is an executive agency sponsored by the DfT.
182 The Receiver of Wreck was established in 1854. S Dromgoole, "Protection of Historic Wreck: The UK Approach Part II: Towards Reform" (1989) 4 IJECL [*Dromgoole, "Protection of Historic Wreck"*], 95, 98.
183 See 4.2.3(a).
184 *Dromgoole & Gaskell, "Interest in Wreck"*, 149.
185 MSA 1995 s 231(1). "Tidal waters" is defined as "any part of the sea and any part of a river within the ebb and flow of the tide at ordinary spring tides, and not being a harbour" (s 255(1)).
186 MSA 1995 s 232(2).
187 Ibid. s 233(1).
188 Ibid. s 232(4).
189 Ibid. s 233(2). It is also an offence to impede or hinder or attempt to impede or hinder the saving of any vessel stranded or in danger of being stranded, or otherwise in distress, on or near any coast or tidal water; or any part of the cargo or equipment of any such vessel; or any wreck. s 246(3)(a).

said, the Receiver's powers are curtailed in that the Receiver "shall not interfere between the master and crew of the vessel in reference to the management of the vessel unless he is requested to do so by the master".[190] Nor can the Receiver impose any requirement on the master or other person having the charge of a vessel owned or operated by the Royal National Lifeboat Institution.[191]

Given the history of the position of Receiver, there are detailed provisions as to the right of the Receiver to pass over adjoining lands in order to render assistance to a vessel in distress.[192] These provisions allow the Receiver to pass and repass, including using vehicles, over the adjoining lands without interruption by the owner or occupier of the land and to deposit any cargo or other articles recovered from the vessel on that land.[193] Indeed, it is an offence for the owner or occupier to impede the Receiver in these endeavours.[194] While the Receiver is directed to do as little damage as possible in exercising these powers, the landowner or occupier has a charge on the vessel, cargo or articles recovered for any damages, and which can be recovered in the same manner as salvage is recoverable under the Act.[195]

In these circumstances, it may not necessarily be the Receiver of Wreck that actually goes to the incident and fulfils these powers and duties, as s 231 of the MSA 1995 provides that they may be fulfilled by any officer of customs and excise or any principal officer of the coastguard, who may be treated as an agent of the Receiver.[196] However, an officer discharging such functions is not entitled to any fees payable to the Receiver, nor can the officer be deprived of any right to salvage to which he would otherwise be entitled.[197]

Also reflecting its historical origins, the Act provides that owners of any vessels, cargo or articles shall be entitled to compensation if that property is "plundered, damaged or destroyed" by persons in circumstances in which those persons commit the offence of riot or, in Scotland, of mobbing and rioting.[198]

4.5.2 Receiver of Wreck's function: salvage

The Act also gives the Receiver a role in salvage operations. Section 226 provides that where salvage is due to a salvor in certain circumstances, the Receiver shall detain the relevant vessel, cargo, equipment or wreck where the wreck has not yet been sold as unclaimed.[199] The circumstances that give rise to this power of detention, is if the salvage is due in respect of services rendered in assisting a vessel, or in saving life from a vessel or in saving the cargo owner and equipment of a vessel.[200] It appears that the duty to detain is mandatory in these circumstances.[201] However, modern practice is such that these issues are

---

190 MSA 1995 s 232(3).
191 Ibid. s 232(1A).
192 Ibid. s 234.
193 Ibid. s 234(1).
194 Ibid. s 234(7).
195 Ibid. s 234(4)–(6).
196 Ibid. s 231(2)–(3).
197 Ibid. s 231(4).
198 Ibid. s 235.
199 Ibid. s 226(1).
200 Ibid.
201 *The Fulham* [1899] P 251; *Brice*, 301.

usually resolved by way of contract and the Receiver usually requests information about items recovered under a salvage contract and liaises with owners as the salvage process and the award are settled.[202] It may however, be that the Receiver of Wreck is involved and recovered salvaged wreck or objects detained. This detention lasts as long as the salvage reward is unpaid or process is issued to arrest or detain the property by the court,[203] or security is provided.[204] The Receiver has the power to sell this detained property in certain circumstances, usually when the salvage award is simply not paid within a certain period.[205] The Receiver may also appoint a valuer to value property when the parties to the salvage dispute request the Receiver to do so.[206] The Receiver may also assist in the apportionment of a salvage award as between salvors when the aggregate amount of the award is less than £5,000.[207]

4.5.3 Receiver of Wreck's function: dealing with wreck

The day-to-day activities of the Receiver of Wreck are concerned primarily with fulfilling duties with respect to dealing with wreck. Section 236(1) of the MSA 1995 provides that any person who "finds or takes possession of wreck" in UK waters or brings wreck found elsewhere into UK waters, must "if he is the owner of it, give notice to the Receiver stating that he has found or taken possession of it, and describing the marks by which it may be recognised" or "if he is not the owner of it, give notice to the Receiver that he has found or taken possession of it and, as directed by the receiver, either hold it to the receiver's order or deliver it to the receiver".[208] Not only is it an offence to fail to report a find to the Receiver, but a finder who is not the owner shall forfeit any claim to salvage[209] and be liable to pay twice the value of the wreck to the owner if claimed or, if unclaimed, to the Crown or any other person entitled to the wreck.[210] For an offence to have been committed, the failure must be one that constitutes a criminal and wrongful attempt to detain the wreck and defraud the rightful owner of his rights.[211] As 'wreck' these provisions cover the vessel, its cargo and other artefacts that come from the vessel. Nevertheless, s 237 addresses cargo and other artefacts that have been separated from the vessel and impose similar obligations and penalties. This is designed to address instances where the vessel itself may not have

---

202 See 3.5.3.
203 MSA 1995 s 226(2).
204 Ibid. s 226(3).
205 Ibid. s 227(2).
206 Ibid. s 225.
207 Ibid. s 228.
208 Under the MSA 1894 s 518, there was an obligation to deliver the wreck to the Receiver, but this requirement was removed and the present text in paragraph (b) was inserted by the Merchant Shipping (Registration etc.) Act 1993 Sch 4 para 22. Indeed, the policy now is that in most cases the salvor will be asked to hold the material to the Receiver's order. Wreck and Salvage Law, www.gov.uk/guidance/wreck-and-salvage-law.
209 See *The Zeta* (1875) 21 TLR 648. The salvor will still be entitled to salvage, even though not complying with this section, if in the end, the property is returned to the owner. See *Brice*, 306.
210 MSA 1995 s 236(2). The Receiver currently requires, as a reasonable period, that notice be given within 28 days after the recovery of wreck. The 28 days begins on the date the item reported to the Receiver of Wreck is actually recovered. Wreck and Salvage Law, www.gov.uk/guidance/wreck-and-salvage-law. By way of comparison, the Treasure Act 1996 requires finds to be reported within 14 days of the find.
211 *Brice*, 306; *Kennedy & Rose*, 525.

been wrecked, but cargo has been washed overboard or thrown overboard as jetsam, and which then washes ashore. It might also cover situations where cargo escapes a wreck and is washed ashore. It is these reporting requirements that seek to prevent an improper detention of the property and to enable the Receiver to establish legal entitlement to the wreck.[212]

Section 236 of the MSA 1995 requires a person who "finds or takes possession" of a wreck to report it to the Receiver of Wreck. The duty to report appears quite clearly to apply both to the taking possession of wreck and merely finding a wreck. Finding in this sense might include locating a wreck using remote sensing equipment or actual discovery whilst diving. In either case, it is very unlikely that finders will report the mere discovery of a wreck, and few would even know of this obligation, even within the diving community. Given the amount of recreational diving that occurs on or around the numerous wrecks of the UK, the Receiver of Wreck is likely to be inundated with reports if mere finds in this sense, were required to be reported. As such, the Receiver of Wreck describes the 'finder' as someone who needs to report their recoveries and the reporting form assumes recovery of objects.[213] The "date found" on the report is usually then the date that items have been recovered, and not the date when the wreck might first have been located underwater.[214] Those who locate a wreck site and do not recover any item do, at times, report these to the Receiver of Wreck. This may be the case where the salvor wishes to record the find and its location to be used as evidence in any later proceedings once any recovery operation begins. While the Receiver of Wreck will note these, the 'find' does not give rise to any possessory right or any right as salvor in possession.[215]

While the failure to report the recovery of objects is an offence, it is not an offence of strict liability in the sense that the failure to report must have been one that amounts to a wrongful attempt to take possession of the wreck so as to defraud the rightful owner of the wreck.[216] It appears then that there have been few prosecutions for a failure to report. Indeed, the first prosecution for a failure to report the recovery of objects as required in ss 236 and 237 was in 2014. In that case, two divers pleaded guilty of failing to report material recovered from a number of wrecks over a 13-year period, including a number of bronze cannons, propellers, ingots, copper, lead, zinc and numerous piece of equipment. The wrecks dated from at least 1807 and included a number of military vessels such as German U-boats *U-8, UC-64* and *UB-40*.[217] More recently a Dutch company was successfully prosecuted for offences in relation to the recovery of copper and steel from the wreck of the *Harrovian*, sunk off the British coast by *U-69* in 1916.[218]

In addition to the offence and other consequences of a failure to report a find or possession of wreck, it is also an offence to take wreck, to which the Act applies, into any foreign port and sell it (which includes the vessel, cargo, equipment and any other object from the

---

212 Dromgoole & Gaskell, "Interest in Wreck", 150.
213 "MSF6200 Report of Wreck and Salvage", Wreck and Salvage Law, www.gov.uk/guidance/wreck-and-salvage-law.
214 See also 3.5.3.
215 See 3.5.1.
216 *Brice*, 306.
217 M Prynne, "Divers Prosecuted for Keeping Wreck Salvage", *The Telegraph* (15 May 2014), www.telegraph.co.uk/news/uknews/crime/10833889/Divers-prosecuted-for-keeping-wreck-salvage.html.
218 www.gov.uk/government/news/master-and-owner-charged-for-illegal-salvage-of-sunken-vessel.

vessel).[219] It is not merely the taking into the foreign port that is an offence, but that it is sold in the foreign port. Owners that merely recover their own property and take it into a foreign port are not therefore committing an offence, but should the owner then sell it, for scrap for example, then it might come within the remit of this offence. Reeder, however, suggests that it is most unlikely that the offence is directed at such a disposal.[220] Moreover, while there have been suspicions that breaches have occurred, there has been no prosecutions for this offence.

It is also an offence to board or attempt to board any vessel which is wrecked, stranded or in distress without the permission of the master.[221] Indeed, the master may forcibly repel any attempt to board.[222] This presupposes that the master is still in control of the vessel, but since wreck is defined to include derelict, the better interpretation of this offence is one where a person boards contrary to the direction of the master, rather than merely without the master's permission. If this were not so, all salvors who board vessels in order to render a salvage service without having first obtained the master's permission would be caught by this provision, which is unlikely to have been the intent.[223]

The Receiver must, within 48 hours of taking possession of wreck, record the appropriate details of any wreck and, if it is believed to exceed £5,000 in value, to inform the chief executive officer of Lloyd's in London.[224] The latter allows insurance interest to take notice of the wreck. On receipt of such a notice, the chief executive officer of Lloyd's must post the notice in "some conspicuous position for inspection".[225] In practice the Receiver of Wreck enters the details of the recovery in its Droit database within 48 hours and makes most of this information available to interested parties. Information protected by the Data Protection Act 2018, and information submitted as Commercial in Confidence are not released, nor is the exact location of a wreck, merely the general area. This has usually been sufficient for the owner to be able to identify its interest in the wreck and objects recovered.

Wreck recovered and reported to the Receiver of Wreck is seldom actually taken into the Receiver's possession. When the report is received, the Receiver of Wreck usually directs the finder to hold the objects recovered on providing an indemnity to the Receiver.[226] This is subject to the objects being held in a secure location and the objects not requiring specialised conservation.

The owner of any wreck in the possession of the Receiver (or held by the finder on the Receiver's directions) must establish its claim to the wreck within a period of one year from the time when the wreck first came into the Receiver's possession.[227] For wrecked foreign ships and cargoes, the owner may be represented by the "appropriate" consulate. In relation to the vessel it is the consulate to which ship "belonged" or, in the case of cargo, the consulate of the nationality of the owner.[228] In practice, it appears that the owner

---

219 MSA 1995 s 245.
220 *Brice*, 310.
221 MSA 1995 s 246(1).
222 Ibid. s 246(4).
223 This appears to be suggested by *Brice*, 311.
224 MSA 1995 s 238(1).
225 Ibid. s 238(3).
226 The reverse of the finder report form provides for this.
227 MSA 1995 s 239(1).
228 Ibid. s 239(3).

need merely come forward and assert the claim within the one-year period, and may be given more time to establish that claim to the Receiver's satisfaction. Once the claim has been established the owner is entitled to possession following payment of any salvage, the Receiver's fee and expenses.[229] The Receiver, however, is given the power of sale in certain circumstances. If the wreck is worth less than £5,000, its value makes storage uneconomical or it is so damaged or of such a perishable nature that it cannot be kept, then the Receiver may sell at any time.[230] The proceeds will then be paid to the owner when claimed, less salvage and expenses. The Receiver may also sell wreck in her possession within the year if it is unlikely that any owner will establish a claim to the wreck within that year and the Receiver has not been given, by a person claiming to be entitled to the wreck, a notice relating to the place where the wreck was found over which entitlement exists.[231] The Receiver also has the option of making an advance to the salvors on account of any salvage that may become payable. The Receiver may attach conditions to the payment, and may decide upon the amount. In many cases, the Receiver simply returns recovered objects to the salvor in lieu of salvage.[232]

If no claim is made to the wreck, either by an owner or a claimant deriving a claim from the Crown,[233] the Receiver shall sell the wreck and, after deducting fees, expenses, VAT and such amount of salvage as the Secretary of State may determine, pay the proceeds into the Consolidated Fund for the benefit of the Crown.[234] "Delivery of wreck or payment of the proceeds of sale of wreck by the receiver" discharges the Receiver from all liability in respect of the delivery or payment.[235]

As discussed above, the Act creates a number of offences, including a failure to report a find or taking possession of wreck, and for taking a wreck into a foreign port and selling it.[236] It is an offence to conceal any wreck[237] and to deface or obliterate any mark on a vessel, as well as to wrongfully remove or carry away any part of any wreck or any part of a vessel, its cargo and equipment where the vessel is in danger or is stranded or in danger of being stranded.[238]

The Receiver is entitled to a fee for the services rendered and to be reimbursed for any expenses arising from those services.[239] In addition to the usual rights and remedies for the recovery of such expenses and fees, the Receiver has the same rights and remedies as those

---

229 Ibid. s 239(1).
230 Ibid. s 240(1).
231 This provision relates to situations where the Crown has granted the right to unclaimed wreck to another person, such as a manorial lord: see ibid. s 241. Such persons must provide the Receiver with a notice giving details of their entitlement: ibid. s 242.
232 Provision is made for disputes as to title to unclaimed wreck to be determined by courts having Admiralty jurisdiction.
233 MSA 1995 s 242.
234 Ibid. s 243(6) also provides that the proceeds may be paid to the Duchy of Lancaster and Duchy of Cornwall when so entitled.
235 Ibid. s 244(1).
236 Ibid. ss 236(2)–(4), 245.
237 The Act makes provision for the Receiver to obtain a search warrant in such cases. Ibid. s 247.
238 Ibid. s 246(3).
239 Ibid. s 249(1)–(2).

a salvor has in respect of salvage due to him.[240] This appears to create a statutory form of maritime lien.[241]

4.5.4 Salvage of or by State vessels

Salvage law, with some exceptions, applies to salvage services in assisting any State vessels, or in saving life therefrom, or "in saving any cargo or equipment belonging to Her Majesty in right of Her Government in the United Kingdom', in the same manner as if the ship, cargo or equipment belonged to a private person".[242] The exceptions relate to the power of the Receiver of Wreck to detain and sell salved property or to appoint a valuer of such property,[243] and to a prohibition of proceeding *in rem*.[244]

This does not specifically include wreck, but refers only to Her Majesty's ships. Nevertheless, it appears that wrecks of ships (and cargo on board) continue to be regarded as ships for this purpose. Not surprisingly, much that is reported to the Receiver of Wreck are objects from military wrecks, both of the UK and of other nations. It is understood that in many cases the MOD has simply returned recovered material to the salvor in lieu of salvage.[245]

4.5.5 Modern practice of Receiver of Wreck

The position of Receiver of Wreck arose in the days of numerous casualties of wooden sailing vessels that necessitated a mechanism to control the plundering of wrecked vessels by local communities.[246] The Act therefore provides for an active and broad range of activities on the part of the Receiver. The modern Receiver of Wreck's function are described by the Receiver itself more modestly, being responsible for "processing incoming reports of wreck" and ensuring that "the interests of both salvor and owner are taken into consideration by research and establishing who own the wreck and liaising with the finder and owner, and other interested parties such as archaeologists and museums".[247] Although the Receiver of Wreck service covers modern casualties,[248] in practice its services are rarely called upon as first responder. Corporate ownership of modern ships, organised salvage facilities and the existence of SOSREP and the coastguard capable of coordinating search-and-rescue activities have largely removed the need for a Receiver of Wreck where there are recent casualties.[249] However, SOSREP and the coastguard's immediate functions relate to the protection of life and the

---

240 Ibid. s 249(3).
241 *Brice*, 299.
242 MSA 1995 s 230(1). Conversely, where a State's vessel renders a salvage service, it is entitled to a salvage award in the same way that a private salvor is rewarded. MSA 1995 s 230(2). In relation to wreck removal of State vessels, see 11.1.3.
243 MSA 1995 ss 225, 226 and 227.
244 Crown Proceedings Act 1947 s 29.
245 See also *Dromgoole, "Protection of Historic Wreck"*, 50.
246 *MCA Napoli Response*, 34.
247 Ibid., 32.
248 MSA 1995 s 243(2).
249 Ibid. s 228.

environment, and while the protection of property also falls within its concern, the Receiver of Wreck's function in looking after property owners interests does ensure that it has a role to play in casualties. As such, all property recovered in such a casualty is required to be reported to the Receiver of Wreck, and the Receiver may seek to ensure that owners are reunited with that property. Nevertheless, the Receiver of Wreck no longer fulfils the functions it had in the days of wooden ships, and is more concerned with dealing with casualties of the past. Indeed, it has been referred to as the "coroner of the seas".[250] Reflecting this the Receiver of Wreck service was significantly simplified when a single Receiver, based in Southampton, replaced a number that were based locally around the coast of the UK.[251]

4.6 Coastguard and wreck claims

Her Majesty's Coastguard is part of the MCA within the DfT, as is the Receiver of Wreck. The MSA 1995 addresses the role of the coastguard in relation to wreck in ss 231 and 250. Section 231 provides that, in respect of the Receiver of Wreck's functions where a vessel is in distress,[252] the coastguard may fulfil these functions. While the duty of the coastguard includes assisting vessels in distress, today its primary role is with respect to communications and surveillance and using these in alerting rescue services and assisting in the coordination of the rescue. Depending on exactly what role the coastguard plays in the event of a vessel in distress, it appears that it might be able to claim salvage. This depends on the extent to which the coastguard will be considered a volunteer with respect to the functions fulfilled and its public duty. However, while there appears to have been some successful claims in the 19th century,[253] the policy today appears to be that the coastguard will not assert a salvage claim.[254] The possibility that the coastguard is entitled to salvage is nevertheless allowed for in s 250 MSA 1995.

Section 250 sets out rights of the coastguard for remuneration for certain services, being merely when "services are rendered by any officers or men of the coastguard service in watching or protecting shipwrecked property the owner of the property shall pay in respect of those services remuneration according to a scale fixed by the Secretary of State". In these circumstances, provided that the services were not declined by the owner of the property or his agent at the time they were tendered or that salvage has been claimed and awarded for the services, the coastguard is entitled to remuneration.[255] This remuneration is recoverable by the same means, paid to the same persons, and accounted for and applied in the same manner as fees received by the Receiver of Wreck.[256]

---

250 The Receiver of Wreck, BBC History, www.bbc.co.uk/history/ancient/archaeology/marine_receive_01.shtml.
251 The Merchant Shipping (Registration, etc.) Act 1993 amended the 1894 Act in order to allow for this change to take place (see now MSA 1995 s 248(2)).
252 MSA 1995 ss 232–235. See 4.4.1.
253 *The Charlotta* (1831) 2 Hagg 361; *The Clifton* (1834) 3 Hagg 117; *Silver Bullion* (Cargo ex Sir Robert Peel) (1854) 2 Spinks E&A 70.
254 *Brice*, 71.
255 MSA 1995 s 250(1)–(2).
256 Ibid. s 250(3), referring to the Receiver of Wreck's fees determined in accordance with s 249.

4.7 Wreck protection legislation

4.7.1 Protection of Wrecks Act 1973

The Protection of Wrecks Act was adopted in 1973 as an interim measure to control access to historic wreck sites, particularly as rival salvors were competing for access to sites, leading not only to violent clashes in some cases but also to hasty recovery of objects that not only destroyed the archaeological sites but also led to the recovered objects being left with the Receiver of Wreck without any conservation, leading to their rapid deterioration.[257] Essentially the Act did no more than regulate access to certain sites, but leaving salvors granted an excavation licence with a salvage claim for recovered items, to be reported to the Receiver of Wreck in the usual way. With this interim measure in place, a Wreck Law Review Committee was established to propose new legislation, but following the Committee's 1974 report, which was never published, no legislation was ever proposed.[258] This 'interim' Act therefore continues to govern the protection of historic wreck.

The purpose of the Act, then, is to protect certain wrecks and the sites of such wrecks lying in UK territorial waters[259] from interference by unauthorised persons. If the Secretary of State is satisfied that a site "is, or may prove to be, the site of a vessel lying wrecked on or in the seabed" and "on account of the historical, archaeological or artistic importance of the vessel, or of any objects contained or formerly contained in it which may be lying on the sea bed in or near the wreck, the site ought to be protected from unauthorised interference, he may by order designate an area round the site as a restricted area".[260] The intent is to specifically nominate certain wreck sites that will be subject to this protective regime and to then regulate access to the wreck sites through the issuance of licences. Only specific wreck sites of clear archaeological or historical value are designated. Before designating a wreck site, the Secretary of State must consult with "such persons as he considers appropriate having regard to the purposes of the order" unless he is satisfied that the case is one in which an order should be made as a matter of immediate urgency.[261] By 2019, only 69 wreck sites had been designated, ranging from an early bronze age site,[262] through the middle ages[263] to wrecks of the early 20th century.[264]

---

257 *Dromgoole, "Protection of Historic Wreck"*, 35–36. For a salvor's account of the issues arising and a view of the Act when adopted, see R Morris, *HMS Colossus: The Story of the Salvage of the Hamilton Treasures* (Hutchinson 1979).

258 *Dromgoole, "Protection of Historic Wreck"*, 35. See also A Flinder and S McGrail, "The United Kingdom Advisory Committee on Historic Wreck Sites" (1990) 19 *Int J Nautical Archaeology* 93; A Firth, "Making Archaeology: The History of the Protection of Wrecks Act 1973 and the Constitution of an Archaeological Resource" (1999) 28 *Int J Nautical Archaeology* 10.

259 Protection of Wrecks Act 1973 s 3(1) defines "United Kingdom waters" to mean "any part of the sea within the seaward limits of United Kingdom territorial waters and includes any part of a river within the ebb and flow of ordinary spring tides"; and further provides that the term "the sea" "includes any estuary or arm of the sea; and references to the sea bed include any area submerged at high water of ordinary spring tides". See also MSA 1995 s 313(2)(a), which defines "United Kingdom waters" as "the sea or other waters within the seaward limits of the territorial sea of the UK".

260 Protection of Wrecks Act 1973 s 1(1).

261 Ibid. s 1(4).

262 The Erme Ingot site off Devon. See www.historicengland.org.uk/listing/the-list/list-entry/1000054.

263 Such as the Pwil Fanog wreck off Anglesey, Wales. See http://cadw.gov.wales/historicenvironment/protection/maritimewrecks/wrecksnwreck/wreckswales/?lang=en.

264 Such as the *UC-70* sunk in 1918, the *Holland V* sunk in 1912 and the *HMSub A1* sunk in 1911. See https://historicengland.org.uk/listing/what-is-designation/protected-wreck-sites/.

The size of the designated area is as the discretion of the Secretary of State, with the only limitation being that it cannot extend above the high water mark of the ordinary spring tide.[265] In that designated area, it is an offence to tamper with, damage or remove any part of the wreck or objects from the wreck, to carry out diving or salvage operations or use equipment for those purposes directed to the exploration of the wreck or to removing objects from the site, or to drop something like an anchor that if it were to fall on the site of a wreck (whether it so falls or not), would wholly or partly obliterate the site or obstruct access to it, or damage any part of the wreck, otherwise than under the authority of a licence.[266] It is not an offence should any of this occur in the course of any action taken by someone without a licence, for the sole purpose of dealing with an emergency of any description; in exercising, or seeing to the exercise of, functions conferred by or under an enactment on him or a body for which he acts; or out of necessity due to stress of weather or navigational hazards.[267]

A licence is only granted to persons who are competent, and properly equipped, to carry out salvage operations in a manner appropriate to the historical, archaeological or artistic importance of the wreck or objects from a wreck and who have a legitimate reason for doing so.[268] Conditions and restrictions may be set and revoked, and work done contrary to this is to be regarded as work done without a licence.[269] Even the owners of a historic wreck can be stopped from exercising their rights to dive on or remove property without a licence. While the Act merely requires a licence to undertake any of the activities listed in the Act, the discretion to impose specific condition in the licence has resulted in four different forms of licence being created: a visitor licence, a survey licence, a surface recovery licence and an excavation licence.[270] These can be revoked.[271] In practise, licences are not issued by the Secretary of State directly but by the relevant National Heritage Agency, being Historic England, Historic Scotland, Cadw (the Welsh historic monuments executive agency) or Environment and Heritage Service of Northern Ireland.[272] In 2013, section 1 of the Protection of Wrecks Act 1973 was repealed in Scotland and those sites previously designated under the Act were designated as Historic Marine Protected Areas under the Marine (Scotland) Act 2010, or de-designated.[273]

The Act applies in concert with the MSA 1995 such that recovered material is dealt with in accordance with the wreck provisions of the MSA 1995, such as the reporting requirements with the Receiver of Wreck, and the consequent right of the crown to abandoned wreck and the rights of the "salvor" to a salvage reward. It is often the case that licences of

---

265 Protection of Wrecks Act 1973 s 1(2).
266 Protection of Wrecks Act 1973 s 1(3) provides that it is an offence to cause or permit any of those things to be done by others in a restricted area, otherwise than under the authority of such a licence. S 3(4) provides that a "person guilty of an offence . . . shall be liable on summary conviction to a fine of not more than £400, or on conviction on indictment to a fine; and proceedings for such an offence may be taken, and the offence may for all incidental purposes be treated as having been committed, at any place in the UK where he is for the time being".
267 Protection of Wrecks Act 1973 s 3(3).
268 Ibid. s 1(5).
269 Ibid. s 1(5)(c).
270 Wreck and Salvage Law, www.gov.uk/guidance/wreck-and-salvage-law.
271 Protection of Wrecks Act 1973 s 1(5)(b).
272 Wreck and Salvage Law, www.gov.uk/guidance/wreck-and-salvage-law.
273 Currently eight wrecks are designated in Scotland: http://marine.gov.scot/information/designated-wrecks. See also www.gov.uk/government/uploads/system/uploads/attachment_data/file/303275/wrecks_designated_as_Historic_Marine_Protected_Areas_in_Scotland.pdf.

designated sites, particularly those designated decades ago, are not professional archaeologists but the original divers who found the site, whether by accident or design.[274] Though the various licences grated will require archaeological supervision of all activities, the licensee's continue to have a claim to wreck under the MSA 1995. Excavation licences now are not readily granted and justification for recovery in archaeological terms is required.

The Protection of Wrecks Act 1973 is not, in fact, an Act directed only at historic wreck but also addresses dangerous wrecks. While dangerous wrecks are 'protected', it is in fact a mechanism to safeguard those at risk from dangerous wreck rather than the protection of the wreck itself. The Act provides that the Secretary of State may designate an area around a wreck where it poses a potential danger to life or property because of anything contained in it.[275] The order must identify the vessel and the wreck site, and prohibits the entry into such a zone without a licence. Two wreck sites are currently designated as dangerous sites: the *SS Richard Montgomery* in the Thames Estuary[276] and the *SS Castilian* off Anglesey, both sunk during World War II with significant quantities of munitions on board.[277] A person guilty of an offence under section 1 or section 2 above shall be liable on summary conviction to a fine of not more than £400, or on conviction on indictment to a fine; and proceedings for such an offence may be taken, and the offence may for all incidental purposes be treated as having been committed, at any place in the UK where he is for the time being.

4.7.2 Protection of Military Remains Act 1986

The Protection of Military Remains Act 1986 was adopted to protect the wrecks of military vessels that had sunk with the loss of its crew from unwanted interference. In the wake of the naval losses suffered by the Royal Navy in the Falklands War,[278] sensitivity was heightened following unauthorised recovery of material from *HMS Hampshire* as well as allegations that divers had inappropriately handled human remains during the government-sanctioned salvage of the cargo of *HMS Edinburgh*.[279] In the case of *HMS Hampshire*,[280] the salvage was undertaken without the knowledge or consent of the government.[281] Despite originally being called the "War Graves Bill", the Act does not protect the wreck

---

274 S Dromgoole, "United Kingdom", in S Dromgoole (ed), *The Protection of the Underwater Cultural Heritage: National Perspectives in Light of the UNESCO Convention 2001* (Martinus Nijhoff Publishers, 2006) [*Dromgoole, "United Kingdom"*], 324.

275 Protection of Wrecks Act 1973 s 2(1).

276 See www.gov.uk/government/publications/receiver-of-wreck-protected-wrecks and, for annual survey reports, see www.gov.uk/government/publications/the-ss-richard-montgomery-information-and-survey-reports.

277 The *MV Braer* off Shetland has been de-designated.

278 A number of Royal Naval vessels were sunk around the Falkland Islands, including *HMS Ardent, HMS Antelope, HMS Coventry, HMS Sheffield, SS Atlantic Conveyor* and *RFA Sir Galahad*.

279 M Williams, "War Graves and Salvage: Murky Waters?" (2000) 5 IJML [*Williams*], 151. S Dromgoole, "Military Remains on and around the Coast of the United Kingdom" (1996) 2 IJMCL [*Dromgoole, "Military Remains"*], 23, 28. On the recovery of human remains in contemporary wreck removal operations, see 13.1.3.

280 *HMS Hampshire* is historically important, as Lord Kitchener was lost in its sinking.

281 A German consortium had applied to the MOD for permission to dive on and film the wreck, but this was refused. However, since there was no legal basis to prevent this, the consortium went ahead and raised a number of objects from the wreck, including personal belongings. *Dromgoole, "Military Remains"*, 29. See also *Williams*, 152.

as a grave, nor is the term 'war grave' used, but achieves a similar result by protecting the known wreck or wreck site.[282]

The purpose of the Act is to "secure to the protection from unauthorised interference of the remains of military aircraft and vessels that have crashed, sunk or been stranded and of associated human remains".[283] The Act therefore protects the wrecks, and by association, human remains. The Act provides that the Secretary of State may designate a specific vessel that sank or was stranded on military service on or after 4 August 1914 as one subject to the Act.[284] Aircraft do not have to be designated and are covered by a blanker protection regime in that all are automatically protected places. The aircraft or designated wreck's location does not have to be known for it to be designated, though wherever that place is, it is a "protected place" under the Act.[285] This allows for wrecks to be protected prior to them being discovered and interfered with. So, for example, two British submarines have been designated as protected vessels despite their positions not being known. The *E-50* was lost without trace with all 30 crew in February 1918, and has yet to be found, though an estimated sinking position is identified on charts.[286] The *G-8*, which simply went missing in the same month somewhere in the North Sea with all 30 crew, has also not yet been found.[287] The location of the majority of vessels listed as "protected" sites is, however, known. These "protected" wrecks are protected in that it is an offence to tamper with, damage, move, remove or unearth remains or to enter any hatch or other opening in any of the remains which enclose any part of the interior of a vessel without a licence.[288] However, for someone to commit this offence their actions must be accompanied by a belief, or having had reasonable grounds for suspecting, that they are engaged with the remains of a vessel which has crashed, sunk or been stranded while in military service.[289] Since "protected wrecks" are named wrecks whose location may not be known, those who accidentally come across the wrecks will not be guilty of an offence unless there is sufficient evidence that makes it clear that it is indeed a military wreck covered by the Act. As such, the Act also specifically prohibits diving or salvage operations that will, or is likely to involve an act that constitutes an offence.[290] However, merely diving on a wreck that is a protected place does not constitute an offence, provided that there is no interference with the wreck itself. For example, *K-17*, a "protected wreck", is a popular dive site and regularly visited and filmed.[291]

The Act also provides for the Secretary of State to designate a specific area as a "controlled" site, being an area which appears "to contain a place comprising the remains of, or of a substantial part of . . . a vessel which has so sunk or been stranded".[292] The scope is

---

282 *Williams*, 153.
283 Protection of Military Remains Act 1986 Chapter 35.
284 Protection of Military Remains Act 1986, s 1(2)(a) and 1(3)(a). It also applies to any aircraft which has crashed (whether before or after the passing of this Act) while in military service; s 1(1).
285 Protection of Military Remains Act 1986, s 1(6).
286 Wreck Site, www.wrecksite.eu/wreck.aspx?16075.
287 Wreck Site, www.wrecksite.eu/wreck.aspx?16136.
288 Protection of Military Remains Act 1986, s 2(2) and 2(3).
289 Ibid., s 2(1)(b).
290 Ibid., s 2(3)(b).
291 See www.youtube.com/watch?v=7nFUYhxB3T8; www.youtube.com/watch?v=Ghv4Llq2Z5Q.
292 Protection of Military Remains Act 1986, s 1(2)(b).

broader than that of protected places in that it concerns aircraft and vessels that have sunk or stranded on military service within the last 200 years.[293] The controlled sites, however, relate to a specific vessel and because their exact location is known, they are protected in relation to that known place. It is an offence to tamper with, damage, move, remove or unearth remains or to enter any hatch or other opening in the wreck that encloses any part of the interior without a licence.[294] The Act also specifically prohibits diving or salvage operations that aim to identify those wrecks that may be subject to the Act.[295] Any interference without a licence is an offence of strict liability.[296] On controlled sites there is therefore an effective ban on diving and salvage operations without a licence.[297] Licences granted by the Secretary of State may include conditions, which may be particularly important in relation to human remains that might still exist.[298] For example, a licence to explore the wreck of *HMS Vanguard*, a controlled site, was granted in 2016 in preparation for the 100th anniversary of its sinking that took 677 of its crew with it.[299]

The controlled site or protected place need not be in UK waters, and could be in international waters provided it is a British vessel to which the Act applies.[300] The British submarine *E-18*, for example, lost without trace in May 1916 with all 30 crew, was found by a Swedish marine survey company in 2009 in international waters off the coast of Estonia.[301] Nevertheless, in 2012 *E-18* was designated a protected place. British vessels in the territorial sea of any other nation, however, cannot be designated or subject to a controlled site, as they then lie within the exclusive jurisdiction of the coastal State.[302]

While a protected place must be of a vessel sunk on or after the outbreak of World War I, or within 200 years for a controlled site, it must be a vessel that was "on military service". Importantly, this is defined in the Act to mean a vessel "in service with, or being used for the purposes of, any of the armed forces of the UK or any other country or territory".[303] In *R (On the Application of Fogg) v The Secretary of State for Defence*,[304] the relatives of a chief petty officer lost on the *SS Storaa* successfully challenged the Secretary of State's decision not to designate the *SS Storaa* on the basis that it was not on military service when sunk. The *SS Storaa* was an armed merchant vessel in convoy when sunk by enemy action in 1943. The court held that in the definition of military service, which provides that a vessel shall be regarded as having been in military service when it is "in service with, or being used for the purposes of, any of the armed forces of the UK" includes merchant

---

293 Ibid., s 1(4)(a).
294 Ibid., s 2(2) and 2(3).
295 Ibid., s 2(3).
296 Ibid., s 2.
297 Dromgoole, "Military Remains", 23, 32.
298 Protection of Military Remains Act 1986, s 4.
299 Scapa Flow divers reveal new images of *HMS Vanguard* wreck, *Express* (19 January 2017), www.express.co.uk/news/world/756218/hms-vanguard-warship-scapa-flow-ministry-of-defence?utm_source=-feedburner&utm_medium=feed&utm_campaign=Feed%3A+daily-express-news-showbiz+%28Express+%3A%3A+News+%2F+Showbiz+Feed%29; Wreck Site, www.wrecksite.eu/wreck.aspx?10477.
300 Protection of Military Remains Act 1986, s 1(2)(b).
301 Wreck Site, www.wrecksite.eu/wreck.aspx?16067.
302 Protection of Military Remains Act 1986, s 1(2).
303 Ibid., s 9(2).
304 [2006] 2 Lloyd's Rep 576.

vessels that are in service with vessels such as warships. Following this judicial review, the *SS Storaa* was designated, as were a number of other 'non-warships'. *HMS Calgarian*, for example, a passenger and mail steamer requisitioned and owned by the navy and armed as an armed auxiliary cruiser when it was sunk by a torpedo from *U-19* with the loss of 49 of its crew has been designated a protected wreck;[305] as has the *Creosol*, a Royal Fleet Auxiliary tanker, sunk off Sunderland on 7 February 1918 with the loss of 2 crew. Vessels requisitioned but still owned by private owners at the time of the loss have also been designated, such as the *Duke of Albany*, a passenger and cargo ship used as an armed boarding ship when torpedoed with the loss of 24 of its crew.[306] So too the *Mendi*, a privately owned passenger ship used to carry troops when it sank after a collision, with the loss of 636 lives, almost all of which were troops from the South African Labour Corps.[307] One of the youngest wrecks protected is that of the requisitioned merchant ship *Atlantic Conveyor*, sunk after being damaged in the Falklands War in 1982.[308]

The Act also applies to foreign vessels, whether designated or within a controlled site, provided then that the vessel is in British waters.[309] A number of German U-boats from both World Wars have been protected: *UB-81* as a controlled site and *U-1018, U-1063, U-12, U-714* and *UB-65* as designated vessels.

The first designations under the Act only took place in 2002, 16 years after its promulgation. It appears that following its promulgation, there was "a very widespread, but erroneous belief within the diving and ex-service community that the 1986 Act conferred automatic protection on 'war graves', a misapprehension which the MOD understandably, felt helped to prevent intrusion and which it did little to dispel".[310] By 2000, however, the growth in interference with these wrecks was such that designation was finally resorted to. By 2017, 66 vessels had been designated as protected sites and 12 controlled sites designated.[311]

The scope of the Act is unnecessarily limited. There is no reason, for example, why it could not apply to the wrecks of foreign vessels beyond the British territorial sea. It could for example, include the protection of German vessels lost during the Battle of Jutland from interference from British nationals or from activities undertaken from British vessels. This is so since the Act only applies to British nationals and British vessels beyond its own territorial sea.[312] This however has created a concern that while British nationals and British vessels are prevented from interfering with British wrecks beyond British waters, such as those off Jutland, nationals and vessels of other nations may interfere with these sites with some impunity, notwithstanding that they are subject to sovereign immunity.[313]

---

305 Wreck Site, www.wrecksite.eu/wreck.aspx?376.
306 Wreck Site, www.wrecksite.eu/wreck.aspx?11864.
307 Wreck Site, www.wrecksite.eu/wreck.aspx?1271.
308 Other vessels lost in the Falklands War protected by the Act are *HMS Sheffield* and *RFS Sir Galahad*. *HMS Ardent* and *HMS Antelope* are protected under the Falkland Islands Protection of Wreck Ordinance 1977.
309 Protection of Military Remains Act 1986, s 1(3)(b) (cf Merchant Shipping and Maritime Security Act 1997 s 24).
310 *Williams*, 152.
311 Protection of Military Remains Act 1986 (Designation of Vessels and Controlled Sites) Order 2012 No. 1110.
312 Protection of Military Remains Act 1986, s 3(1).
313 Dromgoole, "Military Remains", 23, 33.

Where other States have legislation that also protects such vessels, the risk is minimised. Unfortunately, few other States do have such legislation.

The Merchant Shipping and Maritime Security Act (MSMSA) 1997 addresses the issue of the protection by foreign wrecks beyond the UK territorial sea by providing that the Secretary of State may, by statutory instrument, give effect to any international agreement which relates to the protection of such wrecks, and to which the UK is party.[314] The statutory instrument may include designating a wreck or an area in which a wreck is situated as one to which access is restricted or prohibited without a licence issued by the Secretary of State, as well as the necessary enforcement measures commensurate with such a designation.[315] Naturally, the Act only creates offences of interference of wrecks in UK waters or on board a UK registered vessel, or for UK nationals that commit offences in international waters aboard foreign-flagged vessels. The Act defines wreck as "the wreck of any ship other than a ship which, at the time it sank or was stranded, was in service with, or used for the purposes of, any of the armed forces of the United Kingdom or any other country or territory".[316] The Act is not intended to cover those subject to the Protection of Military Remains Act 1986 (or foreign States' equivalent Acts, eg US Sunken Military Craft Act 2004). It was designed specifically to protect the final resting place of victims of merchant wrecks, rather than to protect military wrecks, or indeed to historic wrecks for their historic value. Its intent was to enable the UK to give effect to agreements concerning wrecks such as the *Estonia* and the *Titanic*.

The ferry *Estonia* sank in 1994 in the Baltic Sea with the loss of almost 900 lives, and there was great concern that remains might be disturbed by divers. In 1995, the governments of Estonia, Finland and Sweden reached an agreement to protect the wreck by prohibiting any activities that would disturb the peace of the final resting place of those who went down with the vessel.[317]

The MSMSA 1997 did enable the Secretary of State to give effect to the 2000 Agreement Concerning the Shipwrecked Vessel RMS *Titanic* concluded with the US, France and Canada.[318] However, the agreement has not come into force, though both the UK and US have adopted legislation that essentially gives effect to the agreement.[319] The UK Protection of

---

314 Merchant Shipping and Maritime Security Act 1997 s 24(1). See *Gaskell, MSMSA 1997*, 28/86-26/88.
315 Merchant Shipping and Maritime Security Act 1997 s 24(2).
316 Ibid. s 24(8).
317 See IMO Circular Letter No. 1859, 16 November 1995.
318 *R.M.S. Titanic*—International Agreement www.gc.noaa.gov/gcil_titanic-intl.html.
319 The UK ratified the Agreement on November 6, 2003 (Order No. 2496, 2003) which comes into force on the date on which the International Agreement enters into force in respect of the UK. The US signed the Agreement on June 18, 2004, subject to acceptance following the enactment of implementing legislation. This has not yet occurred. The earlier *RMS Titanic* Maritime Memorial Act of 1986 (US) predates the Agreement and is insufficient to give effect to it. Nevertheless, in 2017 the Consolidated Appropriations Act did require any salvage activity to be subject to the Agreement. See further NOAA, www.gc.noaa.gov/gcil_titanic-ref.html. See S Dromgoole, "The International Agreement for the Protection of the *Titanic*: Problems and Prospects" (2006) 37 ODIL [*Dromgoole, "Titanic"*], 1; M Aznar and O Varmer, "The *Titanic* as Underwater Cultural Heritage: Challenges to its Legal International Protection" (2013) 44 ODIL [*Aznar & Varmer*], 96; O Varmer and C M Blanco, "The Case for Using the Law of Salvage to Preserve Underwater Cultural Heritage: The Integrated Marriage of the Law of Salvage and Historic Preservation" (2018) 49 JMLC [*Varmer & Blanco*] 401.

Wrecks (*RMS Titanic* Order)[320] in principle allows salvage, but subject to the limitations provided for in the Agreement and set out in the order.[321]

4.7.3 Ancient Monuments and Archaeological Areas Act 1979

If wreck material comes from non-tidal waters, it is treated as if it was found on land and governed by the Ancient Monuments and Archaeological Areas Act 1979.[322] This Act provides for the scheduling of monuments of national importance and regulates access to scheduled monuments. A monument is defined as "(a) any building, structure or work, whether above or below the surface of the land, and any cave or excavation; (b) any site comprising the remains of any such building, structure or work or of any cave or excavation; and (c) any site comprising, or comprising the remains of, any vehicle, vessel, aircraft or other movable structure or part thereof which neither constitutes nor forms part of any work which is a monument within paragraph (a) above".[323] Furthermore, this applies to a "monument situated in, on or under the sea bed within the seaward limits of UK territorial waters adjacent to the coast of Great Britain".[324]

Without the consent of the relevant Secretary of State,[325] it is an offence to demolish, destroy, remove, alter or repair a scheduled monument.[326] The Secretary of State will take advice from the relevant agency, being Historic England, Historic Scotland or Cadw.[327] The policy underpinning the application of the Act is twofold; first, to provide *in situ* protection for monuments such that excavation licences are rarely granted; and secondly, to allow and encourage public access.[328] This policy has been used to protect those wrecks where public access is encouraged whilst still maintaining a strict prohibition on activities that have a physical impact on the wreck. This is exemplified by the scheduling of seven German warships scuttled at Scapa Flow in 1919.[329] These wrecks are popular recreational diving sites and a boon to the economy of the Orkney Islands, and as such, public access

---

[320] Order No. 2496, 2003.
[321] See 6.8. See further *Dromgoole, "Titanic"*, 13–16.
[322] Wreck and Salvage Law, www.gov.uk/guidance/wreck-and-salvage-law. Other legislation such as the Treasure Act 1996 may also apply.
[323] Ancient Monuments and Archaeological Areas Act 1979 s 61(7).
[324] Ibid. s 53(1). See also ss 17(10), 24(3AA) and 45(40) with reference to the territorial sea in the Act.
[325] Secretary of State for DCMS.
[326] Ancient Monuments and Archaeological Areas Act 1979 s 2.
[327] Ancient Monuments and Archaeological Areas Act 1979 s 53(2) provides that the "entry in the Schedule relating to any monument in territorial waters shall describe the monument as lying off the coast of England, or of Scotland, or of Wales; and any such monument shall be treated for the purposes of this Act as situated in the country specified for the purposes of this subsection in the entry relating to the monument in the Schedule". The Act does not apply to Northern Ireland, though similar provisions are contained in the Historic Monuments and Archaeological Objects (Northern Ireland) Order 1995.
[328] *Dromgoole, "United Kingdom"*, 326.
[329] Wreck and Salvage Law, www.gov.uk/guidance/wreck-and-salvage-law. The wrecks scheduled are *Konig, Kronprinz Wilhelm, Markgraf, Burmmer, Dresden, Karlsruhe* and the *Koln*. Eight fishing vessels lost in the late 19th and early 20th centuries in Aberlady Bay, East Lothian, and an unknown 18th-century wreck in Bamburgh Castle Beach, have also been scheduled. See www.gov.uk/government/uploads/system/uploads/attachment_data/file/303271/Scheduled_Ancient_Monuments.pdf.

was encouraged.³³⁰ Scheduling these wreck as monuments thus offered an advantage over listing pursuant to the Protection of Wrecks Act 1973 as the latter's licensing requirements would have had to name the divers entitled to visit the site. Despite the Act describing monuments as "ancient", there is no time period requirement in the Act and recent heritage can be scheduled. Moreover, rather than applying merely to shipwrecks, as the Protection of Wrecks Act does, the Ancient Monuments and Archaeological Areas Act 1979 applies to all forms of underwater cultural heritage such as aircraft or tanks lost overboard.

4.7.4 Comparative US approach to protection of historic wreck

Many States have adopted national legislation that provides some form of protection for wrecks of historical, archaeological or cultural importance, irrespective of ownership.³³¹ In many respects though, the US had similar concerns with respect to wreck in its waters and more especially with their own wreck, particularly warships, in international waters or in other State's waters. A brief review then of the US position is instructive; particularly, as will be seen in Chapter 6, both States share similar concerns with the application of the UCH 2001.

The US has a rich heritage of wrecks and a considerable salvage industry, including amateur 'treasure hunters'. In the 1970s considerable judicial activity considered the rights of salvors, finders, owners, the individual states of the US and of the federal government. Early statutory mechanism used to provide some protection for historic wreck include the National Historic Preservation Act, which provides for the National Register of Historic Places and which imposes a form of regulation that can prevent interference with a wreck. It has been used sparingly for shipwrecks but has been used to protect the *San Diego* and the *Comoran*.³³² The degree of protection offered by listing might be somewhat modest. The *Comoran*, for example, was listed in 1975, but is a popular dive site that has suffered significant disturbance, and while having been archaeologically mapped, it has not been extensively studied.³³³ Following a series of disputes as to whether finders were entitled to ownership of abandoned wreck, the US federal government adopted the Abandoned Shipwreck Act in 1987.

The Abandoned Shipwreck Act 1987 was partly a response to the decision in *Treasure Salvors Inc v The Unidentified, Wrecked and Abandoned Sailing Vessel*,³³⁴ in which the

---

330 Dromgoole, "United Kingdom", 328.

331 On the national laws of Australia, China, France, Greece, Ireland, Italy, Poland, South Africa, Spain, Sweden, Turkey, the UK and the US as at 1999, see S Dromgoole (ed), *Legal Protection of the Underwater Cultural Heritage: National and International Perspectives* (Kluwer Law International, 1999), and for an updated consideration of the national law in light of the 2001 UCH Convention (see Chapter 6) for Australia, China, Finland, France, Greece, Ireland, Micronesia, the Netherlands, New Zealand, Norway, Poland, South Africa, Spain, Sweden, the UK and the US as at 2006, see S Dromgoole, *The Protection of Underwater Cultural Heritage: National Perspectives in Light of the UNESCO Convention 2001* (Martinus Nijhoff, 2006) [*Dromgoole, "UNESCO Convention"*].

332 J Delgado and O Varmer, "The Public Importance of World War I Shipwrecks: Why a State Should Care and the Challenges of Protection", in U Guérin, A Rey Da Silva and L Simmonds, *The Underwater Cultural Heritage from World War I: Proceedings of the Scientific Conference on the Occasion of the Centenary of World War I* (UNESCO, 2015) [*Delgado & Varmer*], 108.

333 *Delgado & Varmer*, 108.

334 [1978] AMC 1404 (*Salvors I*), [1981] AMC 1529 (*Salvors II*), [1981] AMC 1857 (*Salvors III*).

court found that the Crown's prerogative to wreck had not been inherited and was not a part of US law.[335] The Act vests title in the federal government to any abandoned shipwreck found either embedded in or resting on the submerged lands of a US State and which is included in or determined eligible for inclusion in the National Register of Historic Places. This claim only targets wrecks that are believed to be historically or archaeologically important.[336] This claim to State ownership rests on the owner having abandoned ownership, thus avoiding any complications in relation to the taking or confiscation of private property—an issue of considerable importance in the US. Other States have not been so concerned and have asserted State ownership over vessels of a certain age without addressing any possible existing ownership rights, in order to protect the historical and archaeological importance of the wreck. South Africa, for example, simply asserts ownership of all wreck over 60 years old.[337]

Few States have addressed the issue of protection of military vessel specifically. Most State have adopted legislation that indirectly protects vessels that have sunk with the loss of crew by including them in a larger category of historic wrecks. The only State other than the UK to specifically consider the issue is the US. The Sunken Military Craft Act addresses the protection of both US military craft and those of foreign nations within US waters.[338] It prohibits any activity directed at such military craft without a permit. US Naval policy has been to reject applications for a permit to salvage warships when they contain the remains of deceased servicemen.[339]

4.8 Sovereign immunity and wrecks

As is evident from the preceding discussion, States have considerable power in relation to wrecks in their territorial waters. This reflects the international law that a State has complete and absolute jurisdiction within its territory, subject to limitations set out in international law itself eg in relation to jurisdiction over ships engaged in innocent passage within the territorial sea.[340] The State has both the power to make laws (legislative jurisdiction) and the power to enforce those laws (enforcement jurisdiction) within that territory. The State also has jurisdiction over its nationals and ships flaying its flag outside of its territory.[341]

If the other party to a dispute is another sovereign State, the territorial sovereign must waive its exclusive jurisdiction, thereby granting the other sovereign State immunity from its enforcement jurisdiction. This sovereign immunity has its origin in the notion that all sovereigns are equal and one sovereign should not therefore be subject to the jurisdiction of another.[342] Originally this immunity was absolute and was applied to cover all acts of the foreign State within the territory of the other State, as well as the sovereign's property

---

335 See 4.3.1.
336 See *Varmer, "United States"*, 351.
337 *Forrest, "South Africa"*, 247.
338 *Varmer, United States"*, 367.
339 J Harris, "The Protection of Sunken Warships as Gravesites at Sea" (2001) 7(1) OCLJ 75, 123.
340 See 5.4.2.
341 It was on this basis that the court had jurisdiction *in personam* to grant an injunction against the defendants in relation to the salvage of the *Tubantia*, even though the wreck lay in international waters. *The Tubantia* [1924] P 78, 86. See further *Kennedy & Rose*, 49–63.
342 R Higgins, *Problems and Process: International law and How We Use It* (Clarendon Press 1994) 78.

in the other State, including, for example, State vessels. However, as States became more engaged in commercial activities, the application of this doctrine of absolute immunity was replaced with the concept of a restrictive theory of immunity that distinguished between those acts that a State undertakes in its capacity as sovereign and those of a private nature, such as commercial transactions. The latter is not subject to immunity. So, for example, salvage may be regarded as a commercial act as it is not an act characterised as one that only a State can perform. It is, however, not always clear on what basis a distinction could be made between acts of State and commercial acts by a State, particularly as political ideologies ascribe different functions to the State.[343]

In the UK, the question of sovereign immunity is subject to this international law[344] and the State Immunity Act 1976 as well as by statutes of general application, such as the Crown Proceedings Act 1947.

This principle of sovereign immunity applies to State property or property controlled by the State, and it is therefore pertinent to State's vessels and those under control of the State, such as chartered vessels or those requisitioned during a war.[345] In the case of warships and those of the naval auxiliary, such as State-owned tankers, it is clear that this function is that of a sovereign and thus capable of attracting sovereign immunity.[346] This was reflected in the 1926 Brussels Convention for the Unification of Certain Rules Concerning the Immunity of State-owned Ships. Other international conventions also allow for such immunity, including the London Dumping Convention[347] and the WRC 2007.[348]

This sovereign immunity is also reflected throughout UNCLOS.[349] In Art 95 of UNCLOS, headed "Immunity of Warships on the High Seas" provides that "[w]arships on the high seas have complete immunity from the jurisdiction of any State other than the flag State". This immunity is extended, by Art 96, to vessels that are not warships but that are being used on governmental non-commercial service.[350] Article 32 also provides that "nothing in this Convention affects the immunities of warships and other government ships operated for non-commercial purposes".[351] In practical terms, it means that these vessels cannot,

---

343 J Crawford, "International Law and Foreign Sovereigns: Distinguishing Immune Transactions" (1983) *British YIL* 89. A number of States have adopted legislation which attempts to make the distinction clearer. The US Foreign Sovereign Immunities Act 1976, 26 U.S.C. s 1330, for example, asserts that "under international law, States are not immune from the jurisdiction of foreign courts in so far as their commercial activities are concerned, and their commercial property may be levied upon for the satisfaction of judgements rendered against them in connection with their commercial activities". See also State Immunity Act 1978.

344 See also European Convention on State Immunity 1972 (Cmnd. 5081).

345 *The Schooner Exchange v McFaddon* (1812) 7 Cranch 116. In this case, the plaintiffs claimed ownership of a French naval vessel that entered a US port. The US Supreme Court dismissed the case on the basis of French "State immunity".

346 The *Parlement Belge* (1880), 5 PD 197. See more recently *The ARA Libertad Case (Argentina v Ghana)* [2012] ITLOS Rep 21.

347 LC 1972 Art 10(4).

348 WRC 2007 Art 4(2).

349 UNCLOS Art 32, 95, 96, 236.

350 UNCLOS Art 96, headed "Immunity of Ships Used Only on Governmental Non-commercial Service" states that "ships owned or operated by a State and used only on governmental non-commercial service shall, on the high seas, have complete immunity from the jurisdiction of any State other than the Flag State".

351 See also UNCLOS Art 236, which provides that "[t]he provisions of this Convention regarding the protection and preservation of the marine environment do not apply to any warship, naval auxiliary, other vessels or aircraft owned or operated by a State and used, for the time being, only on government non-commercial service".

for example, be stopped and searched by vessels of another State, nor can the flag State be prosecuted in another State for any of the actions of that vessel that may be contrary to the laws of the prosecuting State.[352] Immunity for warships as property of a State of a "military character or in use or intended for use in the performance of military functions" is also provided for in Art 21(1)(b) of the 2004 UN Convention on Jurisdictional Immunities of States and Their Property; though this convention has yet to come into force. Nevertheless, it illustrates the possible scope of State immunity.

This immunity is extended to the salvage of such vessels.[353] Art 14 of the Salvage Convention 1910[354] simply provided that the Convention "does not apply to ships of war or to Government ships appropriated exclusively to a public service".[355] This means that any salvor that saved a vessel that is subject to sovereign immunity cannot bring a salvage claim before the court of another State. This is also reflected in Art 4 of the Salvage Convention 1989, which provides that

> this Convention shall not apply to warships or other non-commercial vessels owned or operated by a State and entitled, at the time of salvage operations, to sovereign immunity under generally recognized principles of international law unless that State decides otherwise.

Similarly, unless the State consents,

> no provision of this Convention shall be used as a basis for the seizure, arrest or detention by any legal process of, nor for any proceedings in rem against, non-commercial cargoes owned by a State and entitled, at the time of the salvage operations, to sovereign immunity under generally recognized principles of international law.[356]

However, in relation to warships or other non-commercial vessels owned or operated by a State, a State party may elect to 'opt in' and apply the Convention to these vessels.[357] While the Convention imposes a duty on the State to inform the Secretary-General of IMO of this election and the terms and conditions of such application, this is not a precondition for the election to take effect. The UK does not appear to have informed the Secretary-General of such an election.[358] However, the UK does appear to have elected to apply the Convention to its warships and other non-commercial vessels owned or operated by a State in s 230 of the MSA 1995. Section 230(1) provides that the law relating to salvage, whether of life or property applies in relation to salvage services in assisting any "of Her Majesty's ships" in the same manner as if the ship, cargo or equipment belonged to a private person. It appears that the UK is eager to encourage salvors to come to the assistance of Her Majesty's vessels when they are in distress. Equally, where services are rendered by a naval or government vessel, the Crown is entitled to claim salvage in respect of those services to

---

352 In the other maritime zones, a modified immunity exists for these vessels.
353 See *The Prins Frederick* (1820) 2 Dod 451, in which immunity was claimed in the case of the salvage of a Dutch naval vessel.
354 Salvage Convention 1910.
355 A Protocol in 1967 attempted to bring government vessels into the Convention regime, but never came into effect. *Kennedy & Rose*, 489.
356 Salvage Convention 1989 Art 25.
357 Salvage Convention 1989 Art 4(2), which provides that "[w]here a State Party decides to apply the Convention to its warships or other vessels described in paragraph 1, it shall notify the Secretary-General thereof specifying the terms and conditions of such application".
358 IMO *Status of Treaties*.

the same extent as any other salvor, and shall have the same rights and remedies in respect of those services as any other salvor.[359] While UK vessels are therefore subject to a salvage claim, limitations do apply. The MSA 1995 does not allow the Receiver of Wreck to detain or sell such property[360] and salvors of government vessels cannot proceed against the vessel *in rem*, and no salvage lien exists.[361] The Crown is, however, liable *in personam* for the salvage claim.

Whether this application of State immunity to warships and other government owned or controlled non-commercial vessels continues to apply after the vessel has sunk is less clear.[362] A number of commentators have opined that sunken vessels cease to be ships and are therefore no longer under the exclusive jurisdiction of the flag State.[363] If this is the case, then Arts 95 and 96 of UNCLOS will no longer apply, and State-owned wrecks will be subject to the same jurisdictional regime as other wrecks. In part, these arguments appear to rest on the notion that a wreck is no longer capable of navigation and therefore no longer a ship. As to warships, it also rests partly on the definition of a warship set out in Art 29 of UNCLOS, which defines a warship as one which is "under the command of an officer duly commissioned by the government of the State . . . and manned by a crew which is under regular armed forces discipline".[364] Clearly a wreck is not so commanded and manned at the time of being a wreck. The Institute of International Law's preliminary report therefore concluded that "a sunken warship cannot rely on the sovereign immunity enjoyed by warships".[365] However, a wreck may be raised and re-enter service, and a temporary lack of command should not be a basis for a wreck losing the status of being a ship, or more specifically, a warship.[366] Other commentators have therefore concluded that a ship remains a ship once wrecked.[367] The jurisdiction of the flag State thus continues, as does immunity. Indeed, a number of states have assumed this to be the case and expressed this view in strong terms. France, for example declared that:

> In accordance with the 1982 United Nations Convention on the Law of the Sea (among others Arts 32 and 236) and Customary Law, every State craft (eg warship, naval auxiliary and other ship, aircraft or spacecraft owned or operated by a State) enjoys sovereign immunity, regardless

---

359 MSA 1995 s 230(2).

360 Ibid. s 230(1).

361 Crown Proceedings Act 1947 s 29. See also Senior Courts Act 1981 s 24(2)(c).

362 L Caflish, "Submarine Antiquities and the International Law of the Sea" (1982) 13 *Netherlands Lawbook of International Law* 3, 25; *Ronzitti* (2011); *Ronzitti* (2015). See also S Dromgoole, "The Legal Regime of Wrecks of Warships and Other State-Owned Ships in International Law: The 2015 Resolution of the *Institute de droit international*" (2016) 25 *Italian Yearbook of International Law* 181.

363 L Migliorino, "The Recovery of Sunken Warships in International Waters" in B Vukas (ed), *Essays on the New Law of the Sea* (Sveucilisnanaklada Liber, 1985), 251; W Riphagen, "Some Reflections on Functional Sovereignty" (1975) 6 *Netherlands Yearbook of International Law* 121, 128.

364 In full, UNCLOS Art 29 reads, "For the purposes of this Convention, 'warship' means a ship belonging to the armed forces of a State bearing the external marks distinguishing such ships of its nationality, under the command of an officer duly commissioned by the government of the State and whose name appears in the appropriate service list or its equivalent, and manned by a crew which is under regular armed forces discipline".

365 *Ronzitti* (2011), 143.

366 See ibid.; *Ronzitti* (2015), 275 (Lady Fox).

367 A Strati, *The Protection of the Underwater Cultural Heritage: An Emerging Objective of the Contemporary Law of the Sea* (Martinus Nijhoff, 1995) [*Strati*], 220, 235; Dromgoole, *Underwater Cultural Heritage*, 134.

of its location and the period elapsed since it was reduced to wreckage (general principle of non-limitation of rights of States).[368]

So too did Germany:

> Under international law, warships and other ships or aircraft owned or operated by a State and used only on government non-commercial service (State ships and aircraft) continue to enjoy sovereign immunity after sinking, wherever they are located.[369]

Britain is in agreement with these States, declaring:

> Under international law, warships, naval auxiliaries, and other ships or aircraft owned or operated by a State and used only on government non-commercial service (State ships and aircraft) enjoy sovereign immunity. State ships and aircraft continue to enjoy sovereign immunity after sinking, unless they were captured by another State prior to sinking or the flag State has expressly relinquished its rights. The flag State's rights are not lost merely by the passage of time.[370]

The question of State immunity and ownership more commonly arises in cases of wrecks that sank some time ago. Not only does this turn on questions of abandonment but also on whether the wreck was in fact a warship. There could be a number of reasons for this uncertainty. A wreck site may be so old that it predates any conception of 'the State' in international law, and no existing State can claim to be the flag State.[371] It may also be that there is simply no historic evidence available to determine ownership of the vessel or its function.[372] Alternatively, the original flag State may no longer exist as a separate entity, but has been broken up into smaller nation States.[373] While there are legitimate security and national intelligence reasons for granting exclusive flag State jurisdiction in the case of recently sunken State-owned vessels, these considerations do not apply to sunken State-owned vessels lost long ago. However, these vessels often have archaeological or historical importance, or may be considered a maritime war grave, invoking governmental interest that might justify the application of sovereign immunity to clothe the wreck in a protective mantle.

The complexity of this issue, and the current uncertainties were such that that Institute of International Law (*Institute de droit international*)[374] was prompted to consider the international legal regime of warships and other State-owned vessel in 2009.[375] Following a draft report in 2011,[376] a Resolution was adopted at the Tallinn Session in 2015.[377] The

---

368 Federal Register, 69/24.
369 Ibid.
370 Ibid.
371 This would apply in particular to vessel of antiquity, and include such famous sites as the *Uluburun*, *Geledonyia* and *Antikythera* wreck sites.
372 This applies to cases such as privateers, as well as to early vessels, such as those of the Vikings.
373 See *Simon v Taylor* [1975] 2 Lloyd's Rep 338.
374 The Institute of International Law (*Institut de Droit International*) was founded in 1873 at an institution independent of any governmental influence which would be able both to contribute to the development of international law and act so that it might be implemented. See www.idi-iil.org/en/a-propos/.
375 Santiago Session in 2007, 9th Scientific Commission. See *Ronzitti* (2011).
376 *Ronzitti* (2011).
377 Institute of International Law, www.idi-iil.org/app/uploads/2017/06/2015_Tallinn_09_en-1.pdf.

purpose of the Resolution is to promote the progress of international law through clarifying the existing law and opining on what the law ought to be if the existing law is uncertain.[378]

Whether or not a ship continues to be recognises as a ship or not, in the absence of a finding of abandonment, a State-owned ship will remain State property even though it may have lost its status of being a ship.[379] In that case it may still attract immunity under the restrictive theory of immunity if it is owned by the State and used for non-commercial purposes.[380] In the case of modern sunken warships, it may be argued that the continuing activity of the State is the guarding of its security and military intelligence, and thus acts of a State (*acta jure imperii*).[381] Arguably this State function might include older wreck where the wreck still contain munitions, historically sensitive information, or, importantly, be the last resting place of service personnel which would qualify as an ongoing State 'activity' or interest in the wreck. Moreover, the very place of the wreck in the history of the flag State may be sufficient to attract that function. This immunity thus rests both on the function that the wreck continues to fulfil, and on State ownership. And as noted in Chapter 3, a number of States have asserted a continuing ownership of warships and other state-owned ships subject only to an express abandonment of ownership. France declared that "[t]he primacy of the title of ownership is intangible and inalienable"; Germany declared that it "retains ownership of any German State ship or aircraft owned by it or the German Reich at the time of its sinking"; Japan declared that "[a]ccording to international law, sunken State ships, such as warships and ships on government service, regardless of location or of the time elapsed remain the property of the State owning them at the time of their sinking unless it explicitly and formally relinquishes its ownership"; and Russia declared that "all the sunken warships and government aircraft remain the property of their flag State".[382] That has not prevented States from attempting to salvage other State's warships, though the clandestine nature of such salvage operations attests to the view that the sunken warships are subject to sovereign immunity.[383] That said, the Institute of International Law Resolution Art 4 provides that "[s]unken State ships remain the property of the flag State, unless the flag State has clearly stated that it has abandoned the wreck or relinquished or transferred title to it".[384] It further provides that "[w]ithout prejudice to other provisions of this Resolution, sunken State ships are immune from the jurisdiction of any State other than the flag State".

The Institute of International Law's 2015 Resolution also provides that "[c]argo on board sunken State ships is immune from the jurisdiction of any State other than the flag State".[385] Even though the cargo on board might be private property; the cargo and ship are

---

378 See *Ronzitti* (2015).
379 See also Federal Register, 69/24.
380 *Ronzitti* (2015), 275 (Lady Fox).
381 See, for example, the salvage of a Russian submarine by the Glomar Explorer discussed in F Eustis III, "The Glomar Explorer Incident: Implications for the Law of Salvage" (1975) 16 *Virginia Journal of International Law* 177 [*Eustis III*]; A Rubin, "Sunken Soviet Submarines and Central Intelligence: Laws of Property and the Agency" (1975) 69 *American Journal of International Law* [*Rubin*] 855; *Collins*, 433.
382 Federal Register, 69/24.
383 Such as the US salvage of a Soviet submarine *K-129* in 1968 using a deep-sea drill ship—*The Glomar Explorer*—as cover for the salvage operation. See *Eustis III*, 177; *Rubin*, 855; *Collins*, 433.
384 *Ronzitti* (2015), 372.
385 Resolution Art 5; *Ronzitti* (2015), 372.

interlinked and one entity for sovereign immunity purposes. This was certainly the recent view of the US Admiralty Court in *Odyssey Marine Exploration, Inc v Unidentified Shipwrecked Vessel*.[386] In this case, the salvage company Odyssey Marine Explorations sought to arrest the wreck of the *Nuestra Señora de las Mercedes* and have the court find that it was the owner of artefacts recovered from the wreck, including 594,000 coins. The wreck itself lay on the Portuguese continental shelf west of the Straits of Gibraltar at a depth of 1,100 meters but the deposit of one artefact from the wreck invoked the US Admiralty Court's constructive *in rem* jurisdiction. However, the *Nuestra Señora de las Mercedes* was a Spanish Royal Navy frigate and, the court held, entitled to immunity from arrest pursuant to the Foreign States Immunity Act.[387] This immunity extended to cargo carried aboard the *Nuestra Señora de las Mercedes* irrespective of its ownership. The ship and cargo were considered one for the purposes of sovereign immunity, and any attempt to interfere with the cargo would be interference with the wreck itself.[388]

The Institute of International Law concluded that irrespective of whether a sunken ship is still a ship to which sovereign immunity applies, the principle applies to State owned vessels used on non-commercial services.[389] It includes not only warships but State owned vessels that support naval ships, such as tankers. It did not, however, address the many vessels chartered for State purposes, such as naval auxiliary ships, troopships, hospital ships, etc where the State did not own the ship but was privately owned. If immunity is predicated on the function fulfilled, and continues to be fulfilled by the ship, then in principle, there is no reason why these ships should not be subject to immunity.[390] This might particularly be the case where the ship sank with some of its crew, and it is the obligation to those crew that invokes the responsibility and therefore associated immunity of the State.

The UK has evoked sovereign immunity in relation to its sunken warships and other non-commercial vessels owned or operated by a State. Indeed, the apparent limitation of the application of sovereign immunity in the UCH Convention has been explained as one for the reason why the UK has not ratified that Convention. However, since these wrecks are derelict and therefore wreck within the meaning of the MSA 1995, s 230(1) of the MSA 1995 applies. As discussed above, s 230 has the effect of applying salvage law to these wrecks "in the same manner as if the ship, cargo or equipment belonged to a private person", ie sovereign immunity will not apply. It is thus difficult to reconcile the position taken by the UK in relation to sovereign immunity with that set out in MSA 1995 s 230.

The more plausible explanation for this inconsistency is that s 230 was intended to apply to ships in immediate danger and which are likely to still be in command, encouraging salvors to go to their assistance. Even those that might have been abandoned and thus derelict would benefit from this assistance. For those long lost and thus clearly derelict, the only way in which these positions can be reconciled is if the declarations made by the UK

---

[386] 675 F Supp 2d 1126 (MD Fla 2009), *aff'd* 657 F3d 1159 (11th Cir 2011).

[387] Foreign States Immunity Act 28.

[388] See further M Losier, "The Conflict between Sovereign Immunity and the Cargo of Sunken Colonial Vessels" (2017) 32 IJMCL 1; J Huang, "Odyssey's Treasure Ship: Salvor, Owner, and Sovereign Immunity" (2013) 44 ODIL 170; *Scovazzi* 1.

[389] The Institute of International Law report and resolutions addressed only State-owned vessels and not those owned by private individuals but operated by the State for non-commercial purposes. *Ronzitti* (2015), 271.

[390] *Ronzitti* (2011), 144; *Ronzitti* (2015), 308 (Lady Fox).

concerning sovereign immunity of these vessels constitutes notice that prior permission to salvage is required, or rather, constitutes an express and reasonable prohibition. The Salvage Convention 1989 provides for such a prohibition.[391] Since these vessels are not likely to be in danger in the same way that modern vessels might be in danger, such a prohibition can be argued to be reasonable.[392] Indeed, the Ministry of Defence and Department of Culture, Media and Sport's 2014 Guidelines on How Existing Policies and Legislation Apply to Historic Military Wreck Sites declares that "Sovereign Immune vessels cannot have salvage services conferred upon them without the consent of the flag State" and "[i]n no circumstances should artefacts be recovered without the written permission of the MoD".[393]

---

391 Salvage Convention 1989 Art 19.
392 The authors are indebted to Professor Michael V. Williams on this point.
393 *Protection and Management of Historic Military Wrecks outside UK Territorial Waters: Guidance on How Existing Policies and Legislation Apply to Historic Military Wreck Sites* (DMCS and MOD, April 2014), 7 and 4, respectively.

CHAPTER 5

Law of the sea and wreck

5.1 Early law of the sea

The international law of the sea developed over hundreds of years, from ancient Phoenician and Roman rules, through the age of exploration and expanding maritime trade characterised by the rise of the Grotian theory of freedom of the high seas, to its eventual codification in four relatively short international conventions adopted in 1958: the Convention on the Territorial Sea and the Contiguous Zone; the Convention on the Continental Shelf; the Convention on the High Seas; and the Convention on Fishing and Conservation of the Living Resources of the High Seas. At the heart of this law of the sea regime was the balancing of right and duties as between coastal States and flag States. Wrecks were not addressed in these conventions and were left to the private realm of admiralty law for two reasons. First, wrecks seldom posed any threat to a coastal State, and indeed were often more of a bonanza to the local community than the cause of any damage. Secondly, once a ship had sunk, the technology did not exist to access or salvage it, save where it sunk in relatively shallow and accessible waters that was subject to the jurisdiction of the coastal State.

Shortly after the adoption of the 1958 conventions, the impact that increasingly large oil tankers might have on coastal States began to emerge, as did concern with other forms of marine pollution.[1] Up to then ships had posed little pollution risk. While coal-burning iron-hulled steamships might have posed a moderate hazard, it was the use of oil to fuel ships that first raised the risk of pollution. There was thus little in the way of customary international law of the sea that addressed the rising problem, and little then to codify in the 1958 conventions.[2] The Convention on the High Seas did require States to regulate pollution from ships, pipelines and seabed operations,[3] but without any content such that States had a very wide discretion in the actual regulation required.[4] Inevitably, in the decade following the adoption of the 1958 conventions, the issue of pollution from a wreck challenged the law of the sea. So too did the advances in technology that allowed access to the continental shelf and then the deep seabed. While aimed primarily at accessing the natural resources of the seabed, shipwrecks were found and this highlighted the jurisdictional uncertainties as to which State could control those activities.

---

1 For an account of these early incidents, see 1.2 and *De La Rue & Anderson*, 7–10.
2 As such, the law addressing marine pollution is governed almost exclusively by treaty law. E Franckx (ed), *Vessel-Source Pollution and Coastal State Jurisdiction* (Kluwer Law International, 2001) [*Vessel-Source Pollution*] 2.
3 Convention on the High Seas Art 24.
4 A Boyle, "Marine Pollution under the Law of the Sea Convention" (1985) 79 AJIL [*Boyle*], 347.

5.2 Polluting wrecks and intervention beyond the territorial sea

In 1967, when the *Torrey Canyon* hit the Seven Stones Reef, the UK claimed only a 3 nm territorial sea.[5] The *Torrey Canyon* lay beyond that, in what was therefore the high seas. This brought into question the right of a coastal State in international law to intervene when a non-flag ship on the high seas posed a pollution threat to the coastal State. Justifications included invoking the principles of self-defence or self-help,[6] on the grounds that such pollution affected the coastal State or threaten its security.[7] Alternatively, it was also argued that the international community's apparent acceptance of the UK's intervention (including using its military) resulted in the emergence of a new rule of customary international law.[8] While such a right may have existed or come into existence, the *Torrey Canyon* disaster certainly raised issues as to the *extent* of this right and highlighted the need for clarification through treaty-based rules. This led to the adoption of the Intervention Convention in 1969.

5.3 Intervention Convention 1969

The preamble of the Intervention Convention 1969 reflects the concern that this neglected issue be addressed but that the solution adopted not interfere with the newly adopted 1958 conventions more than was necessary. It declared that the States parties were:

> Conscious of the need to protect the interests of their peoples against the grave consequences of a maritime casualty resulting in danger of oil pollution of sea and coastlines, convinced that under these circumstances measures of an exceptional character to protect such interests might be necessary on the high seas and that these measures do not affect the principle of freedom of the high seas.

This required a high threshold for State intervention reflected in the core of the convention in Art 1:

> Parties to the present Convention may take such measures on the high seas as may be necessary to prevent, mitigate or eliminate grave and imminent danger to their coastline or related interests from pollution or threat of pollution of the sea by oil, following upon a maritime casualty or acts related to such a casualty, which may reasonably be expected to result in major harmful consequences.

"Maritime casualty" is defined as "a collision of ships, stranding or other incident of navigation, or other occurrence on board a ship or external to it resulting in material damage or imminent threat of material damage to a ship or cargo".[9] "Ship" is defined as "any sea-going ship of any type whatsoever".[10] A ship involved in a maritime casualty so as to leave it a wreck, is included within this definition.

---

5 See 1.2.1.

6 R M'Gonigle and M Zacher, *Pollution, Politics and International Law: Tankers at Sea* (University of California Press 1979) [*M'Gonigle & Zacher*], 143–149.

7 D Bodansky, "Protecting the Marine Environment from vessel-Source Pollution: UNCLOS III and Beyond" (1991) 18 *Ecology LQ* 719, 737.

8 R Churchill and A Lowe, *The Law of the Sea* (3rd ed, Juris Publishing 1999) [*Churchill & Lowe*], 355. See also LEG 69/10/1, 28 July 1993, 13.

9 Intervention Convention 1969 Art II(1). This definition was copied in WRC 2007 as Art 1(3).

10 Intervention Convention 1969 Art II(2)(a).

The Convention does not specify precisely what measures can be taken by the coastal State, essentially limiting such action only by the principle of proportionality of the response to the hazard[11] and by a requirement to enter into consultation with other States affected by the maritime casualty, particularly with the flag State.[12] While limited in this respect, and in the application of the relatively high threshold that the danger be "grave and imminent" before the coastal State can act, the danger may very well emanate from a wreck as a maritime casualty.[13] The wreck need not be one of a tanker but of any ship, except a warship or other State ship[14] that poses such a risk provided though that the risk arises from oil, which means "crude oil, fuel oil, diesel oil and lubricating oil".[15]

The right of intervention applies to the high seas, which in 1969 began where the territorial sea ended, and since there was no general agreement on the extent of the territorial sea, depended on that claimed by each State.[16] Since the intent was to allow coastal State intervention beyond its capacity to do so in the territorial sea, it continues to apply beyond the now agreed 12 nm territorial sea despite the creation of the exclusive economic zone, extending up to 200 nm from the territorial sea baseline.[17]

The limitation of the Intervention Convention 1969 to threats from oil only was quickly realised and a protocol adopted in 1973 to extend it to "substances other than oil".[18] "Substances other than oil" are those enumerated in the list annexed to the Convention, and includes a wider category of oils, liquefied gases, radioactive substances and other noxious substances. Intervention though may arise when a non-listed substance is the issue, as "other substances which are liable to create hazards to human health, to harm living resources and marine life, to damage amenities or to interfere with other legitimate uses of the sea".[19] In this latter case, the intervening party bears the burden of establishing that the substance in question could reasonably pose a grave and imminent danger analogous to that posed by any of the substances enumerated in the annexed list.[20] The list of substances covered in the annex is amended from time to time by resolutions of the IMO's Marine Environment Protection Committee (MEPC).[21]

Although the Intervention Convention 1969 did provide convention rules for coastal State intervention, it remained unclear as to what customary international law might actually exist. That a right of intervention might have existed prior to the adoption of the Intervention Convention 1969 is implied by the IMO in its introduction to the Convention, where it declares that the Convention "*affirms* the right of a coastal State to take such

---

11 Ibid. Arts I and V.
12 Ibid. Art III(a).
13 See LEG 69/10/1, 28 July 1993, para. 12.
14 Intervention Convention 1969 Art I(2).
15 Ibid. Art II(3)
16 Ibid. Art I. See LEG 86/4/1, 27 March 2003, 2.
17 Both Spain and Portugal exercised this right of intervention within 200 nm in the case of the *Prestige* in 2002. *De La Rue & Anderson*, 901. See 1.2.2.
18 Protocol Relating to Intervention on the High Seas in Cases of Pollution by Substances Other than Oil, 1973.
19 1973 Protocol Art 1(2).
20 Ibid. Art 1(3).
21 IMO's Marine Environment Protection Committee (MEPC) amended the list of substances in 1991 (MEPC.49(31), 1996 (MEPC.72(38), 2002 (MEPC.100(48) and 2007 (MEPC.165(56)).

measures on the high seas as may be necessary to prevent, mitigate or eliminate danger to its coastline or related interests from pollution by oil or the threat thereof, following upon a maritime casualty".[22] Furthermore, the existence of a customary international right of a right of intervention might be presumed, as maritime States would not likely have condoned any change to the jurisdictional competencies of States (as set out in the 1958 Convention on the High Seas) when negotiating the Intervention Convention.[23] That certain intervention powers exist as a matter of customary international law is also assumed in the Salvage Convention.[24] Individual States have also taken the view that such a right exists in customary international law. Australia's instrument of ratification was accompanied by a declaration that "no coastal State would refrain from taking whatever action was necessary to protect areas under its jurisdiction from serious environmental damage and . . . this right of a coastal State to intervene on the high seas to protect areas under its jurisdiction is recognised under customary international law".[25] The Intervention Convention 1969 merely codified what was already an existing customary right of coastal State action and gave that right content.[26]

As at 16 November 2018, 89 States with approximately 75.2% of the gross tonnage of the world's merchant fleet are parties to the convention, while 57 States with approximately 53.84% of the gross tonnage of the world's merchant fleet are parties to the 1973 Protocol. While the convention, and to a lesser extent the 1973 protocol, represents a significant number of maritime States, it does mean that more than 100 States, many of which would be coastal States, are not parties to the convention, and many more to the 1973 Protocol, and are thus reliant on their customary international law right of intervention. The UK was one of 31 States to sign the convention and ratify the convention in 1971, coming into force in 1975 as one of the originating 15 States whose ratification was needed to bring it into force.[27] The UK enacted the Intervention Convention 1969 through the Prevention of Oil Pollution Act 1971, now consolidated in the MSA 1995 s 141. The UK ratified the 1973 Protocol in 1979 with it coming into force in 1983 when the number of ratifications reached the required 15.[28]

---

22 Our emphasis. See www.imo.org/About/Conventions/ListOfConventions/Pages/International-Convention-Relating-to-Intervention-on-the-High-Seas-in-Cases-of-Oil-Pollution-Casualties.aspx.

23 *M'Gonigle & Zacher*, 203.

24 Salvage Convention 1989 Art 9, which declares that "[n]othing in this Convention shall affect the right of the coastal State concerned to take measures in accordance with generally recognized principles of international law to protect its coastline or related interests from pollution or the threat of pollution following upon a maritime casualty or acts relating to such a casualty which may reasonably be expected to result in major harmful consequences, including the right of a coastal State to give directions in relation to salvage operations".

25 *IMO Status of Treaties* (November 2018) 231, www.imo.org/en/About/Conventions/StatusOfConventions/Pages/Default.aspx

26 Alan Khee-Jin Tan, *Vessel-Source Marine Pollution* (CUP, 2006) [*Tan*] 182.

27 *IMO Status of Treaties* (November 2018), 231. With its instrument of ratification, the UK noted that it extended the convention to a number of territories, including Bermuda, Anguilla, British Antarctic Territory, British Virgin Islands, Cayman Islands, Montserrat, Pitcairn, Henderson, Duice and Oeno Islands, St Helena, Ascension and Tristan da Cunha, Turks and Caicos Islands, Falklands Islands and Isle of Man.

28 *IMO Status of Treaties* (November 2018) 232.

5.4 United Nations Convention on the Law of the Sea

5.4.1 Development of UNCLOS

The United Nations Convention of the Law of the Sea (UNCLOS) was adopted in December 1982 by a majority vote.[29] It is often described as the "constitution of the oceans". The form this "constitution" takes was the result of two important negotiating principles. First, it was agreed that provisions would be adopted by consensus rather than by vote and, secondly, that the convention would then be a "package deal",[30] that is, reservations would not be permitted and States would have to accept the convention as one package of provisions, "warts and all".[31] Implicit in the package deal concept was the assumption that the minimum interests of a maximum number of States on substantial issues would be met. This would necessitate trade-offs and reciprocal support between various claims.

At the core of UNCLOS is the delimitation of the oceans into a number of maritime zones within which States have differing rights and duties.[32] It reflects the old conflict between freedom of the seas on the one hand and the assertion of some form of control, jurisdiction or sovereignty over ocean spaces on the other. This is usually reflected in the balancing of the rights of coastal States, which decrease the further a zone is from the coastal State's landmass, and the rights of "maritime" or "shipping" States to access ocean spaces, usually for the purposes of navigation that facilitates international trade. This balancing is particularly relevant when ships become wrecks in the various maritime zones.[33] Within this structure, UNCLOS addresses specific issues such as marine scientific research, the protection and preservation of the marine environment, the development and transfer of marine technology, and—importantly—the mechanism for the settlement of disputes between States.

UNCLOS was not only a codification of the international law of the sea but included elements of progressive development, such as the creation of the EEZ. Those provisions of UNCLOS which are regarded as having been codified will therefore be considered as customary international law, and binding on all States irrespective of whether they have acceded to either the 1958 conventions or UNCLOS.[34] Whether any parallel customary international law has developed in other respects will depend on State practice.

The jurisdictional capacity of coastal States and flag States is thus an important conceptual framework that underpins UNCLOS and impacts on the regulation of wrecks. Indeed, UNCLOS addresses very specifically the rights and duties of coastal States in the various

---

29 One hundred thirty States voted in favour of adoption, 17 States abstained from voting (including the UK, Italy, Soviet Union, the German Democratic Republic and the Federal Republic of Germany) and four States voted against adoption (US, Israel, Turkey and Venezuela). None of the four States that voted against the adoption of the Convention is yet a party.

30 See H Caminos and M Molitor, "Progressive Development of International Law and the Package Deal" (1985) 79 AJIL 871.

31 *Vessel-Source Pollution and Coastal State Jurisdiction*, 11.

32 It is a detailed and complex treaty, comprising 320 articles divided in 17 parts together with nine additional annexes.

33 See 5.4.2.

34 As the 1958 Convention has no provisions regarding the preservation and management of objects of a historic or archaeological nature, Arts 149 and 303 of UNCLOS can safely be regarded as examples of progressive development.

maritime zones that begin from the edge of its landmass. It also addresses the conceptual nature of flag State jurisdiction, but not necessarily its content in any detail. Article 91 provides that ships have the nationality of the State whose flag they are entitled to fly, and that it is for each State to decide for itself the conditions for the grant of its nationality to ships, for the registration of ships, and for the right to fly its flag. This required that there be a genuine link between the State and the ship. However, with the emergence of the use of flags of convenience in modern shipping, State practice is no longer consistent with this requirement and it is largely ignored.[35] Shipowners in many States therefore have significant freedom to choose where to register their ships, and thus which flag (and jurisdiction) they will be subject to.[36]

The duty of the flag State is to exercise jurisdiction and control over the ship and its crew in relation to all administrative, technical and social matters.[37] The application of the flag State's law should address issues such as the seaworthiness of the ship, the training of the crew and the protection of the marine environment. The details of these flag State obligations are not contained in UNCLOS itself but are contained in a number of International Conventions adopted under the auspices of the IMO. These include, for example, the Salvage Convention 1989 and the WRC 2007. For the most part, then, UNCLOS is concerned with the rights of ships to navigate in the various maritime zones rather than the content of the flag State's right with respect to the running of the ship or the continuation of those rights once a ship becomes a wreck. Nevertheless, there is a degree of overlap when the running of the ship impacts on the marine environment, particularly in the form of pollution, and Part XII of UNCLOS addresses this in some detail. Whilst UNCLOS is not immutable, as a constitutional framework its provisions are difficult to change and adapt to changing circumstances.[38] The IMO conventions, on the other hand, are more easily amended, particularly in those cases where the tacit acceptance procedure applies.[39]

5.4.2 Jurisdictional regime

Ships are most often wrecked close to shore. In this often-treacherous meeting of land and sea, two important maritime zones exist: internal waters and the territorial sea. The division between internal waters and the territorial sea is determined by the baselines provided for in UNCLOS. The normal baseline is a line that follows the low-water line along the coast

---

35 On ship registration and flags of convenience, see E Watt, *Ship Registration: Law and Practice* (3rd ed, Informa 2018).

36 Some States do limit the ability of their nationals and corporations to register a ship in any other State. See, for example Australia's Shipping Registration Act 1981 (Cth) s 12(1).

37 UNCLOS Art 94.

38 While UNCLOS has not been amended, two subsequent agreements have, in effect, provided an alternative mechanism to supplement the Convention itself: the 1994 Agreement relating to the Implementation of Part XI of the United Nations Convention on the Law of the Sea of 10 December 1982 and the 1995 The United Nations Agreement for the Implementation of the Provisions of the United Nations Convention on the Law of the Sea of 10 December 1982 relating to the Conservation and Management of Straddling Fish Stocks and Highly Migratory Fish Stocks.

39 IMO Conventions that apply the tacit acceptance procedure include SOLAS (Art VIII(b)), MARPOL (Art 16(2)), STCW (Art XII(1)(a)) and Load Lines (Art VI(2)).

as marked on large-scale charts officially recognised by the coastal State.[40] Where this baseline reaches the mouths of rivers, ports or small bays, straight baselines are used so as to generally follow the direction of the shoreline, crossing these maritime spaces and dividing them into two parts. The waters of the bay, river or port on the landward side of the straight baseline is internal waters, with the waters on the other side being the territorial sea. These straight baselines can also be used where the shoreline is deeply indented or has numerous small islands breaking up the general coastline, such that normal baselines would be difficult to measure.[41] Internal waters may therefore be quite considerable, constituting not only ports, rivers and small bays on the landward side of the straight baseline but also the waters between the land and the island where the island lies so close to shore that straight baselines have been used by the coastal State on the outer edges of the islands. The territorial sea is measured from the baseline such that its outer limit is a line 12 nm from the nearest point of the baseline.[42] It is for each State to determine where exactly its baselines lie, including exactly which point constitutes the low-water line.[43] Each coastal State thus has some discretion as to where its internal waters and territorial sea lie. In which zone a wreck lies will depend on the nature of the coastline and therefore whether a normal baseline or straight baseline has been used, and not necessarily how close the wreck actually lies to the shore.

The coastal State has full sovereignty in internal waters as if those waters were part of the landmass. That sovereignty is extended to the territorial sea but subject to UNCLOS and "other rules of international law".[44] Arguably, the most important limitation to this sovereignty provided for in UNCLOS is the concept of innocent passage of ships through this zone.[45] Although the coastal State has limited jurisdiction with regard to ships that are engaged in innocent passage, if a ship is not engaged in innocent passage or has contravened its obligations of innocent passage, the coastal State has full legislative and enforcement jurisdiction.[46] "Innocent passage" requires that the ship's passage be continuous and expeditious,[47] and that it is "not prejudicial to the peace, good order or security of the coastal State".[48] Any other activity not having a direct bearing on passage is deemed to

---

40 UNCLOS Art 3.
41 Ibid. Arts 9–13.
42 Ibid. Arts 3 and 4.
43 The UNCLOS does not indicate, for example, whether this is the mean low-water line or the lowest astronomical tide.
44 UNCLOS Art 2.
45 Passage means "navigation through the territorial sea for the purposes of traversing the area without entering internal waters, or of proceeding to internal waters, or of making for the high seas from internal waters" and is innocent if it is not prejudicial to the "peace, good order or security" of the coastal State. UNCLOS Art 15(1) and 14(4).
46 UNCLOS Arts 19 (criminal jurisdiction) and 20 (civil jurisdiction). *Strati*, 117. The UNCLOS also created a new maritime zone for archipelagic States such as the Philippines and Indonesia. Where the archipelagic State has islands some distance apart, they are permitted to draw straight baselines around the outer edges of those islands, enclosing the waters of the archipelago into a maritime zone—archipelagic waters—over which it has sovereignty. UNCLOS Arts 47–49.
47 UNCLOS Art 18(2). "However, passage includes stopping and anchoring, but only in so far as the same are incidental to ordinary navigation or are rendered necessary by *force majeure* or distress or for the purpose of rendering assistance to persons, ships or aircraft in danger or distress".
48 Ibid. Art 19(1).

be "prejudicial to the peace, good order or security of the coastal State".[49] A wrecked ship is thus not engaged in innocent passage. It is likely that the great majority of wrecks will be found in the territorial sea, and coastal States, in the exercise of their sovereignty, have significant jurisdiction over these wrecks. This sovereignty is, however subject not only to UNCLOS but also to other applicable rules of international law, and it may be that rights of other States, such as flag States, can be invoked.[50]

While the baseline delimits internal waters from the territorial sea, its function is much greater in that it is the pivotal point from which all the other maritime zones are measured. The contiguous zone is that which falls between 12 and 24 nm from the baseline.[51] Established in the 1958 Convention, and repeated in UNCLOS,[52] the contiguous zone is a buffer zone in which the coastal State may exercise the control necessary to prevent infringements of its customs, fiscal, immigration or sanitary laws within its territory or territorial sea; or punish infringements of the above laws committed in its territory or territorial sea.[53] The contiguous zone allows the coastal State to exercise a punitive function by undertaking activities aimed at ensuring the arrest and punishment of those who have infringed the customs, fiscal, immigration or sanitary laws of the coastal State in the territorial sea. This then applies to outward bound ships, being those that have left the territorial sea having infringed the relevant laws of the coastal State, and are in the contiguous zone when intercepted. The contiguous zone does not specifically give rise to any rights and duties that pertain to that zone in its own right, and requires a link between the activities undertaken in that zone and the territorial sea; and more specifically, the regulations of the coastal State that applies to the territorial sea.

The contiguous zones then is a buffer zone directly linked to the right of the coastal State in the territorial sea. The rights and duties of the coastal State to the resources that lie beyond the territorial sea are not governed by the contiguous zone but by the exclusive economic zone and continental shelf that begin where the territorial sea ends. These zones therefore overlap with the contiguous zone; each zone addresses different activities, and provides the coastal States (and flag States) with a different "package" of rights and duties.[54] A State must specifically claim a contiguous zone to assert the rights provided for in UNCLOS.[55] Wrecks found in the contiguous zone, which may be numerous as the zone can be relatively shallow, are therefore subject to a complex jurisdictional arrangement, discussed further below.[56]

The continental shelf is essentially a continuation of the landmass such that it makes up a relatively shallow zone before dropping off rather steeply as the continental slope, then levelling off as the continental rise and meeting the deep seabed. Because of its relative shallowness, it not only supports economically important seafloor fisheries but also makes

---

49 Ibid. Art 19(2)(l).
50 See 4.7.
51 UNCLOS Art 33.
52 Ibid.
53 The creation of this buffer zone was essentially a compromise between those States that favoured a three-mile territorial sea and those who favoured a more extensive territorial sea. D Rothwell and T Stephens, *The International Law of the Sea* (2nd ed, Hart Publishing 2016) [*Rothwell & Stephens*], 83.
54 *Strati*, 160.
55 *Rothwell & Stephens*, 82.
56 See 5.4.2.

access to its mineral, oil and gas resources relatively easy. When technological advances allowed for the exploitation of these resources, States began to make claims to the continental shelf. In 1945, President Truman proclaimed the US continental shelf, and that regime influenced the subsequent international agreement in the 1958 Convention on the Continental Shelf. This recognises that the coastal State has the sovereign right to explore and exploit the natural resources of the continental shelf.[57] By 1969, the right to claim a continental shelf was recognised as customary international law,[58] and subsequent State practise required that the 1958 Convention be updated when UNCLOS was negotiated.

As an extension of the landmass, the physical continental shelf could differ dramatically, with some States having a prolonged shelf while others had little where the shelf dropped very quickly to meet the deep seabed. The UNCLOS regime therefore provides for both a legal continental shelf and a geographical continental shelf. The legal continental shelf, granted to every State, measures out to 200 m from the territorial sea baseline irrespective of the actual geographical continental shelf.[59] As such, States with a geographical continental shelf of shorter than 200 nm effectively have parts of the physical deep seabed as part of their continental shelf. States do not formally have to claim this continental shelf as it is recognised as existing as a matter of law.[60] States that have a geographical continental shelf of longer than 200 nm may claim that geographical continental shelf out to a maximum of 350 nm.[61] The convention provides a mechanism for determining where the continental shelf ends and States claiming a geographical continental shelf are required to submit their delimitation to an international technical body established by UNCLOS, the Commission on the Limits of the Continental Shelf (CLCS), for verification.[62] This regime is of some significance to the regulation of wreck, exemplified in that applicable to one of the most famous of wrecks, the *RMS Titanic*, which lies on the outer edge of the continental shelf of Canada.[63]

The EEZ was first established in UNCLOS, and provides that the coastal State has "sovereign rights for the purpose of exploring and exploiting, conserving and managing the natural resources, whether living or non-living, of the water superadjacent to the sea-bed and of the sea-bed and subsoil" of this zone.[64] It is thus essentially a fishing zone and applies to the body of water above the seabed, and thus is coextensive with, and sits on top of, the continental shelf. To these rights were added sovereign rights with respect to "other activities for the economic exploitation and exploration of the zone, such as the production of energy from water, currents and winds". These rights are clearly sovereign rights and thus reserved exclusively to the coastal State. In the EEZ, the coastal State is also granted

---

57 1958 Convention Art 2(1); UNCLOS Art 77.

58 *North Sea Continental Shelf Case* [1969] ICJ Rep 3.

59 UNCLOS Art 76(1).

60 *North Sea Continental Shelf Case* [1969] ICJ Rep 3.

61 UNCLOS Art 76(5).

62 UNCLOS Annex II. A number of States have now submitted their continental shelf delimitation claims which have subsequently been adopted, including Russia, Brazil, Australia, Ireland, New Zealand, Norway, France, the UK, Japan, Philippines, Denmark, Norway and South Africa. Commission on the Limits of the Continental Shelf, www.un.org/depts/los/clcs_new/commission_submissions.htm.

63 For a detailed discussion of the position of the *RMS Titanic*, see A Ruffman, I Townsend Gault and D VanderZwaag, "Legal Jurisdiction over the Titanic" (1988) 37 *Lighthouse* 23.

64 UNCLOS Art 56(1).

jurisdiction to regulate certain activities, such as the establishment and use of artificial islands, installations and structures, marine scientific research and the protection and preservation of the marine environment.[65] The latter provision—coastal State jurisdiction with respect to the protection and preservation of the marine environment—is made subject to "the relevant provision of this Convention [UNCLOS]"[66] and to "other rights and duties provided for in this Convention".[67] To the extent that the EEZ is coextensive in parts with the continental shelf, the rights set out in the EEZ regime for the seabed and subsoil are exercised in accordance with the continental shelf regime.[68]

Measuring 200 nm from the territorial sea baseline, the EEZ was quickly taken up by coastal States, and with this rapid State practise is now considered to be customary international law.[69] While coastal States were given explicit rights in this zone, the rights of flag States were also expressly provided for[70] and include many which would be regarded as freedoms of the high seas, such as freedom of navigation and the laying of submarine cables and pipelines. The explicit division of rights between the coastal States and other States[71] and the provision for the resolution of disputes[72] have led to the EEZ being described as *sui generis*. This would mean that a matter not addressed in Part V of UNCLOS, so that rights are not ascribed to either the coastal State or other States, is to be determined between competing States "on the basis of equity and in the light of all the relevant circumstances, taking into account the respective importance of the interests involved to the parties as well as to the international community as a whole".[73] Like the contiguous zone, the EEZ must be specifically claimed by a coastal State.[74] There has been an element of creeping jurisdiction in the rights coastal States assert in the EEZ, particularly in the extensions of maritime security regimes and those applicable to pollution and other environmental threats.[75] This impacts greatly on the regime applicable to wrecks, especially in relation to ships on the surface that require access through the EEZ water column to reach a wreck on the seabed.

---

65 Ibid. Art 56(1)(b)(iii).
66 Ibid. Art 56(1)(b). This refers directly to Part XII. See 5.5.1.
67 UNCLOS Art 56(1)(c).
68 Ibid. Art 56(3).
69 *Delimitation of the Maritime Boundary in the Gulf of Maine (Canada/United States of America)* [1984] ICJ Rep 246; *Continental Shelf (Libyan Arab Jamahiriya/Malta)* [1985] ICJ Rep 13.
70 UNCLOS Art 58.
71 Including landlocked States and geographically disadvantaged States, UNCLOS Arts 69 and 70.
72 UNCLOS Art 59.
73 UNCLOS Art 59 reads in full: "In cases where this Convention does not attribute rights or jurisdiction to the coastal State or to other States within the exclusive economic zone, and a conflict arises between the interests of the coastal State and any other State or States, the conflict should be resolved on the basis of equity and in the light of all the relevant circumstances, taking into account the respective importance of the interests involved to the parties as well as to the international community as a whole".
74 It is unfortunate that the aims of creating the exclusive economic zone do not appear to have been realised. It is estimated that three-quarters of global ocean fisheries "are fished at, or beyond, sustainable levels". Moreover, this exploitation continues to be by distant water fisheries, and many of the developing States that had hoped to benefit economically from the creation of the EEZ have found it difficult to establish their own sustainable fisheries industries and equally difficult to actually regulate their EEZs. *Rothwell & Stephens*, 85.
75 See, for example, Spain, Portugal and France's assertion of the right to inspect and expel single hull tankers travelling through their EEZ, as a response to the concerns that arose following the sinking of the *Prestige* in Spain's EEZ in 2002. See *Rothwell & Stephens*, 99.

The high seas are those waters beyond the jurisdiction of the coastal State, that is beyond a States' territorial sea, contiguous zone, continental shelf or EEZ, depending on what a particular State has claimed. In it, all States can exercise the freedom of the high seas. The 1958 Convention on the High Seas and subsequently UNCLOS set out this codified regime and lists a number of freedoms in the high seas, including freedom of navigation, overflight, laying of submarine cables and pipelines, construction of artificial islands and other installations, fishing, and scientific research, subject to UNCLOS's provision on the exact conduct of these freedoms.[76] Ships navigating in this zone are subject to the exclusive jurisdiction of the State in which it is registered and whose flag it is then entitled to fly.[77] While these provisions set out this flag State jurisdictional exclusivity, UNCLOS very specifically makes the point that this applies to warships and ships used only on governmental non-commercial service, declaring that such ships have "complete immunity from the jurisdiction of any State other than the flag State".[78] Whether this continues to apply to such ships after they have become a wreck is problematic.[79]

Only recently has the deep seabed been accessible, particularly for the exploitation of its natural resources. It was this accessibility, and the anticipated riches of the deep seabed, which necessitated international agreement and set in trail the events that would lead to the adoption of UNCLOS. The final regime, however was unpalatable to some States, particularly the US, and continued to be a source of frustration for wider UNCLOS partition.[80] Nevertheless, the deep seabed regime, referred to in UNCLOS as the Area, is subject to a regime that has the International Seabed Authority (ISA) as an international governing body, regulating access to and utilisation of the deep seabed.[81] This access and utilisation of the deep seabed is subject to the overriding principles of the common heritage of mankind,[82] which includes the peaceful use of the deep seabed, a prohibition on appropriation by States and the sharing of benefits of deep seabed mining resources through the management of the ISA.[83]

The ISA is the organ through which States parties to UNCLOS organise and control[84] "all activities of exploration for, and exploitation of, the resources of the Area".[85] "Resources" applies only to natural resources[86] and not to wrecks, and the ISA has no responsibility for wrecks found on the deep seabed.[87] It does, however, have "incidental powers" which are those that are "implicit" and "necessary for the exercise of those powers and functions

---

76 UNCLOS Art 87. For example, freedom to conduct scientific research is made subject to Parts VI and XIII of UNCLOS.
77 UNCLOS Arts 92 and 94.
78 Ibid. Arts 95 and 96.
79 See 4.7.
80 In part, the 1994 Agreement relating to the Implementation of Part XI of the United Nations Convention on the Law of the Sea of 10 December 1982 was an attempt to address these concerns, though the US is still not a party to the Convention. See *Rothwell & Stephens*, 18.
81 UNCLOS Part XII.
82 UNCLOS Art 136.
83 Ibid. Art 137.
84 Ibid. Art 1(1)(3).
85 Ibid. Art 157(1).
86 Ibid. Art 133(a).
87 See LEG 74/5/2, 5 September 1996, Add 1, 4.

with respect to activities in the Area".[88] Where wrecks will be affected by activities that the ISA controls, it might then have some role to play. Indeed, in the evolving ISA Mining Code, for example, regulation 8 of the Regulations on Prospecting and Exploration for Polymetallic Nodules in the Area requires that a "prospector shall immediately notify the Secretary-General in writing of any finding in the Area of an object of actual or potential archaeological or historical nature and its location".[89] The ISA undertakes then to transmit this information to UNESCO.[90] Less explicitly, the ISA does have a responsibility in managing activities to protect the marine environment,[91] and thus has the ability to control the activities of prospectors and other entities that might disturb a wreck that poses a pollution hazard.

5.5 UNCLOS and wrecks

There is no reference to "wreck" or "shipwreck" in UNCLOS at all.[92] To the extent that wrecks are ships, negotiators clearly regarded the issue as one within the remit of the IMO, and that the jurisdictional regime that was created in UNCLOS would apply to wreck in the same way that it applied to ships generally. That is not to say that wreck was completely ignored, and it did arise in two contexts. First, UNCLOS deals generally with the right of intervention for a coastal State when a ship poses a pollution hazard to the coastal State, and amounts to a reconsideration of the issues addressed in the Intervention Convention 1969 and 1973 Protocol. While not specifically mentioning wrecks, these are implied within the meaning of ship. Secondly, wreck, or at least those with an archaeological or historical nature, was first raised in the context of the rights and duties of States to the resources of the deep seabed. This consideration led to the addition of Art 149 in the deep seabed regime, but also led to a broader consideration of similar objects in the other maritime zones.

Raised in UNCLOS in a general way, it is these two issues—wreck as a marine pollution hazard and wreck as an archaeological and historical resource—that necessitated the more detailed regime now contained in the WRC 2007 and the UNESCO Convention on the Protection of the Underwater Cultural Heritage (UCH 2001). Nevertheless, UNCLOS provides the framework within which these subsequent conventions operate.

5.5.1 Marine pollution

Marine pollution from ships occurs in two ways: from accidents, especially sinking and wrecking; and from operational discharges.[93] The regulatory response is to address ship

---

88 UNCLOS 157(2).
89 See also Regulation 35 which extends this to human remains of an archaeological or historic nature, or objects of a similar nature.
90 Decision of the Council of the International Seabed Authority relating to amendments to the Regulations on Prospecting and Exploration for Polymetallic Nodules in the Area and related matters ISBA/19/C/17. The same provisions can be found in the Regulations on Prospecting and Exploration for Cobalt-rich Ferromanganese Crusts in the Area ISBA/18/A/11, and the Regulations on prospecting and exploration for polymetallic sulphides in the Area. ISBA/16/A/12 Rev.1. These are available at www.isa.org.jm/mining-code/Regulations.
91 UNCLOS Art 145.
92 Nor is their reference to ships that have "sunk" or have "stranded" or are "derelict".
93 *De La Rue & Anderson*, 807.

safety standards[94] in general as well as to adopt measures specifically to prevent and control marine pollution.[95] Ship safety standards ought to minimise the number of accidents that occur and a regulatory regime that controls shipping activities ought to ensure that operational discharges do not occur, and when they do, consequences follow.

Part XII of UNCLOS contains a framework for dealing with these issues of marine pollution.[96] It applies to a range of sources of marine pollution from those arising from air- and land-based sources, mining activities on the deep seabed to those from ships (including wrecks).[97] Article 194(3)(b) addresses the scope of the laws that States might take when adopting measures to "prevent, reduce and control pollution", being "measures for preventing accidents and dealing with emergencies, ensuring the safety of operations at sea, preventing intentional and unintentional discharges, and regulating the design, construction, equipment, operation and manning of vessels".[98] This applies to all the maritime zones unless the content suggests otherwise. As such, the provisions in Part XII apply to wrecks that pose a pollution hazard in all maritime zones. Indeed, the rebalancing of the rights of coastal States and those of flag States with respect to ship-sourced marine pollution set out in Part XII was influenced by the wrecking of the *Amico Cadiz* off France in March 1978[99] and the failure of the pre-existing prescriptive jurisdictional capacity of flag States to protect the interests of coastal States was a dominant theme throughout UNCLOS negotiations.[100]

One of the unique features of UNCLOS was the attempt to control the content and standard of regulations to protect the marine environment from pollution by reference to internationally agreed rules.[101] This reference appears throughout the convention as "generally accepted international rules and standards" or a variation thereof. For example, Art 211(1) provides that

> States shall adopt laws and regulations for the prevention, reduction and control of pollution of the marine environment from vessels flying their flag or of their registry. Such laws and regulations shall at least have the same effect as that of generally accepted international rules and standards established through the competent international organization or general diplomatic conference.

UNCLOS imposes an obligation on flag States to adopt such laws, but does not directly address the content of those laws, merely providing a minimum standard to be determined by reference to another body of law, that being the "generally accepted international rules and standards established through the competent international organization or general

---

94 The most important of which are the SOLAS and STCW conventions.

95 The most important of which are MARPOL; the International Convention on the Control of Harmful Anti-Fouling Systems on Ships; and the International Convention for the Control and Management of Ships' Ballast Water and Sediments.

96 The extent to which the framework provides a broad and effective regime is much debated. See for example, *Vessel-Source Pollution*, 3.

97 See LEG 69/10/1, 28 July 1993, 12 in relation to UNCLOS Art 221.

98 UNCLOS Art 194(3)(b).

99 See 1.2.2(a).

100 *Boyle*, 352; *Churchill & Lowe*, 255.

101 The duty to respect generally accepted standards was first adopted in Art 10 of the 1958 Convention on the High Seas with respect to the rules relating to collisions. On the development of this duty see B Oxman, "The Duty to Respect Generally Accepted International Standards" (1991) 24 *NYU J Int Law and Politics* 109 [*Oxman*], 121–129; See also *Boyle*, 352.

diplomatic conference". Unfortunately, while the general intent is clear, its implementation is not. In particular, what is not clear is what rules are actually being referred to in a given instance throughout the convention and what the effect of the reference actually is. The phrase "generally accepted international rules and standards" must be understood against the background of UNCLOS, which was "an agreement between participants to further disagree, a sort of lowest common denominator acceptable to all the parties involved" and that the provisions themselves may thus be vague and ambiguous".[102] Furthermore, the use of the phrase "generally accepted international rules and standards" in Part XII arose to resolve the contest between full coastal State jurisdiction over ship-sourced marine pollution and exclusive flag State jurisdiction. The premise of the solution that is Part XII is that the international law that governs the marine environment and that governing the regulation of ships, though addressed in different international fora (UNCLOS and IMO) and through different instruments, is nevertheless "one single whole" international system. It was assumed that the technical standards themselves would be addressed in existing, or future, conventions adopted in accordance with the international competency granted to the flag State and administered through the IMO. Moreover and importantly, the intent in UNCLOS was to ensure that the intentional rules and standards predominate over national laws and regulations.[103]

Against this background, Art 211 of UNCLOS addressed the international rules and national legislation to prevent, reduce and control pollution of the marine environment from ships. This article addresses both the prescriptive jurisdiction of flag States and that of coastal States. The phrase "generally accepted international rules and standards" appears in Art 211 three times, and on two of those occasions it is followed by the phrase "established through the competent international organization or general diplomatic conference". It is clear that when reference is made to the "competent international organization", this means the IMO, and at the time of negotiations, it appears that the sort of international rules and regulations that might apply were the 1954 Oil Pollution Convention[104] and MARPOL.[105] That is, the rules envisaged were those that apply directly to the vessel and its management, including navigation.[106]

Article 211(1) begins with an obligation on States to cooperate through the IMO as the competent international organisation, or through diplomatic conferences, to establish such rules and standards.[107] Importantly, Art 211(1) does no more than require States to undertake this through the IMO, and says nothing of the scope of application or jurisdictional competencies of States that might arise from any such agreement. What follows in Art 211(2) though is a clear recognition of flag State prescriptive jurisdiction, the obligation is imposed on flag States to adopt laws and regulations for the prevention, reduction and control of pollution of the marine environment.[108] But those laws and regulations shall at

---

102 *Vessel-Source Pollution*, 11.
103 Ibid., 12.
104 International Convention for the Prevention of Pollution of the Sea by Oil 1954.
105 See *Churchill & Lowe*, 255–256.
106 UNCLOS Art 211(1) address these as well as "routing systems designed to minimise the threat of accidents which might cause pollution of the marine environment".
107 See also UNCLOS Art 235(1).
108 Ibid. Art 211(2).

least have the same effect as that of generally accepted international rules and standards established through the competent international organisation or general diplomatic conference.[109] In this application, the international laws and regulations serve as a minimum standard and "gives content and effectiveness to the State's duty to regulate".[110] It thus anticipates, for example, that MARPOL provisions will apply as a minimum standard— provided of course that it can be said to have reached the level of being "generally accepted international rules and standards".

In practice, States that are not party to those conventions that do regulate ship safety and the prevention, reduction and control of pollution of the marine environment from vessels, such as SOLAS, MARPOL and STCW, nevertheless comply with these standards as a condition of entering foreign ports.[111] As such, reference to these conventions in UNCLOS has not proved particularly problematic when applied to flag States. While the degree of implementation by flag States may differ, this then becomes an issue for port State control scrutiny. When a ship flagged in a non-State party to a relevant convention sinks in another State's jurisdiction, the application of the "generally accepted international rules and standards" may be at issue.[112]

The drafting history of Part XII reflects the increasing recognition that flag State jurisdiction was not sufficient to regulate marine pollution and that coastal States ought to be given greater jurisdiction in this respect. This is provided for in Art 211. Since Art 211 applies in all maritime zones and to all ships irrespective of their destination, the negotiations sought to recognise coastal State jurisdiction but at the same time, to limit this in some way so as not to encroach on the recognised flag State jurisdiction, particularly that set out in Art 211(2). While there is no limit on the coastal State's prescriptive jurisdiction in the territorial sea,[113] Art 211, in conjunction with Art 220, recognises the prescriptive jurisdiction of the coastal State in the exclusive economic zone.[114] But the laws and regulations so promulgated by the coastal State are limited to the extent of "conforming to and giving effect to generally accepted international rules and standards established through the competent international organization or general diplomatic conference".[115] In UNCLOS's rebalancing of rights as between coastal States and flag States, this was seen as a necessary safeguard for flag States in acceding to coastal States' demand for greater prescriptive and enforcement capacity, such that the content of the coastal States' laws would be limited by reference to these internationally agreed rules.[116] Franckx described the notion of

---

109 In contrast, the rules for atmospheric and land based pollution, UNCLOS Arts 207(1) and 212(1), merely provide that States should take into account internationally agreed rules, standards and recommended practices and procedures.

110 *Oxman*, 131; *Boyle*, 353. Reference to international laws and regulations as minimum standards also apply in Art 208(3) in that laws, regulations and measures to prevent, reduce and control pollution from seabed activities must be *"no less effective* than international rules, standards and recommended practices and procedures". See also Art 210(6) with respect to dumping that uses the same phrase.

111 UNCLOS Art 211(3).

112 See full discussion in 7.4.1.

113 UNCLOS Art 211(4).

114 Ibid. Arts 211(5) and 220. See further 7.4.1.

115 UNCLOS Art 211(5). See further *Oxman*, 136.

116 *Churchill & Lowe*, 255. See further *The Bosphorus Queen*, 2018 Lloyd's LR 493, 495, holding that State could not impose more stringent measures than those imposed in international law.

"generally accepted international rules and standards" as "an instrument to refer to these technical rules while at the same time securing the pre-eminence of these international rules and standards over national laws and regulations".[117] The intent was to set some limit on the increased coastal State jurisdiction and that "the common ground for these references was the attempt to harmonise national laws and regulations with generally accepted international rules".[118] This reference then serves a limiting function in that it refers to a maximum standard of regulation that "seeks to prevent abuse and the imposition of excessively onerous burdens on foreign ships".[119] This limiting function then is important to coastal States who wish to deal with a wreck in its EEZ that poses a pollution threat.[120] This is particularly so with respect to the scope of the rules that might fall within this maximum standard. What is apparent though, is that Art 211(5) does not purport to give coastal States' wide prescriptive powers and limits these to those required for the purposes of enforcement as provided for in section 6.

It appears then that the rules and standards referred to, whether as a minimum standard when applied to flag States or maximum standard when applied to coastal States, are generally the international "regulations and rules applicable to navigation, the preservation, reduction and control of marine pollution from ships or by dumping".[121] But exactly what rules and standards apply is far from clear. Indeed, while "generally accepted rules and standards" is the phrase used in Art 211, other articles use different phrases, such as "internationally agreed rules",[122] "global rules",[123] "generally accepted international regulations",[124] "generally accepted international regulations, procedures and practices",[125] "generally accepted guidelines, criteria and standards"[126] or "generally accepted international standards".[127] While some writers have limited this to the IMO conventions and their annexes, others have argued that it refers to a wider body of both mandatory and non-mandatory instruments.[128] These might include resolutions, codes, recommended practices and guidelines.[129] Oxman further suggests that it might include the practice of individuals and companies directly involved in the regulated activity.[130] Furthermore, it is not clear what "generally accepted" actually means, or when used in the enforcement provisions, which

---

117 *Vessel-Source Pollution*, 12.
118 Ibid., 19. The semantic differences in the wording of the phrases in different articles were not intentional, and it is generally agreed that these small semantic differences are inconsequential. For example, Art 211(5) refers to generally accepted international rules *and* standards, while Art 21(2) refers to generally accepted international rules *or* standards.
119 See Opinion of Advocate General Kokott in *INTERTANKO and Others v Department of Transport* ECJ C-308/06, 20 November, at paras 67–70. See also *Boyle*, 352.
120 The only exceptions to this general principles are those set out in UNCLOS Art 211(6), allowing for more stringent laws and regulations for areas of particular sensitivity, and in UNCLOS Art 234 in relation to ice-covered areas. See further 5.6.2 and 7.4.1.
121 *Vessel-Source Pollution*, citing Study of the Secretariat, LEG/MISC/1, 10 February 1986.
122 UNCLOS Arts 207(1), 212(1).
123 Ibid. Art 210(6).
124 Ibid. Arts 21(4), 41(3), 53(8), 94(2)(a).
125 Ibid. Art 39(2)(a), 94(5).
126 Ibid. Art 271.
127 Ibid. Art 60(3), 60(6).
128 *Vessel-Source Pollution*, 21, 23–24.
129 Ibid. See also *De La Rue & Anderson*, 813.
130 *Oxman*, 141, 153–155.

are "applicable".¹³¹ A narrow interpretation would limit this to that which has achieved a status of customary international law, while a broader interpretation would require widespread ratification of a particular convention or widespread incorporation of a convention's provisions in national law.¹³² Boyle has argued that it should refer to those conventions that "represent the international community's most recent formulations of relevant rules and standards, provided only that they have been ratified by enough States to enter into force".¹³³ This would place on States parties to UNCLOS a duty to adopt rules and standards contained in other conventions to which they "might not and need not be party" to.¹³⁴ Indeed, States have agreed in UNCLOS to accept, by reference, those international standards.¹³⁵ Nevertheless, given the extent to which States jealously guard their sovereignty, it is not likely that States will readily feel bound by UNCLOS to give effect to IMO conventions to which they are not party. Perhaps more importantly, UNCLOS does not make States bound to the IMO Conventions themselves. At best, their national legislation is required to conform to the same standards the State would have to conform to if they were bound by the relevant IMO Convention. Moreover, it is the generally accepted rule or standard contained in the Convention, and not the acceptance of the Convention itself, which is relevant.¹³⁶

The difficulty remains just which rules, whether reflected in IMO Conventions, other instruments or merely by the shipping industry itself,¹³⁷ might be applicable. As Boyle notes:

> To say that States have a duty to regulate pollution is to beg the question what regulations they must adopt, a question the Convention does not satisfactorily answer. Its use of rules of reference is sensible in principle but flawed in practice by the failure to specify with clarity when existing or future rules and standards become applicable.

That said, the issue is minimised by the extent to which flag States do, for the practical reasons discussed above, adhere to most of the applicable international conventions. Where the issue might arise, arguably it will require consideration of the particular rule in question and the degree to which that rule might be said to have reached the threshold of being "generally accepted".¹³⁸ Its application to wrecks takes on a more pronounced importance in respect to the WRC 2007 and is considered in detail below.¹³⁹

5.5.2 Obligations to report and inform

In rethinking the balance of rights between coastal States and flag States, the extent of coastal State jurisdiction over ships beyond the territorial sea, and particularly those that

---

131 See UNCLOS Arts 217(1), 218(1), 219, 220(1)–(3) and 222. *Vessel-Source Pollution*, 12.
132 *Churchill & Lowe*, 256; *Boyle*, 355.
133 *Boyle*, 356.
134 Ibid.; *Oxman*, 144. See also E Franckx, "Coastal State Jurisdiction with Respect to Marine Pollution—Some Recent Developments and Future Challenges" (1995) 10 IJMCL 253, 254 fn 8.
135 *Vessel-Source Pollution*, 30.
136 *Oxman*, 110, 124; *Vessel-Source Pollution*, 30.
137 *Oxman*, 109.
138 See B Marten, "The enforcement of shipping standards under UNCLOS" (2011) 10 *WMU J Maritime Affairs*, 45.
139 See 7.4.

posed a pollution hazard, was limited. Nevertheless, coastal States were anxious to ensure that at the very least they were informed of any incident that would pose a threat to their coastlines or related interests. UNCLOS therefore imposes on flag States a reporting requirement.[140] Article 198 provides that "[w]hen a State becomes aware of cases in which the marine environment is in imminent danger of being damaged or has been damaged by pollution, it shall immediately notify other States it deems likely to be affected by such damage, as well as the competent international organizations". More specifically, when dealing with marine pollution from ships, Art 211(7) requires that the "international rules and standards" to be adopted by the competent international organisation (IMO) to prevent, reduce and control pollution of the marine environment from vessels "should include inter alia those relating to prompt notification to coastal States, whose coastline or related interests may be affected by incidents, including maritime casualties, which involve discharges or probability of discharges".

A number of IMO conventions do require notification to coastal States of such incidents. SOLAS for example, requires the master of a ship that meets any "dangerous derelict", which may be an abandoned ship or indeed, a wreck, to report its existence by all available means to ships in the vicinity and to competent authorities.[141] The master also has to report the loss or likely loss overboard of any dangerous goods in packaged or solid form to the nearest coastal State.[142] MARPOL also requires masters to report incidents involving harmful substances to the nearest coastal State. Such incidents include not only the discharge or probable discharge of harmful substances, such as oil, but also any damage, failure or breakdown of a ship of 15 meters and above that affects the safety of the ship or of navigation.[143] This then includes incidents where a ship is being or about to be wrecked or sunk. Where the ship is abandoned such that the master cannot make the report, the report must then come from the ship's owner, charterer, manager or operator.[144] Similarly, the OPRC 1990 requires the masters to report any event on their ship involving a discharge or probable discharge of oil to the nearest coastal State.[145] These reporting requirements have been consolidated in the IMO's General Principles for Ship Reporting.[146]

5.5.3 Archaeologically and historically important wrecks

The question of jurisdiction over archaeologically and historically important wrecks arose relatively early in UNCLOS negotiations. In 1970, the Secretary-General submitted a report to the Seabed committee, in which it was suggested that although "wrecks, relics and lost objects lying on the seabed are not resources or at least not natural resources, . . . they

---

140 On mandatory ship reporting systems, see *Vessel-Source Pollution*, 5–11.
141 SOLAS Ch V/31.
142 Ibid. Ch VII/6, VII/7–4.
143 MARPOL Art 8 and Protocol I.
144 MARPOL Protocol I Art I(2).
145 OPRC 1990 Art 4. This was used as a basis for drafting WRC 2007 5(1). See 9.1.3.
146 General Principles for Ship Reporting Systems and Ship Reporting Requirements, Including Guidelines for Reporting Incidents Involving Dangerous Goods, Harmful Substances and/or Marine Pollutants, IMO Resolution A.851(2), 27 November 1997.

may fall under the jurisdiction of the machinery if the recovery of lost objects is regarded as another use of the seabed".[147] From this initiative evolved Art 149, which reads:

> All objects of an archaeological and historical nature found in the Area shall be preserved or disposed of for the benefit of mankind as a whole, particular regard being paid to the preferential rights of the State or country of origin, or the State of cultural origin, or the State of historical and archaeological origin.[148]

This article introduces two key notions concerning the protection of wrecks in international waters. Firstly, that the protection of these archaeologically and historically important wrecks, in its broadest sense, is to be undertaken for the benefit of humankind. Secondly, the notion of preferential rights is introduced. The primary concern here was with the archaeological and historical importance of these wrecks. Unfortunately, the vagueness and ambiguity of Art 149 leaves it with little judicial content.

The UNCLOS negotiation process had different committees considering different maritime zones. The issue of objects of an archaeological and historical nature was raised in the First Committee dealing with the Area and Art 149 drafted for that maritime zone only. The question of jurisdiction over archaeological and historical wrecks was not raised simultaneously in the other committees dealing with the other maritime zones, and only raised in 1979 in the Second Committee tasked with the continental shelf and exclusive economic zone regimes. Agreement could not be reached between those States that wanted to extent coastal State jurisdiction in respect of objects of an archaeological and historical nature protected out as far as possible (particularly some Mediterranean States such as Greece) and those States that wanted to limit coastal State jurisdiction to a general duty which would not extend beyond the territorial sea (particularly the US, the UK and the Netherlands).[149] A compromise was finally agreed to limit coastal State jurisdiction to the contiguous zone, but by that time negotiations on the contiguous zone had been concluded and States were reluctant to reopen the debate on the contiguous zone. The compromise article, Art 303, negotiated late in some haste, was therefore included in Part XVI (General Provisions) of UNCLOS with the jurisdictional extent of the coastal State referred to merely in terms of the jurisdictional capacity given to States in the contiguous zone in Art 33. Article 303 reads:

1. States have the duty to protect objects of an archaeological and historical nature found at sea and shall co-operate for this purpose.
2. In order to control traffic in such objects, the coastal State may, in applying article 33, presume that their removal from the sea-bed in the zone referred to in that article without its approval would result in an infringement within its territory or territorial sea of the laws and regulations referred to in that article.
3. Nothing in this article affects the rights of identifiable owners, the law of salvage or other rules of admiralty, or laws and practices with respect to cultural exchanges.
4. This article is without prejudice to other international agreements and rules of international law regarding the protection of objects of an archaeological and historical nature.

---

147 Doc.A/AC.183/23, 25 UN GAOR Supp. No. 21 (A/8021).

148 UNCLOS Art 1(1)(1) defines the Area as the seabed and ocean floor and subsoil thereof, beyond the limits of national jurisdiction (ie beyond the continental shelf).

149 U.N Doc A/CONF.62/GP/4; U.N. Doc No. A/CONF.62/GP/10. GP/10, 18 August 1980; GP/11, 19 August 1980 and C.2/Informal Meeting/43, 16 August 1979. See further *Dromgoole, Underwater Cultural Heritage*, 32–34; L Caflish, "Submarine Antiquities and the International Law of the Sea" (1982) 13 *Netherlands Yearbook of International Law* [*Caflish*], 3, 16–19.

It imposes a general duty to protect objects of an archaeological and historical nature but with a more specific protective mechanism that would, through a legal fiction, apply only in the contiguous zone. This leaves Art 303 as a whole both complex and ambiguous and the subject of much academic debate. From this significant body of academic literature, the most compelling position is that Art 303 applies to all the maritime zones[150] so that it establishes a general duty to protect objects of an archaeological and historical nature found at sea, requires States to cooperate for this purpose, but which does not affect the rights of identifiable owners, the law of salvage or other rules of admiralty, or laws and practices with respect to cultural exchanges.[151] Article 303(2), however, applies only to the contiguous zone.

To have simply presumed that the recovery of objects of an archaeological and historical nature found in the contiguous zone is tantamount to recovery in the territorial sea would have allowed the coastal State to treat the objects of an archaeological and historical nature in exactly the same manner as it does those objects actually found in the territorial sea. However, this would have resulted in an expanded set of coastal State laws applying to activities in the contiguous zone. In order to ensure that this was not the case, the coastal State laws applicable were restricted to those already recognised in Art 33, namely the coastal State's customs, immigration, fiscal and sanitary laws. Art 303(2) amounts to a rule of law—a true legal fiction rather than a rule of evidence.[152] Any objects of an archaeological and historical nature recovered in the contiguous zone will be presumed to result in an infringement of the customs, fiscal and sanitary laws in the coastal State's territory or territorial sea. This would mean that the recovery itself must be presumed to have occurred in the territory or territorial sea.[153]

Disagreement also exists as to the extent to the coastal State's jurisdiction in the contiguous zone. It has been argued that a literal interpretation of Art 303(2) limits coastal State control to the recovery of objects of an archaeological and historical nature.[154] As such, the coastal State's entire body of cultural heritage law would not apply, only that pertinent to "removal from the seabed" of objects of an archaeological and historical nature. Activities such as diving on a wreck, filming a wreck, or in some way damaging a wreck might not then be subject to coastal State jurisdiction.[155] This has not, however, been supported by subsequent State practice, with a number of States interpreting its powers in the contiguous

---

150 For a summary of this debate see *Dromgoole, Underwater Cultural Heritage*, 34. See also *Strati*, 169; C Newton, "Finders Keepers? The *Titanic* and the 1982 Law of the Sea Convention" (1986) 10 *Hastings International and Comparative LR* 159 [*Newton*]; L Migliorino, "In Situ Protection of the Underwater Cultural Heritage Under International Treaties and National Legislation" (1995) 19(4) IJMCL 483; D Watters, "The Law of the Sea and Underwater Cultural Resources" (1983) 48 *American Antiquity* 813.

151 *Strati*, 169: *Caflish*, 25; B Oxman, "Marine Archaeology and the International Law of the Sea" (1988) 12(3) *Columbia VLA J Law and the Arts* 353 [Oxman, "Marine Archaeology"], 362.

152 *Strati*, 166; *Caflish*, 20; Oxman, "Marine Archaeology", 372. M Nordquist, *United Nations Convention on the Law of the Sea 1982: A Commentary* Vol. 5 (Martinus Nijhoff Publishers, 1989) 161.

153 See *Strati*, 194 fn 47.

154 L Migliorino, "Submarine Antiquities and the Law of the Sea" (1982) 4(4) *Marine Policy Reports* 4. *Strati*, 210. A Arend, "Archaeological and Historical Objects: Implications of UNCLOS III" (1982) 22 *Virginia Journal of International Law* 777 [*Arend*], 799; *Caflish*, 20; B Alexander, "Treasure Salvage Beyond the Territorial Sea: An Assessment and Recommendations" (1989) 20(1) *Journal of Maritime Law and Commerce* 1, 7–8.

155 *Newton*, 187.

zone so broadly that an archaeological maritime zone out to 24 nm is effectively created.[156] In particular, Australia, Brazil, Canada, China, Denmark, Greece, Ireland, the Netherlands and the US extend their domestic protective legislation or domestic licensing and authorisation laws to underwater cultural heritage in the contiguous zone.[157]

Finally, the application of Art 303 to all maritime zones creates an overlap with the provisions of Art 149 with regard the "Area". A potential conflict could arise if both Art 149 and 303 apply in the "Area" as Art 303 specifically retains the law of salvage, so that objects of an archaeological and historical nature may have to be disposed of in order to pay the salvage award. However, Art 149 specifies that the disposal shall be for the benefit of mankind as a whole, which may not be achieved if the articles are disposed of for the salvage award. Since Art 303 falls within the general provisions of UNCLOS and applies to all the maritime zones, whereas Art 149 applies specifically to the Area, then as regards the preservation of objects of an archaeological and historical nature found on the seabed, Art 149 will have preference under the principle *lex specialis derogat legi generali*.[158]

Article 303(4) has been described as Art 303's saving grace, as it "leaves the way open for specific agreement on the underwater cultural heritage".[159] It was intended that Art 303(4) would harmonise the rules of the law of the sea with regard to objects of an archaeological and historical nature with the content of the emerging law of archaeology and cultural heritage.[160] It is in terms of this provision, that a more comprehensive convention to preserve objects of an archaeological and historical nature was concluded: the UCH 2001 Convention.

It is evident that in an attempt to reach consensus and produce a convention, the substantive provisions of Arts 149 and 303 were left vague and ambiguous, which is really not surprising as their drafting was inconsequential compared to the major issues of the negotiating Conference. Yet these articles do represent the only substantive international law applicable to objects of an archaeological and historical nature, and contain general applicable principles.[161] First, while vague and ambiguous, it is evident that States do have a duty to protect or preserve objects of an archaeological and historical nature in various maritime zones beyond coastal State jurisdiction. Secondly, this duty is undertaken for the benefit of humankind.[162] Thirdly, in fulfilling these duties, States are duty bound to cooperate.[163] While the UCH 2001 builds on this existing legal regime, for States not party to the UCH 2001, it is effectively the only international regime that addresses such wrecks. This does lead to some significant problems when a wreck of a non-State party to the UCH

---

156 M Aznar, "The Contiguous Zone as an Archaeological Maritime Zone" (2014) 29 IJMCL [*Aznar, "Contiguous Zone"*], 1, 3.

157 Ibid., 27–28.

158 *Strati*, 312, 324 fn 59.

159 L Prott and P O'Keefe, *Law and the Cultural Heritage: Volume 1, Discovery and Excavation* (Professional Book, 1984) 105.

160 *Oxman, "Marine Archaeology"*, 353, 364.

161 *Strati*, 330–334 includes a summary of the positive and negative factors of the inclusion of Arts 149 and 303 in UNCLOS.

162 *Arend*, 777, 800. Cf *Caflish*, 3, 31.

163 B Oxman, "The Third United Nations Conference on the Law of the Sea: The Ninth Session" (1981) 75 AJIL 211, 240; *Dromgoole, Underwater Cultural Heritage*, 33.

2001 lies within a maritime zone of a State party or vice versa, and is addressed in detail below.[164]

5.6 UNCLOS and jurisdiction with respect to wrecks that pose a pollution hazard

5.6.1 Polluting wrecks in internal waters and territorial sea

The sovereignty of the coastal State extends to the territorial sea up to 12 nm from the baseline, and includes the seabed and subsoil.[165] Ships that become wreck in the territorial sea, by definition, cannot be engaged in innocent passage and are thus subject to the full jurisdictional capacity of the coastal State.[166] This includes the adoption of laws and regulations for the prevention, reduction and control of marine pollution from foreign ships and, it is submitted, the wreck of these ships.[167] This sovereignty is, however subject not only to UNCLOS but also to other applicable rules of international law, such as the UCH 2001 and WRC 2007 for States parties. Moreover, international principles relating to sovereign immunity might also apply in relation to naval ships and other State ships within a foreign territorial sea or inland water. Nevertheless, the jurisdictional capacity of the coastal State in relation to wrecks that pose a hazard are considerable.

5.6.2 Polluting wrecks in EEZ and continental shelf

While wreck in the EEZ and on the continental shelf was not specifically addressed in UNCLOS, the provisions of Part XII will apply to those wrecks that are a source of marine pollution. To the extent that the EEZ is coextensive with the continental shelf (at least up to 200 nm), the rights set out in the EEZ regime for the seabed and subsoil are exercised in accordance with the continental shelf regime. Given that any wreck lying on the seabed may pollute the EEZ, ultimately it is the EEZ regime that is the essential zone for the clarification of rights and duties with respect to polluting wrecks, though the majority of the rights and duties provided for in Part XII apply to both zones.[168]

The creation of the EEZ[169] in UNCLOS required a delicate balancing of coastal State rights with flag State rights. While granting coastal States the exclusive rights to explore, exploit and conserve the natural resources of the EEZ,[170] UNCLOS retained many flag States' high seas rights and freedoms, such as freedom of navigation, overflight and the laying of submarine cables and pipelines.[171] While coastal States were given considerable

---

164 See 6.9.
165 UNCLOS Art 2(1).
166 Ibid. Arts 17–19.
167 Ibid. Art 2011(4).
168 See, however, Art 211(5) and 6(2) that apply specifically to the EEZ.
169 UNCLOS Art 55 sets out the EEZ regime in relation to the coastal State. It provides that "the EEZ is an area beyond and adjacent to the territorial sea, subject to the specific legal regime established in this Part, under which the rights and jurisdiction of the coastal State and the rights and freedoms of other States are governed by the relevant provisions of this Convention". To the extent that the EEZ is coextensive in parts with the continental shelf, the rights set out in the EEZ regime for the seabed and subsoil are exercised in accordance with the continental shelf regime. UNCLOS Art 56(3).
170 UNCLOS Art 56.
171 Ibid. Art 58.

prescriptive jurisdiction with respect to marine pollution caused by a range of sources,[172] this is less so for that emanating from ships. The prevailing view during negotiations was that while marine pollution may have a detrimental effect on the natural resources of the EEZ, pollution measures were more closely aligned to shipping regulation and more a matter for the flag State than the coastal State.

As a starting point, Art 211(1) requires flag States to adopt laws and regulations for the prevention, reduction and control of pollution of the marine environment from ships flying their flag or of their registry. Flag States are obliged to enforce their laws irrespective of where a violation occurs.[173] A flag State may not be aware of a violation when it occurs in another State's water or in the high sea, and any other State may request the flag State investigate any violation alleged to have been committed by a ship flying the latter's flag. If satisfied that sufficient evidence is available to enable proceedings to be brought in respect of the alleged violation, flag States shall without delay institute such proceedings in accordance with their laws.[174] As a ship that becomes a wreck continues to be subject to flag State jurisdiction, implementing laws in relation to marine pollution emanating from the wreck continues to be a matter for the flag State.

Where the flag States then continues to have primacy in addressing marine pollution, coastal States have a much prescribed jurisdictional capacity in these zones. The coastal State's powers to address shipping, including wreck and marine pollution, are limited both in the content of the rules and regulations which can be applied, and in the coastal State's ability to actually enforce these regulations. Art 220 places considerable burdens and limitations on coastal State enforcement of its laws that address marine pollution.[175] Where, for example, "there are clear grounds for believing that a ship navigating in the EEZ . . . has committed a violation of applicable international rules and standards for the prevention, reduction and control of pollution from vessels", the coastal State is restricted to requiring the ship to give certain information so as to establish whether a violation has occurred.[176] Moreover, the coastal State may only take action to inspect such a ship if there has been a substantial discharge causing or threatening significant pollution of the marine environment and "the vessel has refused to give information or if the information supplied by the vessel is manifestly at variance with the evident factual situation and if the circumstances of the case justify such inspection".[177] This inspection power is limited as it is unlikely that a coastal State can detect a discharge and still be able to board the vessel while it is still in

---

172 UNCLOS Art 56 provides that "in the exclusive economic zone, the coastal State has . . . (b) jurisdiction as provided for in the relevant provisions of this Convention with regard to: . . . the protection and preservation of the marine environment".

173 UNCLOS Art 217(1), (4).

174 Ibid. Art 217(6).

175 UNCLOS Art 211(5) provides that "Coastal States, for the purpose of enforcement as provided for in section 6 [including Arts 217–222], may in respect of their exclusive economic zones adopt laws and regulations for the prevention, reduction and control of pollution from vessels conforming to and giving effect to generally accepted international rules and standards established through the competent international organization or general diplomatic conference".

176 UNCLOS Art 220(3). Art 220(4) makes it clear that it is the flag State that has the primary responsibility to enforce this duty to give information.

177 UNCLOS Art 220(5).

the EEZ,[178] and even more so when the ship is a wreck. It is clear that these provisions were drafted with navigating ships in mind, even those in some difficulty and such enforcement measures cannot practically be applied to wrecks.

Coastal States are also limited in their ability to prosecute such violations. The coastal State may only institute proceedings, including detaining a ship, when the incident in the EEZ was a violation resulting in a discharge causing major damage or threat of major damage to the coastline or related interests of the coastal State.[179] While instituting proceedings does not necessarily require that the ship itself be detained, the power is largely based on this detention and following that the power to obtain a bond or other financial security for the ship's release from detention.[180] Clearly, this has little effect when the ship is a wreck. Moreover, Art 228 subjects the coastal State proceedings to flag State pre-emption in enforcement. The coastal State's right to address pollution or threats of pollution emanating from the EEZ was therefore restricted and, for the most part, flag States continued to regulate these matters—a result which shipping interests sought to achieve in limiting, as far as possible, increased coastal State jurisdiction over shipping matters.[181] Not surprisingly, coastal States then have felt that their ability to address wreck that pose a pollution hazard has required further consideration, leading to the adoption of the WRC 2007.

This regime in the EEZ was constructed on the basis that the ship that has caused a pollution incident is "navigating" in the EEZ. This poses some difficulty with respect to wreck, where the ship may, prior to sinking, have committed a pollution offence and thus be subject to some of these provisions; whereas it is more difficult to allege that a ship that has sunk without a pollution incident, but which will pose one in the future, is necessarily caught within these provisions. Moreover, many of these powers are of little use to the coastal State once the ship has become a wreck and pose a pollution hazard. While wreck then was not in direct contemplation in the drafting of these provisions, it was indirectly so when considering the powers of intervention addressed in Art 221.

Furthermore, some debate exists as to whether UNCLOS Art 221 can be invoked to allow wreck removal of foreign ships in the EEZ when the wreck poses only a navigational hazard (and is not a pollution risk itself).[182] It is arguable that any ship posing a navigational hazard invariably also poses a pollution hazard. This debate may extend even further to hazards in the EEZ that are not navigational or polluting, such as a threat to the related interests of a State such as tourism, fishing and cultural rights.[183]

5.6.3 Intervention beyond territorial sea

The adoption of UNCLOS unfortunately did little to clarify the intervention powers of a coastal State. Article 221 of UNCLOS reflects the possibility that customary international law allows a coastal State to take action to protect its interests from hazards in and beyond

---

178 *Tan*, 213.
179 UNCLOS Art 220(6). See further *The Bosphorus Queen*, 2018 Lloyd's LR 493 (also giving effect to EU Directive 2005/35/EC.
180 UNCLOS Art 220(6), (7).
181 *Tan*, 212.
182 See eg LEG 86/4/1, 27 March 2003, para 14.
183 See 1.2.4 regarding the *Rena*.

its territorial sea, and recognises the convention rights conferred in the Intervention Convention.[184] Article 221 provides that nothing in UNCLOS

> shall prejudice the right of States . . . to take and enforce measures beyond the territorial sea proportionate to the actual or threatened damage to protect their coastline or related interest, including fishing, from pollution or threat of pollution following upon a maritime causality or acts relating to such a casualty, which may reasonably be expected to result in major harmful consequences.[185]

"Maritime casualty" is defined in a substantially similar way to that in the 1969 convention, being "a collision of vessels, stranding or other incident of navigation, or other occurrence on board a vessel or external to it resulting in material damage or imminent threat of material damage to a vessel or cargo".[186] While the term "maritime casualty" does not refer specifically to wreck, it is so broadly defined as to include wreck.[187] Art 221 does, however, suffer from some important interpretational problems. It is drafted in such a way that it does not purport to introduce any new rights, but ensures that the rights pursuant to customary and treaty-based international law are maintained. It does, though, give these rights some content and appears to provide a lower threshold for coastal State intervention than that required by the Intervention Convention 1969 by not requiring that there be "a grave and imminent danger" of pollution before a coastal State can intervene.[188] Some support for this view is revealed by the negotiating history of Art 221. A draft version had included the threshold phrase "a grave and imminent danger" but had been omitted after objections from a number of States, particularly France following its experience with the *Amoco Cadiz* in 1978. The French view was that it may be too late to prevent or minimise pollution damage if the coastal State had to wait for this threshold to be reached before acting.[189] This suggests that Art 221 indeed provides a substantive right of intervention different to that provided for in the Intervention Convention, and reflects the development of environmental law since 1969. An alternative interpretation[190] is that the threshold contained in the Intervention Convention 1969 may well apply notwithstanding the omission of the phrase "a grave and imminent danger", if emphasis is placed on the fact that Art 221 specifically sets out to maintain rights "pursuant to international law, both customary and conventional". It is submitted that the better view is the former.

Article 221 applies the power of intervention to wrecks that pollute or threaten to pollute the coastline or related interest of the coastal State. Two important thresholds apply to the threat of pollution. It must be a threat that may *reasonably* be expected to result in *major* harmful consequences. On the facts of any particular case there may well be significant latitude in the application of these thresholds. As long as a wreck contains some pollutants when sunk that may escape at some time in the future, there is a reasonable expectation of

---

184 LEG 69/10/1, 28 July 1993, para. 11.
185 A similar provision exists in the Salvage Convention 1989 Art 9.
186 Intervention Convention 1969 Art II(1), which uses "ship" rather than "vessel", but in all other respects the definition is the same.
187 See LEG 75/5/2, 5 September 1996, Add 1, 3. Indeed, this definition of "maritime casualty" is used in the WRC 2007 to qualify which wreck will be covered by the WRC 2007 regime. WRC 2007 Art 1(4). See 8.2.1(a).
188 LEG 85/3/1, 17 September 2002, para. 3.
189 See the Correspondence Group on Wreck Removal: LEG 75/6/1, 14 February 1997, 7.
190 Provided by one member of the IMO Correspondence Group: LEG 75/6/1, 14 February 1997, 7.

some harm. If that ship sinks in a place where it may constitute a navigational hazard, and it contains pollutants, then arguably the first threshold is also met. The IMO Secretariat, in consultation with the United Nations Division of Ocean Affairs and the Law of the Sea (DOALOS), noted that:

> any wreck posing a threat to navigation will almost certainly also pose a threat to the environment. This is because even if a ship colliding with a wreck is not carrying oil or another hazardous cargo, it will be carrying fuel oil, which can cause serious environmental damage if it spills into the sea. Furthermore, a wreck may cause other types of environmental damage, such as smothering marine organisms, breaking up coral reefs, and if it is large enough, interfering with spawning and breeding areas. Problems could also be posed by the leaching of TBT paint and the discharge of harmful organisms in ballast water.[191]

The major harmful consequences that "may reasonably be expected to result" might arise either because of the *chance* of a collision with the wreck, or the risk of harm *if* there is a casualty is high, or both.[192] Meeting the second threshold—that *major* harmful consequence will result—is perhaps more difficult to anticipate and heavily fact specific—facts that the coastal State may not necessarily have at hand at the time the decision to intervene needs to be made. Environmental law should allow a margin of appreciation for States, recognising their difficulty in weighing up the risks. There might be cases where no reasonable person could imagine major harm from pollution,[193] but increasingly these may well be the exception rather than the rule. Although shipowners and flag States may face difficulties in practice in establishing that a State has exceeded the rights recognised under Art 221, there will always be the protection that the coastal State action must be proportionate and reasonably necessary.[194]

5.6.4 Hazards that are not navigational or polluting

The "related interests" of a State are recognised in Art 221 if they are threatened by *pollution*, but what if those interests are threatened in some way by the existence of the wreck itself? Those interests might include fishing (where the wreck might foul nets), tourism (at a diving site) or perhaps cultural rights, eg of indigenous peoples.[195] Interests such as these would not fall within Art 221, as there is no "pollution" threat. The same considerations would apply to a decision by a State to raise a wreck for political reasons, eg to meet public opinion after pressure from relatives of those drowned in a ferry accident.[196] If the premise

---

191 LEG 86/4/1, 27 March 2003, para 14. The danger of TBT contaminating the marine environment is exemplified in the grounding of the Chinese flagged *Shen Neng 1* on Douglas Shoal in the Great Barrier Reef on 3 April 2010. Similarly, the grounding of the *Rena* gave rise to concerns over TBT including the effect of leaving the wreck *in situ* with a TBT sub-layer extant. See *Ngāi Te Hapū Inc & Anor v Bay of Plenty Regional Council* [2017] NZEnvC 073.
192 Eg the *Tricolor* sinking. See 1.2.5(b).
193 Eg where a wreck might only foul fishing nets.
194 UNCLOS Art 221(1).
195 One of the consequences of the *Rena* sinking in New Zealand has been a claim by Maori under the Treaty of Waitangi and the Resource Management Act 1991 that all remains of the wreck should be removed from Astrolabe Reef. See 1.2.4.
196 The South Korean Government, for example, spent $110 million to raise the ferry *Sewol* in 2017, three years after it sank with the loss of 304 passengers, mostly schoolchildren on a trip. See BBC (16 April 2015),

of Art 221 is to recognise that the coastline or related interests, including fishing, should be protected from the *pollution* consequences of a casualty, why should there not also be protection for other consequences of the casualty in the EEZ—provided that any action taken is proportionate and reasonably necessary? It is the casualty that is the common factor. It may be noted, though, that there have been considerable developments in the recognition of cultural rights, including intangible cultural heritage.[197] It seems likely that claims to protect indigenous cultural heritage are most likely to arise in territorial waters rather than the EEZ, but it is not inconceivable that such interests may become more widely recognised in the future.

As noted in Chapter 1, the cultural heritage interests of indigenous groups in the reef upon which the remains of the wreck of the *Rena* lay required a delicate and balanced approach. This included the novel use of trusts to provide funds for the removal of as much of the wreck as possible and the Environment Courts ruling that the *mauri*—or life force of the reef—was capable to recovering despite some wreck remains being left on the reef. The *Rena* certainly raised interests in the wreck—or at least the wreck site—that had not readily been anticipated by either the shipowner and its insurers or the coastal State, New Zealand.

5.7 OPRC 1990

Against this constitution of the oceans, UNCLOS, a number of international agreements have been concluded that address aspects of the protection of the marine environment that includes those emanating or caused by wrecks, and which have been or will be address in other parts of this work.[198] In terms of framework agreements, note needs to be taken of the OPRC 1990.[199] This Convention reflects the need for global and regional cooperative mechanism to prepare for and address oil spills as identified and encouraged in UNCLOS.[200]

---

www.bbc.com/news/world-asia-32297010 and www.bbc.com/news/world-asia-39361944. Similarly, the UK government searched for the wreck of the super trawler *Gaul*, which disappeared in 1974 with its crew of 36, giving rise to conspiracy theories given its sinking in the Barents Sea at the height of the Cold War. See further https://britishseafishing.co.uk/the-loss-of-fv-gaul/.

197 See eg L Lixinski, *Intangible Cultural Heritage and International Law* (OUP, 2013).

198 See eg CLC 1992, FUND 1992, Bunkers Convention 2001 and HNSC 2010 in 2.6, and LC 1972 and OSPAR Conventions in 14.1 Further applicable agreements are summarised in "International Assistance and Co-operation", https://assets.publishing.service.gov.uk/government/uploads/system/uploads/attachment_data/file/338795/130715_International_Assistance_and_Co-operation.pdf.

199 In part, the OPRC 1990 followed concerns raised after the *Exon Valdez* disaster. The UK has given effect to the OPRC 1990 under the MSA 1995 s 1, as amended by the Merchant Shipping and Maritime Security Act 1997, and the Merchant Shipping (Oil Pollution Preparedness, Response and Cooperation Convention) Order 1997 (1997/2567) and delegated legislation, in particular in the Merchant Shipping (Oil Pollution Preparedness, Response Co-operation Convention) Regulations 1998 (the OPRC Regulations), SI 1998/1056, as amended by the Merchant Shipping (Oil Pollution Preparedness, Response and Cooperation Convention) (Amendment) Regulations 2001 (2001/1639) the Merchant Shipping (Oil Pollution Preparedness, Response and Co-operation Convention) (Amendment) Regulations 2015 (SI 2015/386). See also eg the Government's "Guidance Oil and Gas: Offshore Emergency Response Legislation" (2013, updated 2018), www.gov.uk/guidance/oil-and-gas-offshore-emergency-response-legislation#the-merchant-shipping-oil-pollution-preparedness-response-co-operation-convention-regulations-1998.

200 UNCLOS Arts 97–206.

Parties to the OPRC 1990 undertake, individually or jointly, to take all appropriate measures to prepare for and respond to an oil pollution incident,[201] being the discharge of oil that "poses or may pose a threat to the marine environment, or to the coastline or related interests of one or more States, and which requires emergency action or other immediate response".[202] Its scope is relatively broad in that it applies to ships, including hydrofoil boats, air-cushion vehicles, submersibles and floating craft of any type as well as "offshore units", being "fixed or floating offshore installation or structure engaged in gas or oil exploration, exploitation or production activities, or loading or unloading of oil".[203] While the 1990 Convention applies only to oil broadly defined,[204] a Protocol to the OPRC 1990 was adopted in 2000 to apply to essentially the same regime to hazardous and noxious substances (OPRC-HNS Protocol).

In term of preparedness, each State party is required to develop a National Contingency Plan to respond to an oil spill incident.[205] To implement the plan, a State needs to have an organisational structure to respond to an oil spill, effective channels of communication and appropriate levels of equipment and training in their deployment and use. Each State is also required to ensure that ships and offshore units carry an oil pollution emergency plan.[206]

The reporting procedures require each State party to ensure that masters and persons in charge of offshore units' report oil pollution spills, both from their ships and platforms and those observed from their ship or platform. In the case of ships, the report is to be made to the nearest coastal State and in the case of offshore platforms to the coastal State to whose jurisdiction the unit is subject.[207] This reporting obligations extends to port authorities, State inspectors and aircraft pilots.[208] The observed spill in these cases may very well emanate from a wreck, whether recent or one that might have sunk some time ago but is only now leaking bunker fuel or cargo.

On receiving a report, the State is to confirm whether it is an oil pollution incident; assess the nature, extent and possible consequences of the incident; and then, without delay, inform all States whose interests are affected or likely to be affected by such oil pollution incident of the incident and all known facts.[209] This reporting obligation continues until the action taken to respond to the incident has been concluded or until joint action has been decided by such States.[210]

---

201 OPRC 1990 Art 1(1), (3). The Convention does not apply to any warship, naval auxiliary or other ship owned or operated by a State and used, for the time being, only on government non-commercial service. However, each Party is to ensure that such operate "so far as is reasonable and practicable" with this Convention. OPRC 1990 Art 1(3).
202 Ibid. Art 2(2).
203 Ibid. Art 2(3) and (4). Cf WRC 2007 Art 1(2), which excludes floating craft and floating platforms, when such platforms are on location engaged in the exploration, exploitation or production of sea-bed mineral resources. See 8.2.1(g).
204 OPRC 1990 Art 2(1) defines oil as "petroleum in any form including crude oil, fuel oil, sludge, oil refuse and refined products".
205 Ibid. Art 6.
206 Ibid. Art 3.
207 Ibid. Art 4(1), (2).
208 Ibid. Art 4(c)–(e).
209 Ibid. Art 5(1).
210 Ibid. Art 5(1)(c).

Cooperation lies at the heart of the OPRC 1990. It requires States parties to cooperate and provide advisory services, technical support and equipment for the purpose of responding to an oil pollution incident (subject to their capabilities and the availability of relevant resources), when requested by another State.[211] To make sure that one State can provide these resources to another State, each State is required to ensure that ships, aircraft, equipment and personnel can enter and leave the relevant State with ease and no undue customs or immigration limitations.[212] As such, these procedures are part of the national plan that needs to be addressed before an oil spill incident occurs.

When one State requests assistance from another State, the issue of cost becomes an important consideration. The Annex to the OPRC 1990—which forms an integral part of the Convention—addresses this sensitive issue of costs. States are encouraged to enter into bilateral or multilateral agreements that addresses the issues of costs prior to any spill incident, and many have done so through regional agreement such as the Bonn agreement.[213] Where no agreement exists, the Annex provides that Parties shall bear the costs of their respective actions in dealing with pollution, but if the action "was taken by one Party at the express request of another Party, the requesting Party shall reimburse to the assisting Party the cost of its action".[214] The requesting Party may cancel its request at any time, but in that case it shall bear the costs already incurred or committed by the assisting Party.[215] States are required to cooperate in determining these costs and to ensure that they are fairly calculated. Importantly, these provisions do not prejudice the rights of Parties to recover from third parties the costs of actions to deal with pollution or the threat of pollution under other applicable provisions and rules of national and international law.[216] This includes the WRC 2007 such that any cost recoverable from a shipowner and/or its insurer pursuant to the WRC 2007 may be used by the claiming State to reimburse some other State for actions taken that are covered by the WRC 2007 in relation to the wreck.

The Convention provides for the IMO to play an important coordinating role, including with the dissemination and sharing of research results into relevant oil pollution spills responses[217] and the transfer of technology and capacity building in States.[218] The OPRC 1990 also encourages the conclusion of bilateral or multilateral agreements for oil pollution preparedness and response. A number have been concluded in various regions, including the Bonn Agreement for cooperation in dealing with pollution of the North Sea by oil and other harmful substances 1983, as amended in 2001.[219]

---

211 Ibid. Art 7(1).
212 Ibid. Art 7(3).
213 Ibid. Annex Art 1(a).
214 Ibid. Annex Art 1(a)(i).
215 Ibid.
216 Ibid. Annex Art 4.
217 Ibid. Art 8; see ibid. Arts 4(2), 5(2) and 9(1).
218 Ibid. Art 9.
219 See www.bonnagreement.org. The Secretariat has a detailed three volume manual of 34 chapters to assist with operational matters, eg that there be a lead State. There are detailed provisions in Chapter 27 on deciding on a place of refuge, based on a "rational approach". This builds upon IMO Assembly Resolution No A.949(23)) and Art 20 of Directive 2002/59/EC.

CHAPTER 6

Underwater cultural heritage

6.1 Protection of historic wrecks

With much improved diving technology and the advent of self-contained underwater breathing apparatus (SCUBA) that allowed sports divers to access increasing deeper waters beginning in the 1950s, historic wrecks were being found and salvaged.[1] The UK was at the forefront of recognising the importance of protecting the historical and archaeological value of many old wrecks. The Protection of Wrecks Act 1973 was one of the first national regimes to specifically address this emerging value of wrecks.

Once deep-sea search, survey and diving technology allowed access to international waters, the need arose to address this issue at an international level, first at UNCLOS negotiations from the late 1960s to 1982 when it was adopted, and then at UNESCO where an international instrument was drafted that dealt specifically with the protection of historic wrecks and other important underwater cultural heritage. This chapter deals specifically with this conventional regime and its underlying rationale.

6.2 Development of UCH 2001

The Convention on the Protection of the Underwater Cultural Heritage (UCH 2001)[2] was adopted at UNESCO on 2 November 2001 and came into force on 2 January 2009 after the 20th instrument of ratification.[3] UCH 2001 protects historic wrecks and other forms of heritage from unregulated salvage, excavation and destruction with the loss of its archaeological and historical value.

The protection of historic wrecks had been addressed during negotiations that led to UNCLOS, but because it had been raised late in negotiations and was of lesser interest to those that were at the forefront of negotiations, it received little attention. Nevertheless, two articles did touch on the issue: Arts 303 and 149. Unfortunately, while these articles did impose a "duty to protect objects of an archaeological and historical nature found at sea" they did little to explain how this was to be achieved and merely exhorted States to "cooperate for this purpose".[4]

A failed attempt to provide a more detailed protective regime for historic wrecks at the Council of Europe in the 1980s led the International Law Association (ILA)[5] taking up the

---

1 On the pioneers of this technology see T Norton, *Stars Beneath the Sea: The Pioneers of Diving* (Carroll & Graf, 2000).

2 As at 1 April 2019 there were 61 States parties.

3 UCH 2001 Art 27.

4 UNCLOS Art 303(1). On Art 303 and 149 see *Strati*, 169; *Forrest, Protection of Cultural Heritage*, 329–333; *Dromgoole, Underwater Cultural Heritage*, 36–47.

5 Founded in 1873, the ILA is a private non-governmental organisation of persons interested in international law.

issue in 1994. An ILA committee on Cultural Heritage Law produced a draft convention that was passed on to UNESCO for consideration.[6] Annexed to the draft was the Charter on the Protection and Management of Underwater Cultural Heritage[7] produced by the International Council on Monuments and Sites (ICOMOS),[8] which set out benchmark standards for underwater archaeology. UNESCO convened a number of inter-governmental meetings between 1998 and 2001 and UCH 2001 was finally adopted in November 2001. While the Director-General of UNESCO had urged the meeting to agree the draft by way of consensus, this could not be achieved, and it was approved by a majority vote.[9]

6.3 Aim of UCH 2001

UCH 2001 essentially seeks to take historic wreck and other underwater cultural heritage out of the wreck and salvage law regimes and have them treated as archaeological sites.

This is reflected in the preamble. With technological advances that allow access to the ocean's depths coupled with an increased public interest, historic wrecks and other forms of heritage are increasingly being threatened by unauthorised activities directed at it. In particular, the preamble reflects recognition of the threat posed by increasing commercial exploitation of underwater cultural heritage, and in particular by certain activities aimed at the sale, acquisition or barter of underwater cultural heritage.

UCH 2001, then, is concerned with imposing archaeological standards on the investigation and excavation of underwater cultural heritage, the extraction of such activities from the salvage regime and the implementation of this regulated regime by States when that heritage lies beyond a State's territorial seas.[10] A number of States have not, however, become party to UCH 2001, including the UK and the US. To understand the rationale behind UCH 2001 and the debate that exists in the UK and US in particular as to its utility,

---

6 For a detailed discussion of the ILA draft, see P O'Keefe, "Protection of the Underwater Cultural Heritage: Developments at UNESCO" (1996) 25 *Int J Nautical Archaeology* 169 and J Blake, "The Protection of the Underwater Cultural Heritage" (1996) 45 ICLQ 819.

7 The ICOMOS Charter was ratified by the 11th ICOMOS General Assembly, held in Sofia, Bulgaria, 5–9 October 1996.

8 Established in 1964 ICOMOS is a non-governmental organisation with special observer status at UNESCO, and whose primary function it is to advise inter-governmental organisations of the steps necessary to conserve the monuments and sites of the world.

9 Eighty-seven States voted in favour of the Convention, four States (The Russian Federation, Norway, Turkey and Venezuela) voted against adoption, while 15 States abstained (including Brazil, Columbia, France, Germany, Greece, Israel, the Netherlands, Paraguay, Sweden, Switzerland, the UK and Uruguay. The US, not being a member of UNESCO at the time, had no right to vote. For a comprehensive discussion of the negotiating history of each article of the Convention, see R Garabello, "The Negotiating History of the Convention on the Protection of the Underwater Cultural Heritage", in R. Garabello and T. Scovazzi (eds), *The Negotiating History of the Convention on the Protection of the Underwater Cultural Heritage: Before and After the 2001 UCH Convention* (Leiden: Martinus Nijhoff, 2003), 89. For an article by article discussion of the Convention, see P O'Keefe, *Shipwrecked Heritage: A Commentary on the UNESCO Convention on Underwater Cultural Heritage* (2nd. ed. Institute of Art and Law, 2014).

10 The Institute of International Law 2015 Resolution provides significant support for the Convention, endorsing the 100-year cut-off, recognises that *in situ* preservation should be the preferred initial approach, indicating that States shall take the measures necessary to prevent or control commercial exploitation or pillage of sunken State ships, which are part of cultural heritage, that are incompatible with the duties set out in this Article as well as in applicable treaties. *Ronzitti* (2015), 371.

a more detailed discussion of the relation between the law of salvage and historic wrecks is necessary.

6.4 Salvage and historic wrecks

While wrecks have been recovered or salvaged mainly for their economic value, some were recovered for their historic or archaeological interest,[11] particularly in the Mediterranean.[12] The finds of ancient material were sporadic and mostly fortuitous, and although of archaeological and historical interest did not give rise to any systematic enquiry. The invention of SCUBA in the 1940s ushered in an era in which archaeologists could take to the water and led to archaeological excavation in the relatively calm and clear waters of the Mediterranean.[13] However, at the same time, the advantages of SCUBA meant that increasing number of sports divers were gaining access to wrecks. Professional salvage companies too began to specifically target historic wrecks for recovery using all the new diving technologies at their disposal, including not only SCUBA but also the use of prop washers, sonar and underwater metal detectors. Very quickly recovery operation could be divided into those which were archaeological excavations in the strict sense and those that were salvage operations. Examples of the former have steadily grown since the excavation of the 3,000-year-old *Cape Gelidonya* wreck in the 1960s. The excavation of the *Mary Rose*, beginning in the late 1960s and culminating in the remarkable raising of the hull in 1982, stands as a pivotal point in the development of underwater archaeology. Similarly, the raising of the Swedish warship *Vasa*, sunk in 1628 and raised in 1961, is perhaps the last we will see of a wreck recovered whole rather than excavated underwater. In Canada, the excavation of a 16th-century Spanish galleon in Red Bay, Labrador, reflects further developments in sound archaeological practice, and in this case, an example of *in situ* preservation, with large parts of the wreck conserved underwater for the benefit of further investigation by future generations.[14]

A very different picture emerges from a number of other recovery operations which exhibit questionable archaeological practices, if any at all; motivated as they are by the economic value of the recovered artefacts. Historic wrecks lying in various parts of the world have yielded significant commercially valuable artefacts. In many cases, the salvage of cargo has reaped rewards valued in millions. In 1971, the US salvage company Treasure

---

11 In 1446, material from two ancient Roman vessels lying at the bottom of Lake Nemi in Italy was recovered for their historical interest. J Blot, *Underwater Archaeology: Exploring the World Beneath the Sea* (Thames and Hudson, 1995) [*Blot*], 14.

12 In 1900, Greek sponge divers discovered a wreck at Antikythera, near Crete. They recovered not only a number of amphora dating from between 80 and 70 bc, but also a number of rare bronze and marble statues. *Blot*, 32–33; see also GF Bass, "Marine Archaeology: A Misunderstood Science" (1980) 2 *Ocean Yearbook* 137; JP Delgado (ed), *Encyclopaedia of Underwater and Maritime Archaeology* (British Museum Press, 1997) [*Delgado, Encyclopaedia*], 31–32. JN Green, *Maritime Archaeology: A Technical Handbook* (Elsevier Academic Press, 1990).

13 In 1960, George Bass became the first archaeologist to learn how to dive and, in cooperation with Peter Throckmorton, began the excavation of a late bronze-age wreck (approximately 1200 bc) off Cape Gelidonya, Turkey. *Throckmorton*, 24–32. For more on the history and development of underwater archaeology, see *Bass; Throckmorton*.

14 *Delgado, Encyclopaedia*, 336.

Salvors, Inc located the wrecks of the Spanish galleons *Nuestra Señora de Atocha* and the *Santa Margarita*, off the Marquesas Keys in Florida.[15] These wrecks eventually yielded a cargo worth millions and began a series of protracted legal battles over ownership and attempts by the State of Florida to protect the historical and archaeological value of the recovered material and the site itself.[16] This treasure salvage industry continues to find and recover cargo at the expense of the site's historical and archaeological value. The recovery of a cargo of Chinese porcelain from the Dutch East Indiaman *Geldermalsen*, sunk off the coast of Indonesia in 1752 and a number of other similar vessels carrying porcelain, have been salvaged for the sale of that cargo rather than for the vessel or cargo's historic or archaeological value.[17] The more notorious recoveries are those of the cargo of coins from the steamship *Central America* sunk in 1857 off the coast of the US;[18] and that of the *Nuestra Señora de Mercedes*[19] sunk in 1804 off the coast of Gibraltar. More recently, the salvage and sale of a cargo of rare pottery recovered by a commercial salvor from the wreck of an Arab dhow sunk in ad 830, known as the Belitung wreck, has caused significant controversy and a re-examination of the application of salvage law to historic wrecks.

6.4.1 Maritime archaeology and salvage

Archaeologists have argued that the application of salvage law to historic wrecks, or in some jurisdictions such as the US, the law of finds, is incompatible with the realisation of the archaeological, historical or cultural value embodied in the wreck.[20] This is so as salvage law encourages the recovery of historic wrecks, when it may be the case that the wreck might be better preserved by being left *in situ* and that when recovery is undertaken, inappropriate techniques are used so that valuable historical and archaeological information is lost.[21] It is also argued that the sale of salvaged material leads to the splitting up of

---

15 On the excavation of the wreck of *the Nuestra Señora de Atocha* and *Santa Margarita*, see RD Mathewson, *Archaeological Treasure: The Search for the Nuestra Señora de Atocha* (Seafarers Heritage Library, 1983); J Smith, *Fatal Treasure* (Wiley & Sons, 2003).

16 See *Forrest, Protection of Cultural Heritage*, 294–296; Dromgoole, *Underwater Cultural Heritage*, 185–186; T Scovazzi, "Sunken Spanish Ships before American Courts" (2018) 33 *International Journal of Marine and Coastal Law* [*Scovazzi*] 1.

17 *Forrest, Protection of Cultural Heritage*, 296–298. See also M Hatcher and A Thorncraft, *The Nanking Cargo* (Hamish Hamilton, 1987).

18 *Forrest, Protection of Cultural Heritage*, 297–298; Dromgoole, *Underwater Cultural Heritage*, 189. For an account of the salvage, see G Kinder, *Ship of Gold in the Deep Blue Sea* (Atlantic Monthly Press, 1998).

19 *Scovazzi*, 29–36.

20 E Clément, "Current Developments at UNESCO Concerning the Protection of the Underwater Cultural Heritage" (1996) 20 *Marine Policy* 309; R Elia, "US Protection of Underwater Cultural Heritage Beyond the Territorial Sea: Problems and Prospects" (2000) 29 *Int J Nautical Archaeology* 43; R Elia, "The Ethics of Collaboration: Archaeologists and the Wydah Project" (1992) 26 *Historical Archaeology* 46. For a more detailed discussed of the arguments for and against commercial recovery of historic wreck, see JP Sweeney, "An Overview of Commercial Salvage Principles in the Context of Marine Archaeology" (1999) 30 JMLC 185; O Varmer, "The Case against the 'Salvage' of the Cultural Heritage" (1999) 30 JMLC 279; DK Abbass, "A Marine Archaeologist Looks at Treasure Salvage" (1999) 30 JMLC 261; *Varmer & Blanco*, 401.

21 The preservation of the archaeological value of a wreck is not, in itself, a requirement of the law of salvage and the determination of a salvage award. See *Morris v Lyonesse Salvage Co. Ltd (The Association & The Romney)*, [1970] 2 Lloyd's Rep 59, 61 (Adm Ct). US courts have taken a variable approach to the issue. See *Cobb Coin Co., Inc v The Unidentified Wrecked and Abandoned Sailing Vessel*, 549 F Supp 540, 559 (SD Fla 1982);

the archaeological assemblage that undermines future historical research. At the extreme it is also argued that recovered material should quite simply not be subject to economic exploitation and that they should not be subject to private ownership.[22] While these are seen as the undesirable consequences of the application of salvage law to historic wrecks, a more principled objection exists. That is the extent to which historic wreck are in marine peril—a condition precedent for the application of salvage law.

Salvage is most often sought by vessels in distress, usually vessels that have been caught in bad weather conditions or which have suffered structural or engine failure, and risk running aground or foundering. In the case of historic wrecks, this concept of danger has long past, with the vessel having sunk many years before the salvage operation. Once sunk, however, the threat of physical destruction may continue as the vessel and its cargo begins to disintegrate from the immediate forces of nature and the inevitable degeneration over time. It may also be in danger from deliberate destruction because it is causing a hazard to navigation. However, the remains may reach a stage of equilibrium in the surrounding marine environment, and little or no further degradation will occur in the future.[23] This is particularly so in deep water, where, due to low levels of light and oxygen, organic material is often very well preserved.

However, "marine peril" has been interpreted more broadly than merely the threat of physical destruction. As long as the vessel, or more commonly its cargo, might still be of economic value and can be recovered, the failure to reap this value might itself be said to constitute a peril. US admiralty courts, above all, have had to consider the issue. In *Treasure Salvors I*,[24] the court held that "marine peril includes more than the threat of storm, fire, or piracy to a vessel in navigation".[25] In *Platoro Ltd, Inc v The Unidentified Remains of a Vessel*,[26] a US district court took a very wide interpretation of marine peril in relation to the remains of several Spanish vessels that had sunk off the coast of Texas in 1555. The court held that, as a matter of law, marine peril will exist simply where a ship's location was unknown. The physical preservation of the artefacts was therefore not a consideration in determining the existence of marine peril. Similarly, in *Cobb Coin Co. v Unidentified, Wrecked and Abandoned Sailing Vessel*,[27] a case concerning the salvage of the 1715 Spanish Plate Fleet, the court stated that "[b]ecause the defendant vessel was still in marine peril

---

MDM Salvage, Inc v Unidentified, Wrecked and Abandoned Sailing Vessel, 631 F Supp 308, 310–311; *Klein v Unidentified, Wrecked and Abandoned Sailing Vessel*, 568 F Supp 1562, 1568 (SD Fla 1983); *Columbus-America Discovery Group, Inc v Atlantic Mutual Insurance Company*, 42 F Supp 1327, 1990 (ED Va 1990); 974 F2d 450 (4th Cir 1992). See further *Varmer & Blanco*, 401–424. On salvage awards generally see 2.7.7, and on right acquired by salvors see 3.5.

22 See further *Forrest, Protection of Cultural Heritage*, 313–320.

23 See J Barto Arnold III, "Some Thought on Salvage Law and Historic Preservation" (1978) 7 *Int J Archaeology* 174. See also S McLaughlin, "Roots, Relics and Recovery: What Went Wrong with the Abandoned Shipwreck Act of 1987" (1995) 19 *Columbia-VLA Journal of Law and the Arts* 149, 182.

24 *Treasure Salvors, Inc v Unidentified, Wrecked and Abandoned Sailing Vessel*, 569 F2d 330, 337 (5th Cir 1978).

25 See also *Martha's Vineyard Scuba Headquarters, Inc v Unidentified, Wrecked and Abandoned Steam Vessel*, 833 F2d 1059 (1st Cir 1987).

26 *Platoro Ltd, Inc v The Unidentified Remains of a Vessel*, 614 F2d 1051, 1055–56 (5th Cir 1980); 1981 AMC 1087, 1102–03.

27 *Cobb Coin Co. v Unidentified, Wrecked and Abandoned Sailing Vessel*, 549 F Supp 540, 561, 557 (SD Fla 1982).

of being lost through the action of the elements or of pirates and was not being successfully salved when the plaintiff undertook its salvage operation, it was subject to a marine peril for purposes of the plaintiff's salvage claim".[28] More recently, in *Columbus-America Discovery Group, Inc v Atlantic Mutual Insurance Co*,[29] the court concluded that "historically, courts have applied the maritime law of salvage when ships or their cargo have been recovered from the bottom of the sea by other than their owners", thus implying the existence of marine peril.

Quite the opposite conclusion was reached in *Subaqueous Exploration & Archaeology Ltd v The Unidentified, Wrecked and Abandoned Vessel*.[30] The court had to determine whether salvage law was to apply to the recovery of three Spanish vessels and one British vessel of the 18th or 19th century in the State of Maryland. The court held that "marine antiquities which have been undisturbed for centuries" are not proper subjects of salvage because they are not in marine peril. A somewhat different approach was taken in *Klein v Unidentified, Wrecked and Abandoned Sailing Vessel*,[31] when the court acknowledged that marine peril was required for a successful salvage claim but extended the peril to include that posed to the historic and archaeological value of the wreck. The court concluded that the salvors had, by failing to take steps to preserve the archaeological and historical value of the wreck, put the wreck in greater danger than it had been when undisturbed.

The issue has not arisen in the UK in quite the same manner. Section 255 of the MSA 1995 defines wreck as including "jetsam, flotsam, lagan and derelict found in or on the shores of the sea or any tidal water". Derelict is a vessel that has been abandoned at sea by the master and crew, without an intention of returning to her (*sine animo revertendi*) or hope of recovery (*sine spe recuperandi*)[32] and applies equally to vessels afloat and vessels sunk.[33] Importantly, wreck has been held to be a legitimate subject of salvage and, as derelict, includes sunken wrecks, modern and ancient.[34] Indeed, in the UK the application of salvage law to wreck is more likely to turn on the question of whether the wreck was abandoned and therefore derelict, rather than whether there was marine peril.[35]

Few other jurisdictions appear to have had to address this issue directly, though some examples do exist. For example, in the Canadian case *Her Majesty the Queen in Right of Ontario v Mar-Dive Corporation et al*,[36] the court held that a historic wreck embedded in the bottom of Lake Erie was not in marine peril. The court went on to note that it

---

28 See also *Wiggins v 1100 Tons, More or Less, of Italian Marble (The Clythia)*, 186 F Supp 452 (ED Va 1960); *Thompson v One Anchor and Two Anchor Chains*, 221 F 770 (WD Wis 1916); *Eads v Brazelton*, 22 Ark 499 (1861).

29 *Columbus-America Discovery Group, Inc v Atlantic Mutual Insurance Company* [1995] AMC 1985, 2007 (4th Cir). See also *E.L. Soba v Fitzgerald* [1997] AMC 2254.

30 *Subaqueous Exploration & Archaeology Ltd v The Unidentified, Wrecked and Abandoned Vessel*, 577 F Supp 597 (D Md 1983).

31 *Klein v Unidentified, Wrecked and Abandoned Sailing Vessel*, 758 F2d 1515 (11th Cir 1985).

32 *The Aquila* (1798) 1C Rob 36, 165 ER 87; *Cossman v West* (1887) 13 App Cas 160, 6 Asp MLC 233 (PC); *Bradley v Newsom* [1919] AC 16 (HL); *The Tubantia* (1924) P 78, 18 Ll L Rep 158. See further *Kennedy & Rose*, 104–107.

33 HMS *Thetis* (1834) 2 Knapp 390 (PC); 3 Hagg 229, 166 ER 390; *The Tubantia* (1924) P 78, 18 Ll L Rep 158; *The Lusitania* [986] QB 384.

34 *Kennedy & Rose*, 106. See 3.3.1.

35 *Morris v Lyonesse Salvage Co Ltd (The Association and The Romney)* [1970] 2 Lloyd's Rep 59. See 3.3.1.

36 *Her Majesty The Queen in Right of Ontario v Mar-Dive Corporation et al*, 1997 AMC 1000.

might, however, be in danger from the salvage activity itself, especially from the unskilled recovery of artefacts. Other States evince a broader approach by considering that historic wreck of an archaeological nature fall outside maritime law and the law of salvage, not only because they are not, in the salvage law sense, in marine peril, but also because their archaeological or historical importance is incompatible with the commercial nature of salvage law. For example, the Singapore High Court in *Simon v Taylor*[37] rejected the application of salvage law to wreck of historic importance as the operation was motivated simply by commercial interests. Similarly, the High Court of Ireland, in *In re La Lavia, Juliana and Santa Maria de la Vision*[38] concluded that the wreck of three Spanish vessel sunk in 1588 "passed out of the realms of commercial maritime law and into archaeology law long before they were found as Streedagh in 1985".[39] The courts are not alone in their disagreement on the meaning of marine peril and the consequent application of salvage law to historic wreck and commentators on the subject are equally divided.[40]

6.4.2 UK position on salvage and historic wreck

As discussed in Chapter 3, historic wrecks are included within the definition of derelict and therefore subject to the salvage regime as provided for in the MSA 1995.[41] Further, as discussed in 4.7.1, the Protection of Wrecks Act 1973 provides a regulated access regime to certain historic wrecks deemed to be of "historical, archaeological or artistic importance".[42] Essentially the Act did no more than regulate access to certain sites,[43] but leaving salvors granted an excavation licence with a salvage claim for recovered items, to be reported to the Receiver of Wreck in the usual way. That said, licences are now seldom granted unless there is an archaeological reason for excavation or the site is in some danger. Nevertheless, salvage law nominally still applies, and continues to apply for those sites that were designated shortly after the Act, where salvors were engaged at the time of designation in recovery and might continue to recover material. The same applied to wrecks subject to the Protection of Military Remains Act.[44]

This application of salvage law (though somewhat modified for 69 historic wrecks and 79 military wrecks) continues to apply. Indeed, the UK government has enforced its salvage orientation in dealing with military vessels in international waters, including to those of archaeological importance. In 2002, for example, the MOD entered into a salvage contract with US salvors to recover material, including significant amounts of gold bullion, from *HMS Sussex*, sunk in 1694. The agreement provided for the salvor—Odyssey Marine Explorations—to be awarded 80% of the appraised value of recovered material for the

---

37 *Simon v Taylor* [1975] 2 Lloyd's Rep 338 (Singapore High Ct 1974).
38 *In re La Lavia, Juliana and Santa Maria de la Vision* [1996] 1 Irish Law Reports Monthly 194.
39 As quoted in N O'Conner, "Ireland", in S Dromgoole (ed), *The Protection of the Underwater Cultural Heritage: National Perspectives in Light of the UNESCO Convention 2001* (Martinus Nijhoff Publishers 2006) 127, 133.
40 See G Brice, "Salvage Law and the Underwater Cultural Heritage" (1996) 20 *Marine Policy* 337, 339; D Owen, "Some Legal Troubles with Treasure: Jurisdiction and Salvage" (1985) 16 JMLC 139, 145.
41 See 2.7.2.
42 Protection of Wrecks Act 1973 s 1(2)(a).
43 Sixty-nine sites in 2019 across the UK.
44 See 4.7.2.

first $45 million, growing progressively less as more in value was recovered until receiving 40% for that over $500 million.[45] While adherence to archaeological standards were purported to be part of the conditions for the salvage operation, it nevertheless amounted to salvage and was roundly criticised by archaeological groups in the UK and around the world.

The MOD then again entered into a contract with the same salvage company for recovery of material from *HMS Victory*, a predecessor of Lord Nelson's *Victory*, sunk in 1744.[46] Further contracts have been entered into between DfT and Odyssey Marine Exploration for the recovery of cargo from merchant vessels, including the *Gairsoppa* sunk in 1941 and *Mantola* sunk in 1917, both by U-boats. However, the reaction of the archaeological and cultural heritage community, particularly following the *HMS Sussex* and *HMS Victory* contracts, was such that the various branches of the UK government have effectively imposed a moratorium on new contracts. That said, salvage law continues to underpin the UK's legal regime to historic wrecks, both as a matter of admiralty law and contractually.

6.4.3 Salvage Convention and historic wreck

The Salvage Convention 1989 provides that a State may "reserve the right not to apply the provisions of this Convention . . . when the property involved is maritime cultural property of prehistoric, archaeological or historic interest and is situated on the sea-bed".[47] The default position therefore is that the international Salvage Convention applies to historic wreck, unless specifically excluded by a State party. The UK did enter a reservation in this respect, but has not given full effect to it in its national legislation.[48] In effect, the UK has reserved the right to give effect to this reservation but has so far not chosen to do so. This cautious approach effectively renders the reservation one that amounts to a reservation to enter a reservation in the future. Until then, the common law of salvage applies, as amended by the national legislation of the UK. A conflict might arise for States party to the UCH 2001 that have not entered a reservation to the Salvage Convention.[49]

6.5 Defining "underwater cultural heritage"

Against this background, UCH 2001 then attempts to take historic wrecks and other underwater cultural heritage out of the salvage regime (and the law of finds) and have a regulated cultural heritage orientated regime apply. To do so, the scope of cultural heritage needed to be addressed.

---

45 S Dromgoole, "Murky Waters for Government Policy: The Case of a 17th Century British Warship and 10 Tonnes of Gold Coins" (2003) 28 *Marine Policy* 189, 190.
46 D Alberge "Archaeologists Accuse MoD of Allowing US Company to 'Plunder' Shipwreck", *Guardian*, www.theguardian.com/uk/2012/may/06/hms-victory-shipwreck-odyssey-excavation.
47 Salvage UCH 2001 1989 Art 30(1)(d).
48 Schedule 11 Part 2 para. 2 MSA 1995 does not exclude the salvage of historic wreck or other underwater cultural heritage from its application. Over a third of States parties to the Salvage Convention 1989 have entered a reservation in accordance with Art 30(1)(d), including Australia, Bulgaria, Canada, China, Croatia, Ecuador, Estonia, Finland, France, Germany, Iran, Jamaica, Mexico, the Netherlands, New Zealand, Norway, Poland, Russia, Saudi Arabia, Spain, Sweden, Tunisia, Turkey and Ukraine. *IMO Status of Treaties* November (2018).
49 See further *Dromgoole, Underwater Cultural Heritage*, 204–206.

"Underwater cultural heritage"[50] is defined in the Convention as

> all traces of human existence having a cultural, historical or archaeological character which have been partially or totally underwater, periodically or continuously, for at least 100 years such as:
>
> (i) sites, structures, buildings, artefacts and human remains, together with their archaeological and natural context;
> (ii) vessels, aircraft, other vehicles or any part thereof, their cargo or other contents, together with their archaeological and natural context; and
> (iii) objects of prehistoric character.

This definition begins with the exceptionally broad "all traces of human existence". This does, however, begin to act as a limitation on the scope of UCH 2001 in that it does exclude non-human resources, such as paleontological material. It would also exclude natural features that have some cultural significance to a people.[51] The wide scope of "all traces of human existence" is then qualified by three important criteria.

First, it is only that which has "a cultural, historical or archaeological character". A significant point of contention which arose during negotiations was whether the definition should provide for blanket inclusion of all traces of human existence that have been underwater for over 100 years or whether a significance requirement should be introduced. Some States argued strongly in favour of the latter, and were able to have included in the definition the phrase "cultural, historical or archaeological character" as a qualifying criterion. The interpretation of this phrase is not altogether clear, as a number of States held the view that all that has been underwater for 100 years will have such characteristics by definition, and therefore blanket inclusion is provided for. There is therefore scope for each contracting State to apply some evaluative criteria to limit the scope to that which is considered significant.

Secondly, rather than dealing comprehensively with the kind of objects that might be considered cultural heritage, UCH 2001 focuses on the environment in which the cultural heritage is found by limiting it to that which is "partially or totally underwater, periodically or continuously". The use of the four descriptors leaves four possibilities. Most underwater cultural heritage will be totally underwater continuously, especially that which rests in international waters far from the coast. However, a significant proportion of underwater cultural heritage lies in shallow waters or waters subject to great tidal variations. "Partially", coupled with "continuously", will cover that which has a component submerged whilst another part remain above water at all times, such as the wreck of the *USS Arizona* in the shallow water of Pearl Harbor, Hawaii.[52] "Partially" and "periodically" is exemplified

---

50 The term "underwater cultural heritage" is of relatively recent origin, having been first used in Recommendation 848 (1978) of The Council of Europe, to mean "all remains and objects and any other traces of human existence located entirely or part in the sea, lakes, rivers, canals, artificial reservoirs or other bodies of water, or recovered from any such environment, or washed ashore". See *Strati*, 10.

51 During negotiations, the Archaeological Institute of America had unsuccessfully called for an expanded definition to include non-human archaeological objects, such as Paleo-Indian sites. Reprinted as "Comments of the Archaeological Institute of America on the UNESCO Draft Convention on the Protection of the Underwater Cultural Heritage" (1998) 7 *Int J Cultural Property* 538; *Prott & Srong*, 174.

52 Though not having been submerged for over 100 years, it does illustrate the way in which a vessel may be partially submerged.

by the wreck of the VOC vessel *Amsterdam* at Hastings, UK, part of which is exposed at low tide.

Thirdly, underwater cultural heritage is only that which has been submerged for 100 years. This period is somewhat arbitrary and based more on administrative pragmatism than on archaeological, cultural or historical significance. It follows consensus during negotiations that objects older than 100 years are more likely than not to be archaeologically or historically significant.[53] Whilst UCH 2001 does not indicate from what point in time this period is to be measures, it may be presumed, given that one of the aims of UCH 2001 is to promote *in situ* preservation, that this should be calculated from the time that any activity is directed at the underwater cultural heritage, and not merely from the time of discovery. While the definition suggests that only that which has actually been submerged, partially or totally, for 100 years is covered, given rising sea levels, the risk arises that archaeological sites will become inundated but fall outside the scope of UCH 2001.[54]

The scope of the definition is further restricted by the use of the listed examples, from "sites, structures, buildings, artefacts and human remains" to "objects of prehistoric character". The lists serve only as examples of what is most likely to be found underwater and be of cultural, historical or archaeological character. It is therefore not an exhaustive list of underwater cultural heritage, but does act to limit the possible scope, acting as it does to create a generic classification. Finally, the definition excludes pipelines and cables placed on the seabed, as well as any installations other than pipelines and cables placed on the seabed and still in use.[55]

6.6 Non-commercialisation and salvage

The elimination of the law of salvage (and the law of finds) to underwater cultural heritage is addressed in UCH 2001 itself and in the Annex of UCH 2001 that set out the rules of good archaeological practice.[56] Rule 2 of the Annex provides that:

> The commercial exploitation of underwater cultural heritage for trade or speculation or its irretrievable dispersal is fundamentally incompatible with the protection and proper management of underwater cultural heritage. Underwater cultural heritage shall not be traded, sold, bought or bartered as commercial goods.

It is clear that this rule attempts to ensure that artefacts cannot be regarded as commercial goods. However, this rule has been qualified in that it goes on to declare that his Rule cannot be interpreted as preventing

   (a) the provision of professional archaeological services or necessary services incidental thereto whose nature and purpose are in full conformity with this Convention and are subject to the authorisation of the competent authorities;
   (b) the deposition of underwater cultural heritage, recovered in the course of a research project in conformity with this Convention, provided such deposition does not prejudice the

---

53 A number of States have used time periods as a criteria for protection, including the Netherlands (50 years); Australia (75 years); Denmark (100 years); Norway (100 years); Sweden (100 years); and Greece (all underwater cultural heritage dating from prior to 1453, and those from 1453 to 1830 on the advice of the Archaeological Council).
54 The pre-inundation archaeological regime may continue to apply.
55 UCH 2001 Art 1(1)(b) and (c).
56 See 6.8.

scientific or cultural interest or integrity of the recovered material or result in its irretrievable dispersal; is in accordance with the provisions of Rules 33 and 34; and is subject to the authorisation of the competent authorities.[57]

Rule 2(a) reflects the difficulty of divorcing the provision of commercial services during an excavation from the justification of an excavation. Professional archaeologists are paid to undertake scientific investigations, thus possibly making their activity economic in nature. Similarly, the provision of services, such as the supply of diving equipment, remote sensing devices etc, could all be supplied by a commercial enterprise.[58]

While the first sentence of Rule 2 is an attempt at clarity on the issue, Rule 2(b) muddies the water considerably. The failures to define "deposition" and identify the place of deposition creates unfortunate ambiguities. This subsection requires that a collection of cultural heritage can be deposited in either a private or a public collection (together with the project archive as far as possible), and that such a deposition shall not be considered as the commercial exploitation of underwater cultural heritage. Reflecting the non-commercialisation of underwater cultural heritage, Rule 2(b) could be viewed as an exception to the general rule, so that a collection of underwater cultural heritage, excavated according to the remaining rules in the Annex, and with appropriate authorisation from a State's competent authority could be sold, as a collection, to a private or public museum, for a profit. This would seem to be at odds with Art 2(7), which embodies the general principle that underwater cultural heritage "shall not be commercially exploited". In such circumstance, the general principle should dictate the interpretation of the rule, which leaves the exceptions in Rule 2 ambiguous at best, but more probably void for inconsistency.

UCH 2001 addresses the application of salvage law (and the law of finds) to underwater cultural heritage in Art 4:

> Any activity relating to underwater cultural heritage to which this Convention applies shall not be subject to the law of salvage or law of finds, unless it:
>
> (a) is authorised by the competent authorities, and
> (b) is in full conformity with this Convention, and
> (c) ensures that any recovery of the underwater cultural heritage achieves its maximum protection.

Article 4 is structured in a similar way as to Rule 2 of the Annex on non-commercialisation of underwater cultural heritage, in that it opens with a clear rule, which is then made subject to exceptions which have the effect of negating not only the clarity of the opening rule but the very essence of the rule itself. In this case, Art 2 provides that salvage law will not apply, but that, if it is in full conformity with the Convention (which includes the Annex) it may be applied. Given that the application of salvage law to the recovery of underwater cultural heritage is fundamentally incompatible with professional archaeological practice

---

[57] Rule 33 states: "The project archives, including any underwater cultural heritage removed and a copy of all supporting documentation shall, as far as possible, be kept together and intact as a collection in a manner that is available for professional and public access as well as for the curation of the archives. This should be done as rapidly as possible and in any case not later than 10 years from the completion of the project, in so far as may be compatible with conservation of the underwater cultural heritage". Rule 34 states: "The project archives shall be managed according to international professional standards, and subject to the authorisation of the competent authorities".

[58] CLT-2000/CONF.201/10, Paris, 7 July 2000, 2.

as expressed in the Annex, it is difficult to see how salvage law could be conducted so as to conform to the Convention.

This, however, was an intentional 'constructive ambiguity'. The application of salvage law to underwater cultural heritage was the subject of complex and protracted negotiations and in an attempt to reach consensus and compromise, the three additional sections were added, leaving the article as a whole vague and susceptible, intentionally, to alternative interpretations. It was hoped this would encourage greater State ratification of UCH 2001.

6.7 Activities to be regulated

The main thrust of UCH 2001 is to deal with those who specifically target underwater cultural heritage and not those that inadvertently or incidentally affect underwater cultural heritage, such as commercial fishing or cable-laying that only incidentally affect it.[59] Nevertheless, UCH 2001 does touch on the issue, which is expressed in conventional terms as "activities which, despite not having underwater cultural heritage as their primary object or one of their objects, may physically disturb or otherwise damage underwater cultural heritage".[60] States are required to "use the best practicable means at its disposal to prevent or mitigate any adverse effects that might arise from activities under its jurisdiction incidentally affecting underwater cultural heritage".[61] This article leaves the determination of the "best practicable means at its disposal" to each individual State.

6.8 Good archaeological practice

In the case of activities intentionally directed at underwater cultural heritage, UCH 2001 introduces, as Rules in the Annex, the principles of best practice in underwater archaeology.

Underwater archaeology differs from terrestrial archaeology in a number of ways. Firstly, due to the marine environment, underwater cultural heritage is often very well preserved, though extremely fragile, requiring long, expensive and complex conservation techniques. Secondly, in the case of wrecks, the wreck and its contents can be considered a 'time capsule' to the extent that, at the time of sinking, the wreck captures a point in time in history. All the artefacts at the site will have the same time reference, improving their contextual interpretation. Preservation *in situ* and the integrity of an underwater cultural heritage collection are therefore paramount concerns. Thirdly, the nature of the marine environment dictates the use of techniques and tools different from those used by archaeologists in terrestrial excavation. Indeed, for excavation on the deep seabed, the techniques and tools are also vastly different from those used in shallower depths.[62] Derived from equipment developed for commercial activities such as oil exploration, the equipment needed for a deep-sea excavation is extremely complex and expensive.

---

59 Comments of Canada working paper distributed at the Second Meeting of Governmental Experts, UNESCO Headquarters, Paris, 19–24 April 1999.
60 UCH 2001 Art 1(7).
61 Ibid. Art 5.
62 For example, apparently the first deep water archaeological excavation using only remotely operated vehicles was undertaken on the wreck of a 1622 Spanish caravel, 1,300 ft down in international waters off the coast of Florida, in the 1980s. See N Pickford, *The Atlas of Ships Wrecks and Treasure* (Dorling Kindersley 1994) 54.

The Rules in the Annex[63] sets out the benchmark standard for underwater archaeological excavations and concerns matters such as project design, standards of preliminary investigations, project methodology and techniques, project timetabling, competence and qualifications of personnel, material conservation, site management, project documentation, curation of project archives and the dissemination of project results.

A guiding principle of the Convention, contained both in Art 2 and in Rule 1 of the Annex, is that *in situ* preservation of underwater cultural heritage "shall be considered as the first option before allowing or engaging in any activities directed at this heritage". This principle reflects the recognition that before the underwater cultural heritage is disturbed or recovered, an appropriate archaeological investigation is undertaken according to the Annex, and that any decision to disturb or recover underwater cultural heritage is taken "for the purpose of making a significant contribution to protection or knowledge or enhancement" of underwater cultural heritage.[64] The principle of *in situ* preservation does not therefore mean that underwater cultural heritage is never recovered; only that it is recovered for a sound reason, and only after appropriate pre-disturbance archaeological investigation has been undertaken.

6.9 Jurisdictional structure

UCH 2001 addresses jurisdiction in three ways. First, it requires States to "take all practicable measures to ensure that their nationals and vessels flying their flag do not engage in any activity directed at underwater cultural heritage in a manner not in conformity with this Convention".[65] The use of this jurisdictional competency is not controversial, but may be of limited utility in protecting underwater cultural heritage given the ease in which these jurisdictions might be avoided, and the difficulty of compliance by flags of convenience and the ease at which the flag may be changed from one flag of convenience State to another.

Secondly, UCH 2001 requires States parties to "take measures to prohibit the use of their territory, including their maritime ports, as well as artificial islands, installations and structures under their exclusive jurisdiction or control, in support of any activity directed at underwater cultural heritage which is not in conformity with this Convention".[66] The intent is clear. If all States close to an unregulated excavation were party to the Convention, then those recovering the underwater cultural heritage contrary to the Rules in the Annex would have no place to refuel their vessels, obtain supplies or land the recovered material. While this may not deter the largest salvage capable vessels, it will certainly minimise interference by smaller operations. Exactly what measures can be taken is left to each State party. These measures though, will need to take into account the obligations of States to seize underwater cultural heritage in its territory that has been recovered in a manner not in

---

63 The Annex was based substantially on the 1996 ICOMOS Charter. The Annex is an integral part of the convention. UCH 2001 Art 33.
64 UCH 2001 Annex r 1.
65 UCH 2001 Art 16.
66 Ibid. Art 15.

conformity with this Convention⁶⁷ and to impose sanctions for violations of those measures it has taken to implement UCH 2001.⁶⁸

Thirdly, UCH 2001 utilises the jurisdictional structures provided for in UNCLOS to protect underwater cultural heritage in all maritime zones. This is reflected in Art 3:

> Nothing in this Convention shall prejudice the rights, jurisdiction and duties of States under international law, including the United Nations Convention on the Law of the Sea. This Convention shall be interpreted and applied in the context of and in a manner consistent with international law, including the United Nations Convention on the Law of the Sea.

This jurisdictional structure then is based on UNCLOS maritime zones and is to be interpreted consistency with UNCLOS. This includes Arts 303(4) and 322 of UNCLOS that anticipates clarification and expansion of UNCLOS regime in future agreements.⁶⁹

6.9.1 Internal waters, archipelagic waters and territorial sea

Within internal waters, archipelagic waters and territorial sea, the coastal State has, as an exercise of its sovereignty, the exclusive right to regulate and authorise activities directed at underwater cultural heritage.⁷⁰ Nevertheless, the coastal State, by becoming a signatory to the Convention, becomes duty-bound to apply the rules of the Annex in these maritime zones.⁷¹

The coastal State's exclusive jurisdiction to regulate underwater cultural heritage in these zones is not without controversy. Art 7(3) provides:

> Within their archipelagic waters and territorial sea, in the exercise of their sovereignty and in recognition of general practice among States, States Parties, with a view to cooperating on the best methods of protecting State vessels and aircraft, should inform the flag State Party to this Convention and, if applicable, other States with a verifiable link, especially a cultural, historical or archaeological link, with respect to the discovery of such identifiable State vessels and aircraft.

A number of States (especially the UK and the US) have objected to the exercise of this jurisdiction as 'exclusive', and to the obligation that the territorial State 'should', rather than 'must' inform the flag State of the discovery. In other words, this is seen as a direct challenge to the continued sovereign immunity of warships and other non-commercial governmental vessels.

While the territorial sea and internal waters are the most likely place to find underwater cultural heritage, they may also be found in rivers and other bodies of water. To the extent that recovery of underwater cultural heritage ought to be conducted in accordance with Rules in the Annex, the UCH 2001 provides that "[w]hen ratifying, accepting, approving or acceding to this Convention or at any time thereafter, any State or territory may declare that

---

67 Ibid. Art 18.
68 Ibid. Art 17.
69 See V Cogliati-Bantz and C Forrest, "Consistent: The Convention on the Protection of the Underwater Cultural Heritage and the United Nations Convention on the Law of the Sea" (2013) 2(3) *Cambridge International and Comparative Law Journal* [*Cogliati-Bantz & Forrest*] 1.
70 UCH 2001 Art 7(1). See for example, UK Protection of Wrecks Act 1973 and Protection of Military Remains Act 1986, 4.6.1 and 4.6.2.
71 UCH 2001 Art 7(2).

the Rules shall apply to inland waters not of a maritime character". This applies to rivers, lakes, dams and similar bodies of water.[72]

6.9.2 Contiguous zone

Art 8 of UCH 2001 provides that "States Parties may regulate and authorize activities directed at underwater cultural heritage within their contiguous zone. In so doing, they shall require that the Rules be applied".[73] This allows the State to extend its protective regime out a further 12 nm from the edge of the territorial sea (24 nm, from the territorial sea baseline—usually the low-water mark on shore). An increasing number of States are taking the opportunity to do so, providing for an expanded protective regime.[74]

6.9.3 Continental shelf and EEZ

While it was clear that on the continental shelf and exclusive economic zone UNCLOS did not grant the coastal State rights or duties with respect to underwater cultural heritage, it was recognised that the coastal State was best placed to provide surveillance and policing measures for underwater cultural heritage found in these zones, and should take the position of a coordinating State in determining how the underwater cultural heritage should be protected. The resulting jurisdictional structure of UCH 2001 relies on the principles of nationality and flag State jurisdiction rather than on any extension of coastal State jurisdiction over maritime zones beyond the contiguous zone. As the coastal State did not have exclusive sovereignty in these zones, the rights of the flag State were to be given greater regard than in the territorial waters of the coastal State. The resulting balance is that "no activity directed as State vessels and aircraft shall be conducted without the agreement of the flag State and the collaboration of the Coordinating State".[75] The regime is divided into two parts, the first dealing with reporting and notification in the exclusive economic zone and on the continental shelf[76] and the second with the implementation of the protection regime to underwater cultural heritage in these areas.[77]

With regard to notification and reporting, a complex system is structured to ensure that all interested States will be notified of the discovery of, or plans to undertake any activities directed at, underwater cultural heritage in these maritime areas. Coastal States are required to ensure that their nationals or vessels flying their flag report finds or intended activities to it.[78] Other States whose nationals or flag vessels find or intend to undertake activities directed at underwater cultural heritage on another State's continental shelf or exclusive economic zone are required to report to its competent authorities and to the authorities of the coastal State. Alternatively the other State need only require that the report be made

---

72 The waters surrounding crannogs in Europe and especially in Scotland have revealed significant underwater archaeological finds.
73 Art 8 begins with the phrase: "Without prejudice to and in addition to Art 9 and 10, and in accordance with Art 303, paragraph 2, of UNCLOS".
74 See further *Aznar, "Contiguous Zone"*, 1.
75 UCH 2001 Art 10(7).
76 Ibid. Art 9.
77 Ibid. Art 10.
78 Ibid. Art 9(1)(a).

to it and it undertakes to inform the coastal State.[79] States are then bound to inform the Director-General of UNESCO of any finds or reports of intended activities directed at underwater cultural heritage, who in turn informs all other States of any reports received.[80] Any State with a verifiable link, especially a cultural, historical or archaeological link with the underwater cultural heritage in question, may then declare its interest in being consulted on how the underwater cultural heritage may be effectively protected.[81]

In term of providing for a preservation regime in conformity with UCH 2001 for underwater cultural heritage on a coastal State's continental shelf or exclusive economic zone, the coastal State is not granted exclusive jurisdiction but rather is designated as the "co-ordinating State" in the preservation regime.[82] As such, it is responsible for the coordination with all other interested States in the protection regime and may implement the agreed measures of protection, including the conducting of preliminary research and all subsequent authorisation allowing activities directed at the underwater cultural heritage.[83] Furthermore, UCH 2001 allows the coastal State to take all practical measures to prevent immediate danger to underwater cultural heritage, include looting, before consultations with interested States take place.[84] These practical measures are, however, limited to the extent that they are in conformity with existing powers of coastal States in international law. This may therefore only apply to its nationals and flag vessels and to other nationals or vessels only with the agreement of their State. The coastal State only has the power to unilaterally prevent or authorise activities directed at underwater cultural heritage on its continental shelf or exclusive economic zone in order to prevent interference with its sovereign rights and jurisdictions as provided for by international law,[85] including UNCLOS.

In 2018 the first attempt to implement this regime was initiated by Italy when it informed UNESCO of the discovery of several cultural heritage sites, including wrecks ranging from the Roman era to the World Wars, on the Skerki Banks, located between Sicily, Sardinia and Tunisia, and lying on the continental shelf of Tunisia.[86] These sites are at risk from uncontrolled fishing and non-regulated passage of tankers and container ships over the sites. Tunisia and France declared an interest in cooperating to implement the UCH 2001 and establishing a mechanism to address the protection of these sites. This will provide an important case study on how UCH 2001 might operate in practice.

6.9.4 The Area

With regard to underwater cultural heritage found in the Area, which is defined as "the seabed and ocean floor and subsoil thereof, beyond the limits of national jurisdiction", the system for reporting, notification and implementation of the preservation regime is substantially similar to that applicable to the continental shelf and exclusive economic zone,

---

79 Ibid. Art 9(1)(b).
80 Ibid. Art 9(3), (4).
81 Ibid. Art 9(5).
82 Ibid. Art 10(3).
83 Ibid. Art 10(5).
84 Ibid. Art 10(4).
85 Ibid. Art 10(2).
86 UCH 2001 Scientific and Technical Advisory Body STAB 9th meeting report UCH/18/9.STAB/11, 8 June 2018.

except that as there will not be a coastal State to assume the role of coordinating State, all States which have expressed an interest in being a party to a preservation regime will elect one State to act as the coordinating State.[87] When the vessel found in the Area is a State vessel, the exclusive jurisdiction of the flag State is recognised.[88]

While this system of coordinated jurisdiction was a necessary compromise on which to base the protection regime, it is unfortunate in that it is overly bureaucratic and potentially time consuming. The implementation of a timely and effective protection regime may be hampered by the necessity of agreeing upon the regime by any number of States. The determination of which States will be able to participate in discussion on the regime is also hampered by uncertainties regarding the basis for the determination of a verifiable link to the underwater cultural heritage and the body responsible for this determination. Given the international nature of seafaring, it is possible for a number of States to have such a link, requiring complex negotiations on the structure of a protection regime amongst numerous States.

6.10 Regulatory and deterrent regime

6.10.1 Competent authorities and authorisation

The Rules in the Annex are standards of good archaeological practise that need to be applied to the investigation and excavation of underwater cultural heritage. For this to be effective, some body needs to evaluate the planned investigation or excavation to ensure that it complies with these standards.[89] UCH 2001 therefore imposes a duty on States to

> establish competent authorities or reinforce the existing ones where appropriate, with the aim of providing for the establishment, maintenance and updating of an inventory of underwater cultural heritage, the effective protection, conservation, presentation and management of underwater cultural heritage, as well as research and education.[90]

It is the competent authority that is to authorise activities directed at underwater cultural heritage in a manner consistent with UCH 2001.[91] In some jurisdictions, this may include the competent authority ensuring that while elements of salvage law or the law of finds may apply to the excavation of underwater cultural heritage, the competent authority only authorise such an excavation if it is "in full conformity with this Convention", and "ensures that any recovery of the underwater cultural heritage achieves its maximum protection".[92] This applies in a State's internal water, archipelagic water, territorial sea and contiguous

---

87 UCH 2001 Arts 12 and 13.
88 Ibid. Art 12(7).
89 A number of UNESCO Conventions and recommendations require the establishment of some authority to oversee the protection of cultural heritage. See for example, Arts 12–17, 1972 UNESCO Recommendation Concerning the Protection at National Level of the Cultural and natural Heritage Arts 12–17; Arts 5, 13 and 14, the 1970 Convention Arts 5, 13 and 14; 1954 Hague Convention Art 7 and 15; and World Heritage Convention Art 5.
90 UCH 2001 Art 22. States parties have to communicate the names and addresses of their competent authorities to the Director-General of UNESCO.
91 UCH 2001 Art 4 and Annex r 1, 2, 9–13 and 34. See further *Dromgoole, Underwater Cultural Heritage*, 308–312.
92 See generally *Dromgoole, Underwater Cultural Heritage*, 312–320.

zone.⁹³ In areas beyond coastal State jurisdiction, this authorisation will be granted by the "co-ordinating State", which in the case of underwater cultural heritage on the continental shelf will ordinarily be the coastal State.

6.10.2 Public awareness and training

While the tasks of the competent authority are largely set out in the Rules in the Annex, a number of obligations imposed on States party to UCH 2001 are likely to fall within the remit of the competent authority. This includes giving effect to Arts 20 and 21.

Article 20 of UCH 2001 is arguably the most important tool for the preservation of underwater cultural heritage.⁹⁴ This article simply requires that States "take all practical measures to raise public awareness regarding the value and significance of underwater cultural heritage and the importance of protecting it under the Convention". The mandatory requirement of creating a public awareness policy would supplement the requirement that States cooperate in the provision of training in underwater archaeology. The establishment of training facilities such as those envisaged in Art 21 are not only extremely expensive but also highly technical. Very few developing States have the resources or expertise to establish such facilities. Many of these States will require aid from developed States, particularly those with a rich tradition in underwater archaeology and underwater cultural heritage conservation. Thus Art 21 includes an obligation to cooperate in the transfer of technology relating to underwater cultural heritage. It is, however, unlikely that some States will allow the transfer of certain technology related to activities directed at underwater cultural heritage where the technology is connected with the defence industry.⁹⁵ As such, the transfer of technology will be on terms agreeable to the transferring State.

6.10.3 Sanctions and seizure

Article 17 requires States to impose sanctions for violations of measures it has taken to implement the Convention.⁹⁶ These are to be "adequate in severity to be effective in securing compliance with UCH 2001 and to discourage violations wherever they occur and shall deprive offenders of the benefit deriving from their illegal activities". It is left to the State to determine exactly what the sanctions might be. One, though, which is intended to act as a sanction and a significant deterrent, is the obligation to "take measures providing for the

---

93 UCH 2001 Arts 7 and 8.

94 Education and public awareness are important features of many international conventions aimed at the protection of the world cultural and natural heritage. See, for example, 1970 Convention, Art 10, 1954 Hague Convention Art 7 and 1956 UNESCO Recommendations Art 12.

95 For example, Dr Ballard has made extensive use of US naval vessels and technology, particularly the nuclear submarine NR-1 to search for underwater cultural heritage. See "Titanic Man Finds World's Oldest Ships 1,000 ft Down", *The Sunday Times* (27 June 1999).

96 The enforcement of international cultural heritage laws relies mostly on non-criminal sanctions such as the return, restitution and forfeiture of stolen goods. See J Nafziger, "International Penal Aspects of Protecting Cultural Property" (1985) 16 *Int Lawyer* 835; C Bassiouni, "Reflections on Criminal Jurisdiction in International Protection of Cultural Property" (1983) 10 *Syracuse J Int Law and Commerce* 281.

seizure" of underwater cultural heritage in its territory recovered in a manner not conforming with the Rules in the Annex.[97]

This obligation to take measures to seize applies not only to underwater cultural heritage recovered in those maritime zones over which that State has either jurisdiction (eg territorial sea) or control as the coordinating State (eg exclusive economic zone), but also underwater cultural heritage brought into the State's territory. This would include underwater cultural heritage excavated in some other maritime zone and then brought directly into the seizing State's territory. It also applies to that excavated and landed in another State and then brought into the seizing State's territory. A problem that might arise occurs when the underwater cultural heritage that has been seized by a particular State has an identifiable owner. The national laws of the State will therefore have to determine the rights of the owner in these circumstances.[98]

When exercising the right to seize underwater cultural heritage in accordance with Art 18(1), a State is under a duty to "record, protect and take all reasonable measures to stabilise" the underwater cultural heritage.[99] Importantly the duty is to "stabilise" underwater cultural heritage, not 'conserve' it.[100] Conservation of marine artefacts can be a costly and time-consuming activity, and to require all States to provide such a facility may be an onerous burden. To "stabilise" recovered artefacts might imply a less onerous duty than to 'conserve', being a short-term solution to mitigate deterioration rather than long-term conservation. The article also does not impose a mandatory duty, but rather requires a State to take all "reasonable" measures to stabilise artefacts. What "reasonable" measures are will depend on the coastal State's infrastructure, technical expertise and facilities, etc. Developing States may need the expertise of UNESCO and other interested States if the artefacts in these situations are to be conserved. Thus, Art 18(3) requires the seizing State to notify all other States that might have an interest in the underwater cultural heritage of its seizure, as well as UNESCO, and cooperate for the conservation of the underwater cultural heritage.[101]

Having "recorded, protected and conserved" the underwater cultural heritage, the seizing State will have to decide on the ultimate disposition of these artefacts. Article 18(4) provides that

> a State Party which has seized underwater cultural heritage shall ensure that its disposition be for the public benefit taking into account the needs of conservation and research; the need for re-assembly of a dispersed collection, the need for public access, exhibition and education and the interests of any State with a verifiable link, especially a cultural, historical or archaeological link, to the heritage concerned.

As Art 2(3) requires that underwater cultural heritage be preserved for the benefit of humanity, Art 18(4) attempts to give effect to this when a State has seized underwater cultural heritage. These terms are broad and thus subject to the seizing State's interpretation and implementation.

---

97 UCH 2001 Art 18(1). See generally *Dromgoole, Underwater Cultural Heritage*, 330–334.
98 In this case, the choice-of-law rules will be determined by the national courts. See 3.2.1.
99 UCH 2001 Art 18(2).
100 Earlier drafts of UCH 2001 had used the phrase "conserve" rather than 'stabilise'. See CLT-2000/CONF.201/8, Paris, 5 July 2000.
101 UCH 2001 Art 18(3).

THE LAW OF WRECK

6.11 International cooperation

The duty to cooperate is evident in the preamble,[102] in the general principles of the UCH 2001[103] and in a number of other provisions, including in relation to the enforcement of sanctions,[104] in information sharing,[105] in the provision of training in underwater archaeology[106] and in the jurisdictional structure established to deal with underwater cultural heritage beyond coastal State jurisdiction.

Article 19 reflects the extent of cooperation required. It imposes a duty on States to cooperate in the protection of underwater cultural heritage, which includes collaborating in the investigation, excavation, documentation, conservation, study and presentation of such heritage[107] as well as sharing information regarding discoveries of underwater cultural heritage, illicit excavations, scientific methodologies and technologies relating to underwater cultural heritage and legal developments in States to advance the protection of underwater cultural heritage.[108] It was realised that information regarding discoveries of underwater cultural heritage might endanger it if made public. As such, when such a risk occurs, States are required, as far as their national legislation allows, to keep such information confidential.[109]

Underwater cultural heritage, whether found in international or coastal waters, often has an international character, either in the origins of the vessel, its components, crew, cargo or trading routes. As such, it may be of archaeological, historical or cultural interest to a number of States. It is therefore incumbent on any State engaged in any activity directed at underwater cultural heritage, or authorising such activity, to endeavour to cooperate with any other State that might have an interest in that heritage. Such a State is referred to as a State with "a verifiable link, especially a cultural, historical or archaeological link", to the underwater cultural heritage. The interest of such a State is specifically referred to in relation to the seizure of underwater cultural heritage by a State[110] and in the regimes created for the territorial sea,[111] continental shelf and exclusive economic zone[112] and in the Area.[113] This mechanism, however, is poorly constructed. UCH 2001 does not give any direction as to how such a link should be ascertained, or by whom. For underwater cultural heritage found in the Area, this difficulty is compounded in that States are also required to pay regard to "the preferential right" of States with a cultural, historical or archaeological link to the underwater cultural heritage.[114] This notion of preferential rights derives from Art 149 of UNCLOS. However, as the derivation of any meaning from Art 149 has proved

---

102 UCH 2001 preamble tenth recital.
103 UCH 2001 Art 2(2).
104 Ibid. Art 17(3).
105 Ibid. Art 19.
106 Ibid. Art 21.
107 Ibid. Art 19(1).
108 Ibid. Art 19(2).
109 Ibid. Art 19(3).
110 Ibid. Art 18.
111 Ibid. Art 7(3).
112 Ibid. Art 9(5)
113 Ibid. Art 11(4), 12(6).
114 Ibid.

impossible,[115] its inclusion in UCH 2001 only goes to heighten difficulties in determining which States should be party to any cooperative protection regime—clearly inviting disputes.

6.12 Other agreements

Article 6 of UCH 2001 encouraged States to enter into bilateral, regional or other multilateral agreements or develop existing agreements, for the preservation of underwater cultural heritage consistent with UCH 2001 or which provides better protection of underwater cultural heritage than those adopted in UCH 2001. States with a verifiable link, especially a cultural, historical or archaeological link, to the underwater cultural heritage concerned, are especially encouraged to be part of such agreements.[116]

A number of States, most notably European, Latin American and Caribbean States, were concerned that UCH 2001 would not adequately protect underwater cultural heritage in certain regions and wished to ensure that more stringent protective measures could be introduced on a regional basis. The establishment of international agreements, whether bilateral or multilateral, global or regional, are a natural aspect of international law. As such this provision does not provide States with any rights or duties they do not already possess in international law. Nevertheless, promotion of regional agreements may enable certain objectives of UCH 2001 to be realised, such as assistance in the creation of public awareness and training.

The protection of the cultural heritage has been the subject of a number of regional agreements. Whilst not confined to underwater cultural heritage, the 1992 European Convention on the Protection of the Archaeological Heritage reflects such a regional approach.[117] States have, though, more often entered into agreements to protect or regulate the recovery of specific wrecks. For example, Sweden, Finland, Estonia, Latvia, Poland, Denmark, Russia and the UK concluded a multilateral agreement to protect the wreck of the *MS Estonia* that sank in 1994 in the Baltic with the loss of 852 lives.[118] More famously, the UK, US, France and Canada concluded an agreement to protect and regulate the recovery of artefacts from the *Titanic*.[119] However, the agreement has not come into force, though both the UK and US have adopted legislation that essentially gives effect to the agreement.[120] The agreement draws much from UCH 2001, particularly as the Annex of the agreement follow closely the Annex to UCH 2001. However, the agreement is not entirely consistent with UCH 2001 in

---

115 See C Forrest, "A New International Regime for the Protection of Underwater Cultural Heritage" (2002) 51(3) ICLQ 511, 513–514; *Dromgoole, Underwater Cultural Heritage*, 29–36.
116 UCH 2001 Art 6(2).
117 *Dromgoole, Underwater Cultural Heritage*, 83.
118 "Agreement Regarding the *M/S Estonia*" reprinted in (1996) 20 *Marine Policy* 355.
119 *R.M.S. Titanic*—International Agreement www.gc.noaa.gov/gcil_titanic-intl.html.
120 The UK ratified the Agreement on November 6, 2003 (Order No. 2496, 2003) which comes into force on the date on which the International Agreement enters into force in respect of the UK. The US signed the Agreement on June 18, 2004, subject to acceptance following the enactment of implementing legislation. This has not yet occurred. The earlier *R.M.S. Titanic* Maritime Memorial Act of 1986 (US) predates the Agreement and is insufficient to give effect to it. Nevertheless, in 2017 the Consolidated Appropriations Act, 2017 (Public Law 115–31) did require any salvage activity to be subject to the Agreement. See further NOAAwww.gc.noaa.gov/gcil_titanic-ref.html. See also *Dromgoole, "Titanic"*, 1–31; *Aznar & Varmer*, 96–112; *Varmer & Blanco*, 401.

that it recognises the application of salvage law to the *Titanic*, though subject to significant regulation. These include that artefacts are not recovered from inside the hull where human remains might be disturbed,[121] that the recovered artefacts be kept together as a single collection[122] and that recovery comply with the rules set out in the Annex to the Agreement.[123] The UK Protection of Wrecks (*RMS Titanic* Order)[124] in principle allows salvage but subject to the limitations provided for in the Agreement and set out again in the order.

States have, though, more often entered into bilateral agreements to protect or regulate the recovery of specific wrecks. These more often than not involve warships or government non-commercial vessels, and include for example, the agreements between US and France with respect to the *La Belle*, a French vessel sunk in US territorial waters 1686 and the *CSS Alabama*, a US warship sunk of Cherbourg in 1868; the agreement between Canada and UK with respect to the *HMS Erebus* and *HMS Terror*, sunk in 1848; the agreement between UK and Africa with respect to the *Birkenhead*, a UK vessel sunk in South African territorial waters in 1852; and the agreement between the Netherlands and Australia with respect to the VOC wrecks *Vergulde Draak, Batavia, Zeewijk* and *Zuitdorp* off Western Australia.[125]

6.13 Warships and other State-owned vessels

State vessels,[126] particularly warships, of the past clearly fall within the definition of underwater cultural heritage in UCH 2001 and should therefore be recovered in an archaeologically sound manner.[127] However, as discussed in Chapter 4, considerable problems continue to bedevil the recognition of sovereign immunity to such vessels, as well as questions of ownership and abandonment. These issues arose during negotiations, and indeed, were at the forefront of many of the negotiating difficulties and subsequent reluctance, and refusal, of some States to vote in favour of UCH 2001, and to subsequently become a party.

The resulting provisions regarding State vessels reflects these difficulties. The general principles of UCH 2001 include Art 2(8) which merely states that

> Consistent with State practice and international law, including the United Nations Convention on the Law of the Sea, nothing in this Convention shall be interpreted as modifying the rules of international law and State practice pertaining to sovereign immunities, nor any State's rights with respect to its State vessels and aircraft.

Given that the question of the abandonment and sovereign immunity of sunken warships is, to some extent, uncertain, this general principle simply maintains the uncertainty status quo. UCH 2001 does, however, go some way in determining what, for the purposes of the

---

121 Titanic Agreement Art 4.
122 Ibid. Art 3.
123 Ibid.
124 Order No. 2496, 2003.
125 See 4.7.
126 A "State vessel" is "defined in UCH 2001 Art 1.8 as any "warship, naval auxiliary, other vessel or aircraft owned or operated by a State for non-commercial purposes".
127 For example, the majority of wreck designated as being of historical or archaeological importance for the Protection of Wrecks Act 1973 are warships. See V Fenwick and A Gale, *Historic Shipwrecks: Discovered, Protected and Investigated* (Tempus Publishing, 1999).

Convention, a warships or other State vessel is. The definition contained in UCH 2001 declares that

> "State vessels and aircraft" means warships, and other vessels or aircraft that were owned or operated by a State and used, at the time of sinking, only for governmental non-commercial purposes, that are identifiable as such, and that meet the definition of underwater cultural heritage.

It is clear that only those State vessels that can be identified as such are subject to the State vessel regime of UCH 2001.[128] Those that cannot be clearly identified as State vessels will therefore be regarded as ordinary underwater cultural heritage to which UCH 2001 applies. While this does not solve the problems associated with the determination of whether a wreck is indeed that of a State vessel, the shifting of the onus of proof onto a State to clearly be able to identify it as such ensures that all questionable wrecks are included in the normal regime.

While most States agree with these principles, it is the manner in which State vessels have been addressed in the territorial sea, and to some extent the EEZ/continental shelf, that is problematic for States such as the UK and the US. The final compromise reached in Art 7(3) requires the coastal States to inform the flag State of the discovery of any of the latter's State vessels in the former's territorial waters.[129] The coastal State is clearly recognised as having exclusive jurisdiction in its territorial waters and that there is therefore no question of requiring the coastal State to defer to the exclusive jurisdiction of the flag State with regard to State vessels. But a number of States (especially the UK and the US) have objected to the exercise of this jurisdiction as "exclusive", and to the obligation that the territorial State "should", rather than 'must' inform the flag State of the discovery.[130] In other words, this is seen as a direct challenge to the continued sovereign immunity of warships and other non-commercial governmental vessels.

This objection does not, however, go directly to the issue of sovereign immunity. Indeed, neither this nor any other prescriptive rule in UCH 2001 refers to sovereign immunity.[131] Rather, the term "sovereign immunity" is used in Art 13 in relation to modern vessels that might discover underwater cultural heritage and, due to that immunity, are not required to report their finds as provided for in UCH 2001. Moreover, UCH 2001 does not make any changes to the concept of sovereign immunity. To the extent that there may be some disagreement as to its application to underwater cultural heritage, this general principle simply maintains the uncertainty status quo. Article 7(2), then, does not limit any existing obligation or restriction that the coastal State might have in relation to another State's state vessel in its territorial sea. The flag State may continue to rely on the concept of sovereign immunity in relation to such a vessel. But, as a term of UCH 2001, the coastal State "should" inform the flag State of such a discovery for the clearly stated purpose of

---

128 The Royal Navy Loss List, lists 3,486 Royal Naval losses between 1605 and 1945. Of these, 34.8% were lost in the UK territorial sea, EEZ or continental shelf; 44.5% in waters of other States; and 20.7% in the Area beyond coastal State jurisdiction. UK UNESCO 2001 Convention Review Group, *The UNESCO Convention on the Protection of the Underwater Cultural Heritage 2001: An Impact Review for the United Kingdom* (2014) 42.
129 UCH 2001 Art 7(3).
130 See 6.9.1.
131 UK UNESCO 2001 Convention Review Group, *The UNESCO Convention on the Protection of the Underwater Cultural Heritage 2001: An Impact Review for the United Kingdom* (2014) [*UNESCO Review, Underwater Cultural Heritage*] 41.

"cooperating on the best methods of protecting [the] State vessel". The application of the principle of sovereign immunity to such a vessel would not be inconsistent with this purpose. Moreover, the exhortation to inform the flag State relates only the discovery of a State vessel, and not to any activities to be directed at such a vessel. As such, UCH 2001 does not address directly the issue of sovereign immunity as it applied to activities directed at State vessels in the territorial sea.[132]

Importantly, it is not ownership of a vessel that dictates whether it falls within UCH 2001's definition of State vessel, but rather its use. More specifically, its use "at the time of sinking". This qualification is important as it is not necessarily a qualification that exists in customary or conventional international law dealing with sovereign immunity. For example, the Salvage Convention 1989 does not use this qualification, but rather provides that "warships or other non-commercial vessels owned or operated by a State entitled to sovereign immunity at the time of salvage operations" are immune from the terms of the Convention. The effect of the qualification "at the time of sinking" is arguably to expand those vessels that could be considered State vessels in UCH 2001 terms. That is because it would freeze the vessel's purpose at the time of sinking and no subsequent changes would alter the purpose at that time. Importantly, no change of ownership would undermine the recognition of a wreck as a State vessel, nor would the fact that the wreck no longer holds any technological, intelligence or other military function.[133] That the State function might change to that of a war grave would also not undermine the scope of that definition.[134]

The best way to protect State vessels is by cooperation between the coastal State and the flag State. The UCH 2001 therefore provides that the information passed to the flag State concerning the discovery of the State's vessel is undertaken "with a view to cooperating on the best methods of protecting State vessels and aircraft".[135] While the exclusive jurisdiction of the coastal State is recognised, this article must be read with the general principles, which provides that the UCH 2001 does not modify "the rules of international law and State practice pertaining to sovereign immunities, nor any State's rights with respect to its State vessels and aircraft".[136] While issues with abandonment and sovereign immunity might still exist, they are not directly affected by the UCH 2001, and thus no obstacle to State ratification.

A number of State vessels sunk in the course of battle with the loss of service personnel.[137] The concern is that these vessels should either not be disturbed, or if so, should be given appropriate respect. Warships that have sunk within the last 100 years will not fall within the scope of underwater cultural heritage, and will therefore not fall within the scope of the Convention. Any attempt to protect such a vessel in international waters will have to make use of bilateral or a further multilateral treaty. However, vessels that have

---

132 *UNESCO Review, Underwater Cultural Heritage*, 47–48.

133 So, for example, the wrecks of *HMS Aboukir, HMS Cressy* and *HMS Hogue*, very likely sold by the UK to salvors, would nevertheless be State vessels for the purpose of the UCH 2001 (and now Protected Places under the Protection of Military Remains Act). See *UNESCO Review, Underwater Cultural Heritage*, 52.

134 Though it would then be important to the Salvage Convention 1989 as the State function giving rise to immunity "at the time of salvage operations" would be recognition of the State's obligations and interest in the wreck as a maritime war grave.

135 UCH 2001 Art 7(3).

136 Ibid. Art 2(8).

137 For a discussion of the status of war graves in the UK, see *Williams*, 151.

been submerged for more than 100 years may also contain human remains,[138] or sank with the loss of life, especially those of World War I. The archaeological recovery of these vessels according to the rules in the Annex ensures that human remains are removed with due respect in accordance with standards.[139] As such, the general principles of UCH 2001 require State parties to ensure that proper respect is given to all human remains located in maritime waters.[140]

6.14 Implementation through UNESCO

As the Secretariat to UCH 2001, UNESCO provides a forum for the meeting of States parties and the meeting of the Scientific and Technical Advisory Body established by the States parties in 2009.[141] UNESCO also assists States parties in the implementation of the decisions made at these meetings and facilitates information exchange, particularly through organising regional and national meetings.

The Scientific and Technical Advisory Body fosters the development of scientific underwater archaeology and site protection. One of its first tasks was to adopt a Code of Ethics for Diving on Submerged Archaeological Sites, applicable to all divers in States parties and nationals of States parties. It also made recommendations on how to review national legislation protecting underwater cultural heritage, ensuring harmonised implementation of UCH 2001 in national law. The advisory body has provided direct assistance and advice to States on particular underwater cultural heritage, especially that at risk from commercial exploitation or from other threats.[142] This has included, for example, an investigation in Haiti on what had been thought to be the discovery of the wreck of Christopher Columbus' *Santa Maria*[143] and in Madagascar on what was thought to be the wreck of Captain Kidd's *Adventure Galley*.[144] Both investigations revealed that the commercial interests in the sites had misidentified them.

6.15 State practice

Having been adopted by a vote rather than by consensus, concerns arose as to whether the convention would ever enter into force, given the decision of many key States such as the UK, France and Germany to abstain from voting. Nevertheless, UCH 2001 did come into force on 2 January 2009, three months after the 20th ratification—that of Barbados.[145]

---

138 Though there are exceptions. Human remains have been found to exist on underwater cultural heritage sites, especially wrecks, which were lost over 100 years ago. For example, human remains were discovered on the site of the *Mary Rose*, which sank in 1545.

139 Reference may be made to the International Council of Museums Code of Ethics (1986) and the Museums Association (UK) Code of Ethics for Museum Professionals (1977, amended 1987) which require ethical and legal consideration to be given to recovery of human remains.

140 UCH 2001 Art 2(9). On the recovery of human remains in contemporary wrecks, see 13.1.3.

141 Meeting of States Parties to the Convention on the Protection of the Underwater Cultural Heritage UCH/09/2.MSP/220/4, 15 September 2009 Resolution 5 MSP.1.

142 See www.unesco.org/new/en/culture/themes/underwater-cultural-heritage/.

143 It was found to be a wreck of a later date. STAB Report
     www.unesco.org/new/fileadmin/MULTIMEDIA/HQ/CLT/images/Haiti-STAB-en.pdf.

144 It was found in fact to be merely remain of the old port construction of Sainte-Marie: www.unesco.org/new/fileadmin/MULTIMEDIA/HQ/CLT/pdf/Rapport_Madagascar_EN_public.pdf.

145 UCH 2001 Art 27.

There are a number of States who view the UCH 2001 favourably but have not yet ratified it, such as Australia, the Netherlands, Germany and the Republic of Ireland, primarily due to the need to amend national legislation together with the administrative inertia that arises from the low priority many cultural heritage issues have within many States' international convention ratification processes.[146]

While other States may also not be party to the Convention, these do not have the same interest as the US and UK, both of which have significant underwater cultural heritage in their waters but also significant wrecks lying in international waters or in other States' waters.

6.15.1 US position

The US was not a member of UNESCO at the time negotiations were taking place but did send a large observer delegation.[147] While not entitled to vote, the US delegation did indicate that it would not have voted in favour of the Convention, though it did support the Rules in the Annex.[148] Its concerns centred on the compatibility between the UCH 2001 and UNCLOS—despite the US not being party to UNCLOS—and concerns with the extent to which UCH 2001 supported sovereign immunity. Moreover, the US has arguably the largest historic wreck salvage industry, and one of those salvors—Odyssey Marine Exploration—has been active in European waters and is involved with a number of controversial operations associated with British vessels, such as *HMS Sussex*, *HMS Victory* and the *Gairsoppa*. Nevertheless, US federal law is, in many respects, consistent with the Convention, particularly the Abandoned Shipwreck Act and Sunken Military Craft Act,[149] as well as a number of other federal laws that apply directly or indirectly to underwater cultural hertiage.[150]

However, this does not extend to activities by US salvors in waters outside the US but made subject to US admiralty jurisdiction through the employment of the fiction that any part of the wreck brought into the jurisdiction of the US Admiralty Court represent the wreck itself such that the whole wreck is then subject to US admiralty jurisdiction. In such cases the US law of salvage and finds is applied. In determining the salvage award, US admiralty courts have taken into account the extent to which the salvor has applied

---

146 On Ireland's position, see S Kirwan, "Ireland and the UNESCO Convention on the protection of the Underwater Cultural Heritage" (2010) 5 *J Maritime Archaeology* 105.

147 Indeed, the US had the largest delegation during negotiations, and the most diverse delegation membership, drawing members from various federal government departments as well as salvors in the private sector.

148 UNESCO Doc UCH/09/2.MSO/220/4 REV., Annex, 12. See further *Varmer, "United States"*, 351; O Varmer, J Gray and D Alberg, "United States: Responses to the 2001 UNESCO Convention on the Protection of the Underwater Cultural Heritage" (2010) 5 *J Maritime Archaeology* 129; *Varmer & Blanco*, 401; S Dromgoole, "Reflections on the Position of the Major Maritime Powers with Respect to the UNESCO Convention on the Protection of the Underwater Cultural Heritage" (2013) 38 *Marine Policy* [*Dromgoole, "Reflections UNESCO"*] 116.

149 See D Bederman, "Congress Enacts Increased Protections for Sunken Military Craft" (2006) 100 AJIL 649.

150 Such as the Antiquities Act, Archaeological Resources Protection Act and National Marine Sanctuaries Act.

underwater archaeological techniques to the recovery operation, but not to the extent required of the UCH 2001.[151]

6.15.2 UK position

The UK abstained from voting in favour of UCH 2001 and, despite supporting its objectives and recognising the need for an international regulatory regime, cited three specific concerns.[152]

The first relates to warships and State vessels and aircraft used on non-commercial service and what the UK saw as "*competing claims* of the Sovereign Immunity enjoyed by Flag States on the one hand and jurisdictional claims of Coastal States on the other".[153] This concern was particularly acute in relation to Art 7(3),[154] in that it recognises the exclusive jurisdiction of the coastal State in its territorial waters and that the obligation that the coastal State has with respect to informing the flag State of the discovery of a State vessel is not mandatory. The use of the word "should", rather than 'must', the UK argued, "erodes the fundamental principles of customary international law, codified in UNCLOS, of Sovereign Immunity which is retained by a State's warships and vessels and aircraft used for non-commercial service until expressly abandoned by that State". In other words, UCH 2001 was seen as a direct challenge to the continued sovereign immunity of warships and other non-commercial governmental vessels.

A review of this position has, however, questioned this and concluded that the UCH 2001 does not pose any threat to the continued recognition of sovereign immunity to State vessels.[155] The report notes that UCH 2001 quite explicitly does not make any changes to the existing international law of sovereign immunity reflected quite clearly in Art 2(8) which provides that nothing in UCH 2001 shall be interpreted as modifying the rules of international law and State practice pertaining to sovereign immunities. So, while Arts 7(2) and 10(7) do set out how States deal with State vessels in the territorial sea and EEZ/

---

151 See J Nafziger, "The UNESCO Convention on the Protection of the Underwater Cultural Heritage: Its Growing Influence" 2018 (49) JMLC 371, 375–379; On the US national protective regime see *Varmer, "United States"*, 351.

152 Reprinted as Appendix 1.1: UK Explanation of Vote on the UNESCO Convention *on the Protection of the Underwater Cultural Heritage*, 31 October 2001 in *UNESCO Review, Underwater Cultural Heritage*, 87. On the UK explanation of vote, developments in the UK and future prospects, see M Williams, "UNESCO Convention on the Protection of the Underwater Cultural Heritage: An Analysis of the United Kingdom's Standpoint" (The UNESCO Convention for the Protection of the Underwater Cultural Heritage: Proceedings of the Burlington House Seminar, London, October 2005) 2; H Roberts, "The British Ratification of the Underwater Cultural heritage Convention: Problems and Prospects" (2018) 67 ICLQ 833; R Yorke, "The UNESCO Convention and the Protection of Underwater Cultural Heritage in International Waters: The United Kingdom Situation" (2010) 5 *J Maritime Archaeology* 153 [*Yorke, "UNESCO Convention"*]; J Gribble, "The UNESCO Convention and the Protection of Underwater Cultural Heritage 2001: An Impact Review for the United Kingdom: Project Design" (2011) 6 *J Maritime Archaeology* 77; M Aznar, "The Legal protection of Underwater Cultural Heritage: Concerns and Proposals" in C Espósito, J Kraska, H Scheiber and Moon-Song Kwon, *Ocean Law and Policy: 20 Years under UNCLOS* (Brill Nijhoff, 2017) [*Aznar, "Underwater Cultural Heritage"*] 124; Dromgoole, *"Reflections UNESCO"*, 116.

153 Authors' emphasis added.

154 And also in relation to Art 10(7) as applied in the EEZ/continental shelf.

155 *UNESCO Review, Underwater Cultural Heritage*.

continental shelf, respectively, they are subject to the overriding principles of sovereign immunity. These principles are not diluted or abrogated by the provisions of UCH 2001 and can continue to be invoked by the UK. This is further supported by the Institute of International Law's[156] 2015 Resolution on The Legal Regime of Wrecks of Warships and Other State-Owned Ships in International Law, which provides that "sunken State vessels are immune from the jurisdiction of any State other than the flag State", and in Art 7 that the rights of a coastal State in its territorial waters are without prejudice to the immunity of State vessels are provided for in Art 3.[157]

Sovereign immunity is an immunity from the coastal State jurisdiction and thus a limitation on that State. While it is international law, it does nevertheless pit one jurisdictional capacity against another and acts to rein in coastal State powers—something coastal States are not inclined to welcome. While the UK might wish to use sovereign immunity as a protective shield when State vessels lie in other State's waters, this is not the most advantageous mechanism to promote respect and the protection of these wrecks.

The UCH 2001 is, above all, a Convention that creates a regime of State cooperation. It is a foundational principle as set out in Art 2(2)[158] and applied in the territorial sea,[159] the EEZ/continental shelf[160] and the Area,[161] and with respect to information sharing,[162] training[163] and the enforcement of sanctions.[164] It is difficult to see how such a regime could undermine the protection of State vessels or offer much more than the potentially divisive application of sovereign immunity to wrecks in other State's waters.

The second concern the UK had with UCH 2001 was that it appeared to require that it "extend the same very high standards of protection to all underwater archaeology over 100 years old". It contended that as there were about 10,000 wrecks in the UK territorial sea, it was neither "possible nor desirable to extend legal protection to all of them". Even the qualification that UCH is only that which has "a cultural, historical or archaeological character" could not dissuade the UK from taking the position that only "significant" underwater cultural heritage should be subject to a conventional regime.

The UK appears to have misunderstood the scope of the convention, or at least to have interpreted UCH 2001 through the lens of its own approach to heritage management rather than on the Convention's own terms.[165] As explained in Chapter 4, the Protection of Wrecks Act focuses on specific historic wreck considered to be "important and unique examples

---

156 The Institute of International Law (*Institut de droit international*) was founded in 1873 at an institution independent of any governmental influence which would be able both to contribute to the development of international law and act so that it might be implemented. See www.idi-iil.org/en/a-propos/.

157 *Ronzitti* (2015) 371.

158 See also the 11th preambular recital.

159 UCH 2001 Art 7.

160 Ibid. Arts 9(5), 10.

161 Ibid. Arts 11(4), 12.

162 Ibid. Art 19.

163 Ibid. Art 21.

164 Ibid. Art 17(3).

165 See in detail *UNESCO Review, Underwater Cultural Heritage*, 55–70. For a history of the development of the UK's policy and legislation see A Firth, "UK Safeguarding of Underwater Cultural Heritage: Factual Background", *Unpublished briefing paper for BA/HFF Steering Committee on Underwater Cultural Heritage* (Ffordr Ref: 16200. Tisbury Ffordr Limited, 2014) 1–4.

of underwater cultural heritage".[166] The Act is site orientated and regulates all activities on each site, including those that do not disturb the site, and many cases, even access to the site. The UK then assumed that the UCH 2001 would thus require this regime to be replicated for every site in its territorial waters (estimated at about 10,000, when in fact it is more like 1,000).[167] But the UCH 2001 does not require this. What the UCH 2001 does is regulate activities directed at underwater cultural heritage.[168] As the 2014 Impact Review so neatly points out, "it is not the number of wrecks within a State party's territorial sea that is critical for implementing the 2001 Convention, but the number of activities directed at such sites".[169] As such, it requires the Convention, and especially the Annex, to be applied when an activity is to be directed at a site. If there is no intention to direct an activity at the site, then nothing is required. There would not therefore be any significant increase in administrative responsibilities or costs for the UK to implement the UCH 2001 in terms of site management.[170]

The third concerns raised by the UK related to the relationship between the UCH 2001 and UNCLOS, particularly with respect to the possible powers granted to the coordinating State, which is most likely to be the coastal State, with respect to underwater cultural heritage on the continental shelf.[171] It is clear that the UCH 2001 does address issues that were not addressed in UNCLOS, but this is not necessarily the issue since UNCLOS, whilst a constitution for the oceans is not set in stone and includes a mechanism that does allows for future development in matters covered by the Convention. Article 311 expressly allow for a matter to be regulated by another international agreement as *lex specialis* and allows for its parties to conclude *inter se* agreements modifying its terms. Moreover, it does not prejudice agreements that are *compatible* with it and do not affect the rights and obligations of other parties to UNCLOS. That a new Convention may be negotiated is not only reflected in Art 303(4) but is expressly provided for by Art 311.[172] To this extent the UCH 2001 is compatible with UNCLOS;[173] a view which is apparently supported by the General Assembly of the United Nations which, in its 2012 Resolution on Ocean Governance, noted:

> the recent deposit of instruments of ratification and acceptance of the 2001 Convention on the Protection of the Underwater Cultural Heritage calls upon States that have not yet done so to consider becoming parties to that Convention, and notes in particular the rules annexed to that Convention, which address the relationship between salvage law and scientific principles of management, conservation and protection of underwater cultural heritage among Parties, their nationals and vessels flying their flag.[174]

---

166 *UNESCO Review, Underwater Cultural Heritage*, 87.
167 Ibid.
168 UCH 2001 Art 1(6).
169 Ibid. 55.
170 This might entail, for example, the use of pre-disturbance surveys, something that is not necessarily mandated by the UCH 2001; Ibid. 58.
171 See *Cogliati-Bantz & Forrest*, 1; Dromgoole, "Reflections UNESCO", 119.
172 *Cogliati-Bantz & Forrest*, 545–551.
173 A Gonzalez, "Negotiating the Convention on Underwater Cultural Heritage: Myths and Reality", in R Garabello and T Scovazzi, *The Protection of Underwater Cultural Heritage: Before and After the 2001 UNESCO Convention* (Martinus Nijhoff, 2003) 116–121.; Dromgoole, "Reflections UNESCO", 116; Aznar, "Underwater Cultural Heritage", 124, 134.
174 GA Res A/Res/66/231, 5 April 2012. See also the European Community support for the Convention: Commission of the European Communities *EC Green Paper: Towards a Future Maritime Policy for the Union: A European Vision for the Ocean and Seas*, COM (2006) 275 final, Vol II—Annex (7 June 2006).

In this light, there have been a number of calls for the UK to ratify the Convention.[175] However, the UK government has struggled to respond to the issue and had to deal with a range of controversial decisions in recent years. Part of the controversy lies in the fact that while the UK has three concerns with the UCH 2001 'main text', it has no concerns with the Rules in the Annex and has adopted these as government policy.[176] This, however, has not been consistently implemented by the MOD leading to significant controversy over the salvage contract entered into with commercial salvors for the recovery *HMS Sussex*,[177] *HMS Victory*[178] and *HMS Gloucester*.[179] Similarly, the DfT too concluded salvage contracts with the same salvage company (Odyssey Marine Exploration) in relation to the salvage of merchant vessels lost during war, the *Gairsoppa*[180] and *Mantola*,[181] with terms inconsistent with the Rules in the Annex. These two ministries, together with Treasury and the Department of Culture, Media and Sport,[182] have been engaged in policy review in relation to these 'government assets'. An early response was the publication of the Department of Culture, Media and Sport and the MOD Guidelines on "Protection and Management of

---

175 In 2005, a seminar hosted by the Society of Antiquities of London (Burlington House) considered the UK position and, convinced that the UCH 2001 ought to be ratified by the UK, called on the government to re-evaluate its position. The Joint Nautical Archaeology Committee, *The UNESCO Convention on the Protection of Underwater Cultural Heritage: Proceedings of the Burlington House Seminar October 2005*, 41. The Burlington House Declaration of 28 October 2005 is also restated in Yorke, *"UNESCO Convention"*, 155. See also UK National Commission for UNESCO, *UNESCO Convention on the Protection of the Underwater Cultural Heritage: Next Steps for the UK government* Policy Brief 17, March 2015 and British Academy/Honor Frost Foundation Steering Committee on Underwater Cultural Heritage *2001 UNESCO Convention on the Protection of Underwater Cultural Heritage: The Case for UK Ratification* (March 2014): http://honorfrostfoundation.org/wp/wp-content/uploads/2016/04/2001-Convention-The-Case-for-Ratification-FINAL.pdf and www.unesco.org.uk/wp-content/uploads/2015/05/UKNC-Policy-Brief-17_Underwater-Cultural-Heritage_March-2015_REVISED.pdf.

176 *Protection and Management of Historic Military Wrecks outside UK Territorial Waters: Guidance on How Existing Policies and Legislation Apply to Historic Military Wreck Sites* (DMCS and the Ministry of Defence, April 2014) 4–5. See also UK National Commission for UNESCO, *UNESCO Convention on the Protection of the Underwater Cultural Heritage: Next Steps for the UK Government*, Policy Brief 17, March 2015, 3, 11 See also Parliamentary answer by M Lancaster, Minister of State for the Armed Forces, 6 June 2016 c 38932. The UK explanation supported this position by declaring that "[t]he procedures for the protection of underwater archaeology adopted in the Annex are those which are already followed by the United Kingdom with regard to the designation of wreck sites within its territorial sea and internal waters". See further *Dromgoole, Underwater Cultural Heritage*, 36–47.

177 Sunk in 1694.

178 Sunk in 1744 with the loss of over 1,000 crew. In 2019, the charity Maritime Heritage Foundation, to whom the *HMS Victory* was gifted, initiated Judicial Review proceedings in relation to the MOD's refusal to grant permission for excavation of the wreck. See *"HMS Victory*: The English Channel's 'abandoned shipwreck'", www.bbc.com/news/uk-england-47044932.

179 Sunk in 1682.

180 Sunk in 1941 by a U-boat. The conclusion of the salvage contract between the DfT and Odyssey Marine Exploration for the salvage of the *SS Gairsoppa* was a debacle. The DfT had to settle a claim for £16 million by another salvage company in relation to the botched tender process that awarded Odyssey Marine Exploration. Moreover, Odyssey Marine Exploration retained almost £5 million that the MOD is considering pursuing in a legal action. See Parliamentary answers by R Goodwill, Minister of State for Transport, 5 June 2015 c 515; J Hayes and Minister of State for Transport, 10 July 2017 c 2324.

181 Sunk in 1917 by a U-boat.

182 Now the Department of Digital, Culture, Media and Sport.

Historic Military Wrecks outside UK Territorial Waters" in 2014.[183] While indicating that in response to the 2014 Impact Review, the UK position would be reconsidered, in 2017, the Department of Digital, Culture, Media and Sport announced that such a review would be deferred while it focused its efforts and resources on "delivering new and more immediate priorities".[184] In this light, it is unlikely that the UK will ratify the UCH 2001 in the foreseeable future.

6.16 Conclusion

While the UCH 2001 may lack clarity in many respects and includes provisions as the non-commercialisation of underwater cultural heritage and the inclusion of State vessels in the regime that a small number of States find problematic, it should be welcomed as the first international regime to provide a protective framework for the world's underwater cultural heritage, and pave the way for the development of an effective protection regime for underwater cultural heritage beyond coastal State jurisdiction. This is particularly so in regard to underwater cultural heritage on the continental shelf, where it is expected a great amount of underwater cultural heritage will be discovered in the near future due to further advancements in diving and underwater technology.

---

183 *Protection and Management of Historic Military Wrecks outside UK Territorial Waters: Guidance on How Existing Policies and Legislation Apply to Historic Military Wreck Sites* (DMCS and the Ministry of Defence, April 2014)
file:///H:/2016%20Wreck%20Books/Protection_and_Management_of_Historic_Military_Wrecks_outside_UK_Territorial_Waters__April_2014.pdf.
184 House of Commons HC DEB, 31 October 2017. cWS.

PART II

WRECK REMOVAL CONVENTION 2007

CHAPTER 7

Wreck Removal Convention 2007

Creation

7.1 Need for a Wreck Removal Convention

The *Torrey Canyon*[1] disaster provoked a review of a wide range of matters associated with wrecked ships, oil pollution, ship safety and "[t]he extent to which a State directly threatened or affected by a casualty which takes place outside its territorial sea can, or should be entitled to, take measures to protect its coastline, harbours, territorial sea or amenities, even when such measures may affect the interest of shipowners, salvage companies and insurers and even of a flag government".[2] Included within this was the extent to which this might be applied to wrecks.

Wreck removal was not, however, a new phenomenon when the *Torrey Canyon* became a wreck. Wreck removal has taken place whenever wrecks have proved to be some form of hazard, particularly at port entrances or within ports themselves, and usually arose because the cost of removing the hazardous wreck exceeds the 'salvage' value of the wreck.[3] Addressing issues such as who should move the wreck, and perhaps more importantly, bear the costs of wreck removal, was dealt with at a national level or even local level given the location of the wreck.[4] The localised effect of wrecks had meant that it had never been addressed at an international level until the *Torrey Canyon* sank.

Following the *Torrey Canyon*'s wrecking, it was not clear what powers States had to require that action be taken in respect of the wreck beyond its territorial sea, unless they can exert some form of commercial, rather than legal, pressure.[5] If a State then wanted to bear the costs of removal itself, it is unlikely that an owner would object and insist that its vessel be left alone. The owner would normally be happy for anybody to assume rights of possession or ownership. The problem though remained that the powers of States, in international law, to deal with and regulate wrecks off their coasts, was unclear.[6] Such doubts arose in numerous incidents following the *Torrey Canyon*, including the sinking of the *Mont Louis*

---

1 See 1.2.1.
2 C/ES. III/5 8 May 1967, 5.
3 See *Smit Tak Offshore Services v Youell* [1991] 2 Lloyd's Rep 420.
4 See eg *The Putbus* [1969] P 136 and 11.1.2.
5 See, eg *Smit Tak Offshore Services v Youell* [1991] 2 Lloyd's Rep 420.
6 States such as the Netherlands and Germany experienced considerable difficulties with wreck lying beyond their territorial seas, posing a hazard to navigation or to their coastlines or economic interests, and attempted to regulate their removal without any clear national or international mandate to do so: LEG 75/6/1, 14 February 1997, Annex, 3.

and its nuclear cargo just outside Belgian territorial waters in 1984.[7] While Belgian authorities had issued a wreck removal order, it was not clear that they had the authority to do so. Moreover, concern existed over the extent to which shipowners could be forced to pay the costs of wreck removal and related operations, and to maintain appropriate insurance to cover those costs.

Most wrecks which pose navigational or pollution hazards tend to lie in the territorial waters of States. States have generally created national laws giving authority to remove such wrecks, and have tried various ways to shift the costs to shipowners. Powers to sell a wreck have proven to be of little use where the removal costs far exceed any remaining value; if there had been a net value, salvors and shipowners would usually undertake the work themselves. National laws, even in the 19th century, responded by creating strict liability regimes for shipowners.[8] The problem is that States have often had to bear the expense themselves where the shipowner is insolvent. In many cases, the shipowner will be a single ship company with few assets other than the (now valueless) ship, apart from possible hull insurance proceeds. Even a valid legal claim may be difficult to maintain against a foreign single ship company, with many other creditors, that refuses to respond. So, for example, the removal of the *MV Anna Broere* in 1988 cost the Dutch government 11 million Dutch guilders and that of the *MV Nordfrakt* 8 million Dutch guilders.[9] Similarly, in 1997, the Belize registered cargo ship *An Tai* sank in Port Klang, Malaysia. The wreck was both a navigational and pollution hazard and the authorities ordered the shipowner to remove the wreck. The owner ignored the order, necessitating State action to remove it and disperse the pollutants, at a cost to the Malaysian authorities of 18 million ringgits. This cost could not be recovered from the shipowner, or its insurer, which indicated that there were 'reservations' to the insurance cover (presumably including wreck removal).[10] The UK too has had this experience, being unable to recover the £1.25 million cost of removing the wreck of the Antigua and Barbuda registered general cargo ship *Lagik*, and removing the resulting pollution, when she broke her back and blocked the port of Wisbech for 44 days in 2000.[11]

These legal gaps and uncertainties arose again in 2002 when the Norwegian-flagged vehicle carrier *Tricolor* was struck by the Bahamian-flagged container ship *Kariba* in the French EEZ some 20 miles north of the French coast in the English Channel.[12] As a result

---

7 See N Gaskell, "Lessons of the Mont Louis Part One: Prevention of Hybrid Accidents" (1986) 1 IJECL [*Gaskell, Mont Louis Part One*] 117, 149; also 10.8.1, 10.9.3.

8 See eg LEG 63/5 18 May 1990 and LEG 74/5/2/Add 1, 5 September 1996. The UK legislation is typical and has had to deal with issues such as the identity of the person liable when ownership changes after the ship is wrecked: see 11.1.2, 11.1.3.

9 Between 1987 and 1994, the Netherlands government had to remove at least 12 wrecks located just outside the territorial sea. LEG 74/13 22 October 1996, para 35. For other examples of wrecks that required removal, see LEG 75/6/1, 14 February 1997, Annex, 1.

10 See LEG 83/5/2, 14 September 2001; LEG 83/14, 23 October 2001, 18. Note Malaysia's subsequent accession to the WRC 2007 and the enactment of its Merchant Shipping (Amendment and Extension) Act 2011.

11 UK DfT Consultation Document "UK Implementation and Ratification of the Nairobi International Convention of the Removal of Wrecks (2007)" http://webarchive.nationalarchives.gov.uk/20091003113932/; www.dft.gov.uk/consultations/archive/2008/removalofwrecks2007/. See also 11.1.2(b).

12 See "Crash Ship Crew 'Oblivious' of Wreck", *BBC World News*, http://news.bbc.co.uk/2/hi/uk_news/2620957.stm. See also A Clennell and J Henley, "Fuel Tanker Hits Sunken Ship in Channel", *Guardian*,

of the collision the *Tricolor* sank and became a total loss, but it proved to be a significant navigational hazard in one of the world's busiest shipping lanes. Indeed, two other vessels subsequently collided with the wreck. On 16 December 2002, the *Nicola* hit the wreck of the *Tricolor* and had to be towed off using tugs. Similarly, on 1 January 2003, the cargo ship *Vicky* hit and was stuck on the wreck of the *Tricolor* for some hours. While French authorities ordered the *Tricolor* to be removed, doubts existed as to the authority of a coastal State to regulate the removal of wreck in its EEZ. The sinking of the *Hyundai 105* in the busy shipping lane in Indonesian waters in the Strait of Singapore further illustrated the pollution and navigational hazards posed by wrecks.[13]

Throughout this period, from the sinking of the *Torrey Canyon* to the *Tricolor*, the IMO was engaged (at various levels of commitment) with the issue of wreck removal. Existing national legislation had dealt with the issue at a local level for some time, and the need for consistency in maritime law meant that the fundamental principles embedded in this national law was a starting point for considering an international convention on wreck removal.

As noted in Chapter 5, there is uncertainty as to the scope of a coastal State's intervention powers in customary international law, a lack of clarity in the existing convention regimes (Intervention Convention 1969[14] and UNCLOS[15]) and an apparent 'gap' in delimiting a coastal State's powers in relation to wreck beyond the territorial seas.

To fully understand the WRC 2007, it is necessary to consider the prolonged drafting process of the Convention and the difficult international law questions which bedeviled it.

7.2 Development of WRC 2007[16]

7.2.1 Initial negotiations 1967–1990

Following the grounding of the *Torrey Canyon*, IMCO convened an extraordinary session on 8 May 1967 to address issues arising from the incident. Included amongst them, as Item 16, was the issue of compensation and compulsory insurance.[17] Where appropriate, these issues were to be studied in consultation with other interested international agencies.[18] An interested entity was the CMI, which met later that same month, and established an International Sub-committee to consider the issues arising from the incident. An important element of the IMCO response was the establishment of an Ad Hoc Legal Committee to consider many of the issues arising, which met, for the first time, on 21 June 1967. The Ad Hoc IMCO Legal Committee asked the CMI to cooperate on Item 16 and a joint meeting was held later that year. By the time a working group of the CMI International Sub-committee met in Rome on 4–5 October 1967, the French claims arising from the *Torrey Canyon*

---

www.theguardian.com/uk/2003/jan/02/jonhenley. For details of the recovery operation, see www.tricolorsalvage.com.

13 LEG 92/13, 3 November 2006, 7.
14 See 5.3.
15 Particularly in relation to UNCLOS Art 221.
16 See R Shaw, "The Nairobi Wreck Removal Convention" (2007) 13 JIML 429, 431.
17 C/ES.III/5 8 May 1967. See also LEG 140/14, 16 January 2017.
18 C/ES.III/5 8 May 1967, 1.

were estimated at 40 million francs.[19] The report produced a questionnaire for member associations, also drawing attention to the fact that States viewed IMCO as the appropriate forum, rather than the commercially focused CMI, to address the range of issues arising from the incident.[20] The questionnaire responses were considered by the working group and it reported to the CMI International Sub-committee[21] that most had opposed strict liability and opted to retain limitation of liability in order to facilitate insurance coverage. A preliminary draft of a convention emerged[22] at the Tokyo Conference in April 1969.[23]

By that time IMCO had produced a draft convention. It did not, however, fully address all wreck removal issues. The focus at this stage was concerned mostly on hazards to navigation caused by wrecks. The Spanish Maritime Law Association produced a draft convention, prepared by Professor Santiago Yzal, "on the elimination of shipwrecked vessels on the high seas which might be a danger to navigation". An unofficial and undated English translation of this French document was made available by the IMCO Secretariat in 1969.[24] The Yzal draft did not contain draft articles but was more of a commentary setting out principles, under broad headings, of what might be covered. It contained some novel features which were not to be seen again, eg the idea that contracting States might have the ultimate obligation to remove wrecks, the costs being incurred in proportion to their tonnage in a particular year.[25] In reality, it was more of a discussion document than a serious basis for drafting, but it did highlight a number of issues that recurred later in discussions, eg the need to identify the waters in which a regime would apply,[26] the need for reporting and how to decide who did what with the wreck.

In May 1969, wreck was not yet an item on the Legal Committee's work programme.[27] Later that month, the Federal Republic of Germany's delegate drew the attention of the IMCO Council[28] to the Yzal draft convention proposal, which had apparently been circulated by the CMI to member States. In October 1969, the IMCO Assembly did not place wreck removal on the priority list for the Legal Committee for 1970–1971, owing to a lack of information on progress in studies about the subject, but did invite the Legal Committee itself to decide when it would be appropriate.[29] The IMCO Secretariat then presented three general questions on salvage and wreck for consideration at the eighth session of the

---

19 International Sub-committee *Torrey Canyon* [TC-2, 10–67], 96. On 25–26 September, WG II of IMCO Legal Committee also made a study.

20 International Sub-committee *Torrey Canyon* [TC-2, 10–67], 98.

21 Vol III [TC 20, 3–68], 144, 146.

22 Vol IV 1968, [TC 22, 8–68], 132. The draft included a compromise reverse burden of proof. It was also noted that liability insurance was in practice compulsory for ships with mortgages.

23 1969 Vol V. Also Documentation 1970, Vol I. where a text was adopted, 76 [TC–T-26]. IMCO's conference was in November 1969; see 90.

24 LEG VII/7, 12 December 1969, Annex.

25 It also suggested that a bureau be established in London to coordinate information. The idea of a centralised body to collate information, separate from State administrations, was suggested again later. But the IMCO Secretariat was quick to point out how impractical that would have been, even for IMCO: LEG XIX/2/4, 18 June 1973, 2. But cf LEG XIX/5, 29 June 1973, para 61.

26 It talked of "free waters" over which no State had jurisdiction, ie the high seas.

27 LEG VI/6, 6 May 1969, para 41 et seq.

28 IMCO C XXII/SR.3, 31 July 1969, 8.

29 Report of Administrative, Legal and Finance Committee: A VI/WP.6, 28 October 1969, 4.

Legal Committee:[30] (i) salvage on the high seas and in territorial seas; (ii) "the law relating to the removal of wrecks which may cause danger to navigation" on the high seas and in territorial seas; and (iii) the law relating to access for ships to territorial seas for salvage and wreck removal. Environmental salvage issues were ultimately dealt with in the Salvage Convention 1989, but in 1969 the Secretariat's focus on wreck seemed mainly to emphasise the essentially private relations between the parties performing wreck removal services.

It was at the 11th Session of the Legal Committee in January 1972 that the Committee first proposed that consideration be given to adding the substance of wreck removal to its future work programme and the matter was added to the agenda for the upcoming session.[31] At this stage the subject was abbreviated as "wreck removal and related issues", as it was also thought to embrace salvage and the right to intervene on the high seas. All these issues (covering issues of both public and private law) are related, but ultimately needed to be dealt with in separate instruments.

For the 12th Session in April 1972, the Secretariat provided a summary of previous steps and reproduced the Yzal draft.[32] More significant was the somewhat tentative submission by Liberia of its own draft convention.[33] Not surprisingly, it bore little resemblance to the Yzal draft (although paying lip service to it), and was set out in the usual form of draft articles. It is significant that the accompanying commentary recognised that the public and private law issues were "inextricably intertwined".[34] The 1972 Liberian draft was strongly focused on hazards to navigation (ie affecting property and lives), although the *Torrey Canyon* context in which the Legal Committee had been established had clearly linked ship safety to pollution. The 1972 Liberian draft required notification of hazardous wrecks to affected States, but also to IMCO. It firmly placed obligations on coastal States to remove wrecks in their territorial waters, but on the high seas required cooperation between a variety of States. It repeated the notion that IMCO could have a coordinating role when requested by Contracting States, and proposed a simple liability provision based on fault and allowing for limitation of liability. In retrospect, this draft gives the impression of a move by a flag State to head off increased shipowner liabilities in favour of increased State responsibilities.

That 12th Session considered the Yzal and Liberian drafts but, not surprisingly, concluded that further input was needed from States in the form of answers to five detailed questions (and sub-questions).[35] Broadly these covered the definition of hazardous wreck; the obligations of States and shipowners for publicity, physical removal and liability for costs; whether States had a right to remove a wreck, even with no obligation to do so; rights of recourse against States who have not fulfilled responsibilities to remove wrecks; and the relationship between any wreck instrument and the CLC 1969,[36] the Intervention

---

30 LEG VII/7, 12 December 1969, 2.
31 LEG XI/12, 18 January 1972, para 22.
32 LEG XII/4, 8 March 1972.
33 LEG XII/4/1, 24 March 1972, as supplemented by technical observations by the Secretariat in LEG XII/4/2, 6 April 1972.
34 LEG XII/4/1, 24 March 1972, 2.
35 LEG XII/8, 25 April 1972, 10.
36 See 2.6.2.

Convention 1969[37] and the 1957 LLMC.[38] This was a fairly perceptive appraisal of the key issues, and the Committee requested the Secretariat to circulate a questionnaire on a list of questions and issues. Thus began a fact finding process that was to be repeated over the years, sometimes as an excuse to delay action, but also as a recognition that the subject matter was more complicated than it might have seemed.

As to what would happen after the questionnaire, Liberia later stated that it had been decided at the 11th Session that the whole subject matter might then be sent to the CMI for its expert advice.[39] Such a decision does not appear to have been recorded formally in the Report of the Legal Committee[40] and Liberia may have hoped that a less radical outcome might be expected from a body composed of private individuals representing lawyers and business. Significantly the Legal Committee concluded that a number of important questions were being raised at the inter-governmental level, so that CMI collaboration could be considered later.[41] This is perhaps another of the markers since that era of the gradual move away from maritime law being regarded as largely a matter of private law dealt with by private lawyers to one of public law that is properly the function of government.[42] The rise of the environmental movement is also evidence of how non-commercial interests needed to be reflected in addition to private interests and governments.

By the 17th Session in January 1973, the Secretariat felt confident enough to advise the Council that it might be possible to hold a diplomatic conference on wreck removal in 1974 and also to have one on liability for passengers in the same year.[43] This contest for priority would eventually be won by the passenger convention.

The replies to the Secretariat's 1972 questionnaire[44] were presented for consideration at the 19th Session in June 1973.[45] Those replies gave rise to extensive discussion at that session of the key principles for any convention, and the Committee identified eight main questions:[46] geographical scope of application; definition of wreck; definition of hazardous wrecks; obligations about notification; obligations about marking; obligations on removal; liability for costs of removal; and civil liability of damage caused by hazardous wrecks. It is of interest that all of these, apart from the last, ultimately formed part of the WRC 2007.

The Report about the discussion of these questions[47] shows that this was the first time that the Legal Committee can be seen to have been actively involved in the real detail of the subject matter. It also shows that, once the detail was examined, there were wide

---

37 See 5.3.
38 See 2.5.1.
39 Rather in the manner that the CLC 1992 had been dealt with previously: LEG XII/4/1, 24 March 1972, 2.
40 LEG XI/12, 18 January 1972.
41 LEG XII/8, 25 April 1972, 12.
42 It was also something noted by the CMI itself in 1967: International Sub-committee Torrey Canyon, [TC 2, 10–67], 98.
43 LEG XVII/5, 28 December 1972, 4. Cf the Report of the Legal Committee LEG XVII/7, 31 January 1973, 13. See 2.3.1.
44 The extensive responses of 11 States are contained in LEG XIX/2, 15 April 1973. There are also some ten Addenda of States and NGOs which submitted responses too late for inclusion in LEG XIX/2 (numbered eg LEG XIX/2/Add.1 etc) and four related documents.
45 Although it had been hoped that they would have been considered at the 14th Session in September 1972.
46 LEG XIX/5, 29 June 1973, 2–3.
47 LEG XIX/5, 29 June 1973, 3–20.

divergences of view on possible solutions. At this scoping stage of convention negotiations, such differences are to be expected; while some issues later become of less significance,[48] other key ones kept recurring. These included its geographical extent, whether more than navigational hazards should be encompassed; how to secure financial claims; and how cargo hazards should be dealt with.

To resolve some of these issues, the Legal Committee decided to establish a Working Group of eight States to prepare draft articles, taking into account the earlier Yzal and 1972 Liberian drafts and the replies by governments and others, as well as discussions in the Committee.[49] The Working Group met in December 1973. The US had already taken a lead in presenting a rather extensive set of draft articles.[50] A number of the features of this 1973 US draft may be noted. First, this draft went into considerable detail about the minutiae of how a wreck should be determined as being hazardous. Secondly, it suggested a form of full liability (without limit), but in accordance with a proposed schedule of fixed (ie liquidated) costs to be set out in a schedule. Thirdly, it addressed directly the issue of how to secure the payment of costs by the establishment of an international fund from which States could seek reimbursement of expenses not otherwise recovered,[51] an idea initially raised in the Legal Committee.[52] The US proposal envisaged a Fund loosely resembling the IOPC Fund,[53] but which was to consist of an initial amount of US$100 million, contributed to by a very complicated system depending on proportions both of the total registered tonnage of contracting States and their gross national product. This would be topped up by annual contributions calculated in a similar manner. While this was no doubt a worthy attempt to focus attention on the detail of how such a fund might operate, it was not clear which States would agree to join up to such a fund; indeed, the US was careful to point out that the model did not necessarily reflect its official position, and one wonders how seriously it was expected to be taken.

The Report of the Working Group[54] reveals a bewildering range of views on almost every issue. The distinct impression given is that the Working Group was overwhelmed by all the various alternatives, especially in respect of the proposed fund.[55] Moreover, a Drafting Group established to consider draft articles[56] made it clear that it did not have the time to consider the articles (largely based on the US draft that it eventually annexed to the Working Group's Report).[57] The combination of complexity of subject matter and lack of time was to recur.

---

48 Eg dealing with wrecked aircraft; or whether particular systems for notification were needed; or whether the convention would be retrospective; whether IMCO should have a coordinating role.
49 LEG XIX/5, 29 June 1973, 2. The States were Argentina, France, India, Liberia, Norway, UK, US and USSR. LEG/WG(WR).I/4, 12 December 1973.
50 LEG/WG(WR).I/2, 22 October 1973.
51 This can be contrasted with compulsory insurance—both concepts used contemporaneously in the CLC 1969 and the Fund Convention 1971.
52 LEG XIX/5, 29 June 1973, para 50.
53 See 2.6.2(b).
54 LEG/WG(WR).1/4, 12 December 1973.
55 See eg LEG/WG(WR).1/4, 12 December 1973, 5.
56 Consisting of Norway (chair), France, Liberia, US, UK: LEG/WG(WR).1/4, 12 December 1973, para 5.
57 LEG/WG(WR).1/4, 12 December 1973, 7.

The 20th and 21st Sessions in 1974 were almost completely engrossed with a possible passenger liability convention and regulations for the new IOPC Fund, but the Report of the Working Group was raised by the Secretariat. The latter's Note hinted at the level of possible disagreements disclosed by the Working Group when it suggested a series of eight issues on which further guidance might be needed from States.[58] These largely repeated the eight questions of principle raised by the Committee at the 19th Session. In effect, it seems that the Committee had difficulty in using the Working Group's draft as providing immediately workable or attractive answers; indeed, in retrospect it seemed to be presenting a number of blind alleys.

At the 21st Session, the Secretariat had been requested to gather yet more information, eg about existing wrecks and costs.[59] To some extent this was revisiting the earlier questionnaire presented at the 19th Session the previous year, but was relevant to the issue about whether States themselves were to have direct responsibility for removal. Twenty-three responses were received and presented at the 24th Session in November 1974.[60] The UK was the first to reply, indicating that it had information about 10,000 wrecks, 2,000 of which were of some hazard to surface navigation.[61] Figures were given for the annual cost of buoyage, and the example of the *Texaco Caribbean* was given where the cost of wreck removal was £339,000 (some of which was recouped by a salvage award).[62] It is quite clear from the figures that there were thousands of wrecks worldwide, many of which posed navigational hazards, the majority of which seemed to be within territorial waters (assumed then to be three nautical miles). The discussion at the 21st Session returned to the eight questions of principle, albeit as dealt with in the Working Group's draft; but the complexity of the issues was also coming up against the pressure of self-imposed deadlines. This was most evident in the decision to concentrate for the time being on a limited scope, ie navigational hazards only on the high seas (not the territorial sea), and to cover ships but not cargoes.[63] There was still some attraction to placing the responsibility for determining any hazard in a centralised body (eg IMCO, International Hydrographic Organisation (IHO) or the International Association of Marine Aids to Navigation and Lighthouse Authorities (IALA)),[64] but there was uncertainty about whether a similar solution was needed for the actual responsibility for marking, notification and removal.[65] There was also a host of possibilities raised about State obligations to pay unrecovered costs in default of owners paying; these included the State of Registry, the State closest to the wreck, or the coastal State most directly affected.[66] A wreck fund was kept as a possibility, although many had started to recognise its impracticality, while the possibility of applying a convention to existing wrecks was kept open.[67] The Secretariat was also requested to prepare some draft articles

---

58 LEG XXI/4, 11 January 1974.
59 A request was sent by the Sec General in February 2014: LEG XXII 3/1, 18 March 1974.
60 LEG XXIV/3/1, 24 September 1974.
61 LEG XXII 3/1, 18 March 1974.
62 The *Texaco Caribbean* collided with the *Paracas* in the English Channel on 11 January 1971. She exploded, split in two and sank with the loss of eight lives.
63 LEG XXI/5, 8 February 1974, 7–8, 11.
64 LEG XXI/5, 8 February 1974, 8.
65 LEG XXI/5, 8 February 1974, 8–9.
66 LEG XXI/5, 8 February 1974, 12.
67 LEG XXI/5, 8 February 1974, 14.

itself—in reality an indication of the failure of the Working Group. Although based in part on the 1973 Working Group draft, the 1974 draft convention that was produced by the Secretariat for the 22nd Session[68] can perhaps be viewed as the first whose form,[69] language and content could be used as a basis for serious further negotiation. It brought to the fore the principles of compulsory insurance by then enshrined in the CLC. The idea of a wreck fund to cover excess costs was relegated to two short paragraphs with no detail, and never seriously resurfaced.

Wreck removal was next considered at the 24th Session in November 1974, when the Secretariat presented a revised draft convention (with an amended Art 1),[70] along with the results of a questionnaire to governments on existing wrecks. In fact the issues were not considered in detail in the limited time available, although there was a preference to widen the scope of the Secretariat's revised 1974 draft convention to cover all wrecks posing a hazard to navigation, ie to have a wide geographical scope.[71] Given this preference it was clearly felt that States would need to rethink their own views, and indeed whether the time was ripe for a convention at all, eg in 1976.[72] Just to add to the choices, States were also asked to consider many of the other 'scope' issues, eg costs and liabilities, environmental hazards, and dispute settlement. The Legal Committee came back to wreck in the 26th Session in 1975, but other issues were now coming onto its agenda. At the 26th Session the Secretariat was encouraged yet again to collect material on national laws, despite having collected it in 1974.[73]

In looking back at these early discussions of the Legal Committee it seems obvious that it was adopting a rather over-ambitious set of goals.[74] In 1973 there was optimism that it could deal with passengers *and* wreck for a diplomatic conference in 1974. Indeed, the eighth regular session of the Assembly had approved such a conference in principle, but left it to the Council to determine if it were feasible.[75] The 22nd Session had hardly covered draft Art 1 before it recognised that the 1974 target was unrealistic.[76] This is hardly surprising, given that many delegations were also involved in the third UNCLOS conference in Caracas from June to August 1974. That itself raised issues about geographic scope.[77] It was recognised that "wreck removal and related issues" also related to limitation of liability, and a diplomatic conference for the latter was scheduled for 1976.[78] In January 1975, the Secretary-General had invited States to comment on their position on future work on

---

68 LEG XXII/3, 18 February 1974.

69 Eg in the use of sub-headings and square brackets for alternative versions.

70 LEG XXIV/3/1, 24 September 1974; LEG XXIV/3/1/Add 1, 3 October 1974; LEG XXIV/3/1/Add 2, 26 October 1974; LEG XXIV/3/1/Add 3, 4 November 1974; also LEG XXIV/3/2, 20 September 1974.

71 LEG XXIV/6, 18 November 1974, 19–20.

72 LEG XXIV/6, 18 November 1974, 21.

73 LEG XXIV/3/3, 28 October 1974; LEG XXIV/3/3/Add 1, 4 November 1974; LEG XXIV/3/3/Add 2, 1 November 1974; LEG XXIV/3/3/Add 3, 12 November 1974.

74 See eg the Report of the Legal Committee in LEG VI/6, 6 May 1969, where its priority list included HNS, combined transport, seabed exploration and the environment.

75 LEG XXI/4, 11 January 1974, 2.

76 LEG XXII/5, 1 April 1974, 2.

77 LEG XXIV/6, 18 November 1974, 19.

78 This was to produce the LLMC 1976. See 2.5.1.

wreck and related issues,[79] and States were encouraged[80] to come to the 26th Session in April 1975 ready to decide on future action. In the list of possible diplomatic conferences, the Secretariat had wreck as a possibility for 1976 or 1978, but vying with a number of other candidates (now including an HNS convention).[81] Only three States replied directly to the Secretary-General.[82] In the 1975 discussions, the majority of delegations took the view that the subject was important and deserved to be on the work programme of the Legal Committee.[83] They concluded, however, that in view of the difficulties which had come to light, "it did not appear that the time was ripe to proceed immediately with a preparation of a convention of the type that the Legal Committee had concluded would be necessary".[84] It was decided to keep the matter on the work programme for 1978 and beyond but "to leave the decision as to when to re-commence active consideration to a later stage".[85] The decision would be taken in the light of international developments, including UNCLOS. The recommendations were endorsed by the Council in 1975.[86] By 1976, the Legal Committee concluded that its consideration of a wreck removal convention should be "deferred until the Committee felt the time had arrived when more progress could be made".[87] While the issues remained on the Legal Committee's long-term work program, it would be almost 15 years later when that time arrived.

During the intervening years, UNCLOS was adopted, but ultimately did not specifically address the question of wreck.[88] It did, though, in Art 221, reaffirm the right of a coastal State to intervene in cases where a ship, situated beyond its territorial seas, posed a pollution threat to its coastline or related interests.[89] Furthermore, it also introduced a new maritime zone, the EEZ, which was to prove central to the final version of the WRC 2007.

7.2.2 Renewed negotiations 1990–2002

The Legal Committee returned to wreck removal in 1990 when progress was reviewed.[90] As a result, in 1993 Belgium, Germany, Greece, the Netherlands and the UK urged further action.[91] Shortly thereafter, three of these States (Netherlands,[92] Germany[93] and the UK)

---

79 LEG XXVI/3/1, 1 April 1975.
80 LEG XXVI/3/, 20 December 1974.
81 LEG XXVI/6, 10 March 1975, 13; also LEG XXVI/8, 11 April 1975, 14–15.
82 LEG XXVI/3/1, 1 April 1975; LEG XXVI/3/1/Add 1, 4 April 1975.
83 LEG XXVI/8, 11 April 1975, 6.
84 LEG XXVI/8, 11 April 1975, 20.
85 LEG XXVI/8, 11 April 1975, 20.
86 C XXXIV/7, 14 April 1975; C XXXIV/SR.1, 2 June 1975; A IX/SR.315, A IX/SR.9, 6, A IX/c.1/2, 4.
87 LEG XXXI/7, 17 September 1976.
88 See 5.5.
89 See 5.6.3.
90 LEG 63/5, 18 May 1990.
91 LEG 69/10/1, 28 July 1993.

92 Given its geographical orientation, the Netherlands has had to deal with a number of wrecks lying beyond its territorial sea which have posed a hazard to navigation, and which had to be removed at State expense. LEG 75/6/1, 14 February 1997, Annex, 1.

93 For examples of wrecks lying beyond the territorial sea that have posed navigation hazards in Germany, see LEG 75/6/1, 14 February 1997, Annex, 1–2.

produced an initial draft convention for consideration.[94] This draft proved to be the framework for the final WRC 2007. The core components of this draft were the power of a coastal State to remove a wreck located beyond its territorial sea which posed a danger to navigation or to the marine environment, with the option of applying this regime to its territorial seas, and the imposition of strict liability on the shipowner for the removal of the wreck underpinned by a system of compulsory insurance for wreck removal. Following a further review of national legislation, undertaken by the CMI, the possibility of applying the WRC 2007 to the territorial sea was also supported on the basis that existing national laws exhibited significant similarities and that the application to the territorial seas would therefore not undermine national practice but rather contribute to greater uniformity.[95] This sparked a debate that was to continue right up to the final conclusion of the Convention.

Wreck removal faced a battle to force itself up the IMO agenda. In 1996 there was a diplomatic conference which agreed the HNSC 1996[96] and the LLMC 1996. Work on those relegated wreck removal further down the priority in the Legal Committee agenda. The completion of the work might have opened a window to consider wreck removal, but by that time two other important items were also being considered by the Legal Committee: bunker spills and death and injury of passengers. The priority to be assigned within the Legal Committee to deal with particular agenda items is a difficult political issue, given the inevitably differing national priorities of States. As a compromise, the Legal Committee attempted to deal with all three issues at each of its sessions with equal priority. This led, unfortunately, to too many issues being considered, and the debates were too cursory to allow for satisfactory progress. As a result, development was stalled on all three agenda items. While wreck removal had started off as a priority item, the many difficulties and contentious issues arising on the subject resulted in a change in agenda priorities. Delegates realised that the bunker issue was the easiest on which to gain consensus, and decided to press ahead with that as a priority.[97] This ultimately led to the Bunkers Convention being adopted on 23 March 2001.[98]

Thereafter, most delegations felt that wreck removal was a lower priority than the need to provide an updated liability regime for passengers. Drafting work then concentrated on the Athens Convention, which was adopted on 1 November 2002.[99] Meanwhile, the attack on the World Trade Center in New York in 2001 had shifted the priority to security issues, and wreck removal was again relegated to allow for adoption in 2002 of the International Ship and Port Facility Security Code (ISPS Code),[100] and the production of a 2005 Protocol to the Convention for the Suppression of Unlawful Acts Against the Safety of Maritime Navigation 1988 (SUA Convention 1988).[101] With the conclusion of its maritime security

---

94 LEG 73/11, 8 August 1995.
95 LEG 75/6/2, 14 February 1997.
96 See 2.6.4.
97 See N Gaskell, "Decision Making and the Legal Committee of the International Maritime Organization" (2003) 18 IJMCL [*Gaskell, "Decision Making"*] 155.
98 LEG/CONF 12/19 of 27 March 2001: entry into force on 21 November 2008.
99 LEG/CONF 13/20 of 19 November 2002; entry into force on 23 April 2014. The amended instrument is known as the Athens Convention 2002.
100 As an addition to SOLAS 1974, as amended. See also *Gaskell, "Decision Making"*, 160–161.
101 Protocol entry into force 28 July 2010.

related work, the Legal Committee was finally able to give full attention to completing the drafting of the WRC 2007.

7.2.3 Drafting 2002–2007

In fact, in the period from 1997–2002 significant drafting work had been undertaken, with the Netherlands as coordinator of the correspondence group, but discussion at the Legal Committee seemed to raise more problems and divisions, and delegations were not able to focus on solutions. A decisive point was reached in 1999, when the correspondence group proposed abandoning liability provisions altogether in order to garner support for a scaled down convention dealing only with removal powers.[102] This reflected a tension between those who saw the WRC 2007 mainly as a public law environmental treaty, and those who placed it as part of the IMO work on financial security for claims. By 2002, though, there was sufficient confidence for the Netherlands, as lead nation, to produce a revised consolidated draft with the liability provisions reinstated.[103] Work on this draft then proceeded on an article by article basis until the IMO Legal Committee decided at the 92nd Session in October 2006 that the draft was ripe for a diplomatic conference in Kenya in 2007.

The general IMO expectation is that delegations should try to avoid bringing up new issues at a diplomatic conference (although they are entitled to do so), so that the conference can concentrate on voting on the major issues of principle which have largely been fully articulated in the Legal Committee. One of the continuing conceptual difficulties had always been how far various draft proposals were compatible with the law of the sea, and also how far the WRC 2007 could be drafted so as to apply to the territorial sea. It was only through a special effort in early 2007 by a Correspondence and Drafting Group, led by Germany,[104] that a compromise was reached on the highly contentious territorial sea extension. This compromise paved the way for the adoption of the WRC 2007 at the diplomatic conference in Nairobi in May 2007.

With its adoption (and coming into force in 2015), the issue of its standing in the international legal order; its relationship with existing IMO conventions and the position of wrecks of non-State parties requires consideration, particularly as these issues had been much debated during the long gestation period of the convention and the complicated final negotiations.

7.3 WRC 2007 and the international legal order

The WRC 2007, as an IMO convention, takes its place within the IMO suite of conventions that fulfil the IMO's mandate to regulate "the safety, security and environmental performance of international shipping".[105] At the same time, it is subject not only to UNCLOS as the "constitution of the oceans", but also to general principles of international law, and as a convention, to the Vienna Convention on the Law of Treaties. Its place within this

---

102 LEG 80/5, 10 September 1999. It appears that the UK was one of the instigators of this proposal, in order for some progress to be made.
103 LEG 84/4, 18 February 2002. See 10.2.
104 See LEG/Conf.16/12, 24 April 2007.
105 Introduction to IMO www.imo.org/en/About/Pages/Default.aspx.

international legal order is of some import in understanding its scope, its limitations and, importantly, how States parties and non-State parties to the WRC 2007 interact.

7.3.1 WRC 2007 and general principles of international law

A fundamental principle of international law reflected in the Vienna Convention Art 34 is that a "treaty does not create either obligations or rights for a third State without its consent".[106] The application of this fundamental principle to the WRC 2007 means that non-State parties are not bound by its terms.

While a non-State party may not have given consent to be bound through ratification of or accession to the WRC 2007, that State may be bound by customary international law that mirrors or arises out of the WRC 2007, or through its terms applying through some other consent path.[107] This might include through being a State party to UNCLOS. In particular, UNCLOS provides, in Art 211(1) that in adopting rules and regulations for the prevention, reduction and control of pollution of the marine environment "[s]uch laws and regulations shall at least have the same effect as that of generally accepted international rules and standards established through the competent international organization or general diplomatic conference".[108] If the WRC 2007 can be said to be "generally accepted international rules and standards", then it might bind a non-State party. This possibility is dealt with in depth below.

7.3.2 WRC 2007 and UNCLOS

As the constitution of the oceans, UNCLOS is the framework within which all the IMO conventions operate. The WRC 2007 ensures the primacy of UNCLOS and customary international law of the sea.[109]

Nevertheless, UNCLOS was by the 1990s viewed as having struck a less than ideal balance between coastal States and flag States with respect to marine pollution.[110] Unlike the regimes established in the CLC 1969, Fund Convention 1971 or Bunkers Convention 2001, the WRC 2007 sought to rebalance the rights and duties of States as set out in UNCLOS with regard to wrecks in the EEZ. Moreover, UNCLOS is silent on the issue of wrecks which pose a navigational hazard in the EEZ. As such, the WRC 2007 needed to address both a gap in UNCLOS regime and to reconfigure the right and duties of States

---

106 The treaty is regarded as reflecting customary international law. See A Aust, *Modern Treaty Law and Practice* (CUP, 2000) [*Modern Treaty Law*] 10.

107 Vienna Convention Art 11 provides that "[t]he consent of a State to be bound by a treaty may be expressed by signature, exchange of instruments constituting a treaty, ratification, acceptance, approval or accession, or *by any other means if so agreed*" (own emphasis). See further *Modern Treaty Law* 90.

108 See 5.5.1.

109 WRC 2007 Art 16. The heading to Art 16, referring to "other conventions and international agreements" does not quite match its content. See 7.4.3. UNCLOS is, today, regarded largely as reflecting customary international law.

110 E Franckx "Coastal State Jurisdiction with Respect to Marine Pollution—Some Recent Developments and Future Challenges" (1995) 10 IJMCL 253; D Bodansky, "Protecting the Marine Environment from Vessel-Source Pollution" (1991) 18 *Ecology LQ* 719; A Nollkamper, "Agenda 21 and Prevention of Sea-Based Marine Pollution: A Spurious Relationship" (1993) 17 *Marine Policy* 537.

in the EEZ. Indeed, early on in the drafting of the WRC 2007, five interested delegations prepared a document for the Legal Committee that concluded that UNCLOS "seems to indicate that there is still need for an international instrument on wreckremoval [*sic*] in addition to the already existing rights of coastal State intervention as regards maritime casualties which may reasonably be expected to result in major harmful consequences for the marine environment".[111] The inadequacy of UNCLOS with respect to wrecks was thus acknowledged. However, as an existing convention, UNCLOS could not easily be altered. The difficulty, and indeed, success of drafting and bringing UNCLOS into force meant that it was politically impossible to seek to modify UNCLOS itself. However, as a framework convention, it is not immutable and the regime it creates is subject to adaptation and change over time.[112] The IMO Secretariat noted that:

> While the development of IMO regulations should always take into account the provisions of [UNCLOS] and be compatible with them, this is quite different from arguing that, where [UNCLOS] is silent on a matter, it is beyond the scope of the Organization to adopt international regulations on a subject. To concede that would effectively amount to a freeze in the development of the law in this field and would unduly restrict IMO's ability to carry on with its global mandate.[113]

The form that adaption could take was another international convention—the WRC 2007—one that would be consistent with the principles underlying Art 41 of the Vienna Convention. Article 41, headed "Agreements to Modify Multilateral Treaties between Certain of the Parties Only", provides:

> Two or more of the parties to a multilateral treaty may conclude an agreement to modify the treaty as between themselves alone if: (a) the possibility of such a modification is provided for by the treaty; or (b) the modification in question is not prohibited by the treaty and: (i) does not affect the enjoyment by the other parties of their rights under the treaty or the performance of their obligations; (ii) does not relate to a provision, derogation from which is incompatible with the effective execution of the object and purpose of the treaty as a whole.

UNCLOS does indeed provide for the modification of its provisions (and of the convention itself[114]), allowing States to adopt measures in a multilateral convention that has the effect of altering the balance of interests as between themselves.[115] Article 237 of UNCLOS "authorises the conclusion of special conventions containing specific obligations for the protection and preservation of the marine environment".[116] The WRC 2007 does, however,

---

111 LEG 69/10/1, 28 July 1993 (Belgium, Germany, Greece, the Netherlands and the UK), para. 14.
112 *Vessel-Source Pollution*, 3.
113 LEG 86/4/1, 27 March 2003, 4.
114 UNCLOS Art 312.
115 That the IMO could address the rights and duties of States in the EEZ and territorial sea governed by UNCLOS was noted by the IMO Secretariat, in consultation with the UN DOALOS: "the [UNCLOS] should rightly be viewed as a framework convention and not as a barrier to the development of regulations which, even if not concluded in [UNCLOS], are elaborated in pursuance of IMOs paramount objectives of ensuring safety of navigation and preventing marine pollution. The proposed wreck removal convention is a case in point". LEG 86/4/1, 27 March 2004, page 3, para 11.
116 The IMO Secretariat, in consultation with the UN DOALOS noted: "A new IMO Convention to remove environmental hazards posed by wrecks would be in conformity with UNCLOS as it would fall within the provisions of Art 237, which authorises the conclusion of special conventions containing specific obligations for the protection and preservation of the marine environment" LEG 86/4/1, 27 March 2004, 3.

go beyond the protection of the marine environment to address issues of safety of navigation[117] and may not therefore be fully covered by Art 237.[118] Nevertheless, UNCLOS at least in part envisages further conventional regimes that may amend the balance provided for as between contracting States of the new agreement.

Furthermore, specific articles of UNCLOS either envisage broad power to address the issue of environmental protection in the EEZ or defer to agreement being reached in other fora. Article 56(1)(b)(iii), for example, establishes coastal State jurisdiction to protect and preserve the marine environment in the EEZ, while Art 192 establishes a general obligation for States to protect and preserve the marine environment. Article 194(3)(b) further elaborates on this broad duty by providing that States shall take measures to minimise to the fullest possible extent pollution from vessels, in particular measures for preventing accidents and dealing with emergencies, ensuring the safety of operations at sea, preventing intentional and unintentional discharges". So too, Arts 211 and 221 empower States to address issues of marine pollution from vessels.[119]

While these articles may suggest the development of the law of the sea through new international instruments that elaborate on the powers of States, Art 311 of UNCLOS is of much greater breadth in addressing conventional regimes adopted after UNCLOS entered into force. Art 311(2) states:

> This Convention shall not alter the rights and obligations of States Parties which arise from other agreements compatible with this Convention and which do not affect the enjoyment by other States Parties of their rights or the performance of their obligations under this Convention.

The negotiating history of Art 311(2) suggest that it arose to address the relationship between UNCLOS and existing conventions, particularly those that dealt with navigation and overflight in what would become the EEZ.[120] That said, it is not so restrictively worded and could be applied to agreements entered into after UNCLOS came into force. Its focus is on the terms of UNCLOS and the concern that it not alter rights and obligations of States parties which arise from the other agreement, but requires that the other agreement be both compatible with UNCLOS and not affect the enjoyment by other States parties of their rights or the performance of their obligations under UNCLOS.

Article 311(3) also addresses the relationship between UNCLOS and other international instruments:

> Two or more States parties may conclude agreements modifying or suspending the operation of provisions of this Convention, applicable solely to the relations between them, provided that such agreements do not relate to a provision derogation from which it is incompatible with the effective execution of the objectives and purpose of the Convention, and ... that the provisions

---

117 Noting the possible connection between the two in LEG 86/4/1, 27 March 2003, para 14 and IMO Doc. LEG 87/4/1, 8 September 2003, para. 8.

118 See LEG 86/4/1, 27 March 2003, page 3, para 16. States expressed the view that Art 221 of UNCLOS does not fetter the development of new rules intended to empower coastal States to remove wrecks which constitute an impediment to safety of navigation. See LEG 84/14, 7 May 2002, page 8, para 34.

119 LEG 86/4/2, 28 March 2003, 2.

120 M Nordquist, *United Nations Convention on the Law of the Sea 1982: A Commentary*, Vol. V (Martinus Nijhoff, Dordrecht, 1989) [*Nordquist*], 239.

of such agreements do not affect the enjoyment by other States parties of their rights or the performance of their obligations under this Convention.[121]

Consistent with the Vienna Convention this allows for the adoption of a multilateral Convention on the basis that it will not bind non-State parties without their consent.[122] As such, while the new WRC 2007 regime might alter the balance of interests set out in UNCLOS, as between parties to the WRC 2007 it does not have the effect of altering or contradicting the provisions of UNCLOS itself which includes Art 311(2) and (3).[123] As the WRC 2007 allows the coastal State not only to remove a wreck located in the EEZ that poses a hazard to the coastal State, but also to require the shipowner to remove the hazard (and potentially the wreck) and at the shipowner's expense (and which requires flag States to impose extra obligations on their shipowners to address this liability),[124] it clearly does affect the balance between the rights of the flag State and the coastal State as set out in UNCLOS.[125] This re-balancing of rights and duties under UNCLOS is reflected in Art 9(10) of the WRC 2007 which provides that "State Parties give their consent to the Affected State to act under paragraphs 4 to 8 [of Art 9, which grants coastal States certain powers of wreck in the EEZ] where required".[126] This is essentially an acknowledgment that flag States have ceded to coastal States certain powers granted to flag States under UNCLOS for States parties to the WRC 2007.

While it is not entirely clear whether it is Art 311(2) or 311(3) that supports the adoption of the WRC 2007, the most cited sub-paragraph during negotiations for the WRC 2007 was Art 311(3).[127] This appeared to rest on the basis that since the WRC 2007 introduces greater coastal State rights than existed under UNCLOS, and provides that flag States agree that coastal States exercise some of the rights exercised by flag States under UNCLOS, this amounts to an agreement "modifying or suspending the operation of provisions of this Convention (UNCLOS), applicable solely to the relations between them". Irrespective of which sub-paragraph supports the WRC 2007, it has a significant effect on how the regime operates in relation to wrecks of non-State parties. Against this background, the need to assert the primacy of UNCLOS and of customary international law was raised throughout negotiations, particularly by the US.[128]

---

121 Unfortunately, UNCLOS negotiations did not make a clear distinction between the scope of application of subparagraphs 2 and 3. Indeed, described as a "difficult article", Nordquist noted that the subparagraphs 2 and 3 "may well give rise to disputes concerning their interpretation or application": *Nordquist*, 243.

122 Vienna Convention on the Law of Treaties Arts 34 and 41.

123 LEG 91/39, 16 August 2006, page 30.

124 WRC 2007 Arts 9 and 10.

125 Eg in UNCLOS Arts 56, 58, 194, 211 and 220. See also Leg 92/4/8, 15 September 2006, page 2, para 7.

126 See 9.2.

127 The Netherlands delegation stated that "in its final form [the WRC 2007] must be consistent with the [UNCLOS], including Art 311(3), which, consistent with the Vienna Convention on the Law of Treaties, requires, inter alia, that agreements among States Parties to UNCLOS not affect the enjoyment by other States Parties of their rights or the performance of their obligations under UNCLOS". LEG 91/39, 16 August 2006, page 30. See also LEG 87/4, 7 August 2003, repeated in LEG. 89/5, 17 August 2004; LEG 89/5/3, 24 September 2004. See also LEG 89/16, 4 November 2004, page 20, para 124; LEG 91/3/1, 24 March 2006, page 1, para 2.

128 See eg LEG92/4/8, 15 September 2006; LEG/Conf.16/6, 1 March 2007, 1; LEG/Conf.16/7, 15 March 2007; LEG/Conf.16/8, 15 March 2007.

7.3.3 Avoidance of overlap with other IMO conventions

The WRC 2007 was adopted against the constitutional background of UNCLOS and as part of a complex matrix of IMO conventions that address a range of issues on marine pollution and threats to the coastal State. The WRC 2007 deals with potential overlaps with these existing conventional regimes in two ways.

First, Art 4(1) excludes from the scope of the WRC 2007 measures taken under the Intervention Convention 1969. This is of some importance given the difficulties of applying the thresholds for coastal State intervention.[129] The Intervention Convention 1969 provides that a coastal State may act only in cases of grave and imminent danger from pollution.[130] The WRC 2007, on the other hand, will apply to pollution hazards that fail to meet the threshold required by the Intervention Convention 1969. Where, however, the Intervention Convention 1969 threshold is reached, either convention could be relied upon. Which a State will choose will depend on the advantages each regime offers in the particular circumstances.

Secondly, the WRC 2007 ensures that the liability of a shipowner will only ever be determined in accordance with one particular convention.[131] In the event of a marine casualty that gives rise to a wreck, the hazard posed to the environment will usually arise from the oil carried on board, whether as bunkers or cargo, and from noxious and hazardous substances carried as cargo (including on rare occasions, nuclear cargo). A number of existing international regimes address liability in these situations, including the CLC 1992 and Fund 1992; HNSC 2010; Bunkers Convention 2001; Convention on Third Party Liability in the Field of Nuclear Energy 1960; or the Convention on Civil Liability for Nuclear Damage 1963.[132] While these conventions address the liability arising from pollution caused by substances on board a ship, rather than the ship itself, some overlap may occur to the extent that the removal of the wreck itself might fall within the scope of preventative measures covered by the CLC 1992,[133] the HNSC 2010[134] and the Bunkers Convention 2001.[135] The WRC 2007 therefore aims to ensure that liability does not arise under both the WRC 2007 and one of these conventions by excluding the operation of the WRC 2007 where one of these specific four conventions applies and is in force.[136] The concern that underpinned this was not only the risk of allowing double recovery of claims, but also to avoid leaving any gaps in these liability regimes, ensuring that a claim could be dealt with either under the WRC 2007 or the other applicable conventions, or conventions where an overlap occurred.[137] Moreover, where there was an overlap between the WRC 2007 and any another convention, the WRC 2007 ought not to allow a claim where such a claim would have been excluded under any other convention. Where more than one other convention was applicable, the intent was also to limit the number of possible legal proceedings and to allow all wreck removal

---

129 See LEG74/13 22 October 1996, 11; LEG 85/3/1, 17 September 2002, 2. See also 4.2.3(a).
130 See 5.3.
131 See 10.9.2.
132 See 10.9.3.
133 CLC 1992 Art I(7).
134 HNSC 2010 Art 1(7).
135 Bunkers Convention 2001 Art 1(7).
136 WRC 2007 Art 11(1).
137 LEG 87/17, 23 October 2003, 14. See also HNSC 2010 Art 4(3) and Bunkers Convention 2001 Art 4(1).

THE LAW OF WRECK

claims to be addressed through the WRC 2007 at the same time.[138] This, however, really depends on what advantages the WRC 2007 might give a State claimant over those available under any other regime.[139]

Similarly, where the measures undertaken under the WRC 2007 amount to salvage, under either national law or an international convention, such law or convention will govern the question of remuneration or compensation payable to the salvors.[140]

7.4 WRC 2007 and non-State parties

7.4.1 Wrecks of non-State parties in territorial sea

In 1993, when a coalition of States began agitating for a more active consideration of the drafting of a wreck removal convention, it was their view that any "new instrument would not be aimed at the establishment of new rights of coastal States but at the uniform regulation of wreck removal activities".[141] This uniformity was directed particularly at wreck in the territorial sea.

Article 2(3) of UNCLOS recognises coastal States' sovereign rights in their territorial sea, subject only to UNCLOS itself and "other rules of international law". This has generally been regarded as giving a relatively unfettered discretion to address dangers and hazards in these waters, including the ability to order shipowners to remove a wreck or to pay for the costs of such removal if undertaken by State authorities.[142] States have been reluctant to be bound by any convention that would limit these powers in any way. Nevertheless, on the question as to whether Art 2(3) is merely descriptive or operates as a reservation, the Arbitral Tribunal in the 2015 *Chagos* Arbitration[143] considered that though the English text of UNCLOS was ambiguous, "the balance of the authentic versions favours reading that provision to impose an obligation".[144] As such, UNCLOS plays a role in the balancing of interests in the territorial sea and subjects the coastal State's sovereignty to the terms of UNCLOS.

That said, the question of the application of the WRC 2007 to the territorial sea was not described in negotiations as an issue about the scope and extent of State rights of intervention. Rather, it was formulated as an attempt to ensure uniformity in national maritime law and enable coastal States, when they remove hazardous wrecks, to recover associated costs. Once an 'opt-in' compromise had been reached, the mechanism which was used to "shore up" existing coastal State rights in the territorial sea proved to be rather complex.

At the outset, when addressing the right of a coastal State to opt in, the WRC 2007 specifically provides that it does not limit pre-existing State rights with regard to wreck other than measures relating to locating, marking and removing of a wreck.[145] Wreck that falls

---

138 LEG 88/4, 16 February 2004, Annex 3, 7.
139 See 10.9.
140 WRC 2007 Art 1(2). See 10.9.1.
141 LEG 69/11, 12 October 1993, 19.
142 See, for example, the review of State powers under national legislation in LEG 63/5, 18 May 1990, Annex 2, 7–16; also LEG 69/10/1, 28 July 1993, para 7.
143 In the *Matter of the Chagos Marine Protected Area Arbitration*, Award 18 March 2015. The case did not involve wreck removal but, *inter alia*, the creation of a marine protected area.
144 Para 500 et seq.
145 WRC 2007 Art 3(2).

outside of the scope of the Convention, or measures taken by coastal States beyond the scope of the Convention for wreck covered by the Convention, are still to be determined by coastal State law.[146] Article 3(2) specifically provides that Arts 10, 11 and 12 (addressing the extent of the shipowners liability, compulsory insurance and direct action against the insurer) will apply only to the locating, marking and removal of wreck, and will not apply to any other measures a State may take in relation to a wreck in its territorial sea. This at least ensures that the scope of the liability to be borne by shipowners and their insurers is uniform, notwithstanding the powers of a State to address wreck as an exercise of their sovereignty in the territorial sea. The articles addressing the reporting, marking and removal of wreck do, however, themselves contain provisions which many States regarded as incompatible with the existing sovereign rights that could be exercised with respect to a wreck within their territorial waters. The WRC 2007 therefore provides in Art 4(4) that a number of provisions will simply not apply in the territorial sea.[147]

This 'opt-in' regime was agreed late during negotiations, but the extent to which the debate concerning the application of the convention to non-State parties is equally applicable in the territorial sea as is the case in the EEZ. As such, the WRC 2007 does not apply as between a coastal State party and a non-State party whose vessel constitutes a wreck in the territorial sea. That is to say that the WRC 2007 itself is not the source of any rights, duties or powers that a coastal State may exercise in relation to a wreck of a non-State party to the Convention. The consequence is that the advantages and disadvantages of being a party to the WRC 2007 apply only to the extent that the Convention is applicable. This is consistent with the interpretation of Art 2(3) of UNCLOS with respect to the nature of the coastal State's sovereignty and the view of the Legal Committee that "the wreck removal convention will not bind, and will not be applicable to, non-Parties who have not consented to be bound, in accordance with the Vienna Convention on the Law of Treaties".[148]

An important consequence of this would be that the coastal State would not be constrained by any unforeseen limitations that might arise in its application in the territorial sea if the wreck concerned was flagged by a non-State party.

It is important to note here that this conclusion does not address the rights, powers and duties that exist in customary international law or pursuant to any other international law instrument, such as the Intervention Convention 1969 or UNCLOS. It is clear that coastal States have extensive rights in relation to wreck in the territorial sea; many, if not most of these may coexist with the rights and duties that arise from participation in the WRC 2007 with respect to a vessel of another State party. It is worth reiterating the point that the question of the application of the WRC 2007 to the territorial sea is not, therefore, an issue of State rights of intervention but rather an issue of uniformity in national maritime law.

7.4.2 Binding nature of WRC 2007 for non-State parties and wreck in EEZ

General principles of international law, the Intervention Convention 1969 and UNCLOS provide some powers for coastal State intervention in order to prevent pollution resulting

---

146 LEG/CONF.16/12, 24 April 2007, Annex 2.
147 See 8.4.
148 LEG.92/13, 3 November 2006, page 18, para 4.71.

from a casualty (including a casualty that becomes a wreck) in the EEZ, but the exact scope of these powers is uncertain.[149] Indeed, throughout the negotiations for the WRC 2007, views differed as to the extent to which the coastal State had a right to take action against a foreign wreck in the EEZ—particularly in respect of non-pollution hazards—and was one of the reasons for adopting the WRC 2007.[150]

As discussed in Chapter 5, while UNCLOS provides (in Part XII) a role for coastal States in the prevention, reduction and control of pollution of the marine environment from vessels, this is minimal and left largely to flag States to address.[151] Furthermore, existing international law, including UNCLOS, does not expressly confer, confirm or deny powers of a coastal State to take action in relation to wrecks in the EEZ, or other maritime zones beyond the territorial sea, which pose a navigational hazard, or some hazard other than pollution which might affect the interests of a State.[152]

The WRC 2007 addresses these gaps in the international regime. The WRC 2007 is not inconsistent with UNCLOS to the extent that its adoption is support by Art 311, but it does alter the balance of interests between coastal States and flag States set out in UNCLOS, as between parties to the WRC 2007.[153] This is so since coastal States were given limited jurisdiction with respect to taking measures to "prevent, reduce and control pollution", being technical measures as envisaged in Art 194(30)(b),[154] reflected most clearly in the limited enforcement capacity to enforce these technical measures as set out in Art 220.[155] Article 211(5), unlike Art 211(4) which recognises extensive coastal State jurisdiction in the territorial sea, limits coastal States' jurisdiction to the enforcement of those technical measures, and requires that in doing so, the enforcement measures it takes are no more stringent than the "generally accepted international rule and standards" applicable to that enforcement.[156] As such, the WRC 2007 does impact upon existing flag State rights under UNCLOS, grants coastal States rights not provided for in UNCLOS and does, in the words of Art 34 of the Vienna Convention "create either obligations or rights for a third State" which must be consented to before being binding on that State.[157] To the extent that wreck removal in the EEZ, other than in cases provided for in the Intervention Convention 1969, UNCLOS or under customary international law, is likely to be regarded as falling within the exclusive jurisdiction of the flag State, the WRC 2007 cannot grant to the coastal State any powers over such a wreck unless the flag State is also a party to the WRC 2007. For States parties to the WRC 2007, such powers are consistent with the rights and duties of flag and coastal States within the EEZ as provided for in UNCLOS and supported by the

---

149 See 5.3, 5.5.
150 See eg LEG 74/5/2/Add. 1, 5 September 1996, 5 (CMI); LEG 86/4/12,27 March 2003 (IMO Secretariat); LEG 87/4/1, 8 September 2003, para 6 (UK, Japan, US).
151 UNCLOS Art 217. See 5.5.1.
152 See eg LEG 74/5/2/Add 1, 5 September 1996; LEG 86/4/12, 27 March 2003; LEG 87/4/1, 8 September 2003, para 6; LEG 92/13, 3 November 2006, Annex 4; LEG/Conf.16/6, 1 March 2007; LEG/Conf.16/7, 15 March 2007; LEG/CONF.16/8, 15 March 2007.
153 See also LEG 86/4/1, 27 March 2003, 2–4.
154 See 5.5.1.
155 See 5.6.2.
156 UNCLOS Art 211(5).
157 As to the extent to which this prejudices existing State rights under UNCLOS and the application of UNCLOS Art 311 to WRC 2007 see 7.4.4.

provisions of the WRC 2007 itself. This does not prejudice the rights and duties of non-State parties.[158]

That the WRC 2007 does alter the balance of rights and duties for flag and coastal States set out in UNCLOS, and that consent is required for this alteration, is reflected in the WRC 2007.[159] Article 9, which grants coastal States powers not provided for in UNCLOS, specifically adds that "States parties give their consent to the Affected [coastal] State to act under paragraphs 4 to 8 [reporting, locating and removing a hazard], where required".[160] This consent arises from being a party to the WRC 2007 and "does not require any action or implementation on the part of the flag State; it is simply a statement of fact and will apply automatically when a State becomes a party to the convention".[161] The corollary of this provision is that the flag State has not given such consent if it is not a party to the WRC 2007. Indeed, the US concluded that "[w]hile States are free to join the [WRC 2007] and consent, through being a party to that convention, to subject their flag vessels to the enhanced authority of coastal States provided under that convention, States that do not join it have not consented to the enhanced authority of coastal States provided under that Convention".[162] This was acknowledged by the IMO Legal Committee when it noted that "the wreck removal convention will not bind, and will not be applicable to, non-Parties who have not consented to be bound, in accordance with the Vienna Convention".[163] This is also reflected in the view of the lead nation in the intersessional consultations, the Netherlands, when declaring that "it is not the intention for the [WRC 2007] to permit a State to take action against wrecks of non-State parties".[164] This does beg the question as to what the scope of 'take action' entails, as a distinction could be drawn between the State requiring the shipowner of a non-State party to remove a wreck as opposed to making the shipowner liable for the costs incurred by the Affected State in removing the wreck.

As the Legal Committee had accepted by 2006 that the WRC 2007 would not bind non-State parties, the issue became how best to express that principle.[165] While a number of States, led by the US, did propose to make this explicit by referring to "wrecks of States Parties" in the EEZ, the majority of States' delegates viewed this as unnecessary as it was implicit in the draft text and subject to Art 34 of the Vienna Convention that provides that a treaty cannot bind a third State without its consent.[166] This wrangling about the appropriate

---

158 Note also that WRC 2007 Art 2(4) provides that application of the WRC 2007 within the EEZ shall not entitle a State party to claim or exercise sovereignty or sovereign rights over any part of the high seas.
159 See also WRC 2007 Art 2(2) and 2(3). See 9.2.5(e).
160 WRC 2007 Art 9(10).
161 LEG 87/4/1, 8 September 2003, 3 (submitted by UK, Japan and US).
162 LEG92/4/8, 15 September 2006, 2.
163 LEG92/13, 3 November 2006, 18; LEG 87/4, 7 August 2003, Annex 3, 2. See also the US position: LEG 91/3/1, 24 March 2006, 2; LEG92/4/8, 15 September 2006; LEG/CONF.16/18, 17 May 2007, 1.
164 LEG 89/5, 17 August 2004, Annex 3, 5. See also the position of Brazil, France, the UK and US that "State Parties may only take measures allowed under the [WRC 2007] to remove the wrecks of *other States Parties*". Original emphasis. Leg 89/5/3, 24 September 2004, 1.
165 LEG 92/13, 3 November 2006, para 4.71.
166 LEG92/13, 3 November 2006, 18. The US (unsuccessfully) proposed a clause that read "Except as otherwise provided in this Convention, this Convention shall apply only to wrecks of State parties in the Convention Area". LEG/Conf.16/6, 1 March 2007, 1. The proposal was unsuccessful as States regarded it as unnecessary. See also LEG 91/3/1, 24 March 2006, 1; LEG 91/12, 6 May 2006, 15; LEG 91/WP.5, 26 April 2006, 1; LEG/Conf.16/7, 15 March 2007. Alternatively, a submission by Brazil, France, the UK and the US had proposed to

wording served to bury the underlying issue, namely the extent to which a coastal State did have rights over wreck in the EEZ (irrespective of what the WRC 2007 may say).[167] In some ways, the focus on coastal State rights in respect of hazards from "non-pollution" wrecks diverted attention from the other important aspect of the WRC 2007, namely the ability to impose financial costs on shipowners and to insist on compulsory insurance for liabilities in the EEZ. Nevertheless, the debate about the ability of the WRC 2007 to affect the rights of non-State parties continued right up to the diplomatic conference.[168] This has led to some degree of uncertainty as to just what an Affected (coastal) State can do in relation to wrecks of non-State parties in its EEZ and in relation to relevant parties such as the shipowner and insurer.[169]

7.4.3 Coastal State action and non-State party wrecks in EEZ

Coastal States have jurisdiction with respect to wrecks that pose a pollution hazard in the EEZ in accordance with customary international law, the Intervention Convention and UNCLOS. The WRC 2007 adds to these rights, clarifying many for those States party to the WRC 2007. For example, whilst UNCLOS and the Intervention Convention provide powers of intervention when a major pollution incident arises, there will be no such powers for navigational hazards which do not give rise to serious pollution hazards, or for threats to other interests.[170] Naturally, the reverse is true. If the flag State is a party to the WRC, but the coastal State is not, the coastal State will not be able to intervene in cases not covered by the existing international law, and certainly could not take advantage of the obligations imposed on the shipowner.[171]

This, at least, appears to have been the majority position during negotiations, such that coastal States had limited jurisdiction under international law to take such action without the consent of the flag State.[172] Coastal States are, however, usually eager to assert jurisdiction over wrecks that pose a hazard and may do so without clearly distinguishing the basis for the assertion of that jurisdiction,[173] whether that be UNCLOS, the Intervention

---

amend Art 2 of the draft to read "State Parties may take measures established under this Convention in relation to the removal of wrecks *of other States Parties* posing a hazard within the Convention area". Original emphasis. LEG 89/5/3, 24 September 2004, 2

167 The US gave specific examples of how it thought that the WRC 2007 would be exceeding that which would be permissible under customary international law as reflected in UNCLOS: see LEG/Conf.16/6, 1 March 2007; and LEG/Conf.16/7, 15 March 2007. See also LEG 89/16, 4 November 2004, 24.

168 See in particular the trenchant views of the US in LEG/Conf.16/6, 1 March 2007 and LEG/Conf.16/7, 15 March 2007, which also referred to its earlier submissions; and those of Cyprus in LEG 92/13, 3 November 2006, Annex 4.

169 See UNCLOS Art 229 which provides that nothing in UNCLOS "affects the institution of civil proceedings in respect of any claim for loss or damage resulting from pollution of the marine environment". See 10.2.7(b), 11.3.2.

170 When it is not possible to identify the flag State of the wreck, no practical obstacle will prevent the coastal State from intervening.

171 See further 7.4.6.

172 See eg LEG 74/5/2/Add 1, 5 September 1996, 5 (CMI); LEG 86/4/12, 27 March 2003 (IMO Secretariat); LEG 87/4/1, 8 September 2003, para 6 (UK, Japan, US).

173 See the UK's assertion of jurisdiction in 11.3.3.

Convention 1969 or a customary international law related eg to necessity.[174] It may make it difficult then to determine whether a coastal State's exercise of jurisdiction in relation to a wreck of a non-State party is in anyway related to the WRC 2007. This is especially so in relation to the shipowner and insurer's liability.[175]

On a more practical level, there will be few occasions when a shipowner or flag State would object to a coastal State removing a wreck that does pose a hazard to the coastal State,[176] certainly when the removal is paid for by the coastal State and neither the shipowner, the shipowner's insurer nor the flag State is required to pay. Moreover, commercial trading imperatives necessitate shipowner's obtaining the necessary insurance cover and certification to allow entry into ports of non-State parties to the WRC 2007.[177]

7.4.4 Insurance cover and non-State party wrecks in EEZ

A key element of the WRC 2007 is the requirement that shipowners of vessels flagged in States parties have insurance cover for wreck removal, and that claimants have direct access to the insurer for any liabilities arising under the WRC 2007.[178] The manner in which this has been dealt with in the WRC 2007 illustrates the extent to which the WRC 2007 may only apply to States parties, and the limitations that therefore may exist with respect to ships of non-State parties.

Even if the non-State party flag State of a wreck consents to its removal in the EEZ, the shipowner may have no insurance to cover the costs of locating, marking and removing the wreck. The obligation to have insurance cover for wreck removal is provided for in Art 12(1) of the WRC 2007, providing that the "registered owner of a ship of 300 gross tonnage and above and *flying the flag of a State Party* shall be required to maintain insurance".[179] Ships flagged in a non-State party would not be bound by the provisions of the WRC 2007, including Art 12(1), and the reference then to the ship "flying the flag of a State Party" merely acknowledges this as a flag State obligation. Referring to the CLC 1992, Tan argues that the term, "wherever registered", means that "even if a vessel's flag state is not a party to the CLC [1992], the vessel must adhere to the insurance requirement if it wishes to trade with [a] CLC [1992] contracting state".[180] *De la Rue & Anderson* concur, stating that "[t]echnically insurance is compulsory only for ships registered in CLC 1992 States [as provided for in Art VII(1)]; however, it will also be needed for other ships if they are to trade to states which are parties to the convention".[181] While only States parties to the CLC 1992 and Bunkers Convention 2001 are required to ensure that shipowners whose vessels flying their flag have appropriate insurance to cover the relevant liabilities, commercial pressures have necessitated that almost all shipowners carry such insurance. The same applies to the WRC 2007, and if there is widespread adoption of the WRC 2007

---

174 See 5.2.
175 See 7.4.6.
176 For example, Italy, the flag State of the *Torrey Canyon*, apparently did not object to actions taken by the UK. See 1.2.
177 See further 7.4.6 and 10.8.
178 See 10.2 and 10.8.
179 Our emphasis. WRC 2007 Art 12(1).
180 *Khee-Jin Tan*, 300.
181 *De La Rue & Anderson*, 125.

by coastal States, then certification will be required somewhere and shipowners will be obliged to carry appropriate insurance in order to engage in their usual shipping activities.

Article 12(12) addresses a further obligation for States parties, one that does not apply to those ships registered in that State party, but to foreign ships, wherever registered, that enters its ports. Article 12(12) provides:

> Subject to the provisions of this article, each State Party shall ensure, under its national law, that insurance or other security to the extent required by paragraph 1 is in force in respect of any ship of 300 gross tonnage and above, *wherever registered*, entering or leaving a port in its territory, or arriving at or leaving an offshore facility in its territorial sea.

The wording of Art 12(12) is based substantially on Art VII(11) of the CLC 1992,[182] and as such did not receive much debate during negotiations of the WRC 2007. Nevertheless, the extent to which this imposes obligations on a non-State party arises in respect of the italicised phrase above.

The phrase "wherever registered" reflects the extent of a coastal State's port jurisdiction by requiring a vessel flying the flag of a non-State party that enter its port to have the same insurance cover as that of a vessel flying the flag of a State party.[183] This allows a vessel flying the flag of a non-State party to obtain certification from another State that is a party to the WRC 2007.[184] On the assumption that the phrase "wherever registered" was intended to require such insurance certification for all vessel entering the port, including those of a non-flag State, a possible problem arises. Both the CLC 1992 Art VII(11) and the WRC 2007 Art 12(1) refer to the insurance in relation to the "liability for pollution damage under this Convention" and "to cover liability under this Convention", respectively.[185] Arguably, liability under the WRC 2007 only arises in respect of ships flagged in a State party. If the flag State of the vessel entering the port is not a party to the relevant convention, then no liability arises under that convention, and as such, while insurance certification exists, it does not extend to the relevant incident given that no liability in that respect arises in relation to wrecks of a non-State party. In the case of the WRC 2007, then, the insurance cover might not extend to anything a coastal State purported to do as a party to the WRC 2007 in relation to the non-State party vessel in the EEZ. This conclusion is thus consistent with the general view of the Legal Committee that "the wreck removal convention will not bind, and will not be applicable to, non-Parties who have not consented to be bound, in accordance with the Vienna Convention".[186]

Article 12(12) then is underpinned by the coastal State's sovereignty and merely requires that, as a WRC 2007 obligation, the State ensures that all ships entering its ports has an appropriate insurance certificate. Technically that insurance coverage can only apply to

---

182 CLC 1992 Art VII(11), reads: "Subject to the provisions of this Article, each Contracting State shall ensure, under its national legislation, that insurance or other security to the extent specified in paragraph 1 of this Article is in force in respect of any ship, wherever registered, entering or leaving a port in its territory, or arriving at or leaving an off-shore terminal in its territorial sea, if the ship actually carries more than 2,000 tons of oil in bulk as cargo". This was also repeated in the Bunkers Convention 2001 Art 7(12).

183 See 10.2.7(b) and 10.8.4(a).

184 WRC 2007 Art 12(9). See 10.8.3.

185 This phrase does not appear in the Bunkers Convention 2001 Art 7(1) though its wording has the same effect.

186 LEG.92/13, 3 November 2006, page 18, para 4.71.

liabilities arising under the WRC 2007. This, however, is an impractical solution, particularly with respect to the EEZ, and coastal States are likely to make entry into their ports conditional on the ship having the appropriate insurance cover, but also on that ship assuming liability for wreck removal in the EEZ. This might include incidents that took place before the ship entered the port (such as having lost containers overboard). This raises important practical considerations for shipowners wishing to visit ports of States parties when the flag State is not a State party, and is considered in depth in Chapter 10. In essence, national law in the coastal State may recognise that the voluntary issuance of a WRC 2007 insurance certificate may create a direct liability under that law and the shipowner might also be treated as having accepted the imposition of liability upon it.[187]

7.4.5 WRC 2007 as generally accepted international rules and standards

Article 38 of the Vienna Convention provides that "[n]othing [in the convention] . . . precludes a rule set forth in a treaty from becoming binding upon a third State as a customary rule of international law, recognized as such". Indeed, UNCLOS is now regarded as reflecting customary international law, including those provisions making reference to "generally accepted international standards" or similarly worded provision.

The Netherlands raised the issue of application of the WRC 2007 to wrecks of non-State parties through both this mechanism and through customary international law. The delegation declared:

> If the wreck's flag State is not a party to the wreck removal convention and this convention has entered into force, the convention would be considered as an international standard or provision adopted through the competent international organisation, i.e. the IMO. The wreck removal convention would then constitute customary/conventional international maritime law and its provisions could be applicable to wrecks of a non-State party within the meaning of Art 38 of the Vienna Convention.[188]

This incorrectly conflates the two concepts. Art 38 of the Vienna Convention gives no meaning to "customary international law", raising only the possibility that a convention's provision might also become binding on a State through the separate and distinct process of customary international law. That phrase is addressed to some extent in Art 38 of the Statute of the ICJ when declaring as a source of law "international custom, as evidence of a general practice accepted as law". While a full discussion of the nature of customary international law is beyond the scope of this work, the WRC 2007 as a whole does not mirror customary international law, and though in theory is might evolve to be so, this evolution is not likely to occur very quickly.[189]

While "generally accepted international rules and standards" may have some similarity to customary international law in that evidence may be found in the practice of States, it

---

187 See 10.8.
188 LEG 86/4/2, 28 March 2003, 2.
189 In response to this position, the IMO Legal Committee report indicated that "[s]ome delegations expressed their reservations regarding the applicability of the prospective [WRC 2007] to wrecks of flag States which were not parties to the convention. In so doing some of these delegations expressed the view that the matter was more complex than was set out in document LEG 86/4/2, paragraph 11 in which it was noted that the [WRC 2007] could apply to those States as a customary rule of international law". LEG 86/15, 2 May 2003, 8, para 28.

is broader in that the practice of others than a State may be relevant, and arguably will have a lower threshold to make it relevant: being merely an accepted standards rather than being considered a legal obligation "accepted as law". That said, the position of the Netherlands raises the prospect of the WRC 2007 being applied to wrecks of a non-State party in a coastal State party's EEZ.[190] Importantly, this prospect arises from the fundamental principle that treaties do not bind non-State parties, but that parties to UNCLOS may have, through that treaty, have agreed to adopt the WRC 2007 as "generally accepted international rules and standards" for the prevention, reduction and control of pollution of the marine environment.

As discussed in 5.5.1, the concept of "generally accepted international rules and standards" is vague, ambiguous and subject to differing interpretations. At least as it is used in Art 211, which addresses marine pollution, it requires two criteria to be met: (a) that the laws in question are laws and regulations for the prevention, reduction and control of pollution of the marine environment; and (b) that they be generally acceptable.

7.4.5(a) Laws and regulations for the prevention, reduction and control of pollution
The rules and standards referred to do not necessarily encompass an entire convention, but more specific provisions that fall with the scope of rules and standards for the prevention, reduction and control of pollution of the marine environment. It is clear from UNCLOS Art 194(3)(b) that the kind of laws and regulations envisaged as necessary to prevent, reduce and control pollution are those relating to the operation of ships; being "measures to prevent accidents and dealing with emergencies, ensuring safety of operations at sea, preventing intentional and unintentional discharges, and regulating the design, construction, equipment, operation and manning of vessels". Art 211(2) then imposes this most clearly on flag States. As to coastal States, Art 211(3) provides for the adoption of such laws in relation to port entry and, tellingly, in Art 211(4) only to the territorial sea. As far as the EEZ in concerned, Art 211(5) applies the standard of "generally accepted international rules and standards" only in relation to enforcement as set out in Art 220.[191] As discussed in 5.5.1, this enforcement is in relation to breaches of those coastal State laws giving effect to these "generally accepted international rules and standards" and is significantly limited and constrained. It should be recalled that the phrase "generally accepted international rules and standards" in Part XII arose to resolve the contest between full coastal State jurisdiction over ship sourced marine pollution and exclusive flag State jurisdiction by assuring flag States that coastal States would not assert greater obligations that these. As such, it is doubtful whether those rules that address liability for wreck removal and the insurance arrangements to cover that liability (as opposed to removal of the hazard itself and the obligation to report the hazard[192]), could meaningfully be said to be rules for the "prevention, reduction and control of pollution" as envisaged in Part XII of UNCLOS.[193]

---

190 While UNCLOS Art 56(1)(b)(iii) does grant the coastal State jurisdiction with respect to the protection and preservation of the marine environment, these are subject to the relevant provisions of UNCLOS (ie Part XII) and other rights and duties provided in UNCLOS. See 5.5.1.
191 See also UNCLOS Part XII, Arts 223–233.
192 See UNCLOS Art 211(7).
193 See particularly the restrictive scope of those rules reflected in Art 194(3)(b)(iii) and Art 211(1).

7.4.5(b) Generally acceptable

Assuming that rules found within WRC 2007 could fall within the scope of rules and standards for the *prevention, reduction and control* of pollution, to be binding these rules must have reached the threshold of being "generally accepted". As discussed in 5.5.1, there is no agreement of what this threshold actually is. To reiterate Boyle's conclusion, the "use of rules of reference is sensible in principle but flawed in practice by the failure to specify with clarity when existing or future rules and standards become applicable".[194] Given the significant debate concerning the application of the convention to States parties only, it is questionable whether the WRC 2007 as a whole could be said to have reached this threshold. Merely being adopted at IMO is not likely to be sufficient, nor is its coming into force. However, given its amorphous nature, it is open to States to argue that "generally accepted rules and standards" that reflect and support some of the provisions of the WRC 2007 have emerged. This is certainly the case for coastal State intervention when the wreck poses a pollution hazard. Somewhat more difficult may be the exercise of the power to direct the shipowner of a wreck of a non-State party to remove the wreck. The greatest difficulty, however, is with respect to imposing liability on the shipowner and insurer of a wreck of a non-State party (and where no insurance certificate has been obtained from another State party). That said, many of the features of the WRC 2007, such as strict liability of the shipowner, the shipowner's defences, direct action against the insurer and limitation of liability are all features of the CLC 1992, Bunkers Convention 2001, to some extent the Athens Convention 2002 and at least in part the HNSC 2010. Since the WRC 2007 is based on these preceding conventions, particularly the CLC 1992, it is worth pausing to consider the extent to which the CLC 1992 applies to non-State parties and its relevance to the WRC 2007.

The similarity between the liability and insurance aspects of the WRC 2007 and those of the CLC 1992 and Bunkers Convention 2001[195] might suggest a broader interpretation such that it could apply to vessels of non-State parties. However, the WRC 2007 differs to the CLC 1992 and Bunkers Convention 2001 in some important respects. The WRC 2007 seeks to alter the balance between the rights and duties of coastal States and flag States provided for in UNCLOS,[196] as well as imposing liability for aspects of wreck removal and the requirement of the shipowner to have compulsory insurance. The power of a coastal State to require compulsory insurance certificates for ships passing through the EEZ is already circumscribed by the general provisions in UNCLOS that addresses the balance of interests in the EEZ.[197] The powers given to a coastal State to enforce compulsory insurance

---

194 *Boyle*, 357.
195 LEG/CONF 12/19, 27 March 2001.
196 In this respect, the CMI noted, in 1996, that "[a]s new specific rights would in effect be created it would be desirable that any convention should attract wide consensus". LEG 74/5/2, 5 September 1996, Add.1, 5.
197 The origins of the Bunkers Convention 2001 and the Athens Convention 2002 (and to some extent the WRC 2007) were in general a desire to ensure that shipowners should be obliged to have compulsory insurance cover for all maritime claims. The proposal had gradually been watered down, so that compulsory insurance would only be considered in specific contexts (eg passenger, bunker and wreck removal claims). For these reasons, the UK drafted a set of non-mandatory "Guidelines on Shipowners' Responsibilities in Respect of Maritime Claims" ("*Guidelines on Shipowners' Responsibilities*"), which was approved by the IMO Assembly: Resolution A.898(21), adopted 25 November 1999. These are designed to give guidance to shipowners and States to the effect that there should be insurance coverage for ships of 300 tons and above, at least up to the limits in the LLMC 1976 (or 1996). There is some dispute as to how far port States can impose compulsory insurance

requirements (eg CLC 1992 Art VII(11)) relate only to ships entering or leaving ports in its territory (or offshore terminals in the territorial sea) and do not extend directly to allow the coastal State to check on certificates of ships in the EEZ exercising their freedom of navigation.[198] It was in this context that the US strongly urged that the WRC 2007 needed to address expressly the position of flag States that were *not* party to the WRC 2007.[199]

The liability in the WRC 2007 is a great deal more limited than that of the CLC 1992 and Bunkers Convention 2001 and seeks only to cover the cost of aspects of wreck removal by the Affected State, rather than creating a specific liability regime for damages arising from a pollution incident. Arguably, the CLC 1992 and Bunkers Convention 2001 pollution liability regimes are built upon existing coastal State rights under UNCLOS, and as such, are to some extent limited only by the geographical scope of the conventions.[200] That the WRC 2007 does indeed impact on the balance of interests set out in UNCLOS is supported by the inclusion in the WRC 2007 of Arts 15 and 16. The former reiterates the dispute settlement provision of UNCLOS, while the latter stipulates that "[n]othing in this Convention shall prejudice the rights and obligations of any State under the United Nations Convention on the Law of the Sea, 1982, and under the customary international law of the sea". Neither the CLC 1992 nor the Bunkers Convention 2001 addresses the question of the relationship with UNCLOS. This is borne out by the degree of concern expressed by States during negotiations as to this relationship between the WRC 2007 and UNCLOS.

It is debatable whether aspects of the WRC 2007, such as the strict liability of the shipowner and direct action against an insurer, can reasonably be said to be "generally accepted international rules and standards" within the scope of Part XII UNCLOS so as to support the exercise of coastal State jurisdiction (as required in the WRC 2007 in relation to non-State party wrecks in the EEZ).[201] The difficulty is that it may be hard to find instances of where a coastal State has had directly to address the issue,[202] particularly given the commercial imperatives that require shipowners to hold insurance in order to enter ports of State parties. It might also be the case that the existence of eg CLC Art VII(11)

---

requirements to meet the guidelines, but international law seems to be moving to an increased recognition of the importance of such insurance. It is arguable that national legislation could be used to give effect to the Guidelines; eg in the UK under MSMSA 1997s 16.

198 The extent to which States can require compulsory insurance for ships transiting territorial waters (eg in traffic separation schemes) is more controversial. It appears that many States have already introduced insurance requirement, but these are generally limited to circumstances such as port entry, and the UK MSA 1995 s 192A specifically excludes from the requirement ships exercising the rights of passage (although it would seem to include fishing vessels).

199 For the strongest view in support of this view, see the US Statement at the diplomatic conference: LEG/Conf.16/18, 17 May 2007. See also LEG/Conf.16/6, 1 March 2007 and LEG/Conf.16/7, 15 March 2007.

200 The US adverted to this problem by suggesting that it would be beyond customary international law for a coastal State to impose financial costs on foreign shipowners where this was not related to a condition for port entry. It added that "several IMO conventions have been elaborated to fill that gap, most recently [the Bunkers Convention 2001]". LEG/Conf.16/7, 15 March 2007, largely repeating submissions in LEG 92/4/8, 15 September 2006, 3. Other conventions presumably included the CLC 1992, HNSC 2010 and Athens Convention 2002. See further CLC 1992 Art VII(1); See also Bunkers Convention 2001 Art 7(1).

201 See 5.5.1.

202 The CLC itself may not provide much guidance, because the IOPC Fund may always have been available to pay all of the claims under the Fund Convention Art 4(1)(a). Moreover, the only relevant practice under the CLC would be after the coming into force of the CLC 1992 in May 1996 when the CLC was extended into the EEZ.

and WRC 2007 Art 12(12) whereby shipowners voluntarily obtain a Convention insurance certificate to cover liabilities under the particular convention, and the insurer voluntarily provides one, creates the necessary jurisdictional scope for the coastal State to give effect to the WRC 2007. In those circumstances, it could be argued that any State would not be in breach of international law if it recognised such a voluntary liability in its national law.[203]

7.5 Cooperation

As the CMI pointed out, "[v]ery often the effectiveness and success of a wreck removal operation will be much dependent upon co-operation of state parties".[204] Indeed, so important is this issue that it was addressed in the Salvage Convention 1989, which provides, in Art 11 that:

> A State Party shall, whenever regulating or deciding upon matters relating to salvage operations such as admittance to ports of vessels in distress or the provision of facilities to salvors, take into account the need for co-operation between salvors, other interested parties and public authorities in order to ensure the efficient and successful performance of salvage operations for the purpose of saving life or property in danger as well as preventing damage to the environment in general.

While not as extensive, this sentiment is reflected in the WRC 2007 as a general principle, requiring States parties to "endeavour to co-operate when the effects of a maritime casualty resulting in a wreck involve a State other than the Affected State".[205] While this exhortation may appear somewhat modest, it should be viewed against the constitutional cooperative schemes already created by UNCLOS and OPRC 1990, and the many bilateral and multilateral (particularly regional) cooperative schemes that have resulted therefrom, such as the cooperative schemes that already exist such as the Bonn Agreement for Cooperation in Dealing with Pollution of the North Sea by Oil and Other Harmful Substances.[206]

7.6 Convention form

The WRC, like all international Conventions, contain a number of articles that address the "administrative" mechanisms for making the convention work, usually contained in the final clauses. This includes the process for signature, ratification accession or acceptance of the WRC 2007,[207] the process of denouncing the WRC 2007,[208] its entry into force,[209] the place of depositary of the WRC 2007 (IMO)[210] and its official languages.[211] Other important parts of the Convention are its preamble and annex.

---

203 See 10.8.4(a).
204 LEG 78/4/1, 13 August 1998, 7.
205 WRC 2007 Art 2(5). Introduced in LEG 91/3, 16 February 2006, Annex 1, 3.
206 See www.bonnagreement.org.
207 WRC 2007 Art 17.
208 WRC 2007 Art 19.
209 WRC 2007 Art 18. See 7.6.2.
210 WRC 2007 Art 20.
211 WRC 2007 Art 21, being Arabic, Chinese, English, French, Russian and Spanish languages.

7.6.4 Preamble

The WRC 2007 contains a relatively short preamble of five recitals.[212] These form part of the Convention and can be used as an aid to interpretation, and are therefore worth considering.[213] Recital 1 merely explains the need for the Convention, being that "wrecks, if not removed, may pose a hazard to navigation or the marine environment". This does of course misplace the objective of the Convention, in that it requires the hazard posed by the wreck, and not necessarily the wreck itself, to be removed. Nevertheless, it serves to make it clear that wrecks may pose a hazard to the marine environment and to navigation.

The third recital notes that wrecks may (and usually are) located in the territorial sea. This serves as notice that the scope of the Convention does take the territorial sea into account.

Recitals 2 and 4 essentially address the same thing—the need for uniform international rules to address the removal of the hazard and the allocation of liability. Recital 2 however, concentrates on the need for international rules—ie the WRC 2007 itself. Recital 4 follows the reference to the territorial sea and addresses the benefits from uniform regimes—that is national laws. In other words, recital 4 urges States to consider opting in such that uniform national laws will then apply both in the EEZ (the Convention's primary scope) and the territorial sea. Recital 4 extends and implements recital 2.

The fifth recital is important as it addresses the relationship between the WRC 2007 and UNCLOS. Again, this is rather modest in that it merely notes the importance of UNCLOS and customary international law and "the consequent need to implement the present Convention in accordance with such provisions". As discussed above, the relationship between UNCLOS and WRC 2007 required delicate drafting and concessions between States parties—such as that contained in Art 9(10)[214]—such that no stronger a recital could have been made. Nevertheless, this does, importantly, sit the WRC 2007 within this international constitutional framework despite some disagreement as to its exact terms.

7.6.5 Entry into force requirements

The WRC 2007 came into force on 14 April 2015, 12 months after the 10th ratification or similar method of being bound—that of Denmark. While the number of States needed to bring the Convention into force is entirely depended on the negotiating States, ten is a common number.[215]

Unlike many IMO Convention, there is no tonnage requirement needed to bring it into force. The US had considered that this failed to recognise the need for flag States to be part of the regime for it to be effective.[216] However, given that the WRC 2007 addresses in the main the rights and duties of Affected States (ie coastal States) rather than flag States, the tonnage requirement would have held the coastal States to ransom in that the large flag States could have dictated the timing of the Convention coming into force—and indeed

---

212 See LEG91/WP.1, 24 April 2006, 1.
213 Vienna Convention on the Law of Treaties Art 31.
214 See 7.3.2.
215 Ten was required to bring into force the Athens Convention 2002 as well as the LLMC 1996.
216 LEG/CONF.16/19, 23 May 1997, 1.

the very fact of it coming into force. In any event, many of the large flag States, such as Panama, Bahamas, Liberia, Malta, the Marshall Islands and the UK are party to the WRC 2007.[217]

7.6.6 Dispute settlement

The 2005 draft of the Convention merely provided that State parties would "settle any dispute between them concerning the interpretation or application of the Convention by negotiation, enquiry, mediation, conciliation, arbitration, judicial settlement, resort to regional agencies or arrangements or other peaceful means of their own choice".[218] By 2006, it was felt that merely providing for "agreed" or "diplomatic" means of settling disputes was insufficient and that some compulsory mechanism be utilised to ensure that a party could submit a dispute to an international court or tribunal and obtain an enforceable judgment or award.[219] Moreover, the concern that the WRC 2007 be consistent with UNCLOS, and the desire by many negotiating States to ensure that the WRC 2007 was couched in UNCLOS terms, resulted in a proposal to incorporate the UNCLOS dispute settlement provision into the WRC.[220] Part XV of UNCLOS, which had been subjected to long and detailed negotiations, was regarded as flexible in terms of the alternatives provided for as well as being capable of incorporation into the WRC 2007 without States having to be party to UNCLOS.[221] Indeed, in slightly different form, Art 287 of UNCLOS has substantially been copied into other international conventions, so as to form a consolidated "overall international systems of rules on the law of the sea".[222] A more detailed provision was then sourced from the UCH 2001,[223] which had been negotiated in the context of an agreement that too needed to be "consistent" with UNCLOS but in a "non-maritime" forum.[224] This detailed provision was substantially accepted and became Art 15 of the WRC 2007.[225]

As much of the content of this article is discussed in the context of UNCLOS and other Conventions that have incorporated it, there is no need for a full discussion here, but in brief, the dispute settlement provision is as follows. First, States are to resolve any dispute "through negotiation, enquiry, mediation, conciliation, arbitration, judicial settlement, resort to regional agencies or arrangements or other peaceful means of their choice". Secondly, if no settlement is possible within a reasonable period of time,[226] the provisions relating to the settlement of disputes set out in Part XV of UNCLOS shall apply *mutatis mutandis*, whether or not the States party to the dispute are also States parties to UNCLOS. This was of particular concern to the US given that it is not a State party to UNCLOS (as are Norway and Turkey).

---

217 See 11.2.
218 LEG 90/5, 2 February 2005, Annex 1, 13.
219 LEG92/4/1, 8 August 2006, 1.
220 LEG92/4/1, 8 August 2006, 1.
221 UNCLOS Part XV, see in particular Art 287.
222 LEG92/4/1, 8 August 2006, 2.
223 See 6.2.
224 LEG92/WP.6/Rev.1, 19 October 2006, 1; LEG 92/13, 3 November 2006.
225 But see US concerns, LEG/CONF.16/18, 17 May 2007, 2.
226 This is not to exceed 12 months after one State party has notified another that a dispute exists between them. WRC 2007 Art 15(2).

The dispute settlement provisions of UNCLOS are comprehensive and complex and includes a State party choosing one of a number of particular dispute settlement options. The choses are the settlement of a dispute by the International Tribunal for the Law of the Sea, the International Court of Justice, or a specially constituted arbitral tribunal.[227]

Where a State that is party to UNCLOS has elected a particular option that option will then apply to the WRC 2007 as well, thus mirroring the UNCLOS provision for that State. However, the State may, when ratifying, accepting, approving or acceding to the WRC 2007, or at any time thereafter, choose another of UNCLOS procedures that will then apply to the WRC 2007.[228] Where a State to the WRC 2007 is not a party to UNCLOS, and will not therefore have made any election amongst the UNCLOS options, then the WRC 2007 allows that State to make one of those elections as if it were a party to UNCLOS and that election will then apply to the WRC 2007.[229]

7.6.7 Annex

Attached to the WRC 2007 as an Annex is a pro forma "Certificate of insurance or other financial security in respect of liability for the removal of wrecks" to be issued in accordance with Art 12 WRC 2007.[230] The certificate provides for the details of the ship, the insurer and of the security needed to comply with the WRC 2007 to be detailed. It is a basic and straightforward certificate that provides both the minimum information necessary and a basis for uniformity across jurisdictions.

7.7 Participation

The diplomatic conference to negotiate the WRC 2007 was held from 14 to 18 May 2007 in Nairobi, Kenya. Sixty-four States[231] participated together with a number of observer missions from key industry groups such as the International Chamber of Shipping, the International Association of Ports and Harbours, the International Salvage Union and the International Group of P&I Clubs.

As late as 1999, the International Chamber of Shipping (ICS) questioned the necessity of adopting a wreck removal convention.[232] Moreover, if the draft was considered necessary, the ICS were opposed to its application to pollution or environment hazards and the compulsory insurance regime, and considered the general scope of the convention, particularly

---

227 UNCLOS Art 287.
228 WRC 2007 Art 15(2).
229 WRC 2007 Art 15(4).
230 See LEG/CONF.16/20, 23 May 2007, Annex.
231 Participating States were Algeria, Antigua and Barbuda, Argentina, Australia, Bahamas, Bangladesh, Belgium, Benin, Brazil, Bulgaria, Burundi, Canada, Chile, China, Cuba, Cyprus, Denmark, Egypt, Estonia, Finland, France, Germany, Ghana, Greece, India, Indonesia, Iran, Ireland, Italy, Japan, Kenya, Kuwait, Latvia, Liberia, Lithuania, Madagascar, Malaysia, Malta, Mauritius, Mexico, Morocco, the Netherlands, Nigeria, Norway, Papua New Guinea, the Philippines, Poland, Portugal, Qatar, Republic of Korea, Russian Federation, Saudi Arabia, Singapore, Somalia, South Africa, Spain, Sweden, Turkey, Ukraine, UK, Tanzania, US, Vanuatu and Venezuela. LEG/CONF.16/21, 22 May 2007.
232 LEG 79/5/1, 19 March 1999, 1.

in its application of related interest of States, to be unnecessarily vague.[233] It might appear, then, that major flag States would have little incentive to ratify the WRC 2007, as their ships may already be subject to State law in territorial waters and for entry into port, and there appears to be no reason for them to increase their potential liabilities to cover those in the EEZ.

Somewhat surprisingly, many flag States such as Panama, Liberia, Malta and the Marshall Islands have become party to the WRC 2007 such that it covered 32.9% of the world's merchant fleet from only ten States on its entry into force, and has since increased to 42 States covering 72.43% of world merchant tonnage.[234]

---

233 LEG 79/5/1, 19 March 1999, 1.
234 As at 21 February 2019: www.imo.org/en/About/Conventions/StatusOfConventions/Pages/Default.aspx. See 11.2.

CHAPTER 8

Wreck Removal Convention 2007

Scope

8.1 Introduction

In order to settle the scope of the wreck removal regime, two important issues required determination, both of which were subject to great debate. The first was to determine which wrecks would fall within the convention regime; this required a clear definition of "wrecks that pose a hazard". The second concerned the geographical scope of the convention and its effect on the balance of rights and duties of States that exists in customary and treaty-based international law.[1] This debate as to the geographical scope, which finally settled on the EEZ also allowed for a voluntary extension to the territorial sea via an "opt-in" provision. This was not only a hotly debated aspect of the scope of the WRC 2007 but led to a complex shoring-up of the rights and duties of coastal States in the territorial sea.

8.2 Wrecks that pose a hazard

While titled the "wreck removal convention", the intent in fact is to address hazards that emanate from, or are caused by, some wrecks rather than targeting all wrecks.[2] The concept of hazard therefore lies at the core of the Convention, but the convention itself is concerned with the wreck as the source of that hazard. As such, both "hazard" and "wreck" needed to be clearly defined, as they operate in tandem to set the scope of the convention. The co-determinative nature of these two definitions also required other terms to be clearly defined, specifically that of "ship", "marine causality" and "removal". These are interlinked in a quite intricate way which requires a rather complicated, step-by-step approach to understand the scope of the Convention.

8.2.1 Defining "wreck"

As discussed in Chapter 3, defining wreck is no easy task. In light of that difficulty, it is not surprising that there was "endless debate at every IMO Legal Committee meeting"[3] about

---

1 See 5.4.2 and 7.7.4.4.
2 Indeed, Poland had proposed that the title of the convention be changed to the "Convention on Elimination of Hazard Posed by Wrecks". LEG 92/4/6, 15 September 2001, 1.
3 P Griggs, "Wreck Removal: Draft Convention" (2006) *CMI Yearbook 2005–2006* [*Griggs, Convention*] 379.

delimiting those wrecks that, if constituting a hazard, should be subject to a wreck removal regime. The resulting broad definition of wreck was finally agreed on:[4]

"Wreck", following upon a maritime casualty, means:
  (a) a sunken or stranded ship; or
  (b) any part of a sunken or stranded ship, including any object that is or has been on board such a ship; or
  (c) any object that is lost at sea from a ship and that is stranded, sunken or adrift at sea; or
  (d) a ship that is about, or may reasonably be expected, to sink or to strand, where effective measures to assist the ship or any property in danger are not already being taken.

To fully understand the scope of this definition, is it necessary not only to consider the scope of many of the terms and phrases used in it, but also a number of things that were excluded from the definition, and therefore fall outside the WRC 2007 definition of what is a "wreck". These are dealt with in turn.

8.2.1(a) Maritime casualty

As a starting point, not all wrecks are subject to the WRC 2007 regime; only that "following upon a maritime casualty". A "[m]aritime casualty" is defined in the WRC 2007 as "a collision of ships, stranding or other incident of navigation, or other occurrence on board a ship or external to it resulting in material damage or imminent threat of material damage to a ship or its cargo".[5] This definition is not new and was first drafted as Art II(1) of the Intervention Convention 1969, and then substantially reproduced in Art 221(2) of UNCLOS.[6] The generality of this definition (at least in UNCLOS) allows for a broad interpretation.[7] Whilst a collision or stranding of a ship is relatively clear, an "incident of navigation", "an occurrence on board a ship" or an occurrence "external to it" cover a range of possible factual circumstances. In this light, a ship becomes a wreck in circumstances that are *ipso facto* a maritime casualty.[8] As such, the only limitation inherent in this qualification to wreck subject to the WRC 2007 regime is that the incident gives rise to "material damage or imminent threat of material damage to a ship or its cargo". It is thus more concerned with what the consequences of an incident are rather than the cause of the incident. The focus is clearly on the hazard rather than the events which give rise to the hazard.

---

4 WRC 2007 Art 1(4). To some extent this definition influenced the Institute of International Law's definition of "wreck" and "sunken State ship" in its 2015 Resolution on *The Legal Regime of Wrecks of Warships and Other State-Owned Ships in International Law*. Article 1(1) provides that "wreck" means sunken State ship which is no longer operational, or any part thereof, including any sunken object that is or has been on board such ship"; and Art 1(2) that "sunken State vessel" means "a warship, naval auxiliary or other ship owned by a State and used at the time of sinking solely for governmental non-commercial purposes. It includes all or part of any cargo or other object connected with such a ship regardless of whether such cargo or object is owned by the State or privately. This definition does not include stranded ships, ships in the process of sinking, or oil platforms". See *Ronzitti* (2015), 371.

5 WRC 2007 Art 1(3). See also MSA 1995 s 137(9). For a more detailed consideration about how far the definition extends to cargo removal, see 8.2.1(d) and 10.6.

6 UNCLOS Art 221(2) uses the term "vessel" rather than "ship" in its definition of "maritime casualty". See further *Nordquist Volume IV*, 309–314.

7 *Nordquist, Volume IV*, 313.

8 Richard Shaw, "The Nairobi Wreck Removal Convention" (2007) 13 *Journal of International Maritime Law* 429 [*Shaw*], 434.

This definition of maritime casualty does however have some limiting effect. It does not, for example, apply to ships sunk for operational reasons, or dumped.[9] It is also not clear at first blush whether it includes ships abandoned by its crew and left floating and adrift.[10]

8.2.1(b) Sunken or stranded ship

The first of the four categories of "wreck" is a "sunken or stranded ship".[11] Whether a ship has stranded[12] or sunk is merely an evidentiary issue, and no further guidance on this is provided in the WRC 2007.

The term "ship" is defined in the WRC 2007 in broad terms,[13] being "a seagoing vessel of any type whatsoever" and, in a non-exhaustive list of examples, includes "hydrofoil boats, air-cushion vehicles, submersibles, floating craft and floating platforms, except when such platforms are on location engaged in the exploration, exploitation or production of sea-bed mineral resources".[14] While "seagoing vessel"[15] excludes vessels used exclusively for river-going,[16] all other seagoing vessels are included within this broad definition, including vessels that do not navigate under their own power being merely "floating craft" such as a "dumb" barge.[17] It also, by way of example, includes hydrofoil boats, being those that use a foil to lift the hull out of the water once the ship has gained sufficient speed.

It also includes air-cushioned vehicles, ie hovercraft. These craft are used extensively in some jurisdictions, particularly in the English Channel and other European waters. They are not, however, always treated in the same way as a conventional ship or vessel eg LLMC 1976 does not apply to "air-cushioned vehicles".[18] Reference then in the WRC 2007 Art 10(2) to the right to limit liability in accordance with the LLMC 1976 would mean that no limitation can be provided for in relation to air-cushioned vehicles unless by way of national legislation[19] or some other international regime.

The WRC 2007 will apply to the wreck of all these seagoing vessels no matter their size. Although small craft of less than 300 gt are not required to maintain insurance cover for wreck removal,[20] the WRC 2007 applies to them in all other respects.[21]

---

9 LEG 84/14, 7 May 2002, 8. Ships sunk for operational reasons are address in the 1972 Convention for the Prevention of Marine Pollution by Dumping of Wastes and other Matters Art IV and 1996 Protocol Art 4. LEG 85/3, 17 August 2002, Annex 2, 3. See 14.1.2(a).

10 See 8.2.1(f) and 11.4.

11 WRC 2007 Art 1(4)(a).

12 For a technical explanation of the condition, see eg American Society of Naval Engineers and JMS Naval Architects and Salvage Engineers, *Marine Casualty Response: Salvage Engineering* (Kendall/Hunt, 1999), Chapter 5.

13 See also MARPOL Art 2(4).

14 WRC 2007 Art 1(2).

15 See 10.2.7.

16 LEG/CONF.16/12, 24 April 2007, Annex 1.

17 See 10.2.7 and G Gauci, "The International Convention on the Removal of Wrecks 2007—A Flawed Instrument?" (2009) JBL 203, 206.

18 See Art 15(5)(a), and 2.5.2.

19 Hovercraft are regulated in UK by the *Hovercraft Act* 1968, and included in the MSA 1995 wreck regime, see *Hovercraft (Application of Enactment) Order* 1972 (SI 1972/971) Art 8(1) and see 11. See further *Kennedy & Rose*, 125.

20 WRC 2007 Art 12(1).

21 LEG 74/5/2, 20 August 1996, Annex 2.

8.2.1(c) Objects from ships
The WRC 2007 further defines "wreck" to include "any part of a sunken or stranded ship, including any object that is or has been on board such a ship".[22] The intent here appears twofold: first to include cases where a ship has broken into separate parts such that each part can still be dealt with as a wreck as if it were a whole, and secondly to ensure that all objects associated with the ship, including crew and passenger belongings, tackle and equipment, form part of the single whole—the wreck—captured by a combination of Art 1(4)(a) and (b) read together. The objects referred to, then, must be those found with that part of the ship. This includes cargo, including the carcasses of animals.[23] There is no mention in the WRC 2007, though, about bodies and human remains and it is difficult to see that they are "objects".[24] Objects no longer found with the ship, or part of the ship, are covered in the following section.

8.2.1(d) Objects and cargo lost at sea
The third "category" of wreck reflects these separate components in that it includes within the definition of wreck "any object that is lost at sea from a ship and that is stranded, sunken or adrift at sea".[25] The ship itself may not be wreck, but anything that was at one time on the ship at sea may be "wreck".[26] Both this and the reference to "any object that is or has been on board such a ship" in Art 1(4)(b) raise the possibility of cargo being included in the definition of wreck. Indeed, the most likely objects to be washed overboard from a ship, without any mishap to the ship itself, is cargo. This would include cargo such as logs and especially containers, both of which might lie mostly submerged but still afloat, making them treacherous navigational hazards.[27] This inclusion of cargo within the definition of wreck was a key point of negotiation and is discussed in detail in Chapter 10.

Wreck is often said to include flotsam, jetsam and lagan.[28] To the extent that these arise from a maritime casualty, they will fall within the definition of wreck in the WRC 2007. However, things deliberately thrown overboard where no maritime casualty exists is not wreck, but rather regarded as objects dumped overboard and subject to anti-dumping laws such as the LC 1972 and LC Protocol 1996.[29]

8.2.1(e) Effective salvage of ships about to sink or strand
The WRC 2007 applies to ships in a particular condition, being "sunken or stranded". While neither is defined, there is not likely to be any difficulty in determining when a vessel is in either condition, and the ordinary meaning of the terms in relation to the evidence ought to resolve the issue. During negotiations, a number of States were concerned to ensure that the convention allowed States to take action in respect of ships that had not

---

22 WRC 2007 Art 1(4)(b).
23 See 10.6
24 It is not clear if the position in the other official languages makes this any clearer, eg with "*objet*" in French. Cf the discussion of "objects" in relation to cargo: see 10.6.2.
25 WRC 2007 Art 1(4)(c).
26 LEG 78/4/2, 14 August 1998, 2.
27 LEG 87/4, 7 August 2003, Annex 1, 2.
28 See 3.1.
29 *Berlingieri*, 80. See 14.1.2.

yet sunk or stranded, but might do so.[30] The difficulty with this is that it not only deals with ships that are not wrecks, but then possibly interferes with the application of salvage law and the scope of the Salvage Convention 1989.[31] The place of a salvor in the wreck removal regime was of great importance, and during negotiations it was clear that salvors were regarded, in many States, as first responders whose capacity and capability ought not to be restricted in the negotiated outcome. On the other hand, a number of States wanted the capacity to deal with ships that were not yet wrecks but might become so.

An early approach to this problem was to include within the scope of the convention not just wrecks but also a ship that was a "casualty", being a ship "becoming or which may reasonably be expected to become a wreck by reason of: (a) collision, stranding or any other incident of navigation; or (b) other occurrence on board the ship, or external to it resulting in material damage, or imminent threat of material damage, to the ship".[32] A later alternative was to include a provision that allowed a State to take preventative measures in relation to a ship that may become a wreck,[33] much in the same way that the CLC 1992 allows for States to undertake preventative measures.[34] The debate turned on the point at which the convention should include ships that were not yet wrecks but may become so, but should not hamper the activities of salvors. The solution was to include ships that might become a wreck in the sense of being stranded or sunk, but only if no salvage activities were underway at that point in time. The result is that the fourth "category" of wreck is "a ship that is about, or may reasonably be expected, to sink or to strand", with the proviso that "no effective measures to assist such a ship or property in danger is not already being taken".[35]

This proviso reflects the Legal Committee's recognition of the rights of salvors in possession and attempts to entrench these rights in the WRC 2007, since it is generally accepted that it is beneficial to all concerned that encouragement be given for the salvage of wrecks. This proviso is, however, limited in that it only applies when a ship "is about, or may reasonably be expected to sink or strand". As soon as it has sunk or stranded, it is a wreck for the purposes of the WRC 2007 irrespective of any salvage activity. Such vessels are usually those to which salvage services are rendered and, in order to facilitate such salvage by not interfering with such activity, the definition only applies when no "effective" measures to assist such a ship or property in danger is not already being taken.[36]

Effective salvage activity will therefore take the casualty out of the scope of wreck for the purposes of the WRC 2007. It may be difficult to determine exactly when this occurs, given the uncertainty, for example, as to when an abandoned vessel still afloat is "about" to either sink or strand, and whether the assistance provided is "effective". This value judgment lies with the Affected State, which may therefore intervene if it considers that the measures are not effective and thus the wreck poses a hazard. The Affected State may

---

30 LEG 79/5, 10 February 1999, 3.
31 See 2.7.1.
32 LEG 79/5, 10 February 1999, 3.
33 LEG 82/5/1, 15 September 2000, 3.
34 CLC 1992 Art II(b). *Berlingieri*, 122.
35 WRC 2007 Art 1(4)(d).
36 WRC 2007 Art 9(5). The word "effective" was added to the definition at the insistence of the CMI and International Salvage Union. *Shaw*, 434.

however be liable to the salvor if its interference is unjustified.[37] This delicate balance recognises the importance of salvage services in dealing with hazardous wreck and encouraging such services by not interfering with the rights of a salvor in possession. As such, where effective salvage in underway, the Salvage Convention 1989, and not the WRC 2007, may govern the activities of the salvor.[38]

8.2.1(f) Derelict and abandoned ships

Throughout the debate on including within the scope of wrecks those vessels that were not yet wreck in the sense of being sunk or stranded, but might become so, was the place of abandoned vessels or, in salvage terms, derelict. An abandoned vessel is "derelict" when it is abandoned at sea by the master and crew, without any intention of returning to it (*sine animo revertendi*) or hope of recovery (*sine spe recuperandi*).[39] While it includes ships still afloat, it is also applied to vessels that have sunk.[40] As such, sunken derelict is included in this definition of wreck as a sunken ship. No mention, however, is made of a ship that is a floating derelict or abandoned. Earlier drafts of the convention had included derelict in the definition of wreck.[41] Indeed, the 1996 CMI review of national legislation revealed that "legislation in most countries defined wreck as "vessels that are sunk, stranded or abandoned".[42] However, in these earlier attempts to address wrecks, being vessels that have sunk or stranded as well as those that "may reasonably be expected to become a wreck" the draft convention had provided a definition for "wreck" and another for "casualty" such as "drifting ships with engine problems" and those that "may reasonably be expected to become a wreck".[43] This would include, but not be limited to, those abandoned by its crew. However, a number of delegations at the 78th Legal Committee "expressed concerns about the inclusion of drifting ships in the draft WRC 2007".[44] What is not clear is whether this applied to a manned drifting ship or only to abandoned drifting ships. By 1999, the Legal Committee had decided to combine the definitions of "wreck" and "casualty".[45] This had the effect of making "casualty" a subset of "wreck", significantly broadening the power of the Affected State over ships that were, for example, manned ships that had simply broken down. An attempt was made to narrow the scope by referring to the latter as "uncontrolled ships"[46] or to a "ship not under command".[47] An alternative proposal was to limit the scope of the convention to "wreck" as then defined as to exclude casualty, but to allow a State to

---

37 Richard Shaw, "The Nairobi Wreck Removal Convention" (2007) 13 JML 429, 434.

38 That is, if the relevant State is party to the Salvage Convention 1989. That Convention may apply to activities of salvors that are also governed by the WRC 2007 where the registered owner or the Affected State engages a salvor to remove a hazardous wreck. See 12.1.1. Note that in the territorial sea, an Affected State may retain greater rights in national law: see 8.4.1.

39 *Kennedy & Rose*, 104. See 3.3.

40 HMS *Thetis* (1834) 2 Knapp 390 (PC); 3 Hagg 229, 166 ER 390; *The Tubantia* (1924) P 78, 18 Ll L Rep 158; *The Lusitania* [986] QB 384. See 3.1

41 LEG/WG(WR).I/4, Annex Art A, 12 December 1973.

42 LEG 75/6/2, 14 February 1996, 5.

43 LEG 79/5, 10 February 1999, 3.

44 LEG 78/11, 2 November 1998, 12.

45 LEG 80/5, 10 September 1999, 2.

46 LEG 81/6, 25 February 2000, 2.

47 LEG 82/5/1, 15 September 2000, 2. This was inspired by the term used in COLREGS rule 3.

take preventative measures in relation to ships that may reasonably be expected to become a wreck".[48] This was in part inspired by the ability to take preventative measures pursuant to the CLC 1992.[49] With the inclusion of "a ship that is about, or may reasonably be expected, to sink or to strand, where effective measures to assist the ship or any property in danger are not already being taken" within the definition of wreck, abandoned ships were simply ignored and their place in the definition left in some doubt.

That the definition might have intended to exclude floating abandoned ships could be supported by the fact that a ship that is merely abandoned by its crew—perhaps where it is more a liability than an asset to the owner—may not have been involved in a maritime casualty in the narrow sense.[50] Indeed, an unsuccessful attempt had been made to include abandoned vessels in the definition of maritime casualty.[51] The explanation given was that it had been clear from the outset that the convention "would deal with wrecks following a maritime casualty" as defined in the Intervention Convention 1969 and UNCLOS.[52]

A broad interpretation of "incident of navigation" in the definition of maritime casualty might include the abandonment of its crew with the resulting inability to be navigated, thus posing an imminent threat of material damage. Similarly, the abandonment of the crew could fall within "or other occurrence". However, this does not cure the requirement that the floating derelict or abandoned ship be about to or may reasonably be expected to sink or strand.[53]

It might be argued that this unnecessarily narrows the scope of the convention. The threshold was not intended to be used to narrow the definition of wreck in this sense, but rather to act as a threshold when applied in conjunction with the requirement that "effective measures to assist the ship or any property in danger are not already being taken". It might be assumed that a floating and drifting derelict would at some stage strand or sink, and at all times would be a navigational hazard, and would thus fall within the definition of wreck.[54] This appears to accord with the view of the Legal Committee when dealing with an earlier definition of "casualty" such that floating vessels, and vessels that have capsized but still afloat, would fall within the scope of the Convention.[55] Moreover, the result of an expended interpretation would align with the inclusion in the definition of wreck of any object, such as cargo, from a ship "adrift at sea". It would also be consistent with the LLMC 1996, which in Art 2(d) makes claims "in respect of the raising, removal, destruction or the rendering harmless of a ship which is sunk, wrecked, stranded *or abandoned*, including anything that is or has been on board such ship", subject to limitation of liability.[56]

---

48 LEG 82/5/1, 15 September 2000, 3.
49 CLC 1992 Art II(b). *Berlingieri*, 122.
50 See 10.5.1(a), 11.4.
51 LEG 89/5, 17 August 2004, Annex 3, 1.
52 LEG 89/5, 17 August 2004, Annex 3, 1. Intervention Convention 1969 Art II and UNCLOS Art 221(2).
53 See 10.5.1.
54 See LEG75/6, 31 December 1996, 5 for support to include "drifting ships"; within the scope of "wreck'". See also LEG 89/5/2, 10 September 2004, 2, where CMI declared that it understood this article to "cover the position where a vessel has been abandoned and represents a hazard"'. See also 10.5.1(a).
55 LEG 78/4/2, 14 August 1998, 4.
56 Own emphasis.

This, however, is likely to be regarded as too generous an interpretation and does not seem to accord with the general intent of Art 1(4) in addressing wrecks following a maritime casualty.[57]

8.2.1(g) Fixed and floating platforms

A vast array of different platforms, drilling rigs, offshore mobile units, installations and other structures are utilised in the exploration and exploitation of seabed mineral resources. To what extent some of these should be subject to the IMO's remit and the extent to which they should be assimilated with ships, has evolved over the course of the IMO's standards setting remit, and continues to be a vexed question.

Under UNCLOS Art 60, coastal States are granted rights within the EEZ in respect of installations and structures, including the right to remove abandoned or disused facilities to ensure safety of navigation, and with due regard to the marine environment.[58] As such, coastal States have considerable regulatory control over these platforms when on location. IMO conventions have therefore largely sought to exclude platforms and similar structures from their scope when they are engaged in the exploration and exploitation of the resources of the seabed and the ocean floor and the subsoil thereof. Nevertheless, when these installations and platforms are being moved to or from their operating location, they have been brought within the scope of some IMO conventions. The scope of the Intervention Convention 1969 defines "ship" as "any sea-going vessel of any type whatsoever", but excludes those engaged in the exploration and exploitation of the resources of the sea-bed and the ocean floor and the subsoil thereof.[59]

The Salvage Convention 1989 takes a substantially similar approach, but in different form. It defines "vessel" as "any ship or craft, or any structure capable of navigation"[60] which could also include many forms of fixed or floating platforms. However, in a separate article the Salvage Convention 1989 provides that it "shall not apply to fixed or floating platforms or to mobile offshore drilling units when such platforms or units are on location engaged in the exploration, exploitation or production of sea-bed mineral resources".[61] The exclusion of fixed or floating platforms or to mobile offshore drilling units[62] when so engaged means that when not engaged and being towed to location, for example, they will fall within the definition of "vessel" and are a subject of salvage.[63]

Fixed and floating platforms are included within the definition of ship in MARPOL, defining a "ship" as "a vessel of any type whatsoever operating in the marine environment

---

57 See 10.5.1(a), 11.4 and on the difference between abandonment and dumping, 14.2.
58 UNCLOS Art 60(3).
59 Intervention Convention 1969 Art II(2)(b). In full it defines a "ship" as "(a) any sea-going vessel of any type whatsoever, and (b) any floating craft, with the exception of an installation or device engaged in the exploration and exploitation of the resources of the sea-bed and the ocean floor and the subsoil thereof".
60 Salvage Convention 1989 Art 1(b).
61 Salvage Convention 1989 Art 3.
62 For a definition of mobile offshore drilling units, and their regulation, see IMO MODU Code, Res A.414(XI), 1979 as amended by MSC/Circ.561, Res A.649(16) as amended by MSC/Circ.561 and Res MSC.38(63) and Res A.1023, 18 January 2010.
63 *Kennedy & Rose*, 148. See however, LEG 91/3, 16 February 2006, Annex 3, 1, in which the Netherlands delegation concludes that the Salvage Convention 1989 excludes fixed platforms from the definition of "ship" in the Salvage Convention 1989.

and includes hydrofoil boats, air-cushion vehicles, submersibles, floating craft and fixed or floating platforms".[64] Indeed, MARPOL does regulate certain aspects of "fixed and floating drilling rigs when engaged in the exploration, exploitation and associated offshore processing of sea-bed mineral resources and other platforms".[65]

These three conventions then appear to contemplate certain structures being included within their remit. Not surprising then, so too did the first drafts of the WRC 2007, defining "ship" to include "fixed or floating platforms" and "mobile offshore drilling units",[66] except those on location engaged in the exploration, exploitation or production of sea-bed mineral resources. The inclusion of these within the WRC 2007 was however much debated. The 1996 CMI review of national legislation revealed little consistency as to whether platforms were included in their national wreck removal regimes,[67] and there was some inconsistency with the IMO conventions. For example, as discussed above, while the Intervention Convention 1969, MARPOL and the Salvage Convention 1989 evince some inconsistency, yet contemplate some inclusion, the LLMC 1976 quite explicitly excludes application to "floating platforms constructed for the purpose of exploring or exploiting the natural resources of the sea-bed or the subsoil thereof".[68] This appears to apply to floating platforms being towed, or underway under its own power as well as when on station exploring or exploiting the natural resources of the seabed or the subsoil.[69]

Against this inconsistency and the ongoing concern during negotiations to exclude from its scope anything "engaged in the exploration, exploitation or production of sea-bed mineral resources", there was a clear recognition that platforms and similar structures being taken to and from location posed a significant risk that the convention ought to deal with.[70] In 1990, for example, the Norwegian jack-up offshore platform *West Gamma* capsized under tow, and the work to ensure sufficient keel clearance above the wreck cost the German government 11.6 million Deutschmarks.[71] The towage of these structures were sufficiently prevalent and of concern, that the Maritime Safety Committee adopted Guidelines on the Safety of Towed Ships and other Floating Objects including Installations, Structures and Platforms at Sea in 1993.[72]

In 2002, the definition of wreck, for the first time, deleted reference to fixed platforms or offshore mobile units, though retained reference to "floating platforms", though with the exception of those "on location engaged in the exploration, exploitation or production of sea-bed mineral resources".[73] This amendment was explained as being in line with Art 3 of the Salvage Convention 1989 and several reasons were advanced for this change. The first

---

64 MARPOL Art 2(4).
65 MARPOL Annex I, reg 21.
66 LEG 74/5, 17 June 1996, Annex Art 1(1), substantially replicating MARPOL Art 2(4).
67 LEG 75/6/2, 14 February 1996, 5.
68 LLMC 1976 Art 15(5)(b).
69 Like the other "ship" excluded from the LLMC 1976—air-cushioned vehicles (see above)—this means that reference to the LLMC 1976 limitation of liability in WRC 2007 Art 12(2) does not apply.
70 LEG 67/8, 29 June 1992.
71 LEG 75/6/1, 14 February 1997, Annex 1 and J Vinnem, *Offshore Risk Assessment* (2nd ed, Springer, 2007), 258.
72 Res A.765(18), 4 November 1993. This has been supplemented by Guidelines for Safe Ocean Towage MSC/Cir.883, 21 December 1998.
73 LEG 85/3, 17 August 2002, Annex 2, 2.

was that "in other maritime conventions (such as the Intervention Convention 1969 Art II paragraph 2 and the Salvage Convention 1989 Art 3), fixed platforms are not included in the definition of 'ship'".[74] This appears to be a poor justification. While it might be true that the Intervention Convention 1969 does not mention "fixed platforms", it also does not mention floating platforms either, and provides no basis for distinguishing between the two. Similarly, the Salvage Convention 1989 refers to both fixed and floating platform in Art 3, and to the extent that this merely excludes those on location, they are included in the definition of "vessel".

The second justification for excluding fixed platforms is perhaps more convincing. Fixed platforms on location engaged in the exploration, exploitation or production of seabed mineral resources are not covered by the P&I Club insurance regime.[75] Moreover, as they are excluded from the LLMC 1996, so their exclusion is warranted in a regime that addresses liability and insurance issues.[76]

The reference to fixed platforms in Art 1(2) is by way of an inclusion in the definition of ship, being "a seagoing vessel of any type whatsoever". By definition then, a floating platform is a ship. The result is that floating platforms not on location or on location but not engaged in the exploration, exploitation or production of seabed mineral resources, are then subject to the WRC 2007. When engaged in exploration or exploitation they are excluded from this regime as they are subject to national legislation and licensing conditions and an overlap with these and the WRC 2007 was considered undesirable.[77] The most all-encompassing interpretation then would define a "floating platform" as any platform afloat at the time that a determination as to whether it is a wreck is required.

8.2.1(h) Wrecked warships and other government non-commercial ships
While a "warship or other ship owned or operated by a State and used, for the time being, only on Government non-commercial service" may be a wreck, the WRC 2007 does not apply to such a wreck unless that flag State decides otherwise.[78]

Drafts of the WRC 2007 had included a definition of warship[79] by incorporating a reference to Art 29 of UNCLOS that defines a warship as

> a ship belonging to the armed forces of a State bearing the external marks distinguishing such ships of its nationality, under the command of an officer duly commissioned by the government of the State and whose name appears in the appropriate service list or its equivalent, and manned by a crew which is under regular armed forces discipline.

The aim was to ensure that decommissioned warships, which are not infrequently lost under tow and cause navigational hazards were included within the WRC 2007.[80] For

---

74 LEG 85/3, 17 August 2002, Annex 2, 2. See also LEG91/3, 16 February 2006, Annex 3, 1.
75 LEG 85/3, 17 August 2002, Annex 2, 2. See also LEG91/3, 16 February 2006, Annex 3, 1.
76 LEG 91/3, 16 February 2006, Annex, 3. See also LEG 74/5/2, 20 August 1996.
77 LEG 74/5/2, 20 August 1996, Annex 2, 2.
78 WRC 2007 Art 4(2). A similar exclusion applies to Part XII of UNCLOS, Art 235. The WRC 2007 Art 4(3) replicates the Salvage Convention 1989 Art 4(2), by declaring that "[w]here a State Party decides to apply this Convention to its warships or other ships as described in paragraph 2, it shall notify the Secretary-General thereof specifying the terms and conditions of such application".
79 LEG 91/3, 16 February 2006, Annex 1, 3.
80 LEG 74/5, 17 June 1996, Annex, 2, 11.

example, the Russian warship *Vitse-Admiral Drozhd*, decommissioned in 1990, sank under tow in 1992.[81] Similarly, the US submarine *SS-331*, decommissioned in 1970, sank while under tow near Cape Flattery, Washington,[82] and the US guided missile destroyer *Benjamin Stoddert*, decommissioned in 1992, sank under tow in 2001 in the Pacific.[83] However, since the term "warship" will necessarily be interpreted in accordance with UNCLOS, this specific incorporation was unnecessary[84] and, as a matter of consistency, the exclusion provided for in the Salvage Convention 1989[85] was substantially adopted in the WRC 2007. In this context, it means that decommissioned warship will no longer satisfy the definition of warship and are thus covered by the WRC 2007. That said, a decommissioned warship may still be a "ship owned or operated by a State", and thus fall outside of the scope of the WRC 2007. It thus becomes important, on a case-by-case basis, for a decommissioned warship being towed to have its status clarified as this does give rise to some difficulties in the provision of insurance cover, and presumably the tug will arrange cover for the tow on a commercial basis.

8.2.1(i) Aircraft

Early drafts of the WRC 2007 had included aircraft[86] within its scope and some States had supported their inclusion. The 1996 CMI review of national legislation revealed that some States, such as Argentina, Germany, Japan and Denmark, did expressly include aircraft in their wreck removal regime, while others such as Canada, India, Italy, Netherlands, Sweden, Belgium and Liberia did so by implication merely by providing for a wide range of objects that might be hazardous.[87]

However, it had been pointed out that the international regime that applies to aircraft is substantially different to that applicable to ships, and that the resulting wreck removal regime might not address issues such as limitation of liability, insurance cover and financial security in the same way.[88] By 1997, a number of States had expressed reservations about the inclusion of aircraft,[89] and sought advice from the International Civil Aviation Organisation (ICAO). ICAO noted that the Convention on Civil Aviation addresses issues relating to aircraft accident and incident investigation and which require the removal of a wrecked aircraft, including from water.[90] Aircraft, though, are usually recovered as part of the incident investigation by the State responsible for the accident investigation.[91] Moreover, some liability issues are addressed in the Convention on Damage Caused by Foreign Aircraft to Third Parties on the Surface. In light of ICAO's comments, the Legal Committee decided to exclude aircraft from the scope of the convention.[92] The WRC 2007 does not therefore

---

81 http://128.121.102.226/shipind.html.
82 www.uboat.net/allies/warships/ship/3077.html.
83 www.navysite.de/dd/ddg22.htm.
84 LEG 91/12, 9 May 2006, 8; LEG 91/12, 9 May 2006, 8.
85 Salvage Convention 1989 Art 4.
86 See LEG XII/4, Annex Art II, 8 March 1972; LEG/WG(ER).I/4, Annex Art A, 12 December 1973.
87 LEG 75/6/2, 14 February 1996, 5.
88 LEF 74/5/2, 20 August 1996, Annex 2, 2.
89 LEG 75/11, 29 April 1997, 12.
90 Convention on Civil Aviation, Annex 13, Standards 3.2, 5.1, 5.2 and 5.6.
91 LEG 77/5/1, 19 March 1998, 1.
92 LEG 77/11, 28 April 1998, 12.

apply to incidents such as the wreck of the Malaysian Airlines MH 370 that disappeared in 2014, even if it was found to be a navigation or pollution hazard (which is unlikely).

8.2.2 Defining "hazard"

The very object of the WRC 2007 is to grant a State the power to take measures to remove a hazard posed by a wreck, which may necessitate removal of the wreck itself.[93] The concept of "hazard" lies at the core of the Convention and required careful delimitation. Indeed, the Legal Committee were concerned that the resulting definition be clearly defined to ensure that the convention was "a worthwhile instrument and practical to enforce".[94] Originally restricted only to navigational hazards,[95] it was considerably broadened by building on existing liability regimes that addressed maritime hazards to the marine environment.[96] This had been a controversial extension at first, as there was a view that pollution issues were already covered by the CLC 1992 and Fund Conventions and that the Bunkers Convention 2001 and HNSC 2010 were also applicable to both ships and cargo respectively. The 1996 CMI review of national legislation, however, revealed that most States' wreck removal regimes extended beyond navigational hazards to include pollution and other environmental threats.[97]

There is a very close relation though between a navigational hazard and a threat to the environment, as a wreck that does pose a navigational hazard invariably poses a threat to the environment. Should an actual navigational incident occur and a ship collide with a wreck, there might not only be the loss of bunker fuel from one or both vessels, but other environmental threats might also occur, including the smothering of reefs by the ships or their cargo, the leaching of TBT paint into the environment, the discharge of harmful invasive organisms from the loss of ballast waters and the interference of spawning and breeding grounds for marine fauna.[98] While a number of States attempted to restrict the scope of the convention to navigation hazards, the broader view prevailed. In part this was supported by a review of national legislation on wreck removal by the CMI that revealed that, of the States considered, most defined a "hazard" to extend beyond mere navigational

---

93 WRC 2007 Art 2(1).
94 LEG 78/4/2, 14 August 1998, 2.
95 LEG XII/4, 8 March 1972, Annex, 1; LEG/WG(WR).I/4, 12 December 1973. For examples of wreck ordered removed as they posed a threat to navigation, such as the *Robel* and *A.M. Vella*, see T Redding, *Best Endeavours: Inside the World of Marine Salvage* (ABR Company Ltd, Bradford on Avon, 2004), 239–241.
96 LEG 75/6/2, 14 February 1997, 9. The wreck of the *Hyundai 105*, for example, posed a considerable navigation and pollution hazard in the Strait of Singapore: LEG 92/13, 3 November 2006, 7. On the other hand, the bitumen cargo in the wreck of the *Singapura Timur*, lying at a depth of 47 m in the busy shipping lane in the Straits of Malacca, was not considered a pollution hazard, as the wreck was likely to stay intact for over a hundred years, and the bitumen, when it was finally exposed to the sea, would not leach components or float to the surface. See *De La Rue & Anderson*, 998.
97 LEG 75/6/2, 14 February 1996, 9.
98 LEG 86/4/1, 27 March 2003, 3; LEG 86/4/2, 238 March 2003, 3. The definition of "harmful substance" under MARPOL substantially reflects the nature of the hazard provide for in the WRC 2007, being defined to mean "any substance which, if introduced into the sea, is liable to create hazards to human health, to harm living resources and marine life, to damage amenities or to interfere with other legitimate uses of the sea, and includes any substance subject to control by the present Convention": MARPOL Art 2(2).

hazards to include pollution and other environmental issues.⁹⁹ The resulting definition of hazard is any condition or threat that "poses a danger or impediment to navigation" or "may reasonably be expected to result in major harmful consequences to the marine environment, or damage to the coastline or related interests of one or more States".¹⁰⁰

This definition is not without difficulty. In an earlier form, the article merely defined a hazard as "any condition or threat of danger or impediment to surface navigation, to the marine environment, or to the coastline or related interests of one or more States".¹⁰¹ The inclusion of anything other than a navigational hazard was controversial, and an attempt was made to impose a higher threshold for the existence of a hazard in cases other than a navigational hazard by adding the word "significant" to qualify "damage".¹⁰² This was later changed to "substantial" rather than "significant" damage.¹⁰³ The concern had been to ensure that incidents giving rise to minor damage were excluded.¹⁰⁴ This was later changed to "major harmful consequences", a term which originates in the Intervention Convention 1969.¹⁰⁵ However, in an attempt to clarify this threshold and to differentiate it from that applied in the Intervention Convention 1969, the higher threshold was applied only to the marine environment, leaving the coastline and related interests requiring merely a threat or condition of damage arising from the wreck to constitute a hazard. While it is not clear why this occurred, a plain reading of the article suggests that for a condition or threat to constitute a hazard as far as the coastline or related interests are concerned, there need only be a reasonable expectation of damage rather than the higher standard of a reasonable expectation of major harmful consequences that applies in respect of the marine environment.

8.2.3 Defining "related interests"

While dangers posed to navigation and to the marine and coastal environment lie at the heart of the need for wreck removal, the definition of hazard includes a rather broader interest of States, referred to as "related interests". These interests include "(a) maritime coastal, port and estuarine activities, including fisheries activities, constituting an essential means of livelihood of the persons concerned; (b) tourist attractions and other economic interests of the area concerned; (c) the health of the coastal population and the well-being of the area concerned, including conservation of marine living resources and of wildlife; and (d) offshore and underwater infrastructure", directly affected or threatened by a wreck.¹⁰⁶ With the exception of "offshore and underwater infrastructure", the definition merely replicates that contained in the Intervention Convention 1969. Unsuccessful proposals had been made to include more explicit references to certain interests, such as the hazard to fishing and fishing gear and to such things as "artificial waterworks", being dykes, artificial dunes and

---

99 See eg LEG 74/5/2, 20 August 1996, Annex 2, 4.
100 WRC 2007 Art 1(5). For the hazard to fishing vessels, see 10.5.1.
101 LEG 74/5, 17 June 1996, Annex, 2.
102 LEG 76/5, 8 August 1997, Annex, 2.
103 LEG 78/4/2, 14 August 1998, at 2, using the term "*substantial* physical damage" rather than "significant".
104 LEG 77/11, 28 April 1998, 14.
105 Intervention Convention 1969 Art 1.
106 WRC 2007 Art (6). See also UNCLOS Art 60 in relation to rights of States with respect to the construction of artificial islands, installations and other structures in the EEZ.

channels.[107] Other than these unsuccessful attempts, there was not as much debate on the scope as might have been expected, and conformity with the Intervention Convention 1969 was largely supported. Arguably the only interest that did cause some debate very early on in the negotiations was that of the State's fishing industry,[108] and which is clearly covered in the breadth of related interests in Art 6. That said, the turning point really is on the existence of a hazard, which by definition will reveal what it is that is at risk rather than too concentrated a consideration of that interest itself.[109] Nevertheless, despite this broad and potentially all-encompassing "related interest", its scope has been subject to some debate. In the case of the *Rena*, the extent to which the cultural interests of a State were impacted on by a wreck arose.[110]

8.2.4 Defining "removal"

"Removal" is defined to mean "any form of prevention, mitigation or elimination of the hazard created by a wreck. 'Remove', 'removed' and 'removing' shall be construed accordingly".[111] It is clear then that it is the hazard, rather than the physical wreck, that is to be removed.[112] Nevertheless, in many cases the easiest way to remove the hazard will to removal the wreck itself, as reflected in the very title of the WRC 2007 and many of its terms, eg Art 9 is titled "Measures to facilitate the removal of wrecks".

8.2.5 Defining "Affected State"

From the first drafts of the WRC 2007, the State at the heart of the "wreck removal regime" was "the State whose interests are most directly affected by the wreck".[113] At the time this term was being used, the geographic scope of the convention was being hotly debated, but there appeared at least to be some recognition that this referred to a coastal State that was, as the State whose interests are most directly affected by the wreck, likely to be the closest coastal State to the wreck. The ensuing debate over the geographic scope of the convention rested necessarily on UNCLOS and the maritime zones provided therein, but at the same time this idea of the Affected State was central to the ongoing evolution of the powers of a State to take action when faced with a hazardous wreck. However, once the geographic scope of the convention was settled effectively as the EEZ,[114] then the power of the State in relation to wreck removal was necessarily that of the EEZ State.[115] Unfortunately, rather than simply recognising this, the WRC 2007 retains the idea and language of "the State whose interests are most directly affected by the wreck" by using the term Affected

---

107 LEG 77/11, 28 April 1998, 13.
108 LEG XII/4, Annex Art II, 8 March 1972.
109 See 9.2.2, 10.5.1(b) and 10.5.1(d).
110 See 1.2.4. See also discussion at 10.5.1(d) in relation to a State's interests in bodies still within a wreck.
111 WRC 2007 Art 1(7).
112 See 9.2.5 and 10.2.5.
113 See eg LEG 74/5, 7 August 1996, Annex 5.
114 See 8.3.1.
115 Indeed, one draft of the convention had proposed using the term "coastal States" as "the State in whose convention area the wreck is located". LEG 88/416 February 2004, Annex 3, 1.

State, but defining it to mean the "State in whose Convention area [EEZ] the wreck is located".[116]

This use of the term "Affected State" rather than "coastal State" to describe "the State in whose EEZ the wreck is located" is unfortunate.[117] It appears that "coastal State" was avoided because it has a specific meaning under existing public international law.[118] Yet "coastal State" is not a term defined in UNCLOS, and is used in its natural sense to mean a State with a coastline.[119] It is so used simply as a starting point from which the territorial baselines, and all subsequent maritime zones, are defined. As such, "coastal State" is used to describe the State adjacent to the specific maritime zone being addressed. Curiously, though, given that the term "coastal State" was avoided because it appeared to have a specific meaning in international law, the WRC 2007 does in fact use the term in a very general sense in Art 1(6) to mean any State with a coastline whose "related interests" are directly affected or threatened by a wreck. As discussed earlier, with the exception of "offshore and underwater infrastructure" this definition of "related interests" merely replicates that contained in the Intervention Convention 1969, including using the term "coastal State" rather than "Affected State".[120] In a sense this is fortuitous, since the WRC 2007 has packaged the "related interests" into the definition of hazard which threatens not only the Affected State in whose EEZ the wreck is to be found, but any other State.[121]

The choice of the term "Affected State" has a related disadvantage. In waters such as the Mediterranean, the Baltic and the South China Seas, a wreck may pose a hazard to a number of States simultaneously. It may even be that it is not the State in whose EEZ the wrecks lie that is most affected, but its neighbours. In terms of a hazard from a wreck, the Affected State may very well not be the State affected; and the "coastal State" whose interests are affected may not be the "coastal State" (as used in UNCLOS) in whose EEZ the wreck is found.[122] The use of the term "coastal State", to describe the State in whose EEZ the wreck is found, would have been wholly consistent with the use of the term in UNCLOS.[123] The term "coastal State" is also used in other IMO Conventions. MARPOL, for example, uses it both in relation to jurisdiction over platforms and in relation to the duty of the master to report incidents involving harmful substances to the nearest coastal State.[124]

---

116 First defined in LEG 90/5, 21 February 2005, Annex 1, 4. See also LEG 90/5, 2 February 2005, Annex 2, 1.

117 WRC 2007 Art 1(10). The CMI had recommended using the term "coastal State" throughout the WRC 2007. See LEG 90/5/2, 2 March 2005, 1. See also LEG 91/12, 9 May 2006, 8, in which the committee took note of some States' concerns that the use of the terms Affected State and coastal State could lead to confusion.

118 *Griggs, Convention*, 378.

119 The term is first used in UNCLOS Art 2(1), which provides that "the sovereignty of a coastal State extends, beyond its land territory and internal waters and, in the case of an archipelagic State, its archipelagic waters, to an adjacent belt of sea, described as the territorial sea".

120 Intervention Convention 1969 Art II(4). In early drafts the term used had been "any State", and there had also been proposals to limit this only to State parties, that are also coastal States LEG 79/5, 10 February 1999, Annex, 2.

121 WRC 2007 Art 1(5).

122 WRC 2007 Art 2(5). States parties shall endeavour to cooperate when the effects of a maritime casualty resulting in a wreck involve a State other than the Affected State.

123 While it is submitted that the term "coastal State" could have been used, the term "Affected State" will be used in this book to ensure consistency with the actual terms of the WRC 2007.

124 MARPOL Art 2(5) and Art 8 and Protocol I, Art V(1).

The WRC 2007 therefore envisages the State in whose EEZ the wreck is to be found taking action where the wreck threatens not its coastline but that of another State, and therefore requires that States parties "endeavour to co-operate when the effects of a maritime casualty resulting in a wreck involve a State other than the Affected State".[125] This cooperation may be particularly necessary when a wreck in the EEZ of the Affected State poses a grave and imminent danger to the other State, but a lesser danger to the Affected State. While not in its EEZ, the former State may be entitled to take action in respect of the wreck in accordance with the Intervention Convention 1969 while the Affected State may take action in accordance with the WRC 2007.[126] This necessarily requires careful cooperation.

8.3 Scope of WRC 2007

8.3.1 Geographical scope

The WRC 2007 was a response to hazards posed to a coastal State from wreck beyond its territorial waters, as was the case of the *Torrey Canyon* in what was then the high seas.[127] Earlier versions of the draft WRC 2007 had therefore provided variously for application "on the high seas",[128] in "international waters"[129] or "beyond the territorial sea".[130] The possibility of limiting it to the continental shelf was also raised.[131] The development of a wreck removal regime applicable on the high seas necessarily would require a rebalancing of the rights of coastal States with those of flag States—a matter of concern to many maritime nations.

The creation of the EEZ provided a more practical basis for the scope of the WRC 2007 as it granted to the coastal State sovereign rights to its natural resources and jurisdictional competency in relation to a range of matters. These included the protection and preservation of the marine environment, while at the same time maintaining freedoms of the high seas, such as navigation.[132] Furthermore, given the difficulties in agreeing upon any intrusion on the freedom of navigation on the high seas in relation to security matters,[133] the EEZ provided not only a compromise solution, but also some uniformity with similar liability regimes.[134] Some preference for allowing its application to the continental shelf,

---

125 WRC 2007 Art 2(5).

126 Regional cooperative schemes may also apply, eg when the *Mont Louis* sank off the coast of Belgium, but outside of the Belgian territorial sea, resulting in a bunker oil spill. Some assistance was provided by the UK in accordance with the Bonn Agreement: see www.bonnagreement.org/eng/html/welcome.html and *Gaskell, Mont Louis Part One*, 119.

127 At the time, the territorial waters of the UK extended out 3 nm.

128 LEG XIII/4, 8 March 1972, Annex, 1; LEG/WG(WR).I/4, 12 December 1973, Annex, 3.

129 LEG 63/5, 18 May 1990, Annex, 1.

130 LEG 73/11, 8 August 1995, Annex, 3. The continental shelf had also been considered a possible geographical limitation for the scope of the convention. See 78/4/2, 14 August 1998, Annex, 3. The State which would be empowered to act would have been the State closest to the wreck: see LEG 78/4/2, 14 August 1998, 3.

131 See LEG77/11, 28 April 1998, 13.

132 UNCLOS Arts 56, 58.

133 See further H Hesse and N Charalambous, "New Security Measures for the International Shipping Community" (2004) 3 *WMU J Maritime Affairs* 123; R Balkin, "The International Maritime Organisation and Maritime Security" (2006) 30 *Tulane MLJl* 1.

134 Eg CLC 1992 Art II(a), HNSC 2010 Art 3(b), Bunkers Convention Art 2(a).

which would have allowed for a geographical extension in those cases where the continental shelf exceeded the 200 nm limit of the EEZ, persistent for some time.[135] The major advantage of using the continental shelf appears to be that it arose as a matter of law and did not require any express proclamation.[136]

Ultimately a preference was made for the EEZ rather than the continental shelf for the sake of uniformity and clarity.[137] This, in part followed that set out in the HNS Convention,[138] CLC 1992[139] and Bunkers Convention 2001.[140] The "Convention area" is therefore defined as "the EEZ of a State Party, established in accordance with international law".[141] By "international law", the WRC 2007 refers indirectly to UNCLOS, though it also recognises that the EEZ may be a creation of customary international law.[142] If the State party has not declared an EEZ, then the WRC 2007 provides that the Convention area will be an area beyond and adjacent to the territorial sea extending not more than 200 nm from the baselines from which the territorial sea is measured. This amounts to an area that the State would have if it did declare an EEZ in accordance with UNCLOS.[143] To this extent, the WRC 2007 does apply to the high seas in some cases.[144] Since both on the high seas and in the EEZ the application of the wreck removal regime would amount to an intrusion on the existing freedom of navigation, the Convention mandates that State parties have, by being party to the Convention, given consent for the State in whose EEZ (or area of the high seas that would constitute their EEZ if one was declared) the wreck is located, to take acts to remove, or have a wreck removed, at the registered owner's expense.[145]

Where the Affected State has declared an EEZ, no problem arises, including the possibility of any overlapping EEZ claims. Where the Affected State has not declared an EEZ, the intention is not to endorse a regime that operates parallel to UNCLOS's EEZ regime,[146] but merely to recognise an area that would exist if an EEZ were established through UNCLOS. It is thus one that extends 200 nm from the territorial sea baseline as this is the manner in which the territorial sea is established in accordance with international law, ie UNCLOS.

As discussed earlier, while this geographic scope of the WRC 2007 is based on the framework of rights and duties of the coastal States as provided for in UNCLOS, the WRC 2007 refers to that State as the "Affected State" rather than the "coastal State". While this does not cause any significant problem in interpretation it is, as discussed earlier, unfortunate as, in relation to a hazard from a wreck, the Affected State may very well not be the

---

135 LEG 77/11, 28 April 1998, 13; LEG 78/4/2, 14 August 1998, 2.
136 UNCLOS Art 77(3).
137 LEG 78/11, 2 November 1998, 10.
138 HNSC 2010 Art 3(b). LEG 78/11, 2 November 1998, 10.
139 CLC 1992 Art II(a)(ii). *Berlingieri*, 125.
140 Bunkers Convention 2001 Art 2(a)(ii).
141 WRC 2007 Art 1(1).
142 *Libya v Malta*, [1985] ICJ (3 June).
143 WRC 2007 Art 1(1). UNCLOS Part V, Arts 55–75 address the EEZ.
144 Throughout the remainder of this book, the term EEZ, when used in the context of the WRC 2007, will mean both the EEZ of a State party, established in accordance with international law or, if a State party has not established such a zone, that part of the high seas "equivalent" to the EEZ.
145 WRC 2007 Art 9(10). As to its application to wrecks of non-State parties, see 7.4.
146 LEG 87/4, 7 August 2003, Annex 4, 1.

State affected; and the "coastal State" whose interests are affected may not be the "coastal State" in the UNCLOS sense.

In those situations where the "Affected State" is not the State most affected by the wreck, the "Affected State" may nevertheless act if the wreck poses a hazard to "one or more States".[147] It does not, however, have a duty to do so pursuant to the WRC 2007, but does have a duty to "endeavour to co-operate when the effects of a maritime casualty resulting in a wreck involve a State other than the Affected State".[148] Importantly, the other State need not be a State party to the WRC 2007.

The WRC 2007 does not address the powers of the State most affected by a wreck that lies in the convention area of another State. At least where it lies within 200 nm of the coast of the "Affected State", the Intervention Convention 1969 will apply, as will customary intentional law. Where the "State most affected by a wreck" and the "Affected State" are party to the WRC 2007, Art 2(5) does give rise to an obligation to "endeavour to co-operate", but this article is unlikely to be the source of any cooperation in these circumstances.

8.3.2 Temporal scope

The WRC 2007 does not expressly state that it applies only to casualties and wrecks which have occurred *after* the entry into force of the Convention for a particular State. Clearly, the WRC 2007 cannot create retrospective liability on a shipowner, eg for costs incurred before that date.[149] Although Art 3(1) applies the WRC 2007 widely to "wrecks in the Convention area", the public law obligations envisaged by the WRC 2007, eg reporting, are generally designed for contemporary wrecks. This means that a State does not have duties to warn under Art 7 about every pre-existing wreck of which it becomes aware. There is a possible argument that the WRC 2007 may be applied if the *hazard* caused by a wreck arises *after* the WRC 2007 entered into force (or at least *continues* before and after that date), even though the *casualty* occurred beforehand.[150] Such an interpretation may sit uneasily with the drafting of the WRC 2007 and was not addressed directly in the *travaux préparatoires*. Coastal States would have to rely on existing rights in international law in relation to these wrecks, perhaps using the WRC 2007 as a template for action.[151]

8.4 Extension of the WRC 2007 to territorial sea

8.4.1 Coastal State rights in territorial sea

In practice, the majority of wrecks that do pose a pollution hazard, and the great majority that pose a navigational hazard, are to be found in the territorial sea. Under UNCLOS Art 2(3), coastal States have sovereign rights in their territorial sea, subject only to UNCLOS

---

147 WRC 2007 Art 1(5).

148 WRC 2007 Art 2(5). This duty to "endeavour to cooperate" was inspired by UNCLOS Art 123 that concerns cooperation of States bordering enclosed and semi-enclosed sea. LEG 86/4, 25 February 2003, Annex 2, 1.

149 Vienna Convention Art 28. There is, in any event, a six-year time limit from the date of the casualty for a costs claim: see WRC 2007 Art 13.

150 See S Dromgoole and C Forrest, "The 2007 Nairobi Wreck Removal Convention and Hazardous Historic Shipwrecks", [2009] LMCLQ 92 [*Dromgoole & Forrest*] 104–106.

151 *Dromgoole & Forrest*, 106.

itself[152] and other rules of international law". This has generally been regarded as giving a relatively unfettered discretion to address dangers and hazards in these waters,[153] including the ability to order shipowners to remove a wreck or to pay for the costs of such removal if undertaken by State authorities.[154] In the *Chagos* Arbitration,[155] the Tribunal was asked whether UNCLOS Art 2(3) is merely descriptive or operates as a reservation, ie giving rise to obligations (and limitations) for the coastal State. The Tribunal considered that the English text of UNCLOS was ambiguous and that "the balance of the authentic versions favours reading that provision to impose an obligation".[156] In that context, it might be asked whether there is a developing notion that responses by a State should be proportionate and reasonable, as is required *beyond* the territorial sea under the Intervention Convention 1969 and UNCLOS Art 221, and within the territorial sea under IMO liability conventions such as the CLC 1992 and now the WRC 2007. This might be relevant to wreck removal orders that appear excessive.

On any analysis, there are extensive rights in the territorial sea, and States have been reluctant to be bound by any convention that would limit them in any way. For example, following the *Amoco Cadiz* disaster in 1978,[157] it was not surprising that calls for an extension of the Intervention Convention 1969 to cover incidents in the territorial sea were rejected, as it would have undermined the unfettered discretion of States to intervene.[158] The question of the application of the WRC 2007 to the territorial sea was not, therefore, an issue of coastal State rights of intervention, but rather an issue of uniformity in national maritime law.

State practice in the territorial sea "reveals many differences in States' interpretation of their powers",[159] but there has been relatively little discussion about the extent to which UNCLOS or "other rules of international law" may impose restrictions on wreck removal powers in the territorial sea.

8.4.2 *Application of WRC 2007 to territorial sea*

From the outset of negotiations for the WRC 2007, there was a division between States about whether it ought to apply to the territorial sea as well as to the EEZ.[160] There was support for the application of the WRC 2007 to the territorial sea after the CMI conducted

---

152 Eg the right of innocent passage and immunities of public vessels: UNCLOS Arts 17 and 24.
153 Although UNCLOS does not expressly deal with wreck removal, Art 21 allows the coastal State to adopt laws and regulations relating to innocent passage in respect of the "safety of navigation", which would clearly include wrecks positing navigational hazards. See 5.4.2.
154 See, for example, the review of State powers under national legislation in LEG 63/5, 18 May 1990, Annex 2, 7–16; also LEG 69/10/1, 28 July 1993, para 7.
155 *In the Matter of the Chagos Marine Protected Area Arbitration*, Award 18 March 2015. The case did not involve wreck removal but, *inter alia*, the creation of a marine protected area.
156 *Chagos* Arbitration, para 502; see also paras 500–514.
157 See 1.2.2(a).
158 *De La Rue & Anderson*, 903.
159 LEG 74/5/2/Add 1, 20 August 1996, 2.
160 LEG 63/5, 18 May 1990, 12–27.

a survey of national legislation.¹⁶¹ This revealed that, while the law in different States had developed "to differing degrees of sophistication", the laws "follow more or less the same pattern", suggesting a possible basis for introducing greater uniformity within the territorial sea.¹⁶² Support for such greater uniformity came not only from a number of States but also from important industry participants, including the ICS and the International Group.¹⁶³

The question of the application of the WRC 2007 to the territorial sea was not only a matter of establishing uniformity in national approaches to wreck removal, but also an issue of consistency with UNCLOS.¹⁶⁴ A number of provisions set out in the various drafts of the WRC 2007 contained restrictions on the exercise of powers by the coastal State that were objected to by a number of States. They were concerned that the resulting regime would ultimately weaken coastal States' powers to address hazardous wreck within waters over which they exercised sovereignty. While a number of States were opposed to any application of the WRC 2007 to territorial seas, further disagreement concerned how such an application might be achieved; whether mandatorily or through an "opt-in" or "opt-out" provision.

The possibility of States opting in and applying the WRC 2007 regime to wreck in territorial waters was a feature of the initial 1995 draft submitted by Germany, the Netherlands and the UK.¹⁶⁵ Subsequent drafts also provided for the application of only certain provisions of the WRC 2007 to territorial waters when opting in, to ensure that State sovereignty in the territorial waters would not be watered down by certain of the WRC 2007 provisions.¹⁶⁶ In 2005, however, the option of opting in or out was removed from the draft on the basis that nothing prevented any State from applying the WRC 2007 to its territorial waters if it so wished.¹⁶⁷ This, however, overlooked the difficulties that would arise with respect to applying the compulsory insurance provisions within the territorial sea to a foreign vessel whose flag State was also a party to the WRC 2007. The application of the WRC 2007 to the territorial sea was therefore reintroduced in late 2006,¹⁶⁸ leading to yet another round of negotiations as to the geographical scope of the convention.¹⁶⁹ An extraordinary effort in early 2007 enabled a number of States to propose, successfully, a regime which allowed for States to opt in to a modified regime;¹⁷⁰ this ensured the exclusion of any limitations that might have applied to coastal States in exercising powers in their territorial sea.¹⁷¹ On this basis, the WRC 2007 ultimately was restricted to the EEZ, but allowed States (through

---

161 The first survey, conducted in 1974–5 is reported in LEG XXXI/2, repeated in LEG 63/6, 18 May 1990 Annex 2; and the second, conducted in 1996, is reported in LEG 75/6/2, 17 February 1997.
162 LEG 75/6/2, 14 February 1997, 3–4. See also LEG 74/5/2, 20 August 1996, Annex, 7.
163 LEG/CONF.16/5, 27 April 2007.
164 LEG 77/5, 13 February 1998, 3.
165 LEG 73/11, 8 August 1995, Annex, 3.
166 LEG 88/4, 16 February 2004, Annex, 4.
167 LEG 90/15, 9 May 2005, 35. See also LEG/CONF.16/INF.2, 14 May 2007, 3.
168 LEG 92/4/3, 11 September 2006, 1.
169 LEG/CONF.16/11, 27 March 2007. Submission by the US and Turkey to ensure the WRC 2007 applied to the EEZ without any opt-in provision.
170 LEG/CONF.16/12, 24 April 2007.
171 LEG/CONF.16/12, 24 April 2007.

notification to the Secretary-General of the IMO)[172] to extend the application of the Convention to wrecks located within their territory, including the territorial sea.[173]

Perhaps because of the late stage in the negotiations in which this compromise was concluded, the mechanism of "shoring up" existing coastal State rights in the territorial sea is rather complex. At the outset, when addressing the right of a coastal State to opt in, the WRC 2007 specifically provides that it does not limit pre-existing State rights with regard to wreck other than measures relating to locating, marking and removing of a wreck.[174] Wreck that falls outside of the scope of the WRC 2007, or measures taken by coastal States beyond the scope of the WRC 2007 for wreck covered by it, are still to be determined by coastal State law without reference to WRC 2007.[175] In case this was not entirely clear, Art 3(2) provides that Arts 10, 11 and 12 (addressing the extent of the shipowner's liability, compulsory insurance and direct action against the insurer) will apply only to the locating, marking and removal of wreck, and will not apply to any other measures a State may take in relation to a wreck in its territorial sea.[176] This at least ensures that the scope of the liability to be borne by the shipowners and their insurers is uniform, notwithstanding the powers of States to address wreck as an exercise of their sovereignty in the territorial sea.

The articles addressing the reporting, marking and removal of wreck do, however, themselves contain provisions which many States regarded as incompatible with the existing sovereign rights that could be exercised with respect to a wreck within their territorial waters. The WRC 2007 therefore provides in Art 4(4) that a number of WRC 2007 provisions will simply not apply in the territorial sea, eg, restrictions on the coastal State's powers, such as having to inform the State of a ship's registry (and registered shipowner) that it has determined the wreck to be hazard, or having to enter into any negotiations with any parties as to how the wreck might be removed.[177] Importantly, the Art 4(4) exclusions also include any limitation on the extent of the coastal State's intervention if the shipowner removes the wreck, or in the manner in which the State removes a wreck itself.[178] Further, WRC 2007 Art 4(4)(b) imposes restrictions on the ostensible freedom of the shipowner to contract with any salvor provided by Art 9(4),[179] by making it subject to the national law of the Affected State.[180] For instance, the Affected State's national law may require all wreck removal in the territorial seas to be undertaken by a specific salvor, or a State owned

---

172 WRC 2007 Art 3(2).
173 WRC 2007 Art 3(2) specifically adds that "[w]hen a State Party has made a notification to apply this Convention to wrecks located within its territory, including the territorial sea, this is without prejudice to the rights and obligations of that State to take measures in relation to wrecks located in its territory, including the territorial sea, other than locating, marking and removing in accordance with this Convention".
174 WRC 2007 Art 3(2).
175 LEG/CONF.16/12, 24 April 2007, Annex 2.
176 See also 10.5.4.
177 WRC 2007 Art 9(1).
178 WRC 2007 Art 9(5) and 9(7). See also the exclusions of Art 9(8), 9(9) and 9(10); and 10.5.4. Further exclusions include Art 2(4), which, in its application to the EEZ, prohibits the claiming of sovereignty or sovereign rights over any part of the high seas, and Art 15, which relates to the international dispute settlement mechanism.
179 See 8.4.2, 9.2.5(e); cf 4.2.3(a), 11.2.2, 11.3.3(d).
180 WRC 2007 Art 4(4)(b) modifies Art 9(4) in its application to the territorial sea. See also 10.5.4.

salvor.[181] Article 4(4) is notable, though, for what is *not* mentioned, in particular Art 2(2) and (3) requiring that measures taken shall be proportionate and not beyond what is reasonably necessary.[182] Given that Art 4(4)(a) specifically excludes "Article 2, paragraph 4", it can only have been intended that the other paragraphs of Art 2 should continue to apply if the WRC 2007 is extended into territorial waters. The restrictions thereby imposed on States may be particularly significant in the decision whether to extend or not.[183]

---

181 LEG/Conf/16.12, 24 April 2007, Annex 2. See also the International Group paper "The 92nd Session of the IMO Legal Committee: The Draft Wreck Removal Convention", October 2006, www.igpandi.org/News+and+Information/News/2006.

182 See 9.2.5(e), 10.2.4, 10.8.

183 See 11.2.2.

CHAPTER 9

Wreck Removal Convention 2007

States' rights and duties

9.1 Flag State obligations

The WRC 2007 is essentially a regime that applies between an Affected State and a ship's owner, operator and insurer. As an international convention, however, it requires agreement between coastal States, whose interests are affected by a wreck, and flag States that regulates the conduct of the shipowner and/or ship operators. As seen in Chapter 7, the granting of wreck removal powers to a coastal State in a maritime zone (the EEZ) in which freedom of navigation prevails required a delicate balancing of the obligations and powers of coastal States with those of flag States. Naturally, flag States that become parties to the WRC 2007 will need to ensure that the convention is implemented domestically to impose on shipowners and ship operators the obligations embodied in it. To that end, the obligations discussed below that apply to the shipowners and operators are derived from the obligations of the flag State. Flag States are, however, also directly involved in the wreck removal regime. The regime that applies when a wreck occurs thus involves, at various stages, both flag and coastal (Affected) States.

9.1.1 State of a ship's registry and flag State

UNCLOS provides that a ship shall sail under the flag of one State only[1] and that ships have the nationality of the State whose flag they are entitled to fly.[2] The State whose flag the ship flies is to exercise "effective jurisdiction and control" over the ship as to social matters, safety and other public law requirements.[3] Not surprisingly, early drafts of the WRC 2007 used the term "flag State", meaning a State whose flag a ship flies and is entitled to fly".[4] However, in 2002 this was changed to "State of the ship's registry" in order to bring it into line with the CLC 1992,[5] Bunkers Convention 2001[6] and HNSC 2010.[7] By "State of the ship's registry", is meant "in relation to a registered ship, the State of registration of the ship and, in relation to an unregistered ship, the State whose flag the ship is entitled to fly".[8]

---

1 UNCLOS Art 92. See also High Seas 1958 Art 6.
2 UNCLOS Art 91. See also High Seas 1958 Art 5.
3 UNCLOS Art 94. See also High Seas 1958 Art 6.
4 See eg LEG 80/INF.2 19 September 1999, 4.
5 CLC 1992 Art 1(4).
6 Bunkers Convention 2001 Art 1(10).
7 HNSC 2010 Art 13.
8 WRC 2007 Art 1(11).

The distinction between the "flag State" and the "State of a ship's registry" is, in terms of the WRC 2007 and the conventions on which it is based, underpinned by the concept of registration, with the "State whose flag the ship is entitled to fly" applying to unregistered ships. This is not how UNCLOS understands the term "flag State" and indeed, this distinction in particularly problematic when applied to bareboat chartered ships. A ship that is subject to a bareboat charterparty may be registered in the State of the charterer for the duration of the charterparty, or indeed in a third State where national law allows this, and then entitled to fly the flag of that State. In this case, the State of the ship's original (or underlying) registry may suspend that registration for the duration of the bareboat charterparty. The ship might therefore be registered in two States, albeit that one of the registrations is suspended. Given that the ship may be subject to a number of different consecutive short-term bareboat charters, from a regulatory point, the original or underlying registration ought to be the effective registration. This, however, would give rise to the "flag State"—at any particular point in time—being different to that of the ship's (underlying) registry. This distinction between flag State and the State of registration was addressed in the 1986 Convention on Conditions for Registration of Ships,[9] which provides that flag State means "a State whose flag a ship flies and is entitled to fly" while State of registration means "the State in whose register of ships a ship has been entered". This is followed by Art 12(1) that provides that a "State may grant registration and the right to fly its flag to a ship bare-boat chartered-in by a charterer in that State for the period of that charter" while Art 11(5) then provides that "[i]n the case of a ship bare-boat chartered-in, a State should assure itself that right to fly the flag of the former flag State is suspended". This duality is also recognised in Art 16 of the 1993 International Convention on Maritime Liens and Mortgages. To avoid these difficulties in the drafting of the WRC 2007, Germany unsuccessfully sought to revert back to the use of the phrase "flag State".[10] Unfortunately, this debate has left its mark on the WRC 2007 in that both reference to the flag State, or more accurately, the State party whose ship is "entitled to fly its flag"[11] or "flying its flag"[12] and the phrase "State of the Ship's registry" appears.[13] It is the reference to "flag" in Arts 5(1), 12(1) and 12(11) that is problematic as the WRC 2007 definition of "State of the ship's registry" means "in relation to a registered ship, the State of registration of the ship and, in relation to an unregistered ship, the State whose flag the ship is entitled to fly", which would suggest that these Arts apply only to unregistered ships. In the context of the WRC 2007 this is patently not the case and "flag State" or the like ought to be interpreted as applying to both registered and unregistered ships. Indeed, this work uses the more conventional term "flag State" in this wider sense. As to its application to bareboat chartered ships, the WRC 2007 leaves the determination to each specific case.[14]

---

9 Not yet in force.
10 LEG 85/3/2, 16 September 2002, 1.
11 WRC 2007 Art 12(11)
12 WRC 2007 Arts 5(1) and 1291).
13 WRC 2007 Arts 2(3), 9(1)(a), 9(1)(b), 9(8), 12(2), 12(5), 12(7) and 12(14).
14 See further Ademuni-Odeke, *Bareboat Charter (Ship) Registration* (Kluwer Law International, 1998); R Coles and E Watt, *Ship Registration: Law and Practice* (2nd ed, Informa, 2009).

9.1.2 Flag State obligations

As discussed in Chapter 5, the flag State has the primary role in addressing and regulating ship sourced marine pollution in the EEZ and high seas.[15] As such, the WRC 2007 required flag States to concede some of this power to Affected States when becoming a party to the WRC 2007.[16] Nevertheless, the flag State still has a number of important roles in giving effect to the WRC 2007 through the regulation of ships flying its flag. The first flag State's duty is set out in Art 12 and requires the flag State to promulgate the necessary laws to ensure that the registered owner of its ships have appropriate compulsory insurance provisions in place to cover wreck removal subject to the WRC 2007. To the extent that this requires the flag State to impose such burden on shipowners, this is covered in detail in Chapter 10, and the manner in which the UK has done so is covered in Chapter 11.

While flag States have much to do with the insurance provisions, they have less to do with the actual process of wreck removal; this being within the primary remit of the Affected State. Nevertheless, the flag State has two important roles to play; the first in ensuring that masters and operators of their ships report wrecks to the Affected State[17] and the second in cooperating with the Affected State in the process of wreck removal. The first duty falls squarely on the flag State, while the second is an adjunct to the wreck removal undertaken by, or subject to, the Affected State.

9.1.3 Reporting

While the WRC 2007 ostensibly applies to wrecks that pose a hazard, a precautionary approach is taken that assumes that a wreck *may* pose a hazard and therefore imposes obligations on parties prior to the determination of whether the wreck actually poses a hazard. It requires that "a State Party shall require the master and the operator of a ship flying its flag to report to the Affected State without delay when that ship has been involved in a maritime casualty resulting in a wreck".[18] Importantly, the duty to report is not conditional on the ship becoming a hazard, but merely requires that the ship has been involved in a maritime casualty resulting in a wreck.

The reporting obligation only arises when a ship has been involved in a maritime casualty.[19] This obligation is thus similar to those found in MARPOL and OPRC 1990. In MARPOL, the master is required to report incidents involving harmful substances to the nearest coastal State.[20] Such incidents include not only the discharge or probable discharge of harmful substances, such as oil, but also any damage, failure or breakdown of a ship of 15 m and above affecting the safety of the ship or of navigation. This then includes incidents where a ship is being or about to be wrecked or sunk. Where the ship is abandoned such that the master cannot make the report, the report must then come from the ship's owner,

---

15 See 5.5.1.
16 WRC 2007 Art 9(10). See 7.3.2.
17 WRC 2007 Art 5.
18 WRC 2007 Art 5.
19 See 8.2.1(a) as to the meaning of "maritime casualty". In relation to the UK approach to ships merely abandoned, without being involved in a maritime casualty, see 11.4.
20 MARPOL Art 8, and Protocol I, Art V(1).

THE LAW OF WRECK

charterer, manager or operator.[21] Similarly, the OPRC 1990[22] requires the master to report any event on his/her ship involving a discharge or probable discharge of oil to the nearest coastal State.[23] SOLAS also requires a master to report the loss or likely loss overboard of any dangerous goods in packaged or solid form to the nearest coastal State.[24] These reporting requirements have been consolidated in the IMO's General Principles for Ship Reporting.[25] Given these existing reporting obligations, some debate had revolved around whether the convention ought to require yet another reporting obligation. Instead of doing so, there was a proposal to merely include the following: "[r]ecalling further the reporting requirements of SOLAS, MARPOL 73/78 and OPRC Conventions are applicable under this Convention with respect to reporting and locating wrecks".[26] Moreover, these provision are likely to be regarded as "generally accepted international rules and standards" for the prevention, reduction and control of pollution in the marine environment as provided for in UNCLOS Art 211(7). Ultimately, however the view was that there ought to be some reporting obligation, though exactly who would be obliged to make this report, and in what circumstances, were subject to much debate.

9.1.3(a) Who must report

The role of the owner of the wreck is central to the obligation to remove the hazard and because of this the owner, in early drafts of the convention, had the duty to report. However, this was a reporting obligation originally to inform the flag State, who would then channel such a report through the IMO to other States.[27] This was changed to report to the affected coastal State, but the role of the shipowner prevailed for some time.[28] Given that the flag State plays no role once a wreck has occurred, it is understandable why this was removed; though the CMI was of a view that the obligation of the shipowner to report to the flag State ought to remain.[29] In 2003, the ICS pointed out that "in modern shipping management practice the registered owner is not normally in charge of the day-to-day operation of the ship and, accordingly, might not be able to comply with" an obligation to report.[30] Given that early reporting is essential to the avoidance of a hazard, the obligation is imposed on those most immediately connected with the operation of the ship—the master[31] and operator.[32] However, the registered owner will bear the financial liability for any wreck removal. As such, the obligation of the master

---

21 MARPOL Protocol I Art I(2).
22 See 5.7.
23 OPRC Art 4. This was used as a basis for drafting WRC 2007 5(1).
24 SOLAS Ch VII/6 and VII/7–4.
25 General Principles for Ship Reporting Systems and Ship Reporting Requirements, Including Guidelines for Reporting Incidents Involving Dangerous Goods, Harmful Substances and/or Marine Pollutants, IMO Resolution A.851(2), 27 November 1997.
26 LEG 82/5/1, 15 September 2000, 4.
27 LEG 74/5, 17 June 1996, Annex Art IV(2). The CMI had supported a requirement that the shipowner have an independent duty to report a casualty. LEG 87/4/1, 13 August 1998, 5.
28 See change in LEG 87/17, 23 October 2003,8 & Annex 1, 5.
29 LEG 74/5/2, 20 August 1996, Annex 2, 8; LEG 90/WP.6, 25 April 2005.
30 LEG 87/17, 23 October 2003, 8.
31 LEG 89/5/4, 24 September 2004, 1.
32 LEG 90/15, 9 May 2005, 29–30.

and operator to report includes giving the name and the principal place of business of the registered owner.[33]

The importance of the obligation to report by the master and operator, and the channeling of the duty and liability for the wreck removal to only one party—the registered owner—required that these entities be clearly defined given the myriad structures of ownership and operations of ships in the modern shipping industry. "Registered owner" is defined in Art 1(8) as "the person or persons registered as the owner of the ship or, in the absence of registration, the person or persons owning the ship at the time of the maritime casualty.[34] However, in the case of a ship owned by a State and operated by a company which in that State is registered as the operator of the ship, "registered owner" shall mean such company.[35] "Operator of the ship" "means the owner of the ship or any other organization or person such as the manager, or the bareboat charterer, who has assumed the responsibility for operation of the ship from the owner of the ship and who, on assuming such responsibility, has agreed to take over all duties and responsibilities established under the International Safety Management (ISM) Code, as amended".[36] As Shaw notes, the reference to the ISM Code within the WRC 2007 is unusual since there is no guarantee that a party to the WRC 2007 will be a party to SOLAS that embodies the ISM code.[37] Fortunately, SOLAS is almost universally accepted, and therefore the issue is unlikely in practice to be problematic. That said, the ISM code applies to vessels of 500 tons or more, whereas the WRC 2007 applies to all vessels, thus leaving something of a gap in the regime when it comes to identifying the operator of vessels of less than 500 tons.

So the obligation to report falls on the master *and* operator of the ship.[38] This ensures that a report will be received and removes the risk that one party assumes that the other has fulfilled this obligation. However, to the extent that either the master or the operator of the ship has fulfilled the reporting obligation, the other shall not be obliged to report.[39] This is perhaps unfortunate in that obliging both to report ensures that a report is made to the Affected State without any confusion as between the master and the operator as to who will made the report or whether a report had been made. On the other hand, this does not prevent both the master and operator making a report, and relieving one party of the obligation might ensure that only one report is received and the Affected States is not left with possibly two conflicting reports. On balance, however, two reports are likely to be more beneficial to the Affected States than one.

---

33 WRC 2007 Art 5(2).
34 See 9.1.1, 10.2.2.
35 WRC 2007 Art 1(8).
36 WRC 2007 Art 1(9).
37 *Shaw*, 434.
38 This reporting requirement already exists under MARPOL when a risk arises that harmful substances may be discharged into the sea, though it does not apply to reporting the wreck itself: MARPOL Art 8, and Art I of Protocol I, "Provisions Concerning Reports on Incidents Involving Harmful Substances". It is most likely that the State agency responsible for receiving reports from its flagged vessels under MARPOL will also receive reports under the WRC 2007.
39 WRC 2007 Art 5(1).

9.1.3(b) What must be reported and to whom

Together with deciding who was to report a maritime casualty resulting in a wreck, was whether this obligation was limited to reporting only in the case of one's own vessel that results in a wreck, or whether a broader reporting requirement should be imposed such that any maritime casualty resulting in a wreck discovered by the reporting entity needs to be reported. SOLAS, for example, requires the master of a ship who meets any "dangerous derelict" to report its existence by all available means to ships in the vicinity and to competent authorities.[40] This broader approach prevailed for a long time during negotiations, it being "evident that the reporting requirement is that for the shipowner's own vessel as well as for any other wreck encountered following a maritime casualty".[41] This would have reflected a similar approach to that taken in UCH 2001 Art 9(1)(b), where the master has a duty to report the discovery of any historic wreck within another State's EEZ to its authority, which will communicate that discovery to the EEZ State.[42]

However, once the entity making the report was settled on the master and operator of the ship rather than the registered owner, the scope of the obligation to report was retracted to the master's ship itself. The resulting obligation in Art 5(1) of the WRC 2007 is unfortunately a narrow obligation as it does not require the master of a ship to report a maritime casualty involving other ships or a ship that has been abandoned.[43] Nor does it apply to the master of a vessel, for example, that discovered cargo floating at sea, such as a container, that is wreck pursuant to the Art 1(4)(c).[44]

To which State the report was to be made had also been contentious during negotiations. Like the MARPOL, OPRC 1990 and SOLAS conventions, an initial position had been taken to require the report to be made to the nearest coastal State. In the end, whilst not using the terms "coastal State", the effect of reporting to the State in whose EEZ the wreck is to be found ensures that the WRC 2007 is consistent with these existing reporting obligations.

Whether the wreck is a hazard is a matter to be determined by the Affected State. To this end, the master or operator of the ship is required to provide it with all the relevant information necessary to determine whether the wreck poses a hazard, including the precise location of the wreck; the type, size and construction of the wreck; the nature of the damage to, and the condition of, the wreck; the nature and quantity of the cargo, in particular any hazardous and noxious substances; and the amount and types of oil, including bunker oil and lubricating oil, on board.[45]

9.1.3(c) Practical difficulties in reporting

Although the WRC 2007 contains this duty to report, it is not necessarily the case that all wreck will be reported. While in most cases the master will quickly become aware of the development of a wreck resulting from a marine casualty with regard to his ship, this is not necessarily the case. A container washed overboard at night will amount to a wreck

---

40 SOLAS Ch V/31. See also UNCLOS Art 198.
41 LEG 87/4, 7 August 2003, Annex 3, 2.
42 See 6.9.3.
43 The CMI did suggest the broadening of this obligation. LEG 74/5/2, 20 August 1996, Annex 2, 8.
44 See 8.1.2(d).
45 WRC 2007 Art 5(2).

since it is an "object that is lost at sea from a ship and that is stranded, sunken or adrift",[46] having resulted from an "occurrence on board a ship or external to it resulting in material damage . . . to its cargo".[47] In those parts of the world where there are a number of coastal States whose maritime jurisdictions are in very close proximity, it may be that the master, on becoming aware of the loss, will not necessarily know exactly where it was lost, and therefore which State is likely to be the Affected State. Given the imperative language used in Art 5, a duty exists to report to any potentially Affected State the existence of the wreck and a prudent course of action would be to report to all possible Affected States. There are likely to be many occasions where wreck is not reported, for numerous reasons. It is also noteworthy that there is no obligation to report the discovery of a wreck, such as an abandoned hulk or the source of pollution arising from an existing wreck.

Reporting may occur by other parties and/or reach the Affected State indirectly. Where there is a significant casualty, the Affected State might first become aware of it through the Global Maritime Distress and Safety System (GMDSS), and the nearest satellite station receiving the distress signal may not necessarily be situated in the Affected State.[48] While this may occur, it does not affect the obligation of flag States to ensure that masters and operators report to the Affected State pursuant to Art 5(1) of the WRC 2007. Some assistance in doing so it provided by the IMO through its Marine Assistance Service. This service, established in 2003, is a mechanism through which States share information and contact details about their own marine assistance services so that masters, ship operators and other persons can make contact as necessary.[49]

9.1.4 Cooperation in process of wreck removal

The flag State has a number of obligations with respect to cooperating in the process that leads to the removal of the hazard emanating from a wreck. Article 9(1) requires the Affected State to notify the flag State of its determination that a hazard exists with respect to a flag State's wreck, and to then consult the flag States (and other affected States) regarding measures to be taken in relation to the wreck. The degree of the flag State's cooperation in this consultation is not addressed, though for States parties to the WRC 2007, it arguably raises an obligation, at the very least, not to deny the Affected State's fulfilment of its obligations under Art 9(1). Moreover, a general principle of the WRC 2007 provides that States parties "shall endeavour to co-operate when the effects of a maritime casualty resulting in a wreck involve a State other than the Affected State".[50] This general principle had, as the "other" State, in mind those that might be threatened by a wreck in some other State's EEZ. It is not, however, so restrictively drafted and a broad interpretation would include the flag State as the "other" State.

The flag State itself has no other direct role to play once the measures to facilitate the removal of the wreck has been agreed upon, and the primary obligations for the removal falls on the shipowner. However, the flag State does have an obligation "to take appropriate

---

46 WRC 2007 Art 1(4)(c). See 8.2.1(d).
47 WRC 2007 Art 1(3). See 8.2.1(a).
48 See LEG 79/11, 22 April 1999, 10.
49 MSC.5/Circ.13/Rev.2, 9 November 2015, 1.
50 WRC 2007 Art 2.

measures under their national law to ensure that their registered owners comply with" the obligations to remove the wreck provided in Art 9(2) and the obligation in Art 9(3) to provide the "competent authority of the Affected State with evidence of insurance or other financial security as required by article 12".[51]

9.2 Affected States' powers and obligations

9.2.1 Warning

Upon being informed of the existence of a wreck, whether from the master or operator of the ship (or both) or any other source, the Affected State is immediately placed under an obligation to "use all practicable means, including the good offices of States and organizations, to warn mariners and the States concerned of the nature and location of the wreck as a matter of urgency".[52] This obligation applies to all wrecks of which the Affected State becomes aware, and not only those that might constitute a hazard. At least in its application to the territorial sea, this duty mirrors that contained in UNCLOS which, in requiring the coastal State not to hamper the innocent passage of foreign ships, also requires that the coastal State give appropriate publicity to any danger to navigation of which it has knowledge.[53] This accords with the ICJ's judgment in the *Corfu Channel Case*[54] that the coastal State should not knowingly create hazards to navigation in its territorial sea.[55] The duty to report wreck in the EEZ is thus an extension of that contained in UNCLOS, and in particular, that contained in Art 211(7) which requires that, through the competent international organisation (IMO), international rules and standards be established which require that the coastal State be promptly notified of any maritime casualty which involves a discharge or probable discharge that may affect the coastline or the coastal State's related interests.[56]

The question arises as to whether any failure by the State to warn mariners can give rise to liability to the owner of a ship that collides with a wreck. Similar questions have arisen in national law and may depend on whether an authority was under a duty of care and was negligent in that respect as determined by the applicable national law.[57] It may also be possible to argue that a State has a liability to other States in international law[58] for failing to warn (or mark) a wreck, but this is an area of some uncertainty and would not be of immediate help to the shipowner whose ship collided with the wreck.

---

51 The UK does not appear to have given effect to Art 9(2) in respect of UK ships in the waters of other States parties, although it has done so in respect of insurance certificates under Art 9(3): see 11.3.3(c) and (e).
52 WRC 2007 Art 7(1).
53 UNCLOS Art 24(2).
54 *United Kingdom v Albania*, [1949] ICJ Rep 4.
55 LEG 74/5/2/Add.1, 5 September 1996, 2.
56 As well as MARPOL Art 8 and Protocol I, Art V(1), and OPRC 1990 Art 4.
57 See 2.4.2.
58 See eg the International Law Commission, "Articles on the Responsibility of States for Internationally Wrongful Acts" [*ILC Articles on State Responsibility*], as attached to UNGA Res A/RES/56/83 (28 January 2002) and UNGA Draft Resolution UN Doc A/C.6/71/L.28 (7 November 2016).

9.2.2 Determination of hazard

Having been informed of the existence of a wreck within its EEZ, the Affected State must determine whether the wreck poses a hazard, with reference to a range of non-exclusive factors relating to the ship, its cargo and its geographical position. These are set out in the WRC 2007 as follows:

(a) the type, size and construction of the wreck;
(b) depth of the water in the area;
(c) tidal range and currents in the area;
(d) particularly sensitive sea areas identified and, as appropriate, designated in accordance with guidelines adopted by the Organization, or a clearly defined area of the exclusive economic zone where special mandatory measures have been adopted pursuant to [UNCLOS Art 211(6)];
(e) proximity of shipping routes or established traffic lanes;
(f) traffic density and frequency;
(g) type of traffic;
(h) nature and quantity of the wreck's cargo, the amount and types of oil (such as bunker oil and lubricating oil) on board the wreck and, in particular, the damage likely to result should the cargo or oil be released into the marine environment;
(i) vulnerability of port facilities;
(j) prevailing meteorological and hydrographical conditions;
(k) submarine topography of the area;
(l) height of the wreck above or below the surface of the water at lowest astronomical tide;
(m) acoustic and magnetic profiles of the wreck;
(n) proximity of offshore installations, pipelines, telecommunications cables and similar structures; and
(o) any other circumstances that might necessitate the removal of the wreck.

These factors should be taken into account in determining whether the wreck poses a hazard as defined in the WRC 2007, and for the purposes of the WRC 2007. That is, there must exist a condition or threat that (a) poses a danger or impediment to navigation or (b) may reasonably be expected to result in major harmful consequences to the marine environment, or damage to the coastline or related interests of one or more States.[59] Importantly, this determination is different to that which might need to be made for the purposes of giving effect to some other international Convention, such as the CLC 1992 or Intervention Convention 1969, since the threshold for determining the existence of the hazard is different. The CLC 1992, for example, requires that a "grave and imminent threat of causing" marine pollution exist before a State may undertake preventative measures, and which might include wreck removal. Indeed, the very intent of the WRC 2007 is to provide coastal States with a remedy when wrecks do not satisfy the higher CLC 1992 threshold.[60]

---

59 WRC 2007 Art 1(5).
60 Oman, for example, pointed out that in the ten years prior to 1993, six ships had been wrecked and then abandoned by their owners along their coastline, but because they could not be said to pose a 'grave and imminent

Importantly, the Affected State is required to determine whether the wreck poses a hazard, not merely whether it poses a hazard to *it*. It may be that the wreck poses a hazard to a State other than the Affected State. The general principles of the WRC 2007 therefore require that States parties "shall endeavour to co-operate when the effects of a maritime casualty resulting in a wreck involve a State other than the Affected State".[61]

The list of criteria to be taken into account in determining if the wreck poses a hazard are not exhaustive, nor mandatory as they are only those that "should" be taken into account. These criteria are uncontroversial and eminently sensible. The last criteria, set out as Art 6(o), though, is somewhat misplaced. It is "any other circumstances that might necessitate the removal of the wreck".[62] The intent was to allow the Affected State to take into account unforeseen factors or circumstances not listed in Art 6 when determining whether a wreck poses a hazard.[63] The wording, however does not achieve this intent, and essentially reverses the logical flow of Art 6. This is because Art 6 sets out the mechanism to determine whether the wreck constitutes a hazard, from which then flows the removal of the wreck. This criterion reverses this logic by identifying some reason to remove the wreck, and this then is one of the factors (according to Art 6) that determines if there is a hazard.[64] Nevertheless, given the context of the other criteria, and the need in most cases to consider these other criteria, this is not likely to be problematic in practice.[65]

The WRC 2007 does not address the issue of the shipowner's possible response to the Affected State finding that the wreck constitutes a hazard and any ability to challenge this finding. This, including the consequences of a finding that the wreck does constitute a hazard, would fall to be determined in accordance with the national law of the Affected State.

9.2.3 Locating the wreck

Article 8 of the WRC 2007, headed "Locating Wrecks" is something of a misnomer, as it does not necessarily require the wreck to be located. Following the obligation of masters and operators to report a maritime casualty involving the ship that results in a wreck to the Affected State, the duty to determine whether the wreck constitutes a hazard falls to the Affected State.[66] However, before doing so, the Affected State has an obligation to warn others of the wreck. So, Art 7(1) provides that, on "becoming aware of a wreck, the Affected State shall use all practicable means, including the good offices of States and organizations, to warn mariners and the States concerned of the nature and location of the wreck as a matter of urgency". As such, the Affected State does not have to locate the wreck, but merely take steps to warn others of its existence.[67] This is a precautionary measure that follows the

---

danger' no claim could be made pursuant to the CLC 1992 or Fund 1992, and the cost of the wreck removal had to be borne by Oman. LEG 70/9, 25 November 1993.

61 WRC 2007 Art 2(5).
62 WRC 2007 Art 6(o).
63 LEG 91/3, 16 February 2006, ANNEX 3, 4.
64 LEG 91/3, 16 February 2006, ANNEX 3, 4.
65 See 10.5.1(b).
66 WRC 2007 Arts 6 and 7. Some delegations had wanted to impose the duty to locate and to mark a hazardous wreck on the shipowner. LEG 85/4, 17 August 2002. Annex 2, 8.
67 Locating a wreck in open, deep waters can be exceptionally difficult. Even if the wreck is located, it might also be difficult to determine its precise location, and where that might be at the intersection of the different

report of a maritime casualty resulting in a wreck from the master and operators of ships.[68] This obligation to warn others of the wreck is not restricted to only those made known to the Affected State by the master and operator of a casualty, but of any wreck of which the Affected State becomes aware.[69]

If the Affected State has reason to believe that a wreck poses a hazard, the obligation to locate the wreck is heightened, but still qualified, as the Affected State is to take all "practicable steps" to establish the precise location of the wreck.[70] The Affected State need not determine that the wreck does pose a hazard, but only that it has a reasonable belief that it does. So, for example, once the Affected State becomes aware of a wreck that carries a dangerous cargo which leads to a reasonable belief that it may pose a hazard, the obligation to take all practical steps to locate that wreck is enlivened.

9.2.4 Marking the wreck

Once a wreck has been located, the Affected State is also to take all reasonable steps to mark the wreck.[71] This obligation to take steps to mark a wreck in the EEZ imposes on the Affected State a new obligation in relation to the EEZ not contained in UNCLOS and, given the geographical scope of the EEZ, may be an onerous duty notwithstanding that only "all *reasonable* steps be taken".[72]

The reasonable steps to be taken to mark the wreck then require that the Affected State take "all practical steps" to "ensure that the marking conforms to the internationally accepted system of buoyage in use in the area where the wreck is located".[73] The physical mechanism of marking the wreck site is usually that set out by the IALA.[74] At the time the *Torrey Canyon* sank, and the IMO began to consider wreck removal, there was no international buoyage system. The closest system was one that had been proposed in Geneva in 1936, which had reserved green buoys for marking wrecks.[75] By 1971, there was an urgent need to adopt an internationally unified system. The problem had been exemplified by the inability to adopt a buoy to mark a number of wreck in the Dover Strait that was not recognised by all the different flag States plying those waters, with consequential collisions.[76] With the negotiation of wreck removal at IMO, the Maritime Safety Committee addressed the issue

---

maritime zones, such as the EEZ and high seas, it has consequences for the application of the WRC 2007 to that wreck. See further 10.5.5.

68 WRC 2007 Art 6(a).

69 LEG 91/3, 16 February 2006, Annex 1, 6. For possible liabilities for failure to mark a wreck, see the discussion on warning in 9.2.1.

70 WRC 2007 Art 7(2).

71 WRC 2007 Art 9.

72 Emphasis added.

73 WRC 2007 Art 8(2).

74 IALA is a non-profit, international technical association, established in 1957. It encourages its members to work together in a common effort to harmonise aids to navigation, including buoyage, worldwide and to ensure that the movements of vessels are safe, expeditious and cost effective while protecting the environment. www.iala-aism.org/about-iala/.

75 LEG/WG(WR). 1/2/1, 3 December 1973. See also Ship Inspection, "IALA Maritime Buoyage System"; www.shipinspection.eu/index.php/home/k2-item-view/item/322-dock-water-allowance-dwa.

76 Ship Inspection, "IALA Maritime Buoyage System"; www.shipinspection.eu/index.php/home/k2-item-view/item/322-dock-water-allowance-dwa.

and, by 1973, endorsed a temporary IALA buoyage system while further attempts were made to secure an international unification of buoyage systems.[77] By 1976, uniformity was impossible, but agreement was reached on two slightly different systems, to be applied in different geographic regions, though contained in one code: the IALA Maritime Buoyage System.[78] Some amendment was made in 2010 including introducing new buoys such as the Emergency Wreck Marking Buoy.[79] This buoy is placed as close to the wreck as possible, or in a pattern around the wreck, and within any other marks that may be subsequently deployed.[80] SOLAS requires contracting States to make use of aids to navigation where appropriate and, in order to obtain the greatest possible uniformity in aids to navigation, "to take into account the international recommendations and guidelines when establishing such aids".[81]

Where the wreck is buoyed, the Affected State "shall promulgate the particulars of the marking of the wreck by use of all appropriate means, including the appropriate nautical publications".[82]

Importantly, a literal reading of this article suggests that it is not the wreck site itself that is to be marked, for example on a chart, but rather that of the buoy that marks the wreck. Since the obligation to mark the wreck with a buoy is not absolute, for example, where the wreck lies in waters that simply make it impractical to buoy,[83] no obligation appears to arise to mark the existence of the wreck. In those circumstances there is no obligation to promulgate the particularly of the wreck site itself. Nevertheless, the Affected State may, in those circumstances, resort to other forms of marking the wreck site, such as noting its location on nautical charts.

In the UK, Trinity House published Notices to Mariners that may contain wreck information. For example, when the general cargo ship *Fluvius Tamar* sank 5 nm northeast off Ramsgate in 2017, a temporary exclusion zone was imposed by SOSREP and the wreck marked. The Notice to Mariners contained a description of the international standard

---

77 IMO SN/Circ.65, 8 January 1973; MSC/Circ.151, 16 October 1973.

78 System A applies in Europe, Australia, New Zealand, Africa, the Gulf and some Asian Countries, while System B applies in North, Central and South America, Japan, Republic of Korea and Philippines.

79 IALA Recommendation O-133 on Emergency Wreck marking Buoy, December 2005. www.iho.int/mtg_docs/International_Organizations/IALA/IALA_Recommendation_O-133.pdf.

80 IALA recommendation O-133 details the specification of the Emergency Wreck Marking Buoy. The Emergency Wreck Marking Buoy is designed to provide high visual and radio aid to navigation. The buoy itself is a pillar or spar buoy, with between 4 and 8 blue and yellow vertical stripes of the same size, fitted with an alternating blue and yellow flashing light with a nominal range of 4 nautical miles where the blue and yellow 1 second flashes are alternated with an interval of 0.5 seconds. It may also have an upright yellow cross top-mark. The light characteristic was chosen to eliminate confusion with blue lights to identify law enforcement, security and emergency services. It may also have the word wreck painted on it. The Emergency Wreck Marking Buoy is maintained in position until: the wreck is well known and has been promulgated in nautical publications; the wreck has been fully surveyed and exact details such as position and least depth above the wreck are known; or a permanent form of marking of the wreck has been carried out. Trinity House. www.trinityhouse.co.uk/mariners-information/navigation-buoys/emergency-wreck-buoys.

81 SOLAS Ch 5 reg 13.

82 WRC 2007 Art 8(3). Trinity House published Notices to Mariners.

83 LEG 79/11, 22 April 1999, 11.

marker buoys used around the wreck, the coordinates of the wreck and of the four buoys, the light sequence of the buoys and the details of the radar beacon on the one buoy.[84]

9.2.5 Removal of the wreck

Article 9, which sets out the "measures to facilitate the removal of wrecks", was drafted with relative ease and the essential framework established early in the long negotiations.[85] What was subject to debate was to which ships the regime would apply, and the particular concern to delimit as clearly as possible the dividing line between salvage and wreck removal. The concerns was that the granting of wreck removal powers to an Affected State might in some way limit the actions of salvors with the risk that salvors may not wish to respond to an incident.[86] As discussed in Chapter 8, this resulted in the definition of wreck excluding from its scope a ship that is about, or may reasonably be expected, to sink or to strand, where effective measures to assist the ship or any property in danger *are already being taken*.[87] Importantly, the right of the coastal State pursuant to the WRC 2007 only arise when dealing with a "wreck".[88]

9.2.5(a) Hazard notice

On determining that the wreck poses a hazard, the WRC 2007 then imposes an obligation on the Affected State to "immediately inform the State of the ship's registry and the registered owner" of this determination and then to "proceed to consult the State of the ship's registry and other States affected by the wreck regarding measures to be taken in relation to the wreck".[89] As such, the first point of contact between the Affected State and the shipowner is not a wreck removal order or the setting of any wreck removal deadlines but notice of the hazard.[90] Indeed, ideally this notification and then consultation ought to result in the shipowner "voluntarily" removing the wreck without any intervention from the Affected State.

Within this consultation process, the Affected State is granted certain powers with regard to arranging the removal of the wreck. Having determined the nature of the hazard, the Affected State is to determine a reasonable deadline within which the wreck is to be removed, and then to inform the registered owner, in writing, of this deadline.[91] Further, the Affected State must specify that if the registered owner does not remove the wreck within this deadline, it may remove the wreck at the registered owner's expense.[92]

In cases where the hazard posed is so immediate and severe that it is not practicable to set time frames for the removal of the wreck and immediate action is required, the

---

84 Trinity House 2/2017 Wreck "Fluvius Tamar"; www.trinityhouse.co.uk/notice-to-mariners/2/2017-wreck-fluvius-tamar.
85 LEG 76/5, 8 August 1997, Annex 7.
86 Tony Redding *Best Endeavours: Inside the world of marine salvage* (ABR, 2004) vii.
87 Own emphasis.
88 Cf the position of the CMI that the right now reflected in WRC 2007 Art 9 ought to relate "to a situation where a ship is in distress, but has not yet become a wreck". LEG 74/5/2, 20 August 1996, Annex 2, 9.
89 WRC 2007 Art 9(1). The article substantially replicates Intervention Convention 1969 Art III(a).
90 LEG 79/11, 22 April 1999, 13.
91 WRC 2007 Art 6.
92 WRC 2007 Art 9(6)(b).

Affected State must inform the registered owner in writing that it intends to intervene immediately.[93] The Affected State can then "remove the wreck by the most practical and expeditious means available consistent with considerations of safety and protection of the marine environment".[94]

The WRC 2007 does not address the issue of the shipowner's possible response to the Affected State finding that the wreck constitutes a hazard. The ICS had called for the inclusion of an article that would "enable the shipowners to contest the reasonableness of the decision by the Affected State to order or carry out the wreck removal. If such a decision were successfully challenged, the shipowners would not be liable for payment of any compensation and in certain circumstances might be entitled to claim compensation from the State". This proposal was unsuccessful and the matter left to the applicable national law.

9.2.5(b) Scope of "removal"

Once the Affected State has determined that the maritime casualty is a wreck, and one that constitutes a hazard, the central provision of the WRC 2007 comes into play. That is, the "registered owner shall remove a wreck determined to constitute a hazard".[95] Unfortunately, this statement is not as clear as it might appear at first sight. It suggests that having determined that a wreck constitutes a hazard; the wreck itself must be removed. Indeed, the first draft of the WRC 2007 envisaged just that, with the wreck either being moved or destroyed where "destruction" meant the "deliberate fragmentation short of removal from the depths of the sea, so as to dissipate any possibility of hazard" and "removal" meant "their being raised from the seabed to the surface or brought ashore either intact or fragmented, even though such wrecks sink again at another spot in such a manner as no longer to be a hazard".[96] The final definition of "removal", however, is defined as "any form of prevention, mitigation or elimination of the hazard created by the wreck".[97] It is the hazard, rather than the physical wreck, that is to be removed. In many cases, for example, the wreck itself may not need to be removed, but its bunkers and perhaps cargo may need to be pumped out or leaks sealed.[98] For a wreck that poses a navigational hazard merely marking the wreck may be sufficient to remove the hazard, and an early draft of the convention had defined "removal/elimination" to include "marking" the wreck.[99] More usually, though, the wreck is removed or steps taken in relation to the wreck so that it no longer poses a navigational hazard. For example, to remove the navigational hazard caused by the wreck of the *Assi Eurolink* in the busy shipping lane off

---

93 WRC 2007 Art 9(6)(c).
94 WRC 2007 Art 9(8).
95 WRC 2007 Art 9(2).
96 LEG XII/4, 8 March 1972, Annex Art III. In a 1996 survey of national legislation, only the Irish legislation specifically referred to the rendering harmless of the wreck rather than its specific physical removal or destruction. LEG 75/6/2, 14 February 1997, 9.
97 WRC 2007 Art 1(7).
98 See for example, the *Tanio* 1.2.2(a) and *Estonia* 1.2.2(b) and 2.3. See further 10.2.5 on liability for full or partial removal.
99 LEG/WG(WR).I/4, Annex Art A, 12 December 1973.

the Netherlands, the salvors resorted to dredging under the wreck to lower it and ensure sufficient water depth between the wreck and the surface.[100] The wreck itself remained. The very title of the WRC 2007, and the convenient shorthand of "wreck removal" can be slightly misleading in this respect; and there is scope for some confusion about what must be removed owing to the interplay of Arts 1(7), 1(6) and 9.[101] In Art 9 in particular, it might have been clearer to have linked the term "remove" to the "hazard" rather than the "wreck". This is an example of where the complex linking of the individual Art 1 definitions requires close textual analysis; but, standing back, the aims are tolerably clear. That is, the WRC 2007 deals with removing hazards emanating from wrecks and not simply wrecks. Throughout this work, the phrase "wreck removal" or "the removal of a/the wreck" is used in this sense.[102]

9.2.5(c) Removal of hazard by a salvor

In most cases the shipowner will respond to the notice to have the wreck removed, usually by engaging salvors to do so. The agreement reached between the shipowner and the salvor is a matter for the contracting parties. They might enter into a specific contract drafted between them for that particular purpose or make use of existing standard form contracts such as Wreckhire or Wreckfixed.[103] Whilst unlikely, the wreck removal may simply be based on salvage law, possibly underpinned by the Salvage Convention 1989[104] depending on whether the relevant States are party to the Salvage Convention 1989. Where that State is also a party to the WRC 2007, the Salvage Convention 1989 and WRC 2007 should apply to a specific incident "through a harmonious interpretation of their existing provisions".[105]

One of the issues that arises is the shipowner's freedom to choose the salvor. Earlier drafts included the phrase "irrespective of flag" to qualify the salvors chosen by the shipowner.[106] Many felt that this qualification was unnecessary as the existing wording provided that the shipowner "may contract with *any* salvors".[107] However, in some States, the cabotage system, or State salvor monopoly, would not have allowed this.[108] With the possibility of opting into the convention's application to the territorial sea, this was seen as a significant disincentive to opt in.[109] Ultimately the Legal Committee decided to leave out the phrase "irrespective of flag", leaving the phrase "with any salvor or other person to remove the wreck" to be interpreted in light of national law.[110]

---

100 See 2.5.9(e).

101 See for example the use of the phrase "remove a wreck" in Arts 2(3), 9(2) and "remove the wreck" in Arts 4(4)(b), 9(4), 9(6)(a), 9(6)(b), 9(7) and 9(8).

102 See also 10.2.8.

103 These are BIMCO standard form contracts: www.bimco.org. See Chapter 13.

104 See 2.7.

105 LEG 77/5, 13 February 1998, 5. See also LEG90/5/1, 10 February 2005, 1–4. See also 10.9.1.

106 See eg LEG 78/4/2, 14 August 1998, Annex Art VII(3).

107 The ICS commented that a justification for adopting a convention might be in recognising 'the right and duty of the shipowner to remove ships and wrecks by his own means or by the assistance of any available salvor *irrespective of flag*' (own emphasis). LEG 74/5/3, 13 September 1996. Own emphasis. See also LEG 78/4/2, 14 August 1998, 4.

108 See *Kennedy & Rose*, 35.

109 LEG 78/4/2, 14 August 1998, 4.

110 LEG 78/11. 2 November 1998, 13.

When the shipowner has engaged a salvor, the wreck removal is essentially left to the salvor. However, before the wreck removal commences, the Affected State may lay down conditions for the removal but "only to the extent necessary to ensure that the removal proceeds in a manner that is consistent with considerations of safety and protection of the marine environment".[111] This limited right of intervention continues after the removal has commenced.[112] It effectively gives some recognition to the rights and duties of salvors in possession of a wreck, and is an attempt to protect the shipowners and salvors from unreasonable interference by the Affected State. That said, as to whether the standards laid down, or intervention by the Affected State, goes beyond what is necessary for considerations of safety and protection of the marine environment is left to be dealt with by national law, invariably that of the Affected State. The Affected State then has considerable, but not absolute, control over the wreck removal process.

The right of intervention provided in Art 9(5) might include dispossessing a salvor and taking over the wreck removal operations itself, or through appointment of its own salvor.[113] This might occur both where a voluntary salvor's measures are not effective, so as to render the casualty a wreck,[114] and when a shipowner's appointed salvor's measure are inconsistent with considerations of safety and protection of the marine environment. Particular concern was raised by the CMI with respect to the voluntary salvor being dispossessed, particularly since the determination as to whether that salvor's measures were affective lies exclusively with the Affected State, and any obligation by the Affected State to enter into consultations about the wreck does not include the salvor.[115] The option to include either a provision that addressed salvor's involvement in the consultative process, or one that addressed compensation for salvors (or both) was unsuccessful, leaving them to be dealt with by the applicable national law.

9.2.5(d) Removal of hazard by the Affected State

If the registered owner does not remove the wreck within the deadline set or the registered owner cannot be contacted, the Affected State may then remove the wreck by the most practical and expeditious means available, consistent with considerations of safety and protection of the marine environment.[116] The State can either undertake the removal itself or contract with a private salvor to do so. The same might apply where the Affected State has dismissed an existing owner appointed salvor or a voluntary salvor and taken over the wreck removal operations. Moreover, to the extent that the Salvage Convention 1989 might be applicable, Art 5(1) of that Convention ensures that it will not "affect any provisions of national law or any international convention relating to salvage operations by or under the control of public authorities".[117] The Affected State then has absolute control over the wreck removal operations, subject to the principles of proportionality and reasonableness.

---

111 WRC 2007 Art 9(4).
112 WRC 2007 Art 9(5).
113 LEG 89/5/2, 10 September 2004, 2.
114 WRC 2007 Art 1(4).
115 LEG 90/5/1, 10 February 2005, 3.
116 WRC 2007 Art 9(7).
117 Salvage Convention 1989 Art 5(1). See *Kennedy & Rose*, 35. See also LEG 89/5/2, 10 September 2004, 4.

9.2.5(e) Proportionality and reasonableness

The new removal powers granted to the Affected State in its EEZ, particularly with the extended definition of hazard in Art 1(5) and compulsory insurance, raised concerns amongst flag States and their shipowners about excessive actions by Affected States. A key part of overall compromise package in the WRC 2007 was some protection against this risk and it is found in the "Objectives and General Principles" set out in Art 2 of the WRC 2007. Article 2(2) requires that measures taken by the Affected State "shall be *proportionate* to the hazard" and Art 2(3) adds that "[s]uch measures shall not go beyond what is *reasonably necessary* to remove a wreck which poses a hazard and shall cease as soon as the wreck has been removed; they shall not unnecessarily interfere with the rights and interests of other States including the State of the ship's registry, and of any persons, physical or corporate, concerned".[118]

This principle of proportionality was modelled on that found in the Intervention Convention Art V(1)[119] and influenced by various articles in UNCLOS.[120] There is no explicit provision in the CLC 1992, but the IOPC Fund applies a proportionality test in practice. As part of the investigation into the *Prestige* sinking,[121] the IOPC Secretariat reported on previous IOPC Fund incidents involving sunken wrecks.[122] The main questions, in the seven cases considered, concerned removal of oil from the wrecks rather than the separate raising of the hull itself (eg along with the cargo). In two Korean cases, the *Yuil No.1* and *Osung No.3*, Dr Måns Jacobsson, the Director of the IOPC (a distinguished international maritime lawyer) stated[123] that:

> the question of whether and, if so, to what extent, the cost of any operations to remove the oil from the wrecks was admissible for compensation would have to be decided on the basis of the criteria laid down in the 1969 Civil Liability Convention and the 1971 Fund Convention and adopted by the 1971 Fund Assembly, *ie that the operations were reasonable*[124] *from an objective technical point of view and that the relationship between the costs and the benefits derived or expected were reasonable.*[125]

The Affected State under the WRC 2007 does not therefore have a completely unfettered discretion in managing the removal of a wreck within its EEZ. This is reflected throughout Art 9.[126]

---

118 WRC 2007 Art 2(3). The provision substantially replicates Art V(2) of the Intervention Convention 1969, although the further detail found in Art V(3) has not been followed in the WRC 2007; nor has the imposition of liability for damages caused to others through disproportionate measures taken in response to the danger or hazard (see the Intervention Convention 1969 Art VI).
119 Intervention Convention 1969 Art V(1) provides that "[m]easures taken by the coastal State in accordance with Article I shall be proportionate to the damage actual or threatened to it". LEG 81/6, 25 February 2000, 2.
120 Including UNCLOS Arts 56(2); 78(2); 194(4) and 225. See LEG 81/6, 25 February 2000, 2.
121 See 1.2.2 and 10.2.4.
122 92FUND/EXC.30/9/2, 29 September 2005: see para 15 for the *Tanio* incident.
123 92FUND/EXC.30/9/2, para 2.2.5.
124 See also the criteria now included in the IOPC Fund's *Claims Manual* (October 2013 ed), paras 3.1.5, 3.17.
125 Emphasis added.
126 See 10.2.

9.2.5(f) Overlap with preventative measures

Once it was determined that the WRC 2007 was to apply to pollution and other environmental threats[127] the possibility of conflict with the CLC 1992, Bunkers Convention 2001 and HNSC 2010 arose.[128] The CLC 1992, for example, provides for "preventative measures" to be undertaken, meaning any "reasonable measures taken by any person after an incident has occurred to prevent or minimize pollution damage".[129] Wreck removal could fall within the CLC 1992 "preventative measures" regime. The WRC 2007 then deals with this by providing that the registered owner shall not be liable to the extent that liability for costs would be in conflict with the CLC 1992, HNSC 2010 or Bunkers Convention 2001.[130] The phrase "in conflict with" causes some difficulty. A number of different phrases had been used in early versions of this clause to explain the relationship between the WRC 2007 and these other conventions. The first had simply provided that the WRC 2007 would "not apply to pollution damage as defined" in these conventions.[131] The intent had been "to avoid overlap as well as double recovery".[132] This was amended to exclude liability for the cost of locating, marking and removing a wreck under the WRC 2007 "if, and to the extent that, the owner is liable" under one of the other conventions.[133] This considerably narrowed the scope of the exclusion as is arose only once the shipowner was liable pursuant to one of these conventions, and thus addressed merely the issue of double recovery. This was reinforced in a further clarification that read "the shipowner is liable to pay compensation"[134] and then to "liability in respect of costs".[135] These were clearly aimed at avoiding double claims, though the issue was expressed as having to address whether the WRC 2007 should be designed to avoid gaps, "so that claims are dealt with either under the [WRC 2007] or under the other liability regimes" and "the need to avoid claims that are excluded under the other liability regimes being admissible under the [WRC 2007].[136] Finally, the phrase "liability for such costs would be in conflict with" these conventions was proposed,[137] and while subject to debate[138] it was finally settled and agreed upon.[139]

De La Rue and Anderson suggest that "[i]n effect this means that if and to the extent that costs claimed from the registered owner under the WRC 2007 constitute 'damage', 'pollution damage', or costs of 'preventative measures' within the meaning of those regimes, these will govern the owner's liability rather than the [WRC 2007]", provided the relevant convention is applicable. This does not simply address the issue of double recovery, but

---

127 LEG 76/5, 8 August 1997, Annex 2.
128 LEG 76/5/1, 8 August 1997, 2.
129 CLC 1992 Art I(7).
130 WRC 2007 Art 11(1).
131 LEG75/6/1, LEG 76/5, 8 August 1997, Annex 5.
132 LEG 75/6/1, 14 February 1997, 7.
133 LEG 77/5, 13 February 1998, 3 and 7.
134 LEG 78/4/2 14 August 1998, Annex 8. See also LEG 80/INF.2, 10 September 1999, 10.
135 LEG 86/4, 25 February 2003, Annex 8.
136 LEG 87/17, 23 October 2003, 14. See also LEG 89/5, 17 August 2004, Annex 1, 8.
137 LEG 90/5, 2 February 2005, Annex 1, 9. The CMI appeared to have some concern with the use of the word 'conflict' but had withdrawn its comment at some point. See LEG 90/15, 9 May 2005, 39.
138 LEG 91/12, 9 May 2006, 11.
139 LEG/CONF.16/3, 13 November 2006, 7.

ensures that any overlap is governed by the other regime rather than the WRC 2007. As such, any wreck removal that overlaps with "preventative measures" will not be covered by the WRC 2007, and will be subject to the other convention including its limitation of liability. Increasingly, the CLC 1992 and Fund regimes have seen States allow private claims for compensation to be dealt with prior to State claims, particularly when the claims might exceed the funds available, largely for internal political purposes. The consequence in this context is that the State cannot "save" its wreck removal claims for recovery under the WRC 2007 when they fall within the CLC 1992 and or Fund, or some other liability convention.

9.2.5(g) Cost of wreck removal

The WRC 2007 Art 10(1) merely provides that "the registered owner shall be liable for the costs of locating, marking and removing the wreck". Nothing more is said there about these costs.[140] The 1996 CMI review of national legislation revealed that few States addressed the issue. Canada, Norway and the Netherlands did, requiring those costs to be reasonable, with the Netherlands legislation in particular providing that the costs be "reasonable, necessary, useful and effective".[141] Reflecting this sentiment, the ICS had sought to introduce an amendment to the draft WRC 2007 that would qualify these costs to those "reasonably made and incurred". This reflected the concern in relation to payments of salvage rewards, the need for a safety net in LOF and the subsequent attempt to address the issue in Art 14 of the Salvage Convention 1989.[142] The CMI also raised the possibility of including more detailed provisions modelled on those that address costs in the CMI Guidelines on Oil Pollution Damage.[143] However, the WRC 2007 provisions followed the CLC 1992 and HNSC 1996, to the extent that neither contained an express "reasonableness" qualification.[144] While the ICS proposal was not successful,[145] there are other provisions in the WRC 2007 that achieve broadly the same effect, eg that measures taken by the the Affected State must be proportionate and not more than reasonably necessary.[146] The resolution of the costs issue will ultimately be one for the national laws of the relevant jurisdiction in which those costs are claimed.

9.2.5(h) Ownership of wreck and power of sale

The WRC 2007 does not address the ownership of the wreck removed by the Affected State, nor that of a State's power of sale of the wreck to defer its removal costs. The 1996 CMI review of national legislation revealed that many States provided for an express power of sale, but that there was less consistency when dealing with title to these wrecks. That is, it was not clear whether the original owner's title prevailed such that, on sale, any proceeds that exceed the wreck removal cost were then due to the original owner, or vested

---

140 See 10.2.4.
141 LEG 75/6/2, 14 February 1996, 14.
142 See 2.7.9.
143 CMI Yearbook 1994, 199. See http://comitemaritime.org/Guidelines-on-Oil-Pollution-damage/0,2726,12632,00.html.
144 LEG 76/5/1. 8 August 1997, 4.
145 LEG 74/5/3, 13 September 1996, 4.
146 See Art 2(2) and (3): and 10.2.4.

in the State. In a number of States, title of sold wrecks remained with the owner, subject in some jurisdictions to the power to limit liability or abandon the wreck.[147] These issues were reflected in earlier drafts of the WRC 2007, which provided that "a State which has undertaken the removal of a wreck . . . is empowered to sell any property so recovered in order to recover the costs of removal. . . . Any surplus from the proceeds of sale shall be paid to the owner".[148] The CMI view, expressed in 1998, was that these issues were "far from the core" of the convention; and given the great variety of ownership variations across States, it ought to be left out of the draft convention and dealt with on a national basis.[149] This view ultimately prevailed.[150]

9.2.5(i) State obligation to remove
The first draft of the WRC 2007 proposed a novel mechanism for ensuring the removal of a hazardous wreck. It provided that, in circumstances where the owner of the wreck could not be found or the wreck was not identifiable, the obligation to remove the wreck "falls upon all the Contracting Parties" and "shall be bound to undertake the elimination on a pro rata basis of the gross tonnage registered in respect of each Party as at the 1 January of the appropriate year".[151] The WRC 2007, however, is couched in terms of wreck removal "powers" rather than "duties". This was reflected in the 2005 draft when "may" was added to qualify the power of the Affected State to remove the wreck.[152]

The obligation to remove may, at least in the territorial sea, be subject to the UNCLOS regime. Article 24(1) provides that "[t]he coastal State shall not hamper the innocent passage of foreign ships through the territorial sea except in accordance with this Convention"[153] and, in Art 24(2), "[t]he coastal State shall give appropriate publicity to any danger to navigation, of which it has knowledge, within its territorial sea."[154] As such, a duty may arise to remove a hazard in the territorial sea, or at least to manage the risk it poses, in accordance with other international law obligations.

9.2.5(j) State liability
The question of the liability of the State for wrongful performance of its obligations was raised early on in negotiations.[155] In part this was inspired by Art VI of the Intervention Convention, which provides that "[a]ny Party which has taken measures in contravention of the provisions of the present Convention causing damage to others, shall be obliged to pay compensation to the extent of the damage caused by measures which exceed those

---

147 LEG 75/6/2, 14 February 1996, 5.
148 LEG 77/5, 13 February 1998, Annex, Art VII(6).
149 LEG 78/4/1, 13 August 1998, 8.
150 See 11.3.4(c).
151 LEG XII/4, Annex Art V, 8 March 1972.
152 WRC 2007 Art 2(1). LEG 90/5, 2 February 2005, Annex 1, 8.
153 UNCLOS Art 24(1) also provides that, in relation to the duty not to hamper innocent passage, the coastal State shall not (a) impose requirements on foreign ships which have the practical effect of denying or impairing the right of innocent passage; or (b) discriminate in form or in fact against the ships of any State or against ships carrying cargoes to, from or on behalf of any State.
154 LEF69/10/1, 28 July 1993.
155 LEG/WG(WR).I/WP, 15 December 1973.

reasonably necessary to achieve the end mentioned in Article I". However, it was also noted that neither the CLC 1992 nor the HNSC 2010 addresses the issue.[156]

An early proposal was to limit this to cases of gross negligence.[157] In 1996, this was further limited in that the draft WRC 2007 provided that "[t]he State is not liable for damage resulting from the removal of wreck".[158] The following year this was amended somewhat to read "[t]he State is not liable [towards parties having an interest in wreck] for damage resulting from the removal of the wreck". This was meant to deal with issues such as that which arose in the removal of the wreck of the *Anna Broere* in the North Sea in 1988.[159] The wreck removal operation required the ship to be split into two, resulting in a greater loss to the owner than would have been the case if it had been recovered in one piece. The owner, however, was not compensated by the Netherlands for his loss and during negotiations was keen to ensure that such potential liability was expressly excluded.

The CMI sub-committee pointed out that national laws as to liability differed considerably, so much so that the matter ought to be left to national law and not addressed in the WRC 2007 itself.[160] Moreover, there was concern that the mere mention of State liability in a Convention might be a disincentive to State ratification.[161] Eventually this was accepted and any reference to State liability was excluded.[162] It is thus left to the national law to deal with.

9.3 State powers in territorial sea

The WRC 2007 articles covering reporting, marking and removal of wreck contains provisions which many States regarded as incompatible with the existing sovereign rights that could be exercised with respect to a wreck within their territorial waters. The WRC 2007 therefore provides in Art 4(4) that a number of WRC 2007 provisions will simply not apply in the territorial sea, eg restrictions on the coastal State's powers, such as having to inform the State of a ship's registry (and registered shipowner) that it has determined the wreck to be a hazard, or having to enter into any negotiations with any parties as to how the wreck might be removed.[163] Importantly, the Art 4(4) exclusions also include any limitation on the extent of the coastal State's intervention if the shipowner removes the wreck, or in the manner in which the State removes a wreck itself.[164] Further, WRC 2007 Art 4(4)(b) imposes restrictions on the ostensible freedom of the shipowner to contract with any salvor provided by Art 9(4), by making it subject to the national law of the Affected State.[165] For instance, the Affected State's national law may require all wreck removal in the territorial

---

156 LEG 78/11, 2 November 1998, 11.
157 LEG/WG(W).I.4, 12 December 1973.
158 LEG 74/5, 17 June 1996, Annex Art VI(7).
159 LEG 78/4/2, 14 August 1998, 5.
160 LEG 74/5/2, 20 August 1996, Annex 2, 10.
161 LEG 78/11, 2 November 1998, 11.
162 LEG 78/11, 2 November 1998, 11.
163 WRC 2007 Art 9(1).
164 WRC 2007 Art 9(5) and (7). See also the exclusions of Art 9(8), (9) and (10). Further exclusions include Art 2(4), which, in its application to the EEZ, prohibits the claiming of sovereignty or sovereign rights over any part of the high seas, and Art 15, which relates to the international dispute settlement mechanism.
165 WRC 2007 Art 4(4)(b) modifies Art 9(4) in its application to the territorial sea.

seas to be undertaken by a specific salvor, or a State owned salvor.[166] Art 4(4) is notable, though, for what is *not* mentioned, in particular Art 2(2) and (3) requiring that measures taken shall be proportionate and not beyond what is reasonably necessary. Given that Art 4(4)(a) specifically excludes "Art 2, paragraph 4", it can only have been intended that the other paragraphs of Art 2 should continue to apply if the WRC 2007 is extended into territorial waters. The restrictions thereby imposed on States may be particularly significant in the decision whether to extend or not.[167]

---

166 LEG/CONF16.12, 24 April 2007, Annex 2. See also the International Group paper "The 92nd Session of the IMO Legal Committee: The draft wreck removal convention" October 2006, www.igpandi.org/News+and+Information/News/2006.

167 See 10.5.2.

CHAPTER 10

Wreck Removal Convention 2007

Shipowners' and insurers' liabilities

10.1 Introduction

The WRC 2007 creates a variety of public law rights and duties for States and shipowners.[1] This chapter is more concerned with the intersection between such public law issues and the WRC 2007 provisions creating liabilities that will affect shipowners and their insurers. These provisions are mainly designed to benefit States faced with wreck removal operations, but they use essentially private law mechanisms to ensure that the cost of dealing with wrecks is backed by liability and insurance provisions.

From the operational perspective, once a shipowner has been required to remove a wreck in the EEZ that constitutes a hazard, or (more accurately) to remove the hazard, it is entitled under Art 9(4) to "contract with any salvor or other person to remove the wreck determined to constitute a hazard on behalf of the owner".[2] These operational and contractual issues about the removal involve questions of where the law of salvage overlaps with that of wreck removal (whether or not under the WRC 2007), and also involve significant issues of contract law. They are dealt with in Chapter 12.[3]

This chapter will therefore concentrate mainly on Arts 10–13, concerning the liability position of shipowners and insurers in relation to the locating, marking and (particularly) removal of wrecks, but in places it will also need to make reference to related articles, eg Arts 1 and 9.

10.2 Registered shipowner's liability for costs

Art 10(1)[4] creates a civil liability of the registered shipowner for the costs of locating, marking and removing a wreck, but although the liability provision (Art 10(1)) is relatively straightforward,[5] it has to be read with other provisions—especially the definitions in Art 1. The approach in the following sections will be, first, to describe the essential components of liability (and defences) and, secondly, to consider some of the triggers to that Art 10 liability created by Arts 1 and 9.[6]

---

[1] See Chapters 8 and 9.
[2] Note that this choice may be restricted in territorial waters by Art 4(4)(b): see 8.4, 11.2.2, 11.2.3, 11.3.2, 11.3.3(c).
[3] See also 10.9.1, 2.7.
[4] See the MSA 1995 s 255G: 11.3.4(a).
[5] See 10.2.1.
[6] See 10.5.

10.2.1 Strict liability for costs

Art 10 of the WRC 2007 follows the pattern of other IMO liability conventions[7] by creating a strict liability regime, although by 2007 this was hardly controversial as it reflected most State laws on wreck removal. The introduction of a liability regime in the EEZ distinguishes the WRC 2007 from the Intervention Convention 1969,[8] and in itself arguably extends the power of the coastal State beyond that which existed in international law.[9]

Strict liability is shorthand for liability without proof of fault. It is not absolute liability, for there are limited defences in Art 10(1)[10] and, in particular, the imposition of strict liability has usually been accompanied by limitation of that liability to fixed amounts.[11] It is somewhat artificial to separate the liability and defence components of Art 10(1), but it is perhaps helpful to give some simple examples of what strict liability means. Thus, the registered shipowner will be liable if the ship is wrecked as a result of:

- a collision with another ship, even where the latter is 100% at fault;
- grounding on an uncharted rock:[12]
- a breakdown of the ship's engine or equipment (despite proper maintenance);
- the parting of a towing line during a towage operation;
- the cargo shifting in heavy weather[13] so that the ship is holed or capsizes;
- an explosion or fire involving dangerous cargo that has not been properly declared by the shipper.[14]

In each of the examples, the registered shipowner will be liable even if it took all care possible, and employed the best master, crew and sub-contractors. Of course, in many of these examples there will often be fault of the shipowner (or those for whom it is responsible), eg when the master of the *Costa Concordia* navigated too close to the island of Giglio.[15] If there is fault of a pilot, the shipowner would normally be responsible for that pilot's faults in maritime law,[16] and the same would apply under the WRC 2007 Art 10.[17]

In many circumstances it may be that third parties are at fault, eg other shipowners, charterers, cargo owners, stevedores, ship repairers or port authorities. The registered shipowner will seek a recourse claim against these third parties if their conduct constitutes a tortious wrong or a breach of contract.[18]

---

7 See 2.6.2–2.6.4.
8 See 5.3.
9 See 7.3, 7.4.
10 See 10.3.
11 See 10.7, 10.8.5.
12 Assuming that there is no wrongful act of a Government under Art 10(1)(c): see 10.3.3.
13 Assuming that the heavy weather here is what might generally be described as a 'peril of the seas', and not that falling within Art 10(1)(a): see 10.3.2.
14 Cf 2.1.6.
15 See 1.2.5.
16 See the Pilotage Act 1987 s 16 and *Oceangas Gibraltar Ltd v Port of London Authority (The Cavendish)* [1993] 2 Lloyd's Rep 292.
17 Eg when the pilot took the cruise ship *Mikhail Lermontov* too close to shore and the ship sank after striking a submerged rock: see 1.2.2, 2.3.1.
18 See Art 10(4) and 10.2.2. As to whether a recourse claim could be made against the State claimant, see 10.3.3.

10.2.2 Persons liable to pay costs

It is only the registered shipowner that is liable for the costs *under* the WRC 2007 Art 10(1). Indeed, under Art 10(3),[19] claims cannot be made against the registered shipowner[20] for the costs of locating, marking and removing the wreck "otherwise than in accordance with the provisions of" the WRC 2007.[21] A national law claim for such costs (eg under general tort law or statute) could be contrary to the WRC 2007. This does not prevent a non-WRC 2007 claim being made against the registered shipowner for sums that are *not* costs of locating, marking and removing the wreck.[22] It is arguable that national legislation giving a power to bring a claim against the shipowner for wreck removal expenses is separate from (and different to) a power to sell the wreck; the former would have to be in accordance with the WRC 2007, while the latter may not be contrary to Art 10(3) as it is not a claim made "against the registered owner".[23] A related, and difficult, question is how far Art 10(3) can operate when claims may be made under another convention, eg the costs of removing bunkers or cargo.[24]

The WRC 2007 does not have an express provision to deal with what happens if two ships are wrecked, eg after a collision, and when it is not possible to separate the costs relating to each. The UK enacting legislation fills this gap by applying the principle of joint liability for those costs that are not severable;[25] this is a sensible implication of what can be presumed to have been intended by the convention.[26] Moreover, while the Art 10(1) liability regime is strict, Art 10(4) preserves such rights of recourse that the registered shipowner might have against third parties.[27] As such, a registered shipowner may pursue a tortfeasor for costs arising out of liability for the wreck removal, eg where the wreck resulted from a collision involving negligent navigation of the other ship.[28] Similarly, the registered owner may claim damages in contract where the wreck resulted from an order from a charterer to go to an unsafe port, or from the shipment by a cargo owner of undeclared dangerous goods.[29] Such claims will also be subject to the legal rules applicable to any tort or contract action.[30] It will be important to take account of the extent to which these claims would be subject to limitation of liability.[31] Thus, a claim to recover (unlimited) multimillion-dollar

---

19 Added at the diplomatic conference: see LEG/CONF.16/13, 23 April 2007.

20 Under the WRC 2007 Art 1(8) this expression includes a person owning an unregistered ship: see also the MSA 1995 s 255R(4), 11.3.4.

21 Art 10(3) mirrors the first sentence of the CLC 1992 Art III(4), but does not contain the CLC's channelling provisions as set out in the remainder of Art III(4): see 2.6.2(a), and as discussed below. The MSA 1995 Part 9A does not appear to make an express reference to Art 10(3): see 11.3.4.

22 Eg for environmental or economic loss falling outside Art 10(1): see 10.2.4.

23 See 9.2.5(h). For a discussion of how the UK MSA 1995 Part 9A deals with this issue, see 11.3.4(a).

24 See 10.9.2.

25 See 11.3.4(a).

26 Ie the equivalent to the CLC 1992 Art IV, first sentence.

27 WRC 2007 Art 10(4): see also 11.3.4(a).

28 See 2.4.

29 See 2.1.7(a)–(c), 2.1.6.

30 In the case of contract, this will include risk allocation clauses (eg exclusions, limitations, indemnities and benefit of insurance terms) of the type commonly to be found in maritime commercial contracts such as charterparties, bills of lading, towage contracts and stevedoring/handling contracts.

31 See 2.5. It should be noted that the recourse claims against charterers and cargo owners may not be subject to limitation under the LLMC, while the claim against the colliding ship depends on whether it is characterised as a wreck removal claim: see 2.5.4(d).

wreck removal costs against a colliding ship[32] will depend upon proof of negligence, but the third party shipowner may be entitled to limit its liability for the recourse claim.[33]

Note that although the WRC 2007 Art 1(9) contains a definition of "operator of the ship" this is not relevant to liability.[34] The operator, eg a ship's manager, is merely under a duty in Art 5 to report the wreck. The WRC 2007 does not have the channelling provisions of the CLC Art III(4) or the HNSC 2010 Art 7(5).[35] These expressly prevent claims falling within those conventions (eg for "pollution damage" under the CLC) being brought against employees, pilots, charterers, salvors or those taking preventive measures.[36] The absence of such provisions in the WRC 2007 means that it is theoretically open for the costs of locating, marking and removing a wreck to be brought outside the WRC 2007 against persons other than the registered owner. Such actions would not, of course, have the benefit of the compulsory insurance and direct action provisions of Art 12, but they may still be backed by insurance.[37] Whether persons such as those listed were liable in national law would be another matter, but it is possible that actions for negligence or nuisance could be brought in some circumstances.[38] This might be relevant where, for instance, a ship was wrecked after a charterer ordered it to an unsafe port, or a cargo owner shipped undeclared dangerous cargo, or there was a collision caused by another ship's negligent navigation.[39] In such cases, if the registered owner of the wreck was able to limit liability, the State claimant may seek to 'top up' its claim from other defendants.

10.2.3 *Persons who can claim costs*

Unlike other IMO liability conventions which create direct rights for individual claimants,[40] the WRC 2007 only creates rights for *States*. This is because Art 10(1) makes the shipowner liable for the "costs of locating, marking and removing the wreck *under* articles 7, 8 and 9". These articles are all expressed in terms of the rights and obligations of the "Affected State". It may well be that this State does incur direct costs itself, but there could be many circumstances in practice where removal costs are incurred immediately by independent State agencies, or even private bodies or corporations legally separate from the State (eg privatised port corporations). In most circumstances these bodies would be treated, for the international law purposes of the WRC 2007, as having undertaken actions and incurred the costs on behalf of the State. Care may be needed in drafting national

---

32 See eg the *Chitra* wreck, 10.2.5.

33 Art 2(2) of the LLMC 1976/1996 states that claims in LLMC Art 2(1) (eg under sub-para (d) or (e) for wreck or cargo removal) shall be subject to limitation whether brought by way of recourse or indemnity under a contract or otherwise: see also 2.5.4(c).

34 Cf the more extensive list of persons liable created by the Bunkers Convention 2001 Art 1(3): see 2.6.3.

35 See 2.6.2(a), 2.6.4.

36 Unless those concerned are guilty of intent or recklessness: see the CLC 1992 Art III(4) (tailpiece).

37 For example, charterers might have P&I cover: see 2.9.6(b).

38 For the common law position, see 2.4.2, 11.1.1, 11.3.4(c).

39 See 2.1.7(a)–(c), 2.1.6, 2.4.1, 2.4.3.

40 Eg under the CLC/Fund Conventions, the Bunkers Convention 2001 and the HNSC 2010, those who suffer pollution damage may claim. This includes not only States (with clean-up costs) but also persons who have suffered property or economic losses such as fishers. Similarly, under the Salvage Convention 1989, salvors have individual claims for a reward and under the Athens Convention 2002, passenger claimants have rights to compensation for injury. For channelling of liability, see 10.2.3 and 10.8.5.

implementing legislation to ensure that appropriate provisions deal with any issues about delegation or entitlement to sue under the Affected State's legal system.[41]

10.2.4 Costs recoverable

The liability under Art 10(1) is quite simply for the "costs" of locating, marking and removing the "wreck" under Arts 7, 8 and 9. It is important not to ignore the potentially considerable costs in locating and marking the wreck.[42] So far as "removal" is concerned, it must be recalled that this is defined in Art 1(7) as referring to "any form of prevention, mitigation or elimination of the hazard created by a wreck" rather than simply to the removal of the "wreck" itself.[43]

There is no separate definition of "costs"—unlike other conventions which define the type of "damage" recoverable.[44] It follows that the WRC 2007 does not allow for recovery of any environmental damage or economic losses caused by a wreck (eg losses to "related" industries such as tourism and fishing), other than the costs involved in preventing, mitigating or eliminating the hazard (including clean-up costs). The costs of environmental impact assessments may be necessary in order to check that a hazard has been eliminated, and in some circumstances the only way to "mitigate" a hazard may be to undertake a degree of reinstatement (or some form of alternative relief or improvement). Otherwise, the emphasis is on removing a negative (the hazard), rather than providing some form of more positive environmental compensation. Economic loss claims would have to be brought under the other conventions, eg for pollution damage[45] or at common law.[46] The definition of "related interests" in Art 1(6)[47] acts only to trigger the right of removal. It may well be that there are rights of recovery for such losses under national law,[48] or other IMO liability conventions, eg where there is loss from the wreck of a cargo of oil, HNS or bunkers.[49] In such circumstances it may be necessary to consider possible overlaps between the conventions.[50]

Although it is not strictly a defence, as such, the shipowner will not be liable for the cost of measures taken by States which are not "proportionate" to the hazard[51] or, seemingly, if the measures exceed what is reasonably necessary to eliminate the hazard.[52] This means that there must be limitations on the costs incurred by a State if they are to be recoverable.

---

41 See eg ss 255F and 255G of the MSA 1995: 11.3.4(a).

42 Note also the references to "practicable" means or steps in Arts 7 and 8; these must be read together with the proportionality criterion: see also 10.5.5, 10.5.6, 9.2.5(e).

43 See 8.2.2.

44 See eg the CLC 1992 Art I(6): see 2.6.2(a).

45 Eg under the CLC 1992 for oil pollution from tankers (see 2.6.2(a)); under the Bunkers Convention 2001 for bunker oil pollution (see 2.6.3); under the HNSC 2010, when in force, for pollution from HNS (see 2.6.4). For overlaps between these conventions and the WRC 2007, see 10.9.2.

46 Eg in negligence or nuisance, with the *Torrey Canyon* problems: see 1.2.1(b), 2.6.1, 2.6.4, 2.5.

47 See 8.2.3.

48 See 2.4.1–2.4.3, 11.1.1.

49 See eg 2.6.2(b), 2.6.3, 2.6.4.

50 See 10.9.

51 Art 2(2): see 9.2.5(e), 10.9.2(a), and cf 8.4.1, 8.4.2 (proportionate criterion to apply in territorial waters if State has opted in).

52 Art 2(3). Note again the interplay of "removing" in Art 10(1) with the definition of "removal" in Art 1(7) which refers to elimination of the hazard, rather than the wreck: see 8.2.2, 9.2.5.

It follows that all parts of a wreck need not *necessarily* be removed.[53] It also requires attention to be paid to the potential hazards if any remains are left on the seabed. This was an issue with the *Rena*, where indigenous interests argued for all remains of the wreck to be removed (for cultural reasons), even where the costs of such removal might otherwise appear disproportionate.[54] States may well have rights to remove the wreck themselves, but the question of costs recovery poses slightly different issues. Intangible cultural heritage may well be a "related interest" within Art 1(5) and 1(6),[55] but the response to that must still pass the proportionality test in Art 2(2).[56] It does not seem possible to argue that there is a presumption that all traces or remains of the wreck *must* be removed. Each case will turn on its own facts, although it is becoming increasingly difficult to argue against full removal.[57]

The wreck of the *Prestige*[58] raised issues of proportionality in the context of the Fund Convention 1992.[59] In 2004 efforts were made to remove the estimated 13,100 mt of cargo remaining on board the fore part, and 700 mt in the after part. A total of 13,000 mt was removed from the fore part, but no attempt was made to remove the oil in the after part;[60] in neither case does it appear that there was a raising of the remaining wreck of the hull from the seabed. The Spanish government determined to remove all possible remaining oil from the sunken fore part of the hull, and claimed for the cost of doing so.[61] Experts were appointed to report on (i) the technical reasonableness of the operation, including whether the relationship between those costs and the benefits derived or expected was reasonable, and (ii) on the ecological and social necessity to deal with the wreck. Based on the detailed studies, the IOPC Fund Director advised that "the costs of the operation to remove the oil were disproportionate to any potential economic and environmental consequences of leaving the oil in the wreck".[62] This approach was ultimately endorsed by the IOPC Executive Committee and it was decided that this part of the claim should not be paid.[63] That conclusion was controversial for Spain, but was a reflection of international practice as declared by a body of States. It should be recalled, though, that costs recoverable under the WRC 2007 will not be assessed initially by such an international body, but will ultimately be decided by the courts of the State where the claim is brought.[64] Moreover, the pollution

---

53 See eg 4.2.2, but also 10.2.5.
54 An application was made under the Resource Management Act 1991 (NZ) for a resource consent to leave the remains of the *Rena* wreck and debris on the Astrolabe Reef: see 1.2.4(e).
55 See 8.2.3, 9.2.5.
56 See 9.2.5(e), 10.9.2(a), 10.8.6. This is also consistent with a more general approach to the recognition of indigenous rights where proportionality may be relevant: see the decision of the Supreme Court of Canada in *Tsilhqot'in Nation v British Columbia* [2014] SCC 44, [87].
57 See further the incidents analysed in 10.2.5.
58 See 1.2.2.
59 See the discussion at 9.2.5.
60 IOPC Fund *Annual Report* 1996, 112.
61 €109.2 million, later reduced to €24.2 million (apparently after an EU subsidy). Previous costs in relation to oil removal in 2003 which were admissible were €33.1 million: 92FUND/EXC.32/6, 2 March 2006, para 3.2.60.
62 92FUND/EXC.30/9/2, para 3.26, although noting that 1992 Fund's admissibility criteria did not take social, non-economic effects into account.
63 See 92FUND/EXC.32/4/Add.1, 7 February 2006; 92FUND/EXC.32/6, para 3.2.80.
64 See 1.2.2(a) and the decision of the Spanish Supreme Court in the *Prestige* case.

mischief covered by the CLC and Fund is arguably narrower in scope than the "hazard" under the WRC 2007.

The Review produced by the IG of P&I Clubs' Large Casualty Working Group[65] did conclude that where there are disproportionate or unreasonable requirements imposed by States, the owner or Club should really consider challenging such action in the courts. It is perhaps significant that the Review drew specific attention to the fact that the hazard criteria set out in the WRC 2007 Art 6, might be useful in mounting such a challenge. It is clear that the Clubs regard such restrictions on State action as important given "instances where States have made unreasonable and disproportionate demands of shipowners and their insurers",[66] and the Clubs see the WRC 2007 as providing "a legal framework that should promote consistency between signatory States".[67]

The attitude of the Clubs to the WRC 2007 is well summarised by one of their leading experts, who had been involved in many of the most significant recent wreck removal operations,[68] and who summarised some of the restrictions on State power outlined above: "These are welcome developments in the light of recent instances where states have made unreasonable and disproportionate demands of shipowners and their insurers. These were situations where either the perceived benefits (usually environmental) of demands made did not justify the expense involved, or where national economic interests were given primacy over operational efficacy and proper cost control".[69]

10.2.5 Full or partial removal?

The expression "removal" has a natural meaning which suggests taking the whole of the hull and cargo away from the site of the wreck but, as noted,[70] the WRC 2007 Art 1(7) now provides a special definition of "removal" that emphasises mitigation or elimination of the *hazard*. The references to proportionality and reasonableness in Art 2(2) and (3) recognise that there is not an absolute presumption of full removal, but that a balancing exercise will be needed.[71] International practice recognises that there may be other methods of eliminating the hazard that is sought to be avoided, which may mean that total removal is not inevitable.[72] In 1996, France drew the attention of the IMO Legal Committee to some of the alternatives, eg:[73]

> by neutralising (pumping out) the cargo or holds which constitute the hazard. This is what happened after the *Tanio* accident in 1980[74] and it is what is being done with the holds of the

---

65 See 1.4.
66 S Kendall-Marsden, "Wreck Removal and the Nairobi Convention", *International Tug & OSV* (March/April 2015), 44 (available at www.standard-club.com/media/1750190/ito-marapr-p44.pdf).
67 *Kendall-Marsden & O'Donnell, Major Casualty Management*, 2.
68 Including *Chitra* and *Costa Concordia*.
69 S Kendall-Marsden, "Wreck Removal and the Nairobi Convention", *International Tug & OSV* (March/April 2015), 44.
70 See 9.2.5(b) and 10.2.4.
71 See 10.2.4.
72 See also 4.2.2.
73 IMO Doc LEG 74/5/1, 7 August 1996.
74 See 1.2.2(a).

Estonia.[75] It is a point concerning which dialogue between the owner of the wrecked ship and the coastal state is vital, since the kind of measure to be taken for neutralising the danger falls within the competence of the coastal state.

As part of the *Rena* litigation, the New Zealand Government commissioned London Offshore Consultants (LOC) to provide a report showing international comparisons of ten wreck removal operations where wreck removal orders had been issued.[76] One of the purposes was to see how far "full" removal was required. In eight of these operations there had apparently been entire (or nearly entire) removal.

Thus, the *Coral Bulker* (16,725 gt) went aground in 2000 in Portugal with a timber cargo.[77] After an initial salvage contract to remove pollutants, an US$8 million wreck removal operation involved cutting the ship into sections for removal by land via a breakwater. Small sections of shell plating were left entangled in a breakwater as it was too dangerous to remove them.

The car carrier *Tricolor* (49,792 gt) sank in 2002 after a collision in the English Channel about 20 miles from the French coast.[78] Oil removal was undertaken under a modified wreck removal contract, and a Wreckstage contract was agreed in 2013 with final removal taking place by 2014 at a cost of US$54.7 million.[79] The contractual requirement was for everything above 1 m² to be removed, including cargo[80] (although a car cargo would not be expected to move from the site as much as containers).

The container vessel *CP Valour* (15,145 gt) grounded in a World Heritage Site in the Azores in 2005.[81] After removal of 400 mt of bunkers and all the container cargo, the ship was lightened (eg by removal of main engines and much superstructure). After nine months aground the hull was refloated, but sank soon after (at a holding ground about 15 miles off the coast), leaving small sections of scrap at the original site.[82] Authorities required monitoring for five years to ensure no debris remained. Small sections of shell plating remained on the seabed. Wreck removal (and LOF/SCOPIC) costs were US$44.6 million.[83]

---

75 See 1.2.2(b) and 2.3.2.

76 See "Report on the comparisons between Rena and other wreck removal operations in recent years" (9 July 2014) [*LOC Report*]: www.crownlaw.govt.nz/assets/Uploads/Reports/wreck-removal-report-3.pdf. Also www.crownlaw.govt.nz/publications/reports/ for the text of the five reports undertaken by LOC, and AG Cabinet Paper, [108–111], Appendix 7 for a summary table of the casualties. We are grateful to LOC for permission to refer to the *LOC Report* for basic details of the ten incidents described below; additional information is provided, as noted.

77 See *LOC Report*, 25–27.

78 See *LOC Report*, 28–29.

79 International Group Club figures, quoted in *Herbert, Challenges*, 23.

80 See I Brynildsen. "Tricolor—The collision, sinking and wreck removal", 178 Gard News Insight (2005) www.gard.no/web/updates/content/51625/tricolor-the-collision-sinking-and-wreck-removal; also 2.4.2 (fn 505).

81 See *LOC Report*, 30–32.

82 See also MAIB Investigation Report, "Report on the investigation of the grounding of the vessel CP Valour" Report No 22/2006; "'CP Valour' Removal Completed", www.maritimejournal.com/news101/tugs,-towing-and-salvage/cp_valour_removal_completed. Cutting up the ship *in situ* was not an option owing to location and lack of local infrastructure and it took six weeks to mobilise equipment from Europe. Owing to the shallow location, a jackup rig had to be used to remove containers onto a moored barge, from whence they were transported to Lisbon. Rotting produce in the cargo holds produced H2S, which restricted safe access by workers: see www.youtube.com/watch?v=jfiJrSMaAcY.

83 International Group Club figures, quoted in *Herbert, Challenges*, 23.

The RoRo *Rokia Delmas* (32,924 gt) went aground off La Rochelle in France in 2006.[84] After removal of the bunkers the ship was cut in sections and everything above 1 m^2 was removed pursuant to a French government wreck removal notice.[85] The costs were US$73 million.[86]

The *MSC Napoli* (UK, 2007[87]), was believed to have been removed in its entirety according to contractual terms requiring removal of all material above 1 m^2. The costs were US$135 million.[88]

The bulk carrier *Fedra* (35,886 gt, in ballast) ran aground in Gibraltar in 2008 after an engine failure and delay in taking salvage assistance.[89] It lost about 200 mt of bunkers. The accommodation block and aft section of the vessel were cut up *in situ* for removal while the forward section of the vessel was refloated and later broken up for scrap in Gibraltar.[90] The total costs of removal and SCOPIC were US$66 million.[91]

The container ship *MSC Chitra* (33,113 gt), was severely damaged after a collision off Mumbai in August 2010, while carrying 1,219 containers, 2,662 mt of fuel oil, 283 mt of diesel and 88,040 litres of lube oil.[92] Over 300 containers were lost overboard (including 31 with dangerous goods such as aluminium phosphide), there was pollution and the port was closed for a number of days.[93] The ship was partly submerged and extensive efforts were made to remove cargo and pollutants. Attempts to sell the vessel to local shipbreakers apparently failed, given its state, and the ship was eventually refloated in March 2017, towed to sea and scuttled in international waters in 2017.[94] The removal and SCOPIC costs were US$102 million.[95]

The container ship *MSC Al Amine* (8,631 gt) went aground in Tunisia in 2005, spilling bunkers, but was refloated and delivered to a local dry dock.[96]

In two instances recorded in the *LOC Report*, there had been a partial removal, or the wreck remained on the seabed. The fully laden Panamanian bulk carrier *New Flame* (26,824 gt) was beached off Gibraltar after a collision in 2007.[97] Its stern remained afloat and, after bunkers were removed, an attempt was made to cut the hull into two parts. In a storm, the stern then sank in very difficult water conditions (which extended operations by 147 days and cost an additional US$30 million). Before the hull was lifted about 32,000 mt of the

---

84 See *LOC Report*, 33–34.
85 ITOPF, 24 October 2006: www.itopf.com/in-action/case-studies/case-study/rokia-delmas-france-2006/.
86 International Group Club figures, quoted in *Herbert, Challenges*, 23.
87 See 1.2.4 and *LOC Report*, 35–37.
88 International Group Club figures, quoted in *Herbert, Challenges*, 23. See also 1.2.4(c) and (d).
89 See *LOC Report*, 42–43.
90 Government of Gibraltar, "Report on the Investigation of the Grounding of the *MV Fedra*"; ITOPF, Ocean Orbit (November 2009), 2.
91 International Group Club figures, quoted in *Herbert, Challenges*, 23.
92 See *LOC Report*, 44–45.
93 www.fortunes-de-mer.com/old/rubriques/liens%20et%20contacts/detailsactualites/MSC_Chitra_2010.htm.
94 See 14.1.2(b).
95 International Group Club figures, quoted in *Herbert, Challenges*, 23.
96 See *LOC Report*, 46–47. As the *LOC Report* acknowledges, this was not really a wreck removal operation, but one for successful salvage where there was no cargo lost; to that extent it does not really belong in the list of eight examples of "full" wreck removal. See also http://wwz.cedre.fr/en/Resources/Spills/Spills/MSC-Al-Amine.
97 See *LOC Report*, 38–39.

42,200 mt of scrap steel cargo were removed to Portugal in ten shipments. The engine room was lifted in a single 3,000 mt lift and the stern section was carried to Belgium on a barge for scrapping.[98] The remains of crushed double bottoms and shell plating amounted to about one third of the lightweight of the wreck, but were allowed to remain as there was a clearance of 17.7 m and the site was below a cliff where there was no danger to navigation. The removal and SCOPIC costs were US$177 million.[99]

The passenger ship *Sea Diamond* (22,412 gt) grounded and sank in 2007 off the island of Santorini in Greece.[100] The lack of local equipment meant delays in attempting bunker removal from the hull lying in 140 m of water. Although some oil was removed, the hull remains complete on the seabed where it is apparently not a risk to navigation. Costs were US$57.9 million in 2014, although full removal (if possible) would be considerably more expensive.

There are other more recent examples than those cited in the *LOC Report* where full or partial removal was an issue, eg the bulk carrier *Smart* (77,240 gt) that ran aground and eventually broke into three pieces in Richards Bay, South Africa, in August 2012.[101] Salvors removed the fuel, without spillage, and some 10,000 mt of coal slurry. The aft section was stripped of pollutants and in October 2013 sunk 28 miles off the bay. A tender process to lighten and refloat the fore section was won by a different contractor. After refloating it was towed some 1,000 nm to sea and sunk in December 2014. "[T]he remaining mid-section was cut down and buried at the beginning of September 2015, with rehabilitation of the seabed completed immediately thereafter".[102]

By contrast, when the *Baltic Ace* sank in busy waters off Rotterdam in 2013, the entire hull and debris were removed in 2014–2015.[103] A large salvage grab was used to retrieve debris off the bottom, including vehicles and parts from those of the 1,400-vehicle cargo that had fallen from the cut sections; divers were used to clear any remaining waste.[104] It may be that a car carrier's cargo could present fewer problems of removal than a large container ship with thousands of containers of diverse products, but this removal operation was estimated to cost €67 million.[105] Similarly, after the *Costa Concordia* was removed, there were extensive efforts to remediate the site by removing debris. An Italian university has

---

98 See eg, www.titansalvage.com/What-We-Do/Response-and-Results; www.crowley.com/news-and-media/press-releases/titan-salvage-removes-accommodations-block-from-sunken-ship-new-flame-in-gibraltar/; www.joc.com/new-flame-wreck-removal-success-gibraltar-titan-removes-more-50000-tons-scrap-cargo-and-wreckage.

99 International Group Club figures, quoted in *Herbert, Challenges*, 23; *Swedish Club P&I Guidelines 2012*, 17.

100 See *LOC Report*, 40–42.

101 www.nepia.com/news/press-releases-area/north-pi-club-delivers-mv-smart-wreck-removal-on-budget-through-a-collaborative-approach/; http://gcaptain.com/mv-smart-salvage-wraps-up-in-south-africa/.

102 www.nepia.com/news/press-releases-area/north-pi-club-delivers-mv-smart-wreck-removal-on-budget-through-a-collaborative-approach/ http://gcaptain.com/mv-smart-salvage-wraps-up-in-south-africa/. See also 14.3.

103 See 14.3.

104 See "Baltic Ace Wreck Removal", interview and video, Boskalis website, https://magazine.boskalis.com/issue03/baltic-ace-wreck-removal [*Baltic Ace Wreck Removal*]. A total of 460 m³ of fuel oil had already been removed from the hull and superheated water was then used to flush the tanks three times to remove all sticky remains.

105 www.bonnagreement.org/news/baltic-ace-update-and-video/. For the limitation issues, see 2.5.9(c).

been engaged to work on site restoration, eg replanting seagrass and coral and monitoring the wreck site for five years.

There is not enough information provided in these examples to draw very broad conclusions, eg as to developing State practice. They do illustrate that, where possible, there had been compliance with 'full' wreck removal notices. Each case will depend on its own facts, particularly the location and the safety of operations, and the examples did not present the same magnitude of costs as the *Rena*. What can be said is that States are becoming more assertive in favour of full removal than they might have been in the past—particularly where the wreck is in sensitive waters.

10.2.6 Unusual and difficult locations

Ships may become wrecks in environmentally sensitive areas in any part of the world, but the ability to deal with them may vary depending on how remote those areas are from developed world facilities and resources. The *Rena* was an example of a wreck in a developed country[106] but where major infrastructure was not immediately available, and where the location was itself tricky. In remote islands, with even less infrastructure, the problems are exacerbated—particularly for developing States.

The *Oceanus* was a virtually new coal carrier carrying 70,000 mt of coal that grounded on a reef off the island of Satawal (in the Federal States of Micronesia) in 2014. It was ultimately refloated, but it was first necessary to offload 14,000 mt of cargo into a ship chartered in Singapore (which itself needed to be rigged with equipment such as portable tracked cranes and fenders). The only way to remove cargoes like this may be by a slow grab discharge, in this case taking 12 days. In other locations it may be very difficult safely to position discharging equipment, or for that equipment to deal with waterlogged cargo.[107]

Another example of the difficulties involved with remote islands concerns the Maltese registered *MS Oliva*, a 40,170 gt bulk carrier en route from Brazil to Singapore with a cargo of 65,264 mt of soya beans, that ran aground and was wrecked in 2011 on Nightingale Island, part of the UK Overseas Territory of Tristan da Cunha. There was no airstrip and it was five days' sailing for an LOF salvage tug from South Africa, but the vessel broke up before it arrived. Vessels were chartered to bring in pollution response equipment to deal with the estimated 1,400 mt of bunkers that were lost. Residues were bagged and carried by helicopter to one of the ships for disposal in Cape Town. There was also concern to install bait stations to prevent rats getting to previously rodent-free islands and decimating the seabird population (in excess of 2 million breeding pairs).[108] Fisheries were closed for a considerable period and there were fears that spilled soya beans might have affected lobsters in the area. A commercially confidential settlement was reached with the owners and P&I Club (Gard), but it does not appear that the wreck was removed.

---

106 See also the *Shen Neng 1*, which went aground on the Great Barrier Reef but was ultimately saved: see 2.6.4, 10.6.4, 10.2.6.
107 Cf the *Smart*: 10.2.5, 14.1.2.
108 See Joint Nature Conservation Committee (JNNC) http://jncc.defra.gov.uk/page-5824-theme=textonly, and www.tristandc.com/newsmsolivahome.php; ITOPF presentation, www.pcs.gr.jp/doc/esymposium/2012/2_dr_franck_laruelle_ppt_e.pdf. See also the Maltese Marine Safety Investigation Report No. 14/2012.

Where removal is required and possible in such locations it can be very expensive. The newly built Maltese-registered container ship *Kea Trader* (25,145 gt) went aground on the Durand Reefs some 140 nm off New Caledonia in July 2017.[109] Some 750 mt of bunkers were removed by the initial LOF salvage contractor, and many containers had to be lifted off by helicopter. By September the ship was a CTL, attempts to refloat it failed and it eventually broke in two after heavy storms in November. The salvor continued in a caretaker role[110] to deal with unpumpable residues and removed nearly 700 containers. After a tender process, a wreck removal contractor was appointed in March 2018. Further bad weather caused further delays and operations were expected to continue well into 2019, The delays and difficulties are expected to make this one of the most costly removal operations falling initially on the P&I Club, Skuld, and owner Lomar (a large, reputable group).

A UNESCO World Heritage Site was threatened in the Galapagos in 2014 when the Ecuadorian flagged reefer ship *Galapaface* (1,183 gt) ran aground while departing the island of San Cristobal. After removal of 19,000 gallons of bunkers, other pollutants and cargo, it was refloated by the use of external flotation tanks. The weather and condition of the ship meant that a tow to the coast could still present unacceptable environmental risks, as the ship might sink or capsize in an uncontrolled manner. The Ecuadorian government therefore issued a permit for the ship to be towed 20 miles east of the Galapagos Marine Reserve (GMR) and scuttled in 2,500 m of water.[111] Scuttling was also the option utilised for the *Floreana*, which went aground in San Cristobal in 2015. The ship was refloated by contractors after repairs to the hull, the sealing of tanks and removal of cargo and other pollutants (including fluids from fuel and hydraulic lines). *Floreana* was then towed outside the GMR and scuttled in 3,000 m of water.

10.2.7 Ships covered

10.2.7(a) Types of ship

As already seen, the WRC 2007 Art 1 applies to the "wreck" of a "ship".[112] The definition of "ship" in Art 1(2) is much wider than that in some other maritime conventions,[113] and this wide definition has to recalled when interpreting the WRC 2007. This will be of particular importance for both liability and insurance purposes.

Art 1(2) can be divided into an opening definition of ship consisting of nine words and then a list of examples. The opening words are "'ship' means a seagoing vessel *of any type whatsoever*". The italicised words are further extended by the list of examples. There is

---

109 See eg, www.nouvelle-caledonie.gouv.fr/content/download/4734/36723/file/20180711%20DP%20KT%20un%20an.pdf, https://worldmaritimenews.com/archives/tag/kea-trader/.
110 See 12.3.1.
111 Ecuador was not a party to the London Convention 1972 or the LC Protocol 1996: see 14.1.2.
112 See 8.2.1(b).
113 See eg the LLMC Arts 1, 15(5): 2.5.2, where floating platforms are not subject to limitation of liability. There is extensive literature on the definition of the word "ship" in maritime law, but it is important to note that each definition (or use of the word) has to be read in the context of the convention or statute to which it applies. For a recent comparative analysis, see S Gahlen, "Ships Revisited: A Comparative Study" (2014) 20 JIML 252. See also *Gaskell, MSA 1995*, 21/320; S Rainey, "What is a 'Ship' under the 1952 Arrest Convention?" [2013] LMCLQ 50.

no restriction here though as to the size of the vessel, eg with a minimum tonnage,[114] but there is a restriction through the reference to "seagoing".[115] It seems that the adjective is overriding in the sense that it applies to all the vessels identified in in the list in Art 1(2); eg a "submersible" must also be seagoing. This word 'seagoing' is an unfortunate expression as it is inherently unclear what it means, but is used in other conventions, such as the LLMC. It is partly designed to reflect the fact that maritime conventions normally apply to international transit between States, thereby excluding domestic (ie intra-state voyages and craft that cannot go to sea).[116] But the WRC 2007 does not have any restriction about the nature of the voyage being undertaken.[117] Moreover, the late addition of Art 3(2)[118] means that a State can apply the WRC 2007 to wrecks "located within its territory, including the territorial sea".

The first ambiguity is what is meant by "sea" in "*sea*going"? It can fairly confidently be stated that a ship wrecked in the EEZ will be a seagoing ship; on any approach the EEZ will be part of a sea and the ship must have been sea*going* to get there. More difficult is how far the "sea" extends towards land. It cannot mean the 12-mile territorial limit, because that would conflict with Art 3(2) above, and is essentially a geographical expression.[119] There are many regulatory instruments that divide waters into different categories of sea for the purposes of limiting the navigation of small craft not fully equipped for the rigours of the ocean. Thus, passenger craft may be restricted in their navigation under SOLAS to smooth or partially smooth waters.[120] But these definitions are not referred to in the WRC 2007 and are of limited help. The "sea" will almost certainly exclude internal waters eg in the non-tidal parts of rivers, but if one was to approach the matter by considering the broad notion of 'perils of the sea' most major ports can be affected by storms. And States that extend the operation of the WRC 2007 into territorial waters will want the convention to apply in such waters.

But what is a sea*going* ship? It might be said to involve one or more of these features, ie it is a ship that (i) is physically capable of going to sea, (ii) is legally capable of going to sea or (iii) in practice actually does go to sea. The English case law in other contexts suggests that it is the last criterion that is most significant.[121]

The resolution of the seagoing ship question will ultimately be one for national courts, who may be expected to apply a sensible purposive interpretation, although they may need

---

114 Cf Art 12(1) which for insurance purposes imposes a threshold of 300 gt: see 8.2.1(b), 10.8.2.

115 It might be thought that the reference to "vessel" was also restrictive, ie pointing to some form of hollow receptacle, as this might have excluded platforms or rafts, but the former (at least) are covered by the list of examples.

116 Canada has extended its Wrecked, Abandoned or Hazardous Vessels Act 2019 Part 1 (Removal of Wrecks) to craft that are not seagoing: see s 15(1).

117 Unlike say the Hague/Visby Rules Art X (see 2.1.5), or the Athens Convention 2002 Art 2 (see 2.3.1).

118 See 8.4.

119 See 8.3.1.

120 The Merchant Shipping (Safety of Navigation) Regulations 2002 (SI 2002/1473, as amended) reg 2(1) defines categories of waters specified as seagoing for the purposes of SOLAS; they mean "going beyond the limits of waters of categories A, B, C and D, as categorised in Annex 1 to the MCA's 2002 SOLAS V publication" (solasv.mcga.gov.uk/). These refer generally to rivers, canals and estuaries which (for Category D) means those where the significant wave height could not be expected to exceed 2 m at any one time.

121 See *The Sea Eagle* [2012] 2 Lloyd's Rep 37, summarising the case law, including *Salt Union Ltd v Wood* [1893] 1 QB 370: see also 2.3.1.

to be careful to ensure that they are giving an international interpretation not one solely conditioned by national appreciations. The main problem is the application of the expression to small craft operating in territorial waters. In practice, it may be that this is a problem that is more theoretical than practical, especially where ships under 300 gt are not required to carry WRC 2007 insurance certificates.[122] It may be advisable for States to expand upon the definition in their national law when implementing the convention.

The second part of Art 1(2) expands upon the breadth of the opening words by giving non-exclusive examples of the "vessel of any type whatsoever"—provided they are seagoing. Taken together with that wide introduction, the list provides an extensive definition that would include tankers, cargo ships, passenger ships, tugs, supply boats and hovercraft. In the light of current debates about how far IMO conventions apply to maritime autonomous surface ships (MASS),[123] it does not appear that the mere fact that what is otherwise a "seagoing ship" is autonomous would prevent it falling within the definition in Art 1(2) of the WRC 2007. There are issues about how far any object could be a "ship" if it does not have humans on board and in control, but unmanned barges and platforms already clearly fall within the wide definition of "ship" in Art 1(2). So the extent of the WRC 2007 is more likely to focus on the whether there are any 'things' that do not fall within the very wide expressions such as "seagoing vessel of any type whatsoever" or "floating craft".

"Submersibles" are specifically mentioned, but these come in many different types. It seems likely that most would pass the test of being" seagoing", although some may be designed only for calm port or inland waters. There may be large entirely self-sufficient craft with a separate certificate of registration (ie like a submarine).[124] Submersibles may be crewed, operated remotely or fully autonomous.[125] In some circumstances, these craft may be better considered as functionally part of a 'mother' ship, eg where they may be attached by umbilicals (for power and communication). Here, if the submersible were lost (but not the mother ship) the submersible would not be the "ship" for the purposes of the WRC 2007, but would probably fall within Art 1(4)(c) as being an "object that is lost at sea from a ship".[126] There would still need to be a "maritime casualty" within Art 1(3), but the loss of a submersible would probably be "an occurrence . . . external [to the mother ship]".[127]

---

122 Of course, a very small ship would be highly unlikely to cause the sort of "hazard" covered by Art 1(5), but it should be recalled that even anchors or sunken containers can be a hazard to navigation in shallow waters.

123 See eg LEG 106/8/1 11 January 2019, summarising developments in the various IMO Committees; also LEG 106/8/2 (22 January 2019) for a proposal by 12 States and the International Group for a scoping exercise into how MASS might be relevant to conventions emanating from the IMO Legal Committee, eg those dealing with liabilities.

124 Although they may not meet the tonnage threshold of 300 gt under Art 12(1) for insurance purposes: see 10.8.2.

125 Cf E Brown and N Gaskell, *The Law Relating to Autonomous Underwater Vehicles* (Society for Underwater Technology, 2000), 81–136. There seems to be no reason why fully autonomous seagoing submersibles ould not be covered by Art 1(2) of the WRC 2007.

126 See further, the discussion about Art 1(4) and cargo in 10.6. Similar considerations would apply to parts of ships more generally, eg anchors.

127 The "occurrence" would need to result in "material damage or imminent threat of material damage to a ship or its cargo" within Art 1(3). It would seem unduly literal to say that as the occurrence was to the submersible, there was not damage or threat to "the [mother]ship"; the submersible should either be considered to be part of the ship, or cargo.

The Art 1(2) definition would also cover the more unusual floating craft that are found at sea, including the heavy lift cranes and sheerlegs (often mounted on barges) that are used to raise wrecks![128]

The Art 1(2) definition also includes "floating platforms", such as oil rigs and gas platforms. This is an important distinction as such platforms could be significant hazards to navigation and may contain much polluting material. As there is no international convention creating liability for pollution from such platforms, neighbouring States might find that they have few remedies available.[129] The ability to be able to raise such platforms is an improvement in international law. However, Art 1(2) borrows a provision used elsewhere[130] to create a demarcation between maritime law regimes and those applying to the offshore industry. Although this division is artificial in environmental terms, it represents a distinction that is reflected in regulatory provisions and in the insurance markets. A floating platform will not therefore fall within the WRC 2007 when it is "on location engaged in the exploration, exploitation or production of seabed mineral resources". In effect, the WRC 2007 will only apply to wrecks when the platform is in transit, ie where there is a maritime risk. The WRC 2007 could therefore apply to floating platforms that are being towed to shore for dismantling and are wrecked on the way.[131] Note however, that if a rig or platform is being carried on a barge, it is the latter that will be the "ship" and the platform will be cargo within Art 1(4).[132]

There have been questions about whether the many varieties of craft used in the offshore industries are to be treated as ships in maritime law; these craft include FPSOs and FLNGs, some of which are enormous and can cost billions of dollars.[133] Under the WRC 2007 they would almost certainly fall under the alternative description of floating platforms. In such a case, though, they would fall outside the WRC 2007 if they are "on location", as above. To that extent, it might be more advantageous for Affected States to argue that they were ships, where the "on location" requirement does not apply. There might then be an additional question of interpretation, whereby the owner of the craft argues that if the craft falls within the definition of "floating platform" that excludes the possibility that it can also be a "ship"; ie that the wording of Art 1(2) intends to provide for mutually exclusive categories.

Most warships would fall within Art 1(2), but note that they will normally be excluded from the WRC 2007 by Art 4(2).[134]

There may well be 'things' that are not within the Art 1(2) definition. In 2017, a number of pipes broke loose while being towed in the North Sea; they were not being carried on any barge but were floating as sealed units. It would take a very wide definition of "vessel"

---

128 There is a separate issue as to how to measure the gross tonnage of such barges, which are not designed to carry cargo and which might have a minimal tonnage: see 2.5.5(a), 2.8.2 and the MSA 1995 s 255J(6), 11.3.3(e).

129 See the Montara incident discussed in *Gaskell, Liability and Compensation Regimes: Pollution of the High Seas*, 238–240. Note now the effect of the Offshore Safety Directive 2013 which could apply the Environmental Liability Directive 2004 to such incidents within the EU: see 2.6.5.

130 The Salvage Convention 1989 Art 3 which similarly only allows salvage when a platform is in transit and not on location: see 2.7.6 and *Gaskell MSA 1995*, 21/380.

131 See 10.2.8, 14.7.3.

132 See 10.6.

133 Eg, Petronas' *PFLNG Satu* reputedly cost approximately US$10 billion: see www.offshore-technology.com/features/biggest-flng-tankers/.

134 See 8.2.1(h).

for them to be included, but it appears that they were prepared for a seagoing voyage and were hollow, sealed objects.[135] In 2014, an Au$7 million Oceanlinx 3,000 mt wave power generator sank off the South Australian coast while under tow. This was the second prototype to founder and its owner went into liquidation, leaving State authorities to deal with the remains.[136] It appears this generator was mounted on a solid concrete base, intended to be fixed to the seabed, but while under towage was supported by airbags (which were punctured). On the assumption that the structure was incapable of floating of its own accord, it might have been difficult to describe it as a "floating" platform if it depended upon temporary flotation supports. Given the broad aims of the WRC 2007, it is submitted that a wide construction should be given to the expression "floating platform" so as to cover such unusual structures which are designed to float temporarily.[137] By contrast, the *Costa Concordia*[138] would surely have continued to be classified as a vessel after raising—even though supported by extensive sponsons for its voyage to a recycling yard.

The WRC 2007 makes no reference to aircraft and would not therefore apply to the loss at sea of aircraft like the MH 370 in 2014.[139] This would be true even if the aircraft was lost in shallow waters where it might be a threat to navigation. Seaplanes and float planes would not be covered, nor any civil versions of the wave-skimming Russian Ekranoplan. UK law treats hovercraft for some purposes as if they were aircraft,[140] but they are expressly included within Art 1(2) as "air-cushion vehicles". If an aircraft were being carried as cargo on a ship and was lost overboard, then it would be within the WRC 2007.[141]

10.2.7(b) Ships flagged in non-State parties

A more fundamental issue concerns whether there can be liability at all in respect of ships flagged in non-State parties.[142] It seems clear that international law could be used by such a flag State to object to the application in the EEZ (at least) of certain WRC 2007 provisions to its ships; eg the obligation to report a wreck (Art 5(1)), and possibly an order for the shipowner to remove the wreck (Art 9(2)). There may be some doubt as to whether the creation under Art 10(1) of a civil liability for costs in respect of such ships could be justified on more general grounds, eg based on developing international norms for liability systems designed to protect the environment.[143] However, there is a possibility that an Affected State dealing with a wreck in its EEZ could be faced by an assertion from a shipowner whose ship is flagged in a non-State party that the WRC 2007 simply does not apply to it. The authors are not aware of any instance where such a defence has been raised in relation to the CLC and there may well be an assumption

---

135 See 11.3.5. If the WRC 2007 did not apply, national wreck removal provisions might be needed: see 11.3.4.
136 After partial dismantling the intention was to leave the base as an artificial reef: see eg http://mobile.abc.net.au/news/2018-09-26/wrecked-wave-generator-to-become-artificial-reef/10307436?pfmredir=sm; also 14.1.4, 14.2.
137 There would be difficulties though in calculating a tonnage for such a craft so as to trigger the compulsory insurance requirements of Art 12(1): cf the MSA 1995 s 255J(6), 11.3.3(e).
138 See 1.2.5(b).
139 See 13.2.3.
140 See 2.3.1.
141 See 10.6.
142 See the full discussion in 7.4.
143 See 7.4.5.

in practice that it is not available.[144] Whether such a defence succeeds may also depend upon the way that the WRC 2007 has been enacted in national law;[145] coastal States may simply take a robust view that they are entitled to create civil liability in such cases. It appears that the UK has not made a distinction between ships of different flags.[146] It is understood that the Netherlands has applied the WRC 2007 to all ships wrecked in its EEZ, irrespective of flag,[147] so as to exercise powers of removal and cost recovery against any ships wrecked in the EEZ. Similarly, it is understood that Sweden, when implementing the WRC 2007 into Swedish law,[148] made no distinction (from the perspective of liability of shipowners and insurers) between ships from States parties and ships from non-parties. The WRC 2007 is now found in a new Chapter 11a of the Swedish Maritime Code.[149]

In any event, it may also be possible to argue that an insurer could be directly liable to pay for wreck removal costs under the WRC 2007 if it has voluntarily agreed to a request from the registered shipowner to provide WRC 2007 cover for ships of non-State parties and that a WRC 2007 certificate has been issued accordingly.[150]

10.2.8 Completion of removal under WRC 2007

The WRC 2007 Art 1(7) provides: "'Removal' means any form of prevention, mitigation or elimination of the hazard created by a wreck. 'Remove', 'removed' and 'removing' shall be construed accordingly".[151]

This provision defines "removal" in a way that is broader than mere physical removal[152] and emphasises in a number of places that the WRC 2007 is concerned with removing a wreck that "poses a hazard"[153] or "constitutes a hazard.[154] The linkage between "wreck", "removal" and "hazard" is significant because when Art 10(1) sets out the simple liability rule that the registered shipowner is liable for the costs of "removing the wreck" it speaks about more than physical removal of the ship from a particular location. The obligation is to prevent, mitigate or eliminate the hazard. Until that is achieved, the registered owner is still at risk for costs.[155] The obligation does not therefore cease on wreck *raising*, but at what stage *does* the registered shipowner's liability for "removal" cease? In other words,

---

144 Of course, the more States that become parties to a convention like the CLC, the less likely it is that an objection can be raised.
145 See eg 11.3.2(b), 11.3.4(a).
146 See 11.3.4(a).
147 See 11.2.1; cf 7.4.5; also 10.2.7(b), 10.8.4(a).
148 See Bill 2016/17:178.
149 Sjölagen 1992:1009. The language follows that in 1969 CLC and the 1971 Fund Convention (Bill 1973:140), which was in turn followed in preparation of the Swedish legislation implementing the Bunkers Convention 2001 (Bill 2012/13:81) and the HNSC 2010 (Bill 2017/18:268) when in force.
150 See 10.8.4(a).
151 See 9.2.5(b).
152 And see abandonment issues: 8.2.1(f), 10.5.1(a), 11.4, 14.22.
153 See eg Arts 2(1), 2(3), 7(2); and 8.2.1, 8.2.2, 9.2.2.
154 See eg Art 8(1), 9(1), 9(3), 9(4).
155 As might be its insurer under the direct action provisions: see 10.8.4.

when can the owner (or insurer) say that we have now prevented, mitigated or eliminated the hazard?

Common sense indicates that once a ship is raised or refloated, there is still a danger that it may sink again. If that were to occur in the same location, then presumably in most cases there would still be the same "hazard" as before the raising. That is relatively easy to assess in terms of hazard to navigation, but maybe less so in relation to threat of "major harmful consequences to the marine environment, to the coastline, or related interests" of a state within Art 1(5).[156] A wreck that was a threat to navigation and the environment may have had significant amounts of bunkers removed before raising, but the moment it is raised the threat to navigation will largely have gone. At that stage, if the remaining bunkers and other pollutants are removed, is the raised wreck still a "hazard"? In most cases of raising or refloating, the wreck is still very vulnerable and there is obviously a risk, albeit variable, of another sinking.[157] But where the remains of the hull are lifted onto a heavy lift ship or barge, the risks are much less, as the remains are now merely the cargo for which the heavy lift craft is designed.[158] At that moment, do the obligations and liabilities of the WRC 2007 still 'bite'; ie can it be argued that there is no longer a hazard that attracts the powers given by the WRC 2007?

A State may robustly reply that the operations should be regarded as one continuous whole from the inception of the original plan and that at least until the wreck is taken away from its EEZ there has been no removal, ie the hazard has not been "eliminated" within Art 1(7). This may be easier to argue where a hull is raised and is being towed to a scrapyard, as with the *Costa Concordia*, than with the heavy lift example, above. The resolution of this issue is very fact specific, but some care may be needed to ensure that there is not an overly wide interpretation of "removal" and "elimination" within Art 1(7). Article 2(3) makes it clear that the measures taken by a State in relation to the removal of a wreck shall not only be reasonably necessary but "shall cease as soon as the wreck has been removed". Given the link between "removal" and "hazard", it is clear that once the hazard has been eliminated, the powers given by the WRC 2007 should cease. In this particular sense, there is a distinction between 'removal' and 'disposal', and the WRC 2007 does not regulate the latter.[159]

The distinction between 'removal' and 'disposal' is not easy to make, but it is hard to see that a State has the right under the WRC 2007 to dictate in all circumstances when and where the ship is disposed of once it has been removed. A State may specify disposal, eg scrapping or recycling, at a national facility largely for economic reasons. It is difficult to see that this is reasonable, eg if more expensive than a foreign facility, but it may be justifiable if a shorter voyage reduces the hazard of the wreck sinking again (or polluting

---

156 See 8.2.3, 10.5.1.
157 This is not fanciful as there will be so many uncertainties about the true state of the wreck and whether, temporary repairs will last: eg the difficulties with the *MSC Napoli* after initial refloating, see 1.2.3(b). The movement of the refloated *Costa Concordia* with the assistance of buoyancy pontoons (see 1.2.5) was obviously a highly delicate operation based on complex engineering calculations and there may have been legitimate doubts about the extent to which the ship was suitable for a prolonged voyage to a cheaper recycling location.
158 See 14.7.3 for disposal voyage contracts.
159 For disposal, see Chapter 14 generally.

more).[160] Where it is clear that scrapping or recycling must take place at a foreign facility, it is also difficult to see that the Affected State can dictate which of these facilities should be used, unless again there are increased hazards in relation to one particular route.

Alternatively, the registered owner (or insurer) may have a change of plan as to what it is best to do with the wreck, eg where there have been complications with one or more disposal facilities, or where it is planned to transfer ownership of the wreck after raising.[161] The Affected State, which will probably have been deeply involved with the original plan, may now try to insist that the disposal voyage follows that plan. Obviously, it can use its territorial sovereignty to deny access to its ports for a heavy lift ship and may, for instance, forbid the scrapping of the hull in its ports. But where the heavy lift ship is on route to a foreign port it seems doubtful that the Affected State can use the WRC 2007 to insist on a particular route being taken,[162] or that the voyage be to a particular foreign port or location. It would seem that a State's powers under the WRC 2007 cease once the wreck has been taken outside the "Convention area" of that State, ie the EEZ under Art 1(1). At that stage the wreck would certainly have been removed, whether under tow as a dead ship or as cargo on a heavy lift ship.

In these circumstances, the State may need formally to rely on more general intervention powers, either in national law (eg in territorial waters)[163] or international law,[164] or to point to other powers, eg in relation to waste disposal.[165] In practice, it may be difficult to dispute the right of a State in its EEZ; once the convoy is outside the EEZ it is difficult to see that the Affected State has any real interest or, possibly, power to influence the voyage.[166]

After the ship has been removed from the EEZ, arrangements for an ultimate destination (and then for scrapping or recycling) would be a commercial matter.[167] Even here, the distinction between 'removal' and 'disposal' may assume importance, as Club cover may only extend to removal of the hull and not its disposal.[168] If that is the case, there may be a real practical difficulty where there is a dispute as to whether the shipowner should itself bear some of the costs of a 'disposal voyage'. It seems unlikely that a Club would want to try to dissect the costs of a contractual disposal voyage from the wreck site to a recycling facility, but it might do so if the shipowner declined to use a nearby yard and preferred to have a long voyage, eg to Europe from an Asian wreck site. In any event, a wreck removal

---

160 Where the wreck is in territorial waters and the Affected State has opted to apply the WRC 2007 there (see 8.4.2), it may be entitled to use Art 4(4)(b) to impose requirements as to the contractor that is to be used; in the EEZ, Art 9(4) restricts this ability; in both areas there is a restriction as to the conditions that may be imposed: see 9.2.5(c), 10.5.2, 11.2.2, 11.3.3(c).

161 See 14.7.1.

162 Unless of course, the stages or track of that route themselves raised particular safety or environmental risks within Art 9(4), eg where the heavy lift operation took place in dangerous shallows near a sensitive reef. Here the initial danger would probably not yet have ended.

163 See eg 4.2.3.

164 See Chapter 5.

165 Eg in relation to transboundary waste shipments or recycling: see 14.4, 14.5.

166 Again, though, there may be powers in relation to waste disposal or recycling, whose precise ambit is uncertain: see Chapter 14. The shipowner and insurer may consent to a State's wishes in order to avoid threats of criminal prosecution.

167 See 14.7.

168 See 2.6.5(b), although cargo disposal may be covered.

contractor engaged to remove a wreck from a wreck site will want to know what is the ultimate destination, and who will be paying.[169]

10.3 Defences to shipowner liability

As noted, the liability is strict, not absolute.[170] Article 10(1)(a)–(c)[171] make use of boilerplate exceptions to liability found in maritime liability regimes such as the CLC; these defences were originally designed in part to facilitate the participation of the insurance industry, particularly the P&I Clubs.[172]

In the CLC context, the operation of the exceptions means that the shipowner is not liable for oil pollution, but (apart from war) the IOPC Fund would then be liable for the whole of the loss down to the first dollar.[173] It is important to note that the WRC 2007 (like the Bunkers Convention 2001) is a single-tier liability convention; if the shipowner can rely on the exceptions, there is no second-tier 'fund' that can respond to pay for wreck removal, nor is the compulsory insurer liable.[174] Moreover, as already seen,[175] claims against the registered shipowner cannot be brought otherwise than in accordance with the WRC 2007, eg in negligence or nuisance, or some other national law.[176] Nobody apart from the registered shipowner can be liable *under* the convention, but there is no 'channelling' provision[177] that prevents claims outside the WRC 2007 against persons other than the registered owner.[178]

Article 10(1) provides the formal defences to liability. Note also that shipowners will be able to resist claims (ie have defences in a more general sense) which do not satisfy the necessary triggers to liability.[179] Likewise, the shipowner will not be liable for the cost of measures taken by States which are not "proportionate" to the hazard or if the measures exceed what is reasonably necessary to eliminate the hazard.[180]

---

169 See 14.7.3.

170 And obviously it only extends to objects, events and interests within the Art 1 definitions, so it does not apply to non-seagoing vessels, or to warships (unless there is a State declaration under Art 4(3)).

171 See the MSA 1995 s 255G(2): 11.3.4(a).

172 See generally, *De La Rue & Anderson*, 98–105; also, F Berlingieri, *International Maritime Conventions*, Volume III (Informa, 2017) [*Berlingieri Vol III*], 134.

173 See 2.6.2(b).

174 The insurer can rely on the same defences as the shipowner: see Art 12(10), and 10.8.4(b).

175 See 10.2.2.

176 See Art 10(3). The second sentence of this provision preserved the rights of opt-in States to make claims in respect of their territory and territorial sea that were *not* claims for locating, marking and removing wrecks; ie they could maintain their rights to claim for environmental loss from pollution, whether under the IMO conventions or national law.

177 Cf the CLC 1992 Art III(4), see 2.6.2(a); also the HNSC 2010 Art 7(5), see 2.6.4.

178 As explained in 10.2.2, this means that claims might be brought against others involved in wreck, such as charterers or cargo owners, eg basing the claim on negligence or other national law: see eg 2.1.6, 2.1.7(a)–(c).

179 See 10.5; eg that there is a defined "hazard", see 8.2.2.

180 See Art 2 and 9.2.5(e), 10.2.4.

10.3.1 War and terrorism

10.3.1(a) War

There is an exception from liability under Art 10(1)(a) when the registered owner proves[181] that the maritime casualty that caused the wreck "resulted from an act of war, hostilities, civil war, insurrection". The war exception reflected the exclusion of war risks from marine liability policies in the 1960s at the time the CLC 1969 was agreed, but such cover is now available on the market.[182] The exception would cover State on State action. Internal national actions against a State could also be excepted, eg if protesters sank a ship as part of anti-government demonstrations, but this might also fall within Art 10(1)(b).

The wording in the exception in Art 10(1)(a) differs from that in Art 10(1)(b) and (c) in that it uses the words "resulted from" rather than "wholly caused by". It is hardly likely that a shipowner will have caused a war or hostilities, but it is possible that a choice of route is made through waters known to be at risk of attack, as happened in the Iran-Iraq War in the 1980s when freight rates were very attractive to owners. If that attack materialises, it would seem that a maritime casualty still "resulted from" the belligerent acts, even though it might have been negligent or even reckless to take the particular course into the area of risk. There may still be issues of causation, though, even with the words "resulting from",[183] eg where a ship goes aground and is wrecked while trying to take avoiding action because of possible threats (that have not yet materialised) from shore-based militias. Here, there may also be poor navigation, or a panicked appreciation of the risk, and a court might be persuaded that the wreck did not "result from" the warlike circumstances—which could be viewed merely as part of the history of the casualty. A court may be more likely, though, to consider that the exception applies if the navigator is acting under the extreme pressure of the warlike circumstances.

What may loosely be described as the 'war exception' is fairly broad, so as to cover actions by groups, but it might not cover all individual uncoordinated acts of terrorism, or those that are not directed at a particular State or States. During the Iran-Iraq War in the 1980s, ships transiting the Persian Gulf were subject to missile attacks, not necessarily directed at ships of the belligerents, although with the effect of disrupting their trade. Where these were State authorised, they might fall in the war exception. In 2019 there have been attacks on shipping in the Gulf made from unidentified sources that might have been indirectly instigated or encouraged by a State. It may be more difficult for these to fall within "war", but might be "hostilities", although they more naturally may be considered as third party damage within Art 10(1)(b).

10.3.1(b) Third party damage

A separate exception from liability is in Art 10(1)(b), where the shipowner proves[184] that the maritime casualty "was *wholly* caused by an act or omission done with intent to cause

---

181 The burden of proof is clearly on the registered shipowner. This means that if that burden cannot be satisfied, the owner will remain strictly liable.

182 See M Miller, *Marine War Risks* (3rd ed, Informa, 2005); *De La Rue & Anderson*, 99; and 2.9.6(a) and (b).

183 See *De La Rue & Anderson*, 99 and cf 2.9.2(c).

184 The burden of proof is again clearly on the registered shipowner, so that if that burden cannot be satisfied, the owner will remain strictly liable. This proof issue is particularly important given the use of the word "wholly".

damage by a third party". A third party could be any individual, eg pirates, or someone with a grudge against the shipowner.[185]

It is not clear if "third party" here can include an action by crew members that could be considered as barratry,[186] ie when acting for their own interests and not on behalf of the owner. "Third party" is used in contradistinction to "registered owner", so the exception could not apply to deliberate scuttling by that owner through the agency of the crew.[187] This is an issue that is common to all the IMO liability conventions and a common answer should be found, reflecting assumptions made in the negotiations for each. The 'boiler-plate' exceptions are derived from the CLC 1969 Art III(2)(b) where they were designed to except uninsurable risks.[188] The 1969 diplomatic conference offers no other clue as to the meaning of the words,[189] and they have not been altered in any of the subsequent IMO conventions.

Although the exceptions have been described as the "British exceptions",[190] it is necessary to give them an independent international interpretation, and it is not enough simply to say that the employee is acting beyond the contract of employment. As a matter of principle, barratry has always been a risk assumed by H&M (and cargo) insurers[191] and the wilful misconduct of the crew (without connivance of the owner) would not normally be regarded as the wilful misconduct of the owner—even in P&I cover.[192] It may be relevant that barratry did not fall within a "malicious damage" insurance clause,[193] but otherwise it might seem unusual for there to be a defence where insurance has been traditionally available and where the shipowner acts through the crew and other employees. If it is accepted that the exceptions to strict liability ought to be construed narrowly, the exception should be interpreted so as not to apply to actions by those for whom the owner is responsible; ie

---

185 Such malicious damage would be an "occurrence" causing a "maritime casualty" within Art 1(3): and see 8.2.1(a).

186 See 2.1.5(a) (fn 113), 2.9.2(c) (fn 1235).

187 This would be wilful misconduct of the shipowner and would therefore enable the insurer to have a defence to any direct action claims: see 10.8.4(c) and (d).

188 See Official Records of the International Legal Conference on Marine Pollution Damage (IMCO, 1973) [*Official Records 1969*], eg 596–7; D Abecassis, *The Law and Practice Relating to Oil Pollution from Ships* (1978, Butterworths) [*Abecassis, 1st edition*], 182.

189 Most of the liability debates at the 1969 diplomatic conference were about whether to have Alternative A (reverse burden of proof), as opposed to Alternative B (strict liability). Alternative A of the original draft text would have made the owner liable unless it could show there was no fault of its servants. Alternative B originally only had the war and contributory negligence defence until the UK introduced (in WP.35 on 24 November 1969) the text of what (with minor alterations) became Art III(2)(b): see *Official Records 1969*, 596–597. The crucial final choice between alternatives was deliberatively left to the end of the conference and the UK compromise was basically accepted later that day: see *Official Records 1969*, 726–738. Such debate as there was in the short time available was about other aspects of liability (eg establishing a Fund) and it does not appear that there was any debate at all on what became Art III(2)(b).

190 See LEG/CONF/C.2/WP.35, 24 November 1969: see *Official Records 1969*, 597.

191 See *Arnould* 1168–1169, 1240, 1224; also 2.9.2(a). Cf also *The Lady M* [2018] Lloyd's Rep Plus 22, [2019] 2 Lloyd's Rep 109 2.1.5(a), fn 108.

192 See *Arnould*, 1109; *Hazelwood & Semark*, 212–213; 10.8.4(d). Wilful misconduct provisions in Club rules generally refer only to the "member" and not to the crew: see eg Gard Rules for Ships 2018 r 72. Clubs may specifically exclude cover for non-marine personnel, emphasising the normal liability for crew acts: see eg Gard Rules for Ships 2018 r 56.

193 Cf D Gunasekera, *Civil Liability for Bunker Oil Pollution Damage* (Peter Lang, 2011), 211–212.

the crew and other employees (eg ashore) would not be treated as third parties.[194] It does not appear that issue has been finally settled by an authoritative decision and the contrary is still arguable.[195]

A similar, but slightly different, issue arises in respect of charterers, eg if a bareboat charterer arranged for the scuttling of the ship. Such a charterer is technically a third party to the registered owner, but not (in a broader sense) to the vessel. Given that the registered owner has voluntarily delegated the operation of the vessel to the charterer, and would generally be liable under Art 10(1) for a wreck while the ship is under the control of the charterer, the better view may be that the exception would not apply here either. This would be consistent with the overall aim of the WRC 2007 to provide a remedy to States on a strict liability basis, but with very narrow defences.[196]

The Art 10(1)(b) exception should cover most acts of terrorism, eg where a bomb is planted on a ship, but the catch with this provision is that the shipowner bears the burden of proving that the maritime casualty was caused *wholly* by the act of the third person. Any contributory negligence by the shipowner, such as a lapse in the application of the ISPS Code, could render the shipowner liable under the WRC 2007.

The uncertainty about whether terrorism was excepted was a cause of concern to both shipowners and their insurers, as war risks are not normally covered within P&I cover but are subject to separate market insurance.[197] Attempts by the International Group and the International Chamber of Shipping (ICS) to have the word "terrorism" explicitly included in the exclusion clause failed to obtain the support of States, largely because such an attempt had been rejected in the Athens Convention 2002.[198] Ironically, a set of Guidelines had to be agreed in late 2006 before the insurance market was willing to insure passenger ships against war and terrorism risks.[199] This all came too late for the WRC 2007, and (despite the size of the *Rena* and *Costa Concordia* removal operations) the insurance market was apparently not as adamant about wreck removal liabilities alone, as opposed to those also involving large passenger ships.[200] International Group members agreed in 2014 that they would issue WRC 2007 "Blue Cards" to enable shipowners to obtain certificates from States

---

194 However, note that this was apparently not the intention of the UK government at the drafting stage of its implementing legislation: see 11.3.4(a).

195 Cf the US Oil Pollution Act 1990, s 1003(a) which provides similar limited defences to liability to those under the IMO conventions and specifically refers to a "third party, other than an employee or agent of the responsible party": see *De La Rue & Anderson*, 201.

196 A separate question would then arise as to whether the insurer would be able to rely on the defence of wilful misconduct of the registered owner under the policy, and as allowed by Art 12(10). If the shipowner cannot rely on the Art 10(1)(b) exception for the charterer's malicious damage it is possible that the insurer cannot rely on the charterer's wilful misconduct to deny direct liability: see 10.8.4(c) and (d).

197 See 2.9.6(b) and (d); *Hazelwood & Semark*, 179; *De La Rue & Anderson*, 747–748,

198 LEG 85/11, 5 November 2002, paras 29–37, LEG 92/4/4, 15 September 2006; LEG 92/13, 3 November 2006, 16–17; LEG 93/13, 2 November 2007, paras 7.7–7.12; LEG/CONF 16/15, 27 April 2007.

199 See 2.3.5.

200 The scope for terrorist access to general cargo ships is also probably less than with a large cruise liner: see 2.3.5.

parties.[201] This means that if terrorism liabilities do not fall within the Art 10(1) exceptions, the Clubs will effectively front those claims in the first instance.[202]

10.3.2 Natural phenomena

There is also an exception in Art 10(1)(a) when the registered owner proves that the maritime casualty that caused the wreck resulted from a "natural phenomenon of an exceptional, inevitable and irresistible character". The relevant causative wording in Art 10(1)(a) is again "resulted from" rather than "wholly caused by", but this is perhaps less significant than with war[203] because the shipowner has to prove inevitability and irresistibility. A phenomenon will not be irresistible if it could be avoided by having a seaworthy ship, appropriate voyage planning and proper navigation.

The "natural phenomenon" phrase is the international language to deal with circumstances beyond human control. However, it is clearer and much more specific than the traditional common law exceptions of "Acts of God" or "perils of the sea"[204] and is designed to ensure that there is no exception to liability merely because the wreck resulted from bad weather. The usual example given of "exceptional" circumstances within the provision is the case of a tsunami which overwhelms a ship. By contrast, although cyclones may be examples of exceptional sea states, they are not usually "inevitable and irresistible" because ships can often take avoiding action.[205]

The severe storm conditions that led to the wreck of *The Ocean Victory* in 2006[206] were "abnormal" in the context of a charterparty, and the combination of long waves and northerly gales may well have been "exceptional" and unexpected, but that would not automatically bring them within the arguably stricter test in the WRC 2007 Art 10(2)(a). It was significant in that case, though, that the vessel was effectively trapped in the port by a fairway that became unnavigable, whereas to remain was also dangerous. To that extent the wreck may well have been inevitable and irresistible,[207] even though the risk was foreseeable. In the future, it may well be necessary for vessels using the particular port to take extra precautions in similar forecast conditions, eg by leaving port earlier.

After the tanker *Nakhodka* was wrecked in the Sea of Japan in 1997, the shipowner sought to rely on the natural phenomenon exception (in the CLC) by bringing evidence that exceptional and unexpected wave heights had been experienced. There was counter evidence that the ship was in a seriously dilapidated condition and therefore unseaworthy

---

201 See eg Gard Circular 8/14, November 2014; ie contrary to the usual P&I Club practice of not providing primary war risk cover. Members may need to indemnify the Club to the extent that they actually have separate war risks cover that might respond to the wreck liability.
202 See eg the Swedish Club Rules 2018/2019, rule 12(e), and 2.9.6(d); also *De La Rue & Anderson*, 749–750.
203 Cf 10.3.2(a).
204 Cf 2.1.5(a).
205 This commonly occurs in the Far East, eg in Hong Kong.
206 [2017] 1 Lloyd's Rep 521: see 2.1.7(a)–(c), 2.5.4(d), 2.5.4(a).
207 The same test is applied in Art 3(3)(a) of the Bunkers Convention 2001, and this exception could presumably have applied to the *Ocean Victory*'s bunkers had that convention then been in force and had Japan been a party: see 2.6.3.

(ie the casualty was not "inevitable"). This would ultimately have been a question of fact for Japanese courts, but the case was settled without any final determination of the matter.[208]

10.3.3 Government negligence

10.3.3(a) Government navigational aids

A further exception is in Art 10(1)(c) if the shipowner proves that the casualty that caused the wreck "was *wholly* caused by the negligence or other wrongful act of any Government or other authority responsible for the maintenance of lights or other navigational aids in the exercise of that function". The usual examples are where lighthouses or leading lights have stopped working, or navigational buoys are wrongly placed in a channel, or charts fail to show hidden rocks or shoals. There appears to be no reason why "navigational aids" could not include electronic aids.[209] The exception would not apply simply because there was a failure of such navigational aids. The action has to be negligent or wrongful,[210] and relate not to the creation or installation of such aids,[211] but to failures in *maintenance*, eg where the authority delayed in repairing an aid or, more generally, had no institutional structures for checking on and responding to such failures. The mere fact that a chart does not show a reef or rock will not of itself be wrongful, as hydrographic surveys may not purport to be comprehensive, but failing to update a chart can be a failure of maintenance.[212] The failure has to be that of a government which is responsible for the aids, eg a Shipping Department or "other authority" such as Trinity House.[213]

It will not be enough for the shipowner to show that there was a defective light or buoy and that this might have caused the wreck; the burden is very much on the shipowner to show that this was not *a* cause, but the *whole* cause of the ship being wrecked.[214] The exception would not apply if good navigation should have coped with the defective aid, eg through the keeping of a proper lookout, or even if the wreck was caused by a collision with another ship that was guilty of poor navigation when reacting to the defective aid.

10.3.3(b) Government negligence generally

The Art 10(1)(c) exception only operates in relation to "aids" and does not operate merely because a government has been negligent in some other respect, eg in failing to properly

---

208 See IOPC Funds, *Annual Report 2002*, 65–66. This dispute was an action by the IOPC Fund against the shipowner for the latter's contribution to the claims paid to pollution victims under the Fund Convention 1992: see 2.6.2(b). Had there been a case under the WRC 2007, the shipowner's successful defence would have meant that the Affected State would have received no costs.

209 Eg "MAtoN" electronic warning systems: see 11.3.5 (fn 327); also the MSA 1995 s 252(3A), 11.1.3(a). See also *De La Rue & Anderson*, 104.

210 "Wrongful" might refer to a higher standard of care imposed by national law, eg if that created an absolute duty: cf *De La Rue & Anderson*, 103, who suggest that the standard should be an international one, independent of national law.

211 See also *De La Rue & Anderson*, 103–104, citing *The Irish Stardust* (Fed Ct, Canada) [1977] 1 FC 485, [1977] 1 Lloyd's Rep 195.

212 See *De La Rue & Anderson*, 101–102, citing the Swedish Supreme Court case of *The Tsesis* in 1977.

213 See 11.1.3(b).

214 Cf *Cenargo Navigation Ltd and Merchant Ferries Ltd v Harbour of Carlingford Lough Improvement Commissioners (The Merchant Venture)* [1997] 1 Lloyd's Rep 388, where buoys were out of position but it was held that a vessel grounded through negligent navigation.

dredge a channel.[215] Unlike the CLC Art III(3), the WRC 2007 has no general defence of contributory negligence against the State that is claiming for its costs of locating, marking and removal. By implication, this suggests that such general contributory negligence could not formally be used by the shipowner to defend a WRC 2007 claim, even if it were framed as a matter of causation.[216] This might also be relevant in the sort of case where State authorities decline to provide a place of refuge to a ship that has suffered a maritime casualty and the ship is subsequently wrecked.[217] But could it counterclaim, eg on the basis of negligence under national law? Such an action would not be prevented by Art 10(3), which only refers to claims against the shipowner. Such a counterclaim could be the exercise of a right of recourse as allowed by Art 10(4). The difficulty would be in deciding whether the government was a "third party" in these circumstances. It could be argued that the absence of a general contributory negligence provision shows that a "third party" contemplates someone other than the registered shipowner or claimant State and that to allow such a counterclaim would undermine the strict liability provision and limited defence allowed by Art 10(1)(c).[218]

10.4 Time limits

While it is not necessary that the hazard to the coastal State arises contemporaneously with the maritime casualty, the WRC 2007 Art 13 does set a time limit for claims to recover costs from the registered owner or insurer.[219] This provision is similarly structured to other IMO liability conventions in providing that the action may be "extinguished" (not merely subject to a procedural bar). An action must be brought "within three years from the date when the hazard has been determined in accordance with this Convention". Thus, once a hazard has been assessed[220] the State must be aware that the clock has started ticking. Article 6 does not actually specify when the State has to determine that a hazard exists, or the form that the determination should take. However, Art 9 requires that once a determination takes place the Affected State shall immediately notify the flag State and registered owner. That notification is not the determination itself, so strictly the three-year time limit should run from an earlier date than the notification, although in practice they may well be contemporaneous. If the Affected State makes a determination, but fails to notify the flag State or registered owner of that determination,[221] is there a determination "in accordance

---

215 This was an allegation after the grounding of the *Nissos Amorgos* in Venezuela in 1997, but the defence was raised in relation to bulletins about recommended drafts although it was not ultimately successful: see eg IOPC Funds, *Annual Report 1998*, 93; IOPC Funds, *Annual Report 2001*, 80; IOPC Funds, *Incidents Involving the IOPC Funds 2013*, 78–85; *De La Rue & Anderson*, 104, 702.

216 However, the Affected State would still need to show proportionality and reasonableness: see 9.2.5(e), 10.2.4.

217 Cf (in the context of the CLC) *De La Rue & Anderson*, 703–704 and also 905–921. In the *Prestige* case the Spanish Supreme Court declined to reduce liability for alleged negligence of public officials in refusing to provide a place of refuge: see Cassation Appeal/606/2018, 1.2.2(a).

218 The MSA 1995 s 255T refers widely to preserving "any claim . . . against *any other person*" (emphasis added).

219 For the UK, see the MSA 1995 s 255H, 11.3.4(a).

220 See 9.2.2.

221 For the effect of this failure as to liability, see 7.3 and 7.6.

with this Convention" so as to provide a starting point for the time limit? As the determination is separate from the notification, the absence of the latter does not mean that there has been no determination at all. It follows that it may be necessary to investigate the internal processes of the State to assess whether there has been a determination that can be seen to take into account the criteria in Art 6. It would be good practice[222] for States to issue a formal document headed "Determination under the WRC 2007", because otherwise there might be difficulty in pinpointing a particular administrative decision as a determination.

Of course, it is likely to be the Affected State that wants the time limit to start from as late a date as possible, and it may claim that the determination was made ten years after the wreck. Indeed, the Affected State may fail to make a determination at all, but later wants to claim for costs of location, marking and removal. For these reasons, Art 13 partly follows the CLC precedent by providing that in no case shall an action be brought after six years from the date of the maritime casualty that resulted in the wreck. The CLC, though, uses the trigger of the date "of the incident which caused the *damage*".[223] The WRC 2007 Art 13 provision may require a sharp focus on the definition of maritime casualty[224] to see when the time starts to run. The Art 1(3) definition actually lists a series of possible events that might cause a casualty, eg there might be a collision, followed by a stranding and then later an occurrence on board (such as an explosion), leading to the "wreck" in Art 1(4).[225] For this reason, Art 13 provides that where the maritime casualty consists of a series of such occurrences (eg a collision followed by a stranding[226]), the six-year period runs from the date of the first "occurrence".[227]

The expression "occurrence on board a ship or external to it" in Art 1(3) is rather vague, and the need to find the first occurrence could encourage arguments that it covers a wide variety of circumstances. Some of these might be quite remote in time from the collision or stranding. For instance, consider a decision by the master at the port of loading to overload the ship; a failure by the chief engineer on a previous voyage to properly repair and engine part; a failure by a marine superintendent to ensure the correct chart software is installed; and a failure by the ship's managers to appoint a properly qualified master. Maritime lawyers are familiar with many such examples where an earlier event may be causative of a later loss,[228] but it would be somewhat perverse to make a time limit run from an event so removed from the immediate scene of an incident. This is particularly so where the six-year time bar is also designed to deal with the situation where a State may not actually know about the wreck until some years after a sinking (or at least its precise location), but may have been put on notice by reports of a casualty. It would be quite uncertain if a State had to speculate about some of the occurrences mentioned above which are effectively hidden from it. For those reasons, the better approach would be to take a narrow or purposive

---

222 For other instances of a good practice checklist, see 10.5.3(a).
223 Art VIII; emphasis added.
224 As defined in Art 1(3): see 8.2.1(a).
225 See 8.2.1.
226 Somewhat confusingly, a "stranding" appears both as an example of a maritime casualty in Art 1(3) and also as a *consequence* of that casualty in the definition of a wreck in Art 1(4). This would not seem to prevent it from being an "occurrence" for the purposes of Art 13 if it can be regarded as an incident of navigation.
227 Note that under Art 1(3) the collision, stranding or other incident of navigation are all treated as an "occurrence".
228 Cf 2.9.2(c), 2.4.2, 2.1.5(c).

THE LAW OF WRECK

approach to the interpretation of Art 1(3), which refers to the occurrence "resulting in material damage or imminent threat of material damage to a ship or its cargo". The words "resulting in" should be taken to have a degree of immediacy, as does the word "imminent", and an occurrence should normally be something that is sufficiently serious, observable or discoverable to be able to cause "material damage". An element of common sense is needed to prevent the time limit from being a trap for States.[229]

Nevertheless, the time bar could present practical difficulties for States in recovering costs, not only when they do not know of (or are not informed about) a wreck, but also in particular where the removal operation may take many years. For these reasons, it may be prudent for the State to bring a protective action to be within the time bar. Such an action ought (as a matter of prudence) to join both the registered owner and the liability insurer.

Finally, it should be recalled that the Convention was not designed to cover wrecks from before the date of its entry into force on 14 April 2015.[230] This means that an Affected State can only apply the Convention to wrecks occurring after the entry into force of the WRC 2007 for that State. For example, it cannot within one year of adopting the WRC 2007 claim to apply it to a wreck sunk two years previously (on the basis that it is within the three-year time limit).[231] For the avoidance of doubt, enacting legislation should make it clear to which wrecks the WRC 2007 applies.

10.5 Triggers to liability

The existence of Art 10(1) liability is conditional on the claimant satisfying a number of what may be described as 'triggers' created by Arts 1 and 9. To some extent the discussion on triggers reprises matters introduced in Chapters 8 and 9,[232] but now they need to be considered in the slightly different context of civil liabilities.

10.5.1 Art 1 triggers

The liability created by Art 10(1)[233] is dependent upon the claimant State satisfying all the triggers to action or liability articulated in Art 1, eg that there be a "ship", "maritime casualty", "wreck" or "hazard" (and, for the EEZ, that the wreck posed a hazard in the "Convention area").[234] It follows that, by way of example, if a ship was not wrecked following a maritime casualty there can be no liability for the costs involved in locating, marking or removing it.

10.5.1(a) Abandonment and WRC 2007 liability
If, for instance, the ship was merely abandoned in a port owing to insolvency, the State would not be able to claim for the costs of "removing" the vessel, in the sense of getting

---

229 See also the discussion in 10.5.1(a) about whether an occurrence has to be a fortuity.
230 See Art 18, noting that it enters into force for States three months after adoption by that State: and see 7.6.2.
231 Such a State could of course rely on its previous legislation.
232 Eg 8.2, 9.2.5.
233 See 10.2.
234 See eg 8.3.1, 9.2.2.

rid of it.[235] In one sense it might be a worthless 'wreck', but it is not a "wreck" under the convention as there has not been a maritime casualty. Even if the condition of the abandoned ship deteriorated so that it slowly took on water and sank, there would probably still not be a "maritime casualty" within Art 1(3). Lack of maintenance alone does not appear to create a maritime casualty, eg where there is a failure to replace a stern shaft seal known to be leaking. What would be needed would be some other "*occurrence*" on board a ship or external to it, "resulting in material damage or imminent threat of material damage to [the] ship or its cargo". There is a degree of vagueness in the expression,[236] though, and it might be possible to argue that at some stage the abandoned vessel could be said to suffer an occurrence on board when its shell plating was so rusted through that it resulted in material damage, ie a hole sufficient to cause the ship to sink. But this does not seem to be really what Art 1(3) was designed to cover, which was an identifiable (usually fortuitous) event of some kind rather than gradual deterioration *in situ*. Moreover, it might be difficult to describe such gradual sinking as a "stranding or other incident of navigation"[237] within Art 1(3).

Of course, if the abandoned ship were overwhelmed by a storm, or was driven ashore after an anchor failure, then that would seem to satisfy the test. While it may be true that deliberate sinkings for operational reasons[238] are not covered, fraudulent scuttling (as opposed to dumping) is slightly more problematic. It might be hard to describe the deliberate opening of seacocks as an "occurrence" in the sense of a fortuity,[239] but sinking by explosion might seem to come closer. It may well be that the type of occurrence needed is likely to be fortuitous rather than deliberately created with a view to causing a casualty. Even if scuttling were considered to be a maritime casualty it would not assist the claimant State much, as the registered owner is likely to be insolvent and the compulsory insurer would have a defence of wilful misconduct.[240]

10.5.1(b) Proof of hazard

A key factual issue will be whether there was a "hazard" within Art 1(5).[241] In relation to hazards to navigation in Art 1(5)(b), the issue would be decided largely by the expert evidence of hydrographers and master mariners depending, for instance, on the depth of water, its location to main channels and the draft of ship likely to be in the area. In some circumstances it might be safer and more proportionate merely to mark the wreck, eg if it were located close to a rocky shore where ships would not be expected to navigate. Authorities in developed States will have considerable experience in making such balancing judgments,

---

[235] Even if it had a low value, or the costs of removing and selling it exceeded any sale or scrap value. See 8.2.1(f), 11.4, 14.2.
[236] See also 8.2.1(a), 10.4.
[237] As noted in 10.4, "stranding" appears both as an example of a maritime casualty in Art 1(3) and also as a *consequence* of that casualty in the definition of a wreck in Art 1(4). This would not seem to prevent it from being an "occurrence" for the purposes of Art 13 *if* it can be regarded as an incident of navigation. It would be difficult to treat a gradual sinking from lack of maintenance of an abandoned dead ship in a harbour as an incident of navigation. See also 8.2.1(a) and (b).
[238] Eg dumping of an existing wreck at sea: see 14.1–14.2. See also 8.2.1(a).
[239] Cf 14.1.2(b).
[240] See Art 12(10), 10.8.4(c) and (d).
[241] See 8.2.2, 9.2.2.

eg through Trinity House in the UK.[242] Developing States may have less experience, but would need to obtain independent evidence.

10.5.1(c) Hazard to fishing vessels

What constitutes a "hazard" from a wreck raises particular problems in relation to fishing vessels.[243] There is no separate definition of "navigation" in the WRC 2007, but when such vessels are moving with deployed fishing nets there is clearly "navigation" of that ship. It might be argued that, if the only threat from a wreck on the seabed is that nets may be caught in it, there is no "danger" to navigation as such, merely the loss of or damage to equipment ancillary to the fishing vessel. This is an unrealistic argument as the snagging of nets can sometimes cause the vessel to girt or to capsize.[244] In any event, it seems difficult to dispute that the "threat" of nets snagging would pose an "impediment" to navigation within Art 1(5)(a). There could, though, be questions of fact as to the expected depth of fishing operations, eg for drag net trawling, as the risk of snagging could be largely theoretical.

In any event, a hazard can now include a condition or threats that can be expected to result in major harmful consequences to the "related interests" of one or more States.[245] Although the hazard to fishing gear was not explicitly included in the Art 1(6) definition of "related interests", there is a clear reference to "fisheries activities" in Art 1(6)(a). This expression might more easily be applied to aquaculture activities such as salmon farms or oyster beds, but an area where normal fishing takes place could be described as a fishery. Here, though, it must still be shown that the condition or threat passes the "major harmful consequences" hurdle. This criterion does not apply to the navigation hazard in Art 1(5)(a), where there need only be a "danger" or "impediment" whose seriousness is not prescribed.[246] To that extent, there may still be a need in some circumstances to rely on Art 1(5)(a), rather than (b).

10.5.1(d) Other hazards and human remains

Article 6 lists many criteria that a State should take into account in determining if there is a hazard. These mostly relate to safety of navigation and the protection of the environment, and that is consistent with later references to removal in Art 9(4) and (5). Article 6(o) is a catch-all that refers to "any other circumstances that might necessitate the removal of the wreck". An instinctive English response is to interpret this *sui generis*, but care must be taken not to take a national approach when interpreting an international instrument,[247] especially one that uses a broad concept like "any circumstances".[248] It is also not so easy to isolate or identify the generic criteria in Art 6. Most of the criteria listed in Art 6 relate to safety and the environment, but sub-paragraph (i) relates to the "vulnerability of port

---

242 See 11.1.3(b), 11.3.5.
243 See also 8.2.3, in relation to the hazard to fishing as a related interest in Art 1(5)(b) and 1(6).
244 The *Dianne* is an example where a national wreck removal order in Australia was justified in 2017 on the basis that a small sunken vessel presented a risk to navigation, "specifically navigation of the area by fishing ships that are towing fishing equipment on the sea floor": see Notice of 26 October 2017 issued by the Gladstone harbour master under the Transport Operations (Marine Safety) Act 2004 (Qld) s 91; also 13.2.3.
245 See Art 1(5), 1(6): and 8.2.2, 8.2.3.
246 The measures taken would still need to be reasonable and proportionate within Art 2: see 9.2.5(e), 10.2.4.
247 See 11.3.1.
248 But note the controversial debates during drafting: see 9.2.2.

facilities". Although this could refer to physical danger, it can also reasonably encompass economic and social factors such as the need to keep a port open for business and employment. Moreover, the definition of "hazard" also takes into account the broad "related interests" of a State.[249] There are two consequences of this analysis. First, in deciding whether a wreck should be located, marked or removed[250] a State may take into account a wide range of factors. Secondly, the potential restrictions on a State's powers in Art 9(4) and (5) (ie to safety and the environmental factors) only relate to the *manner* in which the removal operation (once decided upon) is to be carried out in the EEZ.[251] Further the Art 9(4) and (5) restrictions do not apply to the decisions taken in relation to locating and marking the wreck.[252]

In relation to the first consequence of a wide interpretation of the catch-all criterion in Art 6(o), the question is whether there is any limit upon it, especially taking into account "related interests". One example might be where the State wants to locate and (possibly) remove the wreck because of the presence of bodies on board.[253] In most cases, there will also be other hazards within Art 6, but suppose that the State determines that the wreck is sunk in very deep water in the EEZ and there is little or no risk to the environment in that particular area, eg from bunkers from a small fishing vessel;[254] it may even be that the wreck is so deep that it cannot be removed at all. The State may be under social and political pressure from relatives of the seafarers at least to locate the wreck so that they can get what is sometimes called 'closure'. That pressure may also relate to finding out the cause of the wreck,[255] but even in order to begin investigations or formal inquiries the wreck has to be located. The wording of Art 6(o) would preclude its use if *location* were the only aim, as it refers to circumstances that might "necessitate the *removal*" of the wreck. Moreover, it seems doubtful if the desire of relatives to recover bodies would of itself "necessitate" such a removal. Even if a State argued that it was necessary for social reasons, the shipowner could still argue that the costs were disproportionate.[256]

In relation to the *manner* of wreck removal, the effect of Art 9(4) seems to be that in the EEZ a State could not apply conditions about how a ship was to be raised[257] if they were imposed in order to preserve human remains and did not relate to safety or protection of the environment. Of course, those phrases could be interpreted widely so as to cover public health concerns about handling bodies, and in practice contractors would always be sensitive about human remains.[258] The issue would assume significance if the most cost effective way to raise the wreck was by cutting it up, whereas the relatives and State might want

---

249 See 8.2.2, 8.3.3.
250 Whether under Art 9(2) or using the default powers in Art 9(7) or (8).
251 For territorial waters, see the effect of Art 4(4) and 10.5.4.
252 See 10.5.5, 10.5.6.
253 It does not appear that the WRC 2007 specifically includes human remains in the definition of a ship: see 8.2.1(c). On that basis there might be no liability for the costs of their removal, but the main issue here is whether their existence can be a related interest affected by the wreck. Cf also 3.2.4, 13.2.3.
254 Eg the FV *Gaul*: see 13.2.3.
255 See 4.3.
256 See 9.2.5(e), 10.2.4. One of the factors in raising the wreck of the *Sewol* in one piece was apparently concerns of relatives, and this may well have made the task more difficult and expensive: see also 13.2.3.
257 Or, under Art 9(5), when it would intervene.
258 See also 13.2.3.

the wreck to be raised in one piece so as to preserve human remains. In territorial waters, though, the restrictions in Art 9(4) would not apply owing to the operation of Art 4(4),[259] so a State would have more power to impose conditions about bodies.[260]

10.5.2 Art 9 triggers: EEZ and territorial waters differences

The liability created by Art 10(1) makes a link to Arts 7 (locating wrecks), 8 (marking wrecks) and 9 (wreck removal). It is the link with Art 9 that will be considered first. There are public law requirements of Art 9,[261] but most of these were designed as safeguards for wreck removal in the EEZ where flag States were arguably giving up rights and wanted to protect their owners. While there may be debate about whether these provisions are too onerous on Affected States,[262] it is clear that their application to territorial waters (under Art 3(2)) would have been a major restriction on what States considered to be their existing rights. For this reason, Art 4(4) was inserted so as to remove many of the State obligations in Art 9. The broad effect of Art 4(4) is to create the possibility of two separate regimes for wreck removal,[263] depending on whether the wreck is in the EEZ or territorial sea. As the wreck removal liability provisions in Art 10(1) refer back to Art 9,[264] this means that it is now necessary to consider the removal obligations in these two geographical areas separately[265] (although the provisions in relation to wreck removal notices in Art 9(6) are largely common). In practice most wrecks will occur in territorial waters, but the EEZ will be considered first as this was the default position with which Arts 7–9 were designed to deal.

10.5.3 Recovery of wreck removal costs: EEZ

Although Art 10(1) creates a general liability on the registered owner to pay for the costs of removing the wreck, Art 10(1) refers back to the "costs of . . . removing the wreck *under* [Art] 9". The question arises as to whether compliance by an Affected State[266] with all the requirements in Art 9 are also pre-conditions of liability under Art 10 (and thus later against the insurer under Art 12(10)).

Article 9(1) requires the Affected State to inform and consult the flag State, but this is designed primarily as a public international law obligation between States and it seems inconceivable that failure to do so would preclude the Affected State from bringing (in

---

259 See 10.5.4.
260 But if, in applying the WRC 2007 to territorial waters, it had reinserted Art 9(4) and other provisions excluded by Art 4(4) it might have reapplied the restricted safety and environment criteria: see 10.5.4 and in the UK the MSA 1995 s 255E, 11.2.2, 11.2.3.
261 See Chapter 8, eg 8.3, 8.4.2; Chapter 9, eg 9.1.3(b), 9.2.5, 9.3.
262 See 7.4.
263 This in turn, requires a State to make decisions as to how it will enact the WRC 2007 in national law: see 11.2.2. A failure to reintroduce some of provisions (eg default removal powers) back into the territory and territorial sea could create problems for States: see 11.2.3.
264 Unlike the position in relation to locating and marking a wreck: see 10.5.5, 10.5.6.
265 This also means that at an early stage it may be important for all parties to be aware of the exact location of the wreck and whether it is in the territorial sea, EEZ or on the high seas.
266 As defined in Art 1(10).

effect) a private law costs claim against the shipowner (or insurer). Is the position any different in relation to notices under Art 9(6)?

10.5.3(a) Wreck removal notices
Although the WRC 2007 does not use the expression "wreck removal notice", Art 9(6) performs some functions of this traditionally used document, and it is convenient to use the expression as shorthand.[267] Article 9(6) sets out three obligations on the Affected State in relation to wreck removal notices.[268] The first (Art 9(6)(a)) requires an internal judgment by the Affected State as to a reasonable deadline to remove the hazard.[269] This follows from the previous requirement in Art 6 that there must be a conscious assessment of the hazard. The second and third obligations require notice to be given to the registered owner: Art 9(6)(b) requires the owner to be told of the deadline, and of the Affected State's power to remove the wreck at the owner's expense if the deadline is not met; Art 9(6)(c) requires the owner to be told that the State "intends to intervene immediately in circumstances where the hazard becomes particularly severe". Both of these are designed to provide advance notice of the risks to the owner if it does not take action itself; they will be obvious to most experienced owners, but might be necessary for those (eg fishing boat owners) who have had no experience of a major casualty. It is not clear if the information in Art 9(6)(c) needs to be given at the same time as that in Art 9(6)(b). As a 'consumer' type warning notice, this would make sense, but it appears that there is no reason why the Art 9(6)(c) information could not be given later in a separate notice.[270]

Although the wording of Art 10(1) does not expressly make compliance by an Affected State with Art 9(6) a pre-condition of liability under Art 10(1), it is a reasonable interpretation that this is the intended effect of the word "under" in Art 10(1).[271] The reason is that the notice contains a clear timeline for action by State and registered owner in relation to removal. This means that a State may need to take care that it does give the appropriate notices[272] (bearing in mind the time limits in Art 13). Most P&I Clubs would, in practice, not expect to respond unless there was a wreck removal notice issued by the relevant State[273] and this practice seems broadly consistent with Art 9(6).[274]

---

267 Although, in some respects the requirements of Art 9(6) are much narrower than that which would be expected in a typical national wreck removal notice, in that Art 9(6) says nothing about the manner of removal. The extent to which the WRC 2007 allows a State to insist on how the operation is to be conducted (ie beyond a bald instruction to remove with a deadline) is limited by Art 9(4): see 10.5.3(a) (below), 9.2.5(c), and 10.1, 10.9.1. The better view is probably that Art 9(6) sets out minimum requirements for a wreck removal notice. The UK has expressly used the concept of the "wreck removal notice" in the MSA 1995 s 255D(2): see 11.3.3(c).

268 See also 9.2.5(a).

269 Note that the reference to hazard is broader than to mere removal of the hull: see Art 1(5) and 8.2.2, 9.2.2.

270 See 10.5.3(c).

271 Note however the fall-back power of an Affected State under Art 9(8): see discussion below and 9.2.5(a). This power seems to make a discussion about whether Art 9(6) is a pre-condition largely irrelevant, but only where there is a need for "immediate action" under Art 9(8). Note also how the position could be different where removal takes place in territorial waters: see 10.5.4.

272 It would be sensible to draw up an internal administrative checklist based on Art 9.

273 *Standard Club, Major Casualty Management*, 2; also *LOC Report*, 10.2.5. See also 2.9.6(d), 10.8.4.

274 But it should be noted that there may be circumstances (possible rare) where the owner cannot be contacted for a notice to be served. Here the State may incur costs itself under Art 9(7) and then claim them directly against the insurer under a combination of Art 10(1) and Art 12(10). Likewise, where a State has to take "immediate

Article 9(4) assumes a timeline in which the owner takes action before receiving any wreck removal notice, although it recognises that the State may lay down conditions for the removal.[275] Once such owner-initiated removal operations have commenced, Art 9(5) allows a State to "intervene", but again subject to the same criteria. Article 9(6) follows these provisions somewhat awkwardly. In practice, it seems likely that the issuing of a traditional wreck removal notice will elide these three provisions in the sense that the notice will order removal, set a deadline and impose conditions as to how the removal operation is to be conducted. Indeed, it is quite common for a series of notices to be issued as the removal operation progresses.[276] What the WRC 2007 does now is to impose restrictions on the extent to which the State can control the manner of removal. There is infinite scope for debates about what is "necessary" and, although the burden is on the State, it is likely that a national court will be sympathetic to the State's appreciation of what is necessary, especially in relation to protection of the environment (which is an elastic concept). Whether a wreck is a hazard to navigation is much more likely to be a technical nautical question.[277]

There are at least five factual situations that a State may face after serving a wreck removal notice under Art 9(6). First, the owner may respond (with its insurer) and take removal action, eg by engaging contractors itself in accordance with the primary obligation in Art 9(2). In these circumstances the owner and insurer retain a degree of primary control over operations, subject to an Affected State's rights to intervene.[278] Here there should be little difficulty in serving a notice and any disputes will really be about the extent of any operations,[279] which will normally be paid for directly by the owner or insurer.

Secondly, despite a wreck removal notice, the owner may not remove the wreck within the deadline given.[280] In these circumstances Art 9(7) provides that the Affected State may remove the wreck itself and claim the costs from the owner under Art 10(1) (and insurer under Art 12(10)). The proviso is that it uses the "most practical and expeditious means available, consistent with considerations of safety and protection of the marine environment".[281] The reference to these requirements reflects owners' and Clubs' concern that States are making ever increasing demands for "full removal" if the technology allows.[282] It may have been more practical and expeditious to have cut the *Costa Concordia* into pieces, rather than effect a complete refloating, but a State like Italy could point to the environmental factors.[283] While this will be a matter ultimately for a court in the forum concerned,

---

action" under Art 9(8). To this extent, the Club cannot simply stand apart until a formal notice is issued, whatever may have been the previous practice. See the following discussion of Art 9(7) and Art 9(8); also 10.5.3(d)–(e), 9.2.5(d).

275 Subject to them being "necessary to ensure the removal proceeds in a manner that is consistent with considerations of safety and protection of the marine environment".
276 For the UK position, see 11.3.3(d).
277 For hazards other than those concerned with safety and the environment, see 10.5.1(b).
278 Under Art 9(4) and (5), and later under Art 9(7) or (8). In practice, these State powers are likely to be highly intrusive, but under Art 9(4) are now conditioned by criteria of reasonableness as to safety and protection of the environment.
279 Eg as to whether they are proportionate and reasonably necessary under Art 2: 9.2.5(e), 10.2.4.
280 For deadlines, see 10.5.3(d).
281 See also 9.2.5(a) and (d).
282 See 1.4, 10.2.5, 10.8.6.
283 See 1.2.5.

the WRC 2007 now gives the owners and insurers the ability say that the measures must be reasonable and proportionate under Art 2. In appropriate circumstances this may permit an argument that it would be quite disproportionate to spend US$80 million to bring up the last remains of a ship.[284]

Thirdly, if the registered owner "cannot be contacted", Art 9(7) again provides that the State may remove the wreck itself[285] and claim the costs from the owner under Art 10 (and insurer under Art 12(10)). This power of the Affected State can be triggered when (for whatever reason) it has proved impossible to contact the owner at all at its registered address, eg to serve a wreck removal notice. The inability to contact the owner could also arise after a wreck removal notice has been issued and served (under Art 9(6)), eg where the owner indicates some initial cooperation, but later on ceases to respond to requests from the State. This may be because the single ship company owner has become insolvent, eg where an H&M claim is denied.[286] Both of these instances are exactly the sort of circumstances where the direct action protection of Art 12(10) is important for the State. Where there is a breakdown in communication (perhaps temporary) with an owner after a notice has *already* been served, there is a chance that the owner might still be seeking to fulfil its obligations. Here the State might still be advised to wait until its deadline had expired before intervening to remove the wreck itself, unless perhaps the evidence is compelling that the owner will not respond.

Fourthly, if there is a dispute about the extent of wreck removal needed, the State may decide to perform some additional wreck removal itself. This might occur where the owner and insurer have paid (or undertaken to pay) for what they consider to be reasonable and proportionate costs (under Art 2), but the Affected State requires a higher standard.[287] In these circumstances, it would (in the EEZ) have to satisfy the additional hurdles in Art 9(5), 9(6), 9(7), or 9(8). If it was able to do so, it could claim the costs from the owner under Art 10(1) (and insurer under Art 12(10)).

Fifthly, Art 9(8) provides a fall-back provision for the Affected State where it considers that it needs to take "immediate action" to remove the wreck. In these circumstances it may remove the wreck itself,[288] claim the costs from the owner under Art 10(1) (and insurer under Art 12(10)). The power under Art 9(8) can be exercised whether or not removal operations have been underway on the part of the owner and (apparently) irrespective of whether a wreck removal notice has been given under Art 9(6). What is necessary for "immediate action" will vary greatly. A clue is given in Art 9(6)(c), where there is a reference to "circumstances where the hazard becomes *particularly severe*".[289] The implication is that there is a change of circumstance of some kind, whether caused by outside factors such as the weather or state of the wreck, or the ability of the wreck removal contractor. It

---

284 See 10.2.5. Cf the *Rena*, 1.2.4(e), and the *Fedra*, 10.2.5.
285 Again, provided it uses the "most practical and expeditious means available, consistent with considerations of safety and protection of the marine environment".
286 See eg 2.9.2 and 2.9.5.
287 Thus, a State may require "full removal" rather than partial removal of the hull, cargo and debris: see 10.2.5.
288 Again, provided it uses the "most practical and expeditious means available, consistent with considerations of safety and protection of the environment".
289 Emphasis added.

is not clear if "particularly" in Art 9(6)(c) is meant to limit the effect of the requirement for "immediate action" under Art 9(8). On balance, the Art 9(6)(c) reference should be taken for what it is—merely general information to an owner about the possible use of powers—and therefore should be treated as a mere example.

There is an obligation, though, in Art 9(8) to inform the flag State and the registered owner of the need for such immediate action. The question is again raised as to whether that is merely an obligation owed to the flag State in public international law or is a pre-condition for any claim under Art 10(1) against the owner (and therefore under Art 12(10) against the insurer).[290] The language does suggest that this is certainly a pre-condition, at least in public international law, but where immediate action is necessary it would seem hard to preclude a State from bringing a civil claim for costs against the owner (or insurer) simply because one or other of flag State or owner was not contacted.[291] A civil law approach would be to enquire whether the failure to notify was in any way causative of increased costs by the Affected State (for which the owner would otherwise be liable under Art 10), although that would also raise the difficult question of whether the owner could counterclaim for any losses it suffered as a result of the failure to notify (eg through contractual liabilities it would otherwise have avoided).[292] The alternative view is that the provision should be strictly enforced as being one of many deliberately insisted upon by flag States to provide some counter to the new extension of State power into the EEZ. If this view were correct it would provide a sharp contrast to the position in relation to wreck removal in territorial waters where Art 9(8) does not apply.[293] Still, for the reasons given, it would be better if the provision was not interpreted as a pre-condition to civil liability, especially as that would create a possible trap for Affected States that were trying to do their best in an emergency.

There are a number of other issues that arise out of the particular wording of Art 9(6).

10.5.3(b) Notice in writing

Article 9(6) refers to a notice "in writing". Traditionally, this would take the form of a document calling itself a "wreck removal notice" or something similar. There is no requirement that this document be in *paper* form and, given modern means of communication, an electronic message in writing ought to be satisfactory.[294] This might involve a question for the law of the forum, but it is submitted that an email or fax should suffice, provided they are sent to an appropriate address.[295]

---

290 See 10.5.3.

291 And particularly where it proves impossible to contact the owner: see also 10.5.3.3(c).

292 See also 10.5.3(d), where it is submitted that it is unlikely that Art 9 was intended to create direct civil liabilities to owners. For rights of recourse, see Art 10(4) and 10.3.3.

293 See 10.5.4.

294 It is arguable that a text message sent to a mobile phone might also comply, although this would seem to be a rather unusual way of imparting such important information, especially if it cannot be proved that the message was ever received. States would be well advised to serve a paper document wherever possible as a back up.

295 Also relevant might be national legislation to give effect to the UNCITRAL Model Law on Electronic Commerce 1996 or the UN Convention on the Use of Electronic Communications in International Contracts 2005.

10.5.3(c) Informing registered owner

Article 9(6)[296] refers to the need to "inform the registered owner", but the question arises about how and to whom the information is to be given. Article 9(11) states that the information has to be given to the "registered owner identified in the reports referred to in [Art 5(2)]". Article 5 is the provision requiring a master and operator to report to an Affected State that the ship has been involved in a casualty resulting in a wreck.[297] Under Art 5(2), the report is supposed to provide the name and principal place of business[298] of the registered owner. If such a report is made, the Affected State complies with its Art 9(6) obligations by using the information given.[299]

Although Art 9(11) uses the word "shall" in relation to the Affected State's obligation to give notice to the owner identified in Art 5(2), it does not say what the Affected State is supposed to do when no Art 5 report has been made, eg where the Affected State has become aware of the wreck through other means. The absence of a report might occur for a variety of reasons, eg because the master, hopefully but unreasonably, does not yet consider his grounded ship is a wreck, or because the ship has sunk with all hands, or because a container has been washed overboard.[300] In any event, there may well be a delay and the State may feel the need to take immediate action. It can be said that some of the well-ordered procedures of Arts 5–9 presuppose that there is plenty of time for taking the required actions. While this may be true when a ship is wrecked in circumstances where it is clear that there will need to be a long drawn out removal operation to remove a hazard to navigation, the reality is that in most circumstances there is a need to act urgently to protect the environment, eg by removing bunkers.

In these circumstances, it will surely be necessary for the Affected State to use the registered address of the shipowner as found from other sources.[301] The question then arises as to whether the wreck removal notice information can be given to employees of the owner (such as the master), or agents (including ship managers, local ship's agents or even lawyers or insurers)?[302] A literal view is that all notices do have to be served on the registered owner personally, eg where it is a company that will be its registered address (usually abroad). Again, this may be a matter for the law of the forum,[303] but it is submitted that a court should not take an overly technical approach to communication in circumstances where urgency may be vital and the Affected State should not have to arrange for notices to be hand delivered in, say, Liberia when reliable representatives are available locally.

---

296 And the related Art 9(8).

297 See 9.1.3.

298 Although Art 5(2) does not say so expressly, it is a reasonable interpretation that an address would be required, not merely a statement such as "Liberia".

299 If for some reason a wrong name or address was given by master or operator, the shipowner could not complain that it had never formally received the Art 9(6) notice. The possibility of inaccurate information being given (innocently or negligently) is not fanciful, as confusion can be caused where there are complicated company structures involving related entities with similar sounding names.

300 See also 9.1.3(c).

301 Using publicly available sources, such as IMO's Global Integrated Shipping Information System (GSIS), the European Equasis database, or one of the commercial finding databases.

302 Where there is a Memorandum of Understanding (MOU) between the International Group and the State, the Club which is identified as insurer should certainly expect to cooperate in forwarding a notice: see 10.8.6.

303 Which may have general procedural rules about service of notices on companies.

Traditionally, wreck removal orders would be served on the master personally, and such service should comply with Art 9(6), as should service on an alternative senior officer in the absence of the master. Likewise, if there are reliable agents who must be presumed to be in contact with the registered owner, then service on them should also suffice.[304] Those agents should include ship's managers (who may be de facto operators of single ship companies) and port agents (eg where the ship has recently called at a port of the Affected State); it is more doubtful if service via insurers or lawyers ought to be effective (at least where they do not agree to accept the notice).

10.5.3(d) Deadline
Article 9(6) requires the Affected State to set a reasonable deadline and to inform the shipowner of it. If the shipowner does not remove the wreck by the deadline then, under Art 9(7), the State may remove the wreck itself; the costs of this can then be claimed against the owner under Art 10(1) (and against the insurer under Art 12(10)). The deadline requirements present a number of practical problems for the State. In practice, what the State really wants to know is whether the owner and its insurer are going to front up and agree to undertake (and pay for) the removal themselves. Such an acknowledgement of responsibility is an important practical concern for the Affected State as it will determine whether the State has itself to start engaging contractors. Article 9 contains no requirement on the shipowner to give such an acknowledgement. Instead the "deadline" referred to is one by which the removal operations are to be *completed*.

Even at an early stage of the casualty, but when it is clear that the ship is a total loss, it may be envisaged that the operation may take months or years.[305] The consequence of the shipowner not completing the removal of the wreck by the deadline is that it triggers the Affected State's right under Art 9(7) to undertake the removal work itself. The problem is that the wording of Art 9(7) (on its own) apparently means that the State cannot undertake the removal itself until that deadline has expired. If the removal operation is estimated to take, say, 12 months, this would mean that the State could not start removal operations until that period had expired. This is highly unlikely to be politically acceptable to a State, unless the wreck is in a remote location with little or no environmental impact—a circumstance that itself is increasingly unlikely. Where ships are aground on most coastlines, an Affected State will want immediate responses. Article 9 provides two solutions for the Affected State in these circumstances. The first is Art 9(7) where "the registered owner cannot be contacted"; this provides an alternative trigger for the power of the State to remove the wreck.[306] The second is Art 9(8), where immediate action is required.[307]

---

304 Again, it would be good practice to serve a copy later, eg by registered post, to the registered owner's address. This would be particularly so where a notice is to be served under Art 9(7).

305 It is clear from the examples considered in Chapter 1 and 10.2.5 that (once salvage is impossible) wreck removal operations need time for planning, environmental assessments and mobilisation of equipment—even before operations start: see also 13.1. Then the period of removal and disposal may take a considerable time, depending eg on the amount of cargo or debris. The removal of a container ship such as the *Chitra*, aground in a port, could take a minimum of six months: see 10.2.5, 14.1.2(b). More complicated cases could take years, as seen with the *Rena* (see 1.2.4) and *Costa Concordia* (see 1.2.5).

306 See 9.2.5(d), 10.5.3(a).

307 See 9.2.5(a), 10.5.3(a).

Article 9(6) does not specify the consequences of the State setting an unreasonable deadline. In those circumstances, the owner would expect to have public law defences, eg a defence to any criminal charge for failing to obey a wreck removal notice,[308] or the ability to bring an administrative law action seeking to annul the notice.[309] In the latter case, the owner could request that a reasonable deadline be given. More difficult would be the question as to whether there could be any civil law consequences of an unreasonable order. Although Art 10 does not provide any relevant contributory negligence defence,[310] if the deadline was not reasonable or proportionate within Art 2, then that would appear to provide a restriction on the extent to which the State could recover its costs under Art 10. Otherwise it is difficult to see that Art 9 is intended to provide the owner with an independent claim arising from loss caused by the giving of an unreasonable deadline, eg where contractors billed the owner for the costs of mobilising additional and unnecessary equipment.

10.5.3(e) Determination of hazard by a State

There is an additional complication here. Article 9, essentially a public law provision, refers to circumstances where the Affected State "*determines* that a wreck constitutes a hazard".[311] Following that "determination" the registered owner has an obligation to "remove"[312] the wreck, and this is later linked to the liability provision, Art 10. How far can it be said that once a State makes a "determination", that is *conclusive* of the fact that there was a hazard that needed eliminating? The provision does not say that the determination is to be made by a court, but seemingly is an administrative act by the State. Such an administrative act is a necessary trigger to further administrative action under Art 9, but there is no indication in the WRC 2007 that the determination is meant to be conclusive thereafter and not open to challenge. It is submitted that the proper interpretation of these linked provisions is that such a determination is subject to challenge on the basis that it is not in conformity with the rest of the WRC 2007; so, for instance, it would be open to the shipowner to dispute whether there was a hazard within Art 1(5), or whether the removal of every trace of the wreck was proportionate within Art 2(2) or reasonably necessary under Art 2(3).[313]

What if the Affected State fails to make a determination of the hazard? This might be relevant to the time limit,[314] but does that have any effect on liability? The absence of notification of the hazard under Art 9(1) surely means that the registered owner's obligations in Art 9(2)–(4) cannot be triggered, but does it also affect the right of the Affected State in Art 9(6)–(8)? Article 6(a) presupposes that a determination has been made and without that it is not possible to set a deadline; or, more accurately, the deadline could be challenged as being invalid, or at least unreasonable. If there is an invalid or unreasonable deadline then

---

308 Assuming that the State had created a criminal offence in that regard. In the UK, see the MSA 1995 s 255D, 11.3.3(a), (f).

309 The ability to do so would vary according to the jurisdiction concerned. In the UK, there would seem to be the possibility of bringing a claim for judicial review.

310 See 10.3.3.

311 See 9.2.2, and also 10.5.1(b).

312 Again, recalling that the expression is slightly misleading as it must be read with the wide definition of "removal" in Art 1(7) which refers to the removal of a hazard, rather than the wreck itself: see 8.2.2, 9.2.5, 10.2.4, 10.2.5.

313 See 9.2.5(e), 10.2.4.

314 See 10.4.

the power of the State to take action itself under Art 9(7) might only be triggered if the owner cannot be contacted. As submitted above, breach by the State of these obligations could give rise to administrative law action (eg to quash the order setting the deadline) but would this be a bar to the civil claim for costs under Art 10(1) on the basis that the costs were not incurred "under" Art 9? That would seem to be a hard sanction for the State in not fulfilling its public law duty under Art 9(1)(a), and the better view may be that the main sanction is in public law, but that any extra costs would have to be borne by the State (eg if the owner can prove that it could have removed the wreck more cheaply itself). In any event, Art 9(8) provides a backstop for a State, allowing it to take action, but again by giving notice.[315]

10.5.4 Recovery of wreck removal costs: territorial waters

Where a State has not opted to extend the WRC 2007 to its territorial waters (ie its internal waters and territorial sea) its ability to recover wreck removal costs will be entirely dependent on its existing national law,[316] but without the advantage of the compulsory insurance and direct action provisions.[317]

Where the State has opted to extend the WRC 2007 to its territorial waters,[318] it will be able to take advantage of the liability provisions in Art 10[319] and the direct action insurance provisions in Art 12(10).[320] The question arises as to whether the triggers for that liability are the same as those for when the wreck is in the EEZ.[321] Article 2(3) preserves the sovereign rights of such States to take measures in their territorial waters[322] but in its last sentence provides that the "provisions of articles 10, 11 and 12 of this Convention shall not apply to any measures so taken other than those referred to in articles 7, 8 and 9 of this Convention".[323] This rather convoluted sentence presumably means that the liability articles (10, 11 and 12) *only* apply to measures that are taken under the operative articles (7, 8 and 9). In the context of the present discussion, that means that Arts 7–9 will still operate as 'triggers' for the liability provisions for wrecks in territorial waters.

In principle, therefore, the same triggers will apply as discussed in relation to the EEZ.[324] However, Art 4(4) provides that a number of WRC 2007 provisions will not apply at all in territorial waters, and that one will only apply in a modified form.[325] Article 4(4) makes no mention of Arts 7 and 8, so the triggers for costs liability in respect of locating and marking wrecks will be the same in territorial waters as in the EEZ.[326] Article 4(4) therefore affects wreck removal in territorial waters.

---

315 See 9.2.5(d), 10.5.3(a).
316 See 8.4.1, 11.1.
317 See 10.8.
318 See 8.4.2, 9.3.
319 See 10.2.
320 See 10.8.4.
321 See 10.5.2 and 10.5.3.
322 See 8.4.1.
323 See 8.4.2.
324 See 10.5.3.
325 See 8.4.2.
326 See 10.5.5, 10.5.6.

It is convenient to deal first with Art 9(4), the provision modified by Art 4(4)(b). The latter makes the ostensible freedom of the shipowner to contract with any salvor provided by Art 9(4) subject to the national law of the Affected State.[327] Although this does not directly affect the liability for costs, it may do so indirectly if the shipowner is obliged to use a more expensive local contractor.

It is Art 4(4)(a)(ii) that expressly provides that Art 9(1), (5), (7), (8), (9) and (10) will *not* apply at all in territorial waters; ie it is only Art 9(2), (3), (4), (6) and (11) that *do* apply in territorial waters. The broad intention of the omissions was to avoid imposing restrictions on the public international law rights that States would otherwise exercise in their territorial waters.[328] Thus, it was not meant to disadvantage such States, but what effect does the omission of the five sub-paragraphs have on the liability provisions?

The omission of the public international law obligation in Art 9(1) should have no effect on liability.[329] Similarly, the omission of Art 9(10) only relates to international law rights.[330] The omission of Art 9(9) also relates to a largely international law obligation, there imposed on flag States. It should have little direct effect on liability, although if a shipowner does not remove the wreck under Art 9(2) this may force the Affected State to intervene; likewise a failure to provide insurance details under Art 9(3) will hamper the State's ability to use the direct action provisions of Art 12(10).[331] The omission of Art 9(5) means that a State can intervene in the removal operations being undertaken by the registered shipowner and its contractors on grounds that go beyond safety and the protection of the marine environment, eg to include local economic factors.[332] Again, this could affect the overall costs of the removal.

It is the omission of Art 9(7) and (8) that presents the most problems for States. Both provisions relate to (and preserve) any pre-existing default rights of a State to take actions in its own territorial waters. But if they do not apply in such waters then they cannot trigger the liability provisions of Art 10(1) that refer specifically to liability for removing the wreck "*under* articles 7, 8 *and* 9" (emphasis added). This would mean that neither the shipowner (under Art 10(1)) nor its compulsory insurer (under Art 12(10)) would have any liability for the costs that an Affected State incurred using the express default powers in

---

327 See 8.4.2, 9.2.5(e). It seems that the restriction as to national law only applies to the choice of contractor in the first sentence of the (amended) Art 9(4) and not to the second sentence: see 11.3.3(c). This means that the State can *only* set conditions of the removal operations undertaken by the shipowner and its contractor that are consistent with safety and environmental protection.

328 See 8.4.1, 8.4.2.

329 As Art 9(1) is not a trigger for liability in the EEZ: see 10.5.3, 10.5.3(c), (d).

330 Ie Affected States would not need consent from another State to take actions in its own territorial waters.

331 It is strange that Art 9(9) is excluded from territorial waters, as it should be important for an Affected State to be able to rely on other States parties to ensure that the obligations under Art 9(2) and (3) are complied with—whether in the EEZ or territorial waters. As a matter of international law, a potential Affected State could not reinsert this obligation in its national law so as to bind that other State; this appears to be a gap in the WRC 2007. The UK does not appear to have given effect to Art 9(2) in respect of UK ships in the waters of other State parties, although it has done so in respect of insurance certificates under Art 9(3): see 11.3.3(c) and (e).

332 If we are correct in the assumption in fn 324 and 11.3.3(c), this creates an apparent anomaly in that the State would be bound to apply only the safety and environmental criteria when setting conditions for the removal (under Art 9(4)), but that once removal had commenced, it could then intervene on wider grounds. This might be an argument for disregarding the literal and grammatical English meaning of the amended Art 9(4). However, there is a distinction between the State intervening itself and imposing conditions for removal by others.

Art 9(7) and (8). This is a potential trap for States when enacting the WRC 2007, and it is important that they reintroduce these provisions in respect of territorial waters.[333] If they do so it might be arguable that this would only be of effect in national (rather than international) law and therefore could not trigger the WRC 2007 liabilities of shipowner and insurer. An Affected State probably does not need the WRC 2007 to create obligations on the shipowner in its territorial waters, whereas the insurer's liability in Art 12 is very much tied to the application of the convention. Nevertheless, it would defeat the whole intention of the WRC 2007 provisions relating to the opt-in to territorial waters if a shipowner or insurer was in a better position in such waters than in the EEZ. Courts of States parties that exercise the opt-in, like the UK, should give full effect to Arts 10 and 12 in territorial waters *if* Art 9(7) and (8) have been reinstated in national law.[334]

10.5.5 *Recovery of costs of locating wrecks*

The triggers for the recovery of costs for locating wrecks are more straightforward than for removal. Article 10(1) refers back to the "costs of locating . . . the wreck *under* [Art] 7". Unlike Art 9 (wreck removal),[335] there is no distinction made between locating wrecks in the EEZ and territorial sea.[336]

The question arises as to whether compliance by a State with all the requirements in Art 7 is also a pre-condition of liability under Art 10, and thus later against the insurer under Art 12(10). The obligation to warn in Art 7(1) is directed to ships other than the one wrecked. Any reasonable and proportionate costs in publicising the warning would be admissible under Art 10(1). The only other relevance to the owner of the wrecked ship might be if, owing to a failure by the State to warn other mariners, another ship collided with the wreck. Any claim by the owner of that ship would not arise under the WRC 2007, but would be an ordinary collision action based on negligence. Assuming that the owner of the wrecked ship had reported it to the Affected State,[337] it would probably have no liability to the other ship if the wreck had arisen through no fault of its own; but if the sinking had been caused by negligence then that could still be a cause of liability to the other ship (subject to any contributory negligence).[338] It might be possible to make a claim against the State authority for any negligence or breach of duty by it in relation to the warning.[339]

The second possible trigger to liability for the costs of locating a wreck is in Art 7(2). Here a State has to take "*all* practicable steps" to establish the "*precise* location" of the wreck.[340] Depending on the information (if any) provided by the master and operator of the wrecked ship[341] the locating of the wreck might be a difficult, time consuming and

---

333 See 11.2.2, 11.2.3.
334 See the MSA 1995 s 255F, and 11.3.3(c) and (d).
335 See 10.5.3, 10.5.4.
336 This is because the carve out provisions in Art 4(4) do not extend to Art 7: see 10.5.2.
337 Under Art 5 (see 9.1.3), and the MSA 1995 s 255B (see 11.3.3(a)).
338 See 2.4.2.
339 See 2.4.2, 9.2.1, 9.2.3.
340 Emphasis added. See also 9.2.3 and *Berlingieri Vol III*, 90.
341 See Art 5 and 9.1.3.

expensive exercise.[342] The reference to "all" suggests that the only limit to this exercise is whether or not it is physically possible, but there are two limitations. First, the proportionality principle applies to the measures taken.[343] Secondly, the Affected State has to have "reason to believe" that the wreck poses a hazard, and that presupposes a "determination" under Art 6.[344] In other words, a State would not be able to recover the costs of locating a wreck if it instantly contracted for a search and location operation without having assessed if it was necessary, taking into account the criteria in Art 6. In a practical sense, this trigger should not be too great a burden for a State to satisfy in most cases concerning wrecks that pose a threat to safety, the environment or related interests.

Likewise, where a ship loses an anchor,[345] the State may have a difficulty in knowing exactly where it is on the seabed. Without this information it will have difficulty in making an assessment as to whether it poses a hazard or not. This is most likely to occur in coastal waters or harbours where there could be a risk to navigation. Again, the burden on the State of showing it had "reason to believe" that the anchor poses a hazard should not be high. But it would presumably have to make an estimate from the information provided by the ship as to a broad area in which the anchor might lie and determine the chance of that posing a risk; otherwise there could be disproportionate costs involved in looking for a 'needle in a haystack'. Similarly, where containers are washed overboard they could drift in an even wider area, but here the hazard might be more apparent, not only to safety but also to the environment. A single sunken container might be equally difficult to find, especially in the EEZ, but again the question will come down to a reasonable assessment of the hazard.

Where the State wishes to locate the wreck for different reasons, eg only in order to find or remove bodies, there may be doubts about whether this is a "hazard' within Art 7(2), at least in the EEZ.[346]

10.5.6 *Recovery of costs of marking wrecks*

The triggers for the recovery of costs for marking wrecks are also more straightforward than for removal. Article 10(1) refers back to the "costs of marking the wreck *under* [Art] 8". Again, unlike Art 9 (wreck removal),[347] there is no distinction made between marking wrecks in the EEZ and territorial sea.[348]

The question again arises as to whether compliance by a State with all the requirements in Art 8 is also a pre-condition of liability under Art 10(1), and thus later against the insurer under Art 12(10). Article 8(1) provides the familiar trigger that the State must

---

342 See eg the *YM Efficiency* that lost 81 containers off New South Wales on 1 June 2018. Australia had to contract for an underwater search and assessment by Remotely Operated Underwater Vehicle (ROUV) and, after a search of 578 km^2, 66 containers were located by August 2019, 5 had been removed and 15 were yet to be located: see 1.3.2. Australia put out a tender for recovery operations but, as it is not yet a party to the WRC 2007, it would have to seek cost recovery from owners under national law.
343 See Art 2(2) and 9.2.5(e), 8.4.2, 10.2.4.
344 See 9.2.2.
345 Ie part of a ship within Art 1(4)(b): see 8.2.1(c). See also S Kendall-Marsden, "Wreck Removal Liability Unravelled", *International Tug & OSV* (May/June 2017), 62.
346 See 10.5.1(b).
347 See 10.5.3, 10.5.4.
348 This is because the carve-out provisions in Art 4(4) do not extend to Art 7: see 10.5.2.

determine that there is a "hazard" before marking a wreck.[349] The obligation on the State under Art 8(1) is to take "all reasonable steps" to mark the wreck; there would be no liability under Art 10(1) for taking unreasonable steps and, in any event, any steps would have to be proportionate.[350] The reference in Art 8(2) to a State taking all practicable steps to use internationally accepted markings would be relevant if a State claimed for costs of markings that were not so accepted. Such costs might not be claimable if there was an internationally accepted system that could have been used. Rather than denying a State all recovery, it would be appropriate to award its actual costs up to the amount that would have been appropriate using international standards; it should not be able to recover the amount by which its own costs exceeded such an amount. Article 8(3) requires a State to promulgate, ie publicise, the particular markings used. These costs would be recoverable if proportionate.

10.5.7 Recovery of wreck removal costs: high seas

The authors are not aware of any attempt to remove a wreck (or its cargo) for navigational or environmental reasons when the wreck is situated beyond the EEZ of any State. There are, though, increasing instances of the salvage (or finding) of historic wrecks or those which may contain valuable cargo.[351] The WRC 2007 does not extend beyond the EEZ.[352] The negotiations to apply the WRC 2007 to the EEZ raised enough objections, eg to creeping jurisdiction, as to suggest that any further extension would be controversial.[353] Article 2(4) expressly states that the application of the WRC 2007 in the "Convention Area" (ie the EEZ) "shall not entitle a State party to claim or exercise sovereignty or sovereign rights over any part of the high seas".

This means that, as a matter of public international law, any question of wreck removal under the high seas would have to be decided according to general principles under UNCLOS, in particular those relating to protection of the marine environment under Part XII. These would mostly fall on flag States, eg obligations to prevent, reduce and control pollution by dumping.[354] There is also a more general obligation under Art 211(2) on flag States to adopt laws for their ships aimed at preventing, reducing or controlling pollution and to enforce such laws.[355] These are to have at least the same effect as generally accepted international rules and standards established by bodies such as the IMO. This might be a basis for a State to apply WRC 2007 type provisions in respect of its own ships wrecked on the high seas, but the concentration in UNCLOS is more on recognising State rights to intervene when maritime casualties are likely to affect that State's coastline or related interests, rather than the high seas itself.[356] Articles 235–236 place general obligations on States about responsibility and liability caused by marine pollution, and to cooperate in

---

349 See 8.2.2, 8.2.3, 9.2.2, 10.5.1(b)–(d), 10.5.3(e).
350 See Art 2(2) And 9.2.5(e), 8.4.2, 10.2.4.
351 See Chapter 3, 4.6, Chapter 6.
352 See Arts 1(1) and 2(4).
353 See 7.3, 7.4.
354 See UNCLOS Arts 210, 216; also 5.5.1.
355 See 5.5.1 and Art 217.
356 See Art 221 and 5.4–5.6.

developing international law on compensation (eg through the sort of compulsory insurance mechanisms adopted in the WRC 2007).

It appears, therefore that there is a gap in international law about how to deal with locating, marking and removing a wreck located on or under the high seas. Indeed, this appears to be part of a wider gap in relation to high seas governance, including the provision of compensation for high seas pollution.[357] At present there appears to be no international provision directly requiring a shipowner to remove a wrecked ship situated under the high seas,[358] or requiring it to pay for the costs of an operation carried out by a State. A fundamental question will always be whether one State has sufficient standing to remove a wreck flagged in another State, let alone seek to recover the costs of such an operation. While there may be scope to try to develop principles of State liability in international law,[359] their application to wreck removal seems far off. National wreck law of the flag State could be extended to its ships on the high seas, but most States will be reluctant to expose their shipowners to the potential costs of such an operation. UK law does not place such an obligation on an owner, certainly not under the MSA 1995 Part 9A[360] or, it would seem, under any other legislation or common law principles.

Moreover, there is a broader argument that such international or national wreck raising provisions are not necessary (at least in respect of navigational hazards), and that in most cases removal of a wreck from the bed of the high seas will be either impossible or disproportionately expensive. Still, the technological and engineering capacity to remove wrecks has advanced way beyond that which might have been imagined a generation ago. What would the international maritime community do if a ship carrying a massively polluting cargo sank in the high seas, in an area of environmental significance to the heritage of mankind?[361]

10.6 Cargo removal under the WRC 2007

10.6.1 Uncertainty in the WRC 2007?

The WRC 2007 is surprisingly unclear about "cargo removal" as distinct from "hull removal". As already seen, the definitions in Art 1 are interlocked in a quite complex way. The first trigger (Art 1(3)) is that there must be a "maritime casualty" to a ship which, for example, threatens the ship "or its cargo". The second trigger for State action is that there has to be a "wreck" of a ship within Art 1(4):

---

357 See *Gaskell, Liability and Compensation Regimes: Pollution of the High Seas*, 235–241.
358 It might be possible to argue that national legislation could achieve this effect: cf the *Rena*, 1.2.4.
359 See the *ILC Articles on State Responsibility*.
360 See 11.3.4(a).
361 Cf the position under Annex VI to the Protocol on Environmental Protection to the Antarctic Treaty on Liability Arising from Environmental Emergencies 2005 (not yet in force): *Gaskell, Liability and Compensation Regimes: Pollution of the High Seas*, 254–259.

"Wreck", following upon a maritime casualty, means:

(a) a sunken or stranded ship; or
(b) *any part* of a sunken or stranded ship, *including any object that is or has been on board such a ship*; or
(c) *any object that is lost at sea from a ship* and that is stranded, sunken or adrift at sea; or
(d) a ship that is about, or may reasonably be expected, to sink or to strand, where effective measures to assist the ship or any property in danger are not already being taken.[362]

This definition is designed to exclude ships that are in temporary difficulty,[363] but is otherwise fairly widely drafted. The liability provision (Art 10(1)) refers only to "wreck" and not to cargo, so the Art 1(4) definition is crucial. It seems axiomatic that "removal" of the hull of a sunken ship from the seabed must also include what is in the wreck as it is raised, including the cargo; but the omission of the word "cargo" in Art 1(4) is unfortunate, particularly as the word is used elsewhere in the WRC 2007.[364] This might seem to raise the question whether the WRC 2007 can apply to the removal of the cargo *independently* of what happens to the hull.

The only wording that could directly extend to cargo is the reference in Art 1(4)(b) and (c) to an "object". While a container, a truck, a drum, or a heavy lift oil rig loaded on deck, might all be "objects", there is an immediate difficulty in the English language of applying the word "object" to bulk cargoes, such as liquid chemicals, fertiliser, iron ore, wheat, or coal. While each lump of coal or grain of wheat might be an "object", this is stretching the language; even more so if one has to consider particles of ore or fertiliser.

There is also a textual difficulty in Art 1(4)(b). The Art 1(4)(b) reference to "part of a ship" must refer to the physical structure of the ship itself, such as masts and superstructure. Cargo is never "part of a ship" (except conceivably when oil residues settle semi-permanently in tanks and pipelines). The final phrase of Art 1(4)(b) can be read by reference to the meaning of "part"; ie the "object" in mind could be something functionally similar to "part" of a ship. An "object that is or has been on board" a ship might include a generator, auxiliary pumps, hatch covers, derricks, radar antenna, anchor chains, or drums of lubricating oil which are functionally part of the equipment of a ship but which may not be permanently connected to it (or which may be supplied after final construction). It is perfectly logical for wreck removal powers to extend to such objects when they have become separated from the hull of the ship on the seabed, but still represent a hazard, eg where an anchor and chain is separated from the ship but still poses a navigational threat.

If this is the meaning of the word "object" in Art 1(4)(b), it would be logical to apply the same meaning to Art 1(4)(c) which is best read as referring to the situation when the ship *itself* has *not* sunk or stranded, but where the "object" is lost in some way (eg washed overboard). That object (eg the anchor or drum) only becomes "wreck" if it is "stranded, sunken or adrift at sea". It is difficult to see that a lost object could be anything other than "stranded, sunken or adrift", so the latter expression is probably best viewed as clarifying a wide view of "lost", to ensure that the WRC 2007 can apply to drifting hazards.

---

362 Emphasis added.
363 While Art (5) provides a further restriction by excluding minor "hazards".
364 The word "cargo" appears only in Arts 1(3), 5(d) and 6(h), mostly in relation to determining whether there is a "hazard".

This interpretation of Art 1(4) has so far made no reference to cargo, except by implication where a ship is raised with cargo in it. The hazardous nature of the cargo is clearly a "hazard" contemplated by Art 1(5)(b): indeed, the threat to the environment of related interests can only be from the cargo in the vast majority of cases. But the question is not whether there is a hazard that triggers the operation of the WRC 2007 but whether the removal provisions operate when it is *only* the cargo that is being removed.

What if cargo is lost from a ship which does not itself sink, eg where containers are washed overboard, or there is a hull fracture resulting in the spilling of a part cargo of coal, iron ore, or liquid chemical? Similarly, what if the ship sinks, and the cargo spills onto the seabed, so that it has to be removed separately from the hull; or where the hull itself is not removed, but only cargo removal actions are taken or ordered? It would be highly surprising if the WRC 2007 did not extend to such operations,[365] but the rather awkward language of Art 1(4), and the absence of a reference to the word "cargo" in it, allows such an argument to be raised.

As the issue is central to the purposes of the WRC 2007, it is important to demonstrate that any doubts are unfounded. A consideration of the history of wreck removal provisions and the *travaux préparatoires* of the WRC 2007 will show that WRC 2007 liability extends not only to the removal of the hull of a ship, but also to cargo that has been on the wrecked ship and floats clear (or sinks); cargo that remains in (or is dispersed from) the wrecked hull where the latter is not a navigational or other hazard; and cargo (such as containers) washed overboard from a ship that is not itself wrecked.

10.6.2 Cargo removal: history

There is a longstanding practice in some States[366] of applying wreck raising, removal and destruction powers to cargo as well as hull. The original UK MSA 1894 s 532 expressly provided that the provisions of the Act relating to wreck removal (ss 530–531) "shall apply to every article or thing or collection of things being or forming part of the tackle, equipments [*sic*], *cargo*, stores or ballast of a vessel in the same manner as if it were included in the term 'vessel'".[367] Although these powers were triggered only by an "obstruction or danger to navigation", and not the wider category of "related interests" under the WRC 2007, there seems little doubt as a matter of interpretation that this power extended to the removal of wrecked cargo, independently of the sinking of a ship.[368]

---

365 Although it must be acknowledged that similar doubts may exist in respect of how far national legislation (such as s 229 of the Navigation Act 2012 (Cth, Australia)) covers cargo lost overboard where the ship itself is not wrecked, or whether the cost of cargo removal is effectively covered by intervention powers.

366 See LEG 75/6/2, 14 February 1997, 5–7.

367 Section 252(3) of the consolidating MSA 1995 is to like effect: see 11.1.3(a). Note also in s 255 the definition of "wreck" for the MSA 1995 Part 9 includes "jetsam, flotsam lagan and derelict" (eg covering cargo washed overboard or lost); *Kennedy and Rose*, 94–96. For the position after the enactment of the UK Wreck Removal Act 2011, see 11.3.

368 By contrast, it seems doubtful if the MSA 1995 s 252 allows for the recovery of cargo which has been lost overboard from a ship which has not itself become sunk, stranded or abandoned: see 11.1.3(a), 11.3.5.

Early drafts of the WRC 2007 dealt only with navigational hazards, and the definition of wreck referred only to a "wrecked or derelict ship, or parts or appurtenances thereof".[369] Not surprisingly, there was only a passing mention of cargo as a possible navigational hazard. By 1995, the German, Netherlands and UK draft for a convention had introduced the wider definition of hazard extended to include environmental risks (including "related interests"), and the definition of wreck became a "sunken or stranded ship, or any part thereof, including anything that is or has been on board a ship".[370] At this stage there is little indication that any particular thought had been given to cargo,[371] but it was recognised in a Report by the CMI that this wording might extend to cargo.[372] The concern here was mainly about overlaps with other conventions,[373] but the Report is quite clear that the definition "covers only cargo, etc., which is or has been on board a sunken ship". The assumption was clearly that cargo was included in the expression "*anything* that is or has been on board a ship", but that there was an initial requirement that the ship be wrecked.

The CMI suggested that a clarification may be needed to include cargo, etc[374] in relation to ships that might reasonably be expected to result in a wreck, and further consideration ought to be given as to whether to include lost cargo from a ship that is not a wreck. Perhaps more significantly, the International Chamber of Shipping (ICS), representing shipowners, commented that the above wreck definition "would include cargo, containers and bunkers".[375] That definition is materially identical to the WRC 2007 Art 1(4)(b), apart from the words "any object" in the latter.[376] The shipowners were clearly alive to the potential of cargo removal being covered by the wording and were anxious to restrict the possibility by restricting hazards to navigational risks only. Moreover, the ICS introduced for the first time the corollary to liability for wreck removal made necessary by the cargo, namely that cargo should be required to contribute to removal costs.[377]

In 1997 the IMO Correspondence Group presented a number of options for development of the convention, including the environmental risk option. In listing the types of "wrecks/ships" which might be covered, attention was drawn to a number of options that would need consideration: drifting ships ("option 1.c.i"); "coverage of *objects* which have been on board ships and which may pose the same danger as a wreck" ("option 1.c.ii"); wrecked aircraft, and offshore installations.[378] No specific reference was made to cargo, but this (apparently first) mention of "objects" which have been on board was expressly related

---

369 See eg the draft presented to the 24th Session of the IMCO Legal Committee in LEG XXIV/3, 20 September 1974, explained and reproduced by the Secretariat for the 63rd Session in 1990 in LEG 63/5, 18 May 1990, Annex 1.

370 LEG 73/11, 8 August 1995, Annex, 2.

371 This was at the time of the drafting of the HNSC when its outcome in relation to hazardous cargo was uncertain, and when the position of bunkers had yet to be finalised (see eg LEG 73/12, 12 July 1995).

372 LEG 74/5/2, 20 August 1996, Annex, 3.

373 Now dealt with by the WRC 2007 Art 11: see 10.9.

374 Ie to include bunkers, not then regulated by a separate liability convention.

375 LEG 74/5/3, 13 September 1996, 2. ICS proposed the deletion of the words "or has been", ie accepting that cargo in a wreck was subject to the draft convention, but opposing any application to cargo no longer in a wreck.

376 Note the different language of WRC 2007 Art 1(4) which refers to "any object": see 8.2.1(c) and 10.6.2 (below), 10.6.3.

377 LEG 74/5/3, 13 September 1996, 4.

378 LEG 75/6/1, 31 December 1996, 5–6.

to the HNSC and CLC, which themselves deal with cargo loss, and seems to have had no particular significance.

At the 75th Session of the Legal Committee in April 1997, the majority of States expressed a preference for the extension to environmental risks and "related interests",[379] which must naturally have included cargo. Although there was no specific discussion of cargo removal, an overwhelming number of States favoured options 1.c.i and 1.c.ii. The assumption seems to have been that "objects" referred to cargo, although the actual draft convention at that stage still used the word "anything".[380]

In 1997, the question of how far cargo interests should be obliged to contribute to the costs of removal was again raised, as part of the familiar arguments of shipowner interests that burdens should be shared between ship and cargo.[381] The debate continued[382] until 2003, when it was recognised that such an attempt would raise too many complex issues of law and practice and the concept was rejected.[383] The present significance is that such a discussion must have been predicated on the notion that cargo removal was within the contemplation of the convention and might be exclusively or mainly related to the nature of the cargo.[384] Moreover, in April 1998, the Legal Committee agreed that the current definition of wreck "had to be amended to make it clear that the draft convention applies to any cargo lost from a ship and not only from a wreck".[385] This is the clearest indication that the drafting intention was for wreck to include cargo which might need to be removed independently of any hull removal. To achieve that result, wording was proposed "including anything that is on board such a ship" and "lost from a ship".[386] This wording was accepted by the Legal Committee, but the Committee only "noted" the submission of one delegation that "another approach would be to specifically mention the term "cargo" in the definition of wreck".[387] It is a pity that this submission was not accepted, but the context does not indicate any intention to *reject* the notion, given the way that the coordinator of the Correspondence Group presented its draft, above, to the Legal Committee.

By 1999, for the 79th Session of the Legal Committee, the definition of "wreck" was proposed as "a sunken or stranded ship, or any part thereof, including anything that is on

---

379 Ie option 1.b.iii: LEG 75/WP.1, 24 April 1997, 15.

380 See the Report of the Correspondence Group to the 76th Session in October 1997, LEG 76/5, 8 August 1997. One submission was not to include "objects" which have been on board ships as these would fall under the concept of "preventive measures" under the CLC and HNSC. Again, the preventive measures can only have been in relation to cargo pollution under these conventions.

381 As they are under the CLC and Fund Convention (see 2.6.2(a), 2.6.2(b)) and the HNSC 2010 (see 2.6.4), and to some extent the Salvage Convention 1989 (see 2.7.7(b)), but not under the Bunkers Convention 2001 (see 2.6.3).

382 See eg LEG 76/5, 8 August 1997, 7; LEG 77/5, 13 February 1998, 6; LEG 78/11, 2 November 1998, 11; LEG 79/5, 10 February 1999, para 17.

383 See LEG 86/15, 2 May 2003. The earliest drafts (eg LEG 74/5, 17 June 1996, Annex) used the CLC Art III(5) provision preserving any rights of recourse by the shipowner against third parties such as cargo interests, and this was confirmed in Art 10(5) of the WRC 2007.

384 LEG 78/11, 2 November 1998, 12.

385 LEG 77/WP.3, 23 April 1998, para 71.

386 LEG 78/4/2, 14 August 1998, 2. The intention of the expression "lost from a ship" was to identify the origin of the object that will be in the ship, but to exclude objects that might have been landed and sometime later being wrecked.

387 LEG 78/11, para 84.

board such a ship or which is stranded, sunken or in danger at sea and lost at sea from a ship". It was noted that this definition reflected option 1.c.ii, from the 75th Session and "includes objects which have been on board ships (such as cargo) and which may pose the same risks as a wreck".[388] Again it was confirmed that the additional wording clarified that "the draft WRC applies to cargo lost from a ship and not only from a wreck".[389] The Legal Committee postponed discussion of the definition of wreck, including a new proposal,[390] but once again the ICS urged that cargo be made to contribute to wreck removal where a State has determined a hazard exists, "solely by reason of the nature and quantity of the cargo on board".[391]

The work of the Correspondence Group appeared to be at a decisive point (if not quite in crisis), as its report for the 80th Session in 1999[392] proposed abandoning altogether the liability provisions in a scaled down draft WRC. In part, it seems that this was because of difficulties such as deciding upon cargo contributions, especially where the nature and quantity of the cargo alone was decisive in determining what constitutes a hazard under what became Art 6(h) of the WRC 2007. While the Legal Committee worked on the draft Bunkers Convention, the Correspondence Group seemed to be going round in circles, and little substantive progress was made between the 81st and 84th Sessions in 2000–2001,[393] after a formal Working Group was also established. At the 84th Session in 2002, the Netherlands produced its revised consolidated draft with the liability provisions reinstated.[394]

This draft is significant for two reasons. First, it proposed a new Art 11(2) whereby the owner of cargo was to pay compensation in respect of the costs of measures undertaken because the wreck was determined to be a hazard "by reason of its cargo". This proposal provoked strong reactions for and against, but it foundered largely because similar problems about cargo liability were disclosed during the HNSC 1996 negotiations[395] and there was apparently an absence of any real cargo liability insurance market.[396] Accordingly, at the 85th Session in October 2002, the cargo liability provision was removed when the Netherlands presented a compromise revised consolidated text.[397] Despite subsequent attempts by shipowners to raise the question of whether "cargo interests should contribute

---

388 LEG 79/5, 10 February 1999, Annex, fn 1.
389 LEG 79/5, 10 February 1999, para 17.
390 From the Chairman of the Correspondence Group: LEG 79/WP.2, 20 April 1999, which tried to combine definitions of wreck and casualty to deal with the drifting ship problem in what ultimately became WRC 2007 Art 1(4)(d).
391 LEG 79/11, 22 April 1999, para 93.
392 LEG 80/5, 10 September 1999.
393 LEG 81/5, 15 September 2000; LEG 81/12, 6 November 2000; LEG 82/5, 12 September 2000; LEG 82/12, 6 November 2000; LEG 83/5/1, 12 September 2001; LEG 83/14, 12 October 2001; LEG 84/4, 18 February 2002; LEG 84/14, 7 May 2002.
394 LEG 84/4, 18 February 2002: and see 7.2.
395 The HNSC 1996 and 2010 avoided the problem of trying to impose liability on individual cargo owners by adopting the IOPC Fund approach of having a second tier of liability, with an HNS Fund, contributed to by cargo interests in all contracting states on the basis of a post-event levy spread pro rata across relevant cargo importers.
396 LEG 84/14, 7 May 2002, 11; LEG 85/3, 17 August 2002; LEG 85/11, 5 November 2002. See in particular, the doubts expressed by the International Union of Marine Insurers (IUMI), LEG 86/15 2 May 2003, para 36.
397 LEG 85/3, 17 August 2002

to payment of compensation in situations involving the removal of wrecks carrying dangerous or hazardous substances"[398] there was no support for reinserting such a provision.[399]

Secondly, it was the 2002 revised consolidated text where the change from "anything" to "any objects" first appeared in what became WRC 2007 Art 1(4).[400] This transition apparently resulted from an (undocumented) informal meeting of States in July 2002. The authors do not have access to submissions made to this meeting, but the changed wording seems not to have been of particular significance as it was not formally explained in the documentation provided to the Legal Committee, or later, as having brought about a major change of interpretation to the English text.[401] By contrast, the French text consistently referred to "tout objet *se trouvant ou s'étant trouvé à bord d'un tel navire*" both in the early drafts of the wreck definition,[402] and *after* the change in the English wording from "anything" to "any objects".[403] Apart from the fact that "*objet*" may have a slightly wider meaning than in English,[404] this consistency strongly supports the proposition that no major change was intended when the English wording was altered. English was the language of the original document presented by the lead nation, the Netherlands.

For the 89th Session in 2004, a suggestion was made to the Working Group that Art 1(4)(c) was unnecessary as Art 1(4)(b) already covered objects at sea that are lost from a ship. The Netherlands (as lead nation for the intersessional negotiations), commented that the sunken or stranded ship itself was covered in subparagraph (a); parts of, or objects that have been on board, the sunken or stranded ship (eg the mast of the ship, or ship's stores) were covered in subparagraph (b); and an object lost at sea from a ship in subparagraph (c) covered "eg a container, that is itself sunken, adrift or stranded".[405] There was no specific reference to or approval, of this Netherlands explanation in the Legal Committee at the 89th, 90th, 91st and 92nd Sessions[406] where the attention on Art 1(4) was focused on the wording of subparagraph (d). For the 91st Session, the Netherlands presented the latest version of the draft convention, with Art 1(4)(a)–(c) unchanged, with the statement "Text approved by the Legal Committee as was reflected in document LEG 95/5".[407] The absence of any challenge to this explanation (or any later amendment) suggests that the delegations at the Legal Committee, and subsequent diplomatic conference, found no fault with it. It is not unreasonable to suppose that they accepted it, or at least the underlying assumptions in it, namely that cargo removal was covered within Art 1(4)(b) and (c).

---

398 Eg LEG 86/15, 2 May 2003, para 36.
399 Ibid., Annex 2, 6.
400 LEG 85/3, 17 August 2002, Annex, 2.
401 Eg in the notes to LEG 85/3, 17 August 2002, Annex, 2, or LEG 86/4, 25 February 2003.
402 See eg LEG 84/4, 18 Février 2002, 2. Emphasis added.
403 See LEG 85/3, 17 Août 2002, 2; and in the text adopted in the Final Act of the Nairobi Conference itself, LEG/CONF.16/19, 23 May 2007.
404 Thus, "*objets trouvés*" might perhaps be translated as "lost [or found] *property*".
405 LEG 89/5, 17 August 2004, Annex 3, 2.
406 LEG 89/16, 4 November 2004, LEG 90/15, May 2005, LEG 91/12, 9 May 2006, LEG 92/13, 3 November 2006, 18. Nor was this identified as an outstanding issue: LEG 90/WP.8, 26 April 2005.
407 LEG 91/3, 16 February 2006, Annex 1, 1, Annex 2, 1. This statement that the text had been approved was accepted without comment in the report of the Legal Committee, LEG 91/12, 9 May 2006, para 13.

10.6.3 Cargo removal: conclusion

This extensive examination of the purpose of Art 1(4) has been made to resolve a doubt that might be raised about an issue central to the WRC 2007 as a result of some uncertainty with the English wording. That doubt can now be resolved, although it is somewhat surprising that it was not expressly answered in the text of the WRC 2007.

The repeated references, particularly by shipowner interests, to the environmental problems presented by cargo (including attempts to make cargo contribute to compensation), establish that the Legal Committee was fully aware that wreck removal necessarily included cargo removal. Moreover, this hazard was particularly identified in the WRC 2007 Arts 1(3), 1(5)(b) and 6(h). It is regrettable that the word "cargo" was not specifically included in Art 1(4), as suggested by one delegation; this omission was not out of a desire to exclude cargo, but almost certainly because all concerned had cargo in mind at all times. There is no support in the *travaux* for an argument that the use of the word "objects" was intended to exclude some or all cargo, as this would undermine a substantial basis on which the WRC 2007 was negotiated, ie that it did apply to cargo. Indeed, it follows from the Netherlands' explanation of Art 1(4)(c) that "object" should be interpreted broadly to cover all cargo (and bunkers). This assumes that an "object" in subparagraph (c) is different to that in subparagraph (b), but is consistent with a more general expression closer to the original wording "anything",[408] and such an assumption is supported by the development of the French text.

If an alternative textual justification is needed, it might be possible to suggest that the word "including" in Art 1(4)(b) of the WRC 2007 should not be interpreted narrowly to refer only to a functional "part" of a ship such as equipment and machinery,[409] but more broadly in the sense of "as well as"; or "part" may be construed more widely to include cargo.

Either way, in our opinion, these *travaux* show conclusively that cargo removal[410] is covered by the WRC 2007, so as to create liabilities for the costs involved. Further, there is no reason why the WRC 2007 provisions should not also apply to cargo being removed independently of any hull removal; such cargo removal is a contemplated result of a maritime casualty within Art 1(3), and falls within Art 1(4)(c).

10.6.4 Cargo removal: liability beyond existing conventions

The conclusion, above, does have consequences that may not be immediately apparent. The wider definition of "related interest"[411] may allow for greater scope of recovery, eg where

---

408 Indeed, it might have been preferable if the word "property", used in Art 1(4)(d), had been used throughout Art 1(4). Sub-para (d) was added in LEG 85/3 at the same time as the change of wording from "anything" to "any object". The wording in (d) is clearly intended to reflect that in the Salvage Convention 1989 Art 1, and was inserted as part of the move to avoid overlaps between the conventions (see 10.9). It is submitted that there is no reason to suppose that that there is any particular reason for the decision to use "any objects" rather than "property" other than the usual difficulties of drafting in intersessional Working Groups where time is short, proposals are introduced piecemeal, English is not the first language of all, and concentration is upon the bigger issues. See generally *Gaskell, Decision Making*.
409 Although this might be the more literal or grammatical reading in English, see 10.6.1.
410 In the wide sense in Art 1(7).
411 See 8.2.3.

a cargo (such as coal, or iron ore) is not hazardous to health, but may have major harmful consequences for fishing and tourism, or marine living resources. Thus, although coal is not covered by the HNSC 2010,[412] it may be arguable that coal spilled onto the Great Barrier Reef could involve "major harmful consequences to the marine environment" within Art 1(5)(b) of the WRC 2007. Loss of a coal cargo is not fanciful. On 19 August 2013, the 77,240 gt Panamanian bulk carrier *Smart* ran aground and broke up in Richards Bay, South Africa, while carrying a cargo of 147,650 mt of coal (and around 1,900 mt of bunkers).[413] Salvors removed the fuel, without spillage, and some 10,000 mt of coal slurry, but most of the cargo was lost overboard or later removed for dumping (some of it in a state of pulp).[414] Likewise, the coal carrier *Oceanus* (with 70,000 mt of coal) grounded on a reef off the island of Satawal (Federal States of Micronesia) in 2014.[415]

The possibility that this wide definition of hazard may create removal liability in relation to coal (and other bulk solids excluded from the HNSC) was adverted to by the CMI in 1998.[416] The IUCN noted at the same time that there might be other substances not covered by the liability conventions (CLC and HNSC, and now Bunkers Convention), such as plastics and grains, and that there may be events such as wrecks smashing into coral reefs.[417] When the coal carrier *Shen Neng 1* went aground on the Great Barrier Reef in 2010, it spilled a small amount of bunkers but damaged the reef, while leaving an estimated 750 kg of toxic paint flakes (containing tributyltin). In the event there was no loss of coal cargo as the vessel was refloated[418] but, in the absence of any applicable convention (or local legislation) to deal with reef damage, a remediation claim for up to Au$125 million had to be brought in negligence.[419] That claim was settled for Au$39.5 million—in effect on the basis of the ship's LLMC limit.[420] Had there been a complete wreck of the ship, involving coal being deposited on the reef, the environmental claim would certainly have been much

---

412 Controversially it was excluded from the HNSC 1996 as not being hazardous, and no change was made in the HNSC 2010: see 2.6.4.
413 See also 10.2.5.
414 www.nepia.com/news/press-releases-area/north-pi-club-delivers-mv-smart-wreck-removal-on-budget-through-a-collaborative-approach/. Operations were expected to take up to 550 days. See eg, www.wrecksite.eu/wreck.aspx?212669.
415 See 10.2.6 and www.youtube.com/watch?v=N1YXsV6553w. In this incident, 14,000 mt of cargo was able to be offloaded by a slow grab discharge process, so that the ship was not ultimately wrecked but was eventually refloated and proceeded to port.
416 LEG 78/11, para 52.
417 LEG 78/11, para 55.
418 If coal had been lost there could have been no liability under the HNSC 2010 (even if in force) as coal is excluded: see 2.6.4.
419 See *Gaskell, Liability and Compensation Regimes: Pollution of the High Seas*, 240–241.
420 See 2.5 generally. It was assumed that this was either a property damage or infringement of rights claim (under LLMC Art 2(1)(a), or (c)) and not a wreck removal claim (under LLMC Art 2(1)(d)) for which there would have been no limitation under Australian law, given the wreck removal limitation opt-out: see 2.5.8. It seems to be at least arguable that the opt-out could have applied as a claim to remove the paint flakes could be "in respect of . . . the rendering harmless of a ship which is . . . stranded, including anything that is or has been on board such ship" (within LLMC Art 2(1)(d)). There was no direct liability of the P&I Club, which in any event disputed the need for such extensive remediation, so the State's settlement (mid-trial) was no doubt a pragmatic compromise. It also appeared that an attempt to prove multiple limitation "occurrences" was likely to fail on the evidence given: see 2.5.6(b).

higher, but it seems that the LLMC 1996 limit would not then have applied.[421] The problem though, is that there could have been no direct action against the insurer.[422]

An important distinction between liability under the HNSC 2010 and that under Art 10 of the WRC 2007 is that the former would extend to pollution damage and economic losses, while the WRC 2007 only covers location, marking and removal costs.[423]

Still, the conclusion that the WRC 2007 extends to cargo removal, even when the hull is not removed, may have far reaching consequences. The ability to recover cargo removal costs (potentially without limit)[424] means that hazardous substances other than oil could be removed under the strict liability and compulsory insurance regime of the WRC 2007 even before the HNSC 2010 comes into force. Most obviously, this could extend to the container cargo of a sunken or stranded ship (eg the *MSC Napoli* and the *Rena*).

10.7 WRC 2007 and limitation of shipowners' liability

The general concept of limitation of liability has already been discussed.[425] In the negotiations for the WRC 2007 there appear to have been no serious proposals to create stand-alone limits to mirror those in the CLC 1992 and HNSC 1996. Part of the reason was undoubtedly the existence of the LLMC Art 18 power of reservation in relation to wreck and cargo removal claims.[426] Rather, the WRC 2007 reflects in some ways the linkage solution in the Bunkers Convention 2001.[427]

The WRC 2007 Art 10(2) provides that "[n]othing in this Convention shall affect the right of the registered owner to limit liability under any applicable national or international regime, such as the [1976 Limitation Convention]". In other words, the WRC 2007 provides no limit of liability for shipowners, but instead refers the issue to national law (which may or may not allow limits for wreck and cargo removal claims), or any limitation convention to which a State may be party. It follows that States which are considering the adoption of the WRC 2007 need to ensure that their general limitation law is appropriate; ie that effect is given to the LLMC 1996 Art 18 powers of reservation, so that there is no limit for WRC 2007 liabilities.[428]

The LLMC 1996 Art 6(1)(b) limits[429] are, however, relevant in one crucial respect to the WRC 2007. They are used to calculate the maximum direct liability of the shipowner's

---

421 On the basis that this would have been an opted out claim clearly falling within LLMC Art 2(1)(e)) "in respect of the removal, destruction or rendering harmless of the cargo of the ship".

422 As Australia is not yet a party to the WRC 2007 and it only entered into force in 2015.

423 See 10.2.4 and 10.9.2(b). Note that the Environmental Liability Directive 2004 might apply in relation to environmental damage from HNS: see 2.6.5. For possible overlaps between the Directive and the WRC 2007, see 10.9.2.

424 See 10.7, 2.5.8. Under the WRC 2007, in addition to removal costs there could also be costs of locating and marking, where appropriate: see 10.5.5, 10.5.6.

425 See 2.5, especially 2.5.4(b), 2.5.4(c); see also 2.6.2(a) (CLC), 2.6.4 (HNSC) and 10.8.5 (insurer's limits).

426 See 2.5.8. Suggestions that the WRC 2007 should prevent States from using the opt-out were not accepted: see LEG 75/6/1, 14 February 1997, and *Martinez Gutierrez*, 198.

427 See 2.6.3.

428 See 2.5.8 and 11.2.3.

429 Eg in the examples shown in Tables 5 and 6 in 2.5.6(a).

insurer under the WRC 2007 Art 10.[430] The figures produced by Art 6(1)(b) can vary significantly, particularly for small to medium sized ships, and that variance should be borne in mind when considering the extent of the insurer's direct liability.

10.8 Compulsory insurance

The strength of the IMO maritime liability regimes, of which the WRC 2007 is a part, lies in a combination of the strict liability of the shipowner *and* the requirement that shipowners carry insurance (or other financial security) to cover such liability.

10.8.1 Need for compulsory insurance

There need to address liability and compulsory insurance regimes in the EEZ had become apparent over many years,[431] eg following the removal of bunker oil and nuclear waste cargo from the 1984 wreck of the *Mont Louis* which lay just outside of Belgian territorial waters. The owner of the wreck had apparently refused to pay the US$2.5 million cost of the removal on the basis that no existing international regulations required it to do so.[432] A central consideration for those States that initially proposed a wreck removal convention was not only the desire to be able to remove a wreck which posed a hazard, but also to ensure that there were financial resources to do so.[433]

Wreck removal can be exceptionally expensive, as recent disasters have shown. The International Group review of major claims showed that the 20 most expensive wreck removals in the decade to 2012 amounted to some US$2.5 billion, and were increasing.[434] The removal of the wreck of the *MSC Napoli*[435] cost approximately US$135 million; the removal of the cargo and wreck of the *New Flame*[436] cost approximately US$177 million; and removing the cargo and hull of the *Rena*[437] cost about US$650 million. These costs, however, are dwarfed by those relating to the *Costa Concordia*, which are estimated to total in excess of US$1.5 billion.[438]

Most P&I Clubs have long had specific cover for wreck removal, where that removal is compulsory by law.[439] In the case of the four wrecks above, the ships were entered with P&I Club members of the International Group.[440] In negotiations for the WRC 2007, the

---

430 See 10.8.5.

431 See 7.1.

432 See 7.1, 10.9.3 and *Gaskell, Mont Louis Part One*, 149; cf N Gaskell, 'Lessons of the Mont Louis Part Two: Prevention of Hybrid Accidents' (1986) 1 IJECL 269. The requirement of a legal obligation is also consistent with Club practice even where the WRC 2007 does not apply: see 2.9.6(d).

433 See also *Griggs, Wreck Removal Draft Convention*, 382.

434 See 1.4 and *Herbert, Challenges*, 21.

435 See 1.2.3.

436 See 10.2.5.

437 See 1.2.4.

438 Including passenger and other claims: see 1.2.5(c).

439 See 2.9.6(d).

440 Market insurers may also be involved in wreck cases. Thus, in 2013 the 86,692 gt Bahamian-flagged containership *MOL Comfort* split in two (like the *MSC Napoli*), but was apparently insured by a pool of Japanese insurance companies: see www.lloydslist.com/ll/topic/mol-comfort/.

International Group initially denied any real need for compulsory insurance.[441] Despite this assertion, in an age of single ship companies with no other assets, States, especially developing States, have traditionally had major resource problems in removing wrecks without the full backing of insurers.[442]

Two specific examples were raised during the negotiations. In 2000, the Netherlands claimed it was unable to recover the €9.6 million costs of removing the wreck of the *Iugo*, where the single ship shipowning company "evaporated" and the P&I insurer, not a member of the International Group, invoked the 'pay to be paid' clause.[443] In 2003, the International Group insurer of the single ship shipowning company of the *Assi Eurolink* threatened to invoke the 'pay to be paid' clause unless the government dropped part of its claims.[444] The clause is relevant in order to understand what the WRC 2007 aims to achieve, but also to assess the position of States who choose *not* to adopt the WRC 2007, or not to apply it in territorial waters.

10.8.2 Introduction to WRC 2007 Art 12

Article 12 of the WRC 2007 makes it compulsory for the registered owner to have insurance[445] or other financial security[446] in a similar manner to other IMO liability conventions, including the CLC 1992, the HNSC 2010, the Bunkers Convention 2001 and the Athens Convention 2002. Moreover, like these conventions, there can be direct action against the insurer.[447]

10.8.2(a) 300 gt threshold
The registered owner of a ship of "300 gross tonnage and above"[448] is required to maintain insurance or other financial security to cover liability under the WRC 2007,[449] but not exceeding an amount calculated in accordance with Art 6(1)(b) of the LLMC 1996 (as

---

441 In the context of the reliability of insurers and direct action, the International Group stated in 2001 that "so far as we are aware, there has been no case where a Club in the International Group has failed to respond in respect of liability for wreck removal, where that liability has been established under domestic law": LEG 83/5, 12 September 2001.

442 See 7.1. See also the *Sewol* wreck in 2014, where it appears that the wreck removal insurance was not enough to cover the costs (and there may also have been policy defences), although Korean direct action provisions may have assisted claimants generally: see I Kim, "Sewol Accident and its Legal Implication" (paper delivered at University of Hong Kong, 22 January 2015) [*Kim, Sewol Accident*] 11–13; also 13.2.3, 13.2.2.

443 LEG 86/4/2, 28 March 2003, 4 and 2.9.6(c). See also the MV *Tycoon* wreck in Australia in 2012: 13.3.1.

444 LEG 86/4/2, 4. The International Group disputed this specific criticism in LEG 86/15, 2 May 2003, para 22. See also 2.5.9(e), 9.2.5(b),11.2.2.

445 For the general insurance position of others involved in the casualty, eg charterers, colliding ships, see 2.9.

446 Such as a guarantee from a bank or similar institution. It is not known how far such bodies provide financial security under the IMO liability conventions, but it is assumed to be rare and that WRC 2007 certificates are overwhelming backed by insurers (particularly P&I Clubs).

447 See 10.8.4.

448 The WRC 2007 does not separately define tonnage, but it should be assumed that this applies to the gt measured under the Tonnage Convention 1969: see 2.5.6(a). States ought to define this in their enacting legislation: see eg the MSA 1995 s 255J(6), 11.3.3(e).

449 In some circumstances the WRC 2007 insurance cover may be greater than that under existing Club policies. Some Club Rules do not specifically mention the costs of "locating" a wreck, although they do cover "marking": see eg the Standard Club's P&I Rules 2018/19 r 3.11, 2.9.6(d).

amended).⁴⁵⁰ Even where the Affected State has entered a reservation (ie opt-out) under Art 18 of the LLMC, allowing it not to apply the LLMC to wreck and cargo removal,⁴⁵¹ this does not affect the shipowner's obligation *under the WRC 2007* to maintain insurance only up to the LLMC 1996 levels. So, while a shipowner may be liable for the full costs of the wreck removal, the insurance cover might be insufficient to cover this,⁴⁵² leaving the shortfall payable directly by the shipowner. Should the shipowner be unable to pay this shortfall, the Affected State may have to bear that financial burden.⁴⁵³

The 300 gt threshold also poses problems for States, as many ships (eg fishing vessels) will be below this level. In these circumstances, while there might be a liability of the shipowner⁴⁵⁴ there would be no insurance cover to protect the State. What happens if a ship under 300 gt actually *does* have liability insurance for wreck removal costs? This would obviously not attract the compulsory certificate provisions within and related to Art 12(1), but the first sentence of Art 12(10) creates a right of direct action for "costs arising under this Convention" against the insurer "providing financial security for the registered owner's liability". There is no mention of the certificate here, or the 300 gt threshold. A literal interpretation would mean that an insurer that *did* "cover liability under this Convention" (Art 12(1)) might be directly liable to the Affected State. It seems unlikely that an insurer would indeed provide cover not simply for "wreck removal" but also expressly for "liabilities under the WRC 2007",⁴⁵⁵ although it is not impossible. The better view is probably to regard Art 12 as an integrated whole, so that Art 12(10) can only have been referring to insurance consequences "under this Convention", thereby excluding insurance cover that was under the 300 gt threshold for which no Convention certificate was issued. This would mean that an Affected State would have to rely on its own general direct action insurance legislation, if any.

10.8.2(b) Ships without a tonnage measurement
It is possible that a craft falling into the wide definition of ship in Art 1(2)⁴⁵⁶ may not be capable of having a gross tonnage in order for Art 12(1) to apply. This may well be only a theoretical problem and, in any event, is a matter within the expertise of ship surveyors, naval architects and the classification societies. The WRC 2007 does not itself define gross tonnage but, by incorporating the reference to Art 6(1)(b) of the LLMC 1976 (as amended) it will thereby attract the application of LLMC Art 6(5). Art 6(5) provides a definition of gross tonnage for LLMC Art 6 calculations by using the tonnage measure system of the International Convention on Tonnage Measurement of Ships 1969—in respect of which tonnage certificates are issued.

It should be noted that gross tonnage is a measurement of volume, not weight. It is conceivable that some platforms (or possibly seagoing rafts) that fall within Art 1(2) of

---

450 WRC 2007 Art 12(1): see further 10.8.5.
451 See 2.5.8.
452 Bearing in mind the increasing costs of wreck removal by reference to the limits illustrated by Tables 2.5 and 2.6: see 2.5.6(a).
453 Subject to such stratagems as attempted in the *Prestige* litigation: see 1.2.2(a). 2.9.6(b), 10.8.5(g).
454 There is no tonnage threshold for *liability*, but the ship must be" seagoing": see 10.2.7.
455 In the terms of the Annex to the WRC 2007 as required by Art 12(2).
456 See 8.2.1(b), 10.2.7.

the WRC 2007 cannot be measured under the 1969 tonnage measurement system. It would seem that under Art 2(1) of the WRC 2007 such craft might be ships (within Art 1(2)) but would not be of "300 gross tonnage *and above*"; they would either have a very low gross tonnage or none at all. On that basis they would not need to have compulsory insurance. This could be a serious issue if there were very large platforms that did not have a tonnage as they could obviously present navigational hazards if wrecked. When problems occurred with the LLMC 1976 and ships that had not been measured under the then relatively new Tonnage Convention 1969, provisions were made in English law for such older ships to be remeasured for the purposes of the 1969 Convention using the "best evidence available"—in effect an estimate.[457] The combined WRC 2007/LLMC/Tonnage Convention 1969 provisions do not require that a ship actually has a tonnage certificate. Article 6(5) of the LLMC simply refers to the calculation of gross tonnage according to the rules in Annex I of the Tonnage Convention 1969. It does not seem possible, though, to attempt a calculation after the ship has become wrecked as it would be too late for a shipowner to obtain an insurance certificate under WRC 2007 Art 12(1).

10.8.3 WRC 2007 compulsory insurance certificates

The WRC 2007 provides for the issuance of a certificate attesting that insurance or other financial security is in force. The detailed requirements for the contents of that compulsory insurance certificate are set out in Art 12(2), largely modelled on the CLC 1992 Art VII(2),[458] and a certificate example is set out in an Annex to the WRC 2007.[459] A State party is not to permit any ship entitled to fly its flag to operate at any time unless a certificate has been issued or certified by the appropriate authority of that State.[460] At the same time, "each State Party shall ensure, under its national law, that insurance or other security . . . is in force in respect of any ship of 300 gross tonnage and above, wherever registered, entering or leaving a port in its territory, or arriving at or leaving an offshore facility in its territorial sea".[461] This is the provision which gives some protection to a coastal State through port state control measures, but there seems to be no power to require the ship of a non-State party to carry insurance if it is merely exercising rights of innocent passage.[462]

---

457 See the Merchant Shipping (Liability of Shipowners and Others)(Calculation of Tonnage) Order 1986 (SI 1986/1040) reg 2, and *Gaskell, The Amount of Limitation*, 45–49.

458 Eg WRC 2007 Art 12(2)(f), requiring the name and principal place of business of the insurer and "where appropriate" the place of business where the insurance was established (ie issued). It would be "appropriate" where the insurance was issued in a branch office or agent's office which was different from the insurer's seat: see *Berlingieri Vol III*, 147. Art 12(2) requires some useful extra information by comparison with the CLC, such as the duration of the insurance cover and the IMO ship identification number.

459 LEG/CONF.16/19, 23 May 2007. Art 12(7) requires the flag State issuing the certificate to "have regard" to guidelines adopted by the IMO on the financial responsibility of registered owners: see IMO Assembly Resolution A21/Res.898 and IMO Circular Letter No 3464 (2 July 2014), LEG 101/11/2, 14 March 2014. The WRC 2007 diplomatic conference also adopted a Resolution inviting the IMO's Legal Committee to develop a model for a single insurance certificate which may be issued by States parties in respect of each and every ship under the relevant IMO liability and compensation conventions, including the WRC 2007: LEG/CONF.16/20, 23 May 2007.

460 WRC 2007 Art 12(11) and 12(2).

461 WRC 2007 Art 12(12).

462 See 7.3, 7.4.3.

The WRC 2007 improves on the CLC model by dealing with the practical difficulty for a coastal State in knowing if a wrecked ship which had been transiting the EEZ has any insurance.[463] Once the Affected State has determined that a wreck constitutes a hazard, it should inform the registered owner, thereby setting in motion the steps that may be taken for the removal of the hazard. At this point, the registered owner or other interested party must "provide the competent authority of the Affected State with evidence of insurance or other financial security".[464]

The flag State need not issue the certificate itself, and may authorise any institution or organisation recognised by it to issue the certificate[465] on the basis that it "shall fully guarantee the completeness and accuracy of the certificate so issued and shall undertake to ensure the necessary arrangements to satisfy this obligation".[466] An exception exists in cases where a ship is flagged by a non-State party to this Convention. In order to ensure that a ship flying the flag of a non-State party can, for example, enter a State party's port, it may provide an insurance certificate issued by any State party. This facilitates trade and access to ports of a State party by vessels flagged in non-State parties. This certificate will not, however, be backed by the flag State's guarantee as to its completeness and accuracy. Nevertheless, "certificates issued and certified under the authority of a State Party shall be accepted by other States Parties for the purposes of this Convention and shall be regarded by other States Parties as having the same force as certificates issued or certified by them, even if issued or certified in respect of a ship not registered in a State Party".[467]

Given that a certificate issued by a State party to a ship flagged in a non-State party might not then be backed by the flag State's guarantee, the WRC 2007 provides a safeguard of sorts in explicitly allowing a State party to request, at any time, "consultation with the issuing or certifying State should it believe that the insurer or guarantor named in the certificate is not financially capable of meeting the obligations imposed by this Convention".[468] The WRC 2007 sets out a range of conditions for the certificate, relating to issues such as ensuring that the certificate is not invalidated,[469] that it is carried on board each ship,[470] and

---

463 There may be particular risks with ships which are being towed to another State for scrapping, where the departure State is not a party to the WRC 2007. In 2013, the *Emsstrom* sank off the coast of the UK whilst under tow to a breaker's yard in Turkey: see www.wrecksite.eu/wreck.aspx?190866. Three months after the sinking, UK authorities still could not make any contact with the owners of the vessel. The vessel was probably not insured; see S Tatham, "Game-Changing" Aspect to Wreck Removal", *Tugadvise*, www.tugadvise.com/resources/articles/game-changing-aspect-to-wreck-removal/. See also W Greenwood, " 'Questions Remain' over Sinking of Ship in Tor Bay", *Western Morning News* (15 April 2014).

464 WRC 2007 Art 9(3).

465 WRC 2007 Art 12(3)(a). Further, Art 12(3)(b) provides that where a State has authorised an institution or organisation to issue the certificate, it must notify the Secretary-General of: "(i) the specific responsibilities and conditions of the authority delegated to an institution or organization recognized by it; (ii) the withdrawal of such authority; and (iii) the date from which such authority or withdrawal of such authority takes effect".

466 WRC 2007 Art 12(3)(a).

467 WRC 2007 Art 12(9). See also 11.3.3(e).

468 WRC 2007 Art 12(9).

469 WRC 2007 Art 12(6).

470 WRC 2007 Art 12(5). That is unless the State party which issues the certificate has notified the Secretary-General that it maintains records in an electronic format, accessible to all States parties, attesting the existence of the certificate and enabling States parties to discharge their obligations under the Convention, Art 12(13).

that it is recognised by all States parties.[471] As with the Bunkers Convention, there were potentially significant administrative burdens on the early ratifiers of the WRC 2007 as they may have been pressed to issue certificates for ships of non-State parties. Difficulties have arisen about whether certificates for ships registered in a bareboat registry should come from the registry State or the flag State (or both) and these have had to be addressed by IMO Resolution.[472]

10.8.4 Direct action and insurer defences

The key insurance provision in Art 12 is Art 12(10);[473] it provides that any claim for costs arising under the WRC 2007 may be brought directly against the insurer or other person providing financial security for the registered owner's liability.

10.8.4(a) Nature of direct liability

The concept of the insurer's direct liability is so well known from the CLC[474] and its progeny that it is taken for granted. But its precise nature still needs to be understood. The insurer will normally provide insurance cover to the shipowner for a variety of risks, and these can include risks under the IMO liability conventions[475] The insurer typically issues the owner with a so-called "blue card" that confirms that the insurer is covering risks under the particular convention, here the WRC 2007.[476] The insurer voluntarily consents for the registered shipowner then to apply to a Contracting State to issue a certificate under Art 12(2) that identifies the insurer as the person providing the security. A direct action claim under Art 12(10) is not strictly a claim *under* the policy of insurance (or member's entry in a Club). Nor is it strictly a claim *under* the WRC 2007 certificate issued by the State. The certificate is an international attestation that the issuing State has satisfied itself that financial security exists and therefore becomes a passport to enable the shipowner to visit Contracting States.

However, the issuing of the certificate also acts as a trigger to enable the Art 12(10) direct action claim. That claim is one under the convention itself or, more particularly, under the law of the Affected State giving effect to the WRC 2007. By voluntarily agreeing to provide the financial security, the insurer brings itself under the liability rules of Art 12(10). As the opening words of that provision make clear, "[a]ny claim for costs arising under this Convention may be brought directly against the insurer". Although the WRC 2007 facilitates a claim by an Affected State that relates to the underlying policy, it creates a *sui generis* liability according to the terms of the Convention itself. Thus, the policy

---

471 WRC 2007 Art 12(9).
472 Resolution A.1057(27), adopted on 30 November 2011, based on discussions in the Legal Committee: LEG 98/13/2, 18 February 2011.
473 Itself largely boilerplate text as used in other IMO liability conventions, eg in the CLC Art VII(8).
474 See *De La Rue & Anderson*, 127.
475 See 2.9.6(b) and (d).
476 See the Amended Guidelines for Underwriters on Issuing Blue Cards (10 October 2014) issued by Clubs to members as a circular, eg Steamship Mutual Circular of November 2014 dealing with entry into force of the WRC 2007; also *De La Rue & Anderson*, 126; and 10.3.1(b).

provisions are only relevant in so far as allowed by Art 12(10).[477] In fact, Art 12(10) makes no reference to contractual policy provisions at all, but merely refers to the "defences" that might be available to the registered owner or insurer itself.

An immediate question of interpretation arises as to the meaning of "costs arising under this Convention" and in particular as to the vexed question as to how far the WRC 2007 can apply to ships registered in non-State parties.[478] If the proper interpretation of the convention in international law is that it cannot apply to create liabilities in the EEZ in respect of a ship registered in a non-State party,[479] then an insurer might be able to say that there can also be no direct liability "under the Convention".

Even here a contrary argument may be maintained, based on the interpretation of Art 12(12) which specifically requires that ships "wherever registered" that enter or leave the ports of States parties should have insurance "to the extent required by [Art 12(1)]". What is the point of this insurance if it is not available to respond to the very incident which the insurer has declared to the Issuing State that its insurance will cover and which is relied on by other States parties in relation to that ship?[480] The reference to "to the extent" means that the reference back to Art 12(1) only relates to the calculation of the level of financial security and not to its reference to a ship flying the flag of a State party; indeed, given that Art 12(12) expressly applies to ships wherever registered, there would otherwise be a contradiction. The express mention in Art 12(1) of a ship flying the flag of a State party is directly related to the obligations of a State party itself; ie it must ensure that its own ships have the insurance. It says nothing about the situation where ships of non-State parties *voluntarily* agree to take out insurance to cover costs claimed under the WRC 2007. This voluntary action could be considered as a waiver of any defence by the shipowner itself that the WRC 2007 could not apply to it as the ship was not registered in a State party. Even if this is wrong, it is still arguable that the only way to give any sense to Art 12(12) is that it is a recognition that an insurer that voluntarily agrees to offer WRC 2007 cover does so irrespective of the flag of the ship. This is what is relied upon by States parties that allow ships to enter or leave their ports on the basis of the WRC 2007 certificate.[481] It then follows that, provided all the other triggers to liability apply,[482] the insurer of a such a ship would be directly liable to the Affected State, subject to the other provisions of Art 12(10).[483]

---

477 This means that it is largely irrelevant if the specific policy cover, eg under P&I Club Rules, is actually less extensive than the WRC 2007 liability as the insurer will be liable under the WRC 2007 for the full liabilities under the convention itself: see 2.6.5(d).

478 See 7.4, 10.2.7(b).

479 See eg 7.4.3–7.4.6.

480 One reason for the equivalent CLC provision was the fear that ships of Contracting States would otherwise be at a competitive disadvantage (eg by comparison with uninsured ships): see eg the comments of the German and Dutch delegations, *Official Records 1969*, 505 (LEG/CONF/4/Add.1, 17 October 1969), 702 (LEG/CONF/C.2SR.14, 21 November 1969). An early commentator on the CLC noted that a degree of uncertainty about the meaning of the insurance provisions may have arisen because of their late acceptance at the 1969 diplomatic conference when there may have been insufficient time to consider them properly: see *Abecassis, 1st edition*, 206–207. Ironically, later conventions developed by the IMO Legal Committee have not made significant alterations to these provisions as negotiators have been reluctant to tinker with a formula that has apparently worked and, in practice, ships trading internationally (wherever registered) will need certificates.

481 Non-State parties could not, of course, rely on the certificate.

482 See 10.5.

483 See 10.8.4(b).

The resolution of this crucial question about the application of the WRC 2007 may also depend upon how the convention has been enacted in the national law of the Affected State. It may have created liability of the registered shipowner in its territorial waters and, by accident or design, applied the same provisions in its EEZ. It may similarly have given effect to the direct liability trigger without reference to the flag of the ship concerned. It may also have dealt with the question of whether such a State party can rely on the certificate where it exists as a trigger to direct action, even when the ship is wrecked while transiting the EEZ without having had to produce the certificate at the ports of an Affected State. As a matter of principle, it is the existence of the certificate for a particular ship that will trigger the insurer's direct liability, not the fact that it has ever been produced.[484]

10.8.4(b) Insurer defences

The insurer can invoke defences available to the registered shipowner under the Convention,[485] including:

- The CLC type defences in Art 10(1)[486] for war, third party damage,[487] or government failures in respect of navigational aids.
- Claims brought outside the Convention, eg in national tort law.[488]
- The exceptions to liability in Art 11, relating to claims under other conventions.[489]
- Limitation of the registered owner's liability under any applicable national or international regime.[490]
- Defences on the basis that the convention is not applicable, eg that there is no maritime casualty, wreck, or hazard within Art 1.[491]

The insurer can also invoke the following defences of its own:

- A cap on its own Art 12(10) liability under the WRC 2007 according to the amount specified in Art 12(1).[492]
- The "wilful misconduct" of the registered owner.[493]

---

484 See the UK enactment in the MSA 1995 s 255P(1)(b) that refers only to the existence of wreck removal insurance.

485 See also E Machum and F Metcalf, "Will Insurance Cover That? A Review of the Challenges Faced by Coastal States Seeking to Recoup Costs for the Removal of Wrecks under the Nairobi Wreck Removal Convention", in Chircop et al (eds), *The Regulation of International Shipping: International and Comparative Perspectives* [*Machum & Metcalf, Will Insurance Cover That?*], 227, 238–247.

486 See 10.3, noting their very restrictive application.

487 See 10.3.1(b) for terrorism and the position of the Clubs.

488 See Art 10(3).

489 See 10.9.

490 See Art 12(10). See eg the LLMC which, under Art 1(6), provides that an "insurer of liability for claims subject to limitation in accordance with the rules of this Convention [ie the LLMC] shall be entitled to the benefits of this Convention [ie the LLMC] to the same extent as the assured himself". But note the wreck removal opt-out available to States under LLMC Art 18(1) reservation procedure: see 2.5.8. Thus, if the shipowner cannot limit "himself", neither can the insurer (under the *LLMC*): but see also 10.8.5(d).

491 See eg 10.5.1.

492 The nature of this 'cap' is explained in 10.8.5(a), and it operation in 10.8.5(d)–(f).

493 See 10.8.4(g)–(h).

In considering "wilful misconduct", it is necessary to decide first, what the expression means when it is used in Art 12(10); and secondly, what meaning will be given to it in an English court applying the WRC 2007.

10.8.4(c) Wilful misconduct as used in Art 12(10)

Article 12(10) states that the insurer "may" invoke "the" (not "a") defence of wilful misconduct. This seems to suggest that the defence is to be found elsewhere, eg in national insurance law (such as the MIA 1906 s 55(2)(a)) or expressly as a term in the policy of insurance. It is possible that the national law of a contracting State (or the governing law of the policy) has no explicit wilful misconduct defence, although many States may refer to the MIA s 55(2)(a) as an influential source to fill any gap. It is also possible that the policy (eg of a local fixed premium liability insurer or in Club rules) has no equivalent express wilful misconduct provision.

Where there is no national law or express policy term, it might be relevant to enquire whether Art 12(10) itself creates a free-standing defence of wilful misconduct. The reference to "may invoke" could mean that this is an option open to the insurer *if* it has such a defence in its policy, or if national law allows one. Alternatively, "may invoke the defence" could mean that the WRC 2007 provides a free-standing defence of its own, although that may not be the obvious meaning of the language. The reference in Art 12(10) is boilerplate text, derived from the CLC 1969, that was part of a general policy of preventing or restricting insurers from relying on existing policy defences. Whether Art 12(10) creates a free-standing defence or not, the question arises as to what are the parameters of "wilful misconduct" in the Convention.

If the insurer is allowed to rely on the defence of "wilful misconduct" as defined by the policy, there could be real problems for a WRC 2007 claimant. The insurance policy (or P&I Club's rules) may give a very wide meaning to the expression, or give the power to a Club's board to decide if there has been such misconduct.[494] It would surely be contrary to the WRC 2007 to give the final say on the meaning of the expression to a Club's board and to have any dispute about that decision made subject to the Club's arbitration clause. There must be some limit on the extent of a "wilful misconduct defence" under the WRC 2007. An English court should refer to the MIA definition of "wilful misconduct" as that is applicable by default in English law as a matter of public policy,[495] but should not refer to policy conditions that restrict it, eg by taking away from the courts the final decision on the meaning of the expression. Courts in other States parties might also apply minimum standards for the defence.[496]

10.8.4(d) Wilful misconduct in English law

The expression "wilful misconduct" has a long history in English marine insurance.[497] There are two elements if the insurer is to establish the wilful misconduct defence: first,

---

494 See eg the Standard Club's *P&I Rules 2018/19* r 6.19, and 2.9.6.(b) (fn 1445).
495 See *Arnould*, 1107.
496 And, if appropriate, as influenced by the seminal MIA definition in s 55(2)(a) – perhaps even as interpreted by the English courts: see 10.8.4(h).
497 See eg *Arnould*, 1107–1115; *De la Rue & Anderson*, 127, 742–743; also 2.9.2(a), 2.9.2(c), 2.9.3(d), 2.9.6(a)–(b).

what is the level or type of "misconduct" required; secondly, which individual person must be guilty of that misconduct?

For the first element, it is clear that there must be deliberate or reckless conduct causing the casualty, not mere negligence, and the most obvious example is deliberate scuttling.

It is the second element that can give rise to most difficulty. The misconduct must be committed by the insured. Under the WRC 2007, this is the registered owner. Although that person might possibly be an individual (eg with a fishing vessel), it is almost invariably the case that the ship is owned by a company. In that case, it is necessary to identify wilful misconduct by one or more persons who are equivalent to the owner, and it is not usually enough to point to the wilful misconduct of a crew member such as the master[498] (except eg in the case of owner-masters). There has been much English case law on whose actions, in a corporate structure, are taken to be those of a company: sometimes called a rule of attribution. Much of that case law is in relation to the similar issue of whose misconduct can deprive the shipowner of the right to limit liability under the limitation of liability conventions.[499] In essence, it is necessary to find misconduct of someone who is the directing mind and will of a company, or who (at board level) is taking the type of corporate decisions that would be taken by an individual owner. Even more difficult is the type of case where those at the senior level delegate their functions to those further down the chain. It is clear that where a single ship company delegates key operational functions to a firm of ship managers, a court will look for misconduct in the management company, especially as the only employee of the registered owner might be an accountant in a flag of convenience State.

The need to point to someone high up in the corporate hierarchy is familiar to English maritime lawyers, but care needs to be taken when dealing with other legal systems. The English insistence on attributing misconduct to higher levels of management is not one that may be immediately obvious in other systems, especially those with little maritime law heritage, where it may be easier to argue that wilful misconduct of the master or a crew member is to be attributed to the registered owner under ordinary principles of vicarious liability.[500]

However, there is also an underlying issue of policy that may influence a decision: courts have often been willing to 'break' limitation where shipowners are in effect trying to avoid the full extent of their liabilities; in the present context, insurers are trying to prove wilful misconduct as a means to avoid direct action liability, so a national court may be less willing to find that misconduct lower down the corporate ladder is sufficient to constitute "wilful misconduct *of* the registered owner". An attempt to break limitation by proving intent or recklessness of the shipowner is therefore a dangerous tactic, as the same level of misconduct could enable the insurer to avoid the policy and direct action liability.

---

498 Eg "barratry": see 2.1.5(a). This means that the shipowner may be liable for the acts of the crew member, but that the insurance cover would not be lost. In the context of the WRC 2007 and direct action, there might be strict liability of the shipowner if the wreck was caused by some malicious act by a crew member; there might be no defence of the shipowner under Art 10(1)(b) (see 10.3.1(b); and the insurer could not have a defence to any direct action claim.

499 See 2.5.7.

500 Cf 10.3.1(b) where it is submitted that barratrous acts of the crew do not fall within the Art 10(1)(b) exception to liability; also 11.3.4(a) for the position under the MSA 1995 s 255G.

In ordinary casualties caused by navigational error the defence of wilful misconduct is rarely relevant, because of the difficulty of proving deliberate or reckless conduct at the requisite corporate (rather than shipboard) level. Insurers will always *consider* the possible defence, eg where there are obvious issues of unseaworthiness that might raise suspicions of deliberate scuttling.[501] In a wreck case, the question of scuttling will be of significance both to the H&M insurer and the liability insurer, particularly where there is an old ship, with a low value, or where the owner is in financial trouble. Scrapping voyages may raise such concerns, as the owner may have little incentive to keep the ship seaworthy. Still, mere negligence in the planning or preparation would not be wilful misconduct. Thus, when two Maersk supply ships, under tow to a scrapyard, sank as a result of bad weather (compounded perhaps by poor planning in the towing make up)[502] it is highly unlikely that any case of wilful misconduct could have been run by an insurer. With less reputable owners, suspicions might have been greater.

There may also be difficulties of interpretation where the wilful misconduct is that of a bareboat charterer, rather than the registered owner. If the registered owner is strictly liable for a deliberate scuttling by the charterer,[503] there will not be wilful misconduct of the assured under the certificate required under Art 12 (although there will almost certainly be P&I cover for the charterer in respect of the vessel).[504] On that basis, the insurer would not be able to resist a direct action claim against it for the strict liability of the shipowner.[505]

10.8.4(e) Prohibition of other insurer defences

The most significant provision in Art 12(10) is its prohibition of other insurer defences, whether under general law (eg insurance or commercial law) or the policy (including the P&I Club entry).[506] The second sentence of Art 12(10) expressly prevents the insurer from relying on the bankruptcy or winding up of the registered shipowner, but the penultimate sentence is phrased more widely: "the defendant shall not invoke any other defence[507] which the defendant might have been entitled to invoke in proceedings brought by the registered owner against the defendant".[508] The main intention of these provisions is to avoid the problem for claimants of the insolvent (often single ship) company.

In particular, the restriction on "any other defence" available to the insurer is a mechanism to ensure that P&I Clubs cannot rely on the 'pay to be paid' clause[509] for the WRC

---

501 See also 2.9.5(a).
502 See 14.3.
503 See 10.3.1(b).
504 See 2.9.6(b).
505 Cf 2.9.2(d).
506 For general description of P&I Club policy cover and defences, see 2.9.5.
507 "Other" than the wilful misconduct defence: see 10.8.4(c) and (d).
508 Article 12(10) uses the "defendant" to refer to "the insurer or other person providing financial security for the registered owner's liability". The alternative financial security, such as a bank guarantee, is referred to in Art 12(1) and is based on the original formula in the CLC 1969. At the time it was not clear whether the alternative might be used, for instance, by States which (for economic reasons) preferred their own shipowners not to use foreign insurers, but to rely on some national solution (for State owned and operated commercial ships see Art 12(14)). It is not known how far, if at all, such alternatives are used in practice to satisfy the requirements of the IMO direct action conventions, but it is assumed that virtually all 'blue cards' are issued by traditional liability insurers (eg P&I Clubs or fixed premium insurers).
509 See 2.9.6(c).

2007 claims brought directly against them.[510] The Clubs have, however, been clear that "policy defences and exclusions will continue to apply in the usual way in respect of liabilities arising otherwise than under Certificates".[511]

Further, the liability cap[512] provided by Art 12(10) to the insurer will mean that the wreck removal exposure of insurers could be much less than under the CLC 1992 or HNSC 2010;[513] it may also be lower than their exposure under recent casualties to which the WRC 2007 did not apply, such as the *Rena* and *Costa Concordia*.[514]

10.8.5 Relationship of WRC 2007 insurance liability cap and LLMC limitation

The potential limits on recovery from an insurer under the WRC 2007 need some further examination, as the liability and limitation structures under the CLC and HNSC systems are different to that in the WRC 2007.[515] The CLC and HNSC have comparatively straightforward stand-alone liability *and limitation* systems. They specifically provide that an insurer that is sued directly may take the benefit of these stand-alone limits, even if the shipowner itself could not.[516] Further, both expressly provide that the insurance sums provided by the insurer "shall be available exclusively for the satisfaction of claims" under the convention.[517] This means that other claimants after a major wreck, eg cargo owners or commercial suppliers to an insolvent shipowner, could not try to obtain an injunction to freeze these proceeds in order to satisfy their claims.

The WRC 2007, like the Bunkers Convention 2001, has a problematic link to other national or international limitation of liability regimes, including the LLMC 1996.[518] Unlike the Bunkers Convention 2001, where most pollution claims against the owner might be limitable under the LLMC 1996,[519] limitation for the primary liability of the owner under the WRC 2007 (ie wreck removal) may be expressly subject to the LLMC opt-out.[520] It is therefore necessary to discuss the nature of the insurer's liability cap under the WRC 2007 Art 12 and its relationship to any traditional limitation of liability by the insurer. In this discussion it must be borne in mind that the discussion of the WRC 2007 itself is complicated because States may apply widely differing limitation provisions to sit alongside it; this is particularly the case with the enactment of the WRC 2007 in the UK.[521]

---

510 This is but one example of policy defences that would be unavailable; others would include breaches of express policy warranties, or unseaworthiness unless that involved wilful misconduct of the assured: cf *The Star Sea* [2001] 1 Lloyd's Rep 389.

511 Eg Gard Circular 8/14, November 2014. For example, the 'pay to be paid' clause might be applied to a cargo claim against the shipowner arising from the shipwreck, or to wreck removal claims in States which are not party to the WRC 2007.

512 See 10.8.5(a), (d), (e), (f).

513 See Table 2.5 (LLMC 1996), 2.5.6(a). Cf Table 2.7 (CLC), 2.6.2(a); Table 2.10 (HNSC 2010), 2.6.4.

514 See 1.2.4, 1.2.5, 10.8.1, 10.8.6.

515 See also, *Martinez Gutierrez*, Chapter 6.

516 See the CLC 1992 Art VII(8), HNSC 2010 Art 12(8).

517 See the CLC 1992 Art VII(9), HNSC 2010 Art 12(9).

518 See 10.7.

519 See the MSA 1995 s 168 in the UK, and 2.4.4(b): also *Gaskell, Bunkers Limitation*.

520 See 2.5.8.

521 See 11.3 generally, and 11.3.4(b) in particular.

10.8.5(a) Nature of the insurer's liability cap

In considering the potential limits on recovery from an insurer two separate limits should be noted. First, there is the individual limit of liability of a shipowner, eg under the LLMC 1996. This will often not be available in wreck removal cases, owing to the LLMC opt-out.[522] Where the WRC 2007 applies, the shipowner may well therefore have a liability that is unlimited.

Secondly, if the compulsory insurer is sued directly under Art 12(10) of the WRC 2007, its liability is capped by Art 12(10) at the applicable LLMC 1996 limit as set out in the WRC 2007 Art 12(1). This was thought necessary to avoid potentially unlimited liability of the insurer under the certificate.[523] The cap is provided by Art 12(10) itself, but although the provision phrases this as allowing the insurer to "limit liability" this can be misleading. Article 12(10) provides that the insurer can take advantage of the registered shipowner's limits under ordinary limitation law; that issue will depend upon applying rules (external to the WRC 2007) about traditional limitation of liability.

10.8.5(b) Shipowner and insurer limiting for wreck removal

The first scenario is where the limitation law of an Affected State allows the shipowner to limit, eg under a national law or a national application of a convention such as the LLMC 1976 or 1996; *and*, in relation to the LLMC, the Affected State has *not* chosen to use Art 18 of LLMC 1976 or LLMC 1996 to opt out of limitation for wreck removal.[524] Thus, any wreck removal claim against the *shipowner* would seem to be subject to the normal LLMC 1976/1996 Art 6(1)(b) limits in States parties to those conventions.[525] On the basis that the shipowner can limit liability, Art 12(10) makes it clear that the insurer "may invoke" this defence, eg by establishing a limitation fund. That is, the WRC 2007 Art 12(10) allows the defence; the WRC 2007 *itself* cannot declare that an insurer has the right to limit under a particular national or international regime.[526] It seems to be merely permissive, ie by providing that it would not be a breach of a State's obligations under the WRC 2007 Art 12 for it to allow an insurer to invoke limitation under another regime. This would have the effect that the limited amount may have to be shared pro rata with other claimants, eg those having collision or cargo damage claims. As there is no separate portion of an LLMC limitation amount reserved for wreck removal (unlike for injury or death claimants)[527] then all 'property' claims would share and be pro-rated.[528]

---

522 See 2.4.8.

523 See eg LEG 74/5/3, 13 September 1996, 4.

524 See 2.5.8. This appeared to have been the case with the *Rena* (at least as a matter of treaty law, as New Zealand had not made the appropriate reservation with the IMO): see 1.2.4(d). Likewise, with the *Sea Diamond* as Greece had not exercised the opt-out: see 10.2.5.

525 See 2.5.4(c).

526 Although national law implementing the WRC 2007 could presumably achieve this in relation to national limitation rules, it could not extend any international convention to which that State was a party. While the LLMC 1976 and 1996 Art 1(6) both provide that an insurer of liability is also entitled to limit, this provision did not appear expressly in earlier limitation conventions—which was presumably why it was included in the LLMC, ie to take account of direct liability legislation.

527 Note also other 'carve-outs' permitted by LLMC Art 15, eg for ships under 300 gt, or for nationals of non-State parties.

528 The idea of different categories of claimant having to share with the 'primary' claimants did not arise under the CLC as there was only one type of claimant, ie those claiming for CLC pollution damage against

When the WRC 2007 Art 12(10) allows the *insurer* to "invoke the defences" to which the shipowner would be entitled "including limitation of liability", it is permitting the insurer to take advantage of another limitation regime; ie the WRC 2007 deems there to be a maximum liability of the insurer *under the WRC 2007* on the basis that the shipowner could limit liability under the Affected State's law. On this basis, it may be strictly irrelevant that the insurer has an independent right to limit under the LLMC Art 1(6), but the fact that the insurer can so limit means that the Affected State is not in breach of any international obligations to other LLMC (or WRC 2007) State parties.

All this means that the insurer would, in effect, still be subject to one limitation amount for all maritime claims arising out of the incident, eg as constituted by a limitation fund established under Chapter III of the LLMC 1996. The normal rules for distribution of money from that fund would be applied; ie the wreck removal claim would be one of many 'property' claims against the fund, including those from cargo owners whose goods were lost in the wreck.[529] This linkage of the WRC 2007 to other limitation regimes will often have a serious effect upon the recovery of full compensation for wreck removal claims.[530]

10.8.5(c) Applicable national or international regime
The Art 12(10) reference to "limitation of liability under any *applicable* national or international regime" would clearly include those limits applied under the law of the Affected State that it applied to the wreck removal claim. Berlingieri took the view that where a ship is registered in a State party, the applicable regime should be that in force in the State party in which the ship is (or was) registered and that should also be the case if there is a direct action against the insurer.[531]

What is not clear under Art 12(10) is whether the reference includes allowing limitation "applicable" in a State *other* than that applying the WRC 2007 to a wreck in its own jurisdiction. The WRC 2007 does not have its own jurisdictional rules, unlike the CLC and Fund regime, so jurisdictional matters would appear to be a matter for each State party. Where that State is party to the LLMC, the extent to which that State may recognise limitation actions in another State will depend on its interpretation of the LLMC, eg whether it is bound to recognise such a limitation fund in that State.[532]

It is arguable that the direct action provision in Art 12(10) can be interpreted as meaning that it envisaged limitation, as a defence to a WRC 2007 claim, *only* being "applicable" in the Affected State whose courts are hearing the WRC 2007 liability claim and according to its own limitation law.[533] This would be consistent with a unitary interpretation of the WRC 2007 and may well accord with the assumptions of many State parties that had focused on linkage to the LLMC 1996 as the fall-back position. The intricacies of limitation law

---

stand-alone limits. The linkage problems in the WRC 2007 have also caused similar problems of interpretation under the Bunkers Convention: see *Gaskell, Bunker Pollution*, 491–492.

529 See 2.4.4(c) and 2.5.4(a). For examples of the limits available for all these 'property' claims, see Table 2.6 (2.5.6(a)).

530 Similar linkage problems apply to the Bunkers Convention, whose Art 7(1)) is materially similar to the WRC 2007 Art 12(10).

531 See *Berlingieri Vol III*, 88.

532 See also 2.5.9 and 2.5.9(f).

533 Something similar was suggested in an early draft of the Bunkers Convention 2001: see *Gaskell, Bunkers Limitation*, 478 and LEG 73/12/1 (12 September 1995).

would have been keenly appreciated by the shipowners and Clubs during the diplomatic negotiations, but the possibility of limitation forum shopping would have been less obvious to many State negotiators.[534]

The preamble to the Bunkers Convention 2001 recognised the importance of establishing strict liability for oil pollution which is linked to an appropriate limitation of the level of that liability".[535] No such preambular statement appears in the WRC 2007, probably because of the opt-out. The focus of the discussions on limitation for insurers in the Bunkers Convention 2001 was very much on the maximum level of insurance cover required, eg where there was no applicable insurance regime, rather than in preserving potentially lower limitation rights through forum shopping.[536]

There is also a difference between Art 6 of the Bunkers Convention 2001 and Art 10(2) of the WRC 2007. The former states that nothing in the convention shall affect "the right of the shipowner *and the person or persons providing insurance* . . . to limit liability"[537] under the national or international regime. In the WRC 2007 Art 10(2) the italicised words do not appear and the only right preserved is that of the registered owner (which includes the shipowner). What Art 12(10) then does is to refer to defences of the insurer to a claim under the WRC 2007 itself, eg in the Affected State, which might suggest that the defence is one that is allowed by the "applicable" limitation law of *that* State. On that basis, there would be no scope for the shipowner and insurer to be able to forum shop to the limitation rules of another State that has lower limits than the Affected State (or which is a 'non-reservation' State).[538] To put it another way, the Affected State would not be obliged to recognise the limitation regime in another State unless it was bound to by international law[539] or a regional regime.[540]

The contrary argument would be that by referring to "any" applicable national or international regime, that included foreign limitation actions—given that the concept of divided liability and limitation proceedings is an established practice. The view of the shipowners and insurers would be that this is one of the consequences of agreeing to limitation by reference, as opposed to having stand-alone limits. If that is right, it arguably reflects a defect in the protections of the WRC 2007 caused by an unwillingness to alter the LLMC 1996 when the Bunkers Convention 2001 and WRC 2007 were agreed.

10.8.5(d) Insurer's liability cap if shipowner cannot limit
The shipowner may not be able to limit liability for a variety of reasons. One may be that the Affected State is not party to any limitation convention and has no provisions in national law that would allow the shipowner to limit. Another reason might be that under

---

534 The matter is complicated because the WRC 2007 provision was effectively borrowed from the Bunkers Convention 2001.
535 See Recital 5 and LEG 78/WP.4 (21 October 1998).
536 See eg LEG 79/6/1 (12 February 1999), 2.
537 Emphasis added.
538 See 2.5.8.
539 Eg if it was still party to both the LLMC 1976 and LLMC 1996, so that it had obligations to different State parties. See also 2.5.1.
540 Eg within the EU: see 2.5.9(e).

the LLMC it has been guilty of intentional or reckless conduct within the LLMC Art 4.[541] Then the insurer might, through Art 12(10), have faced an unlimited liability under the WRC 2007. For that reason, the insurer's WRC 2007 Art 12(10) liability is capped, but according to a calculation in Art 12(1) that itself links to the "LLMC 1976, as amended" [ie the LLMC 1996].[542] Although Art 12(10) refers to the defendant insurer's ability to "limit liability", that will not necessarily be decided according to ordinary limitation principles (eg with constitution of limitation funds etc), as the Affected State may have no limitation law at all; Art 12(1) merely utilises by reference a calculation from the LLMC 1996. For that reason, the expression 'cap' has been used here to avoid confusion; it is a cap within the WRC 2007, not a limit under the LLMC 1996. The result is to produce a single mandatory calculation based on the LLMC 1996 figures.[543] By contrast, Art 10(2) merely preserves the existing rights of a shipowner to limit under regimes "such as" the LLMC 1976, or LLMC 1996; Art 10(2) is an inclusionary rather than a mandatory formula. For States that do have national limitation laws, eg based on the LLMC, it seems to be open to them to give effect to the cap by linking it to that national limitation law.

Where the WRC 2007 differs from the Bunkers Convention 2001 is that there is an additional reason why the "registered owner is not entitled to limit liability"[544] for wreck removal. This is because an Affected State has exercised the wreck removal opt-out in the LLMC.[545] It is here that the Art 12(10) cap should be relevant even in an LLMC State, because the insurer would be entitled to rely on the cap in the WRC 2007.

It should be noted here that in enacting the direct liability provisions the UK has not directly incorporated the Art 12(1) cap into its implementing legislation. This has raised the question about whether the UK has enacted the possibility of a direct action against an insurer without limit (or cap), although that clearly was not the intention. The legislator appears to have taken the view that there was no need to make a specific reference to Art 12(1) or 12(10) in relation to direct action as the insurance certificate issued in accordance with the convention must carry with it the Art 12(1) cap. This is perhaps more a question of UK statutory drafting rather than one of principle under the WRC 2007.[546]

Apart from this UK position, assume that there are no limitation forum shopping issues and the entire claim is being heard in an Affected State under the WRC 2007. If the shipowner *cannot* limit liability for wreck removal in that State,[547] Art 12(10) of the WRC 2007 creates an independent obligation for the insurer, but with a cap fixed in relation to (but technically separate from) national limitation law. Whether it is entirely separate may depend on the way that the Affected State has enacted Art 12(10) of the WRC 2007 and whether it has chosen to link it to its national law, eg under the LLMC 1996.

If it has *not* linked it, this insurer's cap under Art 12(10) does not seem to operate as a 'limitation fund' that has to be shared with other claimants (eg for cargo loss or collision

---

541 See 2.5.7. Here the insurer will also usually have a defence if there is wilful misconduct, as this defence is expressly preserved by the WRC 2007 Art 12(10): see 10.8.4(c) and (d); also *Martinez Gutierrez*, 199.
542 As to whether the reference is to the LLMC in force internationally or in a particular State, see 10.8.5(b).
543 See the examples in Tables 5 and 6: see 2.5.6(a).
544 See the WRC 2007 Art 12(10), third sentence.
545 See 2.5.8.
546 See 11.3.4(b) for a discussion of the difficulties of resolving the matter in UK law so as to give the intended effect to the WRC 2007.
547 Eg because of the State's LLMC 1996 Art 18 opt-out: see 2.5.8.

damage). Indeed, there is no provision for the insurer to establish a 'fund' at all under the WRC 2007. It would appear that the whole amount would be available to the wreck removal claimant. There would be no WRC 2007 'limitation fund' to which other claimants (eg cargo owners) could be referred. If separate cargo or collision claims arising from the same incident were brought against the shipowner then these would be subject to limits in the ordinary way (eg under the LLMC 1996). In this sense, the insurer may have to put up a normal limitation fund for the collision and cargo claims and, in effect, a separate (but identical in amount) 'fund' (ie sum) under the WRC 2007.[548]

One possible argument against this conclusion as to the nature of the cap is that the CLC 1992 and HNSC 2010 have express provisions that sums provided under the compulsory insurance provisions "shall be available exclusively for the satisfaction of claims under this Convention".[549] It might be said that the absence of this provision in the WRC 2007 shows that the WRC 2007 Art 12(10) cap was not intended to be exclusive, particularly as in many ways the WRC 2007 follows the Bunkers Convention 2001. An exclusivity provision did appear in draft Art 7(9) of the Bunkers Convention in 1999.[550] It was deleted by the Legal Committee "on the basis that insurance meeting the obligations under the proposed convention would not necessarily be limited to cover for bunker oil damage".[551] Whether this was fully understood by all delegations or not, it does suggest that the Bunkers Convention 2001 recognised that the insurance was not exclusive and the WRC 2007 followed this model. This, however, may have been a conclusion that focused on insurance to cover the liability of the *shipowner* that *was* able to limit.[552] Where the shipowner is unable to limit, and Art 12(10) operates to create an independent cap on the *insurer's* direct liability, the exclusivity issue should not be relevant. On this analysis, and in the absence of any contrary guidance in the *travaux préparatoires*, the WRC 2007 Art 12(10) cap can be interpreted as being exclusively available to the wreck removal claimants. Such an interpretation probably comes closer to the deal most States thought was on offer in relation to the insurer's liability; ie a guaranteed amount but capped to benefit the insurer.

However, if the LLMC State has chosen somehow to link the WRC 2007 Art 12(10) cap to its own limitation law then, in effect, it has decided not to fully exercise the LLMC Art 18 opt-out in respect of insurers. They would then be entitled to limit under the national law implementing the LLMC and the shipowner would establish a limitation fund in the normal way, and this would be available to meet all 'property' claims.

Where the Art 12(10) cap operates, the amounts directly available from the insurer under the WRC 2007 Art 12(1) calculation may not be enough to cover a large wreck removal claim.[553] For any excess costs, the shipowner would still be liable without limit (eg because of the effects of the opt-out), so a State might legitimately seek to 'top up' the amount received directly from the insurer by pressing on with a claim against the shipowner. Of

---

548 This actually comes close to the result in Dutch law where there is a separate fund for wreck removal claims, apparently in an identical amount to the general 'property' limitation fund: see 2.5.9(c). Indeed, one reason why the shipowner and insurer might wish to forum shop for limitation is to avoid the exclusive interpretation of the Art 12(10) cap by finding a jurisdiction where there is no LLMC opt-out: see 2.5.8 and 2.5.9.
549 See the CLC 1992 Art VII(9); HNSC 2010 Art 12(9).
550 See Leg 79/6/1, 12 February 1999.
551 See LEG 79/11, 22 April 1999, 18.
552 Ie the situation in 10.8.5(b).
553 See eg Table 2.6: 2.5.6(a).

course, this may face the usual problems in dealing with insolvent single ship companies, but there may be circumstances where a shipowner has assets. In theory a shipowner could ask its Club to use its 'omnibus rule'[554] to apply discretionary cover in excess of the direct action cap, eg if it is a member in 'good standing'. The political risk for a Club is that such discretionary cover, if made known, would encourage the large *Rena* or *Costa Concordia* type claims that Clubs had hoped to avoid by the WRC 2007 Art 12(10).[555]

Could an insurer seek to avoid the WRC 2007 Art 12(10) liability and cap in State X through the establishment of a limitation fund in State Y? The only advantage in doing this would be if both State X and Y were party to the same limitation convention. If both were party to the LLMC 1976, this would produce much lower limits than available under the LLMC 1996 Art 6(1)(b). There would be no advantage in the insurer looking to State Y unless State X had exercised the LLMC Art 18 opt-out (ie it was a 'reservation state') and State Y had not opted out. Then State X might be faced with an argument that it was bound to recognise the limitation fund in State Y and that the insurer was entitled to limit[556] to the lower LLMC 1976 figures.[557] This raises again the whole issue of limitation forum shopping,[558] and how far the WRC 2007 allows for reference to a limitation regime in another State.[559] The example above refers to the LLMC 1976, but the same issues could arise with the LLMC 1996. Given that the insurers fought for a cap in WRC 2007 Art 12(10) (connected to the LLMC 1996) it would seem somewhat surprising if they could avoid the direct liability in State X under the WRC 2007 by forum shopping elsewhere.[560] The courts of State X might be persuaded to enforce the Art 12(10) liability and cap and not recognise the LLMC fund elsewhere.[561]

10.8.5(e) Calculating Art 12(1) cap: which LLMC version?
When Art 12(1) refers to the LLMC 1976 "as amended", does it mean as amended at the IMO or as amended according to the law of a particular state, eg that of the forum? And does the amendment have to be in force internationally? This may depend upon whether the State has linked the Art 12(10) cap to limitation under the LLMC 1996 in its national law (eg under the LLMC 1996).[562] Where that is done there is no problem as the national law will reflect the LLMC 1996 limits. LLMC 1976 States should legislate to give effect to the higher cap in the WRC 2007 Art 12(1) in circumstances where there is no shipowner right to limit under the LLMC 1976.

The original LLMC 1976 Art 20 allowed for the convention to be "revised or amended" at a diplomatic conference. Where there is only a revision of limitation amounts a conference can be convened under Art 21. There are different provisions in the two articles as to

---

554 See *Hazelwood & Semark*, 191–193, and 2.9.6(b).
555 Normally, a Club would only apply any discretion to reimburse after all litigation against the member has been concluded: see, eg the Standard Club, "Discretionary Claims: An Overview", June 2018.
556 Under LLMC 1976/1996 Art 1(6).
557 And where the fund would be shared with other claimants, as in 10.8.5(b).
558 See 2.5.9.
559 Cf 10.8.5(b).
560 If both States were also parties to the WRC 2007 it might be easier to argue, as a matter of treaty law, that Art 12(10) only referred to the limitation rules of the Affected State in which the claim was heard, on the basis that (as between them) this superseded any different interpretation of the LLMC: cf 10.8.5(b).
561 For some of the policy issues, see 2.5.9(f).
562 See 10.8.5(d).

the number of States necessary to convene the conference and on voting. The LLMC Protocol 1996 was convened under Art 20, and the LLMC 1996 ensued.[563] So, for the purposes of Art 12(1) of the WRC 2007, the LLMC 1976 "as amended" would clearly include the LLMC 1996 which has been in force internationally since 2004.[564]

The distinction between amendment and revision may appear as significant, given the WRC 2007 Art 12(1) reference to amendment only, and not to revision. The difficulty is that the 1996 Protocol introduced a quicker tacit amendment procedure in order to increase limits and, as has been seen, these were increased internationally in 2012 with effect from 2015.[565] Can it be argued that the WRC 2007 Art 12(1) reference to "as amended" only refers to the figures in the original 1996 Protocol and not to those revised in 2012 (or any time thereafter)?

There is a fairly standard express provision in the 1996 Protocol itself, Art 13, dealing with "revising or amending" the 1996 Protocol (as opposed to the 1976 Convention). Article 8 of the 1996 Protocol, though, is headed "Amendment of Limits" and its ten paragraphs outlining the rapid mechanism for increasing limits all refer to amendments. The 2012/2015 increases in the LLMC 1996 limits were agreed under this procedure. It follows that the distinction between revision and amendment in the original LLMC 1976 is not carried through in the LLMC 1996. So, the WRC 2007 Art 12(1) must be taken to refer to the LLMC 1996 limits as increased by any rapid amendment decision, but only when these are internationally in force; ie from 8 June 2015 (not 2012), and not from 30 November 2016 when they came into force for the UK.[566]

This result seems more likely to be the intention of the drafters of Art 12(1) which was ambulatory, but needed an internationally certain method of calculation for the WRC 2007, whether States are party to LLMC 1996 or not; indeed, such ratification or accession is irrelevant. It should be recalled that Art 12(1) of the WRC 2007 is designed for States party to the WRC 2007, but those States do not need to be party to the LLMC 1996.[567]

It may seem unfortunate that there can be a difference between the treatment of the wreck removal claimants in the two scenarios,[568] but the second and third sentences of Art 12(10) presuppose that the insurer can *either* rely on the shipowner's limit (eg under LLMC 1976/1996), *or* (where the shipowner cannot limit) on the fall back cap in Art 12(1). On this basis the Art 12(1) cap *only* comes into operation when the shipowner cannot itself limit.[569] If there is an anomaly, it is an inevitable consequence of the linkage of the WRC

---

563 See 2.5.1.
564 It seems clear that the reference to the LLMC 1976 "as amended" refers to the LLMC Protocol 1996 (which created the LLMC 1996) as it is in force internationally and not to whether the LLMC 1996 is in force in a particular State. Such an interpretation would undermine the certainty of the provision for risk management.
565 See 2.5.6(a).
566 See 2.5.6.
567 This is clear from Art 12(10) which itself acknowledges that general limitation of liability regimes may apply through national law, with the LLMC 1996 being merely an example. Cf the Bunkers Convention 2001 Art 7 which was a model for Art 12 of the WRC 2007; see also *Gaskell & Forrest*, 48–49 and, eg, LEG 77/11, 28 April 1998, 19.
568 Ie where the shipowner can limit (see 10.8.5(b)) and where it cannot (see 10.8.5(d)).
569 To this extent, the authors, have deliberately changed the emphasis that appeared in [2016] LMCLQ 49, 105. If there is any "anomaly", it arises out of the drafting of the WRC 2007 Art 12(10) and can be cured by State action, as indicated in the next paragraph.

2007 to the LLMC 1996, as opposed to there being stand-alone WRC 2007 wreck removal limits. If the insurer can take advantage of the shipowner's right to limit liability for wreck removal, that is a consequence of a State failing to take advantage of its ability under the LLMC 1996 Art 18 to opt out of limitation of liability for wreck removal claims. In any event, it is clear that States may need to be absolutely clear how they legislate for the cap in national law, eg whether to link it or not.

10.8.5(f) Calculating the Art 12(1) cap: sdr conversion
There is a final drafting problem, however. At some stage in the claims process the Art 12(1) calculation has to be performed. It will produce a figure in special drawing rights (sdrs) and they must be converted into a national currency. That will presumably be needed in the national currency of the Affected State, whether or not legal proceedings are actually commenced in a court of that State. The LLMC 1996 Art 8 provides that conversion shall take place "at the date the limitation fund shall have been constituted, payment is made, or security is given". LLMC States should have provided a mechanism for translating sdr figures into national currency,[570] but that is a calculation under and for the LLMC. If the interpretation of Art 12(1) of the WRC 2007 in 10.8.5(d), above, is correct, the calculation under Art 12(1) is not *necessarily* one *under* the LLMC 1996 (as a convention, enacted in national law) but could be a stand-alone cap merely called up by the international version of the LLMC 1996.

On that basis, national LLMC 1996 provisions converting the sdr calculations might not seem to be strictly applicable to the calculation required under the WRC 2007, unless the enacting legislation for the WRC 2007 clearly links them to the LLMC 1996. Moreover, the WRC 2007 Art 12(1) refers only to Art 6(1)(b) of the LLMC 1996, and not to Art 8, quoted above. A better view would be that when Art 12(1) refers to the "amount calculated *in accordance* with Art 6(1)(b) of the [LLMC 1996], as amended", it allows reference to associated provisions of the LLMC 1996 that relate to or interpret Art 6. Article 8 of the LLMC is actually a provision defining the "unit of account" (ie sdr) in Art 6, and so for that reason it is a necessary component of Art 6 to which it is legitimate to refer when interpreting the WRC 2007 Art 12(1). Still, it would be good practice, when enacting the WRC 2007, to have a provision making clear how and when[571] the limitation amount is to be converted. This will be particularly important for WRC 2007 States who are not party to the LLMC 1996.[572] In the absence of such provisions, national courts will no doubt do their best and might apply LLMC 1996 principles by analogy. In any event, where claims are settled without court proceedings, parties will need to agree on a settlement date and, under LLMC 1996 Art 8, that is the date for conversion.

---

570 See the MSA 1995 Sch 7, Part II para 8, although the UK has not specifically applied this to the WRC 2007 Art 12(1) cap: see 11.3.4(a).

571 The date of translation in LLMC proceedings will normally be when a limitation fund is established but, as explained, Art 12 (1) and (10) are not really true limitation provisions and there is no mechanism under the WRC 2007 for a limitation fund to be established. The UK enactment in s 255G of the MSA 1995 does not address this issue, as it makes no reference at all to the cap or figures in Art 12(1).

572 Korea, Jordan, Morocco, Panama, St Kitts and South Africa are not party to the LLMC 1976 or 1996; the Bahamas, Iran, Nigeria, and Singapore are party to the LLMC 1976: *IMO Status of Treaties* (November 2018).

10.8.5(g) Direct action outside WRC 2007 to avoid Art 12(1) cap

The right of the insurer to have a cap on liability was part of the package under which the P&I Clubs agreed to provide compulsory insurance certificates, although its protection might be seriously undermined if State courts fail to give effect to it, as appears to have happened in the Spanish Supreme Court's 2018 decision in the *Prestige* litigation in the context of the CLC 1992.[573] The Supreme Court found that the London P&I Club was liable for all the oil pollution damages caused by the incident, including moral and environmental damages, beyond the CLC limit of €22.8 million and up to the limit of its policy of US$1 billion.[574] This appears to be quite contrary to the direct action provisions of the CLC to which Spain and France are parties and it remains to be seen how far the judgment can be enforced against the Club which is unlikely to have assets in Spain.[575] Such litigation is, of course, an indication that States can be unhappy with the operation of limits of liability even though they may have agreed to a particular convention.

It might be thought that there is an immediate treaty problem to such litigation for State parties. This is because the wording of IMO liability convention direct action provisions (including the WRC 2007 Art 12(10)) typically states that "any claim for costs arising under this Convention may be brought directly against the insurer", and continues "[f]urthermore, even if the registered owner is not entitled to limit liability, the [insurer] may limit liability to an amount equal to [the LLMC 1996 Art 6(1)(b)]". Does this mean that if there was an unlimited liability judgment against a shipowner and the State then brought a claim against the insurer using *any* direct action provision (eg under any national direct action insurance statute), then the insurer could limit; or does it mean that *only* a direct action claim based on the certificate of insurance under Art 12 is subject to the insurer cap?

As a matter of interpretation, the answer is not immediately obvious. An absolute nature of the cap might be easier to defend in the context of the CLC which, in Art III(4), prevents non-convention claims (eg in tort) for pollution damage within the CLC, whereas there are no equivalent channelling provisions in the WRC 2007.[576] Given that the liability conventions form part of a compromise, one of whose elements was to sign-up the shipowners and P&I Clubs to the applicable liability regime, it is arguable that a good faith interpretation[577] of WRC 2007 Art 12(10) would bind a State party to the WRC 2007 to restrict any wreck removal direct action claim against the insurer to the LLMC 1996 cap provided by Art 12(1).

10.8.6 P&I Club practice after entry into force of WRC 2007

The 2011–2012 policy year produced the first and third largest ever claims on the International Group pool, and it is clear that the *Costa Concordia* and *Rena* payouts had a significant impact on the International Group's reinsurers. Despite such events being viewed as challenging for the market, it appeared that the International Group was able to achieve

---

573 See 1.2.2(a).
574 Supreme Court (Penal Chamber), Cassation Appeal/606/2018; IOPC Funds, *Annual Report 2018*, 16, IOPC Funds, IOPC/APR19/3/2, 15 March 2019.
575 See also 2.9.6(c).
576 See 10.2.2.
577 See the Vienna Convention, Art 31(1).

generally favourable reinsurance renewal terms for the 2015–2016 policy year, ie after the WRC 2007 came into force.[578] Since then the reinsurance loss experience has been "acceptable to reinsurers".[579]

The reinsurance package is complex,[580] but for 2019–2020 involves an individual claiming Club retaining a first layer of liability itself (to US$10 million); a lower pool layer shared with the other Clubs (between US$10 million to US$50 million); an upper pool layer (from US$50 million to US$100 million, with a claiming Club retention of 7.5%). From US$100 million to US$3.1 billion, there is a Group GXL (general excess of loss) reinsurance programme in three GXL layers.[581] There is separate a separate US$1 billion of cover available for oil pollution claims, a figure that was targeted by the Spanish Supreme Court in the *Prestige* litigation.[582] For chartered entries there is US$350 million cover limit.

There have been suggestions that wreck removal cover should be restricted, or separated as a class of risk with its own costs attached, but that does not appear to have happened yet. This may be partly because the incidence of shipwreck is random across ship types, and shipowner members of Clubs realise that an uninsured wreck liability could be catastrophic. In any event, there is a clear incentive to reduce wreck removal claims when it seems that they will increase in number and cost.

Will the entry into force of the WRC 2007 signal a change of attitude by the Clubs and their shipowner members? At the start of the drafting of the WRC 2007 the shipowners and Clubs were sceptical about whether any new liability convention was needed, but by the end of the negotiations had apparently come round to the need for action, largely in the name of uniformity of maritime law—a laudable aim in itself. There may be a more pointed reason for the shipowners and Clubs to be urging strongly that there should be widespread adoption of the WRC 2007, and particularly its extension into national waters.[583] In this context, somewhat disingenuously, the International Group pointed out that "Claims subject only to the jurisdiction of national legislation cannot be brought under WRC [2007] certificates and there can be no reliance on the compulsory insurance provisions in article 12".[584]

Perhaps the Clubs and other insurers are hoping to use the existence of the WRC 2007 to change the practice, apparently applied in cases such as the *Rena* and *Costa Concordia*, of standing behind the shipowner without using the 'pay to be paid' clause to avoid unlimited liability.[585] In future, why could the Clubs not say to a *State party* to the WRC 2007, "We rely on the Art 12(10) cap as agreed in the WRC 2007, but of course you can sue the shipowner if you want (without recourse to us)". The Clubs might be more likely to inform a *non-State party* to the WRC 2007 (which hopes for a large *Costa Concordia* or *Rena* level of payout) that if the State wanted to sue the Club directly it should have adopted the WRC

---

578 See International Group of P&I Clubs, *Annual Review 2014/15*, 11–12. See also 1.4.
579 See International Group of P&I Clubs, *Annual Review 2017/18*, 10.
580 See www.igpandi.org/reinsurance.
581 The International Group also uses a captive reinsurer, Hydra, to cover part of the upper pool layer (eg 92.5%).
582 See 1.2.2(a).
583 See LEG 101/8/4, 21 February 2014.
584 Ibid., 3.
585 Cf the unintended uncertainty in the UK about whether there is unlimited direct insurance liability for wreck (hull) removal claims: see 11.3.4(b).

2007, and that (not having done so) it will have to seek its remedy against the shipowner itself (which, by the way, will be establishing a limitation fund in another State).

The International Group has been actively working on agreeing MOUs with States' maritime administrations to improve cooperation and streamlining response activities following a major wreck casualty.[586] The Clubs have made it clear, though, that they would not issue Blue Cards for liability regimes that might differ from the WRC 2007 regime.[587] While the Clubs are unlikely to refuse to cooperate with non-State parties, it would not be surprising if they played hard ball about potentially huge claims for removal without limits, with the ultimate threat of leaving a State to its remedy against the shipowner or trying to overcome the 'pay to be paid' rule. The Club might then compromise by offering settlement on WRC 2007 terms, ie with capped insurer liability, and it may only be on such terms that it might agree to start cooperating by paying claims directly to wreck removal contractors.

While there is no evidence to suggest that Club and shipowner support for the WRC 2007 is part of a cunning coordinated plan to reduce liabilities, it does seem that the Clubs and their members may have achieved what they failed to do with the HNSC 1996, ie to create a *de facto* linkage of a new liability regime with the general limits of liability under the LLMC.[588] To the surprise of some observers, the WRC 2007 has received early adoption by significant open registry (or flag of convenience) States including Liberia, Panama, Cyprus and the Bahamas. This is surely confirmation that the shipowners see the WRC 2007 as being to their advantage, probably because they hope that ever increasing wreck removal claims will in future be restricted in practice to the sums that the Clubs will pay out under Art 12(10).[589]

If this is a correct analysis, the WRC 2007 may not be such a boon to coastal States as might have been hoped. While the provisions operating in the EEZ provide additional protection, the decision to extend the WRC 2007 to territorial waters may present a real dilemma for States. The extension would certainly impose proportionality and reasonableness restrictions as to the type of operation possible, and in practice the liability payments would be capped, although guaranteed. The retention of national law in territorial waters may leave scope for wide powers to raise wrecks, even for political reasons, and with the prospect of the level of costs recovery evident with the *Rena* and *Costa Concordia*; but there is no assurance that Clubs and shipowners will be so obliging now that the WRC 2007 is in force. If the *Baltic Ace* litigation is a guide,[590] shipowners and Clubs may well seek to

---

586 See 1.4 and eg International Group, *Annual Review* 2014/15, 13. Although the draft MOU excludes any legal obligations, it sets out principles of cooperation on joint training activities (pre and post incident), and encourages the early identification of key individuals for the mutual dissemination of information after an incident. An MOU was signed with Australia, for instance, in October 2014.

587 See LEG 101/8/4, 21 February 2014.

588 The option of having stand-alone shipowner limits for wreck removal in the WRC 2007 was never likely to be acceptable to States, but it might have been possible to agree an independent insurance cap at higher levels than those under Art 6(1)(b) of the LLMC 1996.

589 It has been suggested to the authors that there is a more prosaic reason for accession by such flag States, namely the desire not to lose out on the fees payable for the issue of insurance certificates which would otherwise be received by other State parties. While there may be some truth in this, it is hardly a reason to accede to a convention that was not otherwise seen as beneficial.

590 See 2.5.9(c).

THE LAW OF WRECK

use limitation forum shopping so as to take advantage of States that are party to the LLMC 1976 or 1996, but have not made the wreck removal opt-out.[591]

For States, the choice will be whether it is better to have a bird in the hand than two in the bush. The linkage of the WRC 2007 insurance liability to the LLMC 1996 means that the levels of the general LLMC 1996 Art 6(1)(b) figures are even more important than before. Shipowner States succeeded in resisting the highest possible increases in those limits when they were last considered at IMO in 2012.[592] Those limits cannot now be reconsidered until at least 2020.[593] While coastal States can be advised to adopt the LLMC 1996 (with the 2015 increases),[594] they may find that they end up footing the bill for rather more of major wreck removal incidents than they had hoped for during the 40 years of negotiations on the WRC which first started after the *Torrey Canyon* incident in 1967.

10.9 Overlaps with other maritime liability regimes

It has already been noted[595] that Art 11 "Exceptions to Liability" deals with liability overlaps by giving priority, in effect, to existing liability conventions. It is now necessary to consider this provision in more detail, starting with liability to pay for salvage.

10.9.1 Overlap with Salvage Convention 1989

A potential overlap between the WRC 2007 regime with salvage law was raised in negotiations for the WRC 2007, especially in relation to drifting ships.[596] Article 11(2) solves this by recognising that salvage law generally, including the Salvage Convention 1989, largely deals with the appropriate payment *to* salvors, rather than costs incurred *by* States. Thus, issues about payment for salvage (ie services to assist a vessel and cargo in danger) will be governed by salvage law, eg under the Salvage Convention 1989.[597] The WRC 2007 Art 9(4) allows the registered owner to engage a salvor.[598] Under the Salvage Convention 1989 Art 13, salvors will be paid for saving a vessel or its cargo; in the event of success (or partial success) the need for a State's WRC 2007 claim will be diminished. There can be a claim for a traditional salvage reward even if cargo is recovered from a wreck which is stranded, or even after it sinks to the seabed.[599] A salvor that partly saves property, eg by

---

591 See 2.5.8.
592 See 2.5.6(a).
593 LLMC 1996 Protocol, Art 8(6). Nineteen years elapsed between the LLMC 1996 and the 2015 increases, and there were 20 years between the LLMC 1976 and the 1996 Protocol.
594 States may also be well advised to ensure that they have direct action provisions (operating as an independent statutory claim) available against an insolvent shipowner: cf 2.9.6(c). This will enhance the possibility of a direct action claim against an insurer, eg in respect of ships flagged in non-State parties in transit but without WRC 2007 certificates.
595 See 7.3.3.
596 Eg LEG 80/11, 25 October 1999, para. 120. See also 7.3.3, 8.2 (especially 8.2.1(e)), and 10.6.1.
597 See 2.7.
598 Or "other person", eg a wreck removal contractor engaged under a wreck removal rather than a salvage contract. The provision does not seem to recognise that a salvage contract may also be made with the cargo owners, although in practice this is most often done through the agency of the ship's master: see *Gaskell, 1989 Salvage Convention*, 15–17.
599 Eg in this case, a non-perishable cargo.

offloading most of the cargo intact, will be rewarded by its owners from the value of that property.[600] Anything left behind, eg the hull and any cargo still in it, may be subject to the WRC 2007 regime.[601]

If the salvor succeeds in removing hull and or cargo which is of little value, it will obtain no traditional salvage reward under the Salvage Convention 1989 Art 13, but may be entitled to special compensation under Art 14, payable by the shipowner.[602] It is well recognised that some Art 14 operations, or those undertaken under the provisions of salvage contracts (such as the LOF 2011 and the SCOPIC 2018) may shade commercially into wreck removal; ie there becomes a stage when it is recognised in practice that salvage of valuable property has ended and removal of valueless property will begin.[603] In theory, salvors should not be out of pocket where Art 14 or SCOPIC apply but, in any event, a salvor that is out of pocket will not be able to make a direct, independent WRC 2007 claim for the costs it has incurred, as the WRC 2007 Art 10 is linked to actions of the Affected State in Art 9(8).[604] Of course if the State engages a salvage contractor on salvage or wreck removal terms, the salvor's rights will be governed by that contract.

10.9.2 Overlap with maritime pollution liability conventions

While the WRC 2007 does not expressly deal with environmental clean-up costs, in some circumstances such costs may be recoverable under it when there is a possibility of removal of the cargo (or contents) of a ship.[605] Then, the WRC 2007 can clearly be applied in a State party, but the issue is more complicated if that State is also party to one or more of the CLC 1992, Fund Convention 1992, or Bunkers Convention 2001 (or the HNSC 2010 when in force).

The question of any overlap of the WRC 2007 with these maritime pollution liability conventions involves an interpretation of their relationship in public international law, but at a practical level it raises three particular issues. The first is whether the WRC 2007 and the other convention can be seen to produce separate liabilities for different types of loss; here there is no overlap. The second issue is whether claimants can 'double dip' by claiming the same amount twice; not surprisingly, this will generally not be possible. The third issue is subtly different, as it involves asking whether there can be a claim for the same type of loss or damage, using two conventions in a complementary way so that the overall claim never exceeds the actual proven loss. In the event of large claims, in particular, there may be an applicable limit of liability under (or in relation to) one of these conventions, which a claimant might want to 'top-up' by having access to the other. This may be particularly relevant where there is no effective limit of the shipowner's liability under the WRC

---

600 See 2.7.7.
601 The WRC 2007 does not specify what is to happen to any property which is removed, ie where it has a residual value, albeit less than the costs of removal. There is no express power to sell it (eg for scrap), although it is possible this may be implied as part of the removal process or be allowed under national law. In any event sums would need to be set off against costs. See also the UK position, 11.3.4(c).
602 See 2.7.9(b).
603 See also 11.3.4(a), 12.3.
604 See also 10.2.3, 11.3.4(a).
605 See 10.6.4.

2007 when a State has made a reservation under the LLMC.⁶⁰⁶ This may trigger a 'conflict' defence by the shipowner.

Article 11(1) of the WRC 2007 provides that there is no Art 10 liability for wreck removal costs to the extent that this would be in "conflict" with three maritime pollution liability conventions:⁶⁰⁷ the CLC [1969 or 1992], the HNSC 2010, and the Bunkers Convention 2001.⁶⁰⁸ This means that one starts with these other conventions so that, for example, the costs of removing oil cargo or bunkers from a wrecked tanker might fall under the CLC rather than the WRC 2007; or under the HNSC 2010 for the removal of HNS cargo from a chemical tanker; or under the Bunkers Convention 2001 for removal of bunkers from a wrecked container ship. In practice, it may often not make much difference which convention applies as it is likely that the same insurer will cover all liabilities.⁶⁰⁹ However, given the different scope of application for the various conventions there is room for uncertainty as to what exactly is a "conflict" in Art 11(1).

Before looking at the conventions mentioned in Art 11(1) it is appropriate to mention possible overlap with the EU's Environmental Liability Directive 2004.⁶¹⁰ The latter has provisions designed to avoid overlap with the CLC 1992, the Fund Convention 1992 and the Bunkers Convention 2001, but obviously does not mention the later WRC 2007. It may be thought that there is no possibility of a conflict as the WRC 2007 does not provide compensation for environmental damage. However, the costs of removing a wreck or debris from a wreck might in some circumstances be considered as a form of remediation under the Directive.⁶¹¹ Although it creates a wider category of person liable than merely the registered owner (as under the WRC 2007), it expressly preserves rights to limit liability under the LLMC in national law.⁶¹² Even if a claim for environmental damage in relation to a wreck was brought under the Directive, the nature of that liability might be categorised as one under the LLMC Art 2(1)(a) or (c) and therefore subject to limitation. The difficulty is that the rendering harmless of a ship or its cargo (eg with debris), would fall within LLMC Art 2(1)(d) or (e) and be subject to the limitation opt-out.⁶¹³

10.9.2(a) Conflict with CLC 1992

If an oil tanker sinks with its cargo and bunkers, the cost of removing them can be considered as "preventive measures" and therefore oil "pollution damage" within the CLC 1992.⁶¹⁴ Where the cargo and bunkers are removed by pumping directly from the sunken tanker, it is difficult to see that the costs of raising the tanker's hull would normally be admissible under the CLC 1992, but they would be within the WRC 2007; this is an

---

606 See 2.4.8. The present discussion ignores the question of the solvency of the shipowner but assumes that the compulsory insurer can limit under the WRC 2007 Art 12(10) to the amount referred to in Art 12(1): see 10.8.2, 10.8.5.
607 For the nuclear liability conventions, see 10.9.3.
608 Art 11(1) also requires that they are "applicable and in force": that presently excludes the HNSC 2010.
609 For uncertainty regarding the IOPC Fund liability, see 10.9.2(a).
610 See 2.6.5.
611 It appears that there would be no defence under the Directive if the environmental damage arose from obeying an order under the WRC 2007 Art 9(2) to remove a wreck: see 2.9.5.
612 See Art 4(2) and see 2.5.
613 See 2.5.8.
614 See 2.6.2(a).

example of separate and distinct liabilities. If it were necessary to prevent pollution from cargo or bunkers still in its tanks by refloating the tanker (or otherwise removing it[615]) then this could still fall under the CLC even though there was incidentally a wreck 'removal'. Unless the oil could not be removed from the wreck once refloated, any later removal of the hull might not be within the CLC, but certainly could be within the WRC 2007.[616] In these examples, the CLC limit would apply to the CLC claim, and the limit applicable to the WRC 2007 claim would depend upon the application of Art 10(2),[617] eg, the LLMC 1996 limits might apply, or a State may have opted out of wreck removal limits altogether.[618]

Where the pollution liability falls completely on the shipowner under the CLC, eg where the CLC limits are not exceeded, it is clear that the CLC will take priority in the sense that if the claims are recoverable under the CLC they will not be recoverable under the WRC 2007. Again, the obvious instance would be where the oil cargo is pumped out of a tanker in order to prevent oil pollution damage within the CLC. Where the claims are greater than the CLC limits, there are two scenarios: first, the claimant may seek to 'top up' its claim from the WRC 2007; secondly, the claimant may seek recourse from the IOPC Fund.[619]

A 'topping up' issue might arise where the CLC limit applies to an expensive cargo or bunker removal operation, eg for a small tanker, but the claimant makes an (unlimited)[620] WRC 2007 liability claim for cargo and bunker removal costs. Here it could be argued that there is a "conflict" between the conventions if the shipowner's entitlement to a CLC limit was being avoided by the making of the WRC 2007 claim. The conflict could arise because it might be said that the WRC 2007 was being used as a top-up to the CLC liability for an identical loss. Alternatively, it could be argued that there is no conflict, as all that has happened is that the CLC has been fully utilised according to its terms, and there is no attempt to create extra CLC liability; the WRC 2007 is being used in a complementary manner, and so there is no conflict. While it is true that there would be no overlap allowing for double recovery, the difficulty with the alternative view is that if the costs claimed under the WRC 2007 fall exactly within the definition of "pollution damage" under the CLC Art I(6),[621] then a claim in excess of that against the shipowner would be in breach of the CLC Art III(4),[622] as it prevents any claim against the shipowner "otherwise than in accordance with" the CLC.[623]

---

615 Of course, if the tanker still had a commercial value, the refloating exercise might well be a salvage service.
616 Although for ultimate disposal see 10.2.8 and Chapter 14, eg 14.7.1.
617 See 10.7.
618 See 2.5.8.
619 Logically, it might be thought that the Fund issue should come first, but there might be States which are only party to the CLC 1969 or 1992 and not the Fund Convention 1992; moreover, there are particular problems caused by the fact that the Fund Convention is not specifically listed in the conflict provision, Art 11(1) of the WRC 2007.
620 Ie it is assumed that the State has made the wreck removal opt-out reservation: see 2.5.8. If the LLMC applied to the WRC 2007 claim, it would always produce a lower limit of liability than the CLC for the same size of ship: cf Table 2.5 (see 2.5.6(a)) and Table 2.7 (see 2.6.2(a)).
621 See 2.6.2(a) and (b).
622 See 2.6.2(a).
623 Article 10(3) of the WRC 2007 is a similar provision in that it prevents an Art 10(1) WRC 2007 claim against the registered owner otherwise than under the WRC 2007 (although it does not appear to have been

If it were possible to identify a type of clean-up or removal operation for the cargo and bunkers of a tanker that was *not* within the CLC pollution damage definition, but *was* within the WRC 2007, then there would not be a conflict in allowing such a claim under the WRC 2007.[624] It will be recalled that under the WRC 2007 Art 1(7) "removal" means any form of prevention, mitigation or elimination of the hazard[625] and, applied to cargo and bunkers, this would seem to be practically identical with "preventive measures" under the CLC. This can clearly overlap (and conflict) in so far as both cover removal and clean-up operations.

The CLC 1992 Art I(7) imposes a reasonableness criterion on preventive measures to reduce pollution. The IOPC Fund has applied a proportionality test in deciding whether the costs of removing the last remaining tonnes of oil cargo from a wreck are admissible.[626] Would it be a "conflict" to try to apply the WRC 2007 to pay for the costs of removing those last drops of oil? It is doubtful if there is a practical and legal distinction between the CLC and the WRC 2007, given the latter's own requirements of proportionality and "reasonable necessity",[627] although the focus in both is slightly different; the WRC 2007 focuses on removal of the "hazard" caused by the wreck, whereas the CLC focuses on preventing oil pollution damage. If there was a distinction, it might be argued that, as these additional expenses were not "pollution damage" within the CLC, a suit outside the CLC would not fall foul of the CLC Art III(4), and therefore there would be no conflict. By contrast, it would not seem possible for a State claimant to elect to use the WRC 2007 for all the oil raising and removal expenses so as to reserve the CLC resources for, say, environmental and private economic loss claims; that would appear to be a conflict. As already noted, it would not appear to be a "conflict" if the CLC payment was for the removal of all or most of the oil cargo (leaving the hull on the seabed as it was no longer an environmental risk), and then the WRC 2007 was used to pay for raising the hull (with the last remnants of oil cargo) on the basis that it was a navigational hazard under the WRC 2007.

The second issue concerns overlap between the WRC 2007 and the Fund Convention 1992. Where there is an oil tanker that is wrecked, the IOPC Fund may also have liabilities under the Fund Convention 1992 and its liability and funding are separate to those under the CLC.[628] Article 11(1)(a) of the WRC 2007 does not actually list the Fund Convention 1992 for the purposes of conflicts. In a literal sense, there is no conflict as a claim against the IOPC Fund is not against a shipowner—unlike that in the WRC 2007—although in a broader sense it may be a claim for the same (or similar) damage.[629] Given the high limits of liability under the Fund Convention 1992 (and the existence of the Supplementary Fund 2003),[630] these are likely to be enough to cover the type of removal or clean-up operations that might fall within the WRC 2007, so there may be no need to try to have recourse to

---

enacted in the UK, see 11.3.4(c)). There is no breach of this provision if a claimant brings a cargo removal costs claim against the shipowner under the CLC as this claim is preserved by the very terms of Art 11(1).

624 Cf 14.6.3.
625 See 8.2.2, 9.2.5(b), 10.5.1(b), 10.6.
626 See 9.2.5(e), 10.2.4.
627 See Art 2(3); also 10.2.4, 10.5.1.
628 See 2.6.2(b).
629 The liability under the CLC and Fund is wider in the sense that it covers "pollution damage" not for the costs of locating, marking and removal. The overlap is because the WRC 2007 can include cargo removal.
630 See 2.6.2(c).

the latter for 'topping up' purposes. But where there are likely to be very large economic loss claims that might exceed the liability of the Fund (eg in States not party to the Supplementary Fund 2003), there might again be tactical advantages from a State's perspective in trying to route cargo clean-up (ie removal) claims through the WRC 2007. Where the CLC and Fund Convention operate together, with the shipowner limiting under the CLC and the Fund covering amounts in excess of this, it is unclear if any attempt to use the WRC 2007 for cargo and bunker clean-up expenses would create a "conflict" with the CLC. There would not be a double recovery as different losses would be claimed under each convention, but a WRC 2007 claim against the shipowner would still appear to fall foul of the CLC Art III(4), as explained above.

Moreover, the chapeau to the liability provision in the Fund Convention 1992, Art 4(1), refers specifically to the Fund's liability to pay for pollution damage as defined in the CLC 1992, and where full and adequate compensation under the CLC has not been possible. To this extent the CLC and Fund regimes are interdependent and this perhaps reinforces the view that there would probably be a "conflict" with the CLC if the WRC 2007 were deemed to apply to wreck removal costs that would otherwise have fallen within the Fund Convention 1992 Art 4(1)(c).

The situation is slightly different under the Fund Convention 1992 Art 4(1)(b) and (c), as the Fund may have to bear 100% of the pollution damage claim, eg where there is a "natural phenomenon" such as a tsunami causing the wreck, or where the shipowner's insurance does not respond to a CLC claim.[631] Here it is more difficult to say that under Art 11(1)(a) of the WRC 2007 there is a "conflict" with the CLC, certainly in relation to the tsunami example, as the exceptions from liability are practically identical in the CLC 1992 and WRC 2007.[632] This means that the Fund would still be liable for all of the costs[633] that fell within the Fund Convention 1992 for dealing with the wreck of a tanker (and its cargo and bunkers), after a tsunami or the failure of insurance.

10.9.2(b) Conflict with HNS Convention 2010

As noted, the WRC 2007 Art 11(1) does not presently apply to the HNSC 2010 as the latter is not in force. If and when it does enter into force, there will be similar conflict issues as with the CLC, above. One difference is that the HNSC 2010 deals with the liability of the shipowner and the HNS Fund in the same instrument. This means that there is not the ambiguity, as with the Fund Convention 1992, as to why the latter was not specifically listed in the WRC 2007 Art 11(1).[634] It seems that there would be a conflict with the HNSC 2010[635] for any WRC 2007 top-up claim that related to the clean-up or removal of cargo that fell within the list of substances in the HNSC 2010.

---

631 See 2.6.2(b).

632 Ie the reason why the IOPC Fund has to pay to the first sdr or dollar is because the shipowner has a defence under the CLC, so there could be no 'topping up' liability (limited or not) under the WRC 2007 as the same defence would apply. And if the shipowner were insolvent and the insurer did not respond under the CLC, then the same would apply to any WRC 2007 claim.

633 Up to the Fund's limits: see 2.6.2(b). The same arguments would seem to apply to the Supplementary Fund 2003.

634 See 10.9.2(b).

635 See the HNSC 2010 Art 7(4) for the equivalent provision to the CLC Art III(4).

For substances not within the HNSC 2010, eg coal, there would be no conflict with using the WRC 2007 for cargo removal. Further, as has been noted already,[636] prior to the entry into force of the HNSC 2010, the WRC 2007 may fill an important gap in relation to cargo removal and clean-up. One of the most important areas where the WRC 2007 might be invoked by States is wrecks involving the sinking of container ships having on board many hazardous or noxious cargoes.[637] These are the types of liability which are meant to be covered by the HNSC 2010 but, crucially, while the convention is not yet in force, there would be no "conflict" in applying the WRC 2007 to remove those cargoes. What the WRC 2007 does not cover, however, are the type of economic losses of the fishing and tourism industries that would be compensated within the HNSC 2010.

The practical difficulty, if the HNSC 2010 enters into force, will be to separate those costs that relate to HNS goods in some containers, from those relating to the removal of non-HNS goods in other containers. Where the recovery and removal operations are financed directly by the shipowner or Club, the issue really becomes relevant where limits of liability might operate (and eg how these may affect other 'property' claimants). Where a State incurs recovery and disposal costs to prevent HNS damage, it should be able to rely on the HNSC 2010 with its relatively generous limits.[638] Where the packaged goods do not fall within the HNSC's list of HNS, the State will have to rely on the WRC 2007, but again subject to whether any LLMC 1996 limits will operate. This probably means that rather detailed records may need to be kept during recovery operations so that costs can be apportioned if required.[639] This may be time consuming, expensive and often difficult, eg where containers may contain a mixture of HNS and non-HNS cargo. Indeed, such record keeping may also be needed when the HNSC 2010 operates in States that have not adopted the WRC 2007.

10.9.2(c) Conflict with Bunkers Convention 2001

As the CLC and Fund regime apply to the cost of clean-up of tanker bunkers, the Bunkers Convention 2001 will be relevant to the removal of bunkers from the wrecks of other categories of ships. Although Art 1(3) of the Bunkers Convention 2001 makes a wider category of persons liable (in addition to the registered shipowner), Art 3(5) has a similar provision to the CLC Art III(4), in that it prevents claims for bunker pollution damage within the Bunkers Convention 2001 from being made against this wider category "otherwise than in accordance with" that convention. Therefore, it seems that there would be a "conflict" within Art 11(1) of the WRC 2007 if the latter were used to claim bunker removal or clean-up costs that fell clearly within the Bunkers Convention 2001.

As most claims under the Bunkers Convention 2001 will be subject to limitation of liability,[640] these claims will usually share in the general 'property' limitation fund, along

---

636 See 10.6.4.
637 The cost of locating and removing these is rising considerably: see 1.2.3 and Gard, "Bigger consequences for container loss at sea" Insight, 4 June 2015.
638 See eg Tables 11 and 12: see 2.6.4.
639 A similar exercise is needed to deal with the overlap between the Salvage Convention 1989 and both the Bunkers Convention 2001 and the CLC and Fund regime: see 2.6.3, 2.6.2(a).
640 Both the Bunkers Convention 2001 Art 6 and the WRC 2007 Art 10(2) leave limitation to contracting States, eg to apply the LLMC1996, so there is no direct conflict in relation to limits: see 2.6.3, 10.7.

with wreck removal claims under the WRC 2007.[641] The difficulty, again, would be where the Bunkers Convention 2001 claims were limited, but those in respect of wreck (including bunkers) removal were subject to the LLMC 1996 opt-out.[642] As both conventions leave limitation of liability open to States, it might be argued that there could be no conflict if a WRC 2007 claim were used to top up the amounts available under the Bunkers Convention 2001. However, it seems that the better view, again, is that once the claim was of a type falling within Art 3 of the Bunkers Convention 2001, it could not be brought under the WRC 2007 as that would be in breach of the Bunkers Convention 2001 Art 3(5); that would create a conflict within the WRC 2007 Art 11(1).

10.9.3 Conflict with nuclear liability conventions

There are two conventions dealing with nuclear liabilities: the Paris Convention 1960[643] and the Vienna Nuclear Damage Convention 1963. The WRC 2007 Art 11(1) gives the same priority to the nuclear liability conventions as it does to the three maritime conventions; ie the WRC 2007 does not create a liability for costs if that would create a conflict with the named conventions that are applicable and in force. The nuclear conventions put liabilities for Chernobyl type disasters on States and the operators of nuclear facilities (eg nuclear reactors), rather than on shipowners or the carriers of nuclear cargoes.[644] The applicability of these conventions is beyond this book as they are so specialised and, perhaps, politicised.[645] There may be doubts, though, as to their applicability to certain low-level nuclear wastes; eg cargoes of spent fuel for reprocessing of the kind involved in the *Mont Louis* incident in 1984,[646] or perhaps medical radioactive material or wastes. Such low level wastes may be more dangerous for their chemical toxicity rather than any radioactivity. When the HNSC 1996 was being negotiated it was decided to exclude radioactive material of class 7 falling either in the IMDG Code (as amended) or in Appendix B of the Code of Safe Practice for Solid Bulk Cargoes (as amended).[647] It is possible that some low level wastes may not be within any of these liability conventions. To the extent that they are not, the WRC 2007 may apply in relation to their removal.

---

641 Except for States that have made the wreck and cargo removal opt-out: see 2.5.8.
642 See 2.5.8.
643 For 1997 liability increases see LEG 76/12, 17 October 1997, 15.
644 The Brussels Convention on the Liability of Operators of Nuclear Ships 1962 has not been relevant as it applies to the operators of nuclear-powered civil ships, and these have not been developed: see generally, P Konz, "The 1962 Brussels Convention on the Liability of Operators of Nuclear Ships" (1963) 57 AJIL 100.
645 See eg G Handl, "High Seas Governance Gaps: International Accountability for Nuclear Pollution", Chapter 7 of *High Seas Governance: Gaps and Challenges*.
646 See 7.1, 10.8.1; also N Gaskell, "Lessons of the Mont Louis Part Two: Compensation for Hybrid Accidents" (1986) 1 IJECL 269
647 See now the HNSC 2010 Art 4(2)(b) which is unchanged: also *Gaskell, MSMSA 1997*, 28/64–28/65; and 2.6.4, 2.9.6(b).

CHAPTER 11

National wreck removal law and the MSA 1995 Part 9A

11.1 Wreck removal in national law

This chapter will first consider wreck removal law in the UK as it developed for nearly 150 years before the UK decided to consider the adoption of the WRC 2007. Secondly, it will address the accession choices open to States that want to accede to the Convention and enact it in their national laws. Thirdly, it will consider the method that the UK has used to give effect to the Convention through the enactment of the Wreck Removal Convention Act (WRCA) 2011. As will be seen, much of the older legislation has been retained as a means of incorporating its structures into the functional scheme envisaged by the 2011 Act. Finally, consideration will be given to the practical problems presented by ships that are 'abandoned' without having been involved in a casualty.

11.1.1 Introduction

A significant portion of this book is devoted to the wreck removal solutions provided by the WRC 2007. There will still be many circumstances where there is relevant national wreck removal law that may exist separately to, or in conjunction with, the WRC 2007. The WRC 2007 will not apply to States that are not a party to the convention, but even in State parties the WRC 2007 may apply only in the EEZ[1] and not in territorial waters.[2] Where a ship is wrecked off the coasts of a State not party to the WRC 2007 it may be necessary to apply the national wreck removal law of that State with its various advantages and drawbacks.[3] There is obviously scope for a wide variety of national solutions,[4] although surveys by the CMI (and IMO)[5] have indicated that there were many common features, and highlighted general legislative questions that needed to be answered in the WRC 2007; they will also be relevant in those States that are not party to WRC 2007. These questions include:

> (i) To which craft do the powers apply? (ii) Is liability strict or based on negligence? (iii) Who is liable, the shipowner, or others such as demise charterers? (iv) Is the question of ownership (and liability) settled at the date of the casualty (eg sinking) or the date of the removal operation

---

1 For wreck on the seabed under the high seas (beyond the EEZ) see 7.3, 10.5.7.
2 See 8.3, 8.4, 9.3, and 11.2.2.
3 See *Machum & Metcalf, Will Insurance Cover That?*, 227, 230–235.
4 It may be that such wreck law is found in national or local (eg harbour) legislation, or has an overlay of more recent (general) national environmental law—as was the case with the *Rena*: see 1.2.4. See also Canada's compendious Abandoned or Hazardous Vessels Act 2019 which gives effect to the WRC 2007, but also deals with abandoned ships: and see 11.4.
5 See 7.1, 7.2.

(that may be much later)? (v) Are there any general defences available to the shipowner? (vi) Is the shipowner entitled to limit liability? (vii) What is the position of the insurer (if any)?

In England, the common law gradually developed to recognise that a harbour authority might bring a claim for wreck removal costs as damages for negligence[6] or (possibly) in public nuisance.[7] In the 19th century, it came to be recognised that harbours would benefit from stronger and clearer statutory protection to deal with the practical problem of dealing with wrecks, eg if sunk without fault. A typical approach taken in traditional wreck removal provisions can be seen in the UK legislation applicable before the UK enacted the WRCA 2011 to give effect to the WRC 2007.[8] This older legislation consisted of local legislation applied in individual ports and nationally applicable provisions applied through the Merchant Shipping Acts. This UK legislation is instructive of the practical legal problems that have been faced by public authorities in dealing with wreck removal and is still in force.[9]

11.1.2 UK local harbour legislation

11.1.2(a) Harbours Docks and Piers Clauses Act 1847 s 56

Many ports and harbours in the UK were developed at a time before the existence of modern planning laws and, in practice, Private Acts of Parliament were needed to authorise infringement of private rights[10] and to create new rights and powers. To save time, and to bring some uniformity, the Harbours Docks and Piers Clauses Act (HDPCA) 1847 contained model provisions for incorporation into local harbour Acts[11] Section 56 of the HDPCA 1847 is such a provision, commonly incorporated,[12] and was designed to deal with the problems facing harbour authorities having to deal with wrecked or stranded vessels blocking access, or posing a danger to other vessels.[13] It provided that the "harbour master may remove any wreck . . . to the harbour, dock, or pier, or the approaches to the

---

6 See eg *Dee Conservancy Board v McConnell* [1928] 2 KB 159, 164–166, 169; *Marsden and Gault*, 552–553 and 2.4.2. See also *The Putbus* [1969] P 136, 150, 153, [1969] 1 Lloyd's Rep 253. In *The Putbus* Phillimore LJ considered (obiter), at 155, that the right of the Crown to claim removal costs rested on its ownership of the subsoil of a particular waterway, implying that there might be a limitation on the right to claim removal costs by a harbour authority that did not own the subsoil. Such a principle might be relevant if the authority was claiming for economic losses caused by a blockage in the port (see 2.4.3), but does not appear to have been accepted in the case law on wreck *removal* by authorities.

7 See *Rose v Miles* (1815) 4 M&S 101, *Tate & Lyle Food Distribution Ltd v Greater London Council* [1983] 2 AC 509; *Marsden and Gault*, 553–554; also 2.4.3.

8 See 11.3.1.

9 The WRCA 2011 left these pre-existing wreck provisions largely untouched: see 11.3.4(c).

10 Eg though compulsory purchase, or interference with rights of navigation that might give rise to an action for public nuisance.

11 See eg the Medway Ports Authority Act 1973 s 4.

12 See eg the Poole Harbour Revision Order 2012 (SI 2012/1777), Art 3.

13 Users of a port may be bound by contractual undertakings to the port authority, eg that the customer warrants that the ship is seaworthy and is covered by P&I insurance for third party risks including pollution and wreck removal: see eg Associated British Ports Standard Terms and Conditions of Trade, cl 6.2(a). The problem is always that the personal contractual action may be difficult to enforce against a foreign single ship company whose ship is wrecked.

same . . . and the expense of removing any such wreck . . . shall be repaid by the owner".[14] It also allowed the harbour master to detain the wreck for security and, on non-payment of the removal expenses on demand, the harbour master could sell the wreck to cover those expenses. Any amount left over after the reimbursement of the expenses was held by the harbour authority to be paid to the owner when demanded.

Unusually for the time, this provision created a form of strict liability[15] on the "owner". However, in *The Crystal*[16] the House of Lords held that the removal expenses may only be levied against the person who was the owner of the wreck at the time that the expenses were incurred by the harbour authority. In this case, the shipowners had abandoned the wreck to their insurers as a total loss *before* the expenditure was incurred.[17] This divestment of ownership was said to have occurred because the shipowners "had abandoned the vessel as derelict on the high seas, without any intention of resuming possession or ownership" by giving a notice of abandonment to the underwriters and by notifying the authority of this.[18] It is not clear if the underwriters had accepted the notice of abandonment and had elected to take over ownership of the property.[19] Had they done so, the decision is more understandable, but it is unlikely today that the mere giving of the notice (without an acceptance by the underwriter) would allow the "owner" to argue that it ceased to be the owner for the purposes of the legislation. To do so would be to allow persons statutorily liable to evade their liabilities, and the decision may well have been influenced by the dislike of 19th-century commercial judges for statutory strict liability provisions.[20]

Further, if the owners had divested themselves of title, there has been an open question as to whether the harbour authority could then have claimed directly against the underwriters, on the basis that they had become the "owner". While liabilities at common law in relation to wreck do not necessarily depend on ownership and may be incurred by persons other than the owners of wrecks,[21] the question under legislation like s 56 is ultimately one of statutory interpretation.[22]

---

14 The section made no reference to the separate removal of cargo: cf the MSA 1995 s 252 and 11.1.3(a); also 10.6.

15 See also the HDPCA 1847 s 74, and 2.4.1.

16 *Arrow Shipping Co Ltd v Tyne Improvement Commissioners (The Crystal)* [1894] AC 508.

17 See 2.9.4(c).

18 Per Lord Herschell LC at p 519. Lord Watson at p 520 considered that the effect of abandonment "had divested the [shipowners] of all proprietary interest in the wreck".

19 The MIA 1906 ss 63 and 79 give an underwriter the right to assume ownership, but do not automatically vest title: see 2.9.4(c). The usual practice of underwriters is not to accept a notice of abandonment where there is an alleged constructive total loss, for the very reason that underwriters do not want to assume liabilities as owners.

20 Cf *River Wear Commissioners v Adamson* (1877) 2 App Cas 743, a case on s 74: see 2.1; see also *Dromgoole & Gaskell*, 185–186.

21 An action in negligence may lie against persons who have assumed duties in relation to the marking of a wreck, or those, such as harbour authorities, who may have such a duty imposed on them by law: see eg *The Tramontana II* [1969] 2 Lloyd's Rep 94, *The Kylix and the Rustringen* [1979] Lloyd's Rep 133.

22 In *The Chevron North America* [2002] 1 Lloyd's Rep 77 the House of Lords held that "owner" in s 74 of the HDPCA 1847 referred to the "registered owner", but this was in the context of deciding whether a bareboat charterer could be liable. An insurer that accepts a notice of abandonment may be unlikely to register ownership of a wrecked ship, but it is submitted that it could still be an "owner" for the purposes of the HDPCA 1847.

11.1.2(b) Modern local harbour legislation

The solution to *The Crystal* problem was to amend (or produce) local legislation so as to refer to the owner of the vessel at the time of the sinking, stranding or abandonment. This has been commonly done in applicable legislation in UK ports,[23] although it can sometimes be difficult to trace all such legislation in some ports. There may be a long accretion of private Acts dating back to the 19th century; they may not be easily or publicly available, or collated in a coherent fashion, and may have been affected by nationalisation and privatisation.[24] Extensive powers exist under the Harbours Act 1964 s 14 for the government to issue a 'Harbour Revision Order' (HRO) to repeal or supersede obsolete provisions in local legislation.[25] Such powers are in addition to more general operational powers given to harbour masters to give directions to ships entering, leaving or within their harbours.[26] Local harbour bye-laws tend to deal with normal operational matters within the port, and create offences,[27] but do not generally create substantive wreck removal powers as these are found in the principal legislation.

The Port of London Authority Act 1968 is a relatively clear example of legislation that does not incorporate the HDPCA 1847, but uses similar principles.[28] By s 120, as amended, the Port Authority is given the ability to cause a vessel to be raised, removed, blown up or otherwise destroyed if it is, or is likely to become, an obstruction, impediment or danger to the safe and convenient navigation or use of the Thames or the docks, or parts of them. There is power to sell the vessel and its cargo and retain proceeds to cover expenses, or to proceed against the owner of the vessel at the time of the sinking, stranding or abandonment as a debt.[29] The Authority is required to give 48 hours' notice of intention to use the powers,[30] giving the shipowner the ability to dispose of the vessel itself.

Not even modern local legislation could adequately deal with the problem caused by the absence of an internationally backed compulsory insurance provisions. In 2000, the *Lagik*, an Antigua and Barbuda registered ship with a steel cargo, grounded on the River Nene and broke her back and became a CTL. The port of Wisbech was closed for 44 days. The *Lagik* was abandoned by her owners, and the UK spent about £1.25 million to remove it without being able to make any recovery from the owners or insurers. The fear of what might have

---

23 See eg the Medway Ports Authority Act 1973 s 46(6) which altered the application of ss 252 and 253; the Act also incorporates the HDPCA 1847.

24 See eg the Mersey Docks Acts Consolidation Act 1858.

25 See the public register: www.gov.uk/government/collections/harbour-orders-public-register; also 11.1.3.

26 See eg s 52 of the HDPCA 1847 s 52; s 40A of the Harbours Act 1964 (inserted by s 5 of the Marine Navigation Act 2013); also the Dangerous Vessels Act 1985 and the Dangerous Substances in Harbour Areas Regulations (SI 1987/37); for intervention powers, see 4.8.3, 5.3.

27 See eg Associated British Ports bye-laws at www.abports.co.uk/About_ABP/ABP_ByeLaws/.

28 See also the Medway Ports Authority Act 1973 s 46 which was expressly framed around the MSA 1894 ss 530 and 532.

29 If this is not successful, the Authority may be able to proceed against a person whose name appears as owner in the last licence or certificate of registration issued by the Authority Prior to the LLMC 1976, the framing of the liability as a debt, and not damages, was used as one reason to deny limitation of liability under the MSA 1894 s 503. The LLMC 1976/1996 now Art 2 allows limitation whatever the basis of liability, but has a special reservation for wreck removal: see 2.5.4(c) and 2.5.8.

30 Section 120(5) allows a notice to be displayed at the Authority's head office if the shipowner's place of business is unknown or out of the UK.

happened at Felixstow was one of the arguments raised in Parliament in favour of enacting the WRC 2007.[31]

11.1.3 Merchant Shipping Act 1995

The Removal of Wreck Act 1877[32] enacted more generally applicable powers of wreck removal than the local HDPCA 1847. These powers were re-enacted in the MSA 1894 ss 530–531, which in turn were re-enacted in the MSA 1995 ss 252–253.[33]

11.1.3(a) Harbour authorities: s 252

Section 252 of the MSA 1995 Act[34] provides that where a vessel is sunk, stranded or abandoned[35] in any harbour, a harbour authority[36] or conservancy authority[37] is given the power (a) to take possession of, raise, remove, or destroy the whole or any part of a vessel, (b) to "mark the location of"[38] the vessel and (c) to sell any vessel, or part of it, raised or removed. The powers only arise where, in the opinion of the authority, the vessel is, or is likely to become, "an obstruction or danger to navigation (or to lifeboats).[39] This means that the power to remove did not arise for an environmental threat, or for an abandoned wreck which is merely an eyesore.[40] Where the vessel, or that part which is raised, is sold, the authority is entitled to the reimbursement of its expenses out of the proceeds of sale, retaining any surplus in trust for the benefit of the owner.[41] Section 252(3) treats everything removed from a wreck as part of the common fund, be it the vessel itself or tackle,

---

31 See Dr T Coffey, Hansard Vol 252 col 590, 18 March 2011. Official Report, Wreck Removal Convention Public Bill Committee, 7 February 2011, c 4. See also 7.1.
32 See *Kennedy & Rose*, 689.
33 These provisions were left largely untouched by the WRCA 2011: see 11.3.4.(c).
34 Re-enacting the MSA 1894 s 530. Section 252(10) of the Merchant Shipping Act 1995 provides that the various powers are additional to each other.
35 See also 11.4.
36 Defined in the MSA 1995 s 313(1) (as amended by the MSMSA 1997 Sch 6 para 19) to refer generally to those entrusted with general harbour functions and more particularly to a "statutory harbour authority" or the "proprietor". The former refers to an authority within the meaning of the Harbours Act 1964 (or the Harbours Act (Northern Ireland) 1970; the latter concept reflects private ownership of some ports and was reinstated by the MSMSA 1997 after being omitted from the 1995 consolidation.
37 Defined in the MSA 1995 s 313(1) to include those entrusted with the function of conserving, maintaining or improving the navigation of a tidal water (as defined in s 255): see eg the Chichester Harbour Conservancy established under the Chichester Harbour Conservancy Act 1971. The Environment Agency acts as a conservancy authority for a number of rivers.
38 The Marine Navigation Act 2013 s 11 inserted this more general phrase in s 252(2)(b) to reflect the importance of "location" in the WRC 2007, and in a new s 252(3A) clarified that that the location could be marked by "(a) buoys, lights or other physical devices" and "(b) the transmission of information about the location". This allows for electronic warnings about wrecks, eg a message to appear on an electronic chart display or radar set to keep clear from a particular zone, as a first response before more traditional physical marks are installed. Although there is power to mark the location, there is no express power actually to undertake the activities to actually "locate" the wreck in the first place. Such power may arise under a harbour authority's more general functions; see also s 197A and the power of GLAs, 11.1.3(b), 11.3.5.
39 See s 252(1). The provision does not envisage that cargo could be an obstruction.
40 This is generally also true of most of the harbour legislation. Where the WRC 2007 applies, the position is now different: see 8.2.2, 8.2.39.2.2, 9.2.5, 10.5.
41 See the MSA 1995 s 252(4).

equipment, cargo, stores or ballast. An innocent cargo owner may then find that it is subject to an authority's statutory right that can defeat its proprietary rights.[42] It is doubtful whether s 252 allows for the recovery of cargo which has been lost overboard from a ship which has not itself become sunk, stranded or abandoned.[43]

Although s 252 does not require any proof of fault, it has always been defective in that, unlike the HDPCA 1847 s 56,[44] it does not give the authority an independent cause of action to sue the shipowner for any of its operational expenses in removing a wreck. This is relevant when the wreck has no value out of which the expenses could be paid. Harbour and conservancy authorities may thus need to rely on the HDPCA 1847 s 56, if it is incorporated, or upon special legislation applicable to the particular harbour. Local statutes[45] and modern HROs[46] now often modify s 252 to give an express power to claim expenses from the owner of the vessel,[47] usually providing that appropriate notice is to be given before s 252 powers are exercised against an owner.[48] Such HROs may also have a provision protecting Crown interests in wrecks and dealing with "unserviceable vessels".[49]

There is nothing in s 252, though, to replace any common law liability (eg for negligent navigation) that the owner might have for the expenses incurred by the harbour authority, and such liability cannot be avoided by abandonment of ownership.[50] The MSA 1995 does not generally apply to Royal Navy ships, but can (by Order in Council) apply to UK "Government ships", eg Royal Fleet Auxiliaries.[51] The extent to which the legislation applies to foreign warships and other State vessels will depend on issues of sovereign immunity.[52]

11.1.3(b) General lighthouse authorities: s 253
Section 253 of the MSA 1995[53] was designed to deal with sunk, stranded or abandoned vessels in those areas where there is no harbour or conservancy authority with the relevant

---

42 See also 3.2.3.
43 By contrast with the MSA 1894 (see 10.6.2), the MSA 1995 s 252 used a different drafting technique whereby the general removal powers are only triggered if a vessel is first sunk, stranded or abandoned. At that stage removal powers can be used, including powers in relation to "other property" such as cargo. See also 11.3.5.
44 See 11.1.2.
45 See eg the Chichester Harbour Conservancy Act 1971 ss 43–44.
46 Made under the Harbours Act 1964 s 14: see 11.1.2(b).
47 See eg Art 33(2) of the Comhairle nan Eilean Siar (Ardveenish) Harbour Revision Order 2000 (SI 2000/233) [Ardveenish Order 2000], applying to a modernised small fishing harbour in the Outer Hebrides. Similar provisions appear to have been adopted in other harbours in the UK, see eg Arts 25–27 of the Maryport Harbour Revision Order 2007 [Maryport Order] (SI 2007/3463) for a small port in Cumbria: see also 11.1.3(b), 11.4.
48 "Owner" is usually defined in these HROs as the person who was the owner of the vessel at the time of the sinking, stranding or abandonment: see eg the Portland Harbour Revision Order 1997 (SI 1997/2949) Art 14.
49 Art 33(1) the Ardveenish Order 2000 provides that ss 252 *and* 253 "shall have effect" subject to such additional provisions; see also the Maryport Order, which only applies to s 252; and see 11.4.
50 See eg *Dee Conservancy Board v McConnell* [1928] 2 KB 159.
51 See ss 308, 309 and *Gaskell, MSA 1995*, 21/315–21/316. The Ardveenish 2000 Order Art 34 is an example of a common modern provision imposing restrictions on the exercise of powers in relation to wrecks in which the Crown is interested, eg Royal Navy vessels that are sunk, stranded or "abandoned by design".
52 See also 4.7. For the exclusion of warships and Government non-commercial vessels by the WRC 2007 Art 4(2), see 8.2.1(h).
53 Re-enacting the MSA 1894 s 531, but with new subss (2)–(4). The powers therefore also include the ability to "mark the location" of the wreck and to use electronic methods to transmit information: see fn 38.

powers. Here, the same powers that exist under s 252[54] are given to a general lighthouse authority (GLA) by s 253(1).[55] The area in which the GLA can exercise this power is described in somewhat archaic language in s 253(1)(a) as "in any fairway or on the seashore or on or near any rock, shoal or bank in the United Kingdom or any of the *adjacent seas or islands*". The latter expression, in particular, has caused uncertainty as to how far out to sea the powers can be exercised; it dates from an era before the EEZ was created and may well be restricted to territorial waters. There are also doubts about how far the powers apply to cargo that is washed overboard without the ship sinking. Both of these difficulties will be clarified by applying the WRC 2007.[56] The *Crystal* defect, revealed in s 252, was remedied for the GLAs under s 253(2) and (4) by the addition of a power for the GLA to recover the full amount of its expenses from the owner of the vessel at the time of the sinking, stranding or abandonment.[57]

There are three GLAs: Trinity House (for England and Wales); the Commissioners of Northern Lighthouses (Scotland) and the Commissioners of Irish Lights (Northern Ireland).[58] The GLAs have general responsibility under the MSA 1995 Part VIII, eg to superintend and manage buoys and unmanned radio beacons,[59] within their respective areas and "adjacent seas and islands" to each of their areas. The reference to "seas" includes seas in an area specified under s 129(2)(b);[60] ie the area for which the UK has jurisdiction for the prevention of pollution from ships—in effect the EEZ. The GLAs do not have general responsibilities for the areas governed by "local lighthouse authorities", eg statutory harbour authorities exercising powers within the limits of a port.[61] Statutory harbour authorities have their own powers to carry out operations in their ports, eg marking or lighting.[62] However, although the GLAs cannot install buoys and beacons in a harbour authority's area, they may do so if directed by the Secretary of State (for Transport), eg in the interests of general navigation.[63] This might be because the local harbour authority did not have the facilities or experience to do so.[64] It is acknowledged that the GLAs have significant

---

54 See 11.1.3(a).

55 There may be circumstances where the powers of harbour authorities within their areas are limited by modern HROs, eg in respect of Crown vessels: eg the Ardveenish 2000 Order Art 34. Such provisions usually make clear that the limitation of such powers does not operate to authorise the GLA to use its powers under s 253 to fill the gap: see Art 34(7).

56 See 11.3.5.

57 See the MSA 1995 s 253(2)(b), originally added by the MSA 1988 Sched 5. It is not clear why similar revisions were not made to s 252, but it may have been because of the existence of the HDPCA 1847 s 56 and local legislation.

58 See the MSA 1995 Part VIII, s 193 (as amended). Trinity House also has responsibilities in respect of Gibraltar and the Channel Isles: see s 193(5) and *Gaskell, MSA 1995*, 21/18–21/19.

59 See the MSA 1995 ss 193(1), 195; s 223(1) provides that buoys and beacons "includes all other marks and signs of the sea" and their appurtenances.

60 See s 193(6), inserted by the Marine Navigation Act 2013 s 8(1).

61 See the MSA 1995 s 193(2), (3) and s 197(2). This division of powers was made originally by the Ports Act 1991: see *Gaskell, MSA 1995*, 21/18–21/19.

62 See the MSA 1995 s 201, as amended.

63 See the MSA 1995 s 197(3). For the hierarchy between the GLAs and local lighthouse authorities see DfT, "Draft Marine Navigation Bill: Consultation Document" (May 2008) [*Marine Navigation Bill Consultation 2008*], 19.

64 For the GLA functions in relation to wreck removal under the MSA 1995 Part 9A regime, see 11.3.4(c), 11.3.5.

knowledge and expertise about deciding whether a wreck is likely to become an obstruction or danger to navigation, particularly Trinity House as it has to deal with relatively shallow waterways (eg the English Channel), whereas wrecks off the west coast of Scotland and Ireland tend to be in deeper water. "Factors affecting safety of navigation include the clearance depth over the site at lowest astronomical tide; the depth of water in the area; the type, size and construction of the vessel; traffic density and frequency; the proximity of shipping routes; the type of traffic; and the topography of the seabed. Decisions about wreck removal or dispersal are inextricably linked to the danger presented by the wreck".[65]

11.2 Accession choices for States

11.2.1 Merits of the WRC 2007

In deciding whether to ratify or accede to the WRC 2007 a State will have to question whether it was necessary for the IMO to produce the convention at all. That would entail an examination of its own current wreck removal laws and their adequacy, by comparison with the advantages offered by the WRC.[66]

It is not possible here to provide a complete list of the all the advantages and disadvantages of the WRC 2007. In a broad sense it has achieved some public law advances. The powers of intervention in the EEZ provided for in the WRC 2007 are significant, because for the first time they allow expressly for intervention in relation to wrecks that cause navigational hazards *and* affect other State interests. Moreover, they provide an intervention power in cases where neither the Intervention Convention 1969 nor UNCLOS would apply, by recognising a lower threshold for invoking intervention. For instance, these powers might allow action to be taken in the EEZ when a ship is stranded on a coral reef, or where containers of plastic are lost (threatening living resources and coastal amenities), or where bulk cargoes such as coal or wheat spill from the ship in sensitive waters. Unfortunately, the application of the WRC 2007 in the EEZ may be restricted so that it applies in international law only between States parties,[67] but it is nevertheless a significant new resource for coastal States to protect their interests and a guide for future legal developments.[68] The Netherlands, for instance, has apparently applied the provisions of the WRC 2007 to *all* ships wrecked in its EEZ, using as a justification Art 211(5) and (7) of UNCLOS.[69]

From a private law perspective, it is good to see a strict liability regime for wreck and cargo removal, backed by familiar compulsory insurance provisions. Although there may be overlaps with existing IMO liability conventions, in some circumstances (eg removal of hazardous and noxious cargo) the WRC may provide additional (insured) protection before entry into force of the HNSC 2010 in a way that may not have been fully appreciated.[70] The

---

65 Lord Greenway (an Elder Brethren of Trinity House) speaking at the Second Reading of the Wreck Removal Convention Bill in the House of Lords, Hansard Vol 727, col 1127 (13 May 2011) [*House of Lords, WRC Bill Second Reading debate*].
66 See eg the list of questions posed in 11.1.1; also the CMI and IMO investigations: 7.1, 7.2.
67 See 7.4, but note 10.2.7(b), 10.8.4(a).
68 See also 10.2.7(b), 10.8.5(a), 11.3.1(b).
69 See Netherlands' Act of 14 October 2015 Staatsblad 2015, 399): see also the Nota Van Wijziging ("Amendment Note") from the Netherlands' Government to the Parliament (Tweede Kamer) of 9 September 2019.
70 See 10.6.4.

international community is certainly increasing the harmonisation of its liability regimes, with a longer term possibility of unifying the various conventions.

If the WRC 2007 has succeeded to some extent in providing new and worthwhile rights to States in the EEZ, what of its possible extension to territorial waters?

11.2.2 Should States extend the WRC 2007 to territorial waters?

On the assumption that insurers will be able to rely on the WRC 2007 Art 12(10) cap,[71] there are two important consequences. First, when a State becomes a party to the WRC 2007 it is committing itself, in effect, to a guaranteed but restricted ability to claim for wreck removal costs—albeit with the theoretical possibility of unlimited liability against the shipowner (which in all probability will be a single ship company without assets). Moreover, while national law might give an unfettered right to claim removal costs,[72] adoption of the WRC 2007 will mean that the costs must be proportionate and reasonably necessary,[73] and the ability to impose conditions on salvage operations may be limited.[74]

Secondly, where a State does not become party to the WRC 2007 it may still have its unlimited (but probably worthless) claim against the shipowner, and may continue to have access to any national direct action statute if it can enforce that against a foreign insurer.[75]

Why would a State want to bind itself to the first of these consequences by adopting the WRC 2007 when States such as New Zealand and Italy appear to have made substantial recoveries under existing law, without apparently being affected by any limits of liability? If the Clubs insuring these claims have stood behind the shipowners' practically unlimited liability without relying on the 'pay to be paid' clause,[76] then no special direct action provisions have been needed. The authors are not privy to the detailed negotiations following the *Rena* or *Costa Concordia* casualties, and some caution needs to be exercised before assumptions are made as to who paid what, and why. It may be that the two States have been fortunate in being faced by reputable shipowners who did not want to walk away from their liabilities (or for public relations reasons did not want to be seen to be walking away). Still, busy governments might ask whether any legislation is really necessary. It may be that they should not assume that these cases are the norm,[77] and that insurers may now take a firmer approach with States that have not chosen to adopt the WRC 2007.[78]

---

71 Ie that *Prestige* type parallel actions against insurers ought not to succeed in avoiding that cap: see 2.9.6(c), 10.8.5(g); and that States cannot create unlimited direct action liability of the insurer through exercising the LLMC opt-out: see 2.5.8, 10.8.5(g), but cf 11.3.4(b).
72 Cf 11.1.2, 11.1.3.
73 See Art 2(2) and 2(3): also 9.2.5(e), 10.2.4.
74 See Art 9(4): also 9.2.5(c), 10.1.
75 Cf 10.8.5(g).
76 See 2.9.6(c).
77 Cf the experience of the Netherlands with the *Iugo* and *Assi Eurolink,* where the 'pay to be paid' clause was either applied or used as a negotiating ploy: see 2.5.9(e), and 7.1, 7.2 generally. See also the *Baltic Ace* litigation, 2.5.9(c).
78 See also 10.8.6.

11.2.3 Checklist when adopting the WRC 2007

If a State decides to ratify or accede to the WRC 2007 it will have a number of decisions to make when it implements the convention in national law.

Some decisions may not arise directly under the WRC 2007 itself, eg in relation to limitation of liability which is very much left open by the WRC Art 10(2).[79] Many of the complications and hidden problems in relation to wreck removal claims (and maritime claims in general) revolve around limitation of liability.[80] There are enough drafting problems even in the LLMC 1996[81] for a State to question whether it wants to be a party. The concept of limitation has always been central to maritime law, but is never popular with claimants—especially States that suffer loss. Rejecting limitation altogether may not solve all problems, eg if there is no insurer, but a State will have to weigh up whether the treaty linkage in the WRC 2007 (and Bunkers Convention 2001) is a sufficient reason to reject the limitation conventions and enact its own national limitation laws.[82] Indeed, the reference in the WRC 2007 Art 10(2) to "national . . . regime" almost invites such reconsideration.[83] In any event, LLMC 1976 States (especially those that are not major flag States) need to consider seriously whether to denounce the convention and upgrade to the LLMC 1996.[84] For LLMC 1976 or 1996 States it is important to make sure that they have exercised the right to make the LLMC Art 18 reservation, ie allowing for unlimited shipowner liability for wreck and cargo removal.[85] They also need to ensure that this reservation is then enacted in national law. This holds true even if the States decide not to adopt the WRC 2007, and many small island states are already vulnerable for adopting the LLMC without the reservation.[86] Further, an LLMC State might consider 'clarifying' its limitation procedural rules, eg to state that the insurer's direct liability in the WRC 2010 Art 12(10) is only subject to limitation of liability under the law of the WRC 2007 State itself,[87] and that it will not recognise foreign limitation funds in States that have not exercised the LLMC Art 18 reservation.[88]

In relation to the WRC 2007 itself, drafters will need to integrate the public and private law aspects of the WRC 2007 into a national legal framework. The WRC 2007 cannot simply be implemented by giving it the force of law, without additional provisions. The UK method, discussed below,[89] is not perhaps an ideal model, but it shows the difficulties of the drafter's task. That task may be even more difficult for States with a full federal system.[90]

---

79 See 10.7.
80 See eg 2.5.8 (LLMC opt-out), 2.5.9 (forum shopping) and 10.8.5 (insurer's WRC 2007 cap).
81 There will always be reluctance at IMO to tinker too much with the LLMC, no matter how sensible are any reform suggestions: see eg *Martinez Gutierrez*, Chapter 8.
82 See also 2.4.9(f).
83 Italy, for example, is not party to the LLMC 1976 or 1996.
84 Cf the problems in the *Rena*: see 1.2.4(d), 2.5.8.
85 See 2.5.8.
86 Eg Comoros, Cook Islands, Samoa, St Lucia, Niue, Palau: see 2.5.9(e).
87 Cf 10.8.5(c) and (d).
88 See 2.5.9(e) and (f).
89 See 11.3.1.
90 Cf Malaysia's Merchant Shipping (Amendment and Extension) Act 2011 and Canada's Wrecked, Abandoned or Hazardous Vessels Act 2019.

The most obvious legislative choice is whether to extend the WRC 2007 into territorial (and internal) waters.[91] As the WRC 2007 provisions are limited to "seagoing" ships[92] consideration will be needed as to which wreck removal provisions will apply to non-seagoing ships, eg in internal waters.[93] There may be other structures or objects that are wrecked at sea but do not fall within the WRC 2007, eg floating pipes and fixed offshore platforms.[94] The same issue arises with ships that are abandoned without a "marine casualty" necessary to trigger the application of the WRC 2007.[95] All these areas not falling within the WRC 2007 may mean that pre-existing wreck removal laws should be retained, or at least properly integrated with the WRC 2007.[96] The State may decide that it needs to retain a power to sell wrecks.[97]

Further, where the State has opted-in to extend the WRC 2007 inwards from the EEZ, it will need to take account of the WRC 2007 Art 4(4) under which a number of provisions do not apply at all in its territory[98] and one provision is made subject to the national law of the State.[99] These exclusions were designed not to diminish a State's rights, but to recognise and preserve the wider rights that States can exert in their territory and territorial sea by comparison with the EEZ. In respect of these excluded provisions a State is presumably free to impose its own requirements, or to reapply those in the WRC 2007. It is particularly important for a State to ensure that it has reinstated the power to remove a wreck itself under Art 9(7)–(8), as a failure to do so will mean that it will not be able to trigger the liability provisions in Art 10, or the compulsory insurance provisions in Art 12(10).

This last problem was one of a number of potential legislative traps for a State highlighted by Patrick Griggs (past President of the CMI),[100] mostly to do with the consequences of opting to extend the WRC 2007 into territorial waters and the effect of Art 4(4).[101] These traps include: being careful not to enact special measures about wrecks in their territorial waters that might conflict with the WRC 2007;[102] recognising that the obligation to inform and consult with other State parties when a hazard is assessed only applies in the EEZ and not territorial waters;[103] allowing opt-in States to retain national intervention powers in the territorial sea, although recognising that there are restrictions on State intervention in

---

91 See Art 3(2)–(5); also 8.4, 11.2.2, 11.3.2.

92 See Art 1(2); also 2.5.2, 10.2.7.

93 See 11.3.4(c). Canada has extended provisions in its Wrecked, Abandoned or Hazardous Vessels Act 2019 to craft that are not seagoing.

94 See 10.2.7.

95 See 8.2.1(a), 10.5.1(a), 11.4, 14.2.

96 Cf 11.3.4.

97 This is not covered by the WRC 2007: see 9.2.5(h), 10.2.2, 11.3.4(c).

98 See Art 4(4)(a) excluding Art 2(4), Art 9(1), (5), (7)–(10); also 8.4, 10.5.2, 10.5.4–10.5.6.

99 See Art 4(4)(b) modifying Art 9(4); also 8.4, 10.5.4.

100 See P Griggs, "The Wreck Removal Convention 2007 (WRC 2007)—legislative traps" [*Griggs, Legislative Traps*] (2015) 10 Shipping and Transport International, 10 (currently available from publisher Guthrum House's website www.stl-mag.co.uk/content-from-previous-issues).

101 He also notes the international law obligations that do not apply (or are not relevant) in territorial waters, eg about dispute resolution (Arts 15, 4(4)(a)(iii)), automatic consent (Art 9(10)) and exercising sovereignty over the high seas (Art 2(4)).

102 See Art 3(2); and cf 11.3.1.

103 See Art 9(1); and 8.4.1.

wreck removals in the EEZ;[104] ensuring that the default power to step in, remove the wreck and charge the owner is applied in territorial waters;[105] ensuring that ships flying their flag comply with obligations generally, but also that all shipowners have to remove wrecks and provide insurance details in territorial waters;[106] Griggs rightly emphasises that mere incorporation of the WRC 2007 in national law is not enough because of these traps.

11.3 MSA 1995 Part 9A

11.3.1 UK method of enactment of WRC 2007

11.3.1(a) Wreck Removal Convention Act 2011

The UK had been an early international supporter of the WRC 2007, but before implementing it the DfT issued a consultation document in May 2008,[107] and a response in October 2008.[108] There had been plans to enact the WRC 2007 in a draft Marine Navigation Bill 2008,[109] but that Bill was delayed for reasons unconnected with the WRC 2007.[110] Indeed, in 2008 a powerful Select Committee Report had endorsed most of the proposals about the WRC 2007, although expressing some concerns eg about the financial effects on GLAs.[111] Eventually, the WRC 2007 was hived off into a separate Wreck Removal Convention Bill 2010.[112] With virtually no amendments,[113] and all party support, it became the Wreck Removal Convention Act (WRCA) 2011. The UK acceded to the WRC 2007 on 30 November 2012. Some preparatory provisions took effect from 5 February 2015, and the remainder of the WRCA 2011 came into force on the same date as the WRC 2007 itself, namely 14 April 2015.[114]

The WRCA 2011 only contains two sections; s 2 is the formal short title and commencement provision; s 1 is the main operative provision and contains five subsections which

---

104 See Arts 9(5) and 4(4)(a)(ii).
105 See Arts 9(7), 9(8) and 4(4)(a)(ii); also 11.3.3(d).
106 See Art 9(9), 9(2) and (9(3).
107 DfT, "Consultation on: The UK Implementation and Ratification of the Nairobi International Convention on the Removal of Wrecks, 2007" (May 2008). see *DfT Consultation on Implementation of WRC 2007*.
108 See DfT, "Summary of Responses to the Consultation on the Draft Marine Navigation Bill" (October 2008) [*DfT, Summary of Responses 2008*], 19–30: see https://webarchive.nationalarchives.gov.uk/20090224120926/www.dft.gov.uk/consultations/closed/marinenavbill/responses.pdf. This document contains the most comprehensive discussion of the Government's position in relation to what later became Part 9A of the MSA 1995.
109 See *Marine Navigation Bill Consultation 2008*; *DfT, Summary of Responses 2008*.
110 See the later Marine Navigation Act 2013, referred to elsewhere in this book.
111 See House of Commons Transport Committee, "Ninth Report of Session 2007–08, "The Draft Marine Navigation Bill" (19 July 2008) [*Transport Committee Ninth Report 2008*]; also House of Commons Transport Committee, Seventh Special Report of Session 2007–2008, "The Draft Marine Navigation Bill: Government Response to the Committee's Ninth Report of Session 2007–08" (15 October 2008), 8–10; see also 11.3.5.
112 Introduced as a Private Member's Bill in 2010 but with tacit Government support, as the Bill was prepared on behalf of the DfT. It is telling just how much merchant shipping legislation has had to be introduced in this way over the last 30 years.
113 The meaning of S 255S(1) was clarified; see 11.3.3(g).
114 See the Wreck Removal Convention Act 2011 (Commencement) Order 2015 (SI 2015/133), and the Marine Information Note (MIN 499 (M+F)), December 2014. See also *Kennedy & Rose*, 701–716.

amend the MSA 1995. Thereafter, one can largely ignore the WRCA 2011 and concentrate on the amended MSA 1995, especially a new Part 9A.[115]

The UK's enactment of the WRCA 2011 is one example of how to deal with some of the issues, discussed in 11.2.3, that arise when a State gives effect to the WRC 2007 in national law. In Griggs' view the UK has avoided the traps he identified when it enacted the WRCA 2011,[116] although it will be apparent that there are still drafting problems[117] and it may have been rather generous to declare that the UK comes out of the implementation exercise "with flying colours".[118]

11.3.1(b) Incorporation of WRC 2007

The methods of enacting maritime law conventions in the MSA 1995 have varied. For instance, with conventions such as the Athens Convention 2002, the LLMC 1976/1996 and the Salvage Convention 1989 the technique was used of giving the "force of law" to the respective conventions as contained in "Part I" of Schedules to the MSA 1995.[119] "Part II" of the Schedules contained necessary adjustments to national law in order to make the conventions work in the domestic context. The advantage of such a technique is that it takes the reader directly to the text of the convention itself. The alternative is to rewrite the convention into traditional UK drafting language.[120] This method carries with it the danger of creating subtle differences between fully debated convention language and the enacting statute, as well as the risk of omitting some provisions.[121]

The method of giving effect to the WRC 2007 is not to give it the force of law directly. Instead, there is a slightly curious hybrid method that makes incidental reference to the WRC 2007 in a number of places (without any single clear statement about its full application in UK law), but otherwise uses 'statutory English' to give effect to the Convention. Section 1 of the WRCA 2011 inserted a new self-contained Part 9A[122] into the MSA 1995, although this is not supported by any substantive section in the main text of the MSA 1995.[123] Part 9A contains 21 new sections (numbered from s 255A–255U), along with a new "Schedule 11ZA" which contains the full text of the WRC 2007 itself. What is lacking is any express provision that incorporates the whole convention in this schedule

---

115 For the sake of completeness, note that the WRCA 2011 s 1(3) inserts three technical references into the MSA 1995 s 306(2A)(c) (orders not subject to annulment); s 1(5) includes a reference to the WRCA 2011 amendments into the MSA 1995 s 315(2)–(6) (power to extend the MSA 1995 to relevant British possessions).

116 *Griggs, Legislative Traps*, 13.

117 In particular in relation to Arts 10(3), 11(2) and 12(10): see 11.3.5(a), 11.3.5(b). There is also uncertainty as to the extent to which it applies to ships of non-State parties: see 7.4.

118 *Griggs, Legislative Traps*, 13.

119 See eg s 183 (and Sch 6), s 185 (and Schedule 7), and s 224 (and Schedule 11) respectively.

120 Although it does depend on the drafter making all appropriate adjustments: see eg *Kennedy and Rose*, 252–257.

121 An unfortunate example is the awkward enactment of the CLC and Fund Conventions in Part VI of the MSA 1995: N Gaskell, "The Interpretation of Maritime Conventions at Common Law", in J P Gardner (ed), *United Kingdom Law in the 1990s* (London, 1990), 218, 219. Errors have had to be corrected piecemeal: see eg the Merchant Shipping (Pollution) Act 2006 s 3 (time limits under the Fund Convention 1992).

122 For reasons that are not entirely clear, Arabic numbering has been used for "Part 9A", whereas the other Parts of the MSA 1995 use Roman numbering.

123 Cf s 183 giving the force of law to the Athens Convention 2002 in Sch 6; s 185 giving the force of law to the LLMC 1996 in Sch 7; s 224 giving the force of law to the Salvage Convention 1989 in Sch 11.

by reference.[124] The original draft Marine Navigation Bill 2008[125] merely contained those sections in what is now Part 9A and did not have the convention in a schedule at all. Many of the draft sections 'rewrote' expressions in the WRC 2007 into 'legal English'.[126] Part 9A as finally enacted in 2011 has largely removed definitional rewriting and s 255R(1) (the interpretation section) now requires that expressions used in Part 9A "shall be construed in accordance with Article 1"[127] of the WRC 2007.[128]

This reference *only* to Art 1 of the WRC 2007, not to the whole convention, is rather awkward—especially as the Art 1 definitions are closely linked, and (not surprisingly) essential, to the remainder of the WRC 2007 provisions. A reader may have a nagging concern about whether every particular provision in the WRC 2007 is made effective through this method of incorporation. Indeed, this was the tenor of one of the consultation responses to the draft Marine Navigation Bill 2008, that pointed out nine instances where the draft Bill did not give effect to the WRC 2007.[129] While the final 2011 legislation reflects more of an effort to give express effect to the WRC 2007,[130] it has done so in a way that is piecemeal and difficult to relate to some issues raised by the original text[131] and it is submitted that it would have been much clearer to have used the "Part I" and "Part II" method of the Athens Convention 2002, the Salvage Convention 1989, and the LLMC 1996.[132] It is difficult to criticise the drafter without a full knowledge of the instructions given and it is possible that the technique chosen[133] was a way to avoid dealing expressly with the difficult international law questions, eg about how far the WRC 2007 can be applied to ships of non-State parties.[134] In fact, Part 9A provides no clear answer to all of those questions, whether by accident or design.[135]

---

124 With respect, Griggs is only partly right to suggest that there has been an "incorporation" by reference: see *Griggs, Legislative traps*, 13.

125 See the *Marine Navigation Bill Consultation 2008*, 50–59.

126 The definition section of the draft Marine Navigation Bill 2008, cl 255S(1), was the most egregious example in that it even rewrote the crucial Art 1(5) definition of "hazard".

127 Yet s 255R(2) uses the expression "accident" to describe what is called a "maritime casualty" in Art 1(3) of the WRC 2007, although the content is identical. This may be in order to be consistent with other MSA 1995 provisions, eg Sch 3A para 22(1).

128 Abbreviated in the Act as the "Wrecks Convention", presumably to align with the "Bunkers Convention" in the MSA 1995. In the book we have preferred the shorter WRC 2007 to reflect an international, rather than solely UK, perspective.

129 See *DfT, Summary of Responses 2008* 22–23, with Government replies to four of them. Such concerns may have been one of the reasons for creating Sch 11ZA and s 255R(1) through the WRCA 2011. Even so, there are still worrying examples of WRC 2007 provisions not mentioned in the new Part 9A: see 11.3.1 (below).

130 And it must be assumed that this is what is intended in order to give effect to international obligations.

131 While the WRCA 2011 is not quite as bad as the attempt to give effect to the Limitation Convention 1957 in 1958 legislation roundly castigated by the Court of Appeal in *The Putbus* [1969] P 136, the echoes of that criticism can be heard when reading the 2011 Act.

132 Ie of putting the text of the WRC 2007 in a schedule Part I and placing the substance of ss 255A-255U in a schedule Part II.

133 The drafting technique was foreshadowed by the Government in 2008 on the slightly nebulous basis that including the whole of the Convention's text would have required the addition of a number of new enabling and enforcement provisions: see *DfT, Summary of Responses 2008*, 21–22.

134 See 7.4.4, 10.2.7(b), 10.8.4(a).

135 Wreck reporting only applies to ships registered in States parties: see 11.3.3(a). There is no such *clear* differentiation in relation to wreck removal by the registered owner or Secretary of State: see 11.3.3(c) and (d). Nor is the position any clearer in relation to liability: see 11.3.4(a) and (b).

Specific sections in the new Part 9A do refer to the substantive text of the WRC 2007 in a variety of ways. For example, s 255B requires wreck reports to include information "mentioned in" WRC 2007 Art 5(2); s 255C(2) requires that the UK "complies with its obligations" under Arts 7 and 8; s 255D(2) refers to compliance with Art 9(2) and (3); s 255D(3) refers to matters "set out" in Art 9(6); s 255E(2) requires removal conditions to be "in accordance" with Art 9(4) of the WRC; s 255F(1) allows for removal "in the circumstances set out" in the WRC 2007 Art 9(7) or (8);[136] s 255G(3) refers to a convention "listed" in Art 11(1); s 255R(5) requires that the Secretary of State "take into account" matters in the WRC 2007 Art 6; and s 255S(2) refers to ships "specified" in Art 4(3).

By contrast, there is no specific reference to other provisions, eg Arts 9(1)[137] or 9(10).[138] These latter omissions might be explained on the basis that the obligations exist at the international law level (like Art 15) and need not be dealt with in national legislation. Similarly, there is no mention of Art 9(9) which places an obligation on States parties to ensure that ships flying their flags comply with Art 9(2) and (3), ie to remove a wreck that is a hazard, and to provide an Affected State with a copy of the WRC insurance certificate. Although s 255D(2) refers to Art 9(2) and (3), it is clear from s 255D(1) that it does so only in relation to wrecks in the UK's Convention area. There appears to be no express obligation on UK ships to remove a wreck in another WRC 2007 State's waters, as required by Art 9(9) and (2). By contrast, ss 255J, 255K and 255M do impose obligations on UK ships in relation to having insurance and producing insurance certificates if they are outside the UK.[139] There are many places where the Part 9A provisions do not make clear whether they apply to all foreign ships, or only to ships flying the flag of a State party.[140] There is also some ambiguity in respect of Art 9(4).[141] Potentially more serious omissions appear to be those in relation to Art 2,[142] Art 10(3)[143] and Art 11(2),[144] while the absence of a mention of Art 12(10) in s 255P creates uncertainty about whether insurers are exposed to unlimited liability.[145]

The reader has to be aware that, although it should be assumed that the WRC 2007 provisions in Schedule 11ZA are applicable to the UK as a State party, the method of enactment means that it is necessary to refer to the numbered sections of Part 9A to see exactly how the WRC 2007 will operate in UK law.[146]

---

136 Section 255G(2) also refers to exceptions "set out" in the WRC 2007 Art 10(1).
137 Ie the obligation to consult with the flag State for wrecks in the EEZ.
138 Ie the deemed consent, when entering into the WRC 2007, for Affected States to take action in the EEZ.
139 See 11.3.3(e). Note though that the obligation under Art 9(3) to provide an insurance certificate to the other State is met only indirectly: see s 255M(3) and 11.3.3(e).
140 Each provision needs to be examined separately, although the solutions are not always certain: see eg 11.3.3(c), 11.3.3(d) and 11.3.4(a). See the international law issues discussed in 7.4. In a number of places Part 9A makes reference to a "Wrecks Convention State", but this is only in the context of wreck insurance: see eg s 255N(1).
141 See 11.3.4(a).
142 Requiring proportionality and reasonableness in relation to costs: see 9.2.5(e), 10.2.4, 11.3.4(a).
143 Ie preventing parallel actions against the registered shipowner: see 10.2.2, 11.3.4(a).
144 Dealing with the overlap between the WRC 2007 and the Salvage Convention 1989: see 10.9.1, 11.3.4(a).
145 Ie the insurer's right to a cap on liability calculated according to Art 12(1): see 10.8.5, 11.3.4(b).
146 A number of relatively minor amendments have already been made to the provisions inserted by the WRCA 2011. These are footnoted in the text of Part 9A as reproduced in Appendix 2 of this book and, where relevant, are commented upon further in this chapter.

When considering a convention such as the WRC 2007, the UK courts will recognise its international character and genesis so as to reflect uniformity and comity,[147] so that it is interpreted "unconstrained by technical rules of English law, or by English legal precedent, but on broad principles of general acceptance".[148]

11.3.2 Extension of WRC 2007 into UK territorial waters

The decision to allow States to opt in to a modified application of the WRC 2007 in territorial waters has already been addressed.[149] The WRCA 2011 was enacted before the entry into force of the WRC 2007 (on 14 April 2015) and while the UK had yet to make a final decision whether to exercise the option. Accordingly, s 255R(6) of the WRCA 2011 allowed the Secretary of State by order to describe, from time to time, the UK's "Convention Area" within Art 1(1) of the WRC 2007; ie the extent to which the UK would extend the operation of the WRC 2007 under Art 3(2) from the EEZ to territorial waters. On the UK's accession on 30 November 2012, it declared that it would apply the Convention to wrecks located within its territory, including the territorial sea.[150] This was effected in UK law by the Merchant Shipping (United Kingdom Wreck Convention Area) Order 2015,[151] Art 2 of which defines the UK's "Convention Area" as comprising "(a) the United Kingdom", "(b) United Kingdom waters"[152] and "(c) the United Kingdom's exclusive economic zone".[153] The reference in (a) to the "United Kingdom" is broad enough to include those UK waters to the landward side of the baseline of the territorial sea;[154] these are the "internal waters" of a State.[155] In practice, the baselines may be drawn across the mouths of bays or rivers, so by referring to the "United Kingdom" the order includes ports, harbours and rivers.[156]

In applying the WRC 2007, the UK has also had to deal with the consequences of Art 4(4) which prevents the application of a number of provisions in its territory and territorial sea.[157] These would have placed some restrictions on the actions that a State like the UK could otherwise take,[158] but also would have provided some positive rights. In both cases a

---

147 See the Vienna Convention 1969, Arts 31–33. This includes considering the *travaux préparatoires*: see Art 32.
148 *James Buchanan & Co Ltd v Babco Forwarding & Shipping (UK) Ltd* [1978] AC 141, 152, [1978] 1 Lloyd's Rep 119; also *Fothergill v Monarch Airlines Ltd* [1981] AC 251, 281–282, [1980] 2 Lloyd's Rep 295.
149 See 8.4.
150 *IMO Status of Treaties* (November 2018).
151 SI 2015/172.
152 The MSA 1995 s 313(2) defines this to mean "the sea or other waters within the seaward limits of the territorial sea of the United Kingdom". See also the Territorial Sea Act 1987, the Territorial Sea (Limits) Order 1989 (SI 1989/482).
153 See the Marine and Coastal Access Act 2009 s 41 and the Exclusive Economic Zone Order 2013 (SI 2013/3161) which came into force on 31 March 2014.
154 See fn 89.
155 Under UNCLOS Art 8.
156 The WRC 2007 though, will only apply to "seagoing" vessels: see Art 1(2) and 10.2.7. This means that in these internal waters, in particular, it may be necessary to rely on the HDPCA 1847 s 56, the MSA 1995 ss 252–253 and local harbour legislation: see 11.1.2(a), 11.1.3, 11.3.5.
157 See 11.2.3, 8.4.
158 Eg the imposition of conditions for removal under Art 9(4), the power to intervene in Art 9(5).

State is free to reinstate these provisions in relation to its territory or territorial sea under its international law entitlements as a coastal State. Part 9A does not give a clear (ie separate and express) treatment of how these exclusions will operate but, in general, the UK has not made a distinction in Part 9A between those obligations and rights that will apply in its EEZ as opposed to its territory or territorial sea. In effect, the intention appears to have been to apply essentially the same regime to its whole UK "Convention area". This has required it to add back in the positive rights in relation to removing the wreck itself under Art 9(7) and (8),[159] and therefore the right to charge the registered owner the costs of so doing.[160] What is rather unclear is the extent to which provisions are intended to apply to all ships, or only to those of States parties.[161]

In short, the UK has given the WRC 2007 a very wide geographical application.[162] The UK's accession declared that the "Convention was extended to the Isle of Man (excluding its territory and territorial sea) with effect from 14 April 2015, to Gibraltar with effect from 16 April 2015 and to the Cayman Islands with effect from 7 February 2017".[163]

11.3.3 Part 9A administrative provisions

Most, but not all, of the 21 sections in Part 9A deal with mainly administrative or public law issues.[164] Given that the WRCA 2011 was intended to implement the WRC 2007, it is not necessary to add to the previous analysis of the WRC 2007 in this book.[165] The MSA 1995 Part 9A now provides the public law structure to support implementation in the UK. Most provisions of the WRC 2007 refer to the "registered owner", but that is defined widely in Art 1(8) to include the persons owning an unregistered ship.[166] Note also the provisions in relation to Government ships.[167] The expression "ship" as used in the WRC 2007 and Part 9A is wider than that applying elsewhere in the MSA 1995.[168] Part 9A makes many references to actions or decisions by the "Secretary of State", ie for Transport, but in practice most of the powers in relation to wreck will be delegated to the SOSREP.[169]

---

159 See 11.2.3; s 255F and 11.3.3(d).
160 See 10.5.3(a), 10.5.3(c)–(e); s 255G and 11.3.4(a).
161 This problem is addressed in 11.3.3 and 11.3.4.
162 It is convenient to mention here that s 315(2)–(5) (granting power to the UK to extend the MSA 1995 to relevant British possessions), has effect so that it includes references to Part 9A: see the WRCA 2011 s 1(5).
163 *IMO Status of Treaties* (November 2018). Gibraltar and the Cayman Islands declared that they would apply the Convention to wrecks located within their territories, including their territorial seas.
164 See 11.3.4 for private law liability issues.
165 See Chapters 7–10.
166 See 9.1.3(a), 10.2.2. The MSA 1995 s 255R(4) provides that references in Part 9A to "ships registered in a State" include unregistered ships entitled to fly the flag of that State. The expression "registered in a State" appears literally only in the compulsory insurance provisions, but it is assumed that s 255R(4) was intended to apply more generally, eg when Part 9A refers to the "registered owner", eg in the liability provisions in s 255G.
167 See s 255S, giving effect to the WRC 2007 Art 4(2) and 8.1.2(h), 11.3.4(g).
168 See the WRC 2007 Art 1(2) which includes floating platforms and hovercraft: see 8.2.1(b), 10.2.7, 10.8.2(b); Cf the MSA 1995 s 313 definition, "ship includes every description of vessel used in navigation".
169 See 4.2.2.

11.3.3(a) Wreck reports

Section 255B gives effect to Art 5 of the WRC 2007 by specifying when and to whom wreck reports are to be made. Following the principle of flag State responsibility, reporting obligations under s 255B(1) are placed on those responsible for a UK ship involved in an "accident"[170] in a "Convention area".[171] Reports have to be made "without delay" to the Secretary of State (for wrecks in the UK Convention area), or to a foreign government when in its area.[172] The responsibility for reporting falls on the "master" or "operator" of a ship.[173] A "master" is defined in the MSA 1995 s 313(1) to include those (other than a pilot) having command or charge of the ship. In the event of a wreck where the master is incapacitated, the duty could fall on a senior surviving officer. An "operator" is defined in the WRC 2007 Art 1(9),[174] and means the owner, ship manager or bareboat charterer that has assumed responsibility for operation of the ship. It is possible that others might have assumed control of the ship, eg salvors, but Art 1(9) looks to those who have assumed responsibility under the International Safety Management (ISM) Code. Only one of these persons is obliged to make a report.[175] Although the exact form of the report is not specified it must contain the information listed in the WRC 2007 Art 5(2), eg the name of the registered owner, the location of the wreck and the nature of the wreck and its cargo.[176] A failure to report a wreck is an offence.[177]

As the WRC 2007 puts the reporting obligations on ships registered in States parties, it places no obligation to report on ships registered in non-State parties. The UK has not sought to apply an obligation on such ships to report, either in the EEZ or in the territory or territorial sea.[178]

11.3.3(b) Locating and marking wrecks

Section 255C places an obligation on the Secretary of State to ensure that the UK meets its WRC 2007 Arts 7 and 8 obligations[179] of locating and marking wrecks in the UK "Convention area". The mechanism for the UK to do so will usually be for the Secretary of State to give a mandatory direction[180] to a GLA,[181] a harbour authority or a conservancy authority.[182] The scope of the direction is merely to take "specified steps" within their respective areas, but a direction may also require the authority to exercise (or not exercise) its powers under

---

[170] See s 255R(2); WRC 2007 Art 1(3); 8.2.1(a), 10.5.1.
[171] See s 255R(1); WRC 2007 Art 1(1). Ie the territorial waters and EEZ for the UK: see 11.3.2.
[172] See s 255B(1)–(3).
[173] See s 255B(1) and (4).
[174] See 9.1.3(a).
[175] See s 255B(6) and 9.1.3(a).
[176] See s 255N(5) and 9.1.3(b). The draft Marine Navigation Bill 2008 had omitted a reference to Art 5(2).
[177] See s 255B(7).
[178] This appears to be a recognition that otherwise there might be a breach of general principles of UNCLOS, as recognised by the WRC 2007 Art 16: see 7.4.
[179] See 9.2.3, 9.2.4. The draft Marine Navigation Bill 2008 had an additional (somewhat inelegant) requirement that the "Secretary of State thinks that the wreck poses a hazard". This requirement is now subsumed by the reference to Arts 7 and 8, which is certainly a drafting improvement.
[180] See s 255C(3), (7).
[181] See also 11.1.3(b), (c), 11.3.5.
[182] See also 11.1.2, 11.1.3(a).

the MSA 1995 ss 252 and 253.[183] The notice to the authority has to be in writing, but it may be that the SOSREP[184] has to act immediately at the scene of a wreck and gives the direction by telephone; in such a case the direction has to be confirmed in writing as soon as reasonably practicable.[185]

There is no restriction in s 255C to wrecks of ships that are registered in States parties to the WRC 2007. There merely has to be a "wreck"[186] in the "Convention area". The reference to the WRC Arts 7 and 8 could be said to raise by implication the larger international law question as to how far the convention applies to the ships of non-State parties (at least in the EEZ),[187] but as a simple matter of interpretation of a UK statute there appears to be no restriction intended in s 255C. At one level this is not surprising as the locating and marking obligations are State obligations, although ultimately their costs might fall on owners and insurers.[188]

11.3.3(c) Removal by registered owner
Section 255D is the key provision to give effect to the UK's powers to require a registered owner to remove a wreck under the WRC 2007 Art 9,[189] and is supplemented by s 255E. The Secretary of State has to satisfy the WRC 2007 triggers, eg that there has been accident to a "ship" as a result of which it, or anything from it,[190] has become a wreck in the UK Convention area,[191] and that this poses a hazard.[192]

Section 255D(2) creates the UK concept of a "wreck removal notice" as a mechanism for complying with the general notification obligations owed to the registered owner under the WRC 2007 Art 9(6) when the owner is required to remove a wreck and provide insurance details under the WRC 2007 Art 9(2) and (3).[193] The formality of such a notice is helpful to insurers, in particular.[194] All reasonable steps must be taken to give the notice, which may not be easy with a foreign shipowner. The form and contents of the notice are as set in the WRC 2007 Art 9(6),[195] eg that it be in writing, set deadlines and state the intention of the State to intervene immediately itself when the hazard becomes severe. It is an offence

---

183 See s 255C(4) and 11.1.3. The extent of the GLA's powers in the EEZ have been confirmed by an amendment to s 255C(4) made by the Marine Navigation Act 2013 s 8(2)(a): see 11.3.4(c). The draft Marine Navigation Bill 2008 had a specific reference to the type of marks to be used, but this is now to be found in s 252(3A).

184 See 4.2.2.

185 See s 255C(6).

186 See Art 1(4).

187 See 7.4.4, 10.2.7(b).

188 See 11.3.4(a) and (b).

189 See 9.2.5 and 10.5.

190 Including cargo: see the analysis in 10.6.

191 As noted in 11.3.1, this provision does not impose an obligation on UK registered ships to remove a wreck in the Convention area of *another* State party, seemingly in breach of the UK's obligations under the WRC 2007 Art 9(9).

192 Sees 255D(1); 8.2.2, 9.2.2.

193 Rather unhelpfully, Art 9 did not itself give a specific expression for the information obligations it created: see also 9.2.5(a), 10.5.1(b), 10.8.6.

194 See 10.8.6.

195 See s 255D(3); 10.5.3(b).

for the registered owner to fail, without reasonable excuse, to comply with a notice by the specified deadline.[196]

Article 9(4) of the WRC 2007 contains two separate provisions about how the registered shipowner is to undertake the wreck removal. The first sentence of Art 9(4) allows the shipowner to appoint its own salvor or wreck removal contractor; the second sentence allows the Affected State to impose conditions for the removal.[197] Section 255E(2) expressly allows the Secretary of State to "impose conditions as to the removal of the wreck in accordance with [Art 9(4)]". This seems to refer only to the second sentence, not the first (which has nothing to do with "conditions"). That leaves some doubt as to whether the first sentence has been effectively incorporated at all into the UK legislation, although it is a binding part of the WRC 2007 in respect of the EEZ. That doubt is exacerbated as the first sentence is qualified by Art 4(4)(b) in respect of the territory and the territorial sea (not EEZ), by the words "[s]ubject to the national law of the Affected State".[198] It might be argued that the absence of any clear reference to the first sentence was a conscious decision by the UK not to apply that sentence in UK law, but that would not explain why there would be no reference to it applying in the EEZ. In its response to a comment that the original Marine Navigation Bill made no reference to Art 9(4), the government replied that this point "does not need to be reflected in the draft legislation because the owner's freedom to contract with any salvor or person in such circumstances is, and will remain, unrestricted".[199] It appears that whatever meaning is given to s 255E(2), it does not draw any distinction between the EEZ and the other parts of the UK "Convention area", ie territorial waters.

Section 255E(2) certainly gives effect to the second sentence of Art 9(4) by allowing the Secretary of State (eg via the SOSREP) to impose conditions as to how the shipowner (or contractor) undertakes the wreck removal "*if* the Secretary of State *has* given a registered owner a wreck removal notice".[200] The conditions are circumscribed by Art 9(4) of the WRC 2007,[201] ie requiring that conditions imposed by a State should only relate to "safety and the protection of the marine environment". It is arguable that Art 9(4) places a restriction on the otherwise wide powers in international law after a casualty (at least in the EEZ),[202] by requiring that the conditions imposed by a State should only relate to "safety

---

196 See s 255D(4).

197 See 10.5.2, 10.5.4.

198 See 8.4.2. A natural reading of the paragraph is that these additional words apply only to the first sentence and not to the whole paragraph. The point is significant if the Affected State wants to set conditions that go further than safety or the environment and include, eg, economic considerations. For an apparent anomaly caused by an interpretation that the national law proviso only applies to the first sentence, see 10.5.4.

199 See *DfT, Summary of Responses 2008*, 22–23, 25. Apart from being a general statement of policy, it does not resolve the question of whether such an order could be given under the general intervention powers in Sch 3A: see 4.2.3(a) and cf *Mount Isa Mines Ltd v The Ship "Thor Commander"* [2019] 1 Lloyd's Rep 167 [309].

200 Emphasis added, suggesting that the wreck removal notice has to be issued first and cannot contain the conditions. This seems impractical, and it may be more convenient to supply the conditions in the wreck removal notice, or at least contemporaneously with it. The more sensible interpretation is that conditions cannot be imposed *unless* there is a wreck removal notice, but that if a wreck removal notice is issued then it may contain the conditions. If this is wrong, the conditions would have to be formally served in a separate notice, albeit that the original wreck removal notice might refer to them being provided. See also 10.5.3.

201 See s 255E(2); 9.2.5(c), 10.5.2, 10.5.4.

202 See eg 5.3.

and the protection of the marine environment".²⁰³ This would seem to preclude a State from insisting for largely nationalistic or economic reasons that the wreck removal contractor use local sub-contractors or facilities.²⁰⁴ However, the safety or environment criteria are potentially very wide (eg so as to justify a shorter voyage to a local facility) and the day to day reality is that the shipowner will have to deal with the Affected State about many matters in its own waters, so there may be doubts as to the practical extent of the Art 9(4) restrictions. These restrictions would seem to be allow fewer conditions to be imposed than those that might be applied under the wide Sch 3A general intervention powers.²⁰⁵ There is a separate offence if the registered owner fails, without reasonable excuse, to comply with a condition.²⁰⁶ There is no offence committed by a wreck removal contractor under s 255E, although it is possible that there may be offences for failing to obey general intervention directions issued under the MSA 1995 Sch 3A.²⁰⁷

Section 255D(1) applies to a "ship" wrecked in the UK's "Convention area", and (as with s 255C(1)) there is nothing in that subsection that restricts its application to a "ship" registered in a State party.²⁰⁸ This conclusion is rendered slightly uncertain by s 255D(2) which requires the "registered owner to comply with the obligations imposed on registered owners by [the WRC 2007 Art 9(2) and (3)]". If the WRC 2007 provisions only apply to ships registered in State parties,²⁰⁹ there would be no "obligations" to attach to ships registered in non-State parties. It might be possible to read s 255D(2) as focusing on the Secretary of State's obligations in relation to giving a wreck removal notice, and the extent of its general requirements under Art 9(2) and (3), rather than upon the obligations of the registered shipowner; in this reading, there is merely a reference to what a wreck removal notice should instruct a registered shipowner to do, whatever the flag of the ship.²¹⁰ It is regrettable that there may be uncertainty over this issue as it is vital to know whether the obligation to remove a wreck under Art 9(2) can apply to any ship.²¹¹ Section 255D makes no attempt to distinguish the powers available in the EEZ from those in the territory or territorial sea, where arguably a State could impose stricter removal obligations. By contrast, the obligation in Art 9(3) to provide to the Affected State an insurance certificate "as

---

203 The draft Marine Navigation Bill 2008 cl 255E(2) did not refer to Art 9(4) but only to a risk to safety or of "environmental pollution". The latter was potentially narrower than the WRC 2007 provision and also Art 1(5)(b).

204 The dismantling of the *Costa Concordia* took place in Italy. Note that the first sentence of Art 9(4) restricts the extent to which the State can anyway insist on a particular contractor in the EEZ, but that this sentence does not apply in territorial waters unless it has been reintroduced by that State: see Art 4(4)(b) and 10.2.8.

205 See 4.2.3. On normal principles it might be expected that the Sch 3A powers would be subject to any restrictions in the later (more specific) WRC 2007 Art 9(4) and s 255E. When a State opts to apply the WRC 2007 in its territorial waters, Art 3(2) declares this to be without prejudice to State powers *other than* locating, marking and removing them. However, Art 4(1) states that the WRC 2007 does not apply to measures taken under the Intervention Convention 1969 (and its 1973 Protocol), which seems to preserve the latter's primacy in the EEZ; note also the effect of the MSA 1995 s 108A, which appears to give general primacy to Sch 3A: see 4.2.2.

206 See s 255D(4).

207 See 4.2.3(e), (f).

208 Although in international law it will only be State parties who could complain about non-compliance with the WRC 2007.

209 See 7.4.

210 Similarly, it can be said that there are no restrictions as to the flag of the ship in s 255E, dealing with conditions for wreck removal.

211 See also the discussion in 11.3.4(a).

required by Art 12" would seem to apply only to ships registered in States parties.[212] For reasons of overall policy, there are good reasons to apply s 255D to all ships.[213] If s 255D does not apply to ships registered in non-State parties then the UK would have to rely on the pre-existing UK legislation.[214]

11.3.3(d) Removal in default by UK itself

As the WRC 2007 gives rights to States, rather than individuals, s 255F(1) allows the UK (through the Secretary of State) to remove a wreck itself, in the default circumstances set out in the WRC 2007 Art 9(7) and (8).[215] As s 255F(1) refers to the UK's "Convention area",[216] this means that the UK has reinstated the application of Art (7) and (8) to its territory and territorial sea, as these would otherwise have been excluded by Art 4(4)(a)(ii).[217] While this 'trap' in enacting the WRC 2007 has been avoided, s 255F fails to make clear whether it applies to ships of any flag, or only those of States parties. The language in s 255F is very general, but its "default" powers are linked to the failure of the shipowner to remove the wreck under the "obligations" arising under s 255D. That section itself is unclear as to whether it applies to all ships, or only those registered in States parties,[218] but the sensible interpretation may again be that s 255F has no restriction as to the flag of the ship that is wrecked.

The UK could perform the removal task by using any central resources, eg the Royal Navy or Coastguard, or by the DfT engaging contractors directly. In practice, it may make more sense for the removal task to be performed (or at least coordinated) by those authorities that have traditionally done so. Accordingly, s 255F(2) allows the Secretary of State (eg via the SOSREP) to direct[219] that the s 255F(1) power be exercised by a GLA, a harbour authority or a conservancy authority. The direction can only be given in relation to that authority's area.[220] This direction is mandatory for the authority concerned,[221] which seems to mean that it does not necessarily need to seek additional authority in the local or national legislation setting out its general powers, eg under the HDPCA 1847 s 56, or in the MSA 1995 ss 252 and 253.[222] Unlike s 255C,[223] s 255F makes no mention of the powers in the MSA 1995 ss 252 and 253, but it may well be convenient for them to be used.[224]

---

212 See Art 12(1) and note the different treatment in Art 12(12) (port state control" which applies to ships wherever registered.
213 See also the discussion in 11.3.4(a).
214 See 11.1.2, 11.1.3 and 11.3.4(c).
215 .Eg if the registered owner does not meet a deadline for removal, or where immediate action is required. See s 255F; 9.2.5(d), 10.5.1, 10.5.3(d).
216 Ie to UK internal waters, territorial sea and EEZ: see 11.3.2.
217 See 11.3.2.
218 See 11.3.3(c).
219 In writing, or confirmed in writing as soon as possible: see s 255F(5).
220 See s 255F(3). But note that it seems possible for a local harbour or conservancy authority to engage a more experienced GLA to perform that task: see 11.3.5.
221 See s 255F(6).
222 See 11.1.2, 11.1.3.
223 See 11.3.3(b).
224 See 11.3.5.

11.3.3(e) Compulsory insurance certificates

The MSA 1995 Part 9A contains eight provisions that are designed to give effect to the compulsory insurance provisions of the WRC 2007 Art 12.[225] These are mostly administrative in nature,[226] following the pattern of similar provisions governing other liability conventions with compulsory insurance.[227]

Article 12(1) puts the obligation upon the flag State to ensure that ships of 300 gt[228] (and over) have insurance "wreck removal insurance", but Art 12(12) applies port state control to ships of any flag, even if not registered in a State party. This distinction is recognised in s 255J, by requiring UK ships to have that insurance (backed by a certificate) when entering or leaving ports anywhere in the world;[229] foreign ships (of any flag) must have the insurance and certificate when entering or leaving a UK port.[230] There is recognition of wreck removal insurance certificates issued in a foreign WRC 2007 State.[231] The UK is given the power to issue its own certificates[232] for UK ships, and for foreign ships that are not registered in a WRC 2007 State[233] (as they will need certificates to use ports in WRC 2007 States). In the consultation on the draft Marine Navigation Bill 2008 there was a draft s 255O(3)[234] enabling the Secretary of State to refuse to issue a certificate if there were doubts as to whether the wreck removal insurance would "cover the owner's liability under s 255G". A consultee raised the question as to whether this would mean that a certificate would be refused if the insurance was not unlimited, ie because the owner would have unlimited liability owing to the LLMC opt-out.[235] The government agreed that the certificate should not be refused because the Bill achieved an LLMC Art 6 limit for the insurer because of the reference to "wreck removal insurance" that was defined [in what is now s 255JJ(7)] to be insurance satisfying Art 12.[236] The government agreed to see if the point needed clarification, and in the final MSA 1995 s 255J the draft subsection (3) was completely deleted. That solved the issue about refusal of the certificate, but it presaged an even more difficult issue in relation to whether the insurer could have a limit (or cap) at all.[237]

Offences are created for contravening s 255J,[238] and for failing to have a wreck removal insurance certificate on board under s 255M.[239] The UK has an obligation under Art 9(3)

---

225 See 10.8.
226 The direct action provisions are dealt with separately in 11.3.4(b).
227 Eg the CLC 1992, the Bunkers Convention 2001, the HNSC 2010, the Athens Convention 2002: see 2.6.2(a), 2.6.3, 2.6.4, 2.3.5.
228 Tonnage is to be measured in the UK by using the same method as applies to the LLMC: see s 255J(6), Sch 7 Part II, para 5(2) and 2.5.6(a).
229 Ie giving effect to Art 9(11): see 11.3.1.
230 See s 255J(3). The references to entering or leaving a port in a State include references to "arriving at or leaving an offshore facility in the territorial sea of that State", although the powers of detention are not applicable there: see s 255R(3) and 11.3.3(f).
231 See s 255J(4)–(5), s 255R(7).
232 These may be electronic: see s 255Q.
233 See s 255N. There is also a power to make regulations about the cancellation of certificates: see s 255O.
234 The equivalent section in Part 9A as enacted is now s255N, but without the provision being discussed.
235 See 2.5.8, 10.8.5.
236 See *DfT, Summary of Responses 2008*, 27–28.
237 See 11.3.4(b).
238 See s 255K and 11.3.3(f).
239 See s 255M(4) and 11.3.3(f).

and (9) to ensure that UK ships produce insurance certificates to other Affected States. It seems that the UK gives effect to this by requiring the certificates to be produced to UK officials, rather than directly to the other State.[240] There are exemptions in respect of certain government ships.[241]

11.3.3(f) Offences and enforcement

Part 9A creates a variety of offences in order to support the enforcement of the public law duties under the WRC 2007, eg: failure to report a wreck;[242] failure to comply with a wreck removal notice within the specified deadline;[243] failure to obey conditions in such a notice;[244] failure to have insurance when entering or leaving ports.[245] There are variations in the persons liable to prosecution. It is the registered owner that is guilty of offences for failure to comply with a wreck removal notice or associated conditions.[246] The wreck reporting offence can be committed by the master or operator.[247] The persons liable for failing to insure are the master *and* operator; ie each are guilty of an offence.[248] It is the master who is guilty for not having on board, or producing, an insurance certificate.[249] In all these offences, the punishment on indictment is an unlimited fine. The punishment on summary conviction was originally a maximum fine of £50,000, but this was replaced in 2015 by an unlimited fine.[250]

A power to detain ships is provided in s 255L if there is an attempt to navigate out of a port without the appropriate insurance, but this does not apply to detention in offshore facilities in the territorial sea.[251]

11.3.3(g) Government ships

Section 255S gives effect to the WRC 2007 Art 4(2) and (3) dealing with warships and other ships owned and operated by States, but used for non-commercial purposes "only"[252] (eg carrying equipment for the armed forces).[253] The WRC 2007 excludes its application to

---

240 See s 255M(3).
241 See s 255S and 11.3.3(g).
242 See s 255B(7).
243 See s 255D(4).
244 See s 255E(4).
245 See s 255K.
246 See s 255D(4), s55E(4).
247 If one of them makes a report the other cannot be guilty (see s 255C(6)), but it is arguable that if neither of them make a report both could be guilty as the "or" was not meant to be disjunctive: cf *Federal Steam Navigation v Department of Trade and Industry (sub nom The Huntingdon)* [1974] 1 WLR 505. However, note the use of "each" in s 255K(1), although this formulation does not have to cover the same alternatives as s 255C.
248 See s 255K(1). For "operator" see the WRC 2007 Art 1(9) and 9.1.3(a).
249 See s 255M(3).
250 See the Legal Aid, Sentencing and Punishment of Offenders Act 2012 (Fines on Summary Conviction) Regulations 2015 (SI 2015/664), Sch 4 para 27(11). On the cancellation of an insurance certificate any person who fails to deliver it up can be guilty, but the punishment is only a fine on summary conviction up to level 4 of the standard scale: see s 255O(2)–(3).
251 See s 255R(3).
252 The word "only" was added after the Committee stage in the Commons to comply more precisely with the WRC 2007: see Hansard, Public Bill Committee (7 February 2011), "Wreck Removal Convention Bill", 4.
253 See 8.1.2(h); also 4.7 on sovereign immunity generally.

such ships unless the State decides otherwise, in which case it must notify the IMO of any applicable terms and conditions. Section 255S confirms that Part 9A does not apply to such ships, unless a State has made a notification to the IMO. The compulsory insurance certification provisions of s 255K[254] do not apply to "exempt ships" as defined by s 255S(4). Such ships should have an equivalent certificate issued by the State stating that the ship is owned by the State[255] and that any liability will be met up to the limits in Art 12(1)—ie an acknowledgement of State liability.

11.3.4 Part 9A liability provisions

In order to give full effect to the WRC 2007, Part 9A also makes necessary adjustments to existing private maritime law; eg to deal with liability (for the costs of locating, marking and removing wrecks), as well as compulsory insurance and direct action.

11.3.4(a) Liability for UK wreck costs

Section 255G is designed to give effect to the WRC 2010 Art 10, although there is no express incorporation of it.[256] The section applies where the necessary triggers under the WRC 2007 have been satisfied as set out in s 255G(1); ie there has been an accident[257] causing the wreck of a ship or its cargo[258] in the UK's "Convention area",[259] and costs have been incurred in locating, marking and removing wreck.[260] Those costs are recoverable from the registered owner under s 255G(2).

Unfortunately, there is no reference in s 255G to the WRC 2007 Art 2, in particular the provisions relating to proportionality of costs and the requirement that measures should not go beyond what is reasonably necessary.[261] These were vital to the overall package in the WRC 2007[262] and the omission is the more remarkable because it was specifically adverted to in consultations on the 2008 Bill.[263] Although the government had agreed to re-examine the issue, it does not appear that any changes were made. Some of the provisions in Art 2 relate to solely international law obligations, but the proportionality and reasonableness principles go directly to the liability for costs. The absence of an express reference in s 255G means that it is necessary to conduct a tedious paper trail through Part 9A to see if there is some obscure link.[264] Unlike with other convention provisions where

---

254 See 11.3.3(e).
255 There can be offences under s 255M for failing to have on board, or to produce, a certificate.
256 There is an indirect reference, ie to the *exceptions* in Art 10(1)(a)–(c). Section 255G does not expressly reference the triggers under Arts 7–9 (see 10.5), but simply refers to ss 255C (locating and marking) and 255F (removal in default). Section 255F(1) refers only to Art 9(7) and (8), not to other provisions in Art 9.
257 See s 255R(2); WRC 2007 Art 1(3); 8.2.1(a), 10.5.1.
258 As the new Part 9A s 255R adopts the definitions in Art 1 of the WRC, including that of "wreck" in the WRC Article 1(4), there should be no doubts in UK law that Part 9A covers cargo removal: see 10.6.
259 See s 255R(2); WRC 2007 Art 1(3); 8.2.1(a), 10.5.1, 11.3.3(a).
260 Under ss 255C (see 11.3.3(b)), or s 255F (see 11.3.3(d)).
261 See 9.2.5(e), 10.2.4, 8.4.2.
262 See eg 10.8.6.
263 See *DfT, Summary of Responses 2008*, 22.
264 The key expression in Art 2(2) and (3) is "measures" taken by the Affected State. The only reference to this in Art 1 (whose provisions must be used under s 255R(1) in construing Part 9A) is in Art 1(4)(d), but here it is referring to measures taken by *others* such as salvors. "Measures" is used in the title of Art 9 and in Art 9(1)

possible links can eventually be discovered,[265] we have been unable to find how these key principles are implemented in the UK legislation. To some extent, an assessment of costs in UK law might always be said to involve reasonableness, although "proportionality" is a more specific concept. The best that can be said is that the principles are part of the UK's international obligations to which a court should endeavour to give effect; at least there is no indication in Part 9A that they should *not* be used.

Section 255G(2) also applies to the owner of an unregistered ship.[266] It will not apply to warships and other ships being used by a State for non-commercial purposes, eg if owned and operated by non State parties to the WRC 2007.[267] State parties can opt to have the convention apply to such ships. Otherwise, ships owned by a State, and operated by a company registered in that State as an operator, will be treated as a registered shipowner.[268] Wreck Convention States will be treated as having submitted to the jurisdiction of a court where proceedings are brought to recover costs from it.[269]

Like a number of other provisions in Part 9A, s 255G does not make clear whether it applies only to ships registered in States parties, or to all ships; nor does it distinguish (in this regard) between wrecks in the EEZ and elsewhere in the UK's "Convention area". Other States have not made the distinction either.[270] As a matter of State policy, this seems to be an appropriate solution (at least in respect of cost recovery) which develops international law. This option could have been available to the UK, but it is not at all clear that it has been exercised. Although s 255G(1)(a) applies the section simply to a "ship", s 255G(1)(b) requires that costs were incurred "*complying with* [s 255C or s 255F]".[271] It has already been suggested that there may be some uncertainty about how far those provisions apply to ships registered in non-State parties.[272] While there is no doubt that that there is liability for wreck removal costs in the whole of the UK "Convention area" for ships registered in State parties, it cannot therefore be said with complete certainty that s 255G creates such a liability in respect of ships not registered in State parties. Yet it is quite clear that under s 255J(3)[273] *any* foreign ships must have WRC 2007 insurance to enter or leave UK ports. It would be rather absurd if they were obliged to have insurance where there was no underlying liability,[274] and that may be a reason to interpret s 255G widely.[275] If there is no

---

(b) and 9(9), both of which relate to international law obligations and neither of which is mentioned in Part 9A: see 11.3.1(b).

265 See Art 12 and 11.3.4(b).
266 See s 255R(4) and the WRC 2007 Art 1(8); also 9.1.3(a).
267 See s 255S(1), the WRC 2007 Art 4(2) and 11.3.3(g).
268 See the WRC 2007 Art 1(9) and s 255S(6).
269 See s255S(7); also 4.7.
270 See the example of the Netherlands and Sweden: 10.2.7(b). Cf s 18(c) of the Canadian Abandoned or Hazardous Vessels Act 2019.
271 Emphasis added, ie not complying with the equivalent *WRC 2007* provisions.
272 See 11.3.3(b), 11.3.3(f).
273 11.3.3(E).
274 As noted in 10.2.7(b), it does not appear that such arguments about the flags of ships have been used in relation to liabilities under the CLC 1992. Whatever may be the position in international law, the shipowner and insurer will have to deal with the national law enactment. Note that s 255P(1) also makes no distinction between ships of different flags: see also 10.8.4(a) and 11.3.4(b).
275 There is no clear guidance in the documentation relating to the Marine Navigation Bill 2008, or in the limited debates on the WRC Bill 2011, or in the Explanatory Memorandum used during debates and attached to

s 255G liability, that would also carry over to direct liability actions against insurers,[276] and the UK would then have to rely on the pre-existing legislation[277] which cannot oblige the shipowner to remove the wreck in the EEZ and which is not backed by insurance.

It is important to note that the liability in UK law is not to any person or public authority that incurs costs in locating, marking and removing a wreck. Apart from the case where the wreck is removed directly on behalf of the Secretary of State under s 255F(1),[278] s 255G(1)(b) restricts claims for costs to where they have been incurred in complying with a specific *direction* under ss 255C or 255F.[279] In other words there is a high degree of central government control over who may claim the costs and, by deduction, who will actually perform the tasks of locating, marking and removal. This satisfies any *locus standi* issues in domestic law arising from the fact that obligations under the WRC 2007 are owed to the State, *not* individuals or private companies.[280] Under s 255G(2) the right to recover costs is granted to the "person who incurred the costs". This would include, for instance, the DfT itself, the Royal Navy or Coastguard; or those to whom directions have been given, eg GLAs, port authorities and conservancy authorities. Claims to recover costs under the WRC 2007 through s 255G cannot, therefore, be made by those who act independently of the Secretary of State; this is quite unlike a salvage claim where volunteers are entitled to be rewarded.[281] In some circumstances, the recovery and 'removal' of valuable property may give rise to a salvage claim under the Salvage Convention 1989,[282] but the extent to which State or local authorities are entitled to claim salvage will depend on the application of Art 5 of that Convention.[283]

Section 255G(3) gives effect to Art 11(1) of the WRC 2007 and makes it clear that there is no liability for costs if that would conflict with other liability conventions, eg the CLC 1992,[284] the HNS Convention 2010,[285] and the Bunkers Convention 2010,[286] or the nuclear liability conventions.[287] There is, curiously perhaps, no specific mention in the new MSA 1995 Part 9A of Art 11(2) of the WRC 2007, dealing with overlap with the Salvage Convention 1989. It might have been helpful at least to have clarification that a UK court should give effect to Art 11(2),[288] but otherwise the question of overlap will have to be

---

the WRCA 2011. All that can be said is that none of the speakers voiced an opinion that the powers to remove wrecks and recover costs were limited to ships of particular flags; indeed, the assumption appeared to be that they were not.

276 See s 255P(2) and 11.3.4(b).
277 See 11.1.2, 11.1.3 and 11.3.4(c).
278 See 11.3.3(d).
279 See 11.3.3(b) and (c).
280 See 10.2.3. This is also relevant where ports have been privatised.
281 See 2.7, eg 2.7.1, 2.7.4.
282 As preserved by the WRC 2007 Art 11(2): see 10.9.1. For how Part 9A deals with any conflicts between the WRC 2007 and the Salvage Convention 1989: see the discussion of s 255G(3), 11.3.4(a) (below).
283 See 4.4.4 and *Kennedy and Rose*, 279–301.
284 See 2.6.2(a), 10.9.2(a).
285 See 2.6.4, 10.9.2(b). As the Art 11(1) exceptions only apply when the listed convention is applicable and in force, there would be no conflict as yet with the HNSC 2010.
286 See 2.6.3, 10.9.2(c).
287 See 10.9.3.
288 Note that s255G(3)(c) does give the Secretary of State power to specify by order other provisions in respect of which there might be a conflict. No such order has been made.

answered by applying general principles.[289] It might be argued that, under s 255G, a salvor or wreck removal contractor is a "person" who literally has incurred costs in complying with ss 255C and 255F relating to the location, marking and removal of wrecks. In fact, the right to claim costs is that of the authority with the primary duties under those sections and not those who are sub-contracted to perform work. The same reasoning would seem to apply to voluntary salvors who incur costs that are not recompensed fully under the Salvage Convention 1989.[290]

The WRC 2007 does not itself deal with the question of what happens if two ships are wrecked, eg after a collision, and it is not possible to separate the costs relating to each.[291] Section 255G(4) makes them jointly liable for the total costs if they cannot reasonably be separated. It seems that this joint liability is most likely to be relevant in relation to the costs of location, marking and preparation for removal of both vessels (eg diving surveys).[292] The actual costs of raising are more likely to be severable, unless the two vessels are so intertwined that it is necessary to bring them up together. Section 255T preserves the WRC 2007 Art 10(4) rights of recourse,[293] eg after a collision[294] or under the terms of a charterparty.[295]

The defences in WRC 2007 Art 10(1)[296] are recognised by s 255G(2). The draft Marine Navigation Bill 2008 had rather unnecessarily set these out in a separate s 255H, which was sensibly removed for the WRCA 2011.[297] However, in that draft s 255H(4)(b) the intentional damage exception in Art 10(1)(b) was reworded so that there was no reference to "third party". Instead it referred to the intentional damage caused by "a person other than the owner who . . . was not a servant or agent of the owner". In other words, it purported to clarify the ambiguity in the WRC 2007 provision, by making it clear that the shipowner could not rely on the exception if there was barratrous conduct of the crew.[298] In its response to a question raised in consultations, the government response was "We do not intend to make the owner liable where the person who is a servant or agent of the owner is not acting on behalf of the owner and will examine the need to refine the drafting".[299] No reason was given for the policy position, but the whole of the draft s 255H ("Exceptions") was removed from the legislation and replaced by the simple reference in s 255G(2) to the WRC 2007 Art 10(1)(a)–(c). This was consistent with the general systematic move to refer to more WRC 2007 provisions,[300] and (despite the government response) it is hard to draw a clear inference that the later deletion was intended to change the result of the previous

---

289 See 10.9.1.
290 See 10.9.1. Note the uncertainty about how far the UK has enacted the first sentence of Art 9(4), allowing the shipowner to engage a contractor to remove the wreck: see 11.3.4(a).
291 See 10.2.2.
292 This mirrors s 153(6) in relation to CLC liability.
293 See 10.2.1, 10.2.2, 10.3.3.
294 See 2.4.
295 See eg 2.1.7(a)–(c).
296 See 10.3.
297 The subsequent sections were therefore renumbered, ie s 255H is now the time bar provision.
298 See 10.3.1(b).
299 See *DfT, Summary of Responses 2008,* 26, 29.
300 See 11.3.1.

drafting either way. On that basis the answer will depend on an interpretation of the WRC 2007 itself.[301]

Section 255G(5) preserves the exercise of rights (if any) to limit liability under the LLMC and the MSA 1995 s 185; ie s 255G(5) does not grant or create any rights to limit *itself*.[302] The WRC 2007 Art 13 time bar is given effect by s 255H.

11.3.4(b) Direct action against insurer

Section 255P aims to give effect to the direct action provision in the WRC 2007 Art 12(10).[303] If there is an entitlement to recover from the registered shipowner then s 255P(2) allows the claimant to make a claim against the insurer. Accordingly, the Third Parties (Rights against Insurers) Act 2010 does not apply in relation to "any wreck removal insurance to which a [WRC 2007] insurance certificate relates".[304]

Section 255P(1) is more precise than the WRC 2007 in that it requires three triggers before a direct action claim. First, there must be an accident to a ship as a result of the ship or anything from it has become a wreck in the UK's "Convention area".[305] Secondly, the ship must have had wreck removal insurance. Thirdly, there has to be a wreck removal insurance certificate in relation to the insurance. The last provision, in particular, emphasises that the liability of the insurer arises from its voluntary acts[306]—not only in providing the underlying insurance cover, but in giving the master a manifestation of that insurance to be used as a key to enter the waters of States parties.

As with other provisions, there is a doubt about how far s 255P can apply to ships flagged in non States parties.[307] To some extent, the insurer's liability will follow that of the shipowner,[308] but the terms of s 255P(1) seem to be expressed in wide and unequivocal terms with no hint that there is a restriction based on the flag of the ship.[309] As noted above,[310] there seems to be little point in requiring foreign ships to have wreck removal insurance if it cannot be called upon. While insurers might be able to raise the flag of the ship in order to assert that there should be no liability of the registered shipowner,[311] it could also be argued against them that there is no international law problem with making the insurer liable on the basis of a certificate that it has voluntarily given and which, under s 255P(1), contains no flag restrictions. It is not possible, though, to argue that *if* the WRC 2007 does not apply

---

301 In 10.3.1(b) it is tentatively submitted that the Marine Navigation Bill 2008 draft s 255H(4)(b) was a correct interpretation of Art 10(1)(b), but one respondent to the consultation considered that it was a significant restriction: see *DfT, Summary of Responses 2008*, 29.

302 For such rights, see 2.5.4(c), 2.5.8. For the linked question as to whether an insurer can limit, see 11.3.4(b).

303 See 10.8.

304 See s 255P(7); also 2.9.6(c). It follows that the only direct action claim is against an insurer that has issued a WRC 2007 certificate under s 255P, not under the 2010 legislation (or its predecessors).

305 See also 11.3.3(a) for discussion of this trigger.

306 See 10.8.4(a), 10.8.5(a).

307 See 10.8.4(a).

308 See 11.3.4(a).

309 Section 255P(1)(b) simply requires that the ship "had" wreck removal insurance. These is no restriction here that this had to be an insurance that was produced while entering or leaving UK ports. It could equally apply, in its terms, to any ship that was transiting through the UK Convention Area.

310 See 10.8.4(a), 11.3.4(a).

311 See 7.4.4, 10.2.7(b) for the arguments for and against; also 11.3.4(a).

to shipowners of non-State parties, the insurers could still be independently liable[312] in UK law because s 255P(2) appears to tie the liability of the insurer to the *entitlement* to recover costs from the shipowner. The argument is thus circular, and the insurer's liability will depend on the underlying liability of the registered shipowner.[313]

The shipowner's wilful misconduct defence is confirmed,[314] as well as the defences available to the shipowner,[315] eg under the WRC Art 10(1)[316] and the time bar under Art 13.[317]

Section 255P(5) and (6) deal with the key issue of whether an insurer can limit liability in respect of the direct action. They must be intended to give effect to Art 12(10),[318] but they do not adopt identical language to the WRC 2007. This may be important given the dual nature of the limit or cap on liability that has been discussed in relation to the WRC 2007.[319] Section 255P(5) allows the insurer to limit liability for direct action claims under s 255P(2) "to the same extent as the registered shipowner may limit liability by virtue of [the MSA 1995 s 185][320] (or would be able to limit liability by virtue of that section if it were not for [the MSA 1995 Sch 7 Part 2 para 3]". The use of the expression "to the same extent" is rather ambiguous. It mirrors language in Art 1(6) of the LLMC 1996 whereby "an insurer of liability for claims subject to limitation in accordance with [the LLMC 1996] shall be entitled to the benefits of this Convention to the same extent as the assured himself". Because s 255G(5) (in Part 9A) appears in the same Act as the LLMC 1996 (in Sch 7) the drafter can link the two provisions, so that the one can be read with (or modify) the other. When s 255P(5) then talks about the insurer limiting "to the same extent", it seems to be accepting that the insurer is entitled to limit under the LLMC (via LLMC Art 1(6) and s 185). It has previously been argued that this would not be contrary to the WRC Art 12(10).[321] It follows that when the insurer claims to limit, any limitation fund would be shared pro rata between the wreck removal claimants (under s 255G) and any other property claimants.[322] What s 255P(5) does acknowledge, though, is that the insurer will be affected in exactly the same way as the registered shipowner by the opt-out in Sch 7 Part 2 para 3, ie that claims to remove the ship are not subject to limits although, for the UK, there would be limits for cargo removal claims.[323]

But there appears to be a glaring omission here, because s 255P(5) makes no reference to the third sentence of the WRC 2007 Art 12(10) when the latter refers to the backstop or cap calculated in accordance with Art 12(1).[324] In s 255P(6) it is said that the insurer "may limit liability whether or not the accident is caused by an act or omission mentioned in

---

312 See the argument in 10.8.4(a).
313 See 11.3.4(a) where it is suggested that, as a matter of interpretation of s 255G, there is no restriction on shipowner liability based on the flag of the ship.
314 See s 255P(3) and 10.8.4(c) and (d).
315 See s 255P(4).
316 See s 255G(2) and 10.3
317 See s 255H and 10.4.
318 See 10.8.5.
319 See 10.8.5(a) and (b) and compare with 10.8.5(d).
320 Giving effect to the LLMC 1996: see 2.5.
321 See 10.8.5(b).
322 See also 2.5.6(a).
323 See 2.5.4(c) and 2.5.8.
324 See 10.8.5(d).

[LLMC 1996 Art 4][325] as set out in Part 1 of Schedule 7". This clearly reflects the position that the intent or recklessness of the shipowner will not deprive the insurer of the right to limit.[326] What s 255P(6) does not go on to say is what limit would then apply; it seems to have assumed that it must be the limit applying by virtue of the LLMC 1996, in the same way as with s 255P(5). It is respectfully submitted that this misunderstands the nature of the reference at the end of the third sentence of Art 12(10) when it refers back to the amount calculated in accordance with Art 12(1). It has been argued earlier that this cannot create a limit of liability *under* the LLMC, but is an entirely separate deemed cap under the WRC 2007 Art 12(10).[327] Depending on how national linkage is made to the LLMC, this capped amount might not be shared with other claimants under the LLMC fund.[328]

If we are right that the WRC 2007 Art 12(10) deals separately with limits under the LLMC and with the cap in Art 12(1), what are the consequences for the UK with the drafting of s 255P(5) and (6)? On a plain reading, the absence of any reference at all in those provisions to the backstop in Art 12(1) means that when the insurer is sued directly for a wreck (ie hull) removal claim, it should be treated in exactly the same way as a shipowner—ie there would be no limit at all. A conclusion that the UK has managed to create unlimited direct action insurer liability for most wreck removal claims would be quite contrary to the intention of the WRC 2007, because the backstop was arguably needed for more circumstances than to deal with Art 4 of the LLMC alone.[329]

In fact, the prospect of such unlimited liability was clearly brought to the government's attention in the consultation phase and its response was that "[i]t is not our intention that that should affect an insurer's ability to benefit from the limits in article 6(1) (b) of LLMC 1976 as amended, as that is the limit of insurance cover required under Article 12 of the ICRW".[330] It agreed to re-examine the point during drafting, but no further change was made. On what basis was the drafter confident that the drafting had achieved the evident aim? The clue appears to be in the reference to limit of insurance cover "required under Art 12" and is related to the government's view as to the nature of the liability under the insurance certificate.[331]

The argument appears to be that the LLMC Art 6 limit (ie in Art 12(1)) is achieved by first going to the reference to "wreck removal insurance" and "wreck removal insurance certificate" in s 255P(1)(b)–(c); secondly, then going to s 255R(2), which refers the

---

325 See 2.5.7.
326 It also follows s 165(3) in relation to the CLC, also s 165(4B) in respect of the Bunkers Convention 2001 (see the amendments made by the Bunkers Regulations 2006).
327 See 10.8.5(d).
328 See 10.8.5(e) and (f).
329 If this is a drafting omission in s 255P, it may have arisen because of the assumption that the WRC 2007 direct action provisions are practically identical to those under the Bunkers Convention 2001 (where there is no equivalent of the LLMC Art 18 opt-out), and that it was only necessary to deal with the situation where the shipowner was guilty of intent or recklessness. That this was a key assumption appears from the Explanatory Note to the draft Marine Navigation Bill 2008: see *Marine Navigation Bill Consultation 2008,* 72, paras 66–68. Likewise in the Explanatory Note to the eventual WRCA 2011: see paras 34–37.
330 See *DfT, Summary of Responses 2008,* 28. This clearly refutes any suggestion that there was a deliberate intention for there to be unlimited *insurer* liability. Previous Government comments had not distinguished between unlimited liability for shipowner and insurer: see *Transport Committee Ninth Report 2008,* 28.
331 See the discussion in 11.3.3(e) in relation to a draft s 255O(3).

meaning of those expressions to s 255J(7); thirdly, applying the definitions in s 255J(7), in particular that "wreck removal insurance" is that "satisfying the requirements of Article 12". This trail assumes that when the third sentence of Art 12(10) provides that the insurer "may limit" to the Art 12(1) amount, the result is achieved through the inherent nature of the certificate rather than from positive legislation giving effect to the provision. The actual certificate of insurance issued by the State (based eg on a Club's Blue Card) has to follow a model in an Annex to the WRC 2007,[332] which merely certifies that "there is in force . . . a policy of insurance or other financial security satisfying the requirements of article 12". Yet it might be said that there is a difference between the issuing of a certificate and a substantive limit or cap that needs positive legislation, especially where Art 12 has not been expressly incorporated.[333] Given the expressed intention of the legislator, and the aims of Art 12, it seems highly unlikely that a UK court would apply s 255P without the backstop calculated under Art 12(1), even if the textual justification is questionable. Nevertheless, it is regrettable that a simple clarifying provision was not provided in s 255P to remedy a problem caused by failing to fully incorporate the WRC 2007, and Art 12 in particular.

If the somewhat tortuous interpretive path, described above, means that the insurer has an inherent cap within the policy for circumstances where the shipowner cannot limit, this still presupposes that the sum available is a policy cap, not a limit of liability under the LLMC. There is no limitation fund and the amount would be entirely available to the wreck claimant.[334] This issue was effectively raised by another respondent to the consultation, who observed that the approach taken in the 2008 Bill was equivalent to the setting up of a separate wreck limitation fund envisaged by the MSA 1995 Sch 7 Part II para 3(1).[335] This would have entailed such a fund as an alternative to unlimited *shipowner* liability and has been used by other States such as the Netherlands. The s 255P solution clearly only relates to an amount available from the *insurer* via a policy rather than a separate fund. The government confirmed that such a fund was not the method being used to implement the WRC 2007 and that until an order was made setting up such a fund the shipowner would have unlimited liability.[336]

By contrast, if the insurer can limit for a cargo removal claim under the LLMC Art 2(1)(e),[337] that sum would have to be shared by all property claimants against an LLMC 1996 Art 6(2) fund, as s 255P(5) and (6) seem to assume that this would be a normal limitation claim for the insurer (even if the shipowner had been guilty of intention or recklessness).

---

332 See Art 12(2).
333 The reference to Art 12 in ss 255J(7) and 255Q(1) could be said merely to describe the type of insurance cover and certificate. Section 255S(4) does expressly refer to the Art 12(1) limits, but *only* in the context of exempt (ie Government) ships.
334 See 10.8.5(d). The legislation does not expressly say how this policy cap is to be calculated, given that it is not an LLMC 1996 fund: see 10.8.5(e). The UK courts would have to imply that the appropriate calculation into sdrs is to be made as if it were done under the LLMC 1996 as enacted in the MSA 1995 Sch 7. This would only create problems if there were another increase internationally in the LLMC 1996 limits and the UK (again) failed to give effect to this increase in time: see 2.5.6.
335 See *DfT, Summary of Responses 2008*, 29.
336 Ibid.
337 The UK has *not* exercised the LLMC opt-out in respect of LLMC Art 2(1)(e): see 2.5.8. For differences as to the exact meaning of the LLMC 1996 Art 2(1)(e), see 2.5.4(c).

11.3.4(c) Relationship with existing UK wreck removal laws

The MSA 1995 Part 9A has largely left untouched the existing powers in relation to wreck removal given to harbour and conservancy authorities under the HDPCA 1847 s 56, other local harbour legislation and the MSA 1995 s 252.[338] Similarly, the powers of GLAs under the MSA 1995s 253 are retained.[339] This creates an apparent overlap between these existing provisions and the WRC 2007 provisions in the new Part 9A. The new s 255C(3) creates free standing obligations on the various authorities to locate and mark wrecks,[340] although s 255C(4) specifically references the ability of the Secretary of State (eg via the SOSREP) to require the authority to exercise its powers under the MSA 1995 ss 252 or 253. By contrast, s 255F(2) also creates free standing entitlements on the named authorities to recover costs under s 255G, but makes no reference to the HDPCA 1847 s 56, local harbour legislation or the MSA 1995 ss 252 or 253. This raises the question as to why the liability provisions in such legislation were not repealed or fully integrated with the WRC 2007 provisions.

It is quite clear from the WRC 2007 Art 10(3) that no claim for costs can be brought against a registered owner "otherwise than in accordance" with the convention.[341] This would typically preclude actions against the registered owner at common law[342] or under some local statute, eg: if they imposed liabilities for costs on the registered owner beyond those agreed in the convention; or removed the agreed defences; or provided a different time bar; or removed the procedural hurdles as to notification in Art 9. Unfortunately, there appears to be no specific provision in the enacting legislation in the MSA 1995 Part 9A that gives express effect to the WRC 2007 Art 10(3).[343] This may be a consequence of the piecemeal way in which the WRC 2007 has been given effect,[344] or possibly an oversight, but it still seems highly unlikely that the UK was intending to be in breach of Art 10(3) by allowing parallel actions outside the WRC 2007. Indeed, there might be little point in so doing as only WRC 2007 compliant claims would enable the compulsory insurance provisions to operate.

A functional interpretation of Part 9A is that it leaves the existing wreck removal legislation (eg in the HDPCA 1847 s 56, other local harbour legislation and the MSA 1995 ss 252–253) to be available in circumstances where the WRC 2007 does *not* apply.[345] Examples of that would be where there was a wreck of a non-seagoing ship;[346] or where the wreck occurred without a "maritime casualty"[347] (eg where it was abandoned);[348] or if Part 9A is not applied to foreign ships flagged in a State not party to the WRC 2007.[349] There

---

338 See 11.1.2, 11.1.3(a).
339 See 11.1.3(b) and 11.3.6.
340 See 11.3.3(b).
341 See also 10.2.2.
342 See eg *Dee Conservancy Board v McConnell* [1928] 2 KB 159.
343 Cf the MSA 1995 s 156(1) in relation to the CLC 1992 and also the Bunkers Convention 2001 (see the amendments made by the Bunkers Regulations 2006).
344 See 11.3.1.
345 This appears to have been the intention of the Government: see *DfT, Summary of Responses 2008*, 24.
346 See 10.2.7, 8.2.1(b) and cf the discussion in 2.3.3. The WRC 2007 would be applied in UK internal waters, including ports, harbours and rivers, but only to a seagoing vessel: see 11.3.2.
347 See the WRC 2007 Art 1(3); ie an "accident" in the MSA 1995 Part 9A: see s 255R(2) and 8.2.1(a).
348 See 11.4, 14.2.
349 This issue is discussed in relation to Part 9A in a variety of places, eg 11.3.3(b), 11.3.3(c, 11.3.3(d), 11.3.4(a).

may also be circumstances where (for whatever reason) no Secretary of State's direction is made under ss 255C or 255F.[350] An example might be where there is a small ship that poses a local danger to navigation, of the kind typically dealt with by GLAs, but not meriting the national intervention of the SOSREP.[351] Further, unlike the older UK legislation, the WRC 2007 does not provide for any power of sale of a wreck.[352] This is probably because during the negotiations for the WRC 2007 it was thought that most wrecks that were likely to be covered by the convention would have little or no value, or that an additional remedy was not needed as a result of the compulsory insurance provisions designed to cover costs. It seems that the powers of sale given by the pre-existing legislation have survived the UK's enactment of the WRC 2007, as they do not involve a claim *against* the registered owner so as to fall foul of the WRC Art 10(3); they resemble more a claim against (or in respect of) the vessel itself. Similarly, a claim made at common law against a person *other* than the registered owner, eg a salvor or time charterer,[353] would not be precluded by Art 1(3), nor would any statutory provision that created liabilities on, eg, a bareboat charterer.[354]

Alternatively, it could be argued that the pre-existing legislation can simply be viewed as providing an additional (or cumulative) basis of authority for carrying out wreck removal work directed under Part 9A. The difficulty with that is to explain why there is a reference to the MSA 1995 ss 252 and 253 in s 255C(4), but not in s 255G.

However, on the assumption that there is a real division of legal functions between Part 9A and the pre-existing legislation, care needs to be taken that any 'wreck removal notice' is given under the authority of Part 9A and invokes the WRC 2007, rather than *only* the HDPA 1847 s 56, or other local legislation, or the MSA 1995 ss 252–253. The risk is that a notice that only mentions the older legislation might not trigger the WRC 2007 compulsory insurance provisions.[355]

What is clear from s 255I, though, is that any costs incurred by a GLA in complying with a direction under s 255C (location and marking), or s 255F (wreck removal), are to be paid out of the General Lighthouse Fund (GLF)[356]—but only if an action to recover the costs has not been fully successful under s 255G.

11.3.5 GLAs and wreck removal under Part 9A

The general functions of GLAs have already been described in the context of the MSA 1995 s 253.[357] It is now appropriate to consider their functions after the entry into force of

---

350 As required by s 255G(1)(b).
351 See also 11.3.5.
352 See 9.2.5(h); also 10.2.2.
353 Assuming, eg, that a duty of care existed in respect of a negligent salvor, cf *The Tojo Maru* [1972] AC 242, and 2.5.5, 2.7.4; or a charterer that ordered a ship to an unsafe port or loaded dangerous cargo (see 2.1.7(a)–(c), 2.5.4(d).
354 The HDPCA 1847 s 56 the MSA 1995 s 253 only create liabilities of the "owner": cf *The Chevron North America* [2002] 1 Lloyd's Rep 77, and see 11.1.2, 11.1.3; local HROs also seem to follow this pattern: see 11.1.2(b). For unregistered ships see the WRC 2007 Art 1(8) and the MSA 1995 s 255R(4); also 9.1.3(a).
355 Note also the Club position on national wreck removal laws and liabilities arising other than under WRC certificates: see 10.8.4(e).
356 See 11.3.5.
357 See 11.1.3(b).

the MSA 1995 Part 9A. In the debates prior to the enactment of the WRCA 2011, some concerns had been expressed that the SOSREP was more likely to be concerned about the environmental aspects of wreck, rather than the wreck of a small craft in the estuary to a port and that the SOSREP might interfere where the GLA had particular expertise in marking and may already have exercised powers under the MSA 1995 ss 252–3.[358]

In the case of wreck, the SOSREP[359] may decide that Trinity House has the expertise and equipment ready to locate and mark the wreck in a prompt and efficient manner and issue a direction to do so under the MSA 1995 s 255C.[360] Section 255C was amended by the Marine Navigation Act 2013 s 8(2) to make clear that that the GLA has the s 253 powers throughout its area, ie including the EEZ.[361]

Although the GLAs have a variety of statutory functions under Part VIII of the MSA 1995, these have generally been expressed as powers, eg to mark wrecks, rather than duties.[362] However, as seen, under s 255C the Secretary of State can direct the GLA to take action in relation to locating and marking a wreck, and under s 255F can direct that the GLA actually remove the wreck.[363]

While the GLAs would prefer to deal with wrecks first and worry about costs afterwards, there have sometimes been difficulties about how operations were to be financed by government—even though under s 253 unrecovered wreck removal expenses were to be paid out of the GLF.[364] Section 255I of the MSA 1995 now makes it clear that when the GLA complies with a direction under ss 255C (locating and marking) or 255F (removal) its costs shall be paid out of the GLF to the extent that they are not recovered from the shipowner under s 255G.[365] There were some hopes that the £5 million wreck reserve in the GLF might be reduced,[366] as British shipowners have always been concerned about having to fund the GLF through dues to pay for wreck removal of foreign ships.

The GLAs have increasingly been encouraged to use their spare capacity commercially and their powers were extended first in 1997.[367] The 1997 powers were restricted to the use of physical "assets" rather than personnel.[368] The Marine Navigation Act 2013 extended

---

358 See *Transport Committee Ninth Report 2008*, 27, 34.
359 See 4.8.2.
360 See 11.3.3(b).
361 See the MSA 1995 s 193(6), as inserted by the Marine Navigation Act 2013, s 8(1); also 2.2.2 and 11.1.3(b). The Marine Navigation Act 2013 s 8(2) also deleted s 255C(5).
362 See the MSA 1995 ss 197 and 253. Cf the duty in relation to the inspection and management of those (apparently few) local lighthouse authorities that are not harbour authorities.
363 See 11.3.3(b) and (d).
364 MSA 1995 s 253(3). The GLF, regulated by s 211, is financed by light dues (ie a tax) levied under s 205 against shipowners using UK ports and is usually collected by customs officers in the ports. See generally, Gaskell, *MSA 1995*, 21/225–21/231. Local lighthouse authorities can levy local light dues under s 210. Harbour authorities have wide general powers to charge local dues on ships, passengers and goods: see eg the Harbours Act 1964 ss 26–39, as amended.
365 The MSA 1995 s 255I adds that s 213 will still apply to require that the GLA supply estimates to the Secretary of State (eg to the DfT).
366 Lord Mackenzie, *House of Lords, WRC Bill Second Reading debate*, col 1132.
367 In a new s 197(8)–(11), added by the Merchant Shipping and Maritime Security Act [MSMSA] 1997 s 19, but since repealed by the Marine Navigation Act 2013 s 9(2).
368 Gaskell, *MSMSA 1997*, 28/80–28/81.

and clarified these commercial powers by adding a new s 197A to the MSA 1995.[369] The GLAs now have the power to hire out assets, or provide commercial consultancy, provided that there is no conflict of interest with their general statutory functions.[370] The specific consent of the Secretary of State is needed, but there is now much more flexibility as the consent can be general or specific, and prospective or retrospective.[371] There is also more financial flexibility as the GLA is able to access the GLF[372] to support its commercial contracts, and can ask the Secretary of State to approve capital expenditure, eg to be used in addition to an existing asset for a hire contract.

All these financial changes are particularly relevant to wrecks, because not only can the GLA respond to directions from the SOSREP (or requests from a local harbour authority) using its own resources in the first instance, but it could also contract-in extra equipment. In theory, it could agree directly with shipowners (or their insurers) to perform those locating, marking and removal functions for which shipowners (and their insurers) will have responsibilities under the WRC 2007.[373] Moreover, the increase in jurisdiction from 12 miles out to the EEZ has removed doubts about whether it was ultra vires for Trinity House to mark wrecks in the North Sea.

It is understood that this new flexibility is working well under the MSA 1995 Part 9A, with the SOSREP in effect taking responsibility for new wrecks, while the GLAs continue to superintend the buoys of existing wrecks.[374] There is a good working relationship between the GLAs and the SOSREP that has been underpinned by a Memorandum of Understanding between the GLAs and the DfT.[375] In practice, the SOSREP will consult with the GLA, eg Trinity House, about whether a danger to navigation exists after a wreck. The SOSREP can then direct the GLAs to mark the wreck or remove the wreck—as happened with two ships in 2017. One was the Barbados flagged *Fluvius Tamar* (2,876 gt), carrying 3,800 mt of magnesium oxide, wrecked in the North Sea about 35 miles off Ramsgate. Trinity House was able to respond without being concerned about internal government discussions about finance.[376] Similarly, when the small tug *MV Ella* was also wrecked and removed in 2017,[377] it was Trinity House that called for tenders for her removal, knowing that, as the shipowner appeared to have been uninsured, Trinity House's expenses would fall on the

---

369 Inserted by the Marine Navigation Act 2013 s 9.
370 Under s 195.
371 See s 197A(6), which also allows the consent to be subject to conditions.
372 See s 197A(3)(a). Sums received must be paid into the GLF: see s 197A(3)(b).
373 Of course, it could simply perform the services under the SOSREP's direction and then bill the shipowner or insurer directly for their liability under s 255G. It may be that in some circumstances a contractual arrangement might produce a quicker cash flow, but the GLA would seem to be more secure if it always has a direction from the SOSREP, whether or not it makes an agreement with a shipowner.
374 See 4.2.2 for SOSREP approaches to wreck removal.
375 This had been foreshadowed by the Government when concerns were raised about whether the GLAs would have the resources to respond to SOSREP directions: *DfT, Summary of Responses 2008*, 24.
376 The wreck, in a busy shipping lane, was eventually removed by Ardent later in 2017, after being refloated and towed to Rotterdam: see ISU, Salvage World (October 2017), 7; also Trinity House Notice to Mariners 26/2017 notifying that four emergency wreck marker buoys had now been removed.
377 See 4.2.2 and eg Trinity House Notice to Mariners 37/2017, replacing 27/2017 that had informed mariners that a racon had been fitted to the northern of four emergency buoys. The total value of the wreck removal contract was £534,000: www.government-online.net/salvage-wreck-mv-ella/.

GLF.[378] There is also close cooperation between the three GLAs, eg where it may not be clear exactly where a ship is wrecked.[379] It may well be that the GLAs are more suitable for dealing with relatively small vessels, such as the ones above, whereas it seems unlikely that they would themselves be in a position to undertake or coordinate wrecks such as the *MSC Napoli*.[380] Here the SOSREP may act directly through the MCA, eg under s 255F(1), by engaging contractors itself rather than directing a GLA to engage contractors.[381]

One area of concern with s 253, in particular, is how far it can apply to items that have been lost from a ship that itself is not sunk, stranded or abandoned,[382] eg where a heavy lift deck cargo falls overboard and sinks after the ship takes an unexpected list, creating a navigational hazard. Floating cargo is a more pressing problem. In 2017, 14 giant plastic pipes (2 m in diameter and up to 480 m in length) were under tow when a container ship severed the tow line and 12 pipes drifted away in the North Sea.[383] A more common example is where containers are washed overboard, but continue to float and be a danger to navigation. It is practically impossible to mark each container,[384] although there is close liaison with the Coastguard to provide as much information as possible to mariners. Where the carrying ship is not itself wrecked, a strict reading of s 253 might not extend to allow recovery of any expenses for locating or marking such cargo. However, provided that there was a "maritime casualty" within the WRC 2007 Art 1(3),[385] there would seem to be liabilities under the WRC 2007 in respect of such cargo.[386] As the WRC 2007 creates rights for *States*, the SOSREP could presumably issue a direction to the GLA under ss 255C and 255F to undertake location, marking and removal activities, or alternatively, the SOSREP could agree with the GLA that this be done and, if there were any doubts, retrospective consent could be given to any agreement.[387]

11.4 Abandoned ships

When a ship is wrecked as a result of a casualty, its owners may abandon the wreck as worthless and seek to avoid any subsequent liability; as seen, this is a typical situation for which national wreck removal provisions are designed.[388] There may be other

---

378 See 4.2.2 for how the MSA 1995 s 255F(2) applied.
379 See also s 254.
380 See Lord Greenway, *House of Lords, WRC Bill Second Reading debate* col 1130; also 1.2.3.
381 See also *DfT, Summary of Responses 2008*, 26.
382 See also 11.1.3(a).
383 Some pipes were washed shore, but all were eventually removed and taken for recycling in Denmark: see eg www.scotline.co.uk/pipes-washed-norfolk-beach/ and 10.2.7(a)
384 The International Association of Lighthouse Authorities (IALA) has issued IALA Recommendation R1016, *Mobile Marine Aids to Navigation (MAtoN)* (1st ed, 2017), which recognises the development of MAtoN for, inter alia, "drifting wrecks (eg container, debris)". These could flash, but also beam a laser light into the sky (without interfering with aircraft).
385 See 10.6. Eg that there was an "incident of navigation" (such as heavy seas), or an "occurrence on board" the ship (such as a list caused by shifting cargo or ballast) resulting in "material damage or threat of material damage to a ship or its cargo". The ship itself could be threatened (cf the *Pacific Adventurer* 2.6.3), eg if immobilised, but the floating containers would certainly be "cargo" damaged or threatened.
386 See 10.6.
387 See s 197A(6).
388 See 11.1.1–11.1.3.

circumstances where there has been no casualty, as such, but where the vessel has in effect been dumped—not in the sense of being scuttled,[389] but merely 'abandoned' (usually in harbours, rivers or on coastlines). While this may occur with large trading ships, it is much more likely to be a problem involving small vessels, eg old fishing boats or pleasure craft. There may well be little or no hazard to navigation or the environment, but the vessel may simply be a nuisance or an eyesore on a beach or inlet. As such, it may fall to local authorities or private shoreline property owners, many with little experience of maritime law, to try to dispose of the vessel. Disposal of wreck is discussed more generally in Chapter 14, where abandonment and dumping is contrasted,[390] but in the absence of a "maritime casualty" the WRC 2007 will not apply,[391] so it will be a matter for national law whether there are remedies for 'abandonment' in this sense.[392]

In the UK, the MSA 1995 s 252 and 253 expressly apply not only to vessels that are sunk or stranded, but also to those that are "abandoned".[393] However, the remedies under that section are only triggered when the relevant harbour or conservancy authority is of the opinion that the vessel is, or is likely to become, "an obstruction or danger to *navigation* or to lifeboats engaged in lifeboat service in that harbour or water or approach thereto". This would not cover the vessel that is merely an eyesore or nuisance in a wider sense.[394] There may be powers of a receiver of wreck to take possession of a wreck and sell it,[395] but these tend to be in respect of vessels with inherent value. Likewise, in harbours there may be an *action in rem* against a vessel that has a value,[396] or a property owner may have to resort to common law remedies, eg for trespass.

Otherwise it may be necessary to look for regulatory powers in local harbour legislation, eg to give harbour masters powers to order that derelict ships be moved. The Port of London Authority Act 1968 s 120(1) expressly applies to abandoned vessels, but does require them to become, eg, an "impediment . . . to the safe and *convenient* navigation of the Thames or the docks, or part thereof". The word "convenient" may be particularly relevant to abandoned craft, particularly as they may affect navigation in only "part" of the river or docks. A clearer example of modern local legislation is found in the Ardveenish Order 2000. It gives powers to the harbour master to "remove, sell, destroy or otherwise dispose of any vessel laid by or neglected as *unserviceable*" and to recover the proceeds as a debt from the owner.[397] These powers are given in addition to those under the HDPCA 1847 s 57 which provides that "[no] vessel which shall be laid by or neglected as unfit for sea service shall be permitted to lie within the limits of the harbour . . . but the harbour-master may cause every such vessel to be, at the expense of the owner thereof, removed from the harbour".[398] It is

---

389 See 14.3, 14.5.
390 See 14.2.2.
391 See Art 1(3), 8.2.1.(a) and (f), 10.5.1(a).
392 New Zealand's Environmental Resources Act covers both dumping and abandonment: see the *Rena*, 1.2.4.
393 See 11.1.3(a).
394 Nor the wider "related interests" now covered by the WRC: see 8.2.3.
395 See s 240 and 4.5.3.
396 See eg *Ballantrae Holdings Inc v The Ship Phoenix Sun* [2016] FC 570 (Fed Ct Canada).
397 Art 35: see SI 2000/233 and 11.1.3(a). Art 34 places restrictions on the harbour authority's powers in respect of naval ships "abandoned by design". See also the Maryport Order (SI 2007/3463) Arts 27 and 26.
398 The removal is to "any part of the strand or sea' shore, or other place where the same may, without injury to any person, be placed". The section also laid down a mechanism for claiming the charges for removal

also possible that environmental regulatory offences may be committed by a vessel owner (if traced), eg for an unlicensed deposit of material.[399] See also the Southampton Harbour Bye-Laws 2003 which prohibit the abandonment of a vessel on the banks or shores of the port, or the destruction of any wreck without the permission of the harbour master.[400]

In Canada a number of studies have highlighted both the extent of the abandonment problem, but also the legislative gaps.[401] A 2012 government survey found that there were 397 abandoned or derelict vessels with cost estimates for removing them varying from Can$1,500-$3,000 for a small vessel to several hundred thousand dollars for larger craft.[402] Abandoned ships will require administrative and legal costs, eg in tracing ownership, as well as the more familiar costs necessary for any wreck removal (eg access to sites, environmental assessments, waste disposal). Machum has provided an analysis showing that the core challenges in identifying legislative gaps in Canada included: difficulties in identifying the vessel owner; limited and discretionary scope of the legislation; limited authority and funding of the coastguard; right of arrest and sale is only as good as the value of the ship; overall fragmentation of the regulatory system.[403] Canada's Abandoned Boats Program has provided Can$6.85 million for abandoned boat assessment, removal and disposal, and for research and education initiatives. Funding has already been approved to assess 87 boats for a total of $267,560, and to remove 44 boats for a total of $597,993.[404]

Canada has responded to try to close some of these gaps in the Wrecked, Abandoned or Hazardous Vessels Act 2019 that received Royal Assent on 28 February 2019. The Act is a comprehensive enactment that is intended in Part 1 to give effect to the WRC 2007, but also to update Canada's law on salvage (Part 3) and wreck more generally.[405] In particular there is a Part 2 (Vessels and Wrecks of Concern) that deals with aspects of abandonment. Thus, s 30 prohibits the owner of a "dilapidated vessel"[406] from leaving it on a shore for a period of 60 consecutive days. Section 32 prohibits an owner from abandoning a vessel, and abandonment will be presumed if it is left unattended for two years; s 33 prohibits an owner from letting a vessel become a wreck by reason of failing to maintain it; s 34 prohibits a person in charge of a vessel from knowingly causing it to sink or partially sink or to be stranded or grounded, including on the shore. Various powers are granted to the relevant Minister to enforce these provisions, eg to sell, destroy or otherwise dispose of

---

by "summary complaint" before a Justice of the Peace (or sheriff), with a power of sale (but not apparently of destruction). It is not surprising that its ancient language was supplemented in the Ardveenish Order 2000 and the Maryport Order 2007.

399 Eg under the Marine and Coastal Access Act 2009: see 14.1.4(b).

400 Bye-laws 51 and 58.

401 See particularly, E Machum "Abandoned and derelict ships: where do we go from here?" (17 June 2016), published on Canadian Maritime Law Association website: www.cmla.org/papers.php), citing Transport Canada, *Study of the Extent of Abandoned and Derelict Vessels in Canada*, November 2012: avicc.ca/wp-content/uploads/2013/12/TransportCanada_Report_AbandonedDerelictVesselReport_Feb202013.pdf.

402 Transport Canada, *Study*, 5. Presumably, most of the larger craft would be normal 'wrecks'.

403 E Machum "Abandoned and derelict ships: where do we go from here?, 8–14; cf the questions in 11.1.1.

404 See Transport Canada: www.tc.gc.ca/eng/marinesafety/abandoned-boats-wrecks-4454.html.

405 Late amendments in the Senate added protection for ocean war graves.

406 This means a vessel that meets any prescribed criteria and (a) is significantly degraded or dismantled; or (b) is incapable of being used for safe navigation: see s 27.

a vessel that is abandoned and to deal with wrecks generally,[407] but there are also fairly comprehensive penalty provisions in s 90 (albeit designed to promote compliance and not to punish). Although the Act does not always clearly distinguish between where the WRC 2007 applies and where the national law provisions operate,[408] it does represent a modern attempt to deal with matter not covered by the conventions.

States may end up funding removals of abandoned vessels on an ad hoc basis,[409] but one national solution (not adopted in the UK) is to create a specific fund for removing abandoned and derelict vessels. Such a fund has been used in some US States.[410] Thus, the Washington State Department of Natural Resources (DNR) Derelict Vessel Removal Program[411] is financed from a fund partly contributed to by the State but also from various vessel registration fees.[412] Since 2002, more than 580 abandoned or neglected vessels have been removed from Washington waterways, although some of these are of the type that might be expected to be covered elsewhere by normal national wreck removal legislation. Contingency funds have sometimes been created by governments for dealing with marine incidents[413] or to pay for marine infrastructure,[414] but where they are financed by levies on shipping they are not popular.

Similar issues have arisen in Australia, where a 'War on Wrecks' has been declared by the State of Queensland to remove derelict vessels from its coastal waterways (adjacent to the Great Barrier Reef). An Au$20 million fund has been created for a five-year programme with 96 wrecks already removed, contracts or plans to remove another 225, and a further 252 identified.[415] In 2017 alone, three derelict ships were removed at considerable cost, two of which had been driven aground by cyclones.[416]

---

407 Section 27 uses a wide definition of hazard in Part 2, based on that in the WRC 2007 Art 1.5 (see 8.2.2); ie not limited to navigational issues but also including any other interest, including the health, safety, well-being and economic interests of the public.

408 S 47 does give priority to the WRC 2007 provisions in Part 1 in the event of any conflict, but (rather unusually) s 17 gives priority to Part 2 of the Act if there is any inconsistency with the WRC 2007.

409 In the US, NOAA has a Marine Debris Program that can provide grants to remove vessels: see https://response.restoration.noaa.gov/oil-and-chemical-spills/oil-spills/abandoned-and-derelict-vessels.html. NOAA has also launched an Abandoned and Derelict Vessel (ADV) InfoHub to provide information for each US coastal State, including details on legislation and funding: https://marinedebris.noaa.gov/discover-issue/types-and-sources/abandoned-and-derelict-vessels.

410 Information in this para derived from E Machum "Abandoned and derelict ships: where do we go from here?, 18.

411 Washington State Department of Natural Resources, *Recovering Derelict Vessels*. Available at: www.dnr.wa.gov/programs-and-services/aquatics/recovering-derelict-vessels.

412 See also the Derelict Vessels Removal Account (DVRA) at www.dnr.wa.gov/publications/aqr_dv_guidelines_0716.pdf?v4nftj.

413 Australia has a 'Protection of the sea levy' to pay for its National Plan for Maritime Environmental Emergencies (cf 4.8) and to provide a relatively small fund for clean-up costs which cannot be attributed to a known polluter. Canada has a successful Ship-Source Oil Pollution Fund, which can deal with contingencies, but only applies to oil pollution and not to the wider problems of wreck removal: www.tc.gc.ca/eng/marinesafety/oep-ers-regime-funds-1119.htm#ssop.

414 Eg under the GLF for Trinity House: see 11.3.5.

415 Maritime Safety Queensland, "Taskforce continues gaining ground in war on wrecks" 7 March 2019.

416 *Whitsunday Magic*, 34 m steel sailing ship removed in December 2017 (broken up and removed at a cost of Au$805,000); 39-year-old motor ship (towed for local recycling at acost of Au$957,000); see Queensland Parliament, Estimates Hearing, Transport and Main Roads, 27 July 2018, 27.

Finally, it should be noted that even if there is a statutory liability in national law to pay for the costs of dealing with an "abandoned" vessel, it is potentially subject to limitation of liability.[417]

---

417 Under the LLMC Art 2(1)(d) as a "claim in respect of the . . . removal . . . of a ship which is . . . abandoned" (see 2.4.4), unless a State has reserved the right to exclude Art 2(1)(d) from the list of limitable claims (see 2.5.8).

PART III

WRECK REMOVAL CONTRACTS

CHAPTER 12

Transition to wreck removal

Salvage and SCOPIC

12.1 Salvage and wreck removal

12.1.1 Introduction

When there is a casualty, it is most likely that, before any application of the law relating to wreck removal, it will be necessary to consider whether the principles of salvage law will apply. This is because the ship and cargo owners will be hoping that their valuable property can be saved. Of course, a casualty might immediately become a wreck, eg where a ship sinks, but even here the sunken ship and cargo might still have a positive value if raised. In this general sense, salvage activities to remove this valuable property could be called a form of wreck removal.

It is necessary, though, to be clear about the legal principles that could apply, as there are many conceptual differences between salvage and wreck removal. The main distinction is that salvage is a unique principle for rewarding voluntary efforts to save property at sea, where the underlying right of the salvor is independent of contract;[1] the salvor is rewarded on a no cure no pay basis out of the value of the property saved.[2] Wreck removal usually involves a positive regulatory duty on shipowners to remove a hazard, while arrangements to facilitate that removal will usually depend upon a separate contract with a wreck removal contractor whose payment basis may be agreed in a variety of ways. While those differences have always existed, the last 30–40 years have seen a greater focus both on the distinctions between the concepts and also on the transition between a salvage service and wreck removal. The legal differences also reflect quite different commercial considerations, and the identification and management of the transition has assumed an increasing importance—not only for the private commercial interests but also for governments overseeing operations and considering their intervention powers. It is necessary first, though, to consider the application of salvage law to wreck removal. The general principles of salvage law have been outlined already.[3]

12.1.2 Salvage contracts: commercial and legal choices

12.1.2(a) Initial considerations

There are a number of contractual choices that face those whose ships are in distress and that might become a wreck. In the initial phase of a casualty (when human life has been

---

1 Although there can be salvage contracts, see 12.2.2 and 2.7.2.
2 See 2.7.1, 2.7.7.
3 See 2.7.

safeguarded), all will be focused on saving the vessel and cargo. This is where consideration will need to be given as to whether a salvage service can to be performed. The master of the ship may need such urgent assistance that he needs to contact any potential salvor who can reach his ship in time to save it. The initial question for such a master will be whether to simply accept the services on a no-contract 'salvage convention'[4] basis, or to agree a particular contract. In an age of relative ease of communication, the reality is that (save in the most immediate situation of danger where there is a potential salvor nearby) most masters will contact their owners[5] for advice. Those owners will at some stage contact their H&M insurers (possibly through their insurance brokers), but in the first stages of a casualty they will need to provide immediate advice to the master. Best practice has usually been thought to involve leaving the final word on safety decisions to the master on the spot, but there is an obvious conflict of interest for the owners. Apart from the huge commercial dislocation caused by a casualty, the owners will naturally be thinking about how to keep down the costs of responding to it. Both master and owners may be fearful of the potentially high cost of a salvage reward, even though this may largely be covered by insurance.[6]

The state of the ship may well determine whether immediate assistance is required from whichever potential salvor can first reach the site of the casualty. In these circumstances the first responding salvor may well have a negotiating advantage. Although it will have a duty to assist in saving life, it will have no obligation to perform salvage services.

12.1.2(b) Salvage contract or not?

A salvor might start to perform salvage services before there is any agreement on a contract, especially if it considers that there is a low risk of the ship being wrecked. In such a case the salvor would know that, even in the absence of a contract, it would still have a right to a 'salvage convention' Art 13 reward. If, later, a contract is signed it is likely that the contract form would cover the services which had already been performed.[7] In practice, though, salvors may be wary about starting salvage services without an express agreement as they may be able to foresee jurisdictional and enforcement difficulties, especially when the casualty is located in certain States.

Most professional salvors would probably seek to perform services under a contract such as the LOF, incorporating an arbitration clause; this would at least settle the place where any dispute would be heard. The choice of contract may well depend upon the location of the casualty and nationality of the salvor; there may be cabotage restrictions or the salvor may prefer to use a local salvage contract[8] rather than a more internationally acceptable contract such as the LOF—particularly if it was desired to secure local (rather than London) arbitration.

---

4 See 2.7.3 for the use of this expression.
5 In the case where the registered owner is a single ship company, with perhaps only one or two nominal directors, operational decisions will usually be taken by ship managers (either a separate company in a related group which manages all the group's ships, or an independent firm of ship managers).
6 For examples, see 2.7.7(a), 2.9.2(a), 2.9.3(c).
7 See the LOF 2011 cl E.
8 Eg a Japanese or Turkish form.

12.1.2(c) Salvage contract or a towage contract?

Where the danger of the ship being completely wrecked is a little more remote, the shipowners may well try to exercise more control over negotiations with potential salvors. The ship may have been immobilised by an engine failure in open seas; while a drifting ship can be in 'danger' for salvage purposes in English law,[9] there may be more time for the shipowners to contact a number of potential salvors to obtain better terms.[10] One obvious option for the shipowner is to see if any owner of a tug or supply boat is willing to enter into a (non-salvage) towage contract. Here, a daily rate towage hire contract,[11] or a lump sum towage contract[12] may be agreed. The advantage to the shipowner is that it may have more control over the length of the operation (eg by a specific agreement to tow to a particular port), and the costs may more easily be estimated (rather than being left open to the opinion of an arbitrator applying Art 13 principles). The attraction of a possible cost saving has to be weighed against the transfer of risk that is involved. In a salvage service (eg under contract) the salvor runs the risk that the ship under tow will deteriorate further and be wrecked: under the no cure no pay principle the salvor will be paid nothing. Under a daily rate towage hire contract, the tugowner will be entitled to be paid the agreed amount for each day of the service.[13]

From the perspective of the potential salvor, there are also commercial and legal consequences if the shipowner raises the alternatives of a salvage contract or a towage contract. A professional salvor will usually be more attracted to the salvage option, as it is in the risk business and will be prepared to rely on its expertise to succeed in the operations and so earn a high salvage reward. The simple equation faced by the professional salvor is that the more likely the ship in distress will be wrecked and totally lost, the more likely it is that the shipowner will want a no cure no pay contract; the shipowner will pay nothing if the ship is so wrecked but if, by some feat of skill, the salvor succeeds in saving something of value, then that will be better for the shipowner than having nothing if the ship is completely wrecked. By contrast, if the salvor's professional opinion is that it is very unlikely that a stranded ship and cargo can be saved, then it does not make sense for the salvor to sign up to an onerous, expensive and ultimately unrewarded salvage operation. Salvors can 'sniff' if a CTL likely and so may prefer a daily rate contract, or to move immediately to a wreck removal contract.[14] It is in this context that Art 14 of the Salvage Convention, or (more likely) SCOPIC, may provide some incentive for the salvor to agree to perform salvage services.[15] The salvors may agree to an LOF, but will want to invoke SCOPIC from day one so that they are not faced with having control of a wreck nobody wants.[16]

---

9 Danger is mostly a question of fact, so it will be necessary to assess matters such as the state of the weather and how close the ship is to a dangerous shore. Some assumptions will also need to be made as to the future, eg whether the ship's engines can be fixed fairly quickly. See *Kennedy & Rose*, Chapter 5.

10 There may be more time to negotiate with such salvors when a ship is firmly aground in circumstances where it is clear that it will probably be there for some considerable time: see eg cases such as the *MSC Napoli* and the *Rena*: see 1.2.3, 1.2.4.

11 Eg Towhire 2008.

12 Eg Towcon 2008.

13 Towhire 2008 cl 3(b)(iii) provides that the hire will continue after the loss of the tow until the tug arrives at its destination (with a maximum period of 14 days).

14 See 13.6.

15 See 2.7.9(b) and (c).

16 See also 2.8.1.

12.1.2(d) Non-professional contractors

Different factors may influence the contractual preferences of those who operate ships which have towage capabilities (eg operators of harbour tug or supply boats), but who are not in the business of being professional salvors. Such a commercial operator, although attracted to the prospect of a lucrative occasional salvage job, may more instinctively be happier with the guaranteed income from a towage contract—perhaps with the added attraction of being able to charge higher than normal daily rates (or lump sum). Some sub-contracts contain a clause whereby the sub-contractor undertakes to the salvor that neither it nor any of its sub-contractors, nor their servants or agents, will make any claim against the casualty for salvage.[17]

There is a potential risk for an operator that is not a professional salvor (including eg a passing cargo ship) if it does agree to a 'no salvage' contract with the owner of the ship in distress. If the ship to which the service is being offered is, as a matter of law and fact, in 'danger' then it may not be possible to deprive the master and crew of the assisting ship of their independent right to claim salvage.[18] The MSA 1995 s 39 prevents an employment contract from forbidding seafarers[19] to claim salvage,[20] although those employed on salvage tugs can renounce their rights (and their employment contracts will commonly provide for them to receive a percentage of any sums recovered by the salvage company).[21]

A further alternative for an operator that is not a full time salvor is to act as a sub-contractor to a professional salvor, especially if the operator has the advantage of having the assets (eg ships, barges or other equipment such as heavy lift equipment or pumps) in the right location. In such a case the sub-contractor may be in a strong position to drive a hard bargain as to daily rates, and it may prove difficult for the salvor later to claim that the agreement was entered into under economic duress or a mistake.[22] In such a sub-contract, the salvor will assume the financial risk of being legally liable to pay the sub-contractor on a daily rate—even if the salvage operation as a whole is unsuccessful because the ship and cargo are wrecked and become a total loss. In the latter case, the no cure no pay principle means that there will be little or no salvage reward, but the salvor will still have to pay its sub-contractors. This is a risk that the professional salvor may be willing to accept, given the high salvage reward it would hope to obtain.[23]

---

17 See Salvhire 2005 cll 6.4 and Salvcon 2005 cl 8.4, which are mainly designed for professional salvage companies, but they also restrict the ability to claim for special compensation under Art 14 of the Salvage Convention 1989, or for payment under SCOPIC. Cf Towhire 2008 cl 19 which merely restricts the tugowner's ability to claim salvage during the towage contract.

18 See eg *The Leon Blum* [1915] P 290.

19 The MSA 1995 s 39 does not apply to the master of a ship, presumably because he is thought to be in less need of protection than the crew, and s 41 (giving the master an equivalent lien for wages) does not seem to extend to giving protection against renouncing salvage rights by contract.

20 Standard 'no salvage' contracts may contain indemnities in case such an independent claim is made: see eg Salvhire 2005 cll 6.4, 16.

21 Cf *The Texaco Southampton* [1983] 1 Lloyd's Rep 94 (NSWCA): see also *Gaskell, MSA 1995*, 21/421.

22 See 12.1.2(e).

23 Note that under LSSAC 2014 cl 17.2 an LOF salvor is entitled to use sub-contractors, while remaining primarily liable.

12.1.2(e) Sub-contractor commercial pressure: duress and frustration

The main salvor may be at a commercial disadvantage when it needs to arrange a sub-contract to provide local services. After the *Rena* went aground on 5 October 2011,[24] Svitzer was appointed the next day as an LOF salvor, and SCOPIC was invoked.[25] On that day it sought to charter a small tanker to offload the bunkers. The only ship immediately available was the *Awanuia*, owned by Seafuels, that was on long term charter to Z Energy to supply bunkers in the Auckland area. Under some pressure from the authorities at Maritime New Zealand,[26] Svitzer agreed (under protest) to a very expensive short term charter of the ship at up to NZ$200,000 a day from Seafuels (who arranged a separate contract of release to compensate Z Energy for breaking its charter).[27] The ship was not off hire until 18 November 2011 when an invoice for $8.9 million was issued.

A salvor faced with such demands might naturally be concerned that it would have to pay the full hire up-front and that any future salvage reward might not fully reflect such expenses. Moreover, in the event of a SCOPIC claim, it might be met with a defence that these "out of pocket" expenses were not "reasonably paid".[28] Svitzer later claimed to have the charter with Seafuels set aside on the basis of duress. The claim was dismissed, largely because Svitzer was acting under a variety of pressures[29] and had actually renewed the charter a number of times.

The court left open, as arguable, the extent of its powers to strike down (or reopen) express terms of the charter under the inherent equitable jurisdiction of an Admiralty Court, or Art 7 of the Salvage Convention 1989.[30] The question of whether either jurisdiction extends beyond the direct salvage contract (here between Svitzer and Daina) is controversial. *Kennedy & Rose* argues[31] that the power under Art 7 to annul or modify terms of a contract, eg where the payment is in an excessive degree too large, can apply to sub-contracts made between salvors and third parties (and even to towage contracts)—provided that there are "salvage operations".[32] With respect, it may be doubted whether the very extensive powers of Art 7 of the Convention were ever intended to extend beyond salvage

---

24 See 1.2.4(a).

25 *Svitzer Salvage BV v Z Energy Ltd* (reissue) [2013] NZHC 2584 (20 December 2013), [2014] 1 Lloyd's Rep Plus 19; *Svitzer Salvage BV v Z Energy Ltd* (recall) [2013] NZHC 3541 (20 December 2013); *Svitzer Salvage BV v Z Energy Ltd* [2012] NZHC 1650 (20 Jul 2012). For SCOPIC see 2.8.9(c) and 12.3.

26 Apparently including a threat to 'requisition' the vessel under the Maritime Transport Act 1994 s 100: *Svitzer Salvage BV v Z Energy Ltd* (reissue) [2013] NZHC 2584 [10]. The *Awanuia* was registered in New Zealand, but whether such powers of requisition exist under intervention powers can be open to dispute, especially with foreign flagged vessels: see 4.2.3(a), 5.3.

27 There were also concerns about a demand that all title to the bunkers would pass to Seafuels and then to Z Energy (which agreed to dispose of it through its own facilities). This itself raised issues of ownership of the bunkers (belonging to *Rena*'s owners) and the ability of the salvors to agree to such a term.

28 See SCOPIC 2018 cl 5(iii) and 2.8.9(c).

29 Including a direction from Maritime New Zealand that SCOPIC was not to be terminated without its consent: see also the *MSC Napoli*, 1.2.3.

30 The Case was apparently settled before the substantive issue could be argued: see B Marten, "Third Party agreements in the salvage context" [2014] LMCLQ 497 [*Marten, Third Party Agreements*].

31 397, and also 377–399.

32 See Art 6(1) which applies the Salvage Convention 1989 "to any salvage operations save to the extent that a contract otherwise provides expressly or by implication". "Salvage operation" is defined in Art 1(a).

contracts proper, including even a sub-contract on *salvage* terms,[33] as opposed to sub-contracts which are not for salvage—such as the sub-charter with Seafuels which (as is typical) had a 'no salvage' provision. One problem with the wider interpretation is that there may be many contracts with some sort of connection to salvage operations, and it is rather difficult to see that the wide and general unfair terms powers in Art 7 were intended to extend much beyond the typical situation where the salvor demands a high fixed price salvage payment from a ship in danger.[34] On that basis, the ordinary principles of contract law will apply to sub-contracts such as that agreed by Svitzer, including principles of duress, non-disclosure, misrepresentation,[35] mistake[36] and frustration.

In *The Sea Angel*[37] a salvor chartered a small tanker to shuttle oil cargo from the tanker *Tasman Spirit*, which grounded near Karachi in July 2003, to a larger storage tanker. What was meant to be a 20 day time charter was extended by some 108 days as a result of the unlawful detention of the vessel by the port authorities to back a demand for some US$11 million in respect of clean-up expenses.[38] The salvor failed in a claim for frustration of the charter, partly because SCOPIC placed the risk of detention on the salvors.[39] It is not entirely clear if the salvor was entitled under SCOPIC to be reimbursed for these expenses on the basis that they were reasonably paid, or whether the frustration claim was indirectly supported by the shipowner (and Club) who would be liable under SCOPIC.

12.1.2(f) Subcontracting on salvage basis

The alternative for both parties is for the sub-contractor to be engaged by the salvor on a 'salvage' basis; ie no cure no pay. Here the sub-contractor becomes, in effect, a form of joint salvor, sharing in the risks and rewards. This type of arrangement is much more likely where the sub-contractor is *itself* a professional salvor. It may, for example, have provided initial services at the scene of the casualty but failed to be selected as the contractual salvor by the owners. It is primarily for these situations that the ISU drafted its own salvage sub-contract, currently the ISU Sub-Contract (Award Sharing) 2001. This is designed for use when the main salvage contractor is engaged on LOF terms and the sub-contract largely mirrors the LOF provisions, eg for arbitration in London. It provides for any salvage reward received by the head salvor to be shared with the salvage sub-contractor, in an amount decided by the arbitrator.[40]

---

33 Eg the ISU Subcontract (Award Sharing) 2001: see 12.1.2(f).

34 For this narrower view of the extent of Art 7, see *Gaskell, MSA 1995*, 21/388, and *Marten, Third Party Agreements*.

35 See eg *The Unique Mariner* [1978] 1 Lloyd's Rep 438, *The Unique Mariner* (No 2) [1979] 1 Lloyd's Rep 37; *Gaskell, Lloyd's Open Form and Contractual Remedies*.

36 See eg *Great Peace Shipping Ltd v Tsavliris International Ltd (The Great Peace)* [2002] EWCA Civ 1407, [2003] QB 679, [2002] 2 Lloyd's Rep 653; *Kennedy & Rose*, 373–400.

37 [2007] EWCA Civ 547; [2007] 2 Lloyd's Rep 517.

38 Such a claim would expect to fall within the CLC 1969 or 1992, but Pakistan only acceded to the CLC 1992 in 2005: see also 2.6.2(a).

39 Under what then cl 9(iii), but now SCOPIC 2018 cl 9(ii): see 12.3.4(c).

40 As a result of an incident where the head salvor became insolvent, some clauses were added to the standard contract providing that salvage sums received by the head salvor are to be held on trust for the sub-contractor. See cll 4, 9, 2(d)(e).

The key distinction, then, is between salvage contracts such as the LOF 2011 (and award sharing sub-contracts such as the ISU Sub-Contract (Award Sharing) 2001) and those other contracts which provide for maritime services where the contractor is paid in the ordinary way, eg by way of lump sum or daily rate hire. These service contracts may be in a variety of forms, eg Towcon, Towhire, Salvcon, Salvhire, but (whatever the description) they are not proper salvage (no cure no pay) contracts. Indeed, there is no reason why a subcontract cannot be on the basis of any amended charterparty form, but experience has shown that the special forms (whether drafted by BIMCO or the ISU) are an appropriate basis for the provision of services, inter alia, to assist with casualties.

In practice, a salvor first on the scene could offer to take immediate action to assist—knowing that even if later superseded[41] by a contracted salvor it would still be entitled to a share of salvage remuneration for the efforts that it had taken to assist the casualty. The problem is that the first potential salvor may make it clear that it will be engaged on a salvage operation (eg under LOF), but the casualty's master may delay accepting such assistance under instruction from owners (eg where they may be seeking to engage a tug on a daily rate or other more 'favourable' contractual terms). The time taken by negotiations over contracts could have a serious effect on a casualty if it causes delay to the salvage operation.[42]

12.2 Termination of services[43]

At various stages in operations to assist a casualty a number of parties may wish to terminate their participation, or to end the participation of others. Such a termination may cause concern to other parties, including the non-commercial parties—in particular coastal Affected States. The determination of when or how salvage services may cease is of particular importance in identifying when wreck removal services may start—and assessing the legal incidents of the transition from one to the other. It is necessary to unpick the various legal rights and obligations of the commercial parties[44] and to assess the extent to which States may restrict those rights in order to avoid a shipwreck. The position will be different depending on whether a particular service is being performed under a contract or not.

12.2.1 Salvors operating without a contract

Salvors who are performing voluntary salvage will have their rights and obligations largely defined by the Salvage Convention 1989. The Convention does not contain an obligation on a salvor to perform any salvage services. Article 10 merely provides a duty to render assistance to any "person in danger of being lost at sea". This provision is designed to save life does not create any independent duty to save property, or the environment. Article 8(1) does set out duties of the salvor, including a duty to exercise due care to prevent or minimise damage to the environment, but these are owed only to the owner of the ship (or other

---

41 See 12.2.1.
42 See eg the *Fedra*, 10.2.5.
43 *Kennedy & Rose* 438–454; *Brice* 384–395, 623–627.
44 For the effects of a wreck on other commercial contracts, see Chapter 2; eg bills of lading or charterparties (see 2.1.4, 2.1.7).

property in danger). The wording was deliberately designed so as not to create any more general duties of the salvor to third parties, eg to coastal States to prevent pollution.[45] The duty under Art 8(1)(a) that the salvor owes to the ship and cargo interests is to "carry out salvage operations with due care". Again, this is not open ended; it does not require the salvor actually to salve a ship in distress, merely to use due care in any operations that it decided to perform. Fault of a salvor which results in a ship being wrecked can give rise to a claim for negligence[46] and (apparently) to an action for damages for breach of the Convention.[47] Apart from this, it seems that there is nothing in the Convention that would prevent a salvor from declining to continue with operations that it considered to be too dangerous or uneconomic. In the latter example, a salvor could terminate its services almost at will, although the exercise of "due care" may well require some sort of minimum notice to be given so that the owners of ship and cargo could begin to seek assistance elsewhere. If the ship is later wrecked and totally lost, the salvor would not be entitled to any reward (on the no cure no pay principle). If a later salvor does succeed in saving some valuable property then the terminating salvor might still claim to share in any reward on the basis of contributions it had made to success, but its decision to terminate might in some circumstances be considered as "misconduct" under Art 18 so as to lead to a reduction in any applicable reward.

If it is the ship or cargo owner that decides to terminate the (non-contractual) salvor's service, the position is a little less clear. Article 8(1)(d) requires the salvor "to accept the intervention of other salvors when treasonably requested to so" by the property interests (including the master). The assumption behind Art 8(1)(d) is that the master may consider that the first salvor is not up to the job in some way. It may be that a small tug is the first rescuer on the scene and then later a more powerful ocean going salvage tug arrives and is in a better position to complete the salvage. This could mean that the first salvor receives a much lower salvage reward (by comparison with the intervener).

Article 8(1)(d) goes on to say that if the intervention order was made unreasonably the salvor's reward "shall not be prejudiced". The provision is not without ambiguity.[48] The better view is probably that "intervention" includes complete supersession and termination of the services of the first salvor, as the ultimate control of what happens to the ship should normally be a matter for her master. An able and willing salvor that was unreasonably superseded was entitled to some recompense in the nature of salvage under English Admiralty law prior to the Salvage Convention 1989,[49] and there would appear to be a similar result under Art 8(1)(d).[50] More difficult is whether the first salvor would have a personal

---

45 See *Gaskell, MSA 1995*, 21/389–21/394. Thus, there is nothing in the *Convention* that gives a right to a State to order a tug owner to take, or refrain from taking, any action in order to prevent environmental harm caused by the casualty. However, States may interpret their intervention powers as giving them that right. See 4.2.3(a). 5.3, 12.3.4(c).

46 *The Tojo Maru* [1972] AC 242.

47 *Gaskell, MSA 1995*, 21/389. In both cases it would seem that the salvor would be entitled to limit liability under Arts 1 and 2 of the LLMC 1996: see 2.5.5.

48 See *Gaskell, MSA 1995*, 21/391–21/392.

49 *The Unique Mariner No.2* [1979] 1 Lloyd's Rep 37, *The Hassel* [1959] 2 Lloyd's Rep 82). Gaskell, *Lloyd's Open Form and Contractual Remedies*.

50 It is arguable that, since the enactment of the Convention, it is no longer appropriate to look to the *solatium* referred to in *The Unique Mariner (No 2)* and *The Hassel* as Art 8(1)(c) and (d) could be said to provide exclusive remedies: *Gaskell, MSA 1995*, 21/422.

action for being dismissed if the second salvor failed in its services so that the ship was wrecked (and there was no fund to pay any salvage). The Convention provides no clear guidance, but it is arguable that an action for damages under the Convention could arise.[51]

The absence of a clear provision allowing termination by the ship and cargo interests may be relevant in circumstances other than where there is a possible alternative salvor. It may appear that salvage services are not going to be successful and the ship is about to be wrecked. It might be expected that here a salvor would abandon, ie terminate, the salvage services—as happened with the *Torrey Canyon*.[52] To continue would be a waste of money as there would be little or no salved fund. Where there is some chance of saving part of the cargo from a ship (as with the *MSC Napoli* and *Rena*[53]) the salvor would presumably make an economic calculation about the amount and value of undamaged cargo that it could recover and continue with operations for as long as they seemed worthwhile. In the language of the Salvage Convention 1989 Art 12(1) there would continue to be a "useful result", ie valuable property saved from which a reward could be paid. The introduction of Art 14 of the Salvage Convention 1989[54] altered these assumptions.

Under Art 14(1) a salvor is entitled to special compensation if it "*has* carried out salvage operations[55] in respect of a vessel which by itself or its cargo threatened damage to the environment" and failed to receive an appropriate Art 13 traditional salvage reward. The purpose was to encourage salvors to become involved in eg tanker casualties where it appeared that the ship would become wrecked (or a total loss), but there was a chance of preventing or minimising pollution.[56] It may well have been possible to tow the sinking ship away from a sensitive shore; obviously if cargo could be saved then that would provide a suitable fund for traditional salvage, but the cargo, though transferable, may well have been contaminated. More likely today is the prospect of a container ship such as *MSC Napoli* or *Rena* going aground. There may be many containers of cargo which, although ruined and valueless, might easily be a threat to the environment. The salvor that satisfies Art 14(1) would be entitled to claim its expenses and the increment of up to 30% (or sometimes 100%) of those expenses. That could be a significant amount, with a generous 'profit' element in the form of the increment.[57]

In these circumstances, what is to stop the salvor continuing on with the services, claiming its expenses (and increment) for a seemingly indefinite period in relation to diminishing amounts of cargo? As noted, there is no express provision allowing the shipowner (liable for special compensation under Art 14) to terminate 'Art 14 operations'. Admittedly, the salvor could only claim for expenses that are "reasonably incurred",[58] but there is bound

---

51 *Gaskell, MSA 1995*, 21/393. It seems that such a claim would be subject to limitation under Art 2(1)(c) of the LLMC 1996, as the claim would not be excepted under Art 3(a) as it was not a claim for "salvage".
52 See 1.2.1(a).
53 See 1.2.3, 1.2.4.
54 See 2.7.9(b).
55 Defined widely in Art 1(a) to mean "any act or activity undertaken to assist a vessel or any other property in danger".
56 See 2.7.9(a).
57 Although salvors were unhappy with the calculation of the base expenses as interpreted in *The Nagasaki Spirit* [1997] 1 Lloyd's Rep 323: see 2.7.9(b).
58 See Art 14(3).

to be some uncertainty, delay and expense in settling amounts.[59] That was a particular concern for the P&I Clubs who would be largely responsible for covering the shipowner's Art 14 liabilities. Moreover, the possibility of such continuing operations really blurred the distinction between salvage and wreck removal for which the Clubs were also traditionally liable. Here they were much more used to arranging removal on a contractual basis where they had input into the terms (especially price) and more control over the conduct and extent of operations. The fear, in effect, was that Art 14 might result in a form of wreck removal by stealth; ie salvors who realised that there was a diminishing prospect of a "useful result" (ie salvage of valuable property) might drag out operations in order to earn special compensation.[60] Prior to the introduction of Art 14, salvors would probably have abandoned the salvage operation (as with the *Torrey Canyon*). The limit on the type of service that would qualify for special compensation was that the salvor was carrying out "salvage operations", itself defined in Art 1 as meaning "*any act* or activity undertaken to assist a vessel or any other property [eg cargo] in danger". Provided that the act or activity related to a ship or cargo that threatened the environment, then the expenses involved (and a fair rate for equipment and personnel) could be charged.

There would be an indirect benefit to the shipowner (and Clubs) if pollution liabilities (eg under the CLC) or wreck removal costs could be minimised. This was why it was only shipowners who were made liable to pay special compensation under Art 14; cargo owners would not have been personally liable for pollution caused, eg, by their cargo of oil.[61]

The advantage to the salvor of continuing its services would be that it could be entitled to its costs (plus increment) as a matter of law, rather than by agreement with the owners. To some extent, this was an aim of Art 14 from the environmental perspective. Art 14 was primarily viewed as an incentive for salvors to become involved immediately after a casualty, ie a form of guaranteed future cover for costs where there was an environmental threat. But the incentive was also intended to continue after the start of salvage operations, because that was the purpose of Art 14(2) with its increment designed to reward actions which actually prevented environmental damage (even though no valuable property might be saved). Were there any limits on the services that would qualify for special compensation towards the end of traditional salvage operations, at the stage when it appeared that the ship and cargo would be wrecked (ie a total loss)?

The environmental threats would largely come from the ship's bunkers and its cargo (eg oil, chemicals or hazardous or noxious substances). Attempts to remove these pollutants would obviously fall within the intent of Art 14, especially where they had little or no value to qualify for a salvage reward under Art 13. What is to stop a salvor continuing the services indefinitely in attempts to remove such items, or simply maintaining a full savage team (including vessels and equipment) on site even when there was a diminishing possibility of any reduction of environmental harm. Admittedly, the risk of salvors 'churning'

---

59 See *Bishop*, 75.

60 Such risk concerns are also reflected in the Clubs' concerns about wreck removal contracts: see 13.6.2.

61 Oil cargo interests would only have been affected indirectly because of the contribution by oil importers generally to the second tier IOPC Fund: see 2.6.2(b). The level of contributions would be very small, being spread across the whole industry, as opposed to being imposed on the owner of the particular cargo involved. Further, there are no specific statutory liabilities on cargo owners to remove 'wrecked' cargo, at least in English law: see now the WRC 2007 Art 10, 10.2.2.

expenses was reduced by the definition of "salvors' expenses" in Art 14(3). This required reasonableness both in the incurring of out-of-pocket expenses and in relation to the personnel and equipment actually used. Still, there was scope for disputing how far the criterion of "reasonableness" should balance cost against the type and level of environmental harm that could be minimised. In some cases, the Clubs did not even become aware of a special compensation claims until long after the salvage operations were completed.[62] It was only after the Salvage Convention 1989 had entered into force that it appeared to the shipowners (and Clubs) that there might be no explicit 'haul off' provision, that could enable them easily to bring an end to Art 14 operations. Moreover, given the delicate compromise that had produced the Convention, there was virtually no political possibility at the IMO of easily amending the treaty.[63]

It is in this context that Art 19 becomes significant. This provision was a reworking of Art 3 of the Salvage Convention 1910 which had stated that salvors were not entitled to *any* "remuneration" (ie a traditional salvage reward in 1910) for taking part in salvage operations despite the "express and reasonable prohibition on the part of the vessel". The Salvage Convention 1989 Art 19 preserves the power to give an express and reasonable prohibition, but makes two changes to the 1910 provision. First, it says that the consequence of a failure by the salvor to obey means that the services "shall not give rise to payment under the Convention". The use of the word "payment" clearly includes the possibility of special compensation under Art 14. Secondly, the identity of the persons with power to prohibit services is made more specific than the somewhat general reference to "on the part of the vessel" in Art 3 of the Salvage Convention 1910. The Salvage Convention 1989 Art 19 clarifies that it is the shipowner or master of the vessel which has the Art 19 power, but not the owner of cargo or freight at risk.[64] This reinforces the idea is that it is the shipowner and master who have primary control of operations involving the ship.

The master of the casualty is most likely to exercise the Art 19 power where he has doubts about the capabilities of the salvor to save the ship and cargo. The shipowner will also have these concerns, but may also be concerned about curtailing the possibility of the salvor in 'churning' expenses, as explained above. In both examples, the question of whether a prohibition is "reasonable" will be largely one of fact. The prohibition can apply both to salvage operations that may be about to start and to those which are already underway. To some extent Art 19 needs to be read with Art 8, especially Art 8(1)(d). Article 8 requires the salvors to use due care, and to accept assistance from other salvors. But the overriding power to prohibit further work is reserved to the master and shipowner.

As Art 19 would prevent a salvor from receiving Art 14 special compensation if it disobeyed the order, it would seem to provide a complete answer to shipowner fears of

---

62 See *Bishop*, 85. For this reason, SCOPIC 2018 now includes the ability of the liability insurer (amongst others) to receive daily information about the salvage from a Special Casualty Representative: see 12.3.2. Note also the *Code of Practice between International Salvage Union and International Group of P&I Clubs* (2005), under which the salvor is obliged to notify the Club (at the start of operations or as soon after as is practical) if there is a possibility of a special compensation claim.

63 Subsequent attempts to effect changes to the Convention have received little support in the CMI (see *Bishop*, 105) and have not been accepted by the IMO Legal Committee.

64 Art 19 does include a rather obscure provision allowing prohibitions from owners of other property *not* on board the ship. This might conceivably be the owner of a jetty, oil terminal or offshore platform that considers it might be threatened by the salvage operations: and see *Gaskell, MSA 1995*, 21/422.

churning. A degree of uncertainty can be raised, though, where the salvor claims that its continued operations are "reasonable" because they are designed to prevent or minimise damage to the environment. An example may be where there are still bunkers on board the ship, or a container with drums of pesticide. The bunkers and cargo may well be contaminated and obviously valueless, so as to give no possibility of enhancing the value of the salved fund. It is highly likely that the coastal State will be very keen for the bunkers to be removed first, and also anxious for operations to continue in relation to noxious cargo. Article 19, though, does not spell out what is a "reasonable" prohibition in such circumstances. It does not, for instance, spell out that a prohibition (ie termination) would only be justified where a "useful result" were possible,[65] as provided for in the LOF 2011 cl G.[66] The antecedent of the Art 19 provision, in Art 3 of the Salvage Convention 1910, existed before special compensation was created as a concept. So it is not surprising, perhaps, that it does not spell out in whose interests reasonableness is to be judged. What is reasonable for commercial parties such as the shipowner, may not be reasonable for the "environment", especially given that its protection was one of the drivers of the Salvage Convention 1989. It is arguable that in circumstances such as those involving the bunkers and noxious cargo, above, it would not be a reasonable prohibition to stop the salvor carrying on with operations. Moreover, if there was no direct evidence of 'churning', it might not assist a shipowner's arguments about "reasonableness" if the underlying reason was a more basic desire to be able to control more closely those operations in the transition between salvage and wreck removal (eg by non-salvage contracts with contractors other than the first salvor).

It is largely because of such the uncertainty about termination rights that express termination provisions now exist in the LOF 2011 cl G, as well as SCOPIC 2018 cl 9.[67]

12.2.2 Salvage contracts and the Salvage Convention 1989

The Salvage Convention 1989 does not require that there is any contractual relationship between the salvor and the salved interests; the salvor's reward arises as a matter of law as a result of the performance of successful services. This was the same position in English Admiralty law prior to the Convention. Where salvors do enter into any salvage contract, including an LOF, there is obviously some change in the nature of their relationship with the owners of ship and cargo. Under the pre-Convention Admiralty law, the general maritime law of salvage applied only in so far as it was expressly or impliedly incorporated into the contract.[68] Article 6(1) of the Salvage Convention 1989 now provides that the "Convention shall apply to any salvage operations save to the extent that a contract otherwise provides expressly or by implication". In other words, the Convention (as given the force

---

65 Art 12(2) states that no "payment" is due under the Convention if the salvage operations have had no useful result. "Payment" includes special compensation under Art 14(1)1 (see Art 1(e)) and it might be argued that there could be no useful result, in terms of successful property salvage, to sunken, valueless property. However, Art 14 would seem to fall within the caveat "except as otherwise provided" in Art 1(2).

66 See 12.2.4.

67 See 12.3.4.

68 *The Unique Mariner No.2* [1979] 1 Lloyd's Rep 37, 50–51; *The Tojo Maru* [1972] AC 242; Gaskell, *MSA 1995*, 21/244; Gaskell, *Lloyd's Open Form and Contractual Remedies*.

12.2.3 Termination by LOF salvor

Under an LOF contract the salvor has always undertaken to use its "best endeavours" to salve the ship and other property.[71] In theory, this probably imposed greater duties than under non-contract (ie 'Convention salvage') in that it would arguably have been a repudiatory breach for the salvor to have abandoned the agreed task, eg if there had been a more lucrative job elsewhere. Although the salvor does not guarantee success, perhaps it might have been possible to imply a term that the salvor was not obliged to devote efforts unlimited in expense or time to salve every single item of property, but such a term (allowing termination for uneconomic salvage) would be difficult to apply in practice,[72] especially given the known risks and speculative nature of the contract. For similar reasons, it would be difficult for a salvor to rely on frustration.[73] LOF 2011 cl G[74] now provides for an express right of termination on the giving of reasonable written notice to the shipowner. The right is not so much to terminate the *contract*, but to terminate the *services*. It is a precondition for termination is that there is "no longer any reasonable prospect of a useful result leading to a salvage reward" under Arts 12 and/or 13; ie there is no valuable property to be salved. Again, it would not be a good reason for the contractor to terminate if it merely wanted to undertake more profitable work elsewhere.

More difficult is the case where it was theoretically possible to salve items of cargo, but it would become increasingly expensive to do so. This is where the whole salvage operation is getting close to becoming a wreck removal operation, but not quite yet. It may be obvious that the ship itself is seen to be wrecked and a total loss, while the cargo (or parts of it) is capable of being saved. In principle, the owner of a particular container of cargo in the bottom stack of a stranded ship might assert that the salvor using "best endeavours" could physically remove the cargo, even if to do so would be very expensive. It might be that a weather window had closed so that it was necessary to mobilise a barge for a separate voyage to remove this one container. The cost of that operation might exceed the value of the container and its cargo, but viewed as a total operation the costs of saving all the other containers from the ship may provide a very healthy salved fund from which a reward could be paid. Under normal principles, the overall costs would be a factor in fixing the reward under Art 13.1(f),[75] but it is not the normal practice to separate out the

---

69 See Art 6(3), preserving provisions such as Art 7 (power to nullify unfair contracts) and eg the environmental obligations in Art 8(1)(b) and 8(2)(b).

70 For the application of more general contractual duties, eg arising through statutory implied terms, see *Kennedy & Rose,* 419–438.

71 See now LOF 2011 cl A and 2.1.3(a), 2.7.5.

72 Cf *Kennedy & Rose*, 429.

73 *Brice*, 385–393; *Kennedy & Rose*, 402–406, 445.

74 See also *Brice*, 388–389.

75 Under LSSAC 2014 cl 15, if a container of low value is salved then its value may be omitted from the salved fund and excused from liability, but that is as different issue.

costs or risks for particular cargoes so as to justify different contributions by different salved interests.[76]

It might be thought that LOF 2011 cl G would provide a simple answer for the salvor here, in that it could terminate the services on the basis that there was no longer any reasonable prospect of a useful result in relation to the remaining container. The wording of the provision refers generally to termination of services "hereunder", which would seem to cover services to ship and cargo. But the notice of termination by the salvor needs only to be given to the shipowner and not, apparently, to the cargo interests with whom there may also be contractual obligations. Interestingly, Art 6(2) gives the master or shipowner the right to make salvage contracts on behalf of property such as cargo on board the vessel. It does not say that there is authority to do anything else, eg to terminate the contract or services under it. It might be necessary to consider whether the master can act as an agent of necessity here, or whether the duty of the property owners to cooperate with the salvor under cl F could also include the acceptance of a termination of services by the contractor.

A simpler solution might simply be that once the cargo interests are bound by the LOF they have agreed to all of its provisions, including cl G which allows for the services to be terminated by mere notice to someone other than the cargo owners. At the very least such an interpretation could be inconvenient for cargo owners, in that they may be deprived of knowledge of the termination and have no right to order the termination of services themselves. The alternative interpretation would be that the cargo owners have the contractual right to insist that operations continue even in respect of an apparently uneconomic service.[77] This would amount, in effect, to a form of compulsory wreck (ie cargo) removal under the LOF, which might seem to be contrary to the sensible commercial interpretation of "useful result", either under Art 12 or the LOF 2011 cl G.[78] It may be, though, that the cargo owners have a "reasonable" desire to see that the salvor minimises damage to the environment.[79] Even though they may not be directly liable for pollution[80] they may have political reasons for wanting operations to continue, eg where the cargo owner is based in the coastal State whose waters might be affected by pollution.

12.2.4 Termination by shipowner under LOF

To what extent can the shipowner terminate the LOF salvor's services? In principle, were it not for LOF 2011 cl G, the dismissal of a salvor that was willing and able to perform the engaged service could be treated as a repudiatory breach of contract entitling the salvor to *damages* for breach, and not merely a reward for salvage.[81] Any wrongful dismissal would be treated as a repudiatory breach of contract entitling the salvor to *damages* for breach, and not a reward for salvage, as in the case of a 'pure' salvor. It is arguable that it might

---

76 *Kennedy & Rose*, 617–618, 652–655. Different issues may arise in general average under the non-separation agreement (the Bigham clause) and the YAR 2016 Rule G: see *Lowndes & Rudolf,* 200–203.
77 Cf 12.2.1.
78 Cf LSSAC cl 2, and 12.2.4.
79 Under the Salvage Convention 1989 Art 8(1)(b), see 12.2.1.
80 See 2.6, but note the possibility of liability under the EU Revised Waste Framework Directive: see 14.2.3.
81 On the basis that there was an implied term that a salvor would not be dismissed if willing and able to perform the engaged service: see *The Unique Mariner No.2* [1979] 1 Lloyd's Rep 37.

not have been a breach for a shipowner to dismiss a contractual salvor if there was no longer any property that could realistically be saved. However, the LOF 2011 cl G gives the shipowner (but not cargo owners) the right to terminate the services, provided there is no reasonable prospect of a useful result and written notice is given to the salvor.

Apart from the possibility that a salvor is simply not up to the task, the main reason why a shipowner would want to terminate the LOF is the fear that the salvor may be dragging out the operations in order to earn special compensation under Art 14.[82] The LOF cl D makes clear that the right to special compensation is unaffected by the existence of the contract. Indeed, the arbitration clause, cl I, specifically extends to special compensation as well as the traditional salvage reward. The consequence of termination of the LOF 2011 cl G by the shipowner should mean that the salvor could not make use of the arbitration provisions in relation to expenses claimed for later services.

It is less obvious that the termination, of itself, could prevent the salvor continuing its services and claiming Art 14 special compensation directly under the Convention. A salvor might simply assert that it was entitled to continue services while there was still some property of value to be saved, even if it was likely to be of low value.[83] Given the uncertainty about the legal basis for such action, and the commercial need for major salvors to maintain longer term relationships with the International Group Clubs, it may be unlikely that a salvor would take such an action. This would be particularly so if the salvor was hoping to tender for a wreck removal contract in respect of the ship (and ruined cargo).[84] It is possible, though, that the salvor might not be dealing with an International Group Club, that it was unlikely to be a successful tenderer for the wreck removal and that there was pressure (eg from the coastal State) for services to continue (or be seen to continue for political reasons).

Here, Art 19 again becomes significant in so far as it applies to a contractual salvage. As already explained[85] the provision could extend to "reasonable" prohibitions in relation to Art 14 services; this would mean that even an LOF salvor that ignored the order would lose any potential right to special compensation. Article 6(1) though, allows for a contract to exclude the application of the convention provisions "expressly or by implication". At first sight, this would appear to include the possibility of excluding the application of Art 19, as that is not one of the provisions 'saved' by Art 6(3).[86] This wide interpretation of Art 6 must be treated with some caution[87] but, in any event it would be necessary to examine the salvage contract to see if there had been an exclusion of Art 19. There is no express

---

82 See 12.2.1.

83 See the discussion in paras 23–26, above, noting that there is some doubt about whether it would be reasonable to continue operations solely for environmental reasons.

84 See 13.4.

85 See 12.2.1.

86 See 12.2.2, fn 69.

87 Because it appears to contradict provisions of a public law nature many of which were found in the Salvage Convention 1910 (before Art 6 and its private law implications were under consideration): see eg the duty of assistance in Art 10 of the Salvage Convention 1989 and the MSA 1995 Sch 11 Part II para 3. Although it could be said that Art 19 is mainly dealing with private rights to payment (and thus within the purview of Art 6(1), it is also arguable that Art 19 embodies a wider public policy principle, namely to prevent unconscionable conduct by the salvor which undermines the fundamental control which the master in particular has over operations involving the ship.

exclusion of the article in the LOF 2011 and it is not immediately obvious that an implication is necessary. Indeed, cl G of the LOF 2011 might point against implication as it gives an express power of termination. Unfortunately, cl G is framed entirely in the context of a "useful result" leading to a traditional salvage award under Arts 12 and 13. It does not say that termination can occur even where the salvor is performing services which might prevent of minimise damage to the environment leading to special compensation under Art 14. It might therefore be argued that, by referring expressly to traditional salvage (not special compensation), cl G by implication (under Art 6(1)) does not allow termination under Art 19 where Art 14 services are being performed.

On balance, this seems a rather casuistic argument, and denies the underlying simplicity of cl G which seeks at least to preserve rights of control of master and owner. It might not be in accord with the overriding objective of cl 2(d) of the LSSAC with the requirement to read the provisions in good faith and a business-like manner.[88] If that is correct, Art 19 is not excluded by implication. To the extent, and subject to the reasonableness argument, Art 19 could still enable an owner or master to prohibit Art 14 type operations generally, either during an LOF salvage, or after it had been terminated.

12.3 SCOPIC and the transition from salvage to wreck removal

12.3.1 SCOPIC caretaking role

One reason that SCOPIC came into existence was because the P&I Clubs were unhappy about the lack of control they had over operations involving Art 14, in particular the basis on which payment was to be made.[89] Salvors (particularly those represented by the ISU) were also less than happy about the result in *The Nagasaki Spirit*,[90] and they considered that the decision required an expensive and difficult accounting exercise to establish a "fair rate".[91]

Despite the misgivings of the shipowners and P&I Clubs about the operation of Art 14, experience under it had served to highlight that in some circumstances there was a role for bridging services between the end of the salvage operation (ie when no property of value could any longer be saved), and wreck removal operations. The reason for such a role was because there is often no clear-cut factual break, or distinction, between the two types of operations. It may only be with hindsight that it is possible to recognise at what stage there was no longer any reasonable prospect of saving valuable property. There may be some prospects of success which diminish gradually, eg while the ship remains aground and subject to deterioration by action of wind and waves. It may be that the possibility of refloating a grounded ship becomes increasingly more difficult, although some cargo (eg containers on deck) could still be safely removed before the ship sinks. For all the actors involved (eg

---

88 Although it could be said that cl 2(a) does refer to the need to "prevent or minimise damage to the environment" (words of course used in Art 1(d) of the convention itself.
89 See 2.7.9(b).
90 [1997] 1 Lloyd's Rep 323.
91 The late Geoffrey Brice QC, who did so much on behalf of salvors to negotiate the CMI's Montreal Compromise in 1981, was always adamant that it was intended that "fair rate" should include a profit element, but this view is not really supported by any of the subsequent negotiations at the IMO, or the wording of Art 14.

property owners, salvors and States) there will be a degree of uncertainty about what can happen, and what should happen, to protect their varying interests. In this state of flux, it may be advantageous to have a degree of continuity of service. That continuity is often achieved by ensuring that the initial LOF/SCOPIC salvor is retained for a period of time to provide holding or 'caretaking' services while it is determined what best to do with the wreck.

The services of the salvor might include monitoring of the ship and cargo; maintaining and stabilising their present condition; minimising environmental threats; and undertaking some activities that would be necessary prior to a wreck removal operation. Indeed, once it becomes clear that the ship itself is likely to become a wreck (eg by sinking, or breaking up) it has become standard practice to seek to remove the ship's bunkers, if possible. The Bunkers Convention 2001[92] gave international recognition to the environmental threat from bunkers, eg from an ordinary cargo ship, and States are increasingly keen to insist that bunkers be removed. The stage at which this will be done may well be a matter of contention with salvors and shipowners. Those advising the State will be aware of political pressure to eliminate environmental threats ahead of any need to save property. From the moment when intervention is under consideration, bunker pollution will be seen as an immediate risk that can be ameliorated.[93]

For the salvor, such bunker removal may represent a premature recognition that the ship itself cannot be saved, while possibly diverting resources and attention from that main object. In practice, a salvor may well expect to mobilise a barge or small tanker to off-load bunkers even while salvage operations are underway (as with the *Rena*). If the ship's engine room is still intact, and not flooded, the salvors may want to keep bunkers on board to power the engines in a refloating, or to provide power for lighting and auxiliary equipment to enable pumps to be operated. The shipowner and Clubs will be aware of possible liabilities from bunker pollution, whether the ship is saved or becomes a wreck, and may well concur in (or even insist upon) bunker removal. In practice, it may well be the salvor that is already engaged in salvage operations that is in the best position to undertake actions such as bunker removal. Indeed, if the bunkers are undamaged, they will have a value that can contribute to a salved fund; and bunker removal might also take place while cargo offloading is underway.[94]

Salvors have often complained that their work may be hampered on board a casualty by the presence of large numbers of representatives of commercial interests (let alone State representatives). These persons (including surveyors, engineers and lawyers), may represent the shipowner and cargo owners, but many (if not most) of them will not really be there to assist in the operation of saving the ship—as opposed to gathering evidence. Moreover, the need to take care of the safety of all these people can be a real distraction for salvors, eg if salvage operations become more difficult in bad weather, or the ship catches fire. Ultimately a decision as to who is allowed on board will be a matter for the master (or possibly a salvor in possession), subject to any intervention orders, but underwriters may be suspicious if they are denied access to a casualty. While the development of SCOPIC

---

92 See 2.6.3.
93 See eg 5.3, 4.2.3.
94 For SCOPIC and State intervention, see 12.3.4(c).

adjusted the relationship between the shipowner and salvor, it also involved a recognition by the ship interests (especially the Clubs) that they need to factor in the concerns of others, including the H&M and cargo underwriters.[95] There are two relevant SCOPIC clauses, cll 12 and 13.

12.3.2 Special casualty representative

Clause 12 of SCOPIC 2018 recognises the concept of the "Special Casualty Representative" (SCR). Once SCOPIC has been invoked by the salvor under cl 2, the shipowner can appoint an SCR to attend the casualty. The decision whether to appoint is an option granted solely to the shipowner, although the appointment, qualifications and role of the SCR have been set out in SCOPIC Appendix B.[96]

The role and responsibilities of the SCR are now set out in "Consolidated Guidance Notes on the Role of the SCR" (2018), but in essence, the main role of the SCR is to act as a conduit for information about the salvage operation to the shipowner and other interested parties (including in particular the H&M underwriters and P&I Club). The SCR is appointed from a Panel which has representatives nominated by the International Group, the ISU, IUMI and ICS. The SCR role is meant to be independent of any particular interest and experience has shown that this has been a vital element for the role to work, even though the SCR is selected by the shipowner. In practice, SCRs have great expertise and command respect.[97] The SCR does not have a controlling function; the Salvage Master remains in overall charge of the operation.[98] The SCR does, though, have a right to be kept informed by the Salvage Master, and to be consulted (and may offer advice). It is the information function that is the key. Appendix B requires the Salvage Master to produce a Daily Salvage Report to the SCR which the SCR will copy to Lloyd's, the Club and any "Known Property Underwriters".[99] The Report should contain information about: the salvage plan; the condition of the casualty and any surrounding area; the progress of the operation; the salvors assets and personnel used in operations on that day.[100] The SCR can issue a dissenting report, and ultimately the SCR's Final Salvage Report. All of these reports are distributed to "Interested Parties", so that all the commercial parties will now have contemporaneous access to information and evidence.[101] The assessment of a salvage reward under Art 13, or of special compensation under Art 14, can late be assessed by reference to clear, documented evidence. If there are real objections to the salvage operations these can be raised at the time. The Salvage Master will have to back his judgment as to

---

95 See *Bishop*, 85; also 2.9.5.
96 Currently available is the 1/1/2014 version.
97 They also can be used for expert evaluation under the wreck removal contracts, eg Wreckhire 2010: see 13.6.3(k).
98 Appendix B para 3.
99 Similar daily reports are now used in the wreck removal contracts: see eg 13.6.3(j).
100 Appendix B para 5.
101 Clause 12 of SCOPIC 2018 also makes clear that the SCR cannot be called by SCOPIC parties to give evidence about non-salvage issues, eg as part of a cargo claim against shipowners, or an insurance total loss claim against underwriters. Presumably, this bar would not apply to a claim by the owner of ship or cargo to be indemnified by an insurer for *salvage* liabilities claimed by a salvor.

whether to disagree with the opinion of the SCR. Moreover, the shipowner (and Club) will have contemporaneous information about whether to terminate the salvage operations.[102]

12.3.3 Special representatives

Clause 13 of SCOPIC 2018 also recognises the concept of the "Special Representatives".[103] These were created specifically so that the H&M and cargo underwriters could have their own representatives aboard. In many cases, the underwriters may be satisfied to rely on the independent SCR, but underwriters wanted to ensure that they had the ability to appoint their own representative. Accordingly SCOPIC allows for a limited number of their representatives. There can be a single "Special Hull Representative". If there is more than one hull underwriter, then it is the lead underwriter who can appoint. In addition to the single "Special Hull Representative" there can also be a single "Special Cargo Representative".[104]

The rights of the Special Representatives are set out more fully in Appendix C of SCOPIC.[105] This allows the Special Representatives to have full access to the vessel and to inspect the ship's documents, but only those documents relevant to the salvage operation (as opposed to those that might be handy to defend an insurance claim). Thus, stowage plans and manifests might be relevant, but the ship's rough logs and marked charts might usually only relate to what happened before the casualty. The Special Representatives have an express right to receive a copy of the Daily Salvage Reports and more generally to receive cooperation from the salvage master, the shipowner and the SCR. The SCR should more generally keep the Special Representatives fully informed and in appropriate circumstances should consult with them.[106]

In order to emphasise the point that the purpose of these representatives is to observe and report, SCOPIC 2018 cl 13 specifies that these representatives must be "technical men and not practising lawyers".[107] Of course, there is nothing to stop a surveyor appointed as a Special Hull Representative from taking photographs and gathering evidence from his or her own observations, but the provision is particularly designed to restrict the taking of statements from crew members. While there may be no express right to appoint someone to make such legal investigations, SCOPIC Appendix C para 4 leaves unaffected any other rights ship or cargo interests may have to send "other experts or surveyors" onto the ship for lawful purposes. Given the general powers in maritime law of the master (and salvor in possession), the existence of such "other rights" may perhaps be restricted to express contractual provisions (eg in a H&M policy), or provisions in local law. SCOPIC Appendix C para 5 puts an express contractual limitation on access by providing that where an SCR or Special Representative is appointed, the salvor can limit access to other surveyors

---

102 See 12.3.4(b).
103 Plural; and not to be confused with the similarly named SCR.
104 For cargo insurance, see 2.9.3.
105 Where SCOPIC is *not* invoked, there is no express LOF provision allowing for representation of property interests in LOF salvage cases, although there have been proposals to create a Respondent Interests Salvage Consultant (RISC): see SCR Digest No 5, 1.
106 See "Consolidated Guidance Notes on the Role of the SCR" (2018), 5.
107 Male surely includes female in this instance!

or representatives if he reasonably feels that their presence will "substantially impede or endanger" the salvage operation.[108]

Part of the industry compromise with H&M and cargo underwriters in cl 13 of SCOPIC was to allow a "Special Cargo Representative" to be appointed for cargo interests. In the case of a container ship, by contrast with a bulk carrier, there are likely to be many underwriters but only one cargo representative can be appointed.[109] The SCR may be obliged to consult with a Special Cargo Representative,[110] eg where that person has specialist knowledge of the cargo and how it should be handled.

12.3.4 SCOPIC termination provisions

SCOPIC 2014 had two provisions concerning termination after the salvor had invoked SCOPIC under cl 2. The first, cl 4, related only to the termination of the SCOPIC agreement itself in circumstances where the shipowner has failed to supply the initial security required under cl 3. Clause 4 was accurately headed "Withdrawal", as the consequence of the salvage contractor giving notice under it was that all of the provisions of SCOPIC would cease to apply, and the salvor would revert to its rights under Art 14 of the Salvage Convention 1989.

SCOPIC 2014's main provisions on termination were set out in cl 9. They gave rights to terminate to the salvor and shipowner, subject to a variety of limits—in particular those caused by government restrictions. There was no specific right to terminate given to cargo interests. A revised version of SCOPIC was issued late in 2018, and this has resulted in the salvor's rights of termination and withdrawal being moved to a revised and extended cl 4.

12.3.4(a) Termination of SCOPIC by salvor
SCOPIC 2014 cl 9(i) gave the salvor a right to terminate SCOPIC services *and* the LOF main agreement:

9. Termination

(i) The Contractor shall be entitled to terminate the services under the SCOPIC clause and the Main Agreement by written notice to owners of the vessel with a copy to the SCR (if any) and any Special Representative appointed if the total cost of his services to date and the services that will be needed to fulfil his obligations hereunder to the property (calculated by means of the tariff rate but before the bonus conferred by sub-clause 5(iii) hereof) will exceed the sum of:
(a) The value of the property capable of being salved; and
(b) All sums to which he will be entitled as SCOPIC remuneration

In effect, the right existed when the services became uneconomic, ie when the salvor's past and future costs would exceed the salved value of the casualty and any SCOPIC

---

108 It is not clear if "substantially" is intended to qualify "endanger" as well as "impede", but it is unlikely that there is much difference in any event. The point is that the power of the salvor is not unfettered, as it might have been in the absence of the provision.

109 SCOPIC does not decide how disputes about the appointment of "Special Cargo Representatives" are to be resolved. Presumably any dispute could be covered by the SCOPIC arbitration provision, cl 16.

110 See para 53.

entitlements. This 'haul off' provision did not give the salvor an unfettered right to terminate as a result of mere doubts about the future financial viability of the operation; the requirement was that the total cost "will" exceed the salved value and SCOPIC remuneration. There was no reference to "in the reasonable opinion [or estimate] of the salvor". The salvor faced the risk that a decision to terminate based on a reasonable assumption at the time, eg about salved values, may have been proved wrong if there was later evidence that the values were in fact much higher than expected. The provision seemed to work on the basis of absolute calculations,[111] and commercial parties in shipping know that termination clauses require certainty[112] so that those using them often need to back their judgement.

In SCOPIC 2018 the salvor's withdrawal and termination rights are now contained in an amended cl 4.

4. Withdrawal and Termination by the Contractor

(i) If the owners of the vessel do not provide the Initial Security within the said 2 working days, the Contractor, at his option, and on giving notice to the owners of the vessel, shall be entitled to withdraw from all the provisions of the SCOPIC clause and revert to his rights under the Main Agreement including Article 14 which shall apply as if the SCOPIC clause had not existed. PROVIDED THAT this right of withdrawal may only be exercised if, at the time of giving the said notice of withdrawal the owners of the vessel have still not provided the Initial Security or any alternative security which the owners of the vessel and the Contractor may agree will be sufficient.

(ii) If the owners of the vessel do not provide the Increased Security within 2 working days of the date upon which the reasonable sum for such Increased Security has been agreed between the Contractor and the owners of the vessel or has otherwise been determined by the Arbitrator, the Contractor, at his option, and on giving notice to the owners of the vessel, shall be entitled to terminate the services under both the SCOPIC clause and the Main Agreement. The Contractor will in that event be entitled to payment of all SCOPIC remuneration due up to and including the date of such termination. The assessment of SCOPIC remuneration shall take into account all monies due under the tariff rates set out in Appendix A hereof including a reasonable time for demobilisation after the date of such termination.

Clause 4(i) of SCOPIC 2018 is identical to cl 4 of SCOPIC 2014, and is conditional on the shipowner providing the SCOPIC security required under cl 3. As part of the strictly choreographed procedures, cl 3 requires the shipowners to provide "Initial Security" (as it is now termed), within two working days of the salvor invoking SCOPIC under cl 2. The idea is to give the salvor a quick contractual assurance that it would not have the security difficulties that might arise against an impecunious owner under Art 14.[113] The security is to cover SCOPIC remuneration up to US$3 million (inclusive of interest and costs), and could be a bank guarantee or P&I Club letter. Under cl 4(i), if the "Initial Security" is not

---

111 It might have been difficult to imply words about "reasonable estimate", or that, as a matter of interpretation, the costs calculations were to be made on the basis of the information available to the salvor at the time. Cf the Overriding Objective in cl 2 of the LSSAC which applies to SCOPIC where the latter is incorporated into the main LOF agreement.

112 The provision required written notice by the salvor, with copies to any SCR or Special Representative. Unlike cl 9(ii) (cl 9(i) in SCOPIC 2018), the salvor did not have to give any period of notice before invoking cl 9(i).

113 See 2.7.9(b).

provided, the salvor can "withdraw" from SCOPIC completely. This is not a termination of the underlying contract, ie the LOF incorporating SCOPIC, but is an option granted to the salvor to revert to its legal position as if SCOPIC had not existed. That position would have included a right to Art 14 special compensation, albeit with the perceived limitations of that provision.[114]

Clause 4(ii) of SCOPIC 2018 is new and must be read in the context of the deletion of SCOPIC 2014 sub-cl 9(i), and the existing ability of the salvor to ask for increased SCOPIC security under sub-cl 3(iii), eg where the services are likely to exceed US$3 million. In the 2018 form, this is newly labelled "Increased Security" and sub-cl 4(ii) gives a similar right to the salvor as under sub-cl 4(i), ie if the Increased Security is not provided the salvor can "terminate" the SCOPIC services. Further, the salvor can *also* withdraw from the underlying LOF contract as well.[115] This was the option given by SCOPIC 2014 sub-cl 9(i), but now there is not the much wider right to terminate SCOPIC and the LOF for economic reasons about the overall costs; now the right of termination and/or withdrawal will only arise if the Increased Security is not provided. If the amount of Increased Security cannot be agreed, the issue will be referred to the arbitrator under sub-cl 3(iv). A shipowner (or Club) that did not want to provide the extra security might decline on the basis that it did not really want the additional SCOPIC services at all, eg because it wanted to put out a tender for wreck removal services. It could actually terminate SCOPIC under sub-cl 9(i)[116] but, by declining to provide security, it would effectively pass the decision on termination (and possibly withdrawal) to the salvor. The consequence of such a full withdrawal is that the salvor would be entitled to SCOPIC remuneration up to the time of SCOPIC termination, plus an amount for a reasonable demobilisation time, but it would presumably also cease to have obligations to salve under the LOF. This might not always be to the liking of other property interests, including cargo,[117] but cl G of the LOF already gives the salvor a right to terminate the LOF if there is no longer a prospect of a "useful result".[118]

Where the ship and cargo have become wrecked so that they have little or no value, the salvor has little further incentive to remain, apart from the prospect of SCOPIC remuneration. That remuneration may be attractive, especially if there is no immediate alternative work available. Unless the salvor needs to reposition its assets for other work (eg an existing long-term towage fixture), it might only want to terminate in the unlikely event that the SCOPIC tariff rates did not cover its actual costs. It is that scenario that was specifically covered by SCOPIC 2014 cl 9(i). Now it seems that the salvor's ability to terminate SCOPIC is more restricted, eg where the owner (and Club) want the SCOPIC services to continue, perhaps as a transition to wreck removal. Thus, it seems that the owners (and, indirectly, the Club) can insist on the salvor maintaining a presence under SCOPIC, provided they are prepared to pay and provide security; if they are not the salvor is given

---

114 See 2.7.9(b).
115 See also 12.3.4(c) for implications of the different terminology.
116 See 12.3.4(b).
117 Note also that SCOPIC 2018 cl 4 does not retain the requirement of SCOPIC 2014 cl 9(i) that "written notice" be given to the shipowner "with a copy to the SCR (if any) and any Special Representative". Presumably it was thought that as the cl 4 options are now triggered only by a simple factual issue, ie the amount of security, there is no need for the other interests to be involved in the sort of expert judgments required about the financial viability of the operation.
118 See 12.2.3.

the right to terminate the underlying LOF agreement as well as SCOPIC. However, the effect of SCOPIC 2018 changes is that the salvor has lost one possible counter to the risk of a shipowner unreasonably terminating SCOPIC under cl 9(i) after the salvor had been induced into an unprofitable LOF contract.[119]

12.3.4(b) Termination of SCOPIC by shipowner

Clause 9(ii) of SCOPIC 2014 has been renumbered as cl 9(i) in SCOPIC 2018, but is otherwise identical.

> 9(i) The owners of the vessel may at any time terminate the obligation to pay SCOPIC remuneration after the SCOPIC clause has been invoked under sub-clause 2 hereof provided that the Contractor shall be entitled to at least 5 clear days' notice of such termination. In the event of such termination the assessment of SCOPIC remuneration shall take into account all monies due under the tariff rates set out in Appendix A hereof including time for demobilisation to the extent that such time did reasonably exceed the 5 days' notice of termination.

Clause 9(i) of SCOPIC 2018 gives a right to the shipowner to terminate payment for SCOPIC services after SCOPIC has been invoked by the salvor. The right can be exercised "at any time" thereafter, but the salvor is financially protected to some extent in two ways. First, five clear days' written notice must be given. This will give the salvor time to start planning demobilisation, although presumably immediate demobilisation could not take place after receipt of the notice without the agreement of the shipowner. Secondly, the salvor would be entitled to its SCOPIC remuneration up until the moment of termination. Indeed, the salvor would be entitled to SCOPIC payments after the five days' period if that was reasonably necessary for demobilisation.

This 'haul off' right could be used by the shipowner in circumstances where it (or the Club) has concerns about the salvor incurring unnecessary expenditure,[120] eg where too many assets are being mobilised—especially where it is becoming apparent that a traditional salvage reward is unlikely and where wreck removal operations are imminent. The latter may well require significantly different assets and skills; in particular there may need to be a holding period before wreck removal operations can begin, perhaps with a new contractor.

Unlike SCOPIC 2018 sub-cl 4(ii),[121] there is no right for the shipowner to terminate also the underlying main LOF agreement, unless there was no prospect of a useful result under LOF cl G.[122] The SCOPIC 2018 sub-cl 9(i) notice by the shipowner does not therefore terminate the LOF contract or, strictly, the SCOPIC clause which is incorporated into it. The contractual provisions still continue to apply, according to their terms; it is merely the obligation to make SCOPIC payments that will cease. It might have been thought that once the shipowner invokes SCOPIC 2018 cl 9(i), the salvor would revert to its underlying rights under Art 14 of the Salvage Convention 1989; ie for any subsequent services to protect the environment it could make an Art 14 claim—as provided for in case of withdrawal under

---

119 Cf *Bishop*, 84.
120 *Bishop*, 83.
121 And as in SCOPIC 2014 cl 9(i): see 12.3.4(a).
122 See 12.2.4.

SCOPIC cl 4(ii).[123] The problem is that sub-cl 4(ii) gives the right of reversion expressly, but that is not done in cl 9(i). SCOPIC 2018 cl 1 is quite specific in saying that apart from the circumstances in cl 4, the salvor "may make no claim pursuant to Art 14". As the effect of a cl 9(i) notice by the shipowner is that the underlying contractual terms remain in force (including cl 1), then it seems that there can be no right of reversion to Art 14 while the contract remains in force. Had such a derogation from the prohibition in cl 1 been intended then it would surely have been made express—as in cl 4. Moreover, the contractual exclusion of Art 14 is permitted by Art 6 of the Salvage Convention 1989. It is for this reason that the salvor may itself decide to terminate the services under LOF and SCOPIC.[124]

Again, the effect of SCOPIC 2018 sub-cl 9(i) is not to terminate the contract, but the services under it. It is arguable that the contractual prohibition on Art 14 claims in SCOPIC cl 1 is intended to apply indefinitely once SCOPIC has been incorporated (and unless there has been a withdrawal under cl 4(ii)). This would mean that, as a matter of interpretation, the cl 1 prohibition was intended to apply even after the salvor gave notice of termination under cl 9(i). On balance, it is submitted that this is not what was intended, as the practical effect of termination provisions is that, apart from the continuing obligations about dispute resolution (eg arbitration), the parties do not generally expect SCOPIC to apply to future events. The idea that Art 14 should continue to be available to a salvor after "termination" of SCOPIC would also be consistent with the general aims of the Salvage Convention 1989 in protecting the environment, subject to the restrictions on such claims within the Convention itself.[125]

12.3.4(c) Termination of SCOPIC and State intervention
Clause 9(ii) in SCOPIC 2018 is a renumbered version of cl 9(iii) of SCOPIC 2014, but is otherwise materially similar with a new cross reference to the salvor's termination provisions (which are now wholly in cl 4).

> 9(ii) The termination provisions contained in Clause [sic] 4(ii) and sub-clause 9(ii) above shall only apply if the Contractor is not restrained from demobilising his equipment by Government, Local or Port Authorities or any other officially recognised body having jurisdiction over the area where the services are being rendered.

The LOF and SCOPIC 2018 reflect a contract between commercial companies, to which State authorities are not parties. Until the threat of pollution became apparent, as evidenced by the *Torrey Canyon*, salvage was regarded very much as a matter of property rights to be sorted out between the commercial interests. As has been emphasised already,[126] the last 50 years has undermined that assumption. States will be anxious to monitor salvage operations to prevent pollution and have increasingly used their powers of intervention. One particular aspect has been the increasing insistence by State authorities that salvage operations do not cease without their permission. It is inimical to them that the commercial parties can withdraw because the salvage operations have become too expensive.

---

123 See 12.3.4(a).
124 See 12.3.4(a).
125 See 2.7.9(b).
126 See 2.6.

The rights of the State in these circumstances are not always easy to define, even if the reality is that an intervention order may be given in practice even if it may exceed those powers.[127] Where termination of salvage (or SCOPIC services) is being claimed by the shipowner or salvor, the State may want to intervene whatever the contractual position. There may sometimes be an incentive for the salvor to encourage the State to prohibit demobilisation.

There are a number of dilemmas here. One is the extent to which a State could in effect intervene at all by ordering a foreign flag vessel to perform dangerous operations, eg to prevent pollution. A power was assumed to exist under Australian legislation in *Mount Isa Mines Ltd v The Ship "Thor Commander"*,[128] but its validity (in international law) was not in issue. It seems highly doubtful whether intervention powers could be used to commandeer a foreign flag ship, eg if it was exercising international rights of navigation.[129] Another dilemma is where the State takes a more restricted approach to intervention, by ordering that that contractual demobilisation of salvors shall not take place. The difference in theory is that this is a negative restriction imposed on commercial parties already operating in an area rather than an external imposition of new positive duties on strangers to the disaster. In practice the distinction may be difficult to draw, as an order not to demobilise may in effect require the salvor and its personnel to stay in a dangerous situation. The jurisdictional issues are dealt with elsewhere,[130] but in the context of the salvage contract such powers have been considered as part of the State's legitimate armoury and have been exercised, eg in the UK,[131] New Zealand[132] and Australia.[133]

It is for this reason that what is now SCOPIC 2018 cl 9(ii) was drafted. The provision places a restriction on the ability of the salvor or shipowner to terminate under SCOPIC 2018 cl 9(i) or cl 4(ii) where State authorities apply a restraint on demobilisation. There must be a restraint; imposed by an officially recognised body; and that body must have jurisdiction over the area where the salvage services are being rendered.

A restraint might take many potential forms. A formal intervention order is the most obvious instance falling within cl 9(ii). Before that stage is reached, officials may put forward strong views that salvage operations should continue without demobilisation. Those views may be backed by practical pressure, eg lack of cooperation in agreeing land access to a site. Although SCOPIC must be interpreted in a commercially realistic way, the linkage of restraint to jurisdiction would seem to indicate that the restraint must involve some legal

---

127 See eg *The Sea Angel* [2007] 2 Lloyd's Rep 517, and the examples of State detention of salvage vessels given at [60]. In *The Sea Angel*, an LOF/SCOPIC salvor's vessels were detained, even in circumstances where the operations were moving to a wreck removal stage (performed by another contractor). This demonstrates how the transition from wreck to salvage may not always be clear cut, or at least appreciated as such by State authorities. Individuals employed by shipowners and salvors fear arrest in some States if there is a dispute about operations.

128 [2019] 1 Lloyd's Rep 167 (FC Aust). The ship that obeyed the order to take the casualty in tow was still entitled to salvage as it was treated as a volunteer.

129 The position would be different if the ship had voluntarily commenced salvage operations, although it should not automatically be treated as a salvor merely by responding to an emergency call for assistance and then standing by: see further, 4.2.3(a) and (c), 5.3.

130 See Chapter 5.

131 See the *MSC Napoli*, 1.2.3.

132 See the *Rena*, 12.1.2(e) fn 29.

133 See *Mount Isa Mines Ltd v The Ship "Thor Commander"* [2019] 1 Lloyd's Rep 167, above.

rather than merely practical (or persuasive) basis. Such an interpretation would cause difficulty for the salvor where, for instance, government official instruct naval vessels to block any move away by the salvage vessel in circumstances where the salvor cannot be sure if such an action is legally justified by the public law of the State in question. Moreover, it will probably be very difficult for the salvor to argue that the effect of any delay will be to frustrate the contract: the risk of a State order is one of the risks assumed by the salvor under cl 9(ii).[134]

The body exercising the restraint must be an officially recognised public body such as a national or local government, rather than say a private landowner, or an influential local politician. Port authorities may well be privately owned, but the key is whether they are exercising public functions. As a matter of interpretation, it is assumed that the "jurisdiction" requirement applies not simply to the catch-all "any other officially recognised body" but also to all of the bodies previously listed, ie governments, and local or port authorities. This will be significant, as on this basis all bodies purporting to restrain demobilisation must have "jurisdiction" over the relevant area; otherwise, it would be easier to argue, eg, that any government practical restraint (even if not backed by law) would qualify. It is also assumed that this "jurisdiction" must refer to a power to give a restraining order within the area, rather than simply to a geographic jurisdiction to exercise powers generally.

The consequences of SCOPIC 2018 cl 9(ii) applying are that the respective rights of shipowner and salvor as to SCOPIC "termination" do not apply. For the shipowner, it must keep paying for SCOPIC services (eg through its Club). In the case of the salvor it was also clear under SCOPIC 2014[135] that it could neither terminate the LOF nor the SCOPIC services. The 2018 redrafting of sub-cll 4 and 9 may cause some confusion in terminology. Under SCOPIC 2014, sub-cll 4 was headed (and was expressed in terms of) "Withdrawal", while sub-cll 9 dealt with "Termination". SCOPIC 2018 cl 4 is now headed "Withdrawal and Termination by the Contractor", with the right under sub-cl 4(ii) being expressed as one to "terminate". SCOPIC 2018 sub-cl 9(ii) expressly applies its contractual restriction to "termination" only under sub-cl 4(ii), and not to "withdrawal" as it appears in sub-cl 4(i). From a government's perspective it is not quite clear why the distinction is made, as its concerns about demobilisation may be the same for both—even if the salvor has not mobilised much equipment in the initial stages of the operation to which sub-cl 4(i) naturally applies. In any event, the use of demobilisation restraints by public authorities presents a real practical difficulty for the commercial parties. At least the salvor will still be entitled to some payment, but the shipowner will not want SCOPIC to continue indefinitely.

In effect, the practical effect of a restraint order is that the commercial parties (especially the shipowner and its insurer) cannot walk away from the casualty. In their Large Casualty Working Group 2012/2016 assessment of the costs of large casualties,[136] the Clubs identified the costs caused by State intervention as a significant contributor. It is in this context, in particular, that the Clubs have sought to foster cooperation with States, eg through the Memorandum of Agreement.[137] The answer to the leverage applied by

---

134 See *The Sea Angel* [2007] 2 Lloyd's Rep 517, but frustration may not be impossible to argue: see 12.1.2(e).
135 Sub-cl 9(iii).
136 See 1.4.
137 See 10.8.6.

States is for the shipowner and insurer to present clear plans for pollution prevention and, ultimately, wreck removal.

12.3.5 SCOPIC and preventing pollution from a wreck

As noted in 12.3.1, the ability to continue with SCOPIC services as a form of holding or 'caretaking' exercise can be an advantageous way of bridging to a wreck removal operation especially in relation to pollution prevention.[138] SCOPIC 2018 cl 14 specifically allows for pollution prevention to be remunerated. The classic example would cover the removal of bunkers, but this could also include the recovery of containers, certainly for those cargoes which are hazardous and noxious. It is unclear whether the words "in the immediate vicinity of the vessel" qualify pollution prevention, as well as "removal of pollution". On balance it seems better to restrict the words to the latter. The general aim of SCOPIC (as with the Salvage Convention 1989 itself) is not to provide a regime of pollution compensation; that should be dealt with by the pollution liability conventions such as the CLC 1992 and HNSC 2010 which create direct liabilities for extensive clean-up operations.[139]

The final words of cl 14 are also designed to restrict the extent to which SCOPIC can be seen as a general mechanism to pay for pollution clean-up, as it requires the SCOPIC pollution measures to be "necessary for the proper *execution of the salvage* but not otherwise". The meaning of "*execution of the salvage*" is rather unclear. Removal of bunkers may assist a vessel to be refloated, and skimming of leaking oil (bunkers or cargo) may minimise the risk of a fire. In that way a traditional salvage operation might be assisted. But does the right to payment for pollution measures under cl 14 only apply up to the moment that it becomes clear that a traditional salvage reward will not be possible, eg when ship and cargo are obviously wrecked? Clause 10 reiterates the duties of a salvor to minimise damage to the environment while salving the vessel. "Execution of the salvage" must refer to operations to save the ship and cargo as valuable property and not, as such, to work preparatory to wreck removal. On this basis, a salvor would be well advised to be sure that the shipowner and Club agree that it ought to be paid for pollution prevention work after the ship and cargo have been declared a total loss. Ie the use of SCOPIC here may well be a convenient option for the shipowner but not necessarily an automatic right for the salvor.

Apart from pollution prevention, there may be other services that can usefully be performed under SCOPIC as a bridge to wreck removal operations. The obvious example is of maintaining a sufficient presence to stabilise the ship and cargo before removal operations start. Later wreck removal operations can be made significantly more expensive if the ship deteriorates. This 'caretaking' service may include the maintenance of pumps and other equipment to stop a stranded CTL vessel sinking any further or suffering additional hull damage by shifting. Welding work may be necessary to prevent additional water being taken on board or to prevent further structural damage from cracks. A start may be made in removing those parts of the cargo that are immediately accessible. In the case of containers, those on deck above water may still have a possible value for salvage purposes, but other

---

138 In addition to the similar exercise where there are delays caused by H&M underwriters, see 2.9.5(b).
139 Indeed, where the costs are shared between ship and cargo interests more broadly: see 2.6.2(a)–(b), 2.6.4.

containers which are likely to have suffered water damage could be removed. Arguably, this might all be a form of pollution prevention within SCOPIC.

In order to avoid any disputes between shipowner and salvor as to whether any bridging services are technically within SCOPIC, it is not uncommon to produce a side letter agreeing on a reduced commitment, eg that some pumps and compressors be retained on board the casualty. However Clubs have warned members about using side letters to increasing their liabilities beyond the standard LOF and SCOPIC, without prior Club approval. An example might be a side letter under which a salvor who first endeavours to salvage the ship on "no cure no pay" terms is given a right to "rewind" and reinstate SCOPIC from a time before it was formally invoked.[140]

The LOF salvor may well be content to receive SCOPIC remuneration for these bridging activities, especially as it may be tendering for the wreck removal contract. Even if it does not succeed in its tender, the SCOPIC rates (plus cl 5(iv) bonus) may be sufficiently attractive for it not to try to terminate under SCOPIC 2018 cl 4(ii). By contrast, those paying for SCOPIC (shipowner and insurer) may well want to minimise the time on SCOPIC as many of the wreck removal preparations might be covered under the wreck removal contract in a lump sum package by the new contractor.

Instead of extending SCOPIC 2018, the alternative may simply be to agree a daily rate Wreckhire 2010[141] contract for a particular vessel with the original LOF salvor, anticipating that this will be a temporary 'caretaker' expedient until a full tender process[142] for the removal has taken place. Meanwhile the salvor can then reposition its other salvage assets, eg by demobilising most of the salvage craft and specialist crews. Separate hire contracts can be agreed for specific ancillary tasks.

In any event, a stage will gradually be reached when it is clear to all that a traditional salvage service can no longer continue, at least in respect of the ship. It is likely that meetings will be held with the salvage master and the various representatives of stakeholders. The aim will be to ensure consultation with all rather than interference by all. The shipowner, eg through its Club, will have to make a commercial decision as to whether to authorise a wreck removal operation, who is to perform it and what type of contract to use. These issues will be considered in Chapter 13.

---

140 See eg Gard Member Circular No 12/2017.
141 See 13.6.3.
142 See 13.4.

CHAPTER 13

Wreck removal operations and contracts

13.1 Introduction

13.1.1 Urgency for wreck removal operations

Apart from the gradual transition from salvage to wreck removal, described in Chapter 12, a ship may be wrecked without any prior attempts at (or possibility of) salvage, eg where a vessel founders and sinks quickly. Here it will be fairly obvious that there will be a total loss claim for hull and most of the cargo, and the focus will shift to any responsibilities to raise and remove the wreck on behalf of the shipowner and its insurer (eg the Club).

The speed with which wreck removal preparations (and operations) will be undertaken may depend on the immediacy of any hazards to navigation and threat of pollution. It may well be that a staged operation is necessary, with governments insisting on speedy action to deal with the navigational and pollution issues, while there may be more time needed to assess the necessity for (and feasibility of) any removal of all that remains of the ship (eg with the *Rena*). But 'speedy' is a relative concept, as this may be dependent on the weather, preparation of engineering plans, and negotiation of contracts. In the North Sea it may only be possible to work from April to September, and with the wreck of the car carrier *Baltic Ace*, sunk after a collision off Rotterdam on 5 December 2012, a tender for her removal was only put out at the end of 2013, a contract was awarded in March 2014, and work started in April 2014. By June 2014 the bunkers had been removed and it was not until the end of September in the 2015 season that the wreck was cut up and removed.[1]

13.1.2 Public relations

The wide public and media interest in wrecks, particularly in the immediate aftermath of casualties, has been recognised as being very important—both for governments[2] and the commercial parties.[3]

At the administrative level, civil servants may well have undergone contingency planning, eg under the OPRC 1990,[4] but it is difficult to appreciate the full impact of a wreck. The planning will also involve complex questions as to how to handle coordination between the myriad of local and national agencies that might wish to be involved.[5] In developing

---

[1] See "Baltic Ace Wreck Removal", Boskalis website, https://magazine.boskalis.com/issue03/baltic-ace-wreck-removal [*Baltic Ace Wreck Removal*]; also 10.2.5, 2.5.9(c), 14.3.
[2] See 4.2.4, 4.2.5.
[3] See eg I Brynildsen, "Tricolor—The collision, sinking and wreck removal" 178 Gard News Insight (2005).
[4] See 5.7 and 4.2.1.
[5] See 4.2.4, 4.2.5.

States, the lack of resources and experience also means that public and politicians may be heavily influenced by media reporting.

Most politicians will have had no experience of how to handle a major shipping casualty, and may be acutely concerned about the effect of media reports on their constituents, especially in the fishing and tourist industries. These reports may emphasise issues that are telegenic (eg oil on birds) and demand immediate action. Governments will be under a lot of political pressure to be seen to be doing something,[6] although the nautical and environmental advice may be that it is necessary to wait to see how the casualty develops. It is difficult to explain to the media that once the ship is stranded there may be no easy outcomes and that removal and remediation is a long term process. In the UK, the SOSREP[7] is free from political interference, but may feel the need to be pro-active in dealing with local media and devolved administrations.

From a contractor's perspective, a major wreck will result in a massive number of enquiries from the media and these could distract those staff who already have their hands full with tricky salvage or wreck removal operations.[8] Most major contractors now have plans for handling the media, eg through regular press conferences, often arranged with States. Professional media advisers are often used.

The message that is given out in any briefings is vital. Experience shows that openness about plans and risks is important, and that downplaying the effects of the casualty is likely to be counterproductive. Over-optimistic estimates of when a wreck can be removed are likely to generate unrealistic expectations and increase pressure for immediate action that might be counter-productive. For the wreck removal contractors, it is necessary to separate out questions as to the cause of the incident (and who may be liable) from a more sober message as to the steps that are now necessary to deal with the wreck, in particular minimising environmental threats and what to do with human remains.

13.1.3 *Recovery of bodies*

Salvors will always give priority to saving lives from a ship and, in an appropriate case, life salvage may be rewarded from the salved fund if property is saved in a traditional salvage operation.[9] The commercial salvage position where there are deaths is perhaps a little more obscure. The Salvage Convention 1989 Art 13 criteria for fixing a salvage reward refer specifically to the saving of "life".[10] This would seem to exclude any "success" in saving (ie recovering) bodies. But the Art 13(1) criteria are inclusive, and it may well be a practical necessity to remove bodies in order to save property. In that case, it seems likely that if

---

6 See eg the issue about agreeing to let ships come ashore to a place of refuge, as happened with the *MSC Napoli* (1.2.3(d)), but not with the *Prestige* and other casualties: see *De La Rue & Anderson*, 905–921.

7 See 4.2.2.

8 This can also apply to government officials, eg where key technical pollution control officers are diverted from primary tasks to brief the media: see the criticism after the wreck of the *Sea Empress* (MAIB "Report into grounding and subsequent salvage of the Sea Empress at Milford Haven" (1997), para 16.8).

9 The salvor will be entitled to a "fair share" of the Art 13 reward, and possibly of the special compensation under Art 14: see Art 16. Note also the difficulties where the life saver is not the engaged salvor and see the MSA 1995 Sch 11 Part 2, para 5 and *Gaskell, MSA 1995*, 21/416–21/419, 21/434.

10 See Art 13(1)(e).

there are specific costs involved in dealing with bodies then these can be taken into account by any judge or arbitrator in fixing the Art 13 reward. Where there is no salved fund, it may be possible for the salvor to claim the costs as Art 14(3) special compensation expenses, eg where this is practically necessary before any efforts can take place to minimise pollution, but the position is not entirely clear.[11] The LOF 2011 Box 2 specifically excludes from the salvage agreement the personal effects or baggage of the passengers, master or crew.[12]

The need to consider what to do with any bodies on board the ship is also an additional factor in any wreck removal operation.[13] Sadly, many shipwrecks involve loss of life and the wreck site may be regarded as an unofficial grave. Sometimes there is public pressure for the 'grave' to be 'protected' in some way. There is particular sensitivity with military or wartime graves and the UK has enacted legislation to protect them,[14] but there is no particular legislation protecting as graves the sites of modern commercial wrecks. Where the lives lost are those of foreign seafarers, with no connection to the coastal State, there may be less public interest in what happens to the bodies, so that there is no public pressure to find or remove the wreck (unless it is a hazard). In other cases, there may be pressure to find and raise the wreck to recover the bodies for burial. This can arise where the ship (eg a fishing vessel) is sunk close to its home port[15] but particularly where there is a sinking of a ferry or passenger ship. The number of victims and relatives affected by such modern-day *Titanic* disasters increases the focus on what is to happen with the bodies. At one time, relatives might have been prepared to accept that the seabed was a grave but, as public awareness of wreck raising capabilities increases (especially after the *Costa Concordia*), the pressure increases on authorities to order wreck removal.

The ferry *Sewol* (6,825 gt) sank in 2014 in Korea, with the loss of over 304 lives (mostly children). The casualty was partly caused by poor safety standards for which the State eventually accepted responsibility.[16] There were strong demands from families for the wreck to be raised, although it was in 40 m of water. In 2017, it was finally raised in one piece (which also assisted accident investigation), after great difficulty and expense.[17]

Where a ship is aground, the recovery of bodies may be an unpleasant but relatively straightforward task if there is still access to all parts of the ship. Where the ship is sunk, two separate situations may arise. First, if the ship is to be raised and removed, there may be pressure from families for a priority to be given to searching for and removing bodies before commercial raising and removal operations take place. The removal of bodies in a wreck removal operation is a sensitive and difficult task for divers and contractors. Before wreck raising operations commence, it seems to be accepted practice for great efforts to be made to locate bodies on board and for them to be treated with respect. Instructions to

---

11 *Gaskell, MSA 1995*, 21/416–21/419, 21/434.

12 And see the LSSAC cl 3.2. However, it seems that such personal items are still "property" subject to salvage under Art 1: *Gaskell, MSA 1995*, 21/375.

13 For burial of human remains at sea, see 14.1.4(b).

14 See 4.7.2.

15 See eg the wreck of the fishing vessel *Dianne*, sunk off the Queensland coast in 2017: 13.1.3 (below).

16 See BBC News, "Court rules South Korea must pay for Sewol victims", 19 July 2018; www.bbc.co.uk/news/world-asia-44881841. The ship's captain was imprisoned for life: https://en.wikipedia.org/wiki/Sinking_of_MV_Sewol.

17 See *Kim, Sewol Accident*; also 13.2.2, 10.8.1.

this effect may arise from the wreck removal contract itself, but may more often form part of intervention instructions given by authorities,[18] or ancillary instructions given as part of wreck removal orders. The precise legal basis for such State orders may not always be clear, but it seems likely that disagreements might arise only when the safety of contractors' personnel is at risk, or when the search for bodies will unduly prolong the wreck raising operations (and thus increase costs).

Secondly, a ship may be sunk in circumstances where there is no intention to raise it. This may arise for a variety of reasons; eg because there is no navigational or environmental "hazard"[19] that would trigger a legal obligation to raise and remove the ship; or because the sinking takes place in international waters; or because it is practically impossible to raise the wreck. As noted above, there may be pressure from relatives for bodies to be found, recovered and buried on land, eg so that they can obtain 'closure'. Sometimes, this pressure to recover bodies may also be accentuated by a desire to discover the causes of a shipwreck, eg to assist an inquiry or inquest.[20] Instances include the sinking of the trawler *Gaul* (1,106 gt) in 1974, when extensive and expensive efforts were made to locate the wreck,[21] and the *Sewol* tragedy in Korea in 2014. More recently, the 2014 loss of the Malaysia Airlines Flight MH370 somewhere in the Indian Ocean has prompted hugely expensive location operations, partly financed by Malaysia, Australia and China, and so far unsuccessful.[22]

A number of legal issues arise, both of public and private law. The first is whether any State powers exist, eg under intervention or wreck removal legislation, to order a shipowner or contractor to remove bodies. It is arguable that such general powers may not be exercised where the removal of bodies is unrelated to threats to navigation or the environment. This is most likely to be the case where the ship is wrecked and there is no intention to raise it. Where wreck raising operations are contemplated, common sense and humanity may well require that bodies have to be removed so that contractors can work safely and effectively on the vessel.

States can, of course, decide to pay for wreck removal themselves when a prime motivation is to recover the bodies—irrespective of whether it is necessary to raise the ship for safety or environmental reasons. The difficulty would be when they try to claim those costs from owners.[23] Here owners may have difficulties in contesting the validity of any order, if there is some evidential basis that there was also a safety or environmental "hazard". In February 2018, Maritime Safety Queensland ordered that the sunken trawler *Dianne* (18 m length) be raised from its position 30 m on the seabed five miles from a small local town.

---

18 See eg 5.3, 4.2.3.
19 See 8.2.
20 See 4.3.
21 The DfT had declined to spend £50,000 in 1977, and the wreck was eventually found in 1997 after a TV led expedition, resulting in very expensive MAIB surveys in 1998. Although there were suspicions that the *Gaul* was a victim of the Cold War, a reopened formal investigation found that the sinking occurred during a storm: see the "Report of the Re-Opened Formal Investigation into the Loss of the FV Gaul" (2004); also 4.3, 10.5.1(d). Some human remains were found in 2002 and an inquest was delayed until the formal inquiry was concluded.
22 By 30 June 2017 the estimated costs for the underwater search programme were Au$198 million: see the Australian Transport Safety Bureau, "The Operational Search for MH370 (3 October 2017), 7–8. For removal of the wrecks of aircraft, see 10.2.7(a).
23 See 10.5.1(d).

There was public pressure from families to recover the four unfound bodies of the crew of eight.[24] The removal order was ultimately given by a harbour master under local powers relating to obstruction of navigation on the basis that the wreck presented a risk to trawlers with nets down.[25] The insurers apparently decided not to contest the order, and the vessel was eventually raised and towed to the port of Bundaberg for scrapping, although in an operation that was significantly more expensive than expected. The shipowner or insurer faced with a demand may take into account bad publicity, particularly if it wants to retain business in a particular State or area. This publicity factor can apply eg to insurers of fishing fleets or passenger vessels, but is less likely to be the case with a fixed premium insurer of a single ship bulk carrier.[26]

The WRC 2007 makes no reference to bodies in Art 6 which lists the criteria to be taken into account in determining a hazard. This is not surprising given the definition of hazard in Art 1(5).[27] It is faintly possible that "related interests" in Art 1(6) might be relevant if the presence of bodies on board a sunken ship might affect tourist attractions, eg where creational divers might be dissuaded from swimming near a wreck which was known still to contain bodies. It seems hardly likely that this would qualify in most cases as a "major" harmful consequence within Art 1(5).[28] Even if there were also some slight risk of navigational or environmental hazard, the State would need to overcome the reasonable and proportionate criteria as to costs if it insisted on a full removal mainly to recover bodies.[29] This would be the dilemma facing a State with a wreck such as that of the *Sewol*. The reasonable navigational or environmental response might be to remove bunkers and cargo in situ. If that were so, then any extra costs in ordering a full lifting of the vessel (and in one piece) might fall on the State. In the *Sewol*, that may have been a risk that the State was prepared to bear for political reasons (as there were allegations of failings by State authorities). For the owner and insurer, the pressure to raise may sometimes be irresistible, given that any dispute is likely to be litigated in local courts.

The removal of bodies may also trigger other legislative provisions and the regulatory authorities that administer them.[30] Once a body is within a coroner's area, the coroner may have a duty to investigate a death once it has been reported and will also have a right to possession of the body.[31] The police may be involved, eg if there is a threat of criminal prosecution. They may also be tasked to act on behalf of a coroner to receive bodies, eg for an autopsy, post-mortem or inquest. Any contractor will need to be aware of possible requirements imposed by the police. In States such as Australia, diving operations to recover bodies may well be carried out independently by police divers (as with the *Dianne*), but where a ship is sunk well offshore, eg in the EEZ, police divers might not expect to be involved. The common law will also grant rights of possession of a body to a deceased's personal

---

24 Brisbane Courier Mail 21 February 2018, 10.
25 See the Transport Operations (Marine Safety) Act 2004 (Qld) s 91: see also 10.5.1(c).
26 For public relations see 13.1.2.
27 See 8.2, 9.2.2.
28 See 8.2.2, 8.2.3.
29 See 9.2.5(e), 10.2.4.
30 See generally, H Conway, *The Law and the Dead* (Routledge, 2016) [*Conway*], eg as to registration of deaths (12–13).
31 See the Coroners and Justice Act 2009 and the Coroners (Investigations) Regulations 2013 (SI 2013/1629); *Conway*, 14–15.

representatives.³² While there is no property right in a corpse,³³ there are occasions when legal liabilities might arise through the mishandling of a body where emotional harm is suffered by relatives.³⁴ It seems highly unlikely, though, that a wreck removal contractor would be liable, eg because there was no duty of care to relatives not at the scene of the casualty, or the exigencies of an operation meant that there was no negligence. It is faintly possible that particularly callous treatment of bodies, once recovered, might give rise to liability for psychiatric harm.³⁵

In a wreck removal operation, the question will arise as to whether the contractor is required to perform the work of removing bodies and whether it is entitled to be paid for the operation and ancillary expenses, eg transporting the bodies to shore by suitable means (such as a separate transfer with coffins or refrigerated containers). Where the State authorities have given orders to remove bodies the contractor may dispute the legal basis of such an order,³⁶ especially where an intervention order is addressed personally to the contractor and it might involve some risk to the life of its employees. Wreck removal orders will usually be directed to the shipowner and, if so, the contractor's position will largely be a matter of contract. It may therefore be important that the issue of bodies is dealt with in the specification of the services in the wreck removal contract.³⁷

In at least one casualty, salvage contractors had to remove decomposing carcasses and bury dead cattle after the wreck of a converted livestock carrier.³⁸

13.2 Range of technical wreck removal options

The shipowner and its Club are likely to consult with technical advisers as to what type of operation will be involved. A wide range of possibilities will be canvassed, each dependent on the many variables involved (including the type of ship and cargo, the location, the weather). It is not possible in a legal text to consider all the technical marine engineering issues, but they form part of the context in which commercial and legal decisions are made.³⁹

Is refloating possible? If so, how much preparatory work is needed in relation to the vessel itself, eg to seal leaks, remove oily water in holds, install pumps? It is probably

---

32 See *Conway*, 61–71.
33 See *Conway*, 2–3.
34 See *Conway*, 79–86.
35 Cf R Nwabueze, *Biotechnology and the Challenge of Property* (Ashgate, 2007), 199–202.
36 Cf 4.2.3.
37 Eg in Box 7 of Wreckhire 2010, or in the methods of work in Annex II: see 13.6.3(a).
38 The *Haidar* which capsized and sank in 2015 in Vilo do Conde in Brazil with 5,000 cattle on board: see eg https://portermarinesalvage.com/mv-haidar/. It is not clear if this was a salvage or wreck removal operation. Dead cattle would have no value for a traditional salvage reward, but SCOPIC might be invoked under cl 2 to cover the costs of their removal as a form of pollution prevention within cl 14 (especially as SCOPIC cl 2 excludes the onerous definition of "damage to the environment" in Art 1 of the Salvage Convention). In a wreck removal operation, the cattle would normally be considered part of the cargo that had to be removed, eg to reduce pollution, although it would probably be sensible to specify what is required under Box 7 of the BIMCO contracts, such as Wreckfixed 2010.
39 Sub-contractors who are engaged on particular engineering tasks, eg construction on site of cradles or sponsons, may well be engaged on the basis of general engineering contracts adapted for offshore work: see eg A Constable et al, *Keating on Offshore Construction and Marine Engineering Contracts* (Sweet & Maxwell, 2nd ed, 2018).

unlikely that the ship's engines or generators will be available to provide power, so can this be provided by portable generators or by power lines from support ships? If refloating is not possible because of the extent of damage to the hull, is a partial refloat possible, eg by cutting the ship so that some parts can be sealed and refloated, while others are prepared for loading onto a barge for removal? Significant sections of superstructure (eg accommodation blocks) may be separated and lifted onto barges, using heavy lift equipment.

Where the ship has totally sunk, different and more complex considerations will arise. Investigations will still be made as to whether refloating is a possibility. Underwater repairs may enable the ship to be made watertight so that it can be raised slowly through pumping operations. Flotation devices may also be used to assist this process, and especially where there are too many holes to be sealed. Once the ship (or parts of it) is raised off the seabed it is possible that it is in a fit state to be towed (as occurred with *Costa Concordia,* fitted with sponsons). More likely is that the ship (or parts of it) will be repositioned, eg onto a semi-submersible barge or heavy lift ship. The option of lifting the ship in one piece was chosen for *Costa Concordia*, but other wrecks may need to be cut into sections for removal. This can take longer than expected, eg as a result of weather that had not been forecast. The longer period spent at the scene of the casualty can result in a greater local impact, so this factor has to be balanced against the advantages and risks of trying to tow or move the ship in one piece. All of these activities will involve complex engineering and nautical calculations, which will have to take into account not only the integrity of the ship, pollution minimisation, but also the safety of those involved in the operation. It is all too easy for States and commentators to demand that wrecks be removed, but there are very real risks to the lives of those who have to do the work.

In all cases, there may need to be separate consideration of what to do with the cargo. What will be the effect of the cargo on the removal operation for the ship itself (eg for dangerous cargo), and will there be any pollution risks? Should the cargo be raised with the ship, eg in the case of a bulk cargo? How far can the cargo be removed from the hull, eg bulk liquids in tanks, or containers from a ship which is aground? How will cargo such as containers be removed?

The operations of wreck raising and wreck removal are quite distinct. Once the ship has been raised or refloated it must be disposed of to a place willing to receive it. There will be immediate practical issues, such as how many and what type of tugs will be need to perform the towage to a place of disposal. For many years the option of disposal of a worthless wreck at sea would have been an easy solution.[40] This was the type of option used with the *Castillo de Belver* in 1983[41] and considered for the *MSC Napoli*.[42] Such options may no longer be possible in the light of more recent concerns about what to do with the wreck of the ship (and cargo) and how to dispose of it.[43] There may still be some circumstances, though, where a 'cleaned' hull can be dumped at sea without major environmental harm.[44]

---

40 See 14.1.
41 See eg ITOPF, "Castillo de Bellver, South Africa, 1983" www.itopf.org/in-action/case-studies/case-study/castillo-de-bellver-south-africa-1983/.
42 See 1.2.3(b).
43 See 14.1, 14.5, 14.6.
44 See 14.1.4.

13.3 Responsibility for arranging wreck removal contracts

13.3.1 Shipowner and insurer

Once it is clear that the ship is a total loss, it will be necessary to determine who is going to be responsible for arranging and paying for wreck removal. While most legislation will create liability of the shipowner,[45] the willingness or ability of that owner to respond may vary greatly, especially when it has yet to receive a total loss payment from the H&M underwriters. Where there is a single ship company, the fear that the owner may wash its hands of the casualty is a very real one for States. Such owners may express less interest in dealing with the wreck than the insurers. The advantage, particularly with International Group P&I Clubs, is that they have an advanced network of correspondents (including lawyers) with government contacts. The collective knowledge of the Clubs and their technical experts cannot be underestimated, and in a major casualty that experience can be vital. There may also be a willingness to work with public authorities to produce innovative solutions, as with the *Costa Concordia*.[46]

It is for that reason that the Affected State will be very keen to find out the identity of the ship's liability insurer and the details of any insurance cover.[47] For most large trading ships, it would be common for the H&M insurance to be separate from liability insurance, typically covered by a P&I Club. H&M insurance cover by definition will not normally cover liabilities,[48] so once there is no prospect of saving the vessel, the H&M underwriters are likely to drop out of the picture as regards further operations concerning the wreck (as long as it has no residual value).[49]

Where there has been a salvage operation which moves towards wreck removal it is likely that there will have been time to identify all relevant parties (eg under the LOF/SCOPIC system), but this may not always be so. The ship may have been wrecked without possibility of salvage and so there will have been little time for the commercial interests to come forward. Where there is an International Group Club involved, it is likely that this will be made known to the State, eg if they have agreed an MOU.[50] The Club is likely to take an active interest, at least to minimise liability exposure, eg from pollution.[51] It is sometimes a false supposition that the *only* interest of the insurer is to minimise expenditure in any way. The reputable insurers in the International Group will usually prefer to be involved at an early stage in a major casualty, rather than walking away from it.

The position may be more difficult for a State where the liability insurer is not an International Group member. The shipowner may be entered in a non-International Group Club, but problems may be more likely to occur with fixed premium insurers. These may offer apparently cheaper cover than a Club, and such cover is very common amongst small trading vessels (including fishing vessels) which, despite their size, can cause significant problems for States. For example, after the wreck in Christmas Island of the Panamanian

---

45 See 10.2, 11.1.
46 See 1.2.5(b).
47 See the WRC 2007 Art 9(3); and 9.1.4, 11.3.3(c) and (e).
48 See 2.9.2(b).
49 See 2.9.5.
50 See 10.8.6.
51 See 2.9.6(b).

registered MV *Tycoon* (2,638 gt) in 2012, the Singaporean single ship company owning the vessel (and its Taiwanese managers) apparently failed to take responsibility for its removal. The Australian Maritime Safety Authority (AMSA) paid contractors about Au$5 million to remove it, but the liability insurer (not a P&I Club) allegedly refused attempts by AMSA to settle the claim. That is one reason why compulsory insurance and direct action is important.[52]

13.3.2 State action to engage contractors

Where there is no shipowner or insurer to respond to a casualty, the State may well have to engage individual contractors. Most States will not have the commercial knowledge of, say, an International Group Club, and could be at a disadvantage in understanding the various contract forms on offer. All States will have in-house government legal advisers;[53] but even developed States are unlikely to have specialist maritime commercial legal expertise. For developing States, the knowledge gap is potentially greater. In such cases, the State is well advised to engage maritime industry consultants, to provide technical and commercial advice, and (possibly) a law firm with experience of maritime casualties. Both consultants and lawyers will need to have an international perspective and some experience of dealing with insurers, such as P&I Clubs. It is here, also, that prior communications with Clubs, eg through an International Group MOU[54] may facilitate the communications, especially when access to information is at a premium and public trust[55] will be needed.

13.3.3 Choice of contractor

The choice of wreck removal contractor will be influenced by technical experience and capabilities, but also by price. In relatively straightforward wreck removals the conduct of the whole operation will usually be contracted to a single contractor. As removal operations have required more complex engineering solutions, a consortium of contractors may be involved, perhaps involving a main contractor and a series of sub-contractors. As already noted, one contractor may have undertaken initial salvage operations and then moved to a SCOPIC "caretaker" role, eg under SCOPIC.[56] That contractor may have been initially engaged because it had tugs and other assets immediately available to perform salvage, but when tendering for the wreck removal operation it may face more serious commercial competition—especially as there may be more time for competitors to mobilise equipment.

In some circumstances, the wreck removal operation itself may be split between two or more contractors under different contracts, eg where different parts of the hull present different risks. Typically, the first contractor may be the original salvor engaged under SCOPIC to deal with more straightforward or immediate removal operations for part of a

---

52 See 10.8.
53 These may be scattered between those based in shipping or environment departments, or in Foreign affairs, or a Justice Ministry or Attorney-General's department.
54 See 10.8.6.
55 See also 13.1.2.
56 See 12.3.1, 12.3.5.

ship, while more difficult and time-consuming removal operations for the rest of the ship will be put out to tender. In the *Fedra* casualty, one contractor (which had been on location dealing with another casualty, the *New Flame*) undertook bunker removal, refloating of the bow section and removal of the accommodation block. It appears that this was a SCOPIC operation, as the salvors were not allowed to leave until a wreck removal contractor was on site; a different contractor was engaged on a fixed lump sum basis to remove the wreck of the aft section.[57] By contrast, the car carrier *Baltic Ace* sank in 15 minutes off Rotterdam in 2012 and the removal of the bunkers was part of the wreck removal contract.[58]

13.4 Wreck removal tendering

13.4.1 Tender process

The major salvage and wreck removal contractors will be aware that there is a possibility of a wreck removal operation and may well have instigated contacts with the shipowner and insurer (eg Club). They will be anticipating a tender process and will probably already be identifying assets that may be needed in such an operation, eg tugs, barges, and heavy lift equipment. Some of those assets will be their own; some will belong to competitors, or may be engaged on more general maritime commercial work (such as offshore servicing or installation activities).

The tender process will usually be conducted by the registered owner and its Club, but may be arranged by the Affected State itself. When the car carrier *Baltic Ace* was wrecked, it was the Dutch Ministry of Infrastructure and the Environment (RWS) that put out the tender invitation. The operations manager of Boskalis, whose tender was accepted, stated "This required three plans from the contractor: the execution plan, a risk assessment and an environmental plan. For RWS it is currently quite common to contract on the basis of more than just price, but also taking quality into account".[59]

Where the insurer (eg Club) has become involved at an early stage, it is more likely that an invitation to tender for wreck removal is sent out in the name of the shipowner. The invitees will be contractors well known in the industry and, in any event, will have been identified in the initial technical consultations that will have taken place once it is realised that a wreck removal is needed. As wreck removal has become more complicated, and as competition for work increases, so the time and cost of preparing tenders also increases. In January 1998, the ISU and International Group produced a voluntary Code of Practice on "Formal Tendering Procedures for Wreck Removal/Cargo Recovery that was recommended for use by their respective members. It is a single page document with nine paragraphs. It accepted that Clubs and owners were not bound to seek tenders in all circumstances, and the Club and owners may simply award the contract directly to a contractor of their choice. If there was an invitation to tender it should be accompanied by a draft contract. It set out procedures to ensure that there was a level playing field, eg that all invitees be notified of time extensions, changes to (or clarifications of) specifications. Once the tender time had expired, no further tenders should be accepted. In order to avoid

---

57 See 10.2.5 and the *LOC Report*, 42. See also the *Smart*: 10.2.5.
58 See *Baltic Ace Wreck Removal*; also 10.2.5.
59 Ibid.

playing one set of contractors against another, there should be confidentiality as to a tenderer's prices, methods of work and terms. The successful tenderer may not necessarily be the one with the lowest price, but once a tenderer had been selected the Club and owners were entitled to have further negotiations with that contractor. If no contractor was selected and there was a new tender process, then unsuccessful tenderers would be given the opportunity to retender. In order to avoid anti-competitive conduct (eg price fixing) there should be no discussions about the wreck removal or tender between contractors without the agreement of the Club and owners. Such agreement should not be unreasonably withheld. This might be relevant where contractors may be negotiating for a consortium approach, or for the sub-contracting of equipment.

The issuer of the invitation may decide on the form of contract to be used,[60] as with the technical specifications for the task. The contractor may try to negotiate on a more favourable contractual basis for itself, but this will be more difficult with such a tender process unless its tender has already been accepted. Sometimes tender invitations may be open, so as to allow the contractor to offer a contract with a particular risk profile (eg a staged contract such as Wreckstage 2010) allied to a more competitive price that with a fixed price/no cure no pay contract (such as Wreckfixed 2010). Before considering the standard contracts regularly used,[61] it is necessary to consider moves initiated by the Clubs to improve their (ie owners') contractual position.

13.4.2 Quantitative risk assessment

The International Group's Large Casualty Working Group Review of major casualties[62] had identified that choosing the right contract was an effective mechanism for controlling costs, but that the Clubs needed to ensure that there were "adequate and effective risk transfer mechanisms in contractual terms of engagement".[63] Consideration should be given to the use of "bonus/penalty provisions to improve risk sharing in respect of unforeseen overrun or delays" and a "seamless transition between contracts at the different stages of the operations".[64] Part of the reason for the Clubs' anxieties is undoubtedly the need to reassure reinsurers after the cost blowouts on wrecks like *Rena* and *Costa Concordia*.

To reflect some of these concerns the International Group has been working since at least 2017 to promote the revision of the 1998 Code of Practice to specifically address Quantitative Risk Assessment (QRA).[65] QRA is a process used to facilitate the identification, quantification, mitigation and allocation of risks in project management and has been heavily used in the offshore industry. It signals a move away from individual tendering and towards a team-based approach where an initial stage involves an identification of all risks that might affect the cost of the operation. This envisages potential contractors collaborating with technical experts appointed by the Club to devise risk mitigation measures. The

---

60 Eg daily hire, fixed price/no cure no pay, or staged.
61 Eg Wreckhire, Wreckfixed and Wreckstage: see 13.6.
62 See 1.4.
63 *Large Casualty Working Group Review: Executive Summary*, 2.
64 Ibid. This also drew attention to the difficulties of terminating SCOPIC: see 12.3.4.
65 See S Kendall-Marsden, "Quantitative risk assessment in wreck removal tendering" (June 2017) Maritime Risk International, 18–19.

obvious difficulty for members of the ISU is that they may be obliged to share expertise and knowledge with competitors with no guarantee of later obtaining a contract.

An example given of QRA in practice[66] would be where a wreck is partially embedded, but where additional dredging might later be needed. The technical risk might be mitigated by more detailed initial surveys of the seabed and evaluations of the likely weather conditions for the envisaged period of operations; the costs for such preliminary work might more naturally fall as an expense for the Club. The contractual risk of any additional dredging work could be allocated to the contractor but for an enhanced price, ie a 'risk premium'.[67] From the perspective of some of the major contractors, in particular, this might be the sort of risk they are prepared to accept, given their own appreciation of whether the risk will materialise. By contrast they might be less prepared to accept political risks, which are not subject to technical analysis.[68] In any event, this is a further move towards entrenching the use of fixed price lump sum contracts, albeit with greater advance information, in which there is less scope for claiming additional costs.[69] It may be that a full QRA approach is only needed in major wreck removals, but it signifies a move towards greater preparation and perhaps more delay in starting operations; this may not always be welcome to governments. Whether the QRA approach will be embraced by all contractors, eg ISU members, may depend upon their own size, resources and views about being a 'risk partner', but there is a clear trend by which the Clubs want greater certainty in their (ie owners') wreck removal contracts.

It is anticipated that a first step before any contract revisions is to agree either a revision of the 1998 Code of Practice, or to have a separate QRA Code of Practice for those cases where risk transfer is appropriate. An extensive draft has been produced following consultation with the ISU and technical consultants who are already experienced with QRA and it is hoped that it might be agreed by the end of 2019. The QRA Code of Practice would cover issues such as a description of risk transfer and QRA; introduction to QRA and how to use t in a tendering process, including timing; discussion of types of QRA cases and risk transfer appropriate for utilisation; identification of risks which can be addressed by QRA (weather, technical, political, administrative); limitation on QRA and risk transfer; the role of the technical advisor; identity of QRA providers; and control and ownership of data.

Once the Code of Practice is agreed, attention will turn to producing contractual terms. One option for the Clubs would be for them to draft a new wreck risk contract for use where QRA was used in the tendering process, but it seems to be more acceptable to work within a BIMCO drafting Committee in which all stakeholders can be involved.

BIMCO will probably develop a QRA clause to be inserted into its wreck removal contracts. This may be developed in 2019–2020, but could prove to be controversial for the contractors. The idea, though, is to provide a common starting point when wreck removal contracts are being negotiated.

---

66 Ibid. See also the *Smart* wreck removal, 13.2.2(b).

67 In other circumstances the risk transfer might involve the threat of a contractual penalty provision, eg where the task overruns, or is delayed by unforeseen circumstances.

68 Cf the *Tasman Spirit* wreck in Pakistan in 2013 when contractors' vessels and personnel were detained: also 2.2.2.

69 Eg as is available under Wreckhire 2010 cll 4 and 7: see 13.6.3(d) and (e). Cf Wreckfixed 2010 or Wreckstage 2010: see 13.6.4, 13.6.5.

13.5 Wreck removal and ancillary contracts

Towage contracts, such as BIMCO's Towcon 2008 and Towhire 2008, might be used in some circumstances involving a wreck; eg a where a ship has quickly become a CTL after a grounding or fire, but is still afloat, or can still be refloated fairly easily. The shipowner or Club may arrange for the hull to be towed to a place of disposal, and a contractor may be prepared to do so on the basis of the towage contracts that provide, in effect, for the charter of tugs on a lump sum or daily hire basis.[70]

The BIMCO towage contracts were first introduced in 1985 because of market resistance to the use in offshore operations of the UK Standard Conditions for Towage and other Services 1974. These originally dated back to 1934 and were designed for use in ports, but contained very wide exceptions and indemnities in favour of tug owners.[71] Although the current 1986 version of the form is less draconian, it would be rare to see it used in offshore work. Both Towcon 2008 and Towhire 2008 contain extensive 'knock for knock' provisions designed so that tug owner and shipowner bear the risk of loss or damage to their own vessels.[72]

Alternatively, it may be that in the course of a more complex wreck removal operation the main wreck removal contractor might need the services of a local tug, eg to tow a bunker barge alongside the casualty. The main contractor might then engage the local tug using such a towage sub-contract.[73] The barge might be hired on the basis of Bargehire 2008.[74] Where the main contractor in effect needs a shuttle service to bring out equipment such as pumps or generators to the wreck scene, it might engage a supply boat on terms of the Supplytime 2017 contract.[75] For the disposal voyage a whole range of specialist ancillary contracts are available, eg for heavy lift services.[76] All of these are ancillary contracts that may be used eg by the main contractor, although there is nothing to prevent the shipowner itself from engaging such craft.

13.6 Wreck removal contracts

13.6.1 Introduction to BIMCO wreck removal contracts

Once it has been decided that a wreck removal contractor will need to be hired, consideration will be given as to which form of contract may be used, given freedom of contract.[77] Wreck removal operations have been undertaken on a contractual basis for a long time, but until relatively recently there was no industry-wide standard form contract. It seems that salvage companies would offer wreck removal services on the basis of ad hoc contracts, eg based on a salvage or towage contract.

---

70 See 12.1.2(b).
71 See *Rainey*, Chapter 3 for an authoritative analysis of this as well as other offshore contracts.
72 See *Rainey*, Chapter 4.
73 See 12.1.2(c) and (f).
74 See *Rainey*, Chapter 6.
75 See *Rainey*, Chapter 5.
76 See 14.7.3.
77 It is unlikely that a consumer would make a wreck removal contract, but note 2.7.2 fn 1081 and s 2 of the Consumer Protection Act 2015.

In 1993 the ISU worked with BIMCO to produce two wreck removal agreements, "Wreckcon" and "Wreckhire".[78] These were similar in some ways to the BIMCO standard towage contracts, Towcon and Towhire 1985, in that they provided for a service on a lump sum or daily rate basis. The International Group was unhappy with various aspects of these contractor influenced forms and urged the adoption of a 'no cure no pay' variant. In 1999 BIMCO updated and renamed its two existing wreck contracts so that Wreckstage 99 was the lump sum contract (payable in stages) and Wreckhire 99 was the daily rate contract. It also added a third, Wreckfixed 99, to be a 'no cure no pay' version. By 2009 the International Group was still concerned about the Clubs' cost exposure, particularly with Wreckhire 99 which had apparently become the dominant form used in practice. That concern about cost control has been a consistent feature of the Clubs' involvement both with salvage (through SCOPIC) and wreck removal.[79] Negotiations took place to revise Wreckhire 99 that led to Wreckhire 2010. There were equivalent revisions to the other two contracts, resulting in Wreckstage 2010 and Wreckfixed 2010.[80] The previous versions of these contracts are now largely of historic interest, and the following sections will consider the 2010 contracts. They follow the familiar box format of BIMCO charters, such as Gencon, and offshore contracts such as the towage contracts, Towcon 2008, and Towhire 2008.

Before examining the three contracts and the choice that has to be made between them it is necessary to examine risk sharing in wreck removal contracts in a little more detail.

13.6.2 Allocation of wreck removal risks and costs

In most commercial contracts there is a relationship between the terms on offer and the price for the service. In maritime contracts the relationship is particularly strong, and experience with charterparties has shown that most clauses in a standard form have a distinct heritage, often leading back to a legal decision on a particular wording. The effect of such a decision will have been to place a risk onto a shipowner or charterer. Drafters had had more than 150 years of such recorded experience on which to base their own attempts to allocate what Lord Diplock identified as misfortune risks and fault risks.[81] Misfortune risks will include bad, often unexpected, weather.[82] Fault risks will include negligent operation of craft and equipment, or inadequate technical advice. But the identification of risks may not fall so easily into such a binary characterisation, unless the concept of 'misfortune' is extended to cover everything that is not fault. Some risks may arise because of inadequate knowledge of the true state of affairs relating to the casualty or its position. The condition of the stricken ship's hull may not be fully known before a refloating exercise is agreed or attempted. Where the ship is aground, the exact properties of the rocks or seabed under it may not be immediately apparent. In remote areas, there may not be any reliable data easily

---

78 The titles did not include the date "1993", although it is now convenient to refer to them with this date. See generally *Rainey*, 489–491.
79 See 13.4.2.
80 See *Rainey*, Chapter 10.
81 See *Federal Commerce and Navigation Co Ltd v Tradax Export SA (The Maratha Envoy)* [1978] AC 1, 8; [1977] 2 Lloyd's Rep. 301, 304.
82 See 13.2 and eg the *Rena*, 1.2.4(b).

available relating to normal tidal conditions, or the levels of swell to be expected. And the type or extent of State intervention is often quite unpredictable.

The engineering and other experts will be mainly focusing on what is technically feasible, but all (especially the insurers) will be aware of the costs involved as a result of the different options. Experienced contractors and insurers will have a rough idea as to the cost implications for each of the options. It is obvious that significantly different considerations arise between the raising of a small fishing vessel and a large cruise ship such as *Costa Concordia*.

One risk transfer option that may be attractive to shipowners and their insurers is to separate the wreck raising stage from the disposal of the wreck. Where it is clear that the wreck will have to be recycled, the owners and their insurers will be very keen to sell the raised wreck 'as is'. The buyer might be an ultimate recycling yard, or an intermediate buyer; in some circumstances the wreck removal contractor may itself be persuaded to become a purchaser. The buyer would then take on commercial and navigation risks for the disposal voyage.[83]

It is the level of uncertainty, though, that distinguishes wreck removal contracts from ordinary charterparties for the hire or use of a ship. Although a charterparty is also a type of service, the extent and level of performance provided by the shipowner is relatively clear and circumscribed, eg by the nature of an ordinary trading voyage—although *force majeure* clauses do exist for events that are out of the ordinary. In a wreck removal contract, by contrast, there is an *inherent* degree of uncertainty in the extent (and sometimes level) of service that may be required. In a general sense, the task may become much more difficult that any of the experts could have predicted. That difficulty may result in extra direct expenditure, eg in hiring in additional heavy lift craft, but is most likely to manifest itself in delays. The delays will simply mean that all the contractor's assets will need to be mobilised for a longer period, which naturally means an added cost.

It is the allocation of the risks of unexpected difficulties that lies at the heart of the negotiations about which of the current wreck removal contracts is chosen, and as to any proposed amendments to the standard forms. Here the respective expertise and experience of the contractor and Club will be vital. This balance of knowledge is inherent in many contractual negotiations, where the contractor ultimately has to back its judgment about the risks, their likelihood and its ability to deal with them. In voyage charters, for instance, both parties have to weigh up the amount of time a loading or unloading operation will take in a port when fixing laytime, while making use of contractual provisions to allocate risks of unexpected delays. The distinction with wreck removal, perhaps, is that in many cases the variables as to what is normal, and can be expected, are much greater. In a voyage charter, the parties' own experience (with broker support) can supply most details about the loading or unloading conditions in particular ports, but the variety of conditions that might be faced in a wreck removal operation is almost infinite. Added to which, the ability to obtain precise knowledge of the condition of the wreck is very likely to be limited—by location, weather, and the risks to human life (eg in conducting surveys). This uncertainty all means that the level and extent of the service required is inherently variable.

---

83 See 14.7, in particular 14.7.1.

The questions as to how to cope with uncertainty, and how to allocate risks, lie at the heart of the choice to be made as to which standard form wreck removal contract to use, eg Wreckhire 2010, Wreckfixed 2010 or Wreckstage 2010. Despite the best efforts of the drafters, the forms exhibit a struggle to provide certainty while at the same time also giving the flexibility to deal with changed circumstances. This means that they could be viewed as a recipe for disagreement or, in a collaborative market (where the parties are likely to have future dealings), as a framework which sets out some basic allocation of risk but leaves many questions to be resolved on the basis of commercial common sense as the operations unfold.

As noted,[84] one key feature in controlling wreck removal/SCOPIC costs, identified by the International Group's Large Casualty Working Group Review 2012/2016,[85] was to consider this balance of risks as between contractor and shipowner (and its Club), in particular by the choice of contractual arrangements to be made. Pending any QRA amendments, the Review recommended that Clubs use the 2010 forms (although recognising that earlier versions might still be used).

The current attitude of the Clubs can be seen from a commentary by the North of England P&I Club on the result of the tender process to remove the fore part of the bulk carrier *Smart*.[86] "Titan Salvage won the tendering process to perform the lightening, refloating and scuttling of the partially buried bow section. The contract was unusual because of the extent to which Titan assumed the operational risks associated with the project, so minimising the chances of a cost overrun".[87] The precise extent to which the risks were assumed is confidential, although perhaps a fixed price contract was involved,[88] but the quotation captures the essential commercial issue for contractors and Clubs. The contract for the removal of the wreck of the ferry *Sewol*, in South Korea, went out to tender and was reported to have been agreed for a fixed price of US$73 million, although the actual cost may have increased up to US$130 million.[89] Contractors in such a case could obviously face a loss unless there is renegotiation, or where the contract allows for extra payment as a result of changes to the agreed methods of work.[90] The Korean government was reported to have agreed to pay extra owing to unexpected delays and costs, eg in drilling the seabed under the vessel to install lifting beams, and in preserving the site to assist investigations.[91]

13.6.3 Wreckhire 2010: overview and risk allocation

Having considered the underlying issue of risk allocation, it is now necessary to see in outline how the three BIMCO contracts deal with it. It is convenient to start with Wreckhire 2010, as the daily hire contracts like Wreckhire 93 and 99 had apparently been the most

---

84 See 13.4.2.
85 See 1.4.
86 See 10.2.5. The aft part had been removed by the original salvage contractor, Smit.
87 See www.nepia.com/news/press-releases-area/north-pi-club-delivers-mv-smart-wreck-removal-on-budget-through-a-collaborative-approach/.
88 Eg Wreckfixed, Wreckstage or an amended Wreckhire.
89 See eg https://en.wikipedia.org/wiki/Sinking_of_MV_Sewol, www.maritime-executive.com/article/salvors-to-right-the-sewol-to-search-for-remains.
90 See cl 4 of the three BIMCO contracts: 13.6.3(d), 13.6.4(c), 13.6.5(d).
91 See http://english.donga.com/Home/3/all/26/897308/1.

popular form up until 2010.[92] This may no longer be the case owing to the preference by the Clubs for fixed price contracts,[93] but it is convenient to start with Wreckhire 2010 to illustrate why the Clubs have been concerned about cost control.

The analysis of all three contracts will take a systematic, rather than a clause by clause, approach. Readers can find an authoritative clause by clause analysis in *Rainey*.[94]

13.6.3(a) Basic performance obligations

Wreckhire 2010[95] is subtitled "International Wreck Removal and Marine Services Agreement (Daily Hire)". It has the usual BIMCO Part I box format for commercial details, with 26 pre-printed clauses as Part II.[96] Wreckhire 2010 has some resemblance to the Towhire 2008 towage contract in that they both provide for daily hire and specify extra costs that can be claimed,[97] but the nature of the services they deal with are quite different. The services that the contractor is obliged to perform to the vessel[98] under Wreckhire 2010 are defined in cl 2 by reference to the "Schedule of Personnel, Craft and Equipment" listed in Annex I[99] and a "Method of Work and Estimated Time Schedule" set out in Annex II. The parties are named in Boxes 1 and 2.[100]

The contractor does not guarantee a particular outcome as a result of its services. Clause 2 of Wreckhire 2010 merely requires it to exercise "due care" in rendering the agreed services. This is the language of the Salvage Convention 1989 Art 8(1)(a),[101] rather than the arguably more onerous "best endeavours" required under the LOF 2011 cl 1. There is also an obligation[102] to exercise due care to "prevent or minimise damage to the environment" which also echoes the language of Art 8(1)(b) of the Salvage Convention 1989,[103] but this is qualified in so far as it would not be inconsistent with the nature of the services to be rendered under the contract. That "nature" is set out in Box 7(1), where there may only be a few words (eg "wreck removal"), but it seems that the reference in cl 2 is to the nature of the services looked at more broadly. It is fairly obvious that if the method of work described in Annex II involved removal of bunkers or cargo from the wreck of a sunken

---

92 See *Rainey*, 490.

93 See 13.4.2. Note that all the forms may be heavily amended in practice so that their underlying risk distribution is altered, eg by the amendment and deletion of cll 4 and 7: see 13.6.5 for some more general comparisons between the three forms.

94 See *Rainey*, Chapter 10. Brief clause by clause Explanatory Notes are also available on the BIMCO website: www.bimco.org.

95 For a facsimile of the form, see Appendix 7.

96 In the event of a conflict of terms and conditions in the two Parts, an unnumbered clause in Part I states that the Part I provisions (plus any additional ad hoc clauses) shall prevail over those in Part II.

97 See 13.6.3(b).

98 Clause 1 defines the vessel widely to anything contained in it (or on it) including cargo and bunkers. Although most of the emphasis in the contract is on the hull, the obligations in respect of cargo cannot be ignored, eg when it comes to disposal: see also 13.6.3(i).

99 Under cl 25, the contractor has the right to rotate and replace craft equipment and personnel with equivalents, but must obtain the consent of the "Company Representative": see also 13.6.3(j). Approval cannot be unreasonably withheld.

100 The significance of identifying the parties is dealt with in 13.6.3(b).

101 See 12.2.1.

102 Echoed in cl 24: see 13.6.3(h).

103 See 12.2.2.

ship there is likely to be some pollution, however small. The due care obligation is thus measured by what a reasonable contractor would have done given the state of the vessel, the worksite and the weather. The environmental obligation is repeated in more detail in cl 24, which also requires the contractor to maintain and implement a pollution response plan that meets the requirements both of the "Company Representative"[104] and any "competent authorities" (eg of an Affected State under the WRC 2007).[105]

The contract imposes a variety of obligations to provide information to, or cooperate with, the other party,[106] but there are also other positive performance obligations imposed on the parties. Under cl 5(a) the hirer has to pay for any marking or "cautioning" of the vessel.[107] "Cautioning" is not defined in cl 5(a), but presumably refers to other types of warning than physical marks, eg electronic MAtoN.[108] Clause 5(b) is borrowed almost entirely from the LOF 2011 cl F(i) and entitles the contractor to use the vessel's machinery, equipment and stores free of charge, provided that it is not unnecessarily damaged. Although the wreck will almost certainly be without power to operate its own derricks, winches or pumps, the contractor might be able to rig up an auxiliary power supply and the vessel's anchors and chains could be used to hold her in place if stranded.

The method of work planned in Annex II may already envisage damaging the vessel, eg by cutting it up. In addition, cl 5(c) entitles the contractor to "remove, dispose of or jettison" parts of the vessel or its equipment during the course of the operation. This may involve, eg, the removal of the vessel's accommodation block or other lightening actions.[109] This entitlement is qualified by requiring the approval of the hirer (which cannot be unreasonably withheld), but also permission from the competent authorities. It is increasingly difficult to obtain such permission as States may not allow parts of the wreck to be dumped or abandoned,[110] and may also require all debris and waste to be removed while imposing recycling conditions.[111] The entitlement also has to be considered by the contractor as "reasonably necessary" to perform its services.

Clause 5(c) also allows the contractor to remove, dispose of or jettison cargo, subject to the same requirements of hirer approval and State permission. This can raise slightly different questions as the contractor does not have a direct contractual relationship with cargo interests. As between the contractor and hirer, the contractor does not commit any breach, eg, by jettisoning the cargo in order to succeed with the wreck raising. Where the hirer is also the shipowner, it will probably have sufficient possession of the cargo to be able to authorise the contractor to act, but its responsibility to the cargo owner will be regulated by the contract of carriage.[112] There may be circumstances where the destruction or jettisoning

---

104 See 13.6.3(j).
105 See also 13.6.3(h).
106 See 13.6.3(j).
107 The marking obligation may well be one that falls directly on a State to arrange, eg under the WRC 2007 Art 8: see 9.2.4, 10.5.7. A State could presumably fulfil its obligation to take reasonable steps by allowing the shipowner to undertake the marking, although it is more likely to use its own personnel (eg Trinity House).
108 See 11.1.3(a), 11.3.5.
109 See eg the *Fedra*, 10.2.5.
110 See eg the *Rena*, 1.2.4(e).
111 See eg 10.2.5 and Chapter 14 generally.
112 See 2.1.5 for the extent of those obligation and any defences that might be available.

of some cargo might be a general average act in relation to any other property saved,[113] while any sound cargo that is removed by the contractor under cl 5(c) might theoretically give rise to a salvage claim.[114] Wreckhire 2010 does not contain any express provisions about its relationship with salvage law as it affects cargo and confirms the impression that the form very much emphasises the removal of the hull, without always fully articulating what is to happen with cargo.[115] It might be helpful to have a express provision in all the BIMCO wreck removal contracts (or as a rider) about the extent to which the contractor has any residual rights to salve the cargo.[116]

13.6.3(b) Hire payments and costs

Wreckhire 2010 is a daily hire contract that, under cl 10(a), bases payment to the contractor on a daily rate as set out in Box 11.[117] The hire is irrevocably earned on a day by day basis and is non-returnable, although any overpayments have to be returned within 14 days of the end of the service.[118] The hirer is not allowed to make deductions or set-offs from hire, any monetary claims would have to be brought separately.[119] Under cl 10(g) the contractor has to promptly invoice the hirer for all amounts due under the contracts; late payments may attract interest and may also give a right to terminate the contract.[120]

From the perspective of the contractor, it has the financial assurance of knowing that it will be paid for each day that its craft, equipment and personnel are engaged to work on the wrecked vessel, but it will also want to be sure who is going to be paying the hire. Clause 1 of all three BIMCO contracts, including Wreckhire 2010, describes the two parties as the "contractor" and the "company". The latter is the body named in Box 3,[121] and will usually be the registered owner that has liability insurance cover, eg through a Club, for liabilities arising under the WRC 2007 or national law.[122] It is highly unlikely that the insurer would ever be a principal in the contract, but it clearly will have an enormous influence on its drafting and will probably underwrite any payments to be made under it. There is no reason why the "company" has to be the registered owner. Bareboat charterers will usually have

---

113 See 2.8.

114 See 2.7 and 12.1.2. If there were salvage operations controlled by public authorities, this would not be a bar to the contractor claiming salvage: see the Salvage Convention 1989 Art 5(2). If the Wreckhire 2010 contract specified that the contractor was to be paid at a daily rate to remove cargo, then this could raise the question of whether Art 17 or the complementary Admiralty law operated as a bar. It could be argued that the contract was not entered into before the danger arose, or that the existing contractual duty was not one owed to the cargo interests but to the hirer, but an English court seems more likely to find that a contractual obligation in the wreck removal contract to remove cargo would be a bar to any salvage claims: see *Kennedy & Rose* 224–227, *Gaskell, MSA 1995*, 21/420–21/421.

115 See also 13.6.3(i).

116 Cf Towhire 2008 cl 19, which deals with salvage issues arising under a towage contract.

117 Separate "daily working rates" are set out for craft and equipment (Box 11(i)) and for personnel (Box 11(ii)).

118 See also 13.6.3(c) and (i).

119 See also 13.6.3(g).

120 See 13.6.3(f).

121 In the analysis of these contracts it is usually clearer to use the term 'hirer', but the expression "company" should be taken to refer to the hiring company (not the contractor company).

122 See 2.9.6(d).

liabilities to the owner for wreck removal costs[123] although they may be co-assureds with the same insurer. It may be decided that the bareboat charterer should be the principal, but there may be other entities that the shipowning interests and their insurers want to be the "company".[124] These could even include a buyer of the wreck for the purpose of scrapping or recycling.[125] A more obvious example of a principal other than the registered shipowner would be where an Affected State (including any of its authorities), or a private port owner, was obliged to arrange for the wreck removal because the shipowner was not responding and there was no insurance (eg if the WRC 2007 did not apply).

The contractor would be concerned, though, at its financial exposure if the hirer is a single ship company whose main asset is worthless. In the WRC 2007 this problem is dealt with (for States) by the requirement of compulsory insurance and direct action.[126] In Wreckhire 2010, the contractor is given security though cl 15 which provides that the "Company shall provide on signing this Agreement an irrevocable and unconditional security in a form and amount as agreed by the parties". The mandatory nature of this provision is somewhat undermined by the next sentence which refers to what happens in the event that "initially no security is *requested*". Presumably, the contractor could waive any right to rely on the failure to provide security in so far as created a condition precedent to performance. In any event, a request for security also triggers a right under cl 10(f) for the contractor to terminate the contract where the security is not provided within five banking days following the request.[127] This right to terminate can be exercised "at any time thereafter".[128] Even if there is no initial request, the contractor is allowed by cl 15 to require that it be provided later. Indeed, the clause may require "further security" to be given even if initial security has been provided "when reasonably required" by the contractor.[129] This additional security could presumably arise if there have been changes in the services required or delays caused by adverse weather.[130] The form of security is unspecified but, taking the example of SCOPIC 2018 cl 3(i), it is likely to be either a bank guarantee (which can be expensive to obtain) or a P&I Club letter of undertaking.[131] The amount of the security is also unspecified, by comparison with the

---

123 See 2.1.7(a).

124 Note that cl 16(b) provides that third parties cannot claim benefits under the contract, as allowed under the Contracts (Rights of Third Parties) Act 1999 s 1(1).

125 See 14.7.1.

126 See 10.8.

127 Curiously for such an important issue, the clause does not require that the request be in writing, unlike other notices: cf cl 22(a) and 13.6.3(j).

128 It is possible that the contractor might be estopped from relying on this unlimited right, eg if its words or conduct led the "company" to believe that the contractor would irrevocably give up the right; it is hard to imagine why it would do so.

129 The "reasonably required" criterion does not seem to apply to the initial request for security under the first sentence of cl 15, but the contractor could terminate if there is no agreement. The second sentence runs together the situation where there is no initial request (but a later, first, request is made) and one where there is a request for further (ie additional) security. The second sentence states that the form and amount has to be "agreed by the parties", but the third sentence qualifies this by the "reasonably required" criterion. It might be thought that this qualification was only intended to apply to the request for additional (not first) security, but that is not what it says, so the contractor may have more flexibility at the start of the contract in setting the form or amount of security.

130 See 13.6.3(d) and (e).

131 This is separate from the obligation of the hirer' to maintain insurance from P&I risks under cl 23(b).

initial $3 million in SCOPIC. It would presumably be calculated by taking the daily hire rates and multiplying it by the Estimated Time Schedule in Annex II. Unlike SCOPIC cl 3(iv), cl 15 contains no express reference to arbitration of any dispute about the form or amount of the security, although it could probably fall within the words "any dispute" in cl 21.[132] It is possibly arguable that by leaving the form and amount of the security to be agreed there is a contractual certainty issue (ie an 'agreement to agree'), as this would go beyond asking an arbitrator to interpret what the parties had agreed and might require the arbitrator actually to draft a term.[133]

In addition to the hire payment, cl 10 contains a list of nine specific types of "Extra Costs" that will fall on the hirer (some of which are derived from Towhire 2008 cl 7). Many of these extra costs are external to the parties, eg: port expenses; costs of customs clearance; agency fees; taxes and customs duties (outside of the contractor's State); licensing costs (eg to obtain approvals or permits to work); costs arising from the requirements of governments or unions.[134] Also included in cl 10 are costs that might otherwise be expected to fall on a contractor. These include: the costs of hiring "assisting tugs when reasonably deemed necessary by the contractor or prescribed by port or other authorities";[135] reasonable costs of transporting equipment listed in the Annex I Schedule (eg pumps or chains); and reasonable costs or travel and accommodation for personnel listed in Annex I (eg engineers and surveyors).[136] Moreover, the hirer is also to pay for consumables used in the services including all costs of fuels (eg bunkers), lubricants, materials and stores. In addition, the hirer has to pay for loss or damage to portable salvage equipment, materials and stores.[137] All these costs could be quite considerable, time consuming to estimate in advance and potentially alarming to an insurer that wanted to keep a tight control on overall expenditure. These costs are also supposed to be paid directly by the hirer, but if they are paid by the contractor the latter is entitled to charge a handling charge (at a percentage fee in Box 14) when presenting its invoice. There is separate provision in cl 14 for extra costs of disposal of the vessel.[138]

If there are costs not in the list, they may lie where they fall, eg on the contractor. One example might be in relation to extra costs of dealing with cargo. These costs may well be specified in the method of work in Annex II, but there may be a whole variety of transhipment costs[139] or other costs that may not fit neatly into the cl 13 list. One example may be the not inconsiderable problem of dealing with waste

---

132 See 13.6.3(k).

133 Alternatively, it could be implied that a reasonableness standard should be applied. Although an unenforceable clause could be severed (see cl 26(a)), cl 15 is recognised by both parties as being fundamental to the agreement and, as noted, if security is not supplied when requested the contractor may terminate under cl 10(f).

134 These have to be over and above those costs that would reasonably be incurred by the contractor in normal circumstances. In the case of unions these would presumably include the ordinary crew agreements for vessels, but would not include eg a requirement that particular extra personnel be employed who are nationals of the Affected State.

135 These would be tugs that were not already in the Annex I Schedule of craft.

136 The equivalent costs of the crew of any craft in Annex I Schedule, such as tugs, would not be allowable as extras.

137 By contrast, where craft or other equipment are lost or damaged the hirer is not liable: see cl 16(c) and 13.6.3(g).

138 See 13.6.3(b).

139 See also 2.1.4.

cargo, and it is possible that the contractor might be treated as a "broker" or "waste manager" for the purposes of the EU Waste Framework Directive 2008.[140] It is difficult to see that such costs do fall into the cl 13 list, so care is needed when drafting to clarify who is to pay them. In some circumstances, changes to the condition of the cargo might trigger a change of method within cl 4.[141]

13.6.3(c) Duration of services

Although the financial risk of time overruns essentially falls on the hirer, before agreeing any contract both parties will obviously need to make an estimate as to how long the job will take. Box 11(vi) can be used to guarantee the contractor a *minimum* number of days on hire. Unlike a time charter, which will usually fix an exact time of duration of the contract,[142] Wreckhire 2010 has no formal date as an endpoint, but contains four provisions which relate to the length of the services.

The first, cl 2, incorporates Annex II whose title refers not only the method of work but also to an "Estimated Time Schedule", and presumably an estimated end date will be given. The second is the nomination of a place in Box 8 (supplemented by cl 9) of a place of "Delivery/and or Disposal" of the vessel.[143] The third is the right given in cl 8 for the hirer to "suspend or terminate" the services "at any time", provided that notice is given to the contractor and that the latter is paid for all services rendered. The fourth is that cl 11 allows for the possibility of a bonus[144] to be paid if the contractor completes all the agreed services "to the satisfaction" of the hirer within a date specified in Box 10(ii). Box 10(iii) can be used to give a further, later, date so that a reduced bonus might be payable if the full bonus date is exceeded but the work is completed by the later date. In effect, there is still an incentive for the contractor to expedite work after the first Box 10(ii) date has passed, with the bonus tapering pro rata per day down to zero by the later Box 10(iii) date. There is a further incentive for the contractor not to exploit the daily rate nature of the contract by racking up days without full commitment. If it does not deliver or dispose of the vessel as agreed in Box 8 by the time stipulated in Box 10(iii), the daily working rate of hire for (a) craft and equipment and (b) personnel is reduced by cl 12 to an amount agreed in Box 11(v).[145]

Although most of the provisions in Wreckhire 2010 deal in some manner with risk and cost allocation, cll 4 and 7 of Wreckhire 2010 go to the core of the commercial bargain. They deal respectively with changes to the method of work originally agreed and the consequences of delay. They are also the clauses most likely to be subject to amendment at the drafting stage. They are covered in the following two sections.

---

140 See 14.6.2(a), 14.6.4(a) and 14.6.5(d).
141 See 13.6.3(d).
142 Albeit that there will usually be an agreed express margin (eg a month) either side of the agreed termination date.
143 See 13.6.3(i); also 14.7.3.
144 The amount of the bonus would be set out in Box 10i, and could be a lump sum or a percentage of the total payable under the contract.
145 Where there are "delays" within cl 7 (see 13.6.3(e)) these are not used to affect the dates or periods applied to calculate bonus payments or reduced daily rates: see cll 11(a)(ii) and 12.

13.6.3(d) Changes in services, personnel, craft or equipment

Clause 4, along with cl 7,[146] sits at the heart of risk allocation in Wreckhire 2010. It starts off by pulling together the elements of the bargain, comprising on the one hand the rate of hire to be paid and, on the other, a list of the key services to be provided by the contractor.[147] That list consists of: the nature of the services (set out in Box 7); the personnel craft and equipment to be used (set out in Annex I); the method of work with a time estimate (set out in detail in Annex II); the specifications of the wrecked vessel (set out in Box 4); the condition of the vessel (described in Box 5); the position of the vessel and condition of the worksite (set out in Box 6). A normal time charter would also set out specifications and services to which the charterer is entitled in exchange for hire, but the essential difference with wreck removal is that the nature of the operations required are much more susceptible to change and this naturally will affect the underlying financial risks and assumptions of each party. If the work becomes harder, the contractor may incur extra costs, but the hirer may end up paying for a longer operation than anticipated.[148]

Clause 4 of each of the three BIMCO contracts looks similar, but there are significant differences between them. Wreckhire 2010 cl 4 assumes that additional costs for providing the agreed services will normally fall on the contractor, who has pitched the daily rate to take account of the known and agreed circumstances, but if the contractor can show that there have been substantial changes (before or during its services) it can be entitled to claim for additional costs. Before qualifying for the additional costs, the contractor has to satisfy a threshold and also must follow an agreed procedure.

Clause 4(a), though vital, is difficult to read because of the number both of commas and the word "or", and the use of the word "change" twice but for different purposes. The overriding part is in lines 40–41 where the threshold is a "substantial change" to what the contractor is required to do (ie its "services"[149]), or provide (ie the personnel, craft and equipment[150]). This substantial change must be due to two alternative causes: first, mis-description[151] or "error in the specification"[152] provided by the hirer; or, secondly, because

---

146 See 13.6.3(e).
147 See also 13.6.3(a).
148 How to adjust the hire as a result of delays is dealt with separately in cl 7: see also 13.6.3(e).
149 Although the chapeau to cl 4 pulls together the main elements of the bargain, as described above, the reference to "Services" in cl 4(a) is to only one part of them, as cl 1 defines the expression very narrowly to refer to what is in Box 7. The "Nature of the Services" (in Box 7(i)) appears to require what might be a very general statement, as the box is very small and there is no separate Annex in which a bigger description might be expected. If Box 7(i) contained only a short statement like "raising of the vessel from current position and removal to place of delivery" there is unlikely ever to be any substantial change to its "nature", and this cannot have been intended. It might have been clearer if, eg, the definition in cl 1 included the list in the chapeau to cl 4, or if the reference to "Nature of the Services" in the chapeau became a broad concept (followed by a colon) to describe all of the elements of the list of services and not simply to what is in Box 7, especially as that expression is repeated in cl 4(a)(ii) (although with a lower case "n"): see fn 157.
150 See Annex I.
151 Misdescription by the hirer is separate from error in the specification, but does not seem to refer to *any* misdescription (eg in conversations or emails), but to the descriptions in Box 5 (condition of vessel) and Box 6 (position of vessel and condition of worksite).
152 This must refer to the specification*s* (plural) in Box 4, but presumably not any additional information provided outside of the document.

there has been a "material change" in the position and/or the condition of the vessel or the worksite.

Where there is a misdescription or error by the hirer in the specifications the contractor has to show both that it relied on the misdescription or error and that there is a "substantial change" in what it is required to do or provide. In relation to a "material change" in the position and/or the condition of the vessel or the worksite, this might occur eg where a stranded vessel starts to break up; or where the vessel starts to slip from a reef (as with the *Rena*); or where the seabed on which a wreck rests is affected by tides or build up of mud or rocks. As the definition of "vessel" in cl 1 includes cargo, a material change in the condition of cargo would be relevant. This might occur when sound containers on deck become damaged by heavy weather, or where bulk cargo (or bunker) tanks are breached by movements of the vessel.

The two expressions, "substantial change" and "material change" are used in different contexts, but still provide helpful contrasts. It is unlikely that "substantial" assumes anything like the type of change that would frustrate a contract,[153] but is clearly intended to exclude the risk of normal variations that the contractor must be presumed to have undertaken. Of the two, "substantial" must represent a greater degree of change than "material", while "material" must at least represent more than a minimum degree of change of circumstances. In between these two extremes it is probably not helpful to try to define the expressions too much further without reference to specific facts, but there is obvious scope for differences of opinion and uncertainty. Ultimately, any dispute may have to be resolved provisionally by expert evaluation (and ultimately by mediation or arbitration),[154] although wherever these dispute mechanisms are used (in respect of changes) cl 4 places an express obligation on the contractor to continue to provide the services.[155]

The clause also requires that the substantial change to the contractor's performance has occurred without the fault of the contractor. The wording is phrased as a pre-condition to any claim for increased costs, but this would seem somewhat disproportionate if there was only a minor failure by the contractor. It is arguable that that "fault" should be interpreted causatively, so that rather than it resulting in a compete bar to a claim there could be an assessment of any extra costs (or time) and an appropriate apportionment. In relation to misdescriptions or errors, the fault of the contractor might simply be in failing to identify the problem in the documentation at an earlier stage in the operations, but in most circumstances (unless the error is blindingly obvious) it would still be labouring under the difficulties caused by the hirer. In relation to the change of condition of the worksite or vessel, the scope for contractor fault is obviously greater, eg if there is a lack of monitoring to allow early action, or a failure to activate pumps. There may be many circumstances where 'but for' the fault the change would not have happened at all—or at least it is very difficult to estimate what would have happened without the fault. Here, there would be a heavy evidential burden on the contractor to show that the fault was not causative.

Assuming that the contractor has passed the threshold for claiming additional costs, cl 4 obliges the parties to follow a set procedure. First, under cl 4(a)(i) the contractor has to

---

153 See also 13.6.3(f).
154 See 13.6.3(k).
155 Subject to the suspension or termination clause, cl 8: see 13.6.3(f).

give notice in writing to the hirer "forthwith" of the additional estimated costs.[156] Secondly, under cl 4(a)(ii) if any changes to the "nature of the Services" are agreed between the parties the hirer has to draft a "variation order" which both parties must then sign.[157] Thirdly, under cl 4(a)(iii) both parties must consult each other "without delay" to try to agree the amount of any additional costs.[158] If they agree, the amount is entered in the variation order; if they do not agree then any dispute may again have to be resolved provisionally by expert evaluation (and ultimately by mediation or arbitration).[159]

It is possible that the changes in circumstances make the contractor's services *easier*, rather than harder. Here the hirer can seek to have a *reduction* of the hire, but is not entitled to make an immediate deduction.[160] Again, agreed changes have to be drafted into a signed variation order and the parties "without delay" must consult to agree the amount of the reduction in hire. Any dispute may again have to be resolved provisionally by expert evaluation (and ultimately by mediation or arbitration).[161]

13.6.3(e) Delay

In a similar way to a time charter, Wreckhire 2010 places the underlying risk of delay on the hirer, but cl 7 mitigates that risk by allowing for the hire to be reduced in a number of circumstances. Where the delay is caused by external factors there is to be a hire adjustment. Those factors could be adverse weather, heavy seas or "any other reason outside the contractor's control", eg government intervention.[162] If the external factors mean that no services can be performed at all, the contractor will get a pre-agreed "standby rate" (as set out in Box 11(iii) or (iv)), as opposed to the normal full daily working rate (as set out in in Box 11(i) or (ii)). If the services are reduced, the rate payable has to be adjusted to an agreed figure in between the two rates.

If a delay is caused by breakdown of the contractor's equipment (or non-availability of its personnel) cl 7(b) requires the parties to consult so as to agree on the amount of time

---

[156] It is not clear what the sanction would be if the notice was not given promptly. It seems unlikely that a delay would be intended to operate as an absolute bar to claiming any extra costs as presumably it is in the contractor's interest to seek payment quickly. If the delay was in some way causative then this may be a "fault" of the contractor, as already discussed.

[157] The wording of cl 4(a)(ii) is somewhat confusing, although the aim is tolerably clear, ie to require agreed changes (to what the contractor has to do) to be put into a signed variation order. It starts off by referring to "Any and all substantial changes to the nature of such Services", but it is not clear what "and all" adds, if *any* changes at all have to be documented. The reference to "nature" (lower case) can be contrasted to "Nature"(upper case) in line 37 of cl 4; the latter refers to what appears to be a short description of the services in Box 7, but "nature" in cl 4(a)(ii) seems to be used as a more general expression, ie 'type'.

[158] The second and third stages are drafted as though the one will happen after the other, but it seems more likely that the consultation, agreement on changes and costs and drafting of the variation order will take place more or less contemporaneously.

[159] See 13.6.3(k).

[160] See cl 10(d).

[161] See cl 4(c) and 13.6.3(k). Clause 4(c) refers to the reasonableness and quantum of *costs* (ie under cl 4(a)(i) and (iii), but does not seem to make reference to what happens if the parties cannot agree on the *changes* to the nature of the services in 4(a)(ii). It has to be presumed that the changes are so intimately related to the costs that they are subsumed in any reference of a dispute for resolution under cl 20.

[162] See eg 5.3, 4.2.3. Extra costs incurred in dealing with government requirements would be for the hirer to bear under cl 13(f): see 13.6.3(a). Extra costs caused by delays in delivery or disposal are dealt with separately, but will generally be for the hirer: see cl 9 and 13.6.3(i).

lost; for that agreed period the standby rate applies. Where the contractor has sub-contracted in equipment or personnel it is enjoined by cl 7(c) to use "best efforts" to arrange similar back to back standby rates for breakdown or non-availability. These two provisions refer expressly to equipment and personnel, but not to "craft" which are elsewhere treated separately (eg in Annex 1). It would be curious if the absence of a reference to craft means that there is no off-hire type provision when it is one of the craft (not equipment) that has broken down. The standby rate in Box 11(iii) gives a single rate for "Craft and Equipment", but although Part I takes priority over Part II time lost can only be calculated in relation to specific breakdowns. Clause 7(e) avoids unnecessary *de minimis* calculations by providing that cl 7(b) and (c) do not apply to individual delays unless they exceed six consecutive hours; then the standby rate will apply to the whole agreed delay period.

As the claim for reduction of hire will be initiated by the hirer, it is under an obligation to advise the contractor "promptly" of when the standby rates should apply and to follow this up in writing. While the breakdown of equipment might normally be considered a breach by the contractor, the remedy for the hirer is framed in relation to reduction of hire rather than damages for any consequential loss.[163]

It is fairly obvious that there is great scope here for differences of views as to appropriate adjustments for bad weather, or for time lost for equipment being out of action, or personnel being unavailable. In a time charter there may also be hire disputes but, except in extreme cases of non-payment of hire, the shipowner is likely to continue with the contractual voyage (if only because of duties owned to bill of lading holders). In a complex wreck removal operation more immediate answers may be required if the contractor is to continue with all its tasks while payment issues are undecided. For this reason any dispute about the reduced rates may again have to be resolved provisionally by expert evaluation (and ultimately by mediation or arbitration).[164] Unlike cl 4, there is no express provision in cl 7 whereby the contractor is obliged to continue the services while the alternative dispute resolution (ADR) takes place. It is unclear if this is deliberate, because on ordinary contractual principles the contractor would not be entitled to suspend or terminate operations in the absence of an express clause, a breach of a condition (fundamental term) or a fundamental breach by the hirer.[165]

13.6.3(f) Termination or suspension
As with most commercial contracts, eg LOF and SCOPIC,[166] the right to cancel or terminate a contract is an important element of risk minimisation, and it can arise both under the contract and at common law. Under Wreckhire 2010, the contractor's obligations will terminate naturally on the completion of the service,[167] but it is given the express right by cl 10(f) to terminate the contract when the hirer has failed in two ways to meet its financial obligations. The first is where the hirer has not provided security[168] within five banking days of a request to do so by the contractor. The second is where "any amount payable

---

163 See cl 16(e) and 13.6.3(g).
164 See 13.6.3(k).
165 See also 13.6.3(g).
166 See 12.2.3, 12.2.4, 12.3.4.
167 See 13.6.3(c) and (i).
168 See 13.6.3(b).

under" the contract has not been paid within seven days of the "due date". The "amount" refers to hire and also to any extra costs that should be for the account of the hirer, but have been paid for and invoiced by the contractor under cl 13.[169] Like most modern time charters, an 'anti-technicality' provision in cl 10(f) requires the contractor to give at least three working days' written notice of its intention to terminate.

Clause 8(a) gives the hirer very strong rights to terminate or suspend performance of the services by the contractor. These rights can be exercised "at any time" subject to written notice[170] being given to the contractor. Termination might be relevant when the hirer (and its insurer) have lost confidence in the particular contractor, or consider that the overall task has become too difficult or expensive. On termination the contractor is entitled to all hire already due as well as any "additional direct expenses".[171] Demobilisation of craft, equipment and personnel cannot happen instantly, but the contractor is obliged under cl 8(b) to use "reasonable despatch" eg taking into account safety factors. The problem for the hirer is more likely to be orders to prevent demobilisation given by "competent authorities", eg States exercising intervention powers[172] or those arising under the WRC 2007 to require removal.[173] Similar issues have arisen in relation to SCOPIC,[174] and Wreckhire 2010 cl 8(c) deals with the absence of permission by providing that the contractor is to be paid at the standby rates agreed in Box 11.[175] It is also entitled to its reasonable and necessary costs of continuing with the service.[176] The existence of this express provision in cl 8(c) means that even if the deadlock continues for a long time, it will be difficult for either party to claim that the contract has become frustrated—although there must come a time when an indefinite standby of craft, personnel and equipment has become something radically different from that originally contemplated.[177]

Clause 8(a) also allows the hirer to *suspend* the services on the same basis as with termination, above; ie hire already due will be payable, additional expenses may be claimed and standby rates will apply if the authorities do not allow demobilisation. Suspension, though, raises slightly different issues as there is some similarity with cl 7 which allows for standby rates to apply where there have been delays.[178] The difference is that cl 7 refers only to listed circumstances causing delays, while the power in cl 8 for the hirer to suspend operations can occur "at any time" and for any reason of the hirer's. Those reasons might include a desire to 'go slow' while negotiations continue with the Affected State about the extent of removal operations that might be required, or if there are potential disputes with others with whom the hirer may have commercial relations (eg charterers and cargo owners

---

169 See 13.6.3(b).

170 See also 13.6.3(j).

171 The hire would be at whatever rate was then applicable, eg full daily working rate, standby rate or reduced daily rate: see 13.6.3(b). Presumably the expenses would those not already claimable under cl 13: see 13.6.3(b).

172 See 4.2.3, 5.3.

173 See 9.2.5; also 10.2.5 for issues arising where States require full and not partial removal.

174 See 12.3.4(c).

175 See also 13.6.3(e). Note also the obligation in cl 2 to cooperate in obtaining confirmation from State authorities that there has been compliance with any State orders: see also 13.6.3(j).

176 Eg the extra costs set out in cl 13: see 13.6.3(b).

177 See eg *Fibrosa v Fairbairn* [1943] AC 32, *The Nema* [1982] AC 724 and cf 2.1.4(b).

178 See 13.6.3(e).

about exactly what is to happen with the cargo).[179] The other difference with cl 7 is that the latter uses an essentially causative test to calculate adjustments in hire, eg when weather or breakdowns affect some but not all services. By contrast, suspension under cl 8 seems to involve a total suspension of all services,[180] rather than a right to terminate some part of the services. If this was required, the hirer wold presumably need the agreement of the contractor or to show a "material change" under cl 4(b).[181]

It does not appear that the express termination provisions in cll 8 and 10(f) are intended to provide an exclusive code for when termination can take place, so that parties could still claim rights to terminate performance of the contract at common law, eg for breach of a condition (fundamental term) or a fundamental breach (eg if there was a repudiation). This could give rise to potential claims for damages for the lost bargain, were it not for cl 16(e).[182] Moreover, a failure by the hirer to pay the hire on time is unlikely to be treated as a condition.[183]

13.6.3(g) Claims and liabilities

Wreckhire 2010 contains many obligations for the parties, breach of which could be a fruitful source of litigation. A significant protection against excessive financial risk lies for the hirer in the ultimate sanction of terminating the contract for any reason, and the contractor can terminate if the hirer does not meet its financial obligations.[184]

The key risk allocation provision is cl 16, dealing with liabilities for death or injury of personnel, or damage to property, but also for consequential losses. This aims to distribute losses on a 'knock for knock' basis and builds on similar clauses introduced into BIMCO's towage and other offshore contracts. *Rainey* has authoritatively analysed these clauses and case law relevant to them[185] and it would not be useful to repeat his treatment which necessarily goes beyond wreck removal contracts.

It is convenient to start with cl 16(e), dealing with financial and consequential losses, as it applies to non-performance or breaches of any of the terms of the contract, as well as negligence or any other fault of either party (or their servants, agents or sub-contractors). In essence, cl 16(e) aims to exclude liability for all these financial and consequential losses, although attempts to achieve comprehensive wording that will achieve this effect have been difficult.[186] For example, although words such as "whatsoever" and "any breach"

---

179 See also 2.1.3, 2.1.4.

180 There is no reference eg to "*all or part of* the Services" and suspension is treated in the same way grammatically as termination, which surely refers to the totality of the services. The reference to "*the* Services" leads, via the definition in cl 1, to Box 7 which seems to be designed to record a very general description of the nature of the services as a whole rather than the detailed specifications of the method of work found in Annex III.

181 See 13.6.3(d).

182 See 13.6.3(g).

183 See *Spar Shipping AS v Grand China Logistics Holding (Group) Co Ltd (The Star Capella, Spar Vega and Spar Draco)* [2016] EWCA CIV 982 [2016] 2 Lloyd's Rep 447.

184 See 13.6.3(f).

185 See *Rainey*, 125–181 on the related provisions in Towcon 2008 and Towhire 2008 (especially the summary on 157–158), with commentary on Wreckhire 2010 cl 16 at 512–513. See also B Soyer, A Tettenborn, *Offshore Contracts and Liabilities* (Informa Law Routledge, 2015), Chapters 4, 5, 9 (knock for knock clauses) and 6, 7 (exclusion of consequential loss).

186 *Rainey*, 165–171, traces these difficulties in trying to exclude "indirect or consequential loss in previous versions of the BIMCO clauses, and the effect of the changes now in cl 25(c) of Towcon 2008 and Towhire 2008—upon which Wreckhire 2010 cl 16(e) is based.

are used doubts have arisen about whether they can extend to deliberate or repudiatory breaches, although in the context of wreck removal there seems to be no reason in principle why they should not.[187] Loss of profit or use is excluded by cl 16(e)(i) whether it arises directly or indirectly from performance or non-performance of the contract (including negligence). Such financial losses might otherwise be claimed by a contractor if the hirer wrongly refused to accept delivery of the wreck under cl 9[188] and the contractual rates of hire (which would continue under cl 9(a)) were lower than market rates. If the contractor failed to use "due care" under cl 2, or repudiated the contract, it is difficult to see what loss of profit or use would be suffered by the hirer when the vessel was already a wreck, but it is possible that delays might coincide with a market fall in scrap prices, or the loss of an expected recycling contract.

Clause 16(e)(ii) excludes liability for "any consequential loss or damage for any reason whatsoever". Some consequential financial losses might already be excluded under cl 16(e)(i), but cl 16(e)(ii) could cover extra costs as a result of breach, eg if notices were not served appropriately or in time (eg notice of termination by the hirer under cl 8(a)).[189] "Consequential loss" would not seem to cover a primary liability, eg if the contractor unreasonably damaged the vessel's machinery, gear, equipment, anchors, chains, stores and other appurtenances under cl 5(b).[190] The result might be different if cl 16(e)(ii) referred to "consequential loss or damage arising *directly or indirectly*".

Clause 16(a)–(d) is the other part of the knock for knock agreement and, in essence, the hirer will cover losses in respect of its own personnel[191] and the wrecked vessel, while the contractor will bear losses in respect of *its* personnel[192] or *its* owned or hired-in craft or equipment.[193] This result is achieved through sub-clauses containing mutual exclusions of liability, but combined with hold harmless indemnity provisions in case one or other party has been obliged directly to pay for (or reasonably settle) death or injury claims in the first place. The rationale for such 'knock for knock' agreements is usually because it is generally more efficient for property losses to be borne by those who have property insurance, eg H&M cover, so as to avoid litigation costs and the need for additional liability (eg P&I) cover. This simple concept has not always been reflected in judicial decisions which have sometimes acceded to highly technical arguments about particular wordings. *Rainey* has traced the ebb and flow of judicial pronouncements on such clauses,[194] and it suffices here to support a more purposive approach to such clauses in major commercial contracts that recognises a deliberate decision to allocate risks rather than account for faults. This should counter the ingenuity of lawyers in picking apart the wording, but where large sums of money are at stake the possibility for dispute is always high. With these warnings, it may be

---

187 The authors agree with *Rainey*, 179.
188 See 13.6.3(i).
189 See 13.6.3(f).
190 See 13.6.3(a). Liability for this damage might be excluded by cl 16(d), below.
191 These would include servants, agents or sub-contractors of the hirer, eg engineers; also others at the site of operations "for whatever purposes on behalf or at the request of" the hirer, eg government employees or media representatives.
192 Again, including its servants, agents, sub-contractors, or invitees.
193 But not portable salvage equipment, materials and stores as these are allocated as a hirer's 'extra costs' risk by cl 13(h): see 13.6.3(b).
194 See Preface to the 4th edition, xxvii–xxix.

more helpful to give some examples of where the knock for knock provisions could apply in a wreck removal operation, but mention must first be made of limitation of liability.

Unlike Towhire 2008 cl 23(d), Wreckhire 2010 cl 16 makes no reference at all to the right of either party to limit its liability, eg under the LLMC 1996.[195] Limitation could arise in two contexts. First, suppose that contractor's employees were injured while aboard the wreck by the negligence of the hirer, and sued the hirer; those direct claims may be subject to limitation, eg under the LLMC.[196] Secondly, the party liable, eg the hirer, may then make an indemnity claim against the other party, eg the contractor, under Wreckhire 2008 cl 16(a). That indemnity claim would already have had a limit applied to it, in the sense that the direct claims may already have been limited according to the tonnage of the wreck, but the question arises as to whether there is any reason why the defendant to the indemnity claim (here the contractor) could not then seek to rely on its *own* limit of liability.[197]

The effect of *The Cape Bari*[198] is that it is possible to waive a right to limit liability, provided that this is done clearly. General words in a clause, even an indemnity clause, will not achieve this effect and Art 2(2) of the LLMC 1996 allows for limitation even if brought by way of recourse for an indemnity under a contract. It follows that the knock for knock provisions in cl 16 are subject to any right to limit; ie in the example given the contractor would be able to rely on its applicable limit and the hirer would not obtain a complete indemnity. The same result would apply, in reverse, ie if there had been an injury claim brought by an employee of the hirer against the contractor,[199] the latter's indemnity claim against the hirer under cl 16(b) would be subject to the limits of the wrecked vessel.[200]

If a wreck was damaged by contractor's failure to use "due care"[201] any claim by the hirer for damage to the vessel would be directly excluded by cl 16(d).[202] If that contractor's negligence had damaged the cargo on the wreck, and the cargo had successfully sued the

---

195 See 2.5. *Rainey*, 512, explains that the Clubs insisted on the omission out of concerns that they might be obliged to indemnify the contractor in circumstances where a third party sued the contractor and the latter was not entitled to limit.

196 See eg 2.5.4.

197 In the example, the contractor's employees were not operating on any vessel of the contractor so the limit would be that under LLMC Art 6(4) based on a deemed tonnage 1500 gt: see 2.5.5, 2.5.6(a). If the crew members had been injured on a contractor's vessel (eg while handling lines operated negligently by the hirer's personnel on the wreck) it would be the tonnage of that vessel that would be applied.

198 [2016] 2 Lloyd's Rep 469; and see 2.5.5; also *Rainey*, 181, 258–259.

199 Although the latter's direct liability limits may be quite low, given the size of craft being used, so the personal claimant may seek to bring its claim against the hirer as well if it can find joint negligence.

200 Cf if the hirer claimed to limit as a charterer of the *contractor's* craft on the basis that Wreckhire 2010 resembled a time charter. It seems that Wreckhire 2010 is not really a charter of a specific vessel, but a contract for work and services which incidentally involves the use of vessels. If it were considered as a charterer, its claim to limit in respect of third party claims would not be prevented by *The Ocean Victory* [2017] 1 Lloyd's Rep 521: see 2.5.4(d).

201 See cl 2 and 13.6.3(a).

202 Clause 1 includes in "vessel" anything "contained therein or thereon". It is unclear if this would cover the equipment etc mentioned in cl 5(b), above, as opposed to the cargo or bunkers mentioned in cl 1. Given that cl 5(b) also refers to gear and stores, and they are like cargo, it seems that there may be no claim for damage for a breach under cl 5(b). The hirer's remedy would then be restricted to an entitlement to refuse permission for any use of equipment etc that might risk causing unnecessary damage to it. If that refusal were unreasonable, the contractor would presumably be prevented by cl 16 from claiming any additional loss, but would be entitled to normal hire for any delay: see cl 7(a) and 13.6.3(e).

hirer for it (eg as carrier),[203] it would seem that the contractor would be able to rely (as against the hirer) on the exclusion of liability in cl 16(d). This is because it applies to the hirer's "vessel" which, in cl 1, is defined to include the cargo on the vessel.[204]

If the contractor's own craft suffered property damage as a result of some breach or fault by the hirer, that claim would be excluded by cl 16(c). If the contractor was sued by a sub-contractor for property damage caused by the fault of the contractor, the contractor would be prevented from bringing a claim against the hirer by cl 16(c), and the same would apply even if the damage had been partly caused by faults of the hirer.

There are some deliberate gaps in the knock for knock provisions, though. First, cl 16(d) only excludes liability of the contractor in respect of the vessel (ie wreck) and not other property owned by the hirer, including other vessels. Secondly, a claim might be made against the contractor or hirer by a third party *not* associated with the contract; ie someone who is not a servant, agent or sub-contractor of either party. A specific example would be where, owing to the negligence of the contractor, there was damage to the third party's craft (or subsequent wreck removal liabilities in respect of it).[205] In such a case, the contractor might be able to limit its liability, but there is no express provision for any indemnity from the hirer in Wreckhire 2010. The loss would therefore lie where it falls, ie with the contractor, unless there has been a breach by the hirer that would entitle the contractor to claim such loss (and that it is not excluded as consequential loss under cl 16(e)(ii)). The same position would seem to apply if cargo interests sued the contractor for negligent performance of the wreck removal operation. Although the contractor might be able to limit liability[206] there would be no indemnity from the hirer under Wreckhire 2010. Thirdly, separate provisions are made in respect of pollution risks.[207]

A *Himalaya* clause,[208] in cl 17, restricts any attempts by either hirer or contractor to avoid the exclusion and indemnity provisions by suing others such as the employees of the other party, or their subcontractors and affiliated companies. The clause provides that the persons listed (also including the registered owner, ie if the bareboat charterer is the hirer) are entitled to all the benefits of the of the contract, including exemptions and defences.[209]

Clause 19 imposes a number of time limits. First, the claim has to be notified to the other party within 12 months of the termination or completion of the services[210] or 12 months of any claim by a third party (whichever is the later). Then, any suit (including arbitration) must be brought within 12 months of those notifications.[211] Failure to comply operates not only to bar, but also to extinguish, the claim.

---

203 Such a suit might be difficult owing to Hague/Visby or charterparty exceptions: see 2.1.5(b), 2.1.7.
204 This would not seem to be a loss of profit or use by the *hirer* (even though arising indirectly) within cl 16(e)(i), although it is possible that it might be consequential loss within cl 16(e)(ii).
205 See *Rainey*, 512.
206 See 2.5.5.
207 See cl 24 and 13.6.3(h).
208 This is not the latest International Group/BIMCO Himalaya Clause 2014, designed for bills of lading and other contracts, so the 2010 contract may need to be amended.
209 See the sources cited in 2.1.4(a) and *Rainey* 182–183.
210 See cl 8 (see 13.6.3(f)) and cl 9 (see 13.6.3(i)).
211 Opting for mediation does not stop time running: see cl 21(e) and 13.6.3(k).

13.6.3(h) Pollution risks

There are obvious pollution risks in any wreck removal operation, eg from bunkers or the loss of oil (or other cargo). These risks are relevant, not only because the need to remove such potential pollutants can increase the length (and therefore cost) of operations considerably, but also because of additional liabilities. Under Wreckhire 2010, the risk of a lengthier operation generally falls on the hirer[212] and the ability of the hirer to terminate operations may be restricted by the intervention orders of a State.[213] Where there is oil pollution from a wrecked tanker, the liability for pollution clean-up and economic losses will fall on the registered owner under the CLC 1992 and claims cannot be brought against persons undertaking salvage or preventive measures, such as wreck removal contractors.[214] Under the Bunkers Convention 2001 a contractor is not primarily liable for bunker pollution from the wreck, but there is no responder immunity provision preventing actions against them at common law, eg for negligence.[215] Until the HNS Convention 2010 enters into force, the contractor that has to remove HNS cargo (in bulk or in containers) may also find that it is caught up in litigation either as an agent of the owner (ie hirer) or in some circumstances as a party primarily liable for negligence (or possibly under the Environmental Liability Directive 2004).[216]

Clause 24 seeks to deal with these potential liabilities in a way that is not entirely favourable to the contractor. First, cl 24(a) imposes a positive contractual duty to exercise due care throughout the performance of the services[217] to prevent and minimise "damage to the environment".[218] The "due care" can also be assessed by reference to the pollution response plan that the contractor is obliged to create, maintain and implement. Secondly, the hirer is obliged by cl 24(b) to indemnify and hold the contractor harmless "in respect of any and all consequences of any pollution" resulting from discharges or escapes from the wrecked vessel. This would cover pollution of any type (eg from oil, bunkers or HNS) and would extend to claims for clean-up and economic loss. The drawback for the contractor is that the provision continues by stating "except where such pollution arises as a consequence of the negligence of the contractor, its sub-contractors, its agents and/or servants". This means that if the contractor is sued by a third party (eg a State, or fishing or hotel interests) for pollution losses caused by negligence there will be no indemnity from the hirer and the contractor must bear its own loss.[219] The contractor may be able to limit its liability, eg under the LLMC 1996,[220] but will need to rely on its own liability (eg P&I) insurance. What is left unsaid here is whether the hirer can bring a recourse action against the contractor for any pollution liabilities which it has incurred under the IMO strict liability regimes as a result of the contractor's negligence. These regimes leave open the possibility of such recourse

---

212 See 13.6.3(b) and (e).
213 See 13.6.3(f).
214 See the CLC 1992 Art III((4)(d)–(e) and 2.6.2(a).
215 See 2.6.3.
216 See 2.6.5.
217 Ie including any contractual disposal voyage: see 2.6.3(i)
218 Although this phrase is not defined in the contract, it is also used in the LOF 2011 cl B and it would be appropriate to refer to its definition in the Salvage Convention 1989 Art 1(d).
219 This is one reason why under cl 23(a) the contractor warrants that it will maintain full P&I cover, including salvors' liabilities.
220 See 2.5.4(b).

actions[221] and on ordinary contractual principles a breach of the due care obligation (ie a reasonableness standard) would give the hirer a right to claim for losses that are not too remote, including here the likelihood that it would be strictly liable for pollution damage. The hold harmless promise only applies in the absence of negligence and there is no other specific exclusion of liability in cl 24. The exclusion in cl 16(d)[222] only applies to damage to the wrecked vessel itself, although the exclusion in cl 16(e)(ii) of "consequential loss" (even when caused by negligence) would seem to cover the recourse claim. The hirer might argue that cl 16 is a generic clause and should yield to the specific provisions on pollution in cl 24. Clause 24 was added as a new provision to Wreckstage 2010, but there appears to be no conflict with cl 16. First, cl 24 is expressly aimed at preventing an indemnity in respect of third party claims and says nothing about a recourse claim. Secondly, cl 16(e) expressly covers claims against the other party for consequential loss, which this recourse claim would be, so there is no reason why it cannot apply.

The third situation covered by cl 24 is where there is pollution from the contractor's own or hired-in craft. The contractor agrees under cl 24(c) to indemnify and hold harmless the hirer if the hirer was sued for such pollution, eg if under national law the hirer is held liable for the consequences of the negligence of its contractors. This pollution could occur as a result of bunker pollution from tugs and other support craft, but there might also be pollution if a ship sank after transferring bulk or containerised cargo from the wreck. Here, the CLC 1992 might impose liability directly on the registered owner of the transferring ship, but cl 24(c) could possibly be relevant if negligence caused other pollution, eg from HNS.

13.6.3(i) Wreck delivery and disposal

The services will normally be completed when the wrecked vessel is delivered to the hirer at the place agreed in cl 9 (and Box 8); this might be the location of wreck, or a nearby port of refuge, or an ultimate port of disposal for recycling. Disposal of the wreck[223] is a quite separate process from its raising or removal and Wreckhire 2010 cl 9(a) (with Box 8) gives the parties an option whether the wrecked vessel is to be simply delivered to the hirer at an agreed place of "delivery" or at a place for "disposal" (eg a recycling yard). In either case, at this point the hirer has to accept the vessel "forthwith".

The wreck convoy may present the contractor with many potential risks, eg navigational and political. The hirer undertakes that the agreed place of delivery or disposal will be safe and accessible for the vessel, the contractor's craft and hired-in craft. It also undertakes that the place is one where the contractor will be permitted by government or other authorities to deliver or dispose of the wreck. States may impose many conditions and restrictions about the disposal voyage and where scrapping or recycling will take place.[224] Once the contractor has tendered the vessel for delivery any extra costs caused either by the hirer not accepting the vessel forthwith, or (more particularly) where the delivery is prevented or delayed by the government, will fall on the hirer. Many of the extra costs would be for the

---

221 See eg the CLC 1992 Art III(5) and the Bunkers Convention 2001 Art 3(6).
222 See 13.6.3(g).
223 See Chapter 14, eg 14.7.3.
224 These may arise under general intervention powers: see eg 5.3, 4.2.3; they may also arise under modern recycling laws: see 14.5.

hirer in any event under cl 13, eg if an authority required licences, or special safety vessels to be in attendance.[225] Moreover, the appropriate rates of hire will continue.[226]

Where there is an agreed disposal voyage the daily hire will continue until the vessel has been accepted and taken over by the hirer, but Wreckhire cl 14 allocates all extra costs resulting from the disposal to be for the account either of the hirer or another party named in Box 9(i). This other party is likely to be either an intermediate buyer of the wreck or possibly the recycling yard itself. The contractor is given the right by cl 18 to exercise a possessory lien over the vessel[227] for any amounts due under the contract, as well as any costs of exercising the lien. This is in addition to any right to proceed against the vessel, eg in an *action in rem*.

A big risk for a contractor is that the hirer fails to accept delivery so that the contractor becomes stuck with a deteriorating wreck in circumstances where it may be under pressure from a State or local authority to deal with it.[228] Clause 9(b) accordingly gives the contractor default powers to sell or dispose of the vessel without notice or any liability whatsoever in two circumstances. The first is if delivery is not taken within five days of a formal written notice of delivery being tendered. The second is where the contractor forms the opinion that the vessel is "likely to deteriorate, decay, become worthless or incur charges whether for storage or otherwise in excess of its value".[229] The provision might be helpful if the contractor is worried that the extent of deterioration or decay will reduce the vessel's ultimate value below any likely additional charges if the hirer fails to take delivery, but it does not appear to be dependent upon proof that there is a risk that the hirer will not continue to pay the hire or meet the charges.[230] If the contractor is entitled to sell the wreck any sale proceeds must be accounted for to the hirer, but may be set off against sums owing (eg if after refusing to accept delivery the hirer has ceased paying the hire). If there is not enough money from any sale, eg to a recycling yard, to pay the extra charges the hirer will remain liable for any extra charges. In the case of the hirer being a single ship company that was having difficulties in selling the wreck itself, a contractor could become very nervous about whether its bills were going to be paid and would certainly want to seek assurance from the insurer (eg Club) that it was standing behind the contract.[231] The risk may be considered more real if the insurer's liabilities under the WRC 2007 have ceased after the wreck has been "removed" from an Affected State and the insurer is not liable for "disposal".[232]

---

225 See cl 13(e) and (f) and 13.6.3(a).

226 Either at the full, or reduced rate: see 13.6.3(a).

227 Given that the definition of "vessel" in cl 1 includes the cargo and bunkers, the hirer also grants the right of possession over cargo. Whether this right is good as against the cargo owners not party to the contract may depend on the terms of the contract of carriage and, possibly, whether it authorises a sub-bailment on terms (commonly allowed under most container bills of lading).

228 In less socially aware times such a ship used to be described as a maritime leper.

229 See also the more extensive discussion in 13.6.5(g) for Wreckstage 2010 cl 9(d); for Wreckfixed 2010 cl 8(d), see 13.6.4(e).

230 Note that the contractor may have the benefit of security under cl 15.

231 This is where the security under cl 15 would be important.

232 See 10.2.8. The contractor would not be able to maintain an independent claim under the WRC 2007 against the registered shipowner or compulsory insurer as rights are only given to States: see 10.2.3. The Affected State might itself pay the contractor and make a claim, but would need to show that the WRC 2007 continued to apply (ie that the removal operation had not finished).

Clause 9(c) expressly allows for parts of the vessel to be delivered at different times and places. It seems from the wording that the different places (at least) have to be agreed and set out in Box 8. This may not be easy to predict at the time of the contract, when the success of the operation and ultimate place of disposal and delivery will often be unknown. While cl 9(c) expressly includes cargo[233] it is apparent that delivery and disposal of the cargo may take place in many different places. Again, this will usually be impossible to predict at the time of the contract. This may be a subject that requires a later contractual amendment, or a provision allowing for additional places to be nominated.[234]

Clause 9 may well work in practice, but some consideration might be given to distinguishing its treatment of disposal from delivery, and perhaps dealing separately with the issue of cargo, bunkers and other things "emanating from" the vessel.

13.6.3(j) Collaboration and consultation

The dynamic but collaborative nature of this contract for work and services is underlined by provisions that require the parties to consult with each other, eg in cl 2 as to the need for any change in the method of work (or personnel, craft or equipment)[235] and in cl 7(b) as to time lost by breakdowns in the contractor's equipment.[236] There are also requirements to collaborate, eg when cl 2 requires the parties to assist with obtaining confirmation from State authorities that the hirer has complied with wreck removal or other intervention orders issued by them.[237] In other circumstances, consent of one party is required.[238]

A more general consultation obligation is set out in cl 3, requiring that "the methods and procedures to be employed in the Services shall at all times be discussed and agreed between the company and the contractor". The contract refers to the "company representative", although there is no box that specifically identifies a particular individual. This continuous consultation and agreement obligation sits somewhat uneasily with the method of work set out definitively at the time of the contract in Annex II. An open and ambulatory provision risks being declared uncertain as an 'agreement to agree',[239] but cl 3 may simply be recording that changes in methods under cl 4 have to be discussed first before being incorporated in a variation order.[240] Such an order has to be signed by both parties under cl 4(a)(ii) and that conforms with the requirements of cl 26(c) in relation to that waivers more generally.

The hirer undertakes in cl 3 that its company representative will be available to the contractor with full authority to act. The assumption here may be that the company representative is "available" at the worksite and not, eg by phone from head office, because the company representative is entitled to "full and unfettered access at all times to the site

---

233 And the cl 1 definition of "vessel" includes cargo.
234 See also 13.6.5(g) for the discussion of cl 9(b) of Wreckstage 2010.
235 See also cl 4(a)(iii) and 13.6.3(c).
236 See 13.6.3(e).
237 See eg 9.2.5(b), 11.3.3(c), 5.3, 4.2.3.
238 See eg cl 25, where the contractor wishes to rotate equipment.
239 Clause 26(a) allows for the severance of unenforceable provisions, although it seems to contain its own uncertainty when it states that "the unenforceable provision shall automatically be amended to conform to that which is unenforceable under the law". Quite how this is to be done "automatically" is unclear, but the rest of the clause allows for any offending provision to be treated as if it had not been included (ie it can be severed).
240 See 13.6.3(c).

and to the contractor's craft and equipment". This access can only be refused on reasonable grounds by the contractor (eg for safety reasons). The hirer will have more access to information about the structure, layout and operation of the vessel, so cl 3 also allows the contractor during its services to require advice from persons at ships' officer level.

The hirer has to provide sufficient officers who are "fully conversant with the cargo system and/or layout of the vessel" to be in attendance when reasonably requested by the contractor. The most obvious candidates might actually be the master and crew of the vessel itself, unless they are still traumatised by the wreck. Specific information about the ship should also be available from documents in the possession of the hirer, or to which it should have access. Under cl 5(d) the hirer has to use its "best endeavours" to provide the contractor with documents such as plans and drawings of the vessel, cargo manifests and stowage plans. This should be straightforward, although sometimes key documentation may have been destroyed when the ship was wrecked. The hirer may not necessarily be the registered owner, eg if it is a bareboat charterer,[241] so it may have to seek the documentation from the registered owner. The hirer also has to provide "such other information that the contractor may reasonably require". The information and documentation may actually reside with third parties such as classification societies, ship repair yards or even previous salvors, but the contractor is entitled to expect that the hirer will cooperate by seeking out the information and liaising these other companies. In this sense "best endeavours" requires doing more than what is generally reasonable, as it looks to the best that *this* hirer can do (eg using its influence and contacts).

One of the biggest practical problems faced by contractors is gaining information about the cargo and its properties. With bulk cargoes those properties should be apparent by using the description in the manifest and by contacting charterers or shippers, but there are real difficulties in finding out the actual contents of containers, particularly if dangerous goods have been misdescribed in bills of lading.[242] It may also be difficult to identify the owners of such cargo to obtain further information, eg where order bills have been issued and negotiated. The owners of the cargo would expect to contact the contracting carrier[243] after a wreck, but this may not necessarily be the hirer; eg the hirer might be the registered owner (liable under the WRC 2007), but the contracting carrier might well be a charterer.[244] Although cl 5(d) focuses on information available in relation to the ship, such as cargo manifests, the reference to "other information" is not restricted by this but by what the hirer can achieve by "best endeavours". This means that while the contractor may be making its own enquiries, it is entitled to expect that the hirer will also cooperate in making enquiries with parties with whom it has some relationship—whether directly by contract or through a chain of sub-contracts.

As with SCOPIC operations, the shipowner and insurer will want as much information as possible about how the operations are progressing, in part so that they can monitor costs and delays in a contract that puts the underlying risk of such delays on the hirer.[245] Clause 2

---

241 See 2.1.7(a) for the bareboat charterer's liability to the shipowner for the consequences of wreck.
242 See eg the *Rena* and 1.2.(b) and (c), 1.3.2.
243 See 2.1.3(a), 2.1.5(a).
244 See also 2.1.7.
245 See 13.6.3(d).

requires the contractor to supply to the hirer a daily report in the form set out in Annex II. This includes specific boxes for: the vessel, cargo, bunkers and wreck site; the status of the wreck;[246] the weather on location (and forecasts for the next 24 hours and next five days); the services undertaken in the previous 24 hours and those planned for the next 24 hours. There are also extensive boxes detailing the vessels, equipment and personnel and whether they are on hire; on a standby rate; on a reduced rate; off hire; or demobilised, inoperative, damaged or injured. There is a specific box for "areas of concern", dealing separately with health and safety, "environmental" and "other". There are spaces for comments by the contractor's representative and hirer's representative. These might be particularly significant evidentially if there is a dispute about changes and delays under cll 4 and 7 and whether any extra costs are justified under cl 13.

A number of provisions of the contract require notices to be given to the other party in writing.[247] The written requirement assists both clarification and the maintenance of a record (along with the daily reports). In relation to expert evaluation they are an important part of the strict timetable.[248] Clause 22 provides generally how and to whom these notices are to be served. The notices can be delivered in a variety of ways including electronically (if in writing), but unless otherwise agreed, the addresses will be those set out in Boxes 2 and 3. It is therefore important that email addresses are recorded fully in these boxes. It seems unlikely that important messages would be sent by text, but in theory they could be if a mobile phone number was given in Boxes 2 or 3. Debates about when notices are "received" are resolved by cl 22(b) which deems receipt in three circumstances: on the seventh day after a letter is proved to have been posted; on the day of proved transmission, if sent by facsimile or electronically; on the day of proved delivery, if delivered by hand.

13.6.3(k) Arbitration, mediation and expert evaluation

As is normal in commercial contracts there is an arbitration and law clause and, like Towcon 2008 and Towhire 2008, a mediation option. Clause 21 gives the parties three choices: first, under cl 21(a), English law and London arbitration;[249] secondly, under cl 21(b), US maritime law and New York arbitration; thirdly, under cl 21(c), law and arbitration at another place as agreed. The choices are meant to be indicated in Box 15, but cl 21(e) provides that if that box is not "appropriately filled in" the default position is to apply the English option in cl 21(a). Presumably Box 15 will not be appropriately filled in if it is left blank or leaves a reasonable doubt as to which of the choices have been made (especially in respect of cl 21(c)). Unlike the arbitration provisions in the towage contracts, such as Towhire 2008 cl 31(a), Wreckhire cl 21(a) provides for a single arbitrator chosen from the Lloyd's panel of arbitrators and with an appeal to a Lloyd's Appeal arbitrator. Suits in other fora are prohibited, although provisional remedies to obtain security are allowed. Where the claims are up to US$50,000 the arbitration will take place under the LMAA Small

---

246 It is not entirely clear how this relates to the other separate boxes about vessel, cargo and bunkers, unless they are used merely for identification purposes. The status of wreck box presumably refers to general matters such as whether it is stranded, sunk, having bunkers or cargo removed, being prepared for raising, in the process of being raised, being stabilised after raising, being removed from the wreck site for disposal.
247 See eg cll 4(a), 8(a), 10(f); cf the 'request' in cl 15, 13.6.3(b).
248 See cl 21(d) and 13.6.3(k).
249 The analysis in this chapter has assumed that English law will apply.

Claims Procedure, and claims from US$50,000 to up to US$400,000 will be dealt with under the LMAA Intermediate Claims Procedure.

In any event, the parties will be able to opt for mediation under cl 21(d). This follows the pattern of the BIMCO Dispute Resolution clause used in, eg Towhire 2008, and is triggered by one party serving a "Mediation Notice". Participation is voluntary although there is a potential sanction for costs available to the arbitration Tribunal if mediation might have been more efficient. Otherwise, the mediation process is confidential and conversations and information provided on a 'without prejudice' basis so that they would not be disclosed to the arbitrator (unless disclosable under the arbitration process). The parties are reminded by cl 21(e) that the Mediation Notice does not act as bringing suit to stop time running within the time bar provision.[250]

What is more novel in Wreckhire 2010 is cl 20 providing for "expert evaluation". This is intimately related to the potentially contentious risk allocation exercise as to costs, rates and time lost in cll 4 and 7.[251] Indeed, the very uncertainties inherent in these two provisions led to cl 20. Unlike arbitration, the expert evaluation process is meant to take place relatively quickly while the wreck removal operations are continuing and is one involving technical experts and not lawyers. Either party can request expert evaluation and cl 20 then sets out the process and strict time limits that must follow. The party requesting such evaluation has to nominate, in writing to the other party, three experts from the Lloyd's Panel of SCRs established under the SCOPIC regime,[252] and must check that they are willing and available.[253] The other party has 24 hours to select one of these, and the requester then has 12 hours to appoint that person. If no-one was selected the requester can make the choice. Given that notices can be served in a variety of ways, including electronically,[254] it might be advisable for parties to specify that the expert evaluation notices should be sent to more than one address. The parties then have 48 hours to provide short written statements to the Expert, with copies to the other party. The Expert then has 72 hours to notify the parties of any alteration to costs and/or rates,[255] or the adjustment to the daily working rate or time lost,[256] along with providing "short reasons" for the evaluation.

It is not known how this new procedure is working, but it puts great time pressures on all parties, particularly the Expert who may also have a sensitive commercial position as a person regularly used in salvage and wreck removal operations by both parties. The effect of the evaluation, though, is to provide an immediate but not permanent ruling. If the parties agree, they will give effect to any alterations and adjustments. If one party disagrees with the evaluation, the hirer must still give immediate effect to it, but this is only provisional in the sense that cl 20(b) makes it without prejudice to the right to raise the issue again for final determination under cl 21, eg at arbitration.

---

250 Clause 19: see 13.6.3(g).
251 See 13.6.3(d) and (e).
252 See 12.3.2.
253 Clause 20(iv) sets out the rate of remuneration as being that for a SCOPIC salvage master (plus bonus). The requester pays the fee upfront but can claim back 50% from the other party (win or lose).
254 See 13.6.3(J).
255 See cl 4: 13.6.3(d).
256 See cl 7: 13.6.3(e).

The evaluation process is therefore a device in Wreckhire 2010 to prevent the inherent uncertainty about risk allocation and costs from halting the whole operation. But it does not remove the uncertainty and the concerns of the Clubs, in particular, about how the risks are allocated. This is the context for the shipowner or Club to seek to have cll 4 and 7 deleted or heavily amended in order to give effect to QRA principles,[257] or to insist that the parties use one of the other two BIMCO wreck removal forms.

13.6.4 Wreckfixed 2010: overview and risk allocation

13.6.4(a) Introduction and comparison with Wreckhire 2010

Wreckfixed 2010[258] is subtitled "International Wreck Removal and Marine Services Agreement Fixed Price—'No Cure, No Pay'". It follows the form of Wreckhire 2010 in most ways, eg with the Part I box format (albeit with fewer boxes), 22 clauses in Part II (four fewer than Wreckhire 2010) and the same three Annexes. Most of the clauses are identical, or practically identical, although the numbering of some is different.[259]

Thus, there is the same basic allocation of obligations eg to: exercise due care;[260] provide the personnel, craft or equipment set out in Annex I;[261] provide a method of work (Annex II);[262] rotate personnel and equipment;[263] mark the vessel, allow for the use of the vessel's machinery etc, dispose of cargo and make available plans and drawings;[264] obtain permits;[265] and provide security for payment.[266] The knock for knock clause is almost identical,[267] as are other liability provisions[268] and those for dispute resolution.[269] Other clauses are similar to those in Wreckhire 2010, but with key alterations.[270] It is not proposed here to repeat the equivalent analysis already made in respect of Wreckhire 2010, but to highlight

---

257 See 13.4.2.
258 For a facsimile of the form, see Appendix 8. Brief clause by clause Explanatory Notes are also available on the BIMCO website: www.bimco.org. For an authoritative clause by clause analysis, see *Rainey*, Chapter 10.
259 See eg general provisions such as Wreckfixed 2010 cl 1 (definitions) that is the equivalent of Wreckhire 2010 cl 1; Wreckfixed 2010 cl 18 (Notices) is equivalent to Wreckhire 2010 cl 22; Wreckfixed 2010 cl 22 (General Provisions) is equivalent to Wreckhire 2010 cl 26.
260 Wreckfixed 2010 cl 2 (Services) para 1 is equivalent to Wreckhire 2010 cl 2 para 1.
261 Wreckfixed 2010 cl 2 para 3 is equivalent to Wreckhire 2010 cl 2 para 2.
262 Wreckfixed 2010 cl 2 para 4 is equivalent to Wreckhire 2010 cl 2 para 3.
263 Wreckfixed 2010 cl 21 (Rotation) is equivalent to Wreckhire 2010 cl 25.
264 Wreckfixed 2010 cl 5 (Miscellaneous) is equivalent to Wreckhire 2010 cl 5.
265 Wreckfixed 2010 cl 6 (Permits) is equivalent to Wreckhire 2010 cl 6.
266 Wreckfixed 2010 cl 11 (Security) is equivalent to Wreckhire 2010 cl 15.
267 Wreckfixed 2010 cl 12 (Liabilities) is equivalent to Wreckhire 2010 cl 16. Note that Wreckfixed 2010 cl 12(c) line 169 is slightly different in that the hirer is liable for the contractor's portable salvage equipment, materials or stores that are "reasonably sacrificed during the disposal or other operations of the vessel".
268 Wreckfixed 2010 cl 13 (Himalaya clause) is equivalent to Wreckhire 2010 cl 17; Wreckfixed 2010 cl 14 (Lien) is equivalent to Wreckhire 2010 cl 18; Wreckfixed 2010 cl 15 (Time for suit) is equivalent to Wreckhire 2010 cl 19; Wreckfixed 2010 cl 19 (Insurance) is equivalent to Wreckhire 2010 cl 23; Wreckfixed 2010 cl 20 (Pollution) is equivalent to Wreckhire 2010 cl 24.
269 Wreckfixed 2010 cl 16 (Expert evaluation) is equivalent to Wreckhire 2010 cl 20; Wreckfixed 2010 cl 17 (Arbitration and Mediation) is equivalent to Wreckhire 2010 cl 21.
270 In particular, see cl 4 (Changes of Methods), see 13.6.4(c); cl 7 (Termination), see 13.6.4(d); cl 8 (Delivery and disposal), see 13.6.4(e); cl 2 (Services), new second para, and cl 9 (Payment), see 13.6.4(b).

the differences—especially in relation to risk allocation.[271] In general, Wreckfixed 2010 presents a significant risk transfer to contractors and it is not clear how often it is used.

13.6.4(b) Price and risk

The main difference between the contracts is that Wreckfixed 2010 provides in cl 9(a) for a single overall price, fixed in advance and set out in Box 9.[272] By contrast with Wreckhire 2010, it therefore transfers more of the underlying financial risks to the contractor, who has to be sure that its quote is sufficiently comprehensive (and large enough in amount). This means that the hirer has no need for provisions such as cl 7(b) and (c) of Wreckhire 2010 which call for reductions in payments when there are delays caused by breakdowns in the equipment or personnel; these are merely risks that are now subsumed in the overall price. Indeed, Wreckfixed 2010 has no equivalent at all for Wreckhire 2010 cl 7 delay previsions. It is inherent in the idea of a fixed price that adverse events such as bad weather, or sea conditions, or other factors beyond the contractor's control will be at its risk. One consequence of the deletion of cl 7 is that the "company representative" might no longer need to be available to agree so many adjustments, so cl 2 of Wreckfixed 2010 only requires that availability "if reasonably requested by the contractor".[273]

Using the wording of the LOF (and salvage agreements), cl 2 provides that the "services shall be rendered under the principle of no cure, no pay". This means that under the payment clause, cl 9(a), there will be no payment at all unless and until "completion" of the services (described in Box 7 and again defined in an Annex II). The delivery and disposal clause, cl 8 of Wreckfixed 2010, accordingly has some new provisions dealing with extra costs if delivery is not possible including putting some new risks on the contractor when there is government interference with delivery.[274] Given that all of the price is payable right at the end it is particularly important for the contractor that it is able to call on an unconditional and irrevocable security for payment. This is required by cl 11 of Wreckfixed 2010.[275]

In Wreckfixed 2010 the list of specified "Extra Costs" in cl 10 is now for the *contractor* to bear, rather than the hirer as in Wreckhire 2010.[276] These costs are not really "extra" at all since they are included in the price, but cl 10 presumably lists them to provide certainty. They include port expenses; costs of customs clearance; agency fees; taxes and customs duties; licensing costs (eg to obtain approvals or permits to work); costs arising from the requirements of governments or unions, costs of hiring assisting tugs. Clause 10 does not include any reference at all to a number of cost items that were referred to in the Wreckhire 2010 equivalent clause,[277] namely costs of transporting equipment listed in the Annex I Schedule, costs or travel and accommodation for personnel listed in Annex I, and bunkers

---

271 Wreckfixed 2010 is not a contract of hire in the same way as Wreckhire 2010, but for consistency the "Company" (named in Box 3) that enters the contract with the contractor will continue to be referred to as the "hirer" (here of services).

272 The other payment obligations in cl 9 are the same as in Wreckhire cl 10; eg monies are payable without discount (cl 9(b)), invoices are to be issued promptly (cl 9(e)). The termination provisions are also the same: see 13.6.4(d).

273 Cf Wreckhire 2010 c 2: 13.6.3(e).

274 See 13.6.4(e).

275 Equivalent to Wreckhire 2010 cl 15: see 13.6.3(b).

276 Cf Wreckhire 2010 cl 13: 13.6.3(b).

277 Wreckhire 2010 cl 13(g)–(i): see 13.6.3(b).

and lubricants.[278] The reason is that these costs would now naturally fall on the contractor and be within the fixed price. Whether the contractor is liable for waste disposal costs[279] may depend upon the agreed method of work, or whether there has been a change in the condition of the vessel (including its cargo).[280]

13.6.4(c) Changes in services, personnel, craft or equipment
However, the price is not quite 'fixed' for all circumstances. As in Wreckhire 2010,[281] cl 4 of Wreckfixed 2010 also recognises that there may need to be changes to the services originally agreed in the contract, and that these changes should be reflected financially—to benefit both parties. The contractor has to consult with the hirer if there is any need for a "substantial" change in methods of work (in Annex II) or the personnel, craft or equipment (in Annex I).[282] An additional provision in Wreckfixed 2010 cl 2 deals with what happens if there is not sufficient time to have a consultation, or agreement to changes is unreasonably withheld by the hirer. Here, the contractor is entitled to proceed with the changes, subject to approval by any State authorities. This reflects the fact that delays are at the risk of the contractor, and the only real issue is one of whether it is entitled to any extra payments. Although it will be monitoring operations, the hirer is perhaps less concerned about the detailed methods being used than in Wreckhire 2010, as it has entrusted the contractor to complete the agreed service.[283]

Under cl 4(a) the need for changes to methods or personnel, craft or equipment must again arise through (i) misdescription by the hirer, or an error in the specification it supplied, or (ii) a material change in the condition of the casualty, and these changes might involve extra costs. In these circumstances, provided that the changes are "substantial", the contractor has to give notice of the estimated extra costs involved. If agreement is reached the changes (ie what the contractor now has to do that is different) have to be drafted into a variation order signed by both parties. The parties must also consult in order to try to reach agreement about the additional costs to give effect to the agreed changes. Wreckfixed 2010 cl 4(a)(iii) differs from its equivalent in Wreckhire 2010 cl 4(a)(iii) by adding six further lines giving rights to terminate if agreement cannot be reached on the additional costs within five days. Under Wreckfixed 2010 cl 4(a)(iii) either party can "terminate the services"[284] if allowed by State authorities. If the authorities do allow termination, the contractor's right to extra costs is not lost, but will have to be settled later, eg by mediation or

---

278 The equivalent costs of the crew of any craft in Annex I Schedule, such as tugs, would not be allowable as extras.
279 See 14.6.4(a), 13.6.3(b) and 14.6.5(d).
280 See 13.6.4(c).
281 Wreckhire 2010 cl 4: see 13.6.3(d).
282 See cl 2.
283 This is also reflected in the reduced powers of termination under cl 7 (see 13.6.4(d)) and the deletion (for Wreckfixed 2010 cl 3) of Wreckhire 2010 cl 3, para 1, requiring methods and procedures at all times to be discussed and agreed between hirer and contractor.
284 This expression may be contrasted with the rights given in cl 7 to "terminate the Agreement": see 13.6.4(d). It is not clear that any difference is intended. Strictly, rights of termination relate to continued performance, rather than an end to the contract (which does not cease to exist, eg in relation to arbitration and other clauses that may be intended to continue).

arbitration.[285] If the authorities do not allow termination (eg demobilisation) the contractor is obliged to continue with the services as set out in Box 7, but again preserving its right to claim for the extra costs. Where the changed circumstances result in reduced costs, cl 4(b)[286] allows the hirer to seek an equivalent deduction in the costs to be deducted from the fixed price. The parties can again elect to have the reasonableness or quantum of costs resolved provisionally by expert evaluation (and ultimately by mediation or arbitration)[287] but in the meantime the contractor is obliged to continue with the services.

It is apparent that cl 4 requires very close attention to the initial specifications and their relationship to events that might be unpredictable. All this means that the apparent certainty of price in the contract may well be illusory and there is much scope for disagreement. It is for such reasons that the shipowner or Club may well seek to have cl 4 deleted or heavily amended in order to give effect to QRA principles.[288]

13.6.4(d) Termination
The termination provisions in Wreckfixed 2010 have some similarities with Wreckhire 2010. Wreckfixed 2010 cl 9(d)[289] also gives the contractor the right of to terminate the contract if any amounts payable under the contract have not been paid within seven days of the due date, or if the security required under cl 11 has not been paid. Clause 7 is headed "Termination" and does not contain any right of the hirer to suspend the services".[290] This is because the hirer no longer bear the risks of most delays and difficulties. The hirer is given the right by cl 7(a) to terminate the contract, but this right is only exercisable "at any time prior to commencement of mobilisation" of personnel, craft or equipment (whichever occurs first). Even here, the contractor would have incurred preparation costs, but under the no cure no pay principle would not be entitled to any payment. For that reason, cl 7(a) provides that the hirer has to pay a pre-agreed cancellation fee as set out in Box 12.

Given that the financial risk of completing the service is now on the contractor, there is a need to deal with force majeure events, as under Wreckhire 2010 where the hirer has a relatively wide right to terminate if the operation becomes too difficult (and expensive). To some extent this is dealt with in cl 4 where there are substantial changes in the method of work, but there may be circumstances where the services are changed and the hirer agrees to pay the extra costs under cl 4. Then, the contractor has no right to terminate under cl 4(a)(iii) and must continue to work unless it can show that the services (even as changed under cl 4) have become "technically or physically impossible" within cl 7(b). In those limited circumstances the contractor may terminate the contract without further liability.

Even here, the right is not unfettered as the agreement of the hirer is necessary, although it must not be unreasonably withheld. But that consent only becomes necessary if the contractor can fit its situation into the "technically or physically impossible" criteria. The limited nature of the wording emphasises that termination will not be allowed when the services become merely financially difficult for the contractor. Taken literally, even financial

---

285 Under cl 17, identical to cl 21 of Wreckhire 2010: see 13.6.3(k).
286 Practically identical to cl 4(b) of Wreckhire 2010: see 13.6.3(d).
287 Again, under cl 17, identical to cl 21 of Wreckhire 2010: see 13.6.3(k).
288 See 13.6.2(b).
289 Cf the identical provision in Wreckhire 2010 cl 10(f): 13.6.3(f).
290 Cf Wreckhire 2010 cl 8(a): 13.6.3(f).

impossibility would not be enough, eg if the contractor was unable to maintain operations owing to the ever-increasing costs, because of the *expressio unius est exclusio alterius* principle. Although frustration can still apply where there are express force majeure provisions, it would be difficult to envisage too many situations where frustration could still be argued in the light of cl 7(b). An obvious example might be where the services could be completed, but only at great danger to the contractor's personnel or craft eg because of war, civil unrest, or the political opposition of a State. This situation, though, is largely dealt with in cl 8(b) and the contractor is not allowed to terminate, but must take the wreck to another place, during which time it may be entitled to extra costs under cl 8(a), third paragraph.

It may be unlikely that a hirer would want to drive a contractor to insolvency, as it may then have even more problems for itself in finding other contractors. If the hirer did agree to pay more than it was obliged to do under the contract, it might find that it could not object on the basis that there was no consideration for a promise of extra payment,[291] but may still be able later to plead economic duress.[292]

13.6.4(e) Wreck delivery and disposal

Clause 8 of Wreckfixed 2010 is the equivalent of cl 9 of Wreckhire 2010,[293] and broadly covers the same ground, but has a number of additional provisions. These are needed because, as the contractor's remuneration is on a "no cure no pay" basis, it is particularly vital to decide what is to happen if there are problems with completing the services.

As in Wreckhire 2010, the parties to Wreckfixed 2010 can elect to have the vessel accepted at a "Place of delivery" or a "Place of Disposal" and the hirer is again obliged to accept "forthwith". It also undertakes that the agreed place of delivery or disposal will be safe and accessible for the vessel, the contractor's craft and hired-in craft; and that the place is one where the contractor will be permitted by government or other authorities to deliver or dispose of the wreck. The moment of handover could present risks where the contactor has been keeping the wrecked vessel afloat by using its own pumps, compressors or other equipment. Under Wreckfixed 2010 the contractor might be entitled to leave on completion of the service, so cl 8(c) of Wreckfixed 2010 provides that the hirer must use all due despatch to arrange for its own replacement equipment and in the meantime shall pay the contractor reasonable rates for the continued use of its own equipment as well as any additional costs.

Wreckfixed 2010 cl 8 particularly differs from cl 9 of Wreckhire 2010 when the vessel is not accepted by the hirer forthwith. Here the hirer has to bear "all costs incurred[294] by the contractor from the moment of tender for delivery". These would presumably include the sort of costs which would have been charged under Wreckhire 2010 for craft, equipment and personnel as well as additional costs such as obtaining of permits etc.[295] At this point

---

291 On the basis that it had gained a practical benefit, or obviated a disbenefit: see *Williams v Roffey Bros & Nicholls (Contractors) Ltd* [1989] EWCA Civ 5 [1991] 1 QB 1.

292 See *Universe Tankships of Monrovia v International Transport Workers Federation* [1983] 1 AC 366.

293 See 13.6.3(i).

294 This contrasts with "all costs *necessarily* incurred" in cl 9 of Wreckhire 2010. The difference may not make much difference in practice, but should make any burden of proof on the contractor much easier.

295 Ie the more extensive list in cl 13 of Wreckhire 2010 (see 13.6.3(b)), by comparison with the more restricted list in Wreckfixed 2010 cl10 (see 13.6.4(b)). Note that cl 8(d) repeats the remedy given by Wreckhire 2010 cl 8(b), namely that the contractor can sell the vessel (and cargo) if it is not accepted by the hirer: cf 13.6.3(i).

cl 8(a) para 3 separates out the problem of government interference. It provides that if delivery is prevented or delayed by government or other authorities, all costs "necessarily incurred" by the contractor from the tender for delivery shall be for its own account.[296] That is, this forms part of the risks that the contractor undertook in the fixed price contract, even when the government action is completely outside its control. Where there is delay, only, this result is consistent with the treatment of delay generally in Wreckfixed 2010; ie it is normally a contractor's risk. If the delay appears to be prolonged, the financial risk to the contractor is great because it is not being paid any more. Clause 8 gives no clue as to how long the contractor would have to wait. It could only terminate under cl 7(b) if completion becomes technically or physically impossible.[297] That may be difficult to prove in the delay scenario.

Clause 8(b) does give the contractor a possible alternative[298] where "it is considered by the contractor to be impossible or unsafe for the vessel to be delivered or disposed of at the place indicated in Box 6". In those circumstances there are two alternatives. The first is that the hirer nominates an alternative place acceptable to the contractor. If it is unable to do so, the second alternative is that the contractor is "at liberty to deliver or dispose of the vessel[299] at the nearest place it can reach safely and without unreasonable delay". Again, this is dependent upon that delivery or disposable being permitted by the authorities in that new place. If they do, then then cl 8(b) acknowledges that this would be due fulfilment of the contract, allowing the contractor to claim its fixed fee.[300] This option is potentially a useful way for the contractor to avoid indefinitely being stuck with the vessel, although it has to overcome the hurdle of satisfying the impossible or unsafe criteria; also, a wreck that is not wanted by one government is hardly likely to be attractive to another.

Even if it not impossible or unsafe to deliver or dispose of the vessel at the place in Box 8, the hirer may still fail to take delivery—even though the contractor has done all it could to complete the services. Wreckfixed 2010 cl 8(d) therefore adopts the same solution as Wreckhire 2010 cl 9(b),[301] and this will apply if either (i) delivery is not taken within five days of a formal written notice of delivery being tendered to the hirer, or (ii) the contractor forms the opinion that the vessel is "likely to deteriorate, decay, become worthless or incur charges whether for storage or otherwise in excess of its value". In these circumstances cl 8(d) allows the contractor to sell or dispose of the vessel—without notice or any liability

---

296 It is not clear what "necessarily" adds here as if the costs were unnecessarily incurred they would still be for the contractor's account. This may be an accidental incident of splitting up the third sentence of Wreckhire 2010 cl 9(a), when the costs fell on the hirer, or from using the same words in cl 9(a) para 3 of Wreckstage 2010 where the costs are for the account of the hirer: see 13.6.3(i), 13.6.5.(g).

297 See 13.6.4(d).

298 This alternative is not restricted to government action, although it is convenient to mention it in that context. It could also apply where the delivery was impossible or unsafe for other reasons, eg navigational (where there is not the expected draft to allow the wreck convoy to pass).

299 Including its cargo by virtue of the definition in cl 1. See also cl 8(e) allowing delivery of parts of the vessel and eg cargo at different times and places.

300 But there is no provision for any extra payment or expenses, unlike Wreckstage 2010 cl 9(b) para 2, see 13.6.5(g).

301 See 13.6.3(i).

whatsoever.[302] The hirer still remains liable for any shortfall, if there are not enough funds to pay monies due to the contractor.

Another consequence of the fixed price in Wreckfixed 2010 is that there is no need to provide for extra costs of disposal, as in Wreckhire 2010 cl 14. This provision does not appear in Wreckfixed 2010, so if the place of disposal is agreed in Box 8 the contractor will bear the costs of completing the service, including any ancillary costs relating to disposal.

13.6.5 Wreckstage 2010: overview and risk allocation

13.6.5(a) Introduction and comparison with other forms

Wreckstage 2010[303] is similar to Wreckfixed 2010 in that it provides for a single overall fixed price, although it is not subject to the no cure no pay principle. Instead, the form allows for the parties to divide up the overall lump sum into separate payments to be made at key stages in the anticipated operation.[304] It retains a version of cl 4 (change of method)[305] that is similar to both the other forms, but also a cl 7 (delays)[306] that is largely similar to Wreckhire 2010 cl 7. The responsibility for extra costs in Wreckstage 2010 cl 11[307] uses the list in Wreckhire 2010 cl 13, but leaves responsibility for payment open to be decided by the parties[308] at the time of contracting. The termination provisions in cl 8[309] are found also in Wreckhire 2010 cl 8 and Wreckfixed 2010 cl 7. Issues about delivery and disposal in Wreckstage 2010 cl 9[310] are resolved by using elements found both in Wreckhire 2010 cl 9 and Wreckfixed 2010 cl 8.

Other clauses in Wreckstage 2010 are identical or practically identical to those in the other two forms. Thus, there is the same basic allocation of obligations eg to: exercise due care;[311] provide the personnel, craft or equipment set out in Annex I;[312] provide a method of work (Annex II);[313] rotate personnel and equipment;[314] mark the vessel, allow for the use of the vessel's machinery etc, dispose of cargo and make available plans and drawings;[315]

---

302 For the equivalent provision see Wreckhire 2010 cl 9(b): see 13.6.3(i).
303 For a facsimile of the form, see Appendix 9. Brief clause by clause Explanatory Notes are available on the BIMCO website: www.bimco.org. These provide some background as to why particular provisions were adopted or changed, so for the convenience of readers these are reproduced in Appendix 10. For an authoritative clause by clause analysis, see *Rainey*, Chapter 10.
304 See 13.6.5(b).
305 See 13.6.5(d).
306 See 13.6.5(e).
307 See 13.6.5(f).
308 Again, for convenience the expression 'hirer' will be used to refer to the hiring company (not the contractor company).
309 See 13.6.5(f).
310 See 13.6.5(g).
311 Wreckstage 2010 cl 2 (Services) para 1 is equivalent to Wreckhire 2010 cl 2 para 1; and see 13.6.3(a).
312 Wreckstage 2010 cl 2 para 2 is equivalent to Wreckhire 2010 cl 2 para 2; and see 13.6.3(a).
313 Wreckstage 2010 cl 2 para 3 is equivalent to Wreckhire 2010 cl 2 para 3; and see 13.6.3(a).
314 Wreckstage 2010 cl 22 (Rotation) is equivalent to Wreckhire 2010 cl 25; and see 13.6.3(a).
315 Wreckstage 2010 cl 5 (Miscellaneous) is equivalent to Wreckhire 2010 cl 5; and see 13.6.3(a).

obtain permits;[316] and provide security for payment.[317] The knock for knock clause is almost identical,[318] as are other liability provisions[319] and those for dispute resolution.[320]

For convenience, BIMCO's Explanatory Notes to Wreckstage 2010 are included below,[321] partly to help understand why changes were made to Wreckstage 99.

In some ways Wreckstage 2010 sits between Wreckhire 2010 (which has more uncertainty and risk for the hirer[322]) and Wreckfixed 2010 (which imposes more risks on the contractor). It is understood that Wreckstage 2010 has apparently become the industry standard, and often required in tenders. Economists may debate as to which of these three contracts will produce the most efficient result in cost terms. Wreckhire 2010 might encourage a contractor to underquote, knowing that if there are difficulties which makes the job slightly longer then it will still get paid, while if there are substantial changes, then it could ask for a variation in the contract under cl 4. By contrast, a contractor forced to use Wreckfixed 2010 might feel obliged to quote a very high price in order to cover contingencies that might never happen. That is part of the inherent gamble in no cure no pay contracts (with which most contractors will be familiar from salvage work) and upon which they stake their professional expertise and reputation. From the perspective of the shipowner (and Club), Wreckfixed 2010 at least has the advantage of providing clear cost parameters that can be reported back to Club Boards and to reinsurers. In theory it removes the underlying fear of a job where the costs rack up seemingly indefinitely. Of course, the shipowner (and indirectly) the Club will have to bear the risk of insolvency of the contractor. Wreckstage 2010 therefore may provide a more balanced result as it provides a fixed (but staged) price, allows flexibility about extra costs, but (from the contractor's perspective) makes allowance for changes and delays.

In the end the parties may choose to create a contract that is based on one of these three forms, but is heavily amended, eg by taking Wreckhire 2010 but deleting or heavily amending cll 4 and 7, or Wreckfixed 2010 but with cl 4 deleted or altered. Wreckfixed might be more suitable for smallish, relatively straightforward, wreck removals where the contractor has confidence in its ability to estimate risk and price accordingly. Even here, it might seek to have an element of Wreckstage 2010, eg by having a percentage of the fee payable at the stage when cutting chains are attached, and another when the wreck is alongside at the nominated port of delivery. The multiple differences in risk allocation between the three

---

316 Wreckstage 2010 cl 6 (Permits) is equivalent to Wreckhire 2010 cl 6; and 13.6.3(a).

317 Wreckstage 2010 cl 12 (Security) is equivalent to Wreckhire 2010 cl 15; and see 13.6.3(b).

318 Wreckstage 2010 cl 13 (Liabilities) is equivalent to Wreckhire 2010 cl 16; and see 13.6.3(g). Note that like Wreckfixed cl 12(c), Wreckstage 2010 cl 13(c) lines 230–232 are slightly different in that the hirer is liable for the contractor's portable salvage equipment, materials or stores that are "reasonably sacrificed during the disposal or other operations of the vessel". But Wreckstage then adds "unless the contractor is the party responsible for such costs as indicated in Box 12(i)": see 13.6.5(c).

319 Wreckstage 2010 cl 14 (Himalaya clause) is equivalent to Wreckhire 2010 cl 17; Wreckstage 2010 cl 15 (Lien) is equivalent to Wreckhire 2010 cl 18; Wreckstage 2010 cl 16 (Time for Suit) is equivalent to Wreckhire 2010 cl 19; Wreckstage 2010 cl 20 (Insurance) is equivalent to Wreckhire 2010 cl 23; Wreckstage 2010 cl 21 (Pollution) is equivalent to Wreckhire 2010 cl 24; and see 13.6.3(g).

320 Wreckstage 2010 cl 17 (Expert evaluation) is equivalent to Wreckhire 2010 cl 20; Wreckstage 2010 cl 18 (Arbitration and Mediation) is equivalent to Wreckhire 2010 cl 21; and see 13.6.3(k).

321 See Appendix 10.

322 As explained in 13.6.3(b), (d) and (e) in particular.

forms mean that the commercial parties (and any drafters) have to be acutely conscious of how small changes in wording may transfer significant risks. The point is that the standard contract forms, like the wreck removal operations themselves, have a dynamic nature and the final document needs to be looked at as a whole and reassessed for each particular wreck.

13.6.5(b) Payment stages

Under Wreckstage 2010 cl 10(a) the hirer agrees to pay the total lump sum set out in Box 9(i) in Part I of the contract, but cl 10(b) allows for instalments to be paid. These become fully and irrevocably earned at the moment they are due as described in sub-boxes of Box 9.[323] There are actually seven pre-printed boxes to allow for instalments at different stages, but there could obviously be more or fewer as the parties desire. Typically, there will be an amount payable on signing the agreement (see Box 9(ii)). Mobilisation of vessels and equipment might be another common stage (if this did not coincide with signing). Thereafter, there may be a variety of stages including eg: removal of bunkers; attachment of cutting chains; refloating of the wreck; towage to a disposal port; and final delivery or disposition. The more complex the operation, the more likely it is that there are more stages, especially where a considerable amount of work has to be done by the contractor to prepare the seabed or vessel for raising.[324]

The level and frequency of payments could vary greatly, and will be influenced by commercial factors, but the contractor would expect a significant upfront payment and staged payments to coincide with its major expenditure. The shipowner (and Club) would obviously prefer to have the payments more weighted to results, particularly the final removal of the wreck. An example of that would be 10% of the lump sum payable when all craft, equipment and personnel are on site, 10% when the wreck is raised and put on a barge for transport,[325] and the remaining 80% when delivered. Both parties to the contract will normally be highly experienced and able to estimate the likely costs as they will arise.

13.6.5(c) Extra costs

Although three is an agreed lump sum contract, and to that extent the price is fixed, Wreckstage 2010 cl 11 recognises that extra costs can arise and reproduces seven of the nine items on the list in Wreckhire 2010 cl 13.[326] They include:[327] port expenses; costs of hiring assisting tugs; costs of customs clearance and agency fees; taxes and customs duties; costs of licensing, approvals or permits; costs arising from the requirements of governments or unions; costs in respect of portable salvage equipment, materials or stores sacrificed by the

---

323 Cl 10(b) also provides that other monies, eg additional costs under cl 4 or extra costs under cl 11, are fully and irrevocably payable at a rate earned on a daily basis or pro rata: see also 13.6.5 (d) and (c). Late payment after invoice is subject to interest subject to the rate in Box 11: see cl 10(f).

324 Cf the *Costa Concordia*, 1.2.5(b).

325 See also 14.7.3.

326 See 13.6.3(b).

327 Not included in the Wreckstage 2010 cl 11 list are the cost of bunkers, lubricants and transporting equipment and personnel to the wreck site; these are all contractor costs in any event and covered in the lump sum price. The hirer is responsible under cl 2 for providing officers to be in attendance to advise on matters such as the cargo system and layout of the vessel: see also 13.6.3(j).

contractor.[328] Under Wreckhire 2010 these extra costs are borne by the hirer, while under Wreckfixed 2010 they have to be met by the contractor.[329] Wreckstage 2010 cl 11 leaves open the responsibility for paying for these individually itemised costs. At the time of contracting the parties have to decide who pays for what and then record the agreement in Box 12(i) or (ii). If the one party in fact pays for a particular item that is the other's responsibility then it is entitled to be reimbursed and a percentage handling charge is applied as agreed and set out in Box 12(iii).

The responsibility for extra costs as a result of changes to the work method, or as a result of delay, are dealt with in cll 4[330] and 7.[331] Whether the contractor is liable for waste disposal costs[332] may depend upon the agreed method of work, or whether there has been a change in the condition of the vessel (including its cargo).[333]

13.6.5(d) Changes in services, personnel, craft or equipment
Like its sister forms, Wreckstage 2010 also contains a cl 4 dealing with changes that arise, after the contract is signed, in the services, personnel, craft or equipment required to ensure performance of the contract. As already noted, the clause is often at the centre of risk allocation negotiations and is often deleted or amended. Still, it is necessary to understand its unamended meaning, despite the difficulties with the language.[334] Wreckstage 2010 cl 4 is very similar to the same provision in both Wreckhire 2010 and Wreckfixed 2010, but mostly resembles the latter.[335] First, under cl 2 the contractor has to consult with the hirer if the contractor considers that there is any need for a "substantial" change in methods of work (in Annex II) or the personnel, craft or equipment (in Annex I).[336] Secondly, the contractor has to show that, without its fault, there is such a "substantial" change[337] due to (i) misdescription by the hirer, or an error in the specification it supplied, relied on by the contractor, or (ii) a material change in the condition of the casualty.[338] Thirdly, the contractor has to give notice in writing to the hirer "forthwith" of the additional estimated costs. Fourthly, if the hirer and contractor agree that there are substantial changes in the "nature of the services"[339] the hirer must draft a written variation order, signed by both parties. Fifthly, if they have not already done so, the parties should consult each other to put a figure on the additional costs to be added to the lump sum in Box 9(i). Sixthly, if within five days they

---

328 Wreckstage 2010 cl 13(c) (knock for knock liabilities) would normally exclude all liability of the hirer to pay for loss of the contractor's equipment. But the exclusion in the sub-clause would only apply to its "portable salvage equipment, materials or stores" if the contractor was the party responsible for its costs under cl 11; if the hirer was responsible for the costs (in Box 12(ii)) then the hirer would pay for the sacrifice of these items.
329 See Wreckfixed 2010 cl 10, where the list is slightly shorter than in the other two forms: see 13.6.4(b).
330 See 13.6.5(d).
331 See 13.6.5(e).
332 See 14.6.4(a), 13.6.3(b) and 14.6.5(d).
333 See 13.6.5(d)
334 See 13.6.3(d).
335 Albeit there are particular changes in Wreckstage 2010 cl 4(a)(iii), lines 52–56.
336 If there is no time to consult, or if agreement to the proposed changes is unreasonably withheld, the contractor can proceed with the changes: see Wreckstage 2010 cl 2 para 4 lines 19–21, which appear also in Wreckfixed 2010 cl 2.
337 See 13.6.3(d) for a discussion of the implications of "fault", and the meaning of "substantial".
338 See the discussion in 13.6.3(d) on both of these conditions.
339 See 13.6.3(d) for a discussion of the difficulties of interpretation of this expression in cl 4(a)(ii).

cannot reach agreement on the amount of costs, either party is given the right to terminate the whole agreement; if they do so, it does not prejudice the contractor's claim which it can continue to pursue.

At this stage, the parties have to consider the effects of orders to prevent termination (and demobilisation) given by "competent authorities", eg States exercising intervention powers[340] or those arising under the WRC 2007 to require removal.[341] If permission *is* given by the authorities, Wreckstage 2010 cl 4(a)(iii) entitles the contractor to be paid all sums due to be paid.[342] If permission to terminate is *not* given by the authorities, Wreckstage 2010 cl 4(a)(iii) provides that the contractor must be paid by the hirer at a "delay payment rate" as set out in Box 13 during "any standby period". Presumably, the latter expression covers the position while the parties decide how to deal with the veto exercised by the authorities and when no wreck removal work is taking place as a result of the purported termination.

Wreckstage 2010 cl 4(a)(iii) line 55 then continues by adding that the hirer is liable for the contractor's "reasonable and necessary costs of continuing with the services". It is not entirely clear what this means. It could mean that, during the standby period, the contractor could claim for any extra costs in addition to the delay payment rate, but that sits uneasily with the words "continuing with the services". They suggest that the parties have, in effect, accepted that termination cannot happen and that they will have to continue with wreck removal.[343] But, given that there is a fixed price contract, it is difficult to see why the contractor should be able to claim additional costs for continuing with the basic services. The best interpretation is probably that it is entitled to those extra costs that have arisen as a result of the standby, eg if craft and personnel that had been demobilised have to be remobilised and repositioned.

13.6.5(e) Delay

Although Wreckstage 2010 is a fixed price contract, cl 7(a) follows the pattern of Wreckhire 2010 cl 7 by making an allowance in the contractor's favour in the event of adverse weather, heavy seas or any other reason outside the contractor's control. It does so in a slightly different way. Where it is adverse weather or sea conditions that prevent the contractor from progressing the services, there is a minimum number of "unworkable days" as set out in Box 15 before the contractor may claim any extra payment. This *de minimis* provision enables the hirer to prevent the contractor from amassing many small weather breaks in a contract whose fixed price nature essentially puts such weather risks on the contractor. To reflect this, the hirer may prefer to set the Box 15 figure at quite a high percentage of the estimated contract performance time set out in Annex II. Where the delay is from other reasons outside the contractor's control there is no such minimum threshold. Where the contractor can show a delay satisfying the above criteria it is entitled to additional compensation at the "delay payment rate" agreed in Box 13. This may be calculated per working day (or pro rata of such a day) for the time that the contractor is delayed

---

340 See 4.2.3, 5.3; also for SCOPIC, see 12.3.4(c).

341 See 9.2.5; also 10.2.5 for issues arising where States require full and not partial removal.

342 Eg instalments in Box 9(i) (see 13.6.5(b)); extra costs in Box 12 (see 13.6.5(c)); delay payments in Box 13 (see 13.6.5(e); cancellation fee in Box 14 (see 13.6.5(f)).

343 Cf Wreckfixed 2010 cl 4(a)(iii) lines 48–50 where, if termination permission is refused, "the contractor will continue to provide the services . . . without prejudice to his [*sic*] claim for additional remuneration".

in commencing or continuing the services. There is obviously scope for differences both about whether the external factors did prevent the contractor from progressing and as to the time lost thereby.[344]

If there is a breakdown of the contractor's equipment (or non-availability of its personnel), cl 7(b) requires the contractor to consult with the hirer[345] so as to agree on the amount of time lost, if any. The delay payment rate in Box 13 will apply to that agreed period; ie the contractor will be entitled to an extra payment, despite an apparent breach.[346] In order to achieve back to back coverage, the contractor is required by cl 7(c) to use "best efforts" to arrange similar delay payment rates for breakdown of the equipment or non-availability of personnel of any sub-contractors that it has used. Again, there is an obligation to consult with the hirer as to any time lost. It seems that the aim is to allow the contractor to claim from the hirer at the delay payment rate if there is a back to back agreement with the sub-contractor. If the sub-contract contains terms that are more favourable to the contractor (ie if there is a total off-hire clause), the contractor is obliged to pass on any benefit to the hirer.[347] Both cl 7(b) and (c) fail to mention the breakdown of "craft", as opposed to equipment, and this may be an omission.[348] Clause 7(e) provides that cl 7(b) and (c) do not apply to individual delays unless they exceed six consecutive hours; then the delay payment rate will apply to the whole agreed delay period.

By contrast with Wreckhire 2010 cl 7(d), Wreckstage 2010 cl 7(d) requires the *contractor* promptly to advise the hirer (and to confirm in writing) of all periods when it considers that the delay payment rate will apply.[349] In the absence of agreement as to the various reductions and time lost under cl 7 (a), (b) or (c), the issues may have to be resolved provisionally by expert evaluation (and ultimately by mediation or arbitration).[350]

13.6.5(f) Termination

The termination provisions in Wreckstage 2010 are similar to both Wreckfixed 2010 and Wreckhire 2010. Wreckstage 2010 cl 10(e)[351] also gives the contractor the right to terminate the contract if any amounts payable under the contract (eg instalments) have not been paid within seven days of the due date, or if the security required under cl 12 has not been paid. Clause 4(a)(iii) also gives both parties rights to terminate if they cannot reach agreement on additional costs that may be payable.[352]

The termination provisions in cl 8 are taken partly from Wreckhire 2010 cl 8[353] and Wreckfixed 2010 cl 7.[354] Like Wreckfixed 2010, there is no power for the hirer to suspend

---

344 Cf Wreckhire 2010 cl 7(a) where there has to be a separate agreement on how to adjust rates: see 13.6.3(i).
345 Cf Wreckhire 2010 cl 7(b) which puts the obligation to consult on both parties.
346 The hirer's ability to claim damages would probably be restricted by cl 16(e): cf 13.6.3(g).
347 If there are no back to back delay payment terms at all in the sub-contract, and no off hire clause, the contractor may not be able to claim for a delay payment at all, which might seem a rather perverse result.
348 See also the discussion in 13.6.3(e).
349 This may well be done via the contractor's daily reports as required by cl 2 and Annex III.
350 Again, under cl 17, identical to cl 21 of Wreckhire 2010: see 13.6.3(k).
351 Cf the identical provision in Wreckhire 2010 cl 10(f) (see 13.6.3(f)) and Wreckfixed 2010 cl 9(d) (see 13.6.4(d)).
352 See 13.6.5(d).
353 See 13.6.3(f).
354 See 13.6.4(d).

the services but, under cl 8(a) of Wreckstage 2010, the hirer does have the right to terminate the contract at any time prior to commencement of the mobilisation of personnel, craft or equipment (whichever occurs first)—apparently without needing to give notice. On doing so the hirer must to pay a pre-agreed cancellation fee as set out in Box 14.

Again, like Wreckfixed 2010, Wreckstage 2010 cl 8(b)[355] recognises that changes of circumstances may affect the contractor and (assuming that there is no right to terminate under cl 4(a)(iii))[356] the contractor is given right to terminate without further liability if the services (even as changed under cl 4) have become "technically or physically impossible". The agreement of the hirer is necessary, although it must not be unreasonably withheld and there is obvious scope for disagreement here.[357]

Clause 8(c) Wreckstage 2010 is taken from Wreckhire 2010[358] and deals with the circumstance where "competent authorities" refuse to give permission to terminate, and may give orders to prevent demobilisation.[359] The contractor is to be paid at the "delay payment rate" in Box 11 during any standby period. It is also entitled to its reasonable and necessary costs of continuing with the service.

13.6.5(g) Delivery and disposal

The choice of where to deliver the wreck and whether the contract will also deal with disposal involves many commercial calculations and decisions about risk allocation.[360] For example, as Wreckstage 2010 is essentially a fixed price contract, like Wreckfixed 2010, if the place of disposal is agreed in Box 8 the contractor will bear the costs of completing the service, including any ancillary costs relating to disposal. There is no need to provide for any extra costs of disposal, as in Wreckhire 2010 cl 14, provided that everything goes according to plan.

Wreckstage 2010 cl 9 deals with delivery and disposal using provisions that are a mixture of those found in Wreckhire 2010 cl 9[361] and Wreckfixed 2010 cl 8.[362] The starting point is for the parties to agree in Box 8 what is to be the "Place of Delivery". The parties also have the option of naming a "Place of Disposal". In either case, at this point under cl 9(a) the vessel[363] has to be accepted "forthwith" by the hirer and "taken over" by the hirer or its representative at the place of delivery (or disposal). That representative might be a recycling facility. Acceptance presumably involves agreeing that the contractor has fulfilled its obligations to complete the services. Taking over suggests a transfer of possession (even constructive).

Some care is needed in reading cl 9 as it is not always easy to follow where a distinction is being made between the two concepts of delivery and disposal.[364] This is important

---

355 Taken from Wreckfixed 2010 cl 7(b).
356 Eg because the parties have agreed on additional costs.
357 See also the discussion in 13.6.4(d).
358 See Wreckhire 2010 cl 8(c) and the discussion in 13.6.3(f), eg on termination at common law.
359 See 4.2.3, 5.3, 9.2.5, 10.2.5.
360 See 13.6.2, 14.7.1.
361 See 13.6.3(i).
362 See 13.6.4(e).
363 Including any cargo on board: see the definition in cl 1.
364 The last sentence of cl 9(a) tries to solve this by stating that references to "delivery or the Place of Delivery" shall include references to "disposal or the Place of Disposal". This is not a definition within cl 1, but it must

because there is a difference between (i) the *hirer* taking delivery at two different places, eg a "place of delivery" at a wreck site and a "place of disposal" at a recycling yard, and (ii) the *contractor* undertaking to dispose of the wreck. In the latter case the obligation will presumably be set out in the method of work in Annex II (and in any additional clauses), but it will still be necessary to specify a place and time at which the contractor's services are completed for it to be able to claim the last instalment of the lump sum price in Wreckstage 2010. Clause 9 seems mainly to be envisaging the first alternative, because of its references to the hirer accepting, taking over, or taking delivery.[365]

Where the contractor agrees to dispose of the wreck, eg having first undertaken to buy it,[366] there are still two possibilities as to when its services under the wreck removal contract will be fulfilled and it will be entitled to the last instalment. The first would be where the hirer tries to offload any of its direct responsibilities by terminating its involvement at the wreck site, eg once the wreck has been raised. Here it would aim to pay any final instalment at this stage, transfer ownership to a buyer (eg the contractor or a scrap buyer) and rely on that buyer to arrange a disposal voyage. The contractor would then need to know exactly when that last instalment would be paid and this would be achieved by tendering a notice of delivery under Wreckstage 2010 at the wreck site, with the hirer accepting that delivery and then transferring ownership of the wreck. The difficulty with this first possibility is that the hirer has only 'raised' but not 'removed' the wreck. It may therefore face difficulties from an Affected State that wants to be sure of a complete removal operation undertaken by the registered shipowner, but may also face potential continuing liabilities if there is a problem on the wreck disposal voyage.

A second possibility is therefore more likely, in which the vessel may still be sold and transferred at the wreck site, but the contractor's responsibilities under Wreckstage 2010 continue until the wreck is disposed of at a recycling port, place or yard. At this terminus, which needs to be carefully defined, the contractor will earn its final instalment, but the references in cl 9 to the *hirer* accepting, taking over, or taking delivery do not seem to work at this stage—at least in so far as these expressions refer to transfer of possession. In this scenario, that is the last thing desired by the hirer (eg a registered shipowner). Clause 9(a) does, though, allow the hirer to authorise a representative to accept delivery, and this could be the representative of the recycling yard chosen by the contractor (or other buyer). So careful drafting may be needed to ensure that a clear time and place has been identified and to ensure that there is an authorised acceptance and taking over by the hirer within cl 9(a).[367]

---

at least be intended to apply throughout cl 9(a) (and possibly all of cl 9), as the word "delivery" (lower case) does not appear again in the first para. The clarification seems rather unnecessary for the upper case references as "Place of Delivery" appears only once, in cl 9(a) second para, where "Disposal" is already mentioned. The lower case "delivery" does appear six more times in cl 9, but there appears to be some inconsistency as in three places there is also a reference anyway to both "delivery" and/or "disposal" (see cl 9(b) lines 147–148, cl 9(e) line 168). The reference to "notice of delivery" in line 159 should presumably be read to include "notice of disposal", which would be relevant to the form of notice in cl 19(b)(iii).

365 The use of these three expressions in cl 9 may not be entirely consistent; eg "taken over" in cl 9(a) and "taking delivery" in cl 9(d) both seem to involve a change of possession, although perhaps it could be said that "taking delivery" involves both an acceptance and a taking over.

366 See 14.7.1.

367 Such difficulties may be one reason of the opening and closing words of para 1 of cl 9(a), "if applicable".

Wreckstage 2010 cl 9(a) para 2 deals with the navigational and political risks at the place of delivery and/or disposal in the same way as Wreckhire 2010 and Wreckfixed 2010. The hirer undertakes that the agreed place of delivery or disposal will be safe and accessible for the vessel, the contractor's craft and hired-in craft; and that the place is one where the contractor will be permitted by government or other authorities to deliver or dispose of the wreck. Where there is damage to the contractor's (or hired-in) craft, those losses would fall on the contractor by virtue of the knock for knock provisions in cl 13. The contractor's remedy is therefore to decline to deliver at the agreed place if it is impossible or unsafe to do so. That then raises the question of who pays for the costs that would ensue, and also as to what must happen next.

Clause 9(a) para 3 deals with the costs that might arise if delivery (or disposal) is prevented or delayed by the actions of government or other authorities (outside of the contractor's control),[368] but also where delivery has not been accepted "forthwith" by the hirer. All "costs necessarily incurred by the contractor" from the moment of the "tender for delivery" will be for the account of the hirer.[369] There is no separate requirement in cl 9(a) para 3 for (or definition of) a "tender for delivery", but it is obviously in the contractor's interest to provide one.[370] Under the Wreckstage 2010 lump sum contract any delay would be at the risk of the contractor, although delays caused by factors outside its control would entitle the contractor to additional compensation under cl 7(a) at the delay payment rate in Box 13.[371] Clause 9(a) para 4 removes any doubt about the relationship between the costs available under para 3 and the compensation under cl 7(a) by providing that they are to be additional to each other. Where delivery is not prevented but merely delayed by government action, the contractor would still be receiving payment, but it may not be clear how long the delay will be or whether it will become permanent. The contractor might be quite content to wait, but there may come a stage when it wants to leave. It could only terminate under cl 7(b) if completion becomes technically or physically impossible.[372] Impossibility might arise if the government was obviously adamant in refusing entry to the place of delivery (eg as a result of environmental protests), as opposed to be being open to negotiation. If the contractor tried to terminate for reasons less severe than impossibility it might be in breach, although there might come a time after which it could be said that the contract was frustrated.

Clause 9(b)[373] actually deals with what happens next if it is impossible or unsafe for the vessel to be delivered or disposed of at the place indicated in Box 8. First, the contractor

---

368 Th provision is clearly aimed at intervention type orders from the authorities, backed perhaps by the threat of physical or criminal sanctions. It is not necessary that these are legally justified, if there is nothing in practice that the contractor can do to avoid them.

369 Cf cl Wreckfixed 2010 cl 8 para 3: 13.6.4(e).

370 The "tender for delivery" is not described here as a "notice" and would therefore be outside the requirements of cl 19 as to the form of "notices", eg that they be in writing. Somewhat confusingly, cl 9(d) refers to tendering a "written notice of delivery", which *would* trigger cl 19. It must be assumed that cl 9(a) para 3 is referring to the tender of such a "notice of delivery".

371 See 13.6.5(e).

372 See 13.6.5(f).

373 Largely identical to that in Wreckfixed 2010 cl 8(b).

has to consider that it is impossible or unsafe.[374] Secondly, assuming such a judgment has been made, the contractor should then enquire of the hirer if it is prepared to nominate an "acceptable" alternative place; ie acceptable to the contractor. Thirdly, if there is such an acceptable nomination, then cl 9(b) para 2 provides that the hirer will reimburse the contractor for any additional time used at the "delay payment rate" set out in Box 13. The hirer will also be liable to the contractor for any" additional expenses" incurred, eg if there were authorisation or customs fees to be paid in the new place.[375] Fourthly, if the hirer is unable to nominate an alternative place acceptable to the contractor, the latter has a very real problem of what to do with its wreck convoy, especially if has chartered-in heavylift craft or barges to carry the remains of the wreck. Here cl 9(b) of Wreckstage 2010 adopts the same solution as in Wreckfixed 2010, ie the contractor is "at liberty to deliver or dispose of the vessel[376] at the nearest place it can reach safely and without unreasonable delay". This itself is subject to the caveat that the delivery or disposal is permitted by the authorities in the new place. If this delivery or disposal takes place, the financial consequence is that the contractor is deemed to have fulfilled it obligations and will be entitled to any final staged payment. In addition, cl 9(b) para 2 again provides that the hirer will reimburse the contractor for any additional time used at the "delay payment rate" set out in Box 13 and the hirer will also be liable to the contractor for any" additional expenses" incurred. Fifthly, if the authorities do not permit delivery or disposal at he newly nominated place, the contractor will be back at the position in cl 9(a) para 3, above, ie it will still be on the delay payment rate and entitled to addition expenses.

As with Wreckfixed, 2010, even if the hirer (or its representative) has accepted delivery of the vessel,[377] the physical handover to the hirer could present risks where the contractor has been keeping the wrecked vessel afloat by using its own pumps, compressors or other equipment (eg floatation collars). Under Wreckhire 2010, the hirer would presumably keep the hire going until it was able to ensure that replacement equipment was available. Under Wreckstage 2010 the contractor might be entitled simply to leave on completion of the service, so cl 9(c) provides that the hirer must use all due despatch to arrange for its own replacement equipment and operators. In the meantime, the hirer must pay the contractor "reasonable rates" for the continued use of its own equipment as well as any additional costs. Although cl 9(c) does not say so expressly, it seems implicit that the contractor is not entitled to remove its pumps etc until the replacements are in place, for it is being paid all relevant costs. If there was default in payment, the contractor might be able to terminate under cl 10(e).[378] Otherwise, the contractor would not be able to remove its equipment

---

374 This presumably requires a good faith opinion, but may not necessarily be one that is reasonable in the sense that all reasonable contractors would agree with it.

375 It is not clear if there is intended to be a difference between "costs" as used cl 9(a) line 141 and "expenses" in cl 9(b), but they are both probably referring to external costs such as those in cl 11: see 13.6.5(c). It is unclear if the "expenses" include normal operating costs that might be covered in the delay payment rate, such as those listed in Wreckhire 2010 cl 13(g) and (h). The latter relate to bunkers, lubricants and transportation/accommodation costs for personnel. This is not a matter than can be referred to expert evaluation, as that only applies to disputes under cl 4 and 7.

376 Including its cargo by virtue of the definition in cl 1. See also cl 9(e) allowing delivery of parts of the vessel and eg cargo at different times and places, discussed below.

377 Under cl 9(a) line 134.

378 See 13.6.5(f).

and leave simply because there was a delay by the hirer in providing the replacements; at common law, termination of such a term is likely to require a fundamental breach and that would probably involve a very considerable delay.[379]

The contractor still needs a fallback position if the hirer fails to take delivery and it is not impossible or unsafe (within cl 9(b)) to deliver or dispose of the vessel at the place in Box 6. Wreckstage 2010 cl 9(d) adopts the same solution as Wreckhire 2010 cl 9(b)[380] and Wreckfixed 2010 cl 8(d)[381] and allows the contractor default powers to sell or dispose of the vessel and apply any proceeds to reduce sums owed to the contractor, with any remaining proceeds being refunded to the hirer. The sale or disposal power can be exercised without notice or any liability whatsoever and arises in two circumstances. The first is if delivery is not taken within five days of a formal written notice of delivery being tendered. The second is where the contractor forms the opinion that the vessel is "likely to deteriorate, decay, become worthless or incur charges whether for storage or otherwise in excess of its value". The opinion must presumably be formed in good faith and on the balance of probabilities given the information available to the contractor.

The wording of this second power is not entirely clear in a number of respects. The words "deteriorate" and "decay" are not grammatically dependent on the value of the vessel;[382] ie the provision does not say "deteriorate or decay so that so that it becomes worthless". Most wrecks that have been raised will be deteriorating to some extent through rust caused by the internal presence of seawater and other residues, so that there should be a *de minimis* assumption. The provision would apply where the extent of deterioration or decay is likely to pose a serious risk in the mind of a reasonable contractor that the vessel's ultimate value may not be enough to meet any likely additional charges if the hirer fails to take delivery, but it does not appear to be dependent upon proof that there is a risk that the hirer will not meet any final instalment or any additional charges.[383]

There is an additional problem with the wording, as a natural grammatical meaning of the triggers for the two alternative powers (ie non acceptance for five days, or deterioration etc) is that the second one (deterioration etc) creates a free-standing power unrelated to delivery which can apply at any stage of the contract.[384] This might be somewhat surprising given the placing of sub-cl 9(d) in a clause about delivery and disposal and that the default sale and disposal power is exercisable "without notice and without any responsibility whatsoever attaching to the contractor". Moreover, the reference to "storage" suggests that the provision is dealing with an end of contract scenario rather than a type of force majeure event that could happen at any time. The ability to "sell or dispose" of the vessel is also likely to be relevant in a port, but both could arise while at sea—especially where

---

379 Given that the contractor would be paid, it may be difficult to show that it had been deprived of substantially the whole benefit of the contract. The position might be different if, eg the necessary personnel had good reasons to leave.

380 See 13.6.3(i).

381 See 13.6.4(e).

382 The phrase "in excess of its value" relates to the incurring of charges.

383 The provision is without prejudice to other claims that the contractor may have and if there are not sufficient funds from the sale to pay monies due then the hirer is still liable for any shortfall. It may be necessary to check if the security required under cl 12 extends to such charges.

384 Ie it assumes that the first phrase about the five day period in lines 137–138 is entirely separate from it. This view is reinforced by the fact that both phrases begin with the word "if".

the place of "delivery" is not in a port but, eg, at the wreck site. On that basis, "disposal" could include dumping the wreck at sea, provided that this were allowed by an Affected or coastal State.[385] Yet if the trigger was not meant to be freestanding, it could only be relevant as an alternative to waiting five days after a notice of delivery, and that short period may not be sufficient to form a view about whether any charges are "likely" to exceed the value. The clause might be clearer if the two default powers were separated, but the better interpretation at present may be that second power is only exercisable upon completion of the service, eg by tendering of delivery.

If cargo has to be disposed of separately from the vessel this does not fit neatly into the scheme of cl 9 already described, as it seems best suited to "delivery" of the entire wreck at one location. Clause 9(e), though, provides that references in cl 9 to the vessel shall include "parts of the vessel and/or cargo and/or any other thing emanating from the vessel".[386] What cl 9(e) then does is to confirm that "such delivery and/or disposal may take place at different times and in different places (see Box 8)".[387] This draws attention to a need for some careful drafting. If it is known at the time of the contract that the cargo might need to be delivered or disposed of in a different place to the vessel (eg on board a vessel for transhipment, or in a port near to the wreck site) this could be specified in the method of work in Annex II and a separate place of delivery and/or disposal of the cargo could be specified in Box 8. A payment instalment stage may also be created in Box 9 for such delivery and/or disposal. This sort of situation could be envisaged with a container ship, where it is unlikely that the vessel could be refloated from a stranding without first removing the cargo. Where it is not known exactly what is to happen to the cargo at the time of the contract, but it later transpired that it would have to be removed, the contractor may have to rely on a substantial change in the services under cl 4(a),[388] eg based on a material change in the position and/or condition of the vessel. The difficulty for the contractor is that it may not necessarily have incurred additional costs to those that might have arisen if the vessel had been taken (along with the cargo) to its original place of delivery and/or disposal. In such a case, the contractor might be faced by an argument that, in the absence of a pre-agreed instalment for cargo disposal, it would have to wait until the vessel was delivered and/or disposed of before being paid for the cargo delivery/disposal stage. This is where a sensible agreement about changes to be incorporated into a variation order might be appropriate, but the option of expert evaluation (allowed by cl 4(c)) only applies as to reasonableness or quantum of the extra costs, apparently not to whether mere changes to performance are required.

In the context of cargo removal, all three wreck contracts are silent as to the extent to which the wreck removal claimant can make a salvage claim against cargo interests for

---

385 See 14.1.

386 It is not clear if this needed to be said given the wide definition of "vessel" in cl 1 (including anything on or in a vessel, including cargo and bunkers), and it does not seem that "emanating from" adds much to that definition. The reference was probably used to make the final part of the sentence more comprehensible.

387 The reference to Box 8 is added at the end of cl 9(e) by way of cross reference (like other clauses). The Box only refers expressly to the place, not the time, of delivery, so it may depend how the box is filled in to see if it does name the place *or places* of delivery or disposal.

388 See 13.6.5(d).

removing cargo that may still have a value,[389] but almost certainly a contractual obligation in the wreck removal contract to remove cargo would be a bar to any salvage claims.[390]

Overall, while the drafting of cl 9 is generally suitable for straightforward removal and disposal operations, its application to more complicated operations, particularly in relation to different methods of disposal (both of the vessel and its cargo), means that it may need close consideration and, if necessary, amendment.

---

389 Cf Towhire 2008 cl 19.
390 See also 13.6.3(a) and fn 114.

PART IV

WRECK DISPOSAL

CHAPTER 14

Wreck disposal

The WRC 2007 has a special definition of wreck "removal" that goes beyond mere physical removal,[1] but in a practical sense after wreck raising and wreck removal comes wreck *disposal*. The WRC does not itself specify any steps that need to be adopted to ensure the safe disposal of a recovered wreck.[2] There are three main areas of disposal to consider: (i) dumping of ships at sea; (ii) scrapping and recycling of ships; and (iii) waste disposal more generally (including cargo disposal).

This chapter will consider these three issues in that order, ie starting from the specific, before dealing with the general, as that largely reflects the temporal order of wreck disposal. There is a disadvantage in this approach in that the specific issues have to be seen in the context of wider general environmental policies[3] and legislation at international, regional (particularly EU) and national levels. Some of this legislation is overlapping and mind-numbingly complex—even before trying to disentangle those elements specifically relevant to wreck. It is not appropriate in a book on wreck to attempt a general description of all UK and EU marine environmental law,[4] but readers who wish to understand the general legislative position on waste could first consult the material in 14.6.

Owing to the uncertainty concerning Brexit, it should also be noted that references to EU requirements in this book (particularly this chapter) may be subject to change after 31 October 2019 (exit day), eg so as not to apply to the UK. The European Union (Withdrawal) Act 2018 was passed to ensure legal continuity after Brexit. The Act has been amended twice to allow further time for a withdrawal agreement to be struck.[5] In broad terms, the Act contains savings for EU-derived domestic legislation and directly applicable EU legislation, as well as case law, so as to preserve what is described as "retained EU law".[6] By September 2018 the government had issued a large series of planning documents, eg the general "UK government's preparations for a no deal scenario",[7] and including the more specific "Handling civil legal cases that involve EU countries if there's no

---

1 See WRC Art 1(7); also 8.2.4, 9.2.5, 10.2.5 and 10.2.8.
2 Apart from the general objective of the "removal" of a "hazard" in Art 2(1) and as defined in Art 1(5) and Art 1(9) (see 8.2.2, 9.2.5(b), 10.2.8). See also T Puthecherril, *From Shipbreaking to Sustainable Ship Recycling: Evolution of a Legal Regime* (Martinus Nijhoff, 2010) [*Puthecherril*], 128.
3 UK government environmental policies are subject to much flux, but can be found at www.gov.uk/environment/marine-environment; more settled policies from 2010–2015 are at www.gov.uk/government/publications/2010-to-2015-government-policy-marine-environment/2010-to-2015-government-policy-marine-environment.
4 See *De La Rue & Anderson*. Space does not permit full references in this chapter to all devolved legislation.
5 See the European Union (Withdrawal) Act 2018 (Exit Day) (Amendment) Regulations 2019 (SI 2019/718), The European Union (Withdrawal) Act 2018 (Exit Day) (Amendment) (No. 2) Regulations 2019 (SI 2019/859).
6 See ss 1–7 and also the Explanatory Notes to the Act, 7.
7 www.gov.uk/government/publications/uk-governments-preparations-for-a-no-deal-scenario/uk-governments-preparations-for-a-no-deal-scenario.

Brexit deal"[8] and "Upholding environmental standards if there's no Brexit deal".[9] The latter emphasises that the 2018 Act will ensure that all existing EU environmental law continues to operate in UK law, but this may obviously be subject to later Parliamentary changes. Announced changes include a new Environmental Principles and Governance Act, a new statutory body for environmental standards in England and a new statutory statement of environmental principles to guide future government policy.[10] Note that the Merchant Shipping (Miscellaneous Provisions)(Amendments etc) (EU Exit) Regulations 2018[11] make amendments to UK legislation (mainly about safety standards and ship registration) and also revoke some EU retained law (eg relating to institutions such as EMSA). Most of the changes appear to be only indirectly relevant to the subject matter of this book. The content (and extent) of any further changes is heavily contingent on the political landscape post-Brexit. However, the enactment of legislation such as the International Waste Shipments (Amendment) (EU Exit) Regulations 2019[12] would suggest that the underlying law discussed in this chapter will largely be retained. Where possible, references to existing amending legislation introduced to retain EU law have been included throughout this chapter.

14.1 Dumping of ships and cargoes at sea

14.1.1 Introduction

The expressions "scuttling" and "dumping" are often used interchangeably to describe the practice of disposing of wrecks at sea. In the legal world, "scuttling" has tended to be used where there is deliberate wrongful conduct in the commercial sense, eg attempts to defraud owners[13] or insurers.[14] "Dumping" has acquired a legislative meaning[15] and in relation to wreck generally refers to the deliberate actions of owners in order to deal with the practical problems of disposing of the hull, eg in accordance with State permission. However, the distinction between both expressions does not depend upon whether the action is illicit or not, as "dumping" is sometimes used operationally to include illicit disposals by owners and "scuttling" is sometimes used to describe authorised disposals. It is not therefore realistic to maintain a formal legal distinction between the two expressions, unless they are referred to expressly in contracts or legislation, but the suggested differences should be borne in mind.

Before environmental consciousness was awakened by the *Torrey Canyon*, and even during the development of marine environmental law in the decades after 1967, a simple

---

8 www.gov.uk/government/publications/handling-civil-legal-cases-that-involve-eu-countries-if-theres-no-brexit-deal/handling-civil-legal-cases-that-involve-eu-countries-if-theres-no-brexit-deal

9 www.gov.uk/government/publications/upholding-environmental-standards-if-theres-no-brexit-deal/upholding-environmental-standards-if-theres-no-brexit-deal.

10 See also www.gov.uk/government/news/new-environment-law-to-deliver-a-green-brexit.

11 SI 2018/1221.

12 SI 2019/590: see the text to fns 5–12. See also 14.5.2 for 2019 Regulations to give effect to the EU Ship Recycling Regulation 2013. See also the Marine Environment (Amendment) (EU Exit) Regulations 2018 (SI 2018/ 1399) as an example of the hundreds of "EU Exit" SIs.

13 See eg *The Salem* [1983] 1 Lloyd's Rep 342: also 2.9.3(b).

14 See wilful misconduct at 10.8.4, 2.6.

15 And is regulated by the LC 1972 and national implementing legislation: see 14.1.2.

expedient for disposing of a wreck was to take it out to sea and dump it; ie to sink it in deep water where it would not be a navigational hazard. In an era before super-sized ships this was not a surprising option. After all, thousands of ships have lain sunk on the floors of the oceans as a result of maritime disasters and wars. This sort of dumping was a regular option for salvors and, indeed, governments.

Thus, the Greek flagged oil tanker *Christos Bitas* went aground off Pembrokeshire on 12 October 1978, losing some 5,000 mt of cargo. The bulk of its cargo was offloaded into two tankers but some 4,000 mt was lost. The vessel was a CTL and, to avoid extra costs and difficulties (eg in tank cleaning), it was eventually towed by the salvors some 300 miles west of the Fastnet rocks and "scuttled" (with the agreement of the owners). The area selected was apparently clear of fishing grounds and submarine cables. The towage operation of a heavily listing ship was itself somewhat hazardous, and it could well have sunk on route; moreover, by modern standards, it appears that the ship was not fully cleaned before sinking,[16] so that oil, containers and other debris floated clear from the ship. It is not now entirely clear if there was a formal State intervention order, or merely a commercial arrangement with the UK salvor (United Towing), but this was an operation ordered by the Department of Transport, with an escort from *HMS Eskimo*.[17]

The *Christos Bitas* was scuttled following cooperation and consultation with the Irish Republic under the Bonn Agreement for Cooperation in Dealing with Pollution of the North Sea by Oil 1969.[18] The international regulatory framework for the dumping of ships has evolved considerably since the 1970s, with both international and regional agreements.

14.1.2 London (Dumping) Convention 1972/1996

Article 210(6) of UNCLOS sets out very generalised minimum standards for national laws on dumping by reference to global rules and standards, but the main international convention on dumping is the Convention on the Prevention of Marine Pollution by Dumping of Wastes and Other Matter 1972 (LC 1972).[19] This relatively early environmental convention has to be considered separately from its 1996 Protocol (LC Protocol 1996) which takes a radically different approach to dumping. The basic LC 1972 adopts an essentially permissive approach—allowing most dumping provided that there is approval from a Contracting State; the 1996 Protocol effectively prohibits dumping unless substances appear on an approved list.[20] In 2018 the basic LC 1972 had 87 Contracting States (accounting for about 60% of the world's gross tonnage). By contrast, the LC Protocol 1996 has 50 Contracting

---

16 Cf modern hot-tapping techniques used with the *Baltic Ace*: see 10.2.5.

17 See eg http://hmseskimo.org.uk/page13.htm; http://wwz.cedre.fr/en/Resources/Spills/Spills/Christos-Bitas.

18 See now the Bonn *Agreement for cooperation in dealing with pollution of the North Sea by oil and other harmful substances* 1983, as amended in 2001 [Bonn Agreement] and www.bonnagreement.org. See also 5.7 and 4.2.3(e).

19 Sometimes abbreviated as the London Convention, or London Dumping Convention.

20 See the IMO website for the LC 1972 and LC Protocol 1996, www.imo.org/en/OurWork/Environment/LCLP/Pages/default.aspx; *De La Rue & Anderson*, 1000–1014; D VanderZwaag, "The International Control of Ocean Dumping", Chapter 6 of R Rayfuse (ed) *Research Handbook on International Marine Environmental Law* (Edward Elgar, 2015) [*VanderZwaag*].

States, not including some major shipping nations (and most of the open registry States).[21] Although the LC Protocol 1996 takes precedence as between parties to it,[22] this still leaves a great deal of variance internationally[23] and that has encouraged regional solutions.[24] Nevertheless, the international instruments have increasingly set standards in place of unregulated or uncontrolled dumping of ships.

14.1.2(a) London Convention 1972

Article III of the LC 1972 defines dumping to mean: "(i) any deliberate disposal at sea of wastes[25] or other matter from vessels, aircraft, platforms or other man-made structures at sea; (ii) any deliberate disposal at sea of vessels, aircraft, platforms or other man-made structures at sea". This definition would cover the scuttling of ships which have become CTLs while afloat, or of wrecks which have been raised, but Art IV only *prohibits* the dumping of a limited number of waste substances listed in Annex I.[26] This 'black list' includes chemicals such as mercury[27] and industrial wastes. The latter expression excludes vessels, provided that material capable of creating floating debris or otherwise contributing to pollution of the marine environment has been removed to the maximum extent. Unless substances are in the Annex I list, they may be dumped, provided that an appropriate permit is issued by a Contracting State for such 'grey list' substances, which has to take into account factors in Annex III.[28]

The relevance of this to wreck removal is that scuttling is an option under the LC 1972, if an approval can be obtained from a Contracting State and provided that pollutants are removed as far as possible.

In an emergency, as defined in Art V, even the basic requirements of Art IV need not be complied with, provided that dumping appears to be the only way of averting a threat to human life or other vessels and if there is every probability that the damage consequent upon such dumping will be less than would otherwise occur. It is possible that this might be relevant to wreck if, for example, a grounded vessel was on fire, or likely to explode, or likely to sink in a harbour where it would be a hazard to navigation. These instances relate to immediate risks to the vessel and its surroundings. The exception would not apply simply because a vessel itself was at risk of sinking unless further action was taken to saveit, eg by refloating and towage to a recycling facility. Even here, though, the basic LC 1972 would allow dumping if the shipowner were able to get a permit from a Contracting State,

---

21 Eg Greece and Panama are party to the LC 1972, while Liberia is party to neither: see *IMO Status of Treaties* (November 2018). Asia is particularly underrepresented (although China is a party to the LC 1972).

22 See LC Protocol 1996 Art 23.

23 India is a party to neither instrument (cf the *MSC Chitra*, 10.2.5); nor is Ecuador (see the *Galapaface* and *Floreana*,10.2.6). South Africa is a party to the LC Protocol 1996: cf the *Smart*, 10.2.5.

24 See eg 14.1.3; also 14.3–14.6 generally.

25 See the LC 1972 Art III(1)(b)(i) for disposal of normal operational wastes from ships: 14.1.2(b).

26 States are entitled in national law to prohibit the dumping of other substances in their national law: see Art IV(3).

27 Crude oil is also listed but only if "taken on board for the purpose of dumping". This is not likely in a wreck scenario, so an oil cargo would not otherwise be in the prohibited list.

28 Including the characteristics and composition of the matter being dumped the characteristics of the dumping site and other considerations such as possible effects on amenities, fishing and other uses of the sea.

eg the flag State, and probably also of a coastal State if the plan was to dispose of the ship in the EEZ of any State.[29]

14.1.2(b) LC Protocol 1996

The LC Protocol 1996 entered into force in 2006.[30] It applies more general environmental obligations to Contracting States in Arts 2–3, including the precautionary approach to environmental protection from dumping of wastes or other matter. Incineration at sea of wastes or other matter is prohibited,[31] as is the export of wastes or other matter to other countries for dumping or incineration at sea.[32] It is Art 4 that prohibits Contracting Parties from dumping any wastes or other matter with the *exception* of those listed in Annex 1 (sometimes called a "reverse" list). This lists substances that *may* be considered for dumping, including "vessels". Even here, Art 4 requires Contracting Parties to adopt administrative or legislative measures to ensure that issuance of permits and permit conditions comply with provisions of Annex 2.[33] Annex 2 goes into much more detail than Annex III of the LC 1972 about the factors that States should take into account when considering a permit. It is here that the reversed presumption is significant, as particular attention has to be paid to opportunities to avoid dumping in favour of environmentally preferable alternatives. The obvious alternative for ships is recycling.[34] Here it will be necessary to weigh up the real practical options, with the relative risks to be balanced; eg the risk of the vessel accidentally sinking in a sensitive location (eg if refloated for a scrapping voyage) against planned dumping in a site where the environmental and navigational risks have been appropriately audited. States may be expected to apply conditions to any permit, eg to include monitoring. To assist these decisions, the IMO published "Waste Assessment Guidelines under the London Convention and Protocol", which contain specific guidelines for assessment of vessels.[35] The latter were revised in 2016,[36] in particular to take account of the Hong Kong Recycling Convention and its 2015 Guidelines for the Development of the Inventory of Hazardous Materials.[37]

---

29 See also Art VII. In 1972, the rights of States in the EEZ was not yet recognised, but UNCLOS 1982 Part V presumably applies, subject to the emergency exception in the LC 1972 Art V (to which consultation obligations apply): see 14.1.2(a).

30 See L de La Fayette, "The London Convention 1972: Preparing for the Future" (1998) 13 IJMCL 515.

31 Art 5. Note that under Art 1(5) "Incineration at sea" means the combustion *on board* a vessel of wastes. It would not seem to apply to the deliberate incineration of oil or bunkers that had *already* leaked from a vessel, although such a technique of disposing of cargo from a wreck is not generally favoured as a means to reduce pollution.

32 Arts 5, 6. Cf the Basel Convention: see 14.4.1.

33 There is a similar exception for emergencies in Art 8 to that in the LC 1972 Art V (see 14.1.2(a)), as well as more general obligations on application in Art 10: Note the Procedures and criteria for determining and addressing emergency situations 2006: see LC 28/15 Annex 11: www.imo.org/blast/blastData.asp?doc_id=13647&filename=Emergency%20procedures.pdf.

34 See 14.5.

35 2014 edition. An edited version of this is available in zipped form at www.imo.org/en/OurWork/Environment/LCLP/Publications/wag/Documents/2014%20WAGs%20English.zip.

36 See IMO doc LC 38/16, Annex 7: see www.imo.org/en/OurWork/Environment/LCLP/Publications/wag/Documents/2016%20Rev%20Specific%20Guidelines%20for%20vessels.pdf

37 See 14.5.1.

Although these guidelines make no specific reference to the dumping of wrecks,[38] they do emphasise the factors to be taken into account in the comparative risk assessment, eg effects on the environment, human health, and users of the sea; technical and practical feasibility; and economic considerations. There is particular emphasis on recycling using Hong Kong Recycling Convention principles, and reuse of vessels as artificial reefs (eg to encourage tourist diving). The latter will fall outside the scope of "dumping" if it is "placement of matter for a purpose other than the mere disposal thereof".[39] The onus would be on an applicant to show that an artificial reef proposal really was designed for environmental or leisure purposes[40] and this might be very hard if the ship was already a wreck and the owners were obviously looking for a cheap alternative to recycling.[41] The inference might be different where it is a State that has been left with a problem by an insolvent owner.[42]

The various guidelines, including the 2016 IMO Guidelines, make clear that for dumping of ships to take place hazardous materials may need to be destroyed, treated, or disposed of on shore (including by incineration on land). Dump-site selection should be made on a scientific basis.[43] The guidelines also highlight four stages in the permit process: (1) a description of the best environmental practices for the disposal option selected; (2) cleaning of the vessel; (3) inspection/verification by relevant authorities that adequate cleaning has taken place; and (4) the issuance of the permit itself.

It is evident from the guidelines that deliberate dumping of a wreck will almost certainly first require the hull to be cleaned, eg of oil and oily waste; this may even extend to hydraulic fluid from fixed equipment such as winches and cranes. But removal can also extend to any potential contaminants under the LC 1972 and its Protocol including items that might float away (eg bedding and furniture in a passenger ship).

Article 10 of the LC Protocol 1996 requires Contracting States to apply it to ships flying their own flags and also to "vessels . . . believed to be engaged in dumping or incineration at sea in areas within which it is entitled to exercise jurisdiction in accordance with international law". The latter expression could clearly apply to a tug towing a wreck from an EEZ

---

38 They do note the need to repair a vessel at sea (to avoid unexpected sinking) while assessing preparation for waste disposal or transporting it to a disposal location. While this may seem fairly obvious, it may serve as a timely reminder to government officials not used to the urgency sometimes needed in dealing with a casualty. Even with the *MSC Napoli*, a relatively well-managed casualty, delays in deciding upon dumping or recycling contributed to the decision to re-ground the vessel after initial refloating: see 1.2.3(b).

39 See LC Protocol 1996 Art 1.4.2.2.

40 See eg the letter of advice dated 10 December 2013 from Marine Scotland about a proposal to sink a frigate in the Sound of Mull: www.gov.scot/resource/0044/00440180.doc. Although the LC Protocol 1996 does not apply to vessels entitled to sovereign immunity (see Art 10(4)) States are expected to apply appropriate measures for such vessels and the UK does so. An environmental Impact Assessment (EIA) may also be required under the Directive 2011/92/EU of the European Parliament and of the Council of 13 December 2011 on the assessment of the effects of certain public and private projects on the environment (the EIA Directive 2011).

41 Applicants would need to satisfy international or regional guidelines, eg the IMO/UNEP "Guidelines for the Creation of Artificial Reefs": see www.imo.org/en/OurWork/Environment/LCLP/Publications/Documents/London_convention_UNEP_Low-res-Artificial%20Reefs.pdf, and an OSPAR equivalent (2012–3), www.ospar.org/documents?d=7143.

42 Cf the *Oceanlinx* generator: see 10.2.7(a).

43 Eg using the Report of the Joint Group of Experts on the Scientific Aspects of Marine Environmental Protection (GESAMP Reports and Studies No.16—Scientific Criteria for the Selection of Waste Disposal Sites at Sea, 1982): www.gesamp.org/publications/scientific-criteria-for-the-selection-of-waste-disposal-sites-at-sea.

to a place of scuttling; it is rather awkward to refer to a vessel under its own power being "engaged in dumping" itself, but it must also have been intended to cover a self-scuttling operation. It appears that a permit may be needed in practice—not only from a flag State, but also from a State in whose EEZ it is planned to dump the ship.[44]

In many circumstances, sinking the ship (whether it be called scuttling or dumping) will be the cheapest and easiest disposal solution for the commercial parties. It may be that this sort of solution is easier for States to accept where there is a bulk carrier, eg of coal, where the main environmental concern will be the bunkers. If these are removed, and the tanks and lines cleaned (eg with hot water), then there may be fewer objections to scuttling.[45] Such disposal was considered as an option in the case of the container ships *MSC Napoli* and *Rena*,[46] but rejected, although scuttling was used for the *MSC Chitra*.[47] It may not always be clear which factors influence the final decision about scuttling or dismantling, although States will be acutely aware of political pressures, while the owners and Club will be resisting more expensive disposal methods. The *MSC Napoli* and *Rena* are examples where the locations were particularly sensitive for tourist or cultural reasons. It seems that the *MSC Chitra* was regarded as a nuisance (in all senses of the word) and it may have been that the primary need was simply for it to be removed from the environs of Mumbai as soon as possible.[48]

The LC 1972 definition of wastes excludes those "incidental to or derived from the normal operations of vessels".[49] The broad intention was to leave such operational matters to MARPOL, but there have been difficulties of interpretation in relation to spoilt cargoes generally and the disposal of animal carcasses in particular.[50] MARPOL Annex V[51] prohibits the disposal of garbage[52] and applies to "cargo residues",[53] but this is not apt to describe cargo after a grounding, eg a complete hold full of grain contaminated by seawater, or containers of wet electronic goods.

Guidance on the Management of Spoilt Cargoes was issued in 2009 and revised in 2013,[54] and states that such spoilt cargo may be subject to the LC 1972 and LC Protocol 1996 regimes and may require permits both from the flag State and the State in whose jurisdiction (eg EEZ) the dumping would occur.[55] The 2013 Revised Guidance notes that

---

44 See also 10.1.2(a).
45 Se eg the *Smart*, 10.2.5.
46 See 1.2.3, 1.2.4. Both the UK and New Zealand are parties to the LC Protocol 1996. In the *Rena* the State maintained that leaving the wreck *in situ* was a form of dumping under the RMA 1991 provisions relating to abandonment. Although it is difficult to see that this is required by the LC Protocol 1996, a State is free to prohibit other forms of dumping in its waters: cf Art 4(2).
47 See 10.2.5; also 10.2.6, 10.5.1(a) for other examples of dumping of ships.
48 Local shipbreakers may not have wanted to take the vessel because of safety fears over the containers of chemicals still on board: see https://shipwrecklog.com/log/2014/08/recall-msc-chitra/.
49 See LC 1972 Art III(1)(b)(i), LC Protocol Art 1(4).2.1.
50 See *VanderZwaag*, 138–9.
51 See Resolution MEPC.201(62), adopted in 2011 and in force from 2013.
52 Annex V Reg 7 provides the usual exception for emergency and non-routine situations.
53 Ie those cargo residues that cannot be recovered using commonly available methods for unloading: see reg 1.
54 In a joint circular issued by the LC and IMO's MEPC: see MEPC.1/Circ.809 (28 June 2013); LC-LP 1/Circ.58 (3 July 2013).
55 MEPC.1/Circ.809 (28 June 2013), Annex, para 7.

the ideal way to manage cargo spoilt during a voyage would be to offload it from the ship so that it could be managed on land (eg to sell it as distressed cargo for an alternate use, or recycling) or be disposed of in an environmentally safe manner. Dumping at sea should occur only when there is urgency, a lack of land-based facilities or there is a risk of harm to the environment or human health (eg where dangerous gases are given off by rotting food). Paragraph 16 of the 2013 Revised Guidance lists the information that should be included in an application for a dumping permit under the LC 1972 or LC Protocol 1996, eg quantities and property of the cargo, how spoiled, packaging, method of release, dump site, potential effects on health and environment. The Annex to the 2013 Revised Guidance lists 25 examples of spoilt cargoes considered for sea disposal (even if not eventually dumped). The examples include frozen beef in a damaged container, and water ingress to a variety of bulk cargoes such as: magnesite granules, alumina, steam coal, iron ore, fertiliser, stearine that had become semi-solid after failure of heating equipment;[56] and foodstuffs, such as rice, sugar, potatoes, lentils, and wheat.[57] In addition, a table of permits issued between 1984—2009 for sea disposal of spoilt cargoes, as notified to IMO, showed that permits had been issued for eg 24,000 mt of cement (Malta, 2004), 100 tonnes of damaged frozen chicken (Liberia, 2007), and 800 mt of fire-extinguishing water containing coal dust (Liberia, 2000). There were also two spoilt cargoes specifically on board stranded vessels: 15,000 mt of potassium nitrates, sulphates and chlorides (South Africa, 2001) and 10,000 mt of diammonium phosphate (St Vincent & Grenadines, 2003), as well as 3,700 mt of sulphuric acid diluted with seawater on a damaged tanker (Brazil, 1999).

The 2013 Revised Guidance notes that the position about animal carcasses is more difficult. This is because Regulation 4.1.4 of MARPOL Annex V permits the discharge into the sea of animal carcasses generated during the normal operation of a ship, but only if the ship is en route, outside a special area, as far as possible from the nearest land and taking into account IMO guidelines.[58] The 2017 Guidelines for the Implementation of MARPOL Annex V[59] recommend that to comply with reg 4.1.4 the discharge into the sea should take place greater than 100 nautical miles (nm) from the nearest land and in the maximum water depth possible.[60] Discharge of animal carcasses needs to be recorded in the Garbage Record. It is also recommended that animal carcasses should be split or otherwise treated prior to their discharge into the sea, so that they sink.[61]

The distinction between mortalities arising in the "normal operation" of a ship (ie garbage within MARPOL Annex V) and those in excess of this (subject to the LC Protocol

---

56 Cf the Italian flagged chemical tanker *Ievoli Sun* (4,189 gt), wrecked in the English Channel in 2000 with a cargo of some 4,000 mt of styrene which had to be pumped from the seabed.

57 In some circumstances contaminated or infected cargoes may be refused entry into ports. If this was in any way caused by the condition of the cargo on shipment, the shipper may be liable to the carrier for breach of the obligation not to ship dangerous goods under Art IV r 6 of the Hague/Visby Rules: see 2.1.6. This would not apply where the cargo was ruined or infected (eg by mould) as a result of events happening after the casualty, eg where the ship is aground and the cargo cannot be ventilated.

58 See paras 32–34.

59 Resolution MEPC.295(71) (adopted on 7 July 2017), MEPC 71/17/Add.1, Annex 21, 1.

60 Although if a ship is closer to land and there are health risks it is recommended that discharge occur at least 12 nm from land. See 2017 Guidelines para 2.12.5–12.2.6; Revised Guidance 2013, para 34. In the case of a grounded ship with a few dead cattle on board this may not be possible.

61 2017 Guidelines, para 2.12.7.

1996) is not capable of precise calculation, as some deaths can always be anticipated in a normal voyage.[62] In the case of a wrecked and sunken livestock carrier, the carcasses will not be garbage.[63] If some live cattle die while being transferred from a grounded ship (eg to another ship) it is conceivable that their carcasses might be considered as garbage, but this seems unlikely. The alternative to dumping of carcasses at sea is for them to be buried on land, which may well attract different regulatory issues.[64]

14.1.2(c) Civil liability for dumping under the LC Protocol 1996
The LC Protocol 1996 does not itself create any civil liability arising from dumping or incineration, but in Art 15 merely encourages Contracting Parties to develop procedures regarding liability. It seems that little progress has been made on this issue.[65] It is possible that there might be liability (without limit) of a tanker owner under the CLC 1992 if it deliberately scuttled the ship,[66] but the liability insurer would appear to have a defence of wilful misconduct.[67] In these circumstances, the IOPC Fund might respond for pollution damage under the Fund Convention 1992.[68] Likewise, there would appear to be liability (without limit) of the registered owner of a dumped ship for any bunker pollution damage, but a defence for the insurer;[69] here there would be no second tier fund to respond. By contrast, it seems unlikely that deliberate dumping could be considered as a "maritime casualty" so as to give rise to liability under the WRC 2007 for subsequent wreck removal costs.[70] Otherwise, claims might need to be brought under national law, with all the difficulties experienced after the *Torrey Canyon*.

14.1.3 OSPAR Convention 1992

Both the LC 1972 and the LC Protocol 1996[71] encourage regional cooperation. An example is the Convention for the Protection of the Marine Environment of the North-East Atlantic (OSPAR Convention) 1992. It is a regional convention with 16 European parties (including the EU) and was designed to replace the Convention for the Prevention of Marine Pollution by Dumping from Ships and Aircraft (the Oslo Convention) 1972.[72]

Under Art 2 the OSPAR Convention there are general obligations on Contracting States to take all possible steps to prevent and eliminate pollution in the "maritime area".[73] More

---

62 Dead fish, including shellfish, carried on board as cargo, eg on fishing vessels, are considered to be animal carcasses, so the same principles apply to them: Revised Guidance 2013, para 38.
63 Cf the sinking of the *Haidar* in 2015: see 13.1.3, 14.6.4(b).
64 See 14.6.4(b).
65 See *VanderZwaag*, 145.
66 There would appear to be an "incident" under Art I(8), eg if the opening of sea cocks were considered as an "occurrence" (cf 10.5.1), and intentional conduct under Art V(2). See generally 2.6.2(a).
67 Art VII(8); see also 10.8.4(d).
68 Similar considerations might apply to the HNSC 2010, when in force.
69 See Bunkers Convention Art 7(10).
70 But if it was, the insurer would again have a defence of wilful misconduct: see 10.5.1(a), also 8.2.1(a).
71 Arts VIII and 12, respectively.
72 As amended by Protocols of 1983 and 1989. OSPAR is named from a combination of Oslo and Paris (where it was agreed).
73 Defined in Art 1(a) to mean the internal waters and the territorial seas of the Contracting Parties and specified areas of the North East Atlantic. See also the interactive map at https://odims.ospar.org/maps/1134.

particularly, Art 4 places an obligation on the States to "take . . . all possible steps to prevent and eliminate pollution by dumping or incineration of wastes or other matter in accordance with the provisions of the Convention, in particular as provided for in Annex II".

Dumping is defined in Art 1(f) as "(i) any deliberate disposal in the maritime area of wastes or other matter . . . from vessels . . . (ii) any deliberate disposal in the maritime area of . . . vessels". Incineration is defined in Art 1(f) as "any deliberate combustion of wastes or other matter in the maritime area". Annex II Art 2 prohibits incineration and Art 3(1) prohibits the dumping of "all wastes or other matter". The latter expression is not defined[74] but Art 3(2) specifically excludes from it dredged material and "vessels . . . until, at the latest, 31st December 2004". This makes it clear that these provisions would now cover the deliberate scuttling of a wreck, the deposit of waste from the ship (including ruined cargo) and, eg the burning off of cargo or bunkers. There are two exceptions: in case of force majeure due to stress of weather or any other cause,[75] when the safety of human life or of a vessel is threatened (Art 7); or in an emergency where land disposal cannot occur without unacceptable danger or damage (Art 9). These exceptions might apply where a refloated wreck is being towed but its condition deteriorates in the course of a voyage to a recycling or scrapping facility.[76] They would not apply simply because the towage or disposal voyage became more expensive.

There are consultation requirements if transboundary pollution is likely and States have to report on implementation and measures taken.[77] Article 8 addresses a more general issue relevant to wreck removal in that it obliges Contracting Parties "to take appropriate measures, both individually and within relevant international organisations, to prevent and eliminate pollution resulting from the abandonment of vessels . . . in the maritime area caused by accidents". The WRC 2007 can be seen as a response to this obligation.

14.1.4 Dumping and the UK

14.1.4(a) Background

The UK enacted legislation on dumping in the Dumping at Sea Act 1974. This was replaced by Part II of the Food and Environment Protection Act 1985 which in ss 5, 6 required licences for deposits in the sea or incineration at sea. While this Part II still applies to the Scottish inshore region, the various licensing and consent controls were replaced for elsewhere in the UK by Part 4 of the Marine and Coastal Access Act 2009.

14.1.4(b) Marine and Coastal Access Act 2009

The Marine and Coastal Access Act 2009 was a result of a Marine Stewardship Report[78] that set out a "vision for the marine environment".[79] The Act established an independent body,

---

74 But Art 1(o) of the Convention excludes human remains.
75 Ie circumstances beyond the control of a party.
76 Cf the options considered for the *MSC Napoli*: see 1.2.3(b).
77 Arts 21–22.
78 https://assets.publishing.service.gov.uk/government/uploads/system/uploads/attachment_data/file/69321/pb6187-marine-stewardship-020425.pdf.
79 See also the "UK Marine Policy Statement" (2011), www.gov.uk/government/publications/uk-marine-policy-statement. The Statement sets the framework for preparing marine plans and provides high level policy objectives, eg in Marine Protected Areas (MPAs).

the Marine Management Organisation (MMO), to discharge a number of marine functions for English waters and Northern Ireland offshore areas.[80] Part 2 of the Act also defined a "UK marine area" as used in the Act and allowed for an EEZ to be designated.[81] Part 5 allowed for new marine conservation zones and the regulation of other conservation sites. In Part 4 it replaced the various licensing and consent controls in previous legislation.[82] As mentioned, Part 4 now imposes licensing requirements for dumping and scuttling.

Section 65(1) requires a person to have a marine licence to carry on a licensable marine activity. Such an activity means under s 66(1):

1. to deposit any substance or object within the UK marine licensing area, either in the sea or on or under the sea bed, from — (a) any vehicle, vessel, aircraft or marine structure, (b) any container floating in the sea[83] ...
2. To deposit any substance or object anywhere in the sea or on or under the sea bed from — (a) a British vessel, British aircraft or British marine structure, or (b) a container floating in the sea, if the deposit is controlled from a British vessel, British aircraft or British marine structure.
3. To deposit any substance or object anywhere in the sea or on or under the sea bed from a vehicle, vessel, aircraft, marine structure or floating container which was loaded with the substance or object — (a) in any part of the United Kingdom except Scotland,[84] or (b) in the UK marine licensing area.
4. To scuttle any vessel or floating container in the UK marine licensing area.
5. To scuttle any vessel or floating container anywhere at sea, if the scuttling is controlled from a British vessel, British aircraft or British marine structure.
6. To scuttle any vessel or floating container anywhere at sea, if the vessel or container has been towed or propelled, for the purpose of that scuttling, — (a) from any part of the United Kingdom except Scotland, or (b) from the UK marine licensing area, unless the towing or propelling began outside that area.[85]

Although there is no specific mention of "wreck", the list can clearly apply to the type of situation where a contractor is dealing with the consequences of a wreck. Taken together, these provisions cover almost every type of wreck disposal operation connected with the UK that involves depositing, dumping or scuttling at sea of ships, cargoes and wastes from them.[86] It covers not only disposal at sea in the UK marine licensing area, but also (in

---

80 See also, the Marine (Scotland) Act 2010. The regulators for waters elsewhere in the UK are Marine Scotland, Natural Resources Wales, and the Department of Environment's Marine Division (Northern Ireland). The MMO has developed a Geographical Information System (GIS), ie an interactive map, to identify the various inshore and offshore areas: http://defra.maps.arcgis.com/apps/webappviewer/index.html?id=6d5a7b3a1f07440f947d1e31bfaa7d38.

81 Since designated on 31 March 2014 under the Exclusive Economic Zone Order 2013 (SI 2013/3161); see also the Merchant Shipping (Prevention of Pollution) (Limits) Regulations 2014 (SI 2014/3306), as amended. For the continental shelf see the Continental Shelf (Designation of Areas) Order 2013 (SI 2013/3162). For maps of the UK's EEZ and Continental Shelf, see the National Contingency Plan, 8–9: and 4.2.1.

82 The Act replaced Part II of the Food and Environment Protection Act 1985 (FEPA) and Part II of the Coast Protection Act 1949 (excluding Scottish inshore region).

83 The provision is clearly not considering shipping containers washed overboard but, eg, floating skimmer tanks containing oil or dispersants and which might not be considered as vessels. In any event, containers would be "objects" within the s 66(1) list. See further 14.6.5(b).

84 As already noted, separate provisions exist for Scotland.

85 For other parts of s 66 dealing with disposal more generally of wastes from wreck, see 14.6.5(b). Marine licensing is a way that the UK gives effect offshore to the EU Waste Framework Directive 2008.

86 It also covers burial of human remains at sea: see also 13.1.3.

paras 2, 3 and 6) anywhere in seas the world if there is a suitable British connection. Thus, scuttling in international or foreign waters would be covered if it was controlled from a British ship, or if the ship had been towed from the UK or the UK marine licensing area (ie the EEZ).

In the *Rena* litigation, the New Zealand legislation on dumping was applied to any decision to leave the remains of the ship on the seabed after it had involuntarily sunk after the casualty.[87] The tenor of the UK legislation is all about voluntary decisions to dispose of ships and objects at sea and it seems inconceivable that it could be interpreted to apply to a ship and its contents once sunk, eg to create a criminal offence for depositing without licence. In any event, the WRC 2007 would now apply.[88]

Chapter 2 of Part 4 of the 2009 Act sets out various examples where a licence is not required, mostly of no relevance to wreck.[89] Section 74, though, allows the appropriate licensing authority for an area (eg the MMO) to exempt specific activities by order. Various activities are exempt from licensing under the Marine Licensing (Exempted Activities) Order [Exempted Activities Order] 2011.[90] A number of these might potentially affect wreck, and are dealt with below in the context of waste exemptions more generally.[91] Article 9 of the Exempted Activities Order 2011 exempts "salvage activities". This exemption is unlikely to apply to dumping, except in relation to an emergency, eg where a casualty which is taking on water is under tow and the tow line is severed to prevent the tug itself being dragged down, or where it seems the ship will inevitably sink but a decision is taken to sink it immediately in an area away from a more environmentally sensitive area near the coast.[92]

Sections 67–73 of the 2009 Act deal with the licence application process and give wide powers to refuse applications or to grant them subject to conditions.[93] The mere fact that wreck disposal at sea is licensable does not mean that it is automatically allowed. The UK will obviously give effect to the LC Protocol and the OSPAR Convention and guidance issued under them.[94] Factors that need to be taken into account in licensing for a scuttling site will presumably include impacts on: navigation (eg harbour administrative areas, IMO routing measures); cables and pipelines; military activities (eg munitions dumps, MOD danger and exercise areas, military practice areas); heritage issues (eg protected wreck sites or sites protected by the Military Remains Act 1986);[95] Marine Protected Areas (MPAs), including Marine Conservation Zones (MCZs), Special Areas of Conservation (SACs),

---

87 See 1.2.4.
88 See 11.3.
89 Eg related to matters such as harbour works, but note s 83 where Admiralty consent might be required for certain activities in harbours.
90 SI 2011/409, as amended by the Marine Licensing (Exempted Activities) (Amendment) Order 2019 (SI 2019/893).
91 See 14.6.5(b).
92 For the self-service licensing option for low risk activity see 14.6.5(b), but it seems unlikely that this would apply to the type of scuttling undertaken in wreck removal operations.
93 See further, 14.6.5(b).
94 See 14.1.2(a) and eg the list in www.gov.uk/government/policies/marine-environment.
95 See 4.7.2.

Special Protection Areas (SPAs), Ramsar sites and Special Sites of Scientific Interest (SSSIs).[96]

Chapter 3 of Part 4 of the 2009 Act contains various mechanisms for the enforcement of its provisions.[97] Section 85 creates offences for breaching the licensing requirements, but s 86 provides a defence in emergencies, eg for securing safety of a vessel or to save life. These seem unlikely to apply to the type of planned scuttling associated with wreck. There are also defences in s 88 where the activity is in one of the items taking place outside the UK and where it is licensed by another State which is party to the LC 1972, its 1996 Protocol or the OSPAR Convention. Additional enforcement measures include compliance or remediation notices,[98] also backed up with criminal sanctions.

The MMO cautions that other consents for certain activities may be required in addition to a marine licence, eg if the activity is in or next to a site of special scientific interest (SSSI),[99] intrusive works on the seabed within 12 nautical miles of the coast (and some outside) may require consent from the Crown Estate.[100] Lighting and marking requirements may need the agreement of a local harbour authority or Trinity House.

14.2 Dumping or abandonment?

A distinction is sometimes made between dumping and abandoning a ship.[101] In one sense the expressions can be used interchangeably, eg where a ship is dumped underwater and thereby abandoned. But, as seen, dumping is usually reserved for disposing of the wreck on the ocean floor. Abandonment, by contrast, can refer to a case where an owner simply leaves a floating vessel, usually in a port or at an anchorage, because it is uneconomic to continue to operate it.[102] These circumstances may occur where there has been no event that might lead to an insurance claim (or the ship may be uninsured, or have had its cover removed). Unless there has been a "maritime casualty" to the ship,[103] there will be no possibility for the WRC 2007 to apply, eg to enable a State to remove the ship and reclaim the costs against the WRC 2007 insurer.[104] The ship would not be a "wreck" to attract the obligations and liabilities of the owner (or insurer) under the WRC 2007.

---

96 Scientific advice may be available from the Joint Nature Conservation Committee (JNNC) which is the statutory adviser to the UK government and devolved administrations (including overseas territories). It has produced, inter alia, the Coastal Directories—a series of regional reports covering the whole of the UK coast, and over 600 reports some of which consider the effect of wrecks in the marine environment: see http://jncc.defra.gov.uk/page-0.

97 Part 8 of the Act creates "marine enforcement officers" (as appointed by the MMO, but including naval officers) with wide associated powers, including directing a vessel to port and detaining it (s.259). Part 7 of the Waste (England and Wales) Regulations 2011 requires that offshore licensing functions (eg powers of inspection under Part 4 of the 2009 Act or Part 2 of the 1985 Act) for the deposit of wastes at sea are exercised to implement waste management plans and to give effect to relevant principles of the Waste Framework Directive 2008: see 14.6.

98 Ss 90–91; see also Sch 7 for civil sanctions.

99 Natural England may need to be consulted, although consent may not be needed in an emergency.

100 MMO guidance: www.gov.uk/guidance/make-a-marine-licence-application.

101 For abandonment in the different contexts of insurance and ownership, see 2.9.4(c), 3.3.

102 See 11.4.

103 See 8.2.1, 10.5.1(a).

104 Under Art 12(10): see 8.2.1(f), 10.5.1(a).

Yet for the port authority or State, there may be great practical problems in dealing with such abandoned ships.[105] Normally the owner or operator will be insolvent, or on the verge of insolvency and the chance of recovering assets may be difficult, time consuming and costly—especially where there is a foreign owner and the centre of the debtor's main interests is in another State.[106] In the meantime, the ship may be occupying an important berth and causing economic disruption in the port. If the abandonment were caused by the impecuniosity of the owner, rather than the condition of the ship, it is likely that many claimants would come forward with claims against it. These may well include cargo claimants or charterers, but it is also highly likely that a bank would intervene to protect its mortgage.

All these claimants would expect to arrest the ship and obtain a court order for appraisement and sale. Almost certainly, though, the ship will be old and without commercial value except possibly for scrap. The costs of towing it to a scrapping yard may well exceed its residual value—so that it is a constructive total loss in a commercial sense. The longer the ship is abandoned, the more likely it is to deteriorate. This in turn may prompt the authorities to take precautionary measures to ensure its safety and prevent damage to the environment. It may be normal for water to enter the ship's bilges, eg via a tail shaft, and in routine operating circumstances this would be pumped out. By this stage, the ship may well have used all its bunkers so that engines and pumps may not be operating. The authorities may feel obliged to supply power and some form of caretaker maintenance, but with little hope of recompense. Moreover, while it rests afloat, it may well have crew on board who have been equally 'abandoned', especially where there are no bunkers to provide electric power, and food runs out. Remedies for the crew are improving,[107] but local authorities may be under some pressure to provide financial or other assistance to them.

Of course, there might come a stage when the abandoned ship deteriorates so badly that it sinks (or is in serious danger of sinking) and becomes a wreck in a general sense. If there is pollution, eg from bunkers, the State may be covered by the Bunkers Convention 2001 but if the ship has been abandoned for a long time its certificate of compulsory insurance may have expired.[108] Further, unless a State can point to some "maritime casualty" it seems that the WRC 2007 would not apply, as it was not designed to cover sinking by mere poor maintenance.[109]

For these reasons, there is a potential gap in convention protection and States may need to ensure that they have in place national legislation to deal with such abandoned ships.[110] Further, the underlying problem with such national legislation[111] is that it lacks the

---

105 See Basel Convention Conference of the Parties UNEP BC-VII/27 2004; open ended working group.

106 See eg the Model Law on Cross Border Insolvency 1997 Art 17, the Cross-Border Insolvency Regulations 2006 (SI 2001/1030), the EC "Insolvency Regulation", Council Regulation (EC) No. 1346/2000 of 29 May 2000 on insolvency proceedings, and some of the issues that arise in maritime law: M Hafeez-Baig, "The Interaction of the Statutory Right of Action In Rem and the Cross-Border Insolvency Act 2008 (Cth)" (2018) 26 Insolv LJ 22, S Derrington, "The Interaction between Admiralty and Insolvency Law" (2009) 5 ANZMLJ 30.

107 See 2.2.

108 Eg at the usual P&I Club renewal date of 20 February, or because the insurer has given three months' notice of termination to the flag State under Art 7(6) of the Bunkers Convention 2001: see also 2.9 6, 2.6.3. There is a similar provision in Art VII(5) of the CLC 1992 and Art 12(5) of the HNSC 2010: see also 2.6.2(a), 2.6.4.

109 For discussion of arguments to avoid this conclusion, see 10.5.1(a) and 8.2.1(a).

110 See 11.4, 10.5.1(a), 8.2.1(f).

111 See 11.1.

fundamental protection provided by Art 12 of the WRC 2007, namely compulsory insurance and direct action.¹¹² It is almost axiomatic that a claim against the impecunious owner will be pointless, and so the main remedy for the State will be to remove the ship itself, perhaps even destroy it,¹¹³ or to sell the ship and reclaim any expenses from the proceeds of sale.¹¹⁴

14.3 Scrapping of ships generally

Owners might want to dump wrecks where they have no inherent value, or the cost of getting them to a scrapyard would exceed any residual value, or there is a high risk that they would not survive the voyage. Where owners are not allowed to dump the wreck they will need to find a way to dispose of it. This will present a variety of practical and commercial choices. The older terminology used by shipowners has been "scrapping", but other commercial expressions are used such as "demolition" or "shipbreaking" (eg by shipbrokers selling old ships). In the international sphere, "dismantling" or "ship recycling" are now used more generally in legal regulatory instruments and contracts.

The disposal of ships at the end of their useful commercial lives has become more of a problem for shipowners as environmental standards have tightened in the developed world, particularly in dealing with hazardous wastes. Moreover, there is increasing pressure to recycle as much as possible. Commercial pressure to reduce costs has led to the export of industrial wastes to developing States where there may be a lack of regulatory structure, or will, to apply high safety and environmental standards. The international community has reacted in two ways in particular: first, by trying to prohibit such transboundary movements of waste generally under the Basel Convention;¹¹⁵ secondly, by addressing the particular problem of the dismantling and recycling of ships under the Hong Kong Convention.¹¹⁶ At a regional level, the EU has acted to produce legislation to deal with wastes within the EU itself,¹¹⁷ but also to bolster the two international conventions.¹¹⁸

All this legislative activity has produced a mass of sometimes overlapping requirements—none of which are particularly designed to deal with the wreck of ships and their cargoes, although all of them may apply to varying degrees and in different circumstances. It is difficult to disentangle the legislative requirements, but they are having an increasing importance in relation to wreck removal and are posing many additional difficulties for wreck removal contractors—who are already having to cope with the nautical, engineering and environmental problems in actually raising wrecks. The difficulties cannot be ignored and have to be factored into planning for the wreck removal operation. This itself takes an increasing amount of time and is often compounded by having to deal with more government agencies, eg not only a maritime administration to approve the wreck raising, but also an environment agency (and local authorities) to approve of the disposal of the

---

112 See 10.8, and 10.8.4.
113 See eg the MSA 1995 ss 252(2)(a) and 253(1)(b): 11.1.3, also 11.3.
114 See eg the MSA 1995 ss 252(2)(c)–(d), 253(2): 11.1.3.
115 See, 14.4.1.
116 See 14.5.1.
117 See 14.6.
118 See 14.4.2, 14.5.2.

wreck.[119] Owners and operators will examine closely whether the legislation is actually binding on them. It is inevitable that there will be attempts at avoidance, eg through reliance on non-EU flag States.

The practical difficulties are well illustrated by wrecks such as the *MSC Napoli*, the *Rena*, and the *Costa Concordia*.[120] Another example is the car carrier *Baltic Ace*, wrecked off Rotterdam in 2012 while carrying over 1,400 vehicles. The wreck was cut into eight sections and loaded onto four barges, along with some 5,000 mt of smaller parts recovered from the seabed using a large salvage grab. Some 13,000 mt of steel was recovered and the barges were then taken to a nearby recycling yard in Vlaardingen.[121] The *MSC Chitra* and *Smart* casualties[122] show that there may be difficulties in finding scrapyards at a convenient location willing to take the wreck; both were ultimately disposed of at sea.[123]

A 'normal' end of life scrapping voyage may already present risks. In December 2016 two unmanned supply vessels foundered off Ushant, sinking in 200 m of water, while under tow to Turkey where they had been sold to a shipyard for recycling.[124] This was an accident involving a major reputable international company despite preparations lasting four months, but redundancies during the planning operation may have contributed to inadequate towing preparations. In order to keep down costs at the end of a vessel's life, it may be advantageous to have a dead tow (ie where it is unmanned operationally). This itself can increase risks. Moreover, both the ships had residual fluids on board[125] which, according to common practice, were to be disposed of by the shipyard.

This chapter will next consider the two international conventions and their implementation into EU law (in so far as they may relevant to disposing of ships themselves), before looking at the more general EU Waste Framework Directive (which will be more relevant to disposal of cargoes and bunkers).

14.4 Transboundary waste disposal

The movement of waste from one country to another may be relevant to wreck, eg when it is decided to move to other countries the remains of ruined cargo or, possibly, the hull of the ship itself.

14.4.1 Basel Convention 1989

The Basel Convention on Transboundary Movement of Hazardous Wastes and their Disposal 1989 (Basel Convention) was designed to prevent the export of hazardous wastes

---

119 See eg 4.2.
120 See 1.2.3, 1.2.4, 1.2.5.
121 See *Baltic Ace Wreck Removal*; also 10.2.5, 2.5.9(c).
122 See 10.2.5.
123 See also the *Galapaface* and *Floreana*: 10.2.6.
124 Danish Maritime Accident Investigation Board, "Marine Accident Report on Mærsk Battler's loss of tow on 21 and 22 December 2016" (2017). Apparently, a waste disposal certificate had to be obtained before the ship could leave a Danish port, but it is not clear if this was under the EU Waste Shipment Regulation (see 14.4.2).
125 These residues may have been "unpumpable" (EMSA Newsletter No 144, March 2017), but the amounts could still be environmentally significant. Thus, one ship, *Maersk Searcher* (4,013 gt), had 78 mt of waste oil and sludge, 40 mt of fuel/diesel, 22 mt of lubricating oil, 12 mt in bilges, 6 mt of hydraulic oil and 1 mt of base oil (cargo): *Maersk Battler* Report, 28.

generally to non-OECD States.[126] It mainly puts burdens on the OECD States to police their waste exporters, either banning exports of certain wastes altogether or requiring that transboundary movements are notified to all States concerned—often called 'prior informed consent'. Wastes are required to be managed in an environmentally sound manner.[127] Under Art 6, the exporting State[128] has to oblige the generator or exporter of waste (the "notifier") to notify the exporting and importing State of the proposed transboundary movement. The exporting State must prevent movement until the State of import has (i) provided written consent and (ii) confirmed that there is a contract between the exporter and the ultimate "disposer" specifying environmentally sound management of the wastes in question.[129] If an export cannot be completed in accordance with the contractual terms, there is an obligation on the exporter to re-import the goods to the exporting State unless disposal can be achieved in an environmentally sound manner.[130]

The definition of wastes in Art 2.1 of the Basel Convention is very wide: they are "substances or objects which are disposed of or are intended to be disposed of or are required to be disposed of by the provisions of national law". Under Art 2.3, "disposal" covers any operation mentioned in Annex IV, which itself includes landfill, incineration (on land or at sea) and the recycling of metals.[131] The hazardous wastes subject to the Convention under Art 1.1 are those listed in Annex 1 (or considered as hazardous by domestic legislation).

The list of substances covered by the Basel Convention is very long, but of course is predicated on the substance actually being a "waste". The Basel Convention was particularly designed to focus on land-based exporters who, for instance, might transport containers of wastes (using normal shipping lines) which were then in effect dumped in developing countries. There are documentary requirements on those shipping lines,[132] but neither a ship nor its normal cargo would be wastes at the start of the voyage. The Basel Convention does not specifically deal with "ships", wrecks or their recycling at all. But its list of substances covered is in such general language that it might be said to apply in some circumstances.

It seems clear that where ruined cargoes are removed from a wreck and brought to land for temporary storage, before being disposed of elsewhere, the Basel Convention would apply to that subsequent export.[133] More difficult is whether the Convention could apply (i)

---

126 See Basel website: www.basel.int/Home/tabid/2202/Default.aspx. There is a regular Conference of the Parties (COP) which also holds joint sessions with regional convention parties, eg under the Rotterdam Convention on the Prior Informed Consent Procedure for Certain Hazardous Chemicals and Pesticides in International Trade and the Stockholm Convention on Persistent Organic Pollutants: see eg UNEP/CHW.13/28, 16 August 2017.

127 See Art 2.8.

128 Ie the State party from which a transboundary movement of hazardous wastes or other wastes is planned to be initiated or is initiated: Art 2.10.

129 Art 6.3.

130 Art 8.

131 Annex IV D1, D10, D11, R4.

132 Article 6.9 provides that the Parties "shall require that each person who takes charge of a transboundary movement of hazardous wastes or other wastes sign the movement document either upon delivery or receipt of the wastes in question". The "movement document", required under Art 4.7(c), has to contain a list of information set out in Annex VB. The Notes to the Annex advise that the information required on the movement document shall where possible be integrated in one document with that required under transport rules, but it may be difficult to incorporate all the information in a traditional bill of lading or waybill.

133 Eg the containers brought ashore from many casualties, eg the *MSC Napoli*: see 1.2.3.

to that wreck cargo waste from the moment that it is moved from the wreck site to land in a neighbouring State across boundaries,[134] or (ii) to the disposal and recycling of the hull of the ship itself.

To deal with recycling of ships first, there have been many debates within the Conference of the Parties (COP) to the Basel Convention about recycling (or dismantling) of ships generally[135] (and not particularly from wreck sites), especially in view of the hazardous material such as asbestos, PCBs and waste oils that may be on board. This has led to a focus on what to do with waste after recycling, but the position seems to have been unclear on whether and how the Basel Convention applies to a ship planned for normal scrapping and recycling, let alone a wreck that needs to be scrapped and recycled after a casualty. At the COP in 2004 it was accepted that ships could become waste under Art 2,[136] but the underlying scheme of the Basel Convention relied on exporting States for enforcement. Very often, a ship destined for recycling would be flagged in a non-OECD State, or may have been reflagged for one. Scrapping voyages would be very difficult to monitor and could be disguised by organising a bogus penultimate voyage to a non-State party, or organising a sale on the high seas.[137] The so called 'Basel Ban amendment 1995' (restricting export to non-party States) is not in force internationally.[138] The difficulties of application of the Basel Convention to ship recycling generally led the COP to support work with the IMO, which ultimately led to the Hong Kong Convention.[139]

The broader question of whether the Basel Convention can apply to ships and cargoes that are ruined in a wreck is a slightly different one, although dealing with a wrecked hull can present similar environmental risks to end of life ships generally. There is a significant difference between the deliberate export of waste stored on land and the consequences of having to deal with a maritime casualty where once sound items become ruined. Can those items become "waste" in the middle of a voyage? This distinction was at the heart of the controversial *Commune de Mesquier* case dealing with an oil cargo in a different EU context.[140]

The practical relevance of this to wreck removal operations is that if the wreck of a ship and its cargo do constitute "waste", there will be Basel Convention regulatory hurdles (backed by criminal sanctions) for those involved in the removal operation, including recycling. There may also be quite separate civil liability issues, although not at present under the Basel Convention. A Liability and Compensation Protocol was added in 1999, but the Protocol is not in force. However, there may be civil liabilities under EU law.[141]

---

134 This is arguably a transboundary movement within Art 1.3, and probably extends to a State's EEZ (see Art 1.9). See also Art 7 for movements through non-parties.
135 See eg UNEP/CHW.13/28, 16 August 2017, 32–33.
136 UNEP BC-VII/26 and UNEP/CHW.7/33, 25 January 2005, 5–6.
137 See P Heidegger, Dirty and Dangerous Shipbreaking, 17 April 2015, www.iims.org.uk/dirty-and-dangerous-shipbreaking/.
138 By April 2019, only two more States out of 66 needed to adopt it: UNEP/CHW.14/28, 11 May 2019, 9. For the EU position, see 14.4.2.
139 See 14.5.1.
140 See 14.6.3.
141 See 14.6.3.

14.4.2 EU Waste Shipment Regulation 2006

The Basel Convention was implemented in the EU from 1993 and is now governed by the "Waste Shipment Regulation" 2006.[142] This included the Basel Ban amendment 1995 and also gave effect to an OECD decision.[143] The Waste Shipment Regulation 2006 entered into force generally in 2007, and is directly applicable in the UK, but is supplemented by the Transfrontier Shipment of Waste (TSWR) Regulations 2007,[144] which provide for offences and penalties for non-compliance with the EU Regulation and identify the competent authorities for shipments of waste within the UK. There are also administrative guidance documents.[145] The International Waste Shipments (Amendment) (EU Exit) Regulations 2019[146] will amend the TSWR with effect on the day that the UK exits the EU.

The Waste Shipment Regulation 2006 has a wide scope of application in Art 1 so that it applies to shipments of waste: "(a) between Member States, within the Community or with transit through third countries; (b) imported into the Community from third countries; (c) exported from the Community to third countries: (d) in transit through the Community, on the way from and to third countries". It is the references to third countries that gives effect to the Ban amendment 1995 and makes the EU supervision and control wider than that presently covered under the Basel Convention itself.[147]

The Waste Shipment Regulation 2006 covers most types of waste, but excludes the offloading of ships' normal operational waste.[148] In view of the difficulty of deciding whether the Basel Convention applied to ships themselves, a new Art 1(3)(i) was inserted into the Waste Shipment Regulation to exclude ships flying the flag of a Member State falling under the scope of the EU Ship Recycling Regulation 2013.[149] Where that particular Regulation applies, it will govern ship recycling, but there may be circumstances where it does not apply and it may still be necessary to consider whether ships are covered by default in other

---

142 Regulation (EC) No 1013/2006 of the European Parliament and of the Council (OJ L 190, 12 July 2006); slightly amended by the EU Ship Recycling Regulation (EU) No 1257/1013 Art 27: see 14.5.2. The Waste Shipment Regulation is being evaluated for a review by 2020: http://ec.europa.eu/environment/waste/shipments/evaluation_of_the_wsr.htm.

143 Decision of the OECD Council C (2001) 107/final, as amended by C(2004)20.

144 SI 2007/1711, as amended, eg by the Transfrontier Shipment of Waste (Amendment) Regulations 2014 (SI 2014/861) (devolving some powers); see also fn 146. The TSWR apply not only to the UK's territorial sea, but also to areas where the UK has in effect exercised rights within the EEZ and continental shelf: see reg 4(1)(c) and eg the Renewable Energy Zone (Designation of Area) Order 2004 (SI 2004/2668) referring to a Renewable Energy Zone which is coextensive with the limits of the zone within which the UK already exercises jurisdiction with respect to marine environmental matters (see now the under the Merchant Shipping (Prevention of Pollution) (Limits) Regulations 2014 (SI 2014/3306)).

145 See eg Department for Environment Food & Rural Affairs (DEFRA), 'UK Plan for Shipments of Waste', May 2012 (drawn up under the 2007 Regulations), and 'Waste: import and export' (15 April 2016) www.gov.uk/guidance/importing-and-exporting-waste.

146 SI 2019/590. Part 2 of these 2019 Regulations also makes amendments to the current TSWR: see fn144.

147 The Regulation makes no reference to whether it applies not only in territorial waters of Member States but also within their EEZs. A similar issue was left open in the *Commune de Mesquer* case on the Waste Framework Directive 2008: see 14.6.3. Note that the UK supplementary legislation does apply in the EEZ: see fn 144.

148 Provided it is subject to MARPOL.

149 Regulation (EU) No 1257/2013 of the European Parliament and of the Council, Art 27: see 14.5.2. The provision was designed to avoid duplication between the two Regulations, by providing that the Ship Recycling Regulation control regime (see 14.5.2) would take precedence (see Recital 10).

legislation. Ships not covered by the Ship Recycling Regulation 2013 and wastes on board the ship (other than operational wastes which are covered by MARPOL) may therefore be governed by the Waste Shipment Regulation 2006 or the Waste Framework Directive 2008.[150] In one decision of the Rotterdam District Court, a ship was considered waste under the Waste Shipment Regulation 2006 where there was a subjective intention to discard.[151] The Waste Shipment Regulation 2006 will therefore be important where wastes such as ruined cargoes are moved across State boundaries. Where there is a wreck within one EU member State and wastes are disposed of in that State, the more general waste provisions of the Waste Framework Directive 2008 will apply.[152]

The content of the Waste Shipment Regulation follows that of the Basel Convention, eg with requirements to ensure that waste is managed in an environmentally sound manner.[153] Exports of waste from the EU destined for *disposal* are prohibited,[154] unless for EFTA States who are party to the Basel Convention.[155] Export of wastes to non-OECD States for *recovery* (eg recycling) is also prohibited if they are listed in Art 36 (eg hazardous wastes in Annex V).[156] There are also prohibitions on imports of waste other than from Basel Convention parties.[157] Bilateral agreements between EU and non-EU States may allow for imports, eg where it cannot be managed in an environmentally sound manner in the non-EU State, but the Commission has to be notified.[158]

Where shipment is allowed, the level of control varies. For 'green' listed or non-hazardous wastes, the Waste Shipment Regulation imposes general information requirements normally applicable to the shipment of wastes for recovery.[159] But for other wastes, eg certain hazardous wastes,[160] there has to be prior notification[161] and consent[162] of States involved in the shipment, eg the States of shipment and destination. Notification is effected

---

150 See 14.6.
151 District Court of Rotterdam 10/994550–15, 15 March 2018: www.rechtspraak.nl/Organisatie-en-contact/Organisatie/Rechtbanken/Rechtbank-Rotterdam/Nieuws/Documents/English%20translation%20Seatrade.pdf. See also www.nortonrosefulbright.com/en/knowledge/publications/f686f825/seatrade-a-new-approach-to-violations-of-regulations-on-ship-recycling-in-the-european-union;
152 See 14.7.
153 See eg Recital 33 and Arts 24(3), 34(3), 35(3), 36(1), 38(3), 49.
154 Art 34(1). See also Art 40 for exports to overseas territories.
155 Art 34(2) and 35
156 Separate provisions apply in Art 38 to exports to States where the OECD Decision applies: see fn 143. For exports to OECD States, see Art 38.
157 Arts 41–45.
158 Art 41(2). In "emergency situations" that notification can be delayed; this appears to be the only reference to the type of circumstance involved in wreck removal cases, but is of little help. The UK Guidance indicates that in emergencies imports are allowed from any State, provided competent authorities have been informed (or there is a "duly reasoned request" from a non-OECD State), and exports are allowed to Member States and EFTA States; 'UK Plan for Shipments of Waste' paras 12–14. 19–21.
159 See Art 18 and Annex III and IIIA.
160 See Annex IV and V.
161 See Art 4. The "notifier" will be an original producer, but may also be a holder', ie "the producer of the waste or the natural or legal person who is in possession of it" See Art 2(10) and Art 2(15).
162 Art 9.

by the completion both of a "notification document"[163] and a "movement document"[164] for the shipment. The States may also impose conditions for shipment.[165] There has to be a contract between the notifier and consignee[166] which includes the 'take-back' obligations from Basel Convention.[167] Financial guarantees are required eg to cover costs of transport and disposal.[168]

The EU has estimated that there was a 25% non-compliance with the Waste Shipment Regulation and sought to bolster it by requiring stricter inspection systems in Member States.[169] Under the TSWR Regulations 2007[170] the extensive powers of authorised persons given by the Environment Act 1995 s 108 are extended to waste vessels, and the Regulations create a whole series of offences for individuals and companies.[171]

For wrecks within the EU, although there is some doubt as to the extent to which the Waste Shipment Regulation 2006 can apply to the ship itself, there is clearly regulatory pressure for hull and cargo to be disposed of within the EU. EU shipowners might seek to avoid the Regulation by selling the wrecked ship for cash to a foreign company which reflags it and takes it directly out of the EU.[172] There may be difficulties of enforcement against such non-EU shipowners, but shipowners who arrange for the waste to be exported out of the EU from the wreck site may be treated as notifiers[173] and sale transactions designed simply to avoid the Regulation risk being treated as a form of arrangement. In some ways the position of wrecked and ruined cargo taken from a hull is a little different. Shipowners who arrange for such waste to be exported out of the EU from the wreck site may again be treated as notifiers, or possibly brokers[174] on behalf of the cargo owners, or even producers.[175] It would make no difference if the shipowner arranged for this waste to be transported on a non-EU ship, but again there may be difficulties of enforcement against non-EU shipowners.

Wreck removal contractors could also face similar difficulties as they fit more closely the definition of brokers, ie "anyone arranging the recovery or disposal of waste on behalf of others, including such brokers who do not take physical possession of the waste".[176] In any

---

163 See Art 4(1) and Annex IA. Further information required is listed in Annex II Part 1.
164 See Art 16 and Annex IB. Further information required is listed in Annex II Part 2. Annex IC contains specific instructions for completing both the notification and movement documents.
165 Art 10.
166 Art 5.
167 See 14.4.1.
168 Art 6. See Regs 48–49 and Sch 4 of the TSWR Regulations 2007.
169 Regulation (EU) No 660/2014 of 15 May 2014. See also the EU Waste Shipment website, which also includes information about case law: http://ec.europa.eu/environment/waste/shipments/
170 Reg 51, Sch 5.
171 Companies could be liable for an unlimited fine and imprisonment is possible for individuals: see Regs 55, 58.
172 A variation on this device is to send the ship on a sham voyage to a non-EU State, eg in the Middle East, but where it is actually destined for a break-up voyage to India or Pakistan. Duplicate insurance certificates might seek to hide the true last-voyage insurance position. Such arrangements pose risks of criminal prosecutions for those involved, including insurers and brokers.
173 If "under the jurisdiction" of the member state from where the waste is removed: see Art 1(15) and fn 161.
174 See Art 2(13).
175 See Art 2(9) and cf 14.6.4(a).
176 Art 2(13). See also the discussion in 14.6.4.

event, it may well be that in practice it will normally be more convenient for the contractors to bring wrecked and ruined cargo ashore to the nearest convenient port, eg in the EU. The point then is that there will be restrictions on re-exporting it.

14.5 Ship recycling

14.5.1 Hong Kong Ship Recycling Convention 2009

The export of "toxic ships" for scrapping has given rise to much controversy, especially in relation to the beaching of vessels[177] and there have been many concerns among international organisations about the lack of safety and environmental regulation in many of the ship dismantling and disposal industries in developing States. This has led to attempts to restrict disposal by putting obligations on developed states whose companies want to dispose of ships.[178]

The Secretariat of the Basel Convention had produced technical guidelines for the environmentally sound dismantling of ships in 2002, and similar guidelines with a similar purpose had been produced by the ILO and IMO in 2004 and 2005. As noted,[179] the Basel Convention was ill-suited to deal with the particular problems of ships and it became clear to UNEP, the ILO and IMO that concerted action was needed to produce an international instrument to facilitate the safe and environmentally sound recycling of ships generally.

The Hong Kong International Convention for the Safe and Environmentally Sound Recycling of Ships (Hong Kong Convention) 2009 was designed to achieve this aim. It must be noted at the outset that it was not designed to deal specifically with wrecks. Moreover, it is not yet in force, although its principles are implemented in the EU.[180] The Convention focused on three main areas. The first concentrated on the ships to be recycled, in particular their design, operation and (most importantly) their preparation for recycling. The second was to concentrate on the recycling facilities themselves, eg by requiring recycling yards to have a "Ship Recycling Plan". The third was to deal with appropriate enforcement mechanisms.

Some key features of the Hong Kong Convention 2009 that might be relevant to wreck disposal can be outlined here.[181] The Convention puts obligations on flag State parties to ensure that their ships comply with the convention, and that they are surveyed and certified accordingly.[182] The detail is largely set out in the Annex to the Convention which contains "Regulations for Safe and Environmentally Sound Recycling of Ships". Regulation 4 requires States parties to prohibit or restrict the installation or use of certain hazardous

---

177 See eg the controversy over the car carrier *Global Spirit*, which was destined for scrapping in India in 2014 until an NGO pressured environmental authorities in Antwerp to block the export until the owners and operators agreed to send the ship for recycling in Turkey where the 'landing' method was used: www.shipbreakingplatform.org/global-spirit/. The same NGO had previously put pressure on the UK to apply the Basel Convention to the LNG tanker *Margaret Hill* that had been laid up in Southampton in 2009.

178 See eg *Puthecherril*; M Tsimplis, "The Hong Kong Convention on the Recycling of Ships" [2010] LMCLQ 305 [*Tsimplis, Hong Kong Convention*].

179 See 14.4.1.

180 See the EU Ship Recycling Regulation, 14.5.2. Two more States are needed to adopt the Convention for entry into force, but there are other volume criteria to be met.

181 See further *Puthecherril*, 147–167; *Tsimplis, Hong Kong Convention*.

182 See Arts 4, 5.

materials, such as asbestos, or PCBs[183] on its ships. There are also port State control obligations on States parties.[184]

Central to the Hong Kong Convention 2009 is reg 5 which requires all new ships[185] to have on board an "Inventory of Hazardous Materials". Existing ships shall comply as far as practicable not later than 5 years after the entry into force of the Convention, "or before going for recycling if this is earlier". The latter requirement will obviously be highly relevant to wreck disposals for recycling, but compliance with this regulation is supposed to take into account guidelines to be developed by the IMO. Initial guidelines used the expression "green passport" for the Inventory,[186] but more detailed Inventory guidelines have since been produced.[187] The minimum requirement for existing ships is that "a plan shall be prepared describing the visual/sampling check by which the Inventory of Hazardous Materials is developed". It is not clear how onerous this task will be for some wrecks, and the assessment as to what is "practicable" will need a great deal of flexibility where wrecks have been raised or cut into sections for transport on barges. Access to the internals of the wreck may well be dangerous, and it may be time consuming to try to piece together a record from paper sources. It may be that preparing an Inventory is yet another part of the planning process for wreck raising, ie investigations into the ship's records may need to precede the raising. The downside is that this can lead to yet more delay and expense.

In addition to preparing an Inventory, a ship has to be conducted so as to "minimize[188] the amount of cargo residues, remaining fuel oil, and wastes remaining on board" prior to entering the authorised Ship Recycling Facility.[189] Moreover, the ship's readiness for recycling will have to be certified by the Flag State Administration, or an organisation recognised by it (presumably including a classification society). In addition, before recycling a "Ship Recycling Plan" has to be developed by the Facility, taking into account the information provided by the shipowner.

Regulation 1.8 defines "shipowner" to mean the registered shipowner "or, in the absence of registration, the person or persons or company owning the ship or any other organization or person such as the manager, or the bareboat charterer, who has assumed the responsibility for operation of the ship". The final sentence of Reg 1.8 provides that an owner "also includes those who have ownership of the ship for a limited period pending its sale or handing over to a Ship Recycling Facility". Thus, responsibilities may depend on whether the wreck has been sold, eg to the wreck removal contractor or to the scrapyard,[190] Where

---

183 The full list of substances is in Appendix 1 of the Annex.
184 See eg regs 4(2), 8, 9 and *Puthecherril*, 161–2.
185 Defined in reg 1(4), but essentially only covering ships contracted for or delivered after the entry into force of the convention.
186 See eg the Guidelines on Ship Recycling, IMO Assembly Resolution A.962(23), 2003; Guidelines for the Safe and Environmentally Sound Ship Recycling, Resolution MEPC 2010(63), 2012.
187 Guidelines for the Development of the Inventory of Hazardous Materials, Resolution MEPC 269(68), 2015, superseding MEPC 197(62), 2011.
188 The vagueness of this expression has been criticised as failing to ensure the prior removal of hazardous wastes: see *Puthecherril*, 175.
189 There are particular obligations for tankers under Reg 8.4.
190 See 14.7.1.

a wreck has ceased to be registered after it became a wreck,[191] there may be circumstances where a wreck contractor assumes responsibility even if it does not become an owner.

The fact that the Hong Kong Convention 2009 is not yet in force is, in part, a reflection of the practical and political difficulties faced in its drafting, particularly in relation to enforcement. Many recycling facilities are in developing states (eg India, Bangladesh and Pakistan) where the industry supplies much employment, and these States may be reluctant to join a regime that imposes obligations on them to ensure that their ship recycling facilities comply with, and are authorised under, the Hong Kong Convention 2009. Further, the enforcement of any international regime would depend on there being a large number of flag States who would agree to enforce it. As with the Basel Convention 1989, an obvious way around such regulation would be for a single shipowning company to sell a ship at the end of its life to a shell company, which could flag the ship in a State not party to any regulatory system of the Hong Kong Convention 2009 and/or consign the ship to recycling in a non-State party. In theory, the "owner" may be pursued by the original flag State as part of its general obligations under Art 1(1) to give full and complete effect to the convention,[192] but there are doubts about the willingness or ability of some open register States to enforce criminal laws against foreign companies whose employees are outside its jurisdiction.

Shipowners could voluntarily agree to apply Hong Kong Convention 2009 standards through contract, eg by selling the vessel to an intermediary on the basis of BIMCO's Recyclecon 2012 contract, but there may be commercial opposition, eg from prospective buyers.[193] Recyclecon was envisaged by BIMCO as a contract that could be used in the interim before the Hong Kong Convention (with all its State approval requirements) entered into force,[194] but it is more important next to take into account the EU's activity in relation to ship recycling.

14.5.2 EU Ship Recycling Regulation 2013

14.5.2(a) Introduction and entry into force

Given the regulatory difficulties of bringing the Hong Kong Convention 2009 into force, the EU decided to enact the EU "Ship Recycling Regulation" 2013.[195] Its provisions had staggered dates for application, but the whole Ship Recycling Regulation 2013 applies from 31 December 2018.[196] Its purpose is to facilitate ratification of the Hong Kong Convention 2009 by giving effect within the EU to the Convention's provisions and control mechanisms. The Ship Recycling Regulation 2013 takes precedence over the EU Waste

---

191 See 14.7.2.
192 Including using authorised facilities: see reg 8 and Art 3.4, and cf *Puthecherril*, 151, 170–175.
193 See 14.1.1, 14.7.1.
194 See BIMCO's background explanatory note: www.bimco.org/contracts-and-clauses/bimco-contracts/recyclecon.
195 Regulation (EU) No 1257/2013 of the European Parliament and of the Council of 20 November 2013. See M Tsimplis, "Recycling of EU ships: From prohibition to regulation?" [2014] LMCLQ 415.
196 Art 32.

Shipment Regulation 2006 to the extent that the latter applied Basel Convention standards for the recycling of ships themselves.[197]

Like all EU regulations it has direct effect in member States, but still needs national implementing measures in order for it to work administratively and in relation to enforcement. The EU Ship Recycling Regulation 2013 was eventually given effect in the UK by the Ship Recycling (Requirements in relation to Hazardous Materials on Ships) (Amendment etc) Regulations [Ship Recycling Requirements Regulations] 2018.[198] In order to ensure that the EU Ship Recycling Regulation 2013 continues to be effective in the UK as retained EU law after Brexit, the Ship Recycling (Facilities and Requirements for Hazardous Materials on Ships) (Amendment) (EU Exit) Regulations [Ship Recycling Requirements Regulations (EU Exit) Regulations] 2019[199] will take effect on the day the UK exits the EU. These UK Ship Recycling Requirements Regulations (EU Exit) Regulations 2019 merely amend the existing UK provisions giving effect to the EU Ship Recycling Regulation 2013 so that they work as retained EU law, eg so that: references in Art 2 to "ships flying the flag of a Member State" will read as "UK ships"; in Art 3 "Member State or third country" will read as "state"; in Art 5 (in relation to powers) "Commission" will read "Secretary of State". The substantive provisions applying to ship recycling will be the same articles of the EU Ship Recycling Regulation 2013, but derived through UK law including the UK Ship Recycling Requirements Regulations 2018.[200]

14.5.2(b) Scope

The EU Ship Recycling Regulation 2013 generally follows the Hong Kong Convention 2009.[201] Thus, the definitions are broadly similar but sometimes go into more detail.[202] Article 5 requires "new ships"[203] to have the Convention-based inventory of hazardous material, and existing ships to comply "as far as practicable" but anyway by the end of 2020.[204]

It is Art 6 that applies general requirements on shipowners when sending a ship of any age for recycling. Apart from the Convention inspired requirements to supply the recycling facility with all relevant information (including the inventory) there is a specific obligation in Art 6 on shipowners to ensure that all ships destined to be recycled (a) "are only recycled

---

197 See the Ship Recycling Regulation 2013 Art 27, amending the Waste Shipment Regulation 2006 Art 1(3) so that it did not apply to "ships flying the flag of a Member State falling under the scope of" the Ship Recycling Regulation 2013. This means that where the latter does not apply, the former may continue to do so: see 14.5.2, 14.5.3 and 14.4.2.

198 SI 2018/122.

199 SI 2019/277.

200 DEFRA issued an "Overview of ship recycling in the UK" in February 2007, but it is expected that the MCA will issue guidance on the application in the UK of the EU Ship Recycling Regulation 2013 as enacted in the UK Ship Recycling Requirements Regulations 2018.

201 Although merging some of the provisions found in the Convention and its Annex (containing the Regulations).

202 See the definition of shipowner in Art 3(14): 14.5.2 (below).

203 Here specifically defined in Art 3(2) by reference to three criteria, such contracted for after the date of the regulation or delivered 30 months after the date of the Regulation in 2013. Given the expected life of ships, this aspect of the Regulation is only likely to apply to wrecks of relatively new ships.

204 There are different dates for the application of these provisions, as set out in Art 32. Ships destined for recycling have to comply with the inventory requirements, as far as practicable, as from 31 December 2014, but for new and existing ships generally, the relevant date is 31 December 2020.

at facilities that are included in the European List"²⁰⁵ of ship recycling facilities,²⁰⁶ and (b) "conduct operations in the period prior to entering the ship recycling facility in such a way as to minimise the amount of cargo residues, remaining fuel oil, and ship generated waste remaining on board" and (c) hold a "ready for recycling certificate" issued by a designated authority of a Member State prior to any recycling and after receipt of a ship-specific recycling plan developed by the ship recycling facility under Art 7. This ship recycling plan is based on the requirements of the Hong Kong Convention 2009, and has to be approved by the State where the recycling is to take place. There are also requirements in Art 8 as to surveying of ships, with a final survey to be conducted prior to the ship being taken out of service and before the start of recycling. It is at that stage that the flag State Authority issues the ready for recycling certificate, which cannot last for more than five years.

Under Art 3(2) of the Ship Recycling Regulation 2013 the Regulation does not apply to (a) warships, (b) ships of less than 500 gt, (c) ships flagged in and operating throughout their life in waters subject to the sovereignty or jurisdiction of a Member State. The latter two categories are more likely to be scrapped within the EU, rather than being transported abroad but category (c) could cover some quite large ferries.

The Ship Recycling Regulation 2013 does not mention wreck at all, but the definition of "ship" in Art 3(1) means "a vessel of any type whatsoever operating or *having operated in the marine environment*, and includes submersibles, floating craft, floating platforms, self-elevating platforms, Floating Storage Units (FSUs), and Floating Production Storage and Offloading Units (FPSOs), as well as *a vessel stripped of equipment* or being towed".²⁰⁷ The general words emphasised should therefore apply to a wrecked and sunken ship²⁰⁸ as well as to a refloated ship—certainly if it is to be towed for recycling, but also if it were to be carried as cargo on a barge or heavylift craft. On the assumption that the Regulation can apply to a sunken ship, this means that the recycling plan must be created and approved when it may be very difficult to determine key information, eg as to the type and amount of hazardous materials and of waste to be generated by the recycling. There are obligations that might be difficult to satisfy where a ship has been partially dismantled while underwater or aground. Thus, under Art 6(3) owners of tankers are obliged to ensure that tankers arrive at the recycling facility with cargo tanks and pump rooms in a condition ready for

---

205 A UK List will be established in the place of the European List after EU exit day: see Part 2 of the Ship Recycling Requirements Regulations (EU Exit) Regulations 2019.

206 As established by Art 16 of the Regulation, in accordance with standards specified in Art 13. This list can include facilities in third countries (see Art 3(7)), but they will need to be inspected and certified on behalf of the Commission: see Art 15. A technical guidance note about inclusion was published in Commission Communication C/2016/1900. The European List was implemented by Commission Implementing Decision (EU) 2016/2323 of 19 December 2016, C/2016/8507. It contained 18 facilities in Member States, while applications from facilities in third countries were still being assessed. The List was updated by Commission Implementing Decision (EU) 2018/684 of 4 May 2018, but no third country facilities had by then been completed. To deal with the consequences of Brexit, the Commission issued a notice on 28 March 2018 to the effect that UK facilities would no longer appear in the European List (unless specifically extended to them): https://ec.europa.eu/info/sites/info/files/notice_to_stakeholders_brexit_ship_recycling_final.pdf.

207 Emphasis added. The Ship Recycling Regulation does not apply to ships under 500 gt, or warships (or those used in government non-commercial service): see Art 1.

208 Unless it be said that a sunken wrecked ship had ceased to be a ship or vessel at all, which would defeat one obvious purpose of the Regulation: cf 14.7.2.

certification as "safe-for-hot" work. It may be that many preparations for recycling would have to take place after the wreck or parts of it have been raised. It may not be possible to carry out such work at sea and this raises the possibility that the wreck may need to be taken to some intermediate port or facility for such work to be undertaken; ie the equivalent of what would happen to a laid-up ship prior to recycling.

The definition of "ship owner" in Art 3(14) means the registered owner (as with the Convention), but also specifically includes persons "owning the ship for a limited period pending its sale or handover to a ship recycling facility". This appears to be designed to cover commercial practices whereby ownership is transferred to wreck removal contractors immediately after wreck raising, but where it is anticipated that they may immediately transfer ownership of the wreck either to intermediate buyers who deal in scrap, or directly to the recycling yard.[209] In the same way it could apply to scrap buyers to whom ownership is transferred directly as part of a strategy of divestment by the registered owner prior to recycling (whether those are genuine buyers or shell companies). In these examples there may have been a deregistration after the sinking and reregistration may be seen as an unnecessary cost or burden.[210] If the ship is unregistered (or has been deregistered) the Regulation will apply to the owner or others such as ship managers and bareboat charterers who have "assumed the responsibility for operation of the ship from the owner". This could apply to a wreck removal contractor that had undertaken to raise the wreck and take it for recycling.

The key provision, though, that will govern the 'bite' of the EU Ship Recycling Regulation 2013 (especially in wreck cases) is Art 2, as it applies the Regulation, with one exception, to ships "flying the flag" of *Member States*. In international law the nationality and status of ships is defined by UNCLOS Arts 91 and 92, but ship registration is the normal evidence of the right to fly the flag.[211] In relation to wrecks, it is necessary to consider the interplay of the Regulation's flag State requirement with the definition of "ship owner", considered above. It would seem that owners of ships registered in EU Member States would not be able to avoid the Regulation *merely* by transferring the registration to a non-EU State. The Art 6(2) obligations, eg to ensure that ships are only recycled at facilities in the European List, apply to "ships destined to be recycled".[212] This will ultimately be a question of fact, and may be difficult to prove for ships that are nearing the end of their normal commercial lives where a seller could assert that a new foreign buyer might be able to trade the ship at a profit. In the case of wrecks, though, it will be fairly obvious that the ship will have to be taken away for dismantling. There appears to be no geographical restriction within the Regulation itself as to its operation,[213] which means that it could

---

209 See 14.7.1, 13.6.3(b), (i) and 13.6.5(g).

210 See 14.7.2.

211 And see Directive 2009/21/EC of the European Parliament and of the Council of 23rd April 2009 on compliance with flag State requirements, which was part of the Erika III package. It was implemented in the Merchant Shipping (Flag State Directive) Regulations 2011 (SI 2011 No. 2667).

212 Art 3(6) uses a different definition of recycling to that in the Waste Framework Directive 2008, but essentially means the dismantling of a ship at a ship recycling facility in order to recover materials for reprocessing or reuse. For possible offences in relation to Art 6(2), see 14.5.2(c).

213 Save within Art 2(2)(c) which excludes from its operation ships operating solely in the waters of one Member State.

impose obligations in respect of EU flagged ships that sink anywhere in the world and are taken to a recycling facility outside the EU.[214]

The exception to this jurisdictional restriction is the imposition of port state controls on ships flying the flag of third countries which call at ports in member States. These third party ships will be obliged to carry on board an "inventory of hazardous materials".[215] Apart from this, the effect of restricting the EU Ship Recycling Regulation 2013 to EU flagged ships means that the detailed regulatory requirements, derived from the Hong Kong Convention 2009 provisions, will not apply to a foreign flagged ship even if it is wrecked in the EU. If the Ship Recycling Regulation does not apply, then it may still be necessary to consider whether the Waste Shipment Regulation (based on the Basel Convention) might apply.[216]

Even if the Ship Recycling Regulation does not apply technically, the owner of a wreck may be under great pressure from an Affected State in the EU to agree to removal on the basis of its provisions. Here the State may seek to rely on its intervention powers[217] to insist that removal operations incorporate planning for ship recycling and may only approve removal to a local recycling facility (as apparently occurred with the *Costa Concordia*). Whether this is justified may depend upon the application of public law principles and excessive actions might be subject to judicial review. Whether any extra costs associated with using a particular facility can be claimed under the WRC 2007 will depend upon general questions of reasonableness[218] and when "removal" ceases under that convention.[219] One of the aims of BIMCO's Recyclecon 2012 contract for green recycling was to give some assurance to developing States that operations carried out under it were consistent with the Hong Kong Convention 2009 and many of its provisions would assist in ensuring compliance with the EU Ship Recycling Regulation 2013. It seems that it would be suitable, with amendments, to ensure compliance with the Regulation.[220]

14.5.2(c) UK Ship Recycling Requirements Regulations 2018

Article 22 of the EU Ship Recycling Regulation 2013 requires Member States to lay down provisions on penalties for infringement of the Regulation. In the UK, the Ship Recycling Facilities Regulations 2015[221] introduced arrangements which have enabled UK ship recycling facilities to appear on the EU's European List and they also designated various Agencies[222] and the Health and Safety Executive (HSE) to be competent authorities (eg to authorise ship recycling facilities). These Regulations deal only with the facilities

---

214 Provided that it is on the European List of ship recycling facilities.
215 See Arts 2 and 12.
216 See 14.4.2.
217 See 5.3.
218 See 10.2.4.
219 See 8.2.4, 10.2.8 and eg 13.6.3(i), 13.6.4(e), 13.6.5(g).
220 See C. Benedictsen-Nislev, "Rycyclecon—a new standard contract for ship recycling" (2012) 107 BIMCO Bulletin 12, 14: also 14.8.1.
221 SI 2015/430.
222 Eg the Environment Agency (for England), the Natural Resources Body for Wales, the Scottish Environment Protection Agency. See also the separate Ship Recycling Facilities Regulations (Northern Ireland) 2015 (SI 2015/229), which would apply to the Harland & Wolff facility, included in the European List.

themselves, which are already regulated under the EU's Waste Framework Directive 2008 and general health and safety legislation.[223]

Measures to enforce the EU Ship Recycling Regulation 2013 as from 31 December 2018 were introduced by the UK's Ship Recycling Requirements Regulations 2018.[224] Under them it will be the MCA,[225] acting through its normal port state control inspectors, that will have responsibility to apply the survey regime of Art 8 of the EU Ship Recycling Regulation 2013, eg to ensure UK flagged ships have the appropriate surveys and that EU ships have the appropriate documentation to show that they have complied.[226] It will also ensure that EU flagged ships destined to be recycled hold the appropriate documentation; ie that there is a "ship recycling plan" (from a recycling yard) and that prior to any recycling of the ship it has a "ready for recycling certificate" issued by the MCA (or other EU authorities).

The MCA will also exercise its port state control functions[227] arising under Art 12 of the EU Ship Recycling Regulation 2013 by verifying a ship's "inventory of hazardous materials" as required under Art 5. These regulatory powers will apply to UK registered ships and ships of any other flag in UK waters. There were concerns about how burdensome the Art 8 survey would be for MCA inspectors, but it appeared that the DfT took the view that a thorough investigation would not be required if a valid inventory was in place; ie there was to be a largely desk-based exercise. Unless flag States take a stricter approach, the utility of many inventories could be limited if they have been poorly prepared and monitored. Their existence might, though, be of some use to wreck removal contractors (and States) even before recycling, ie when they are assessing the environmental and safety risks in raising the wreck or leaving it on the seabed.

The issue of avoidance of the regulatory powers was raised after 2017 when the DfT published a draft of proposals for what became the Ship Recycling Requirements Regulations 2018. In its regulatory assessment it stated that the "preferred option is to implement all the necessary provisions in the EU Ship Recycling Regulation . . . without gold-plating". It then added that there "is a risk that some shipowners may continue to reflag their vessels to avoid complying with the new regulation, but the financial incentive to do so would be less and would carry a higher risk of reputational damage if they were caught". These justifications are not particularly convincing. In the DfT's 2018 summary of consultation responses it noted one response that "[i]t is not clear how the SI or EU Regulation will prevent late flag changes by ship owners in order to avoid higher compliance costs".

---

223 Eg under the Health and Safety at Work Act 1974 and its delegated legislation.

224 To be replaced on EU exit day by the UK's Ship Recycling Requirements Regulations (EU Exit) Regulations 2019.

225 Or a recognised organisation authorised by it. These could include a classification society, or even officials from BEIS or the HSE, given their knowledge of the oil & gas industry.

226 The powers of the MSA 1995 s 258(1)–(3) are given to the inspector or surveyor, eg to inspect and detain for inspection. Obstruction of an officer is an offence under reg 5 of the Ship Recycling Requirements Regulations 2018.

227 Under the Merchant Shipping (Port State Control) Regulations 2011 (SI 2011/2601), as amended by reg 7 of the Ship Recycling Requirements Regulations 2018. There are powers to detain ships, but note that under the MSA 1995 s 258(1A) powers of inspection cannot be used in relation to "qualifying foreign ships" exercising the UNCLOS rights of innocent passage or of transit through straits. "British" ships (as defined in the MSA 1995 s 1) and fishing vessels are not technically within Part I of the 2011 Regulations, but similar powers are granted by the Ship Recycling Requirements Regulations] 2018 reg 8.

The DfT reply was that the "EU Regulation does not create such an offence, due to the difficulty in linking reflagging to the intention to avoid requirements related to waste shipments or recycling".[228]

It does not appear that the enacted version of the Ship Recycling Requirements Regulations 2018 has closed this specific loophole for owners of EU ships, eg by making reflagging itself an offence. This apparently means that such reflagging of an EU registered wrecked ship could be used to send it directly to States such as India or Bangladesh for disposal,[229] but there are two caveats. First, in a wreck case where it is known fairly early that an EU ship will have to be recycled, the owners might be caught by criminal sanctions because of the Art 6(2) requirement that [EU] "ship owners shall ensure that ships *destined* to be recycled" comply with its three criteria, ie: (a) using recycling facilities on the European List, (b) minimising cargo, bunkers and other wastes on the ship, and (c) having a "ready for recycling certificate". There may be a period of time when it is clear that the ship will have to be recycled, but before ownership is transferred, eg if the wreck removal plan approved by an Affected State envisages recycling but ownership is only transferred after the ship is raised.[230] Here it could be said that the ship is "*destined*" to be recycled, even if all the final details have not been worked out.

The Ship Recycling Requirements Regulations 2018 reg 8 gives effect to obligations in the EU Ship Recycling Regulation 2013 by making the "ship owner" guilty of an offence in a number of circumstances, including non-compliance with Art 6(1)–(4). The offence will apply to a UK ship wherever it is in the world, eg including when it is wrecked and sunk. For ships of other Member States, it applies "when the ship is in port or anchorage in the United Kingdom or in United Kingdom waters". This would not seem to apply to a sunken ship that was wrecked, except eg if it were raised and then anchored. But even here it is not the mere fact of being anchored that counts, but whether it is at a place that is an "anchorage". That expression is not defined, but would include normal waiting places outside a port where ships wait. If a ship had sunk at such an anchorage then reg 8 might apply, perhaps even when he ship is still on the seabed—but at least to a period when, after raising, it was present *at* the anchorage prior to being removed elsewhere. An anchorage could include a place of refuge, such as Lyme Bay to which the *MSC Napoli* was ordered'[231] even if that was not a normal commercial anchorage. The only defence under reg 11 of the Ship Recycling Requirements Regulations 2018 is that the owner "took all reasonable steps to avoid committing the offence" and (assuming that reg 8 applied) this might be difficult to satisfy where the owner was obviously trying to avoid the regulatory requirements by reflagging.

Secondly, it can still be argued that where the Ship Recycling Regulations did not apply, the Waste Framework Directive 2008 and Waste Shipment Regulation might do so by

---

228 See "Summary of Consultation Responses: The Ship Recycling (Requirements in Relation to Hazardous Materials on Ships) Regulations 2018": https://assets.publishing.service.gov.uk/government/uploads/system/uploads/attachment_data/file/701146/SHIP_RECYCLING_CONSULTATION_COMMENTS_19_APRIL_2018.pdf.
229 See also 14.7.2.
230 See 14.7.1.
231 See 1.2.3(b).

default;[232] eg where there is an intention to dispose of an EU ship that is wrecked in European waters and that ship is re-flagged with a non-Member State flag in order to avoid the application of the Ship Recycling Regulation 2013.[233] In those circumstances, compliance with the Waste Shipment Regulation would be necessary.

Such uncertainties might put pressure on those with a business base in Europe, owing to the fear of prosecution under one of the EU regimes, particularly as reg 11 of the Ship Recycling Requirements Regulations 2018 provides that the offences could involve an unlimited fine or, on indictment, an additional two years' imprisonment. The UK would still use its port state control powers to ensure that ships, even flagged in non-EU States, comply with the EU Ship Recycling Regulation 2013, eg by having the inventory of hazardous materials on board.[234] This would be relevant to ships calling normally in the UK, eg prior to any wreck, or if the wreck disposal convoy calls into the UK.

14.6 EU Waste Framework Directive 2008

14.6.1 Background

The transboundary export of wastes and ship recycling have particular regulatory regimes that are relevant as to how to deal with wastes from wrecks.[235] There may be wastes from wreck that are not covered by these specific regimes, and this is particularly true for the wastes from cargoes carried on board ships that are wrecked and that are brought ashore in the territory of the wreck. For such wastes, and general debris recovered from the sea, disposal in landfill sites is a last resort. As with the recycling of ships, there are many practical (and commercial) difficulties in dealing with this general waste from wrecks. Oil and oil residues can sometimes be recycled; in the case of oil cargoes this may be facilitated by the cargo owner which might be an oil company with its own refining facilities or commercial relations with a refiner.[236] Animal carcasses present a particular problem.[237] In 2016, a fire in a cargo of wood pellets (ie biomass) in the *V Due* resulted in significant difficulties and costs in discharging the remains of the cargo for landfill in Liverpool. Such cargoes may actually need to be transhipped to other ports (eg Rotterdam) where there are more cargo disposal facilities. In extreme cases the costs of landfill may be greater than the value of the cargo, whose owners may decline to respond.

States have increasingly imposed regulatory standards for dealing with general wastes and these must now be taken into account in wreck removal cases. As has already been seen,[238] the EU has played a major role in creating legislation to deal with the export of

---

232 See fn 197 and 14.4.2.
233 It is not possible here to examine the possibility of preparatory offences, eg attempts and conspiracies where sham arrangements are made.
234 The Ship Recycling Requirements Regulations 2018 reg 8 creates an offence for the owner or master in failing to have on board a valid inventory of hazardous materials. Offences for non-EU ships are created by reg 9.
235 See 14.4, 14.5, 14.6.5(d). See generally, G Arguello, *Marine Pollution, Shipping Waste and International Law* (Routledge, 2019).
236 This occurred with the *Sea Empress* in 1996, when some oil was transferred to the Milford Haven oil refinery: see also 1.2.2(a).
237 See 14.1.2(b), 14.6.4(b), 13.1.3.
238 See 14.4.2, 14.5.2.

wastes and ship recycling. It has also created much wider and more general legislation on wastes and their disposal, and this is particularly relevant to the regulation in the EU of the disposal of wreck cargoes (as well as bunkers).[239] UK environmental legislation has aptly been described as an "unwieldy legal beast"[240] and problems with legislative coherence, integration and transparency are particularly evident when EU law is involved.[241] Unfortunately, there is much scope for uncertainty about overlap between particular wastes regimes and their application to wreck in particular.

The EU first introduced a legislation on waste disposal through Directive 75/442 (the 1975 Directive).[242] The 1975 Directive was primarily concerned with the safe *disposal* of waste,[243] but since then the regulatory scope has widened to include matters such as *recovery* (eg recycling). That Directive was amended five times[244] before a codified version incorporating those amendments was introduced in 2006 (the Codified Directive).[245]

On 22 July 2002, the European Parliament and Environment Council of Ministers adopted the "Sixth Community Environment Action Programme" which called for the revision of EU law on waste management to promote the sustainable use and management of natural resources and wastes.[246] As a consequence, the Codified Directive was repealed and Directive 2008/98/EC [Waste Framework Directive 2008] was agreed.[247] The Waste Framework Directive 2008 entered into force on 12 December 2008.[248] It re-enacted, revised and repealed the Codified Directive, integrated Directive 75/439/EEC[249] on the disposal of waste oils and integrated a modified version of Directive 91/689/EEC[250] on hazardous waste. The Waste Framework Directive 2008 represents the current position on waste disposal in the European Union. Like all Directives, it needs to be transposed into national

---

239 It may also create liabilities: see 14.6.3.
240 See UK Environmental Law Association, King's College London and Cardiff University, 'The State of UK Environmental Law in 2011–2012: Is there a case for legislative reform?' (May 2012), 2.
241 E Scotford, J Robinson, "UK Environmental Legislation and Its Administration in 2013: Achievements, Challenges and Prospects" (2013) 25 Journal of Environmental Law 3.
242 Directive 75/442/EEC of the European Parliament and of the Council of 15 July 1975 on waste [1975] OJ L 194/39.
243 Ibid., Preamble which read: "the essential objective of all provisions relating to waste disposal must be the protection of human health and the environment against harmful effects caused by the collection, transport, treatment, storage and tipping of waste".
244 See: Directive 91/156/EEC of 18 March 1991 amending Directive 75/442/EEC on waste [1991] OJ L 078/32. Council Directive 91/692/EEC of 23 December 1991 standardizing and rationalizing reports on the implementation of certain Directive relating to the environment [1991] OJ L 377/48. Commission Decision 96/350/EC of 24 May 1996 adapting Annexes IIA and IIB to Council Directive 75/442/EEC on waste [1996] OJ L 135/32. Regulation (EC) No 1882/2003 of the European Parliament and of the Council [2003] OJ L 284/1.
245 Directive 2006/12/EC of the European Parliament and of the Council of 5 April 2006 on waste [2006] OJ L 114/9.
246 Decision No 1600/2002/EC of the European Parliament and of the Council of 22 July 2002 laying down the Sixth Community Environment Action Programme [2002] OJ L 242/1.
247 Directive 2008/98/EC of the European Parliament of the Council of 19 November 2008 on waste and repealing certain Directives [2008] OJ L 312/3 [the Waste Framework Directive 2008].
248 IWaste Framework Directive 2008 Art 42.
249 Council Directive 75/439/EEC of 16 June 1975 on the disposal of waste oils [1975] OJ L 194/23.
250 Council Directive 91/689/EEC of 12 December 1991 on hazardous waste (the Hazardous Waste Directive) [1991] OJ L 377/20.

law, and this gives scope for potential uncertainty but, before considering UK legislation, it is necessary to consider some of its basic provisions.

14.6.2 Overview of Waste Framework Directive 2008

The Waste Framework Directive 2008 sought to:

> clarify key concepts such as the definitions of waste, recovery and disposal, to strengthen the measures that must be taken in regard to waste prevention, to introduce an approach that takes into account the whole life-cycle of products and materials and not only the waste phase, and to focus on reducing the environmental impacts of waste generation and waste management, thereby strengthening the economic value of waste.[251]

14.6.2(a) Definitions

The Waste Framework Directive 2008 has produced its own terminology and has a long list of very wide definitions.[252] Thus:

a *waste* means "any substance or object which the holder discards or intends or is required to discard";[253]
b *waste oils* means "any mineral or synthetic lubrication or industrial oils which have become unfit for the use for which they were originally intended, such as used combustion engine oils and gearbox oils, lubricating oils, oils for turbines and hydraulic oils";
c *waste producer* means "anyone whose activities produce waste (original waste producer) or anyone who carries out pre-processing, mixing or other operations resulting in a change in the nature or composition of this waste";
d *waste holder* means "the waste producer or the natural or legal person who is in possession of the waste"; and
e *broker* means "any undertaking arranging the recovery or disposal of waste on behalf of others, including such brokers who do not take physical possession of the waste";
f *disposal* means "any operation which is not recovery even where the operation has a secondary consequence the reclamation of substances or energy".[254]

There are problems with the breadth of many of these definitions, whose implications for wreck will be considered below.[255] The definition of waste under the Codified Directive had been the subject of criticism.[256] This criticism flowed from the fact that the definition

---

251 Waste Framework Directive 2008 Recital 8.
252 Waste Framework Directive 2008 Art 3.
253 'Hazardous waste' means waste which displays one or more of the hazardous properties listed Annex III "Properties of waste which render it hazardous".
254 "Disposal Operations" are further defined in Annex 1, where para D 7 is "Release to seas/oceans including sea-bed insertion"; see also 14.6.3, 14.6.5(a).
255 See 14.6.5.
256 See eg D Wilkinson, 'Time to discard the concept of waste?' (1999) 1 *Environmental Law Review* 172, [*Wilkinson*] 174–175. M Ráz, 'Being Wasted: Development of Waste Definition in EU Environmental Law' (2010) 11 *Common Law Review* 47.

sought to give the "widest possible field of application" to the word.[257] While the definition of waste under the Waste Framework Directive 2008 remains the same, surrounding provisions provide a little more clarity. For example, Art 6 establishes an "end-of-waste status, ie when waste ceases to be waste following a recovery process (eg recycling).[258] Despite this, there has been ongoing criticism of the definition,[259] which has also been the subject of consideration by the CJEU in the *Commune de Mesquer* case.[260]

14.6.2(b) General duties
The broadest obligation imposed on Member States in the Waste Framework Directive 2008 is through Art 36, whereby they "shall take the necessary measures to prohibit the abandonment, dumping or uncontrolled management of waste". It is this provision which is given effect by the detailed enactments in national laws.[261]

Under Art 12 Member States must ensure that where recovery operations are not undertaken, waste undergoes safe disposal operations.[262] Those operations must meet the requirements of Art 13, ie that waste management must be carried out "without endangering human health, without harming the environment" and, *inter alia*, without risk to water, air, soil, plants or animals.[263]

Article 17 requires Member States to ensure that hazardous wastes are correctly labelled and have appropriate high environmental and health standards in Art 13[264] for production, collection and transportation.

Article 15 of the Directive, a revised version of Art 8 of the Codified Directive, requires Member States to ensure "that any original waste producer or other holder carries out the treatment of waste himself or has the treatment handled by a dealer or an establishment or undertaking which carries out waste treatment operations".[265]

Article 23 requires the issue of "permits" for those intending to carry out treatment of waste although exemptions are allowed by Art 24. It is assumed that most wreck removal contractors will not intend to treat any waste themselves. By contrast Art 26 requires a "register" to be kept by States of (a) businesses that collect or transport waste on a professional basis; (b) dealers or brokers; and (c) those exempt under Art 24. The register is in effect no more than a list, but Art 26(3) allows States some discretion to impose minimum standards for activities that require registration, eg relating to technical qualifications of collectors, transporters, dealers or brokers.

Under Art 14(1) "[i]n accordance with the polluter-pays principle, the costs of waste management shall be borne by the *original waste producer* or by the current or previous

---

257 Explanatory Memorandum referred to in *Wilkinson*, 173.
258 The Waste Framework Directive 2008.
259 UK Environmental Law Association, King's College London and Cardiff University, 'The State of UK Environmental Law in 2011–2012: Is there a case for legislative reform?' (May 2012), 15.
260 See 14.6.3.
261 See 14.6.5.
262 Waste Framework Directive 2008 Art 12.
263 Waste Framework Directive 2008, Art 13.
264 Including action to ensure traceability from production to final destination, as well as record keeping (Art 35) and enforcement (Art 36).
265 Waste Framework Directive 2008, Art 15(1).

waste holders".²⁶⁶ Under the Codified Directive, the liability for the cost of "waste disposal" was placed primarily on the holder, but also on "previous holders or the producer of the product from which the waste came".²⁶⁷ The change may not be all that significant, as Art 14(2) gives some leeway to implementing Member States as to how responsibility for paying for waste management is to be allocated down the chain of producers and distributors, eg by making costs of waste management wholly or partly for the "producer of the product from which the waste came and that the distributors of such products may share these costs".

A forerunner of this costs provision[268] has been controversially used, in the maritime context, to create civil liabilities following an oil pollution casualty.

14.6.3 Commune de Mesquer

The *Commune de Mesquer* case[269] in 2008 provides some guidance on the meaning of waste, albeit that it was decided under the materially similar provisions of the 1975 Directive (as amended). The case was a direct consequence of the sinking of the tanker *Erika* in 1999.[270] As a result of the casualty, oil cargo and bunkers spilled into the sea. The environmental damage caused by the spillage fell squarely within the CLC and Fund Convention 1992 and remedies were available to all the claimants, who in fact had received payments and settled claims on the basis that they would not bring any other actions. The claims against Total (as seller of the cargo and charterer) were probably brought to seek further compensation over the settlement figure against the shipowner which itself no doubt took into account the limits of liability (and perhaps the narrow definition of damage) applicable under the maritime conventions.[271] The claim was brought under the French legislation implementing the Directive that required the producer or holder of waste to dispose of it or have it disposed of in accordance with the legislation.

A claim under the Directive is not one for compensation at large, eg including economic loss,[272] but is for the cost of disposing of the waste. The cargo was a normal cargo of heavy fuel oil, fully meeting all specifications, but the question arose as to whether it could become waste on account of being mixed with water and sediment following its accidental spillage into the sea.[273] The Court of Justice of the EU noted that it was necessary to interpret the definition of waste widely in order to limit its inherent nuisance and harmful effects.[274] It held that the oil cargo was not a waste of itself—it being a relevant factor that

---

266 Emphasis added.
267 See Art 15 of the Codified Directive.
268 In the 1975 Directive.
269 *Commune de Mesquer v Total France SA and Total International Ltd*, Case C-188/07, Judgment of the Court (Grand Chamber) of 24 June 2008, [2] [*Commune de Mesquer*], [2008] 2 Lloyd's Rep 672.
270 See 1.2.2(a) and V Power, "The Commune de Mesquer case" (2013) 19 JIML 486.
271 The Supplementary Fund 2003 was only agreed after the casualty, partly as a result of the Fund Convention's limits being inadequate to cover the many claims: see 2.3.2(c).
272 The Environmental Liability Directive 2004 might now apply to create liability for marine pollution, but specifically excludes the IMO liability conventions: see 2.6.5. It might, though, apply to HNS pollution prior to the entry into force of the HNSC 2010.
273 Commune de Mesquer [28], [55].
274 Ibid. [44], [38].

the goods or materials had an economic value.[275] Although placing particular emphasis on the word "discards" in the waste definition the Court found that an accidental spillage, even involuntary, could be the discard of a burden by the holder.[276] Moreover, even though there was no intention for the holder (eg Total) to produce this waste which was being transported by a third party, the oil could still became waste when it emulsified in water or mixed with sediment.[277] The court declined to rule on whether the Directive applied in a member State's EEZ, because the wastes washed up on land.[278] Once washed up the mixture was no longer capable of being exploited or marketed (eg as an economically valuable product) without prior processing.

From the international perspective, the disappointing part of the decision was that the Court declined to find that the CLC and Fund Convention applied exclusively to the spillage of oil so that the Directive did not apply (or at least would only apply once the oil hits the shore and then had to be dealt with).[279] The international package was a compromise, one of whose tenets was that the compensation available for a spillage was to be exclusive and limited; claims against the shipowner and eg a charterer for pollution damage within the CLC are prohibited.[280] It seems likely that the same result would occur in relation to substances covered by the HNSC 2010, if that enters into force.[281] The court did say, however, that in implementing the Directive it would be open to Member States to give effect to their international commitments under the CLC and Fund Convention so that a shipowner or charterer can only be liable up to the Convention limits.[282] It is in those circumstances that a claim may be made under the Directive against an original producer or, possibly, another holder who might be outside the protections of the CLC (or LLMC).

The issue of who can be a producer or holder was the final issue in *Commune de Mesquer* and will be considered next.

14.6.4 Wreck and the Waste Framework Directive

The *Commune de Mesquer* case shows that although the Waste Framework Directive (even as revised in 2008) is not really designed for the immediate consequences of maritime casualties, it could still be applicable. It could be relevant both to cargo 'wastes' that have to be cleaned up by third parties (as in the case itself), but also to cargo removal undertaken eg by wreck removal contractors who bring "waste" onshore following a shipping incident.[283] This has both practical implications, in that the waste must be disposed of in

---

275 Ibid. [43].
276 Ibid. [47–48], [56], [59].
277 Ibid. [59].
278 Ibid. [60–61].
279 Ibid. [60–63]. See also *Somers & Gonsaeles* and 1.2.2(a).
280 See eg the CLC 1992 Art III(4); 2.3.2(a).
281 See 23.4 and 14.7.4(b) and (c).
282 *Commune de Mesquer* [81].
283 It appears that sound salvaged cargo with an economic value would not be a waste, unless it required reprocessing: cf *Commune de Mesquer* [49]. Of course, a salvor that removes a container may not know it is waste until it is landed and the contents are inspected: see also 14.6.4(a). Where a salvor is engaged under SCOPIC or a wreck removal contract it may well knowingly be removing container waste in order to prevent pollution: cf 2.7.9(c), 12.3.1.

accordance with the legislation, and financial implications in that the costs of compliance and disposal may fall to a party handling the waste.

14.6.4(a) Who are waste producers or holders?
Where bulk or containerised cargo becomes waste as a result of a wreck, it may be difficult to trace the "original producers" of the cargo under the Waste Framework Directive 2008, or at least to make them financially amenable to pay for the costs associated with waste following a shipping incident.

Is an owner of a wreck a "waste producer"? A consideration of the aims of the Directive and the wording might have suggested that an owner of a ship whose operations were designed to carry cargo safely, and whose ship was wrecked without any intention to damage the cargo, was merely a third party transporter who could not possibly be a producer of waste; any waste would be unintentionally caused as a by-product of the fortuity. As noted, Art 14(1) of the Waste Framework Directive 2008 now distinguishes between producer and the "original producer", and leaves the liability of the former to national law. Nevertheless, in *Commune de Mesquer* the court treated the shipowner as a person in possession of the cargo immediately before it became waste, and to that extent was both a producer and a holder.[284]

In *Commune de Mesquer* the court went on to consider whether other previous holders could also be responsible for the cost of disposing of the waste. It was held that it would be possible for a seller-charterer to have "produced" waste if the court reaches the conclusion that "the seller-charterer contributed to the risk that the pollution caused by the shipwreck would occur, in particular if he failed to take measures to prevent such an incident, such as measures concerning the choice of ship".[285] It might be thought that this would be difficult to prove in most wreck cases but, if it were proven, the seller-charterer could be regarded as a previous holder of the waste.[286] This would be particularly relevant to shippers of large quantities of cargo that are lost at sea, but in principle they might be entitled to limit liability.[287]

It might be suggested that salvage and wreck removal contractors become "waste *producers*" in the removal process as they are "anyone who . . . carries out . . . operations resulting in a change in the nature or composition of *this* waste".[288] During cargo removal operations (which may extend over months) a sound cargo may become ruined, eg by the entry of seawater into a container or bulk tank, or by shifting within a container or hold. In that sense the nature of the cargo has changed, but the emphasis on "*this*" waste indicates that a contractor cannot become a producer unless it is dealing with a product that is *already* a waste before operations start on it. This would not seem to apply when the cargo is sound before the start of removal operations, eg with sound containers that have to be removed from a ship that is irremediably aground. If the cargo becomes a waste during removal operations then the contractor might simply become a "waste holder" in possession of waste.

---

284 *Commune de Mesquer* [74].
285 Ibid. [78].
286 Ibid.
287 See 2.3.4, 2.3.10.
288 See Art 3(5). Emphasis added.

In *Commune de Mesquer*, the Court distinguished "the actual recovery or disposal operations, which [the Regulation] makes the responsibility of any 'holder of waste', whether producer or possessor, from the financial burden of those operations, which, in accordance with the 'polluter pays' principle, it imposes on the persons who cause the waste, whether they are holders or former holders of the waste or even producers of the product from which the waste came".[289] While this distinction may not always be clear in wreck cases, it follows that removal contractors who are waste holders must follow any public law requirements as to methods of disposal. Whether they have any additional financial liability to others (eg States) that themselves remove the waste (eg if bulk cargoes or the remains of container cargoes come ashore) will depend on what is meant by "cause the waste". In a literal sense the removal contractor may sometimes have a causative influence, in that while attempting to remove cargo it may become ruined but, as a matter of principle, it seems hard to penalise the responder to a maritime casualty by artificially categorising it as a "polluter" as it did not contribute to the risk that pollution would occur in the first place.[290] It is a different matter to say that, as a holder of waste, it has to follow appropriate procedures.

In any event, the definition of "waste holder" will be of particular concern to salvage and wreck removal contractors, as they can almost certainly come into possession of wreck waste, eg when already ruined cargo (with no economic value) is removed from a ship and taken ashore in the EU. Here they would certainly become a "current or previous waste holder".

It is not clear if the Waste Framework Directive 2008 would apply where cargo waste was removed from a wreck situated in the EEZ of an EU Member State, but then taken for ultimate disposal to a non-member State. Although this was an issue upon which the Court declined to rule in *Commune de Mesquer*, the practice of the court indicates that it is loath to reduce the jurisdictional impact of EU legislation. It should probably be assumed that the Directive could be applied here, unless the Waste Shipment Regulation applied.[291]

In some circumstances wreck removal contractors could also be "brokers", eg when they sub-contract the transport of containers from the wreck site to shore. At that stage the contractors might possess the wrecked cargo. Alternately, it may pass directly into the hands of another third party, eg a terminal or handling facility, or to another carrier for on-carriage. The consequence is that the contractors may have to bear the regulatory hurdle and, in some circumstances, could be liable for waste management costs.

For this reason, the contractors need either to charge sufficient to recover their likely costs, or to provide for an indemnity in their contracts.[292]

14.6.4(b) Relationship with LC 1972/LC Protocol 1996
Unlike its predecessor, the Waste Framework Directive 2008 recognises in Recital 21 the regulatory role of the LC 1972 and 1996 Protocol by stating that "disposal operations

---

289 *Commune de Mesquer* [71]; see also [89].
290 Cf *Commune de Mesquer* [78].
291 See 14.4.2. Note also the English enactment which applies in the EEZ: see 14.6.5(a).
292 In salvage, this should be reflected in the award. Under SCOPIC 2018 cl 5(iii) such costs might be "out of pocket expenses". The ability to claim "extra costs" such as these may vary between the three BIMCO wreck removal contracts. It is doubtful if the costs are within the list in Wreckhire 2010 cl 13, but they may be recoverable if there has been a change of circumstances within cl 4: see eg Wreckhire 2008 cl 16 and 13.6.3(g).

consisting of release to seas and oceans including sea bed insertion are also regulated by international conventions, in particular [the LC 1972]".[293] The use of the word "also" indicates that the Directive can apply to dumping at sea even if already covered by the London Convention, which gives rise to a possible overlap. A view has been expressed that "the international system with respect to dumping at sea will prevail over the Directive"[294] and it might be supposed that the Directive should only apply to dumping if for some reason the Convention or Protocol is inapplicable.

The issue of dumping animal carcasses at sea under the LC 1972 and Protocol has already been noted[295] but their disposal on land may also cause practical difficulties. The *Haidar* was a converted livestock carrier which capsized and sank in 2015 in Vilo do Conde in Brazil with 5,000 cattle on board. Local contractors had to remove decomposing carcasses and bury the dead cattle on land.[296]

14.6.4(c) Relationship with WRC 2007 and LLMC
At first sight there does not appear to be any conflict between the Waste Framework Directive 2008 and the WRC 2007, as the Waste Framework Directive 2008 could be said merely to regulate how a disposal operation required under the WRC 2007 is to be carried out. In this sense they should be complementary. However, it is not inconceivable that the registered shipowner who is liable for removal under the WRC is entitled to limit liability,[297] in circumstances where the compulsory insurance is not sufficient to pay the full claim for clean-up of waste.

As in the *Commune de Mesquer* case, the Waste Framework Directive 2008 might be used as a device to 'top up' the sums available to a claimant where there were convention obligations which included limitation of liability.[298] If a charterer were sued as a producer or holder under the Directive, it should in theory be entitled to limit liability, but that might depend on whether the claim fell within the LLMC reservation.[299] The same issue would arise if a wreck removal contractor were sued as a holder.

14.6.5 Waste disposal: adoption in the UK

As noted, the Waste Framework Directive 2008 has to be transposed into national law, and there is much scope for States to decide exactly how this will be done.[300] Like its predecessors, it has been implemented in the UK through a number of legislative instruments[301]

---

293 See 14.1.1. It is significant that there is no equivalent Recital in respect of the CLC and Fund Convention, a factor that was significant to the court's decision in *Commune de Mesquer* [87–88].
294 See *Somers & Gonsaeles* 57, 82.
295 See 14.1.2(b).
296 See various web reports as to the fate of the ship and cargo: eg https://portermarinesalvage.com/mv-haidar/. Animal carcasses are excluded from the Waste Framework Directive 2008: see Art 2(c). These may be covered by other legislation, eg Regulation (EC) No 1774/2002.
297 See 2.3.10,
298 See 14.6.3.
299 See 2.3.9.
300 See eg Art 14(2), 14.7.2(b) above.
301 These include the Environment Act 1990; the Control of Pollution (Amendment) Act 1989, the Controlled Waste (Registration of Carriers and Seizure of Vehicles) Regulations 1991 (SI. 1991/1624), as amended; the

whose inter-relationship is not easy to follow. It is not possible here to analyse all of these instruments, but an outline will be given of some of the key duties that arise and how they might affect wreck disposal.

14.6.5(a) Waste Regulations 2011

The Waste Framework Directive 2008 has been mainly adopted through the Waste (England and Wales) Regulations 2011 [Waste Regulations 2011],[302] as amended. The instrument transposes the provisions of the Waste Framework Directive 2008 that did not appear in the Codified Directive[303] and amends existing legislation to reflect those provisions that were re-enacted or revised.[304] It is necessary to refer back to the Directive for some definitions, eg of "broker", as these are not separately defined in the Waste Regulations 2011.[305]

The Waste Regulations 2011 introduced a requirement that the appropriate authority[306] evaluate the usefulness of measures set out in Annex IV of the Waste Framework Directive 2008[307] and establish one or more programmes of waste prevention measures.[308] This has been implemented through a series of Department for Environment Food & Rural Affairs (DEFR) publications.[309] The Waste Regulations 2011 also require the appropriate authority to ensure that there are one or more waste management plans containing policies in relation to waste management in England, including the sea adjacent to England as far as the seaward boundary of the territorial sea.[310] In England, it is the Environment Agency that has executive responsibility for waste management.[311]

The Waste Regulations 2011 impose a duty on an establishment or undertaking which imports, collects, transports, recovers or disposes of waste, or which (as a dealer or broker)[312] has control of waste. It must, on the transfer of waste, take all such measures available to it as are reasonable to apply the "waste hierarchy".[313] The waste hierarchy is based on Art 4 of the Waste Framework Directive 2008 and prescribes the methods of handling

---

Waste Management Licensing Regulations 1994 (SI 1994/1056); the Environmental Permitting (England and Wales) Regulations 2010 (SI 2010/675), as amended; the Hazardous Waste (England and Wales) Regulations 2005 (SI 2005/894), as amended; the Hazardous Waste (Wales) Regulations 2005 (S. 2005/1806 as amended); The Town and Country Planning Act 1990 and the Planning and Compulsory Purchase Act 2004. See also the Explanatory Memorandum to the Waste (England and Wales) Regulations 2011 (SI 2011/988), 1–2.

302 SI 2011/988, made under s 2(2) of the European Communities Act 1972 and s 2 of the Pollution Prevention and Control Act 1999. Equivalent provisions exist for other parts of the UK.

303 See Annex 1 of the Waste Regulations 2011 for a table of transpositions.

304 Explanatory Memorandum to the Waste Regulations 2011, 1. See eg amendments to the Hazardous Waste (England and Wales) Regulations 2005, amending Reg 2 to define "the Waste Directive" to mean "Directive 2008/98/EC of the European Parliament and of the Council on waste" (ie the Waste Framework Directive 2008).

305 See Reg 3(2).

306 In England, the Secretary of State (for Environment Food & Rural Affairs): reg 3(1).

307 This gives examples of waste prevention measures.

308 Waste Regulations 2011, reg 4.

309 See eg 'Waste Prevention Programme for England Evaluation of Annex IV measures', December 2013. See also 14.6.5(h).

310 Waste Regulations 2011, reg 7. These programmes and plans have to be reviewed every six years and may be modified from time to time: reg 10.

311 See www.gov.uk/topic/environmental-management/waste.

312 Brokers and dealers of controlled waste must be registered with the Environment Agency: see Reg 25. Note the exemptions in Reg 26.

313 Waste Regulations 2011, reg 12.

waste that should be prioritised. These are, in the following order: prevention, preparing for re-use, recycling, other recovery and finally, disposal.[314] The duty to comply with the waste hierarchy will have implications on the way waste is handled by businesses. This is because it affects the steps businesses take to prevent materials from becoming waste, although notably, material may be treated as waste if it is no longer economical to have it repaired.[315]

Following Art 26 of the Directive, Part 8 of the Waste Regulations 2011 requires registration of carriers, brokers and dealers in "controlled waste".[316] As a result of a CJEU decision in 2005[317] these must include all those who normally and regularly transport waste, whether that waste is produced by them or others. The UK has implemented this requirement in a "light touch" two tier manner.[318] High level professional waste carriers have to register every year, but others (including those carrying their own waste) require a one-off low-cost registration. The wide registration system was really designed to deter fly-tipping on land, and is not easily applied to wreck removal operations.

Registration as a carrier of controlled waste is not required in two circumstances. First, if a "carrier" does not normally and regularly transport controlled waste that is "produced by the carrier itself".[319] Wreck removal contractors may sometimes be carriers with possession of waste; at other times they may be arranging for sub-contractors to carry waste, and in this context might be brokers. Whether a wreck removal contractor "produces" waste in the course of a removal operation is also unclear.[320] Secondly, registration as a carrier of controlled waste is also not needed[321] if the "operator "of a "vessel, floating container or vehicle" has been loaded with waste in circumstances where a marine licence is required[322] or there is a marine exemption order[323] to carry out a specified marine operation.[324] Ie there is no need to register under one set of rules if, in effect, there is licensing under another. The generalised Waste Regulations 2011 therefore defer, to some extent, to the specific marine licensing rules where the UK gives effect offshore to the Waste Framework Directive 2008.[325] The Waste Regulations

---

314 Waste Regulations 2011, reg 12(1)(a)–(e).

315 A Watt, 'Waste and the Waste Hierarchy in Europe' (2012) 26 Natural Resources and the Environment 53.

316 As regulated by the Environmental Protection Act 1990 (with accompanying regulations), 14.6.5(c).

317 *Commission v Italy*, Case C-270/03 involving infraction proceedings on a previous version of the Directive (75/442/EEC, as amended by 91/156/EEC).

318 See Explanatory Memorandum to the 2011 Regulations, paras 7.10–7.11.

319 See Reg 26(1)(a) and Reg 24(5)(e), except where it is "construction or demolition" waste; the context here suggests that this exception refers to buildings rather than ships or their contents. For exemptions generally, see the Environmental Permitting (England and Wales) Regulations 2010 (SI 2010/675) Part 5 and its Schedules which contain a variety of exemptions for certain activities (none of which directly refer to wreck removal). But see 14.6.5(b) in relation to dismantling.

320 See also 14.6.3.

321 See Reg 26(1)(b).

322 Under Part 4 of the Marine and Coastal Access Act 2009 (most of the UK), or Part 2 of the Food and Environment Protection Act 1985 (Scottish inshore area). See 14.1.4(b) and 14.6.5(b).

323 Made under s 74 of the Marine and Coastal Access Act 2009 or s 7 of the Food and Environment Protection Act 1985: see 14.1.4(b) and 14.6.5(b).

324 See Items 1 to 6, or 11 to 13, in s 66(1) of the Marine and Coastal Access Act 2009 (which specifies licensable marine activities) or ss 5, 6 of the Food and Environment Protection Act 1985 (deposits in the sea or incineration).

325 For marine licensing, see 14.1.4(b) and 14.6.5(b).

2011 will be particularly relevant to a wreck removal contractor for those waste operations that do not occur offshore, eg once cargo wastes have been landed onshore for land disposal or recycling.

The obligations on transfer of wastes are set out in Part 9 of the Waste Regulations 2011. As enacted, a formal "waste transfer note" was required, that had to identify the waste and give details about the transferor and transferee. This would include whether they are: the producer, importer or transporter of the waste; or a registered carrier, broker or dealer of controlled waste. Following amendments in 2014, it is now sufficient for "waste information" to be merely in writing, so that alternative documentation, such as invoices, may be used.[326] The transferor and transferee should retain a copy of the information for at least two years.[327]

The enforcement obligations required by Arts 15 and 36 of the Waste Framework Directive 2008 are given national effect through a variety of provisions[328] creating administrative and penal sanctions. These include powers under Part 10 of the Waste Regulations 2011 to issue compliance, stop or restoration notices (backed by criminal sanctions) in respect of duties in relation to waste management and registration of brokers and dealers[329] in controlled waste. Offences for the abandonment, dumping or uncontrolled management of waste are regulated by s 33 of the Environmental Protection Act 1990.[330]

14.6.5(b) Marine waste licensing and exemptions

It has already been noted that a marine licence is required under the Marine and Coastal Access Act 2009 s 65–66 for licensable marine activity, such as dumping of ships.[331] These provisions also require licences for activities connected with waste that also include wreck removal, ie activities under s 66(1):

7. To construct, alter or improve any works within the UK marine licensing area either—(a) in or over the sea, or (b) on or under the sea bed.[332]
8. To use a vehicle, vessel, aircraft, marine structure or floating container to remove any substance or object from the sea bed within the UK marine licensing area.[333]
9. To carry out any form of dredging within the UK marine licensing area (whether or not involving the removal of any material from the sea or sea bed).[334]

---

326 See: the Waste (England and Wales) (Amendment) Regulations 2014 (SI 2014/656), and the Explanatory Memorandum, para 7.1.

327 Waste Regulations 2011, as amended, reg 35(6).

328 See Annex 1 of the Waste Regulations 2011 for a table of transpositions showing the list of the enforcement provisions.

329 For carrier offences, see the Control of Pollution (Amendment) Act 1989 as amended.

330 See also 14.6.5(c) and Reg 12 of Environmental Permitting (England and Wales) Regulations 2010 (S.I. 2010 No. 675), as amended.

331 See 14.1, in particular 14.1.4(b).

332 In theory this might apply to the type of engineering operations in casualties such as the *Costa Concordia*, where piles are driven into the seabed under the hull so as to stabilise it before raising: see also 1.2.5(b).

333 This is the main Item that applies to most hull and cargo removal operations. It would cover all vessels used by wreck removal contractors, in addition to helicopter removals (see eg the *Kea Trader*, 10.2.6), or any form of semi-submersible structure. In this context a "floating container" will most likely refer to oil skimming equipment. The expression "substance or object" is deliberately wide and would extend to aircraft, as well as ships or parts of them (such as anchors), and all types of cargo.

334 Dredging to allow a ship to be refloated, or to ease removal, would be covered. Under s 66(2) "dredging" includes using any device to move any material (whether or not suspended in water) from one part of the sea or sea bed to another part.

10. To deposit or use any explosive substance or article within the UK marine licensing area either in the sea or on or under the sea bed.[335]
11. To incinerate any substance or object on any vehicle, vessel, marine structure or floating container in the UK marine licensing area.[336]
12. To incinerate any substance or object anywhere at sea on — (a) a British vessel or British marine structure, or (b) a container floating in the sea, if the incineration is controlled from a British vessel, British aircraft or British marine structure.[337]
13. To load a vehicle, vessel, aircraft, marine structure or floating container in any part of the United Kingdom except Scotland, or in the UK marine licensing area, with any substance or object for incineration anywhere at sea.[338]

Despite the width of these provisions, various activities are exempt from licensing under the Marine Licensing (Exempted Activities) Order 2011 [Exempted Activities Order][339] — which has been briefly considered earlier in relation to scuttling and dumping of ships.[340] The scheme of the Exempted Activities Order 2011 has resulted in three categories of marine exemption: Category 1 (exemptions where no notification is required); Category 2 (exemptions where *notice* is required); Category 3 (exemptions where positive MMO *approval* is required).[341] Some of the exemptions are designed to avoid overlap with other provisions, eg the MSA 1995 Part 6 provisions on pollution prevention[342] or the Sch 3A intervention powers relating to safety directions.[343] There is also a provision preserving rights of vessels flagged outside the EU in international law.[344]

The Exempted Activities Order 2011 has no *specific* exemption for "wreck removal" and so the general licensing requirements of s 66(1), eg Item 8, could apply to the raising of a ship and its cargo. However, a number of exemptions might apply more generally to wreck removal operations that relate to deposit or removal of "wastes"[345] in, or from, the sea.[346] Unfortunately, for the wreck removal context, there is a degree of overlap in the exemptions and their precise extent is not always clear. Moreover, they are hedged about somewhat in

---

335 This would apply to the use of explosives by contractors to assist in the demolition of a ship underwater, eg where it was necessary to separate part of the hull for raising.

336 Since the *Torrey Canyon* (see 1.2.1), the burning off of oil and other cargoes (or bunkers) is not usually a preferred method of dealing with a wreck, but such activity would now be covered.

337 Here there is a typical flag state restriction imposed worldwide, eg where incineration is "controlled" from a "British ship" (see the MSA 1995 s 1). The other provisions, listed above, apply to any ship (foreign flagged or not) operating in the UK marine licensing area.

338 This would apply where a foreign flag ship was loaded in the UK marine licensing area with the intention that there was to be incineration outside UK waters.

339 SI 2011/409, as amended: see fn 90. The issue of permits and exemptions is regulated by Art 23–35 of the Waste Framework Directive 2008 and its restrictions are reflected in Art 5 of the Exempted Activity Order 2011.

340 See 14.1.4(b).

341 See the MMO Guidance, "Marine licensing exempted activities" (updated 21 December 2018): www.gov.uk/government/publications/marine-licensing-exempted-activities/marine-licensing-exempted-activities.

342 See Art 7 of the Exempted Activities Order 2011; eg provisions covered by MARPOL such as disposal of garbage.

343 See Art 8 of the Exempted Activities Order 2011, and 4.2.

344 Art 37.

345 As defined in the Waste Framework Directive 2008: see Art 3 of the Exempted Activities Order 2011.

346 See eg Items 1 and 8 in the list of substances in s 66(1) of the 2009 Act.

order to comply with the Waste Framework Directive 2008, eg the requirement that a company recovering or disposing of waste must itself be licensed.[347]

Article 9 of the Exempted Activities Order 2011 exempts "salvage activities", ie "an activity carried on, in the course of a salvage operation, for the purpose of ensuring the safety of a vessel or preventing pollution".[348] This will obviously cover attempts to refloat a ship in distress[349] and would also cover some of the pollution prevention activities that might fall within the caretaking role of salvors under SCOPIC or Art 14 of the Salvage Convention 1989.[350] This exemption could also apply to the recovery of containers lost overboard, certainly where they have a value or where they are a substantial threat to the environment.[351] The difficulty is in defining where salvage activities end and wreck removal begins—as these are distinct concepts, albeit that there is a grey area in between.[352] Any distinction between the regulatory treatment of salvage and wreck removal almost certainly relates to the urgency with which operations are needed, eg risks in relation to saving life, property and the environment.[353] This is confirmed by the updated 2018 MMO Guidance which states that the salvage exemption "is not intended to exempt the removal of wrecks or other subjects of archaeological interest". Salvage activities in such cases are only likely to be exempt if a new risk of pollution is identified. Where it is clear that a ship is a CTL and that recovery operations have moved to the longer time schedules involved in a complicated wreck removal operation then the salvage exemption would not appear to apply. Other exemptions might apply, though.

The first is in Art 28 of the Exempted Activities Order 2011 and is headed "Dismantling of ships". It applies the exemption to "a deposit or removal activity carried on as part of dismantling a ship that is waste", but not to "any such deposit to the extent that it falls within item 10" (ie the deposit of explosives). What is not clear is whether this exemption was intended to deal only with the dismantling of ships in facilities in ports and harbours, or whether it can be interpreted more generally to apply to any dismantling of a ship at sea. The latter interpretation of Art 28 might be supported by (i) the reference to explosives (and Item 8), and (ii) the specific definition of "removal activity" as a "reference to an activity

---

347 See the conditions of Art 5 of the Exempted Activities Order 2011, eg that of registration and the need to ensure that the type and quantity of waste involved, and the method of disposal or recovery, are consistent with Art 13 of the Waste Framework Directive 2008. See also the Explanatory Memorandum to the Exempted Activity Order 2011.

348 See also the definition of "salvage operation" in Art 1(a) of the Salvage Convention 1989. Salvage would include firefighting, although this is specifically mentioned in Art 10 of the Exempted Activities Order 2011. There is a separate exemption in Art 32 in relation to activities of the Coastguard in saving life or property. Under Art 24 a conservancy authority, harbour authority, or lighthouse authority do not need a licence to remove obstructions or dangers to navigation.

349 Thus, dredging of a beach or seabed to refloat a ship would be exempt even though dredging would otherwise require a licence under Item 8 of s 66(1). There are a number of exemptions for navigational dredging, eg de minimis principles in Art 18A of the Exempted Activities Order 2011, but these are unlikely to apply to wreck removal operations. Some small-scale dredging may be licensed through a fast track route.

350 See 12.1, 12.3.4, 2.7.9(b) and (c).

351 Within Art 1(d) and 14 of the Salvage Convention 1989.

352 See Chapter 12, especially 12.3.

353 This is consistent with the overriding concerns for safety and the environment in Art 13 of the Waste Framework Directive 2008.

falling within Item 8" of s 66(1) of the Marine and Coastal Access Act 2009.[354] If the Art 28 exemption does apply to wrecks at sea, it would only cover "dismantling" and not the complete raising of a ship; nor would it seem to cover cargo removal.

However, the Explanatory Memorandum to the Exempted Activities Order 2011 explains that the Art 28 exemption "is designed to ensure that ship dismantling is regulated under *Environmental Permitting* rather than under Part 4 of the [2009 Act]" (emphasis added). The idea was obviously to ensure that there is no overlap of regulation, ie an allocation of regulation between agencies, rather than that the activity was to be unregulated. The reference was presumably to the Environmental Permitting (England and Wales) Regulations 2010,[355] which was part of a wider initiative, the Environmental Permitting Programme, designed to streamline approvals (eg under EU Directives including the Waste Framework Directive 2008). Since then, the general regulatory position on ship dismantling has moved on and recycling facilities in the UK are regulated under the Ship Recycling Facilities Regulations 2015.[356] On balance, given the general policy to ensure that hazardous waste activities need licensing, and that most wrecks will contain hazardous materials, it is submitted that it is unlikely that this dismantling exemption was intended to apply generally to wreck dismantling at sea as part of wreck removal operations. This is rather confirmed by the MMO Guidance, above, in relation to the salvage exemption and "wreck removal". On "dismantling" under Art 28, the MMO Guidance simply says that "a licence is not required for a deposit or removal activity carried out as part of dismantling a ship that is waste". This implies that the ship is only "waste" when in a recycling facility, but it has already been seen that EU law may find that a casualty may result in waste being produced at sea.[357]

The next licensing exemption relevant to wreck removal is Art 17B of the Exempted Activities Order 2011[358] which exempts a "removal activity carried on for the purpose of removing any object which has been accidentally deposited on the seabed". If taken literally this exemption would apply to all wreck removal operations where a ship and its cargo has "accidentally" sunk, eg as a result of a collision or stranding. This does not appear to be what was intended by this new provision where the broader context is to exempt relatively small scale or low risk activities. The MMO Guidance states that the exemption "is intended to allow the removal of objects including but not limited to, lost anchors, rock and equipment". It might possibly cover container recovery operations (if these are not within the salvage exemption, above), eg of an empty container lost overboard that might pose a threat to navigation.[359] This is a Category 2 exemption requiring notice; removal must take place within 12 months of the deposit, and it must neither cause a danger to navigation itself nor have a significant effect on a marine protected area.

Another Category 2 exemption is for "removal activity using a vehicle *carried on* by or on behalf of a local authority for the purpose of removing any litter . . . or dead animal

---

354 See Art 6(2)(c) of the Exempted Activities Order 2011, and 14.6.5(b) (above).
355 SI 2010 No. 675 as amended: see also 14.6.5(a).
356 See 14.5.2(c).
357 See 14.6.3.
358 As added by the Marine Licensing (Exempted Activities) (Amendment) Order 2013 (SI 2013/526).
359 See also 10.6.

from a beach (sic)".³⁶⁰ The MMO Guidance seems to go further than the provision in that it applies the exemption to the removal of litter and dead animals even without the use of a vehicle. There is no definition of "litter" in the Order or the Explanatory Memoranda, and the question arises as to whether cargo debris washed ashore could be considered as litter.³⁶¹ There is an overriding environmental requirement in Art 21, ie that the activity must not be likely to have a significant effect on a marine protected area, which indicates that the regulatory burden is not aimed at minor litter removal. It seems likely that the type of recovery undertaken after the *MSC Napoli* casualty³⁶² would go beyond the removal of litter and would need licensing. The Art 21 provision only requires notice to the licensing authority, eg the MMO, of the intention to remove the carcass of a dead animal (not litter), but again the exemption would not apply if there were likely to be significant effect on a marine protected area. This might be relevant where heavy equipment was needed to remove masses of carcasses from a wrecked livestock carrier.³⁶³ A salvor or wreck removal contractor engaged directly by shipowner or Club might not be working "on behalf of" a local authority, except in an indirect sense, so it may be advisable to obtain permission from such an authority in any event.

Activities to recover substances or objects related to an air accident investigation are also exempted and this was designed to deal with aircraft wrecks where urgency may be needed.³⁶⁴

An example of a Category 3 exemption concerns oil spill response and treatment, eg the use of marine chemical and marine oil treatment substances (and recovery equipment such as skimmers and booms), provided that there is a (non-licensing) approval by the relevant licensing authority, eg the MMO.³⁶⁵ The substance must be used in accordance with that approval and specific permission is needed for all uses in or below the surface of the sea.³⁶⁶ Given a need to respond urgently, the MMO will give a formal response within one hour for spills in English waters.³⁶⁷

Given the uncertainties about which wreck removal activities are exempt, it would seem prudent to consult with the relevant regulator, eg the MMO, in relation to significant activities in the UK marine area. There is guidance about licence applications with information about issues such as protected areas.³⁶⁸ Partly because of the complexity and bureaucracy

---

360 Art 21 of the Exempted Activities Order 2011, as amended. The emphasis is added as there appears to be an error in the provision.

361 Cf the MSA 1995 provisions in 4.4.3.

362 See 1.2.3.

363 See eg the *Haidar*, 14.6.4(b). This would contrast with the example of stranded cetaceans given in the Explanatory Memorandum to the Exempted Activities Order 2011.

364 Art 11 of the Exempted Activity Order 2011; see also Explanatory Memorandum, para 7.2(ii).

365 See Arts 15–16 of the Exempted Activities 2011 Order and s 107(2) of the 2009 Act.

366 See MMO, Marine Pollution Contingency Plan (2014, updated 2018), available at https://assets.publishing.service.gov.uk/government/uploads/system/uploads/attachment_data/file/737259/Marine_pollution_contingency_plan_2018.pdf. See also the guidance at www.gov.uk/guidance/clean-an-oil-spill-at-sea-and-get-oil-spill-treatments-approved which gives lists of standing approvals.

367 MMO Guidance, "How we respond to marine pollution incidents": www.gov.uk/guidance/how-we-respond-to-marine-pollution-incidents. See also 4.8.

368 See MMO Guidance, "Make a marine licence application" (updated 2018): www.gov.uk/guidance/make-a-marine-licence-application.

involved with licensing there is now a self-service licensing option for low risk activity.[369] It covers matters such as the removal of litter[370] and other discrete minor objects.[371] It also covers "non-navigational clearance dredging (within a heritage designation or a wreck site elsewhere in the sea)", but it is made clear that the "wreck site" is one related only to the preservation of a historic asset.

14.6.5(c) Environmental Protection Act 1990

The Environmental Protection Act [EPA] 1990, as heavily amended,[372] sets out extensive primary powers in relation to waste. Thus, s 141 gives a power to prohibit or restrict the importation or exportation of waste and s 156 allows for effect to be given by regulations to EU[373] and other international obligations. The main relevance to wreck concerns what happens to waste once it is brought ashore as the EPA 1990 creates duties in respect of "controlled waste" and supplements the Waste Regulations 2011 in respect of enforcement.

Part II of the EPA 1990, dealing with waste on land, adopts the definition of waste in Art 3(1) of the Waste Framework Directive 2008.[374] "Controlled waste" is separately defined to distinguish between household, industrial and commercial waste.[375] Nonetheless, the definitions of household, industrial and commercial waste have been amended to ensure that "the term 'controlled waste' has the same effect as the meaning of 'waste' in the Directive".[376] Indeed, the Controlled Waste (England and Wales) Regulations 2012[377] [Controlled Waste Regulations] classify Directive waste[378] that is not otherwise classified and is from, *inter alia*, a vessel, as industrial waste[379] and also categorises waste oil as industrial waste.[380] It follows that the prohibition on depositing controlled waste (or knowingly causing or permitting the deposit of controlled waste), discussed below, applies to waste that is from a vessel (including, presumably, from a sunken or wrecked vessel).

The EPA 1990 prohibits: first, depositing controlled waste, or knowingly causing or knowingly permitting the deposit of controlled waste in or on any land unless an environmental permit authorising the deposit is in force and the deposit is in accordance with

---

369 See MMO Guidance, "Introduction—self-service marine licensing guidance" (updated 2018): www.gov.uk/government/publications/self-service-marine-licensing/self-service-marine-licensing.

370 Explained as an "accumulation of items and materials below mean high water springs (MHWS)": see MMO Guidance, "Self-service activities table": www.gov.uk/government/publications/self-service-marine-licensing/self-service-activities-table. Cf s 98(5A) of the Environmental Protection Act 1990.

371 See the activity table at www.gov.uk/government/publications/self-service-marine-licensing/self-service-activities-table. This could apply to burials at sea, although note that there are special requirements for the materials and design of coffins to prevent them washing ashore.

372 In particular by the Waste Regulations 2011, see 14.6.5(a).

373 Eg through the various amendments to the Hazardous Waste (England and Wales) Regulations 2005 (SI 2005/894) to comply with the Waste Framework Directive 2008.

374 See eg EPA 1990, s 57(8), s 75(2), as amended by the Waste Regulation 2011.

375 EPA 1990, s 75(4).

376 Explanatory Memorandum, the Waste Regulations 2011.

377 SI 2012/811. Note reg 17 of the Waste (Miscellaneous Amendments) (EU Exit) (No. 2) Regulations 2019 which commences on exit day.

378 Reg 3 of the Controlled Waste Regulations 2012 defines that as meaning anything that is waste within the meaning of Art 3(1) of the Waste Framework Directive 2008 and that is not excluded from the Directive's scope by Art 2(1), (2) or (3).

379 Controlled Waste Regulations 2012 Sch 1, para 2 (No 27 in table).

380 Controlled Waste (Regulations 2012 Sch 1, para 3 (No 8 in table).

the licence; second, submitting waste or knowingly causing or knowingly permitting controlled waste to be submitted to any listed operation that is carried out in or on any land, or by means of any mobile plant and is not carried out under and in accordance with an environmental permit; and, third, treat, keep or dispose of controlled waste or extractive waste in a manner likely to cause pollution of the environment or harm to human health.[381]

Section 34 of the EPA 1990 imposes a duty on any person "who imports, produces, carries, keeps, treats or disposes of controlled waste or, as a dealer or broker, has control of waste, to take all such measures applicable to him in that capacity as are reasonable in the circumstances" to, *inter alia*, prevent any contravention by any other person of s 33 (as discussed above) and to prevent the escape of waste from his control or that of any other person.

The prohibition referred to above arises primarily in relation to operators of waste disposal facilities. However, s 34 has bearing on those seeking to dispose of waste as it requires measures to be taken to ensure compliance.

14.6.5(d) Practical compliance considerations for wreck waste
As a starting point, parties should consider whether the goods being handled need to be discarded. If that is the case, the goods will likely be 'waste' or 'controlled waste' within the meaning of the legislation. Following a shipping incident, damaged cargo may be waste if it is not salvageable. If cargo is damaged but not defective it may not be considered waste.

The relevant party should then consider whether they are a waste holder and therefore owe a duty of care. A shipowner and charterer may be considered a waste producer and therefore a waste holder. A salvor or wreck removal contractor will be a "waste holder" if it takes possession of the waste for the purposes of disposing of it on behalf of the shipowner or cargo owner.[382] Even if the contractor does not take physical possession of the waste, it will be a "broker" if it arranges the recovery or disposal of waste on behalf of others (eg shipowners or cargo owners). It may also be a "waste manager" who is involved in the collection, transport, recovery or disposal of controlled waste.

This may present some difficulties in that a party transferring waste to a carrier or broker must ensure that they are properly registered. It may be unclear whether salvage and wreck removal contractors need to register, but it would seem prudent to do so.[383] Without formal registration by the contractor, the shipowner or charterer may be in breach of their duties. However, a marine casualty involving salvage or wreck removal is a novel situation in that it may be unclear whether the material removed is waste at the time of the operation (particularly where cargo is concerned) and where there is no direct transfer effected by the shipowner to the contractor. This is not a circumstance contemplated by the provisions, but the impact of *Commune de Mesquer* suggests that the CJEU will take the widest possible interpretation of the provisions.

After the waste is brought to shore, the process is relatively straightforward. The waste can be transferred to a registered carrier, broker or dealer. At the time of transferring the

---

381 EPA 1990, s 33.
382 See Art 3(8) of the Waste Framework Directive 2008: 14.6.4(a). This is contemplated in the discussion about waste brokers in the UK: see "Waste Duty of Care Code of Practice" (DEFRA, 2016), 3.
383 See 14.6.4(a) and 14.6.5(a).

waste, the matters set out in reg 35 of the Waste Regulations 2011 as amended must be set out in writing and provided to the transferor.[384]

The Environment Agency has an online register of carriers, brokers and dealers.[385] The transferor should ensure that the carrier, broker or dealer has accurately represented their credentials by searching the register. If a service provider is engaged for the disposal of waste, assurances should be sought that only licenced carriers, brokers and dealers will be engaged.

The Waste Framework Directive 2008 and UK's implementing legislation require businesses to apply the waste hierarchy to minimise the environmental impact of waste. The shipping industry is obliged to follow the waste hierarchy when handling waste brought to shore. Shipowners, charterers, cargo owners or contractors will be obliged to turn their minds to the hierarchy if they import, collect, transport, recover or dispose of waste.

14.7 Commercial choices for wreck disposal

Once it is clear that a wreck will have to be raised (eg as a result of State wreck raising orders) the owners, insurers and contractors will be planning how to dispose of it. In fact, the planning operation is most likely to be one seamless whole, as any plan to raise the wreck cannot really be separated from what is to happen with it afterwards. This can be seen with wrecks such as *Costa Concordia* and *MSC Napoli*, where the method of wreck raising was intimately related to what would happen next to the wreck, eg how safe the buoyed or repaired wreck would be for a particular scrapping voyage.

The commercial choices on wreck disposal mirror those in relation to wreck raising and will depend on the potential scrap value of the wreck and the engineering or nautical risks involved in conveying the wreck to the scrapyard.[386] The higher the scrap value the easier it may be to find a buyer, but the owners and insurers will generally want to be rid of the wreck and its inherent risks as soon as possible.

14.7.1 Sale of wreck

One way to be rid of the wreck is to sell it directly to a scrapyard or recycling facility as close in time to the wreck raising as possible.[387] Alternatively, it could be sold to a cash buying intermediary, but that market might be deterred by the higher than average risks by comparison with the scrapping of a normal ship at the end of its life. The shipowner could create a new special purpose company for it to assume ownership and negotiate a sale to a scrapyard.

---

384 See also DEFRA, "Waste Duty of Care Code of Practice" and 14.6.5(a).
385 Environment Agency, Register of waste carriers, brokers and dealers: https://environment.data.gov.uk/public-register/view/search-waste-carriers-brokers]
386 See 13.2; also 14.2.
387 The owners of the *MSC Napoli* reportedly sold the forward section to Harland and Wolff for £150,000 on payment of a 10% deposit: see R Fletcher, "Storm ahead as Napoli claimants join battle", The Telegraph 28 April 2008.

In some circumstances, the owners may press for a term in the wreck removal contract for the contractor itself to take ownership of the wreck at a certain point,[388] eg at refloating or raising. This contractor will almost certainly be looking for an immediate on-sale and so may become an owner only for a few moments before title is immediately transferred to a scrap buyer. Where the contractor is on a fixed price contract, it would expect to make its profit on that, so that the scrap may be a small part of its financial calculations. Indeed, the deal may involve the buyer obtaining the scrap for free and then chartering a barge itself to complete the voyage to the recycling yard.[389] Alternatively, eg with a large wreck, the contractor may take ownership of the hull from the shipowner under the wreck removal contract and take the risk of world scrap prices by arranging to sell directly to the recycling yard on arrival. The contractor may then need to arrange for a heavylift subcontract[390] for the disposal voyage from the wreck site.

All of these choices present risks and costs for those involved and require careful consideration in the drafting of contracts. A scrapping yard would normally prefer for its risks to start only when the wreck arrives at its yard, but might be more prepared to assume ownership at an earlier stage if the wreck consists, at that stage, of cargo aboard a heavy lift craft; it might be less willing to assume risks involved in a difficult towing operation of a refloated ship. The use of an intermediate company is an obvious device to transfer ownership risks, and for that reason the Affected State may be suspicious, but the transferring owner cannot avoid liabilities already incurred.[391] Where ownership has been transferred by these methods it may be that the new owner becomes the principal in the contract for disposal with the wreck removal contractor. It can clearly complicate contractual arrangements for that contractor if it has, in effect, to have separate contracts for the raising operation and then the disposal process.

The option for the wreck removal contractor to assume ownership of the wreck has obvious attractions, particularly to the shipowner. It means that it can satisfy its wreck removal obligations (under the WRC 2007 or otherwise) yet at the same time pass on the commercial risks of the operation to the contractor. These might not only be the physical risks in the raising operation itself, but also those arising on the disposal voyage and, in addition, the commercial risk of finding a scrap buyer for the wreck. From the contractor's perspective this option presents very different risks to those traditionally borne by salvage and wreck removal operators, but with such wreck removal contracts usually going to tender, there is increasing pressure from the shipowner and Club clients.[392] With the increasing consolidation and specialisation of the major salvage and wreck removal companies[393] there is a certain logic in one company providing a complete service from raising to disposal. Of course, the existing BIMCO contracts already allow for the contractor to assume disposal

---

388 There may be circumstances where even the H&M underwriter becomes an owner, or has an arrangement with the assured as to how to account for any scrap value of a wreck where a CTL payment has been made: see 2.6.4(b).

389 This voyage would be at the risk of the buyer, but the contractor might need to take out insurance (in effect as if on freight) if it was being paid on a no cure no pay wreck removal contract that was only completed on disposal: see eg Wreckfixed 2010, 13.6.4(b).

390 See 14.7.3.

391 See also 10.2.8.

392 See also 13.4.2.

393 See 2.7.4.

responsibilities, and these do not necessarily depend on the contractor assuming ownership of the wreck.

BIMCO produced the RECYCLECON 2012 as a standard contract for the sale of ships for 'green' recycling.[394] It is based on the standard SALEFORM 2012[395] contract for ship sales, but adapted for recycling and is designed to incorporate Hong Kong Convention requirements such as the Inventory of Hazardous Materials, the Ship Recycling Plan and a Statement of Completion. It may be that the greater 'green' administrative and legal burdens posed by the form will actually be a disincentive for its commercial use, especially by the many cash buyer intermediaries who apparently but and on-sell vessels to ship recycling facilities or others for a profit.[396]

14.7.2 Wreck and ship deregistration

In most legal systems, ship registration is regarded as compulsory where there are the necessary links between the nationality of the owning company and the State.[397] In many civil law States it appears that once a ship sinks and is wrecked it may cease to be regarded as a "ship" for many purposes of maritime law.[398] It may follow that a wrecked ship is no longer entitled to be registered as a matter of law and must therefore be deregistered. This may cause complications with the application of the EU Ship Recycling Regulation or Waste Shipment Regulation where the owner of a ship registered in an EU State may want to reregister a ship in order to avoid the Regulations.[399]

This contrasts with the UK, where an *entitlement* to register is set out in the MSA 1995 s 9. Unlike other States, registration is optional in the UK.[400] Section 9(3) gives a discretion to the Registrar to terminate the registration of a ship if it would be "inappropriate" for the ship to remain registered. The detailed provisions for registration and its termination are set out in the Merchant Shipping (Registration of Ships) Regulations 1993[401] (Registration Regulations) and reg 56(1) provides that the Registrar may, subject to service of notices, terminate a ship's registration in the following circumstances:

(a) on application by the owner;
(b) on the ship no longer being eligible to be registered;
(c) on the ship being destroyed (which includes, but is not limited to, shipwreck, demolition, fire and sinking);
 . . .
(d) if, taking into account any requirements of the Merchant Shipping Acts (including any instrument made under them) relating to the condition of the ship or its equipment so far

---

394 Replacing in turn, Salescrap 1987 and Demolishcon 2001: see BIMCO's background explanatory note: www.bimco.org/contracts-and-clauses/bimco-contracts/recyclecon. See also M Strong, P Herring, *Sale of Ships: The Norwegian Saleform* (3rd ed, Sweet & Maxwell, 2016), Chapter 26.
395 See also I Goldrein, M Hannaford, P Turner, *Ship Sale and Purchase* (6th ed, Informa, 2012), Chapter 5.
396 See C Benedictsen-Nislev, "Rycyclecon—a new standard contract for ship recycling" (2012) 107 BIMCO Bulletin 12, 14.
397 See generally, E Watt, Ship Registration: Law and Practice (3rd ed, Informa, 2018); also A Clarke, "Ship Mortgages", Chapter 26 of *Palmer & McKendrick, Interests in Goods* [*Clarke, Ship Mortgages*], 666–7.
398 Cf the application of the Salvage Convention 1989 to sunken ships: *Gaskell, MSA 1995*, 21/376–21/377.
399 See 14.5.2, 14.4.1, 14.4.2.
400 For the reasons, see *Gaskell, MSA 1995*, 21/29–21/30.
401 SI 1993/3138.

as relevant to its safety or to any risk of pollution or to the safety, health and welfare of persons employed or engaged in any capacity on board the ship, he considers that it would be inappropriate for the ship to remain registered;[402]

From this it is clear that an owner can apply to remove a ship from the register. The relevant form[403] requires the owner to declare whether the vessel has been sold (and if so to whom and when), destroyed or registered elsewhere. Where the "destroyed" box has been ticked, the owner has to provide the date of destruction and is supposed then to tick one of four boxes in answer to the question "how was it destroyed?". The boxes are "wrecked", "scrapped, "fire" and "other". It is clearly possible for the registrar to deregister the ship even without an application from the owner, but it is not clear when this would happen. The word "destroyed" is perhaps unusual in the context of wreck, but reg 56(1)(c) makes it clear that this is a wide expression and includes "shipwreck, fire and sinking". The first and last of these are likely to be actual total losses, while "fire" may be more likely to cover a CTL.

It is unlikely that there would be much difference in practice in relation to deregistration between the discretion given to the UK Registrar to deregister and the approach in other systems; it seems highly unlikely that the UK Registrar would decline to deregister a ship once it had been declared by its owner to be wrecked. It seems possible for the Registrar to deregister on receiving information from other sources, eg reliable media reports of a notorious sinking. Apart from oversight, or the possibility of reregistering to avoid the Ship Recycling Regulation 2013 or Waste Shipment Regulation 2008, it is difficult to see why an owner would want to continue the registration of a sunken ship. It might be thought there were advantages if the ship still had a value of some kind and the owner wanted to preserve future sale rights under the particular registration system—even where salvage was unlikely and scrapping was a possibility.

An obvious incentive for an owner to deregister is that registration fees would no longer apply, but that is perhaps relatively insignificant. There may well be other reasons, or at least consequences, which are less obvious. It is possible that others interested in the ship do not yet know of the sinking. Mortgagees of the ship must be notified by the UK Registrar of the deregistration[404] and once the Registrar issues a "closure transcript" under reg 56(2) "the owner shall immediately surrender the ship's certificate of registry to the Registrar for cancellation".[405] Registration may carry with it many public law, ie regulatory, consequences which an owner might want to avoid; although many of a State's jurisdictional power and duties under UNCLOS relate to ships "flying its flag",[406] there is a distinction between nationality of ships and registration.[407] There may be criminal responsibilities even in respect of unregistered ships[408]—provided that the wreck is still a "ship".[409]

---

402 Paras (e)–(h) need not be set out here but relate broadly to circumstances where: the owner has not answered a summons for contravention of the MSA 1995; where penalties under the MSA 1995 remain unpaid; fishing vessels cease to be licensed.
403 MSF4744 (Rev 02/15).
404 Reg 56(2).
405 Reg 56(3).
406 See eg Art 94 of the "Duties of the flag State".
407 See eg Arts 91 and 92 and the discussion in *Gaskell, MSA 1995*, 21/18 et seq.
408 See eg the MSA 1995 ss 16(3), 307.
409 See the MSA 1995 s 311 and cf 10.2.7.

Under the UK system, registration perfects legal title and the registered owner has the absolute power to dispose of the ship, while unregistered interests can exist in equity.[410] If the ship is deregistered from the UK register, the owner's title in English law is not affected, as such, although subsequent dealings may need to refer to the *lex situs*, as explained below.

In a civil law system, such as Greece, deregistration may have the effect that rights in respect of the ship cease to be regulated by the ship's register. Thereafter, the entity that was a "ship", but is now a wreck, could be treated in the same way as any other moveable for the purposes of private international law. This might have the consequence that issues such as ownership rights fall to be dealt with by the *lex situs* (the default position for chattels), rather than the law of the flag or the nationality of the ship.[411] In *The WD Fairway*[412] there was a dispute as to proprietary rights as between the assured and underwriters who had paid out €150 million for a CTL for what was apparently the world's largest trailing suction hopper dredger, wrecked after a collision. The wrecked vessel had been towed to a naval dockyard in Thailand, but the assured had deregistered the vessel and purported to sell it to an associated company to prevent it falling into the hands of commercial competitors. Under English law, the governing law of the policies, the insurers were entitled to assert equitable interests,[413] but it was common ground that the incidence of proprietary interests would need to be determined by the *lex situs*. In phase 1 of the litigation on preliminary issues, there was a question about whether the reference to the *lex situs* would include its rules of private international law. Tomlinson J was inclined (obiter) not to apply the doctrine of renvoi, so that it would be necessary only to refer to the domestic law of the *situs*.[414] It was then necessary to decide *which* was the *situs* of the vessel, in particular whether she was deemed to be situated at its port of registry (eg Holland), or where she was physically situated from time to time (eg Thailand). Dicey[415] favoured the port of registry when the vessel is on the high seas, but the actual *situs* when the vessel was within territorial or national waters.[416] It was agreed in *The WD Fairway* that, *after* deregistration in Holland, any transfer of property would be governed by Thai law as the actual *lex situs*;[417] for transfers *before*

---

410 See the MSA 1995 Sch 1(1) and (2); also *Clarke, Ship Mortgages* 671–2, *Meeson & Kimbell* 349–351, 347–349.

411 See generally, 3.2.1.

412 *Dornoch Ltd & Ors v Westminster International BV & Ors* [2009] EWHC 889 (Admlty); [2009] 2 Lloyd's Rep 191 [80]: also 2.9.4(b).

413 [2009] 2 Lloyd's Rep 191 [60–64].

414 [2009] 2 Lloyd's Rep 191 [89]. On that basis, English law about proprietary interests would be irrelevant to the efficacy of transfer of title, unless eg the law of the situs would look to it. In Phase 1 there was no evidence available about the position in Thai or Dutch law. See further *Dornoch Ltd & Ors v Westminster International BV & Ors (The WD Fairway (No 3))* [2009] EWHC 1782 (Admlty), [2009] 2 Lloyd's Rep 420 [4], [50], where it became clear that Thai law would apply its own domestic law, and that there was no automatic transfer of property rights when a CTL was paid, so that there were no proprietary interests of which the buyer had notice.

415 *Dicey, Morris and Collins on the Conflict of Laws* (15th ed, Sweet & Maxwell, 2006), para 22–058.

416 Tomlinson J also noted that if there was a dispute and the ship was sold by court order, property rights would be transferred irrespective of the place of registry: see [2009] 2 Lloyd's Rep 191 [94].

417 [2009] 2 Lloyd's Rep 191 [95]. To that extent, the tactical deregistration before transfer of ownership was effective. The difficulty in the case was the equitable proprietary interests of the insurers under English law predated the sale to the associated company. In *The WD Fairway (No 3)* [2009] 2 Lloyd's Rep 420 [129–135], though, the sale to the associated company was set aside under the Insolvency Act 1986 s 423, as it was at an undervalue.

deregistration (when the ship was still registered) the *lex situs* in respect of the equitable interests falling short of legal title was the default position for chattels, ie Thai law.[418]

These considerations about governing law may be relevant if owners seek to sell the wreck to contractors as part of a wreck removal process.[419]

14.7.3 BIMCO disposal voyage contracts

After a wreck raising, it will usually be necessary to undertake some sort of separate disposal voyage and whoever remains primarily responsible for that part of the wreck removal[420] will have to arrange that voyage. The three BIMCO wreck removal contracts all allow for the parties to agree not only on a place of delivery of the wreck, but also of its disposal.[421] If the wreck removal contract provides only for delivery, eg at the casualty site after raising, the shipowner (or any wreck buyer) will have to engage contractors to perform a disposal voyage. Where that responsibility has been contractually undertaken by the wreck contractor, eg under Wreckstage 2010, it may simply use its own craft as part of its performance of its wreck removal obligations. If the wreck contractor does not have its own craft available for the task of moving a wreck that has been raised or refloated, it will need to engage sub-contractors to perform that disposal voyage, eg by hiring in tugs using the Towhire 2008 or Towcon 2008 contracts.[422] Alternatively, the wreck contractor or the registered owner of the wreck may turn to one of the BIMCO suite of heavylift or related offshore contract forms.[423] These contracts are fully analysed in *Rainey*[424] so only a brief introduction as relevant to wreck disposal will be given here.

The essential choice for the parties in heavylift contracts concerning wrecks is whether they want to undertake a (relatively) conventional carriage of goods to which the Hague/Visby Rules would apply to give basic protections to the cargo interests (ie owner or shipper), or whether they would prefer to adopt a charter of the heavylift craft (such as Heavycon 2007) that would enable them to agree any terms as to the allocation of risk and liability for the disposal voyage.

---

418 [2009] 2 Lloyd's Rep 191 [103]. Tomlinson J recognised, though, that for questions of legal (as opposed to equitable) title, most legal systems would inevitably look to the law of the place of registration (in this case, Dutch law), as a consequence of their own conflict rules.

419 See 14.7.1.

420 Eg the owner (through its insurer), or a buyer of the wreck. See also 10.2.8.

421 See eg Wreckhire 2010 cll 9, 12 and Box 8 (see 13.6.3(i)); Wreckfixed 2010 cl 8 and Box 8 (see 13.6.4(e)); Wreckstage 2010 Box 8 and cl 9 (see 13.6.5(g)).

422 See 12.1.2(c), 13.5. Here the wreck contractor as principal may have to assume the risk of loss of the tow, as the tug owner should be entitled to rely on the knock for knock provisions in the towage contract, eg Towhire 2008 cl 25: See *Rainey* 125–181. As with all the BIMCO contracts, care will need to be taken to specify who are parties to the contract with the sub-contractor. Is it the wreck contractor, the registered owner, the insurer (unlikely), an intermediate buyer of the wreck, or an ultimate purchaser (such as a scrap yard)? This will be relevant not only in relation to core obligations such as payment, but also because of privity issues: See the Himalaya clauses in BIMCO contracts, eg Towhire 2008 cl 24, and cf Wreckhire 2010 cll 17, 26(b).

423 Where containers have been offloaded from a wreck and taken ashore for storage, as occurred eg with *MSC Napoli* (see 1.2.3), the containers could then be transported by another container ship under ordinary carriage terms. In *MSC Napoli*, MSC itself arranged for one of its ships to pick up intact containers that had been salved. Different carriage arrangements might be needed for damaged containers.

424 Chapter 7.

The use of a specialised contract form for heavylift operations is a major improvement on the previous use by some operators of the Conlinebooking Note[425] which was really designed for bills of lading issued on the Conlinebill forms.[426] Once a bill of lading is issued, the Hague/Visby Rules would normally apply to cargo,[427] either as a matter of law, or because their terms are incorporated into the contract voluntarily using a clause paramount.[428] In practice, bills of lading (as opposed to waybills)[429] may not always be used for such heavylift operations,[430] but if they are issued the parties have to be careful as the mandatory terms of the Rules could conflict with charter terms that might exclude many carrier liabilities. Where the bill is in the hands of the charterer the Hague/Visby Rules would not apply.[431] Once that bill is in the hands of a third party (eg through endorsement and transfer) that person will be entitled to rely on the Rules which, in turn, would invalidate any incorporated charter clause that would derogate from the Rules.[432] Such a situation might arise in the wreck context where the hull of a wreck is being delivered by a heavylift craft to a shipyard that has bought the wreck, eg from the registered owner who shipped it from the wreck raising site. Given the nature of a wreck 'cargo', essentially scrap, it is unlikely to suffer the sort of damage that might occur to conventional cargo—so it may not matter greatly whether the Rules apply or not.[433]

Thus, the most obvious risk for such 'wreck cargoes' (ie shipwrecks being carried as cargo) is when there is a casualty involving the heavylift craft which results in the total loss of the craft and its 'cargo'. The contracting carrier, eg the owner of the craft, would be entitled to exclude any liability under the Rules caused by negligent navigation;[434] the same result can be achieved under the knock for knock provisions of a charter such as Heavycon

---

425 See eg *CPC Consolidated Pool Carriers v CTM Cia Transmediterranea SA (The CPC Gallia)* [1994] 1 Lloyd's Rep 68.

426 In some respects, operations contracted for using a booking note might be considered as similar to a charter and thereby outside the Hague/Visby Rules. In any event, see now Heavyliftvoy, which is derived from the Conlinebooking Note.

427 Note that the Hague/Rules would not apply to "particular cargo" falling within Art VI. This provision is designed to remove the operation of the rules from highly unusual cargoes that present particular risks of carriage, eg oil paintings. It might seem that large risk wrecks still containing bunker and cargo residues would fit this category, but in order to take the carriage outside the Rules it would be necessary for a non-negotiable waybill to be issued.

428 See 2.1.5(a). There may still be issues about whether the Hague/Visby Rules apply, eg if the shipment is not from a contracting State: cf *Parsons Corporation v CV Scheepvaartonderneming "Happy Ranger" (The Happy Ranger)* [2002] EWCA Civ 694, [2002] 2 Lloyd's Rep 357.

429 The Hague/Visby Rules would not apply as a matter of law where a waybill is issued, as it is not a "similar document of title" to a bill of lading: cf a straight bill and *JI Macwilliam Co Inc v Mediterranean Shipping Co SA (The Rafaela S)* [2005] UKHL 11, [2005] 2 AC 423, [2005] 1 Lloyd's Rep 347. This means that if a waybill is issued for heavylift cargo it acts primarily as a receipt for the cargo shipped. Waybill forms commonly incorporate the Hague/Visby Rules by contract, see eg *Bills of Lading: Law and Contracts*, 719.

430 And see eg Projectcon cl 22.

431 See Hague/Visby Rules Art 1(b) and eg *President of India v Metcalfe Shipping (The Dunelmia)* [1970] 1 QB 289, *Bills of Lading: Law and Contracts*, 685–689.

432 See Art III r 8.

433 Cf *Rainey*, 353–356, 416–420 on relative seaworthiness for heavylift craft.

434 See Art IV r 2(a) and 2.1.5(b).

2007. If the 'cargo' was lost or damaged by reason of unseaworthiness[435] or lack of care (not excepted by the Rules), then the carrier might be entitled to rely on the limits in the Rules.[436] The hull of a wreck would almost certainly be a "unit" (not a package) within Art IV r 5 of the Hague/Visby Rules. By contrast, the carrier might allege that the wreck as cargo is "dangerous goods", especially if it has not yet been fully cleaned of all bunkers and cargo. Here the 'cargo' interests (ie owner or buyer of the wreck being carried) will need adequate insurance and/or indemnities.[437]

Heavycon 2007 is a form of voyage charter.[438] It is suitable for the type of heavy lift operations where an entire wreck (or large sections of the hull) are transported on a large specialist float-on, float-off semi-submersible craft of the type operated by companies such as BigLift or Boskalis. The 'wreck cargo' might have buoyancy tanks still attached, or it could itself be on a barge before being floated onto the heavylift ship.[439] Some heavylift ships will be self-geared, while others may utilise separate heavy lift cranes mounted on their own barges. There is the usual freedom of contract granted to the parties to a Heavycon 2007 charter, so that they can include any terms they want, and are not restricted by the Hague or Hague-Visby Rules—unless bills of lading are issued.[440] The Heavyconbill 2016 is the latest version of the bill (designed specifically for the Heavycon 2007 charter). It incorporates the charter terms in cl 1 and applies the HVR to cargo shipped underdeck, while a clause on the face excludes all damage for loss damage or delay for goods shipped on deck.[441] Clause 25 of Heavycon 2007 requires that the use of a bill of lading or non-negotiable waybill should be specifically agreed in Box 25 of the charter. If a bill is issued then it should be on Heavyconbill terms.[442] Heavycon 2007 itself contains the

---

435 As *Rainey* rightly observes seaworthiness obligations are already relative, eg for semi-submersible craft which are, by definition, designed to make cargo accessible to the sea: see 354.

436 In that case the limit might be as low as the equivalent of US $1,841 under the Hague/Visby Rules or US$500 under the Hague Rules: see 2.1.5(e). Under the Hague Rules there would be no alternative weight limit: see *Vinnlustodin v Sea Tank Shipping AS (The Aqasia)* [2018] EWCA Civ 276, [2018] 1 Lloyd's Rep 530 and cf 2.1.5(e). Under the Hague-Visby Rules, by contrast, the cargo owner would have access to the alternative weight limit of 2 sdrs per kg of gross weight of the goods lost or damaged. As this is about $2,765 per tonne there would in practice be no Hague-Visby Rules limit as demolition scrap values do not seem to exceed US$500: cf Hellenic Shipping News, 11 January 2018 www.hellenicshippingnews.com/ships-demolition-prices-skyrocket-on-high-demand/. See also F Gavin, "Heavy lift cargoes—Contractual issues and risk allocation" (2011) 293 Gard News. Nb unlike containers where the "enumeration" of the container's contents is an express measure in Art IV r 5(c) for limitation purposes, the weight recorded in the bill would only be *prima facie* evidence of the wreck cargo lost for the purposes of Art IV r 5(a).

437 Indemnities might be needed for circumstances where the bunker oil leaked from the hull of the wreck being carried as cargo. Here difficult questions might arise as to whether the Bunkers Convention 2001 still applied or not: see 2.6.3 and cf 10.2.8.

438 See *Rainey*, 348–382 and, generally, *Voyage Charters*.

439 This is what occurred with the wreck of the *Sewol* in 2017: see also 13.1.3.

440 Unless bills of lading are issued: see above. As enacted eg in COGSA 1971. The Hague/Visby Rules do not apply to charterparties: see Art V and 2.1.5(a).

441 As allowed by the Hague/Visby Rules: see Art 1(a): *Bills of Lading: Law and Contracts*, 328–331.

442 The Heavycon 2007 cl 25 still refers to the Heavyconbill 2007, but Heavyconbill 2016 itself has all the bill of lading terms required by cl 25. If a non-negotiable waybill is issued, it should be in the Heavyconreceipt form, which also has a 2016 version updating that of 2007. With such a waybill, there is no contractual incorporation of the Hague/Visby Rules, even for underdeck cargo, so this would be appropriate where the parties only wanted a receipt under the charter and did not want to alter the knock for knock liability regime. e

familiar knock for knock provision where the parties allocate risks somewhat mechanically between themselves.[443] The charter refers in cl 1 to the "loading port", including a "place" or "area" and this would need to be specified where the wreck is loaded at the site of the sinking. Although cl 37 allows double banking (eg for transhipment between vessels) it does not expressly allow loading *of* a wreck at sea where the anchorage may not be safe. In order to avoid implied obligations as to the safety of the loading area (or any implied indemnity) an express provision about safety would be appropriate. Likewise, the charterer would probably need to clarify the ambit of the dangerous goods clause (cl 18), but cl 24(b) puts full responsibility on the charterer in respect of pollution damage or clean-up costs originating "from the Cargo or other property of the charterers".[444] The charterers have the obligation under cl 26 to obtain insurance for the cargo, including costs of wreck removal of the cargo.

Heavyliftvoy, issued in 2009, is designed for the type of heavy lift on/lift off operations involving conventional cargo where the transaction is, in effect, a carriage of goods.[445] Under cl 26 the owner assumes no liability for deck cargo, although there is a slightly different provision for US trade. Heavyliftvoy requires in cl 27 that the carrier issues a bill of lading in the Heabyliftbill form[446] incorporating Heavyliftvoy. Again, this would only be a receipt in the hands of the charterer, but in the hands of a third party the Hague/Visby Rules could apply, although the bill again exempts liability for deck cargo. It seems unlikely that Heavyliftvoy would be suitable for the type of wreck removal operations discussed earlier, although it could possibly be used for the transport of oversized cargo that was actually being carried on the wreck itself.

If, instead of a heavy lift ship, a barge is chartered separately to carry parts of the wreck (eg an aft section, or the accommodation superstructure, or salved containers), the parties may wish to use the Bargehire 2008 form.[447] This is in effect a form of bareboat charter, where the risk of loss or damage to the barge falls on the hirer. The barge may then be towed by one of the wreck contractor's own fleet (in fulfilment of its wreck removal contract), or by a tug that is sub-contracted in, eg on the basis of Towcon 2008 or Towhire 2008[448] (depending on whether a lump sum or daily rate contract is required). The towage contracts contain familiar knock for knock provisions under which the hirer assumes responsibility for loss or damage to its vessel (and injury or death of its personnel) and the tugowner is responsible for loss or damage to the tug (and injury or death of the tug's personnel).[449]

Alternatively, it is possible that an offshore contractor will itself offer a tug and barge combination to perform the type of task that might be performed by a single heavylift ship under Heavycon 2007. The Projectcon[450] form, issued in 2006, could be used for this type

---

443 See cl 22(b)) and cf 13.6.3(d). Clause 32 expressly preserves the right of the owner of the heavylift craft to limit its liability, and this reinforces the effect of *The Cape Bari* [2016] 2 Lloyd's Rep 469: see 2.5.4(d).
444 The wording seems to assume that the cargo is owned by the charterer, but this may not be apt to describe a situation where the wreck removal contractor is the charterer and the cargo belongs to the owner of the wreck.
445 See *Rainey*, 383–410; also F Gavin, "Heavy lift cargoes—Contractual issues and risk allocation" (2011) 293 Gard News.
446 There is again an updated Heabyliftbill 2016 version.
447 See *Rainey*, Chapter 6.
448 See *Rainey*, Chapter 7; also 12.1.2(c), 13.5.
449 See *Rainey*, 125–181.
450 See Rainey 410–430.

of wreck removal operation, eg with a specialist semi-submersible barge, although it was designed more for the transportation of awkward cargoes for use in the offshore oil and gas sector. Again, it might also be used for transport of oversize cargo or containers that have been removed from the wreck (and may well be intact) in circumstances where the wreck removal contractor is not able to hire in a barge for use with its own tugs. Like Heavycon 2007, Projectcon has a knock for knock provision (cl 21), and cl 22 expressly states that no bills of lading will be issued (thus avoiding the Hague/Visby Rules), and that there will be no liability for deck cargo.

The WRC 2007 does not apply to offshore platforms, eg when they are on location,[451] but it could apply to floating platforms that are being towed to shore for dismantling and are wrecked on the way. BIMCO has now developed a lump sum offshore structure dismantling contract, "Dismantlecon" for release in 2019. This is very much designed for the decommissioning of offshore platforms rather than wrecks, although its draft sub-title is quite wide, ie "Dismantling, Removal and Marine Services Agreement". There are some similarities between decommissioning and the problems involved in wreck removal and the solutions adopted in contracts such as Wreckstage 2010. The draft contract[452] is not designed to deal with the physical disposal of the structure,[453] and delivery by the decommissioning contractor could take place at the actual offshore worksite once the structure is loaded onto a barge, although it could also take place in a port. The contractor is never intended to become the title owner of the structure; the oil company will be the one that assumes responsibility if the facility is wrecked and has to be removed, while the equivalent provision applies if the contractor's property is wrecked.[454] The contract acknowledges that services are calculated on the basis of a series of documented Assumptions and Information described in an Appendix. This means that revision and variation orders can be used to reflect cost changes, with the use of a construction industry type of expert evaluation adjudication process where variations cannot be agreed (before mediation and arbitration). The circumstances in which the Dismantlecon parties can ask for variations may well be less prescribed than by comparison with those in the substantial change provisions in cl 4 of Wreckstage 2010.[455] It remains to be seen if this sort of solution (also allowing for the correction of inconsistencies in information) will influence the wreck removal contracts that only use arbitration and mediation to resolve disputes.

14.7.4 Rena *trust fund and finality*

Where the wreck cannot be raised at all, the owners and insurers will also be faced with the problem of how to put a stop to the seemingly endless costs involved in removing the

---

451 See Art 1(2) and 10.2.7.
452 For the draft contract, see P Dean, E Bokor-Ingram and M Dow, "Offshore", Chapter 4 of G Eddings, A Chamberlain, R Warder (eds) *The Shipping Law Review* (5th ed, Law Business Research, 2018), 30.
453 For which see Recyclecon.
454 It is not quite clear how the costs and liabilities would be apportioned when a barge owned by the contractor sinks while carrying property owned by the oil company. These provisions are contained within a knock for knock clause, but it is not clear how far this will eventually be modified from other BIMCO clauses.
455 Decom North Sea and Society of Underwater Technology, "Salvage and Decommissioning—Review of New Contract Template Options", 11: http://decomnorthsea.com/uploads/pdfs/training/DNS-SUT-decom-terms-article-draft-rev3-final.pdf.

remains, or rendering them harmless. The State may prefer to have long term monitoring in case there are continuing environmental problems, so as to retain some sort of option of requiring further remediation at a later stage. It is here that questions of cost and proportionality under the WRC 2007 will arise, along with a close examination of which obligation of the owner is enlivened.[456]

This can be seen most acutely in relation to the *Rena*, when the issue of finality of operations (and costs) arose because the shipowner and Club wanted to dump or abandon the last remains of the ship.[457] The rather novel device to end the shipowner's and Club's exposure was to create a separate Astrolabe Community Trust to which ownership of the *Rena*'s remains would pass.[458] The Trust would be given funds to deal with possible future claims, but those funds were related to the final settlement with the State;[459] ie the shipowner and insurer would pay the final agreed sum, but thereafter they would not respond to further claims. The *Rena* was not a WRC 2007 case, where direct liability might prevent the insurer from evading liability, but even under the WRC 2007 a shipowner and insurer may be able to limit or cap liability.[460] In those circumstances, the State may be faced with a finite amount to be able to deal with any remaining problems. These may include the sort of longer term site monitoring and remediation work that is being undertaken with the *Costa Concordia*.[461] While the State might prefer the shipowner and insurer to remain actively involved in the longer term, the use of a trust to achieve finality may have some attractions. The Club might be prepared to make a generous final commercial settlement as part of its exit strategy. The State, if suitably represented as a trustee, might feel it had more direct control of operations and costs (without the continual need to agree items with the Club). Others interested in remediation, eg indigenous groups or environmentalists, might also have the opportunity to participate in decisions about expenditure in a way seen to be separate from government. For the State, that might also be a way to achieve political finality.

---

[456] Ie whether this is a wreck removal or pollution prevention issue, potentially raising the overlap of legislative or convention regimes: see 10.9 and 10.2.8.

[457] See 1.2.4(d) and (e).

[458] See www.astrolabereef.co.nz/astrolabe-community-trust. An application to achieve charitable status was declined on 2 September 2015: Charities Registration Board Decision No 2015-2.

[459] For the full text of the various deeds of settlement, see *Rena: Crown Law 2017 Letter to Ombudsman*.

[460] See 10.7, 10.8.5.

[461] See 1.2.5(b) and (c); also 10.2.5.

APPENDICES

Introduction

It is customary to include long extracts of Conventions, Statutes and Contracts in the Appendices of legal books. Although this can sometimes be convenient for readers, it is increasingly wasteful in an era when most of these materials are easily available on the web—often in more up to date versions than are printed in the books. For this reason, the authors have decided to reduce the Appendices as much as possible.

Accordingly, some useful web links are provided for a range of material that would otherwise have been included in print form. Obviously, these links are subject to change, but simple web searches are all that is necessary to trace most sites.

Nevertheless, key extracts of the Merchant Shipping Act 1995, as amended are reproduced, as listed below. These include the most recent amendments made by the Wreck Removal Convention Act 2011 and the Marine Navigation Act 2013. The full text of the Wreck Removal Convention 2007 is also reproduced (as Sch 11ZA of MSA 1995). One reason for reproducing these materials is that the official UK legislation site (www.legislation.gov.uk) does not yet have an up to date full consolidation available for the MSA 1995, and it can be quite tricky to cut and paste together all the amendments with accuracy. The authors believe that the version in the Appendices is up to date as at 31 December 2018, but readers always need to check for amendments.

Facsimiles of the three BIMCO wreck removal contracts are also reproduced.

Merchant Shipping Act 1995: extracts

The legislation has been lightly annotated with footnotes showing (i) amendments made as at 31 December 2018; (ii) cross references to some of the key parts of the book where the legislation is discussed; (iii) in Part 9A some references to the relevant WRC 2007 provisions.

The annotations are not meant to be comprehensive and readers should also refer to the Index.

1. MSA 1995 Part IX, ss 252–255
2. MSA 1995 Part 9A, ss 255A–255U
3. MSA 1995 Schedule 3A Safety Directions
4. MSA 1995 Schedule 11ZA [Text of the Wreck Removal Convention 2007]
5. Wreck Removal Convention 2007: Annex (Certificate of Insurance)
6. Wreck Removal Convention 2007: Diplomatic Conference Resolutions

BIMCO Wreck Removal Contracts

7. Wreckhire 2010
8. Wreckfixed 2010
9. Wreckstage 2010
10. Wreckstage 2010: BIMCO Explanatory Notes

Links to useful web sites

UK legislation: www.legislation.gov.uk
　　Contains Acts and delegates legislation, but displayed versions are not always fully consolidated. Annotations in the text (and in separate pull-down menus) indicate known amendments.

EU law: www.eur-lex.europa.eu/homepage.html?locale=en
　　www.emsa.europa.eu/: European Maritime Safety Agency:

iLaws: www.i-law.com
　　Informa Law's website for full text of the Lloyd's Reports and books in the Informa Shipping Law Library, as well as journals such as the Lloyd's Maritime and Commercial Law Quarterly (by subscription).

Bailii: www.bailii.org/
　　A site containing free access to most UK decisions, but without the headnote summaries available, eg, in Lloyd's Reports.

BIMCO: www.bimco.org/
　　www.bimco.org/contracts-and-clauses: Free registration available to see draft versions of all BIMCO shipping contracts, including Towcon, Towhire, Wreckstage, Wreckcon, Wreckhire. Subscription necessary for editable versions of contracts

Lloyd's of London: www.lloyds.com/
　　www.lloyds.com/market-resources/lloyds-agency/salvage-arbitration-branch: Includes copies of LOF 2011, LSSAC and SCOPIC 2018.

ISU: www.marine-salvage.com/
　　Includes copies of contracts such as ISU Award Sharing Sub-contract

International Group of P&I Clubs: www.igpandi.org/
　　Group insurance arrangements and links to the websites of all the major Clubs. These in turn publish their Rules annually, as well as many short articles of relevance

IMO: www.imo.org/en/Pages/Default.aspx
　　IMO main website including publications
　　www.imo.org/en/About/Pages/DocumentsResources.aspx: Links to separate IMO Docs site (free access by registration) with records of IMO bodies, eg the IMO legal Committee and diplomatic conferences. Note that the Legal Committee documents are not complete back to 1969, and many of the earlier documents are only available in print form.
　　www.imo.org/en/About/Conventions/StatusOfConventions/Pages/Default.aspx: Status of conventions, updated regularly. Readers wanting access to full texts of all IMO maritime conventions (and associated lists of ratifications) should consult the loose-leaf *Ratification of Maritime Conventions* (Informa)

CMI: www.comitemaritime.org
　　Contains CMI records and documentation going back to 1897 including status of CMI inspired conventions

UNESCO: www.unesco.org/new/en/culture/themes/underwater-cultural-heritage/
　　Contains copy of Underwater Cultural Heritage Convention 2001 and accessible database of national legislation.

APPENDIX 1: MSA 1995 PART IX, SS 252-255

1995 CHAPTER 21

PART IX

SALVAGE AND WRECK

CHAPTER II

WRECK

Removal of wrecks

252 Powers of harbour and conservancy authorities in relation to wrecks[1]

(1) Where any vessel is sunk, stranded or abandoned in, or in or near any approach to, any harbour or tidal water under the control of a harbour authority or conservancy authority in such a manner as, in the opinion of the authority, to be, or be likely to become, an obstruction or danger to navigation or to lifeboats engaged in lifeboat service in that harbour or water or approach thereto, that authority may exercise any of the following powers.

(2) Those powers are —
  (a) to take possession of, and raise, remove or destroy the whole or any part of the vessel and any other property to which the power extends;
  (b) to *mark the location of*[2] the vessel or part of the vessel and any such other property until it is raised, removed or destroyed; and
  (c) subject to subsections (5) and (6) below, to sell, in such manner as the authority think fit, the vessel or part of the vessel so raised or removed and any other property recovered in the exercise of the powers conferred by paragraph (a) or (b) above;
  (d) to reimburse themselves, out of the proceeds of the sale, for the expenses incurred by them in relation to the sale.

(3) The other property to which the powers conferred by subsection (2) above extend is every article or thing or collection of things being or forming part of the equipment, cargo, stores or ballast of the vessel.

(3A) *For the purposes of subsection (2)(b) a location may be marked by —*
  (a) *buoys, lights or other physical devices;*
  (b) *the transmission of information about the location.*[3]

(4) Any surplus of the proceeds of a sale under subsection (2)(c) above shall be held by the authority on trust for the persons entitled thereto.

(5) Except in the case of property which is of a perishable nature or which would deteriorate in value by delay, no sale shall be made under subsection (2)(c) above until at least seven days

---

1 See 11.1.3(a).
2 Words in italics substituted in place of "light or buoy" by Marine Navigation Act 2013 s 11(1).
3 Words in italics inserted by Marine Navigation Act 2013 s 11(2).

APPENDIX 1 MERCHANT SHIPPING ACT 1995 PART IX

notice of the intended sale has been given by advertisement in a local newspaper circulating in or near the area over which the authority have control.

(6) At any time before any property is sold under subsection (2)(c) above, the owner of the property shall be entitled to have it delivered to him on payment of its fair market value.

(7) The market value of property for the purposes of subsection (6) above shall be that agreed on between the authority and the owner or, failing agreement, that determined by a person appointed for the purpose by the Secretary of State.

(8) The sum paid to the authority in respect of any property under subsection (6) above shall, for the purposes of this section, be treated as the proceeds of sale of the property.

(9) Any proceeds of sale arising under subsection (2)(c) above from the sale of a vessel and any other property recovered from the vessel shall be treated as a common fund.

(10) This section is without prejudice to any other powers of a harbour authority or conservancy authority.

253 Powers of lighthouse authorities in relation to wrecks[4]

(1) Where —
 (a) any vessel is sunk, stranded or abandoned in any fairway or on the seashore or on or near any rock, shoal or bank in the United Kingdom or any of the adjacent seas or islands; and
 (b) there is no harbour authority or conservancy authority having power to raise, remove or destroy the vessel;
 the general lighthouse authority for the place in or near which the vessel is situated shall, if in the authority's opinion the vessel is, or is likely to become, an obstruction or danger to navigation or to lifeboats engaged in lifeboat service, have the same powers in relation thereto as are conferred by section 252.

(2) Where a general lighthouse authority have incurred expenses in the exercise of their powers under this section in relation to any vessel, then —
 (a) if the proceeds of any sale made under section 252 in connection with the exercise of those powers in relation to the vessel are insufficient to reimburse the authority for the full amount of those expenses, the authority may recover the amount of the deficiency from the relevant person, or
 (b) if there is no such sale, the authority may recover the full amount of those expenses from the relevant person.

(3) Any expenses so incurred which are not recovered by the authority either out of the proceeds of any such sale or in accordance with subsection (2) above shall be paid out of the General Lighthouse Fund, but section 213 shall apply to those expenses as if they were expenses of the authority falling within subsection (1) of that section other than establishment expenses.

(4) In this section "the relevant person", in relation to any vessel, means the owner of the vessel at the time of the sinking, stranding or abandonment of the vessel.

254 Referral of questions as to powers between authorities

(1) If any question arises between a harbour authority or conservancy authority and a general lighthouse authority as to their respective powers under sections 252 and 253 in relation to any place in or near an approach to a harbour or tidal water, that question shall, on the application of either authority, be referred to the Secretary of State for his decision.

(2) Any decision of the Secretary of State under this section shall be final.

---

4 See 11.1.3(b), 11.3.5.

Interpretation

255 Interpretation.

(1) In this Part —
"receiver" means a receiver of wreck appointed under section 248;
"salvage" includes, subject to the Salvage Convention, all expenses properly incurred by the salvor in the performance of the salvage services;
"the Salvage Convention" has the meaning given by section 224(1);
"salvor" means, in the case of salvage services rendered by the officers or crew or part of the crew of any ship belonging to Her Majesty, the person in command of the ship;
"tidal water" means any part of the sea and any part of a river within the ebb and flow of the tide at ordinary spring tides, and not being a harbour;
"vessel" includes any ship or boat, or any other description of vessel used in navigation; and
"wreck" includes jetsam, flotsam, lagan and derelict found in or on the shores of the sea or any tidal water.

(2) Fishing boats or fishing gear lost or abandoned at sea and either —
   (a) found or taken possession of within United Kingdom waters; or
   (b) found or taken possession of beyond those waters and brought within those waters;
   shall be treated as wreck for the purposes of this Part.

(3) In the application of this Part in relation to Scotland, any reference to a justice of the peace includes a reference to a sheriff.

APPENDIX 2: MSA 1995 PART 9A, SS 255A-255U

PART 9A[1]

WRECK REMOVAL CONVENTION

Preliminary

255A "The Wrecks Convention"

(1) In this Part —
  (a) "the Wrecks Convention" means the Nairobi International Convention on the Removal of Wrecks 2007 done in Nairobi on 18 May 2007, and
  (b) "Wrecks Convention State" means a State which is a party to the Wrecks Convention.
(2) The text of the Wrecks Convention is set out in Schedule 11ZA.

255B Wreck reports[1]

(1) Where an accident[2] results in a wreck[3] in a Convention area,[4] the persons responsible for any United Kingdom ship[5] involved in the accident must report the wreck without delay.
(2) If the wreck is in the United Kingdom's Convention area,[6] it must be reported to the Secretary of State.
(3) If the wreck is in the Convention area of any other State, it must be reported to the government of that State.
(4) The following are responsible for a ship[7] —
  (a) the master[8] of the ship, and
  (b) the operator[9] of the ship.
(5) A report under subsection (1) must include the information mentioned in paragraph (2) of Article 5 of the Wrecks Convention (so far as it is known).
(6) If one of the persons responsible for a ship makes a report under subsection (1) the others are no longer under a duty to make a report.
(7) Failure to comply with the reporting requirement is an offence.

---

1 See the WRC 2007 Art 5; and 9.1.3, 11.3.3(a).
2 See s 255R(2); WRC 2007 Art 1(3); 8.2.1(a), 10.5.1.
3 See s 255R(1); WRC 2007 Art 194).
4 See s 255R(1), (6); WRC 2007 Art 1(1); 11.3.2.
5 See the MSA 1995 ss 1(3), 313(1).
6 See s 255R(6) and the Merchant Shipping (United Kingdom Wreck Convention Area) Order 2015 (SI 2015/172).
7 See s 313(1).
8 See the MSA 1995 s 313(1).
9 See the WRC 2007 Art 1(9).

APPENDIX 2 MERCHANT SHIPPING ACT 1995 PART 9A

(8) A person guilty of an offence under this section is liable *on summary conviction, or on conviction on indictment, to a fine.*[10]

255C Locating and marking wrecks[11]

(1) This section applies where an accident results in a wreck in the United Kingdom's Convention area.

(2) The Secretary of State must ensure that the United Kingdom complies with its obligations under Articles 7 and 8 of the Wrecks Convention (locating and marking of wrecks).

(3) The Secretary of State may, for those purposes, direct any of the following to take specified steps in relation to the wreck if it is within their area — [12]
   (a) a general lighthouse authority;[13]
   (b) a harbour authority;[14]
   (c) a conservancy authority.[15]

(4) A direction may require an authority to exercise or not to exercise a power under section 252 or 253 within their area (*and for this purpose a general lighthouse authority has the powers conferred by section 253 throughout their area*).[16]

(5) ~~For the purposes of subsections (3) and (4) (and, in a case where a direction is given, section 253), a general lighthouse authority's area includes any area that —~~
   (a) ~~is adjacent to the area specified in relation to the authority under section 193(1), and~~
   (b) ~~is within the United Kingdom's Convention area.~~[17]

(6) A direction —
   (a) must be in writing, or
   (b) where it is not reasonably practicable to give it in writing, must be confirmed in writing as soon as reasonably practicable.

(7) An authority to whom a direction is given must comply with it.

255D Removal by registered owner[18]

(1) This section applies where —
   (a) a ship has been involved in an accident as a result of which it or anything from it has become a wreck in the United Kingdom's Convention area, and
   (b) the Secretary of State has determined that the wreck poses a hazard.[19]

(2) The Secretary of State must take all reasonable steps to give a notice (a "wreck removal notice") requiring the registered owner[20] to comply with the obligations imposed on registered owners by paragraph 2 and 3 of Article 9 of the Wrecks Convention (removal of wrecks and production of evidence of insurance).

---

10 Words in italics substituted by the Legal Aid, Sentencing and Punishment of Offenders Act 2012 (Fines on Summary Conviction) Regulations 2015 (SI 2015/664), Sch 4 para 27(11); the maximum fine on summary conviction was previously £50,000.
11 See 9.2.3, 9.2.4, 10.5.6, 10.5.7, 11.3.3(b).
12 See the MSA 1995 193(4); and 11.3.3(c).
13 See the MSA 1995 s 193.
14 See the MSA 1995 s 313(1).
15 See the MSA 1995 s 313(1).
16 Words in italics substituted by the Marine Navigation Act 2013 s 8(2)(a).
17 Subs (5) deleted by the Marine Navigation Act 2013 s 8(2)(b). See 11.1.3, 11.3.3(c).
18 See s 255R(5); WRC 2007Art 9(2); and 9.2.5, 10.5, 11.3.3(c).
19 See s 255R(1); WRC 2007 Art 1(5) and 6; also 8.2, 10.2, 10.5.
20 See s 255R(1); WRC 2007 Art 1(8).

(3) The notice must be in writing and must —
   (a) specify the deadline set under paragraph 6(a) of that Article for the removal of the wreck, and
   (b) inform the registered owner of the other matters set out in paragraph 6(b) and (c) of that Article.
(4) A registered owner who fails, without reasonable excuse, to comply with a notice by the specified deadline is guilty of an offence.
(5) A registered owner guilty of the offence is liable *on summary conviction, or on conviction on indictment, to a fine.*[21]

255E Imposition of conditions about removal[22]

(1) This section applies if the Secretary of State has given a registered owner a wreck removal notice.
(2) The Secretary of State may impose conditions as to the removal of the wreck in accordance with paragraph 4 of Article 9 of the Wrecks Convention.
(3) A condition is imposed by giving notice of it to the registered owner.
(4) A registered owner who fails, without reasonable excuse, to comply with a condition is guilty of an offence.
(5) A registered owner guilty of the offence is liable *on summary conviction, or on conviction on indictment, to a fine.*[23]

255F Removal in default[24]

(1) The Secretary of State may remove a wreck in the United Kingdom's Convention area in the circumstances set out in paragraph 7 or 8 of Article 9 of the Wrecks Convention.
(2) The Secretary of State may, instead of exercising the power under subsection (1), direct that the power be exercised by any of the following —
   (a) a general lighthouse authority;
   (b) a harbour authority;
   (c) a conservancy authority.
(3) A direction may be given to an authority only in relation to a wreck within the authority's area.
(4) ~~Section 255C(5) applies for the purposes of determining a general lighthouse authority's area.~~[25]
(5) A direction —
   (a) must be in writing, or
   (b) where it is not reasonably practicable to give it in writing, must be confirmed in writing as soon as reasonably practicable.
(6) An authority to whom a direction is given must comply with it.

---

21 Words in italics substituted by SI 2015/664, Sch 4 para 27(12); the maximum fine on summary conviction was previously £50,000.

22 See 11.3.3(c).

23 Words in italics substituted by SI 2015/664, Sch 4 para 27(13); the maximum fine on summary conviction was previously £50,000.

24 See 11.3.3(d).

25 Subs (4) deleted by Marine Navigation Act 2013 s 8(3).

APPENDIX 2 MERCHANT SHIPPING ACT 1995 PART 9A

255G Liability for costs[26]

(1) This section applies where —
    (a) a ship has been involved in an accident as a result of which it or anything from it has become a wreck in the United Kingdom's Convention area, and
    (b) costs have been incurred complying with section 255C or 255F (locating and marking and removal of wrecks).

(2) The person who incurred the costs is entitled to recover them from the ship's registered owner unless the owner proves that an exception set out in paragraph 1(a), (b) or (c) of Article 10 of the Wrecks Convention applies.

(3) The owner is not liable for costs under this section if or to the extent that liability would conflict with —
    (a) a convention listed in paragraph 1 of Article 11 of the Wrecks Convention (exceptions to liability),
    (b) an enactment implementing such a convention, or
    (c) any other provision specified by order made by the Secretary of State.[27]

(4) Where the registered owner of each of two or more ships is liable for costs under this section but the costs for which each is liable cannot reasonably be separated, the registered owners shall be jointly liable for the total costs.

(5) This section does not prevent the exercise of the right (if any) to limit liability by virtue of section 185.

(6) An order under subsection (3)(c) may be made only if a draft has been laid before and approved by resolution of each House of Parliament.

(7) An order may include incidental, supplemental or transitional provision.

255H Limitation period[28]

An action to recover costs under section 255G may not be brought after the end of whichever of the following ends earlier —
    (a) the period of 3 years beginning with the date on which a wreck in s removal notice was given in respect of the wreck, and
    (b) the period of 6 years beginning with the date of the accident which resulted in the wreck.

255I Expenses of general lighthouse authorities[29]

Costs incurred by a general lighthouse authority in complying with a direction under section 255C or 255F shall be paid out of the General Lighthouse Fund[30] if or to the extent that they are not recovered under section 255G; but section 213 shall apply as if they were expenses of the authority falling within subsection (1) of that section other than establishment expenses.

---

26 See 11.3.4(a).
27 The WRCA 2011 s 1(3) amends the MSA 1995 s 306(2A)(c) (orders not subject to annulment) by inserting after "223(3)" a reference to s 255G(3)(c).
28 See the WRC 2007 Art 13; and 10.4, 11.3.4(a).
29 See 11.3.4(a), 11.3.5.
30 See the MSA 1995 s 211.

APPENDIX 2 MERCHANT SHIPPING ACT 1995 PART 9A

Insurance[31]

255J Wreck removal insurance

(1) This section applies to ships with a gross tonnage of 300 or more.

(2) A United Kingdom ship may not enter or leave a port in the United Kingdom or elsewhere unless —
   (a) the ship has wreck removal insurance, and
   (b) the Secretary of State has certified that it has wreck removal insurance.

(3) A foreign ship may not enter or leave a port in the United Kingdom unless —
   (a) the ship has wreck removal insurance, and
   (b) there is a certificate confirming that it has wreck removal insurance.

(4) For a ship registered in a foreign Wrecks Convention State the certificate must be one that has been issued by or under the authority of the government of that State.

(5) For a foreign ship registered in any other State the certificate must be one that has been issued —
   (a) by the Secretary of State, or
   (b) by or under the authority of the government of a Wrecks Convention State.

(6) For the purposes of subsection (1) the gross tonnage of a ship is to be calculated in the manner prescribed by order under paragraph 5(2) of Part II of Schedule 7.

(7) In this Part —

"wreck removal insurance" means a contract of insurance or other security satisfying the requirements of Article 12 of the Wrecks Convention, and "insurer" means the person providing the insurance or other security, and

"wreck removal insurance certificate" means a certificate required by subsection (2)(b) or (3)(b).

255K Failure to insure

(1) The master and operator of a ship are each guilty of an offence if —
   (a) the ship enters or leaves a port in contravention of section 255J, or
   (b) anyone attempts to navigate the ship into or out of a port in contravention of that section.

(2) A person guilty of the offence is liable *on summary conviction, or on conviction on indictment, to a fine.*[32]

255L Detention of ships[33]

A ship may be detained if anyone attempts to navigate it out of a port in contravention of section 255J.

255M Production of certificates

(1) This section applies to a ship which is required to have a wreck removal insurance certificate before entering or leaving a port.

---

31 For ss 255J-255Q generally, see the WRC 2007 Art 12 and 10.8, 11.3.4(e), 11.3.5(b).

32 Words in italics substituted by SI 2015/664, Sch 4 para 27(14); the maximum fine on summary conviction was previously £50,000.

33 See the MSA 1995 s 284.

(2) The master of the ship must ensure that the certificate is carried on board.
(3) The master of the ship must, on request, produce the certificate to —
    (a) an officer of Revenue and Customs;
    (b) an officer of the Secretary of State;
    (c) if the ship is a United Kingdom ship, a proper officer.[34]
(4) Failure to comply with subsection (2) or (3) is an offence.
(5) A person guilty of the offence is liable on summary conviction to a fine not exceeding level 5 on the standard scale.

255N Issue of certificates

(1) This section applies where the registered owner applies to the Secretary of State for a wreck removal insurance certificate in respect of —
    (a) a United Kingdom ship, or
    (b) a foreign ship registered in a State other than a Wrecks Convention State.
(2) In relation to a United Kingdom ship, the Secretary of State must issue the certificate if satisfied —
    (a) that the ship has wreck removal insurance in place for the period to which the certificate will relate, and
    (b) that the obligations of the person providing the wreck removal insurance will be met.
(3) In relation to a foreign ship registered in a State other than a Wrecks Convention State, the Secretary of State may issue the certificate if satisfied of the matters in paragraphs (a) and (b) of subsection (2).
(4) The Secretary of State must send a copy of a certificate issued in respect of a United Kingdom ship to the Registrar General of Shipping and Seamen.
(5) The Registrar must make such certificates available for public inspection.

255O Cancellation of certificates

(1) The Secretary of State may make regulations about the cancellation and delivery up of wreck removal insurance certificates issued under section 255N.
(2) A person who fails to deliver up a certificate in accordance with the regulations is guilty of an offence.
(3) A person guilty of the offence is liable on summary conviction to a fine not exceeding level 4 on the standard scale.

255P Third parties' rights against insurers[35]

(1) This section applies where —
    (a) a ship has been involved in an accident as a result of which it or anything from it has become a wreck in the United Kingdom's Convention area,
    (b) at the time of the accident the ship had wreck removal insurance, and
    (c) there is a wreck removal insurance certificate in relation to the insurance.
(2) A person who is entitled to recover costs from the ship's registered owner under section 255G may recover them from the insurer.
(3) It is a defence for the insurer to prove that the accident was caused by the wilful misconduct of the ship's registered owner.

---

34 See the MSA 1995 s 313(1).
35 See the WRC 2007 Art 12(10); and 10.8.5, 11.3.4(b).

(4) The insurer may also rely on any defences available to the registered owner (including section 255H).
(5) The insurer may limit liability in respect of claims made under this section to the same extent as the registered owner may limit liability by virtue of section 185 (or would be able to limit liability by virtue of that section if it were not for paragraph 3 of Part 2 of Schedule 7).
(6) But an insurer may limit liability whether or not the accident is caused by an act or omission mentioned in Article 4 of the Convention set out in Part 1 of Schedule 7.
(7) The following do not apply in relation to any wreck removal insurance to which a wreck removal insurance certificate relates —
    (a) the Third Parties (Rights against Insurers) Act 1930;
    (b) the Third Parties (Rights against Insurers) (Northern Ireland) Act 1930;
    (c) the Third Parties (Rights against Insurers) Act 2010.

255Q Electronic certificates

(1) This section applies if the Secretary of State has given, or proposes to give, notice under paragraph 13 of Article 12 of the Wrecks Convention (electronic insurance certificates, &c.).The Secretary of State may by order make such amendments of this Part as the Secretary of State thinks necessary or expedient for giving effect to the notice.
(2) An order may be made only if a draft has been laid before and approved by resolution of each House of Parliament.[36]
(3) An order may include incidental, supplemental or transitional provision.

Supplemental

255R Interpretation etc.

(1) Expressions used in this Part shall be construed in accordance with Article 1 of the Wrecks Convention.
(2) In this Part —
    "accident" means a collision of ships, a stranding, another incident of navigation or another event (whether on board a ship or not) which results in material damage to a ship or its cargo or in an imminent threat of material damage to a ship or its cargo,
    "insurer" shall be construed in accordance with section 255J(7), "wreck removal insurance" has the meaning given by section
    255J(7),
    "wreck removal insurance certificate" has the meaning given by section 255J(7),
    "wreck removal notice" means a notice under section 255D,
    "the Wrecks Convention" has the meaning given by section 255A(1), and
    "Wrecks Convention State" has the meaning given by section 255A(1).
(3) References in this Part to entering or leaving a port in a State include references to arriving at or leaving an offshore facility in the territorial sea of that State (except in section 255L).
(4) References in this Part to ships registered in a State include unregistered ships entitled to fly the flag of that State.
(5) In determining for the purposes of this Part whether a wreck poses a hazard the Secretary of State must take into account the matters set out in Article 6 of the Wrecks Convention (determination of hazard).

---

36 The WRCA 2011 s 1(3) amended the MSA 1995 s 306(2A)(c) (orders not subject to annulment) by inserting after "223(3)" a reference to s 255Q(2).

(6) The Secretary of State shall from time to time by order describe the United Kingdom's Convention area.

(7) If Her Majesty by Order in Council declares that any State specified in the Order is a party to the Wrecks Convention, the Order shall, while in force, be conclusive evidence of that fact.

255S Government ships[37]

(1) This Part does not apply in relation to warships or ships for the time being used by a State for non-commercial purposes only.

(2) But it does apply to such ships if specified in a notice under paragraph 3 of Article 4 of the Wrecks Convention.

(3) Section 255K does not apply to a ship (an "exempt ship") that is owned by a Wrecks Convention State.

(4) An exempt ship must have a certificate issued by the government of the State concerned and stating —
   (a) that the ship is owned by that State, and
   (b) that any liability under section 255G will be met up to the limits prescribed by paragraph 1 of Article 12 of the Wrecks Convention (compulsory insurance).

(5) Section 255M(2) to (5) applies to such a certificate.

(6) Where a ship is owned by a State and operated by a company which is registered in that State as operator of the ship, references in this Part to the registered owner are references to that company.

(7) In proceedings against a Wrecks Convention State for the recovery of costs under section 255G the State shall be treated as having submitted to the jurisdiction of the court in which the proceedings are brought; but this does not authorise execution, or in Scotland the execution of diligence, against the property of a State.

255T Saving

Nothing in this Part affects any claim, or the enforcement of any claim, a person incurring any liability under this Part may have against any other person in respect of that liability.

255U Power to amend

(1) The Secretary of State may by order amend this Part to reflect any amendment of the Wrecks Convention.[38]

(2) An order under this section may be made only if a draft has been laid before and approved by resolution of each House of Parliament."

---

[37] See 11.3.3(g).

[38] The WRCA 2011 s 1(3) amends the MSA 1995 s 306(2A)(c) (orders not subject to annulment) by inserting after "223(3)" a reference to s 255U(1).

APPENDIX 3: MSA 1995 SCHEDULE 3A SAFETY DIRECTIONS[1]
SCHEDULE 3A[1]

SAFETY DIRECTIONS

Direction following accident: person in control of ship

1 (1) The Secretary of State may give a direction under this paragraph in respect of a ship if in his opinion —
    (a) an accident has occurred to or in the ship,
    (b) the accident has created a risk to safety or a risk of pollution by a hazardous substance, and
    (c) the direction is necessary to remove or reduce the risk.
   (2) The direction may be given to —
    (a) the owner of the ship,
    (b) a person in possession of the ship,
    (c) the master of the ship,
    (d) a pilot of the ship,
         (da) the owner of a hazardous substance in the ship,[2]
    (e) a salvor in possession of the ship,
    (f) a person who is the servant or agent of a salvor in possession of the ship and who is in charge of the salvage operation, or
    (g) where the ship is in, or has been directed to move into, waters which are regulated or managed by a harbour authority, the harbour authority or the harbour master.
   (3) The direction may require the person to whom it is given to take or refrain from taking any specified action in relation to —
    (a) the ship;
    (b) anything which is or was in the ship;
    (c) anything which forms or formed part of the ship;
    (d) anything which is or was being towed by the ship;
    (e) a person on the ship.
   (4) In particular, the direction may require a person to ensure —
    (a) that a ship or other thing is moved or not moved;
    (b) that a ship or other thing is moved or not moved to or from a specified place or area or over a specified route;
    (c) that cargo is or is not unloaded or discharged;
    (d) that a substance is or is not unloaded or discharged;
    (e) that specified salvage measures are taken or not taken;
    (f) that a person is put ashore or on board a ship.

---

1 Inserted by s 2 of the Marine Safety Act 2003. Section 1 of that Act inserted a new s 108A of the MSA 1995 which makes clear that other provisions of the MSA 1995 shall have no effect in so far as they are (i) inconsistent with the exercise of powers under Sch 3A, or (ii) would interfere with a person's compliance with a direction under Sch 3A, or (iii) would interfere with action taken by virtue of Sch 3A.

2 Provision inserted by the Merchant Shipping (Vessel Traffic Monitoring and Reporting Requirements) Regulations 2004 (SI 2004/2110) r 22(1).

Direction following accident: person in control of land

2 (1) The Secretary of State may give a direction under this paragraph in respect of a ship if in his opinion —
  (a) an accident has occurred to or in the ship,
  (b) the accident has created a risk to safety or a risk of pollution by a hazardous substance, and
  (c) the direction is necessary to remove or reduce the risk.
 (2) The direction may be given to a person in charge of coastal land or premises.
 (3) For the purposes of this paragraph —
  (a) a person is in charge of land or premises if he is wholly or partly able to control the use made of the land or premises, and
  (b) "coastal" means adjacent to or accessible from United Kingdom waters over which the public are permitted to navigate.
 (4) The direction may require the person to whom it is given to grant access or facilities to or in relation to the ship or any person or thing which is or was on the ship.
 (5) In particular, a direction may require a person —
  (a) to permit persons to land;
  (b) to make facilities available for the undertaking of repairs or other works;
  (c) to make facilities available for the landing, storage and disposal of cargo or of other things.
 (6) A direction under this paragraph —
  (a) must be given in writing, or
  (b) where it is not reasonably practicable to give it in writing, must be confirmed in writing as soon as is reasonably practicable.

Other direction

3 (1) The Secretary of State may give a direction in respect of a ship under this paragraph if in his opinion it is necessary for the purpose of —
  (a) securing the safety of the ship or of other ships;
  (b) securing the safety of persons or property;
  (c) preventing or reducing pollution.
 (2) The direction may be given to —
  (a) the owner of the ship;
  (b) a person in possession of the ship;
  (c) the master of the ship.
 (3) The direction may require the person to whom it is given to ensure that —
  (a) the ship is moved or not moved from a specified place or area in United Kingdom waters;
  (b) the ship is moved or not moved to a specified place or area in United Kingdom waters;
  (c) the ship is moved or not moved over a specified route in United Kingdom waters;
  (d) the ship is removed from United Kingdom waters.

Action in lieu of direction

4 (1) This paragraph applies where the Secretary of State thinks —
  (a) that circumstances exist which would entitle him to give a direction under this Schedule, but
  (b) that the giving of a direction would not be likely to achieve a sufficient result.
 (2) This paragraph also applies where —
  (a) the Secretary of State has given a direction under this Schedule, but
  (b) in his opinion the direction has not achieved a sufficient result.
 (3) The Secretary of State may take such action as appears to him necessary or expedient for the purpose for which the direction could have been given or was given.

(4) In particular, the Secretary of State may —
  (a) authorise a person to enter land or make use of facilities;
  (b) do or authorise a person to do anything which the Secretary of State could require a person to do by a direction;
  (c) authorise a person to assume control of a ship;
  (d) make arrangements or authorise the making of arrangements for the sinking or destruction of a ship.

Enforcement

5 A person to whom a direction is given under this Schedule —
  (a) must comply with the direction, and
  (b) must try to comply with the direction in a manner which avoids risk to human life.

Enforcement

6 (1) A person commits an offence if he contravenes paragraph 5(a).
  (2) It is a defence for a person charged with an offence under sub-paragraph (1) to prove —
    (a) that he tried as hard as he could to comply with the relevant direction, or
    (b) that he reasonably believed that compliance with the direction would involve a serious risk to human life.

Enforcement

7 A person commits an offence if he intentionally obstructs a person who is —
  (a) acting on behalf of the Secretary of State in connection with the giving of a direction under this Schedule,
  (b) complying with a direction under this Schedule, or
  (c) acting by virtue of paragraph 4.

Enforcement

8 A person guilty of an offence under paragraph 6 or 7 shall be liable *on summary conviction, or on conviction on indictment, to a fine.*[3]

Enforcement

9 (1) Proceedings for an offence under paragraph 6 or 7 may be brought in England and Wales only —
  (a) by or with the consent of the Attorney General, or
  (b) by or with the authority of the Secretary of State.
  (2) Proceedings for an offence under paragraph 6 or 7 may be brought in Northern Ireland only —
  (a) by or with the consent of the Attorney General for Northern Ireland, or
  (b) by or with the authority of the Secretary of State.

Variation and revocation

10 (1) A direction under this Schedule may be varied or revoked by a further direction.
  (2) If the Secretary of State thinks that a direction under this Schedule is wholly or partly no longer necessary for the purpose for which it was given, he shall vary or revoke the direction as soon as is reasonably practicable.
  (3) Where the Secretary of State has given a direction to a person under this Schedule he shall consider any representations about varying or revoking the direction which are made to him by that person.

---

3 Words in italics substituted by SI 2015/664, Sch 4 para 27(16); the maximum fine on summary conviction was previously £50,000.

Procedure

11 (1)　　Where the Secretary of State —
   (a)　proposes to give a direction under this Schedule to a company or other body, and
   (b)　thinks that section 1139 of the Companies Act 2006 (service of documents on company) does not apply, the direction may be served in such manner as the Secretary of State thinks most suitable.[4]

Procedure

12　　A person acting on behalf of the Secretary of State may —
   (a)　board a ship for the purpose of serving a direction under this Schedule;
   (b)　enter land or premises for that purpose.

Procedure

13　　Before giving a direction under paragraph 2 in respect of land or premises the Secretary of State shall, unless he thinks that it is not reasonably practicable —
   (a)　give the person to whom he proposes to give the direction an opportunity to make representations, and
   (b)　consider any representations made.

Unreasonable loss and damage

14 (1)　This paragraph applies where action taken in accordance with a direction under this Schedule or by virtue of paragraph 4 ("remedial action") —
   (a)　was not reasonably necessary for the purpose for which the direction was given, or
   (b)　caused loss or damage which could not be justified by reference to that purpose.
(2)　The Secretary of State shall pay compensation to any person who —
   (a)　suffered loss or damage as a result of the remedial action (whether it was taken by him or someone else), and
   (b)　applies to the Secretary of State for compensation.
(3)　In considering what is reasonably necessary or justifiable for the purpose of sub- paragraph (1) account shall be taken of —
   (a)　the extent of the risk to safety or threat of pollution which the direction was intended to address,
   (b)　the likelihood of the remedial action being effective, and
   (c)　the extent of the loss or damage caused by the remedial action.

Expenses

15 (1)　This paragraph applies where —
   (a)　a direction is given to a person in respect of a ship under paragraph 2, or
   (b)　the Secretary of State relies on paragraph 4 to take or authorise action in respect of a ship in lieu of a direction under paragraph 2.
(2)　The person to whom a direction is given shall be entitled to recover the costs of his compliance with the direction from the owner of the ship.
(3)　A person in charge of coastal land or premises shall be entitled to recover from the owner of the ship costs incurred by him as a result of action taken by virtue of paragraph 4 in relation to that land or premises.
(4)　The Secretary of State may make payments to a person on account of sums recoverable by that person under sub-paragraph (2) or (3).

4　Para 11 substituted by Companies Act 2006 (Consequential Amendments, Transitional Provisions and Savings) Order 2009 (SI 2009/1941) para 152(5).

(5) The Secretary of State shall be entitled to recover from the owner of the ship —
  (a) costs incurred in connection with the giving of a direction;
  (b) costs incurred in connection with action taken under paragraph 4;
  (c) costs incurred under sub-paragraph (4).
(6) A right under sub-paragraph (2), (3) or (5) permits the recovery of costs only in so far as they are not recoverable —
  (a) under another enactment,
  (b) by virtue of an agreement, or
  (c) under the law relating to salvage.

Jurisdiction

16 The Admiralty jurisdiction of the High Court and of the Court of Session shall include jurisdiction to hear and determine any claim arising under paragraph 14 or 15.

Ships to which Schedule applies

17 A direction under paragraph 1 or 2, in so far as it relates to a risk of pollution, may have effect in respect of a ship only if it —
  (a) is a United Kingdom ship, or
  (b) is in United Kingdom waters or an area of the sea specified under section 129(2) (b).

Ships to which Schedule applies

18 (1) Her Majesty may by Order in Council provide that a direction under paragraph 1 or 2, in so far as it relates to a risk of pollution, may have effect in respect of a ship which —
  (a) is not a United Kingdom ship, and
  (b) is not in United Kingdom waters or an area of the sea specified under section 129(2)(b).
(2) An Order in Council under this paragraph —
  (a) may be expressed to apply generally or only in specified circumstances;
  (b) may make different provision for different circumstances;
  (c) may provide for this Schedule to have effect in cases to which the Order in Council applies with specified modifications;
  (d) may contain transitional or consequential provision (including provision amending an enactment).

Ships to which Schedule applies

19 A direction under paragraph 1 or 2, in so far as it relates to a risk to safety, may have effect in respect of a ship only if it is in United Kingdom waters and —
  (a) it is not a qualifying foreign ship, or
  (b) it is a qualifying foreign ship which in the Secretary of State's opinion is exercising neither the right of innocent passage nor the right of transit passage through straits used for international navigation.

Ships to which Schedule applies

20 (1) A direction under paragraph 3 may have effect in respect of a ship only if it is in United Kingdom waters and —
  (a) it is not a qualifying foreign ship, or
  (b) it is a qualifying foreign ship which in the Secretary of State's opinion is exercising neither the right of innocent passage nor the right of transit passage through straits used for international navigation.
(2) A direction may not be given under paragraph 3(3)(d) in respect of a United Kingdom ship.

Ships to which Schedule applies

21   A direction may not be given under paragraph 1(2)(a) to (d) or 3 in respect of —
      (a)   a ship of Her Majesty's Navy, or
      (b)   a Government ship.

Interpretation

22 (1)   In this Schedule —
      "accident" means a collision of ships, a stranding, another incident of navigation or another event (whether on board a ship or not) which results in material damage to a ship or its cargo or in an imminent threat of material damage to a ship or its cargo,
      "action" includes omission,
      "enactment" includes an enactment comprised in, or in an instrument made under, an Act of the Scottish Parliament,
      "harbour authority" has the meaning given by section 151(1),
      "harbour master" includes a dock master or pier master, and any person specially appointed by a harbour authority for the purpose of enforcing the provisions of this Schedule in relation to the harbour,
      "hazardous substance" has the meaning given by sub-paragraph (2), "owner", in relation to the ship to or in which an accident has occurred,
      includes its owner at the time of the accident,
      "pilot" means a person who does not belong to a ship but who has the conduct of it,
      "pollution" means significant pollution in the United Kingdom, United Kingdom waters or an area of the sea specified under section 129(2)(b), and
      "risk to safety" means a risk to the safety of persons, property or anything navigating in or using United Kingdom waters.
  (2)   In this Schedule "hazardous substance" means —
      (a)   oil (within the meaning given by section 151(1)),
      (b)   any other substance which creates a hazard to human health, harms living resources or marine life, damages amenities or interferes with lawful use of the sea, and
      (c)   any substance prescribed by order of the Secretary of State.

Savings

23   Nothing in this Schedule shall be taken to prejudice any right or power of Her Majesty's Government.

Savings

24 (1)   This paragraph applies where action is taken —
      (a)   in respect of a ship which is under arrest or in respect of anything in a ship which is under arrest, and
      (b)   in accordance with a direction under this Schedule or by virtue of paragraph 4.
  (2)   The action shall not —
      (a)   be treated as a contempt of court, or
      (b)   give rise to civil liability on the part of the Admiralty Marshal (including the Admiralty Marshal of the *Court of Judicature*[5] in Northern Ireland)."

---

5 Words in italics substituted by Constitutional Reform Act 2005, Sch 11, Part 3 para 6.

APPENDIX 4: MSA 1995 SCHED 11ZA [TEXT OF THE WRC 2007][1]
SCHEDULE 11ZA WRECKS CONVENTION 1

Preamble:[2]
THE STATES PARTIES TO THE PRESENT CONVENTION,
CONSCIOUS of the fact that wrecks, if not removed, may pose a hazard to navigation or the marine environment,
CONVINCED of the need to adopt uniform international rules and procedures to ensure the prompt and effective removal of wrecks and payment of compensation for the costs therein involved,
NOTING that many wrecks may be located in States' territory, including the territorial sea,
RECOGNIZING the benefits to be gained through uniformity in legal regimes governing responsibility and liability for removal of hazardous wrecks,
BEARING IN MIND the importance of the United Nations Convention on the Law of the Sea, done at Montego Bay on 10 December 1982, and of the customary international law of the sea, and the consequent need to implement the present Convention in accordance with such provisions,
HAVE AGREED as follows:

Article 1
Definitions[3]

For the purposes of this Convention:

1. "Convention area" means the exclusive economic zone of a State Party, established in accordance with international law or, if a State Party has not established such a zone, an area beyond and adjacent to the territorial sea of that State determined by that State in accordance with international law and extending not more than 200 nautical miles from the baselines from which the breadth of its territorial sea is measured.[4]
2. "Ship" means a seagoing vessel of any type whatsoever and includes hydrofoil boats, air-cushion vehicles, submersibles, floating craft and floating platforms, except when such platforms are on location engaged in the exploration, exploitation or production of seabed mineral resources.[5]
3. "Maritime casualty" means a collision of ships, stranding or other incident of navigation, or other occurrence on board a ship or external to it, resulting in material damage or imminent threat of material damage to a ship or its cargo.[6]
4. "Wreck", following upon a maritime casualty, means:[7]
    (a) a sunken or stranded ship; or

---

1 The footnotes contain some limited cross references to where particular articles are dealt with in the text of the book. These are not meant to be definitive and readers should refer to the Index and Table of Contents.
2 See 7.6.1.
3 See Chapter 8, in particular.
4 See 8.3, 11.3.2.
5 See 8.2.1, 10.2.7.
6 See 8.2.1(a), 10.5.1(a).
7 See 8.2.1(a)–(f), 10.2.7, 10.6.

(b) any part of a sunken or stranded ship, including any object that is or has been on board such a ship; or

(c) any object that is lost at sea from a ship and that is stranded, sunken or adrift at sea; or

(d) a ship that is about, or may reasonably be expected, to sink or to strand, where effective measures to assist the ship or any property in danger are not already being taken.

5. "Hazard" means any condition or threat that:
   (a) poses a danger or impediment to navigation; or
   (b) may reasonably be expected to result in major harmful consequences to the marine environment, or damage to the coastline or related interests of one or more States.[8]

6. "Related interests" means the interests of a coastal State directly affected or threatened by a wreck, such as:
   (a) maritime coastal, port and estuarine activities, including fisheries activities, constituting an essential means of livelihood of the persons concerned;
   (b) tourist attractions and other economic interests of the area concerned;
   (c) the health of the coastal population and the wellbeing of the area concerned, including conservation of marine living resources and of wildlife; and
   (d) offshore and underwater infrastructure.[9]

7. "Removal" means any form of prevention, mitigation or elimination of the hazard created by a wreck. "Remove", "removed" and "removing" shall be construed accordingly.[10]

8. "Registered owner" means the person or persons registered as the owner of the ship or, in the absence of registration, the person or persons owning the ship at the time of the maritime casualty. However, in the case of a ship owned by a State and operated by a company which in that State is registered as the operator of the ship, "registered owner" shall mean such company.[11]

9. "Operator of the ship" means the owner of the ship or any other organization or person such as the manager, or the bareboat charterer, who has assumed the responsibility for operation of the ship from the owner of the ship and who, on assuming such responsibility, has agreed to take over all duties and responsibilities established under the International Safety Management Code, as amended.[12]

10. "Affected State" means the State in whose Convention area the wreck is located.[13]

11. "State of the ship's registry" means, in relation to a registered ship, the State of registration of the ship and, in relation to an unregistered ship, the State whose flag the ship is entitled to fly.[14]

12. "Organization" means the International Maritime Organization.

13. "Secretary-General" means the Secretary-General of the Organization.

Article 2
Objectives and general principles

1. A State Party may take measures in accordance with this Convention in relation to the removal of a wreck which poses a hazard in the Convention area.

---

8 See 8.2.2, 10.2.5.
9 See 8.2.3, 10.5.1.
10 See 9.2.5(b), 10.2.5, 10.2.8.
11 See 9.1.1, 10.2.2.
12 See 9.1.1, 10.8.2, 11.3.3(a).
13 See 8.2.4.
14 See 11.3.3.

2. Measures taken by the Affected State in accordance with paragraph 1 shall be proportionate to the hazard.[15]
3. Such measures shall not go beyond what is reasonably necessary to remove a wreck which poses a hazard and shall cease as soon as the wreck has been removed; they shall not unnecessarily interfere with the rights and interests of other States including the State of the ship's registry, and of any person, physical or corporate, concerned.
4. The application of this Convention within the Convention area shall not entitle a State Party to claim or exercise sovereignty or sovereign rights over any part of the high seas.
5. States Parties shall endeavour to co-operate when the effects of a maritime casualty resulting in a wreck involve a State other than the Affected State.

Article 3
Scope of application

1. Except as otherwise provided in this Convention, this Convention shall apply to wrecks in the Convention area.
2. A State Party may extend the application of this Convention to wrecks located within its territory, including the territorial sea, subject to article 4, paragraph 4. In that case, it shall notify the Secretary-General accordingly, at the time of expressing its consent to be bound by this Convention or at any time thereafter. When a State Party has made a notification to apply this Convention to wrecks located within its territory, including the territorial sea, this is without prejudice to the rights and obligations of that State to take measures in relation to wrecks located in its territory, including the territorial sea, other than locating, marking and removing them in accordance with this Convention. The provisions of articles 10, 11 and 12 of this Convention shall not apply to any measures so taken other than those referred to in articles 7, 8 and 9 of this Convention.[16]
3. When a State Party has made a notification under paragraph 2, the "Convention area" of the Affected State shall include the territory, including the territorial sea, of that State Party.
4. A notification made under paragraph 2 above shall take effect for that State Party, if made before entry into force of this Convention for that State Party, upon entry into force. If notification is made after entry into force of this Convention for that State Party, it shall take effect six months after its receipt by the Secretary-General.
5. A State Party that has made a notification under paragraph 2 may withdraw it at any time by means of a notification of withdrawal to the Secretary-General. Such notification of withdrawal shall take effect six months after its receipt by the Secretary-General, unless the notification specifies a later date.

Article 4
Exclusions

1. This Convention shall not apply to measures taken under the International Convention relating to Intervention on the High Seas in Cases of Oil Pollution Casualties, 1969, as amended, or the Protocol relating to Intervention on the High Seas in Cases of Pollution by Substances other than Oil, 1973, as amended.[17]

---

15 See 9.2.5(e), 10.2.4.
16 See 8.4, 7.4.1, 11.2.2, 11.3.2.
17 See 10.9.2(a)

2. This Convention shall not apply to any warship or other ship owned or operated by a State and used, for the time being, only on Government non- commercial service, unless that State decides otherwise.[18]
3. Where a State Party decides to apply this Convention to its warships or other ships as described in paragraph 2, it shall notify the Secretary-General, thereof, specifying the terms and conditions of such application.
4. (a) When a State Party has made a notification under article 3, paragraph 2, the following provisions of this Convention shall not apply in its territory, including the territorial sea:
    (i) Article 2, paragraph 4;
    (ii) Article 9, paragraphs 1, 5, 7, 8, 9 and 10; and
    (iii) Article 15.
  (b) Article 9, paragraph 4, insofar as it applies to the territory, including the territorial sea of a State Party, shall read:
  Subject to the national law of the Affected State, the registered owner may contract with any salvor or other person to remove the wreck determined to constitute a hazard on behalf of the owner. Before such removal commences, the Affected State may lay down conditions for such removal only to the extent necessary to ensure that the removal proceeds in a manner that is consistent with considerations of safety and protection of the marine environment.[19]

Article 5
Reporting wrecks[20]

1. A State Party shall require the master and the operator of a ship flying its flag to report to the Affected State without delay when that ship has been involved in a maritime casualty resulting in a wreck. To the extent that the reporting obligation under this article has been fulfilled either by the master or the operator of the ship, the other shall not be obliged to report.
2. Such reports shall provide the name and the principal place of business of the registered owner and all the relevant information necessary for the Affected State to determine whether the wreck poses a hazard in accordance with article 6, including:
   (a) the precise location of the wreck;
   (b) the type, size and construction of the wreck;
   (c) the nature of the damage to, and the condition of, the wreck;
   (d) the nature and quantity of the cargo, in particular any hazardous and noxious substances; and
   (e) the amount and types of oil, including bunker oil and lubricating oil, on board.

Article 6
Determination of hazard[21]

When determining whether a wreck poses a hazard, the following criteria should be taken into account by the Affected State:
  (a) the type, size and construction of the wreck;
  (b) depth of the water in the area;

---

18 See 11.3.3(g).
19 See 8.4, 11.2.3, 11.3.3, 11.3.4.
20 See 9.1.3, 11.3.3(a).
21 See 9.2.2, 10.5.1(b).

(c) tidal range and currents in the area;
(d) particularly sensitive sea areas identified and, as appropriate, designated in accordance with guidelines adopted by the Organization, or a clearly defined area of the exclusive economic zone where special mandatory measures have been adopted pursuant to article 211, paragraph 6, of the United Nations Convention on the Law of the Sea, 1982;
(e) proximity of shipping routes or established traffic lanes;
(f) traffic density and frequency;
(g) type of traffic;
(h) nature and quantity of the wreck's cargo, the amount and types of oil (such as bunker oil and lubricating oil) on board the wreck and, in particular, the damage likely to result should the cargo or oil be released into the marine environment;
(i) vulnerability of port facilities;
(j) prevailing meteorological and hydrographical conditions;
(k) submarine topography of the area;
(l) height of the wreck above or below the surface of the water at lowest astronomical tide;
(m) acoustic and magnetic profiles of the wreck;
(n) proximity of offshore installations, pipelines, telecommunications cables and similar structures; and
(o) any other circumstances that might necessitate the removal of the wreck.

Article 7
Locating wrecks[22]

1. Upon becoming aware of a wreck, the Affected State shall use all practicable means, including the good offices of States and organizations, to warn mariners and the States concerned of the nature and location of the wreck as a matter of urgency.
2. If the Affected State has reason to believe that a wreck poses a hazard, it shall ensure that all practicable steps are taken to establish the precise location of the wreck.

Article 8
Marking of wrecks[23]

1. If the Affected State determines that a wreck constitutes a hazard, that State shall ensure that all reasonable steps are taken to mark the wreck.
2. In marking the wreck, all practicable steps shall be taken to ensure that the markings conform to the internationally accepted system of buoyage in use in the area where the wreck is located.
3. The Affected State shall promulgate the particulars of the marking of the wreck by use of all appropriate means, including the appropriate nautical publications.

Article 9
Measures to facilitate the removal of wrecks[24]

1. If the Affected State determines that a wreck constitutes a hazard, that State shall immediately:
    (a) inform the State of the ship's registry and the registered owner; and

---

22 See 9.2.3, 10.5.5, 11.3.3(b).
23 See 9.2.4, 10.5.6, 11.3.3(b).
24 See 9.2.5, 10.5, 11.3.2, 11.3.3(c), (d).

(b) proceed to consult the State of the ship's registry and other States affected by the wreck regarding measures to be taken in relation to the wreck.
2. The registered owner shall remove a wreck determined to constitute a hazard.
3. When a wreck has been determined to constitute a hazard, the registered owner, or other interested party, shall provide the competent authority of the Affected State with evidence of insurance or other financial security as required by article 12.
4. The registered owner may contract with any salvor or other person to remove the wreck determined to constitute a hazard on behalf of the owner. Before such removal commences, the Affected State may lay down conditions for such removal only to the extent necessary to ensure that the removal proceeds in a manner that is consistent with considerations of safety and protection of the marine environment.
5. When the removal referred to in paragraphs 2 and 4 has commenced, the Affected State may intervene in the removal only to the extent necessary to ensure that the removal proceeds effectively in a manner that is consistent with considerations of safety and protection of the marine environment.
6. The Affected State shall:[25]
   (a) set a reasonable deadline within which the registered owner must remove the wreck, taking into account the nature of the hazard determined in accordance with article 6;
   (b) inform the registered owner in writing of the deadline it has set and specify that, if the registered owner does not remove the wreck within that deadline, it may remove the wreck at the registered owner's expense; and
   (c) inform the registered owner in writing that it intends to intervene immediately in circumstances where the hazard becomes particularly severe.
7. If the registered owner does not remove the wreck within the deadline set in accordance with paragraph 6(a), or the registered owner cannot be contacted, the Affected State may remove the wreck by the most practical and expeditious means available, consistent with considerations of safety and protection of the marine environment.
8. In circumstances where immediate action is required and the Affected State has informed the State of the ship's registry and the registered owner accordingly, it may remove the wreck by the most practical and expeditious means available, consistent with considerations of safety and protection of the marine environment.
9. States Parties shall take appropriate measures under their national law to ensure that their registered owners comply with paragraphs 2 and 3.
10. States Parties give their consent to the Affected State to act under paragraphs 4 to 8, where required.
11. The information referred to in this article shall be provided by the Affected State to the registered owner identified in the reports referred to in article 5, paragraph 2.

Article 10
Liability of the owner[26]

1. Subject to article 11, the registered owner shall be liable for the costs of locating, marking and removing the wreck under articles 7, 8 and 9, respectively, unless the registered owner proves that the maritime casualty that caused the wreck:
   (a) resulted from an act of war, hostilities, civil war, insurrection, or a natural phenomenon of an exceptional, inevitable and irresistible character;

---

25 See 10.5.2.
26 See Chapter 10, in particular 10.2, 10.5, 10.6, 11.3.4(a).

(b) was wholly caused by an act or omission done with intent to cause damage by a third party; or
(c) was wholly caused by the negligence or other wrongful act of any Government or other authority responsible for the maintenance of lights or other navigational aids in the exercise of that function.[27]

2. Nothing in this Convention shall affect the right of the registered owner to limit liability under any applicable national or international regime, such as the Convention on Limitation of Liability for Maritime Claims, 1976, as amended.[28]

3. No claim for the costs referred to in paragraph 1 may be made against the registered owner otherwise than in accordance with the provisions of this Convention. This is without prejudice to the rights and obligations of a State Party that has made a notification under article 3, paragraph 2, in relation to wrecks located in its territory, including the territorial sea, other than locating, marking and removing in accordance with this Convention.

4. Nothing in this article shall prejudice any right of recourse against third parties.

Article 11
Exceptions to liability[29]

1. The registered owner shall not be liable under this Convention for the costs mentioned in article 10, paragraph 1 if, and to the extent that, liability for such costs would be in conflict with:
   (a) the International Convention on Civil Liability for Oil Pollution Damage, 1969, as amended;
   (b) the International Convention on Liability and Compensation for Damage in Connection with the Carriage of Hazardous and Noxious Substances by Sea, 1996, as amended;
   (c) the Convention on Third Party Liability in the Field of Nuclear Energy, 1960, as amended, or the Vienna Convention on Civil Liability for Nuclear Damage, 1963, as amended; or national law governing or prohibiting limitation of liability for nuclear damage; or
   (d) the International Convention on Civil Liability for Bunker Oil Pollution Damage, 2001, as amended;
   provided that the relevant convention is applicable and in force.

2. To the extent that measures under this Convention are considered to be salvage under applicable national law or an international convention, such law or convention shall apply to questions of the remuneration or compensation payable to salvors to the exclusion of the rules of this Convention.

Article 12
Compulsory insurance or other financial security[30]

1. The registered owner of a ship of 300 gross tonnage and above and flying the flag of a State Party shall be required to maintain insurance or other financial security, such as a guarantee of a bank or similar institution, to cover liability under this Convention in an amount equal to the limits of liability under the applicable national or international limitation regime, but

---

27 See 10.3.
28 See 10.7, 2.5.
29 See 7.5, 10.9.
30 See 10.8, 11.3.3(e), 11.3.4(b).

in all cases not exceeding an amount calculated in accordance with article 6(1)(b) of the Convention on Limitation of Liability for Maritime Claims, 1976, as amended.

2. A certificate attesting that insurance or other financial security is in force in accordance with the provisions of this Convention shall be issued to each ship of 300 gross tonnage and above by the appropriate authority of the State of the ship's registry after determining that the requirements of paragraph 1 have been complied with. With respect to a ship registered in a State Party, such certificate shall be issued or certified by the appropriate authority of the State of the ship's registry; with respect to a ship not registered in a State Party it may be issued or certified by the appropriate authority of any State Party. This compulsory insurance certificate shall be in the form of the model set out in the annex to this Convention,[31] and shall contain the following particulars:
   (a) name of the ship, distinctive number or letters and port of registry;
   (b) gross tonnage of the ship;
   (c) name and principal place of business of the registered owner;
   (d) IMO ship identification number;
   (e) type and duration of security;
   (f) name and principal place of business of insurer or other person giving security and, where appropriate, place of business where the insurance or security is established; and
   (g) period of validity of the certificate, which shall not be longer than the period of validity of the insurance or other security.

3. (a) A State Party may authorize either an institution or an organization recognized by it to issue the certificate referred to in paragraph 2. Such institution or organization shall inform that State of the issue of each certificate. In all cases, the State Party shall fully guarantee the completeness and accuracy of the certificate so issued and shall undertake to ensure the necessary arrangements to satisfy this obligation.
   (b) A State Party shall notify the Secretary-General of:
      (i) the specific responsibilities and conditions of the authority delegated to an institution or organization recognized by it;
      (ii) the withdrawal of such authority; and
      (iii) the date from which such authority or withdrawal of such authority takes effect.
   An authority delegated shall not take effect prior to three months from the date on which notification to that effect was given to the Secretary-General.
   (c) The institution or organization authorized to issue certificates in accordance with this paragraph shall, as a minimum, be authorized to withdraw these certificates if the conditions under which they have been issued are not maintained. In all cases the institution or organization shall report such withdrawal to the State on whose behalf the certificate was issued.

4. The certificate shall be in the official language or languages of the issuing State. If the language used is not English, French or Spanish, the text shall include a translation into one of these languages and, where the State so decides, the official language(s) of the State may be omitted.

5. The certificate shall be carried on board the ship and a copy shall be deposited with the authorities who keep the record of the ship's registry or, if the ship is not registered in a State Party, with the authorities issuing or certifying the certificate.

---

31 See 7.6.4.

6. An insurance or other financial security shall not satisfy the requirements of this article if it can cease for reasons other than the expiry of the period of validity of the insurance or security specified in the certificate under paragraph 2 before three months have elapsed from the date on which notice of its termination is given to the authorities referred to in paragraph 5 unless certificate has been surrendered to these authorities or a new certificate has been issued within the said period. The foregoing provisions shall similarly apply to any modification, which results in the insurance or security no longer satisfying the requirements of this article.
7. The State of the ship's registry shall, subject to the provisions of this article and having regard to any guidelines adopted by the Organization on the financial responsibility of the registered owners, determine the conditions of issue and validity of the certificate
8. Nothing in this Convention shall be construed as preventing a State Party from relying on information obtained from other States or the Organization or other international organizations relating to the financial standing of providers of insurance or financial security for the purposes of this Convention. In such cases, the State Party relying on such information is not relieved of its responsibility as a State issuing the certificate required by paragraph 2.
9. Certificates issued and certified under the authority of a State Party shall be accepted by other States Parties for the purposes of this Convention and shall be regarded by other States Parties as having the same force as certificates issued or certified by them, even if issued or certified in respect of a ship not registered in a State Party. A State Party may at any time request consultation with the issuing or certifying State should it believe that the insurer or guarantor named in the certificate is not financially capable of meeting the obligations imposed by this Convention.
10. Any claim for costs arising under this Convention may be brought directly against the insurer or other person providing financial security for the registered owner's liability. In such a case the defendant may invoke the defences (other than the bankruptcy or winding up of the registered owner) that the registered owner would have been entitled to invoke, including limitation of liability under any applicable national or international regime. Furthermore, even if the registered owner is not entitled to limit liability, the defendant may limit liability to an amount equal to the amount of the insurance or other financial security required to be maintained in accordance with paragraph 1. Moreover, the defendant may invoke the defence that the maritime casualty was caused by the wilful misconduct of the registered owner, but the defendant shall not invoke any other defence which the defendant might have been entitled to invoke in proceedings brought by the registered owner against the defendant. The defendant shall in any event have the right to require the registered owner to be joined in the proceedings.
11. A State Party shall not permit any ship entitled to fly its flag to which this article applies to operate at any time unless a certificate has been issued under paragraphs 2 or 14.
12. Subject to the provisions of this article, each State Party shall ensure, under its national law, that insurance or other security to the extent required by paragraph 1 is in force in respect of any ship of 300 gross tonnage and above, wherever registered, entering or leaving a port in its territory, or arriving at or leaving from an offshore facility in its territorial sea.
13. Notwithstanding the provisions of paragraph 5, a State Party may notify the Secretary-General that, for the purposes of paragraph 12, ships are not required to carry on board or to produce the certificate required by paragraph 2, when entering or leaving a port in its territory, or arriving at or leaving from an offshore facility in its territorial sea, provided that the State Party which issues the certificate required by paragraph 2 has notified the Secretary-General that it maintains records in an electronic format, accessible to all States Parties, attesting the existence of the certificate and enabling States Parties to discharge their obligations under paragraph 12.

14. If insurance or other financial security is not maintained in respect of a ship owned by a State Party, the provisions of this article relating thereto shall not be applicable to such ship, but the ship shall carry a certificate issued by the appropriate authority of the State of registry, stating that it is owned by that State and that the ship's liability is covered within the limits prescribed in paragraph 1. Such a certificate shall follow as closely as possible the model prescribed by paragraph 2.

Article 13
Time limits[32]

Rights to recover costs under this Convention shall be extinguished unless an action is brought hereunder within three years from the date when the hazard has been determined in accordance with this Convention. However, in no case shall an action be brought after six years from the date of the maritime casualty that resulted in the wreck. Where the maritime casualty consists of a series of occurrences, the six-year period shall run from the date of the first occurrence.

Article 14
Amendment provisions

1. At the request of not less than one-third of States Parties, a conference shall be convened by the Organization for the purpose of revising or amending this Convention.
2. Any consent to be bound by this Convention, expressed after the date of entry into force of an amendment to this Convention, shall be deemed to apply to this Convention, as amended.

Article 15
Settlement of disputes[33]

1. Where a dispute arises between two or more States Parties regarding the interpretation or application of this Convention, they shall seek to resolve their dispute, in the first instance, through negotiation, enquiry, mediation, conciliation, arbitration, judicial settlement, resort to regional agencies or arrangements or other peaceful means of their choice.
2. If no settlement is possible within a reasonable period of time not exceeding twelve months after one State Party has notified another that a dispute exists between them, the provisions relating to the settlement of disputes set out in Part XV of the United Nations Convention on the Law of the Sea, 1982, shall apply mutatis mutandis, whether or not the States party to the dispute are also States Parties to the United Nations Convention on the Law of the Sea, 1982.
3. Any procedure chosen by a State Party to this Convention and to the United Nations Convention on the Law of the Sea, 1982, pursuant to Article 287 of the latter, shall apply to the settlement of disputes under this article, unless that State Party, when ratifying, accepting, approving or acceding to this Convention, or at any time thereafter, chooses another procedure pursuant to Article 287 for the purpose of the settlement of disputes arising out of this Convention.
4. A State Party to this Convention which is not a Party to the United Nations Convention on the Law of the Sea, 1982, when ratifying, accepting, approving or acceding to this Convention or at any time thereafter shall be free to choose, by means of a written declaration, one or more of the means set out in Article 287, paragraph 1, of the United Nations Convention

---

[32] See 10.4, 11.3.4(a).
[33] See 7.6.3.

on the Law of the Sea, 1982, for the purpose of settlement of disputes under this Article. Article 287 shall apply to such a declaration, as well as to any dispute to which such State is party, which is not covered by a declaration in force. For the purpose of conciliation and arbitration, in accordance with Annexes V and VII of the United Nations Convention on the Law of the Sea, 1982, such State shall be entitled to nominate conciliators and arbitrators to be included in the lists referred to in Annex V, Article 2, and Annex VII, Article 2, for the settlement of disputes arising out of this Convention.

5. A declaration made under paragraphs 3 and 4 shall be deposited with the Secretary-General, who shall transmit copies thereof to the States Parties.

Article 16
Relationship to other conventions and international agreements[34]

Nothing in this Convention shall prejudice the rights and obligations of any State under the United Nations Convention on the Law of the Sea, 1982, and under the customary international law of the sea.

Article 17
Signature, ratification, acceptance, approval and accession

This Convention shall be open for signature at the Headquarters of the Organization from 19 November 2007 until 18 November 2008 and shall thereafter remain open for accession.

(a) States may express their consent to be bound by this Convention by:
  (i) signature without reservation as to ratification, acceptance or approval; or
  (ii) signature subject to ratification, acceptance or approval, followed by ratification, acceptance or approval; or
  (iii) accession.
(b) Ratification, acceptance, approval or accession shall be effected by the deposit of an instrument to that effect with the Secretary-General.

Article 18
Entry into force[35]

1. This Convention shall enter into force twelve months following the date on which ten States have either signed it without reservation as to ratification, acceptance or approval or have deposited instruments of ratification, acceptance, approval or accession with the Secretary-General.

2. For any State which ratifies, accepts, approves or accedes to this Convention after the conditions in paragraph 1 for entry into force have been met, this Convention shall enter into force three months following the date of deposit by such State of the appropriate instrument, but not before this Convention has entered into force in accordance with paragraph 1.

Article 19
Denunciation

1. This Convention may be denounced by a State Party at any time after the expiry of one year following the date on which this Convention comes into force for that State.

---

34 See 7.3, 7.4, 8.4.
35 See 7.6.2.

2. Denunciation shall be effected by the deposit of an instrument to that effect with the Secretary-General.
3. A denunciation shall take effect one year, or such longer period as may be specified in the instrument of denunciation, following its receipt by the Secretary-General.

Article 20
Depositary

1. This Convention shall be deposited with the Secretary General.
2. The Secretary-General shall:
   (a) inform all States which have signed or acceded to this Convention of:
      (i) each new signature or deposit of an instrument of ratification, acceptance, approval or accession, together with the date thereof;
      (ii) the date of entry into force of this Convention;
      (iii) the deposit of any instrument of denunciation of this Convention, together with the date of the deposit and the date on which the denunciation takes effect; and
      (iv) other declarations and notifications received pursuant to this Convention;
   (b) transmit certified true copies of this Convention to all States that have signed or acceded to this Convention.
3. As soon as this Convention enters into force, a certified true copy of the text shall be transmitted by the Secretary-General to the Secretary-General of the United Nations, for registration and publication in accordance with Article 102 of the Charter of the United Nations.

Article 21
Languages

The Convention is established in a single original in the Arabic, Chinese, English, French, Russian and Spanish languages, each text being equally authentic."

APPENDIX 5: WRECK REMOVAL CONVENTION 2007: ANNEX (CERTIFICATE OF INSURANCE)

ANNEX

CERTIFICATE OF INSURANCE OR OTHER FINANCIAL SECURITY IN RESPECT OF LIABILITY FOR THE REMOVAL OF WRECKS

Issued in accordance with the provisions of article 12 of the Nairobi International Convention on the Removal of Wrecks, 2007

Name of Ship	Gross tonnage	Distinctive number or letters	IMO Ship Identification Number	Port of Registry	Name and full address of the principal place of business of the registered owner

This is to certify that there is in force, in respect of the above-named ship, a policy of insurance or other financial security satisfying the requirements of article 12 of the Nairobi International Convention on the Removal of Wrecks, 2007.

Type of Security ....

Duration of Security ....

Name and address of the insurer(s) and/or guarantor(s)

Name ....

Address ....

....

This certificate is valid until ....

Issued or certified by the Government of ....

....

(Full designation of the State)
OR

The following text should be used when a State Party avails itself of article 12, paragraph 3:
The present certificate is issued under the authority of the Government of ....
(full designation of the State) by .... (name of institution or organization)

APPENDIX 5 WRC 2007: CERTIFICATE OF INSURANCE

At .... On ....

(Place) (Date)

....

(Signature and Title of issuing or certifying official)

Explanatory Notes:

1. If desired, the designation of the State may include a reference to the competent public authority of the country where the Certificate is issued.
2. If the total amount of security has been furnished by more than one source, the amount of each of them should be indicated.
3. If security is furnished in several forms, these should be enumerated.
4. The entry "Duration of Security" must stipulate the date on which such security takes effect.
5. The entry "Address" of the insurer(s) and/or guarantor(s) must indicate the principal place of business of the insurer(s) and/or guarantor(s). If appropriate, the place of business where the insurance or other security is established shall be indicated.

APPENDIX 6: WRC 2007: DIPLOMATIC CONFERENCE RESOLUTIONS

INTERNATIONAL CONFERENCE ON THE
REMOVAL OF WRECKS, 2007
Nairobi, 14–18 May 2007
Agenda item 8

LEG/CONF.16/20
23 May 2007

Original: ENGLISH

ADOPTION OF THE FINAL ACT AND ANY INSTRUMENTS, RECOMMENDATIONS AND RESOLUTIONS RESULTING FROM THE WORK OF THE CONFERENCE

CONFERENCE RESOLUTIONS

Text adopted by the conference

RESOLUTION ON EXPRESSIONS OF APPRECIATION

THE CONFERENCE,

NOTING with appreciation the kind invitation of the Government of Kenya to the International Maritime Organization to hold the Conference in Nairobi,

ACKNOWLEDGING the generous financial and in-kind contribution and excellent arrangements made by the Government of Kenya for the Conference, as well as the hospitality and other amenities bestowed on the participants to the Conference by the Government and the People of Kenya,

ACKNOWLEDGING FURTHER the excellent facilities provided by the United Nations Office at Nairobi (UNON), which greatly facilitated the efficient conduct of the Conference,

1. EXPRESSES its profound gratitude and thanks to the Government and the People of Kenya for their valuable contribution to the success of the Conference;
2. DECIDES, in grateful recognition of this contribution, to designate the Convention adopted by the Conference as the:

   NAIROBI INTERNATIONAL CONVENTION ON THE REMOVAL OF WRECKS, 2007;

3. EXPRESSES FURTHER its thanks to UNON for the facilities provided.

RESOLUTION ON COMPULSORY INSURANCE CERTIFICATES UNDER EXISTING MARITIME LIABILITY CONVENTIONS, INCLUDING THE NAIROBI INTERNATIONAL CONVENTION ON THE REMOVAL OF WRECKS, 2007

THE CONFERENCE,

HAVING ADOPTED the Nairobi International Convention on the Removal of Wrecks, 2007 (hereinafter referred to as "the Convention"),

NOTING that the Convention requires that a compulsory insurance certificate attesting that insurance or other financial security is in force on the same basis as previously established IMO liability and compensation conventions,

MINDFUL that all existing liability and compensation conventions require that a compulsory insurance certificate attesting that insurance or other financial security in force, shall be issued in the form of the model set out in the specific annexes to these conventions,

RECOGNIZING the reduction of administrative costs and further facilitation as regards the issuing of all relevant compulsory insurance certificates by appropriate authorities in States Parties, if in future each and every ship could be provided with a single compulsory insurance certificate,

NOTING FURTHER the urgent priority to implement all the existing liability and compensation conventions,

1. URGES States to ensure, as a matter of priority, the entry into force of the International Convention on Liability and Compensation for Damage in connection with the Carriage of Hazardous and Noxious Substances by Sea, 1996, the International Convention on Civil Liability for Bunker Oil Pollution Damage, 2001, and the Protocol to the Athens Convention Relating to the Carriage of Passengers and their Luggage by Sea, 2002;
2. INVITES the International Maritime Organization (IMO) and in particular the Legal Committee to develop a model for a single insurance certificate which may be issued by States Parties in respect of each and every ship under the relevant IMO liability and compensation conventions, including the Convention;
3. INVITES FURTHER IMO to follow the same procedure as that adopted in relation to the reciprocal recognition of certificates by States Parties to the 1969 and 1992 International Conventions on Civil Liability for Oil Pollution Damage.

APPENDIX 6 WRC 2007: CONFERENCE RESOLUTIONS

RESOLUTION ON PROMOTION OF TECHNICAL CO-OPERATION AND ASSISTANCE

THE CONFERENCE,

HAVING ADOPTED the Nairobi International Convention on the Removal of Wrecks, 2007 (hereinafter referred to as "the Convention"), concerning uniform international rules and procedures to ensure the prompt and effective removal of wrecks and payment of compensation for the costs therein involved,

RECOGNIZING the need for the development of appropriate legislation and the putting in place of appropriate infrastructure for the removal of wrecks which may pose a danger or impediment to navigation, or may reasonably be expected to result in maJor harmful consequences to the marine environment, or damage to the coastline or related interests of one or more States,

RECOGNIZING FURTHER that there may be limited infrastructure, facilities and training programmes for obtaining the experience required in assessing the hazard which a wreck may pose, particularly in developing countries,

BELIEVING that the promotion of technical co-operation at the international level will assist those States not yet having adequate expertise or facilities for providing training and experience to assess, put in place or enhance appropriate infrastructure and, in general, implement the measures required by the Convention,

EMPHASIZING, in this regard, the grave threat a wreck can pose to the safety of navigation and to the marine environment, or both, if not removed promptly and effectively,

1. URGES States Parties to the Convention, Member States of the International Maritime Organization (IMO), other appropriate organizations and the maritime industry to provide assistance, either directly or through IMO, to those States which require support in the consideration of adoption and in the implementation of the Convention;
2. INVITES the Secretary-General of IMO to make adequate provision in its Integrated Technical Co-operation Programme (ITCP) for advisory services related to the adoption and effective implementation of the Convention and, in particular, to address requests for assistance in assessing the safety and environmental hazards of wrecks and in developing appropriate national legislation;
3. INVITES States Parties to the Convention, Member States of IMO, other appropriate organizations and the maritime industry to provide financial and in-kind support to IMO for technical assistance activities related to the adoption and effective implementation of the Convention.

APPENDIX 7: WRECKHIRE 2010
Wreckhire 2010*

Explanatory Notes for WRECKHIRE 2010 are available from BIMCO at www.bimco.org

BIMCO / ISU INTERNATIONAL SALVAGE UNION

WRECKHIRE 2010
INTERNATIONAL WRECK REMOVAL AND MARINE SERVICES AGREEMENT (DAILY HIRE)

PART I

First published 1993. Revised 1999 and 2010
Approved by the International Salvage Union (ISU)

1. Place and Date of Agreement

2. Contractor/Place of Business (Cl. 1)

3. Company/Place of Business (Cl. 1)

4. Vessel Specifications (Cl. 1, 2, 4)

(i) Name	(ii) Flag
(iii) IMO Number	(iv) Place of Registry
(v) Length/Beam/Depth //	(vi) Maximum Draft
(vii) GT/NT/DWT //	(viii) Details and Nature of Cargo
(ix) P&I Club/insurer (Cl. 23 (b))	(x) Any other Vessel details relevant to this Agreement

5. Condition of Vessel (Cl. 2, 4)

6. Position of Vessel and Condition of Worksite (Cl. 1, 2, 4)

7. Nature of Services (Cl. 1, 2, 4, 10(c))

   (i) Nature of services:

   (ii) Compliance with orders of competent authorities (state party to obtain confirmation):

8. Place of Delivery and/or Disposal of Vessel (Cl.9(a), 9(c),12)

9. Extra costs of disposal of Vessel (Cl. 14)

   (i) state which party is responsible for costs and/or division between the parties:

   (ii) handling charge, if applicable (state percentage):

10. Bonus payment/Reduced hire (Cl. 11, 12)

    (i) Amount of Bonus (state either total amount or percentage of the total payable under Agreement)

    (ii) Full bonus (state applicable date or commencement date/event and subsequent period in days for full bonus)

    (iii) Pro rata bonus/reduced hire (state applicable date or commencement date/event and subsequent period in days for pro rata bonus after which reduced hire to apply)

11. Payment and Rates of Hire (Cl. 7, 8(a), 8 (c), 10(a), 12)

(i) Daily Working Rate for Craft and Equipment (Cl.10(a))	(ii) Daily Working Rate for Personnel (Cl.10(a))
(iii) Daily Standby Rate for Craft and Equipment (Cl. 7)	(iv) Daily Standby Rate for Personnel (Cl. 7)
(v) Reduced Daily Rates of Hire (Cl. 10(a), 12) (a) Daily Working Rate for Craft and Equipment: (b) Daily Working Rate for Personnel: (c) Daily Standby Rate for Craft and Equipment:	(vi) Payment of the appropriate Working Rate of Hire is to be made in advance every (state number of days) (a) Commencing from: (b) and continuing until: (c) with a minimum payment of hire in any event (state number

continued

This document is a computer generated WRECKHIRE 2010 form printed by authority of BIMCO. Any insertion or deletion to the form must be clearly visible. In the event of any modification made to the pre-printed text of this document which is not clearly visible, the text of the original BIMCO approved document shall apply. BIMCO assumes no responsibility for any loss, damage or expense as a result of discrepancies between the original BIMCO approved document and this computer generated document.

* Reproduced by kind permission of BIMCO.

APPENDIX 7 WRECKHIRE 2010

(continued)   PART I

(d) Daily Standby Rate for Personnel:	of days hire)
12. Payment Details (Cl. 10(e))	
(i) Currency	
(ii) Bank	(iii) Address
(iv) Account Number	(v) Account Name
13. Time of Payment and Interest (state period within which sums must be received by the Contractor and rate of interest per month) (Cl. 10(g))	14. Extra Costs (state percentage to be applied) (Cl. 13) (i) General handling charge (Cl. 13(a)-13(h)) (ii) Fuels and lubricants handling charge (Cl. 13(i))
15. Arbitration and Mediation (state Cl. 21 (a), 21 (b) or 21 (c) of Cl. 21 as agreed; if 21 (c) agreed, also state place of arbitration (Cl. 21) (if not appropriately filled in, Clause 21(a) shall apply) (c) -	16. Number of Additional Clauses covering special provisions, if agreed

It is agreed that this Agreement shall be performed subject to the Terms and Conditions which consist of PART I, including Additional Clauses, if any agreed, and PART II, as well as Annex I (SCHEDULE OF PERSONNEL, CRAFT AND EQUIPMENT), Annex II (METHOD OF WORK AND ESTIMATED TIME SCHEDULE), and Annex III (CONTRACTOR'S DAILY REPORTS) or any other Annexes attached to this Agreement.

In the event of a conflict of terms and conditions, the provisions of PART I including Additional Clauses, if any agreed, shall prevail over those of PART II to the extent of such conflict but no further.

The undersigned warrant that they have full power and authority to sign this Agreement on behalf of the parties they represent.

Signature (for and on behalf of **the Contractor**)	Signature (for and on behalf of **the Company**)

continued

This document is a computer generated WRECKHIRE 2010 form printed by authority of BIMCO. Any insertion or deletion to the form must be clearly visible. In the event of any modification made to the pre-printed text of this document which is not clearly visible, the text of the original BIMCO approved document shall apply. BIMCO assumes no responsibility for any loss, damage or expense as a result of discrepancies between the original BIMCO approved document and this computer generated document.

APPENDIX 7 WRECKHIRE 2010

(continued)   PART I

ANNEX I (SCHEDULE OF PERSONNEL, CRAFT AND EQUIPMENT)
INTERNATIONAL WRECK REMOVAL AND MARINE SERVICES AGREEMENT (DAILY HIRE)
CODE NAME: WRECKHIRE 2010

Dated:

Vessel:

Schedule of Personnel, Craft and Equipment (Cl. 2, 4 and 13(g))

APPENDIX 7 WRECKHIRE 2010

(continued) PART I

ANNEX II (METHOD OF WORK AND ESTIMATED TIME SCHEDULE)
INTERNATIONAL WRECK REMOVAL AND MARINE SERVICES AGREEMENT (DAILY HIRE)
CODE NAME: WRECKHIRE 2010

Dated:

Vessel:

Method of Work and Estimated Time Schedule (Cl. 2 and 4)

APPENDIX 7 WRECKHIRE 2010

(continued)   PART I

ANNEX III (CONTRACTOR'S DAILY REPORTS)
INTERNATIONAL WRECK REMOVAL AND MARINE SERVICES AGREEMENT (DAILY HIRE)
CODE NAME: WRECKHIRE 2010

Date	Report no
Status of wreck:	

Vessel	
Cargo	
Bunkers	

Status of wreck site:

Weather on location:			
	1200	2400	Forecast next 24 hours
Wind direction & speed (Bft)			
Swell direction & height (m)			
Wave height & max wave height (m)			

Long range forecast (5 days):

Services:
- performed in last 24 hours:

- planned for next 24 hours:

Vessels:					
Name	On hire	Standby rate	Reduced rate	Off hire	Remarks

Demobilised, inoperative or damaged – insert under "Remarks"

Equipment:					
Description	On hire	Standby rate	Reduced rate	Off hire	Remarks

Demobilised, inoperative, consumed, lost or damaged – insert under "Remarks"

continued

This document is a computer generated WRECKHIRE 2010 form printed by authority of BIMCO. Any insertion or deletion to the form must be clearly visible. In the event of any modification made to the pre-printed text of this document which is not clearly visible, the text of the original BIMCO approved document shall apply. BIMCO assumes no responsibility for any loss, damage or expense as a result of discrepancies between the original BIMCO approved document and this computer generated document.

APPENDIX 7 WRECKHIRE 2010

(continued)   PART I

Personnel:					
Name	On hire	Standby rate	Reduced rate	Off hire	Remarks

Demobilised, inoperative or injured – insert under "Remarks"

Areas of concern:
Health & safety
Environmental
Other

Comments:
Contractor's Representative
Company Representative

Signed:			
Company Representative			
Contractor's Representative			
	Name	Position	Signature

Contractor's Daily Reports (Cl. 2).

continued

This document is a computer generated WRECKHIRE 2010 form printed by authority of BIMCO. Any insertion or deletion to the form must be clearly visible. In the event of any modification made to the pre-printed text of this document which is not clearly visible, the text of the original BIMCO approved document shall apply. BIMCO assumes no responsibility for any loss, damage or expense as a result of discrepancies between the original BIMCO approved document and this computer generated document.

6

APPENDIX 7 WRECKHIRE 2010

WRECKHIRE 2010 - International Wreck Removal and Marine Services Agreement (Daily Hire)
PART II

1. Definitions
"Company" means the party stated in Box 3.
"Contractor" means the party stated in Box 2.
"Services" means the services stated in Box 7.
"Vessel" means any vessel, craft, property, or part thereof, of whatsoever nature, including anything contained therein or thereon, such as but not limited to cargo and bunkers, as described in Box 4.
"Worksite" means the position of the Vessel stated in Box 6.

2. The Services
The Contractor agrees to exercise due care in rendering the Services which shall include, if applicable, the delivery and/or disposal of the Vessel. Insofar as it is not inconsistent with the nature of the Services to be rendered under this Agreement, the Contractor will also exercise due care to prevent and minimise damage to the environment.

The Contractor shall provide the Personnel, Craft and Equipment set out in Annex I of this Agreement which the Contractor deems necessary for the Services based upon the Specifications, Condition and Position of the Vessel and Worksite set out in Boxes 4, 5 and 6.

The Contractor's Method of Work and Estimated Time Schedule shall be as described in Annex II, utilising the Personnel, Craft and Equipment described in Annex I.

The Contractor shall consult with the Company if there is any need for substantial change in the Method of Work and/or Personnel, Craft or Equipment. (See Clause 4 (Change of Method of Work and/or Personnel, Craft and Equipment) hereof).

The Contractor shall provide the Company Representative with daily reports in accordance with Annex III.

The party identified in Box 7(ii) of this Agreement shall be given all reasonable assistance by the other party in connection with obtaining confirmation from the competent authorities that the Company has complied with any orders issued by them.

3. Company Representative
The methods and procedures to be employed in the Services shall at all times be discussed and agreed between the Company and the Contractor.

The Company Representative will be available during the performance of the Services with the full authority to act on behalf of the Company. The Company Representative shall have full and unfettered access at all times to the site and to the Contractor's craft and equipment, unless such access is reasonably refused by the Contractor.

In addition, the Company will provide at its sole risk and expense sufficient officers or their equivalents, who are fully conversant with the cargo system and/or layout of the Vessel, and who should be in attendance when reasonably required during the performance of the Services in order to provide advice as and when requested by the Contractor.

4. Change of Method of Work and/or Personnel, Craft and Equipment
The Rates of Hire stated in Box 11 are based upon the Nature of the Services, as set out in Box 7, Method of Work, and Personnel, Craft and Equipment, as set out in Annexes I and II, and the Description, Specifications, Position, Condition of the Vessel and the Worksite, as set out in Boxes 4, 5 and 6.

(a) If before or during the performance of the Services, and without fault on the part of the Contractor, there is a substantial change in the Services, and/or in the Personnel, Craft and Equipment required to undertake the Services due to any misdescription by the Company or error in the specification provided by the Company, upon which the Contractor has relied, or a material change in the position and/or condition of the Vessel or the Worksite:

(i) The Contractor shall forthwith give notice in writing thereof to the Company and of the estimated additional costs to effect the Services;

(ii) Any and all substantial changes to the nature of such Services which are agreed between the Contractor and the Company shall be drafted into a variation order by the Company, which shall be signed by the parties;

(iii) The parties shall, without delay, consult each other to reach agreement on the amount of the additional costs to be added to the Rates of Hire and any agreement shall be incorporated into the variation order.

(b) If, as a result of a material change in the position and/or condition of the Vessel or the Worksite, subsequent to entering into this Agreement, the Services become easier to perform in terms of the work and/or Personnel, Craft and/or Equipment requirements, then:

(i) The Company may, subject to the provisions of Clause 10(d) hereof, seek a reduction in respect of the monies

1

WRECKHIRE 2010 - International Wreck Removal and Marine Services Agreement (Daily Hire)
PART II

payable pursuant to Clause 10(a) hereof;

(ii) All such material changes which are agreed by the Contractor and the Company shall be drafted into a variation order by the Company, which shall be signed by the parties;

(iii) The parties shall, without delay, consult each other to reach agreement on the amount of the costs to be deducted from the Rates of Hire and any agreement shall be incorporated into the variation order.

(c) Alternatively either party may refer the matter to expert evaluation in accordance with Clause 20 (Expert Evaluation) or to arbitration or mediation pursuant to Clause 21 (Arbitration and Mediation) for a decision on the reasonableness and quantum of such costs, or the claim by the Company for a reduction in remuneration, which shall be incorporated into the variation order.

In the event the matter is referred either to expert evaluation or arbitration or mediation the Contractor will continue to provide the Services, without prejudice to any claim for an adjustment to the remuneration.

5. Miscellaneous
(a) The Company shall arrange and pay for any marking of the Vessel and cautioning required. The Contractor shall arrange and pay for any marking or cautioning required in respect of its own equipment during the Services under this Agreement.

(b) The Contractor may make reasonable use of the Vessel's machinery, gear, equipment, anchors, chains, stores and other appurtenances during and for the purposes of these Services free of expense but shall not unnecessarily damage, abandon or sacrifice the same or any property which is the subject of this Agreement.

(c) Subject to approval of the Company which shall not be unreasonably withheld, and subject to it being permitted by the competent authorities, the Contractor shall be entitled to remove, dispose of or jettison cargo, or parts of the Vessel, or equipment from the Vessel if such action is considered by the Contractor to be reasonably necessary to perform the Services under this Agreement.

(d) The Company will use its best endeavours to provide the Contractor with such plans and drawings of the Vessel, cargo manifests, stowage plans, etc., and such other information as the Contractor may reasonably require for the performance of the Services.

6. Permits
All necessary licences, approvals, authorisations or permits required to undertake and complete the Services without let or hindrance shall be obtained and maintained by the Contractor (see Clause 13(e)). The Company shall provide the Contractor with all reasonable assistance in connection with the obtaining of such licences, approvals, authorisations or permits.

7. Delays
(a) Adverse Weather and Other Delays
In the event that the Contractor is prevented from progressing the Services due to adverse weather or sea conditions or any other reason outside the Contractor's control, the Standby Rate (Box 11(iii) and (iv)) shall apply. In such circumstances where there is a partial reduction in Services, there shall be an adjustment to the Daily Working Rate between the Working Rate and the Standby Rate to be agreed between the Contractor and the Company Representative.

(b) Contractor's Equipment and/or Personnel
If there is a breakdown of any of the Contractor's equipment or non-availability of personnel, the Company Representative and the Contractor shall consult each other to reach agreement on the amount of time lost as a result, if any. The Standby Rate shall apply for the agreed period.

(c) Hired-in Equipment and/or Personnel
The Contractor shall use its best efforts to ensure that appropriate standby rates of hire are agreed in any sub-contract agreement in the event of breakdown of their equipment or non-availability of their personnel. If there is a breakdown of equipment or non-availability of personnel, the Company Representative and the Contractor shall consult each other to reach agreement on the amount of time lost as a result, if any. The sub-contract standby rate shall only apply for the agreed period if such standby rates have been agreed with sub-contractors. The Contractor shall pass on to the Company the benefit of any off-hire or reduction in the rate of hire in respect of equipment or personnel hired-in by the Contractor.

(d) The Company Representative shall promptly advise the Contractor of all periods when they consider that Standby Rates shall apply and shall at the same time confirm same in writing to the Company and the Contractor.

(e) Sub-clauses 7(b) and 7(c) shall not apply for individual delays unless such delays exceed six (6) consecutive hours when the Standby Rate shall apply to the whole agreed delay period.

(f) In the event that the parties cannot reach agreement in respect of the applicable reductions in Sub-, 7(b) or 7(c) above to the Daily Rates of Hire or the duration of such reduction, then the issue may

WRECKHIRE 2010 - International Wreck Removal and Marine Services Agreement (Daily Hire)
PART II

be referred to expert evaluation in accordance with Clause 20 (Expert Evaluation) or to arbitration or mediation pursuant to Clause 21 (Arbitration and Mediation).

8. Suspension or Termination

(a) The Company has the right to suspend or terminate the Services to be carried out under this Agreement at any time, provided always that notice of such suspension or termination is given to the Contractor in writing. In such event the Contractor is entitled to be paid all sums due at the time of suspension or termination in accordance with the provisions of Box 11.

(b) Such suspension or termination of the Services will be carried out with all reasonable despatch by the Contractor, subject always to the safety of Personnel, Craft and Equipment involved in the Services. Any additional direct expenses arising as a consequence of the instructions to suspend or terminate the Services shall be for the account of the Company.

(c) If permission to suspend or terminate is not given by the competent authorities, the Contractor shall be paid by the Company at the appropriate rate set out in Box 11 for Personnel, Craft and Equipment during any standby period, and the Company shall be liable for the Contractor's reasonable and necessary costs of continuing with the Services.

9. Delivery and/or Disposal

(a) If applicable, the Vessel shall be accepted forthwith and taken over by the Company or its duly authorised representative at the Place of Delivery indicated in Box 8. References to delivery or the Place of Delivery shall include disposal or the Place of Disposal, if applicable.

The Place of Delivery and/or Disposal shall always be safe and accessible for the Contractor's own or hired-in craft and the Vessel to enter and operate in and shall be a place where the Contractor is permitted by governmental or other authorities to deliver and/or dispose of the Vessel.

In the event the Vessel is not accepted forthwith by the Company or delivery is prevented or delayed by action of governmental or other authorities outside the control of the Contractor, all costs necessarily incurred by the Contractor from the moment of the tender for delivery shall be for the account of the Company, and the Rates of Hire shall continue to be payable to the Contractor.

(b) If the Company fails, on completion of the Services, to take delivery of the Vessel within five (5) days of the Contractor tendering written notice of delivery or, if in the opinion of the Contractor the Vessel is likely to deteriorate, decay, become worthless or incur charges whether for storage or otherwise in excess of its value, the Contractor may, without prejudice to any other claims the Contractor may have against the Company, without notice and without any responsibility whatsoever attaching to the Contractor, sell or dispose of the Vessel and apply the proceeds of sale in reduction of the sums due to the Contractor from the Company under this Agreement. Any remaining proceeds will be refunded to the Company.

In the event that such sale or other disposal of the Vessel fails to raise sufficient net funds to pay the monies due to the Contractor under the terms of this Agreement, then the Company shall remain liable to the Contractor for any such shortfall.

(c) Reference to delivery and/or disposal of the Vessel shall include parts of the Vessel and/or cargo and/or any other thing emanating from the Vessel and such delivery may take place at different times and different places (see Box 8).

10. Payment

(a) The Company shall pay the Contractor the Daily Working and Standby Rates of Hire for Personnel, Craft and Equipment set out in Box 11(i)-(iv) and, if applicable, Reduced Daily Rates of Hire in accordance with Box 11(v).

(b) Such hire shall be fully and irrevocably earned on a daily basis and shall be non-returnable.

(c) Within 14 days of termination or completion of the Services set out in Box 7 the Contractor shall return any overpayments to the Company.

(d) All monies due and payable to the Contractor under this Agreement shall be paid without any discount, deduction, set-off, lien, claim or counterclaim.

(e) All payments to the Contractor shall be made in the currency and to the bank account stipulated in Box 12.

(f) If any amount payable under this Agreement has not been paid within seven (7) days of the due date, or if the security required in accordance with Clause 15 (Security) is not provided within five (5) banking days following the request by the Contractor, then at any time thereafter the Contractor shall be entitled to terminate this Agreement without prejudice to the sums already due to the Contractor and to any further rights or remedies which the Contractor may have against the Company, provided always that the Contractor shall give the

APPENDIX 7 WRECKHIRE 2010

WRECKHIRE 2010 - International Wreck Removal and Marine Services Agreement (Daily Hire)
PART II

Company at least three (3) working days' written notice of its intention to exercise this right.

(g) The Contractor shall promptly invoice the Company for all sums payable under this Agreement. If any sums which become due and payable are not actually received by the Contractor within the period specified in Box 13, they shall attract interest in accordance with the rate set out in Box 13.

11. Bonus
If the Contractor completes the Services to the satisfaction of the Company:
(a)
  (i) before the date or within the period stated in Box 10(ii), the Company shall pay the Contractor the bonus set out in Box 10(i); or

  (ii) on or after the date or outside the period stated in Box 10(ii), but before the date or within the period stated in Box 10(iii), the Company shall pay the bonus set out in Box 10(i) reduced pro-rata on a daily basis from 100 per cent (100%) on the date or period stated in Box 10(ii) down to zero on or after the date or period stated in Box 10(iii).

(b) Delays (Clause 7) shall not affect the dates or periods to be applied for the purposes of this Clause 11.

12. Reduced Daily Rates of Hire
If the Contractor fails to complete the Services and, if applicable, deliver and/or dispose of the Vessel at the place(s) indicated in Box 8 within the period or on or before the date stated in Box 10(iii), the Daily Rates of Hire shall be reduced in accordance with Box 11(v). Delays (Clause 7) shall not affect the dates or periods to be applied for the purposes of this Clause 12.

13. Extra Costs
The following shall be paid by the Company as and when they fall due:

(a) all port expenses, pilotage charges, harbour and canal dues and all other expenses of a similar nature levied upon or payable in respect of the Vessel and the Contractor's own or hired-in craft;

(b) the costs of the services of any assisting tugs when reasonably deemed necessary by the Contractor or prescribed by port or other authorities;

(c) all costs in connection with clearance, agency fees, visas, guarantees and all other expenses of such kind;

(d) all taxes and social security charges (other than those normally payable by the Contractor in the country where it has its principal place of business), stamp duties, or other levies payable in respect of or in connection with this Agreement, any import - export dues and any customs or excise duties;

(e) all costs incurred in obtaining and maintaining licences, approvals, authorisations or permits required to undertake and complete the Services in accordance with Clause 6 (Permits);

(f) all costs incurred due to requirements of governmental or other authorities or unions over and above those costs which would otherwise be reasonably incurred by the Contractor in the execution of the Agreement;

(g) all reasonable costs of transportation of equipment and the travel and accommodation costs of Personnel identified in Annex I, (other than the crews of craft utilised in the Services);

(h) all costs incurred by the Contractor in respect of portable salvage equipment, materials, or stores which are lost, damaged or consumed during the Services;

(i) all costs in respect of fuels and lubricants consumed during the Services, unless included in the Daily Rates.

If any such costs are in fact paid by or on behalf of the Company by the Contractor, the Company shall reimburse the Contractor on the basis of the actual cost to the Contractor plus a handling charge of the percentage amount indicated in Box 14(i) for Clause 13(a) - (h) costs or Box 14(ii) for Clause 13(i) costs, upon presentation of invoice.

14. Extra Costs of disposal of Vessel
All extra costs incurred resulting from the disposal of the Vessel shall be for the account of the party stated in Box 9(i). If the Company is the party stated in Box 9(i) and any such costs are paid by or on behalf of the Company by the Contractor, the Company shall reimburse the Contractor on the basis of the actual cost to the Contractor plus a handling charge of the percentage amount indicated in Box 9(ii) upon presentation of invoice.

15. Security
The Company shall provide on signing this Agreement an irrevocable and unconditional security in a form and amount as agreed between the parties.

If required by the Contractor and also in the event that initially no security is requested, the Company shall

4

WRECKHIRE 2010 - International Wreck Removal and Marine Services Agreement (Daily Hire)
PART II

provide security or further security in a form and amount as agreed between the parties for all or part of any amount which may be or become due under this Agreement. Such security shall be given on one or more occasions as and when reasonably required by the Contractor.

16. Liabilities
(a) The Contractor will indemnify and hold the Company harmless in respect of any liability adjudged due or claim reasonably compromised arising out of injury or death occurring during the Services hereunder to any of the following persons:

(i) any servant, agent or sub-contractor of the Contractor;

(ii) any other person at or near the site of the operations for whatever purpose on behalf or at the request of the Contractor.

(b) The Company will indemnify and hold the Contractor harmless in respect of any liability adjudged due or claim reasonably compromised arising from injury or death occurring during the Services hereunder to any of the following persons:

(i) any servant, agent or sub-contractor of the Company;

(ii) any other person at or near the site of the operations for whatever purpose on behalf or at the request of the Company.

(c) Neither the Company nor its servants, agents or sub-contractors shall have any liability to the Contractor for loss or damage of whatsoever nature sustained by the Contractor's owned or hired-in craft or equipment (excluding portable salvage equipment, materials or stores which are lost, damaged, or consumed during the Services), whether or not the same is due to breach of contract, negligence or any other fault on the part of the Company, its servants, agents or sub-contractors.

(d) Neither the Contractor nor its servants, agents or sub-contractors shall have any liability to the Company for loss or damage of whatsoever nature sustained by the Vessel, whether or not the same is due to breach of contract, negligence or any other fault on the part of the Contractor, its servants, agents or sub-contractors.

(e) Neither party shall be liable to the other party for:

(i) any loss of profit, loss of use or loss of production whatsoever and whether arising directly or indirectly from the performance or non-performance of this Agreement, and whether or not the same is due to negligence or any other fault on the part of either party, their servants, agents or sub-contractors; or

(ii) any consequential loss or damage for any reason whatsoever, whether or not the same is due to any breach of contract, negligence or any other fault on the part of either party, their servants, agents or sub-contractors.

17. Himalaya Clause
All exceptions, exemptions, defences, immunities, limitations of liability, indemnities, privileges and conditions granted or provided by this Agreement for the benefit of the Contractor or the Company shall also apply to and be for the benefit of their respective sub-contractors, operators, the Vessel's owners (if the Company is the demise/bareboat charterer), masters, officers and crews and to and be for the benefit of all bodies corporate parent of, subsidiary to, affiliated with or under the same management as either of them, as well as all directors, officers, servants and agents of the same and to and be for the benefit of all parties performing Services within the scope of this Agreement for or on behalf of the Contractor or the Company as servants, agents and sub-contractors of such parties. The Contractor or the Company shall be deemed to be acting as agent or trustee of and for the benefit of all such persons, entities and Vessels set forth above but only for the limited purpose of contracting for the extension of such benefits to such persons, bodies and Vessels.

18. Lien
Without prejudice to any other rights which the Contractor may have, whether *in rem* or *in personam*, the Contractor shall be entitled to exercise a possessory lien upon the Vessel in respect of any amount howsoever or whatsoever due to the Contractor under this Agreement and shall for the purpose of exercising such possessory lien be entitled to take and/or keep possession of the Vessel, provided always that the Company shall pay to the Contractor all reasonable costs and expenses howsoever or whatsoever incurred by or on behalf of the Contractor in exercising or attempting or preparing to exercise such lien.

19. Time for Suit
Any claim which may arise out of or in connection with this Agreement or any of the Services performed hereunder shall be notified to the party against whom such claim is made, within twelve (12) months of completion or termination of the Services hereunder, or within twelve (12) months of any claim by a third party, whichever is later. Any suit shall be brought within twelve (12) months of the notification to the party against whom the claim is made. If either of these conditions is not complied with, the claim and all rights whatsoever

WRECKHIRE 2010 - International Wreck Removal and Marine Services Agreement (Daily Hire)
PART II

and howsoever shall be absolutely barred and extinguished.

20. Expert Evaluation

(a) If the parties are unable to agree the alteration to costs or rates under Clause 4(a) or Clause 4(b) or the adjustment to the Daily Working Rate or the time lost under Clauses 7(a), 7(b) or 7(c), then either party may request an expert evaluation in accordance with the following procedure:

(i) The party seeking the evaluation shall propose three (3) experts from the persons currently on the Panel of Special Casualty Representatives maintained by the Salvage Arbitration Branch of the Corporation of Lloyd's to the other party in writing having checked that the proposed experts are available and willing to be appointed. The other party may select one of the proposed experts by responding in writing within twenty-four (24) hours. The party seeking the evaluation will then, as soon as possible (and in any event in less than twelve (12) hours) appoint the expert selected by the other party or, if none has been selected, one of the three (3) experts proposed (hereinafter "the Expert").

(ii) Both parties shall provide short written statements to the Expert setting out their arguments within forty-eight (48) hours of their acceptance of instructions and shall provide copies of their statement to the other party.

(iii) The Expert shall, within seventy-two (72) hours of receipt of written statements, advise the parties in writing of the alteration to costs and/or rates or of the adjustment to the Daily Working Rate or time lost. The Expert may also provide short reasons explaining the evaluation.

(iv) The Expert's rate of remuneration shall be the applicable rate plus bonus as set from time to time by the SCOPIC Committee for a Salvage Master. The costs of the Expert shall be paid by the party seeking the expert evaluation, but such party shall then be entitled to recover fifty per cent (50%) of the Expert's fees from the other party.

(b) If the Expert's evaluation is not agreed by both parties, the Company shall in any event make payments to the Contractor calculated in accordance with the evaluation. Such payments shall be on a provisional basis and without prejudice to the parties' rights to seek a determination in accordance with Clause 21 (Arbitration and Mediation).

21. Arbitration and Mediation

This Clause 21 applies to any dispute arising under this Agreement.

(a) *This Agreement shall be governed by and construed in accordance with English law and any dispute arising out of or in connection with this Agreement shall be referred to arbitration in London in accordance with the Arbitration Act 1996 or any statutory modification or re-enactment thereof save to the extent necessary to give effect to the provisions of this Clause.

The reference shall be to a sole arbitrator ("Arbitrator"), to be selected by the first party claiming arbitration from the persons currently on the Panel of Lloyd's Salvage Arbitrators with a right of appeal from an award made by the Arbitrator to either party by notice in writing to the other within twenty-eight (28) days of the date of publication of the original Arbitrator's Award.

The Arbitrator on appeal shall be the person currently acting as Lloyd's Appeal Arbitrator.

No suit shall be brought before another Tribunal, or in another jurisdiction, except that either party shall have the option to bring proceedings to obtain conservative seizure or other similar remedy against any assets owned by the other party in any state or jurisdiction where such assets may be found.

Both the Arbitrator and Appeal Arbitrator shall have the same powers as an Arbitrator and an Appeal Arbitrator under LOF 2000 or any standard revision thereof, including a power to order a payment on account of any monies due to the Contractor pending final determination of any dispute between the parties hereto.

In cases where neither the claim nor any counterclaim exceeds the sum of US$50,000 (or such other sum as the parties may agree) the arbitration shall be conducted in accordance with the LMAA Small Claims Procedure current at the time when the arbitration proceedings are commenced.

In cases where the claim or any counterclaim exceeds the sum agreed for the LMAA Small Claims Procedure and neither the claim nor any counterclaim exceeds the sum of US$400,000 (or such other sum as the parties may agree) the arbitration shall be conducted in accordance with the LMAA Intermediate Claims Procedure current at the time when the arbitration proceedings are commenced.

(b) *This Agreement shall be governed by and construed in accordance with Title 9 of the United States Code and the Maritime Law of the United States and any dispute arising out of or in connection with this Agreement shall be referred to three persons at New York, one to be appointed by each of the parties hereto, and the third by the two so chosen; their decision or that of any two of them shall be final, and for the purposes of enforcing any award, judgement may be entered on an award by any court of competent jurisdiction. The proceedings shall be conducted in accordance with the rules of the Society of Maritime Arbitrators, Inc.

WRECKHIRE 2010 - International Wreck Removal and Marine Services Agreement (Daily Hire)
PART II

In cases where neither the claim nor any counterclaim exceeds the sum of US$50,000 (or such other sum as the parties may agree) the arbitration shall be conducted in accordance with the Shortened Arbitration Procedure of the Society of Maritime Arbitrators, Inc. current at the time when the arbitration proceedings are commenced.

(c) *This Agreement shall be governed by and construed in accordance with the laws of the place mutually agreed by the parties and any dispute arising out of or in connection with this Agreement shall be referred to arbitration at a mutually agreed place, subject to the procedures applicable there.

(d) Notwithstanding 21(a), 21(b) or 21(c) above, the parties may agree at any time to refer to mediation any difference and/or dispute arising out of or in connection with this Agreement. In the case of a dispute in respect of which arbitration has been commenced under 21(a), 21(b) or 21(c) above, the following shall apply:

(i) Either party may at any time and from time to time elect to refer the dispute or part of the dispute to mediation by service on the other party of a written notice (the "Mediation Notice") calling on the other party to agree to mediation.

(ii) The other party shall thereupon within fourteen (14) calendar days of receipt of the Mediation Notice confirm that they agree to mediation, in which case the parties shall thereafter agree a mediator within a further fourteen (14) calendar days, failing which on the application of either party a mediator will be appointed promptly by the Arbitrator or such person as the Arbitrator may designate for that purpose. The mediation shall be conducted in such place and in accordance with such procedure and on such terms as the parties may agree or, in the event of disagreement, as may be set by the mediator.

(iii) If the other party does not agree to mediate, that fact may be brought to the attention of the Tribunal and may be taken into account by the Tribunal when allocating the costs of the arbitration as between the parties.

(iv) The mediation shall not affect the right of either party to seek such relief or take such steps as it considers necessary to protect its interest.

(v) Either party may advise the Arbitrator that they have agreed to mediation. The arbitration procedure shall continue during the conduct of the mediation but the Arbitrator may take the mediation timetable into account when setting the timetable for steps in the arbitration.

(vi) Unless otherwise agreed or specified in the mediation terms, each party shall bear its own costs incurred in the mediation and the parties shall share equally the mediator's costs and expenses.

(vii) The mediation process shall be without prejudice and confidential and no information or documents disclosed during it shall be revealed to the Arbitrator except to the extent that they are disclosable under the law and procedure governing the arbitration.

(Note: The parties should be aware that the mediation process may not necessarily interrupt time limits.)

(e) If Box 15 in PART I is not appropriately filled in, Sub-clause 21(a) of this Clause shall apply. Sub-clause 21(d) shall apply in all cases.

*Sub-clauses 21(a), 21(b) and 21(c) are alternatives; indicate alternative agreed in Box 15.

22. Notices Clause

(a) All notices given by either party or their agents to the other party or their agents in accordance with the provisions of this Agreement shall be in writing and shall, unless specifically provided in this Agreement to the contrary, be sent to the address for that other party as set out in Boxes 2 and 3 or as appropriate or to such other address as the other party may designate in writing.

A notice may be sent by registered or recorded mail, facsimile, electronically or delivered by hand in accordance with this Sub-clause 22(a).

(b) Any notice given under this Agreement shall take effect on receipt by the other party and shall be deemed to have been received:

(i) if posted, on the seventh (7th) day after posting;

(ii) if sent by facsimile or electronically, on the day of transmission; or

(iii) if delivered by hand, on the day of delivery.

And in each case proof of posting, handing in or transmission shall be proof that notice has been given, unless proven to the contrary.

WRECKHIRE 2010 - International Wreck Removal and Marine Services Agreement (Daily Hire)
PART II

23. Insurance

(a) The Contractor warrants that throughout the period of this Agreement it will maintain full cover against normal P&I risks including salvors' liabilities as evidenced by a Certificate of Entry issued by a P&I Club or insurer acceptable to the Company and shall comply with all the requirements of the policy.

(b) The Company warrants that throughout the period of this Agreement it will maintain full cover against normal P&I risks for the Vessel as evidenced by a Certificate of Entry issued by a P&I Club or insurer stated in Box 4(ix) and shall comply with all the requirements of the policy.

24. Pollution

(a) The Contractor shall exercise due care throughout the performance of the Services to prevent and minimise damage to the environment and shall also put in place, maintain and implement throughout the Services a pollution response plan which meets the requirements of the competent authorities and the Company Representative. The Contractor shall provide the Company with a copy of the pollution response plan on request by the Company.

(b) The Company shall indemnify and hold the Contractor harmless in respect of any and all consequences of any pollution which results from any discharge or escape of any pollutant from the Vessel except where such pollution arises as a consequence of the negligence of the Contractor, its sub-contractors, its agents and/or servants.

(c) The Contractor shall indemnify and hold the Company harmless in respect of any and all consequences of any pollution which results from any discharge or escape of any pollutant from its own or from hired-in craft.

25. Rotation and Replacement of Craft, Equipment and Personnel

The Contractor shall have the right to rotate and replace any craft, equipment and personnel with other suitable replacement craft, equipment and personnel subject to the approval of the Company Representative, which shall not be unreasonably withheld.

26. General Provisions

(a) Severability
If, in any legal proceedings, it is determined that any provision of this Agreement is unenforceable under applicable law, then the unenforceable provision shall automatically be amended to conform to that which is enforceable under the law. In any event, the validity or enforceability of any provision shall not affect any other provision of this Agreement, and this Agreement shall be construed and enforced as if such provision had not been included.

(b) Third Party Beneficiaries
Except as specifically provided for elsewhere in this Agreement, this Agreement shall not be construed to confer any benefit on any third party not a party to this Agreement nor shall this Agreement provide any rights to such third party to enforce any provision of this Agreement.

(c) Waiver
No benefit or right accruing to either party under this Agreement shall be waived unless the waiver is reduced to writing and signed by both the Contractor and the Company. The failure of either party to exercise any of its rights under this Agreement, including but not limited to either party's failure to comply with any time limit set out in this Agreement, shall in no way constitute a waiver of those rights, nor shall such failure excuse the other party from any of its obligations under this Agreement.

(d) Warranty of Authority
The Contractor and the Company each warrant and represent that the person whose signature appears in Part I above is its representative and is duly authorized to execute this Agreement as a binding commitment of such party.

(e) Singular/Plural
The singular includes the plural and vice versa as the context admits or requires.

(f) Headings
The headings to the clauses and appendices to this Agreement are for convenience only and shall not affect its construction or interpretation.

APPENDIX 8 WRECKFIXED 2010
Wreckfixed 2010*

Explanatory Notes for WRECKFIXED 2010 are available from BIMCO at www.bimco.org

BIMCO AND MARINE **INTERNATIONAL SALVAGE UNION**

WRECKFIXED 2010
INTERNATIONAL WRECK REMOVAL SERVICES AGREEMENT
(FIXED PRICE – "NO CURE, NO PAY")

PART I

First published 1999. Revised 2010
Approved by the International Salvage Union (ISU)

1. Place and Date of Agreement	
2. Contractor/Place of Business (Cl. 1)	3. Company/Place of Business (Cl. 1)

4. Vessel Specifications (Cl. 1, 2, 4)	
(i) Name	(ii) Flag
(iii) IMO Number	(iv) Place of Registry
(v) Length/Beam/Depth //	(vi) Maximum Draft
(vii) GT/NT/DWT //	(viii) Details and Nature of Cargo
(ix) P&I Club/insurer (Cl. 19(b))	(x) Any other Vessel details relevant to this Agreement

5. Condition of Vessel (Cl. 2, 4)	6. Position of Vessel and Condition of Worksite (Cl. 1, 2, 4)
7. Nature of Services (Cl. 1, 2, 4, 9(a)) (i) Nature of services: (ii) Compliance with orders of competent authorities (state party to obtain confirmation):	8. Place of Delivery and/or Disposal of Vessel (Cl. 8(a), 8(b), 8(e))
9. Payments (Cl. 4, 9(a)) Fixed Price (in figures and words)	10. Payment Details (Cl. 9(c)) (i) Currency (ii) Bank (iii) Address (iv) Account Number (v) Account Name
11. Time of Payment and Interest (state period within which sums must be received by the Contractor and rate of interest per month) (Cl. 9(e))	12. Cancellation Fee (Cl. 7(a))
13. Arbitration and Mediation (state Cl. 17(a), 17(b) or 17(c) of Cl. 17 as agreed; if 17(c) agreed, also state place of arbitration) (Cl. 17) (if not appropriately filled in, Clause 17(a) shall apply) (c) -	14. Number of Additional Clauses covering special provisions, if agreed

It is agreed that this Agreement shall be performed subject to the Terms and Conditions which consist of PART I, including Additional Clauses, if any agreed, and PART II, as well as Annex I (SCHEDULE OF PERSONNEL, CRAFT AND EQUIPMENT), Annex II (METHOD OF WORK AND ESTIMATED TIME SCHEDULE), and Annex III (CONTRACTOR'S DAILY REPORTS) or any other Annexes attached to this Agreement.

In the event of a conflict of terms and conditions, the provisions of PART I including Additional Clauses, if any agreed, shall prevail over those of PART II to the extent of such conflict but no further.

The undersigned warrant that they have full power and authority to sign this Agreement on behalf of the parties they represent.

Signature (for and on behalf of **the Contractor**)	Signature (for and on behalf of **the Company**)

continued

This document is a computer generated WRECKHIRE 2010 form printed by authority of BIMCO. Any insertion or deletion to the form must be clearly visible. In the event of any modification made to the pre-printed text of this document which is not clearly visible, the text of the original BIMCO approved document shall apply. BIMCO assumes no responsibility for any loss, damage or expense as a result of discrepancies between the original BIMCO approved document and this computer generated document.

* Reproduced by kind permission of BIMCO.

APPENDIX 8 WRECKFIXED 2010

Explanatory Notes for WRECKFIXED 2010 are available from BIMCO at www.bimco.org

ANNEX I (SCHEDULE OF PERSONNEL, CRAFT AND EQUIPMENT)
INTERNATIONAL WRECK REMOVAL AND MARINE SERVICES AGREEMENT (FIXED PRICE – "NO CURE, NO PAY")
CODE NAME: WRECKFIXED 2010

Dated:

Vessel:

Schedule of Personnel, Craft and Equipment (Cl. 2, 4 and 7)

continued

This document is a computer generated WRECKHIRE 2010 form printed by authority of BIMCO. Any insertion or deletion to the form must be clearly visible. In the event of any modification made to the pre-printed text of this document which is not clearly visible, the text of the original BIMCO approved document shall apply. BIMCO assumes no responsibility for any loss, damage or expense as a result of discrepancies between the original BIMCO approved document and this computer generated document.

APPENDIX 8 WRECKFIXED 2010

(contiuned)

PART I

ANNEX II (METHOD OF WORK AND ESTIMATED TIME SCHEDULE)
INTERNATIONAL WRECK REMOVAL AND MARINE SERVICES AGREEMENT (FIXED PRICE – "NO CURE, NO PAY")
CODE NAME: WRECKFIXED 2010

Dated:

Vessel:

Method of Work and Estimated Time Schedule (Cl. 2 and 4)

APPENDIX 8 WRECKFIXED 2010

(contiuned)   PART I

ANNEX III (CONTRACTOR'S DAILY REPORTS)
INTERNATIONAL WRECK REMOVAL AND MARINE SERVICES AGREEMENT (FIXED PRICE – "NO CURE, NO PAY")
CODE NAME: WRECKFIXED 2010

Date		Report no	

Status of wreck:

Vessel	
Cargo	
Bunkers	

Status of wreck site:

Weather on location:

	1200	2400	Forecast next 24 hours
Wind direction & speed (Bft)			
Swell direction & height (m)			
Wave Height & max wave height (m)			

Long range forecast (5 days):

Services:
- performed in last 24 hours:

- planned for next 24 hours:

Areas of concern:
Health & safety

Environmental

Other

Comments:
Contractor's Representative

Company's Representative

continued

This document is a computer generated WRECKHIRE 2010 form printed by authority of BIMCO. Any insertion or deletion to the form must be clearly visible. In the event of any modification made to the pre-printed text of this document which is not clearly visible, the text of the original BIMCO approved document shall apply. BIMCO assumes no responsibility for any loss, damage or expense as a result of discrepancies between the original BIMCO approved document and this computer generated document.

APPENDIX 8 WRECKFIXED 2010

(contiuned) PART I

Signed:			
Company's Representative			
Contractor's Representative			
	Name	Position	Signature

Contractor's Daily Reports (Cl. 2)

APPENDIX 8 WRECKFIXED 2010

WRECKFIXED 2010 - International Wreck Removal and Marine Services Agreement
(Fixed Price – "No Cure, No Pay")
PART II

1. Definitions
"Company" means the party stated in Box 3.
"Contractor" means the party stated in Box 2.
"Services" means the services stated in Box 7.
"Vessel" means any vessel, craft, property, or part thereof, of whatsoever nature, including anything contained therein or thereon, such as but not limited to cargo and bunkers, as described in Box 4.
"Worksite" means the position of the Vessel stated in Box 6.

2. The Services
The Contractor agrees to exercise due care in rendering the Services which shall include, if applicable, the delivery and/or disposal of the Vessel. Insofar as it is not inconsistent with the nature of the Services to be rendered under this Agreement, the Contractor will also exercise due care to prevent and minimise damage to the environment.

The Services shall be rendered under the principle of no cure, no pay.

The Contractor shall provide the Personnel, Craft and Equipment set out in Annex I of this Agreement which the Contractor deems necessary for the Services based upon the Specifications, Condition and Position of the Vessel and Worksite set out in Boxes 4, 5 and 6.

The Contractor's Method of Work and Estimated Time Schedule shall be as described in Annex II, utilising the Personnel, Craft and Equipment described in Annex I.

The Contractor shall consult with the Company if there is any need for substantial change in the Method of Work and/or Personnel, Craft or Equipment. In the event that time does not permit such consultation, or agreement to the proposed change(s) is unreasonably withheld, then the Contractor may proceed with such change(s), subject to any necessary approval of the authorities. (See Clause 4 (Change of Method of Work and/or Personnel, Craft and Equipment) hereof).

The Contractor shall provide the Company or the Company Representative, if in attendance, with daily reports in accordance with Annex III.

The party identified in Box 7(ii) of this Agreement shall be given all reasonable assistance by the other party in connection with obtaining confirmation from the competent authorities that the Company has complied with any orders issued by them.

3. Company Representative
If reasonably required by the Contractor a representative of the Company will be available during the performance of the Services with the full authority to act on behalf of the Company.

In addition, the Company will provide at its sole risk and expense sufficient officers or their equivalents, who are fully conversant with the cargo system and/or layout of the Vessel, and who should be in attendance when reasonably required during the performance of the Services in order to provide advice as and when requested by the Contractor.

4. Change of Method of Work and/or Personnel, Craft and Equipment
The Fixed Price stated in Box 9 is based upon the Nature of the Services, as set out in Box 7, Method of Work, and Personnel, Craft and Equipment, as set out in Annexes I and II, and the Description, Specifications, Position, Condition of the Vessel and the Worksite, as set out in Boxes 4, 5 and 6.

(a) If before or during the performance of the Services, and without fault on the part of the Contractor, there is a substantial change in the Services, and/or in the Personnel, Craft and Equipment required to undertake the Services due to any misdescription by the Company or error in the specification provided by the Company, upon which the Contractor has relied, or a material change in the position and/or condition of the Vessel or the Worksite:

(i) The Contractor shall forthwith give notice in writing thereof to the Company and of the estimated additional costs to effect the Services;

(ii) Any and all substantial changes to the nature of such Services which are agreed between the Contractor and the Company shall be drafted into a variation order by the Company, which shall be signed by the parties;

(iii) The parties shall, without delay, consult each other to reach agreement on the amount of the additional costs to be added to the Fixed Price and any agreement shall be incorporated into the variation order. In the event that the parties are unable to reach agreement on the additional costs within 5 days of the Contractor providing details of the extra costs, either party may terminate the Services under this Agreement, without prejudice to any claim the Contractor may have under this Sub-clause 4(a), provided always that such termination is permitted by the competent authorities. If permission to terminate is not given by the competent authorities, then the Contractor will continue to provide the Services set out in Box 7, without prejudice to his claim for additional remuneration.

(b) If, as a result of a material change in the position and/or condition of the Vessel or the Worksite, subsequent to entering into this Agreement, the Services become easier to perform in terms of the work and/or Personnel, Craft and/or Equipment requirements, then:

(i) The Company may, subject to the provisions of Clause 9(b) hereof, seek a reduction in respect of the monies payable pursuant to Clause 9(a) hereof;

(ii) All such material changes which are agreed by the Contractor and the Company shall be drafted into a variation order by the Company, which shall be signed by the parties;

(iii) The parties shall, without delay, consult each other to reach agreement on the amount of the costs to be deducted from the Fixed Price and any agreement shall be incorporated into the variation order.

1

WRECKFIXED 2010 - International Wreck Removal and Marine Services Agreement
(Fixed Price – "No Cure, No Pay")
PART II

(c) Alternatively either party may refer the matter to expert evaluation in accordance with Clause 16 (Expert Evaluation) or to arbitration or mediation pursuant to Clause 17 (Arbitration and Mediation) for a decision on the reasonableness and quantum of such costs, or the claim by the Company for a reduction in remuneration, which shall be incorporated into the variation order.

In the event the matter is referred either to expert evaluation or arbitration or mediation the Contractor will continue to provide the Services, without prejudice to any claim for an adjustment to the remuneration.

5. Miscellaneous

(a) The Company shall arrange and pay for any marking of the Vessel and cautioning required. The Contractor shall arrange and pay for any marking or cautioning required in respect of its own equipment during the Services under this Agreement.

(b) The Contractor may make reasonable use of the Vessel's machinery, gear, equipment, anchors, chains, stores and other appurtenances during and for the purposes of these Services free of expense but shall not unnecessarily damage, abandon or sacrifice the same or any property which is the subject of this Agreement.

(c) Subject to approval of the Company which shall not be unreasonably withheld, and subject to it being permitted by the competent authorities, the Contractor shall be entitled to remove, dispose of or jettison cargo, or parts of the Vessel, or equipment from the Vessel if such action is considered by the Contractor to be reasonably necessary to perform the Services under this Agreement.

(d) The Company will use its best endeavours to provide the Contractor with such plans and drawings of the Vessel, cargo manifests, stowage plans, etc., and such other information as the Contractor may reasonably require for the performance of the Services.

6. Permits

All necessary licences, approvals, authorisations or permits required to undertake and complete the Services without let or hindrance shall be obtained and maintained by the Contractor (see Clause 10(e)). The Company shall provide the Contractor with all reasonable assistance in connection with the obtaining of such licences, approvals, authorisations or permits.

7. Termination

(a) The Company may terminate this Agreement at any time prior to commencement of mobilisation of either the Personnel or the Craft or the Equipment identified in Annex I, whichever may be the first, upon payment of the Cancellation Fee set out in Box 12.

(b) The Contractor, with the agreement of the Company, which shall not be unreasonably withheld, may terminate this Agreement without any further liability if completion of the Services or any agreed change of work under Clause 4 (Change of Method of Work and/or Personnel, Craft and Equipment) hereof, utilising the Personnel, Craft and Equipment set out in Annex I, or any amendment thereto, becomes technically or physically impossible.

8. Delivery and/or Disposal

(a) If applicable, the Vessel shall be accepted forthwith and taken over by the Company or its duly authorised representative at the Place of Delivery indicated in Box 8. References to delivery or the Place of Delivery shall include disposal or the Place of Disposal, if applicable.

The Place of Delivery and/or Disposal shall always be safe and accessible for the Contractor's own or hired-in craft and the Vessel to enter and operate in and shall be a place where the Contractor is permitted by governmental or other authorities to deliver and/or dispose of the Vessel.

In the event the Vessel is not accepted forthwith by the Company all costs incurred by the Contractor from the moment of tender for delivery shall be for the account of the Company. However, in the event that delivery is prevented or delayed by action of governmental or other authorities, even if outside the control of the Contractor, all costs necessarily incurred by the Contractor from the moment of the tender for delivery shall be for the account of the Contractor.

(b) If it is considered by the Contractor to be impossible or unsafe for the Vessel to be delivered or disposed of at the place indicated in Box 8, and the Company is unable to nominate an acceptable alternative place, the Contractor is at liberty to deliver or dispose of the Vessel at the nearest place it can reach safely and without unreasonable delay, provided delivery or disposal at such place is permitted by governmental or other authorities, and such delivery or disposal shall be deemed due fulfilment by the Contractor of this Agreement.

(c) In the event the Vessel is delivered under the control of pumps and/or compressors or other equipment the Company shall with all due dispatch arrange for their own equipment and operators to replace the Contractor's equipment and operators.

Until such replacement the Company shall pay the Contractor for the use of its equipment and operators at reasonable rates as from the day of delivery until and including the day of arrival of the equipment and personnel at the Contractor's base, plus any additional costs relating thereto and incurred by the Contractor.

(d) If the Company fails, on completion of the Services, to take delivery of the Vessel within five (5) days of the Contractor tendering written notice of delivery or, if in the opinion of the Contractor the Vessel is likely to deteriorate, decay, become worthless or incur charges whether for storage or otherwise in excess of its value, the Contractor may, without prejudice to any other claims the Contractor may have against the Company, without notice and without any responsibility whatsoever attaching to the Contractor, sell or dispose of the Vessel and apply the proceeds of sale in reduction of the sums due to the Contractor from the Company under this Agreement. Any remaining proceeds will be refunded to the Company.

In the event that such sale or other disposal of the Vessel fails to raise sufficient net funds to pay the monies due to the Contractor under the terms of this Agreement then the Company shall remain liable to the Contractor for any such shortfall.

(e) Reference to delivery and/or disposal of the Vessel shall include parts of the Vessel and/or cargo and/or any other thing

APPENDIX 8 WRECKFIXED 2010

WRECKFIXED 2010 - International Wreck Removal and Marine Services Agreement
(Fixed Price – "No Cure, No Pay")
PART II

emanating from the Vessel and such delivery may take place at different times and different places (see Box 8).

9. Payment

(a) The Company shall pay the Contractor the Fixed Price set out in Box 9, which amount shall be due and payable upon completion of the Services as described in Box 7.

(b) All monies due and payable to the Contractor under this Agreement shall be paid without any discount, deduction, set-off, lien, claim or counterclaim.

(c) All payments to the Contractor shall be made in the currency and to the bank account stipulated in Box 10.

(d) If any amount payable under this Agreement has not been paid within seven (7) days of the due date, or if the security required in accordance with Clause 11 (Security) is not provided within five (5) banking days following the request by the Contractor, then at any time thereafter the Contractor shall be entitled to terminate this Agreement without prejudice to the sums already due to the Contractor and to any further rights or remedies which the Contractor may have against the Company, provided always that the Contractor shall give the Company at least three (3) working days' written notice of its intention to exercise this right.

(e) The Contractor shall promptly invoice the Company for all sums payable under this Agreement. If any sums which become due and payable are not actually received by the Contractor within the period specified in Box 11, they shall attract interest in accordance with the rate set out in Box 11.

10. Extra Costs

The follwing shall be paid by the Contractor as and when they fall due:

(a) all port expenses, pilotage charges, harbour and canal dues and all other expenses of a similar nature levied upon or payable in respect of the Vessel and the Contractor's own or hired-in craft;

(b) the costs of the services of any assisting tugs when reasonably deemed necessary by the Contractor or prescribed by port or other authorities;

(c) all costs in connection with clearance, agency fees, visas, guarantees and all other expenses of such kind;

(d) all taxes and social security charges, stamp duties, or other levies payable in respect of or in connection with this Agreement, any import - export dues and any customs or excise duties;

(e) all costs incurred in obtaining and maintaining licences, approvals, authorisations or permits required to undertake and complete the Services in accordance with Clause 6 (Permits);

(f) all costs incurred due to requirements of governmental or other authorities or unions over and above those costs which would otherwise be reasonably incurred by the Contractor in the execution of the Agreement.

11. Security

The Company shall provide on signing this Agreement an irrevocable and unconditional security in a form and amount as agreed between the parties.

If required by the Contractor and also in the event that initially no security is requested, the Company shall provide security or further security in a form and amount as agreed between the parties for all or part of any amount which may be or become due under this Agreement. Such security shall be given on one or more occasions as and when reasonably required by the Contractor.

12. Liabilities

(a) The Contractor will indemnify and hold the Company harmless in respect of any liability adjudged due or claim reasonably compromised arising out of injury or death occurring during the Services hereunder to any of the following persons:

(i) any servant, agent or sub-contractor of the Contractor;

(ii) any other person at or near the site of the operations for whatever purpose on behalf or at the request of the Contractor.

(b) The Company will indemnify and hold the Contractor harmless in respect of any liability adjudged due or claim reasonably compromised arising from injury or death occurring during the Services hereunder to any of the following persons:

(i) any servant, agent or sub-contractor of the Company;

(ii) any other person at or near the site of the operations for whatever purpose on behalf or at the request of the Company.

(c) Neither the Company nor its servants, agents or sub-contractors shall have any liability to the Contractor for loss or damage of whatsoever nature sustained by the Contractor's owned or hired-in craft or equipment (excluding portable salvage equipment, materials or stores which are reasonably sacrificed during the disposal or other operations on the Vessel), whether or not the same is due to breach of contract, negligence or any other fault on the part of the Company, its servants, agents or sub-contractors.

(d) Neither the Contractor nor its servants, agents or sub-contractors shall have any liability to the Company for loss or damage of whatsoever nature sustained by the Vessel, whether or not the same is due to breach of contract, negligence or any other fault on the part of the Contractor, its servants, agents or sub-contractors.

APPENDIX 8 WRECKFIXED 2010

WRECKFIXED 2010 - International Wreck Removal and Marine Services Agreement
(Fixed Price – "No Cure, No Pay")
PART II

(e) Neither party shall be liable to the other party for:

(i) any loss of profit, loss of use or loss of production whatsoever and whether arising directly or indirectly from the performance or non-performance of this Agreement, and whether or not the same is due to negligence or any other fault on the part of either party, their servants, agents or sub-contractors; or

(ii) any consequential loss or damage for any reason whatsoever, whether or not the same is due to any breach of contract, negligence or any other fault on the part of either party, their servants, agents or sub-contractors.

13. Himalaya Clause
All exceptions, exemptions, defences, immunities, limitations of liability, indemnities, privileges and conditions granted or provided by this Agreement for the benefit of the Contractor or the Company shall also apply to and be for the benefit of their respective sub-contractors, operators, the Vessel's owners (if the Company is the demise/bareboat charterer), masters, officers and crews and to and be for the benefit of all bodies corporate parent of, subsidiary to, affiliated with or under the same management as either of them, as well as all directors, officers, servants and agents of the same and to and be for the benefit of all parties performing Services within the scope of this Agreement for or on behalf of the Contractor or the Company as servants, agents and sub-contractors of such parties. The Contractor or the Company shall be deemed to be acting as agent or trustee of and for the benefit of all such persons, entities and Vessels set forth above but only for the limited purpose of contracting for the extension of such benefits to such persons, bodies and Vessels.

14. Lien
Without prejudice to any other rights which the Contractor may have, whether *in rem* or *in personam*, the Contractor shall be entitled to exercise a possessory lien upon the Vessel in respect of any amount howsoever or whatsoever due to the Contractor under this Agreement and shall for the purpose of exercising such possessory lien be entitled to take and/or keep possession of the Vessel, provided always that the Company shall pay to the Contractor all reasonable costs and expenses howsoever or whatsoever incurred by or on behalf of the Contractor in exercising or attempting or preparing to exercise such lien.

15. Time for Suit
Any claim which may arise out of or in connection with this Agreement or any of the Services performed hereunder shall be notified to the party against whom such claim is made, within twelve (12) months of completion or termination of the Services hereunder, or within twelve (12) months of any claim by a third party, whichever is later. Any suit shall be brought within twelve (12) months of the notification to the party against whom the claim is made. If either of these conditions is not complied with, the claim and all rights whatsoever and howsoever shall be absolutely barred and extinguished.

16. Expert Evaluation
(a) If the parties are unable to agree the alteration to costs under Clause 4(a) or Clause 4(b), then either party may request an expert evaluation in accordance with the following procedure:

(i) The party seeking the evaluation shall propose three (3) experts from the persons currently on the Panel of Special Casualty Representatives maintained by the Salvage Arbitration Branch of the Corporation of Lloyd's to the other party in writing having checked that the proposed experts are available and willing to be appointed. The other party may select one of the proposed experts by responding in writing within twenty-four (24) hours. The party seeking the evaluation will then, as soon as possible (and in any event in less than twelve (12) hours) appoint the expert selected by the other party or, if none has been selected, one of the three (3) experts proposed (hereinafter "the Expert").

(ii) Both parties shall provide short written statements to the Expert setting out their arguments within forty-eight (48) hours of their acceptance of instructions and shall provide copies of their statement to the other party.

(iii) The Expert shall, within seventy-two (72) hours of receipt of written statements, advise the parties in writing of the alteration to costs. The Expert may also provide short reasons explaining the evaluation.

(iv) The Expert's rate of remuneration shall be the applicable rate plus bonus as set from time to time by the SCOPIC Committee for a Salvage Master. The costs of the Expert shall be paid by the party seeking the expert evaluation, but such party shall then be entitled to recover fifty per cent (50%) of the Expert's fees from the other party.

(b) If the Expert's evaluation is not agreed by both parties, the Company shall in any event make payments to the Contractor calculated in accordance with the evaluation. Such payments shall be on a provisional basis and without prejudice to the parties' rights to seek a determination in accordance with Clause 17 (Arbitration and Mediation).

17. Arbitration and Mediation
This Clause 17 applies to any dispute arising under this Agreement.

(a) *This Agreement shall be governed by and construed in accordance with English law and any dispute arising out of or in connection with this Agreement shall be referred to arbitration in London in accordance with the Arbitration Act 1996 or any statutory modification or re-enactment thereof save to the extent necessary to give effect to the provisions of this Clause.

The reference shall be to a sole arbitrator ("Arbitrator"), to be selected by the first party claiming arbitration from the persons currently on the Panel of Lloyd's Salvage Arbitrators with a right of appeal from an award made by the Arbitrator to either party by notice in writing to the other within twenty-eight (28) days of the date of publication of the original Arbitrator's Award.

The Arbitrator on appeal shall be the person currently acting as Lloyd's Appeal Arbitrator.

No suit shall be brought before another Tribunal, or in another jurisdiction, except that either party shall have the option to bring proceedings to obtain conservative seizure or other similar remedy against any assets owned by the other party in any state or jurisdiction where such assets may be found.

Both the Arbitrator and Appeal Arbitrator shall have the same powers as an Arbitrator and an Appeal Arbitrator under LOF

APPENDIX 8 WRECKFIXED 2010

WRECKFIXED 2010 - International Wreck Removal and Marine Services Agreement
(Fixed Price – "No Cure, No Pay")
PART II

2000 or any standard revision thereof, including a power to order a payment on account of any monies due to the Contractor pending final determination of any dispute between the parties hereto.

In cases where neither the claim nor any counterclaim exceeds the sum of US$50,000 (or such other sum as the parties may agree) the arbitration shall be conducted in accordance with the LMAA Small Claims Procedure current at the time when the arbitration proceedings are commenced.

In cases where the claim or any counterclaim exceeds the sum agreed for the LMAA Small Claims Procedure and neither the claim nor any counterclaim exceeds the sum of US$400,000 (or such other sum as the parties may agree) the arbitration shall be conducted in accordance with the LMAA Intermediate Claims Procedure current at the time when the arbitration proceedings are commenced.

(b) *This Agreement shall be governed by and construed in accordance with Title 9 of the United States Code and the Maritime Law of the United States and any dispute arising out of or in connection with this Agreement shall be referred to three persons at New York, one to be appointed by each of the parties hereto, and the third by the two so chosen; their decision or that of any two of them shall be final, and for the purposes of enforcing any award, judgement may be entered on an award by any court of competent jurisdiction. The proceedings shall be conducted in accordance with the rules of the Society of Maritime Arbitrators, Inc.

In cases where neither the claim nor any counterclaim exceeds the sum of US$50,000 (or such other sum as the parties may agree) the arbitration shall be conducted in accordance with the Shortened Arbitration Procedure of the Society of Maritime Arbitrators, Inc. current at the time when the arbitration proceedings are commenced.

(c) *This Agreement shall be governed by and construed in accordance with the laws of the place mutually agreed by the parties and any dispute arising out of or in connection with this Agreement shall be referred to arbitration at a mutually agreed place, subject to the procedures applicable there.

(d) Notwithstanding 17(a), 17(b) or 17(c) above, the parties may agree at any time to refer to mediation any difference and/or dispute arising out of or in connection with this Agreement. In the case of a dispute in respect of which arbitration has been commenced under 17(a), 17(b) or 17(c) above, the following shall apply:

(i) Either party may at any time and from time to time elect to refer the dispute or part of the dispute to mediation by service on the other party of a written notice (the "Mediation Notice") calling on the other party to agree to mediation.

(ii) The other party shall thereupon within fourteen (14) calendar days of receipt of the Mediation Notice confirm that they agree to mediation, in which case the parties shall thereafter agree a mediator within a further fourteen (14) calendar days, failing which on the application of either party a mediator will be appointed promptly by the Arbitrator or such person as the Arbitrator may designate for that purpose. The mediation shall be conducted in such place and in accordance with such procedure and on such terms as the parties may agree or, in the event of disagreement, as may be set by the mediator.

(iii) If the other party does not agree to mediate, that fact may be brought to the attention of the Tribunal and may be taken into account by the Tribunal when allocating the costs of the arbitration as between the parties.

(iv) The mediation shall not affect the right of either party to seek such relief or take such steps as it considers necessary to protect its interest.

(v) Either party may advise the Arbitrator that they have agreed to mediation. The arbitration procedure shall continue during the conduct of the mediation but the Arbitrator may take the mediation timetable into account when setting the timetable for steps in the arbitration.

(vi) Unless otherwise agreed or specified in the mediation terms, each party shall bear its own costs incurred in the mediation and the parties shall share equally the mediator's costs and expenses.

(vii) The mediation process shall be without prejudice and confidential and no information or documents disclosed during it shall be revealed to the Arbitrator except to the extent that they are disclosable under the law and procedure governing the arbitration.

(Note: The parties should be aware that the mediation process may not necessarily interrupt time limits.)

(e) If Box 13 in PART I is not appropriately filled in, Sub-clause 17(a) of this Clause shall apply Sub-clause 17(d) shall apply in all cases.

*Sub-clauses 17(a), 17(b) and 17(c) are alternatives; indicate alternative agreed in Box 13.

18. Notices Clause
(a) All notices given by either party or their agents to the other party or their agents in accordance with the provisions of this Agreement shall be in writing and shall, unless specifically provided in this Agreement to the contrary, be sent to the address for that other party as set out in Boxes 2 and 3 or as appropriate or to such other address as the other party may designate in writing.

A notice may be sent by registered or recorded mail, facsimile, electronically or delivered by hand in accordance with this Sub-clause 18(a).

(b) Any notice given under this Agreement shall take effect on receipt by the other party and shall be deemed to have been received:

APPENDIX 8 WRECKFIXED 2010

WRECKFIXED 2010 - International Wreck Removal and Marine Services Agreement
(Fixed Price – "No Cure, No Pay")
PART II

(i) if posted, on the seventh (7th) day after posting;

(ii) if sent by facsimile or electronically, on the day of transmission; or

(iii) if delivered by hand, on the day of delivery.

And in each case proof of posting, handing in or transmission shall be proof that notice has been given, unless proven to the contrary.

19. Insurance
(a) The Contractor warrants that throughout the period of this Agreement it will maintain full cover against normal P&I risks including salvors' liabilities as evidenced by a Certificate of Entry issued by a P&I Club or insurer acceptable to the Company and shall comply with all the requirements of the policy.

(b) The Company warrants that throughout the period of this Agreement it will maintain full cover against normal P&I risks for the Vessel as evidenced by a Certificate of Entry issued by a P&I Club or insurer stated in Box 4(ix) and shall comply with all the requirements of the policy.

20. Pollution
(a) The Contractor shall exercise due care throughout the performance of the Services to prevent and minimise damage to the environment and shall also put in place, maintain and implement throughout the Services a pollution response plan which meets the requirements of the competent authorities and the Company, or the Company Representative if applicable. The Contractor shall provide the Company with a copy of the pollution response plan on request by the Company.

(b) The Company shall indemnify and hold the Contractor harmless in respect of any and all consequences of any pollution which results from any discharge or escape of any pollutant from the Vessel except where such pollution arises as a consequence of the negligence of the Contractor, its sub-contractors, its agents and/or servants.

(c) The Contractor shall indemnify and hold the Company harmless in respect of any and all consequences of any pollution which results from any discharge or escape of any pollutant from its own or from hired-in craft.

21. Rotation and Replacement of Craft, Equipment and Personal
The Contractor shall have the right to rotate and replace any craft, equipment and personnel with other suitable replacement craft, equipment and personnel subject to the approval of the Company, or the Company Representative if applicable, which shall not be unreasonably withheld.

22. General Provisions
(a) Severability
If, in any legal proceedings, it is determined that any provision of this Agreement is unenforceable under applicable law, then the unenforceable provision shall automatically be amended to conform to that which is enforceable under the law. In any event, the validity or enforceability of any provision shall not affect any other provision of this Agreement, and this Agreement shall be construed and enforced as if such provision had not been included.

(b) Third Party Beneficiaries
Except as specifically provided for elsewhere in this Agreement, this Agreement shall not be construed to confer any benefit on any third party not a party to this Agreement nor shall this Agreement provide any rights to such third party to enforce any provision of this Agreement.

(c) Waiver
No benefit or right accruing to either party under this Agreement shall be waived unless the waiver is reduced to writing and signed by both the Contractor and the Company. The failure of either party to exercise any of its rights under this Agreement, including but not limited to either party's failure to comply with any time limit set out in this Agreement, shall in no way constitute a waiver of those rights, nor shall such failure excuse the other party from any of its obligations under this Agreement.

(d) Warranty of Authority
The Contractor and the Company each warrant and represent that the person whose signature appears in Part I above is its representative and is duly authorized to execute this Agreement as a binding commitment of such party.

(e) Singular/Plural
The singular includes the plural and vice versa as the context admits or requires.

(f) Headings
The headings to the clauses and appendices to this Agreement are for convenience only and shall not affect its construction or interpretation.

APPENDIX 9: WRECKSTAGE 2010

Wreckstage 2010*

Explanatory Notes for WRECKSTAGE 2010 are available from BIMCO at www.bimco.org

BIMCO / **ISU INTERNATIONAL SALVAGE UNION**

WRECKSTAGE 2010
INTERNATIONAL WRECK REMOVAL AND MARINE SERVICES AGREEMENT
(LUMP SUM – STAGE PAYMENTS)

PART I

First published 1993. Revised 1999 and 2010
Approved by the International Salvage Union (ISU)

1. Place and Date of Agreement	
2. Contractor/Place of Business (Cl. 1)	3. Company/Place of Business (Cl. 1)

4. Vessel Specifications (Cl. 1, 2, 4)

(i) Name	(ii) Flag
(iii) IMO Number	(iv) Place of Registry
(v) Length/Beam/Depth //	(vi) Maximum Draft
(vii) GT/NT/DWT //	(viii) Details and Nature of Cargo
(ix) P&I Club/insurer (Cl. 20(b))	(x) Any other Vessel details relevant to this Agreement

5. Condition of Vessel (Cl. 2, 4)	6. Position of Vessel and Condition of Worksite (Cl. 1, 2, 4)
7. Nature of Services (Cl. 1, 2, 4) (i) Nature of services: (ii) Compliance with orders of competent authorities (state party to obtain confirmation):	8. Place of Delivery and/or Disposal of Vessel (Cl. 9(a), 9(b), 9(e))

9. Payments (Cl. 4, 8(b), 10(a), 10(b))

(i) Lump Sum (in figures and words)	(ii) Amount due and payable on signing this Agreement
	(iii) Amount due and payable on
(iv) Amount due and payable on	(v) Amount due and payable on
(vi) Amount due and payable on	(vii) Amount due and payable on

10. Payment Details (Cl. 10(d))

(i) Currency	
(ii) Bank	(iii) Address
(iv) Account Number	(v) Account Name

continued

This document is a computer generated WRECKSTAGE 2010 form printed by authority of BIMCO. Any insertion or deletion to the form must be clearly visible. In the event of any modification made to the pre-printed text of this document which is not clearly visible, the text of the original BIMCO approved document shall prevail. BIMCO assumes no responsibility for any loss, damage or expense as a result of discrepancies between the original BIMCO approved document and this computer generated document.

* Reproduced by kind permission of BIMCO.

APPENDIX 9 WRECKSTAGE 2010

(continued)   PART I

11. Time of Payment and Interest (state period within which sums must be received by the Contractor and rate of interest per month) (Cl. 10(f))	12. Extra Costs (state percentage to be applied) (Cl. 4(a)(iii), 8(b), 11, 13(c))
	(i) Contractor shall be responsible for and pay for the following extra costs
	(ii) Company shall be responsible for and pay for the following extra costs
	(iii) Handling Charge to be applied, where applicable (state percentage)
13. Delay Payment Rate (Cl. 4(a)(iii), 7, 8(b), 8(c), 9(a), 9(b))	14. Cancellation Fee (Cl. 4(a)(iii), 8(a))
15. Number of Unworkable Days due to Adverse Weather or Sea Conditions (Cl. 7(a))	16. Number of Additional Clauses covering special provisions, if agreed
17. Arbitration and Mediation (state Cl. 18(a), 18(b) or 18(c) of Cl. 18 as agreed; if 18(c) agreed, also state place of arbitration) (Cl. 18) (if not appropriately filled in, Clause 18(a) shall apply) (c) -	

It is agreed that this Agreement shall be performed subject to the Terms and Conditions which consist of PART I, including Additional Clauses, if any agreed, and PART II, as well as Annex I (SCHEDULE OF PERSONNEL, CRAFT AND EQUIPMENT), Annex II (METHOD OF WORK AND ESTIMATED TIME SCHEDULE), and Annex III (CONTRACTOR'S DAILY REPORTS) or any other Annexes attached to this Agreement.

In the event of a conflict of terms and conditions, the provisions of PART I including Additional Clauses, if any agreed, shall prevail over those of PART II to the extent of such conflict but no further.

The undersigned warrant that they have full power and authority to sign this Agreement on behalf of the parties they represent.

Signature (for and on behalf of **the Contractor**)	Signature (for and on behalf of **the Company**)

continued

This document is a computer generated WRECKSTAGE 2010 form printed by authority of BIMCO. Any insertion or deletion to the form must be clearly visible. In the event of any modification made to the pre-printed text of this document which is not clearly visible, the text of the original BIMCO approved document shall apply. BIMCO assumes no responsibility for any loss, damage or expense as a result of discrepancies between the original BIMCO approved document and this computer generated document.

APPENDIX 9 WRECKSTAGE 2010

(continued) PART I

ANNEX I (SCHEDULE OF PERSONNEL, CRAFT AND EQUIPMENT)
INTERNATIONAL WRECK REMOVAL AND MARINE SERVICES AGREEMENT (LUMP SUM – STAGE PAYMENTS)
CODE NAME: WRECKSTAGE 2010

Dated:

Vessel:

Schedule of Personnel, Craft and Equipment (Cl. 2, 4 and 8)

continued

This document is a computer generated WRECKSTAGE 2010 form printed by authority of BIMCO. Any insertion or deletion to the form must be clearly visible. In the event of any modification made to the pre-printed text of this document which is not clearly visible, the text of the original BIMCO approved document shall apply. BIMCO assumes no responsibility for any loss, damage or expense as a result of discrepancies between the original BIMCO approved document and this computer generated document.

APPENDIX 9 WRECKSTAGE 2010

(continued)   PART I

ANNEX II (METHOD OF WORK AND ESTIMATED TIME SCHEDULE)
INTERNATIONAL WRECK REMOVAL AND MARINE SERVICES AGREEMENT (LUMP SUM – STAGE PAYMENTS)
CODE NAME: WRECKSTAGE 2010

Dated:

Vessel:

Method of Work and Estimated Time Schedule (Cl. 2 and 4)

continued

This document is a computer generated WRECKSTAGE 2010 form printed by authority of BIMCO. Any insertion or deletion to the form must be clearly visible. In the event of any modification made to the pre-printed text of this document which is not clearly visible, the text of the original BIMCO approved document shall apply. BIMCO assumes no responsibility for any loss, damage or expense as a result of discrepancies between the original BIMCO approved document and this computer generated document.

APPENDIX 9 WRECKSTAGE 2010

(continued) PART I

ANNEX III (CONTRACTOR'S DAILY REPORTS)
INTERNATIONAL WRECK REMOVAL AND MARINE SERVICES AGREEMENT (LUMP SUM – STAGE PAYMENTS)
CODE NAME: WRECKSTAGE 2010

Date		Report no	
Status of wreck:			
Vessel			
Cargo			
Bunkers			
Status of wreck site:			

Weather on location:	1200	2400	Forecast next 24 hours
Wind direction & speed (Bft)			
Swell direction & height (m)			
Wave Height & max wave height (m)			

Long range forecast (5 days):

Services:
- performed in last 24 hours:

- planned for next 24 hours:

Areas of concern:
Health & safety

Environmental

Other

Comments:

continued

This document is a computer generated WRECKSTAGE 2010 form printed by authority of BIMCO. Any insertion or deletion to the form must be clearly visible. In the event of any modification made to the pre-printed text of this document which is not clearly visible, the text of the original BIMCO approved document shall apply. BIMCO assumes no responsibility for any loss, damage or expense as a result of discrepancies between the original BIMCO approved document and this computer generated document.

APPENDIX 9 WRECKSTAGE 2010

(continued)   PART I

Contractor's Representative

Company's Representative

Signed:			
Company's Representative			
Contractor's Representative			
	Name	Position	Signature

Contractor's Daily Reports (Cl. 2)

APPENDIX 9 WRECKSTAGE 2010

WRECKSTAGE 2010 - International Wreck Removal and Marine Services Agreement
(Lump Sum-Stage Payments)
PART II

1. Definitions
"Company" means the party stated in Box 3.
"Contractor" means the party stated in Box 2.
"Services" means the services stated in Box 7.
"Vessel" means any vessel, craft, property, or part thereof, of whatsoever nature, including anything contained therein or thereon, such as but not limited to cargo and bunkers, as described in Box 4.
"Worksite" means the position of the Vessel stated in Box 6.

2. The Services
The Contractor agrees to exercise due care in rendering the Services which shall include, if applicable, the delivery and/or disposal of the Vessel. Insofar as it is not inconsistent with the nature of the Services to be rendered under this Agreement, the Contractor will also exercise due care to prevent and minimise damage to the environment.

The Contractor shall provide the Personnel, Craft and Equipment set out in Annex I of this Agreement which the Contractor deems necessary for the Services based upon the Specifications, Condition and Position of the Vessel and Worksite set out in Boxes 4, 5 and 6.

The Contractor's Method of Work and Estimated Time Schedule shall be as described in Annex II, utilising the Personnel, Craft and Equipment described in Annex I.

The Contractor shall consult with the Company if there is any need for substantial change in the Method of Work and/or Personnel, Craft or Equipment. In the event that time does not permit such consultation, or agreement to the proposed change(s) is unreasonably withheld, then the Contractor may proceed with such change(s). (See Clause 4 (Change of Method of Work and/or Personnel, Craft and Equipment) hereof).

The Contractor shall provide the Company or the Company Representative, if in attendance, with daily reports in accordance with Annex III.

The party identified in Box 7(ii) of this Agreement shall be given all reasonable assistance by the other party in connection with obtaining confirmation from the competent authorities that the Company has complied with any orders issued by them.

3. Company Representative
If reasonably required by the Contractor a representative of the Company will be available during the performance of the Services with the full authority to act on behalf of the Company.

In addition, the Company will provide at its sole risk and expense sufficient officers or their equivalents, who are fully conversant with the cargo system and/or layout of the Vessel, and who should be in attendance when reasonably required during the performance of the Services in order to provide advice as and when requested by the Contractor.

4. Change of Method of Work and/or Personnel, Craft and Equipment
The Lump Sum stated in Box 9 is based upon the Nature of the Services, as set out in Box 7, Method of Work, and Personnel, Craft and Equipment, as set out in Annexes I and II, and the Description, Specifications, Position, Condition of the Vessel and the Worksite, as set out in Boxes 4, 5 and 6.

(a) If before or during the performance of the Services, and without fault on the part of the Contractor, there is a substantial change in the Services, and/or in the Personnel, Craft and Equipment required to undertake the Services due to any misdescription by the Company or error in the specification provided by the Company, upon which the Contractor has relied, or a material change in the position and/or condition of the Vessel or the Worksite:

(i) The Contractor shall forthwith give notice in writing thereof to the Company and of the estimated additional costs to effect the Services;

(ii) Any and all substantial changes to the nature of such Services which are agreed between the Contractor and the Company shall be drafted into a variation order by the Company, which shall be signed by the parties;

(iii) The parties shall, without delay, consult each other to reach agreement on the amount of the additional costs to be added to the Lump Sum and any agreement shall be incorporated into the variation order. In the event that the parties are unable to reach agreement on the additional costs within 5 days of the Contractor providing details of the extra costs, either party may terminate the Services under this Agreement, without prejudice to any claim the Contractor may have under this Sub-clause 4(a), provided always that such termination is permitted by the competent authorities. In such event the Contractor is entitled to be paid all sums due at the time of termination in accordance with the provisions of Boxes 9, 12, 13 and 14. If permission to terminate is not given by the competent authorities the Contractor shall be paid by the Company at the Delay Payment Rate set out in Box 13 during any standby period, and the Company shall be

APPENDIX 9 WRECKSTAGE 2010

WRECKSTAGE 2010 - International Wreck Removal and Marine Services Agreement
(Lump Sum-Stage Payments)
PART II

liable for the Contractor's reasonable and necessary costs of continuing with the Services.

(b) If, as a result of a material change in the position and/or condition of the Vessel or the Worksite, subsequent to entering into this Agreement, the Services become easier to perform in terms of the work and/or Personnel, Craft and/or Equipment requirements, then:

(i) The Company may, subject to the provisions of Clause 10(c) hereof, seek a reduction in respect of the monies payable pursuant to Clause 10(a) hereof;

(ii) All such material changes which are agreed by the Contractor and the Company shall be drafted into a variation order by the Company, which shall be signed by the parties;

(iii) The parties shall, without delay, consult each other to reach agreement on the amount of the costs to be deducted from the Lump Sum and any agreement shall be incorporated into the variation order.

(c) Alternatively either party may refer the matter to expert evaluation in accordance with Clause 17 (Expert Evaluation) or to arbitration or mediation pursuant to Clause 18 (Arbitration and Mediation) for a decision on the reasonableness and quantum of such costs, or the claim by the Company for a reduction in remuneration, which shall be incorporated into the variation order.

In the event the matter is referred either to expert evaluation or arbitration or mediation the Contractor will continue to provide the Services, without prejudice to any claim for an adjustment to the remuneration.

5. Miscellaneous
(a) The Company shall arrange and pay for any marking of the Vessel and cautioning required. The Contractor shall arrange and pay for any marking or cautioning required in respect of its own equipment during the Services under this Agreement.

(b) The Contractor may make reasonable use of Vessel's machinery, gear, equipment, anchors, chains, stores and other appurtenances during and for the purposes of these Services free of expense but shall not unnecessarily damage, abandon or sacrifice the same or any property which is the subject of this Agreement.

(c) Subject to approval of the Company which shall not be unreasonably withheld, and subject to it being permitted by the competent authorities, the Contractor shall be entitled to remove, dispose of or jettison cargo, or parts of the Vessel, or equipment from the Vessel if such action is considered by the Contractor to be reasonably necessary to perform the Services under this Agreement.

(d) The Company will use its best endeavours to provide the Contractor with such plans and drawings of the Vessel, cargo manifests, stowage plans, etc., and such other information as the Contractor may reasonably require for the performance of the Services.

6. Permits
All necessary licences, approvals, authorisations or permits required to undertake and complete the Services without let or hindrance shall be obtained and maintained by the Contractor (see Clause 11(e)). The Company shall provide the Contractor with all reasonable assistance in connection with the obtaining of such licences, approvals, authorisations or permits.

7. Delays
(a) Adverse Weather and Other Delays
In the event that the Contractor is prevented from progressing the Services due to adverse weather or sea conditions in excess of the number of days set out in Box 15, or due to any other reason outside the Contractor's control, the Contractor shall receive from the Company additional compensation – per working day or pro rata – at the rate set out in Box 13, for the time the Contractor is delayed in commencing or continuing the Services with the customary progress.

(b) Contractor's Equipment and/or Personnel
If there is a breakdown of any of the Contractor's equipment or non-availability of personnel, the Contractor shall consult the Company, or the Company Representative if applicable, to reach agreement on the amount of time lost as a result, if any. The Delay Payment Rate shall apply for the agreed period.

(c) Hired-in Equipment and/or Personnel
The Contractor shall use its best efforts to ensure that an appropriate Delay Payment Rate is agreed in any sub-contract agreement in the event of breakdown of their equipment or non-availability of their personnel. If there is a breakdown of equipment or non-availability of personnel, the Contractor shall consult the Company, or the Company Representative if applicable, to reach agreement on the amount of time lost as a result, if any. The sub-contract Delay Payment Rate shall only apply for the agreed period if such Delay Payment Rate has been agreed with sub-contractors. The Contractor shall pass on to the Company the benefit of any off-hire or reduction

APPENDIX 9 WRECKSTAGE 2010

WRECKSTAGE 2010 - International Wreck Removal and Marine Services Agreement
(Lump Sum-Stage Payments)
PART II

in the rate of hire in respect of equipment or personnel hired-in by the Contractor.

(d) The Contractor shall promptly advise the Company, or the Company Representative if applicable, of all periods when they consider that the Delay Payment Rate shall apply and shall at the same time confirm same in writing to the Company, or the Company Representative if applicable.

(e) Sub-clauses 7(b) and 7(c) shall not apply for individual delays unless such delays exceed six (6) consecutive hours when the Delay Payment Rate shall apply to the whole agreed delay period.

(f) In the event that the parties cannot reach agreement in respect of the applicable reductions in Sub-clauses 7(a), 7(b) or 7(c) above to the Delay Payment Rate or the duration of such reduction, then the issue may be referred to expert evaluation in accordance with Clause 17 (Expert Evaluation) or to arbitration or mediation pursuant to Clause 18 (Arbitration and Mediation).

8. Termination

(a) The Company may terminate this Agreement at any time prior to commencement of mobilisation of either the Personnel or the Craft or the Equipment identified in Annex I, whichever may be the first, upon payment of the Cancellation Fee set out in Box 14.

(b) The Contractor, with the agreement of the Company, which shall not be unreasonably withheld, may terminate this Agreement without any further liability if completion of the Services or any agreed change of work under Clause 4 (Change of Method of Work and/or Personnel, Craft and Equipment) hereof, utilising the Personnel, Craft and Equipment set out in Annex I, or any amendment thereto, becomes technically or physically impossible. In the event of such termination, the Contractor shall be entitled to payment of all monies due in accordance with the provisions of Boxes 9, 12 and 13.

(c) If permission to terminate is not given by the competent authorities, the Contractor shall be paid by the Company at the Delay Payment Rate set out in Box 13 for Personnel, Craft and Equipment during any standby period, and the Company shall be liable for the Contractor's reasonable and necessary costs of continuing with the Services

9. Delivery and/or Disposal

(a) If applicable, the Vessel shall be accepted forthwith and taken over by the Company or its duly authorised representative at the Place of Delivery indicated in Box 8. References to delivery or the Place of Delivery shall include disposal or the Place of Disposal, if applicable.

The Place of Delivery and/or Disposal shall always be safe and accessible for the Contractor's own or hired-in craft and the Vessel to enter and operate in and shall be a place where the Contractor is permitted by governmental or other authorities to deliver and/or dispose of the Vessel.

In the event the Vessel is not accepted forthwith by the Company or delivery is prevented or delayed by action of governmental or other authorities outside the control of the Contractor, all costs necessarily incurred by the Contractor from the moment of the tender for delivery shall be for the account of the Company.

These costs shall be in addition to any delay payment as set out in Box 13.

(b) If it is considered by the Contractor to be impossible or unsafe for the Vessel to be delivered or disposed of at the place indicated in Box 8 and the Company is unable to nominate an acceptable alternative place, the Contractor is at liberty to deliver or dispose of the Vessel at the nearest place it can reach safely and without unreasonable delay, provided delivery or disposal at such place is permitted by governmental or other authorities, and such delivery or disposal shall be deemed due fulfilment by the Contractor of this Agreement.

The Company shall reimburse the Contractor for any additional time used pursuant to this Sub-clause 9(b) at the Delay Payment Rate set out in Box 13, and shall be liable to the Contractor for any additional expenses arising under this Sub-clause.

(c) In the event the Vessel is delivered under the control of pumps and/or compressors or other equipment the Company shall with all due dispatch arrange for their own equipment and operators to replace the Contractor's equipment and operators.

Until such replacement the Company shall pay the Contractor for the use of its equipment and operators at reasonable rates as from the day of delivery until and including the day of arrival of the equipment and personnel at the Contractor's base, plus any additional costs relating thereto and incurred by the Contractor.

(d) If the Company fails, on completion of the Services, to take delivery of the Vessel within five (5) days of the Contractor tendering written notice of delivery or, if in the opinion of the Contractor the Vessel is likely to deteriorate, decay, become worthless or incur charges whether for storage or otherwise in excess of its value, the Contractor may, without prejudice to any other claims the Contractor may have against the Company,

APPENDIX 9 WRECKSTAGE 2010

WRECKSTAGE 2010 - International Wreck Removal and Marine Services Agreement
(Lump Sum-Stage Payments)
PART II

without notice and without any responsibility whatsoever attaching to the Contractor, sell or dispose of the Vessel and apply the proceeds of sale in reduction of the sums due to the Contractor from the Company under this Agreement. Any remaining proceeds will be refunded to the Company.

In the event that such sale or other disposal of the Vessel fails to raise sufficient net funds to pay the monies due to the Contractor under the terms of this Agreement then the Company shall remain liable to the Contractor for any such shortfall.

(e) Reference to delivery and/or disposal of the Vessel shall include parts of the Vessel and/or cargo and/or any other thing emanating from the Vessel and such delivery may take place at different times and different places (see Box 8).

10. Payment
(a) The Company shall pay the Contractor the Lump Sum set out in Box 9, which amount shall be due and payable as set out in Box 9.

(b) Each instalment of the Lump Sum shall be fully and irrevocably earned at the moment it is due as set out in Box 9. Any other monies due under this Agreement shall be fully and irrevocably earned on a daily basis or pro rata.

(c) All monies due and payable to the Contractor under this Agreement shall be paid without any discount, deduction, set-off, lien, claim or counterclaim.

(d) All payments to the Contractor shall be made in the currency and to the bank account stipulated in Box 10.

(e) If any amount payable under this Agreement has not been paid within seven (7) days of the due date, or if the security required in accordance with Clause 12 (Security) is not provided within five (5) banking days following the request by the Contractor, then at any time thereafter the Contractor shall be entitled to terminate this Agreement without prejudice to the sums already due to the Contractor and to any further rights or remedies which the Contractor may have against the Company, provided always that the Contractor shall give the Company at least three (3) working days' written notice of its intention to exercise this right.

(f) The Contractor shall promptly invoice the Company for all sums payable under this Agreement. If any sums which become due and payable are not actually received by the Contractor within the period specified in Box 11, they shall attract interest in accordance with the rate set out in Box 11.

11. Extra Costs
The following shall be paid as and when they fall due by the respective parties as indicated in Box 12:

(a) all port expenses, pilotage charges, harbour and canal dues and all other expenses of a similar nature levied upon or payable in respect of the Vessel and the Contractor's own or hired-in craft;

(b) the costs of the services of any assisting tugs when reasonably deemed necessary by the Contractor or prescribed by port or other authorities;

(c) all costs in connection with clearance, agency fees, visas, guarantees and all other expenses of such kind;

(d) all taxes and social security charges (other than those normally payable by the Contractor in the country where it has its principal place of business), stamp duties, or other levies payable in respect of or in connection with this Agreement, any import - export dues and any customs or excise duties;

(e) all costs incurred in obtaining and maintaining licences, approvals, authorisations or permits required to undertake and complete the Services in accordance with Clause 6 (Permits);

(f) all costs incurred due to requirements of governmental or other authorities or unions over and above those costs which would otherwise be reasonably incurred by the Contractor in the execution of the Agreement;

(g) all costs incurred by the Contractor in respect of portable salvage equipment, materials, or stores which are reasonably sacrificed during the disposal or other operations of the Vessel;

If any such costs are in fact paid by or on behalf of one party by the other party, the party on whose behalf the payment has been made shall reimburse the paying party on the basis of the actual cost to the paying party plus a handling charge of the percentage amount indicated in Box 12(iii) upon presentation of invoice.

12. Security
The Company shall provide on signing this Agreement an irrevocable and unconditional security in a form and amount as agreed between the parties.

If required by the Contractor and also in the event that initially no security is requested, the Company shall

APPENDIX 9 WRECKSTAGE 2010

WRECKSTAGE 2010 - International Wreck Removal and Marine Services Agreement
(Lump Sum-Stage Payments)
PART II

provide security or further security in a form and amount as agreed between the parties for all or part of any amount which may be or become due under this Agreement. Such security shall be given on one or more occasions as and when reasonably required by the Contractor.

13. Liabilities
(a) The Contractor will indemnify and hold the Company harmless in respect of any liability adjudged due or claim reasonably compromised arising out of injury or death occurring during the Services hereunder to any of the following persons:

(i) any servant, agent or sub-contractor of the Contractor;

(ii) any other person at or near the site of the operations for whatever purpose on behalf or at the request of the Contractor.

(b) The Company will indemnify and hold the Contractor harmless in respect of any liability adjudged due or claim reasonably compromised arising from injury or death occurring during the Services hereunder to any of the following persons:

(i) any servant, agent or sub-contractor of the Company;

(ii) any other person at or near the site of the operations for whatever purpose on behalf or at the request of the Company.

(c) Neither the Company nor its servants, agents or sub-contractors shall have any liability to the Contractor for loss or damage of whatsoever nature sustained by the Contractor's owned or hired-in craft or equipment (excluding portable salvage equipment, materials or stores which are reasonably sacrificed during the disposal or other operations on the Vessel, unless the Contractor is the party responsible for such costs as indicated in Box 12 (i)), whether or not the same is due to breach of contract, negligence or any other fault on the part of the Company, its servants, agents or sub-contractors.

(d) Neither the Contractor nor its servants, agents or sub-contractors shall have any liability to the Company for loss or damage of whatsoever nature sustained by the Vessel, whether or not the same is due to breach of contract, negligence or any other fault on the part of the Contractor, its servants, agents or sub-contractors.

(e) Neither party shall be liable to the other party for:

(i) any loss of profit, loss of use or loss of production whatsoever and whether arising directly or indirectly from the performance or non-performance of this Agreement, and whether or not the same is due to negligence or any other fault on the part of either party, their servants, agents or sub-contractors, or

(ii) any consequential loss or damage for any reason whatsoever, whether or not the same is due to any breach of contract, negligence or any other fault on the part of either party, their servants, agents or sub-contractors.

14. Himalaya Clause
All exceptions, exemptions, defences, immunities, limitations of liability, indemnities, privileges and conditions granted or provided by this Agreement for the benefit of the Contractor or the Company shall also apply to and be for the benefit of their respective sub-contractors, operators, the Vessel's owners (if the Company is the demise/bareboat charterer), masters, officers and crews and to and be for the benefit of all bodies corporate parent of, subsidiary to, affiliated with or under the same management as either of them, as well as all directors, officers, servants and agents of the same and to and be for the benefit of all parties performing Services within the scope of this Agreement for or on behalf of the Contractor or the Company as servants, agents and sub-contractors of such parties. The Contractor or the Company shall be deemed to be acting as agent or trustee of and for the benefit of all such persons, entities and Vessels set forth above but only for the limited purpose of contracting for the extension of such benefits to such persons, bodies and Vessels.

15. Lien
Without prejudice to any other rights which the Contractor may have, whether *in rem* or *in personam*, the Contractor shall be entitled to exercise a possessory lien upon the Vessel in respect of any amount howsoever or whatsoever due to the Contractor under this Agreement and shall for the purpose of exercising such possessory lien be entitled to take and/or keep possession of the Vessel, provided always that the Company shall pay to the Contractor all reasonable costs and expenses howsoever or whatsoever incurred by or on behalf of the Contractor in exercising or attempting or preparing to exercise such lien.

16. Time for Suit
Any claim which may arise out of or in connection with this Agreement or any of the Services performed hereunder shall be notified to the party against whom such claim is made, within twelve (12) months of completion or termination of the Services hereunder, or within twelve (12) months of any claim by a third party,

APPENDIX 9 WRECKSTAGE 2010

WRECKSTAGE 2010 - International Wreck Removal and Marine Services Agreement
(Lump Sum-Stage Payments)
PART II

whichever is later. Any suit shall be brought within twelve (12) months of the notification to the party against whom the claim is made. If either of these conditions is not complied with, the claim and all rights whatsoever and howsoever shall be absolutely barred and extinguished.

17. Expert Evaluation

(a) If the parties are unable to agree the alteration to costs under Clause 4(a) or Clause 4(b) or the adjustment to the Delay Payment Rate or the time lost under Clauses 7(a), 7(b) or 7(c), then either party may request an expert evaluation in accordance with the following procedure:

(i) The party seeking the evaluation shall propose three (3) experts from the persons currently on the Panel of Special Casualty Representatives maintained by the Salvage Arbitration Branch of the Corporation of Lloyd's to the other party in writing having checked that the proposed experts are available and willing to be appointed. The other party may select one of the proposed experts by responding in writing within twenty-four (24) hours. The party seeking the evaluation will then, as soon as possible (and in any event in less than twelve (12) hours) appoint the expert selected by the other party or, if none has been selected, one of the three (3) experts proposed (hereinafter "the Expert").

(ii) Both parties shall provide short written statements to the Expert setting out their arguments within forty-eight (48) hours of their acceptance of instructions and shall provide copies of their statement to the other party.

(iii) The Expert shall, within seventy-two (72) hours of receipt of written statements, advise the parties in writing of the alteration to costs or of the adjustment to the Delay Payment Rate or time lost. The Expert may also provide short reasons explaining the evaluation.

(iv) The Expert's rate of remuneration shall be the applicable rate plus bonus as set from time to time by the SCOPIC Committee for a Salvage Master. The costs of the Expert shall be paid by the party seeking the expert evaluation, but such party shall then be entitled to recover fifty per cent (50%) of the Expert's fees from the other party.

(b) If the Expert's evaluation is not agreed by both parties, the Company shall in any event make payments to the Contractor calculated in accordance with the evaluation. Such payments shall be on a provisional basis and without prejudice to the parties' rights to seek a determination in accordance with Clause 18 (Arbitration and Mediation).

18. Arbitration and Mediation

This Clause 18 applies to any dispute arising under this Agreement.

(a) *This Agreement shall be governed by and construed in accordance with English law and any dispute arising out of or in connection with this Agreement shall be referred to arbitration in London in accordance with the Arbitration Act 1996 or any statutory modification or re-enactment thereof save to the extent necessary to give effect to the provisions of this Clause.

The reference shall be to a sole arbitrator ("Arbitrator"), to be selected by the first party claiming arbitration from the persons currently on the Panel of Lloyd's Salvage Arbitrators with a right of appeal from an award made by the Arbitrator to either party by notice in writing to the other within twenty-eight (28) days of the date of publication of the original Arbitrator's Award.

The Arbitrator on appeal shall be the person currently acting as Lloyd's Appeal Arbitrator.

No suit shall be brought before another Tribunal, or in another jurisdiction, except that either party shall have the option to bring proceedings to obtain conservative seizure or other similar remedy against any assets owned by the other party in any state or jurisdiction where such assets may be found.

Both the Arbitrator and Appeal Arbitrator shall have the same powers as an Arbitrator and an Appeal Arbitrator under LOF 2000 or any standard revision thereof, including a power to order a payment on account of any monies due to the Contractor pending final determination of any dispute between the parties hereto.

In cases where neither the claim nor any counterclaim exceeds the sum of US$50,000 (or such other sum as the parties may agree) the arbitration shall be conducted in accordance with the LMAA Small Claims Procedure current at the time when the arbitration proceedings are commenced.

In cases where the claim or any counterclaim exceeds the sum agreed for the LMAA Small Claims Procedure and neither the claim nor any counterclaim exceeds the sum of US$400,000 (or such other sum as the parties may agree) the arbitration shall be conducted in accordance with the LMAA Intermediate Claims Procedure current at the time when the arbitration proceedings are commenced.

(b) *This Agreement shall be governed by and construed in accordance with Title 9 of the United States Code and the Maritime Law of the United States and any dispute arising out of or in connection with this Agreement shall be referred to three persons at New York, one to be appointed by each of the parties hereto, and the third by the two so chosen; their decision or that of any two of them shall be final, and for the purposes of enforcing

WRECKSTAGE 2010 - International Wreck Removal and Marine Services Agreement
(Lump Sum-Stage Payments)
PART II

any award, judgement may be entered on an award by any court of competent jurisdiction. The proceedings shall be conducted in accordance with the rules of the Society of Maritime Arbitrators, Inc.

In cases where neither the claim nor any counterclaim exceeds the sum of US$50,000 (or such other sum as the parties may agree) the arbitration shall be conducted in accordance with the Shortened Arbitration Procedure of the Society of Maritime Arbitrators, Inc. current at the time when the arbitration proceedings are commenced.

(c) *This Agreement shall be governed by and construed in accordance with the laws of the place mutually agreed by the parties and any dispute arising out of or in connection with this Agreement shall be referred to arbitration at a mutually agreed place, subject to the procedures applicable there.

(d) Notwithstanding 18(a), 18(b) or 18(c) above, the parties may agree at any time to refer to mediation any difference and/or dispute arising out of or in connection with this Agreement. In the case of a dispute in respect of which arbitration has been commenced under 18(a), 18(b) or 18(c) above, the following shall apply:

(i) Either party may at any time and from time to time elect to refer the dispute or part of the dispute to mediation by service on the other party of a written notice (the "Mediation Notice") calling on the other party to agree to mediation.

(ii) The other party shall thereupon within fourteen (14) calendar days of receipt of the Mediation Notice confirm that they agree to mediation, in which case the parties shall thereafter agree a mediator within a further fourteen (14) calendar days, failing which on the application of either party a mediator will be appointed promptly by the Arbitrator or such person as the Arbitrator may designate for that purpose. The mediation shall be conducted in such place and in accordance with such procedure and on such terms as the parties may agree or, in the event of disagreement, as may be set by the mediator.

(iii) If the other party does not agree to mediate, that fact may be brought to the attention of the Tribunal and may be taken into account by the Tribunal when allocating the costs of the arbitration as between the parties.

(iv) The mediation shall not affect the right of either party to seek such relief or take such steps as it considers necessary to protect its interest.

(v) Either party may advise the Arbitrator that they have agreed to mediation. The arbitration procedure shall continue during the conduct of the mediation but the Arbitrator may take the mediation timetable into account when setting the timetable for steps in the arbitration.

(vi) Unless otherwise agreed or specified in the mediation terms, each party shall bear its own costs incurred in the mediation and the parties shall share equally the mediator's costs and expenses.

(vii) The mediation process shall be without prejudice and confidential and no information or documents disclosed during it shall be revealed to the Arbitrator except to the extent that they are disclosable under the law and procedure governing the arbitration.

(Note: The parties should be aware that the mediation process may not necessarily interrupt time limits.)

(e) If Box 17 in PART I is not appropriately filled in, Sub-clause 18(a) of this Clause shall apply. Sub-clause 18(d) shall apply in all cases.

*Sub-clauses 18(a), 18(b) and 18(c) are alternatives; indicate alternative agreed in Box 17.

19. Notices Clause
(a) All notices given by either party or their agents to the other party or their agents in accordance with the provisions of this Agreement shall be in writing and shall, unless specifically provided in this Agreement to the contrary, be sent to the address for that other party as set out in Boxes 2 and 3 or as appropriate or to such other address as the other party may designate in writing.

A notice may be sent by registered or recorded mail, facsimile, electronically or delivered by hand in accordance with this Sub-clause 19(a).

(b) Any notice given under this Agreement shall take effect on receipt by the other party and shall be deemed to have been received:

(i) if posted, on the seventh (7th) day after posting;

(ii) if sent by facsimile or electronically, on the day of transmission; or

(iii) if delivered by hand, on the day of delivery.

And in each case proof of posting, handing in or transmission shall be proof that notice has been given, unless

APPENDIX 9 WRECKSTAGE 2010

WRECKSTAGE 2010 - International Wreck Removal and Marine Services Agreement
(Lump Sum-Stage Payments)
PART II

proven to the contrary.

20. Insurance
(a) The Contractor warrants that throughout the period of this Agreement it will maintain full cover against normal P&I risks including salvors' liabilities as evidenced by a Certificate of Entry issued by a P&I Club or insurer acceptable to the Company and shall comply with all the requirements of the policy.

(b) The Company warrants that throughout the period of this Agreement it will maintain full cover against normal P&I risks for the Vessel as evidenced by a Certificate of Entry issued by a P&I Club or insurer stated in Box 4(ix) and shall comply with all the requirements of the policy.

21. Pollution
(a) The Contractor shall exercise due care throughout the performance of the Services to prevent and minimise damage to the environment and shall also put in place, maintain and implement throughout the Services a pollution response plan which meets the requirements of the competent authorities and the Company, or the Company Representative if applicable. The Contractor shall provide the Company with a copy of the pollution response plan on request by the Company.

(b) The Company shall indemnify and hold the Contractor harmless in respect of any and all consequences of any pollution which results from any discharge or escape of any pollutant from the Vessel except where such pollution arises as a consequence of the negligence of the Contractor, its sub-contractors, its agents and/or servants.

(c) The Contractor shall indemnify and hold the Company harmless in respect of any and all consequences of any pollution which results from any discharge or escape of any pollutant from its own or from hired-in craft.

22. Rotation and Replacement of Craft, Equipment and Personnel
The Contractor shall have the right to rotate and replace any craft, equipment and personnel with other suitable replacement craft, equipment and personnel subject to the approval of the Company, or the Company Representative if applicable, which shall not be unreasonably withheld.

23. General Provisions
(a) Severability
If, in any legal proceedings, it is determined that any provision of this Agreement is unenforceable under applicable law, then the unenforceable provision shall automatically be amended to conform to that which is enforceable under the law. In any event, the validity or enforceability of any provision shall not affect any other provision of this Agreement, and this Agreement shall be construed and enforced as if such provision had not been included.

(b) Third Party Beneficiaries
Except as specifically provided for elsewhere in this Agreement, this Agreement shall not be construed to confer any benefit on any third party not a party to this Agreement nor shall this Agreement provide any rights to such third party to enforce any provision of this Agreement.

(c) Waiver
No benefit or right accruing to either party under this Agreement shall be waived unless the waiver is reduced to writing and signed by both the Contractor and the Company. The failure of either party to exercise any of its rights under this Agreement, including but not limited to either party's failure to comply with any time limit set out in this Agreement, shall in no way constitute a waiver of those rights, nor shall such failure excuse the other party from any of its obligations under this Agreement.

(d) Warranty of Authority
The Contractor and the Company each warrant and represent that the person whose signature appears in Part I above is its representative and is duly authorized to execute this Agreement as a binding commitment of such party.

(e) Singular/Plural
The singular includes the plural and vice versa as the context admits or requires.

(f) Headings
The headings to the clauses and appendices to this Agreement are for convenience only and shall not affect its construction or interpretation.

APPENDIX 10: WRECKSTAGE 2010 BIMCO EXPLANATORY NOTES

It might be helpful for readers to see BIMCO's clause by clause Explanatory Notes for Wreckstage 2010,[1] as this form (or lump sum instalment contracts generally) appear to be the most commonly used. In places, brief cross references have been added in footnotes, but the full systematic analysis is found in 13.6.5.

BIMCO's copyright and support is acknowledged. It should be noted that the Explanatory Notes are for general guidance only and help to provide some background as to why particular provisions were adopted or changed, eg from Wreckstage 99. The Notes have no formal status for interpretation and cannot replace a close reading of the wording. Readers who want an authoritative clause by clause analysis should also consult *Rainey*.[2]

Part I box layout[3]

BIMCO Explanatory Notes. Part I of Wreckstage 2010 is largely unchanged from the 99 edition of the form. Box 4 (Vessel Specifications) has been expanded to include the vessel's IMO number and the P&I Club/insurer.

Box 7 (Nature of Services) now requires two fields to be completed: (i) a description of the nature of the services; and (ii) the party responsible for obtaining confirmation of compliance by the Company with the orders issued by competent authorities.

Box 9 (Permits) has been removed as the revised agreement now requires the Contractors to obtain and maintain the necessary permits (with the assistance of the Company as appropriate).

Part II

Clause 1 (Definitions)

BIMCO Explanatory Notes A number of new definitions have been added to the agreement to improve the overall clarity of the form. The new definitions include "Company", "Contractor", "Services" and "Worksite" all of which were terms already used in Wreckstage, but not defined. There is now a consistent use of these defined terms through the Agreement.

Clause 2 (The Services)[4]

BIMCO Explanatory Notes This Clause deals with the Contractors' obligations in providing the agreed services, as well as the provision of personnel, craft and equipment, the method of work, and any change in the method of work, or provision of personnel, craft and equipment. Consistent with the approach taken in the 1989 Salvage Convention, the Contractor is obliged to exercise "due care" when providing the services. Provided that it is not inconsistent with the nature of the services

---

1 BIMCO's Explanatory Notes for Wreckhire 2010 and Wreckfixed 2010 are available on BIMCO's website: www://Bimco.org.
2 Chapter 10.
3 Cf Wreckhire: 13.6.3(a)
4 See 13.6.5(a).

to be rendered, the Contractor must also exercise "due care" to prevent and minimise damage to the environment.

The first paragraph of Clause 2 has been amended to make the delivery and/or disposal of the vessel a "due diligence" type obligation on the part of the Contractor. The previous reference to the Contractor's "endeavour to deliver" has been removed as the obligation to exercise "due care" applies to all of the agreed services under the Agreement, which may also include delivery and/or disposal.

In the last sentence of the first paragraph the Contractor now has to exercise due care to "prevent" as well as minimise damage to the marine environment. This has been done to be consistent with the phrasing used in the newly introduced Clause 21 (Pollution).

Two new provisions have been added at the end of Clause 2. The first requires the Contractor to give the Company Representative, if in attendance at the site, daily reports (the reports to be based on a standard format set out in Annex III (Contractor's Daily Reports)). The second new provision requires assistance to be given to the party named in Box 7(ii) by the other party to assist in obtaining confirmation from the authorities of compliance with their orders.

Clause 3 (Company Representative)[5]

BIMCO Explanatory Notes This Clause provides for a representative of the Company to be available onsite, but only if required by the Contractor. A previous reference to the Company being obliged to provide information to the Contractor has been moved to the final part of Clause 5 (Miscellaneous)

The Clause also deals with the attendance on site, at the Company's risk and expense, of ship's personnel who are fully conversant with the layout of the Vessel and its cargo system in order to provide advice to the Contractors.

Clause 4 (Change of Method of Work and/or Personnel, Craft and Equipment)[6]

BIMCO Explanatory Notes Problems may arise during the operation that require a substantial change of method, equipment, etc. This Clause deals with the circumstances under which the Contractor may seek a variation to the Lump Sum stated in Box 9.

Clause 4 has been substantially restructured and split into three distinct sections. The first section (sub-clause (a)) deals with substantial changes before or during the services resulting in additional costs. The second section (sub-clause (b)) deals the task becoming easier due to a change in circumstances and where the Company can ask for a reduction in the money due to the Contractor. In both cases the parties must agree to a work variation order and to any increase or decrease in costs. In sub-clause (c) provision is made for the parties to resolve any disagreement in respect of sub-clauses (a) and (b) by referring the matter to a new expert evaluation procedure or to mediation or arbitration.

The previous method of referring the matter solely to arbitration was felt to be too slow and inefficient for this type of dispute where it is essential that work is not interrupted or delayed awaiting the outcome of an arbitrator's decision. In any event the Contractor is obliged to continue operations pending the outcome of any evaluation, mediation or arbitration.

Clause 5 (Miscellaneous)[7]

BIMCO Explanatory Notes This Clause, which is largely unchanged from the Wreckstage 99 edition, deals with matters such as the marking of the Vessel; use of the Vessel's machinery and equipment; removal or jettison of parts of the Vessel and/or its cargo, and provision of plans and manifests.

---

5 See Wreckhire cl 3: 13.6.3(j).

6 This clause is central to all three BIMCO wreck removal contracts, but is very complicated. The Notes here are very basic and reference should be made to 13.6.5(d).

7 Cf Wreckhire cl 5: 13.6.3(a).

In sub-clause (d) the strict obligation on the Company to provide the Contractors with plans, drawings and other data/information has been amended to "best endeavours" as the Company may simply not be in possession of some of the requested information. The Contractors are at liberty to request the Company to provide plans, drawings and information (previously, the requirement to provide information was found in Clause 3 (Company Representative)) but such requests must be "reasonable".

Clause 6 (Permits)[8]

BIMCO Explanatory Notes This Clause deals with the need to obtain licences, approvals, authorisations and permits. The Permits Clause previously allowed for either party to be designated as responsible for obtaining permits. This has now been amended to make the Contractor solely responsible for this task although the Company is required to assist where necessary (for example in situations where a particular permit can only be issued to the shipowner or where the submission of certificates held by the shipowner is required). This amendment reflects the reality of salvage operations where the on-site contractor is best placed to obtain the necessary permits.

Clause 7 (Delays)[9]

BIMCO Explanatory Notes This Clause has undergone significant amendment and now offers a much more sophisticated method of dealing with delays encountered during the salvage operation. The previous Clause did not take into account a partial reduction in salvage work, meaning that anything other than full salvage work resulted in the standby rate applying. The new Delays Clause deals with partial standby as well as a full stand-down of services and which rates should apply under each set of circumstances. The provision as amended clearly sets out the position of the parties and which rate should apply in the event of delays whether caused by weather (Sub-clause (a)) or breakdown or failure of the Contractors' equipment or personnel (Sub-clause (b)) or third party equipment or personnel hired in by the Contractor (Sub-clause (c)). As such, the provision more clearly sets out the position of the parties in the event of delays whether caused by weather or breakdown or failure of the Contractors' equipment or personnel or third party equipment or personnel hired in by the Contractor.

Sub-clause (d) places the onus on the Contractor to act swiftly to advise the Company or its on-site representative of any delays to which the Contractor feels the Delay Payment Rate should apply. The Contractor must also at that time inform the Company (or its representative if appropriate) in writing (which would normally be done as part of the daily report and is consistent with obligations under the Lloyd's Form SCOPIC Clause).

Sub-clause (e) excludes from the Delay Payment Rate individual delays of 6 running hours or less duration. This "free time" represents half a working day and is felt by salvors to be a reasonable compromise. However, if the delay exceeds 6 hours then the entire delay period is to count at the Delay Payment Rate.

Sub-clause (f) provides a means of resolving any disagreement as to what rate applies in the different circumstances listed in sub-clauses (a), (b) and (c) or for how long such a rate should apply. If the parties cannot agree on the rate that is to apply then the matter is referred to a new expert evaluation procedure (Clause 17).

---

8 See 13.6.5(a). Cf Wreckhire cl 6: 13.6.3(j).

9 Again, this clause is central to the allocation of risk, but the description is very basic. See 13.6.5(e) for a more detailed treatment.

APPENDIX 10 WRECKSTAGE 2010: BIMCO EXPLANATORY NOTES

Clause 8 (Termination)[10]

BIMCO Explanatory Notes This Clause remains unchanged from Wreckstage 99. It sets out the circumstances under which the Agreement may be terminated by the Company (Sub-clause 8(a)); the manner in which the termination of the Agreement will be carried out by the Contractor (Sub-clause 8(b)); and the situation if permission to terminate the services is not given by the competent authorities (Sub-clause 8(c)).

Clause 9 (Delivery and/or Disposal)[11]

BIMCO Explanatory Notes The Clause has been amended to take account of situations where the Contractors also agree to dispose of the vessel or part of the vessel. "Part" of the vessel includes cargo and bunkers and it is recognised that disposal of such items may take place at different locations and at different times from the disposal of other parts of the vessel.

Clause 10 (Payment)

BIMCO Explanatory Notes The new Payment Clause is the result of the merging of the old Clause 10 (Price and Conditions of Payment) and Clause 11 (Time of Payment and Interest).

Clause 10 is fundamental to the proper working of the Agreement. Sub-clauses (9(a), 9(b) and 9(c) deal with the payment of the agreed Lump Sum in instalments irrevocably earned when due and without deduction; Sub-clause (d) provides for the Lump Sum instalments to be paid in the agreed currency to the stated bank account; Sub-clause (e) gives the Contractor a right of termination in the event that payment is not made in accordance with the terms of the Agreement, or if security is not provided in accordance with the provisions of Clause 12 (Security); and Sub-clause (f) enables the Contractors to charge the Company interest at the agreed rate in the event any sums due and payable are not received by the Contractors within the agreed period.

Clause 11 (Extra Costs)

BIMCO Explanatory Notes This Clause provides for any various extra costs incurred to be for the account of the Company. A new sub-clause (e) obliges the Company to meet the cost of obtaining and maintaining licenses and permits needed to undertake the salvage operation.

BIMCO Explanatory Notes The final paragraph of Clause 11 has been amended to require the Company to reimburse the Contractor for any costs paid on the Company's behalf plus any agreed handling charge.

Clause 12 (Security)[12]

BIMCO Explanatory Notes The Security Clause requires the Company to provide an irrevocable and unconditional security in any form as agreed between the parties. The Company is required to provide satisfactory security to cover monies due to the Contractor. The Contractor may also commence operations without the provision of initial security, but can request it to be provided at a later stage when "reasonably" required. This Clause remains unchanged from Wreckstage 99.

---

10 See 13.6.5(f).
11 Again, this clause is central to the allocation of risk, but the description is very basic. See 13.6.5(g) for a more detailed treatment.
12 See 13.6.5(b).

Clause 13 (Liabilities)[13]

BIMCO Explanatory Notes Clause 13 provides the usual knock for knock provisions common in offshore contracts. Sub-clauses (a), (b), (c) and (d) have been slightly modified to include "sub-contractors" (which reflects the common use by salvors of third party sub-contractors). Sub-clause 13(e) is new and replaces the old consequential losses provision which was felt to be ineffective. The new wording is taken from Towhire 2008 the consequential losses provision of which has been positively received by lawyers previously critical of BIMCO consequential liability provisions.

Clause 14 (Himalaya Clause)[14]

BIMCO Explanatory Notes This Clause is the same as that found in Wreckstage 99.

Clause 15 (Lien)[15]

BIMCO Explanatory Notes This Clause is the same as that found in Wreckstage 99.

Clause 16 (Time for Suit)[16]

BIMCO Explanatory Notes This Clause remains largely unchanged from Wreckstage 99. The previous reference to notification by "telex, facsimile, cable or otherwise in writing" has been deleted because methods and forms of notification are now dealt with by a new Notices Clause (see Clause 19).

Clause 17 (Expert Evaluation)[17]

BIMCO Explanatory Notes Wreckstage 2010 introduces a new method of dealing with certain types of dispute under the Agreement—notably disputes relating to the application of Delay Payment Rates (Clause 7) and the adjustment of costs following a change to the nature of the services (Clause 4). It was felt that the standard BIMCO Dispute Resolution Clause used in most BIMCO forms is simply not well suited to resolving issues that require a more or less on-the-spot decision so that work is not interrupted. Conventional arbitration lacks the infrastructure and expertise to determine such types of disputes. Therefore a two-tier approach to dispute resolution has been introduced.

In the first instance, if the parties cannot agree to additional costs for a change in the nature of the services, or are in dispute as the application of the standby rate, they may refer the disagreement to an "expert evaluator". It is intended that the role of the "expert evaluator" will be assumed by a SCR (Special Casualty Representative) chosen from the Panel of SCRs maintained by the Salvage Arbitration Branch of Lloyd's. Once appointed, the SCR acting as "expert evaluator" will take into account short written submissions provided by each party and then within 72 hours give written advice to the parties as to how costs/rates should be adjusted or how time should be accounted for. The cost of such an evaluation is to be met by both parties.

It is important to note that the evaluation is not binding on either party. The intention is to take impartial advice so as to not delay or further delay the salvage operation. The parties only agree that

---

13 Again, this clause is central to the allocation of risk, but the description is very basic. See 13.6.5(a), but for a more detailed treatment see Wreckhire cl 16: 13.6.3(g).

14 Cf Wreckhire cl 17: 13.6.3(g).

15 Cf Wreckhire cl 18: 13.6.3(g).

16 Cf Wreckhire cl 19: 13.6.3(g).

17 See Wreckhire cl 20: 13.6.3(k).

whatever the SCR proposes is given immediate effect but without prejudicing their right to resolve the dispute by conventional arbitration methods set out in Clause 18 at a later date.

Clause 18 (Arbitration and Mediation)[18]

BIMCO Explanatory Notes The Arbitration and Mediation Clause of Wreckstage 2010 builds on the "Governing Law and Arbitration" Clause in Wreckstage 99 which makes special provision for using Lloyd's Salvage Arbitrators who are experts in resolving salvage related disputes. Consistent with the current BIMCO standard Dispute Resolution Clause, the parties may choose an applicable law and arbitration venue from a choice of English law/London arbitration; US law/New York arbitration; or a choice of law and arbitration as chosen and agreed by the parties.

The Clause incorporates the LMAA's recently introduced intermediate claims procedure to supplement the existing small claims procedure. The Clause also introduces new mediation provision which permits the parties to refer all or part of a dispute, for which arbitration has been commenced, to mediation.

Clause 19 (Notices Clause)[19]

BIMCO Explanatory Notes The notices provision is new but is a provision commonly found in other recently produced BIMCO standard forms. The Clause provides that all notices must be in writing and sent using one of the prescribed formats. The Clause also sets out when notices given under the Agreement take effect depending on the method of communication used.

Clause 20 (Insurance)[20]

BIMCO Explanatory Notes This is another new Clause for Wreckstage and provides for each party to warrant that they have in place appropriate insurance cover.

Clause 21 (Pollution)[21]

BIMCO Explanatory Notes This Clause is also new and requires the Contractor to exercise "due care" to prevent and minimise damage to the environment and have in place an oil spill response plan which meets the requirements of the Authorities and the Company. Sub-clauses (b) and (c) provide knock-for-knock provisions in relation to pollution from the vessel and the Contractor's vessels.

Clause 22 (Rotation and Replacement of craft, equipment and personnel)[22]

This is another new provision that basically gives the Contractor the right to swap resources/equipment in and out of the salvage operation for maintenance and/or fatigue-relief purposes.

Clause 23 (General Provisions)

BIMCO Explanatory Notes This set of clauses covering the enforceability of provisions; third party beneficiaries; no-waiver; and warranty of authority, reflect additional clauses commonly added to wreck removal and other marine service agreements used in the salvage/offshore industry.

---

18 See Wreckhire cl 21: 13.6.3(k).
19 Cf Wreckhire cl 22: 13.6.3(j).
20 Cf Wreckhire cl 23: 13.6.3(j).
21 See Wreckhire cl 24: 13.6.3(h).
22 Cf Wreckhire cl 25: 13.6.3(a).

Annexes

BIMCO Explanatory Notes Annex I (Schedule of Personnel, Craft and Equipment) and Annex II (Method of Work and Estimated Time Schedule) are unchanged from the previous edition of Wreckstage.

A new Annex III has been added to provide a proforma template for the Contractor's daily reports.

INDEX

abandoned ships 559–66; derelict, and 398–400; IMO conventions 312; *MSC Napoli* 15–16; State practical problems 668–9; WRC 2007 liability 464–5
abandonment: derelict 222–4; dumping, or 667–9; financial security 74; notice of 12, 171, 187, 190–193, 195–6, 224, 231–234, 236, 238, 525; ownership, of 224–31; rights, of 222–31; total loss 190–2
Accident Reporting Regulations 2012 266–7
adventurae maris 211–2, 247, 268–9
acquisition: law of the flag 214; ownership of wreck 220–2, 703–5; UCH 2001 326
actual total loss 188–90; bareboat charterer 60–1; constructive total loss 190–19; insurers' rights 231–4, 236–9; ship registry 706; underwriters' decision time 195–6
Aegean Sea 12, 61, 100, 102, 104, 105, 137
Affected States: determining hazards 423–4; locating wreck 424–5; marking wreck 425–7; powers and obligations 422–35; wreck removal 427–35
aircraft 212, 228, 281, 282, 285, 286, 290, 291, 292, 322, 323, 338, 339, 346, 347, 348, 351, 403, 452, 484, 658, 665, 696–7, 700
alternative dispute resolution 619–25
Amoco Cadiz 11, 13, 63, 135, 137, 319, 411
Ancient Monuments and Archaeological Areas Act 1979 285–6
apportionment: collision liability 94–5; GA security 172; sub-apportionment of liability 111; Wreckhire contract 618
Assi Eurolink 121, 123, 126–8, 428, 492, 531
Athens Convention 1974 78; passenger claims 85; UK domestic carriage 89
Athens Convention 2002 78–80: compensation and limits of liability 83–5; compulsory insurance 86–9; domestic carriage 89; liability for death and injury 80–3; passenger claims 89–90; passengers' luggage 85–6; terrorism 459–60; UK domestic carriage 89; WRC 2007 385, 492, 535–8

Baltic Ace 27–8, 104, 119–21, 123, 128, 140, 446, 513, 531, 595, 604, 657, 670
barratry 47, 177, 458, 500, 550
Bargehire 2008 607, 711
Basel Convention 1989: Conference of the Parties 668, 671–2; EU Ship Recycling Regulation 2013 678–9; EU Waste Shipment Regulation 2006 673–6; ship recycling 676–8; wreck disposal 669–72
BIMCO 607–54; Barecon 2017 58–61; Barecon 89 59–60; disposal voyage contracts 708–12; QRA 606; Recyclecon 2012 682, 704–5; subcontracts 572–3; Towcon 2008 607; Towhire 2008 607; Wreckfixed 2010 633–9; Wreckhire 2010 610–33; Wreckstage 2010 639–54
Bonn Agreement: *Christos Bitas* 657; OPRC 1990 323; WRC 2007 387
Brussels I Regulation Recast 55, 56, 89, 90, 118, 120, 124, 203, 204: Art 9 125; Art 45(1)(a) 125, 127; EU jurisdiction 127; *Uno* case 126
Bunkers Convention 2001 141–4; EEZ 409–10; Environmental Liability Directive 2004 150–1; hazard definition 404; HNSC 2010 147; LLMC pollution claims 101, 626; multi-state limitation proceedings 117–19; national law 549–50; pollution damage liability 59, 432, 505; *Rena* legal claims 21–2; salvage 583; ship registry 415; state parties 381, 668; time charterers 63–9; voyage charterers 61; WRC 2007 369, 371–6, 385–7; 490, 492, 496, 502, 507, 520–1; wreck pollution 14–15

carcasses 396, 600, 601, 662, 663, 685, 693, 700
cargo claims 36,-37; 44–56; LLMC, and 99
cargo forwarding costs 39–43; insurance, and 184–188; *see also* carriage contracts
cargo owners/interests: carriage contracts, and 11, 36, 43, 44–56; collision 94–95; directions to 258; insurance and GA 169, 174, 179–188, 189, 194; liability for wreck 56–7, 137; limitation 103, 108, 137, 710; removal by

INDEX

interests 38, 206; practical difficulties after wreck 36; salvage or removal operations 37–9, 108, 166, 182, 194, 255, 271, 574, 580; state immunity 163; waste 685, 702; wreck and 206528, 612; *see also* dangerous goods

cargo problems 30–4; changing environmental focus 30; *see also* container problems, dangerous goods

cargo removal 96: under CLC 140, 518; under WRC 2007 140, 394, 440, 481–490, 530, 532, 547, 552; HNSC 520; limitation, and 100, 102–105, 106, 107, 108, 111, 114–116, 129, 151, 440, 490, 493, 521, 554; lost at sea 396; salvage, and 165, 167, 580, 650; UK and WRC 2007 547, 552, 554; waste, and 690, 691, 696, 699; wreck removal contracts, and 650

carriage claims: forum issues 55

carriage contracts 39–43; termination 41–3; transhipment costs 40

CEFAS: SCU pollution response 265

charterers 58–69; bareboat 58–60; directions, and 256–7; influence on wreck removal 69; limitation 105–106, 109; time 63–9; voyage 61–3

Chitra 440, 443, 445, 474, 658, 661, 670

Christos Bitas 261, 657; *see also* Bonn Agreement

Cita 14

claims subject to limitation: charterers and limitation 105; pollution 100–1; property and personal 99; wreck and cargo removal 102–4

CLC 1969: *Amoco Cadiz* 11–12; hazard definition 363–5; IMCO salvage, disasters 132–4; pollution claims 100; war and terrorism 457–8; WRC 2007 371, 499–501

CLC 1992 133–7; *Aegean Sea* 12; *Amoco Cadiz* 11; bareboat charterer 59; Bunkers Convention 2001 141–17, 157; EEZ 381–3, 431; Environmental Liability Directive 2004 150–1; *Erika* 12–13; Fund Convention regime, and 132–40; hazard definition 404, 423–4; HNSC 2010 130; insurer's liability cap 507–8; LC Protocol 1996 663; multi-state limitation proceedings 117–19; national law 549–51; pollution claims 100–3; pollution risks 626–7; salvage payment 258; SCOPIC 593–4; ship's registry 415–16; time charterer 64; voyage charterer 61; WRC 2007 375, 385–7, 399, 409, 411, 432–5, 490–502, 511–19

CLCS 303–6

CMI: cargo removal 483–7, 489–90; derelict and abandoned ships 398–406; Montreal Compromise 165; national legislation review 433–5, 523–4; Patrick Griggs 533–4; shipowner responsibility to report 418–19; *Torrey Canyon* 9, 131–2; voluntary salvor 430; WRC 2007 development 361–9, 387; WRC 2007 territorial sea application 411–14

coal 30, 54, 103, 147, 242, 295, 446, 447, 482, 483, 489, 520, 530, 661, 662

coastguard: wreck claims 277–8; *see also*, MCA

Collision Convention 1910: proportionate fault rule 94–5

collision liability 90–5: apportionment of liability 94; damages 93; liability 90; wreck and causation 91–2

Commune de Mesquer 672–3, 689–93, 702

compensation: death and injury of passengers 83–4; Maritime Labour Convention 76

Conlinebooking Note 709

constructive total loss 36–7, 189–91, 668; bareboat charterers 60–1; ownership of a wreck, acquiring 220–2; time charterers 66

consumer protection 77, 80, 83, 89, 154, 174, 193, 202, 607

container: problems 30–4; increased size 31; limitation, and 55; lost overboard 30; weight and contents 31; *see also*, dangerous cargo, *MSC Napoli*

contractor, choice of 603

Controlled Waste Regulations: EPA 1990 701

Coral Bulker 444

cost insurance freight: GA security 171–2; sale of good contracts 37

Costa Concordia 27–9, 32; casualty 27; commercial choices for disposal 703; compulsory insurance 491; cost and liability 29, 81, 88, 103, 107, 110, 491, 531, 713; EEZ 454; liability cap 502, 508; limitation forum shopping 128–9; LLMC 1996 97, 110; P&I Club 128–9, 201, 443, 511–13, 605; recovery of bodies 597; removal claims 102–3; removal operation 28, 140, 156, 446–7, 459, 470–1, 474, 601, 641, 670, 696, 703; *Rena* 21, 713; responsibility for arranging wreck removal 602; scrapping 670, 682; shipowner liability 438; vessel classification 452; WRC 2007 comparisons 438, 452, 454, 459, 502, 508, 531, 543

CP Valour 444

crew 70–6; criminalisation of seafarers 71; fair treatment 72; Maritime Labour Convention 2006 73–6; master's concerns after casualty 70

802

dangerous cargo 15, 16, 137, 146, 257, 312, 418, 439, 440, 445; liability under contract for 51, 57–58, 62, 64, 65, 105, 137, 662, 710, 711; liability 37, 150, 556; limitation and 98, 105, 137; misdescription of 31, 51, 440, 630; salvors and 195; WRC 2007, and 425, 438, 439, 440; wreck removal and 601; *see also* HNSC
deadweight tonnage 135, 136, 148
DEFRA 264
Department for Business Energy and Industrial Strategy, 250, 683: offshore installations 250
Department for Transport 250: *Christos Bitas* 657; costs incurred 549, 557; counter-pollution preparedness 250; *Gaul* 598; GLAs and 558; historic wreck recovery, and 332, 354; MAIB, and 266; MSA 1995 Part 9A 534–5, 558–9, 683–4; Odyssey Marine Exploration 332, 354–5; receiver of wreck, and 270; recycling regulation 683–4; shipping inquiries 266–8; SOSREP 260–1; UK coastguard 277; UK default wreck removal 544; WRC 2007 consultation 360, 529, 534, 536, 545, 547, 550, 551, 553, 554, 555, 558, 559
derelict and abandoned ships: WRC 2007 398–400; *see also*, abandoned ships
deviation 50, 69, 185, 199
Dismantlecon 712
disposal legislation: Basel Convention 1989 670–3; Environmental Protection Act 1900 701–2; Hong Kong Ship Recycling Convention 2009 676–8; LC Protocol 1996 659–63, 692–3; London (Dumping) Convention 1972/1996 657–63, 692–3; OSPAR Convention 1992 663–4; Ship Recycling Regulation 2013 678–85; UK Ship Recycling Requirements Regulations 2018 682–5; Waste Framework Directive 2008 685–703; Waste Shipment Regulation 2006 673–6
disposal of wreck 655–714; BIMCO 708–12; commercial choices 703–14; transboundary 670–6
DOALOS 320
Donaldson, Lord 12, 200, 249–50, 257, 262, 265
Dona Paz 15
dumping: abandonment, or 667–9; scrapping of ships 669–70; ship recycling 676–85; ships and cargoes at sea 656–67; SOSREP 250–2; transboundary waste disposal 670–6; Waste Framework Directive 2008 685–703

EEZ: affected state definition 406–8; binding nature of WRC 2007 377–80; casualty consequence protection 321; coastal State action 380–1; creation, UNCLOS 299, 303–5; HNSC 2010; insurance cover 381–3; non-State party wrecks 377–83; pollution threat 310, 316–18; powers over UK 262; territorial waters 134; *Tricolor/Kariba* collision 360–1; UCH 2001 jurisdictional structure 339–40, 351–2; UNCLOS Art 60 400–2; WRC 2007 368, 371–4, 377–80, 384, 385–7, 388
EMSA: maritime accident review 6
Environmental Liability Directive 2004 150–1; HNSC 2010 144; pollution risks 626; WRC 2007 516
EPA 1990 701–2
Erika 12–14, 135, 139, 140, 146, 150, 197, 253, 681, 689
EU: limitation fund recognition 124–7
EU legislation: Environmental Liability Directive 2004 150–1; Offshore Safety Directive 2013 150–1; Rome II Regulation 127–8; Ship Recycling Regulation 2013 678–85; Waste Framework Directive 2008 674, 683, 685–703; Waste Shipment Regulation 2006 673–6; *see also*, Brussels I Regulation Recast
Exempted Activities Order: Art 9 698; Art 17B 699–700; Art 28 698; Explanatory Memorandum 699; Marine and Coastal Access Act 2009 666; marine waste licensing 697
Exxon Valdez 11

Fedra 33, 91, 152, 161, 254, 445, 471, 573, 604, 612, 637
fixed and floating platforms: WRC 2007 400–2
flag State obligations 415–22; cooperation in wreck removal 421–2; reporting 417–21; state of ship registry 415–17
Floreana 448, 658, 670
Frustration 35, 40–43, 49, 171, 185, 572, 579, 592
Fund Convention 1971: *Amoco Cadiz* 11; *Braer* 12; CLC 1992 134; IMCO 132; WRC 2007 371
Fund Convention 1992 138–40; *Amoco Cadiz* 11; *Braer* 12; CLC 1992 132–3, 135; *Commune de Mesquer* 689–90; Environmental Liability Directive 2004 150; *Erika* 12; HNS Fund 149; LC Protocol 1996 663; maritime pollution liability conventions 515–19; *Prestige* 13, 442

Galapaface 448, 658, 670
Gaul 268, 321, 467, 598
general average 169–73; claims 170; cutting away wreck 173; security 171–2

general lighthouse authority: directions, and 549; finances, and 534; locating/marking wrecks, and 540; powers 527–530, 541, 544, 555; SOSREP, and 251; wreck removal, and 528–530, 544, 555–559

Hague Rules: Art III r8 63; Art IV r5 54–5; Art IV r2(a) 66–7; cargo loss claims 68–9; liability for cargo loss or damage 44; liability scheme 45–8; time charterer 66–7; voyage charterer 62–3

Hague/Visby Rules: Article III 50; Article IV 50; Art IV r6 57–8; Athens Convention 2002 78, 82, 84; BIMCO 709–12; burden of proof 50; cargo overboard 49; carriage contracts 40–1; liability for cargo loss or damage 44; liability scheme 45–7; limitation of liability 53–5; proof of loss or damage 51–4; transhipment costs 40–1; voyage charterers 62; wreck cargo 710–11

Hamburg Rules 1978: proof of fault 46

Harbour authority: abandoned wrecks and, 560; buoys, and 529; claims, and 93, 524–5; directions to, 257–8; locating/marking wreck, and 540, 667; wreck removal, and, 527–8, 544, 558, 698

Haven 11

Heavycon 708–12; Heavyconbill, and 710

Himalaya clause 41, 49, 625, 633, 640, 708, 763; *see also,* privity, of contract

HNSC 2010 144–50; Art 7(5) 440; bareboat charterers 59; cargo owner's liability 58; cargo removal 489–90; *Commune de Mesquer* 689; hazard definition 404; liability cap 502, 507; multi-state limitation proceedings 117; pollution claims 100–2, 515–16; pollution threats 432; SCOPIC 593; state liability 435; state of ship's registry 415; time charterers 64; voyage charterers 61; WRC 2007 130, 375, 385, 492, 519–20, 530; wreck and cargo removal claims 103

Hong Kong Convention 2009: Ship Recycling Regulation 2013 679–82; wreck disposal 676–8

human remains 222, 280, 281, 282, 333, 346, 349, 396, 406, 466–8, 479, 596–600

Ievoli Sun 30, 662

IMDG: nuclear liability conventions 521

IMO 375–6; *Baltic Ace* 121; "Blue Cards" 76; Bunkers Convention 2001 143; CLC 99-cruise ship wrecks, reaction to 15; defences of liability 80–1; Environmental Liability Directive 2004 151; EU compensation regimes 14; "Guidelines on Fair Treatment of Seafarers in the Event of a Maritime Accident" 71–3; "Guidelines on Provision of Financial Security in Case of Abandonment of Seafarers" 73, 74–5; "Guidelines on Shipowners' Responsibilities in Respect of Contractual Claims for Personal Injury to or Death of Seafarers" 73; HNSC 1996 145–6; Legal Committee 88, 135; "Liability and Compensation Regarding Claims for Death, Personal Injury and Abandonment of Seafarers" 72–3; liability for pollution following wreck 131–3; MEPC 297; Salvage Convention 1989 289; *Torrey Canyon* 6, 10; UNCLOS, obligations 300, 306, 308; WRC 2007 200

Institute of International Law 231, 290–3, 352, 394

in specie salvage award 245–6

influential wreck casualties 5–29 *see also* cargo problems; other wrecks 14; tanker wrecks; individual ships' names

insurance: cargo cover 179–188; H&M cover 175, 179; liability cover 197–209; practice of underwriters 193–6; total loss 188–193; wreck, and generally 173–5; wreck and passengers 86–8

insurer's rights 231–9; long lost wrecks 237–9; reinsurance 234–5; subrogation 234; to take over property 232–4; war risks 235–7

international conventions: Athens Convention 2002 78–9; Athens Convention 1974 78, 85,89; Basel Convention 1989 670–3; Bonn Agreement 657, 323, 387; Brussels I Regulation Recast 125–7; Bunkers Convention 2001 141–3, 520–1; CLC 1992 133–7, 516–19; Collision Convention 1910 94–5; Fund Convention 1992 138–9; Fund Convention 1971 11, 12, 134, 132, 371; Hague-Visby Rules 1968 40–1, 44, 51–3, 53–5, 710–11; Hamburg Rules 1978 46; HNSC 2010 144–9, 519–20; Hong Kong Convention 2009 676–82; Intervention Convention 1969 296–9; LC Protocol 1996 657–64; LC 1972 657–64, 667; Limitation Convention 1924 96; LLMC 1996 99, 116, 552–3, 554; LLMC 1976 97, 109, 111; London (Dumping) Convention 1972/1996 657–63; Maritime Labour Convention 2006 71–7; MARPOL 308–12, 400–1, 407, 417–18, 420, 661–2; Montreal Compromise 165; OPRC-HNS Protocol 1990 321–4; OSPAR Convention 1992 663–4; Paris Convention 1960 521; Salvage Convention 1910 158, 289, 577–8; Salvage Convention 1989 514–15, 578–9; SCOPIC 2018 167–8,

567–94; Supplementary Fund Protocol 2003 140–1; UCH 2001 315–16, 325–55; UNCLOS 299–321; UNESCO 213, 325–6, 340, 343, 349; Vienna Convention on the Law of Treaties 370–6; Vienna Nuclear Damage Convention 521; Wreck Removal Convention 2007 359–566

Intervention Convention 132, 296–8, 306, 319, 361; 1973 Protocol 252, 262; "Affected State" 410–11; EEZ 380; major harmful consequences 405; maritime casualty 394, 399; proportionality 431; related interests definition 405–8; ship definition 400–2; state liability 434; *Torrey Canyon* 296; WRC 2007 measures 375, 377–8, 423, 438, 530

ISM Code 419

ISU Sub-Contract (Award Sharing) 2001 572, 573

jurisdiction: bills of lading, 39, 53, 55–56; CLC 134; collisions 94; HNSC 2010 149; law of sea and UNCLOS 295, 298, 300–321, 373, 660–661; limitation, 117–11, 504, 507; ownership and possession, 214–215, 221, 242–244; passengers, 90; P&I 202–204; recycling, 678, 680; States and SCOPIC 590–2; UCH 2001 336–349, 415; sovereign immunity, 287–293, 351–352; UK, 262, 265, 351, 529, 548, 558, 571, 673; US and salvage, 350; WRC 2007, 362, 376–387, 407–408, 480, 504, 512

Kea Trader 30, 448, 696

Lagik 360, 526

law of finds 246–7

law of the sea 295–324; Intervention Convention 1969 296–9; OPRC 1990 321–4; polluting wrecks and intervention 296; United Nations Convention on the Law of the Sea 299–321

LC 1972 657–64, 667; objects and cargo lost at sea 396; relationship with 692–3; Waste Framework Directive 2008 692–3

LC Protocol 1996 657–64; Art10 660–1; civil liability for dumping 663; objects and cargo lost at sea 396; Waste Framework Directive 2008 692–3

liability: burden of proof 50; cargo loss or damage 44–55; cargo owner's 56–7; collision liability 90–5; death and injury, for 80–2; *see also* Hague/Visby Rules; insurance cover 197–210; navigation error 48–9; management exception 48–9; pay salvage, to 161; pollution 131–51; proof of loss or damage 51–2; WRC 2007 shipowners' and insurers' 437–522

Limitation Convention 1924 96

limitation of liability 95–130: *Baltic Ace* litigation 119–21; 'breaking' limits 112–13; claims subject to 99–105; craft subject to 97; establishing fund 116; forum shopping 128–30; fund recognition and the EU 124–7; LLMC fund and wreck removal reservation 122–3; multi-state proceedings 117–18; persons entitled 98; policy 128–30; procedure and forum shopping 116–30; salvors and wreck removal contractors 106–8; WRC 2007 128–30

LLMC 1976 97, 109, 111; air-cushioned vehicles 395; floating platforms 401; fund and wreck removal reservation 122–3; opt-out for wreck and cargo removal claims 100, 101, 102, 104, 114–16, 143, 151, 489, 490, 493, 498, 502, 503, 505–8, 514, 516, 517, 521, 531, 532, 545, 552, 553, 554, ; gross tonnage 493–4; limitation of liability 96, 119, 122, 128, 503; major casualty 84; passenger claims 90; *Rena* 21, 26; UK reservation 115, 552, 553, 554; *Uno* Case 126; Waste Framework Directive, relationship with 693; WRC 2007 508–10, 514, 532, 535, 553; *see also* limitation of liability, LLMC 1996

LLMC 1996: Art 1(6) 552–3; Art 2(1)(e) 554; Art 6(2) 554; Art 7 99; Art 10 116; Art 11 116; *Baltic Ace* 120–2; Hague/Visby Rules 53–5; limitation of liability 57, 84–5, 96–7, 109–11, 119, 128, 142–3, 147, 490, 517, 520–1, 624, 626; *MSC Napoli* 17; passengers, wreck and 77; pollution claims 100–2; *Shen Neng 1* 489–90; *The Cape Bari* 624; WRC 2007 399, 402, 492–4, 502–11, 514, 532–8; wreck removal 369; wreck removal reservation 115, 122–5, 130; *see also* limitation of liability, LLMC 1976

LOF 7, 16, 19, 38, 108, 153, 154, 155, 157, 158, 160, 161, 163, 168, 169, 172, 173, 239, 254, 255, 433, 444, 447, 448, 515, 568, 569, 571, 572, 573, 578, 579–82, 586, 588, 589, 590, 592, 594, 597, 602, 611, 612, 620, 674

LSSAC: cl 2(d) 582; LOF 2011 163

Lusitania 216–7, 226–7, 238, 242, 247, 269

Lutine 229, 237–8

MAIB 266

Marine and Coastal Access Act 2009: dumping in the UK 664–7; marine licensing 696, 699; oil recovery equipment 264; Part 4 664; wreck disposal 664–7

marine insurance 173–210; cargo cover 179–87; H&M cover 175–8; insurance cover for liabilities 197–210; practice of underwriters

193–6; role with shipwreck 173–4; Ship Recycling Regulation 2013 674; total loss 188–92, 195–6
maritime casualty: WRC 2007 394–5
Maritime Labour Convention 2006 71–7; compensation 75; financial security for abandonment 74; implementation of financial security provisions 76; indemnity for unpaid wages 75; P&I Club cover 208–9; repatriation costs 74
MARPOL: coastal state 407, 420; LC 1972 661–662; ship definition 400–1; UNCLOS 308–12; WRC 2007 obligations 417–18
Marchioness 15, 79, 267
MCA 250, 263, 264, 277: *MSC Napoli*, and 15, 16, 18, 264–266, 276; Receiver of Wreck 270; recycling 679, 683; reporting accidents 267; SOLAS waters 449; SOSREP and engaging contractors 559
MEPC 297
MIA 1906 174, 198, 232–7; amendments 193; constructive total loss 190–1; s55 177, 199, 499; s57(1) 188; wilful misconduct definition 499
Mikhail Lermontov 15, 438
MOD: 220, 283–4 294, 354
Mont Louis 359–60, 408, 491, 521
mortgagee 178–9, 668, 706
MSA 1995 527–30; general lighthouse authorities s 253 528–30; GLAs and wreck removal 556–9; harbour activities s252 527–8; national wreck removal law 523–66; Part 9A 523–66; Part 9A administrative provisions 539–47; Part 9A liability provisions 547–56; Sch 3A 252
New Flame 445–6, 491, 604
MSC Napoli 15–18, 445; casualty 15, 459; charterers 36, 39, 40, 56, 69, 98, 105, 257; containers 31, 52, 57, 118, 163, 182, 252, 490, 575, 671, 708; insurance 177, 180, 182, 185, 491; legal claims 17, 105, 177, 445, 491, 575; limitation 105, 110; removal operations 16, 254, 445, 454, 601, 660–1, 664, 670–1, 700, 703, 708; response coordination 251, 254, 264–6, 559, 571, 591, 596, 684; YAR 170
MSMSA 1997 284–5
MTA 1994: *Rena* 19, 20–1

NCP 250–1; *MSC Napoli* 265; public agencies 263–4
non-State parties: Athens Convention, and 78, 87; LLMC 503; Basel Convention, and 672; UCH 2001, and 315; Hong Kong Convention, and 678; UNCLOS, and wreck 309; WRC 2007, and 370–1, 374, 376–87, 409; 452–453, 494–497, 503, 512, 513, 514; WRC 2007, UK MSA 1995, and 535, 536, 540, 541, 543, 544, 548, 552,
notice of abandonment 12, 171, 187, 190–193, 195–6, 224, 231–234, 236, 238, 525

Oceanus 446
Oliva 447
OPRC 1990 249, 250, 312, 321–4, 595; coastal states 312; public relations 595; WRC 2007 387, 417–18, 420, 422
OPRC-HNS Protocol 322
OSPAR Convention 1992 663–4, 666–7
ownership 213–22; acquisition 220–2; human remains 222; identification 216–20; choice-of-law 214–5; Crown right 249, 268–70, 272, 279, 286

Paris Convention 1960: nuclear liabilities 521
P&I Clubs 174; Athens Convention 2002 88; availability of cover 197; crew claims 208–10; cover for casualties 197–205; financial security for abandonment 74–5; HNS diplomatic conference 130; Large Casualty Working Group 443; major incident analysis 32–4; Montreal Compromise 165; SCOPIC 2018 167–8, 582–3; shipowner liability 456, 576, 602; spill handling 14; state action 603; tankers 135–6; typical cover for casualties 198–200; WRC 2007 469, 491, 501–2, 511–14; wreck liabilities 204–7; wreck removals 69–70
passengers 77–89: Athens Convention 2002, application of 78–9; claims 89; compensation 83–4; compulsory insurance 86–8; domestic carriage 89; forum issues 89; liability for death and injury 80–2; limits of liability 83–4; luggage 85–6
platforms: decommissioning 712; LC 1972 658; limitation 97–98, 129, 448; OPRC reporting 322; recycling 680; salvage 158, 159, 577; WRC 2007 394, 395, 400–402, 407, 449, 450, 451–452, 493, 494, 533, 539, 712,
polluting wrecks: intervention beyond territorial seas 296; United Nations Convention on the Law of the Sea jurisdiction 316–21
pollution liability 131–51; Bunkers Convention 2001 141–3; CLC 1992 133–7; Environmental Liability Directive 2004 150–1; Fund Convention 1992 138–9; HNSC 2010 144–9; international action after *Torrey Canyon* 131; Supplementary Fund Protocol 2003 140

possession: salvor's right of 239–41, 396; of sunken wreck 241–5; Receiver of Wreck's 272–6; harbour authority 527–8, 717
Prestige 13, 14, 18, 135, 139, 140, 146, 203, 204, 253, 297, 304, 431, 442, 462, 493, 511, 512, 531, 596
Privity 47, 112: actual fault, and 47, 67, 112, 113, 119, 199; of assured 178, 183, 199; of contract, and 108, 708 and *see* Himalaya clause
Projectcon 709, 711, 712
proof of loss or damage 51–3
proportionate action 321
proportionate costs 471, 478, 531, 599
proportionate fault 94
proportionate loss 117
proportionate marking 465, 480
proportionate measures 33, 319, 414, 431, 433, 436, 441, 456, 471
proportionate protection 320
proportionate removal 475
proportionate responses 411
Protection of Military Remains Act 1986 249, 280–5; human remains 222; salvage law 331
Protection of Wrecks Act 1973 213, 249, 278–80; Ancient Monuments and Archaeological Areas Act 1979 285–6; historic wrecks 325, 331–2, 352–3; temporary exclusion zones 262–3
Public relations 595–6

quantitative risk assessment (QRA) 605–606

reasonable measures *see* proportionate action; proportionate costs; proportionate fault; proportionate loss; proportionate marking; proportionate measures; proportionate protection; proportionate removal; proportionate responses
receiver of wreck 270–7
Recyclecon 2012 678, 682, 705, 712
recycling: regulation 683–4; *see also*, dumping, scrapping, ship recycling
refuge, place of 12, 16, 18, 89, 162, 170, 194, 253–4, 265, 323, 462, 596, 627, 684
registered shipowner's liability for costs 437–56; costs recoverable 441–3; liability for costs 437–9; persons to claim 440–1; persons to pay costs 439–40; WRC 2007 437–522
Registration Regulations 1993: ship deregistration, wreck and 705
Rena 18–27, 320, 406, 442, 444, 447, 595, 661, 666; bills of lading, 39, 56, 630; casualty 18–19, 608; charterers 36, 39, 69, 257–8; consent order 24–5; criminal proceedings 71; legal claims 21, 32, 48, 197, 264, 459, 491, 511, 531, 605; legal problems 20, 145, 168, 207, 318, 481, 523, 560, 612; limitation 96, 103, 110, 114, 128–9, 503, 532; practical problems 20, 30, 32, 320–1, 608, 618, 630, 661; salvage problems 168, 569, 571, 575, 583, 591; trust fund and finality 320, 712–14; WRC 2007 comparisons 471, 474, 490, 502–3, 508, 511–13
repatriation costs: Maritime Labour Convention 2006 74
reporting of accidents 267
rights: abandonment 222–31; insurers 231–9; salvors and finders 239–48; state rights 249–94; ownership 213–22
Rokia Delmas 445
Rome II Regulation: Art 15 127–8

Sale: *see also*, wreck (sale of), wreck (sale of goods contracts, and)
Saleform 2012 705
salvage: applicable law 153; environment, and 163–8; equitable jurisdiction 571; frustration of charter 572, 579; *in specie* award 245–6; law of 152–68; liability to pay 161; non-commercialisation of cultural heritage 334–6; of or by State vessels 276; professional salvage and wreck removal contractors 155; receiver of Wreck's function 271–2; reward 159–61, 164; SCOPIC 2018 167–8, 567–94; security for payment 162; ships about to sink or strand 396–8; special compensation 164–6; terminology 154; underwater cultural heritage 327–32
Salvage Association 216, 239
Salvage Convention 1910 158; Art 3 577–8; Art 14 289
Salvage Convention 1989 103, 137, 144, 154–5, 157, 158–9, 167, 294, 398, 514–15, 578–9; Art 1 255–6; Art 3 577; Art 4 289–90; Art 5 430, 549; Art 6 38–9, 578–9, 590; Art 7 571–2; Art 8 573–4, 611; Art 10 573; Art 12 575; Art 13 108, 160, 161–2, 575, 576–7, 596; Art 14 108, 159, 172, 433, 575–6, 586, 589, 698; Art 18 574; Art 19 240, 577–8; Art 20 162; Art 21 162–3; compensation 550; cooperation 387; environmental salvage issues 363; historic wreck 332; IMO international conventions 300; liability salvage 163–4; recovery of bodies 596–600; SCOPIC 2018 168, 586, 589–90, 593, 698; state vessels 348; *Torrey Canyon* 131–2; voluntary salvage 573–8; WRC 2007 400–2, 429, 535–6; WRC overlap 514–15; wreck definition 213; YAR 169

INDEX

Salvcon 2005 570, 573
Salvhire 2005 570, 573
salvors and finders' rights 239–48; finds 246–8; *in specie* salvage award 245–6; possession of sunken wrecks 241–5; rights to possession 239–41
SCOPIC 165, 167–9, 515, 600; Appendix B 584; Appendix C 585; bunkers and caretaking role 144, 254, 582–4, 602, 603–4, 698; cl 1 590; cl 2 584, 587; cl 3 587, 614–15; cl 4 587–92; cl 5 692; cl 9 578, 589–92; cl 12 584; cl 13 585–6; cl 14 593–4; cl 15 172; CTL, and 190;damages, and 60; GA, and 171, 172; limitation, and 108; *MSC Napoli* 16; P&I Clubs, and 32, 33, 199, 205, 444, 445, 446, 572, 577, 608, 610; preventing pollution from wreck 593–4; *Rena* 19, 571; Salvage Convention 1989 154, 155, 158, 188, 254; security 614–5; special hull representative 71, 194; special casualty representative 71, 577, 584–5, 632; special representatives 71, 585–6; termination provisions 571, 578, 586–93, 621; transition from salvage to wreck removal 569, 570, 582–94, 605; waste 690; WRC 2007 515
scrapping 669–70; *see also*, dumping, ship recycling
Sea Diamond 446, 503
Sea Empress 12, 140, 249, 250, 257, 265, 596, 685
seagoing 79, 85, 89, 97, 134, 141, 145, 395, 402, 448–452, 493, 553
Seawheel Rhine/Assi Eurolink case 123, 126–8
Sewol 15, 156, 320, 467, 492, 597, 598, 599, 610, 710
Shen Neng 1 112, 147, 320, 447, 489
ship recycling 676–85
Ship Recycling Regulation 2013 678–85; deregistration 706; Waste Shipment Regulation 2006 673–4
Ship Recycling Requirements (EU Exit) Regulations 2019: Brexit entry into force 679
Ship Recycling Requirements Regulations 2018 679, 682–5
shipowners' and insurers' liabilities: Bunkers Convention 2001 520–1; cargo removal under WRC 2007 481–90; CLC 1992 516–19; compulsory insurance 491–514; defences to shipowner liability 456–62; HNSC 2010 519–20; limitation of shipowners' liability 490–1; LLMC 508–10; overlaps with other maritime liability regimes 514–22; P&I Club 511–14; registered shipowner's liability for costs 437–56; time limits 462–4; triggers to liability 464–81; WRC 2007 437–522, 490–1

single ship company: 19, 56, 74, 77, 102, 113, 128, 132, 135, 142, 183, 187, 202, 360, 471, 500–1, 524, 531, 568, 602–3, 614, 628
Smart 30, 147, 446, 447, 489, 604, 606, 610, 658, 661, 670
SOLAS: coastal states 312; marine environment regulation 309; other ship obligations 259–60; sea definition 449; State obligations 426; wreck reporting 418, 419, 420
SOSREP 12, 261, 265; coastguard, and 276; directions 252–5, 257, 258, 265; exclusion zones, and 263; GLAs, and 426, 556, 557–9; *MSC Napoli*, and 16–18; role 250–252; place of refuge 253–4; power to act 260; public relations 596wreck removal 539, 541, 542, 544, 545, 556, 557–9,
sovereign immunity 287–94
State: non-commercial ships WRC 2007 definition 402–3
State rights 249–94; Affected States' powers and obligations 422–35; coastguard 277–8; flag State obligations 415–22; powers in territorial sea 435–6; receiver of wreck 270–7; shipping inquiries 266–8; sovereign immunity 287–94; UK regulation 249–66; wreck protection legislation 278–87; wreck, to 268–70
sunken or stranded ship: WRC 2007 395–6
Supplementary Fund Protocol 2003 140–1; *Erika* packages 13–14

tanker wrecks 10–14
Tanio 11, 428, 431, 443
Tasman Spirit 71, 572, 606
territorial waters: extension of WRC 2007 530–4; State powers 435–6; WRC 2007 application 410–14
terrorism: Athens Convention 2002 459–60
time charter 36, 45, 58, 62, 63–70, 556, 572; CLC 137; collision 93; dangerous cargo 57; directions, and 256–7; limitation and 105–106, 109; orders to owner 41, 56; salvage of bunkers 161, 165, 257; termination 41–43; unsafe port, and 56
Titanic 237, 238, 243–8, 284–5, 303, 314, 345–6, 597…*Tojo Maru* 47, 106, 107, 143, 153, 556, 574, 578
tonnage: dwt 9, 135; limitation 9, 96, 99, 105, 106, 107, 109, 110, 135, 136, 148, 624, ; WRC 2007 insurance, and 365, 381, 382, 434, 449, 450, 451, 452, 492–4, 545,
Torrey Canyon 6–10; BP charterer, and 7–10; casualty 7; international action after 30, 32, 131–2, 134, 138, 144, 163, 184, 249, 252, 261, 296, 359, 361–4, 408, 425, 514, 656,

808

663, 697; legal claims 8–9, 48, 56, 110, 123, 361–2, 381, 441, 575–6, 590
Towcon 2008 109, 569, 573, 607, 608, 631, 708, 711
Towhire 2008 109, 569, 573, 607, 608, 611, 615, 622, 624, 631, 632, 708, 711
Tricolor 28, 92, 320, 360, 361, 444, 595
TSWR Regulations 2007: wreck disposal powers 674
Tubantia 226, 241–2, 287

UCH 2001 315–16, 325–55; dispute settlement 389; elimination of law of salvage 334–6; international cooperation 344–6; jurisdictional structure 337–41; regulatory regime 341–3; Salvage Convention 1989 332; state practice 349–55; state-owned vessels 346–9; UNCLOS 306, 316; underwater cultural heritage, definition 332–4; UNESCO implementation 349; US approach to historic wreck 286; WRC 2007 420
UK Club Rules 2018: payment first by the Owner 201
UK legislation: Accident Reporting Regulations 2012 266–7; Ancient Monuments and Archaeological Areas Act 1979 285–6; Carriage of Passengers Regulations 2012 89; Environmental Protection Act 1900 701–2; Marine and Coastal Access Act 2009 264, 664–7; MIA 1906 174, 198, 232–7; MSA 1995 252–63, 523–66; MTA Maritime Transport Act 1994 19–21; Protection of Military Remains Act 1986 249, 280–25; Protection of Wrecks Act 1973 213, 249, 278–80; Registration Regulations 1993 705; Ship Recycling Requirements (EU Exit) Regulations 2019: Brexit entry into force 679; Ship Recycling Requirements Regulations 2018 679, 682–5; Ship Recycling Requirements Regulation 2013 678–85; TSWR Regulations 2007 674; Waste Regulations 2011 694–6; Wreck Removal Convention Act 2011 524, 534–5, 550
UK regulation: abandoned ships 559–66; accession choices for states 530–4; dumping 664–7; intervention powers 252–63; local harbour legislation 524–7; marine waste licensing and exemptions 696–701; *MSC Napoli*, response coordination 264–6; pollution preparedness and response 249–50; SOSREP, relationship between public agencies 263–4; role of 250–2; waste regulations 694–6;wreck response, and 249–66
UK territorial waters: rights outside 269–70; rights within 268–9

UNCLOS 299–321; development 299–300; jurisdiction over pollution hazards 316–21; jurisdictional regime 300–6; WRC 2007 371–5; wrecks, and 306–16
underwater cultural heritage 325–58; definition 332–4; good archaeological practice 336–7; implementation through UNESCO 349; international cooperation 355–345; jurisdictional structure 337–41; non-commercialisation and salvage 334–6; protection of historic wrecks 325; regulated activities 336; regulatory and deterrent regime 341–4; state-owned vessels 346–9; state practice 349–55; UCH 2001 325–32; UK position 351–5; US position 350–1; warships 346–9
UNESCO Convention: historic wrecks 213, 325–6, 343; Director-General of 340; implementation of UCH 2001 349; Italian cultural heritage sites 340; ISA reporting 306; UCH 2001 306; US position 350–1; World Heritage Site 448
Uno case 121–3, 126, 128
unpaid wages 75
US Abandoned Shipwreck Act 1987 213, 228–9, 247, 286–7, 350

V Due 254
vessels in distress 270–1
Vienna Convention on the Law of Treaties 370–6; Art 34 371, 378, 379–80; Art 38 383; Art 41 372 ; IMO Legal Committee 379; MSA 1995 741; WRC 2007 382
Vienna Nuclear Damage Convention 521
Voyage charter 36, 43, 45, 61–3, 64, 65, 66, 109, 609, 710; GA 171, 173; CLC 137; dangerous cargo 57; directions, and 256–7; limitation and 105–106, 109; salvage, and 38; unsafe port, and 56; *see also*, Wreckhire 2010

warships: WRC 2007 402–3; *see also*, sovereign immunity
Waste: EU Waste Framework Directive 674, 683, 685–703; transboundary disposal, and 670–676
Waste Framework Directive 2008 674, 683, 685–703; adoption in the UK 693–703; *Commune de Mesquer* 689–90; hire payments 616; Ship Recycling Regulations 684–5; wreck 690–3
Waste Regulations 2011 694–6; Environmental Protection Act 1990 701; practical compliance 703
Waste Shipment Regulation 2006: wreck disposal 673–6

wilful misconduct 113, 136, 138, 176, 177, 178, 182, 183, 184, 187, 196, 198, 199, 207, 458, 459, 465, 498, 499–501, 502, 506, 552, 656, 663, 726, 743
wreccum maris 211–2, 247, 268–9
wreck: cargo position after 36; carriage of goods contracts, and 35–69; collision liability, and 90–4; charterers, and 58–69; crew, and 70–6; definitions 4; disposal 655–714; general average, and 169–73; law of salvage, and 152–68; law of the sea, and 295–324; limitation of liability, and 95–130; marine insurance, and 173–210; maritime law, and 3; non-State parties in territorial sea 376–7; ownership 213–22; passengers, and 77–89; polluting wrecks 296, 316–21; pollution liability, and 131–51; practice of underwriters 193–6; protection legislation 278–94; receiver of 270–7; rights, in relation to 211–48; sale of 9, 191–2, 209, 215, 232, 235, 275, 326, 328, 433–4, 465, 527, 556, 561, 628, 649, 668–9, 672, 675, 677, 681, 703–7; sale of goods contracts, and 37; shipping inquiries, and 266–8; state rights, and 249–94, 268–70; success in preventing 156–7; UK regulations 249–66
wreck cases: *Baltic Ace* 119–21; *Christos Bitas* 657; *Commune de Mesquer* 689–93, 702; *Costa Concordia* 27–9; *MSC Napoli* 15–18, 265; *Rena* 18–25; *Seawheel Rhine/Assi Eurolink* case 126–7; *Torrey Canyon* 6–9, 131; *see also*, individual ships' names
wreck disposal; *see* disposal of wreck
wreck protection legislation: Ancient Monuments and Archaeological Areas Act 1979 285–6; comparative US approach 286–7; Protection of Military Remains Act 1986 280–5; Protection of Wrecks Act 1973 278–80
wreck removal 567–94; ancillary contracts, and 607; contracts 607–54; operations and contracts 595–654; public relations 595–6; range of technical operations 600–2; recovery of bodies 596–600; responsibility for arranging contracts 602–4; salvage, and 567–73; SCOPIC 582–94; tendering 604–7; termination of services 573–82
Wreckfixed 2010: analysis 633–639; comparisons 633, 639–641; limitation waiver 109; risk allocation 610–11; text facsimile 767
Wreckhire 2010 108, 143, 165, 171, 584, 594, 606, 608, 610–632, 692, 708; analysis 610–632; bodies 600; comparisons 633, 634, 635, 636, 637, 638, 639–641, 642, 643, 644, 645, 647, 648, 649; limitation waiver 109; risk allocation 610–11; text facsimile 753
Wreckstage 2010 608, 639–651, 708, 712; analysis 639–651; comparisons 639–641; Explanatory notes 793; limitation waiver 109; risk allocation 610–11; text facsimile 781
WRC 2007 359–566; accession choices for States 530–4; Affected State 406–8; Art 12(1) 508–11; Art 12(10) 499; creation 359–92; development 361–70; EU Waste Framework Directive 2008, relationship with 693; extension/opt-in to territorial sea 376, 377, 393, 410–14, 456, 478, 512, 513, 531, 533, 538; hazard definition 404–5; international legal order, and 370–6; limitation of liability 128–30; non-state parties, and 376–87, 452–3; related interests definition 405–6; removal definition 406; ships covered 448–453;shipowners' and insurers' liabilities 437–522; state territorial waters 530–4; states' rights and duties 415–36; UNCLOS, and 371–5; UK enactment 534–9; wreck definition 393–404; wrecks that pose a hazard 393–408
WRCA 2011 534–5, 550; MSA 1990 Part 9A 539, 557; UK legislation 524; WRC 2007, incorporation of 535–8, 538

YAR 170; cutting away wreck 173; YAR 2016 170–2; YAR 1994 170